PSYCHOLOGY

PSYCHOLOGY

DODGE FERNALD
Harvard University

Prentice Hall, Upper Saddle River, New Jersey 07458

Library of Congress Cataloging-in-Publication Data

Fernald, L. Dodge (Lloyd Dodge)
    Psychology / Dodge Fernald.
      p. cm.
    Includes bibliographical references and index.
    ISBN 0-13-149725-1
    I. Psychology.   I. Title.
BF121.F38 1997
150—dc20   95-19381
                      CIP

Editor-in-chief: Peter Janzow
Director of production and manufacturing: Barbara Kittle
Managing editor: Bonnie Biller
Editorial/production supervision: Mary Rottino
Development editor: Barbara Muller
Manufacturing manager: Nick Sklitsis
Manufacturing buyer: Tricia Kenny
Creative design director: Leslie Osher
Editorial assistant: Marilyn Coco
Interior design: Carmela Pereira
Cover design: Maria Lange
Cover and part opening art: Jose Ortega
Line art coordinator: Michele Giusti
Illustrations: Dartmouth Publishing, Inc.
Photo researcher: Teri Stratford
Acknowledgments appear on pp. 684-685, which constitute an extension of the copyright page.
This book was set in Centaur MT by Black Dot Graphics and was printed by
Webcrafters. The cover and color inserts were printed by Phoenix.

 © 1997 by Prentice-Hall, Inc.
Simon & Schuster / A Viacom Company
Upper Saddle River, New Jersey 07458

Printed in the United States of America
10 9 8 7 6 5 4 3 2 1

ISBN 0-13-149725-1 (Student's edition)
ISBN 0-13-184151-3 (Instructor's edition)

Prentice-Hall International (UK) Limited, *London*
Prentice-Hall of Australia Pty. Limited, *Sydney*
Prentice-Hall Canada Inc., *Toronto*
Prentice-Hall Hispanoamericana, S.A., *Mexico*
Prentice-Hall of India Private Limited, *New Delhi*
Prentice-Hall of Japan, Inc., *Tokyo*
Simon & Schuster Asia Pte. Ltd., *Singapore*
Editora Prentice-Hall do Brazil, Ltda., *Rio de Janeiro*

To the Storymakers

BRIEF CONTENTS

CONTENTS

PREFACE

SOME TIME AGO, WHILE I WAS WORKING ON A MANUSCRIPT AFTER DINNER IN A RESTAURANT, the waitress came to clear the table. As it happened, she cleared my mind a bit, too.

"Are you writing a book?"

I nodded, thinking that she certainly looked like a college student.

"Is it a book with a story," she continued brightly, and then her voice trailed off softly, "or is it the . . . other kind?"

I explained that it was indeed "the other kind."

"Oh," she replied, finishing the table with a dramatic sweep of her wet rag. She left without another word.

At that moment, I had an epiphany—a sudden revelation, an understanding that caused me to change in a fundamental way my view of introductory college textbooks. The student had taught the teacher.

She had not taught me something new, but she had reminded me rather forcefully of a characteristic of the human mind to which I previously had paid little heed.

Psychological research has revealed, I knew, that the human mind is a pattern-making, pattern-recognizing system. Trying to understand the world, our mind seeks meaningful patterns. If there are none, it imposes those of its own. We seek patterns in literature, science, mathematics, and almost everything else, including nonsense syllables.

Psychological research also has shown that we develop many of these patterns by telling stories. We tell them at home, at work, in school, in taverns, in therapy, in the courts, in the media, throughout daily life. They appear in the ancient Odyssey, modern books, picture stories of the Eskimos, and the orations of Samoan "talking chiefs." They pervade mass media in our electronic age. They are found all over the world, wherever there is human life. There is a universality in this mode of expression.

In the pages that follow, therefore, I have used the age-old method of storytelling, employed as a supplement to the topical approach in this otherwise traditional textbook. Guided by the way life is lived, stories are a natural way of thinking about the world, even in science, especially at the introductory level.

I have found this approach useful and entertaining. I hope you do, too. And I like to think that the waitress who inspired me will be inspired by this book.

When we next meet, I certainly expect to say to her, "Hey, thanks for the tip."

Dodge Fernald
Cambridge, Massachusetts

INTRODUCTION

IN COMPLETING THIS MANUSCRIPT, IT BECAME CLEAR THAT, WILLIAM SHAKESPEARE AND PETE JANZOW offered an author conflicting advice. And I had to make a choice.

Shakespeare, in fact, has a warning for anyone planning to make a presentation of any sort: "Hawking and spitting are prologues to a poor voice" (*As You Like It,* 5:3, 12). I am inclined to agree, knowing that every audience is ready to be tired. Nonetheless, Janzow insisted that I do some hawking and spitting about why and how I wrote this book. He said that the reader will want this information. My thoughts are divided here, but my loyalty lies with Pete, a good friend and a model of competence and good judgment in our complex society. The remarks that follow are in deference to his perspective. Oh, yes, and Pete is also editor-in-chief of this book.

• AIMS AND THEMES •

My aims in writing this book can be stated quite simply: to give the beginning student an up-to-date account of contemporary scientific psychology and to provide a narrative context for understanding this rapidly changing field.

The actual writing was not so simple, owing to the unbounded diversity of modern psychology, extending into every corner of human existence. To present the field adequately, I employed an eclectic perspective, recognizing the extensive range of concepts and viewpoints.

To give cohesion to this welter of facts, theories, and scientific studies, I have reiterated at numerous points a widely accepted theme in psychology, the *multiple bases of behavior,* stating that several factors are often influential in any given response. The aim of psychology is to identify these factors and the intricate relationships among them.

Two subordinate themes have been employed to elaborate and extend this approach. The first is a stress on *empiricism,* which states that knowledge is acquired through experience; psychological information is obtained by observation and experimentation. The second is a reminder that psychology is guided by *various theories.* These diverse theoretical views emphasize and encompass the breadth of modern psychology.

• NARRATIVE METHOD •

The major instructional innovation in this textbook is the narrative approach—the telling of stories. It is *the* distinctive feature in this otherwise traditional twentieth-century psychology textbook. The stories that follow are true stories, as far as we know, with one notable literary exception. They have been obtained from the best scientific journals and most reliable mass media.

The objective of science is truth, and therefore the fundamental mode of communication in this book is rational and direct, guided by logical analysis. The narrative method, with its unfolding sequence, serves as a complement. It is a powerful and ubiquitous mode of human thought, possessing the capacity to instruct in ways not possible in traditional scientific discourse. More holistic and contextual, it is a deeply ingrained human tendency, a natural way of thinking about the world (Bruner, 1990).

Support for narrative instruction comes from a wide variety of studies and essays in modern psychology—too numerous to cite fully (Bruner, 1986; Coles, 1989; Epstein, 1994; Fernald, 1987; Mandler & Johnson, 1977). Human beings tell stories not just for entertainment and pleasure but also for comprehension, explanation, memory, interest, and persuasion, as well as for the organization and preservation of their culture (Bruner, 1990; Howard, 1991; Liebes, 1994; Sarbin 1986; Schank, 1990; Vitz, 1990).

The narratives in this book were drawn chiefly from a psychological context. Most are about the work of pscyhologists—their research, teaching, and clinical practice; some are about the lives or families of psychologists; and others arise from psychologist's thoughts about the human condition.

Each chapter of this book relates its own story. You will meet a young man sailing around the world, a drummer battling a rare disease, men walking on fire, and women scaling Mount Everest; you will encounter seventeenth-century monks, a college student who becomes a patient, and pseudopatients who enter a mental hospital; you will find tales of research about obedience to authority and enslavement to the standard keyboard; you will observe learning in schoolchildren, a wild boy from the woods, orphan girls in institutions, and a clever horse in Berlin; you will build with a corps of carpenters and struggle with a dreaming artist; and you will follow the lives of a mother and son, a father and son, and a young couple in love.

Each narrative serves three instructional functions. First, through its appeal to intelligence and emotion, it increases reader interest. The unfolding sequence develops and sustains motivation. Second,

the narrative aids comprehension. It does so by favoring Bacon's rule of one variable, which states that different theories or viewpoints can be best understood when they are compared with respect to the same illustration. Thus, when different theories, methods, or perspectives are presented within a chapter, a single illustration for all of them is provided by the unfolding narrative. Third, the narrative improves memory for the contents of the chapter. Serving as a connecting thread, it gives each chapter a mnemonic framework or structure. In the words of William James, the narrative may become an idea to which the "facts will soon cluster and cling . . . like grapes to a stem" (1890).

• TRADITIONAL INSTRUCTION •

This book has benefited from steady advances in textbook instruction in the United States in the last century. Appearing in two volumes of almost 700 pages each, the first such textbook, William James's *The Principles of Psychology* (1890), contained few sketches, no photographs, no boldface terms, no glossary, and no other instructional aids considered standard practice today. In contrast, the present textbook incorporates numerous contemporary learning aids, evident in scanning the pages. They include photos and graphs and illustrations, chapter summaries, lists of key concepts, questions for class discussion and critical thinking, and a glossary.

There is also a companion to this textbook, the *Student Learning Guide*, offering several aids for the student. First, it contains learning objectives for each chapter, informing the student of the expected learning outcomes. Then it presents an extensive learning-and-practice exercise for every chapter, called programmed instruction, emphasizing the major concepts in the chapter. Programmed instruction is effective for three reasons. It proceeds in small steps, appropriate to the learner's capacity. It requires active responding, ensuring that students are directly engaged in the task. And it provides immediate knowledge of results, informing learners about the adequacy of their responses.

The guide also includes a variety of exam questions, ranging from multiple-choice to matching items. They constitute a self-testing review. With an emphasis on diversity, these questions are designed to assist students in preparing for examinations of all sorts.

• ACKNOWLEDGMENTS •

Deepest appreciation is expressed for the work of Richard A. Chumley, whose intelligence, unfailing good humor, and constant attention to detail played a central role in the successful and timely preparation of the manuscript, including construction of the glossary and references. Clever Hans, the Wild Boy, Skeels's orphans, Jenny, and all the others are in their proper places through his efforts.

In Chicago, Barbara Muller, publishing consultant, set forth a very clear rule for the further refinement of this manuscript: Successful writing is rewriting. With extensive experience, she guided a detailed revision of the text, ever mindful of a tendency throughout the publishing industry: The covers of most books are too far apart.

And finally the edited manuscript reached the publisher's offices, coming under the supervision of a poised and sagacious production editor, Mary Rottino. She ably directed the whole project—manuscript, photographs, line art, and all the rest—through the labyrinthine corridors and across the innumerable desktops that comprise an impressive modern publishing house, Prentice Hall.

Writing a textbook is an instructional task, and here I am clearly indebted to former and current students and colleagues at various universities and colleges in America and Europe. Much of this book reflects my development as a teacher, writer, and psychologist through interactions with them. May they find themselves here in spirit, if not in lettered tribute.

BACKGROUND
AND BASICS

BEGINNINGS

∾

RESEARCH METHODS

∾

BIOLOGICAL FOUNDATIONS

∾

HISTORICAL ANTECEDENTS
Contributing Fields
Scientific Inquiry

FOUNDING OF PSYCHOLOGY
Wundt and Structuralism
James and Functionalism
Calkins's Contributions

SYSTEMS OF PSYCHOLOGY
Biological Approach
Origins of Psychoanalysis
Rise of Behaviorism
Humanistic Psychology
Cognitive Psychology

DIVERSITY IN PSYCHOLOGY
Basic Research
Applied Psychology
Ethics and Principles

I
BEGINNINGS

❧

MR. WILHELM VON OSTEN CUT QUITE A FIGURE IN THAT DUSTY BERLIN COURTYARD, STANDING DEFIANTLY IN HIS LONG WHITE SMOCK BESIDE the red brick buildings. Everyone called him *Mister* von Osten, partly in keeping with the formality of that day, partly out of respect for this elderly, rather eccentric, retired schoolteacher. He wore his long smock even on the warmest days, and a large black hat usually covered his head. His floppy white hair stuck out in all directions beneath its broad brim.

Privileged visitors and a few dignitaries waited expectantly in a small grandstand. For all other spectators, there was standing room only.

When all was quiet, Mr. von Osten moved to the center of the courtyard. Taking a position in front and just to the right of his pupil, he began the performance.

"How much is two and four?" he asked. Hans answered readily.

"How much is three *times* three?" Mr. von Osten spoke the *times* loudly, lest Hans fail to notice that the problem required multiplication. Again, Hans succeeded, and the audience murmured appreciatively.

"What is the square root of 16?" After the last of 4 steady taps, the spectators erupted into hearty applause. After all, Hans was a horse.

A large brown stallion with white socks, Hans could tell time, knew the value of German coins, and remembered the days of the week. He tapped out popular sayings and the answers to spectators' questions by using a special chart that Mr. von Osten had constructed, displaying the letters of the German alphabet in numbered rows and columns. By tapping a pair of numbers, Hans could indicate a specific letter; by tapping several pairs, he could spell a word. He also answered by shaking his head or pointing with his nose.

The horse had become known as Clever Hans, a celebrity throughout Europe and even in the United States, where the *New York Times* carried stories on the wonderful horse. In 1904, letters to the editor of the *Berliner Tageblatt*, the major newspaper in the city, arrived in overwhelming numbers. Readers of the newspaper demanded an explanation. *How* did Hans do it? What might he do next? Mr. von Osten explained that he had given Hans five years of intensive instruction, using the most modern methods available. The horse's ability lay in this careful training (Pfungst, 1911).

This challenge to explain Clever Hans offered early psychology a special opportunity. Psychology might demonstrate to an eager public the breadth and usefulness of its methods, focusing on an unusual problem, a horse in an open courtyard, rather than people in a private laboratory or clinic. In those early days, psychology was chiefly the study of human mental life, but partly through the case of Clever Hans, it began to expand considerably.

Today, the field of **psychology** is defined as the scientific study of human and animal behavior, experience, and mental processes. Its goals are to understand why organisms behave, feel, and think as they do and to apply this knowledge in diverse situations. Psychology is thus involved in all human concerns. It is devoted to creating peace and harmony in a troubled world, to helping the homeless and the underprivileged, to improving our schools, television, and legal systems.

This chapter begins with selected historical antecedents and afterward turns to the founding of psychology. Then, proceeding chronologically, it presents several views or systems of psychology and concludes with an emphasis on the diversity in psychology today.

• HISTORICAL ANTECEDENTS •

In introducing the story of Clever Hans, we are not horsing around. The animal had become a beastly problem in Berlin, disrupting people's thoughts about their universe, prompting nightmares about what might happen next. "Many a young lieutenant," wrote one reporter, "will be embarrassed to put his spurs to the nag which can add better than he" (Block, 1904). "We humans," he continued, "who put so much stock in our knowledge and progress, will do well to pack up our wisdom and with every passing coach horse doff our hats respectfully. Who can say whether or not some secret Socrates lies within that melancholy skull?"

Amid this turmoil, Count Otto zu Castell-Rüdenhausen entered the courtyard and asked Hans the date, thinking it was the seventh of September. Hans tapped eight times, and suddenly the embarrassed Count realized that Hans was right. It was indeed the eighth of the month. On another occasion, Hans was asked to spell a name, and his questioner interrupted, pointing out a mistake. Hans continued anyway, spelling the full name correctly. He was not

wrong; the human being had erred. On these occasions, when Hans proved superior to his questioners, the celebrated horse greatly enhanced his reputation.

The exploits of Clever Hans, occurring early in the history of modern psychology, provoked a great deal of interest, but the subject matter of psychology has interested people throughout the ages. In fact, the word *psychology* is derived from two Greek words: *psyche*, meaning "soul," and *ology*, meaning "study." Prescientific psychology was the study of the soul. Scientific psychology has far broader concerns.

CONTRIBUTING FIELDS

Modern psychology emerged as a scientific enterprise just over a century ago, only a few years before Clever Hans. It appeared first in Germany, stimulated by developments in philosophy, biology, and other academic fields, as well as practical concerns.

PHILOSOPHICAL FOUNDATIONS. One prominent concept in nineteenth-century philosophy was empiricism, an idea many centuries old. According to **empiricism,** from the Greek word for "experience," all knowledge is gained through the senses, directly from experience. Empiricism stresses *observable* phenomena. It emphasizes that ideas are not innate or inborn but rather acquired during our lifetime. This viewpoint can be traced to Aristotle. In taking this position, Aristotle was speaking out against his teacher, Plato, who said that certain ideas are common to all people and thus must be innate.

For almost 2,000 years, the Aristotelian idea was virtually ignored. In the seventeenth century, an important British philosopher, John Locke, revived it. He described the human mind as a *tabula rasa*, a "blank sheet" at birth. The thoughts and ideas that arise during our lives are based on experience and written on this slate. Although this view does not seem new today, it was radical at that time.

An implication of this doctrine is that almost anyone can be made reasonably intelligent. Empiricism was therefore regarded with much favor by educators, including Mr. von Osten, who decided that with appropriate instructions even a horse could be made intelligent. He taught Hans with learning aids of all sorts, including a counting machine, colored cloths, cards with numbers, and cards with letters. He also used a very gradual method, beginning with a simple command, moving the horse's hoof himself, and then offering a carrot. After countless trials of this sort, he gave the command and just touched the hoof—which Hans promptly lifted, thereby receiving a carrot.

Eventually, Mr. von Osten simply spoke the command and pointed; Hans lifted his hoof and received his reward. Finally, much to the trainer's great joy, the command itself sufficed. Hans lifted the hoof and began to tap when the command alone was given (Figure 1-1).

Empiricism also had enormous implications for science, including psychology. If the way to knowledge is through the senses, scientific knowledge must be pursued in this same manner. Observe the event and let the senses tell the story.

The importance of direct observation has been illustrated in a farcical story about another horse and a most controversial discussion in an ancient temple of learning. The quarrel arose over this question: How many teeth are there in a horse's

BERLIN'S WONDERFUL HORSE

He Can Do Almost Everything but Talk— How He Was Taught.

Special Correspondence THE NEW YORK TIMES. BERLIN, Aug. 23.—In an out-of-the-way part of the German capital a horse is now shown which has stirred up the scientific, military, and sporting world of the Fatherland. It should be said at the very outset that the facts in this article are not drawn from the imagination, but are based upon true observations and can be verified by Dr. Studt, Prussian Minister of Education; by the famous zoologist, Prof. Moebius, director of the Prussian

became signs for visible objects, and he used footsteps as signs for his perceptions, according to the same psychic laws as we use a language to make others understand. After Herr von Osten had taught Hans this simple sign language, the foundation for further education was established. He put before him gold, silver, and copper coins, and taught him to indicate gold pieces by one movement of the foot, silver with two, and copper with three steps. When, for example, three coins were placed

FIGURE 1–1 BERLIN'S WONDERFUL HORSE. The *New York Times* special correspondent, Edward Heyn, visited Clever Hans in the courtyard and contributed this account, shown here only in part. The second column describes how Hans tapped with his foot.

mouth? The debate raged for 13 days with no resolution, although all important books and chronicles had been fetched and consulted. On the 14th day, a youthful newcomer called for his elders' attention and offered a preposterous way to answer the question: Go look in the mouth of a horse! Upon hearing this coarse suggestion, his learned superiors were deeply hurt, and they drove him from the temple for declaring such an unholy manner of finding the truth, one that might prove contradictory to the teachings of their forebears. Instead, after many days of strife, the assembly declared unanimously that the problem must remain an everlasting mystery due to the lack of historical, theological, and other evidence (Mees, 1934).

In this satire, the youth's empiricism offered a very different approach from common sense or the word of some authority. A cornerstone of modern science, empiricism is the first principle or theme in this book, appearing intermittently throughout the chapters. It emphasizes a basic aim in psychology: to obtain the answer "straight from the horse's mouth." This effort at direct observation is what separated the upstart friar from his unbending superiors.

EVOLUTIONARY BIOLOGY. One person who made careful observations a half century earlier was Charles Darwin. He completed a voyage around the world and wrote a book about what he had observed, *The Origin of Species* (1859). Specifically, Darwin noted the wide variations in structure and behavior among the species and observed the struggle for existence among them.

Darwin concluded that the organisms that survive are those with variations that enable them to adapt most adequately to their environment. The poorly adapted perish and produce no offspring. This process of natural selection, continued over millions of years, led to the appearance of distinctly different organisms. Darwin developed these ideas into his **theory of evolution,** which states that any given plant or animal species has developed through modifications of pre–existing species, all of which have undergone the process of natural selection.

The theory of evolution had an almost unprecedented influence on scientific and lay thought. It suggested that if human beings are descended from animals, there may be continuity from the animal to the human mind (Darwin, 1859, 1872). Furthermore, the idea of animal instincts led to the question of human instincts and the study of human motivation. If animals are our ancestors and they have instincts, perhaps we have instincts. By pointing out that our psychological as well as structural characteristics evolved from those prehuman organisms, Darwin stimulated enormous interest in the study of human and animal behavior (Innis, 1992).

Darwin's theory prompted Mr. von Osten to decide, quite erroneously, that many animals have a potentially high intelligence, as shown in his work with Clever Hans. This same intellectual capacity, Mr. von Osten added modestly, could be demonstrated in any horse of average ability (Pfungst, 1911).

PRACTICAL CONCERNS. In addition to philosophy and biology, other academic fields also influenced the founding of psychology, especially physics and physiology. Studies in vision and hearing, for example, emerged from investigations of light and sound in physics. Studies of the brain and other mechanisms of behavior evolved from physiology. However, amid these developments in the academic world, certain practical concerns cannot be overlooked.

Especially in the past two centuries, people who experience mental disorders have been regarded as ill or disturbed rather than possessed by the devil. The person first responsible for this change in attitude was a French physician,

FIGURE 1–2 VOYAGE OF THE BEAGLE. Darwin wrote: "When on board *H.M.S. Beagle*, as naturalist, I was much struck with certain facts in the distribution of organic beings inhabiting South America…" Studying the giant tortoises in the Galapagos Islands, Darwin was assisted by sailors from his ship. For careful scrutiny, they used boathooks to turn over these creatures.

Philippe Pinel, who removed the chains from asylum inmates during the French Revolution. By this act, he stimulated a more humane treatment of these individuals and, at the same time, a more scientific approach to problems of personal adjustment.

A century later, another French physician advanced this perspective. Jean-Martin Charcot, a neurologist, reached the height of his practice in the years immediately following publication of the work by Darwin (Figure 1–2). Equally important, Charcot made a lasting impression on one of his students, a Viennese physician, Sigmund Freud (Figure 1–3).

Originally trained in a highly scientific orientation, Freud became a leader in the clinical study of psychological problems. As other physicians and practitioners became interested, they too contributed to the founding of scientific psychology.

But what is science? This term refers to more than the techniques and findings in biology, physics, and chemistry. In a general sense, **science** means "knowing" or "knowledge" but it implies that careful systematic procedures have been followed in obtaining that knowledge. Science is not a particular field of study; rather, it is a system for making discoveries.

FIGURE 1–3 CHARCOT'S DEMONSTRATIONS. Using actual patients, Jean Martin Charcot showed physicians and medical students how to use hypnotic procedures. The bearded figure in the front row wearing an apron is presumed to be Sigmund Freud.

SCIENTIFIC INQUIRY

This system of discovery is sometimes called the **scientific method,** an expression that can be misleading. There are many different scientific methods. One constant task of science is to develop improved methods of research. The fundamental characteristic of science is an attitude—one of demanding evidence. In idealized form, this evidence is obtained in three stages or steps.

STAGES OF THE SCIENTIFIC METHOD.

In the conventional view, scientific research begins by **forming an hypothesis,** which involves making an educated guess or prediction. The investigator develops some tentative explanation about something. In Berlin, many observers hypothesized that Hans's performance was based on trickery by Mr. von Osten, his suspicious-looking owner.

The next stage, **testing the hypothesis,** involves collecting evidence in support or refutation of the prediction. The hypothesis is tested in a laboratory, clinic, or any other place where the behavior occurs. A zoologist named Carl Georg Schillings, widely respected for his adventures with animals and love of fair play, held the trickery hypothesis. He went into the courtyard and tested it by questioning Clever Hans alone, without Mr. von Osten. To his surprise, Hans performed all of the feats attributed to him. Trickery, Schillings concluded, was no longer a reasonable possibility.

In **replicating the result,** the investigation is repeated and the finding re-examined to confirm its accuracy. The essence of a scientific finding, according to many authorities, is that the same result is obtained over and over again in every repetition of the original research. Count zu Castell-Rüdenhausen, a prominent social figure, also tested Clever Hans alone. After a full session, he too declared that no tricks were involved (Pfungst, 1911).

Even these three broad steps are not always followed, however, as when a psychologist merely describes a crowd reaction or a zoologist examines an animal without any hypothesis in mind. Furthermore, some scientists contend that the first stage in research is observation, from which the hypothesis is developed. Others point to the difficulty in determining just when observation begins, for we are observing all our lives. Therefore, they restrict their definition of the scientific method to these three broad stages beyond observation: forming an hypothesis, testing the hypothesis, and replicating the result.

THE RESEARCH REPORT.

Successful scientific inquiry also requires a *research report*, which presents in detail the method, results, and interpretations of the study. If the procedure has been carried out objectively and the report is explicit, other investigators can repeat the research and draw their own conclusions.

Without these reports, there would be no science of psychology, and without a standard format, their use would be greatly complicated. For this reason, guidelines have been prepared. For example, there is a convention for citing the sources used in any report or book in psychology. The author's name and the date of publication appear in parentheses following the material to which the citation refers. As the reader has perhaps noticed already, references to the story of Clever Hans have appeared in this way: (Pfungst, 1911).

Who was Pfungst? What did he do? He was a student in psychology with a special interest in Clever Hans. He appears later in this chapter.

• FOUNDING OF PSYCHOLOGY •

The event usually considered to mark the formal beginning of modern psychology occurred with little fanfare. In the late 1870s, Wilhelm Wundt, a German philosopher and physiologist, was gradually establishing a three-room research laboratory on the top floor of a building at the University of Leipzig. Looking back years later, he chose 1879 as the official date for the founding of his laboratory, not because it was constructed then but because a graduate student completed the first independent research in that year. Owing to his direction of that laboratory and his prodigious handbook on experimental psychology, historians credit Wundt with founding *scientific* psychology and regard his laboratory as its birthplace (Figure 1–4).

WUNDT
AND STRUCTURALISM

A distinctive feature of Wundt's approach was its use of *introspection*, which involves contemplating and reporting on one's own experiences. Introspection itself was not new; anyone who examines or reflects on personal experiences is introspecting.

FIGURE 1–4 WILHELM WUNDT— (1832–1920). Seated with his wife in the middle of the second row, surrounded by psychologists from his laboratory, Wundt celebrated his 80th birthday.

But the people who made observations in Wundt's laboratory were specially trained in introspecting. First, they were instructed how to make their reports. Then they were exposed to some specific stimulation, such as a whirl of color, and afterward they were asked to describe the basic elements of their experience.

For Wundt and his followers, psychology was the study of immediate, conscious experience. Their aim was to analyze human experience much as the chemist analyzes matter into its elements. This psychology was referred to as **structuralism** or *structural psychology*, for its goal was to describe the basic units or structure of human consciousness. Through proper study, the fundamental elements of mental life would be disclosed.

Psychology at this time was defined as the science of conscious experience, and anything that did not lead in this direction was thought to be outside its sphere of interest. Most of the results were subjective, evident only to the experiencing individual, and there was great difficulty in establishing verifiable, repeatable observations. This approach excluded animals and young children, who could not give accurate reports of their experiences. In fact, structuralists would have no research interest in Clever Hans and little interest in the eccentric Mr. von Osten, who might give unreliable reports.

Strictly speaking, Wundt was not solely a structuralist, but his efforts spawned this laboratory work (Figure 1–5). There was a narrowness in this approach, but no comparable opportunity for research existed elsewhere. Thus it attracted students from all over Europe and the United States, making an indelible impact on early American psychology (Benjamin, Durkin, Link, Vestal, & Acord, 1992).

FIGURE 1–5 EARLY LABORATORY APPARATUS. This instrument, used to study reaction time, measured the speed with which a person could stop a falling weight. Prior to each trial, the weight in the center was pulled to its highest point. At a signal, it was released, moving the pointers as it fell, indicating the elapsed time before the person tugged on a wire to stop its fall.

JAMES AND FUNCTIONALISM

One early visitor to Wundt's lab was William James, a young American suffering from an identity crisis. Bright, personable, and witty, he had received an excellent education in the United States and Europe, but he could not decide what he wanted to do with his life. His efforts at finding a vocation ranged from art to zoology, and he wrote that he had four interests: "natural history, medicine, printing, and beggary" (Perry, 1935). College students today can perhaps appreciate his predicament.

After his short visit to Germany, while still preoccupied with the problem of "finding himself," James accepted a modest teaching position in physiology at Harvard University. He began as an unknown except for the growing fame of his brother, Henry, a novelist. Soon, however, William James shifted from physiology to psychology, and in 1875, four years before Wundt, he developed his own laboratory, used for demonstrations rather than research. Thus, the credit for founding scientific psychology is accorded to Wundt. Looking back on these early efforts, James wryly observed: "The first lecture I ever heard on psychology was the one I gave myself" (Perry, 1935).

With poor eyesight and a weak back, James was not inclined to laboratory work. He did studies on memory, thinking, and vision, usually with some practical goal in mind, and presented his views to diverse audiences. These lectures, within and outside the classroom, did a great deal to promote the new field.

Even more important to the future of psychology were James's accomplishments as a writer. When his two-volume textbook *The Principles of Psychology* appeared in 1890, it immediately earned him an international reputation, not only for its science but also for its literary style, and it did a great deal to stimulate interest in psychology. William James is rec-

FIGURE 1–6 WILLIAM JAMES (1842–1910). Of the James brothers, it is said that William, the scientist, wrote like a novelist, and Henry, the novelist, wrote like a scientist.

ognized as the early leader of American psychology, largely because of his writings, which continue to influence the field (Estes, 1991b; Howard, 1993).

James could not find much value in Wundt's structural psychology. In America, he advocated a much broader approach, called **functionalism** or *functional psychology*, which emphasized the functions rather than the content of mental life (Figure 1–6). The concern was with the purposes of mental life, not its nature. The functionalists thought that consciousness should be studied from the standpoint of how its processes are related to the *adaptation* of *any* organism. Wundt asked, "What is mind?" James asked, "What is mind for?"

In short, functionalists were more interested in what mental life does than what it is, a natural view for practical-minded Americans. They used whatever method was helpful or necessary, rather than restricting themselves to a given procedure. Functionalism was a psychology of adjustment, clearly compatible with Darwin's theory of evolution.

Through James's functionalism, psychology gained much of its identity and gradually broadened in scope, for he wrote on such diverse topics as habit, reasoning, instinct, emotion, education, and hypnotism, in addition to mental disorders. His views on emotion still play a role in contemporary research (Mandler, 1990). Modern psychology is broadly functional, including all aspects of mental life and behavior, thanks in no small way to James's efforts. In turn, James found his own identity through his work in psychology.

CALKINS'S CONTRIBUTIONS

One of James's most celebrated students was a college professor, a young instructor at a nearby women's institution. Mary Whiton Calkins, while teaching Greek at Wellesley College, was offered an opportunity to teach psychology and to establish a psychology laboratory there, *if* she could obtain the proper training. Psychology in the 1890s was a new field, and opportunities for students and faculty were limited (Scarborough & Furumoto, 1987).

WOMEN'S ISSUES. Calkins found only two institutions open to graduate study for women, and neither gave access to a laboratory. At age 30, prohibited from entering a laboratory course with men, she obtained private lessons from an instructor at nearby Clark University. Later, as a woman at all-male Harvard University, she needed special permission to study psychology. Her request to work with William James was granted, and she faithfully attended his classes.

Calkins eventually completed all of the requirements for the doctoral degree at Harvard University, but in those days Harvard did not award degrees to women. Instead, it offered a degree from Radcliffe, an affiliated women's college. Calkins refused the award, pointing out that she had not earned the degree from Radcliffe. Even at the out-

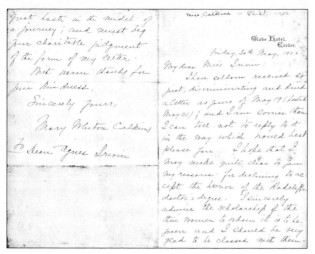

FIGURE 1–7 CALKINS AND WOMEN'S EDUCATION. In her letter of refusal to Dean Agnes Irwin of Radcliffe College, Calkins began: "I have seldom received so just discriminating and kind letter as yours of May 19 (posted May 21); and I am sorrier than I can tell not to reply to it in the way which would best please you. . . ." After stating her view of "the best ideals of education," she added: "You will be quick to see that holding this conviction, I cannot rightly take the easier course of accepting the degree" (H.U. Archives, May 30, 1932).

set of her career, she steadfastly resisted sexism (Figure 1–7).

ATTEMPT AT RECONCILIATION. Two years later, Calkins was elected to membership in the American Psychological Association (APA). This recognition was followed by considerable success in the field, including books and theoretical papers on the psychology of the self. In the process, she developed original experimental methods in the study of memory that are still employed today (Madigan & O'Hara, 1992).

A dozen years thereafter, she was awarded the highest honor in the American Psychological Association. She was elected to its presidency. In her inaugural address in 1905, she attempted to reconcile structural and functional psychology, using the concept of the self, or self-awareness, as the connecting link. The study of the self, she declared, is analyzable into basic elements, as the structuralists would have it, and it is also composed of complex relationships with the environment, social and physiological, which is the functionalists' perspective. In other words, the psychology of self-awareness requires both approaches, an understanding of the basic, structural elements and also a view of one's adjustment to the surroundings.

In Calkins's view, this focus on the self from two directions resolved the controversy: "It harmonizes the truth in the teachings of structural and of functional psychology" (Calkins, 1905).

CONTROVERSY AND SCIENCE. Controversy has played an important role throughout the history of psychology, and attempts to settle it are the basis of much research. Ideas are promoted; the debates begin; and investigations follow. Like the structural-functional dispute, many controversies are never clearly settled, but they serve to stimulate research activity.

While Mary Calkins sought to settle the structural-functional controversy in the United States, psychologists and newspapers in Berlin and America tried to resolve a smaller but more heated psychological question, the intelligence of Clever Hans. Finally, the newspapers invited Professor Carl Stumpf into the arena. As director of the Berlin Psychological Institute, he reluctantly agreed to study Clever Hans. For this purpose, he assembled 13 diverse but uniquely qualified citizens, ranging from schoolteachers to cavalry officers, promptly dubbed the Hans Commission. On September 12, 1904, after two days of questioning the horse in a very careful manner, with its owner sometimes present and sometimes absent, the commission announced its findings: It detected no tricks of any sort.

One disgruntled citizen insisted on another investigation. Someone should call the horse on the telephone (Block, 1904). Carl Stumpf also insisted on further study, this time without a committee of 13, which proved cumbersome. One or two well-trained investigators should be sufficient. Until that time, he was withholding judgment.

• SYSTEMS OF PSYCHOLOGY •

Particularly as seen in the efforts of Wundt and James, a new science often develops through competing theories and positions. Wundt's approach was extremely influential for a few decades, and then it disappeared rapidly as psychology developed different interests and methods.

When a certain broad perspective becomes prominent in psychology, it is often called a model or **system of psychology,** for it guides research and theory for many investigators. A system defines the field of inquiry for its advocates, identifying the problems to be studied and the methods to be used. A new system or model often develops in reaction to previous systems or is embedded in the

spirit of the times. It can attract a large group of adherents, especially if it is sufficiently open-ended to indicate all sorts of research questions for them to pursue (Kuhn, 1962).

Today there are distinctly different systems in psychology, just as there are different systems of religion, politics, economics, and other social institutions. No one perspective can embrace an entire field. Also, there are countless different theories. Somewhat smaller than a system, a **theory** is a set of principles with explanatory value. For example, psychoanalysis is a system of psychology; it offers a framework for approaching the whole field of psychology. Within psychoanalysis can be found a theory of dreams, a theory of neurosis, a theory of childhood sexuality, and so forth, all part of the larger system. Often the terms *systems* and *theories* are used interchangeably, for some theories are broad indeed. In the following discussion, the case of Clever Hans offers a basis for comparisons among five systems: the biological approach, psychoanalysis, behaviorism, humanistic psychology, and cognitive psychology.

BIOLOGICAL APPROACH

Wilhelm Wundt, the first person who, without reservation, could be called a psychologist, regarded the new field as physiological psychology. He considered psychology a descendant of physiology, although his interests and methods sometimes diverted him onto other paths. Even today, there is a tendency to emphasize the kinship of psychology with biology, occasionally to the detriment of psychology's independence and uniqueness (McPherson, 1992).

The basic premise in the **biological approach** is that behavior and experience are most usefully studied in terms of the underlying physical and biochemical structures. These are the mechanisms that

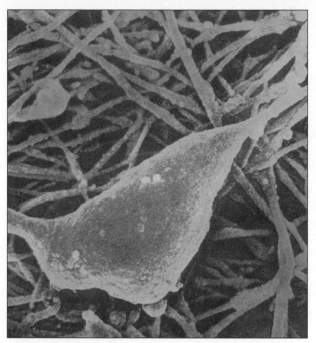

FIGURE 1–8 NEURAL STRUCTURES.
Enlarged many thousands of times, this photograph shows nerve cells in the human brain. Forming an exquisitely intricate network, they underlie the versatility of human behavior.

enable us to respond (Figure 1-8). All of our experiences and information from our own bodies, and all of our reactions to these experiences and sensations, can be studied in the context of brain structures, nerve impulses, genes, hormones, and so forth. Today there is considerable emphasis on neural mechanisms. Hence this approach is also known as *neurobehavioral psychology* or **neuropsychology,** recognizing the role of the nervous system, especially the central nervous system, in relation to behavior and experience.

In studying Clever Hans, the biological approach would focus on the physical structures of the animal and his master. Clever Hans read numbers and letters readily, even without moving his head. What characteristics of his eyes enabled the horse to do so? Hans tapped his answers in much the same way on each occasion, almost as a ritual. Which organs controlled this behavior? And most important, how was the horse able to think? Mr.

von Osten taught the horse. Which mechanisms played a role in this behavior? How did they function? These sorts of questions are prominent in the biological approach.

ORIGINS OF PSYCHOANALYSIS

Some scholars say that Sigmund Freud's psychoanalysis arose as a grand intellectual protest against the rigid social code in his Vienna. A remark by his father illustrates the attitudes of the day and his son's capacities: "My Sigmund's little toe is cleverer than my head, but he would never dare to contradict me!" (Wittels, in Jones, 1957).

Psychoanalysis first appeared late in the 19th century. According to Freud, his most important book was *The Interpretation of Dreams,* published in 1900. Many people therefore regard this date as the beginning of psychoanalysis, although psychoanalytic theory gained a truly international reputation in 1909, when Freud gave five introductory lectures in America (Patterson, 1990).

Freud's basic premise was that behavior can be influenced by events of which we are no longer aware. Wundt claimed that psychology should study conscious experience, but Freud described an unconscious realm, one that could be understood only by careful examination of childhood experiences. For this purpose, he introduced a new method of therapy, the "talking cure," in which the person reclined on a couch and expressed whatever thoughts came to mind. The term **psychoanalysis,** originating with Freud, refers to a theory of personality that focuses on unconscious childhood conflict and also to a method of therapy that attempts to relieve these early conflicts, still influential in the individual's life.

A more recent term, *psychodynamic approach,* is used in both of these ways. It is particularly applicable to modifications of Freud's work, especially

FIGURE 1–9 SIGMUND FREUD
(1856–1939). He is shown here a few years after his trip to the United States in 1909, which gave international recognition to his work. It also enabled him to see a wild porcupine, which he claimed was the second purpose of his trip. Smoking as many as 20 cigars per day, he died from cancer of the jaw.

those approaches that, while recognizing the significance of past conflict, give increased emphasis to the person's *present* social environment.

Freud's revolutionary theory soon developed into a whole system of psychological thought, including many distinct concepts. The most fundamental principle, **unconscious motivation,** states that human behavior is significantly influenced by childhood events of which the individual is no longer aware. Hidden in the deep recesses of the mind, they motivate adult behavior in disguised ways, often sexual or aggressive (Figure 1–9).

Although hardly applicable to Clever Hans, psychoanalysis might have been of value in studying the eccentric Mr. von Osten. What was his motivation for these lonely hours in that dusty courtyard? Why was he so completely consumed with this tedious, forbidding task, shunning the neighbors and all other human contacts? Did the answers lie in long-forgotten childhood experiences, leaving him fearful,

unable to enjoy the company of human beings? Such questions illustrate the psychoanalytic perspective.

The theory of psychoanalysis has been enormously controversial and highly influential in psychology, as well as in medicine, the social sciences, art, literature, and other fields today. Also, it has been modified and adapted since Freud's time (Pedder, 1990). Anyone interested in the ideas that make our modern world distinct from earlier ages must give serious consideration to the psychoanalytic approach.

RISE OF BEHAVIORISM

Somewhat later, another system of psychology arose as a protest against the study of consciousness as developed by Wundt. In simplest terms, the basic premise of early, radical **behaviorism** was that overt behavior is the only suitable topic for study in psychology. Psychologists must concern themselves exclusively with observable phenomena. The study of consciousness is wrong because it is subjective—known only by the experiencing individual. It exists only in someone's mind and cannot be verified by others.

As the leader of this protest movement in 1913, John B. Watson was a colorful, active personality, able to promote the new outlook in diverse ways—through research, a textbook, and the lecture platform. He argued that physicists study phenomena that any trained physicist can observe, not just privately but in common with others of this training. Likewise, biologists study what other biologists can observe. Watson urged psychologists to look outward, like natural scientists, rather than inside their skulls, and to study human beings as objects in nature.

Later, behaviorism acquired another controversial spokesperson, B. F. Skinner, known for his research with rats and pigeons and often misunderstood for his ideas on human learning

(Figure 1–10). He studied animals not to learn about them but to learn about the learning process. Animals are suitable, convenient subjects, especially when their background and environment can be controlled. Skinner continued the behavioristic emphasis on objectivity and stressed the ways in which behavior is developed and sustained by external events (Skinner, 1990). The appearance of food, a smile, or some other favorable event following a certain behavior increases the likelihood that the behavior will be repeated. Such events are called **reinforcement** because they strengthen the behavior that precedes them, increasing the likelihood that the behavior will reappear.

A traditional behaviorist studying Clever Hans or his trainer would focus on observable events, avoiding speculation on what might be happening

FIGURE 1–10 B. F. SKINNER (1904–1990). Even in the later years of his career, Skinner arose at 4:30 a.m., fresh and rested, and immediately resumed research and writing. Accomplishing most of his day's work by midmorning, he enjoyed classical music in the afternoons and evenings.

inside their skulls. In particular, the behaviorist would look for the reinforcements that kept both of these creatures at their seemingly impossible tasks. Mr. von Osten continued his instruction, the behaviorist would argue, because his efforts were reinforced. Step by step, Hans mastered one task, then another, and then another. Hans, in turn, kept on tapping because he received carrots or bread after each correct answer. In short, the behaviorist would emphasize that a system of reinforcement supported the persistent efforts of Wilhelm von Osten, his horse, and anyone else who happened to be involved in this enterprise.

The details of the behavioristic outlook are considered throughout this book, especially in connection with an approach to learning called *conditioning*. For now, it is sufficient to note that there are many behavioristic psychologists today and many opponents of this view, both inside and outside the field. Many modern behaviorists, furthermore, are more willing than Watson and Skinner to consider unobservables, including the workings of the mind (Rachlin, 1991).

❧ HUMANISTIC PSYCHOLOGY

Behaviorism was not the only protest movement. Humanistic psychology arose in the 1960s as a protest against both behaviorism and psychoanalysis. The emphasis in **humanistic psychology** is on the complexity, subjectivity, and capacity for growth of human beings, features often ignored in other systems. In this view, human beings are not ruled by the reinforcement principle in their daily behavior, as behaviorism would have it, and they are not exclusively controlled by deep inner forces dating to bygone years, as suggested in psychoanalysis. Instead, they have free will. They are an extraordinary species with capacities and awareness not found in other animals. Especially significant is the capacity for personal growth.

According to humanistic psychology, human beings must be studied as a unique development on the evolutionary scene, emphasizing the actualizing tendency. The **actualizing tendency** is a fundamental, inborn motivation for growth and fulfillment, arising because human beings, among all species, have a special capacity for controlling their own actions, making choices, and growing from their experiences. Choice is at the very center of human existence, responsible for humanity's greatest achievements—and its most penetrating moments of anxiety. This emphasis on choice and free will stands in marked contrast to the uncontrollable influences postulated in behaviorism and psychoanalysis. Led in this country by Carl Rogers and Abraham Maslow, the roots of this system are deep and diverse (Figure 1–11).

The concern in humanistic psychology is with conscious experience, meaning one's feelings at the present moment, not the unconscious and the past, as in psychoanalysis. And the most important viewpoint is that of the individual, not some particular system of psychology (De Carvalho, 1991). Many contemporary humanistic psychologists regard subjective reality as the only certain reality and therefore the proper topic of study in psychology. To understand a person's response, one must understand how that individual perceives the reality of that particular situation.

The humanistic psychologist would have had no research interest in the wonderful Berlin horse. Concerned with the special capacities and predicaments of human beings, it would not even focus on Mr. von Osten's rewards from training the horse, as in behaviorism, or on his childhood experiences, as in psychoanalysis. Both of these concerns lead in the wrong direction. Humanism instead would attempt to understand Mr. von Osten's thoughts and feelings at the moment, his capacity for making choices, and the ways in which the actualizing tendency was thwarted or enhanced. The human capacity to choose and make plans is a unique endowment, allowing us to select our own way of life. It is also a singular burden, causing anxiety about these choices.

The humanistic trend at times has been called *third-force psychology,* meaning that it represents the most significant system of psychology after behaviorism and psychoanalysis (Smith, 1990). But only history can confirm such a description.

FIGURE 1–11 CARL ROGERS (1902–1987). Raised in rural Minnesota without close friends, Rogers regarded himself as peculiar and a loner. In pursuing these personal issues and his career, he increasingly emphasized the forces of growth within human beings.

❧
COGNITIVE PSYCHOLOGY

Still another approach, the cognitive model, has been highly influential in American psychology in recent decades, despite its lack of a unifying theory. The basic concern in **cognitive psychology** is with mental processes; the focus is on perceiving, remembering, and thinking. Cognition is concerned with knowledge or understanding; cognitive psychology studies the mental processes by which we understand our world. It therefore stands in opposition to traditional behaviorism, which concentrates on overt acts rather than mental processes.

Modern cognitive psychology does not have a single, obvious leader in the sense that Freud promoted psychoanalysis and Skinner guided behaviorism. Nevertheless, a Swiss psychologist, Jean Piaget, became an early, inspirational figure in the study of human cognitive development. He began his academic career as a biologist with a special interest in birds and concluded it as a psychologist-philosopher, interested in the origins of knowledge (Figure 1–12). His pioneering studies of cognition in children have been regarded as lasting contributions to psychological theory (Hilgard, 1993).

Cognitive psychology has been stimulated by advances in computer technology and simulations of human thought, but it is broadly based. Today a guiding principle in cognitive psychology is the concept of **information processing,** which refers to the ways in which human beings and other species obtain, retain, and use information about their world. In the past quarter century, this approach has evolved into a sophisticated experimental science (Leahey, 1992).

Cognitive psychologists would approach Clever Hans as a set of problems in information processing. To what extent could Hans perceive the questions posed by his master? How successful was his memory? Could he actually manipulate symbols? And what about his master, who read the works of Charles Darwin and Annie Sullivan, teacher of Helen Keller? He had a great storehouse of information on horses, mathematics, evolution, and education, all intermixed. How did he retain it? Why did he sometimes become confused? Cognitive psychologists would study Hans and Mr. von Osten in

FIGURE 1–12 JEAN PIAGET (1896–1980). His first published article, on a rare albino sparrow, was well received. Piaget was pleased; he was only eleven years old at the time.

terms of the mental schemes or systems they employed in acquiring, storing, and using information.

Compared to the humanistic approach, cognitive psychology is more scientific and less philosophical. It differs from psychoanalysis in its greater concern with conscious mental life. And cognitive psychology, emphasizing mental processes, differs sharply from traditional behaviorism, which is concerned only with directly observable phenomena.

And here we arrive at the second principle in this book. Psychology is guided not only by empiricism but also by *various theories.* Psychology recognizes and encourages diverse interpretations of its observations. The human condition is far too complex to be encompassed by any single system or theory. Instead, each perspective makes its own special contribution (Table 1-1).

• DIVERSITY IN PSYCHOLOGY •

To satisfy the public and perhaps his own curiosity as well, Carl Stumpf selected two graduate students, Oskar Pfungst and Erich von Hornbostel, to make a more thorough investigation of Clever Hans. Still in his 20s, just beginning a career, Pfungst did not use any particular system of psychology. The different systems were just emerging at that time, and many psychologists today do not limit themselves to one or another.

After assuring themselves that Hans could indeed perform the tasks attributed to him, Pfungst and von Hornbostel turned to their first question. Did Clever Hans produce these answers *by himself?* In other words, they prepared to test the hypothesis that Clever Hans possessed a special intelligence.

This investigation illustrates a fundamental aim in contemporary psychology. Called **basic research,** it seeks to increase our understanding of the world in which we live. The goal is to find out about things. Did Clever Hans have a special mental ability? Can horses really see color? How do human beings think? Why do we forget? In basic research, the focus is on knowledge. Let there be light!

A second aim, called **applied psychology** or *applied research,* attempts to solve practical problems and improve conditions of life. The aim is to make things better for all. How can an understanding of Clever Hans improve the conditions of human life? Of animal life? What are the best ways to teach animals— and children? Applied psychology is concerned with the fruits of science. What is its practical value?

Thus science has a dual aim. Through it, we seek both light and fruit. "Most of us," observed Lord Adrian, "would like both if we can get them."

Today there are approximately 90,000 psychologists in the United States, seeking light or fruit or both. Their work is diverse, but most are employed in one of four settings: academic, medical, private practice, or business and government. The range of interests, abilities, and responsibilities among psy-

SYSTEM	EARLY LEADER	FOCUS
Biological	Wilhelm Wundt	All bodily mechanisms, especially the nervous system
Psychoanalysis	Sigmund Freud	Unconscious conflicts, dating from childhood, influencing adult life
Behaviorism	B. F. Skinner	Development of habits in all species, based on reinforcement
Humanistic	Carl Rogers	The actualizing tendency and capacity to choose a way of life
Cognitive	Several	Perceiving, remembering, thinking; information processing

TABLE 1–1 SYSTEMS OF PSYCHOLOGY

chologists is as broad as society itself. In fact, maintaining the unity of the field stands as a challenge for the whole discipline of psychology (Wand, 1993).

❧

BASIC RESEARCH

Psychologists in basic research obtain and disseminate psychological information. In this country, many of them are members of the American Psychological Association or a newer organization, the American Psychological Society (APS), devoted specifically to the advancement of psychology as a science (Bower, 1992). Psychologists from both organizations have conducted most of the investigations in the body of knowledge now called psychology.

FIELD EXPERIMENTS. When Pfungst and his assistant began work, their aim was pure research—to discover whether the horse truly had the abilities attributed to him. Thus they established two conditions and compared them. In one, called "with knowledge," the questioner always knew the answer to the problem presented to the horse, such as the number printed on a placard. And Hans answered with 98% success. In the other, called "without knowledge," the cards were scrambled face down. The questioner selected a card and, without looking at its other side, held up the card for the horse to tap the number. In these instances, Clever Hans began tapping, then faltered and stopped, tossed his head, and sometimes reared into the air. His overall success on these trials fell to 8%.

Next Pfungst tested Clever Hans in daylight and in darkness. Later he tested him in the open and behind a screen. By these comparisons, Pfungst determined that the correct answer did not come from the horse. Clever Hans knew nothing whatsoever of numbers, letters, coins, or musical tones. When denied a view of his questioner, Hans did not even know his own name.

In fact, Hans was responding to totally unintentional, very tiny visual cues. Exceedingly slight, these subtle signals had completely escaped even the careful scrutiny of the Hans Commission (Pfungst, 1911).

Each questioner, Pfungst discovered, bent forward ever so slightly after presenting the horse with a question and bent backward and upward ever so slightly when the correct tap was reached. Hans was simply responding to these minute visual cues, the start and stop signals. The chief explanation for the horse thus lay with the basic principles of behaviorism. A forward tilt of Mr. von Osten's head was the signal for Hans to start tapping, a backward tilt was the signal to stop, and a carrot or crust of bread was Hans's reward, or reinforcement, for doing so correctly.

In more general terms, Mr. von Osten's head movement was a **stimulus,** the Latin word for "spur," meaning that it initiates some activity. The resulting activity, or consequent event, is called a **response,** which was Clever Hans's tapping or the cessation of tapping. In much of psychology, including behaviorism, the aim is to understand stimulus–response relationships. The research problem is to discover which stimulating conditions lead to which responses.

So perceptive was Hans in noticing these signals, including head movements from side to side and slight turns in one direction or another, that he gave his name to this phenomenon. Communication through slight, unintentional, nonverbal cues is now called the **Clever Hans effect.** Prior to Pfungst's work, these cues had not been reported in scientific research. Yet they are recognized today as unconscious signals in posture, gesture, and vocal tone emitted by all of us in speaking our language (Ambady & Rosenthal, 1992; Scheflen, 1964).

The answer that was sought in the horse was found in his questioner—and in the careful training by Mr. von Osten. In this story of unconscious signaling, we must pin the tale on the horse's past.

If the horse's answer lay with his questioner, then how do we explain those celebrated moments when he proved superior to his human examiner? Further research showed that in these instances, two human errors occurred at the same time, one precisely compensating for the other. A flustered questioner had the wrong answer in mind and gave the signal for it at the wrong time, which was the right moment for the correct answer. These few coincidences greatly enhanced the horse's reputation, and eventually all of this research was reported in a book under the title *Clever Hans: The Horse of Mr. von Osten* (Pfungst, 1911).

LABORATORY INVESTIGATIONS. In one modern study of these unconscious cues, several people were asked to act out six different moods—anger, fear, indifference, seductivity, sadness, and happiness—each of which was videotaped. The tapes were shown to large audiences, who tried to identify the emotion being portrayed. Sometimes the actors were successful, but sometimes their emotional intentions were not at all in harmony with their behavior. One woman tried to display all six moods, but the judges in every instance decided she was angry. Another invariably impressed the judges as seductive, even when she tried to be indifferent. Imagine how difficult life must have been for both of these women if their behavior outside that contrived situation always suggested to others a mood they did not feel (Beier, 1974).

When verbal and nonverbal messages are inconsistent, the nonverbal communication may be closer to the true message. This outcome apparently arises because we can listen to our own words more readily than we can monitor our movements and vocal tones. Thus underlying thoughts and feelings are more likely to emerge in nonverbal ways (Ambady & Rosenthal, 1993).

A detailed analysis of 44 separate research studies showed that successful judgments of the honesty, competency, biases, and effectiveness of others can sometimes be made through very brief nonverbal cues, lasting no more than 30 seconds (Ambady & Rosenthal, 1993). To paraphrase Ralph Waldo Emerson: "What you are speaks so loudly I cannot hear what you say." Or, rather, I know all too well what you are *really* saying.

These laboratory and field studies give only the barest hint of their diversity. Psychologists in basic and applied areas possess markedly varied interests (Figure 1–13). The growth of all specialties during this century has been remarkable (Figure 1–14).

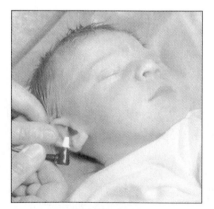

FIGURE 1–13 BASIC RESEARCH. People and animals are studied across the lifespan, as in this example of hearing. The infant's hearing is tested by inserting a probe into the ear. Dolphins are studied for their ability to maintain contact with one another by high-pitched cries, inaudible to the human ear. Among elderly people, hearing loss is studied to understand the effect of aging on the auditory mechanisms.

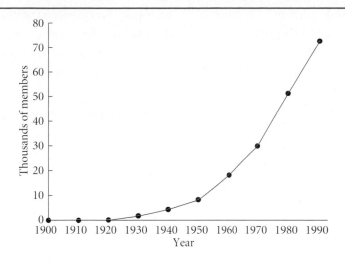

General Psychology	1	Community Psychology	27
Teaching of Psychology	2	Psychopharmacology & Substance Abuse	28
Experimental Psychology	3	Psychotherapy	29
Evaluation, Measurement, & Statistics	5	Psychological Hypnosis	30
Physiological & Comparative Psychology	6	State Association Affairs	31
Developmental Psychology	7	Humanistic Psychology	32
Personality & Social Psychology	8	Mental Retardation & Disabilities	33
Study of Social Issues	9	Population & Environmental Psychology	34
Psychology & The Arts	10	Psychology of Women	35
Clinical Psychology	12	Psychology of Religion	36
Consulting Psychology	13	Child, Youth & Family Services	37
Industrial & Organizational Psychology	14	Health Psychology	38
Educational Psychology	15	Psychoanalysis	39
School Psychology	16	Clinical Neuropsychology	40
Counseling Psychology	17	Psychology-Law Society	41
Public Service	18	Independent Practice	42
Military Psychology	19	Family Psychology	43
Adult Development & Aging	20	Lesbian & Gay Issues	44
Engineering Psychology	21	Ethnic Minority Issues	45
Rehabilitation Psychology	22	Media Psychology	46
Consumer Psychology	23	Exercise & Sport Psychology	47
Theoretical & Philosophical Psychology	24	Peace Psychology	48
Experimental Analysis of Behavior	25	Group Psychology & Psychotherapy	49
History of Psychology	26	Addiction	50

FIGURE 1–14 GROWTH OF PSYCHOLOGY. Since mid-century, membership in the American Psychological Association has increased sevenfold. Divisions of special interest have grown accordingly; there are no divisions numbered 4 or 11 (American Psychological Association, 1994).

APPLIED PSYCHOLOGY

The aim in applied psychology is to use psychological principles for the improvement of the human condition. For instance, our understanding of the Clever Hans effect has been usefully applied in a wide variety of situations: improving family relations, analyzing business negotiations, teaching human language to animals, and studying the cuing of subjects in a research setting (Sebeok, 1985). Most recently, it has proved useful in understanding the seemingly incredible performance of autistic children receiving instruction by means of electronic devices for word processing (Silliman, 1992).

A fuller understanding of applied psychology can be gained from specific examples. These range from peace psychology to sports psychology, from social issues to cultural differences. In recent years, *cultural psychology* has experienced a reemergence in national and international spheres as the need for greater cultural understanding has become increasingly obvious (Shweder & Sullivan, 1993). Among dozens of applied specialties currently recognized by the American Psychological Association, the following concern our environment, health, education, media, and law.

ENVIRONMENTAL PSYCHOLOGY. Among the many people today who pursue careers in environmental protection and maintenance, some have a background in psychology. This specialty, called **environmental psychology,** aims to design physical settings appropriate to successful human living, making them functional and comfortable in a mental, physical, and ecological sense (Stokols, 1992; Sundstrom, Bell, Busby, & Asmus, 1996).

The focus of environmental psychologists can be as specific as a bathroom appliance or as broad as a national forest. In the human-made environment, they work with architects and city planners; in the natural environment, they are involved with biologists and conservationists (Figure 1-15). This diverse employment shows that the traditional boundaries between various fields are becoming less and less distinct (Strathman, Baker, & Kost, 1991).

HEALTH PSYCHOLOGY. Some years ago, psychologists decided that heart disease is related to twentieth-century work habits, and they proposed to test this idea. Specifically, they hypothesized that heart attack was related to the *type A personality,* in which the individual's behavior is generally characterized by ambition, a sense of urgency, and rapid performance of tasks. People lacking in these behaviors were considered the *type B personality,* showing less ambition and only a minor concern with competition or deadlines. More than 250 employed men between the ages of 40 and 60 were identified in one early study, and after 8½ years, follow-up investigations showed that cardiovascular disease was significantly associated with type A

FIGURE 1–15 ENVIRONMENTAL PSYCHOLOGY. Psychologists in city planning distinguish between density, which is the number of people per unit of space, and crowding, which is a feeling of stress in the presence of others. The aim is to make life in high-density areas as comfortable as possible, partly by designing these areas to avoid the sense of crowding.

individuals. They had twice as many fatal heart attacks and five times as many heart problems as type B people (Rosenman et al., 1975). Some later studies confirmed this finding; others did not, pointing instead to the influence of smoking, eating habits, family history of heart disease, and underlying anger, more than ambition. Collectively, these studies show that the social and emotional components of heart disease are highly complex and interrelated. As they become more fully identified, the fundamental goal of prevention becomes more attainable (Strube, 1991b).

The specialty of **health psychology** concerns not only diagnosis, treatment, and prevention of illness but also the critical issue of health education. Heart disease and cancer, the two leading causes of death in the United States, are influenced by smoking, alcohol consumption, and obesity. These risks have been markedly reduced through the contributions of health psychology in changing the norms and attitudes toward risk-related behaviors (Levine, Toro, & Perkins, 1993). Known earlier as *medical psychology* and *behavioral medicine*, health psychology is rapidly becoming a worldwide enterprise (Kinoshita, 1990).

In the future, even humor may find its way into the domain of health psychology, both for prevention and treatment. Laughter decreases stress and also seems to play a role in recovery from disease, relieving symptoms and even diminishing pain. "There isn't much fun in medicine," Josh Billings joshed, "but there is a heck of a lot of medicine in fun."

Like physical exercise, laughter stimulates various internal organs through its vibrations and other movements. The huffing and puffing in a half minute of hearty laughter may even be the equivalent of that in three minutes of rowing (Fry, 1986). Especially among older people, unable to exercise and sometimes beset with unpleasantness, humor may be a matter of laugh or death (Goodman, 1994).

EDUCATIONAL PSYCHOLOGY. "Children are tyrants," one prominent educator has declared, thinking of the crisis in the schools. "They contradict their parents, gobble their food, and tyrannize their teachers." These words were spoken more than two thousand years ago by Socrates.

Subsequent centuries have not changed the view of many educators, who have made numerous suggestions for improvement: deregulate teaching, let students tutor one another, use experts as teachers, diversify the schools, and recognize individual learning styles (Satin, 1990). Among them, the approach that perhaps offers the best chance of encompassing the others is simple and demanding: Make classes smaller. Students in large classes do not receive the attention they need.

The specialty of **educational psychology** seeks to expand knowledge and concern about the teaching–learning process and to apply this knowledge in school and work settings. The focus is on improving instruction and curriculum at all levels, kindergarten through college, as well as in the workplace. Allied professionals in *school psychology* work directly with individual students, particularly those with special needs, usually at the primary and secondary levels.

MEDIA PSYCHOLOGY. Children begin to watch television before they are one year old. By age three they spend an average of four hours per day in this activity. Television is the child's early window to the world outside the home.

What do children learn from looking out this window? The average unrestricted viewer eventually receives more detailed information in how to commit assassination, burglary, and rape than in any other class of activities. By the teenage years, the typical American adolescent has observed several thousand violent assassinations on television. Meanwhile, the research linking television violence and aggressive behavior in viewers has become convincing. Media portrayals of violence influence *both* the attitudes and behavior of youth (Comstock & Strasburger, 1990; Dorr, 1986; Hoberman, 1990).

For children, *all* television is educational. The question is: What are we going to teach? Our great need is for a less violent, more cooperative world, and one way to achieve that society will be through appropriate media for children, especially children's television programs (Comstock & Paik, 1991). The aim of **media psychology** is to understand how electronic and printed information can be used for the public good.

LEGAL PSYCHOLOGY. Psychologists are also employed in diverse ways in the field of law. This work, called **legal psychology**, uses the science of human behavior to improve our system of laws, making them more humane and just. The idea is that a background in psychology can offer an empirical perspective that cannot be obtained through the study of law alone (Small, 1993).

The jury, for example, is often the core of the legal process, and yet it is composed of ordinary citizens unfamiliar with the law. Before each case, they receive standard instructions from the judge's handbook, phrased in legal jargon. How useful are these instructions?

In one instance, college undergraduates simulated jury members exposed to trial proceedings. One group received the standard legal instructions; another received instructions rewritten for greater juror comprehension; and still another group received no instructions. After the trial, all jury members completed a questionnaire based on the facts of the trial and on legal negligence, the issue on which the verdict was to be based. It was found that the decisions of the jurors receiving the rewritten instructions were most in agreement with the intent of the law. Regrettably, the jurors exposed to the standard instructions performed no better than those with no instructions at all (Elwork, Sales, & Alfini, 1977).

Given the existence of so many homeless people today, for example, there is a clear need to improve social institutions. Like all other fields, the law has numerous defects, depicted for centuries by poets and social philosophers. As Anatole France pointed out: "The law, in its majestic equality, forbids the rich as well as the poor to sleep under the bridges" (1894, *The Red Lily*).

These applications of psychology, ranging from law to the media, education, health, and so forth, together with the many areas of basic research, are just a few of the diverse interests in the field today. The numbers and endeavors of psychologists have increased precipitously since the beginning of this century.

❧

ETHICS AND PRINCIPLES

Attempts to understand human behavior have existed since earliest recorded history. Some of them are essentially naïve, as when people explain behavior by reliance on gossip, a fable, or some striking personal characteristic, such as the distance between a person's eyes, the size of the head, or the shape of the body. Mr. von Osten claimed that Hans was particularly intelligent because he had an unusually large forehead, even for a horse. He believed in *phrenology*, which states that a person's character and intelligence can be understood by examining the bumps and contours of the skull. This approach came to a bumpy end; it claimed too much, demonstrated too little, and was abandoned as a useful theory long before Mr. von Osten's day. "Bumpology" had no scientific validity.

How was it determined to be invalid? It was simply a matter of employing the scientific method. Phrenologists hypothesized that agreeableness lay in a bump high on the forehead, memory at the intermediate level, and language close to the eyes. Skeptical investigators tested these hypotheses with various people and found them to be false. Further tests replicated these results. Phrenology's downfall lay not just in the fact that its hypotheses were wrong—but also in the fact that they were testable. They could be *proved* wrong; they were falsifiable.

A theory or explanation that is **falsifiable** at least has the potential to be proved incorrect. It is not so broad and all-encompassing that it covers all possibilities or so vague that it cannot be tested. Some theories of astrology, using the stars, and numerology, using numbers, are not falsifiable. As scientific explanations, they have little value.

FRAUDULENT PRACTICES. It is one matter to adopt an incorrect theory or have an honest misunderstanding of established facts. It is quite another to misrepresent oneself intentionally as a psychologist or other expert, claiming a certain title or background. Unethical practices of this sort are considerably more common than one might expect.

In most states, clinical and counseling psychologists must be certified or licensed by law. The work of **clinical psychology** deals with maladjustment of all sorts, including the diagnosis and treatment of mental disorders. As a specialty within the field of psychology, it shares certain characteristics with *psychiatry,* a specialty within the field of medicine (Table 1–2). In contrast, **counseling psychology** deals with problems in the more normal range, such as vocational problems, adjustment to retirement, and school progress. People misrepresenting themselves as psychologists run the risk of legal penalties, but often they circumvent this legality by adopting some other professional-sounding title. At present, extensive public education seems to be the most promising approach to such problems.

FALSE CLAIMS. Fraud also occurs in manufacturers' claims for products and services, such as tapes for sleep learning, seminars for firewalking,

---

Psychology: the study of all forms of behavior, experience, and mental life.

Clinical psychology: the diagnosis, treatment, and prevention of mental disorders, often emphasizing insight therapy, behavior therapy, and research.

Medicine: the study and treatment of all forms of illness and disease.

Psychiatry: the diagnosis, treatment, and prevention of mental disorders, often emphasizing insight therapy and the prescription of drugs.

TABLE 1–2 CLINICAL PSYCHOLOGY AND PSYCHIATRY. A clinical psychologist earns a Ph.D. in psychology. A psychiatrist, trained in medicine, earns an M.D. Both are concerned with diverse problems of adjustment, offering similar services with somewhat different emphases.

---

and self-help subliminal messages. All of us would like to improve ourselves with little or no effort. Why not, for example, turn on a tape recorder and learn while asleep?

Several early studies of sleep learning produced promising results, and the mass media quickly publicized these claims. Later investigations showed an important shortcoming: The sleepers, who were supposed to be dozing on the job, were not fully asleep. Instead, they had been partially awakened by the recordings. In studies designed to correct this defect, the tape recordings remained on only when patterns of brain waves showed that the subjects were truly asleep. Under these conditions, the sleepers showed no evidence of learning (Emmons & Simon, 1956).

A recent confirmation of these findings showed no memory for lists of words presented during sleep. Partial recall sometimes occurred, but only when the presentation of words was followed immediately by arousal (Wood, Bootzin, Kihlstrom, & Schacter, 1992). One general conclusion remains from most research on topics of this sort: Self-improvement is typically proportional to the effort. Claims to the contrary, whether they concern subliminal messages or psychic secrets, are typically made by unethical people who profit from the false impressions of a gullible public (Moore, 1992).

FALLACY OF THE SINGLE CAUSE. A warning about simple solutions to complex problems is in order here. The **fallacy of the single cause** states that one condition or factor leads to one or more specific outcomes—for example: "Early to bed, early to rise makes a person healthy, wealthy, and wise." In fact, several factors besides one's habitual bedtime inevitably are involved in health, wealth, wisdom, and other conditions of life.

We can express this caution differently. Behind every complex problem there is one answer that is simple, efficient, attractive—and probably wrong. In the study of human behavior and experience, we need great respect for the complexity of the issues.

MULTIPLE BASES OF BEHAVIOR. This concept of multiple causation can be expressed in more positive terms. Known as the **multiple bases of behavior,** it states that behavior is typically influenced by many factors, both within and outside the individual, often in interaction with one another. It is assumed that there is an orderliness among these factors and that their number in any one instance is not infinite. Hence, they are potentially discoverable.

This emphasis on the multiple bases of behavior is the third and final principle in this book. Indeed, it is the *central* principle. Psychology as a field of study is guided by these three principles: empiricism, various theories, and a conviction in the multiple bases of behavior. This textbook describes the factors that seem most important in any given instance and, as far as possible, indicates how they have been identified. In fact, Clever Hans's ability to answer questions of all sorts, even

from spectators, demonstrates the multiple bases of behavior in three realms—physical, personal, and social.

The physical factor lay in the nature of his eyes. How did the *horse* notice the signals when all around him were human beings, their eyes darting hither and yon, unsuccessful in their efforts to find out what was happening? The answer is that Hans's eyes, much larger than ours, contained a larger retina, which was very well suited to the detection task that Mr. von Osten unintentionally had set for him. Like those of any horse, Hans's large eyes also were especially adapted to noticing sudden, slight movements, a vital capacity for wild horses escaping predators. Further, the location of Hans's eyes, one on each side of the head, allowed him to scrutinize the entire scene around him, almost 360 degrees, without moving his eyes or his head and thereby disclosing the direction of his gaze (Figure 1-16).

The personal factor lay in Mr. von Osten's preference for clothes, specifically his broad-brimmed hat. This headgear apparently brought to Hans's attention the slightest change in Mr. von Osten's posture. Any movement of the trainer's head was greatly magnified in the arc transcribed by the edge of his hat. This movement was obvious in the first stages of training, when Mr.

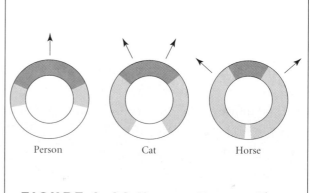

FIGURE 1–16 VISUAL FIELD. The light gray areas show monocular vision; the dark areas show binocular vision; and the arrows show the direction of normal gaze (Walls, 1942).

von Osten bent over to lift or touch Hans's hoof. It was still obvious when he bent forward and pointed. But it went unnoticed by all except the horse when Mr. von Osten, or anyone else, merely asked the question and thought of the correct answer. In certain respects, that hat was the thin thread by which hung this unusual tale (Fernald, 1984).

The social factor lay in the convention that most of us follow whenever we have finished asking a question: tipping the head forward unconsciously, ever so slightly. It is a signal learned from our elders, indicating that we expect a reply, after which we tip it backward again.

And at this point we follow another social convention, giving a tip of the hat to Mr. von Osten for his prodigious effort. He could lead his horse to water but he could not make him think, at least not in the human sense.

• SUMMARY •

HISTORICAL ANTECEDENTS

1. Psychology is defined as the scientific study of human and animal behavior, experience, and mental processes. It emerged as a clearly formulated science just a century ago, stimulated by: empiricism in philosophy, evolutionary biology, and experimental methods in physics and physiology. In addition, there were factors of practical significance, especially attempts to deal with behavior disorders.

2. There is no one scientific method, but the various stages in the scientific process are sometimes identified as forming hypotheses, testing hypotheses, and replicating the results.

FOUNDING OF PSYCHOLOGY

3. The founding of modern psychology is credited to Wilhelm Wundt, who established the first laboratory. He was interested in the study of feelings and sensations, and his students, intending to discover the structure of the mind, developed an early approach to psychology called structuralism.

4. William James, the early leader of American psychology, stimulated the new field by his creative writing and teaching. He inspired the broad development of psychology, emphasizing the functions rather than the structure of mental life, and therefore his approach was called functionalism.

5. Mary Calkins, a student of William James, founded an early laboratory and, through the concept of the self, attempted to resolve the differences between structuralism and functionalism. Amid these activities, she remained a significant advocate for improved educational opportunities for women.

SYSTEMS OF PSYCHOLOGY

6. There are different systems or models of psychology, one of which is the biological approach, based on the view that behavior can be most readily understood by examining neurons, hormones, genes, and other structures of the body. Underlying all behavior are the mechanisms that enable us to respond.

7. Another system, psychoanalysis, states that human behavior is influenced by past events in a person's life of which that individual is no longer aware. The basic concept is unconscious motivation; the basic concern is with childhood conflict.

8. In behaviorism, the emphasis is on an objective approach, stressing the study of overt behavior and its consequences in the environment. This system states that certain events in the environment, called reinforcement, strengthen or support the behavior that precedes them.

9. Another model, humanistic psychology, arose more recently in resistance to both behaviorism and psychoanalysis. Emphasizing humanity's unique capacity for growth and choice, as reflected in the

actualizing tendency, it states that the study of subjective reality in the present moment is the proper topic for psychology.

10. Still another system, cognitive psychology, focuses on the role of mental processes in human behavior, especially perceiving, remembering, and thinking. The chief aim is to understand information processing—the ways in which people obtain, retain, and utilize information about their world.

❧

DIVERSITY IN PSYCHOLOGY

11. There are two different aims in much of modern psychology. In basic research the aim is to increase our understanding of ourselves and the world in which we live. Research psychologists want to find out about human and animal behavior, experience, and mental processes.

12. Another aim in modern psychology is the betterment of humankind, to be achieved through practical applications of psychological knowledge. This approach, called applied psychology, includes many diverse specialties: environmental, health, educational, media, and legal psychology.

13. The central theme of this book, the multiple bases of behavior, states that a given response typically is influenced by a variety of factors. Psychology, as a field of study, is guided by three fundamental principles: empiricism, various theories, and a conviction in the multiple bases of behavior.

• WORKING WITH PSYCHOLOGY •

❧ REVIEW OF KEY CONCEPTS ❧

psychology

Historical Antecedents
empiricism
theory of evolution
science
scientific method
forming an hypothesis
testing the hypothesis
replicating the result

Founding of Psychology
structuralism
functionalism

Systems of Psychology
system of psychology

theory
biological approach
neuropsychology
psychoanalysis
unconscious motivation
behaviorism
reinforcement
humanistic psychology
actualizing tendency
cognitive psychology
information processing

Diversity in Psychology
basic research
applied psychology
stimulus
response

Clever Hans effect
environmental psychology
health psychology
educational psychology
media psychology
legal psychology
falsifiable
clinical psychology
counseling psychology
fallacy of the single cause
multiple bases of behavior

❧ CLASS DISCUSSION/CRITICAL THINKING ❧

A NARRATIVE TWIST
Mr. von Osten's broad-brimmed hat signaled to the horse the slightest movements of the man's head. Suppose the retired schoolmaster had never worn such a hat. Would we know today about the effect named for Clever Hans? If so, how might we have learned about it and what might the effect be called? If not, why not? Defend your answer by citing your own ideas and, if possible, relevant information from the text. ❧

• *Historical Antecedents.* Should the real beginnings of psychology be attributed to the musings of Aristotle on the nature of the soul or to developments in evolutionary biology in the nineteenth century? Explain the reasons for your answer.

• *Founding of Psychology.* What might be some differences between a structuralist's and functionalist's commentary on a baseball game?

• *Systems of Psychology.* Would a person charged with assaulting an abusive spouse want a jury of behaviorists, psychoanalysts, or humanists? Why?

• *Diversity in Psychology.* Describe some specific problem on which psychologists might well work with physicians, lawyers, or educators to improve the public welfare. Focus on joint problem solving rather than on solutions.

❧ TOPICS OF RELATED INTEREST ❧

The major systems of psychology are discussed in several chapters of this book. The biological approach is considered under the biological foundations of behavior (3); psychoanalysis appears in the discussions of memory (8), personality (14), and therapy (16); behaviorism is discussed in the context of conditioning (7), as well as in personality (14) and therapy (16); humanistic psychology appears in personality (14) and therapy (16); and cognitive psychology is the basic perspective in perception (5), memory (8), and thought and language (9).

NATURALISTIC OBSERVATION
Types of Observation
Uses and Cautions

SURVEY METHOD
Use of Questionnaires
Sampling Procedures
Unobtrusive Measures

CASE STUDY
Interviews and Tests
Case History

EXPERIMENTAL METHOD
Classical Experiment
Design of Experiments
Multifactor Studies

RESEARCH IN PERSPECTIVE
Research Ethics
Comparison of Methods

2
RESEARCH METHODS

IN HIGH SCHOOL, THEY CALLED HIM SMART STANLEY. HE READ THE *NEW YORK TIMES,* EDITED THE SCIENCE MAGAZINE, AND KNEW THE ANSWERS TO QUESTIONS THAT PUZzled his classmates.

A lean teenager full of ambition, he was intellectual more than social. Early in life, he began to study questions for which there were no answers (Zimbardo, 1992).

Growing up in New York City, Stanley Milgram was a city person. He loved cities. He observed the movement of crowds, behavior of bystanders, and reactions of strangers. He marveled at the coordination among millions of city dwellers as they read the morning newspapers simultaneously, walked the streets together, and arrived at places on time, all in a relatively confined area. He watched people compete for seats on the subway, positions in waiting lines, machines at the laundromat and, of course, parking spaces.

Growing up during World War II, Milgram was deeply concerned about human aggression, grieving over the destruction of millions of people in Nazi concentration camps. At age 16, just three years after the war, he demonstrated his concern, as well as his capacity for finding out about things. He published his first research article, describing the effects of radiation from the atomic bomb. "It was as easy as breathing," he said of his research. "I tried to understand how everything worked" (Milgram, 1992).

Afterward, Milgram became a part-time photographer, amateur songwriter, inventor of gadgets, and finally a social psychologist. Observing people became his life's work. No matter where he traveled, he used his inquiring mind and roving eye, the tools of his trade. He studied people on the sidewalks, in the streets, and at cafes, as well as in the laboratory. People in any context could serve as his subjects.

In planning an investigation, Milgram sought direct, simple procedures, approaching research as an excursion into the unknown. "It is tentative, indeterminate, something that may fail," he said. It might yield only a confirmation of the obvious, reflecting what we think we already know through common sense. Or it might yield highly significant, unexpected insights (Milgram, 1992).

For two reasons, important research findings in psychology are often considered common sense. First, we are all amateur psychologists more than

we are amateur physicists, chemists, or biologists because psychological issues—our personal relations, individual achievements, emotional experiences, and so forth—are generally more important to us than are the impersonal elements of our environment. Second, common sense supplies several answers for most psychological questions. In most situations, almost any human reaction is conceivable. Thus, the task for scientific psychology is to determine which common sense beliefs are relevant, which are not, and to reconcile contradictions among them. Common sense is *sometimes* supported by research (Kelley, 1992).

This chapter concerns the ways in which psychologists conduct research, showing how they collect or gather information. Specifically, it describes four basic methods: naturalistic observation, the survey method, case study, and the experimental method. As noted in the closing discussion on research in perspective, each of them makes its own special contribution. This chapter does not include the so-called correlational approach, which is *not* a method for collecting information. It is a later phase of the research process, a statistical procedure for analyzing and interpreting information after it has been gathered. Correlation is therefore considered briefly at the end of this chapter and extensively in a later chapter on statistics.

• NATURALISTIC OBSERVATION •

In **naturalistic observation,** the most basic of the four methods, the aim is to study behavior in its usual setting, without asking the subjects any questions or administering any tests. The investigator simply observes and records what happens in the natural environment. For this reason, naturalistic observation is often the first step in a research program.

Each morning for several years, Milgram awaited the commuter train to New York City, and there he observed the same people at the same time, standing in the same places every day. Yet they almost *never* spoke to each other. Fellow commuters, he decided, are like trees, posts, and billboards—regarded as scenery, not as people with whom to talk and exchange greetings. Milgram called these people *familiar strangers,* for they encountered each other daily but never introduced themselves. Instead, they stood in clusters, back to back, staring straight ahead. "I found a particular tension in this situation," he confessed (Milgram, 1992).

TYPES OF OBSERVATION

The basic technique in naturalistic observation is to be a very careful observer. As an eager tourist noted: "You can observe an awful lot just by watching." Yet there are important decisions to be made and subtle procedures to be followed. Among these, the most basic is whether to acknowledge or disguise the research purpose.

OVERT OBSERVATION. In overt observation, the subjects are aware that they are being studied; the research purpose is acknowledged. Milgram sometimes studied familiar strangers by taking photographs of people at train stations, later showing them to commuters, and then asking them whom they recognized. From their responses, he determined that the typical commuter encountered four or five familiar strangers at the station compared with only one or two speaking acquaintances.

Milgram's finding gave a specific, quantified answer. The average New York City commuter had 4.5 familiar strangers in his or her life. As Milgram explained, city people must discourage many potential relationships. "If you live on a country road, you can say hello to each of the occasional persons who passes by; you can't do this on Fifth Avenue" (Milgram, 1992).

But the focal point here is that these commuters knew they were being observed and photographed. Milgram and the other researchers even stated their purpose. Hence, this investigation was an instance of overt observation.

Overt observation may not influence subjects at some distance or subjects who are sleeping, for example, but in other instances this research procedure could be disruptive. Commuters might alter their behavior to impress the observer, or they might avoid the observer, taking a different train. To deal with this problem, the investigator might spend time helping them become accustomed to his or her presence and the research procedure. After the subjects seem to be behaving naturally once again, the actual research begins.

From these observations, Milgram drew a conclusion about familiar strangers. When making a small request, such as asking the time of day, a person is more likely to ask a complete stranger than a familiar stranger—someone never spoken to but seen regularly for years. "Each of you is aware that a history of noncommunication exists between you," he said, "and both of you have accepted this as the normal state." Requesting even a small favor would disrupt this well-established, tacit agreement (Milgram, 1992).

COVERT OBSERVATION. To ensure that the subjects behave in a natural manner, the investigator sometimes uses **covert observation,** in which the individuals being studied do not know they are part of a research project. The investigator can mingle openly with the subjects and then make notes secretly or remain hidden in some way. Of course, this effort to hide one's work may restrict the range of observation.

A question of research ethics emerges immediately. To what extent is a researcher justified in secretly studying commuters, coworkers, or even neighbors? The answer is complex, but it depends on the way in which the unsuspecting individuals are involved, the extent to which they may be affected, whether recordings are made, and so forth. We shall return later to this issue, noting in passing

that even overt observation raises questions about subjects' rights (Pope & Vetter, 1992).

Both methods, overt and covert, are used with animals. Field studies have stimulated much interest in chimpanzees, owing partly to certain similarities to human beings (Figure 2–1). Of course, the most celebrated naturalistic studies are those of Charles Darwin, whose trip aboard the *Beagle* enabled him to make observations of plants and animals around the globe.

◆

USES AND CAUTIONS

Naturalistic observation serves two purposes. It provides an excellent description of certain phenomena, and it can be a rich source of hypotheses. As one investigator commented: "I find that during

FIGURE 2–1 OBSERVATION OF ANIMALS. Dian Fossey conducted extensive studies of wild gorillas in the mountains of Rwanda, Africa. Spending months at the edge of their territory, until they were comfortable in her presence, she gained their confidence by imitating their vocalizations and adopting a submissive posture. Ultimately, she assembled a large mass of information on gorilla habits and characteristics. She found, in fact, that individual adult gorillas possessed quite distinctive personalities (Fossey, 1983).

the long hours of observation in the field, I not only learn about behavior patterns, but I get ideas, 'hunches,' for theories, which I later test by experiments whenever possible" (Tinbergen, 1965).

There is a drawback, however. Naturalistic observation is not notably useful as a source of explanation. It does not identify cause-and-effect relations with any certainty. These must be examined in a more controlled setting, typically with the experimental method. In the study of memory, for example, there has been recent debate over the most fruitful approach, some urging naturalistic observations, others advocating controlled laboratory conditions. This difference of opinion is partly resolved when naturalistic observation is regarded as a good starting point for research but not as a substitute for controlled experiments to reveal the underlying causal factors (Roediger, 1991).

Even as a starting point, the process of naturalistic observation is not as simple and straightforward as it may seem. It presents the investigator with some difficult questions and the constant problem of bias.

QUESTION OF PARTICIPATION. Some years ago, a small religious group in Chicago believed that the world would be destroyed by a series of floods and earthquakes on December 21. They would be saved by flying saucers, they decided, if they followed appropriate rituals, such as removing all metal from their clothing, remaining indoors, and reading the sacred writings. A team of psychologists and sociologists wanted to study them, but the cult did not permit outsiders to observe its activities. Thus, the investigators used their only recourse: They became cult members. Their research method was **participant observation,** in which an investigator joins the people being studied and takes part in their activities, living with them for an extended period, if necessary.

These investigators used *covert* participant observation out of necessity. If they had used *overt*

participant observation, they would have been banished from the premises as disbelievers. If they had not participated, they would not have gained access to the group's activities. They knew their mere presence in the group would tacitly support the members' convictions about world destruction, but there was no alternative.

Our interest here lies in research methods, not the findings, but in passing the reader will be relieved to learn that the world was not destroyed on that December day. And the faith of the cult members was not destroyed either. On December 22 and 23, after some doubt, delay, and debate, the members decided that their Creator had not destroyed the world precisely *because* they had maintained their faith in the face of skepticism from others. Their unwavering loyalty had saved the whole world from destruction (Festinger, Reicken, & Schachter, 1956).

As a rule, researchers do not engage in the daily activities of their subjects. They generally remain apart from the people they are observing, a research procedure called **nonparticipant observation.** Stanley Milgram once observed crowds of pedestrians from a sixth-floor window. These people did not know they were being studied, and Milgram did not participate in their activities. His method was *covert* nonparticipant observation. Later, he stood in the street and openly made notes about the pedestrians: *overt* nonparticipant observation.

PROBLEM OF BIAS. Recognizing several difficulties in naturalistic observation, William James stated that exact procedures for observation could not be established in advance. Rather, he advised the observer: "Use as much sagacity as you possess." He also warned of the great sources of error in this method, especially the intrusions of personal bias (James, 1890).

A **bias** is a preference or inclination that

	ACTIVITY	
	PARTICIPANT	NONPARTICIPANT
OVERT	Waiting with other commuters, taking notes obviously	Standing aside from commuters, taking notes obviously
COVERT	Waiting with other commuters, taking notes secretly	Hiding from commuters, taking notes secretly

DISCLOSURE

TABLE 2–1 TYPES OF OBSERVATION. Two decisions, overt or covert, and participant or nonparticipant, yield four research strategies. The chief issues are ease of observation and disruption of the subjects' behavior.

inhibits objective observation. It results in an inaccurate judgment. A man who is suspicious of people may make biased judgments about strangers. One method for dealing with this problem is to use several observers, assuming their biases are randomly distributed. Another is to train observers carefully. Still another involves the use of remote recording equipment (Pepler & Craig, 1995).

Concerned about this problem, Stanley Milgram had his city observers work in pairs. Sometimes a newcomer and a long-term resident toured the area together, walking side by side down the street, but they made their recordings separately. This way, Milgram had a check or verification on what had taken place, for he believed that the long-term resident, while sensitive to nuances, might have the habit of tuning out many events noticed by the newcomer. City life perhaps required that sort of adaptation (Milgram, 1992).

Using naturalistic observation, Milgram identified the phenomenon of familiar strangers and other habits of city dwellers. But he could not, through observation alone, determine the underlying causal factors. And he typically could not study significant moral issues in detail (Table 2–1).

• SURVEY METHOD •

A research psychologist collecting information may intrude beyond naturalistic observation. Usually the next step is to ask questions. What do you think about this? Why do you do that? When many people are questioned, often by mail, telephone, or in a large group, the procedure is called the **survey method,** which has the advantage of including a large number of subjects.

The origins of this method are usually credited to two illustrious English cousins, Charles Darwin and Sir Francis Galton, the latter well known for his practical discoveries in testing the sensory abilities of human beings and animals. Here, too, William James had a warning: "Messrs. Darwin and Galton have set the example of circulars of questions sent out by the hundreds to those supposed able to reply. The custom has spread, and it will be well for us in the next generation if such circulars be not ranked among the common pests of life" (James, 1890).

∾

USE OF QUESTIONNAIRES

In addition to his studies of conformity among commuters, Milgram's curiosity turned to questions of obedience, and he began giving lectures on this topic. In some lectures, he described a hypothetical situation that involved taking orders for administering electrical shocks to another person. Following the lecture, he employed the survey method with the audience. He wanted to find out what the members thought they would do in that situation. Under orders, how much punishment would they administer to a person who constantly made mistakes in learning a certain task? Here Milgram was asking: What does common sense tell you?

This method of collecting information of course depends heavily on the questions that are asked. A **questionnaire** is a printed form with questions of all sorts, often administered by mail or telephone, sometimes in a direct interview. It is intended to be answered by many people. Some questionnaires are simply a list of reminders to be checked as applicable or not.

TYPES OF ITEMS. These questions or reminders can vary from highly specific to broad and vague. Milgram's questions were specific, for people were asked to indicate how long they would follow orders—that is, how much shock they would administer to someone, under the condition that the strength of the shock would be increased by 15 volts each time the learner performed incorrectly. An exact answer was requested, using a numerical scale on the questionnaire.

In a survey on dental care, specific questions might include: "How many times per day do you clean your teeth?" and "Do you brush with a vertical, horizontal, or circular motion—or with more than one motion?" Each of these is a *structured item*, for there is little leeway in answering. Or the question might be an *open-ended item*, which can be answered in a wide variety of ways, such as: "What is your approach to dental care?" On an open-ended item, people are more likely to reveal what is important to them, but they may include endless details of no significant value. In either case, variations in the wording of the item may substantially influence the response (Table 2–2).

DEVELOPING NORMS. When Milgram administered his questionnaire to college students in New Haven, Connecticut, most of them stated that they would refuse to give any punishment stronger than 150 volts. Middle-class adults and psychiatrists responded the same way. All people in all groups indicated that they would disobey the orders eventually. None would administer the full shock of 450 volts; in fact, no one would proceed beyond 300 volts.

These results can serve as norms, for they are the responses from a large number of subjects. In short, **norms** show how people perform, indicating what is common and rare in a given population. Norms provide a means for interpreting a person's results. We can compare the response of that subject with those of the group to find out whether that subject's response is highly typical, somewhat typical, or rather deviant. Usually, a person's response is most

YEAR	DESCRIPTIVE PHRASE	LABEL
	"HALT RISING CRIME RATE"	"LAW ENFORCEMENT"
1984	69.3%	56.5%
1985	67.3%	57.8%
1986	66.8%	52.9%
	"ASSISTANCE TO THE POOR"	"WELFARE"
1984	64.1%	25.2%
1985	65.2%	19.8%
1986	62.8%	23.1%

TABLE 2–2 WORDING OF QUESTIONNAIRES. During a three-year period, a descriptive phrase *or* a label was used to ask opinions about government spending on law enforcement and welfare. For both topics in all three years, the descriptive phrase generated more public support than the label (Rasinski, 1989).

appropriately evaluated with the norms for his or her age, sex, economic status, and so forth.

❧

SAMPLING PROCEDURES

A critical issue in the survey method is the people asked to respond. These people are typically called a **sample,** which is a number of subjects drawn from some larger group. This larger group, known as the **population,** includes all the people, objects, or events in a particular class. It might be all students in a certain college, as defined by the registrar's office; the general population of the United States, as defined by the census; or all red marbles in a certain toy store, as defined by a count of all the marbles in stock. When any sample accurately reflects the characteristics of a certain population, it is called a **representative sample.** It includes appropriate proportions of tall students, sophomores, men, and so forth, in comparison with the college population.

RANDOM SAMPLING. The most common means of obtaining a representative sample is to develop a **random sample,** in which each subject in the population has the same chance of being included. To obtain a random sample of 20 students, for example, each student in the college is designated by a different number. Then 20 numbers are selected by random drawings or random-digit dialing on the telephone.

While there are other methods, random sampling is the basic procedure for obtaining a representative sample. In fact, randomization is a fundamental principle in any research, from naturalistic observation to the experimental method. As any sample is increased in size, the influence of chance factors generally becomes less. In other words, a large random sample is more likely to be representative of the population than is a small one.

INCIDENTAL SAMPLE. In predicting the outcome of an election or testing a new drug, a representative sample is indispensable. The investigator must know the extent to which the sample reflects the population. In the early phases of some research, however, or if individual differences are not important, the investigator may use an **incidental sample,** which includes anyone who happens to be available and willing to respond. It is for this reason that so much psychological research is based on college sophomores and white rats. An incidental sample is relatively easy to obtain; the danger lies in the conclusions drawn from such a sample.

In administering his questionnaire at his lectures, Milgram obtained incidental samples. Anyone who came to a lecture could complete the questionnaire. To ensure representative samples in other instances, he used a telephone book and city records for the general population of New Haven, culling thousands of names and addresses by random methods.

Even when the sample is representative, some people do not return the questionnaire or refuse to give an interview. Unless adequate substitutes are found, these situations may produce a *nonresponse bias,* in which the findings are invalid or biased due to the lack of returns from the full sample. The people who fail to respond may be against the whole issue, or they may simply have different reactions than those who do reply. These difficulties have prompted considerable research aimed at improving the survey method (Dillman, 1991).

❧

UNOBTRUSIVE MEASURES

Besides the sampling question, there is also the problem of reliability. The investigator cannot be certain that all subjects have responded honestly and carefully to all of the questions. The results merely show what people *say* about their dreams, cereals, sex life, or electric shocks, not what they actually *do.*

In thinking about his questionnaire results, Milgram was impressed by the extent to which college students, psychiatrists, and middle-class adults all said they would disobey orders. They would not administer the highest shock available or even a dangerous shock. "But," Milgram noted, "they show little insight into the web of forces that operate in a real social situation" (Milgram, 1992).

TYPES OF UNOBTRUSIVE MEASURES. Subjects in survey research may try to please the investigator, present themselves in a favorable manner, or complete the task as soon as possible. This problem is called the *guinea pig effect,* meaning that the subjects know they are "guinea pigs"—participants in a research situation. To deal with this problem, survey researchers sometimes employ unobtrusive measures, rather than questionnaires. In **unobtrusive measures,** the investigator collects information from people without disturbing them in any significant way—and without even observing them directly. The subjects do not know they have been included in a research project. The investigator simply examines the traces of their behavior.

For example, some unobtrusive procedures are called *erosion measures,* for they indicate the ways in which people use and wear out the environment. In a library, the dirty, wrinkled, and torn pages tell a story. Those magazines are used. Clean pages and stiff bindings give a very different impression. Investigators also use *accretion measures,* examining the materials people leave behind in corridors and restrooms, such as wrappers, graffiti, and empty bottles and cans. In short, our refuse can be revealing (Figure 2–2).

The use of *archival data* offers still another unobtrusive measure, for an investigator can consult institutional files for all sorts of information, ranging from births and marriages to thefts and accidents. Retrieving this information is unobtrusive, although

FIGURE 2–2 ACCRETION MEASURES.
An observer might make hypotheses about the background and interests of people who read and post notices on this bulletin board.

the process of obtaining it originally perhaps was quite intrusive for the subjects, as when the census taker appeared at the front door. Institutional files have been used, for example, to study the outcome of legal proceedings and techniques of control with disruptive children (Himelein, Nietzel, & Dillehay, 1991; Skiba & Raison, 1990).

The use of unobtrusive measures stands somewhere between naturalistic observation and the survey. It is not traditional naturalistic observation, for the behavior is never observed. It is not a traditional survey either, for the subjects do not know that they have participated in research. Except for the archival method, it offers little information on the people who serve as subjects.

USING UNOBTRUSIVE MEASURES. Bothered by the guinea pig effect with questionnaires, Milgram employed an unobtrusive measure known as the *lost-letter technique,* in which many letters are distributed throughout a city, stamped and addressed but unposted. Anyone who finds one must decide what to do. Mail it? Destroy it? Ignore it? By varying the addresses on the envelopes and calculating the proportion mailed, this survey technique can be used to measure attitudes toward the addressees (Milgram, 1992).

In one instance, Milgram distributed 400 letters in parking lots, streets, shops, and phone booths throughout the city of New Haven. Each letter was addressed to a medical research group, a private individual, or the Communist or Nazi party. Each envelope was coded and sealed in a manner to indicate later where it had been dropped and whether it had been opened. For most Americans, common sense would have predicted that the letters addressed to the Nazi and Communist parties would be least often mailed and most often opened. Milgram's returns showed these results (Milgram, 1992; Table 2–3).

The use of this unobtrusive measure is not as simple as it may seem. First, all letters must be "lost" separately, requiring hundreds of different locations. Milgram once tried dropping them from an airplane, and many never reached a proper destination, landing instead on roofs and in trees. He tried throwing them from cars, only to have many fall in the gutters or be blown away. Moreover, the letters were sometimes found by people who did not read the address—children, illiterates, street cleaners, and some college sophomores.

Second, the method is not useful for asking subtle questions. The finder simply shows an overall attitude, favorable or unfavorable, by mailing or not mailing the letter. This technique is appropriate for measuring positions on either-or questions, such as the abortion issue and sexual orientation (Kunz & Fernquist, 1989; Levinson, Pesina, & Rienzi, 1993). It is not suitable for determining *why* people take one stand or the other.

Milgram was much impressed by the extent to which people mailed the letters, even though no letter contained any such request. These results showed a widespread compliance with an unstated invitation—far greater than he might have anticipated. But again, he could not, through the survey method alone, determine the underlying causal factors. Then he thought again about his questionnaire on electric shocks. When confronted with the actual situation, would these people disobey the order?

• CASE STUDY •

Those answering Milgram's questionnaire said they would refuse to punish the learner. They also believed that other people would disobey. Most people reject unnecessary pain and therefore would not follow brutal orders. The responses of college students, psychiatrists, and middle-class adults all predicted that only 1% or 2% of the general population would obey such orders fully, administering the highest shock available.

In pursuing this question further, we turn to a line of inquiry quite different from naturalistic observation and the survey. It takes place not only in clinics and hospitals but also in businesses, schools, and a wide range of other institutions. Called the **case study,** or the *clinical approach* due to its origin in hospitals and clinics, it refers to diverse psychological techniques carried out with the aim of examining a specific person, group of people, or event in considerable detail.

ADDRESSEE	TOTAL
Medical Research Associates	72
Mr. Walter Carnap	71
Communist Party	25
Friends of the Nazi Party	25

TABLE 2–3 RETURN OF "LOST" LETTERS Letters to the Communist and Nazi parties were least mailed and most often opened: 40% and 32%, respectively (Milgram, 1992).

The case study may concern almost anyone or anything—a religious group, dangerous expedition, or the mayor's office. While it commonly focuses on a problem of personal adjustment, it provides an opportunity to examine relevant factors in the widest possible context (Bromley, 1990).

These procedures for collecting psychological information show two distinct differences from the other research methods. First, the study of the individual plays a more central role. In fact, the case study is sometimes erroneously thought to be concerned exclusively with the individual. Second, this approach usually involves more direct contact with the subjects, as readily reflected in the chief procedures: interviews, psychological tests, and case histories.

INTERVIEWS AND TESTS

In Milgram's research, a woman given the pseudonym Gretchen Brandt was particularly memorable during two long interviews, partly because she spoke with a thick German accent. She had immigrated to the United States several years earlier, but even at age 26 her pronunciation of English often made her words unintelligible.

INTERVIEW PROCESS. Perhaps the most fundamental technique in the case study, the *interview* is a conversation between two people, variously called the *counselor* and *client, interviewer* and *interviewee,* or *therapist* and *patient.* In various ways, the counselor aims to assist the client with some personal problem. In thinking of the interview, we should never overlook the power of words—not only to express our own thoughts and feelings but also to learn about other people and even to influence them. Words, observed Rudyard Kipling, are the most powerful drug used by humanity.

When Milgram interviewed Gretchen Brandt, she showed no signs of tension either by what she said or what she did, such as fidgeting, shifting her position, averting her gaze, or attempting to with-

draw from the interview. She spoke of herself only when asked directly and did so in a firm, simple manner, without stammering or making unwarranted claims or irrelevant comments. She said she was not tense or nervous in any way, and her appearance corresponded well to this claim.

Another interviewee, Morris Braverman, proved to be quite different. Under the same circumstances, his brow furrowed constantly, suggesting that he carried with him many burdens. Throughout most of the interview, he behaved in a carefully controlled, serious fashion. In moments of tension, however, he began to snicker, then laugh, and then wheeze with uncontrollable laughter. At one point, he became visibly agitated trying to stifle his nervous laughter. Almost the same age as Gretchen Brandt, he seemed a great deal older because of his lined face and typically serious manner (Milgram, 1974).

As these descriptions indicate, people in interviews communicate not only with words but also by their actions. The skillful, experienced interviewer uses all available evidence in reaching conclusions based on this method.

PSYCHOLOGICAL TESTS. Perhaps the best-known devices in psychology are psychological tests. For many, they should be classified with taxes, traffic lights, and television, unwanted by-products of an advanced society. For others, they are simply an additional means of gathering information about someone, helping that individual to find his or her most appropriate place in our highly complex society. We shall return to this controversy in later discussions of intelligence.

The reader is undoubtedly familiar with **group tests,** also called *pencil-and-paper tests,* which are administered to many people simultaneously and scored by machine. Each answer is indicated by selecting one of three or four choices and marking it on the printed form.

Most group tests have two significant limitations. The first concerns the test questions, which examinees must read and answer without individual attention from the test administrator. These questions are largely *verbal items,* placing heavy emphasis on the ability to use words, which does not always reflect an individual's personal characteristics or mental ability. In fact, it may simply indicate the person's subculture (Table 2–4). Second, the test administrator cannot be sure that each subject understands the instructions, has suitable motivation, and is in a proper condition to take the test. Such problems can lead to spuriously low test scores.

There is a simple rule for interpreting the results of group tests. High scores probably represent a high level of the trait in question. Low scores do not necessarily indicate a low level. For various reasons, a person may perform far below his or her true capacity.

Less familiar are the **individual tests,** administered to one person at a time. These include inkblots and ambiguous pictures, as well as the more traditional questions. A highly trained examiner observes as the subject responds by speaking or by some other overt actions, rather than by writing. On *nonverbal items,* which do not require the use of words, the subject manipulates puzzles, blocks, and pictures, an approach that can be used to test people with language deficits (Figure 2–3).

Which person has not become an eponym?
    Achilles
    Charles Darwin
    Earl of Sandwich
    Puskas

TABLE 2–4 VERBAL TEST ITEM. To answer this test item, a person must know the meaning of the word *eponym* and possess a background in Western history and culture.

Answer: An eponym is someone whose name is given to something. The tendon connecting the heel bone to the calf muscle is named for Achilles, a hero in Greek mythology; Darwin's name has been given to the evolutionary approach in biology; and the Earl's name is attached to what we now call the sandwich. Puskas, a former Spanish soccer player, is not an eponym.

The advantages of individual tests reflect the drawbacks of group tests. A wide variety of items can be employed, and the examiner can note the subject's efficiency, conviction, and mode of answering. The examiner observes behavior, not pencil marks on an answer sheet, perhaps discovering that the subject is correct but without confidence, brashly incorrect, or has obtained the correct answers for the wrong reasons. To the extent that the test is used in these additional ways, test administration is a time-consuming, expensive, and exacting task.

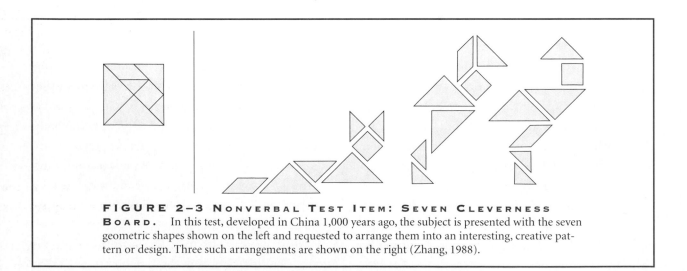

FIGURE 2–3 NONVERBAL TEST ITEM: SEVEN CLEVERNESS BOARD. In this test, developed in China 1,000 years ago, the subject is presented with the seven geometric shapes shown on the left and requested to arrange them into an interesting, creative pattern or design. Three such arrangements are shown on the right (Zhang, 1988).

CASE HISTORY

Sometimes the investigator collects information from several outside sources, such as family, friends, schools, business accounts, and medical records. Whenever detailed social and medical information is combined with an extensive psychological background and assembled in some chronological order, it is known as a **case history.** This history is almost a biography of an individual or, in the case of an event, an account of all relevant incidents.

STUDYING AN INDIVIDUAL. From a research perspective, the intensive study of one individual or event is sometimes known as **idiographic research,** for it attempts to describe the special "lawfulness" of just one person or case. It focuses on the predictable behaviors of *that* individual. Even when several people are studied in this way, individual differences are emphasized; uniformities among people are of less concern (Pelham, 1993).

With Gretchen Brandt, the aim was to understand the ways in which her behavior marked her as different from all other people. Working as a technician in a local medical school, she showed poise and satisfaction with her life. She grew to adolescence in Nazi Germany and World War II, and yet she lived easily within her new culture. This reaction was especially interesting in view of her exposure to Nazi propaganda during her youth. She seemed quite capable of resisting authority that she regarded as evil or wrong.

STUDYING SEVERAL CASES. Sometimes a psychologist conducts a series of studies for some practical purpose and later examines them again, searching for basic principles among them. The aim here is to discern common or universal themes. These studies are called **nomothetic research** because their purpose is to discover general laws of behavior applicable to all human beings in varying degrees. Several case histories, or complete case studies, considered collectively, may reveal unexpected findings about people in general. Most of this book, and indeed most of psychology, is devoted to discovering and understanding these general principles.

Earlier in the history of psychology, controversy arose over the respective merits of the idiographic and nomothetic approaches. Today they are recognized as complementary rather than antagonistic. The idiographic approach develops clinical insights; the nomothetic approach serves in the broader domains of personality, adjustment, and therapy (Lamiell, 1991; Fraenkel, 1995). Both contribute to our knowledge of human behavior.

• EXPERIMENTAL METHOD •

In his naturalistic observations, Milgram noted a high degree of conformity among commuters. In the survey method, he found that almost all subjects claimed they would disobey malevolent authority. Through case studies, he discovered that people differed sharply in response to questions of compliance and obedience, as illustrated by Gretchen Brandt and the others. However, none of this research allowed him to draw conclusions about the *causes* of conformity, compliance, and obedience. For this purpose, he needed still another method—one that would enable him to collect information about cause-and-effect.

The most promising answers to cause-and-effect questions are found in the **experimental method,** in which the chief factors in a research problem are manipulated or controlled in precise ways. For this reason, the experimental method is often considered to stand foremost among the various research techniques in psychology.

CLASSICAL EXPERIMENT

In his effort to accomplish morally significant research in social psychology, Milgram placed an announcement in a New Haven newspaper. It offered a reasonable sum of money for participation in a laboratory study of memory. People with all sorts of occupations returned the newspaper coupon and participated in this research. Among them was a 35-year-old drill-press operator named Jack Washington, a pseudonym.

Unknown to Jack and the others, the true purpose of this research was not to study memory but to identify factors that influence obedience and disobedience. To investigate them, Milgram designed a classical laboratory experiment.

In the **classical experiment,** all potentially influential factors are controlled or held constant except one, which is manipulated. What happens when it is manipulated? One by one, each presumably important factor is tested in this way. In modern multifactor studies, to be considered later, several factors can be examined simultaneously.

MANAGEMENT OF VARIABLES. Any changeable factor or element in research is called a **variable.** It is some condition that the investigator wishes to study. In the classical experiment, the investigator selects for study only one variable at a time. This method follows the **rule of one variable,** in which just one factor is manipulated, or examined, at any given moment. If an effect is observed—that is, if some specific event takes place—it is regarded as a result of the manipulated factor, assuming that other potentially influential factors are held constant.

Milgram studied obedience this way, using three people and an important deception. The real subject, such as Jack Washington, arrived at the laboratory prepared to engage in a study of memory, unaware of any deceit. In a rigged drawing, Jack drew the role of "teacher" and was given the task of administering punishment to a person trying to memorize a list of words. This second person, the "learner," was an accomplice of the experimenter, and he made many mistakes, for which he had agreed to receive electric shocks as punishment. In fact, he never received any shocks—none were administered. But by complaining and pounding the wall he acted as if he were in pain. The third person, the investigator, served as the authority figure, requesting Jack, as the teacher, to administer stronger and stronger shocks for successive mistakes by the learner. These shocks began at 15 volts and ranged up to 450 volts, each labeled with a verbal description on the shock generator (Figure 2–4).

To what extent would Jack Washington and other subjects obey the orders? We have already noted what common sense suggested to most people. On the basis of the questionnaire responses, it seemed that essentially all subjects would disobey the authority.

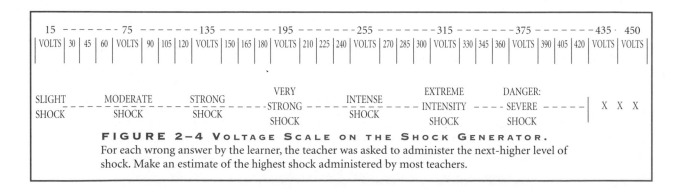

FIGURE 2–4 VOLTAGE SCALE ON THE SHOCK GENERATOR.
For each wrong answer by the learner, the teacher was asked to administer the next-higher level of shock. Make an estimate of the highest shock administered by most teachers.

With the learner strapped to a chair in the next room, Jack began the procedure, shocking the learner for his occasional errors. At the beginning, these errors were infrequent and the shocks mild. At 75 volts, the learner grunted, and at 150 volts his first protests were heard. Jack looked sadly at the authority figure but continued to obey. At 300 volts, the learner hollered: "I absolutely refuse to answer any more. Get me out of here." Yet Jack, following orders, continued to administer stronger and stronger punishment, even when the learner no longer answered.

Finally, when he reached the 450-volt level, the maximum shock available, Jack once again turned to the investigator across the room and asked what to do. He was told: "Continue using the 450-volt switch for each wrong answer. Continue, please." With a dejected expression on his face, Jack resumed his difficult task (Milgram, 1974).

Jack had been completely obedient. He followed all orders—but he was not alone. In several repetitions of this procedure with various subjects, 60% of *all* subjects eventually shocked the learner with the maximum voltage available. They obeyed all orders, showing a wide range of emotions, attitudes, and styles. Some were humble, some were self-assured, and most were deeply concerned about the learner. A minority of subjects resisted the orders before reaching the maximum voltage available. One of them was Gretchen Brandt, who disobeyed at 210 volts. At that point, in a calm but resolute manner, she refused to proceed further, thereby placing herself among the first quarter of all subjects in resisting malevolent authority.

Using this situation and many subjects, Milgram then designed a series of experiments to examine the causal factors in this astonishing obedience. One by one, he manipulated these variables: proximity of the learner, closeness of authority, prestige of the setting, and presence of rebellious peers.

INDEPENDENT AND DEPENDENT VARIABLES. The variable to be manipulated is called an **independent variable** because changes in it are independent of any other aspect of the experiment. It is varied in accordance with the investigator's purpose. If the aim is to discover the influence of the proximity of the learner on the obedience of the teacher, the investigator places the learner at various distances from the teacher. This factor, the distance between learner and teacher, is the independent variable (Table 2–5).

In addition to introducing an independent variable, the experimenter observes and measures the subject's response. This response is referred to as the **dependent variable** because it is the result of the manipulation; its presence or intensity depends

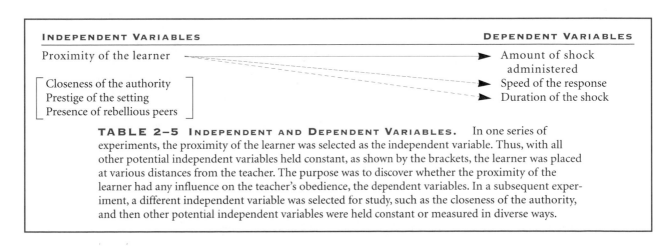

INDEPENDENT VARIABLES	DEPENDENT VARIABLES
Proximity of the learner	Amount of shock administered
Closeness of the authority	Speed of the response
Prestige of the setting	Duration of the shock
Presence of rebellious peers	

TABLE 2–5 INDEPENDENT AND DEPENDENT VARIABLES. In one series of experiments, the proximity of the learner was selected as the independent variable. Thus, with all other potential independent variables held constant, as shown by the brackets, the learner was placed at various distances from the teacher. The purpose was to discover whether the proximity of the learner had any influence on the teacher's obedience, the dependent variables. In a subsequent experiment, a different independent variable was selected for study, such as the closeness of the authority, and then other potential independent variables were held constant or measured in diverse ways.

on the independent variable. In most of Milgram's experiments, the dependent variable was the amount of shock the teacher administered. Instead, it might have been the teacher's speed in administering the shock or the duration of the shock.

As a rule, the independent variable is some stimulus; the dependent variable is some response. A word of caution is in order, however. In many experiments, the independent and dependent variables are more complex and cannot be so readily identified in terms of stimuli and responses.

OPERATIONAL DEFINITIONS. In any research, the variables must be clearly defined. As a rule, scientists use operational definitions for this purpose. An **operational definition** indicates the specific procedures by which something is measured; it depicts the meaning of something in highly explicit, usually *quantifiable* terms.

To study obedience, for example, Stanley Milgram did not use a dictionary definition: "following orders" or "carrying out commands." He devised an experiment with a fake shock generator, explicitly defining obedience as the highest amount of electric shock administered by the subject. Someone who administered 450 volts was more obedient then someone who administered only 300 volts, and so forth. The merit in this definition lies in its clarity and quantification.

Milgram might have studied obedience in other ways. Using the method of naturalistic observation, he might have observed people on city streets, defining obedience as discarding waste in refuse receptables, following pedestrian signals, or obeying laws about public transportation. He might even have used all of these measures together, employing a composite definition. Using the survey method, he could have consulted public records, defining obedience as timely payment of city and state taxes. In another experiment, he could have requested each subject to engage in an extremely boring task, defining obedience as the length of time the subject

persisted in that task (Figure 2–5).

Operational definitions do not necessarily require quantification. For example, how might cohabitation be defined? You may say: "Oh, that's easy—unmarried people living together." But how long must they live together? How regularly?

Instead of setting a time limit, some surveys of cohabitation have used marriage applications to create an operational definition. If the partners for a license gave the same address, their living condition was considered cohabitation. If they gave different addresses, they were not considered cohabitants (Reimann-Marcus, 1992). With this definition there may be some false positives, partners considered cohabitants who were not together

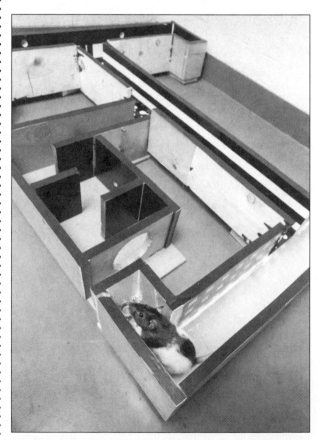

FIGURE 2–5 OPERATIONAL DEFINITION OF INTELLIGENCE. The animal learning this maze begins in the start box, at the upper right end of the maze, and finishes in the goal box, as shown, where it obtains food. Its speed in completing the maze and number of wrong turns are measures of its performance—that is, they m†ay constitute an operational definition of intelligence.

very much, very long, or in a very loving way. And there may be false negatives, partners who lived together romantically but gave different addresses. However, the definition is precise, which is a requirement of scientific research, and no definition can readily satisfy all potential criteria for a complex concept.

This use of operational definitions restricts the scope of any research and the conclusions that can be drawn from the findings. For example, Milgram's research has been questioned on this basis, though studies using a different operational definition have confirmed the overall outcome (Meeus & Raaijmakers, 1986).

❧

DESIGN OF EXPERIMENTS

Following the rule of one variable, subjects in experiments are often studied under two contrasting conditions. There is the **experimental condition,** in which the independent variable is present or manipulated in some degree. There is also the **control condition,** equivalent to the experimental condition except for the independent variable, which is absent or held constant under its normal, nonexperimental circumstances. It is not manipulated. Thus, the control condition provides a basis

for comparison. The investigator assesses the influence of the independent variable by comparing the outcomes under the experimental and control conditions. Unwanted influences should have occurred equally in both conditions, and therefore any difference in the subjects' response must have been due to the independent variable (Table 2–6).

In Milgram's early studies, the learner was placed in another room, where he could not be seen or heard by the teacher. He simply flashed his answers on a screen. This condition can be regarded as the control condition. Then, in successive experimental conditions, the learner was located closer and closer to the teacher. For example, when Jack Washington participated as a subject, the learner sat in an adjacent room, but his cries of pain and resistance were distinctly audible through the wall. For other subjects, the learner sat in the same room, readily visible to the teacher. And in still another condition, the learner sat next to the teacher and received a shock only if the teacher pressed the learner's hand against the shock plate. This tactile condition required the obedient teacher to have physical contact with the learner. These different experimental conditions, in which the proximity of the learner was varied, were compared with the remote or control condition, in which there was no

---

1. Establish the research question: Does proximity of the learner influence obedience?
2. Assign subjects randomly to an experimental or a control condition:

VARIABLES

	Independent Variable	Dependent Variable
Experimental	Learner's cries can be heard	Amount of shock administered
SUBJECTS		
Control	No cries can be heard	Amount of shock administered

3. Collect the results from the experimental group, which heard the learner's cries, the independent variable, and from the control group, which heard no cries.
4. Determine the difference in obedience between the two groups; obedience is the dependent variable.

TABLE 2–6 DESIGN OF AN EXPERIMENT These steps are followed in a traditional experiment. In Milgram's studies, the proximity of the learner made a marked difference. The closer the learner, the less was the obedience.

contact of any sort with the learner. In this way, Milgram investigated the influence of the proximity of the learner on the obedience of the teacher (Figure 2–6).

This overall plan for different conditions is called the *design* of the experiment. It includes the choice of subjects and apparatus, as well as the manipulation of the independent variable, but no issue is more important than the control condition. The chief concern here is control of confounding variables. An *extraneous* or **confounding variable** is any factor that may exert an unwanted influence on the dependent variable, giving the experiment an uninterpretable result.

In Milgram's studies on proximity, suppose the learner in some instances was a child and in others an adult. Then both variables, the learner's age and the learner's proximity, might influence obedience. In this poorly designed experiment, the learner's age would be a confounding variable, producing results which might be confused with those produced by the learner's proximity, the independent variable.

TYPES OF DESIGN. In addition to identifying and manipulating variables, experimenters need to decide how to use their subjects. In one common experimental design, all subjects serve in both conditions, experimental and control. Each subject in the experimental condition is compared with himself or herself in the control condition. In this way, the two conditions should be equal, except for the key factor, the independent variable. This procedure is called the *within-subject design* or *own-control design* because comparisons are made within each subject, who serves under different conditions, providing his or her own control condition.

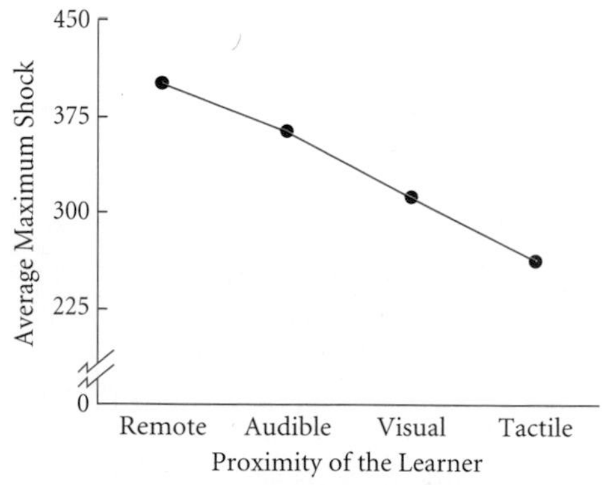

Sometimes the same subjects cannot serve in both conditions. This restriction often occurs when the independent variable extends over a long period of time, as in a program of therapy. If the therapy lasts for two years, the experimental subjects will be two years older and wiser, and they will have completed a program of therapy before beginning the control condition. Hence, the subjects in the two conditions will not be equal. The major method for dealing with this problem involves multiple sets of subjects matched for important characteristics, such as age and sex, each group serving in one condition or the other, experimental or control. This procedure is called the *between-groups design* because the subjects are *randomly* assigned to the experimental *or* control group; then their results are compared.

Milgram debriefed all subjects immediately after the experimental hour, for he did not want them to leave the research thinking that they had really administered pain to someone. Thus, his subjects could not serve as their own control; his method here involved the between-groups design.

Using such procedures, he found that the closeness of the authority also made a great deal of difference. When the experimenter sat just a short distance away, 65% of the subjects obeyed all commands. When the experimenter left the laboratory and gave instructions by telephone or a tape recording, obedience diminished sharply. Only 23% of subjects delivered the highest level of shock, and many subjects surreptitiously administered lower shocks than required, assuring the experimenter by telephone that they were proceeding according to

FIGURE 2–6 PROXIMITY OF THE LEARNER. As proximity to the learner increased, obedience to the malevolent authority decreased (Milgram, 1974).

the original plan (Milgram, 1974).

In the same way, Milgram found that the presence of rebellious peers greatly influenced the subject's obedience. These peers, pretending to be assistant teachers, in fact were accomplices of the experimenter. When they refused to follow orders, the subject refused too. "The effects of peer rebellion are very impressive in undercutting . . . authority," Milgram concluded.

CONTROL OF EXPECTATIONS. In many experiments, the subjects have an expectation about what should happen. Controlling expectations is especially important, for example, in testing the physiological effect of drugs, for the investigator wants to know what benefits are available *apart from* the knowledge that treatment has been received. The experimental group therefore receives the actual drug, and the control group receives a sugar pill, identical in appearance, with no medical properties. This pill, with no active ingredients, is called a **placebo,** which, freely translated, means "I shall please." The aim is to give the control subjects the same set or expectation as that in the experimental group (Figure 2–7).

The placebo effect also occurs in daily life, as well as in research. One former student had been asked to make a mixed drink each evening for his grandfather, who enjoyed the warm, relaxed feeling it provided. One day he confided that, per the doctor's orders, he never spiked the drink, but the thought of vodka certainly satisfied his grandfather.

There is evidence, nevertheless, that a placebo may not be purely psychological. The thought of receiving a certain medication may prompt activity within the nervous system, releasing neurotransmitters that can influence the subject's reactions in significant ways, especially regarding the perception of pain. Further research on the placebo effect is underway in diverse areas of psychology, ranging from education to health (Adair, Sharpe, & Huynh, 1990; Jensen & Karoly, 1991).

Similarly, the experimenter's expectations can be a concern. The experimenter's hopes, habits, and personal characteristics can influence the results of the investigation without his or her knowledge, a condition referred to as **experimenter effects.** The experimenter unconsciously signals to the subjects the response he or she hopes to obtain from them. This unintentional cuing is also known as the *Clever Hans effect,* named for the presumably intelligent Berlin horse that tapped out answers by observing subtle cues from people around him (Pfungst, 1911).

When the subjects' expectations are controlled by preventing them from knowing which treatment they have received, the procedure is called a **single-**

Which pills have medicinal properties?   Which tape allegedly contains a subliminal message?

FIGURE 2–7 USE OF PLACEBOS. One pill has medicinal properties; the other is merely a salt pill. One tape allegedly contains a subliminal message; the other makes no such claim. The concept of placebo, derived from drug studies, now applies to any object, event, or other treatment used to control expectations in research.

blind design. It is illustrated in the use of the placebo. Instead, the experimenter may not know which subjects have received which treatments, again a single-blind design. Sometimes both the experimenter and subjects do not know their treatments, a procedure called a **double-blind design.** In the latter design, neither the investigator nor the subject knows to which group the subject belongs. A third party decides which subjects receive what treatment and codes them so that the experimenter can evaluate each subject's responses without knowing the treatment received. Under these conditions, expectancy cannot create a bias in the research outcomes.

The study of animals offers special possibilities for research design, which is one reason for psychologists' interest in animals. Genetic factors can be manipulated through selective breeding. Environmental conditions can be managed in ways not possible at the human level. Comparisons across species and among different research designs offer a powerful technique for disentangling the diverse determinants of behavior (Timberlake, 1993). Still another advantage is the animals' faster maturation rates. Studies of growth and development often can be completed in a year or two, as opposed to several decades with human beings.

❧

MULTIFACTOR STUDIES

The research procedures just described illustrate the classical experimental design, so called because the earliest experiments were conducted in this fashion, following the rule of one variable. But modern science also recognizes that behavior typically is influenced by more than one factor. For this reason, psychologists often study two or more independent variables together, a procedure made possible with the use of refined statistical methods. Many contemporary investigators prefer these investigations, known as **multifactor studies,** because of their capacity to identify relationships among several different factors or variables. However, the basic procedure is similar to that of the single-factor model.

The interest in multifactor studies lies in their greater efficiency and in the capacity to discover what happens when two or more factors are combined. Sometimes the result is an **additive effect,** meaning that the total influence of all the factors is the sum of their separate influences. No independent variable influences the effect of any other independent variable; the final result is simply their cumulative sum. In Milgram's experiments, the subjects were moderately obedient when the authority figure was nearby and moderately obedient when the learner was in another room. If these effects were additive, both factors together would produce even greater obedience.

In other instances, the result is an **interactive effect,** meaning that the influence of one variable depends on other variables or that the influence of one variable changes with alterations in other variables. Milgram did not examine interaction effects in these experiments, but a dramatic example can be observed in everyday life with the consumption of alcoholic beverages. Mild consumption of alcohol before going to sleep may have no significant effect on a person's health. Similarly, ingestion of phenobarbital, taken to induce sleep, may have no significant effect. But when taken together, even in moderate amounts, they can be fatal (Figure 2–8).

Outside an experimental situation, these mutual influences among variables are known as the *interaction principle,* and their subtleties sometimes escape notice in daily life. In supermarkets, for example, baggers and produce clerks sometimes experience an itch or a rash, especially on the hands and forearms. People working with dairy products or stocking shelves are not afflicted. The reason? Chemicals from certain vegetable products, such as celery and parsnips, are deposited on the skin in minute amounts. But that is not all. The problem appears largely in the summer, occurring through a

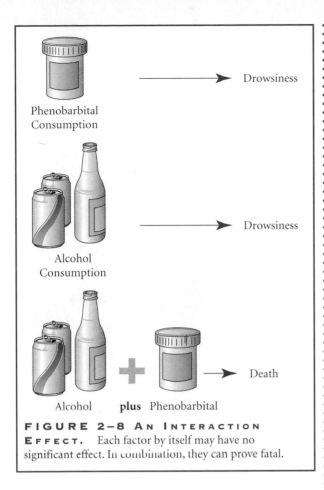

Phenobarbital
Consumption → Drowsiness

Alcohol
Consumption → Drowsiness

Alcohol **plus** Phenobarbital → Death

FIGURE 2–8 AN INTERACTION EFFECT. Each factor by itself may have no significant effect. In combination, they can prove fatal.

combination of the chemical deposits *and* exposure to sunlight. The name of this disorder might cause anyone to itch or scratch: phytophotodermatitis. *Phyto* indicates the plant, *photo* the light, and *dermatitis* the resulting rash. To avoid it, one should work with canned goods, wear long gloves, or stay out of the hot sun.

• RESEARCH IN PERSPECTIVE •

Psychiatrists had predicted that only 1/10 of 1% of Milgram's subjects would give the maximum shock. Instead, approximately 60% did so, obeying fully. Is there any doubt that common sense gave an incorrect answer here? One, of course, might doubt the common sense of psychiatrists. However, graduate students and faculty, college sophomores, and middle-class adults had predicted that only 1% or 2% of subjects would obey completely. The common sense of all these groups was very wrong.

The research subjects, Milgram emphasized, were ordinary people—typical citizens from the professional and working classes. And they obeyed even when no further reason was given except these statements: "The experiment requires that you go on. . . . It is absolutely essential that we continue."

On publication, Milgram's findings generated a wide range of commentary. Many readers thought about the astonishing obedience of the Nazis in carrying out brutal, inhumane orders. More than one critic decided that Milgram had accomplished some of the most morally significant investigations in modern psychology (Elms, 1972). Another described Milgram's work as "a momentous and meaningful contribution to our knowledge of human behavior" (Erikson, 1968). In sharp contrast, another decided that Milgram himself had behaved immorally, duping his subjects and persuading them to perform this distasteful task. No matter what they revealed, his findings were not worth the tension and self-doubt they created in his subjects (Baumrind, 1964). Many others have voiced opinions between these extremes or contributed different interpretations of his findings (Nissani, 1990).

These diverse views offer an opportunity to examine research methods from a broader perspective, focusing on ethical issues and comparisons among the different methods. Depending on the situation, each method has special assets and limitations.

RESEARCH ETHICS

Earlier we asked: To what extent is a researcher justified in secretly studying commuters awaiting their train? Is it acceptable to induce people to mail "lost" letters? Here we ask: Was Milgram's experimental study of obedience justifiable and ethical?

This question of research ethics concerns the

experience of subjects participating in a scientific investigation. It requires the humane and just treatment of all subjects. This issue is regularly raised in animal research by psychologists and the lay public (Timberlake, 1993; Ulrich, 1991). It is also confronted in the clinic, usually by the investigators themselves (Hall, 1991a).

People commuting to work may become subjects in naturalistic observation, but they do not alter their behavior in any way. Ethics should not become an issue, *provided* that the results are managed with discretion and confidentiality. People mailing lost letters go out of their way, but they do so voluntarily, just as they do to assist an elderly person, use a trash can, or help someone with parking. The general rule is that the subject's explicit consent to participate is not required if the behavior in question occurs as part of a normal routine, if there is no coercion, and if the findings are handled in a manner that fully respects the right to privacy.

BASIC ETHICAL QUESTIONS. When Jack Washington participated in Milgram's experiment, he went out of his way, was duped by a rigged drawing for the teacher and learner roles, and received false information about the electrical shocks. These are more fundamental ethical issues.

Such issues are not unique to psychology; they occur in all disciplines. For some people, the entire field of nuclear physics is an ethical issue. In biology, animals are confined to cages and subjected to surgery solely for research purposes. In legal and psychiatric research, ethical issues arise over the question of clients' rights. Even educational research involves ethical considerations, for the procedures sometimes impose researchers' values on the students in the study (Figure 2–9).

The issues in animal rights, for example, are more complex than might be readily apparent, as demonstrated when a cat lover complained that her neighbor's pet boa constrictor devoured kittens. The neighbor replied that the snake merely ate

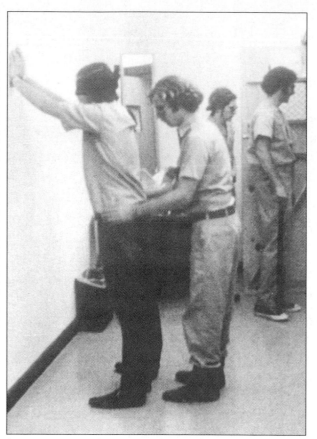

FIGURE 2–9 RESEARCH ETHICS. Issues of moral values and moral behavior underlie all research. When research subjects are exposed to a prison environment, for example, questions immediately arise concerning their physical and mental welfare.

mice and pointed out an advantage of snakes as pets. Having extraordinarily low metabolism, they consume far fewer fellow creatures than the approximately 54 million pet cats in this country. One reason for the cat lover's complaint, of course, is that cats rank higher than snakes on the human list of pet preferences. In killing and preparing cats' food, human beings make attractive packages out of the dead fish, horses, rats, and other animals fed to felines. In short, the animal world pays a high price for our pets, which we keep chiefly for one purpose—affection (Herzog, 1991). And the proper relation of human beings to lower animals, whether in research or relaxation, remains a perplexing ethical issue (Locke, 1992).

One **basic ethical question** in research seems to be this: Does any possible discomfort incurred by all subjects collectively outweigh the gain in alleviation of human and nonhuman problems? Many of Milgram's subjects experienced tension, doubt, and self-recrimination, clearly signs of discomfort. On the other side of the ledger, the obedience of the Nazis played an important role in the pain experienced by millions of people in World War II, and after their capture they did not appear to be cruel and sadistic. Instead, they seemed like ordinary citizens who did what they thought was their duty, which is the way many of Milgram's subjects characterized themselves. After the experiment, they decided that they had to resist authority more effectively in the future. Thus, the question still stands: On balance, was this research justifiable? Was the suffering of Milgram's subjects offset by the gain in understanding obedience to malevolent authority?

This ethical question involves value judgments about the feelings of research subjects. It also involves value judgments about the role of research in society. It extends beyond obedience and disobedience to include legitimate versus illegitimate authority and even benevolent versus malevolent orders (Saks, 1992). Taking a thoughtful ethical stand is a challenging task.

INFORMED CONSENT. Throughout his research, Milgram employed certain procedures to protect the subjects and to provide them with maximum benefit from their participation. These precautions, implemented in all proper investigations today, include informed consent before participation, privacy during participation, and confidentiality on completion of the research (Korn, 1988).

Among these, the most important is **informed consent,** which means that the general nature, risks, and benefits of research participation are explained to each subject before the procedures begin. The subjects are told about the tasks they will be expected to perform, and if they agree to participate, they do so giving informed consent. In Milgram's work, all subjects were informed of the basic experimental procedures at the outset. Each of them signed a consent form, indicating voluntary participation in this research.

An obvious question in informed consent concerns the complexity of the explanation and, in some cases, the need for deception about underlying purposes. Sometimes a less-than-full explanation may be acceptable, providing the subject incurs no other risk by participation. Still another issue is the subject's ability to give informed consent, especially in three populations: elderly people, the mentally disabled, and children. Investigators studying young children typically rely on a proxy from their parents, but each research project, with its unique characteristics, requires special steps to ensure that children's rights are respected (Hughes & Helling, 1991; Krener & Mancina, 1994).

For these reasons, an interdisciplinary ethics committee now must evaluate all federally funded psychological research. The goal is to permit the most useful, productive research without endangering the subjects in any way. The ideal solution to this problem, and one toward which many psychologists are working, is the development of research techniques that rely on the subjects' usual behavior and naturally occurring events rather than on contrived situations and misleading information (Huntingford, 1984; Kelman, 1967).

DEBRIEFING INTERVIEW. At the close of each research session, Milgram interviewed the subject. This procedure is called a **debriefing interview,** and it has a dual purpose: to ensure the maximum benefit for the subject and to obtain any further information that might be useful. Concern for the subjects is paramount, directed not only to ensuring that they are as fit and healthy as they were before the research but also to enable them to profit as much as possible from the experience.

Milgram's debriefing instructions included a meeting between the teacher and the un-harmed learner, as well as extended discussion with the authority figure. During his debriefing interview, Jack Washington explained that he would have discontinued the shocks if he had received a signal from the experimenter. "I did not get a cue to stop," he emphasized. Then he added that he knew the shocks were painful but not dangerous. Earlier in life he had received a very strong, accidental shock to his hand, causing him pain but no permanent damage, and thus he believed the investigator's contention that the shocks were not harmful.

Some weeks later, all subjects received a five-page report, including a questionnaire asking them to express once again their thoughts and feelings about the experience. Altogether, 80% of the subjects recommended more experiments of this nature, and 74% replied that they had learned something important to them personally. For Milgram, this finding constituted the central justification of this research: The participants judged it as acceptable and worthwhile (Milgram, 1974).

~

COMPARISON OF METHODS

The system that we call science is unfinished— always aimed at evaluating and extending the ideas it has generated. Conducting research is like fight-ing the many-headed hydra of Greek mythology. For every head that is cut off, two more grow in its place. In science, the price of getting a head is more work to be done.

This work is accomplished by all four methods, combined and modified in various ways to fit the requirements of a particular research question. We know about Milgram's use of these methods through his collected reports, *The Individual in a Social World* (1992), and his book with a single focus,

Obedience to Authority (1974). In response to contin-ued interest 15 years after publication of the for-mer volume, two of Stanley Milgram's followers, John Sabini and Maury Silver, edited and repub-lished that book as a second edition under his name (Milgram, 1992). These works show how Milgram found ways to collect research informa-tion by using an original mix of methods: observa-tion, the survey, the case study, and, of course, laboratory experiments (Zimbardo, 1992).

STATISTICAL ANALYSES. After collect-ing the information, the investigator's next task is to analyze and interpret it. Sometimes qualitative analysis is involved, requiring considerable wisdom on the part of the investigator. Especially in natu-ralistic observation and case studies, subjective judgments and verbal descriptions may be the only recourse for depicting the findings. More often, quantitative analysis is included, meaning that the information is expressed in numerical units and sta-tistical techniques are employed to assess them. These techniques, discussed in detail in the final chapter, can be categorized as descriptive, correla-tional, and inferential statistics.

Utilized in all research methods, *descriptive statis-tics* characterize or summarize a group of scores, often by presenting just a few numerical values. Usually they include some typical score, such as an average, and some measure of variability, indicating the extent to which other scores differ from the typical score. For example, Milgram found that commuters in New York City had an average of 4.5 familiar strangers in their lives. In one instance, the range was from zero, for a commuter new at the depot, to more than 12 for long-time commuters who recognized almost every "regular" at the station. These numerical values are descriptive statistics.

Instead, an investigator may want to know about the relationship between two sets of scores.

In his studies of pedestrians, Milgram noted that the size of crowds varied considerably according to several factors. We might wonder about the relationship between pedestrians and sidewalk performers. When pedestrians increase or decrease in number, do sidewalk performers also increase or decrease? Answers to such questions involve *correlational statistics*, which indicate the association between two sets of scores. They show whether there is a relationship between the number of pedestrians and the number of sidewalk performers.

Numerically, these relationships can vary from 0.00, meaning no correlation, to +1.00, a perfect positive correlation, or to -1.00, a perfect negative correlation. A correlation of +.60, for example, indicates a direct, rather strong association. As pedestrians increase in number, so do sidewalk performers. A correlation of -.10 indicates a weak, indirect association. As the number of pedestrians increases, the number of sidewalk performers tends to decrease mildly. However, correlational statistics do *not* indicate causality. Both factors *may* be influenced by a third variable, such as the weather or a holiday season.

Finally, *inferential statistics* are used to make a guess, an inference, or a statement of probability about one or several groups of scores. In Milgram's studies of obedience to authority, the subjects were asked to use a 14-point scale to estimate the amount of pain experienced by the learner. For a sample of obedient subjects, the mean was 11.36; for defiant subjects, it was 11.80. Is there a statistically significant difference between these two means? Expressed differently, what might be found with other samples of obedient and defiant subjects? Clearly, Milgram could not test all possible subjects. Inferential statistics allow the investigator to estimate the probability that the same findings would occur if the same experiment were repeated over and over again. Inferential statistics are common in the experimental and other research methods as the investigator tries to determine the reliability of the findings.

To emphasize the basic point once again: Research methods are used to collect information. Diverse statistical methods are used afterward to analyze and interpret this information.

CONTINUUM OF METHODS. When these research methods are compared, they fall to some degree on a continuum of intervention or control. That is, they differ in the extent to which the investigator intervenes in the subjects' lives.

In naturalistic observation, at one end of this continuum, the subjects are studied in their own environment, unaffected by the investigator insofar as possible. In the survey, further along the continuum, the subjects' privacy is invaded to some degree by mail or telephone. Toward the opposite end of the continuum, case studies often take place in a clinic or comparable institution. At the far end of this continuum, opposite from naturalistic observation, the experimental method involves the fullest control and the most intervention. The subject usually enters a laboratory setting, and the investigator manipulates this environment in varying degrees, permitting the most definitive study of cause-and-effect relations.

There are innumerable variations in these methods. A study of animal migration might involve a combination of naturalistic observation and the survey method. Experiments can be conducted in school, at work, and elsewhere in the natural environment. Called *field experiments,* they reflect modifications in the basic experimental design. The overall aim is to find the most useful integration of methods for any topic of inquiry (Banaji & Crowder, 1989; Conway, 1991).

Collectively, these different methods provide a variety of useful approaches to the study of psychological problems. Each has advantages and disadvantages, and each makes a special contribution

METHOD	DESCRIPTION	MILGRAM EXAMPLE	CHIEF ADVANTAGE	CHIEF DISADVANTAGE
Naturalistic Observation	Studying behavior in its usual setting	Observing conformity among commuters at a railway station	Deals with everyday situations and events	May have high potential for investigator bias
Survey	Obtaining information from many subjects by mail, phone, or letters	Administering an obedience questionnaire; distributing "lost" letters	Allows access to a large number of subjects	May yield unreliable or unrepresentative data
Case Study	Conducting an interview, administering tests, preparing a case history	Interviewing Gretchen Brandt, testing her, and developing a case history	Offers opportunity to deal with practical problems and individual cases	May be expensive and not generalizable
Experimental Method	Manipulating and controlling relevant factors for study	Varying the proximity of the learner, closeness of authority, and so forth	Provides for the study of cause-and-effect relations	May involve artificial environments and manipulations

TABLE 2–7 METHODS OF RESEARCH

(Table 2–7). As these diverse methods become more fully developed and integrated, through psychologists' continual search for improved research techniques, we should become more and more skillful in understanding all sorts of behavior, including conformity, compliance, and obedience.

IN CONCLUSION. Milgram's studies prompted him to develop two hypotheses about the performance of women. Traditionally more compliant than men, they might show more obedience. Traditionally more empathic too, they might display more resistance to shocking someone. What do you think? Choose one of these hypotheses before reading further.

When Milgram performed these experiments with women, he found that the level of obedience was virtually identical to that of men. When these experiments were repeated by other investigators in Italy, Australia, Germany, and South Africa, each time with a somewhat different sample of subjects, the level of obedience was as high as that found by

Milgram. In one instance, the subjects were required to administer psychological punishment, rather than physical punishment, harassing and berating an interviewee. Once again, the level of obedience was comparable to that in Milgram's work (Meeus & Raaijmakers, 1986).

These replications have essentially verified Milgram's findings on obedience to authority. Scientists within and outside of psychology therefore regard this work as a rare integration of the humanistic and empirical perspectives and as an extraordinary contribution to the study of moral issues. Panels of experts have selected this research as one of the most important investigations in modern psychology. With the exception of Darwin's book, it was the only single piece of research included in a comprehensive list of terms and concepts depicting basic psychological information (Boneau, 1990).

Milgram showed that what subjects say on a questionnaire may be very different from what they actually do. Further, he showed that social situations can powerfully override personal dispositions in influencing behavior. This conclusion is widely accepted, although personal factors cannot be entirely discounted (Blass, 1991). Finally, he showed that what people do is not necessarily predictable through common sense (Milgram, 1974).

Sometimes common sense is supported by psychological research. These occasions are gratifying, indicating that we learn something about human behavior and experience through daily life. Sometimes common sense is contradicted by psychological research. These occasions are important because scientific research is generally considered the most rigorous and reliable pathway to knowledge. A psychology that consistently opposed common sense would be disturbing, apparently concerned with a different reality than the one we think we know. A psychology that merely supported common sense would be a waste of time. The value of employing diverse research methods in modern psychology is that they increase our chances of distinguishing one from the other.

For his simple, elegant research methods, Stanley Milgram became internationally famous. For his studies of obedience, he was awarded numerous honors, including the prize in socio-psychology offered by the American Association for the Advancement of Science. This series of experiments has been described as one of the few classic studies in social psychology, containing all the elements of a parable: a story line, conceptual simplicity, vivid imagery, and an unexpected outcome (Kotre, 1992).

Stanley Milgram completed these obedience studies while he was still in his twenties. Sadly, this early success was followed by an untimely death many years before it might have been expected. His genius is now to be found frozen in his published works (Sabin & Silver, 1992). He has left us an inspirational legacy in research methods, morally significant findings, and a reminder about our own lives: "We are all fragile creatures, entwined in a cobweb of social constraints."

• SUMMARY •

NATURALISTIC OBSERVATION

1. Naturalistic observation involves the study of behavior in its usual setting. In overt observation the researcher's presence is known to the subjects; in covert observation it is concealed.
2. Naturalistic observation may not appear complex, but it requires considerable training. The investigator must decide whether to participate in the subjects' activities and how to minimize personal bias. This approach is useful for generating hypotheses.

SURVEY METHOD

3. The purpose of the survey is to obtain information from a large number of subjects in an efficient manner. A questionnaire, containing structured or open-ended items, is used and the results may provide norms indicating what is normal or expected for a certain group.
4. The people to whom the questionnaire is administered constitute a sample, which is a group of subjects drawn from a larger group called the population. When a sample accurately reflects the characteristics of a certain population, it is called a representative sample. As a rule, a large random sample is more likely to be representative than a small one.
5. Some surveys are based on unobtrusive measures, in which the subjects never know that they have been included in a research project. The lost-letter technique is a modified unobtrusive measure because the investigator presents potential subjects with a specific stimulus. Most unobtrusive measures provide little knowledge of the sample of subjects.

CASE STUDY

6. The case study describes one person, a group of people, or an event in detail. Extensive information is gained through a series of interviews. Psychological tests also are useful for gathering information.

7. The case history includes social, educational, and medical information, as well as the psychological background, obtained from all available sources. Case histories, interviews, and psychological tests may involve idiographic analysis, concerned with discovering the underlying principles in a given case. They also may involve nomothetic research, which has the purpose of discovering general laws of behavior.

EXPERIMENTAL METHOD

8. The experimental method, involving control or manipulation of variables, is concerned with cause-and-effect relationships. In the classical experiment the investigator manipulates an independent variable, usually a stimulus, and notes its influence on the dependent variable, usually a response.

9. To control disruptive influences, subjects are studied under two conditions, experimental and control, which are equal except for the presence of the independent variable. This variable is manipulated, and then the two conditions are compared. Sometimes the same subjects are used for the experimental and control conditions. In another design, two sets of subjects are used, and they are placed in comparable groups by matching or procedures for randomization.

10. The multiple bases of behavior prompt some psychologists to study the influence of several independent variables simultaneously. These multifactor studies can reveal additive effects, in which the influences are simply cumulative, and interactive effects, in which the influences are interdependent.

RESEARCH IN PERSPECTIVE

11. Research ethics with human beings require informed consent prior to participation, privacy during participation, and complete confidentiality of records at all times. At the end of the research, debriefing is required, in which the aim and research procedures are explained to the subject as fully as possible, and a written report is prepared, designed to enhance the value of the experience for all participants.

12. Each research method has advantages and disadvantages and makes its own contribution to our understanding of human and animal behavior, experience, and mental processes. These methods are used in complementary ways as investigators examine complex psychological questions.

• WORKING WITH PSYCHOLOGY •

❧ REVIEW OF KEY CONCEPTS ❧

Naturalistic Observation
naturalistic observation
overt observation
covert observation
participant observation
nonparticipant observation
bias

Survey Method
survey method

questionnaire
norms
sample
population
representative sample
random sample
incidental sample
unobtrusive measures

Case Study
case study

group tests
individual tests
case history
idiographic research
nomothetic research

Experimental Method
experimental method
classical experiment
variable

rule of one variable
independent variable
dependent variable 0
operational definition
experimental condition
control condition
confounding variable

placebo
experimenter effects
single-blind design
double-blind design
multifactor studies
additive effect
interactive effect

Research in Perspective
  basic ethical question
  informed consent
  debriefing interview

❧ CLASS DISCUSSION/CRITICAL THINKING ❧

A NARRATIVE TWIST

The subjects in Stanley Milgram's obedience studies reacted in a surprising manner—not at all as psychiatrists had predicted. Suppose instead that they had behaved according to expectations. Would Milgram's research then have been largely meaningless? Explain the reasons for your view, including a discussion of psychology and common sense. Would this research have raised ethical issues? Again, explain the reasons for your view.

TOPICAL QUESTIONS

• *Naturalistic Observation.* Suppose that you want to study jaywalking in a moderately large city. Decisions about revealing your purpose offer two approaches to observation, overt and covert. Which approach would you use? Explain your reasons. ❧

• *Survey Method.* Sometimes surveys are administered to college students, and the results are reported as representative of the general population. Are students sufficiently different from one another and sufficiently similar to the general population that they adequately reflect our society? Explain your answer.

• *Case Study.* It has been said that a test merely provides a sample of the subject's behavior. If, instead, the examiner had the opportunity to accompany the subject for 24 hours in daily life, that opportunity would yield more useful information than the test. Do you agree or disagree? Why?

• *Experimental Method.* To what extent are confounding variables part of every type of investigation? Explain the reasons for your view.

• *Research in Perspective.* Describe how each of the four basic research methods might be used in studying the effectiveness of a new pill for the common cold.

❧ TOPICS OF RELATED INTEREST ❧

The design of research includes correlational studies, described in detail in the chapter on statistics (18). Research methods and instruments are also described in the context of biological foundations (3), intelligence and testing (13), and therapy (16).

OVERVIEW OF THE BODY
Organs and Systems
Human Nervous System

NEURAL COMMUNICATION
The Neuron
Nature of the Message
Chemical Foundations

THE HUMAN BRAIN
Brain and Evolution
Subcortical Structures
Cerebral Cortex
Hemispheric Specialization

INTERLOCKING SYSTEMS
Autonomic Functions
The Endocrine System

3

BIOLOGICAL FOUNDATIONS

THE DRUMMER'S SOUL MATE SAT AMONG THE AUDI-
ENCE, AWAITING THE BEGINNING OF THE NIGHT'S
CONCERT. WE SHALL CALL HER SACHA, WHICH MEANS
"helper of humanity," for she was indeed loyal to Ray, supporting him
in all sorts of circumstances.

Imagine the scene. Out on the floor, the bass player flexed his fingers,
his mind seemingly elsewhere. Ray bent over the snare drum, lightly
tapped its head, listened, and tightened a lug. He repeated the process
at the next lug, and the next, moving slowly around the head of the
drum. Reaching the last lug, he banged the drum, jerked his head up,
and swore loudly. The vocalist turned in Ray's direction; the bass player
turned a bit rosy; and Ray turned the last lug on his drum. Sacha did
not change her expression; she simply looked on intently.

As the musicians tuned up for another night of jazz, miraculous activity
was taking place inside their heads. Among the tens of billions of microscopic cells in each brain, with its millions of threadlike connections, innu-

merable nerve networks were transmitting and receiving messages. Traveling faster than 100 miles per hour, they prompted Ray to smile at his audience, to strike the drum again, and to drink a bit of soda, wriggling his tongue to move the residue around in his mouth.

The human brain, capable of mediating all of these activities, can also study itself, as yours is about to do. Referred to as the most intricate mechanism on this planet, it is the only structure sufficiently complex to turn on itself in this extraordinary way. If it were much simpler, making it easier to understand, our thinking probably would be too simple to conduct this inquiry.

In many respects, Ray was just a normal, fun-loving young man who happened to be a very talented musician. He was also athletic, witty, loyal, and persevering, characteristics that raise a vital question. What are the underlying mechanisms that enabled him to respond in these ways? Modern answers to this question form the basis for this

chapter. Indeed, Ray's story is appropriate for this purpose because, due to a specific, rare neurological disorder, addressed later, he provides an excellent example not only of the functions but also of the dysfunctions of these underlying mechanisms. His case is of particular interest in neurospsychology, physiological psychology, and clinical psychology (Sacks, 1987).

With a focus largely on neural structures, we begin this chapter with an overview of the body. Then we examine neural communication, specifically the pathways that connect the chief organs. Afterward, we concentrate on our major integrating organ, the human brain. Finally, we emphasize that the body is composed of interlocking systems.

• OVERVIEW OF THE BODY •

Throughout the animal kingdom, biological mechanisms are studied in terms of organs and systems. The focus is on structures and their relationships.

ORGANS AND SYSTEMS

In the biological sense, an **organ** is a distinct and specific body part specialized to perform a particular function. The ears receive auditory information; the stomach digests food; the brain prompts thoughts about an enjoyable night of jazz. A **system,** in biology, refers to a series of interacting organs and connecting links, making a functional whole. We speak of the auditory, gastrointestinal, and respiratory systems, referring to the interrelated organs that result in hearing, digestion, and breathing, respectively.

BASIC ORGANS. Awaiting her husband's moment to begin, Sacha's sense organs were attuned to incoming cues from the band leader, his fellow musicians, and even the audience. In all of us, some organs are concerned with the intake of information; others are concerned with the management of information; still others are concerned with output.

Within the eyes, ears, nose, and other sense organs are the **receptors,** nerve cells specialized for receiving information and transmitting it to adjacent nerve tissue. They receive information about the external environment: musical sounds, bright lights, and the odor of food. They also receive information about the internal environment: the action of the muscles, condition of the stomach and heart, and so forth. When receptors are acted on by appropriate stimuli, they transmit that information to the brain via the nervous system.

Ray smiled, hunched his shoulders, leaned forward in his chair, and began a light drum roll, signaling the start of the concert. The **effectors** are the muscles and glands that enable the organism to do something, to take some action—that is, to have an effect on the environment. Ray lifted his head and swore again, this time more softly.

Still other organs do not receive information from the environment or take direct action in the environment. They are primarily concerned with activities within the body, especially maintenance and integration functions. Again, the brain is foremost among them. Other vital organs include the heart, lungs, stomach, and so forth.

INTEGRATED SYSTEMS. The complex interactions among these different sorts of organs, for input and output and maintenance, could not occur without intricate, highly differentiated body systems. In human beings, these systems play a central role in communication; foremost among them are the *nerve networks*, also called the *nervous system.*

In the jellyfish, the nerve network is extremely simple, shaped much like a wheel with a hub, an outer rim, and a few spokes. The jellyfish moves in a slow, repetitive fashion, without much variation. The earthworm, at a higher level, has a nervous system with two symmetrical halves, both divided into parts, much like a ladder in appearance. The earthworm can move its different segments separately, allowing it to inch along, extending one part of its body and then another in sequential fashion.

In contrast, vertebrates have extensive concentrations of nerve cells along the backbone and especially in the head. This central pattern, with its countless interconnections, permits a wide variety of specific and distinct actions. An impressive example occurs in human beings, who can execute a roll on the snare drum and simultaneously wink at a friend, performing with a versatility and complexity not found in any other organism.

GENETIC BACKGROUND. The growth of these organs and systems is directed by a code passed on to all of us at the moment of conception. The basic principles of this genetic unfolding, known for some time, are discussed in a later chapter on human development. However, recent investigations with animals suggest that the expression of the genetic code may be more variable than was once thought.

Among a species of African cichlid, a few male fish control virtually all of the feeding territories and access to most of the female fish. These aggressive males are bigger and more brightly colored than their more submissive counterparts. However, once a dominant fish has been displaced by combat or a predator, the newly ascendant fish not only becomes domineering but also develops a bigger body, becomes more brightly colored, and experiences marked growth in its brain and testicles. The brain increase occurs in the hypothalamus, which plays a vital role in feeding, fighting, and mating. Certain cells may grow to six or seven times the size of those in the subordinate fish (Davis & Fernald, 1990).

After its defeat, the displaced male fish swims away and remains largely by itself. Within a few days, its hypothalamus diminishes in size; its bright colors disappear; and even its testicles become reduced in mass. In other words, the social position of the male African cichlid, which is part of its external environment, influences the structure and function of its brain and other organs (Bond, Francis, Fernald, & Adelman, 1991; Davis & Fernald, 1990).

Internal influences on the genetic code were demonstrated when 100 different viruses, easily distinguished from one another, were injected into the developing brains of the fetuses of pregnant rats. This procedure gave the injected cells an unmistakable virus "tag" without influencing the brain development of the fetus. The pregnant rats gave normal births; the newborn pups developed normally; and after an appropriate period, the brains of these young rats were examined to determine the locations of the various tagged cells.

The brain cells produced by the division of a parent cell, or progenitor, had extended in various directions, eventually migrating to very different parts of the brain. Offspring nerve cells from the same parent cell were found in many *different locations* in the upper brain regions and performed *different functions*, relevant to the particular site in which they had become established: vision, hearing, taste, and so forth, depending on the activity in that region of the brain. In other words, the genetic code in a parent cell did not instruct all offspring cells to perform the same task. Their final performance was also influenced by their neighbors' functions (Walsh & Cepko, 1992).

Collectively, these experiments suggest that the development of nerve cells is under the influence of the genes, the external environment, *and* a particular internal environment. Genes certainly do influence development but perhaps not in the rigid manner suggested by earlier studies.

❧

HUMAN NERVOUS SYSTEM

The consequences of inheriting a certain physical structure are most readily observed in the nervous system, which accounts for so much diversity in behavior. At the human level,

for example, it enabled Ray to become a highly accomplished musician, a drummer of real virtuosity. When he played in a weekend jazz band, his wild extemporizations never failed to delight the audience. His unpredictable swearing also attracted an audience from time to time. Over the years, Sacha had learned somewhat to tolerate these unexpected bursts of coarse language. From her perspective as his wife, Ray was just that way.

Ray was also quick in conversation. "Tell me how long drum rolls should be played," an admirer might ask. "The same as short ones" was a likely reply.

Integrating all such activity, the **nervous system** is a coordinating network that regulates internal responses and reacts to external and internal stimulation, transmitting information throughout the body. It is the major integrating system in many animals and human beings, consisting of the brain, spinal cord, and numerous related nerve pathways.

PERIPHERAL NERVOUS SYSTEM.

Peripheral means "outlying," and the **peripheral nervous system** includes essentially all the nerves of the body lying outside the brain and spinal cord. It transmits messages to and from the brain and the spinal cord. Some of these nerves may be quite long. Nerve structures not found within the brain and spinal cord generally belong to the peripheral nervous system (Figure 3–1).

The peripheral nervous system makes connections with two types of organs. The largely involuntary organs include the heart, lungs, stomach, and adrenal glands, and they are controlled by a part of the peripheral nervous system called the **autonomic nervous system.** This subsystem, in turn, has two divisions, the sympathetic and parasympathetic, considered later in this chapter and elsewhere. Suffice it to note here that the sympathetic division prepares the body for emergencies; the parasympathetic division maintains the body in more routine situations. The other part of the peripheral nervous system, the **somatic nervous system,** involves the striated mus-

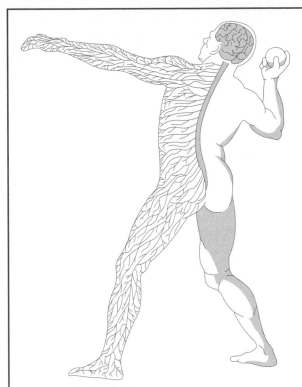

FIGURE 3-1 PERIPHERAL AND CENTRAL NERVOUS SYSTEMS. The peripheral system, extending to and from the body's extremities, is represented in color. The central nervous system, which includes the brain and spinal cord, is shown in black. Neither system is fully depicted here.

cles and sense organs and therefore is responsible for the regulation of most voluntary behavior, providing control and also feeling in diverse parts of the body. It enables students to walk to class, drummers to play their instruments, and professors to write textbooks.

CENTRAL NERVOUS SYSTEM. The brain and spinal cord are the two basic elements of the **central nervous system,** the primary integrating and control center in the human body, receiving impulses from the peripheral nervous system and from its own subdivisions. Integrations of greatest complexity occur in the human **brain,** an exquisitely intricate concentration of nerve tissue enclosed within the skull.

A ropelike structure with the diameter of the little finger, the **spinal cord** is an intricate bundle of nerve fibers extending down the spinal column of organisms with a backbone, serving two purposes. It contains the nerve fibers for reflexes, our most primitive and automatic responses. Through these pathways, it also conveys messages to and from the brain, providing the basis for much more complex reactions.

The ascending and descending pathways to and from the brain form definite spinal tracts, most of which cross over near the brain from one side of the body to the other. Ascending pathways from the left side of the body, for example, cross over to the right side of the brain. Descending pathways from the left side of the brain eventually reach the right side of the body. When a drummer uses his right hand, impulses for this action originate in the left side of his brain—the left cerebral hemisphere—and vice versa.

In the brain, the ascending impulses, in addition to serving involuntary functions, activate the so-called higher mental processes, which include perceiving, remembering, reasoning, and other forms of thinking. After examining the transmission of information throughout the nervous system, we shall consider various parts of the human brain in further detail.

• NEURAL COMMUNICATION •

While Ray was thumping his drums in weekend concerts, a physician in New York City was engaged in more sedentary activity. Dr. Oliver Sacks was studying neurological disorders, defects in the nervous system that disrupt behavior. Interested in diseases and people, he wrote numerous articles on his work, one of which was published in the *Washington Post* (Sacks, 1987). This newspaper account, of course, reached far beyond the scientific community. Sacks thought about the thousands of citizens who might be exposed to it.

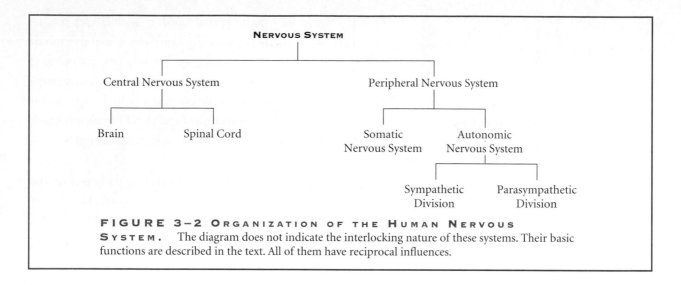

FIGURE 3–2 ORGANIZATION OF THE HUMAN NERVOUS SYSTEM. The diagram does not indicate the interlocking nature of these systems. Their basic functions are described in the text. All of them have reciprocal influences.

☙ THE NEURON

Whether we are thumping drums, writing articles, or thinking about other people, underlying all of our behavior is the **neuron,** a cell specialized for electrochemical communication. The fundamental unit of all nerve tissue, it typically appears in bundles with other neurons. A nerve is a bundle of neurons; collectively, these bundles make up the human nervous system (Figure 3–2).

STRUCTURE OF THE NEURON. Basically, a neuron is composed of three parts. The **cell body** is the central part, containing the nucleus; there are also two types of fibers, slender threadlike structures known as dendrites and axons. The **dendrite,** typically the shorter of these fibers but with innumerable branches, receives impulses and carries them toward its own cell body. The neuron also receives impulses directly at its cell body and sometimes even at the axon. The **axon,** often a very long fiber, characteristically carries impulses away from its cell body toward other neurons. Each neuron has only one axon, which follows the *law of forward conduction,* meaning that it carries impulses only in one direction, away *from* the cell body *to* the dendrites

and cell bodies of other neurons, thereby making connections with those neurons (Figure 3–3).

In many cases, the axon is covered by a substance called the **myelin sheath,** which serves chiefly to insulate one axon from the electrical activities of other axons. It prevents interference among adjacent neurons and speeds the transmission of the impulse. A white, fatty substance, myelin basically covers the gray matter of the neuron itself.

TYPES OF NEURONS. There are three widely recognized types of neurons. The **sensory neuron** transmits messages from the sense organs, such as the ears, tongue, and skin. When such a message reaches the brain, where it is integrated with other messages, we hear, taste, or have other experiences. These neurons are also known as *afferent neurons,* which means "carrying toward" or "input," for they bring information into the central nervous system.

The **motor neuron** transmits impulses away from the central nervous system to the muscles and glands. These neurons initiate actions and create effects, as in striking the drums. Hence, they are also called *efferent neurons,* which means "carrying away" or "output." Both sensory and motor neurons are part of the peripheral nervous system.

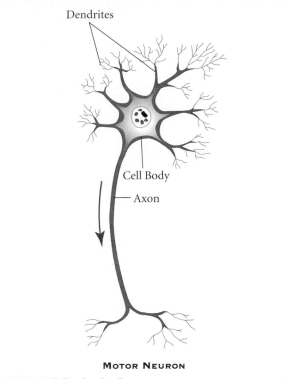

Dendrites

Cell Body

Axon

MOTOR NEURON

FIGURE 3–3 STRUCTURE OF A NEURON. Although neurons have a typical structure, they differ enormously in shape and size. The arrow shows the direction of impulse. Tiny knobs at the ends of the axon make connections with other neurons.

Some nerve impulses entering the spinal cord remain confined to that particular region. These may result in a *reflex*, a relatively simple, automatic response, typically integrated within the spinal cord. If you prick yourself with a pin, you withdraw your hand immediately. You feel pain from the pinprick only afterward, when the message reaches your brain; a reflex occurs faster than the brain can respond. This connection between sensory and motor nerves, known as the simple **reflex arc,** is the basic pattern of the spinal reflex.

Most nerve impulses entering the spinal cord ascend to the brain, and in both locations a third type of neuron is involved. The **interneuron** transmits messages from sensory neurons to motor neurons and also to other interneurons (Figure 3–4). Interneurons not only complete certain reflex arcs; they enable most impulses to ascend the spinal cord, stimulate innumerable circuits within the brain, and eventually prompt other impulses that descend the spinal cord through efferent neurons. Interneurons are thousands of times more common than the other types. When Ray heard about the concert, he did not

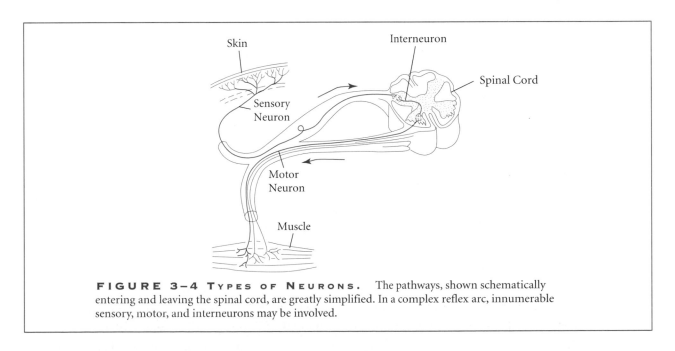

Skin

Interneuron

Spinal Cord

Sensory Neuron

Motor Neuron

Muscle

FIGURE 3–4 TYPES OF NEURONS. The pathways, shown schematically entering and leaving the spinal cord, are greatly simplified. In a complex reflex arc, innumerable sensory, motor, and interneurons may be involved.

respond in an automatic way. Instead, chiefly through interneurons, several brain circuits were aroused as he thought about the opportunity.

~

NATURE OF THE MESSAGE

The neural message is an electrochemical impulse. It travels along the nerve fiber chiefly by means of its electrical properties—through an exchange of electrical charges known as *ions.* This exchange can occur because the covering of each fiber is porous.

The nerve fiber, in effect, is a very tiny but lengthy battery. In its resting state, without stimulation, the fiber carries no message or current. The battery is not in operation. The membrane has positively charged sodium ions outside and positively charged potassium ions inside, but the overall charge is less positive inside than outside. Thus, relatively speaking, the charge inside is negative whenever the fiber is at rest.

In recent years, the passage of charged ions across the cell membrane has been studied by a revolutionary method. The *patch clamp technique* employs an extremely thin tube or pipette made of glass, which can be very tightly sealed to the cell membrane, thereby establishing a small area, or patch, adhering to the tip of the pipette, and this patch can be investigated by chemical or electrical stimulation. With a strong seal, the patch of membrane can even be removed from its cell, or it can be opened into the cell, offering further opportunities for stimulating the membrane and deducing the ways in which ions flow across it, influencing its voltage (Neher & Sakmann, 1992).

RESTING AND ACTIVATED FIBERS. In its resting state, without stimulation, the nerve fiber is said to be **polarized** because it has opposite poles, or charges, on either side of the membrane. This unactivated state is also called the **resting potential** of the nerve fiber as it awaits a stimulus of a certain minimum intensity. A stimulus must be above a certain level of intensity, or threshold, to activate the fiber.

When the resting fiber has been sufficiently stimulated, either by an impulse from a receptor or by activity in adjacent fibers, the membrane becomes more permeable or porous in the region of stimulation. Some closed "sodium gates" of the membrane open very briefly, permitting positively charged sodium ions to flow in for an instant. This part of the nerve fiber, where the positively charged particles have moved inside, is momentarily **depolarized,** or activated. This change prompts positively charged potassium ions to flow out, causing the inside of the fiber to become increasingly negative. Then tiny ionic pumps in the cell restore the normal balance within a few milliseconds, returning that part of the fiber to its original resting state.

This change in voltage passes successively along the length of the neuron, constituting the nerve impulse. In a crude way, the traveling impulse is like a burning fuse on a firecracker. It produces a similar increase in permeability, or depolarization, in the immediately adjacent part of the neuron, causing an influx of sodium particles there, and so on, until the depolarization has traveled the length of the fiber. Its maximum speed in human nervous tissue is 240 miles per hour, and it is fastest in the relatively thick fibers (Figure 3–5).

This brief shift in electrical energy, the nerve impulse, is also called the **action potential,** and all impulses traveling along a particular neuron have the same energy, regardless of the nature or intensity of the activating stimulus. The reason is that a stimulus does no more than release the electrical energy already in the fiber; it does not contribute energy. This property of the neuron, responding at full strength or not at all, is known as the **all-or-none law,** which is illustrated whenever a doorbell is pressed. If you press it hard enough, the bell sounds; if you press harder, it does not sound any louder.

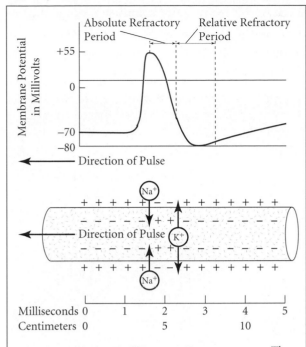

FIGURE 3–5 NERVE IMPULSE. The top of this figure shows the electrical changes in the action potential as it moves along the neuron. The bottom of the figure shows the corresponding chemical changes. Sodium ions (Na) enter the neuron, causing potassium ions (K) to flow outward. This successive release of energy along the neuron constitutes the nerve impulse.

The nerve fiber is like a doorbell in another sense. Most doorbells cannot be reused until the button pops out again. A waiting or recovery period, known as the **refractory period,** is also necessary with the nerve fiber as the sodium and potassium particles return to their original positions, ready for another firing. This refractory period has two phases. Immediately after activation, during the *absolute refractory phase,* no stimulus of any strength can start a nerve impulse. This phase differs from fiber to fiber but it is very brief, usually only about 1/1,000th of a second.

After this phase, there is a progressive increase in sensitivity. During this period, a stimulus that is stronger than normal can produce another response. This interval between the absolute refractory phase and restoration of the normal resting state is known as the *relative refractory phase,* and it lasts a few thousandths of a second.

If a nerve, when it does fire, responds only on an all-or-none basis, how are we able to experience different levels of stimulus intensity? How can we discriminate, for example, between a dim pocket light and the glare of a bright neon sign? The answer lies in the arrangements of nerve fibers, which typically occur in bundles, allowing thousands of fibers to be activated simultaneously, depending on the intensity of the stimulus. The optic nerve, for example, has an estimated 400,000 fibers, and increasing the stimulus intensity can have two effects. It can increase the frequency of discharge in each fiber that responds during the relative refractory phase, and it can activate more and more receptors and fibers.

INTERACTIONS AT THE SYNAPSE.
Musical ability, the capacity for conversation, and all other manifestations of human flexibility are due to a vital feature of the human nervous system. Unlike the jellyfish, in which each fiber is welded to another fiber, and the worm, in which fibers in certain segments are welded together, the ends of nerve fibers in human beings do not make direct contact with each other to form fixed connections. Rather, their endings are simply very close together.

The small space between all adjacent neurons, where the nerve impulse passes from one neuron to another, is called a **synapse.** It is the site at the end of an axon where the stimulation is transmitted to the dendrite or cell body of the adjacent neuron, and it occupies a central position in our understanding of the flexibility of mammalian behavior. At some synapses, nerve impulses are inhibited and go no further. At others, they converge and activate one or many other fibers in the spinal cord and brain. Hence the behavioral outcomes are indeed innumerable.

Here, at the synapse, where several impulses converge, the all-or-none law no longer prevails. Instead, small changes in polarization may occur in the membrane of the receiving cell. A change of this sort is known as a **graded potential** because the size of the shift can vary, depending on the amount and type of information in the incoming message. One shift may be slight, too small to activate the fiber. Another may be larger. Amid this interplay of numerous influences, the graded potential may reach a certain level of intensity. It then stimulates the nerve to fire, producing an action potential.

In other words, transmission of the impulse *along the neuron* follows the all-or-none law. Transmission *from neuron to neuron* follows the principle of the graded potential.

How does the graded potential reach the necessary intensity to fire the neuron? It does so in two ways. Sometimes impulses from several different axons converge at adjacent points on a receiving membrane, causing it to fire, an outcome known as *spatial summation.* Sometimes, as the axons continue to fire in very quick succession, collectively they cause the nerve to fire, a phenomenon known as *temporal summation.*

❧

CHEMICAL FOUNDATIONS

But how does the nerve impulse cross the synapse? It does not jump across, like a spark, as once was thought (Figure 3–6). Instead, the chemical bases of this electrochemical impulse become more significant. They convey the impulse across the synapse to adjacent neurons. In the final analysis, the diversity of human behavior is significantly dependent on these chemical substances.

Consider the diversity in Ray's behavior. At one moment, he reached a frenzied high in a musical improvisation. At another, he enjoyed table tennis, taking much pleasure in his swift reactions. Even opponents agreed that his successful play was marked by very sudden, unexpected shots. "*Frivolous* shots," Ray called them (Sacks, 1987). On still other occasions, he accepted the enticing challenge of revolving doors. For him, they made the world go round. He gleefully dodged in and out of them with lightning

speed and a ready quip, spinning a tale about his fancy footwork. This broad range of activity, from beating drums to beating doors, was made possible by chemical substances in the synaptic spaces.

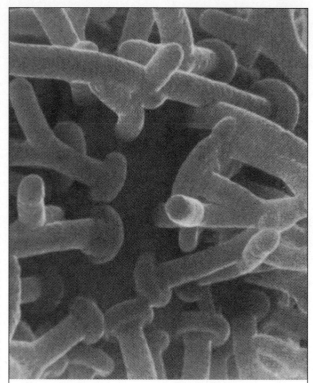

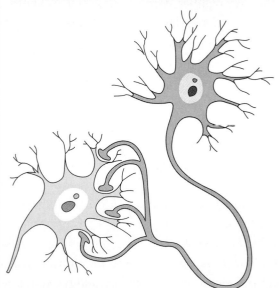

FIGURE 3–6 THE SYNAPSE. A small space, known as the synaptic space, lies between the transmitting axon and the receiving dendrite or cell body, as shown in the drawing and magnified in the photograph.

**OPERATION OF NEUROTRANSMIT-
TERS.** These chemicals are contained in small sacs
or vesicles in the knobs at the ends of axons. Each
of them is called a **neurotransmitter substance,**
meaning a chemical that, when discharged into a
synapse, travels across the space to act on the membrane of the adjacent nerve fiber. One chemical
may depolarize the receiving membrane, causing
activity in that membrane, contributing to an *excitatory reaction.* Another may make the receiving membrane more polarized and therefore more resistant
to firing, contributing to an *inhibitory reaction.* In a
broad sense, there are two kinds of reactions at
synapses, excitation or inhibition, depending partly
on which receptor sites are activated.

More specifically, in traveling across the
synapse, the neurotransmitter substance encounters
a neurotransmitter receptor, which is a site on the
receiving neuron with a specific molecular structure.
If the shape or structure of the transmitter substance matches that of the receptor site, then the
receiving neuron can accommodate that transmitter.
Since different neurotransmitters have different
molecular structures, some fit a particular site,
initiating a reaction or amplifying an effect; others,
at the same site, block the transmission, preventing
further stimulation. Still others do not fit the site
at all. Thus, arousal of a receiving neuron depends
not only on the neurotransmitter chemical but also
on the nature and structure of that receptor site.

This interpretation of synaptic transmission
has been known as the *lock-and-key hypothesis,* meaning
that the shape of the neurotransmitter substance,
the key, must fit the structure of the receiving
membrane, the "lock." And, of course, the key
needs to work in the lock, either through summation or on its own, initiating an excitatory or
inhibitory reaction in the receiving cell membrane.

This release of chemicals into the synapse
occurs in a fraction of a second, with thousands of
neurons firing, resulting in a deluge of neurotransmitters into the synaptic space. Between firings,
those neurotransmitters that remain in the synapse
are drawn back into their sacs once again or otherwise rendered ineffective by various clean-up chemicals also in the system. The whole process is
designed to produce an infinite variety of activating
and inhibiting forces, depending on the chemical
structures of the transmitter substances and receptor sites (Figure 3–7).

Alcohol consumption, for example, blocks certain neurotransmitters responsible for brain activity,
eventually inducing sleep. But it also disrupts the
work of other neurotransmitters, awakening the
person earlier than usual. Certain mind-altering
drugs that cause distortion in perception and consciousness appear to have these pronounced effects
because their chemical structures are similar to

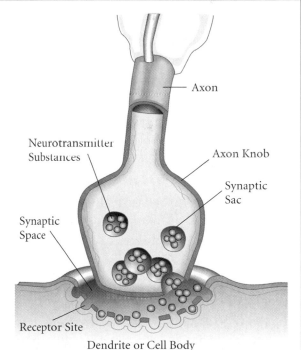

**FIGURE 3–7 TRANSMISSION IN
SYNAPTIC SPACE.** Upon reaching the knob at
the end of the axon, the nerve impulse releases chemical
messengers from small sacs, and these neurotransmitter
substances travel into the synaptic space. If they fit the
molecular structure of the receptor site in a receiving
dendrite or cell body, they cause a voltage change in that
cell, exciting or inhibiting a nerve impulse. If they do not
fit into that molecular structure, they are removed by other
chemicals or return to the original axon.

those of natural neurotransmitters found in the brain. In other words, there are critical differences among the neurotransmitters released in the brain.

The number of different transmitters in the human body is not known at this time, for proposed substances must meet several stringent criteria. Nevertheless, experts have identified 50 or more, and a few have been studied extensively.

PROMINENT NEUROTRANSMITTERS.

Perhaps the most thoroughly studied neurotransmitter is **acetylcholine,** which plays a prominent role in muscular activity. It can be either excitatory or inhibitory. It is excitatory at motor synapses in the peripheral nervous system, important in such activities as making music, playing table tennis, and dodging revolving doors. Certain gases and poisons that produce convulsions or seizures apparently do so by prolonging the action of acetylcholine.

A decrease of acetylcholine in the central nervous system is prominent in **Alzheimer's disease,** a rapid deterioration of brain functions, especially in the elderly. It involves memory loss and disorientation in time and place. The decrease in acetylcholine associated with Alzheimer's disease is well documented, and it correlates with the severity of the disease (McDonald & Nemeroff, 1991).

Operating in a diffuse fashion, the neurotransmitter called **norepinephrine,** also known as *noradrenaline,* is influential in general arousal and mood, as well as in learning and memory. Exerting excitatory influences at synapses for the heart, blood vessels, and genitals, it can result in a highly pleasurable reaction. Amphetamines, stimulating its release, promote an alert, active state.

Another neurotransmitter, apparently related to norepinephrine, acts without such widespread effects. Thus **dopamine** influences emotional reactions, rather than general wakefulness, as well as learning and memory. It too is influenced by amphetamines and reserpine, and it may be a factor in severe behavior disorders, including schizo-phrenic reactions (Goteborgs, 1990). Blocking the transmission of dopamine at synapses, by the administration of chlorpromazine and other drugs, has proved useful in the treatment of psychosis and related mental disorders.

The operation of dopamine illustrates the exquisite complexities among and within neurotransmitters, for it also influences the control of voluntary movements. If dopamine is depleted in motor neurons, the result is slowness and inability to move, as in **Parkinson's disease,** characterized by muscular tremors, rigidity, and loss of voluntary control. This disease occurs primarily in men in later life and may be related to depression (Guze & Barrio, 1991; Oles, 1992). These patients need additional dopamine to become aroused. Sometimes their disease is combated with the administration of L-dopa, called a *dopamine precursor* because it is converted into dopamine.

Some people who are frenetic and highly aroused may profit from lower levels of dopamine, enabling them to act in a more stable, normal fashion. This outcome is achieved by administering a medication that is *antagonistic* to dopamine, meaning that it blocks or impedes the action of dopamine. In contrast, a drug or other substance that triggers or increases the action of a neurotransmitter is said to be *agonistic* to that neurotransmitter.

A light snack before bedtime can lead to increased production of **serotonin,** a neurotransmitter associated with drowsiness, sleep, and food metabolism. It plays a role in food intake and appetite, especially the ingestion of protein, carbohydrates, and even alcohol (Tollefson, 1991). Foods high in carbohydrates, such as spaghetti and bread, enhance the production of serotonin. Turkey also is high in the precursors of serotonin. If you must be an after-dinner speaker, do so only if you can choose the menu: no spaghetti, no turkey, no bread, and so forth. Serotonin operates in several areas of the brain and is known to be related to depression and hypertension, as well as to appetite and sleep (Bonate, 1991).

NEUROTRANSMITTER	GENERAL INFLUENCES	FUNCTIONS AND DISORDERS
Acetylcholine	Excitatory	Muscle movement, emotion, memory, cognitive functions.
Norepinephrine	Excitatory	Arousal, cognitive functions. Excess: mania. Deficit: depression.
Serotonin	Inhibitory	Sleep, appetite, awareness. Deficit: depression.
Dopamine	Inhibitory	Movement, emotional arousal, memory. Excess: schizophrenia.
GABA	Inhibitory	Deficit: seizures
Endorphins	Inhibitory	Suppression of pain.

TABLE 3–1 PROMINENT NEUROTRANSMITTERS. These functions are constantly being confirmed or revised. Additional functions and neurotransmitters are regularly being identified.

In normal functioning, there is an extraordinarily delicate balance among these neurotransmitter influences. One condition in which this balance goes awry is *epilepsy,* a neurological disorder characterized by attacks of convulsive movements, mental malfunction, and sometimes loss of consciousness. One important neurotransmitter in this disorder is **GABA,** an acronym for *gamma amino butyric acid,* recognized as the most widespread inhibitory transmitter.

Given the literally countless neurons in the central nervous system and their innumerable synapses, it is not surprising that the great majority of synaptic events in the brain are inhibitory. Without this inhibition, we would be overwhelmed by torrents of competing and unwanted messages. One might speculate about Ray in this regard. In his sudden, impulsive swearing, and even in other activities, did he sometimes experience a failure to inhibit?

COMPLEXITY OF NEURAL COMMUNICATION. As the delicate chemical messengers of the nervous system, neurotransmitters have produced several unexpected research findings. Early investigators reported that serotonin is associated with sleep; others found that it has no such role. Gradually, it was understood that any given neurotransmitter can serve in diverse ways. Moreover, different neurotransmitters have similar functions.

Serotonin and norepinephrine are both associated with depression; norepinephrine and dopamine influence arousal; acetylcholine and dopamine both play a role in memory and emotion; and so forth (Table 3–1).

Further evidence for the complexity of neural communication comes from the brain chemicals called **endorphins,** so named because they are endogenous, meaning produced in the body, and yet possess properties of morphine, an addictive opiate compound that reduces pain. In short, "endogenous morphines" are natural anesthetics apparently secreted by certain brain cells. They regulate pain by blocking pain signals from the peripheral nervous system. Their production may be stimulated during acupuncture, for example, thereby suppressing the experience of more painful medical procedures. They may operate locally in some situations, as in acupuncture, and more generally in others, when athletes or people in emergencies perform at high levels under otherwise painful circumstances, seemingly unaware of their injuries. These bodily changes have survival value, enabling animals and human beings to escape the immediate danger and then, afterward, tend to their wounds.

There has been some debate over the classification of endorphins as neurotransmitters. Some investigators simply regard them as endogenous opiate compounds produced in greater quantities under conditions of pain or stress. Others believe that they meet the basic requirements for neurotransmitters: chemical substances produced in the presynaptic neuron, released by the nerve impulse, and resulting in excitation or inhibition at the receptor site.

• THE HUMAN BRAIN •

Ray's quick wit and considerable strength of character enabled him to complete school and college. Afterward, he enjoyed a successful marriage, maintained friendships, and held several jobs. When not at work, he succeeded in all sorts of physical endeavors requiring quickness and accuracy. In sports, games, and physical challenges, his timing seemed almost unnatural, beyond the normal range.

Ray also engaged in various mental activities, including reading and writing. One day he read an article in the *Washington Post* that described some unusual behaviors he had experienced himself, and he decided to write to its author. He thought Dr. Oliver Sacks would receive hundreds of such letters, far more than he might answer, but he wrote anyway.

Ray was right. Sacks received many letters, and he gave all but one to appropriate colleagues. He intended to answer that one letter, thinking its author might profit from his assistance.

All of these diverse responses—playing games, reading, writing, thinking, and endless others—are related to developments in the human brain. Variously described as a wrinkled boxing glove, a head of cauliflower and its stalk, and a thick sack crumpled into a small space, the human brain is three pounds of moist rubberiness usefully studied from several viewpoints.

BRAIN AND EVOLUTION

From an evolutionary perspective, study of the human brain is usually considered in terms of its three major divisions: the hindbrain, midbrain, and forebrain. Approaching the brain in this way allows the discussion to proceed from the biological processes we share with other creatures to the mental capacities that uniquely characterize the human condition.

HINDBRAIN. Closest to the spinal cord and oldest of the three divisions in an evolutionary sense is the hindbrain, so named because it appears at the rear of the brain. The **hindbrain** plays a significant role in *vital functions,* such as waking, sleeping, balance, and coordination. One part, the **medulla,** controls digestion, breathing, and blood circulation. An adjacent organ, the *pons,* meaning "bridge," consists chiefly of motor neurons; it connects several structures serving underlying functions in waking and sleeping states, including dreams.

The largest structure of the hindbrain is the **cerebellum,** or "little brain," a major mechanism in maintaining posture and coordinating body movements. Impulses from receptors in the muscles, tendons, and joints provide it with information about movements throughout the body. Integrated in the cerebellum and associated structures, this information prompts return impulses to the muscles, tendons, and joints, initiating the proper adjustive actions. In this manner, when coupled with other organs, the cerebellum plays a role in our capacity to repeat well-practiced motor movements.

Some parts of the cerebellum appear to control movements of the whole body; others concern specific regions. Thus, damage to the central area may cause difficulty in posture and locomotion; damage in more lateral areas may disrupt arm and leg motions and rapidly alternating hand and finger movements. When Ray surprised the members of the band with his unexpected improvisations, the cerebellum played a key role in controlling these movements.

MIDBRAIN. A short segment between the hindbrain and upper brain regions is called the **midbrain,** serving a vital role in *processing information*

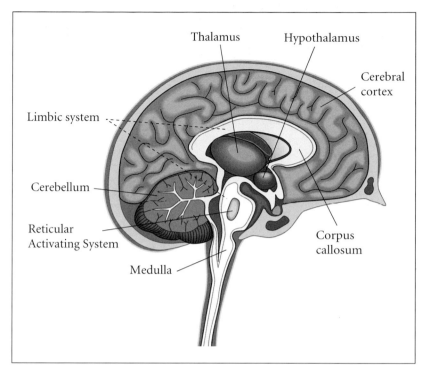

Thalamus   Hypothalamus

Cerebral cortex

Limbic system

Cerebellum

Reticular Activating System

Medulla

Corpus callosum

HINDBRAIN

Medulla: controls digestion and breathing. Example: Bodily processes convert Ray's dinner into assimilable substances.

Cerebellum: coordinates balance and muscle movements. Example: Ray plays a drum roll.

MIDBRAIN

Reticular Activating System: influences the onset of sleep and arousal. Example: Ray dozes off during intermission.

FOREBRAIN

Thalamus: relays incoming and outgoing messages. Example: Sounds of a bass fiddle and guitar are integrated and transmitted elsewhere in Ray's brain.

Hypothalamus: regulates biological activities, including eating, drinking, and many others. Example: Ray begins to feel hungry.

Limbic System: plays a key role in emotion and motivation. Example: On hearing familiar music, Ray feels sentimental.

Cerebral Cortex: guides perceiving, learning, memory, thinking, and voluntary behavior. Example: Ray thinks about meeting Sacha after the concert.

FIGURE III.1 BRAIN STRUCTURES AND FUNCTIONS. This cross-section shows the human brain from the right, indicating its major structures and functions. No one structure is solely responsible for any function; the brain operates in an integrated manner. The loosely defined limbic system, not clearly depicted here, is a group of interconnected structures lying deep beneath the cerebral cortex. The corpus callosum is discussed later.

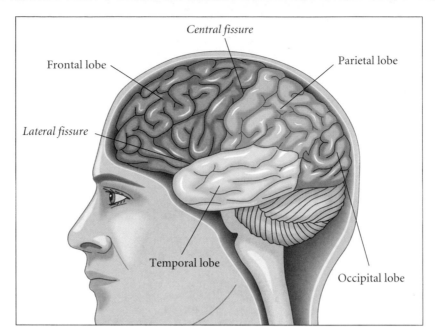

FIGURE III.2 LOBES OF THE CEREBRAL CORTEX. The four lobes, seen here from the left, are divided in some cases by a major crevice or fissure. The frontal and parietal lobes are separated by the central fissure. The temporal lobe is largely separated from them by the lateral fissure. The occipital lobe is not clearly delineated from either of its neighbors.

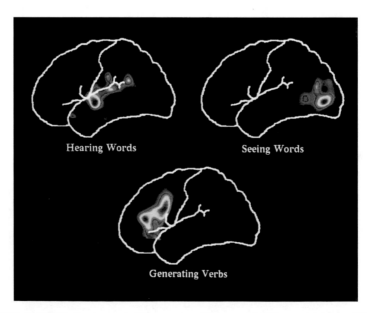

FIGURE III.3 PET SCANS. Different uses of language involve activities in different brain areas, as shown when a person is hearing, reading, or saying words. In these PET images, the red depicts the areas of most activitiy, followed in decreasing order by yellow, green, and then blue.

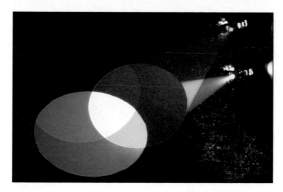

FIGURE IV.1 ADDITIVE COLOR MIXTURE. Combining lights of different colors adds wavelengths to the mixture. The result is some new color or, when all colors are combined, white light.

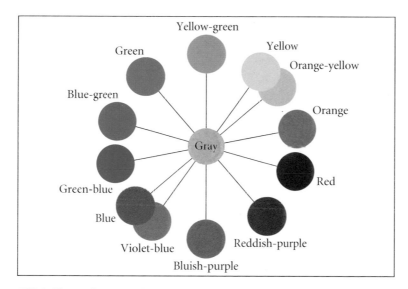

FIGURE IV.2 THE COLOR CIRCLE. The circle represents the color spectrum plus various shades of purple created by mixing red and blue. Mixing complementary colors, opposite one another on the circle, gives gray, but mixing any other pair produced an intermediate hue.

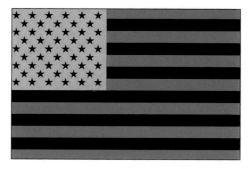

FIGURE IV.3 NEGATIVE AFTERIMAGE. Under bright illumination, gaze steadily for about one minute at the lower right corner of the yellow field of stars. Then look immediately at any white space above or beside the flag. The "Old Glory" you experience is composed of the complementary colors in your visual system, apparently due to receptor adaptation.

NORMAL COLOR VISION

RED-GREEN BLINDNESS

YELLOW-BLUE BLINDNESS

TOTAL COLOR BLINDNESS

FIGURE IV.4 COLOR BLINDNESS. The balloon colors and circular disc patterns below each photograph are shown as they would appear to people with normal color vision, red-green blindness, yellow-blue blindness, and total color blindness. The discs illustrate a test for color blindness. A person with normal color vision would readily perceive the red 48 against the green background, as would a person with yellow-blue blindness. People with red-green or total color blindness would not perceive the number at all.

for the upper brain regions, especially information coming from the eyes and ears. Sometimes the midbrain and hindbrain together are called the *brain stem.* In any case, they share many fibers that have a diffuse, netlike appearance and therefore are called the *reticular formation.* These shared netlike connections are also known as the **reticular activating system,** for they influence the arousal of the whole organism, acting like gates. When you fall asleep suddenly, the reticular activating system has abruptly stopped sending impulses to the many cortical synapses with which it has connections. When you are unable to fall asleep, the reticular system is still active.

The neurons in the reticular activating system vary widely in size. They also have long dendrites with diffuse branches, creating innumerable synaptic pathways, and axons that apparently make connections with their own cell bodies. Poorly designed for transmitting specific information, they appear to be well constructed for arousal and nonarousal.

Chiefly because he was so readily aroused, Ray was successful at table tennis, revolving doors, and repartee, but he also suffered a great deal. At work, he had been fired several times, not for incompetence, but for lack of restraint. At home, his emotional outbursts occasionally unsettled his wife. According to Ray, they were completely involuntary.

Worse yet, Ray was plagued by tics. A *tic* is a sudden, involuntary muscle twitch appearing habitually, usually in the face or extremities. In Ray, they appeared every few seconds, causing him to be severely stigmatized in public (Sacks, 1987).

Recognizing his condition as both a gift and a curse, he called himself "Witty Ticcy Ray." He was the "ticcer of Broadway," prone to "ticcy witticisms and witty ticcicisms" (Sacks, 1987).

All of these reactions—Ray's quickness, tics, and uncontrollable swearing—were influenced by elements of the hindbrain and midbrain. To the knowledgeable person, they suggested a possible disturbance in the midbrain, especially in those parts involved with the emotional aspects of personality. Ray was free from tics, tension, and uncontrollable outbursts only when completely at rest or working in some evenly paced, melodic fashion (Sacks, 1987).

FOREBRAIN. From an evolutionary viewpoint, the **forebrain**—the upper and most recently developed of the three major brain areas—most clearly separates the human brain from those of other animals, for it is fundamentally involved in *perceiving, remembering, and thinking.* The olfactory bulb, concerned with smell, is relatively smaller and less important in human beings than in many other animals, but other structures become larger and more elaborate as we ascend the evolutionary order.

These include, in particular, the *cerebral cortex*—the large, rounded structure at the top of the forebrain, divided into two nearly symmetrical hemispheres. This structure, to which we shall return shortly, allows human beings to recall the past and to ruminate on forthcoming events in ways apparently impossible for other species (Figure 3–8).

Of these three brain divisions, the human forebrain constitutes our greatest advance over all other

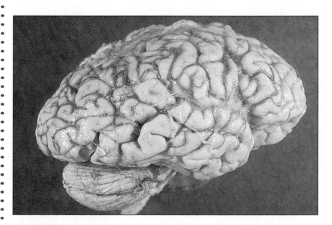

FIGURE 3–8 BRAIN AND EVOLUTION.
Shown from the right side, the forebrain is the large oval mass occupying most of the photo. The midbrain, in the interior, is not shown. The hindbrain is chiefly the lower, smaller oval-shaped region.

species, including other primates. The midbrain, prominent in biological motivation and emotion, is found in all mammalian species. And the hindbrain represents what human beings have in common with even the most primitive aquatic creatures: reflexes and other involuntary functions.

~

SUBCORTICAL STRUCTURES

In further study of the human brain, we turn from the evolutionary perspective to a somewhat simpler distinction between the lower and upper brain regions. The lower regions, at the very center of the brain, are often referred to as **subcortical structures,** for they lie beneath the outer covering, or cerebral cortex, occupying a region just above the spinal cord. These structures, for the most part, are found in the lower part of the forebrain. They play an important role in regulating basic bodily functions, including eating, sexual behavior, and emotional reactions.

RELAY ROLE OF THE THALAMUS.
Among the major subcortical structures, the thalamus, hypothalamus, and limbic system are especially important in emotional behavior and general arousal. The **thalamus,** meaning "inner room," is situated at the very center of the brain, serving as a prominent switchboard for various brain regions. It is, according to many, the brain's finest relay station. With the exception of impulses for smell, which go more directly from the olfactory bulb to the olfactory cortex, the thalamus manages the input from sensory systems throughout the body. It is justifiably called a fundamental link between the external environment and the various parts of the nervous system, especially the cerebral cortex.

The axons of the optic nerve, for example, connect largely with the thalamus, which integrates these visual signals with information already in the system. The thalamus also receives auditory, tactile, and related information from other sensory systems. Then it relays this information to appropriate regions in the central nervous system, especially the cerebral cortex. At the same time, the thalamus is responsive to feedback *from* the cortex, for it has both ascending and descending connections. Especially in the context of sensory input, it deserves its reputation as a relay station.

In addition, the thalamus plays a role in the formation of memories, particularly the reception of new information. It is not evident, however, that it has any significant function in the consolidation and retention of these memories.

REGULATION BY THE HYPOTHALAMUS.
If there is any significance in the old aphorism about not judging a package by its size, then in brain regions it certainly applies to the hypothalamus. The prefix *hypo* means "under" or "lower," and the **hypothalamus,** a very small structure situated just below the thalamus, has a major role in regulating all sorts of biological and psychological activities. It is often said to be critically involved in four fundamental functions: feeding, fighting, fleeing, and—making love. It maintains this pervasive control partly through its influence over the autonomic and endocrine systems, considered at the close of this chapter.

The role of the hypothalamus in eating is evident with damage to its central area, which results in overeating. In contrast, damage to its peripheral regions causes self-imposed starvation. Injury or disease in still other areas can disturb thirst, sexual behavior, and emotional expression.

Not solely responsible for full emotional experience, the hypothalamus is nevertheless a central organ in emotional reactions. Numerous experiments have verified this integrative role of the hypothalamus in emotional behavior.

Overwhelmed by his uncontrollable emotional reactions, Ray was delighted to receive a letter from

Oliver Sacks, author of the article in the *Washington Post* and world-renowned neurologist. Especially interested in disorders of the subcortical structures, including the hypothalamus, Sacks had decided that Ray perhaps was afflicted with an unusual disorder and invited him for a consultation. This disorder, *Tourette's syndrome,* is characterized by tics—repetitive movements or nonword noises—and often by unprovoked swearing, as well (Berecz, 1992). In addition, there may be an impulsive tendency to repeat the words or phrases of other people, or even their gestures (Table 3–2).

The causes of Tourette's syndrome are unknown, but it seems that people with this disorder have an excess of certain neurotransmitters in subcortical regions, particularly dopamine. Just as lethargic patients with Parkinson's disease can be aroused to more normal action by the administration of L-dopa, with its dopamine derivatives, patients with Tourette's syndrome can achieve more normal functioning by blocking this neurotransmitter through administration of haloperidol, known under the brand name Haldol, which is antagonistic to dopamine. When Ray met with Dr. Sacks, the diagnosis of Tourette's syndrome was confirmed. Ray was then tested for responsiveness to Haldol and proved extraordinarily sensitive. He received a prescription for three very small doses daily. Initially this treatment seemed satisfactory, suppressing both the tics and the unpredictable emotional episodes.

LIMBIC SYSTEM. Certain portions of the thalamus and hypothalamus, along with several other organs lying in a circuit along the brain stem, constitute the **limbic system,** which plays a key role in emotion and motivation. The term *limbic* means "border" or "outlying," and this system of organs represents the inner or under border of the cerebral hemispheres. There is still some controversy, however, about just which subcortical organs should be included in this system.

The basic point here is that emotion is not the exclusive function of any specific brain center but rather is the result of an activated circuitry of organs called the limbic system. Within this system our sensory experiences take on an emotional tone. The thalamus, with sensory input, and the hypothalamus, with regulatory functions, are natural contributors to this system. Overall, the limbic system plays an important role in the integration of emotional behavior. Generally, it is slow to turn on, but once turned on, it is slow to turn off.

The *amygdala,* a limbic organ that looks like a large almond, is situated between the thalamus and hypothalamus. It also mediates emotional behavior, and it plays an important role in the emotional aspects of memory. Stimulation with a needle microelectrode implanted in this area has produced aggressive attacks and apparently unpleasant emotions in animals. Electrodes in adjacent areas prompt only a momentary disruption, not a prolonged reaction.

SYMPTOM	DESCRIPTION	ROLE IN DIAGNOSIS	RAY'S CASE
Tics	Involuntary, repetitive movements or noises	Essential	Present
Swearing	Unprovoked foul language	Not essential	Present
Echolalia	Involuntary repetition of someone's words	Not essential	Absent
Onset of illness	Prior to 21 years of age	Essential	Present

TABLE 3–2 DIAGNOSIS OF TOURETTE'S SYNDROME. Swearing and echolalia are not essential for the diagnosis. In severe Tourette's syndrome, there may be imitation of gestures (Comings, 1990).

Oliver Sacks had decided that Ray's uncontrollable outbursts were related to disturbances in the limbic system, including the hypothalamus and amygdala, where the basic emotional determinants of personality are lodged (Sacks, 1987). Ray's symptoms disappeared and reappeared with the presence and absence of a slight amount of medication, which apparently had its strongest impact in this region. Nevertheless, the limbic system is concerned with more than emotion and motivation. It also plays a complex role in learning and memory.

Another area of the limbic system, the *septal area*, was accidentally discovered to play a role in pleasurable emotional experience. Around midcentury, a young psychologist named James Olds, bent on replicating some earlier studies with needle electrodes, apparently used a bent needle, positioning it slightly in the wrong part of the brain. To his surprise, a rat with the improperly implanted electrode, allowed to stimulate itself in the septal area by pressing a bar, eventually did so at the rate of 500 to 5,000 times per hour. Other animals also behaved as if they were experiencing pleasure, some stimulating themselves 2,000 times per hour for a full day, prompting Olds to call this particular brain region the "pleasure center" (Olds, 1956).

Today we know that it is the neurochemical system in the septal area, not the septum itself, that supports this phenomenon. The prominent substances appear to be norepinephrine and dopamine. We also know that human beings examined in a clinical setting apparently do not respond with the same emotional intensity as do animals studied experimentally in a laboratory (Valenstein, 1973).

The nature of these limbic regions is indeed puzzling. Unlike such obviously motivated behaviors as eating and sexual activity, electrical self-stimulation is sometimes not marked by temporary diminution of interest for extended periods. Still further, alcohol and other drugs seem to have a stronger effect in this area than in other brain regions. Thus, it has been hypothesized that its motivating effects may involve some sort of physiological addiction; successive stimulations may increase the craving.

This topic has developed into a broad research field now called *intracranial self-stimulation* (Olds & Forbes, 1981). The most promising findings to date suggest that dopamine may play a critical role (Wise & Rompre, 1989). Overall, this research provides an excellent example of a basic theme of this book: the role of empiricism in modern psychology. Investigators have tried one approach, then another, and another, all based on stimulation of specific areas and direct observation of the behavioral reactions.

CEREBRAL CORTEX

The largest and most obvious aspects of the human brain are structures of the forebrain or upper brain regions, the two cerebral hemispheres. They are vital in learning, memory, and other high-level thought processes. The term *cerebrum,* often applied to the brain as a whole, refers to these two hemispheres. Each hemisphere, for the most part, pertains to the opposite side of the body. The left hemisphere serves the right side; the right hemisphere serves the left.

Our special interest lies in the outer covering, or bark, of the cerebral hemispheres, known as the **cerebral cortex,** which has a smooth surface in most lower animals but contains many folds, or convolutions, in human beings, providing a large neural surface. The significance of these folds becomes readily evident when you imagine trying to place a large piece of thin tissue paper into a small cup. When crumpled, it readily fits. Owing to its important role in higher mental processes, the cerebral cortex is sometimes called our "thinking cap." Much of it is also called the neocortex, meaning "new covering," for it covers other parts of the cortex that are older in an evolutionary sense (Figure III.1 Color).

Structurally, the two hemispheres are separated by the longitudinal fissure, a large crevice that runs from front to rear. In addition, each hemisphere is less obviously divided into four sections or lobes: **frontal lobes,** over the eyes, involved in motor control, as well as cognitive functions; **temporal lobes,** near the ears, for processing of auditory information; **occipital lobes,** at the extreme back of the head, where visual information is processed; and **parietal lobes,** at the top and back of the brain, concerned with body feeling, especially sensitivity in the skin, muscles, and body cavity (Figure III.2).

STUDYING THE CORTEX. There are several ways of studying the subcortical and cortical regions of the brain. Some have been mentioned already, including clinical studies of brain damage in human beings, experimental studies of brain lesions in animals, and electrical brain stimulation. Additional methods permit non-invasive studies of the intact living brain. One of these, called the **electroencephalograph** (EEG), is a device for recording the spontaneous electrical patterns of the brain, sometimes called *brain waves.* Regular and irregular patterns can be detected. This procedure is described more fully in a later chapter on consciousness.

Newer, more dramatic methods use powerful electronic devices that produce photograph-like images of the living brain. These successive images are called *brain scans,* and the device is known as a *brain scanner.* The basic technique is evident in the term *tomography,* which comes from two Greek words. *Tome* means "cutting," for these images cut across different regions of the brain. *Graphein* means "recording." Thus, a *tomograph* is a device that records a series of brain images.

The most common brain scan is *computerized tomography,* called the **CT scan,** or *CAT scan,* produced by successive X-rays of a given location in the head, each from a slightly different angle, fed into a computer. There they are synthesized, giving an in-depth computerized image of the structure of the brain. By combining successive images, each depicting a different slice of the brain, large areas of the brain can be portrayed, thereby revealing evidence of damage from injury or disease.

Another promising method which shows the brain's structure is *magnetic resonance imaging,* called the **MRI scan** because it uses an intense magnetic field to generate these images. When the magnetic field is turned on and off, each brain element has its own particular response, and when these different resonances are combined and analyzed by a computer, they show normal and abnormal brain conditions. These pictures are extraordinarily sensitive and more detailed than those available in the CT scan, and there is no danger from radiation. However, they are also more expensive at this time.

Another tomographic method, the **PET scan,** meaning *positron emission tomography,* requires the subject to ingest a glucose compound that is utilized in the brain. Then the subject engages in various activities, such as talking, solving problems, or relaxing. The brain areas most activated utilize the most glucose and thus reveal the function with which they are most closely associated. This technique receives its name because it shows *positively* charged particles *emitted* from the *tomogram,* or cross section, of the brain. Extremely useful in brain research, it reveals activities in the brain, not just its structure. In other words, the PET scan shows the brain *at work* (Figure III.3).

One review over a five-year period reported the CT, MRI, and PET techniques as equally effective in detecting moderately to severely impaired patients with Alzheimer's disease, often with 100% accuracy. However, with mildly impaired patients, the PET and CT techniques were most accurate (Albert & Lafleche, 1991). In contrast, studies of patients with head injuries showed MRI to be more sensitive than the CT scan for detecting organically based neuropsychological deficits (Wilson, 1990). Thus, the different techniques can serve similar and also different functions.

MOTOR CORTEX. We know that the primary area for controlling body movements is a narrow strip of cortical tissue at the rear of the frontal lobe directly in front of the central fissure, known as the **motor cortex.** Here, the degree of control required for specific body parts is closely related to the size of the brain area involved. The finer and more coordinated the movements, the larger is the cortical region devoted to these movements. The fingers, hands, lips, and tongue occupy large parts of the motor cortex; the arms and legs occupy lesser areas; and the hips and shoulders, which involve the least precision, occupy the smallest areas.

Furthermore, control of the body parts is represented in an inverted sequence with reference to an upright human being. Control of the toes, feet, and legs appears near the top of each hemisphere; the trunk is toward the middle; and the arms, hands, neck, and head are near the bottom.

When Ray moved his feet, dashing through a doorway, impulses occurred at the top of his motor cortex. Impulses were emitted lower down the side when he smiled and boasted about his success. In both cases, the locations were just forward of the central fissure (Figure 3–9).

Within a week after beginning his medication, which was less than 1 milligram daily, Ray returned to the clinic with a black eye, a broken nose, and several disparaging remarks about the medication. "So much for your f——— Haldol," he growled. As it turned out, even these very small doses so interfered with his neural transmission and motor coordination that he had been bashed by a revolving door. His tics, rather than disappearing, simply became slow and extended.

Ray wanted to give up the medication. If there were only two alternatives, he much preferred to be his quicker, sharper "old self," dashing through doorways and winning at table tennis, suffering his accustomed tics and obscenities. Others, however, had higher hopes. Most important, Ray's physician decided that the medication, to be successful, required a new psychological outlook on the part of the patient (Sacks, 1987). Learning perhaps played a role in Ray's behavior.

SENSORY CORTEX. Research on the **sensory cortex,** which receives incoming information, has shown that the primary visual areas are in the occipital lobes and that each eye sends nerve impulses to both lobes. Impulses for auditory experiences are received chiefly in the temporal lobes. Reception by each ear is also represented in both lobes.

The primary cortical area for body feeling is the front part of the parietal lobes. This specialized area is called the *somatosensory cortex* because it mediates feeling within the body. Body feeling, also called **somesthesis,** has two divisions: external or *cutaneous sensitivity*, involving sensitivity to pressure, temperature, and pain on the skin; and internal, including *kinesthesis*, which is the feeling in muscles, tendons, and joints, and also *visceral sensitivity*, the feeling in internal organs and glands. Receptors for these forms of stimulation are located throughout much of the body. Again, the body is represented in an inverted sequence. When Ray felt something underfoot, impulses arrived at the top of his cortex. When the revolving door bashed his nose, messages were sent to the lower portions of his somatosensory area. And again, there is a relationship between the degree of cortical specialization and the performance of the body. The larger the relevant brain area, the greater is the sensitivity in the corresponding body part. In this region of the brain, human beings are largely fingers and palms, lips and tongue (Figure 3–9).

ASSOCIATION CORTEX. As suggested previously, these cortical areas are not the exclusive seat of any movement or experience. Despite our need to discuss them separately, no one area completely controls any complex human reaction. The control is inevitably shared by other areas as well.

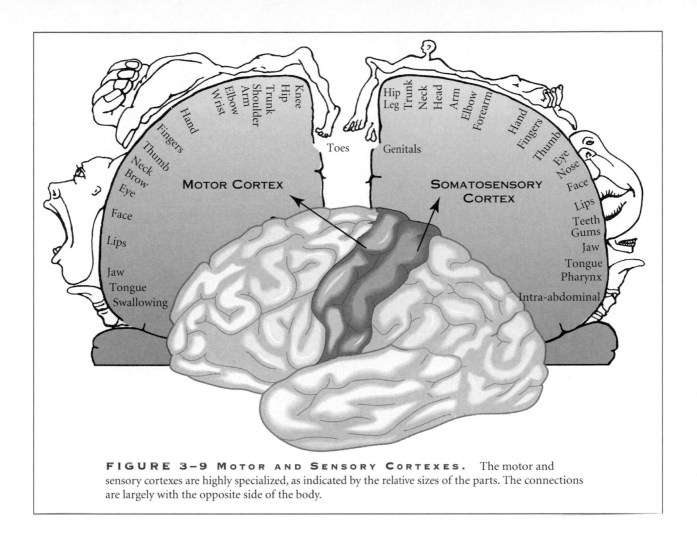

FIGURE 3–9 MOTOR AND SENSORY CORTEXES. The motor and sensory cortexes are highly specialized, as indicated by the relative sizes of the parts. The connections are largely with the opposite side of the body.

Occupying large sections of the human brain around the motor and sensory areas is the **association cortex,** so called because it seems to be involved in the integration of information. It does not receive information directly from the sense organs; instead, data are brought together and presumably analyzed here. Not surprisingly, the association cortex seems to be most significantly involved in memory, language, and other complex mental processes. Knowing a certain piece of music, Ray nevertheless introduced variations. The association cortex was intimately involved in these improvisations.

The significance of the association areas for touch can be illustrated by reference to a *disease* known as *astereognosis,* literally meaning "without tac-

tual knowledge of space." Normally, a blindfolded person asked to handle a small cube has no difficulty identifying this object. But a person with seriously impaired association areas for touch is unable to recognize it by touch alone. Loss of the association tissue causes impressions of touch to lose their meaning. Differences in sharpness and smoothness can be experienced, assuming that the sensory areas remain intact, but they cannot be identified.

When brain disorders involve language functions, we speak of **aphasia,** meaning "without language." This disruption is most likely if the damage is in the left cerebral hemisphere, for language is managed by that hemisphere in most of us. A portion of the frontal lobe, called *Broca's area,* plays a central role in *producing* speech. An afflicted individual makes sense but talks very slowly and with diffi-culty.

A region in the left temporal lobe, known as *Wernicke's area,* is involved in *understanding* speech and making it meaningful. An afflicted individual can-not comprehend language. Or this person may speak fluently but utter statements that are non-sense, completely lacking in meaning. The separate words may be intelligible, but they are used in a jumbled sequence, showing no meaningful relation to each other.

~

HEMISPHERIC SPECIALIZATION

When playing the drums, Ray used both hands simul-taneously, rapidly and rhythmically. In more routine activities, such as taking his medication, one hand held the container while the other unscrewed the top. How did Ray coordinate such movements?

The key organ here is the **corpus callosum,** a large bundle of nerve fibers between the two cerebral hemispheres, joining them at the lower areas of the association cortex. Although it was considered for years to be merely a structural connection, researchers eventually showed that the corpus callosum plays a very important role in coordinating functions in both sides of the body, enabling the hemispheres to coop-erate by sending visual, auditory, and other informa-tion back and forth (Figure 3–10). Later, they showed that what happens in one side of the brain does not necessarily take place in the other. This con-dition, referred to as **hemispheric specialization,** means that the two hemispheres do not perform exactly the same functions; they have somewhat dif-ferent but largely overlapping capacities.

SPLIT-BRAIN RESEARCH. A surgical procedure in which the corpus callosum is com-pletely cut, leaving the two hemispheres joined only at subcortical levels, is called the *split-brain technique.* This unusual procedure eventually led to an impor-tant discovery: that the two hemispheres do not handle the same information in the same way. This condition was suddenly brought to public attention in the 1960s by Roger Sperry and his colleagues, who conducted studies with human subjects after they had under-gone split-brain surgery for severe epilepsy. Afterward, the epileptic activity did not spread to the other hemisphere; there were decreased attacks in the initiating hemisphere; and previously hopeless epileptic cases went for years without seizures (Gazzaniga, Bogen, & Sperry, 1965; Sperry, 1968). Moreover, people with this operation appeared to be essentially normal.

Later, Sperry noted that with the midconnec-tions destroyed, each hemisphere has its own style, storing its own memories and functioning ade-quately alone. Thus a strong case can be made for two consciousnesses or two minds housed in the same skull (Sperry, 1968, 1984). This finding has led to an enormous upsurge of interest in similari-ties and differences in information processing between the two hemispheres (Hellige, 1990).

In one study, split-brain patients were com-pared with normal people for attention to visual stimuli. Different patterns were positioned simulta-neously on each side of the head, and each subject engaged in a visual search task, scanning these pat-terns as rapidly as possible. Split-brain patients per-formed the task faster than normal people, suggesting that each of the surgically separated hemispheres maintained an independent focus of attention during the visual search (Luck, Hillyard, & Mangun, 1989).

NORMAL DIFFERENCES. This research showed that even if the right hemisphere knows the answer in a simple test involving two objects, the split-brain patient cannot *say* the correct answer. The person will reply that he or she does not know or did not see the test objects. The reason is that for most people the *left hemisphere* is more dominant in using words, numbers, and reasoning,

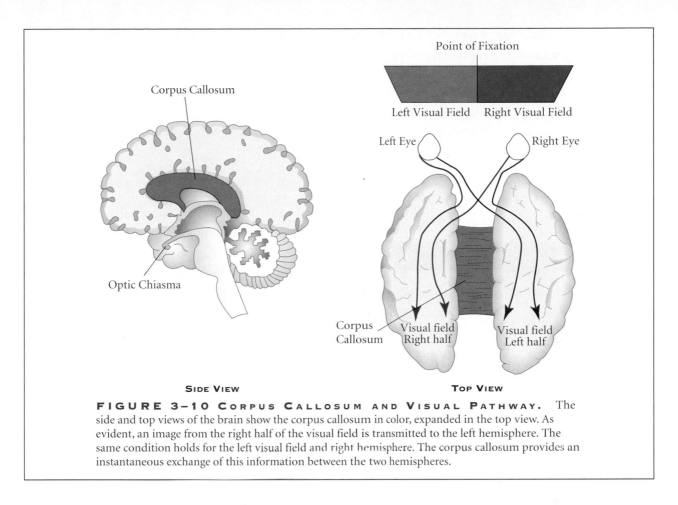

FIGURE 3–10 CORPUS CALLOSUM AND VISUAL PATHWAY. The side and top views of the brain show the corpus callosum in color, expanded in the top view. As evident, an image from the right half of the visual field is transmitted to the left hemisphere. The same condition holds for the left visual field and right hemisphere. The corpus callosum provides an instantaneous exchange of this information between the two hemispheres.

especially spoken language. If you ask the individual to grasp the correct object or point to the correct word instead, the person can do so with the left hand, using the right hemisphere.

The right hemisphere, although generally subordinate in the use of language, also has special capabilities. It can manage only simple numerical problems but, for example, it exceeds the left hemisphere in recognizing faces, important for social responsiveness; in assembling objects, such as blocks and puzzles; and in drawing three-dimensional objects. Split-brain people using the left hand and therefore the right hemisphere assemble objects more readily than when using the right hand and left hemisphere, even when they are naturally right-handed. Thus the *right hemisphere* appears to be the locus of control for synthesizing and utilizing spatial information.

Evidence for this specialization has been obtained in a variety of ways. With split-brain patients, electrical impulses in the left hemisphere increased during language problems and those in the right hemisphere increased during spatial relations problems (McCallum & Glynn, 1979). Among subjects who underwent diverse forms of brain surgery, recognition of the words for songs was related to activity in the left hemisphere; recognition of the melodies was related to activity in the right or both hemispheres (Samson & Zatorre, 1991).

In general terms, the left hemisphere tends to be analytical and logical, concerned with words. The right hemisphere seems more holistic and intuitive, concerned with spatial processes. On this basis, creativity perhaps involves contributions from both hemispheres. In fact, both hemispheres have some competence for many tasks, but they seem to process the information in qualitatively different ways (Hellige, 1990).

Again, a reminder is appropriate. The terms "right-brained" and "left-brained" are grossly inaccurate when used in the same way that we speak of handedness. The cerebral hemispheres are *integrated*. They are separate but complementary information processing subsystems (Hellige, 1993).

• INTERLOCKING SYSTEMS •

Integration is further emphasized when we consider the context in which the nervous system must operate. Directly or indirectly, it becomes involved in routine activities, emergency situations, and maintenance functions, such as growth, conservation of energy, and reproductive reactions. In short, the nervous system has interlocking associations with many other systems of the body. The story of Witty Ticcy Ray emphasizes this point: The biological mechanisms that underlie human behavior and experience are interconnected in exquisitely complex and balanced ways. This integration is also readily evident in the autonomic nervous system and endocrine system, to which we now turn.

And here, a further word about Ray is in order. His physician had decided that Ray's problem was no longer exclusively one of brain malfunction. Over the years, it had become *partly* psychological, as well. There was an interaction between Ray's physiological and psychological conditions; one could not be readjusted without the other.

Ray had a different view. "Suppose you *could* take away the tics," he said. "What would be left? I consist of tics—there is nothing else." Partly joking because he was obviously very skillful in many ways, Ray and his physician struck a bargain. For 3 months Ray would go off the medication, during

which time they would make a deep and patient exploration of Ray's thoughts about himself, his tics and emotional upheavals, and what life might offer without Tourette's syndrome. After this intensive insight therapy, Ray would try the medication once again, taking the same small doses prescribed previously.

Ray proved adept at this self-scrutiny; later, when he began taking the medication again, the result was remarkable. Prepared to understand its effects, he found himself released from a problem that had dominated his life since he was 4 years old. With a freedom from tics he never imagined, he became loved not as a clown but as a valued member of society, joking less but certainly pleasing Sacha and his coworkers more. For nine years, Ray lived with no tics and no emotional outbursts.

These and further details of Ray's life were reported by Sacks in a series of clinical cases with an odd title, *The Man Who Mistook His Wife for a Hat* (1987). This title had nothing to do with Ray. The narrative about Ray, however, was supplemented by a brief conversation with the author, who kept all identities confidential.

AUTONOMIC FUNCTIONS

Regrettably, this more settled life that Ray experienced came at a high cost, at least for him. The drug eliminated his emotional crises and tics, but it also reduced him to an average, competent individual in music, conversation, and sports. His sudden, wild musical improvisations, which formerly arose from a tic or after compulsively striking the drum, no longer appeared. For someone of his earlier talents, life had become routine—too routine and even a bit discouraging (Sacks, 1987).

To experience a stable, routine life, we all depend on several interconnected systems of the body, devoted to respiration, circulation, digestion, urination, and so forth. They provide an appropriate internal environment within which the central and peripheral nervous systems operate, and they also influence behavior. The system chiefly responsible for regulating these involuntary actions, both in routine and emergency situations, is called the *autonomic nervous system* because it was once thought to be completely independent of voluntary control. As the name indicates, it is part of the nervous system and, as the research shows, this earlier conception of total autonomy has changed.

OPPOSITIONAL DIVISIONS. The autonomic nervous system, as noted earlier, is composed of two divisions that operate essentially but not completely in opposition to one another. The **sympathetic nervous system** plays a dominant role in emotion. The heart pounds, gastric and salivary secretions are checked, and adrenaline flows, all in an integrated fashion because the sympathetic division has assumed control. It causes blood vessels of the intestine and stomach to constrict, inhibiting the digestive process. At the same time, it permits more blood to flow to the arms and legs in anticipation of "fight or flight." Indeed, the sympathetic division acts as an *emergency system*, significantly influenced by the hypothalamus.

When the crisis subsides, the **parasympathetic nervous system** resumes control, and the activity of the related organs returns to its usual level. Heartbeat becomes more normal, saliva appears in the mouth, and blood flows more readily in the stomach. This division serves as a *routine system*, providing for normal body functioning.

When Ray was fleeing from revolving doors, the sympathetic division was dominant. When he was resting from these labors, the parasympathetic division became ascendant.

The traditional conception of the sympathetic and parasympathetic divisions as completely involuntary has been brought into question on two bases. First, there are numerous reports of voluntary control of blood circulation and breathing, brought about through forms of meditation, and they have been at least partially verified. Second, similar control has been achieved by subjects in experiments on biofeedback (Wallace & Benson, 1972). Together, these findings show that the autonomic nervous system, which is part of the peripheral nervous system, is partly under the control of the central nervous system.

AUTONOMIC FUNCTIONS AND BIOFEEDBACK. Biofeedback is not a system in which some chemical or electrical impulse is delivered to the body. Instead **biofeedback** occurs when information about body functions is made available to the brain. Typically, an electronic monitoring device is used that, for example, indicates the heart rate or blood pressure. The question is this: Can people who receive feedback about their biological processes thereby control these processes?

The sympathetic nervous system, for example, initiates blood flow in certain parts of the body, including the brain. When an individual is constantly tense, the blood supply to the brain may become extreme, contributing to migraine headaches. For this reason, some patients susceptible to these headaches receive training in biofeedback. Monitoring devices sound a tone whenever the blood flow decreases by a certain amount, enabling subjects to become more aware of this relaxed state. With this procedure, some subjects achieve lowered cerebral blood flow and report fewer migraine headaches (Sturgis, Tollison, & Adams, 1978).

Nevertheless, the daily human environment is infinitely more varied than a medical setting. Patients sometimes cannot maintain control in the home (Engel, 1972). Furthermore, the patient's expectation about the therapist or the treatment may play a significant role in the outcome of biofeedback procedures (Borgeat, Elie, & Castonguay, 1991). For many problems, such as heart disease and cancer, the biofeedback procedure is not clearly superior to more traditional treatments, especially relaxation and cognitive therapy (Johnston, 1991; Figure 3–11).

When used for a very different specific purpose—problems of muscular control—biofeedback has been quite successful, comparing very favorably with other treatments. For example, after sustaining severe head injuries, five patients displayed both fecal and urinary incontinence. Following a biofeedback program of neuromuscular re-education, all of them developed complete continence, voiding normally and regularly (Tries, 1990).

❧ THE ENDOCRINE SYSTEM

The second great communication network within the body, after the nervous system, is the **endocrine system,** composed of a series of interlocking glands that secrete fluids directly into the bloodstream. Both systems are feedback systems, both involve contact with the environment, and both are critical for adaptation (Drickamer & Vessey, 1992). Among the differences between them, speed of reaction and breadth of distribution are most important. The nerve impulse travels rapidly and must stay within the limits of the axons and dendrites. The endocrine system generally has a slower and broader influence. Its secretions, carried by the blood, travel to various parts of the body, where they typically have a maintenance function pertaining to growth, general vigor, and other long-range developments.

While at least a dozen endocrine glands have been identified, eight are well known today, including the placenta, which appears only in the pregnant female. Four have special significance for physiological psychology: the pituitary, thyroid, gonads, and adrenals. These tiny glands have incred-

FIGURE 3–11 BIOFEEDBACK.
In treating headaches, electrodes attached to the facial muscles sound a tone when muscle tension decreases in that area.

ibly small secretions, yet they form an interlocking system to the extent that disturbance in any one of them may lead to malfunctioning of the others. These glandular secretions, called **hormones,** ensure fundamental chemical activities within the whole organism. For example, they influence body growth, the utilization of food, energy expenditure, and reproductive reactions. They are involved in almost every aspect of body functioning.

ENDOCRINE GLANDS. The most important gland, in the sense of influencing others, is the **pituitary gland,** a small structure located just below the center of the brain. It is attached to the hypothalamus and sometimes considered part of the brain. Its location is not surprising, for in many ways it is regulated by hypothalamic activities. Often called the *master gland,* its front, or anterior, portion influences the secretions of several other endocrine glands, including those for sexual behavior and physical growth. The dwarf may have an underactive and the giant an overactive pituitary gland. The rear, or posterior, portion of this gland, through hormones exchanged with the hypothalamus, maintains a complex interaction with the central nervous system (Figure 3–12).

General body vigor is affected by the pituitary and also by the **thyroid gland,** lying at the base of the neck. The thyroid hormone is thyroxin. Lack of this hormone early in life can result in inactivity and cretinism, a condition of various bodily defects and low intelligence. Undersecretion at later ages often produces lethargy. Both conditions can be corrected by injection of thyroxin. In contrast, oversecretion seems to result in tension, which can be diminished through surgery.

The testes in men and the ovaries in women, situated in the genital area and collectively known as the **gonads,** are key factors in sexual behavior. They produce hormones responsible for the major physiological changes that occur at puberty; they contribute significantly to accompanying psychological development; and they continue to influence sexual responsiveness throughout adulthood. Normal adult sexual behavior can occur in their absence, although typically at a reduced rate.

Still another hormone from the pituitary, the adrenocorticotropic hormone or ACTH, stimulates the **adrenal glands,** which are located in the back of the abdomen below the rib cage, immediately above the kidneys. They have two basic parts. The adrenal medulla, inside the gland, secretes *adrenaline,* another name for **epinephrine,** which serves to increase energy in emergencies and other emotional situations. The adrenal cortex, on the outside, has diverse influences. When there is inadequate secretion in the adrenal cortex, there may be widespread changes in personality. The individual often becomes weak and lethargic, loses the appetite for food and sexual activity, and suffers a widespread breakdown of physiological functions. In contrast, overactivity in this part of the adrenal gland may produce sexual maturity at an unusually early age.

HORMONAL AND NEURAL COMMUNICATION. The major communication networks in the human body involve both hormonal *and* neural messages. In fact, certain chemical substances act as both hormones and neurotransmitters. Endocrine and neural tissues are connected by multiple bidirectional pathways (Daruna & Morgan, 1990).

The pituitary gland, through the discharge of ACTH, stimulates the adrenal gland, which in turn discharges several additional hormones. The pituitary also secretes the gonadotropic hormone, act-

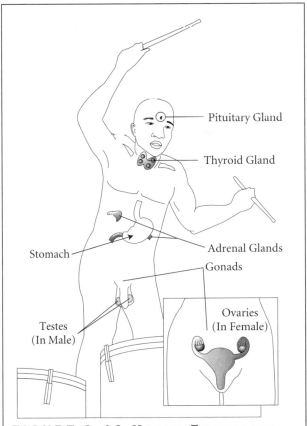

FIGURE 3–12 MAJOR ENDOCRINE GLANDS. These four glands, with vital implications for behavior, are interconnected in various ways.

ing on the gonads, which release their own hormones, regulating male and female sexual behavior. In both cases, the pituitary gland, part of the endocrine system, is activated by the hypothalamus, considered part of both the endocrine and nervous systems. The chief but not exclusive control of these interlocking systems lies in the brain, sending messages based on feedback it receives from other parts of the systems.

For Ray, this concept of interlocking systems was all too apparent. Medication made him a more normal citizen. "Sober, solid, square," he said of himself. It also made him a dull musician and a dim wit. With the drug, the favorable and unfavorable components could not be separated (Sacks, 1987).

One day Ray came to a momentous two-part decision. He would stay on medication throughout the working week. He thereby remained calm and deliberate Monday through Friday, making life easier for Sacha, himself, and his colleagues at work. Slower and more deliberate in thought and action, he experienced no emotional crises.

Especially costly in this decision was his loss of musical talent, both as a means of economic support and as a mode of self-expression. Without full freedom in his music, Ray forfeited his soul, his energy, and his enthusiasm for life. Hence, Ray made another decision—to avoid the Haldol on weekends. He "let fly" instead, becoming witty, ticcy, and inspired. At these times, Ray delighted himself and his companions with improvisations on the drums and bold shots at table tennis.

In looking at his double life, Ray noted that neither of his selves was completely free. One was controlled by the disorder, the other by its treatment. Normal people, he said, have a natural balance; he had to be content with an artificial balance (Sacks, 1987).

However, Ray had achieved a balance of a different sort, a balanced outlook on life. In his admirable, jocular style, he realized that sometimes he had to suffer his adversity, and sometimes he could put his "bold biological intruder" to advantage, using it for sudden, brilliant excursions into the worlds of music and conversation and also, of course, through revolving doors.

• SUMMARY •

OVERVIEW OF THE BODY

1. Organs perform specific functions; systems involve interacting organs. Genes, the basic determiners of heredity, are largely but not entirely responsible for our physical characteristics and contribute to other characteristics.

2. The chief integrating system of the body is the nervous system One part, the peripheral nervous system, is essentially a transmitting system; it sends impulses to and from the central nervous system. It includes the autonomic nervous system and the somatic nervous system. The central nervous system consists of the spinal cord and brain. The spinal cord is responsible for sending impulses to and receiving impulses from the brain.

NEURAL COMMUNICATION

3. There are various types of neurons in the human body. Some are sensory; they enable us to become aware of our environment and the condition of our own bodies. Others are motor; they enable us to respond, to take some action. In addition, the nervous system includes countless interneurons, which make other connections that can result in a wide range of behavior.

4. The nerve impulse is an electrochemical change in the nerve fiber, and it operates on an all-or-none principle. The synapse, which is the junction between neurons, plays a most important role in the flexibility of human behavior. Conditions at

the synapse operate according to a graded potential.

5. At the synapse, the action potential, or nerve impulse, releases a chemical substance into the synaptic space. This substance, a neurotransmitter, exerts an excitatory or inhibitory influence on the adjacent neuron. The action of these neurotransmitters—acetylcholine, norepinephrine, dopamine, serotonin, GABA, and others—can be influenced in many ways by internally produced and externally administered chemical substances.

THE HUMAN BRAIN

6. From an evolutionary perspective, the human brain can be considered in three sections. The hindbrain plays a central role in many vital functions: digestion, breathing, blood circulation, posture, and coordination. The midbrain processes sensory information and is also designed for arousal of the whole organism. The forebrain, the newest of the three major sections, clearly separates the human brain from those of other animals.

7. Portions of the brain near the spinal cord and midbrain are called the lower brain centers, or subcortical structures, for they lie beneath the cortex. The thalamus, at the center of the brain, serves as a relay station, especially for sensory impulses. The hypothalamus plays an important role in regulating all sorts of behaviors, including eating, fighting, fear reactions, and sexual behavior.

8. The cerebral cortex has specialized areas in each of four lobes. Visual areas are located in the occipital lobes, auditory areas in the temporal lobes, and areas for body feeling in the front part of the parietal lobes. Voluntary motor activities are mediated in the back part of the frontal lobes. These lobes also have association functions relating especially to the higher mental processes, including language.

9. In split-brain research, the cerebral hemispheres are separated by cutting the corpus callosum. The results suggest some important differences between these consciousnesses. These differences involve analytical and logical functions in the left hemisphere and holistic and perhaps intuitive functions in the right hemisphere.

INTERLOCKING SYSTEMS

10. The interlocking nature of human physiology is illustrated in the autonomic nervous system, which has connections with the endocrine system, the central nervous system, and the peripheral nervous system. It has two divisions: the sympathetic operates in emergencies, and the parasympathetic is dominant in routine functioning.

11. The endocrine system communicates by secreting hormones. It regulates growth, helps control the body's energy, and plays an important integrative function. Disturbances in any one of the endocrine glands may have widespread repercussions in physical structure and behavior.

• WORKING WITH PSYCHOLOGY •

REVIEW OF KEY CONCEPTS

Overview of the Body
organ
system
receptors
effectors
genes
nervous system
peripheral nervous system
autonomic nervous system
somatic nervous system
central nervous system

brain
spinal cord

Neural Communication
neuron
cell body
dendrite
axon
myelin sheath
sensory neuron
motor neuron

reflex arc
interneuron
polarized
resting potential
depolarized
action potential
all-or-none law
refractory period
synapse
graded potential
neurotransmitter substance

acetylcholine
Alzheimer's disease
norepinephrine
dopamine
Parkinson's disease
serotonin
GABA
endorphins

The Human Brain
hindbrain
medulla
cerebellum
midbrain
reticular activating system
forebrain

subcortical structures
thalamus
hypothalamus
limbic system
cerebral cortex
frontal lobes
temporal lobes
occipital lobes
parietal lobes
electroencephalograph (EEG)
CT scan
MRI scan
PET scan
motor cortex
sensory cortex
somesthesis

association cortex
aphasia
corpus callosum
hemispheric specialization

Interlocking Systems
sympathetic nervous system
parasympathetic nervous system
biofeedback
endocrine system
hormones
pituitary gland
thyroid gland
gonads
adrenal glands
epinephrine

❧ CLASS DISCUSSION/CRITICAL THINKING ❧

A NARRATIVE TWIST

When Witty Ticcy Ray began using Haldol, his extraordinary quickness and fine muscular coordination disappeared. Dr. Sacks then requested him to undergo several months of insight therapy, and thereafter Ray achieved an improved adjustment to the medication. Suppose that Ray had refused the insight therapy but continued taking Haldol. Simply by attempting each day to cope with his altered physical condition, would he eventually have adapted in essentially the same way? Might some other experience have promoted this adaptation? Defend your view. ❧

TOPICAL QUESTIONS

• *Overview of the Body.* Investigators often use studies with animals as windows to the human condition. Cite an instance in which this procedure might be useful, referring to a specific animal or a specific organ or system.

• *Neural Communication.* Consider our national telephone system as an analogy to neural communication in human beings. Indicate the assets and limitations of this analogy.

• *The Human Brain.* Does it seem possible that the CT, PET, or MRI scan will yield further understanding of intracranial self-stimulation? If not, why? If so, which technique may prove most useful? Why?

• *Interlocking Systems.* Complete this analogy: The pituitary gland is to the endocrine system as the —— is to the central nervous system. Select one alternative and defend your answer: reticular activating system, thalamus, hypothalamus, cerebral cortex.

❧ TOPICS OF RELATED INTEREST ❧

Numerous references to the biological bases of behavior appear throughout this text. The chief discussions occur with respect to sensation (4), interpretation of dreams (6), the memory trace (8), motivation (10), emotion (11), and human development (12).

Experiencing the World

SENSATION

PERCEPTION

&

CONSCIOUSNESS

&

AWARENESS OF STIMULATION
Responding to Stimulation
The Detection Question
The Discrimination Question
Signal Detection Theory

TRADITIONAL SENSES
Visual Ability
Capacity for Hearing
Sense of Smell
Taste Sensations
Sensitivities of the Skin

PROPRIOCEPTIVE SENSES
Kinesthesis
Visceral Sensitivity
Sense of Balance
Passive Motion

SENSATION AND PERCEPTION
Intersensory Perception
Extrasensory Perception

4
SENSATION

∾

AS THEY DROVE OUT TO THE SAN GABRIEL MOUNTAINS ON A NOVEMBER EVENING, BERNARD AND BILL WERE MORE THAN COMPANIONS ENJOYING THE COUNTRY-side. A pair of professors from the University of California in Los Angeles, they were headed for firewalking.

Bernard Leikind, a physicist, wanted to investigate the physics of firewalking. His friend Bill McCarthy, a psychologist, intended to explore the psychological aspects. Together they might shed some light on this ancient practice of treading across hot coals.

They had been enticed to this scene by newspaper accounts of firewalking extolling the importance of a self-help seminar and other psychological practices. Bill had read about these seminars in advertising brochures. They claimed that in just one session people could eliminate addictions, develop good study habits, become stunning lovers, and walk on fire. From a very different perspective, Bernard simply wanted to test a brash hypothesis: Firewalking was no hot feat. Anyone could do it *without* the seminar. The seminar participants, he had decided, paid a few hundred dollars for no real benefit. The key factors were simply principles of physics.

Firewalkers in Sri Lanka and other far-off lands claimed to feel no pain because they engaged in meditation. Bernard believed that methods of thought control perhaps diminished the pain somewhat, but basically they gave people the courage to try. The laws of physics determined whether they would get burned.

When the pair arrived at the parking lot of the designated hotel, Bernard immediately sat in the grass and kicked off his shoes, preparing for the night ahead. "Tough soles don't burn," he said to himself, not without some apprehension.

His friend Bill, in a more relaxed mood, mingled with the crowd moving into the hotel. After evaluating the psychological aspects of the self-help seminar, he would watch Bernard and the others from the sidelines, careful to stay out of the pits to observe more carefully. Besides, after testing his hypothesis, Bernard might need someone to drive his car home for him that night (Leikind & McCarthy, 1985).

As this adventure suggests, the focus of this chapter is on **sensation,** the processes by which we become aware of stimulation. Sensation consists of the most primitive experiences from the sense organs. The eyes, ears, nose, tongue, and skin are **sense organs,** providing information about our environment. It is important to understand the operation of the senses and sense organs because everything we know about ourselves and our world comes through the senses. Sensation is the first step to intelligent behavior.

This exploration of firewalking by Bernard and Bill involves a wide spectrum of concepts in this area and it contains this underlying message: Our sensory systems are active, and through the information they obtain, they become interrelated, exploring the environment in a coordinated manner. The idea that our senses function in a passive, isolated fashion, merely receiving information, is a myth.

We begin with awareness of stimulation, for we are not responsive to all of the events in our environment. Afterward, we turn to the processes by which this information is obtained, focusing on the five tra-

ditional senses: vision, hearing, smell, taste, and touch. There are others, particularly sensory capacities that make us aware of our own bodily states, and next we examine these, the proprioceptive senses. Finally, at the end of the chapter, we compare two fundamental and related processes, sensation and perception.

• AWARENESS OF STIMULATION •

Bernard remained for a while in the parking lot, uneasy that his nickname might be prophetic. Everyone called him Bernie.

He waited while the workers prepared two large bonfires in the nearby grass. In the quiet darkness, he felt his heart thumping and noticed the rustle of leaves in the woods, more aware than usual of these slight noises.

Everything we know about ourselves and the world around us comes through the stimulation of sense organs and related neural mechanisms. Likewise, almost everything we do depends, first of all, on information encoded in neural messages from our sense organs. Awareness of stimulation is the starting point. Meaningful behavior is impossible without such information.

RESPONDING TO STIMULATION

We can describe this process of obtaining information about the world as a sequence with four phases, beginning with stimulation of the sense organs. This sequence includes collector mechanisms, receptor mechanisms, transmission mechanisms, and coding mechanisms.

The **collector mechanisms** gather and channel information in some way. They do not record it. For example, the *pinna* of the ear, which is the visible and folded flesh outside the head, aids in the collection of sound waves, but it does not record them. The variable opening in the eye, called the

pupil, controls the amount of light that enters, but it does not register that light. The purpose of these mechanisms is to provide an optimal stimulus for the next phase.

The **receptors** are highly specialized nerve cells within the sense organs, sensitive to specific types of information, that convert physical stimuli to neural impulses. For light waves the receptors lie in the retina, at the back of the eye. The inner portion of the ear contains receptors for sound waves. Basically, receptors change a physical stimulus into a neural message.

In the third phase, nerve impulses are transmitted from the receptors to the brain. The neural mechanisms responsible for this transmission follow the **law of specific nerve energies,** which states that an individual's experience is a function of the particular nerves that are stimulated, *not how* they are stimulated. A knock on the ear may prompt you to hear a ringing sound because auditory nerves have been stimulated directly, not because sound waves have stimulated your eardrum. You may "see stars" following a blow to the head, activating optic nerves without stimulation of the retina. The key element in any sensation is the particular nerves that are firing, including their destination, not the type of stimulation that causes them to fire.

In the final phase, the nerve impulse reaches the brain, after which we hear, or see, or have some other experience, depending on which neural mechanisms are stimulated. This whole distribution process in the brain is sometimes called **neural coding,** referring to the ways in which neural impulses are distributed throughout different areas of the brain. In the visual cortex, for example, some neurons apparently respond to certain frequencies of light waves, others to different frequencies; some may respond primarily to shape cues, others to movement cues. Studies of neural coding aim to discover how we derive information from the different rates and patterns. An analogy might be made to the outsider trying to understand telegraphic messages in Morse code. What is the system? What are the patterns? And what meanings do they have?

THE DETECTION QUESTION

Out in the parking lot, a thin wisp of smoke drifted in Bernie's direction. Did he smell it? An insect buzzed in the woods. Did Bernie hear it? In the *detection question,* the problem is to discern or become aware of a very slight stimulus. It represents the starting point in awareness of stimulation.

Imagine that a man has crept into a quiet, dark room where you are sitting. Would you be aware of his presence just by the ticking of his watch? Or by his breathing? Or by some odor from his body? These questions concern the detection of stimuli.

ABSOLUTE THRESHOLD. The level of intensity at which a certain form of stimulation can just be detected is known as the **absolute threshold.** It is the lowest intensity detectable by a given individual. In determining this threshold, an individual is given a number of trials, and the absolute threshold is the lowest level detectable on 50% of these trials. For example, detection on 80% or

STIMULUS	THRESHOLD
Vision	A candle seen at 30 miles on a dark, clear night.
Hearing	The tick of a watch under quiet conditions at 20 feet.
Taste	One teaspoon of sugar in 2 gallons of water.
Smell	One drop of perfume diffused into a 3-room apartment.
Touch	The wing of a bee falling on your cheek from a distance of 1 cm.

TABLE 4–1 ABSOLUTE THRESHOLDS. The values are estimated from laboratory research (Brown, Galanterr, Hess, & Mandler, 1962).

20% of the trials is well above or well below the absolute threshold, respectively (Figure 4–1).

The absolute threshold varies among different people and within the same individual from time to time, depending on fluctuations in mood and physiological conditions. These individual variations can be offset by studying a large number of people. Then investigators obtain information on absolute thresholds in general (Table 4–1).

With our population growing steadily older, there has been interest in determining absolute thresholds at the later life stages. During much of adulthood, thresholds increase—that is, sensitivity decreases, a condition widely recognized for vision and hearing (Figure 4-2). This decline has also been demonstrated in laboratory tests of smell and taste. Young adults perform significantly better than people in midlife, and those in midlife perform better than the elderly (Stevens, 1989). At all ages, incidentally, the absolute threshold rises more slowly for taste than for smell (Cowart, 1989). In other words, as we grow older, we taste better than we smell—relative to the earlier years.

SUBLIMINAL ADVERTISING. The Latin word for "threshold" is *limen;* stimulation just below the absolute threshold is occasionally referred to as

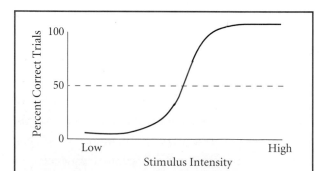

FIGURE 4–1 DETERMINING A THRESHOLD. When the stimulus intensity is very low, the individual rarely detects it, as shown in black. When it is presented at a very high intensity, the subject detects it on every trial, also shown in black. At some intermediate level, it is detected on approximately 50% of the trials, as shown in the colored portion of the graph.

FIGURE 4-2 ABSOLUTE THRESHOLDS AND AGING. In vision, the thresholds for focus and color discrimination increase slowly after early adulthood.

subliminal. Much public concern has arisen over **subliminal advertising,** in which a message is presented so rapidly or at such a low level of intensity that it cannot be detected, and yet it allegedly influences perception. Self-help audiotapes with subliminal messages are widely sold today as a convenient, efficient means of achieving all sorts of desirable outcomes—including weight loss, a better memory, and decreased anxiety. The audible content of these tapes consists of relaxing classical or popular music or the sounds of nature, especially surf and woodlands. Are these tapes effective?

In one study, two such tapes were selected, one allegedly improving memory, the other improving self-esteem. The 237 adults serving as subjects completed two pretests, one on each characteristic, and then listened to one of the tapes each day for 1 month—a period specified by most manufacturers as sufficient to produce the desired effect. Unknown to the subjects, the label on each tape had been *randomly* assigned. Some subjects listened to a memory tape correctly labeled, others to a memory tape labeled as self-esteem. Similarly, some

self-esteem tapes were correctly labeled; others were labeled as memory. The investigators justified this procedure on the grounds that all subjects had expressed interest in both tapes and had agreed to serve in either condition.

The results were quite clear. There were no subliminal effects on the posttests 1 month later. Regardless of the label, correct or incorrect, on memory or self-esteem, the claimed outcomes for *subliminal* effects failed to appear, although many subjects had the illusion that the tape had produced its labeled effect. They thought the claim had been supported—even though no substantial evidence for such an outcome has yet appeared in scientific research (Greenwald, Spangenberg, Pratkanis, & Eskenazi, 1991).

What might be a fundamental problem with all allegedly subliminal advertising, if it were attempted? First, among the more dominant stimuli in our daily environment, it could not readily compete for our attention. It would be too fragile. Second, the popular audience is composed of countless different people, and an advertiser can never be certain that the message is just barely below the absolute threshold for each person. The presumably appropriate level must be determined individually for *each* person in *each* context. At this time, we need have no underlying anxiety about underlying messages.

TERMINAL THRESHOLD. The absolute threshold is the point at which a stimulus of increasing intensity is first noticed. The **terminal threshold,** at the other end of the scale, is that point at which the normal sensory response changes to pain. The terminal threshold can be produced by strong light, loud sound, extreme heat, or any other stimulus that becomes painful.

While sitting in the parking lot, Bernie worried that the heat of the fire *might* reach his terminal threshold. If it did, that would be the end of his firewalking career. It would be terminal right there,

SOUND	DECIBELS	DANGER
Rocket launching pad	180	Inevitable
Rock concert, in front of speakers	120	Immediate
Truck traffic, noisy appliances	90	After a few hours
Conversation, sewing machine	60	—
Quiet library, soft whisper	30	—

TABLE 4–2 THE TERMINAL THRESHOLD. For most individuals, the terminal threshold appears around 120 decibels.

at the moment of pain. With this thought, he went back to the hotel and began thumbing the pages of Kittel's *Thermal Physics.* "Perhaps," he mused, thinking back on his college days, "I missed something" (Leikind & McCarthy, 1985).

The terminal threshold has a subtle but critical place in environmental pollution. Through the foods organisms eat, the water they drink, and the air they breathe, chemical agents enter their bodies. For every species, there is a point at which this accumulation of foreign chemicals results in physical and behavioral malfunctioning, disrupting the stability of our physiological and psychological processes (Russell, 1988). This point, the onset of disease, is truly a terminal threshold (Table 4–2).

In addition to the terminal threshold, the normal sensory response is limited in another respect, which does not involve pain or physical injury and therefore is not properly called a terminal threshold. All sense organs respond only to a limited range of stimuli. There are stimuli for which we have no receptors. One *nanometer* is one-billionth of a meter, and the human eye does not respond to wavelengths greater than 700 nanometers. A *hertz* is a unit of sound equal to one cycle per second, and the human ear does not respond to frequencies greater than 20,000 hertz. In these instances, there is no sensitivity at all.

☙

THE DISCRIMINATION QUESTION

Suppose that you turn on a light in a well-lit room. Would a friend notice the change? If someone turns down the bell on the telephone slightly, would you notice that the ring is softer? In the *discrimination question,* the problem is to notice a very slight difference or change in stimulus intensity or quality. As the participants in Bill's self-help seminar waited in the conference room of the hotel, the temperature gradually increased due to the body heat from many people. Did they notice the change? These questions involve a comparison between two stimuli.

DIFFERENCE THRESHOLD. The smallest perceptible difference between two stimuli of the same type is known as the **difference threshold.** This difference, determined in the laboratory by a series of tests, can just barely be detected by the individual on 50% of the trials.

If three candles are burning in a room and one more is added, there will be a readily noticeable difference in illumination for a human being with normal vision. If 100 candles are burning and one more is added, there may be a barely perceptible or **just noticeable difference,** called a *j.n.d.,* which is another expression for the difference threshold. Now suppose that 200 candles are burning and we add another. No matter how much a person is prepared to perceive the difference, he or she cannot do so. The change in illumination is not a j.n.d.; it does not reach the difference threshold (Figure 4-3).

The difference threshold is a common concern in daily life. When you use outdated yeast in making a delicate bread, you hope the change in texture is below the difference threshold. When you ask someone to increase the volume on your stereo set,

SENSE	STIMULUS	RATIO
Hearing	Pitch, at 2,000 hertz	.003
Vision	Brightness, at 1,000 photons	.016
Touch	Heaviness, at 300 grams	.019
Smell	Rubber, at 200 olfactories	.104
Taste	Saline, at 3 moles/liter	.200

TABLE 4–3 DIFFERENCE THRESHOLDS. Each ratio, known as the Weber ratio, indicates the difference threshold (Boring, Langfeld, & Weld, 1948).

FIGURE 4–3 DIFFERENCE THRESHOLDS AND EXPERIENCE. Thresholds sometimes can be lowered through practice. The wine taster, with extensive training, can make discriminations among odors and flavors not possible for people with less experience.

you expect a change above your difference threshold.

WEBER'S LAW. As these examples suggest, the size of the difference threshold, or j.n.d., depends on the initial stimulus intensity. With a slight stimulus, a mild change is noticeable; with a strong stimulus, a change of much greater magnitude is necessary if it is to be noticed. This finding, that the size of the difference threshold is a constant fraction of the standard stimulus, is known as **Weber's law**, named for E. H. Weber, a German physiologist who investigated this principle.

In studies of Weber's law, one stimulus is referred to as the *standard stimulus.* Then other stimuli are compared with it to discover the size of the difference that is just barely detectable. If the standard or original intensity is 100 and the smallest noticeable difference is 1, then the ratio is 1:100 or .01. To produce a j.n.d. in brightness with 500 candles, for example, we must add one candle for every 100, or a total of 5 more candles. The increase or decrease must be a constant fraction of the standard intensity.

The Weber fraction varies with different organisms, and it depends on which sensory process is involved. In typical experiments, a larger fraction is required for detecting a change in brightness than for detecting a change in pitch. It also differs with extreme intensities, being constant only within the intermediate range of stimulation (Table 4–3).

Modern laboratory studies have supported Weber's law, but outside the laboratory numerous pressures and distractions disrupt our attention to specific stimuli. Hence, the various thresholds and Weber's law are not adequate to explain people's judgments about changes in inflation, salaries, and related financial matters (Batchelor, 1986; Champlain & Kopelman, 1991). These perceptions, occurring amid the commotion of daily life, are more readily understood in the context of signal detection theory, which suggests some modification in the classical view.

SIGNAL DETECTION THEORY

According to **signal detection theory,** the detection of stimulation depends not only on the sensitivity of the subject but also on the conditions for making the judgments. The issues of expectation and motivation are involved, sometimes rendering the concept of threshold imprecise or arbitrary (Green & Swets, 1966).

Suppose that you are seated in a dark room prepared to detect a dim, brief flash of light. On each trial you must decide whether or not it has occurred. How would you answer on the control trials, in which no stimulus is presented?

If you believed that the light would appear on almost every trial, you would guess affirmatively. If you knew that it would appear only occasionally, you would guess in the negative. In other words, your response would be influenced by your expectation in that situation.

Similarly, suppose you received 25 cents every time you noticed the flash. Then you probably would guess that the light appeared on the control trials. Suppose you were required to pay the experimenter $5 or to lick hundreds of postage stamps every time you incorrectly thought you perceived the light. How would you react in doubtful cases? You would guess "No."

Collectively, these examples indicate that the detection or discrimination question involves two different processes, a sensation task and a decision task. Performance on the *sensation task* depends on the intensity of the stimulation and sensitivity of the subject. Performance on the *decision task* depends on the subject's expectation and motivation, sometimes called a response bias. The term **response bias** means that the subject has a predetermined tendency to answer one way or the other, a decision that is influenced by factors *apart from* the stimulating condition. In a political survey, for example, liberals tend to respond to the questions in one way and conservatives in another.

For the air controller or meteorologist, missing an image on the screen may be a vital mistake. Falsely detecting an image where there is none may be embarrassing or costly, but it probably will not have disastrous consequences. Hence, the radar operator is likely to err in the latter direction. Suppose you are working out in the garden and expect a phone call at 3:00 P.M. As the hour approaches, the expectation of the call increases. Hence, you are more likely to think you heard the telephone ring.

In the contemporary approach, prompted by signal detection theory, the threshold is viewed as variable, depending on complex cognitive and motivational processes that influence the individual's response. Signal detection theory emphasizes the diversity of these factors (Commons, Nevin, & Davison, 1991).

• TRADITIONAL SENSES •

The noise level was well above Bill's absolute threshold when he entered the crowded conference room for the self-help seminar. There he found 80 or so seminar participants listening to rather loud, upbeat music and chatting freely among themselves, an atmosphere clearly designed to develop a sense of comradeship. Eventually, a powerfully built group leader stood up and exhorted the participants to have confidence and patience. Everyone could succeed simply by staying with the group and following his lead. They were all kindred souls. If they followed his advice, they *would* succeed.

Meanwhile, Bernie returned to the parking lot and took out a pyrometer to measure the heat. What he found was a bit chilling—a reading of more than 1,500 degrees Fahrenheit. He was even a bit gratified that, before leaving home, he had phoned his physician for advice on first aid—just in case (Leikind & McCarthy, 1985).

Bernie's experience here, as he watched the glowing coals send burning embers floating into the November sky, illustrates that at least three disciplines are involved in the investigation of sensory processes. Sensation begins with a problem in physics, for some physical energy, such as light waves, is emitted by the fire; then there is a physiological condition as this energy is combined with other neural activities in the brain; and finally, there is the psychological experience, an awareness of the glowing coals. Sensation involves physical, physiological, and psychological events.

At the pits, all five of the **traditional senses** informed Bernie about the fire: vision, hearing, smell, taste, and touch. Recognized since the time of Aristotle, they receive considerable research attention today, but other senses are important too, as noted later in the chapter. In fact, Bernie did not actually taste the fire; he tasted its smoke. And he had not yet touched it, but his cheeks, forehead, and other skin areas already felt warm.

∾

VISUAL ABILITY

Horses, pigeons, frogs, and people differ markedly in **visual sensitivity,** meaning responsiveness to the energy of light waves. The horse excels in the breadth of its visual field, which is almost 360 degrees. The pigeon excels in visual acuity, which is the capacity to see small details, the sharpness of vision. The frog is highly adapted to the detection of movement, particularly by small flying insects. And human beings possess notable color vision, more varied than that in most species and far greater than that of their typical pets.

Light waves, the physical stimulation for visual experience, are considered to be radiant energy emanating from a source. The **wavelength** in this stimulation is the distance between two adjacent crests. The human eye is attuned only to a narrow range of light wavelengths, from approximately 400 to 700 nanometers. Waves outside this narrow range of visible light fail to excite the eye. Within this range, the shorter wavelengths are perceived as

violet, the intermediate ones as blue, green, and yellow, and the longer ones as red. The experience of **hue,** which refers to what we commonly call color, is largely a function of wavelength.

We do not always see in color. Visual phenomena also can be described in terms of intensity or *brightness,* which means that the stimulus may vary from dark to light. Even a yellowish hue may be dark or light. This experience is correlated chiefly with wave *amplitude,* which is the size of the wave.

Finally, colors vary in richness or *purity.* The purest colors are the most highly saturated—the reddest reds, the yellowest yellows, and so forth— as determined by several physical properties of light, including the mixture of different wavelengths. When we speak of purity, we are referring to the degree to which any given hue differs from gray of the same brightness (Table 4–4).

Although we do not have names for all of the hues, a human being with normal color vision can discriminate approximately 150 different hues. When the brightness and saturation dimensions are included, it is not surprising to find that we have the capacity for thousands of color experiences.

OPERATION OF THE EYE. As Bernie watched the dancing flames, light rays entered his eye through the **pupillary opening,** which varies in size automatically, depending partly on the amount of light available. When the light intensity is low, the opening is large to allow as much light as possible to enter the eye. When the intensity is high, the

PROPERTY	EXPERIENCE
Wavelength	Hue
Wave amplitude	Brightness
Mixture	Purity

TABLE 4–4 PHYSICAL PROPERTIES OF VISUAL EXPERIENCE. Our visual experiences are more complexly determined than is indicated in the table.

opening is small to protect the eye from overstimulation. This dilation or constriction is brought about through reactions of the **iris,** which gives color to the eye and serves a regulatory function analogous to that of the diaphragm of a camera (Figure 4–4).

As the light enters the eye, the next mechanism is the **lens,** which gives the image a sharp focus. It does so by automatically changing its shape or curvature, a reaction known as **accommodation.** After passing through a transparent liquid that fills the space behind the lens, the light waves fall on a light-sensitive surface known as the **retina,** which contains the receptors necessary for vision. When these receptors are stimulated, impulses are carried to the brain, arousing visual experiences.

The human retina, which in limited ways is analogous to the film in a camera, has millions of receptors of two basic types. The **rods,** located toward the periphery, are sensitive only to the brightness of light, and their number is estimated at 120 million. Patterns of black, white, and gray are experienced in extreme peripheral vision, which serves best for night vision and to help us to notice objects and events deserving of closer attention. In contrast, the **cones,** of which there seem to be 6–7 million, mediate color vision. Less dense toward the periphery, they are heavily concentrated in a small area near the center of the retina called the **fovea,** responsible for the clearest images and fullest experience of color (Figure 4–5).

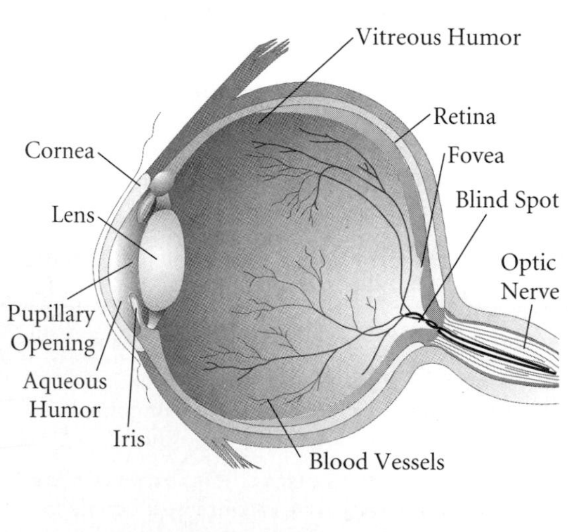

The retina also has a **blind spot,** where vision is completely absent because the optic nerve takes up this space on the retina, leaving no room for rods and cones. Here, in the **optic nerve,** certain nerve fibers leave the eye for connections elsewhere, carrying impulses to the brain. This visual defect is not significant because the blind spot for each eye involves a slightly different part of the visual field. Furthermore, the head and eyes are constantly in motion, permitting a visual image to change its location on the retina. On these bases, this deficiency goes undetected except in careful scrutiny (Figure 4–6).

VISION AND THE BRAIN. The nerve impulses traveling toward the brain along the optic nerve eventually follow either of two pathways through the thalamus, the brain's chief switchboard and relay mechanism. These separate routes make possible the contribution and integration of various details from the visual scene. In this condition, known as **parallel distributed processing,** different types of information, even about the same stimulus, are handled simultaneously in different regions of the brain. One route seems to contribute information about shape and color; the other apparently conveys information about the movement and location of the object and serves a coordinating function (Livingstone & Hubel, 1988).

After passing through stages and substages, these visual messages reach the brain. Here they stimulate the cells in the visual cortex. These cells are highly specialized, so much so that they are

FIGURE 4–4 STRUCTURE OF THE EYE. The humors help the eye keep its shape. The retina is shown in color.

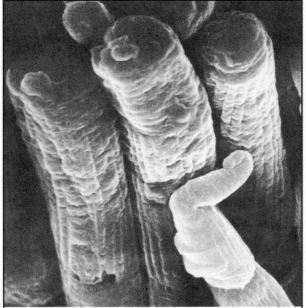

CHARACTERISTIC	RODS	CONES
Prevalence	120 million	7 million
Location	Outside fovea	Especially in fovea
Optimal function	In dim light	In bright light
Degree of acuity	Low	High
Color sensitivity	Black, white	Black, white, color

FIGURE 4–5 RODS AND CONES.
Named for their shapes, these visual receptors differ in important ways, some of which are indicated here.

often referred to as **feature detectors,** which are cells that respond only to a highly specific feature

or characteristic of a visual stimulus, such as a straight edge, an angle, brightness, or movement of a spot. This specialization has been demonstrated through studies of the visual cortex in various animals, including cats, monkeys, and frogs (Hubel & Wiesel, 1962, 1979; Maturana, Lettvin, McCulloch, & Pitts, 1960).

Somehow, these specific visual features are united or combined in the brain to form the coherent images of normal visual experience. Just how this synthesis is accomplished is almost beyond speculation at this point, for there may be far more than two pathways. Some investigators speculate about the kinds of information in these parallel systems, one involving specific wavelengths and therefore mediating color, the other including all wavelengths and thus perhaps playing a fundamental role in movement and other visual experiences (Shapley, 1990).

ADAPTATION. The concept of **adaptation** means that behavior changes according to the setting, as the individual adjusts to the situation. There is a gradual increase in visual sensitivity, for example, under conditions of low illumination, known as *dark adaptation.* After the lights are turned off at bedtime, the room appears absolutely dark,

FIGURE 4–6 BLIND SPOT. Close the left eye and look straight ahead at Bernie's shoes with the right eye. Then, beginning at about 20 inches, move your head slowly toward the book until the coals disappear. At that position, the image of the coals is falling on the blind spot, the point on the retina where there are no receptors because the optic nerve occupies this space.

but one gradually sees more clearly, even though the illumination has remained constant. This improvement is due partly to pupillary dilation but chiefly to chemical changes in the rods that make us more sensitive to weak visual stimuli. As Bernie sat in the dark parking lot, his vision improved for both reasons.

In contrast, a gradual decrease in sensitivity with bright illumination is referred to as *light adaptation.* Again, the eye adjusts to the prevailing light intensity partly as a result of the pupillary reaction but largely because of a chemical reaction in the cones. A person emerging into the intense glare of a fire or sunlight on icy snow gradually becomes accustomed to this condition through the photochemical reaction.

IMPORTANCE OF STIMULUS CHANGE.

Although we do not notice it, our eyes are constantly moving. These tiny, incessant eye movements, called **saccadic movements,** are enormously important in human vision in two ways. First, by concentrating different parts of the image on different areas of the retina, they play a role in the clarity of vision. Second, they keep us capable of responding to the visual image, a capacity that soon fades without change in stimulation.

The role of saccadic movements in maintaining the visual image was demonstrated when a tiny projector was mounted on a contact lens placed over the subject's eye. Thus, the eye movements caused both the contact lens and the projector to move, but the image projected back onto the retina never changed. Within a minute, the unchanging image could not be seen, and it did not reappear until there was some change in stimulation (Riggs, Ratliff, Cornsweet, & Cornsweet, 1953).

Most birds do not have saccadic movements, and those that eat motionless objects are constantly moving themselves, perhaps to prevent an unchanging image. Those that consume moving prey often remain motionless, partly to avoid detection, like the crane stalking the frog. But perhaps they also remain motionless for another reason—to promote a fading of the image of the prey, thereby causing the prey's movements to be more readily observed (Cornsweet, 1970).

These conditions of adaptation in animals and human beings point to an important property of many sensory systems. They are generally more responsive to changing than to unchanging stimulation.

Another illustration of this need for stimulus change occurs in the phenomenon known as the *Ganzfeld effect,* involving a completely uniform color field. *Ganzfeld* means "entire field." When someone is steadily exposed to a completely blue field, for example, uninterrupted by shapes or other colors, the blue gradually disappears. This effect can be obtained by placing well-fitted halves of plastic table tennis balls over the eyes and illuminating them by a slide projector equipped with a colored filter. Your author was once exposed in this way to a homogeneous field of red. The red faded to a neutral brown-gray after a few minutes—and then interest in the demonstration faded too.

COLOR MIXTURE.

Theorists attempting to explain color vision have been confronted with a difficult question. When factors of brightness and purity are added to hue, human beings have the capacity for hundreds of thousands of different color experiences. How does our visual system provide this immense versatility?

The answer seems to lie partly in the mixture of colors. When the artist mixes yellow and blue pigments or the printer overlaps yellow and blue ink, the result is green. This procedure, surprisingly, is called **subtractive color mixture** because the outcome depends on the light absorbed from the spectrum rather than what is reflected. The yellow pigment absorbs all wavelengths except those for yellow and green. The blue pigment absorbs all wavelengths except those for blue and green. When these pigments are mixed, the yellow and blue reflectances are canceled by each other, leaving only green. For the most part, however, subtractive color mixture produces relatively few different hues because wavelengths are absorbed from the mix.

Mixing light produces a very different outcome from mixing pigment. Here the process is known as **additive color mixture** because each light adds a different reflectance, or wavelength, to the final outcome. Thus, an additive mixture of all colors gives the experience of white light (Figure IV.I Color). The reason is that the human eye cannot detect or separate the individual wavelengths that have been combined in the additive mixture. By using a wedge-shaped lens called a prism, white light can be broken down into the full spectrum, thus showing that it is composed of all colors.

The important point for color theorists lies in these additive mixtures. Except for colors widely separated on the spectrum, additive mixtures typically give a new hue falling between the component hues. A mixture of blue and green gives blue-green. A mixture of blue and red gives blue-red, which we call purple or violet, depending on how much blue is included. Mixing red and yellow produces orange, and so forth (Figure IV.2). If more than two hues are used, still further colors can be obtained. In summary, additive mixtures can yield an endless array of colors.

THEORIES OF COLOR VISION. In the additive mixture of color, theorists have found a means of explaining our capacity for hundreds of thousands of different color experiences. This view, called **trichromatic theory,** assumes that there are three types of cones especially responsive to the long, intermediate, and short wavelengths. Studies of vertebrate retinas have supported this view, indi-

cating that color is mediated by three different cones that appear to correspond to the red, green, and blue wavelengths (MacNichol, 1964). This mixture presumably takes place in the brain on the basis of diverse signals from these three types of cones, making possible any color experience. Yellow, for example, would be experienced by simultaneous stimulation of red and green cones in approximately equal units. Orange would arise from stimulation of somewhat more red than green cones.

A different approach, **opponent-process theory,** postulates three different pairs of receptor mechanisms, with the members of each pair working in opposition. These pairs respond to red-green, yellow-blue, or black-white stimulation. The red-green pair, working in opposition, cannot send messages about red and green simultaneously and, in fact, we never see reddish-greenish light. Similarly, the yellow-blue pair cannot mediate these two hues at the same time, and yellowish-bluish light is not encountered.

It is further speculated that when the yellow-blue pair is stimulated by yellow, it develops increasing sensitivity to blue and decreasing sensitivity to yellow. This same reciprocity is assumed for the other pairs, and electrophysiological evidence lends support to this view (Boynton, 1982). According to opponent-process theory, excitation of one color opposes excitation of the other.

This approach offers an interpretation of the visual **afterimage,** the existence of a color experience after the hue is no longer observed. When you look at a bright green image, the color sensation remains for a moment after you cease looking, an outcome called a *positive afterimage.* It occurs because receptor processes continue for a moment following cessation of the stimulation. This carryover is soon replaced by an image of the complementary color, known as the *negative afterimage,* which will have a reddish hue in this case. The receptor cells for the complementary color apparently are inhibited by the green and then fire in a counterreaction when the green is removed. This pairing of red-green, yellow-blue, and black-white afterimages offers evidence for opponent-process theory (Figure IV.3).

How do we reconcile these different theories, each supported by some research? Overall, the evidence favors a combination of both approaches. The trichromatic theory seems appropriate at the receptor level. Three types of cones have been identified in the retina, and they correspond to different points on the color spectrum. The opponent-process theory appears more relevant in higher neural activities, nearer the brain. The phenomena of afterimages and even color blindness support this theory (Hurvich & Jameson, 1957). Together these two theories, one closer to the receptors, the other closer to the brain, offer a rather broad account of color vision. Attempts at this synthesis have been in progress since the first quarter of this century (Niall, 1988).

The condition of *color blindness,* the total absence of color experience, is a rare phenomenon among human beings. It is also called **achromatic vision,** meaning "without color." A person with this defect is a **monochromat,** experiencing only degrees of gray, which is a mixture of black and white. Usually, however, the individual can see some colors, prompting the expression *color weakness.*

Among these deficiencies, attributed to defects in the cones, the most common is the inability to discriminate between reds and greens of the same brightness, experienced by about 1% of women and more than 5% of men. Yellow-blue blindness is less frequent. A person of either type is called a **dichromat** because the individual's color sensitivity is limited to two hues, usually yellow and blue. When one hue is absent, the opposing or complementary hue is typically absent as well, providing further evidence for the opponent-process view. To be adequate, theories of color vision must explain why many more people suffer red-green than yellow-blue blindness and why the periphery of the

human retina is not as sensitive to red-green as to yellow-blue (Figure IV.4).

❧
CAPACITY FOR HEARING

Vision and hearing are the so-called *higher senses* among human beings, not because these organs are located near the top of the head but because they typically provide the most information regarding survival. The other senses are important too, especially in selecting foods, but looking and listening furnish more detailed information, particularly about distant objects and events.

Listening to their leader in the conference room, the seminar participants obtained information about firewalking, a matter of safety if not survival. Then they listened to their own rhythmic clapping, thereby increasing their motivation for the adventure ahead. As they filed out of the conference room, they shouted encouragement to each other.

Out in the parking lot, the would-be firewalkers circled the fresh sod on which two bonfires of wood crackled furiously in separate pits. Following their leader, they closed their eyes and imagined themselves completing a successful firewalk. Then each student made a fist, thrust it up, and shouted into the night sky: "Yah!" "Yahooo!" "I did it!" Afterward, all of the students, Bill among them, returned to the conference room to hear further instructions (Leikind & McCarthy, 1985).

Sitting alone in the darkness, Bernie listened to these activities. Sound waves, the physical stimulus for hearing, were produced by vibrations from the shouting and transmitted through the air to his eardrums. When the resulting nerve impulses reached his brain, he experienced hearing, or **auditory sensitivity,** as hearing is more formally known.

The sound of the crackling wood also stimulated Bernie's auditory nerve fibers, as did the scraping of tongs and shovels while the attendants stoked the blazes. These sounds gave rise to *noise*, for they involved irregular vibrations. The thud of a log thrown on a fire is also a noise because it produces a heterogeneous sound with no regularity. In contrast, a *tone* involves regular, or periodic, vibrations. It is more pleasant and homogeneous, often with a typical pitch, as in a person's voice or the sound of a musical instrument. In short, irregular and regular vibrations produce noise and tone, respectively.

The **frequency** of vibrations is the number of vibrations per second, also called wavelength. The experience of *pitch*, which is the relative position of a tone on a scale, is determined partly by the frequency of vibrations. Low, regular frequencies produce a tone of low pitch; high, regular frequencies produce a tone of high pitch. The human ear is attuned to frequencies ranging from 20 to 20,000 hertz, but it is most sensitive between 2,000 and 4,000 hertz.

The *loudness* of a sound is primarily a function of the sound pressure activating the eardrum. It depends on the wave amplitude—that is, the degree of displacement of the air molecules, resulting from displacement of the vibrating body from its resting position. As an example, consider the difference in displacement between a lightly plucked guitar string and one that is vigorously struck.

Vibrating bodies also vibrate complexly. The harp string vibrates as a whole, producing a predominant pitch known as the fundamental tone. At the same time, it vibrates in sections—in halves, thirds, fourths, and so forth—and these vibrations are called partials, producing overtones. All complex musical instruments give off many overtones in addition to the fundamental. This complexity of mixture determines the *timbre,* or quality, of a sound. A harp and a horn playing the same tone make different sounds because of the different mixtures (Table 4–5).

Thus, the chief properties of light and sound

PROPERTY	EXPERIENCE
Wavelength	Pitch
Wave amplitude	Loudness
Mixture	Timbre

TABLE 4–5 PHYSICAL PROPERTIES OF AUDITORY EXPERIENCE. Our auditory experiences are more complexly determined than is indicated in the table.

can be compared. Pitch and hue are partly a function of wavelength. Loudness and brightness are both aspects of wave amplitude. And timbre corresponds to purity; both are types of mixtures. There is some parallelism in the two realms.

OPERATION OF THE EAR. The human ear is divided into three regions—the outer, middle, and inner ears. The major structures of the **outer ear,** apart from the folds of skin outside the head, are the auditory canal and tympanic membrane. When sound waves travel through the canal, they cause the tympanic membrane, or **eardrum,** to vibrate, activating mechanisms of the middle ear. For this reason, the outer ear is called a collecting system.

The **middle ear** is chiefly an amplifying system. The vibrating eardrum activates the **ossicles,** three small bones of the middle ear—the hammer first, next the anvil, and then the stirrup. The stirrup presses against the oval window.

The **oval window** marks the beginning of the **inner ear,** and its movements exert pressures on a liquid in a snail-shaped canal called the **cochlea.** Within this canal is a structure known as the **basilar membrane,** which contains the tiny *hair cells* that are the receptors for hearing, somewhat analogous to the rods and cones in the retina. Whenever the liquid in the canal moves in response to movements of the oval window, it induces these hair cells to bend, sending impulses to the brain via the auditory nerve, which result in hearing. In this respect the inner ear is a converting system, changing the mechanical motions of

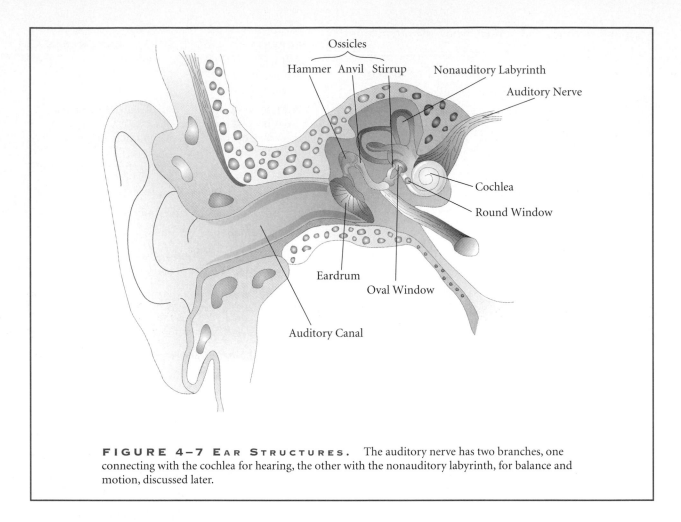

FIGURE 4–7 EAR STRUCTURES. The auditory nerve has two branches, one connecting with the cochlea for hearing, the other with the nonauditory labyrinth, for balance and motion, discussed later.

the oval window into electrochemical impulses (Figure 4–7).

In passing, the function of the *round window* should be noted. Located at the base of the cochlea in human beings, it makes no direct contribution to hearing but absorbs the pressures created by the oval window, its counterpart at the other end of the cochlea canal. A push of the stirrup on the oval window produces movement in the liquid, or *endolymph,* which bends the hair cells. This movement is relieved by an outward bulge of the round window, acting as a safety valve (Figure 4–8).

THEORIES OF HEARING. In hearing, as in color vision, there are two major theoretical positions, one of which is place theory. According to

place theory, different frequencies of vibration arouse different regions of hair cells on the basilar membrane, and the resulting impulses go to different regions of the auditory cortex. Pitch depends on the place in the membrane that is most activated and also on the place in the auditory cortex that receives the resulting nerve impulses. This assumption, that there are precise cortical localizations for high-pitched and low-pitched sounds, has yet to be verified.

Loudness, according to this theory, depends on the spread of disturbance in either direction from the activated area of the basilar membrane. Two tones of the same pitch would activate the same fibers, but if the tones differ in intensity, the range of activated fibers would be greater for the louder sound (Warren, 1984).

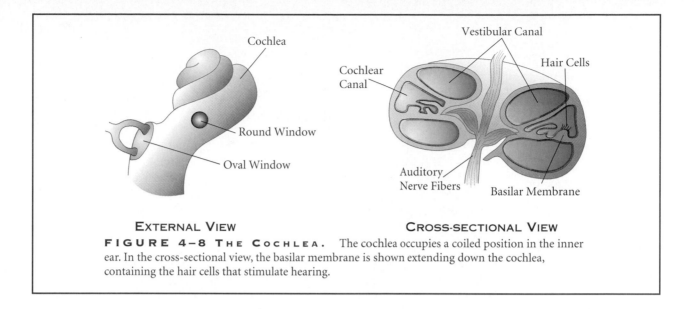

EXTERNAL VIEW   CROSS-SECTIONAL VIEW

FIGURE 4–8 THE COCHLEA. The cochlea occupies a coiled position in the inner ear. In the cross-sectional view, the basilar membrane is shown extending down the cochlea, containing the hair cells that stimulate hearing.

A second theory, based on the rate of firing of neurons, is called **volley theory,** suggesting that nerve fibers work in groups, producing successive, simultaneous discharges. Volley theory is appealing because a high-pitched sound should cause the same neuron to fire more rapidly. However, there is a limit to how fast a neuron can fire. No single fiber in the auditory nerve can respond more frequently than 1,000 times per second. How, then, can we readily hear sounds at 4,000 hertz?

By suggesting that nerve fibers work in groups, the volley theory attempts to take this problem into account. One group of fibers is discharged by one sound wave, another group by the next. The first group, on account of the absolute refractory period of .001 second, cannot respond to the second wave, but with different groups of fibers involved, some fibers are always available to respond. Collectively, the fibers can exceed the maximum for each fiber; they can respond at a rate as high as 5,000 impulses per second, with different groups of fibers contributing to different impulses. Also, some fibers, because of their greater excitability, contribute to more volleys than do other fibers. Pitch, according to volley theory,

depends on the frequency of volleys rather than the frequency carried by the individual fibers (Wever, 1949).

Loudness is thought to increase as more fibers participate in each volley. A large sound wave might activate 100 instead of 50 fibers, producing more impulses per volley without changing the frequency of the separate volleys.

As in vision, place and volley theories are not necessarily incompatible. Volley theory may play a major role in mediating the lower frequencies, up to 4,000 or 5,000 hertz, and place theory may be more significant at higher frequencies.

❧

SENSE OF SMELL

The senses of smell, taste, and touch are often considered the *lower senses* at the human level. This description does not mean that they are necessarily less acute, for it is impossible to make comparisons across the different senses. Rather, it means that they are generally less important for survival. The sense of smell does not alert us to predators, as it does with animals, although it may put us on guard when certain foods are unfit to eat and warn of such dangers as fire, gasoline, and ammonia. Bernie

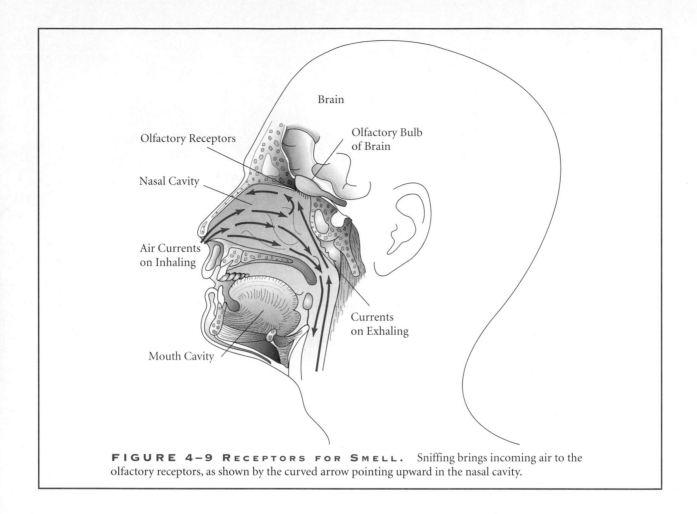

FIGURE 4–9 RECEPTORS FOR SMELL. Sniffing brings incoming air to the olfactory receptors, as shown by the curved arrow pointing upward in the nasal cavity.

Labels in figure: Brain; Olfactory Receptors; Olfactory Bulb of Brain; Nasal Cavity; Air Currents on Inhaling; Currents on Exhaling; Mouth Cavity

noticed the bonfire partly through **olfactory sensitivity,** as the sense of smell is called, but this detection depended significantly on the direction and strength of the wind.

RECEPTORS AND BASIC ODORS. The receptors for smell in human beings are long, threadlike structures extending from the olfactory bulbs and other brain centers down into the nasal cavities. They lie in the **olfactory epithelium,** a thin layer of tissue at the top of the nasal cavity, above the main current of air moving from the nostrils to the lungs. Sniffing is helpful in identifying an odor because then the odorous currents are more likely to reach these remote receptors (Figure 4–9).

One theory of smell, called the **stereochemical theory,** assumes that we experience an odor when airborne molecules of various shapes fit into similarly shaped sockets in the receptors. Molecules from substances with the odor of musk, for example, may have a particular shape and therefore fit into a socket of that shape, while floral molecules fit into their own kind of socket (Amoore, Johnston, & Rubin, 1964). The analogy here is another *lock-and-key hypothesis,* in which the molecule from the musk odor, for example, serves as the key. It must fit into the receptor site, the lock, if that particular olfactory experience is to occur.

However, there has been little success in identifying the basic odors. For human beings there are fourfold and fivefold classifications, and one popular approach includes six types: flowery, fruity, spicy, resinous, smoky, and putrid.

SUBTLETIES OF SMELL. Standing near the fires, waiting for the seminar participants to emerge again from the conference room, Bernie was stimulated by more than sight and sound. The embers gave off the unmistakable smell of burning wood, and odors, as we know, have a marked capacity to evoke emotions and memories. There is sentiment in scent, perhaps because the olfactory bulb is located relatively close to certain subcortical structures involved in emotion, motivation, and other forms of arousal. In any case, do not sniff at the role of smell in daily life. Delicate fragrances and foul odors can exert a powerful influence on human experience.

On the practical side, smell plays a subtle but important role in our enjoyment of the environment, as was demonstrated in door-to-door research in New York State many years ago. Three pairs of identical stockings were scented with attractive odors, one pair was left unscented, and then 250 women were asked individually to select the pair they preferred. More than 50% chose a narcissus-scented pair, and approximately 20% selected each of the other scented pairs; the pair with the natural odor was preferred by less than 8% of the group. When each subject was asked afterward, it was evident that only 2% even noticed that the stockings had been scented, although the smell was readily discernible (Laird, 1932).

Odors from animals and human beings also can operate in subtle fashion. Many mammals secrete odorous substances called **pheromones,** which serve a communication function among members of the same species and sometimes even between species. Animal pheromones are widely recognized; they provide signals about sexual readiness, food sources, territorial boundaries, and so forth. Among human beings, their existence and function are considerably more doubtful.

Unlike vision and hearing, human olfaction typically detects only one stimulus at a time, the strongest available. Weaker odors are masked by the most powerful one, a phenomenon much appreciated by those who wish to become more alluring through perfume, hide telltale odors with breath mints, or simply make certain environments more pleasant by use of air fresheners.

TASTE SENSATIONS

The sensation of taste, known as **gustatory sensitivity,** plays a most important role in the human condition. It too is of survival value, sometimes warning us about substances dangerous to human consumption. The adequate stimulus for taste, as for smell, is some type of chemical energy. These two senses therefore are sometimes referred to as the *chemical senses.* For smell, a substance must be gaseous or airborne; for taste, it must be soluble.

RECEPTORS AND BASIC TASTES. Our taste buds, containing the taste receptors, lie in the crevices between the papillae, which are the many slight elevations on the tongue's surface. Seeping into these crevices and then into the pore of a taste bud, the chemical substances constituting our foods thereby reach the taste receptors.

Taste had little to do with Bernie's adventure, but as he well knew, the mouth goes a bit dry in situations of fear. This lack of saliva diminishes our capacity for taste because the chemical substances remain in a solid state. They do not flow into the deeply embedded receptors.

We experience four basic tastes: bitter, sour, sweet, and salty. The receptors at the back of the tongue are particularly sensitive to bitter, those at the sides to sour, and those at the tip to sweet. Still others, scattered all over the tongue except at the center, are most sensitive to salty substances. Those at the tip appear especially sensitive to salt (Linschoten & Kroeze, 1991).

The ways in which we mediate the many tastes available to us are still a mystery, but all of our gus-

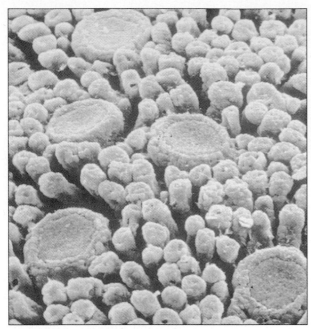
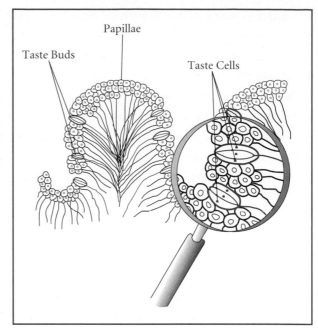

FIGURE 4–10 RECEPTORS FOR TASTE. Each taste bud has numerous cells, not just two or three, and each of the cells has its own nerve fibers. For purposes of illustration, the drawing has been simplified. The photo shows the surface of a frog's tongue, highly magnified, revealing the disc-shaped papillae.

tatory experiences seem to arise through the interaction among these four fundamental flavors. According to **pattern theory,** the taste conveyed by any given fiber depends on the activity of other fibers. If a certain fiber is activated, the taste may be salty, but if nearby fibers are also activated, the taste may be sour. The role of the adjacent nerve tissue is emphasized in this theory, but there is still debate even on the primary tastes (Figure 4–10).

A MULTISENSORY EXPERIENCE. Taste, as we know, is influenced by vision and smell. With the eyes closed and the nostrils blocked, lemon juice is sensed merely as sour and cola as bittersweet. Temperature is important too, for coffee and other drinks taste quite differently at different temperatures. Still other substances, such as cauliflower and broccoli, vary in taste depending on whether they have a smooth or rough texture.

The food processing industry uses such knowledge to increase our appetite for its products.

Canned tomatoes, pistachio ice cream, and fancy pastries are served with color additives, appealing to vision. Breakfast cereals are said to go "snap, crackle, pop," suggesting auditory experiences that indicate a freshness in this fibrous food. Sandwiches at fast-food chains offer beef in very thin slices, making chewing and swallowing easier, thereby appealing to sensitivities of the muscles and joints, to which we turn later.

❧

SENSITIVITIES OF THE SKIN

Up at the firewalking seminar, at nearly one o'clock in the morning, the preparations reached their peak. The leader gave his final instructions; the participants took off their shoes and stockings; and the whole group once again trooped out of the conference room together. This time they broke into a spontaneous chant: "Yes, yes, yes." This chant, accompanied by clapping, was clearly a wishful answer to the question on everyone's mind: "Can I do it without getting burned?"

Moving around the pits, the unperturbed workers continued to spread the coals into two thin beds in the grass, each approximately eight to ten feet in length. Close to the fires, the heat on the eyes and skin was intense, forcing the crowd to move backward and the shovelers to work carefully. This contrast with the cool night air and wet grass made everyone well aware of the sensitivities of the skin (Leikind & McCarthy, 1985).

A small expanse of thin tissue, our skin represents a very delicate and important part of life. It is the chief grounds for intimacy; it holds us together, at least physically; and it defines our boundaries. We know where we begin and end by the limits of our *integumentary system,* meaning the skin, hair, nails, and other external covering. This term comes from the Latin word for "cover."

There have been attempts to identify the primary skin experiences in human beings. An oyster on the tongue, for example, involves pressure; oyster soup usually involves temperature and, if it is too hot, pain. These three experiences—pressure, temperature, and pain—are known as **cutaneous sensitivity,** meaning that they arise through the skin. In the past they have been referred to collectively and imprecisely as the *sense of touch,* but sensory psychologists, interested in understanding these distinct experiences and the underlying mechanisms, emphasize the differences among them.

PRESSURE AND TEMPERATURE. Nevertheless, relatively little is known about the underlying receptors for pressure sensitivity in human beings. The experience of light pressure is induced by stimulation of a hair follicle, but free nerve endings at early or late stages of growth also may be responsible. The experience of heavy pressure involves tissues lying beneath the skin's surface; Pacinian corpuscles are subcutaneous and relatively numerous, and therefore they are considered recep-

tors for this experience. Here again, the concept of adaptation is relevant. The Pacinian corpuscles are responsive only to changes in pressure; under steady pressure, they do not respond (Figure 4–11).

Explorations of the human skin have told us more about the distribution of these receptors than about their mode of operation. The experience of light pressure is greatest on the most mobile parts of the body, which are at least four or five times more sensitive than the less mobile parts, such as the back. The lips and tips of the fingers serve very well indeed in explorations based on touch.

The structural bases of temperature sensitivity are not well known either, although human beings and many animals are sensitive to warmth and cold just a few degrees above or below normal body temperature. Free nerve endings and the microscopic blood vessels that run to every part of the skin are currently mentioned as possible mediators.

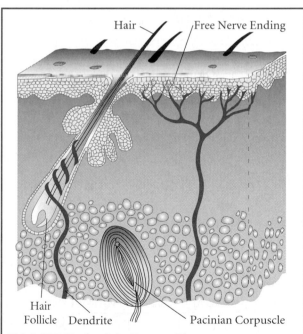

FIGURE 4–11 SKIN RECEPTORS. Dendrites around hair follicles and unknown mechanisms mediate light pressure. Pacinian corpuscles, located beneath the skin's surface, apparently are the receptors for heavy pressure. Free nerve endings are responsible for temperature and pain sensitivity.

Throughout most of the body, the receptors for cold are much more numerous than those for warmth, but they are not evenly distributed. There are many more cold spots per square centimeter on the tip of the nose, for example, than on the forearm. The receptors for warmth have been studied in two places of vital importance, the palm of the hand and sole of the foot, involving comparisons between young and old human beings. As might be expected from knowledge of other thresholds, elderly feet are markedly less sensitive than young feet to warmth (Kenshalo, 1986).

PUZZLE OF PAIN. Among all of the senses of the skin, pain has been especially puzzling, partly because it does not seem to operate in the direct way of the other sensory systems. For example, the intensity of pain is not necessarily in proportion to the degree of bodily harm. As Bernie knew, there were instances in which firewalkers had been burned yet felt no pain at the time. Pain, furthermore, is altered by a number of psychological states, including expectation, anxiety, and motivation. And finally, direct surgical intervention, aimed at cutting the nerve pathways assumed to mediate pain, often has been unsuccessful. In numerous instances the pain has persisted, sometimes accompanied by new pains (Melzack, 1987).

These puzzling conditions are not entirely surprising, for pain serves quite a different purpose from the other senses, providing information on harmful events, regardless of the type of stimulation. One condition of pain is the stimulation of free nerve endings found just beneath the skin surface almost everywhere on the body. Some of these nerves appear to transmit pain without being associated with any other sensory process. Pain is not experienced in the cerebral cortex and certain visceral organs, where there are no free nerve endings.

The most prominent attempt to explain the puzzle of pain is the **gate control theory,** which states that certain nerve fibers at the back of the spinal cord act as a barrier, or gate, for the flow of pain impulses into the brain. They do so by giving priority to nonpain impulses arriving at the gate at the same time. These nonpain impulses, presumably from the skin, occupy the same nerve pathways by which the pain impulses would have been transmitted. In other words, the pain impulses from the peripheral nervous system are blocked before they enter the central nervous system (Melzack, 1987).

Rubbing, squeezing, and kissing the injured spot, it is argued, lessen the pain not only for psychological reasons but also because these more pleasant sensations around the injury occupy the pathways to the brain, decreasing the transmission of pain impulses. Acupuncture may operate in much the same manner. The long, very thin needles used in this traditional Chinese treatment are inserted at key points in the tissue and sometimes slowly rotated. The prickly feelings they elicit apparently prompt inhibitory activities by occupying the potential pathways for pain.

It is speculated that the gate also may be closed from above, by the brain, as well as from below, by competing incoming impulses. In human beings and animals, the perception of pain may be blocked by stress, suggestion, and general excitement. Attention and distraction are well-known factors in analgesia through hypnosis.

• PROPRIOCEPTIVE SENSES •

We began this chapter with the topic of awareness of stimulation, emphasizing the questions of detection and discrimination. Then we examined the traditional sensory capacities oriented to external sources of energy: vision, hearing, smell, taste, and the various skin sensitivities. They are sometimes called *exteroceptive senses,* for the relevant stimuli are typically outside the body (Table 4–6).

Human beings also have receptors for stimuli inside the body. The *interoceptive* or **proprioceptive** senses provide us with information about conditions within our bodies; the root *proprio* means "belonging to the body." As we turn to four internally oriented senses, a qualification is necessary. Human beings can gain information about their bodies through the exteroceptive senses—such as listening to heartbeats. They can learn about the external world through the proprioceptive senses—experiencing the sudden stop of an elevator in which they are riding. This general distinction between external and internal is useful chiefly for purposes of discussion.

This approach to sensory processes brings us well beyond Aristotle's five senses. The total today stands at eight to twelve, depending on whether certain systems, such as cutaneous sensitivity, are considered one or several senses. It also brings us, at one o'clock in the morning, to the pits of hot coals, where Bill observed from the sidelines and Bernie waited inconspicuously.

The leader of the seminar, standing at the first pit, prepared to lead the way. Exaggerating the instructions he had transmitted to his students, he stood still, breathed deeply and fully, and fixed his gaze upward—to produce a more tranquil state. Then he strode across the pit at an even pace, chanting: "Cool moss, cool moss." Finishing amid shouts from the seminar students, he quickly wiped his feet and then punched into the air in the celebratory routine (Leikind & McCarthy, 1985).

KINESTHESIS

How did this leader manage to walk easily, wipe his feet readily, and then punch into the air in the prescribed fashion? Certainly vision and the skin were partly responsible, but another sensitivity, often taken for granted, was significantly involved. The answer to successful walking and wiping and punching also lies in **kinesthesis,** which is the sense of body movement or position. It guides the limbs in extension or flexion, forward or backward, to one side or the other, through feedback from within the body itself.

Kinesthesis is made possible by receptor mechanisms in the muscles, tendons, and joints. These mechanisms are subject to pressure and release of pressure as parts of the body are moved or held in a firm position; the resulting nerve impulses travel to the brain, providing information concerning the status of our limbs. Other impulses are then sent back to the muscles, tendons, and joints, stimulating further activity. An experienced golfer knows

SENSITIVITY	STIMULUS	RECEPTORS	EXPERIENCE
Visual	Light waves	Rods and cones in the retina	Hue, brightness, purity: color of the embers
Auditory	Sound waves	Hair cells in the basilar membrane	Pitch, loudness, timbre: hiss and crackle of fire
Olfactory	Gaseous substance	Hair cells on the olfactory epithelium	Smoky, putrid, resinous, flowery, fruity, spicy: odor of smoke
Gustatory	Soluble substance	Taste cells in taste buds	Bitter, sour, sweet, salty: taste of thick smoke
Cutaneous	Mechanical or thermal stimulation	Free nerve endings in the skin	Pressure, cold, warmth, pain: texture and heat of the embers

TABLE 4–6 THE TRADITIONAL SENSES.

when she is swinging the club well just by the feeling in her body (Figure 4–12).

VISCERAL SENSITIVITY

While Bernie awaited his turn to step across the coals at 1,500 degrees Fahrenheit, a sensation that he had been feeling mildly all day suddenly became pronounced—"butterflies in the stomach." His lower abdomen felt heavy.

These feelings in the internal organs of the body are called **visceral sensitivity,** for the viscera include the stomach, intestines, kidneys, and various glands. When these organs are stimulated to accelerate or inhibit activity, they send nerve impulses into the central nervous system. Reception of these impulses in the brain underlies visceral sensitivity. These experiences include thirst, hunger, nausea, bladder tensions, sexual tensions, suffocation, and the feeling of fullness.

FIGURE 4–12 ROLE OF KINESTHESIS. Successful body movements are dependent on feedback from muscles and tendons usually learned in gradual fashion.

Visceral sensitivity is given relatively little attention from the standpoint of how it influences experience. In fact, our later discussions of hunger, thirst, and sex show that studies of these activities contribute much more to our knowledge of motivation than to our understanding of visceral experience.

The nausea associated with motion sickness appears attributable to visceral disturbances. Sudden upward movement of the body, as in an elevator, leads to a lag in the visceral organs, exerting pressure on the membranes that keep the intestines in position. Such pulls are not the sole cause, however; motion sickness is also mediated by mechanisms in the inner ear (Clark, 1985).

SENSE OF BALANCE

Around the pits, the aspiring firewalkers wearing pants had bent over to turn up their cuffs. Some sat in the grass to do so. Then, in the darkness, they walked to the edge of the pit. All of these activities—bending, sitting, walking, standing—required more than kinesthesis. Also at work was the **sense of balance,** which means maintaining one's position or equilibrium relative to gravity. The mechanisms that mediate it are part of the inner ear, but they have nothing to do with hearing.

In human beings, the portion of the inner ear that contains the primary mechanisms for balance is called the **nonauditory labyrinth,** meaning that it is not related to hearing and is mazelike in structure. It is nonauditory and labyrinthine. This delicate structure, entirely filled with a liquid, has two types of chambers, vestibules and canals (Figure 4–13).

The vestibules are concerned with the sense of balance, and they are collectively known as the **vestibular system.** The hair cells in this system are the receptors for the position of the head and body. They are weighted with calcium particles, and

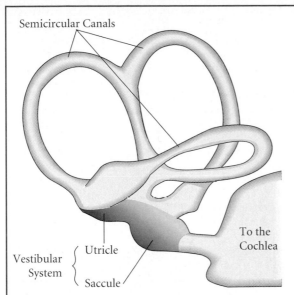

FIGURE 4–13 NONAUDITORY LABYRINTH. There are two parts to the nonauditory labyrinth. The vestibular system, shown in color, includes two saclike structures, the utricle and saccule. It mediates balance—as well as passive linear motion. The semicircular canals, shown in black and white, compose the second part of the nonauditory labyrinth. They serve as receptors for passive rotary motion.

any change in the position of the head causes them to bend in the liquid. Then the aroused nerve impulses go to the brain, and we have a sense of being tilted, horizontal, upside down, or in some other position.

In lobsters, the weighted particles on the hair cells must be replaced periodically as the animal acquires a new shell, and the substances used for this purpose are generally stones and sand obtained from the ocean floor. In some early experiments, conditions were arranged so that no materials other than iron filings were available for replacing the sloughed-off stones, and the animals used them. Later, when a magnet was placed above these aquatic creatures, they rolled over on their backs and remained in this position. This action reversed the normal gravitational pull, which comes from the animal's underside rather than its back, thereby clearly demonstrating

the importance of the vestibular system in the lobster's sense of balance and position in space (Prentiss, 1901).

Bernie knew that vision plays a role in balance, and he took advantage of this fact when it became his turn for a stroll on the coal. The leader made him huff and puff before his first step, but then Bernie, instead of looking up at the heavens, followed some early advice from his mother: "Watch where you're going!" In another three strides he reached the other side, delighted with his achievement. Then he followed another instruction that seemed quite important. He wiped his feet.

Bernie was also disappointed, for the embers had cooled a bit. They felt like warm moss under his feet, not much above the *absolute* threshold. Later, when the workers brought new coals, he jumped to be the first in line, a movement that again required a sense of balance, mediated largely in the vestibular system. This time the embers felt prickly, approaching the *terminal* threshold, and afterward Bernie was afraid to look at his feet. When he did, he found no damage other than one small blister (Leikind & McCarthy, 1985).

Bernie, of course, had cheated on the seminarians. He paid no tuition and took the final exam—twice.

☙

PASSIVE MOTION

Whenever an individual is traveling from one place to another but not actively moving, the condition is called **passive motion.** It occurs in elevators, roller coasters, and automobiles. During their ride back to Los Angeles, Bernie and Bill experienced this form of motion. Bernie had other experiences too. His whole body felt better, including a lighter stomach and more relaxed muscles. As we know from everyday life, especially from riding in vehicles, the proprioceptive senses are often experienced in various combinations.

SENSITIVITY	STIMULUS	RECEPTORS	EXPERIENCE
Kinesthetic	Change in position of body parts	Nerve endings in the muscles, tendons, joints	Movement of body parts: walking across the hot coals
Visceral	Stimulation of intestines, stomach, glands	Unknown receptors in visceral organs	Discomfort, heaviness, tension: feeling butterflies in the stomach
Balance	Body position	Vestibular system	Upright, tilted: standing in the parking lot
Passive motion	Linear motion; rotary motion	Vestibular system; semicircular canals	Change in rate of motion, spinning: riding in a car

TABLE 4–7 THE PROPRIOCEPTIVE SENSES.

Generally, two types of passive motion are specified, the first of which is mediated by the vestibular system. With *linear motion,* we experience a *change* in the rate of straight-line movement, associated with a lag in the adjustment of the hairs in the vestibule. The body or head need not be tipped or turned, as in the sense of balance. Instead, even when the person does not move a muscle, any change in the rate of linear motion through space, in the form of acceleration or deceleration, bends the hairs in the opposite direction, transmitting nerve impulses to the brain.

The other type, *rotary motion,* involves circular movement, and it too is experienced whenever there is a change in rate, though it is mediated by the semicircular canals, the other part of the nonauditory labyrinth. In addition to the vestibule, the nonauditory labyrinth includes three **semicircular canals,** responsible for sensitivity to rotary motion. In the human being, each canal is approximately perpendicular to the others, corresponding to each of the three planes of space. Turning the head in any direction produces movements of hair cells in at least one canal (Figure 4–13).

Human beings are generally exposed only to mild rotary motion, as when a car rounds a curve or some brief spinning motion is involved in a dance or athletics. When the movement is pronounced and sustained, motion sickness can result, and evidence is plentiful that the vestibular system plays a role. In one demonstration, 15 people were exposed to motion in all three planes. Nine of them possessed normal vestibular systems, and they showed symptoms of motion sickness in 78% of the trials. The other subjects had defective vestibular systems. They reported no motion sickness even when directly exposed to a rolling, pitching stimulus (Cheung, Howard, & Money, 1991; Table 4–7).

• SENSATION AND PERCEPTION •

Our study of sensation is almost complete, and Bernie has demonstrated his point. He completed the firewalk successfully without attending the seminar. Bill, in turn, completed his investigation of the seminar without a trip across the hot coals. He noted, incidentally, that most of the seminar participants attempted the walk. No longer tenderfeet, only a few reported blisters. Then Bernie and Bill combined their findings and published an article about this experience. Citing several factors in physics and psychology, they titled their report *An Investigation of Firewalking* (Leikind & McCarthy, 1985).

The physics of firewalking is most readily understood through the analogy of baking a cake. After several minutes in a heated oven, the air and cake and pan are all at the same temperature, approximately 350 degrees Fahrenheit. When you reach in to fetch your creation, you have no hesitation about contact with the oven air, some trepidation about dipping a finger into the cake, and considerable reluctance to touch the pan. The reason is that these different substances, although all at the same temperature, contain different amounts of heat and conduct them to other substances at very different rates of speed. The air has a low heat capacity and poor conductivity; the cake is intermediate; and the aluminum pan has a very high heat capacity and conductivity. You will not bake your hands unless you keep them in the oven air for an hour or so, but you can get burned immediately just by touching the aluminum pan.

Walking on aluminum at 1,500 degrees Fahrenheit would burn you instantly. But wood, ashes, and pot holders—even pumice, used for firewalking in Fiji and Sri Lanka—are extremely poor conductors of heat. So, despite our usual perception of incandescent objects, firewalking is not as dangerous as it might seem—as long as you do not walk too long (Dennett, 1985; Leikind & McCarthy, 1985). As a rule, the total time on the coals for any specific part of the body is no more than two seconds, which means that newcomers to the world of firewalking should be encouraged to complete their stimulating trip promptly.

The study of firewalking shows that our experience of any event, including a trip across the coals, arises initially from our sense organs, but there is no one-to-one correspondence between physical stimulation and psychological experience. In firewalking, the experience arises partly from the stimulation of the glowing embers and partly from other events, including the shouts of spectators, the walker's focus of attention, and the leader's instructions to breathe deeply, to gaze upward, and to concentrate on the cool-moss mantra. These events diverted Bernie's attention, thereby raising his threshold for pain. In responding to them, he was rendered less responsive to the task at hand—or rather underfoot.

Deep breathing played an additional role, not only as a distraction but also in relaxation and pain reduction, as in the Lamaze technique in childbirth. Performed just before the moment of greatest pain, this increased rate and depth of breathing help to reduce the intensity of the experience (Leikind & McCarthy, 1985).

Thus, the full psychological experience of firewalking is based not only on the direct physical stimulation but also on our expectations, motivation, and physiological readiness, and here we encounter an important point about sensation and perception. Perception usually arises from *several* sensory processes, as well as prior events.

In other words, the process called *sensation* consists of primitive sensory experiences, raw and unorganized. They arise at the receptors, where information is originally obtained. In daily life, these sensory experiences are combined with information already stored in the brain. In this complex process, known as **perception,** we add memory, expectation, and other cognitive elements to current sensations, arriving at some interpretation about ourselves and the world around us. The result is a unified experience arising from more than warmth, brightness, and noise. We combine this sensory information with past experience, and we know that we are standing near hot coals amid a band of cheering spectators in front of a zealous leader.

❧

INTERSENSORY PERCEPTION

As a rule, our senses operate in conjunction with each other. They are interrelated—and active. Rec-

FIGURE 4-14 THE SENSES AS INTERRELATED AND ACTIVE. Consider which of these senses are illustrated in the photograph.

ognizing this condition, psychologists often speak of **intersensory perception,** meaning that information is obtained from several senses simultaneously. Then it is added to previously acquired information stored in the brain. These interrelated conditions hold for the traditional and proprioceptive senses (Figure 4–14).

SENSES AS INTERRELATED. During his firewalking, Bernie could feel the heat, hear the cheers, see the coals, smell the smoke, and perhaps even taste it. Through the proprioceptive senses, he could also detect his bodily movements, keep his balance, and notice the "butterflies" in his stomach, all of which collectively provided a very definite intersensory experience.

Eating a meal is an intersensory experience, a composite of gustatory, olfactory, visual, and cutaneous sensitivities. A person tipped backward in a dentist's chair is aware of the situation through what is seen, through what may be heard, and also through information from the semicircular canals and vestibule. People with defective vestibular systems maintain themselves reasonably well in an ordinary environment until they wear blindfolds, and then the defect is obvious.

Kissing is an intimate intersensory experience. It provides opportunities for seeing, hearing, smelling, touching, *and* tasting. Compared to other modes of contact, such as the wave and handshake, it offers a rather complete inventory of another person.

SENSES AS ACTIVE. There is evidence for intersensory perception even in *touch typing,* an inappropriate label because the primary sensation is kinesthetic. The expert typist allegedly never looks at the keyboard, but research shows that typing is a kinesthetic-visual task, especially with regard to accuracy. The skillful typist often steals corner-of-the-eye glances at the keyboard (West, 1967). These reactions show that the senses are both interrelated and active. They *seek information.*

The firewalkers did not sit passively amid all of the activity in their environment. They looked hither and yon, listened to the chants and instructions, moved their bodies, stretched their limbs, and perhaps even sniffed the air, all to find out what was happening. As their story indicates, most of us are actively exploring our environment, using all of the senses available to us. Human beings and other organisms seek changes in stimulation even when they do not perceive themselves to be in peril.

EXTRASENSORY PERCEPTION

For many years in the United States, firewalking has been considered a psychic activity, along with postmortem survival, water dowsing, and other allegedly occult phenomena. One reason is that firewalking was practiced only in distant lands. Not much was known about it in this country. Another reason is that the mind can influence experience. There is no doubt about that. It can make us more tolerant of pain through spiritual, mystic, and other beliefs—although it *cannot* make the feet invulnerable to intense heat.

Among all claims of psychic phenomena, the most popular and widely debated is **extrasensory perception,** or ESP, which is awareness without any sensory basis. Information is obtained without the use of our normally recognized senses. Firewalking is *not* an instance of ESP, for no special awareness is claimed. In fact, almost the opposite is true: There is lack of awareness of the heat of the coals. Nevertheless, the concept of ESP is widely used for almost any inexplicable event or special awareness. It therefore merits attention in the context of sensation.

ANECDOTES, FRAUD, AND PROBABILITIES. In one of their first meetings, Sigmund Freud and Carl Gustav Jung were discussing psychic phenomena when suddenly the bookcase made a noise. Then, for some reason that he was never able to explain, Jung predicted another loud noise. Bang! It occurred just as he spoke, and this event made a profound impression on both of them (Jung, 1963).

Such reports are impressive, especially when given by respected individuals, but the problem with anecdotes is that we do not know the *full details.* Was the original perception accurate? Has the anecdote been distorted in retelling? Noting the unreliability of anecdotal evidence, William James, a very strong believer in psychic experience, lamented his inability to discover an absolutely irrefutable case of ESP. To demonstrate the existence of the supernatural, he pointed out, just one good instance is needed. In more colorful language, he emphasized: To upset the law that all crows are black, we need just one white crow.

Another difficulty in claims of ESP is the widespread incidence of obvious fraud. For this reason, Randi, a nationally recognized magician, has written books, given lectures, and received large grants to expose fraudulent psychics. He has offered $10,000 to any psychic performing a feat that he, Randi, cannot duplicate. To this date, no psychic has even accepted the challenge, much less proved him wrong (Randi, 1982).

More serious cases of fraud have occurred in ESP laboratories. Two decades ago, J. B. Rhine, the foremost American investigator of ESP, declared that dishonesty was no longer an issue in this research (Rhine, 1974b). Three months later, Rhine's successor in the ESP movement, the director of one of the world's leading ESP laboratories, was discovered to be falsifying research results (Rhine, 1974a).

Also, probabilities are used skillfully. One self-proclaimed psychic takes a "psych-up walk" before each ESP performance, and he uses probabilities very cleverly later. In the parking lot before the show, he notes all sorts of telltale signs: a license plate here, a baseball sticker there, twin infant seats in another car. Afterward, in front of the audience, he makes his psychic claims: "I have the feeling there is someone in the audience from Maryland." "Who roots for the Tigers?" "One of you has a special interest in twins." When probabilities are used in this way, augmented by assistance from accomplices and trick equipment, faking ESP is not a difficult task.

Did you know, for example, that with just 30 people in a room, the chances are better than two to one that at least two of them will have birthdays on the same day of the year? And the odds rise above 90% in a group of 50 people (Bergamini, 1971).

AN UNSETTLED ISSUE. A major obstacle in the scientific study of ESP is the lack of a conceptual framework. Despite a century of scientific investigation, there is no useful theory, not even according to the leading figures in this field. The field, in fact, is defined by what it is not; it is anything not otherwise explainable by science. If ESP does exist, we have no adequate approach to interpreting such phenomena, despite continuing efforts to test ESP hypotheses (Gissurarson, 1990; Walther, 1986).

This lack of a theoretical basis has implications for the research methods, which must be aimed at excluding any known sensory channel. As the controls against normal sensory awareness increase, the evidence for ESP usually becomes weaker, a circumstance that is contrary to what one finds elsewhere in science. Usually the expected effect grows stronger as extraneous variables are eliminated.

A notable exception involved a study in mental telepathy with "senders" and "receivers" isolated from one another. In contrast to earlier investigations, the sender viewed highly dramatic images, such as a crashing tidal wave or wildly animated cartoon, while the receiver sat quietly in another room, trying to apprehend this visual image. Later, when shown four different images and asked to select the one that was transmitted, the receiver chose it with a success rate of approximately 32%, well above the expected level of 25%. The probability of a difference this large occurring by chance is extremely low (Bem & Honorton, 1994). This finding, defying statistical odds and using stimulating visual images rather than the geo-

metric patterns of earlier years, will make ESP research more intriguing and perhaps more creative in the future.

A survey of college psychologists showed that they were equally divided on the ESP issue. Approximately one-third viewed ESP as essentially impossible; one-third were uncertain; and one-third regarded ESP as a likely or established fact. But compared with professors in other fields, including other scientists, psychologists were much more doubtful. Only 3% of the natural scientists decided that ESP is impossible (Wagner & Monnet, 1979). Clearly, people from different backgrounds, including different research experience, have very different views of ESP.

As these investigations continue, we need to remind ourselves of the implications of the ESP perspective. Accepting its underlying assumptions and applying them broadly to the human condition would radically alter the content of modern thought. It would generate a fundamentally different set of explanations about human behavior, profoundly changing our thinking about religion, education, law, medicine, and virtually all other areas of human existence (Adams, 1991).

IN CONCLUSION. With Bernie and Bill safely back at the university, beyond the glowing coals, we should acknowledge another principle of physics and one from physiological psychology as well. In the *Leidenfrost effect*, protection from heat is provided by a thin, watery layer, basically a form of thermal insulation produced naturally through perspiration or artificially by wetting the skin. For this reason, people spit on their fingers before touching a hot iron. For human feet, perspiration is often sufficient to produce this minimal insulation, but for insurance the workers at the firewalking seminar kept the sod around the pits rather damp (Leikind & McCarthy, 1985).

The principle of physiological psychology concerns the timing of the whole event, which began late in the evening and included 2 hours of instruction, used for raising motivation, enlisting cooperation, and, of course, justifying the expense of the seminar. The actual firewalking took place at 1:00 A.M., long past Bernie's usual bedtime, and therefore he was probably less aware of pain. The responsiveness of our bodies is significantly governed by the *circadian rhythm*, meaning that our bodies exhibit a cycle of approximately 24 hours, completing a full wake-sleep span within that period. When it is well past our usual bedtime, bodily functions become depressed, as though the body is trying to sleep. People walking on hot coals in the wee hours of the morning are less likely to feel pain than those hearty souls doing so at high noon.

In addition, responsiveness to pain is governed by endorphins, the body's own pain killers, released at abnormally high levels during times of stress. The presence of all of these factors shows once again the multiple bases of behavior.

However, people who stand or walk barefoot on hot coals for more than a few seconds will get burned regardless of what they are thinking, how deeply they breathe, how much they are sweating, where they walk, when they walk, or what they believe. So, please be careful. And be courteous! Let someone else go first.

Finally, we must add a warning about quick—fix seminars, arising from Bill's investigation. These brief encounters may temporarily enhance self-esteem or prepare people to ignore pain, and there may be other gains too, but without more extensive practical counseling a long-term benefit is unlikely. Worse yet, participants may experience adverse reactions later. Those who attend the seminar but forego the firewalking may develop increased self-doubts. Those who trust their soles to the coals may develop false notions about themselves. Whatever happens, do not go home, call everyone into the kitchen, and take hot pans out of the oven bare-handed. Instead, take a reputable course in physics, psychology, or the sociology of crowds.

With these cautions, we conclude this discussion of sensation, pointing out that Bernie never got burned. But Bill did, in a way. He paid a few hundred dollars for that fear seminar. In that sense, he was "taken over the coals" by the seminar leader.

• SUMMARY •

AWARENESS OF STIMULATION

1. All that we know of the world comes to us through stimulation of the sense organs, a process called sensation. Four structures are involved: collector, receptor, transmission, and coding mechanisms.
2. To be perceived, a stimulus must be above a certain level of intensity known as the absolute threshold. For a stimulus not to be painful, it must be below a certain level of intensity known as the terminal threshold.
3. The difference threshold concerns sensitivity to a difference between stimulus intensities. In the normal ranges of intensity, it follows Weber's law, which states: The least amount of change in a stimulus that can be noticed is a constant fraction of that stimulus.
4. Signal detection theory deals with the problem of a subject's response bias in making judgments about stimulation, including expectation and motivation. It is concerned with influences on the judgment process.

TRADITIONAL SENSES

5. The human eye focuses an image on a light-sensitive surface known as the retina, which contains rods for black-and-white vision and cones for color vision. The trichromatic theory of color vision pos-

tulates that there are three types of cones, especially responsive to red, green, and blue wavelengths. The opponent-process theory also postulates three types of receptor pairs for complementary colors: red-green, yellow-blue, and black-white.

6. The stimuli for hearing are sound waves causing the bending of small hair cells at the basilar membrane. The movement of these cells arouses nerve impulses that travel over the auditory nerve to the brain. According to the place theory of hearing, certain regions of hair cells are especially attuned to certain vibration frequencies. According to the volley theory, nerve fibers operate in groups, and the experience depends on the frequency of volleys.

7. Smell plays a subtle role in everyday life, especially in its contribution to what is usually considered to be taste. The olfactory receptors are located high in the nostrils and are stimulated only by odorous substances.

8. Gustatory sensitivity at the human level consists of four primary qualities: salty, sour, sweet, and bitter. The receptors are small cells located in buds within the walls of the papillae of the tongue. Olfactory and cutaneous cues are also important in taste.

9. Cutaneous sensitivity to light pressure is mediated by hair follicles and other mechanisms; heavy pressure is perhaps mediated by the Pacinian corpuscles. Specialized receptors for warmth or cold have not been clearly identified and verified. Pain sensitivity, also not well understood, appears to be mediated, at least in part, by free nerve endings.

PROPRIOCEPTIVE SENSES

10. Kinesthetic sensitivity results from activation of receptors in the muscles, tendons, and joints. Muscular activities and posture therefore provide their own feedback, which underlies the automaticity of well-established motor responses.

11. Visceral sensitivity involves feelings of heaviness or "butterflies" in the organs of the body cavity. They are related to both motivation and emotion, as well as to motion sickness, and are perhaps caused partly by pressures on the membranes supporting these organs.

12. Our sense of balance or equilibrium, such as being right side up or upside down, is based on activities in the nonauditory labyrinth of the inner ear. Hair cells in two small chambers, collectively known as the vestibular system, provide this information.

13. Awareness of linear motion, which is passive motion in a straight line, also arises through events in the vestibular system, and the only adequate stimulus is a change in the rate of movement. Sensitivity to rotary motion comes from another part of the nonauditory labyrinth. Hair cells in the semicircular canals are stimulated to bend one way or the other, transmitting impulses to the brain. Again, a change in motion is the adequate stimulus.

SENSATION AND PERCEPTION

14. Awareness usually involves intersensory or multisensory perception. Our information about the world at any given moment is based on several sense organs typically seeking information and also on data previously stored in the brain. The various sensory systems operate in an interrelated and active manner.

15. Extrasensory perception (ESP) implies perception without the use of any currently known sense organs. This phenomenon has been questioned on the basis of anecdotal reports, the problem of fraud, use of probabilities, and difficulty in establishing useful theory and research procedures.

• WORKING WITH PSYCHOLOGY •

❧ REVIEW OF KEY CONCEPTS ❧

sensation	*Awareness of Stimulation*	receptors
sense organs	collector mechanisms	law of specific nerve energies

neural coding
absolute threshold
subliminal advertising
terminal threshold
difference threshold
just noticeable difference (j.n.d.)
Weber's law
signal detection theory
response bias

Traditional Senses
traditional senses
visual sensitivity
wavelength
hue
pupillary opening
iris
lens
accommodation
retina
rods
cones
fovea
blind spot
optic nerve

parallel distributed processing
feature detectors
adaptation
saccadic movements
subtractive color mixture
additive color mixture
trichromatic theory
opponent-process theory
afterimage
achromatic vision
monochromat
dichromat
auditory sensitivity
frequency
outer ear
eardrum
middle ear
ossicles
oval window
inner ear
cochlea
basilar membrane
place theory
volley theory
olfactory sensitivity

olfactory epithelium
stereochemical theory
pheromones
gustatory sensitivity
pattern theory
cutaneous sensitivity
gate control theory

Proprioceptive Senses
proprioceptive senses
kinesthesis
visceral sensitivity
sense of balance
nonauditory labyrinth
vestibular system
passive motion
semicircular canals

Sensation and Perception
perception
intersensory perception
extrasensory perception (ESP)

❧ CLASS DISCUSSION/CRITICAL THINKING ❧

A NARRATIVE TWIST.

Imagine that Bernie had a mystical outlook on life, believing in all sorts of psychic phenomena, ESP, and other occult activities, rather than the principles of physics. Would this outlook have influenced his physical experience of firewalking? Would it have influenced his psychological experience? Take a position in each instance. Provide information and ideas to defend each viewpoint. ❧

TOPICAL QUESTIONS.

• *Awareness of Stimulation.* To avoid the misery of taking a cool shower, a bather always starts with hot water, even on the warmest days, and then very gradually decreases the temperature—almost fooling her skin into thinking that the water is still warm. Does this situation depict the difference threshold, the absolute threshold, or both? Explain your answer.
• *Traditional Senses.* In what ways

might adaptation both threaten and aid the survival of a shipwrecked crew or lost adventurer in the Arctic Circle?
• *Proprioceptive Senses.* Describe how kinesthesis and cutaneous sensitivity might be at work during sleep.
• *Sensation and Perception.* How are the processes of sensation and perception functionally inseparable? How are they functionally independent? Is the attempt to make a distinction between them useful? Explain your view.

❧ TOPICS OF RELATED INTEREST ❧

The question of subliminal advertising extends into the issue of embedded messages, discussed in the next chapter (5). Nerve

impulses in the retina and cochlea are transmitted to the occipital and temporal lobes of the cerebral cortex (3). The nature of the nerve

impulse is discussed in the context of neural communication (3).

ATTENDING TO STIMULATION
Selective Attention
Divided Attention

ORGANIZING THE PERCEPTUAL FIELD
Primitive Organization
Form Perception
Perceptual Constancy

INTERPRETING PERCEPTUAL INFORMATION
Depth Perception
Perception of Movement
Experiencing Illusions
Perception of People

INFLUENCES ON PERCEPTION
Perceptual Set
Role of Learning

5
PERCEPTION

GROUP OF FRENCH HUNTERS IN THE CAUNE WOODS OF AVEYRON, FRANCE, FINALLY CLOSED IN ON THEIR PREY, A WILD BOY WHO HAD BEEN RUNNING FREE and naked in the forest for some years. After pulling him from a tree he had climbed to evade their pursuit, they assigned him to the care of a neighboring widow. He escaped within a week. Wandering through the country-side in the most rigorous weather, he was captured again and this time transferred to Paris. Ministers and scholars in the capital city had requested a scientific study of this savage, thinking it would shed some light on the development of the human mind.

He was called the "Wild Boy of Aveyron," and his arrival along the banks of the Seine in 1800 aroused two quite different expectations. Some people were anticipating Rousseau's noble savage in all his dignity. After a few months' education, he would give a most interesting account of life in the wilds. Others looked forward to the boy's astonishment at the wonders of Paris. He would be profoundly impressed with modern clothing, furniture, buildings, and modes of transportation.

Both groups were disappointed.

Visitors to the Wild Boy encountered instead a dirty, frightened creature who crawled and trotted like a wild beast. About 12 years old, he spent most of his time rocking back and forth like an animal in the zoo. No sound left his mouth except for an infrequent growl from the back of his throat. Finding a dead bird, he stripped off its feathers, opened it with his fingernail, smelled it, and then threw it away. He scratched and bit those who opposed him but otherwise was largely indifferent to everything and everyone in his new environment (Itard, 1807).

The famous French physician Phillippe Pinel, renowned for developing positive attitudes towards mental illness, was the first to examine the boy thoroughly. Dr. Pinel thereupon declared that the Wild Boy was an incurable idiot and that his wildness was probably overestimated. In Pinel's opinion, the poor creature was the product of a decidedly subnormal mentality. He was a man-animal or perhaps a man-plant, for his only development beyond that of the flower was locomotion. His behavioral deficiencies lay in his defective intelligence.

A much younger physician, Jean-Marc-Gaspard Itard, requested a meeting with the boy, an historic occasion in the Luxembourg Gardens. The boy wore only a gray, loose-fitting robe like a nightshirt, which he tore from his body at the first unguarded moment. He said nothing, appeared deaf, and gazed distantly across the gardens. Sitting across from him in a long coat and tie, with ruffles and cuff links, Itard looked kindly on the boy. At age 26, he had just come to Paris in search of a career, and the boy's condition aroused his interest. Little did either of them know that they had, at that moment, joined their lives in a long and difficult search (Lane, 1979).

And little did writers and observers of that day appreciate the unflagging efforts of a third person in this joint venture. Today, with greater understanding of the contribution of the daily caregiver, we pay special tribute in this instance to Madame Guerin, who became the boy's guardian and daily companion.

After examining the boy briefly, Itard took a bold view, quite different from that of the renowned Pinel. The Wild Boy's subnormality, he declared, was due to his lack of experience in

human civilization. If carefully trained in a normal environment, the boy would show corresponding gains in mental life. Itard staked his youthful reputation on this opinion and sought permission from the Ministry of Interior to begin a treatment that would produce a normal child.

According to Itard, the Wild Boy was a *feral child,* meaning that he was totally uncivilized from living in the wilds, perhaps in the company of animals. Approximately 50 such cases have been recorded, most in scant detail, some apparently as hoaxes (Malson, 1972). Among them, the story of this boy from France is the most widely accepted as scientifically sound (Table 5–I).

Specifically, Itard planned to increase the boy's perceptual, intellectual, and emotional responsiveness, thereby enabling him to take his rightful place in human society. The starting point would be perception, the gateway to knowledge, the portal of the mind, the avenue to a fuller intellectual and emotional life. Permission was granted, and Itard began his treatment. As it turned out, this treatment formed the roots of modern educational and behavioral psychology, as well as psychological testing.

Our concern in this chapter is with **perception,** the process by which we select, organize, and interpret stimuli, thereby gaining an understanding of ourselves and our environment. In doing so, we combine sensory information with information already stored in the nervous system, as memory.

Name	Date	Age
Hesse wolf-child	1344	7
First Lithuanian bear-boy	1661	12
Irish sheep-child	1672	16
Wild Boy of Aveyron	1799	11
Amala of Midnapore	1920	2
Kamala of Midnapore	1920	8

TABLE 5–1 CASES OF FERAL CHILDREN   This partial list shows the date and estimated age of each child at the time of capture (Malson, 1972).

The term **sensation,** as we saw in the previous chapter, refers to a more basic condition; it is raw experience, direct from the sense organs. Sensation and perception overlap considerably, but the process of perception involves more cognitive activities. In perception, we derive some meaning based on sensation *and* prior experience.

The citizens of Paris expected the young boy to perceive the excitement and nuances in their sophisticated environment, but such was not the case, at least initially. The Wild Boy saw and heard the city, but these events were little more than sensations for him. He had insufficient prior experience to find meaning in the colors, shapes, odors, and sounds. Itard's attempt to train him therefore provides a useful narrative, illustrating the contributions of innate and acquired factors in human perception.

Three phases of perception are considered in this chapter: attending to stimulation, organizing the perceptual field, and interpreting perceptual information. At the end of the chapter, we note that, among all of the influences on perception, learning plays a central role. It helps us to find meaning in this "blooming, buzzing confusion," as William James once called the infant's environment.

• ATTENDING TO STIMULATION •

Less than five feet tall, with straight brown hair and a round face, the Wild Boy looked at the world with deep, dark eyes. His well-tanned skin showed numerous scars on his arms and legs, neck and face. Outdoors, he trotted barefoot, restrained by a leash. Inside, he roamed the house like a prisoner. At mealtimes, he dragged his food into a corner, kneaded it, and chewed only with his incisors. Otherwise, the Wild Boy paid little attention to human civilization .

OBJECT/EVENT	RESPONSE
Food	Avoided all prepared foods
Drink	Rejected all liquids except water
Clothing	Resisted clothes, including shoes
Furniture	Ignored beds; slept on the floor
Speech	Paid no attention to words
Music	Insensitive to all melodies

TABLE 5–2 THE WILD BOY'S RESPONSE TO HUMAN SOCIETY

FIGURE 5–1 SELECTIVE ATTENTION.
If one neural channel becomes prominent—as when a particular odor arouses a dog, the responsiveness of other channels may be diminished. Impulses from the primary stimulation appear to activate the reticular formation in such a manner as to block irrelevant sensory input.

Itard thus began to increase the range of stimuli to which the boy attended. The process of **attending** involves a readiness to perceive. It is an active process, an orientation toward certain stimulation, often involving an adjustment of the sense organs. To respond properly to human civilization, the boy needed to attend properly to all sorts of events (Table 5–2). For the most part, we perceive only those aspects of the environment to which we attend.

SELECTIVE ATTENTION

Attending is based significantly on interests and motivation; we attend to stimuli relevant to our needs and desires. When Itard began his lessons, the Wild Boy paid no attention at all to the shrillest human cries or words of any sort, even with sharp differences in intonation. They meant nothing to him. Owing to the importance of speech in daily life, improved attention to these sounds was considered indispensable.

Giving exclusive attention to something, focusing on one aspect of the environment and shutting out others, is called **selective attention**. This term may seem redundant, but shortly we shall turn to divided attention, in which we try to focus simultaneously on two or more events (Figure 5–I).

ADJUSTMENTS IN ATTENDING. In the first weeks of training, Itard used the simplest

objects and colors, but still the Wild Boy attended only to stimuli associated with his earlier life in the forests. Spying a large earthen plate with many foods, he grasped only the potatoes, which he had eaten previously. At the sound of a walnut cracked behind him, he immediately turned around, and he invariably tried to smell anything that was given to him, even objects we would consider without odor. In the streets of Paris, he constantly picked up pebbles and pieces of dry wood, discarding them only after holding them to his nose.

The process of attending involves adjustments in the brain, muscles, and sense organs in exquisitely complex and reciprocal fashion, each modifying the other. Adjustments in the brain, for example, require cooperative activity among millions of neurons, especially in the cortex.

When a person sniffs an odor, the molecules carrying this scent are detected by receptor neurons in the upper passages of the nose. The intensity of the stimulation is indicated by the number of receptors activated and the nature of the odor by the specific site stimulated. This pattern of receptor activity is then transmitted to a lower region of the brain known as the *olfactory bulb,* which synthe-sizes the information. The bulb then sends its own messages up to the *olfactory cortex,* which disperses signals throughout other brain areas, including the *frontal cortex.* Some of these go by way of the *thala-mus,* a relay center and switchboard. Others go to the *limbic system,* which contributes elements of memory and emotion and combines this mass of information with incoming messages from other

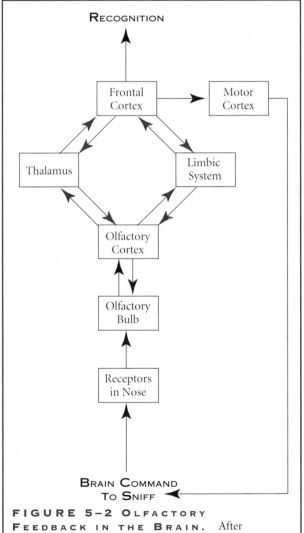

FIGURE 5–2 OLFACTORY FEEDBACK IN THE BRAIN. After information about an odor leaves the olfactory bulb, a high degree of interaction occurs among other parts of the brain, as indicated in color. Similar feedback loops could be identified for other sensory systems (Freeman, 1991).

sensory systems. On the basis of these intricate interconnections, the odor may be recognized, the brain may send a message to sniff again, or it may initiate some other message (Figure 5–2).

The outcome, a meaning-laden perception, is based on what seems to be chaos in the brain—activity so complex that it appears random. Of course, it has a hidden order, demonstrated in the capacity of massive groups of neurons to shift simultaneously and abruptly from one complex pat-tern of activity to another in reaction to seemingly insignificant changes in stimulation (Freeman, 1991).

Adjustments in the muscles, in response to any signal from the brain, are especially evident when someone stoops to look at something on the ground or leans forward to listen more carefully. The Wild Boy holding a pebble to his nose, the dog pointing, and the cat crouching to pounce on its prey all illus-trate sustained attentive postures.

Obvious adjustments of the sense organs occur when someone displays tracking movements of the eyes while watching a ball game. In tasting, we sometimes move a substance around in the mouth so that it falls on different parts of the tongue. Other changes in the sense organs are not learned, and some are too subtle to be readily observed. These include, for example, dilation of the pupils and changes in the skin's electrical activity.

Despite all of these adjustments, we can attend to only a few of the many stimuli to which we are regularly exposed. To which stimuli, therefore, do we attend?

STIMULUS CHARACTERISTICS. A stim-ulus catches our attention partly because it is rele-vant to conditions within us, such as biological motives and personal interests. It also catches atten-tion through its own special characteristics. Adver-tisers use high-intensity stimuli to catch attention. For this reason, we see full-page ads, billboards, and skywriting. Among all of these factors, however, prior experience exerts a profound impact. It influences both our selective exposure to certain stimuli and our interpretation of them (Cohen & Chakravarti, 1990).

The best location for a visual stimulus, when not directly in front of the eyes, is the upper portion of a page or screen. That part receives more attention than the lower part, and the left side receives more attention than the right, at least in the Western world, where people read from left to right and top to bottom.

Color attracts more attention than black and white, and movement attracts more attention than a stationary stimulus. In addition, the novelty of a stimulus is important. A familiar item in unexpected surroundings or an unfamiliar item in common surroundings usually catches attention.

EMBEDDED MESSAGES. Is it possible for advertisers to catch our attention without any obvious stimulus at all? One alleged procedure is called *subliminal advertising* because the message or stimulus is presumably below awareness yet somehow influential. This possibility, received with much excitement in midcentury, has little research support, partly because each of us has a different threshold, or limen, and all of us vary from day to day. Flashing on a screen an advertisement that would be both subliminal and effective on a large scale appears highly unlikely, and evidence has been negative (Moore, 1985). There is no need to fear these hidden persuaders, at least at this point.

In another procedure, advertisers presumably influence us by messages skillfully obscured in a visual display. These stimuli are called **embedded messages,** for they are purposely indistinct or hidden in some larger context, allegedly influential without the viewer's awareness. A photographic ad for a certain brand of beer, for example, shows a rumpled napkin or discarded vest. Within the folds of the cloth, if you look carefully—or possess a

vivid imagination—there may be a sexual symbol, promoting your interest in the advertised product. If you look carefully enough, then the merchants have achieved their purpose. You have attended to the advertisement, although the presumably potent stimuli, if present at all, certainly are not subliminal. They are above threshold, and you have taken the time to find them (Figure 5–3).

One study tested the claim that the word *sex*, when embedded in a pictorial advertisement, increases viewers' memory for that ad. In a set of slides depicting vacation scenes, the word *sex* was embedded several times in each slide. Nonsense syllables, such as *vib* and *res,* were embedded in another

FIGURE 5–3 EMBEDDED FIGURES.
Viewers are prompted to make this search not only by the challenge but also by the alleged image.

set of the same slides, using the same locations, and the control slides contained no embedded messages. The subjects observed these slides and then, two days later, observed them again, along with completely new slides. The subjects were asked to indicate which slides they had seen previously, and they showed no greater recognition for the *sex*-embedded slides than for the slides with nonsense syllables or no message at all. None of the subjects reported anything unusual about the slides, although they could detect the embedded messages after they were pointed out (Vokey & Read, 1985).

Instead of worrying about subliminal or embedded messages, our concern should be with the obvious, sometimes obnoxious, advertisements, which are all too detectable. These overt persuaders prompt most of us to buy far more goods than we can afford or use or store or even discard (Zanot, Pincus, & Lamp, 1983).

DIVIDED ATTENTION

Sometimes attention is not so concentrated. The Wild Boy always noticed the weather, and his appetite never abated. A sudden gust of wind and a bowl of potatoes competed for his attention. Similarly, a modern partygoer, engaged in a boring dialogue, at the same time tries to eaves-drop on a nearby conversation. This process of attending simultaneously to two or more events is called **divided attention.** To what extent is it possible? Can we really do two things at once? Everyday experience suggests that most people can indeed walk and chew gum at the same time.

TASKS IN THE SAME MODALITY. In one instance, subjects were asked to listen to two different messages simultaneously, one in each ear. To ensure that they attended to one of the messages, they were required to repeat it word for word as it appeared. After performing this task, they did not even know whether the other message had included nonsense syllables or a foreign language (Cherry, 1953). In a variation of this experiment, the subjects watched two films presented simultaneously on the same screen, one superimposed over the other. In one film, people were slapping hands; in the other, they were playing ball. The subjects were instructed to attend to one of the games by indicating each occurrence of a given event. Again, it was found that they had essentially no memory of the other events (Neisser & Becklen, 1975).

Except for the basic features of the nonattended communication, such as the sex of a speaker or the number of players, the subjects could not simultaneously monitor two sequences in the same sensory modality. That level of comprehension, involving *what occurred* in each situation, was simply too difficult.

TASKS IN DIFFERENT MODALITIES. Two factors facilitate divided attention. While listening to a caller on the telephone, you can simultaneously admire a painting or taste a pudding. Dual attention is most readily achieved when different sensory modalities are involved (Pashler, 1990).

The other factor is the extent to which one stimulus can be responded to routinely. While playing some very well remembered tunes, the pianist can also attend to the decor of the room and perhaps even nearby conversation. But as one habit increases in strength, the case for divided attention weakens. Attention simply shifts to the novel task. When full attention is required for both tasks, lapses occur for one or the other on the order of milliseconds, but they go unnoticed. The conversation, game, or business is resumed as memory smoothly bridges the gap (Pashler, 1992).

Studies of asymmetry in the cerebral hemispheres add to the complexity of this issue. Each hemisphere has a processing capacity partly independent of the other, one more analytic, the other more holistic. To the extent that they involve separate processing, it may be inappropriate to think of attention as a single, undifferentiated response (Hellige, 1990).

PERCEPTION AND THE UNCONSCIOUS. Studies of divided attention have prompted a new perspective on unconscious mental life. Focused on attention and perception, it contrasts with an older, more theoretical perspective prominent in studies of motivation and personality.

The older focus is called the psychoanalytic or *motivational unconscious,* for it is concerned with past events that have emotional or motivational significance for an individual. These experiences arouse anxiety, and therefore they have been pushed out of awareness and into the realm of the unconscious. In contemporary terms, the motivational unconscious has been wryly described as "hot and wet" because its contents appear in expressions of lust, anger, fear, competition, and related manifestations (Kihlstrom, Barnhardt, & Tataryn, 1992).

From a very different perspective, some psychologists today speak of a *cognitive unconscious,* referring to the apparent role of nonconscious processes in perception and learning. This form of the unconscious is not concerned with long-forgotten events but rather with current stimulation, especially events that are barely perceptible or perceptible but unnoticed. Compared with the motivational unconscious, the cognitive unconscious is "cold and dry" because it is more rational and more closely bound to reality (Kihlstrom, Barnhardt, & Tataryn, 1992). Some of the evidence for it has been mentioned already in connection with the absolute threshold, which includes a region of uncertainty, and certain ambiguities in divided attention. The cognitive unconscious seems to be simpler intellectually and more severely limited than the motivational unconscious portrayed in psychoanalysis (Greenwald, 1992).

Speculated to be at the edge of consciousness,

the cognitive unconscious has not yet generated impressive research support. (Holyoak & Spellman, 1993). It does, however, continue to intrigue some investigators and fuel the imagination of an interested public.

• ORGANIZING THE PERCEPTUAL FIELD •

Gradually, the Wild Boy became more receptive to his new environment. Still without modesty or manners, he no longer tore off his nightshirt, which covered most of his scars, variously counted at 23 to 26. Taken for walks, or rather scampers, he no longer needed a leash. Beside the measured gait of Madame Guerin, his scurrying mode of locomotion was an obvious remnant of his life in the wild.

Perceptually, he had made progress too, attending to human objects and recognizing patterns among them. In one series of training tasks, with a bandage over his eyes, the boy was induced to give a signal on each occasion that a sound differed from the preceding one. Striking diverse objects and using his own voice in varied ways, Itard eventually enabled the boy to take genuine pleasure in discriminating these sounds. In fact, the boy, still completely mute, began to come to Itard with the bandage in hand, his way of requesting further training (Figure 5–4).

Some forms of stimulation require no such training. Instead, they automatically arouse similar perceptual experiences in all of us. They appear to be independent of previous experience. In a word, they seem largely innate. We now turn to the first of these fundamentals of perception.

∾

PRIMITIVE ORGANIZATION

Something that is primitive is not readily reducible to something else. It is, instead, original, basic, or primary. Hence, the concept of **primitive**

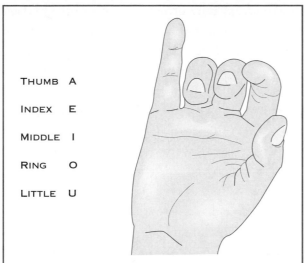

THUMB	A
INDEX	E
MIDDLE	I
RING	O
LITTLE	U

FIGURE 5–4 TRAINING THE WILD BOY. Without language, the Wild Boy needed a way to indicate which sound he had heard. Itard trained him to raise a specific finger for each vowel.

organization refers to aspects of perception that are determined by the fundamental, inborn characteristics of the sense organs and nervous system. It would be difficult, perhaps impossible, to prove that these perceptual tendencies are inborn, but animals, children, and preliterate people, which would include the Wild Boy, behave as if the stimulating properties were the same for them as for normal adults.

Even in these primitive stages, however, perception is not simply the act of recording a stimulus. It is a dynamic event. The brain obtains information through the sense organs, delves into its own environment—its store of memories and motivations—and then modifies the incoming message to suit its particular purposes (Freeman, 1991).

PERCEIVING FIGURES. In our simplest perceptions a figure, or pattern, is perceived as having a certain contour, and it stands out against a background, or ground. There is a certain theme and its surroundings, which comprise a **figure–ground relationship.** The sound of a trombone is heard as a figure against a background of conversations; a bird is seen as a figure against the clouds. Figure–ground discrimination is so basic that it is usually considered the starting point in organized perceptual experience.

Figure–ground relationships are determined partly by the intensity of the stimulus. A sudden, loud clap of thunder or flash of lightning inevitably becomes the figure for a moment, not the background. Figure–ground relationships are also influenced by the process of attending. If you are attending to conversations, then the voices become the figure and the trombone music is the background. If you focus on the clouds, you may not even notice the bird at all.

Eagerly shelling kidney beans with Madame Guerin, the Wild Boy tossed each bean into a pot, and occasionally one fell to the floor. He watched it, retrieved it, and then placed it with the others to be cooked. For him, the fallen bean was a figure, standing out against a background of the floor.

As you read this page, you focus on the black print, not the white paper. The separation of figure from ground is accomplished readily, apparently as an unlearned response.

More important for understanding perceptual processes are the *impossible figures* in which figure–ground relations are altered (Figure 5–5). These outcomes can be induced by clever drawings in which part of the visual image appears to be *both*

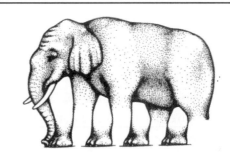

FIGURE 5–5 IMPOSSIBLE FIGURE. The legs of the elephant at times appear to be the figure, at times the ground. The outcome depends on the viewer's point of fixation—at the shoulders or feet of the elephant.

the figure and the ground. They can also be observed in *reversible figures,* in which part of the visual image is viewed as *either* the figure or the ground. After viewing such an image for a few moments, it shifts automatically from one interpretation to the other (Figure 5–6).

According to one explanation, these unintentional shifts are the result of stimulus satiation in the central nervous system. With prolonged observation the neural mechanisms become progressively more fatigued, and the shifts to new stimulation take place more frequently. Human beings confined to an unchanging environment seek sensory variation, which is perhaps imposed on them in these automatic shifts. A different explanation focuses on the activity of the sense organs, which do not passively receive stimulation. The regular reversals, according to this viewpoint, are the efforts of our visual apparatus to make sense of the data. We are asking ourselves: "Is it this? Or this?" We actively seek to understand our environment.

To test the second hypothesis, the ambiguity of the reversible figure was reduced. With no other change, the reversals presumably would be less frequent, for the pattern would be more readily interpreted. This result was obtained when subjects touched a potentially reversible three-dimensional cube, thereby gaining assurance about which corner was closest and which was most distant. The reversals immediately decreased, suggesting that the influential factor was not fatigue but rather a proper understanding of the environment (Shopland & Gregory, 1964).

These demonstrations and this research with impossible and reversible figures show a fundamental characteristic of our perceptual systems: They attempt to construct *meaningful* images out of whatever information becomes available to them.

GROUPING PRINCIPLES. Stimulation usually has several parts, and therefore the next question concerns their organization. Here the relevant principles are known as **perceptual grouping,** in which the parts are perceived according to various patterns, depending on their specific properties. These principles are also called *Gestalt* principles, after the German word for "shape" or "configuration." Emerging from Gestalt psychology, they emphasize the perception of whole patterns or whole situations, regarded as greater than or different from the sum of their parts. A Wagnerian opera is much more than the tones of the separate instruments, available to any composer. The beauty and meaning come from their interactions.

In Gestalt terms, these interactions are called *emergent properties* because they are not inherent in the parts of the figure. Rather, they arise through the relationships among the parts.

According to the **principle of similarity,** stimuli that are alike tend to be grouped together. When Itard trained the Wild Boy's sense of touch, he used this principle. He put a mixture of chestnuts, acorns, and coins into an opaque vase and made the boy bring forth all items of a similar shape, which he did readily, even when Itard added metal letters (Figure 5–7).

The **principle of proximity** refers to the tendency to perceive stimuli near one another as

FIGURE 5–6 REVERSIBLE FIGURE.
Sometimes you see a white vase against a dark background; sometimes you see two dark faces against a white background.

GROUPING PRINCIPLES	ILLUSTRATIONS	NEW PRINCIPLE

Similarity. The dark and light squares are grouped together on the basis of shading.

Similarity

Common Region

Proximity. The triangles comprise four groups. They are not seen as one scattered group.

Proximity

Closure. The drawings are generally perceived as five incomplete rectangles, although no figure is a rectangle.

Closure

Good Continuity. The crossing pattern appears as two gently curving and bisected lines, not as a pair of half-oval, pointed figures just touching one another.

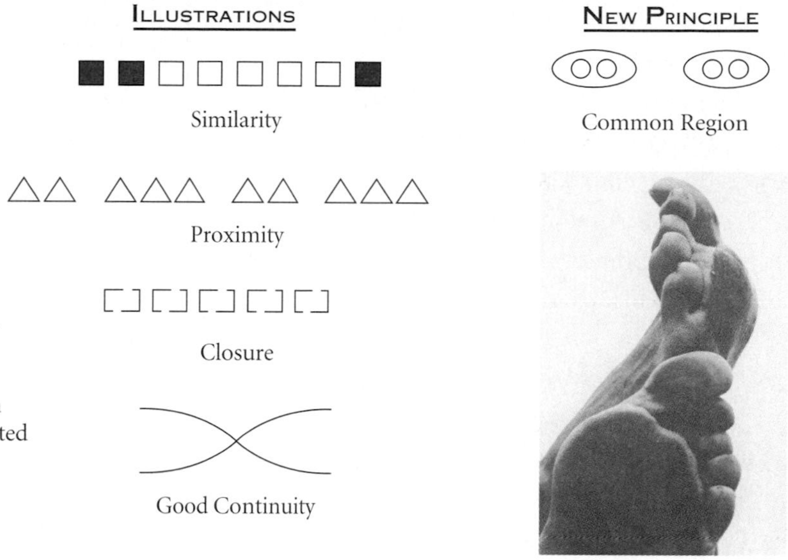

Good Continuity

FIGURE 5–7 PRINCIPLES OF GROUPING. Four original principles, illustrated in the drawings, are present but less evident in the photo of the feet. One newly proposed principle, common region, is illustrated by the toes on each foot (From Freeman, 1990).

belonging together. Ask a friend to listen while you tap twice in rapid succession, wait a while, and tap twice again. When asked how many taps he or she has heard, your listener probably will report two pairs of taps, rather than four altogether.

In teaching the alphabet, Itard used both of these principles, one pitted against the other. He drew on the blackboard two equal circles, one in front of himself and one facing the boy. At six or eight points on the circumference of each circle he wrote a different letter, and then within the circles he wrote the same letters but placed them differently in the two circles. Next, Itard drew lines connecting each letter on the circumference of his circle with its counterpart in the interior of that same circle, obviously following the principle of similarity. Then he requested the Wild Boy to do likewise for the other circle. At first this task was too challenging for the boy,

who wanted to connect the letters on the basis of proximity. Later he used the principle of similarity, no longer influenced by the arrangement of the letters.

The third principle occurs when we cannot perceive the whole figure. Following the **principle of closure,** we make assumptions about the undetected parts, ignoring their absence. A person partly hidden behind a tree is still perceived as a human being, provided that enough of the person is visible. When a band strikes up in the distance, the music is heard only intermittently, but the song is often recognized.

In the last principle, called the **principle of good continuity** or *good form,* any stimulus tends to be perceived as continuing in its established direction. Stimuli that form a continuous pattern are perceived as a whole; they make an obvious or "good" figure (Saariluoma, 1992). If several balloons are clustered together, we decide which contours belong to which balloons on the basis of the natural continuity of the lines.

There are other principles of grouping as well. These principles are used intentionally to render objects less visible, a result known as camouflage. Soldiers in battle, a thief at a cocktail party, and unprepared students who fear being called on in class all try to blend in with their surroundings.

~

FORM PERCEPTION

Perception is not merely active but, more accurately, interactive. It is influenced on one side by sensory input and on the other side by memories and thoughts about the incoming stimulation. Many cognitive psychologists therefore emphasize **information processing,** meaning the fundamental operations used by the human mind in understanding our world. These studies attempt to describe the interactive mental operations by which incoming information influences human behavior and experience (Massaro & Cowan, 1993). In particular, they stress today the concept of **parallel distributed processing,** which states that the brain can manipulate different kinds of information at the same moment. It can engage in simultaneous processing even when the information is distributed in different brain regions.

What takes place in our brains as we seek this information, trying to make sense of a given figure, its ground, or some combination of these events? How do we go about deciding that something has this or that form? In this process, called **form perception,** the task is to determine *what* is being observed.

Invariably, the object has some familiar qualities. Therefore, we typically speak instead of *pattern recognition,* in which the task is to compare incoming information with stored information, determining the similarities and differences. Decisions about incoming information arise from two perspectives, the bottom and top.

BOTTOM-UP APPROACH. Consider the Wild Boy's task in matching the letters in Itard's circles. Or consider your own task in reading this book. In both cases, the problem is letter recognition. In addressing this problem, the **bottom-up approach** begins at the most fundamental level of perception, close to the receptors, attempting to analyze the basic features of the incoming message. This approach to information processing is sometimes referred to as the *direct perspective,* for it *begins with* what is "out there."

The bottom-up approach is illustrated in the role of feature detectors, discussed in the previous chapter. A feature detector is a cell in the organism's visual system that is highly responsive to a specific stimulus. These detectors react to certain visual forms in the environment—a straight edge, brightness, a dark point, and so forth. In reading or identifying letters, the bottom-up approach involves the same sort of analysis, postulating the role of *horizontal detectors* and *curve detectors.* If Itard wrote the letter T on the edge of the circle and the Wild Boy searched for its mate within, the horizontal detector would be activated by the letters E, L, and A, all of which include horizontal lines, but not X and Y, which contain only diagonal and vertical lines.

Then, according to the theory, these horizontal, diagonal, and vertical detectors combine with each other in stimulating what might be called *letter detectors.* Recognition of the letter L would be aroused by a configuration of horizontal and vertical detectors and inhibited by diagonal detectors. The letter A would be aroused by a pattern of horizontal and diagonal detectors and inhibited by vertical and curved detectors. The French word LA would be recognized through stimulation of these two sets of letter detectors, combined in this sequence, and so forth. As evident from this description, approaching the problem this way means that the ultimate conception of the solution becomes extremely complex, based on countless combinations of single, highly specific responses to the original stimulation.

TOP-DOWN APPROACH. From the other direction, the **top-down approach** emphasizes the brain activity in the higher-level thought processes, including expectancy, motivation, and set. This approach is referred to as an *indirect perspective*, for it embodies a constructivist view of the world, stressing that we *impose our perception* on the world out there. In a very general sense, bottom-up processing begins closer to characteristics of the stimulus; top-down processing begins closer to the state of the perceiver.

The top-down perspective is readily illustrated by comparing the pattern recognition of the Wild Boy and Itard. The boy, laboriously studying one letter and then the next, did not use the top-down approach effectively. Seeing the combination LAI, for example, he had no idea about what letter might come next. With no overall sense of these patterns of black and white, he did not anticipate the word for his favorite food.

Itard, in contrast, used rules derived from his experience with the French language. A set of expectancies guided his processing of information. If he saw LAI, he would read LAIT, making an assumption about the fourth letter, for in French LAIT means "milk." A great deal of efficiency presumably is added in the top-down approach.

COMBINED APPROACHES. Both approaches have been used in electronic solutions to everyday problems, such as sorting mail. A bottom-up analysis begins with specific details, such as straight lines and curved lines, parts of the digits in the zip code. A top-down analysis begins with computer recognition of the global features of the item in the mail: envelope, stamp, and address. The process of using television images with bottom-up and/or top-down analysis is called *visual pattern recognition* or *computer vision*. An interdisciplinary field with contributions from neuropsychology and computer science, it has enormous potential for solving practical problems and providing further understanding of visual processes (Banks & Krajicek, 1991).

It seems most likely that human pattern recognition involves both approaches, solving the problem up from the bottom, near the receptors, and down from the top, beginning with the brain. In fact, it can be argued that our high speed of pattern recognition *requires* this parallel distributed processing. With so much information available to us, we need both avenues to understand our world.

Sometimes the bottom-up approach is called *data-driven*, for it begins with the stimulus. Similarly, the top-down approach is said to be *knowledge-driven*, for it commences in the brain. Sometimes we cannot use either direction. The context is ambiguous, inhibiting top-down analysis, and the printed letters are unclear, preventing bottom-up analysis: consider PAPIS. If the third letter were complete, facilitating a bottom-up approach, you could have read the word. If you knew we were referring to the city where Itard trained the Wild Boy, enhancing a top-down approach, you also could have read it.

❧

PERCEPTUAL CONSTANCY

The Wild Boy recognized Itard when the physician was far out in the fields, when he was below a window, and at dusk when he sat in his study enjoying a drink from his favorite decanter. Yet on the boy's retinas the image of Itard was different at these different moments. When he was distant, the image was small. When he was directly below, the

Wild Boy saw little more than a hat. In the dusk, the image was faint. Even when stimuli represent the same object, they can change a great deal as the observer moves about and as conditions of the environment change.

In the midst of all this change and potential ambiguity, it is remarkable that we achieve a stable perception of the world. This capacity for recognizing objects under conditions of different stimulation is known as **perceptual constancy,** of which there are several types. Imagine the domestic crises that might arise if you did not recognize your spouse or significant other when viewing that person in different positions.

TYPES OF PERCEPTUAL CONSTANCY. The hallway door in the home of Madame Guerin appeared rectangular, regardless of the position from which it was viewed. This condition is an example of **shape constancy,** meaning that something is perceived as having the same shape regardless of the perceiver's vantage point. Similarly, the opening in Itard's decanter appeared circular, even though the image was oval when viewed at an angle. This phenomenon occurs whenever an object appears to maintain its form or shape despite

marked changes in the retinal image (Figure 5–8).

When you hold a familiar object close to your eyes and then gradually move it away, the retinal image becomes smaller. But the perceived size of the object does not change greatly under different viewing conditions, demonstrating **size constancy.** Similarly, people far away have a smaller image than those closer to you, but they look about the same size.

A white rabbit in the setting sun reflects orange rays, but it is perceived as white. When the normal hue is perceived, despite changes in lighting, **color constancy** has occurred. Actually, some compromise takes place in all cases. The rabbit appears a little less white than usual, just as people far away, especially if they are unfamiliar, look a bit smaller than their actual stature. All of the constancies involve some degree of compromise between perceiving something as constant and perceiving it as somehow altered due to its place in the visual scene.

Turn a light from high to low while looking at some familiar object. The brightness of the object does not change appreciably with the change in illumination, a phenomenon known as **brightness con-**

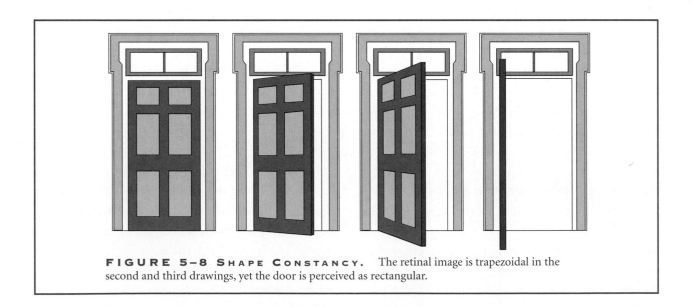

FIGURE 5–8 SHAPE CONSTANCY. The retinal image is trapezoidal in the second and third drawings, yet the door is perceived as rectangular.

stancy. A black belt can be illuminated until the amount of light entering the eye is greater than that received from a white shirt, and yet the belt will still appear black and the shirt white.

All constancy phenomena depend on environmental cues. When these cues are removed, a person far away, for example, appears smaller than is really the case. In the maintenance of constancies, prior experience and knowledge of the context are most important (Figure 5-9).

DISTAL AND PROXIMAL STIMULI. In discussions of perceptual constancy, the term **distal stimulus** refers to the properties of the stimulus out there in the world. It is physical energy at its source, such as the light waves emanating from the figure of Itard at dusk. The term **proximal stimulus** refers to the stimulation at the receptor, the light waves impinging on the Wild Boy's retinas. The difference between these stimuli is created not only by molecules of air as the light waves are scattered but also by the lens of the viewer's eyes, which

refocuses the light, and by the humors and other eye mechanisms as the light passes to the retinas. The paradox, and also the essence of the constancy phenomena, is that the perceived stimulus, influenced by the viewer's expectancy as he or she looks at the world, corresponds not so much to the proximal stimulus, on which it is based, as to the distal stimulus out there. In visual judgments of size, for example, the brain somehow performs a transformation on the proximal stimulus at the retina, thereby recovering the original distal size. This transformation, as expressed in mathematical theory, depends on the angle of the stimulus, its distance, and its orientation (Baird & Wagner, 1991).

The relative constancy of perceived objects is essential in achieving a stable perception of the world. Think of the confusion that would exist if we responded to every aspect of our world in terms of mental images alone. Even the simplest routines of daily life would be almost impossible to accomplish.

FIGURE 5-9 SIZE CONSTANCY. The retinal image of the woman in the white skirt is twice the size of that cast by the woman in the background holding onto the railing. Yet owing to distance cues, the two women are perceived as essentially the same size.

• INTERPRETING PERCEPTUAL INFORMATION •

As the months passed, the Wild Boy's progress was unmistakable. He was not the same lad who had paid little attention to household objects or human speech. At mealtime, he sat at the table with Madame Guerin and ate quite a range of foods. He managed common utensils and certainly knew the meaning of his wooden bowl. Still without speech of any sort, he asked for milk by bringing it to her.

Whenever Madame Guerin's food preparation reached a certain stage, he went to the cupboard, pulled out the tablecloth, and began setting places for the meal. When curious visitors overstayed their leave, he offered them, without mistake, their hats, gloves, and canes and pushed them gently toward the doorway. Itard submitted a report on these early developments, the first of two classic papers, entitling it *De l'Education d'un Homme Sauvage* (1801).

We too have made progress. Perception begins, as we have seen, with the process of attending. Next, there is the problem of organizing these stimuli. Distinctions must be made among the various figures and grounds as we attempt to discover what is being perceived. We now turn more fully to the interpretation of this information, considering such issues as where the object is, whether it is moving, the accuracy of the perception, and so forth.

DEPTH PERCEPTION

One day the indefatigable Madame Guerin took the Wild Boy onto a high platform for the first time, and there was no doubt about his interpretation of that situation. Moving to the edge of the ledge, he was seized by a great fear. Trembling throughout his body, his face wet with sweat, he dragged Madame Guerin away and became calmer only when they reached the bottom of the stairs. The Wild Boy certainly had adequate **depth perception,** which is awareness of the distance, space, or size of objects in the environment.

The human eye has an extremely thin retina, less than half a millimeter thick. It has no significant depth. How, then, did the Wild Boy, or how do any of us, see in three dimensions?

VISUAL DEPTH CUES. The answer, at least in terms of the stimuli we use, is fairly clear. There are numerous *depth cues,* stimuli that provide information on the distance between objects or between the viewer and other objects. They include several common **monocular cues,** observable by just one eye. Chief among these are *interposition,* which occurs whenever one image partially obscures a more distant image; *shadows,* which fall away from

the sunlight, shading the objects farther away; *linear perspective,* in which objects decrease in size and seem closer together as they become more distant; *texture gradient,* in which distant details become hazy due to atmospheric conditions; and *relative size* of the image, which is larger for nearby objects than for distant ones. Each cue provides its own information, but in the natural environment human beings use complex patterns of these stimuli to perceive unambiguously (Stoppers & Waller, 1993; Figure 5–10).

Another monocular cue is derived from the perceived motion of objects. In *relative movement,*

FIGURE 5–10 DEPTH PERCEPTION.
All the psychological monocular cues to depth perception, except movement, appear in this scene of a country road in France.

whenever an object moves by rapidly, it is generally perceived as closer than an object that moves by slowly. When two birds are flying across the horizon at the same speed, the one that is more distant seems to move more slowly.

All of these cues are psychological because they depend on characteristics of the visual image. Still another monocular cue is physiological, arising from the structure and movement of the eyes. In *accommodation,* the curvature of the lens increases for objects close at hand and decreases for more distant objects. Both changes bring the object into sharper focus, providing clearer vision. These adjustments by muscles of the eye provide the brain with information about the relative distance of perceived objects.

There are, in addition, two generally recognized **binocular cues,** requiring both eyes, and both are physiological. In *convergence,* the eyes turn inward as we look at objects. They do so more for nearby objects than for distant ones; therefore, convergence is an effective distance cue only for objects within a short distance of the viewer. These movements prevent blurred vision by placing the image closest to each fovea, where vision is clearest.

Finally, since the eyes have different locations in the head, each eye also obtains a somewhat different view of the same object, as can be experienced by holding up a finger near your face and alternately closing one eye and then the other. The reason is that the right eye always sees more of one side of the nearby object; the left eye sees more of the other side. This difference, referred to as *retinal disparity,* is greater for closer than for distant objects. It too is a useful depth cue, especially for nearby objects, and it may be mediated in the visual cortex by neurons particularly suited for depth information (Ohzawa, DeAngelis, & Freeman, 1990).

The behavior of animals and young children suggests that some of these cues are innate. Animals born with their eyes open and able to move around soon after birth avoid a cliff without prior experience. Human beings cannot be tested until they are able to crawl, but babies' heart rates speed up when they are at a *visual cliff,* in which a glass surface seems to present a sudden drop into space (Figure 5–11). At the age of six months or so, they too avoid this cliff, but considerable learning has already occurred.

FIGURE 5–11 TESTING DEPTH PERCEPTION. This apparatus is called a *visual cliff* because it only looks like a cliff; the thick glass can support a child. The patterned squares at the far end are directly under the glass; at the near end, they extend downward and along the floor. Human infants typically stay on the "shallow" side, suggesting that depth perception is present early in life.

AUDITORY DEPTH CUES. We also per-ceive in three dimensions by using nonvisual cues, as illustrated by blind people. Apart from touch, they rely most heavily on auditory cues; helpful sounds come not only from the objects themselves, as in the motor of a car, but also from reflected sound waves. The echoes of the blind person's foot-steps, from a wall or another obstacle, are most important (Supa, Cotzin, & Dallenbach, 1944).

In general, there are several **monaural cues** for distance, available even to one ear alone. *Loudness,* of course, increases with decreasing distance; *complexity* is also associated with decreasing distance, as when the hum of a motor becomes more intricate on coming closer. Furthermore, nearby sounds, in addition to being louder and more complex than distant ones, seem to fill more space. They take up more *volume,* as is evident when a cannon is fired a few yards away, as opposed to several miles away. Precise laboratory experiments have indicated that monaural cues operate in restricted situations, but it is not clear that they contribute significantly under more realistic conditions (Middlebrooks & Green, 1991).

To determine the *direction* of a sound by hearing alone, rather than its *distance,* we need **binaural cues,** provided by both ears. In these instances, the same sound usually stimulates each ear somewhat differ-ently, owing to the different locations on either side of the head. Stimulation of the ear on the far side of the head, away from the sound, is disrupted because the sound must travel around the head.

In binaural cues, there is a *time difference,* which occurs when the sound reaches the nearer ear before the farther ear. There is an *intensity difference* when the sound stimulates the closer ear more strongly. Finally, there is a *phase difference,* which occurs when the sound reaches the two ears at different points in its cycle, striking the nearer ear at one stage, such as the crest of a wave, and the farther ear at another, such as the trough. Having an ear on each side of

the head is not like having a spare part, as in the case of kidneys. Both ears are essential to locating the direction of a sound only by hearing, called **auditory localization,** just as having two eyes in different positions provides the depth cue of retinal disparity. Auditory localization is relatively poor, however, as is readily evident when you try to find out at night just where the barking dog is located.

Eventually the Wild Boy developed exquisite sensitivity to the sound of the key in his door, even when it was merely touched, and he would run quickly to the place where the sound originated. This ability showed acute hearing but not auditory localization. The Wild Boy knew where to look when he heard the sound, just as you know where to look when the telephone rings or you hear an air-plane.

Our perceptions of depth also come from olfactory, cutaneous, and kinesthetic cues. Smell allows us to determine the direction and distance of odor-giving objects. Temperature sensitivity reveals drafts and gusts of warm air, also indicative of space; other skin senses tell us about the size and shape of objects that we handle without looking at them. Muscle movement plays an obvious role in the perception of depth as we move around in our environment.

❧

PERCEPTION OF MOVEMENT

We perceive movement through the same array of visual, auditory, cutaneous, and other senses, and these experiences are generally pleasant. The Wild Boy took such delight in this activity that he often asked for a ride in the wheelbarrow. He went into the house, took Madame Guerin by the arm, led her to the garden, and put the han-dles of the barrow in her hands. Then, still mute, he climbed into it himself, and his obedient care-giver performed the expected task. Thus, the Wild Boy enjoyed the changing scenery, the jostling motion, and perhaps a sense of power as well (Itard, 1807).

The basic condition for the visual experience of movement is successive stimulation of different visual receptors. As the distal stimulus moves within the visual field, it activates different rods and cones. If an animal is crossing your visual field, its image stimulates one and then the other side of your retinas while other points in the visual field remain stationary.

Sequential stimulation of the receptors also occurs whenever you turn your head and eyes to observe a motionless scene. In this case, information from the relevant muscles in the neck and eyes informs you that the movement is not external. As the brain initiates the signals for head and eye movements and then receives feedback from them, it discounts the changes in location of images on the retinas.

INDUCED MOVEMENT. The visual experience of movement becomes more complex when you are sitting on a stationary train looking out the window. You can see only the train on the next track, and suddenly your train seems to be moving, although you have experienced no jolt at the start. The images are successively stimulating different receptors in your retinas, and there is no feedback from the ciliary and other muscles suggesting that your eyes are moving. Hence, a misperception occurs. You look out the window again and do not experience successive images with respect to a telephone pole, and then you know that the other train is moving. Rarely, however, do we experience movement solely on the basis of retinal cues, without auditory, kinesthetic or other information.

When movement is attributed to a stationary stimulus, it is called **induced movement,** for the perception is induced by another stimulus, which is moving. When you are looking just at the sky on a moonlit but cloudy night, the moon sometimes seems to dart behind the clouds. But again, there is no stationary reference point. When there are tree-tops in the visual field, there is no induced movement; instead, the clouds show real movement.

A special form of induced movement is helpful in visual depth perception. When the viewer is moving and all other objects are stationary, which was the case with the Wild Boy in the wheelbarrow, close and distant objects seem to move in different directions, a condition called *motion parallax.* Distant objects, beyond the point of fixation, seem to move in the same direction as the viewer; those nearer than the point of fixation seem to move in the opposite direction.

THE SEARCH FOR CUES. The cues in our visual perception of movement are not well understood. With minor exceptions, the rate and direction of movement are detected without reliance on the physical characteristics of the object itself. Here we encounter again the concept of *parallel distributed processing.* Different types of information, even concerning the same stimulus, are transmitted to the brain by separate neural pathways and acted on simultaneously in different brain regions. This parallel processing enables us, for example, to perceive the form and movement of an object without confusing one dimension with the other.

In one study, motion-sensitive neurons in the cortex of the monkey were examined for their responsiveness to the physical traits of moving objects. Using a computer screen, these neurons were stimulated by moving patterns of various forms, such as a rectangular pattern of twinkling dots flowing across a background of identical but stationary dots. The perception of movement in such cases depends on the number of dots and their size, as well as the distance among them, and the neurons responded to this movement. However, they were basically insensitive to cues concerning form. This independence of form and movement cues may have an adaptive function. It may permit the uniform perception of motion in objects possessing a wide variety of physical characteristics (Albright, 1992).

It has been proposed that the visual system, in interpreting different pieces of information, constructs an *abstract representation* as an object moves in space or is viewed in different positions, with different lighting, and so forth. This abstract representation, which enables us to maintain perceptual constancy, is readily illustrated in a laboratory demonstration. Imagine that a blue square moves briefly on a screen and then disappears, followed by the appearance of a moving red circle. Under proper conditions, this display is not seen as two different objects appearing one after the other in slightly different locations but rather as a single moving object that changes its color and shape at a certain moment in its history. The salient feature is not the color or shape of the object but the inferred trajectory of the abstract representation. To maintain the integrity of objects in our environment as they move and change, our visual system seems to construct abstract representations of them (Kanwisher & Driver, 1992).

EXPERIENCING ILLUSIONS

Perceived movement can occur even when both the stimulus and viewer are stationary. In a *completely* darkened room, a small, fixed spot of light will appear to move by itself, a phenomenon called the **autokinetic effect.** However, the perceived motion immediately ceases when another light is displayed. One explanation lies in our tiny, involuntary eye movements, which occur whenever we look at the world. Referred to as **saccadic movements,** they take place several times per second, moving the image onto the fovea, in the central part of the retina, which gives the clearest vision. They apparently play a role in the autokinetic effect in somewhat the same way that a moving stimulus results in induced movement. Minute and automatic, they may not signal the brain that the eyes are moving. Without a reference point, we assume that the light is moving instead.

The autokinetic effect is an **illusion**, for it does not correspond to the objective situation as determined by physical measurement. Going to the movies is also an illusion, for there is no actual movement on the screen (Figure 5-12).

For many of us, romance also includes at least

FIGURE 5–12 ILLUSORY MOVEMENT. In motion pictures, the illusion of movement is created by a series of still images shown at the rate of almost 1,500 per minute.

one illusion—a full moon just over the horizon. When low in the sky, it appears up to one-third larger than the same moon overhead. This widespread but incorrect perception of lunar size is called the *moon illusion.*

Atmospheric and other physical conditions are not adequate to explain it, and the moon does not become deflated as it rises. From a physiological perspective, the position of the head, straight up or tilted backward, has been considered influential, but this interpretation is not adequate either. Among the psychological explanations, the role of context is prominently mentioned. The moon on the horizon is judged against roofs, treetops, and other objects in the landscape known to be smaller and closer. When it is overhead, there are no cues for size and distance.

POSSIBLE INNATE FACTORS. The blue square changing into a red circle portrays a phenomenon widely employed by advertisers in everyday life whenever a lighted arrow or dot in a neon sign *seems* to move from one position to another. In this illusion, called the **phi phenomenon,** there is no actual movement but instead a rapid sequence of slightly different still images suggesting movement. When the light seems to move, there are in reality two or several lights, each in a different location, and they go on and off alternately. The interval between the lights cannot be too long, or one light appears to go on and then the other. If it is too short, both lights are seen flashing at the same time. An appropriate interval depends on the space between the lights, their size, and their brightness. When this illusion was first demonstrated experimentally around 1912, the experience was considered so basic yet so impossible to analyze that it was simply designated by a Greek letter—*phi.*

One explanation suggested that the phi phenomenon was due to kinesthetic sensations in the eyes as they looked from one light to the other. These muscle movements somehow produced the illusion. But then an early demonstration was set up in such a way that eye movements could not possibly account for the outcome. Two pairs of lights were used, one above the other, and the perceived movement was left to right in one instance and right to left in the other. Since the eye movements could not occur in two opposite directions at the same time, they could not account for the illusion (Wertheimer, 1938).

The phi phenomenon apparently is dependent on some innate, fixed reaction of the visual system to these particular stimulus relationships. It may ensure that we perceive the motion in objects moving at extreme rates (Rock, 1975).

We all experience this illusion in motion pictures. A still image appears, a shutter blocks all projected light, and then a new frame with a slightly different image moves into place, and so forth. The whole sequence is repeated again and again in extremely rapid fashion, without any objective movement on the screen, which would only be seen as a blur. Instead, the motion picture is a dramatic example of the phi phenomenon.

LEARNING AND ILLUSIONS. Illusions involving distance and shape are even more common than illusions of motion. One group of investigators, believing that learning is important, formulated the *carpentered-world hypothesis.* This hypothesis states that people who live among rectangular doors, tables, walls, platforms, and benches, all constructed with carpenter's tools, develop certain expectancies from this experience, making them especially prone to rectangular illusions. One such illusion is *Sander's parallelogram,* which depicts straight lines of different lengths drawn on a rectangular surface presumably viewed from one side.

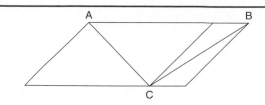

FIGURE 5-13 SANDER'S PARALLELOGRAM ILLUSION. The *AC* diagonal is 16% shorter than the *BC* diagonal. If the image were a table top, the *AC* diagonal would represent a greater distance along the surface than the *BC* diagonal. Thus, they seem about equal. The photo shows the circular huts in the Zulu culture. The cultural emphasis on the circle makes these people less susceptible to this illusion than people from more "carpentered" cultures.

On the basis of the carpentered-world hypothesis, it seems that Sander's parallelogram illusion is more likely to occur among residents of Illinois, for example, than among the Zulus of southeastern Africa (Figure 5–13). The Zulus spend much time outdoors and recognize the circle as the dominant geometric pattern, not only in their huts but also in their grounds and even in their religious ceremonies. When these two groups were compared, the Americans were found to be distinctly more susceptible to this illusion (Herskovits, Campbell, & Segall, 1969).

Altogether, 15 cultures were tested with Sander's parallelogram, and because susceptibility to this illusion was found in all of them, it was concluded that biological factors are clearly involved to some degree. Nevertheless, the large group differences indicate that experience is an augmenting factor. In fact, this narrative of the Wild Boy shows that perception depends on inherited neural structures, including the nature of the sense organs, *and* on prior experience. To the information obtained from the world around us we must add the influence of learning.

In the *Müller-Lyer illusion,* a vertical line with arrowheads pointing outward appears shorter than a vertical line of equal length with the arrowheads pointing inward. This illusion occurs for children and animals, as well as for adult human beings (Figure 5–14). What is the current explanation? It seems that the vertical line with the arrow pointing outward may represent, in terms of past experience, the near corner of a building seen from the outside. The other line,

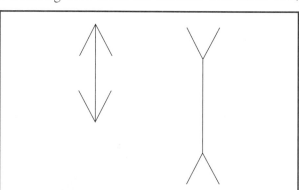

FIGURE 5-14 MÜLLER-LYER ILLUSION. The vertical lines are equal in length. Franz Carl Müller-Lyer, discoverer of this illusion, believed it arose because viewers unintentionally consider the amount of uninterrupted white space beside each vertical line, which is less when the arrow heads point outward than when they point inward.

FIGURE 5–15 INTERPRETATION OF THE MÜLLER-LYER ILLUSION. The vertical center lines are the same length, but the one on the left represents a near corner, the one on the right a far corner. Presumably the far corner is more distant and therefore this line seems longer than the other one.

with the arrow pointed inward, represents the far corner of a building seen from the inside. When two stimuli have retinal images of the same size, and yet one seems more distant, it is assumed to be a larger distal stimulus (Figure 5–15).

These studies with Sander's parallelogram and the Müller-Lyer illusion show the central role of empiricism in the field of psychology. The illusory experience is subjective, known only to the individual, but the people being studied can report their experiences directly, by using words, or indirectly by their behavior, as happens with children and animals. Thus, the phenomenon can be *tested* objectively, even with nonverbal subjects.

✍ PERCEPTION OF PEOPLE

Perhaps the most challenging and important perceptual task for all of us is the perception of people, a topic of considerable interest in the later chapter on social psychology but worthy of mention here. We are endlessly trying to make accurate judgments about other human beings, often with little success. What factors make the perception of people so much more difficult than object perception?

OBSTACLES IN PERCEIVING PEOPLE. First, when we perceive another person, we usually try to determine something more than physical characteristics. In hiring a taxi driver, we want to know whether the person is safe, reliable, and courteous. Psychological characteristics are usually more important than physical conditions.

Itard had curly hair, large brown eyes, and a bold chin, but after the first impression, these physical features are not as important as personality traits. In forming an impression, we make inferences about his motivations, interests, and so forth, combining current experience with previous information. The process is a creative one and also prone to error.

Itard had a broad forehead, but that characteristic does not provide information about his personality. Moreover, there is no significant relationship between the size of one's forehead and one's intellect, and the relationship between body type and personality is also doubtful.

Second, in object perception, the size and shape of the retinal image change as the perceiver moves about in space, but the perceived object itself is relatively stable in most cases. In contrast, the perceived individual moves about, grows older, responds emotionally, develops physically, and acquires new ideas and interests. Observers therefore must alter their perceptions to maintain accuracy. During his captivity, the Wild Boy had grown heavier, stronger, and taller. He wore clothes, including shoes—which diminished his tendency to trot or gallop—and he had some very definite likes and dislikes. Altogether, he was quite different from the dirty, frightened little boy brought from the woods years earlier.

Finally, perception of people is usually a two-way process. When Madame Guerin looked at her table, the table did not look back, but when she met Dr. Itard, he perceived her while she perceived him. This condition might have prompted Madame Guerin to become pleased, angry, or excited, thereby resulting in perceptual distortions. In judging others, we may be distracted by the demands of maintaining a certain impression or self-image (Ambady & Rosenthal, 1992).

INFERENCES ABOUT PEOPLE. In recent years, psychologists have devoted considerable effort in trying to understand how people arrive at the ideas they have about one another. This area of psychology, **attribution theory,** concerns the procedures or implicit rules they use in making inferences about behavior and personality (Schneider, 1991).

Perhaps the most important finding in attribution theory concerns the relatively little weight we tend to give to the circumstances in making judgments about someone else. We tend to perceive the other person's behavior as the result of personality dispositions rather than the situation. The passenger who complains about the bus schedule is likely to be regarded as disagreeable rather than in a hurry. The store customer who loses his money is likely to be considered careless or clumsy rather than as hassled by the small children he is supervising.

None of us needs to be reminded of the difficulty in perceiving other people accurately. Research in this area is now sufficiently ample that it is considered in further detail later. Known as *social cognition,* it constitutes a major area of modern social psychology.

On occasion, Itard filled his favorite decanter with a colorless liqueur, a strong, syrupy alcoholic beverage. This liquid looked much like water, and the Wild Boy, one day with a strong thirst, decided that it was water. He gulped down a whole goblet of this potent, odorless liquid before experiencing any burning sensation. Then, throwing away the glass, he ran howling up and down the corridors like a badly wounded animal, attempting by these actions to divert the pain.

Meanwhile, Itard stood transfixed, unable to offer a helping hand or even words of consolation. Although the boy had developed his perceptual abilities enormously, he still did not understand anything but the simplest language. Itard certainly could not have explained to the boy that he was the victim of a perceptual set.

PERCEPTUAL SET

Earlier we noted that attending is a general readiness to perceive—an overall preparedness to obtain

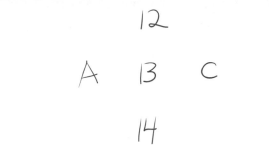

FIGURE 5—16 PERCEPTUAL SET.
Persons exposed only to the column of numbers perceive the middle figure at 13. Those exposed only to the row of letters perceive it as B.

information. A special form of attending, called **perceptual set,** is a readiness to perceive something *in particular* or in a particular way; it involves a certain expectation. In other words, attending is a predisposition to perceive something or anything. A perceptual set is a predisposition to perceive a specific event (Figure 5—16).

For any perceptual set, an endless variety of origins might be cited, but two general categories can be identified: motivational states and prior learning. The Wild Boy certainly was influenced by his thirst, a temporary motivational state, just as a hungry person readily detects the odor of food. The shape of the vessel and the colorless liquid also were contributing factors in the boy's mistake, based on prior experiences. Yet his thirst had to be intense indeed, for he overlooked the strong odor and density of the liquid, cues that might have provided a warning.

There is no doubt that people find in their environments the things they are looking for, the sorts of things they are prepared to see in the first place. As Shakespeare said:

Or in the night, imagining some fear
How easy is a bush suppos'd a bear!
A Midsummer Night's Dream, 5:1

Laboratory evidence for perceptual set is legion. Adults who had not eaten for many hours perceived food and food-related objects where there were none, especially in ambiguous situations (McClelland & Atkinson, 1948). Children from wealthy or poor families tried to indicate the exact sizes of coins. Both groups overestimated them, and the poorer children did so to a greater extent (Bruner & Goodman, 1947). When 49 adults touched the same vibrating surface, some found it pleasurable, others experienced pain. What caused the difference? The stimulation was neutral and harmless, but some subjects had been told it would produce momentarily intense pleasure, others that it would produce momentarily intense pain. When they touched the surface, most of them experienced the reaction they were led to expect (Anderson & Pennebaker, 1980).

We should note in passing that there are two other types of **set,** generally defined as a tendency to respond in a predetermined way. A *motor set* involves a special readiness to respond physically in a certain way, usually based on a muscular posture. Motor sets are commonly observed among athletes just before the game begins. In a *thought set,* there is a readiness to think about something in a certain manner. In one laboratory demonstration, students who solved problems with necessarily complex solutions began to think about all problems in this way, ignoring simpler solutions that would have been successful in other instances (Sweller & Gee, 1978).

In daily life, a perceptual set is likely to occur in adversarial relations, such as political elections, athletic contests, and family arguments. Views about what happened sometimes differ so radically that people seem to be lying, but a more charitable interpretation states that their perceptions were distorted by their hopes and fears, wishes and interests, values and prejudices. As we know, some things must be believed to be seen. Referees, judges, and marriage counselors are appointed to guard against perceptual sets but, being human, they are not completely immune either.

ROLE OF LEARNING

The Wild Boy possessed certain perceptual abilities either present at birth or the result of biological maturation. His survival in the forests and his initial response to his human environment suggested that he was capable of figure–ground relations, perceptual grouping, color discrimination, and other basic dimensions of human perception. In his animal life and later human environment, he acquired a special awareness of stimuli connected with his physical interests, and these outcomes emphasize the role of learning. The sound of a key in the lock, the smell of potatos, and the sight of visitors' hats and canes—these were the events he experienced and about which he thought. In fact, sensation and perception, sometimes referred to as the first causes of behavior, merge imperceptibly with learning, and are influenced by it, as we take our place in human society. The case of the Wild Boy emphasizes the contributions of both factors, inborn and acquired, in human perception.

It is a matter of no small significance that people learn to respond perceptually to stimuli relevant to their interests and expectations. When a society has patterned a person's interests and trained him or her to expect certain things, it has gained a significant measure of control over that person's thought processes. It has also gained a distinct measure of control over the very material on which that thought operates—the experienced data of perception (Bruner 1958).

During five years of the most ingenious instruction imaginable, the Wild Boy greatly increased his perceptual ability, extended his range of ideas, and became interested in human social life. Perceptually, he seemed almost like any normal child—but, alas, the hope for his full education was never realized. Itard and his pupil encountered an insurmountable barrier—

the French language. The boy remained completely mute throughout his life, except for an occasional "Lait" or "Oh! Dieu." These three words were uttered at almost any moment, like a parrot, with no understanding of their significance. And so, with feelings of some satisfaction and deep despair, Itard gave up his laborious efforts. He then submitted to the ministry a second and final report of his work, published years later as the book *Rapports et Mémoires sur le Sauvage de l'Aveyron* (1807).

Unable to transform his pupil into a normal person, perhaps because the boy had missed a vital early exposure to the sounds of human speech, Itard nevertheless achieved a lasting outcome through his methods of instruction. They form the basis today of many practices in special education, behavior therapy, psychological testing, and even the Montessori method with young children.

Designed by Maria Montessori, an Italian physician who openly acknowledged her debt to Itard, the *Montessori method* focuses on perceptual, motor, and intellectual training in preschool children, based on the view that all normal children have a high capacity for self-education. The teacher's role is to provide occasions for the child's self-instruction. One visual exercise promotes the correct arrangement of more than 50 blocks of colors. An auditory exercise involves ringing bells that have the same pitch as bells rung by the teacher. The cutaneous sense is trained with textures ranging from silk to sandpaper. Like the Wild Boy, the child practices with these materials and, when ready, moves to more advanced activities involving not only perceptual but also personal and social skills (Flynn, 1991).

After his extensive instruction, the Wild Boy remained for years in the home of tireless Madame Guerin, grew to manhood, and lived into his forties. All the while Itard was tormented by his lack of speech, which sometimes made the good doctor feel that his labors had been wasted. Over and over, Itard was confronted with this nagging inquiry: "Does the Savage speak? If he is not deaf, why does he not speak?"

At the same time, Itard wondered whether he had been right. Was the Wild Boy unable to speak due to the irretrievably lost opportunity? Or was Phillippe Pinel correct in the first place? Was the boy abandoned and unable to learn because he was significantly retarded? Perhaps the boy instead suffered damage to his speech mechanisms. As Itard indicated in his final report, one long scar across his pupil's neck, at the level of the voice box, appeared to be the work of a human hand.

• SUMMARY •

ATTENDING TO STIMULATION

1. Attending is a readiness to perceive, based on internal states and characteristics of the stimulus. The subtle physiological adjustments in attending include activities in the brain, muscles, and sense organs.

2. The process of attending to two or more stimuli simultaneously is called divided attention. As a rule, human beings are not highly successful in this endeavor unless one of the tasks is simple, the tasks involve different sensory modes, or one of the tasks is habitual.

ORGANIZING THE PERCEPTUAL FIELD

3. Discrimination of figure–ground relationships seems to be the starting point in organized perceptual experience. According to Gestalt principles of perceptual grouping, the parts of a figure, or several figures, are grouped on the basis of similarity, proximity, closure, and good continuity.

4. Form perception concerns detection of the shape of the object being observed. The bottom-up approach begins at the most fundamental level of perception, close to the receptors; the top-down approach emphasizes the brain activity in higher-level processes, including expectancy, motivation, and thinking.

5. Stable perception of the world is also based on perceptual constancy, which is the tendency to perceive any given object as the same, even though it stimulates us in a variety of ways. Important types of perceptual constancy include shape, size, color, and brightness constancy.

INTERPRETING PERCEPTUAL INFORMATION

6. Depth perception arises from the integration of diverse cues from several senses. Monocular cues include interposition, shadows, linear perspective, texture gradient, size of the retinal image, relative movement, and accommodation of the lens. Among the binocular cues are convergence and retinal disparity.

7. Real movement is perceived visually whenever successive areas of the retina are differentially stimulated. The visual detection of movement seems to be independent of the cues for the form and color of the moving object, a condition of parallel distributed processing.

8. An illusion is a perception that does not correspond to the external situation, as indicated by physical measurement. Extensive cross-cultural studies have shown that learning and innate factors both contribute to the illusory experience.

9. Perception of people is more complex than object perception for several reasons. The perceiver tries to determine psychological as well as physical characteristics; the perceived person moves about in space

and changes with time; and if the perceiver knows that he or she is being perceived, perception may be reciprocally influenced.

11. We learn about events that we perceive, and what we perceive is determined partly through learning. Perception and learning merge imperceptibly in the process of human development.

❧

INFLUENCES ON PERCEPTION

10. A perceptual set is a readiness to perceive something in particular, an expectation about what will be perceived. Perceptual sets arise largely on two bases, motivational states and past experience.

• WORKING WITH PSYCHOLOGY •

❧ REVIEW OF KEY CONCEPTS ❧

perception
sensation

Attending to Stimulation
attending
selective attention
embedded messages
divided attention

Organizing the Perceptual Field
primitive organization
figure–ground relationship
perceptual grouping
principle of similarity
principle of proximity
principle of closure

principle of good continuity
information processing
parallel distributed processing
form perception
bottom-up approach
top-down approach
perceptual constancy
shape constancy
size constancy
color constancy
brightness constancy
distal stimulus
proximal stimulus

Interpreting Perceptual Information
depth perception

monocular cues
binocular cues
monaural cues
binaural cues
auditory localization
induced movement
autokinetic effect
saccadic movements
illusion
phi phenomenon
attribution theory

Influences on Perception
perceptual set
set

❧ CLASS DISCUSSION/CRITICAL THINKING ❧

A NARRATIVE TWIST

After his training by Itard, the Wild Boy developed adequate perception in the civilized world. This outcome suggests that he possessed normal perceptual capacities, despite his inability to speak. Suppose the Wild Boy had then returned to the wilds. Overall, how might his new perceptual capacities have served in

that mode of living? Describe some specific circumstances and his probable reactions. Would these newer perceptual capacities have changed gradually? Explain your viewpoint. ❧

TOPICAL QUESTIONS

• *Attending to Stimulation.* Suppose

that you go to a baseball game with your cousin. Internal factors are more influential in your selective attention; external factors are more influential for your cousin. Which events do you observe? Why? Which events does your cousin observe? Why?

• *Organizing the Perceptual Field.* Consider the concept of perceptual constancy. Cite examples to show that it varies under different stimulating circumstances.

• *Interpreting Perceptual Information.*

The autokinetic effect occurs when there are no reference points. In the Müller–Lyer illusion, one line is compared with another. Which illusion seems most strongly based on learning? Why?

• *Influences on Perception.* Are attending and perceptual set most usefully considered as separate and distinct concepts or merely as different points on a continuum? Explain your reasoning.

❧ TOPICS OF RELATED INTEREST ❧

Subliminal messages are also discussed in the chapter on sensation, focusing on their use in advertising (4). The perception of people is a major topic in social psychology, generally approached under the heading of social cognition (17). A perceptual set, when it inhibits problem solving through lack of flexibility in using tools, is known as functional fixedness (9).

STUDY OF CONSCIOUSNESS

SLEEP AND DREAMS
Wake-Sleep Cycle
The Sleeping State
The Dreaming State
Theories of Dreaming

MEDITATION AND HYPNOSIS
Practice of Meditation
Use of Hypnosis

DRUG-INDUCED STATES
Using Drugs
Drug Experiences

NORMAL CONSCIOUSNESS

6
CONSCIOUSNESS

❧

PETRA ROLLED OVER, LAY FACE DOWN, AND REGAINED NORMAL CONSCIOUSNESS SLOWLY. HER FIRST THOUGHT WAS ABOUT HER DAUGHTER'S BIRTHDAY.

Almost immediately, a competing awareness intruded, and Petra smiled a bit, realizing where she was—in a new building. Actually, it was a dilapidated old boarding house, but it was new to her.

Looking around sleepily, Petra stared at the white walls, venetian blinds, and skylight. The room was large and airy, with plenty of sun, ideal for studio art. Then her gaze rested for a moment on her cherished African goddess.

A craftsperson as well as an artist, all Petra's work was highly personal. Dressed in black denim pants and a flannel shirt, with a cup of coffee in hand, she painted about herself and her ethical standards in a whimsical, abstract way. Sometimes she included recognizable elements of human figures, especially her mother. She often painted about procreation in a figurative sense, and for inspiration, she kept on her bureau the African fertility goddess, sculpted from clay.

Petra turned her gaze to the cardboard boxes containing her belongings. Her hat and coat lay on the floor near the bedroom, where she had dropped them, too tired to find a hook or even to fold them. She had simply slept on the floor in the studio. Awakened in the middle of the night by her recurrent nightmare about her daughter, she felt tired and disappointed to be awake again so early in the morning (O'Neill, 1990).

Awareness of one's own existence and surroundings at any given moment is known as **consciousness,** and it includes three dimensions: external, internal, and the self. Petra was aware of the boxes and clothes in the studio of her new apartment; she was aware of her feelings of fatigue and sleepiness; and she was aware of herself as a separate living being, distinct from all other living creatures. As Petra's awareness shows, human consciousness is highly personal. Her states of consciousness in nightmares and drug abuse finally brought her to a psychological clinic.

Human consciousness is discussed in one form or another throughout this book. Here we begin with the study of consciousness and then consider the automatic variations in everyday life, sleep, and dreams. Afterward, we turn to intentional efforts to alter consciousness: meditation, hypnosis, and drug-induced states. These **altered states of consciousness** are characterized by decreased capacity for self-control and logic and by changes in self-

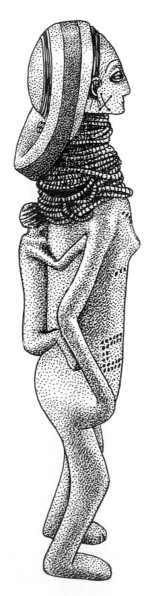

perception. A discussion of normal consciousness concludes the chapter.

• STUDY OF CONSCIOUSNESS •

Of all the topics in modern psychology, the study of consciousness is the oldest, and it has an interrupted history. It began in psychology's first laboratory, in Germany, under Wilhelm Wundt, who decided that conscious experience could indeed be measured. For Wundt the only acceptable method was **analytical introspection,** a systematic effort to observe and classify the basic elements of one's own experience. In short, it meant looking inward under standard conditions.

In one series of experiments, Wundt used a metronome to demonstrate that human consciousness is not confined to events in the outer world. Setting the instrument at a moderate pace, he asked his subject to listen to a few beats and describe the experience. The listener reported an even pace and intensity. Wundt then asked his listener to subjectively emphasize every other beat. With this voluntary emphasis on alternate beats, the subject noticed a new experience, an impression of a more agreeable whole. Wundt declared, and his subjects agreed, that the pleasure was not in itself a part of the beats.

Then Wundt asked his subject to concentrate on any two successive beats in the series. The subject reported that immediately after the first beat there was an expectation of the next one, and this expectation increased until that second beat occurred. At that moment, the strain was released. Then the same sequence of experiences recurred during the next pair of beats. These demonstrations, Wundt declared, showed that the pleasure and strain arose entirely from within the subject (Wundt, 1912).

William James, an American contemporary of Wundt, agreed that the study of consciousness was the chief goal of psychology, but he had a very different approach. More inclined to walking in the park than bending over a laboratory table, he disparaged Wundt's interest in describing the structure—or basic elements—of consciousness.

Influenced by Darwinian thinking, James argued that when consciousness evolved, the new symbolic processes played a vital part in survival. Consciousness should be studied in terms of the ways it helped human beings adapt to their environment.

Consciousness, James declared, is a "teeming multiplicity of objects and relations." Even when consciousness studies itself, it does not appear in bits and pieces but rather as a whole. James therefore spoke of the **stream of consciousness,** meaning that mental life is continuous, always changing, and personal as it flows from one experience to the next (James, 1890). It is not jointed but joined. The words *chain* and *train* do not aptly describe it. Instead, consciousness is viewed more appropriately as a stream or river. Although it is constantly changing, there is nevertheless an inevitable unity in its diversity.

Wilhelm Wundt and William James thus offered contrasting approaches to the study of consciousness. More controlled and narrow, Wundt would be interested in the specific elements of Petra's thoughts and fears during her nightmare. He and his colleagues would take her into the laboratory, train her to give introspective reports, and then record the detailed descriptions of her anxiety and confusion, focusing on each separate reaction. Broader and more speculative, James would study

Petra's nightmare as part of a continuous, ever-changing pattern of responses, studied most usefully in a more holistic fashion, perhaps by analogy or illustration. He would give more emphasis to dynamic relations among the parts of the nightmare and the role it played in her life, including her adaptation to her surroundings.

The task of science is to explain things, and different scientists have different ideas about the adequacy of various explanations. Neither approach offers a complete understanding of consciousness; all human knowledge is incomplete in one way or another. Instead, they provide different types of explanations at different levels of specificity. Many approaches have something of value; most are complementary; and all are limited in some way.

In the first decades of this century, John B. Watson took a position totally opposed to those of Wundt and James. He contended that psychology should give up all investigations of conscious experience, both its contents and its functions. Consciousness, he said, is evident only to the experiencing individual. Entirely private, it cannot be studied scientifically. In a movement called *behaviorism,* Watson led psychology away from the study of consciousness, aiming for greater objectivity in psychological research (Watson, 1930).

From this perspective, the study of Petra's nightmare would be limited to observations of a person sitting up in bed, propped on one elbow, shivering, and so forth, but she would not be asked to describe her thoughts and feelings. Under Watson's influence, and later under that of B. F. Skinner, much of psychology adopted this approach: the study of overt responses, the stimuli that aroused them, and the related physiological mechanisms. Behaviorism became the dominant perspective in American psychology until the 1960s.

By the middle of this century, several converging strands of research led to the reemergence of the study of consciousness in psychology, culmi-

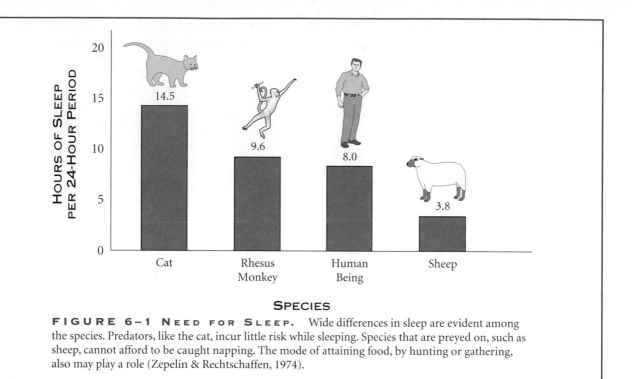

FIGURE 6–1 NEED FOR SLEEP. Wide differences in sleep are evident among the species. Predators, like the cat, incur little risk while sleeping. Species that are preyed on, such as sheep, cannot afford to be caught napping. The mode of attaining food, by hunting or gathering, also may play a role (Zepelin & Rechtschaffen, 1974).

nating in a "cognitive revolution." These investigations, aided by instruments from early advances in the electronic age, included successful measurement of short-term memory, progress in the analysis of language, developments in computer science, and discovery of a method for investigating dreams. Collectively, they gave rise to modern **cognitive psychology,** which is concerned with mental processes of all sorts, conscious and unconscious. Modern cognitive psychologists would be interested in all aspects of Petra's mental functioning, including perception, memory, and all forms of thinking, discussed elsewhere in this book, as well as the variations in consciousness considered in this chapter.

• SLEEP AND DREAMS •

Working intermittently as a waitress, on her feet six to ten hours each evening, Petra was fatigued by her schedule, even as a young woman of 24 years. She did have the daylight hours for painting, and she tried to recuperate through an irregular pattern of eating and resting.

Like most of us, Petra also devoted about one-third of her life to a distinctly diminished state of consciousness—sleep. Think of it: The average person of 60 has spent about 20 years in bed. However, human beings are not the sleepiest species. The cat spends more than half of its life in that mode of consciousness (Figure 6–1).

Prolonged deprivation of sleep can be devastating to our mental functions. It can produce perceptual distortions, depression, anxiety, and even extreme elation. In other words, going without sleep seriously disrupts normal consciousness. Talkathon contestants who stayed awake for 88 consecutive hours became irritable and withdrawn and then developed an intense concern about their mental health (Cappon & Banks, 1960). After a 146-hour tennis match, allowing less than 4 hours of sleep each night, the competitors displayed pronounced intellectual and emotional deficits, although they differed sharply in overt signs of sleepiness and endurance (Edinger, Marsh, McCall, & Erwin, 1990).

WAKE-SLEEP CYCLE

For most people, the daily wake-sleep pattern includes about 16 hours of wakefulness and eight of sleep, but there are marked differences among us. To become fully refreshed, some people require nine or ten hours of uninterrupted sleep. Older people are often rejuvenated after only five or six hours of sleep each night. In contrast, some college students seem to get along very well on just a few hours of wakefulness each day.

This tendency for regular alternation between greater and lesser activity in physiology and behavior is known as the **circadian rhythm,** especially when it refers to a 24-hour period. This term comes from the Latin *circa,* meaning "around," and *diem,* meaning "day." Such rhythms occur in insects, plants, and animals, as well as in people. In human beings, they bring out subtle differences in body temperature, heart rate, and hormonal secretion, as well as the obvious differences in energy expended (Figure 6–2).

The importance of these biological rhythms is evident when light-dark schedules are altered. Variations in periods of illumination, or in the intensity of light, influence the length, type, and duration of sleep in many species, as well as the level of energy. Under constant illumination, laboratory rats sleep an hour longer each day, but cats and fish sleep less under the same condition (Campbell & Tobler, 1984). When human beings are in an isolated environment, without clocks or sunlight, their natural rhythm often drifts toward a 25-hour cycle (Webb & Agnew, 1974).

Flying into space or into another time zone partway around the world produces a change in this rhythm in human beings, resulting in a mental syndrome called *jet lag,* involving slower reaction time, poorer problem-solving capacity, and less concentra-

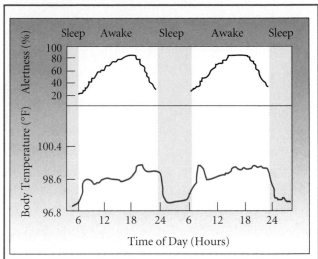

FIGURE 6–2 CIRCADIAN RHYTHM. Alertness and temperature increase and decrease together (Coleman, 1986).

tion. The term is not precise, however. These same reactions appear among people who change their work schedule every few weeks—from daytime hours to the evening shift and then to early morning hours. There is still debate on the rate at which these schedules should be rotated forward in order for workers to become most effective (Wedderburn, 1992; Wilkinson, 1992).

In passing, it should be noted that there is some validity in "Early to bed, early to rise makes one healthy . . ." Body temperature, hormones, and energy rise in the morning. When a person sleeps late into the day, metabolic processes may be depressed, resulting in a groggy, "blah" feeling.

THE SLEEPING STATE

Almost no matter when they go to bed, some people fall asleep immediately. Other need a half hour or more. Petra often needed more, partly because she was worried about her daughter. Her recurrent nightmare involving her baby always woke her, leaving her extremely frightened. Afterward, unable to sleep again right away, she watched late night television or stayed awake making small pieces of jewelry that she enjoyed giving away. She often hung these little gifts on people's doors or draped them over her African fertility goddess.

Regardless of how fast people fall asleep, the pattern for everyone is much the same. Gross body movements and postural changes occur first. These are followed by twitching in the limbs, heavier breathing, and slow rolling of the eyes. At this point, the gentle journey toward sleep has taken the individual into the **hypnagogic state,** which is the interval of drowsiness between waking and sleeping. Special interest has been attached to this state because it includes vivid images, particularly before falling asleep. These images are not dreams; they lack the narrative, unfolding quality of dreams, and they are generally not bizarre.

During the hypnagogic state, a person may experience a pronounced muscle spasm, much more than a twitch. This shocklike reaction, known as the *hypnagogic jerk* or, more formally, **nocturnal myoclonia,** is sometimes so violent that it awakens the individual for a brief, painful instant. Purely physiological, it is apparently unrelated to the mattress, dinner, bedclothes, or even the sleeping partner. It is perhaps stimulated by dream images and motor commands from the lower brain centers, reflecting the ways in which the brain manages the process of entering and leaving the various stages of sleep (Chase & Morales, 1990).

SLEEPING BRAIN. Contrary to popular thought, the sleeping part of the wake-sleep cycle is not necessarily passive. Muscle tension, blood pressure, and heartbeat all decrease during sleep, but we cannot dismiss sleep as a passive, unchanging state.

Several brain mechanisms are actively involved in producing sleep. The thalamus, lower brain centers, and cortex are all part of our sleep system. In particular, a subcortical arousal mechanism called the **reticular activating system** (RAS) plays a prominent role, influencing sleep by ending the transmission of impulses to many cortical synapses. Electrical stimulation of the reticular activating system in animals awakens them immediately, and when this mechanism is inoperative through surgery, the animal remains in a sleepy or drowsy state.

The arousal state of the brain is also influenced by chemical factors called *neurotransmitters,* discussed previously. These substances include acetylcholine, norepinephrine, and serotonin, all of which are secreted in waking life by lower brain centers, and they have ramifications throughout the brain. At sleep onset, the output of acetylcholine and norepinephrine declines. Although it is only vaguely understood, the neurotransmitter **serotonin** may play a special role in drowsiness and sleep, for it is involved in brain circuits that can be inhibitory or excitatory, thus influencing arousal.

Another reason that sleep cannot be considered merely a passive state in the wake-sleep cycle is found in its different stages. One of these, in which dreaming occurs, involves considerable physiological activity.

STAGES OF SLEEP. In investigating these stages, psychologists have employed several electronic devices, including the electroencephalograph, used to detect the spontaneous electrical activity of the brain. These patterns, or brain waves, are detected by electrodes placed on the scalp and recorded by a writing stylus on a moving paper tape. This record of the brain waves is known as an **electroencephalogram** (EEG), in which regular and irregular patterns may be observed (Figure 6–3).

Before entering sleep, when the person is just resting or relaxed, a regular EEG rhythm appears, called *alpha waves.* These waves occur at a rate of 8–12 cycles per second. The individual is awake but relaxed, and then, in a series of gradual transitions, moves into the various stages of sleep, numbered at four or five. In stage I, drowsiness, the EEG becomes a somewhat disorganized pattern of fast

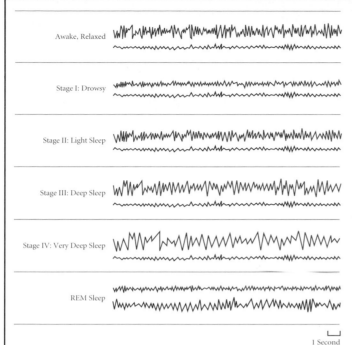

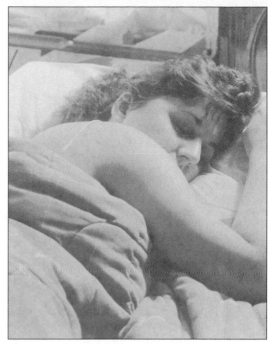

Awake, Relaxed

Stage I: Drowsy

Stage II: Light Sleep

Stage III: Deep Sleep

Stage IV: Very Deep Sleep

REM Sleep

1 Second

FIGURE 6–3 STAGES OF SLEEP. Certain brain waves are typical of each stage, though they may appear throughout the night. Overall, the waves become slower and deeper from stages I through IV. Stage I sleep and REM sleep are much alike in EEG patterns, but REM sleep is also characterized by rapid eye movements, dreams, and difficulty in waking the sleeper. The EEG tracings are shown in red; the REMs appear in black.

waves of low voltage; the regular alpha rhythm largely disappears. The onset of stage II, light sleep, is marked by occasional spindles, which are brief, rhythmic patterns of approximately 15 cycles per second. In stage III, these spindles become mixed with very slow waves of high voltage occurring at the rate of three cycles per second. These slow, deep waves, called *delta waves,* are indicative of deep sleep. In stage IV, also called deep sleep, the delta waves become predominant, appearing in at least 50% and sometimes in 100% of the EEG pattern (Hobson, 1988).

All of these stages reappear predictably, but often in reverse order, from IV back to III and then to II and so forth. One full cycle lasts for approximately 90 minutes, sometimes longer. Then, when stage I should recur, a new phenomenon appears. At this time, the slow, rolling movements of the eyes quicken considerably. They

become **rapid eye movements** (REMs) as the eyes dart in one direction and then in another, in coordinated fashion, under the closed lids. Breathing becomes heavy and irregular, blood pressure increases, and muscles begin twitching. Most surprising, the EEG pattern in this state shows a level of brain activity much like that of someone poised and alert. High-frequency, low-amplitude waves dominate the pattern. This wide-awake profile appears to be incompatible with a sleeping brain, and therefore this REM state is sometimes called *paradoxical sleep.* This expression is also appropriate because a person in the REM state is difficult to awaken.

These characteristics of sleep, which occur in the second and subsequent cycles, are sometimes called stage V, but many investigators simply refer to this sleep as *REM sleep* and to all other stages as *non-REM (NREM) sleep.* Altogether, REM sleep

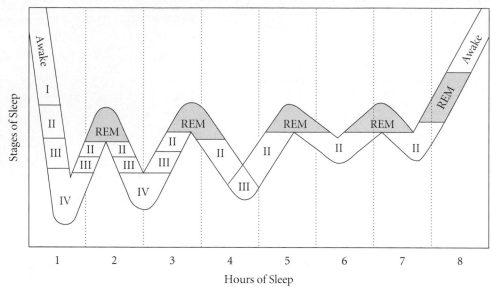

FIGURE 6–4 CYCLE OF SLEEP AND DREAMS. After the first full cycle, stages I–IV, the sleeper generally reverses the sequence, except there is no significant return to stage I. The sleeper enters REM sleep instead, presumably dreaming. As the graph indicates, the deepest sleep, stages III and IV, occur early in the night; the longest periods of dreaming occur toward morning.

appears four or five times during the night, constituting about 25% of the total time spent in sleep. During the first cycle it lasts for about 10 minutes, but this stage grows longer during the night. Toward the end of sleep, it becomes more prominent, sometimes lasting for a half hour or even an hour (Figure 6–4).

DISCOVERY OF REM SLEEP. In the early 1950s, while Eugene Aserinsky was collecting basic facts about sleeping infants, he noted twitches of the arms and legs as each child went to sleep. He also noted the slow, rolling movements of their eyes under the lids, which investigators knew to be prominent just prior to sleep. During one cribside visit, after the slow, uncoordinated, drifting eye movements, his attention suddenly was caught by something else—the rapid, jerky, but coordinated movements in both eyes, similar to those of someone watching a spirited game of table tennis in waking life.

Aserinsky's first reaction was one of disbelief

and surprise that no one had reported these rapid eye movements previously. Immediately, he and a colleague, Nathaniel Kleitman, went to their laboratory and confirmed these movements, painting sleepers' eyelids black and using a flashlight to observe them more carefully. Later, they performed a controlled investigation, using ten subjects who were awakened sometimes during REMs and sometimes when there were no REMs. In each case, the subject was asked to report what he or she had just been experiencing while asleep.

Among 27 awakenings during these movements, 20 revealed detailed memories of dreams, including visual imagery; the other seven produced only the feeling of having dreamed or no dreams at all. Among the 23 awakenings in the absence of these movements, 19 indicated no dreams and four included only a few details. Altogether, almost 80% of the REM subjects reported dreams compared to only 20% of the non-REM subjects. This procedure of awakening people during REM sleep provided the first means for determining accurately and efficiently the incidence and duration of dreams, and it inaugurated widespread research (Aserinsky & Kleitman, 1953).

NATURE OF REM SLEEP. Several characteristics of the REM state distinguish it from the other stages of sleep. In addition to REMs and the alert, high-frequency EEG pattern, breathing becomes irregular and heavy. There is also a loss of normal muscle tension, currently used in some research laboratories as a sign of the onset of the REM period. This limpness of the muscles, even in the face, particularly under the chin, stands in sharp contrast to their condition in the other sleep stages. It appears to serve a protective function, preventing sleepers from acting out their dreams.

There is much evidence for similar physiological activity in animals. Using the REM state as an indicator, psychologists have discovered that pigeons dream, sea turtles do not, and elephants stand up to sleep but lie down to dream. However, dreams and REMs are not perfectly correlated. We can only assume that animals in the REM state are dreaming (Hartmann, Bernstein, & Wilson, 1967; Hobson, 1988).

Among human beings, another physiological reaction suggests that we constantly dream about sex. Changes in blood flow cause erections in men and engorgement of vaginal regions in women, but these reactions occur with any dream content— even when the dreamer is simply conjugating Latin verbs or weeding the garden. The only notable exception to these physiological changes occurs in cases of extreme fatigue. Brain chemistry also may change in REM sleep. The release of acetylcholine and norepinephrine appears to decline to levels even lower than those in non-REM sleep.

The physiological activities during dreaming are so marked that investigators have examined the results of preventing them. This outcome is achieved simply by waking subjects when the REM pattern occurs and then permitting them to fall asleep again.

Cats, rabbits, and other animals deprived of REM sleep, as well as human subjects, immediately spend considerable time in REM sleep when allowed to do so. They make up for the deficit by increasing the REM state from 60% to 160% above normal. This outcome has led researchers to speak of the **REM rebound effect,** meaning that people deprived of REM sleep or dreams must compensate later by dreaming more than usual. There seems to be a *need* for dreaming. People awakened during the REM state show signs of personality disorder and anxiety; those awakened for comparable intervals at other times show fewer adverse effects (Dement, 1960, 1992; Tolaas, 1980).

Different sleep stages may serve different purposes. Deep, slow-wave, non-REM sleep apparently has a restorative function. It allows the body to replace energy diminished during the previous day. REM sleep, in contrast, appears to be more related to circadian rhythms, regulating or reflecting the wake-sleep cycle. Deprivation of REM sleep may interfere with the conservation of energy rather than its restoration. Our stages of sleep each night may be triggered by both sources, the homeostatic mechanisms of restoration and the circadian mechanisms of rhythm and conservation (Borbely, Achermann, Trachsel, & Tobler, 1989).

SLEEP DISORDERS. We have all gone to bed and been unable to sleep. Usually the problem is temporary. The chief causes include stressful daytime activities, mental effort just before retiring, too much coffee or another stimulant, or simply insufficient fatigue. The chief feature in **insomnia** is *chronic* inability to go to sleep or to remain asleep. Young people are more likely to find that they cannot fall asleep within a reasonable period, a condition known as *initial insomnia.* Older people have the other complaint. They awaken too early or too frequently, a sleep disturbance known as *terminal insomnia.* People of all ages complain at times that they have not had restful sleep, and sleeplessness is often overestimated by the alleged insomniac. The condition is considered insomnia only if it continues for at least a month (American Psychiatric Association, 1994).

Petra experienced both types of insomnia. Sometimes she could not fall asleep because she was worried about her daughter; often she could not sleep because she had consumed too much coffee. On other occasions, she found herself wide awake after sleeping for just a few hours, frightened by her nightmare. Unknown to her, consumption of alcohol is also a factor in terminal insomnia. Alcohol blocks certain neurotransmitters responsible for brain activity, thus inducing relaxation and promoting sleep (Sudzak, Glowa, Crawley, Swartz, et al., 1986). At the same time, it disrupts the work of other neurotransmitters, thereby awakening the person earlier than normal.

In particular, alcohol suppresses REM sleep, which is why alcoholics in a detoxification center experience such frequent and terrifying dreams. They are undergoing the REM rebound effect, dreaming more to make up for the earlier dream loss. Drugs, including alcohol, are responsible for numerous sleep disturbances (Table 6–1).

The recommended treatments for insomnia are well known. Avoid concerted mental effort before going to bed. Do not use drugs under the impression that they induce relaxation, for they too interfere with the sleep pattern. Many people adapt to sleeping pills, and in the long run these substances

---

√	Chronic stress: family, health, work, finances
√	Consumption of alcohol, coffee, tea
	Endocrine disorders
√	Concern about insomnia
	New work or school setting
	Temporary anxiety over minor matters
	Consumption of psychoactive drugs
	Jet lag or shift work

TABLE 6–1 DISRUPTION OF SLEEP.
The chief factors, listed in order of their importance for the general public, vary considerably from individual to individual. Those most disruptive for Petra are indicated by the checkmarks (Larson, 1990).

---

may even disrupt sleep (Figure 6–5). Instead, exercise as much as possible during the day; start relaxing a couple of hours before bedtime; and do not go to bed with a completely empty stomach. Consume a warm nonalcoholic drink.

The opposite of insomnia, *hypersomnia,* is the inability to stay awake. The wake-sleep cycle is again disrupted, but the disturbance is in the opposite direction. In a severe case, called **narcolepsy,** the individual experiences sudden, uncontrollable episodes of falling asleep. These recurrent states are usually of short duration, and mild cases may even pass almost unnoticed, as though the individual were simply in a daze or inattentive for a moment. More serious cases can jeopardize the safety of the individual and others. The underlying causes remain unknown, although there is evidence for an inherited predisposition (Dement, 1992).

Some people go to sleep easily and normally but awake tired the next morning, not realizing that they have awakened briefly several times during the night. This condition, **sleep apnea,** arises because breathing is interrupted during sleep, and waking for a moment restores breathing. Most common among overweight men, this disorder occurs because the muscles controlling the air passages become relaxed during sleep. Then the passages may become temporarily blocked by the surrounding tissues. Surgery, certain medications, and weight loss are recommended treatments.

Sometimes people get out of bed after going to sleep and move around without awakening. This disturbance, **sleepwalking,** includes all sorts of activities—eating, dressing, and going to the bathroom, as well as walking around and climbing stairs. It typically does *not* occur during dreams, but rather in stages III and IV, and it continues for no longer than a half hour. At its outset, the person may sit up in bed and engage in some simple, repetitious activity, such as picking at the bedclothes. Then, with a blank look, the person leaves the bed and walks around, typically avoiding obstacles while still asleep.

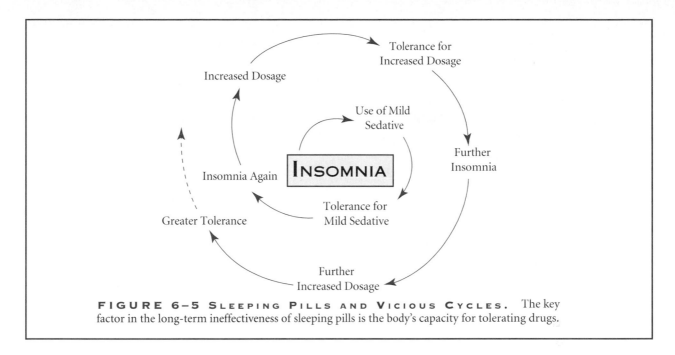

FIGURE 6–5 SLEEPING PILLS AND VICIOUS CYCLES. The key factor in the long-term ineffectiveness of sleeping pills is the body's capacity for tolerating drugs.

THE DREAMING STATE

By waking people during REMs, we now know that nearly everyone has **dreams,** which are images, thoughts, and feelings experienced during sleep. They occur about four or five times during the night and, contrary to belief, do not take place in a momentary flash. They may last a half hour or more, corresponding somewhat to the time required for the activities during waking life, and they grow longer toward morning, which is why, when awakened at that time, you are likely to find that you have just been dreaming. Babies are in REM sleep almost one-third of their lives, although we cannot be certain that they are dreaming. Adults spend one-twelfth of their lives dreaming. In other words, we dream, on the average, two hours each night.

Dreams during the REM state are especially vivid, although the rapid eye movements do not necessarily correspond to what is being dreamed. Dreams also occur in non-REM sleep. These are less frequent and contain less imagery, both visual and auditory.

CONTENTS OF DREAMS. Since discovery of the REM state, dreams are no longer considered completely inaccessible. People keep dream logs, go to dream seminars, and serve as subjects in dream laboratories. One investigator collected thousands of dreams from hundreds of college students. Among the numerous findings, one was quite clear. We dream mostly about the familiar in our lives, the fabric of our existence—an old couch cover, a recent dinner, fences that need to be mended. We dream about ourselves, our family, and our friends, not about famous people or historic events. The settings are our homes, neighborhoods, and schools, not faraway places with strange-sounding names (Hall & Van de Castle, 1966).

Petra's recurrent nightmare about her baby illustrates this tendency to dream about ourselves and our surroundings. Actually, the nightmare had two parts, the first of which took place in an adoption agency. In the dream, Petra brought her baby to the agency and handed her to the adoption nurse. Then she turned around and began walking away. As she did so, the baby began crying and pushed and struggled to escape from the nurse. Still crying, the baby reached out for Petra's soothing

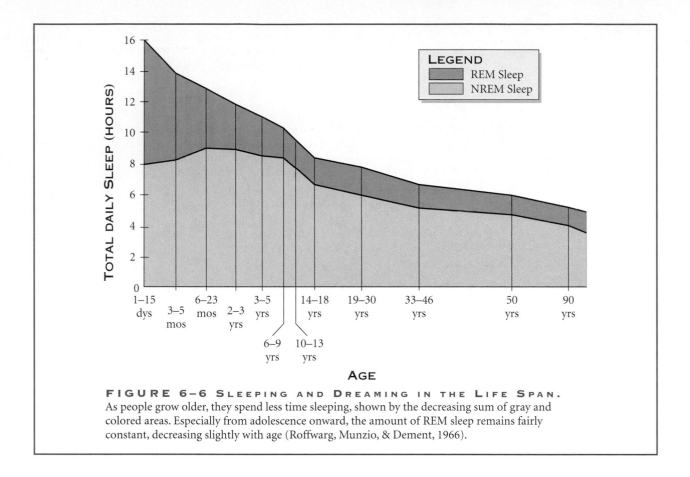

FIGURE 6–6 SLEEPING AND DREAMING IN THE LIFE SPAN.
As people grow older, they spend less time sleeping, shown by the decreasing sum of gray and colored areas. Especially from adolescence onward, the amount of REM sleep remains fairly constant, decreasing slightly with age (Roffwarg, Munzio, & Dement, 1966).

embrace. As the dream ended, Petra ignored the baby and left forever (O'Neill, 1990).

A *nightmare* is a vivid, detailed, frightening dream experience, often characterized by an inability to move, usually awakening the dreamer. It typically occurs late at night, associated with the REM state. A *night terror*, in contrast, is a very sudden awakening, often with a scream, but without vivid imagery. It is not a dream; it is not associated with REM sleep; and, not surprisingly, it occurs in the early hours of sleep (Oswald, 1987).

Petra was terrified by her nightmare because she had never wanted to give her baby up for adoption in the first place. Eight years earlier, at age 16, she had been an honors student in high school, doing very well, and then she became pregnant. Her father forced her to place the baby for adoption, a scene she felt was re-enacted in her recurrent night-

mare. A short time later, her father forced her to leave the home too (O'Neill, 1990).

The chief characters in Petra's dream are herself and her baby. The setting is familiar, the local adoption agency, and the nurse is a minor character, perhaps a stranger. In most of our dreams, even strangers are more common than public figures. If you want to know who is dreaming about you, think of the people who appear in your own dreams. On these bases, it is postulated that waking and dream thoughts blend in some fashion. Our lifestyles influence our dreams, and dreams somehow become part of our daily thoughts. Dreams are a constant element in adult mental life (Figure 6–6).

INFLUENCES ON DREAMS. It is sometimes thought that dreams are influenced by events that occur while we are sleeping. The sleeper dreams about the event instead of being awakened by it. The first recorded experimental studies of this hypothesis occurred in 1861, when a Frenchman named Alfred Maury had simple experiments performed on himself. When the sleeping Maury was pinched, he reported the next morning that he dreamed about receiving medical treatment. When exposed to a heated iron, he dreamed about people with their feet on hot coals (Maury, 1861).

Maury's work prompted a cause-and-effect conclusion: Dream contents are caused by external factors. However, this work suffered from serious defects. Maury set up these experiments himself. He perhaps went to bed thinking about being pinched or exposed to heat.

In fact, Maury's view has not been confirmed by more recent experiments using more precise laboratory techniques. When a sleeper is sprayed with water or exposed to a tone, that person may or may not dream about being wet or listening to music. The dream includes a wide variety of contents not evident in the external stimulation (Dement & Wolpert, 1958; Webb & Cartwright, 1978).

Most investigators agree instead that people dream about recent events that are important to them. To test this hypothesis, the experimental method was used again, but rather than stimulating sleeping people, the investigators exposed the subjects to several types of stimulation *before* they went to sleep. The subjects viewed films that were likely to be stimulating and personal—erotic, violent, athletic, and so forth. Then, awakened at appropriate times, they recorded their dreams. The overall finding was that these stimuli did influence the content of their dreams (Tolaas, 1980).

To what extent are dreamers aware that they are dreaming? The answer to this question varies considerably, not only among individuals but also at different times during an individual's dreams. If no one is present in the dream, then the person may not realize that he or she is having a dream. In contrast, a person dreaming about himself or herself is likely to be aware that dreaming is occurring. Whenever someone is sound asleep and also aware of being in the dreaming state, the condition is called **lucid dreaming,** a concept that is widely debated. The individual presumably possesses a conscious mind in a sleeping brain (Gackenbach & LaBerge, 1988; Walsh & Vaughn, 1992).

THEORIES OF DREAMING

Questions about the reasons for our dreams are still far from answered, and they can be approached in at least two different ways, as physiological or psychological issues. From the physiological perspective, the question concerns the origins of dreams. How do they arise? From the psychological viewpoint, the main issue seems to be function. What purpose do dreams serve?

PHYSIOLOGICAL VIEWPOINT. One approach to the physiology of dreams stresses the human brain as a dynamic whole, a self-sustaining system capable of generating and then analyzing its own information. Specifically, the **activation-synthesis hypothesis** proposes that the brain activates itself through neural activity in the lower brain centers and that these random pieces of information are then combined with memories in the upper brain regions (Hobson, 1988).

In the activation stage, the sleeping brain must somehow turn itself on. It is proposed that this internal activation occurs automatically after a period of sleep of 90 minutes or so. The responsible neurons are presumed to be part of the *reticular activating system,* the basic arousal system in the human brain. In the synthesis stage, the auto-activated brain processes these random signals by interpreting them in terms of information already in storage. The *cerebral cortex* thus becomes the critical brain region during synthesis but, disconnected from the outside world, it lacks the opportunity to test its activities against external realities. It takes the spurts of random signals and weaves them into the best possible story by using information in preexisting memories.

In Petra's dream about the adoption agency, the activation of these impulses came from the lower brain regions, as her brain was turned "on" every 90 minutes or so. This jumble of impulses included images of her baby, the agency, crying, and so forth. Simultaneously, the reticular activating system blocked out other messages, external and internal, which might have disrupted the dream. Then the synthesis of these messages took place in the cerebral cortex, responsible for higher-level symbolic activities. It constructed from this disorganized mass of information a reasonably coherent story or whole, which was the dream Petra experienced.

The activation-synthesis hypothesis does not indicate in any detail how certain neurons are turned on, perhaps by acetylcholine, and the synthesis of the brain stem impulses and cortical memories, if it even occurs, certainly is not understood. The purpose of theory is to guide research; the activation-synthesis hypothesis may prove fruitful in this regard.

FREUDIAN VIEW. Interpretations of dreams from a psychological perspective are much older than the physiological theories, dating to the earliest recorded history. This speculation was enormously augmented by the publication of Sigmund Freud's book *The Interpretation of Dreams* (1900), regarded with some skepticism today. It states that the obvious dream story, known as the **manifest content,** is relatively unimportant. A mask for something more significant, beyond the dreamer's awareness, it reflects unfinished business or events that the dreamer has dealt with in waking life, a view supported by modern research.

The manifest content of Petra's recurrent nightmare concerned her baby, even in the second part, an imaginary scene years after the adoption. In this part of the nightmare, the rejected baby had become a young woman, searching for Petra, her natural mother. Petra's dream depicted their reunion. When they encountered each other, the young woman, screaming wildly, rushed toward Petra in anger because of her abandonment years earlier. She was furious, and her anger was growing stronger and stronger. At this point, Petra inevitably awoke in a state of anxiety (O'Neill, 1990). She reported this dream to the psychologist who assisted her at the clinic.

How would Freud regard this dream?

Freud argued that the manifest content protects the dreamer from threatening thoughts and memories lying beneath its surface. These traumatic experiences, typically from childhood, have become unconscious through the process of *repression,* a form of motivated forgetting. The resulting collection of unconscious, forbidden memories from earlier years forms the **latent content** of the dream, which is its underlying significance. It is a symbolic representation of an earlier problem in the dreamer's life, presumably an unconscious wish.

To ensure that this latent content is kept out of awareness while we are asleep, repression is aided by the dreamwork, which generates a disguise, transforming the threatening latent content into the dream story, or manifest content, using universal and private symbols of all sorts.

The effort to understand the psychological significance of a dream, called **dream interpretation,** is a highly complex and speculative process requiring skill, experience, and a broad fund of knowledge. Moreover, Freud was emphatic on one point: The dream must be understood in the context of the *dreamer's* spontaneous thoughts about it, not in terms of someone else's ideas. Otherwise, the interpretation presumably reveals more about the interpreter than it does about the dreamer.

After his interviews with Petra, the clinical psychologist, using psychoanalysis, speculated that Petra's two-part nightmare depicts the abandonment theme through three generations—from the parents to Petra to her daughter. The first-generation rejection occurred when the parents forced Petra to leave their home. The second-generation rejection occurred when Petra left her child to be adopted. According to psychoanalytic theory, the disguise in these dreams is that the parents, who were the real source of the problem, do not appear at all. At the same time, this omission is a most revealing element of the dreamwork (O'Neill, 1990).

The third rejection occurred only in the dream. Here the daughter, after finally finding her mother, spurns her, further intensifying Petra's concerns about abandonment and loneliness.

These details about Petra's dreams, and other facts in her life, were reported in a research journal under the title *Case Study* (O'Neill, 1990). Additional information was obtained through an interview with the author, who asked that Petra's true identity be concealed in various ways.

JUNGIAN VIEW. A colleague who eventually left Freud's circle, Carl Gustav Jung developed his own brand of psychoanalysis and took a very different view of dreaming. The manifest content, in his opinion, is a mirror, not a mask. It reflects the dreamer's current concerns, often rather openly. The dream is concerned with here-and-now issues, although elements of the past may be evoked.

For Jung, the basic approach to understanding dreams is to expand the contents in any way possible, a process called **amplification of dreams.** For this purpose, he urged the use of an *interior dialogue,* meaning that the dreamer holds an imaginary conversation with the elements in the dream, including people, animals, and even objects and events. During this dialogue, the dreamer plays any and all parts, behaving and speaking in ways that seem appropriate for each element (Jung, 1963, 1964).

In amplifying the nightmares about leaving her baby, Petra might carry out an interior dialogue, expressing to herself the anguish she experienced. She could also include the baby's part, struggling and crying, protesting against the abandonment. The aim would be to discover, in any way possible, what each of the dream images and ideas might mean to her. These amplifications might show that Petra *herself* felt abandoned, just as she had abandoned her baby.

DREAMS AS INFORMATION PROCESSING. A more recent approach continues somewhat along Jungian lines. The **information processing viewpoint** regards dreaming as a process of sorting and sifting, storing and dumping recently acquired information. This review and rehearsal may serve three functions. First, dreams may assist in *problem solving* by playing an active role in the elaboration of current information. Dreaming somehow enables us to organize recent thoughts into coherent forms and perhaps to consolidate previously acquired information (Table 6–2).

When they encountered one another, the young woman, screaming wildly, rushed toward Petra in anger because of her abandonment years earlier. She was furious, and her anger was growing stronger and stronger...

THEORY	EXPLANATION
Activation-synthesis	This dream is the best possible narrative sequence of random messages from the lower brain centers, mixed with information already stored in memory.
Freudian	The nightmare is a disguised expression of aggression against her parents, for Petra is the young woman in this dream, screaming about her own abandonment.
Jungian	Petra's dream rather directly reveals the anxiety she experienced in abandoning her child; here she imagines the child's response to this abandonment.
Information processing	Dreaming plays a role in organizing, remembering, and forgetting information; Petra, perhaps stimulated by the sudden departure of a friend, is sifting and sorting recent experiences for later use.

TABLE 6–2 THEORIES OF DREAMING. The second part of Petra's nightmare is shown at the top of the table. Each theory offers a somewhat different explanation.

Taken at face value, both of Petra's nightmares are attempts to work through her adolescent pregnancy, her abandonment of the baby, and her fears of the child's reaction. The manifest content tells this story.

Second, dreams may play a role in *remembering*, serving as a means of assessing new and old information and deciding whether new information needs to be stored. Redundant information is discarded, and the remainder is processed for storage (Hobson, 1988). It is known that sleep has a beneficial effect on certain memories, possibly because our dreams early in the night seem to be a review of the day's events.

A third possibility goes one step further, arguing that the most basic purpose of dreams lies in *discharging information*—that is, to forget. The idea here is that the brain is a highly complex mechanism, the most intricate structure on earth, managing truly remarkable amounts of information daily, but it needs an opportunity to discharge itself. In this view, dreaming is an unwinding process, releasing superfluous or unwanted information from potential storage (Crick & Mitchison, 1983).

• MEDITATION AND HYPNOSIS •

When we go to bed, we usually intend to sleep and we expect to dream. These changes are regular and inevitable parts of our lives. But in meditation and hypnosis, we make a special effort to change our consciousness.

It is useful to compare meditation and hypnosis, for both altered consciousnesses are brought about by a narrowing of attention, and the object of attention can be much the same. Set or expectation is involved in both cases. Moreover, people who do not want to meditate or to be hypnotized cannot be made to do so. The induction of both processes is under the individual's control.

PRACTICE OF MEDITATION

Meditation usually has one of two purposes—to allow people to relax or to enable them to look differently at themselves or the world. Specifically, the aim of most **meditation** is to achieve a state of deep relaxation or increased awareness, brought about chiefly by the restriction of incoming stimuli (Figure 6–7).

TECHNIQUES OF MEDITATION. In a quiet setting and a comfortable position, the individual adopts one of two fundamental meditation strategies, concentration or mindfulness. In **concentrative meditation,** attention is directed to a single object or event; the focus is on a simple source of stimulation, such as a soft sound or candle. In

FIGURE 6–7 MEDITATION. Tibetan monks, through meditation, apparently have achieved remarkable control over body temperature, respiration rate, and other presumably involuntary responses. A most important factor is practice, not just for months but for decades (Benson et al., 1990).

mindfulness meditation, attention is directed toward a broad awareness of objects and events as they arise spontaneously in consciousness. In both cases, the aims are *relaxation* and *expanded awareness* of any and all contents of consciousness, including special colors, voices, odors, and so forth. The mind, in certain respects, observes itself observing the outside world (Delmonte, 1990, 1995).

The specific techniques vary widely. In traditional *yoga,* meditators concentrate on their breathing and engage in special stretching exercises at the same time.

In the concentrative technique called *transcendental meditation,* the individual induces altered awareness by silently repeating a special syllable or sound, called a *mantra,* over and over again. This sound is usually kept secret, for otherwise it loses its personal significance. Its aim is to provide an adequate focus for the individual's attention.

When she worked intensely on a painting, Petra found she could engage in a form of concentrative meditation, focusing her mind on what she was painting. She even carried on a dialogue with her painting. After working, she sat back quietly and looked for a long time at what she had done— sometimes for almost an hour. In this way, she let her painting speak to her. "It painted back," she said, "giving something back to me."

OUTCOMES OF MEDITATION. The experiential outcomes of meditation are usually reported to be expanded awareness, perceptual alterations, and loss of orientation in time and space. They range from benign, dreamlike fantasies to images of beasts in darkness. At the highest levels, consciousness is reported as blissful and subtle, reaching almost a sensationless state.

Experienced meditators point out that this practice has little effect for the novice or first-time user. At least two years of training are essential if it is to yield any substantial value. The alleged outcome, an unusual sense of well-being and consciousness, is not regularly recognized in traditional Western life (Delmonte, 1990; Halbrook, 1995; Sweet & Johnson, 1990).

Certain physiological changes can be readily assessed, however. In one instance, subjects who had been meditating for approximately two years experienced marked reductions in oxygen consumption, carbon dioxide production, and blood lactate concentrations, all associated with the practice of meditation (Wallace & Benson, 1972). In another, Buddhist monks using advanced meditation practices were able to alter sharply body metabolism and EEG patterns (Benson, Malhotra, Goldman, Jacobs, et al., 1990; Figure 6–8).

It is also clear that meditation can provide therapeutic psychological outcomes. It has been effective for insomnia, anxiety, and borderline hypertension, but not more so than other self-regulation strategies. Whether meditation techniques

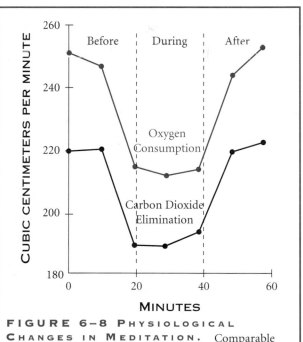

FIGURE 6–8 PHYSIOLOGICAL CHANGES IN MEDITATION. Comparable changes can be generated by other relaxation procedures, as well (Wallace & Benson, 1972).

are unique and distinct from these other procedures, including relaxation and self-hypnosis, is still a question (Dillbeck & Orme-Johnson, 1987; Holmes, 1984). In other words, the psychological benefits have not yet been demonstrated to be significantly different from those that might accrue through regular relaxation, resting, running, or some other diversionary activities.

USE OF HYPNOSIS

Vigorous interest in hypnosis has a relatively short history, especially compared with meditation in the East. It first came to the Western world in

FIGURE 6–9 AN EARLY PRACTITIONER OF HYPNOSIS. Anton Mesmer explained that "animal magnetism" was a physical force, like gravity, and stated that it permeated the universe. The human nervous system was presumed to be especially sensitive to this energy, which he used for therapeutic purposes.

Paris late in the eighteenth century through the work of a Viennese physician, Anton Mesmer. An early psychiatric practitioner in Paris, Mesmer claimed that an "animal magnetism" passed from him to his patients. His method became known as Mesmerism, and he gave his name to our word *mesmerize*, meaning "to hold spellbound," "to enthrall," or "to hypnotize" (Figure 6–9). But Mesmer was unable to hypnotize the French government. It conducted an investigation, disclaimed animal magnetism, and drove Mesmer from the city—although it did not deny that his treatment had a therapeutic effect in many cases (Fancher, 1990).

The commission investigating Mesmer came up with no understanding of how his cures worked and left us with the question of what is meant by hypnosis. The term comes from the Greek word *hupnos*, meaning "sleep," but hypnotized people are not asleep. In a sense, **hypnosis** is a social interaction in which one person, responding to suggestions made by someone else, experiences alterations in perception, memory, and voluntary action. On this basis, there is one clear difference between meditation and hypnosis. Meditators make sustained efforts to *remove themselves from outside influences.* Their concern is with their own thought processes; no significantly involuntary behaviors occur. Hypnotized people show *decreased ability to act on their own;* involuntary changes in memory, behavior, and physiology are induced. In this sense, hypnosis is a more unusual state of consciousness.

SUSCEPTIBILITY TO HYPNOSIS. Two myths about hypnosis can be readily dispelled, one concerning its evil use, the other concerning the hypnotist's power. First, hypnotism cannot be used to coerce people into criminal, sadistic, or other forms of deviant behavior. People cannot be hypnotized against their will, and some cannot be hypnotized at all. Second, the hypnotist does not play a magical role. The real performer is the hypnotized person; the hypnotist serves as an assistant or facilitator.

However, the hypnotist can try to work with people who are most amenable to this procedure. Highly hypnotizable people tend to have supple, vivid imaginations and a distinct capacity for focused attention, evident in the way they can become fully absorbed in reading a book, playing a game, or holding a conversation.

If subjects are known to be extremely easy or difficult to hypnotize, the hypnotist's methods may vary in certain details, but the basic procedure is simple. The subject is given the suggestion of drowsiness and relaxation, and perhaps that he or she is slipping further and further away from voluntary control. At this point any number of additional techniques can be employed, such as asking the person to concentrate on something in a methodical way—an object, a thought, or the hypnotist's words—or to imagine certain bodily sensations. As the person yields control, various hypnotic effects become possible.

CLASSIC HYPNOTIC EFFECTS. Among the behaviors erroneously cited as evidence of the hypnotic state, the "human plank" demonstration is the most famous. Here a person is suspended horizontally between two chairs, one under the head, the other under the feet, while another person stands on his or her stomach or chest, supported only by the rigidity of the first person's body. However, normally healthy people can perform this feat readily without hypnosis. They simply need proper instructions.

The condition of **analgesia,** insensitivity to painful stimuli, is a reliable hypnotic phenomenon, as testified by numerous successes in medicine. It has proven equally or more effective than morphine, acupuncture, and other pain-reducing agents. Again, the outcomes have been most successful with highly hypnotizable subjects.

The most humorous behavior displayed under hypnosis involves **regression,** also called *age regression,* in which a hypnotized person, with adult clothes and adult proportions, behaves as he or she did in an earlier stage in life. The person talks like a child of 5 years, for example, and shows a distinct interest in children's activities (Figure 6–10).

Sometimes, however, the regression is incomplete. In one demonstration, adults are hypnotized and told that they are 2 years old, wearing diapers. They totter about the stage in their street clothes, cooing and babbling amid laughter from the audience. When told that their diapers have suddenly fallen down, most of them quickly cover their lower regions, prompting more howls from the spectators. But this behavior reveals the bare truth—that the subjects are not fully regressed. Most two-year-olds show no such modesty.

The third condition, **hypnotic amnesia,** refers to the subject's inability to remember events that occurred during hypnosis. The hypnotized subject is told that he or she will forget what happens during

FIGURE 6–10 HYPNOTIC REGRESSION.
The actions of this woman, sitting on the floor, sobbing and clutching her blanket, presumably reflect her behavior at a much earlier age.

the trance, and after the hypnotic state is removed, the person cannot recall these events. However, when a certain arbitrary signal is given, the subject's memory improves dramatically; almost all of the events under hypnosis are recalled successfully.

This arbitrary signal, called a *posthypnotic suggestion,* is simply a cue for the previously hypnotized person to recall the earlier events, during hypnosis, or to behave in some other way prescribed by the hypnotist during the trance. On receiving a handshake or kiss, for example, the formerly hypnotized person may sit on the floor or draw a picture. The posthypnotic signal—the handshake or kiss or whatever—need not have any direct relationship to the activity performed by the subject. When asked why he or she sat on the floor, the former subject may become embarrassed and reply: "I really do not know" or "I just felt like it."

The posthypnotic suggestion is not as dangerous as it might seem, however. First, as noted already, people cannot be coerced through hypnosis to perform acts against their will. Second, if the posthypnotic signal is not removed or deleted by the hypnotist, it will not persist as a potential influence for the remainder of the subject's life. Instead, it simply fades away, leaving the subject free from any hypnotic influences.

Despite enthusiastic claims for improved memory under hypnosis, there is no impressive evidence that people, after being hypnotized, can suddenly remember *earlier* events, such as a bank robbery or an unusual musical score. On the contrary, laboratory studies show that hypnosis increases the likelihood of giving incorrect answers to leading questions. Even field studies with police departments, using actual witnesses' and victims' questions under hypnotic conditions, show no beneficial effects of hypnosis on accuracy of memory for events prior to the hypnotic procedure (Kihlstrom, 1985). Despite recent court rulings that allow greater use of hypnosis, there is no substantial evidence that hypnosis improves eyewitness testimony (McMaster, 1990).

CLINICAL APPLICATIONS OF HYPNOSIS. In clinical settings, hypnosis has been directed at a variety of disorders. Treatment outcomes vary a great deal, depending on the characteristics of the person and the nature of the problem. Here we can specify two broad classes of adjustment problems, behavioral and experiential. Overeating, smoking, and drug abuse involve behavior; they are overt habits emitted by the individual. Headaches and asthma are experiences of pain, significantly influenced by neural and hormonal factors. These conditions are less voluntary in the sense that the subject never decided to have headaches or wheezing in the way that someone may decide to have another piece of pie or buy a pack of cigarettes. The aim of hypnotic treatment in the first instance is to alter an undesired behavior. In the second, the aim is to change a painful experience or bodily condition.

It now appears that hypnotic treatment is most useful in the second instance, for modifying the experience of migraine headaches, asthma, warts, and so forth. In the hypnotic condition, the individual may imagine a warm liquid bathing the afflicted area and therefore eliminating the problem. The short-term and long-term goals are the same: to eliminate pain. Hypnosis has been a useful therapeutic intervention in these instances, assisting medical patients in pain control and the resolution of emotional conflicts (Appel, 1990).

With more voluntary behavior, the subject must imagine that some immediately pleasurable activity, such as eating, smoking, or drinking, is now aversive. Addicted people are pitted against themselves. The short-term goal, to consume a certain substance, is at odds with the long-term goal, to break the addiction. In all cases, however, factors other than hypnosis may be influential, such as the subject's expectation of success, support from family and friends, use of adjunctive treatments and, especially, the readiness to change (Wadden & Anderton, 1982).

On this basis, mixed results would be predicted for Petra in hypnotherapy. For the reason just mentioned, her caffeine problem would have a less favorable prognosis than her nightmare, but hypnotizability and motivation would be key factors.

THEORIES OF HYPNOSIS. Among the many theories of hypnosis, two are dominant and quite opposed. According to the *social* viewpoint, the hypnotic condition is essentially a normal state of consciousness in which the subject demonstrates a high degree of control and willingness to engage in certain acts. The subject enters into a contract with the hypnotist and then endures pain, forgets a friend's name, or behaves like a child. In daily life, people behave in these same ways. They endure injury in athletic contests, regress to "puppy love" during television dating games, and perform seemingly impossible feats of strength in emergency situations. The hypnotic subject's suggestibility and motivation are significant factors in attaining the so-called hypnotic condition (Barber, Wilson, & Scott, 1980; Sarbin, 1991).

The social or suggestibility approach argues that there is no need to postulate a special hypnotic state, which involves circular reasoning. A person is said to be under hypnosis when insensitive to pain or acting as a child, and yet when these acts are explained, they are invariably attributed to the hypnotic state. This view is sometimes called **role enactment** because it stresses that the individual is trying to fill a role, to act like a hypnotized person—that is, to be a good subject, as specified by the hypnotist. The chief factors influencing this outcome include the subject's perception of the role, the presence of an audience, and the subject's possession of the necessary skills.

Another theoretical approach postulates two different types of *cognition* in hypnosis. The hypnotic condition is brought about by a shift in brain control. The experience begins in the higher centers, as the individual listens to the instructions and prepares for the hypnotic induction. Afterward, the lower brain centers become more important, influencing what is experienced, remembered, and reported. According to the **dissociation view,** a separation or dissociation occurs between these different levels, and a consciousness beyond immediate awareness assumes control (Watkins & Watkins, 1990).

A hypnotized woman places one hand in a pail of extremely cold water and experiences no significant pain, but physiological measures of heartbeat show little difference from the state in which pain is fully experienced. At some level the subject is responsive to the cold, and when asked to write with the other hand about her experience, she indicates that she is aware of the pain (Hilgard, 1973). These and other demonstrations suggest that part of the individual's consciousness has been separated from normal awareness. It has been called the "hidden observer," for it has access to information otherwise unavailable.

Each of these perspectives can contribute to our understanding of hypnosis. Role enactment, with its parsimony, points to the simplicity with which many hypnotic responses can be explained, but it does not adequately account for other conditions, such as posthypnotic suggestion and the tolerance of extreme pain (Zangwill, 1987). The dissociation view, which points to cognitive factors, reminds us that subjects can be taught to cope with pain. The contact with the hypnotist, which perhaps includes a temporary disruption in the central nervous system, may facilitate these experiences of painlessness.

Both explanations are derived from principles of normal behavior. There is no compelling reason to regard them as incompatible. Social influence is everywhere, and changes in consciousness are too. Hence, the chief issue is the ways in which these theories, separately or together, may stimulate much needed further research.

• DRUG-INDUCED STATES •

Sleep and dreams are natural states; the body responds in a predetermined, rhythmic fashion. Meditation is self-induced and largely self-regulated. Hypnosis is induced by someone else, but the hypnotized person cannot be coerced or otherwise compelled to commit criminal or deviant acts. In drug-induced states, the outcomes are not necessarily controllable or predictable, especially when they involve *street drugs*, concocted illegally in the laboratory and elsewhere, designed to produce certain experiential effects. They may have properties somewhat similar to or extremely different from those of *prescription drugs*, prepared by a pharmacy for use as a medication or remedy. In all cases, the outcome depends on the chemical composition of the drug and its interaction with the specific neurophysiology and psychological makeup of the individual.

Petra had tried to stay away from street drugs. She once abused LSD, and then one night she took an overdose of medication prescribed by her physician (O'Neill, 1990). That incident, together with her nightmares, brought her to the clinic for psychological assistance.

USING DRUGS

It is said that drugs keep this country in trouble, and troubles keep this country in drugs. Drugs are consumed daily by millions of people for all sorts of reasons. Coffee, tea, and cigarettes are used around the clock. Prescription drugs are consumed in the morning, in the evening, and after meals for allergies, pain, and other physical disorders. Diet pills suppress the appetite. Psychiatric drugs control anxiety and depression. Wine, beer, whiskey, and other forms of alcohol are enjoyed before, during, and after dinner, and at night, a sleeping pill may be taken for insomnia.

Our focus here is on drugs employed with the aim of changing consciousness. Any drug that does so, altering consciousness by influencing mental activity, mood, or perception, is known as a **psychoactive substance**. Some of these drugs serve medical purposes as well (Figure 6–11).

PHYSIOLOGICAL RESPONSE. To understand drug use and abuse, an important relationship must be kept in mind. The more direct and immediate the intake, the stronger is the physical reaction. The drug can be taken in any of three major modes: orally, by inhalation, or by injection.

FIGURE 6–11 CHANGING CONSCIOUSNESS. Caffeine is a popular substance for altering attentiveness in minor ways; it retards habituation to repetitive tasks and enhances the appeal of novel stimulation (Davidson & Smith, 1991).

When taken by mouth, the drug is soluble in the stomach, reaches the bloodstream, and then produces a reaction. Occasionally instead, it is inserted into the rectum as a suppository. When drugs are inhaled through the nose and mouth, as in smoking marijuana, snorting cocaine, and also sniffing heroin, this approach avoids the gastrointestinal system. The drugs pass quickly into the bloodstream, producing a more immediate and stronger reaction. Eventually, however, the user reaches a point of adaptation, and then the drug no longer has its earlier effect. To obtain the earlier result, a greater amount must be used or the drug must be incorporated into the bloodstream more rapidly. In the third mode, therefore, the drug is injected directly beneath the skin or into a muscle, and it reaches the bloodstream even more quickly. But after repeated usage, the body adapts once again, and still more potent stimulation is necessary. Then the drug is injected directly into the bloodstream via the vein, called *mainlining*. After this technique has been used for some time, the only recourse against the body's adaptive response is to use more and more potent dosages. At this point, the aim is not only to obtain altered consciousness but also, because the body is physically adapted, to avoid the highly aversive withdrawal symptoms when the drug is not employed.

Ultimately, the chemical substances in psychoactive drugs act on the brain, disrupting neural activity at the synapses. They do so by mimicking the function of the natural neurotransmitters, by prolonging their action, by obstructing the transmitters at the receptor site, or by preventing the transportation of natural transmitters into and out of the synaptic space. Consumption of alcohol, for example, inhibits cell activity at the synapses. Initially, this inhibition seems to have a stimulating effect, for it produces a sense of freedom, release, and relaxation. However, continued consumption produces more and more inhibition, resulting in slower and less coordination. Further consumption

induces stupor. And finally, when neural activity is sufficiently inhibited, the individual falls asleep or becomes unconscious.

Investigations of opium showed that when the brain is regularly exposed to exogenous opiates—meaning pain suppressors from outside the body—it ceases to produce its own internal pain suppressors, the various endorphins. The opiates, acting at specific receptors, have essentially the same molecular shape as endorphins, which are neurotransmitters serving as the body's natural pain killers. By fitting into those receptor sites, heroin and other opiates block the pain. After continued use of opiates, the body stops producing its own endorphins of this type, and more and more drug usage becomes necessary to fill the vacant receptors. If further opiates are not used, then various painful responses occur, including vomiting and chills as the body begins to compensate for its newly acquired need.

PSYCHOLOGICAL RESPONSE. Each use of a psychoactive drug, as well as its habitual use over an extended period, typically shows an initial positive psychological response followed by a negative experience. The immediate positive reaction, which Petra experienced with alcohol and a few other drugs, eventually wears off; then an aversive condition develops, commonly characterized by depression, headaches, dry mouth, or other physical symptoms. Petra's reactions included chest pains and heart palpitations (O'Neill, 1990). In addition, as the drug is employed more and more, each successive usage results in stronger and stronger negative reactions after the drug has been withdrawn. In other words, repeated drug usage reflects in a general way its use in any one specific instance; the long-term result, like the single incident, eventually involves a negative experience.

Both reactions, short-term and long-term, illustrate the opponent-process theory, considered in a later chapter on emotion. After any emotional experience, according to *opponent-process theory,* our feelings do not return directly to normal; rather, when the first feeling subsides, they swing in the opposite direction before becoming normal or neutral once again. If the initial feeling is positive, as in an early response to a drug, it is followed by a second reaction, which is negative. After this negative reaction disappears, the normal state returns. If the initial feeling is negative, as in taking a cold shower, then it is followed by a positive reaction. After this pleasant state disappears, the response returns to its usual baseline level.

A second postulate of opponent-process theory is that with greater and greater exposure to the stimulus, the second feeling becomes stronger and stronger. The regular bather enjoys the follow-up reaction to her cold shower more and more, just as the drug user finds the withdrawal response more and more acute. Opponent-process theory, applicable to numerous areas of human functioning, is one of the major theoretical models proposed to explain drug abuse and to stimulate research (Baker, Morse, & Sherman, 1986).

DRUG DEPENDENCE. These reactions of increasing need for a certain drug and dosage are referred to as **drug dependence** or, more generally, *addiction.* There are two types. In *physical dependence,* the individual has a physiological need for the drug, developed through adaptation of the body after continued drug usage. The two criteria for judging physical dependence are *tolerance,* meaning the amount that can be consumed with reduced or no effect, and *withdrawal symptoms,* referring to the magnitude of the negative reaction when the drug is no longer used. Withdrawal from cocaine or heroin, for example, can include fever, headaches, and ringing in the ears, as well as vomiting, chills, and other symptoms.

An individual on drugs also may develop a *psychological dependence,* meaning that use of the drug has become habitual and important to the individual even though few withdrawal symptoms occur and there is little change in tolerance. Drinking small amounts of coffee regularly is suggestive of psychological dependence. In this case, the individual will go to some effort to maintain the habit, making sure that the cupboard is stocked, watching for coffee breaks at work, and so forth. To the extent that a physiological need also develops, the dependence is physical. Wanting very much to read the newspaper each morning, and feeling upset without it, is a better example of a purely psychological dependence.

DRUG EXPERIENCES

The experiential and behavioral effects of psychoactive drugs are ultimately the result of influences in the nervous system. These influences on synaptic action are highly diverse, a condition that complicates the classification of these drugs. One convenient system includes: depressants, generally associated with diminishing anxiety; stimulants, used to increase alertness; and hallucinogens, consumed to achieve expanded sensory awareness. In turning to these categories, it should be emphasized that the unpredictable dangers from drugs can hardly be overstated (Table 6–3).

DEPRESSANTS. As the name suggests, **depressants are** basically *downers,* inhibiting activity in the central nervous system, thereby decreasing anxiety, pain, and related states. The basic effect is sedation, although these drugs differ in strength and speed of action, some producing an effect in a few seconds, others after several hours. When taken in modest doses, they provide a feeling of tranquility and relaxation.

The most widely used depressant in the Western world, without doubt, is alcohol. Its initial use at parties is well known, resulting in spontaneous,

DEPRESSANTS	EXPECTED EFFECTS	DISRUPTIVE EFFECTS
Alcohol	Relaxation, reduced anxiety and inhibition	Decreased physical and mental functions, cirrhosis, blackouts
Opiates	Euphoria, dreaminess, relief from pain	Nausea, impaired mental ability, convulsions, coma, death

STIMULANTS	EXPECTED EFFECTS	DISRUPTIVE EFFECTS
Amphetamines	Increased arousal, alertness, energy	Restlessness, headaches, delusions, psychosis
Cocaine	Excitement, euphoria, increased energy	Sweating, depression, aggressiveness
Caffeine	Increased attention, quicker reactions, greater alertness	Insomnia, irregular heartbeat, restlessness, increased blood pressure
Nicotine	Unpredictable, ranging from increased relaxation to alertness	Heart disease, cancer, respiration problems, decreased circulation

HALLUCINOGENS	EXPECTED EFFECTS	DISRUPTIVE EFFECTS
Marijuana	Relaxation, pleasant feeling, sensory alterations	Perceptual distortions, nausea, impairment of learning
LSD	Hallucinations, sense of insight, exhilaration	Panic reaction, nausea, emotional upheaval

TABLE 6-3 MAJOR PSYCHOACTIVE DRUGS. The outcomes for individual drug use are never fully predictable. Only the most prominent effects are indicated.

carefree spirits punctuated by some wit and good cheer. On such bases, alcohol may appear to be a stimulant, but in fact it retards the action at certain brain synapses responsible for inhibition and control. If the party continues too long or the guests drink too rapidly, the poor coordination and lack of clarity in thought clearly show that alcohol is a depressant.

At issue here is the amount of alcohol in the bloodstream, which is determined by three basic factors: the drink being consumed, the condition of the drinker, and the rate of consumption. Wine, for example, has less alcohol than whiskey; prior consumption of food or nonalcoholic beverage delays the entrance of alcohol into the bloodstream; and the slow drinker ingests less alcohol per unit of time than does the rapid drinker. The difference between sipping wine slowly on a full stomach and taking shots of whiskey rapidly when tired or hun-

gry lies in the capacity of the body to use, or metabolize, the alcoholic content. When it cannot keep up with the rate of ingestion, the result is drunkenness.

The term **alcoholism** refers to people who have become "problem drinkers," loosely defined as the inability to take only one or two drinks or to go for a day or two without any alcohol at all. An alcoholic, or problem drinker, as defined by the *Diagnostic and Statistical Manual of Mental Disorders* (DSM-IV), is anyone who, for at least a month, is unable to stop using alcohol, despite the consequences of physical disorders, amnesic periods, or disrupted social, occupational, or family life (American Psychiatric Association, 1994). Who are these people? They come from all walks of life, and estimates run to 10 million or more Americans. Alcohol abuse is alarmingly high among teenagers, isolated individuals, and those raised in addicted families. Petra's

LEVEL OF ALCOHOL	TYPICAL BEHAVIOR
.35	Surgical anesthesia, potential death
.30	Barely conscious, no sense of surroundings
.25	Extreme motor disturbance, "wiped out"
.20	Marked disruption of sensory-motor ability
.15	Large delay in reaction time, less caution
.10	Delay in reaction time, impaired motor capacity
.05	Less alertness, impaired judgment
.00	Sober, normal functions intact

TABLE 6–4 ALCOHOL CONSUMPTION AND BEHAVIOR. The usual legal definition of intoxication is .10, which means the blood alcohol level is 1/10th of 1%. At that point, the risk of automobile and other accidents rises sixfold or higher (Ray, 1983).

consumption of alcohol began when she was in her mid-teens, isolated from friends, and living with alcoholic parents. Even in high school, when performing at an honors level academically, she was at risk for this problem (O'Neill, 1990).

Directly or indirectly, alcohol is associated with the most diverse individual disasters in society: accidents, assault, rape, divorce, and death, to say nothing of inefficiency, errors, insults, and psychiatric disorders (Miller & Ries, 1991; Whitlock, 1987). The hangover is a mild form of withdrawal symptoms, and people can die from alcohol poisoning (Table 6–4). Hazards of social drinking by pregnant women have become apparent. Even this level of consumption may be harmful for the offspring (Blume, 1991).

Depressants that inhibit the central nervous system even more markedly are called **opiates,** for they come from the opium poppy and include not only *opium* but also its derivatives, *morphine* and *heroin*. When injected or inhaled, opiates produce a surge of

pleasure and a period of bliss. These drugs are also called *narcotics* because this bliss can become a sleep-like state characterized by numbness and stupor. After some hours the need for another dose arises, and the cycle has begun.

STIMULANTS. The opposite effect occurs with **stimulants,** which arouse the central nervous system, heightening its action and increasing related bodily activities. These *uppers* raise the heart rate, muscle tension, and alertness, giving a general lift or sense of well-being. Overall, they improve the mood, but they differ markedly from each other in their molecular structure and mechanisms of action. Describing these drugs collectively as stimulants does not adequately reflect their differences and complexities.

Certain stimulants, called **amphetamines,** are used to stay awake and improve mental and physical performance. They relieve nasal congestion as well, a therapeutic outcome that led to the discovery of their stimulating properties. Today amphetamines are colloquially called "speed," for they increase the rate of these bodily functions. Sometimes they do so even to the point of inducing a psychotic reaction—meaning a break with reality.

Consuming amphetamines a few times, Petra drank alcohol afterward to recover from the speed. Whatever goes up must come down—one way or another. She engaged in this sequence of abuse while thinking about her baby (O'Neill, 1990). She worried about her daughter's health, where she lived, and whether she might ever search for her mother.

Stimulants, legal and illegal, also include **cocaine,** obtained from the coca plant and consumed via needle, pipe, or pill. A crystallized form, called *crack,* is extremely powerful and used chiefly by smoking. Cocaine induces such a state of bliss and euphoria that a severe dependency can quickly arise (Figure 6–12). Prison sentences are automatic for unauthorized possession; death can be the out-

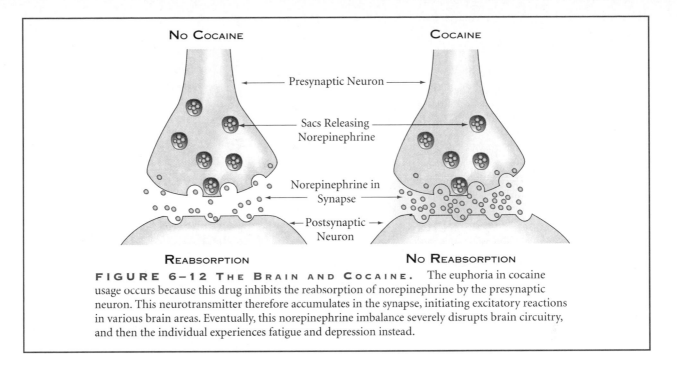

FIGURE 6–12 THE BRAIN AND COCAINE. The euphoria in cocaine usage occurs because this drug inhibits the reabsorption of norepinephrine by the presynaptic neuron. This neurotransmitter therefore accumulates in the synapse, initiating excitatory reactions in various brain areas. Eventually, this norepinephrine imbalance severely disrupts brain circuitry, and then the individual experiences fatigue and depression instead.

come of inappropriate use, chiefly because the drug is so stimulating that it can cause cardiac arrest.

Nicotine and caffeine have mild effects and therefore are widely available, although their influence is more pronounced than might be evident at first glance. When ingested by smoking, nicotine reaches the brain swiftly, stimulating and suppressing various activities. It may affect several neurotransmitters, including acetylcholine, norepinephrine, and serotonin, and it may cause heart and lung disease (Murray, 1991). The expressions "tea time" and "coffee break" show that both of these drinks, containing caffeine, are at the very center of our social lives around the globe.

HALLUCINOGENS. Quite different from the drugs that suppress or stimulate the central nervous system, the **hallucinogens** primarily produce alterations in sensation and perception, heightening or distorting awareness of oneself or the environment. These false perceptions of reality, called *hallucinations*, are typically visual or auditory.

Considered by some a mild hallucinogen, **marijuana** is derived from the hemp plant, usually producing a sense of exhilaration and intoxication when ingested. However, altered consciousness is not inevitable, as emphasized by first-time users who indicate that they experienced nothing different. With practice and a drug of a certain potency, which is very difficult to assess, a person using marijuana might experience *time expansion,* in which a momentary scene seems quite prolonged, and *sensory intensification,* in which colors seem more saturated, shapes more distinct, and variations more noticeable. When these two features are combined, one can understand why a person using marijuana may find extended fascination in some leaf or the face of a clock. While its experiential outcomes are milder than those of most other illegal drugs, the dangers to physical well-being are still unclear (Akers, 1992).

Some years ago, **lysergic acid diethylamide (LSD)** was referred to as a *psychotomimetic* drug, meaning that it produces psychoticlike symptoms, such as hearing unspoken voices and seeing nonexistent events. The idea of psychotic induction also

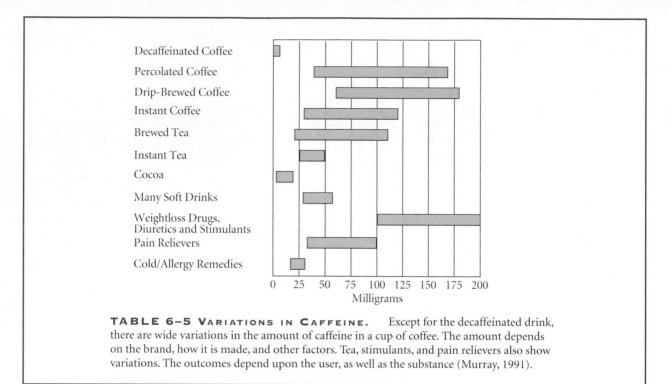

Decaffeinated Coffee
Percolated Coffee
Drip-Brewed Coffee
Instant Coffee
Brewed Tea
Instant Tea
Cocoa
Many Soft Drinks
Weightloss Drugs, Diuretics and Stimulants
Pain Relievers
Cold/Allergy Remedies

0 25 50 75 100 125 150 175 200
Milligrams

TABLE 6–5 VARIATIONS IN CAFFEINE. Except for the decaffeinated drink, there are wide variations in the amount of caffeine in a cup of coffee. The amount depends on the brand, how it is made, and other factors. Tea, stimulants, and pain relievers also show variations. The outcomes depend upon the user, as well as the substance (Murray, 1991).

came partly from the use of LSD in clinical work, especially for controlling severely depressed and hyperactive patients. Later, when LSD was used in experiential settings, it was referred to as *hallucinogenic,* a term that is not completely accurate either. The visual reactions often have a substantial basis in reality. Sometimes LSD is known as *psychedelic,* a neutral word meaning "mind-manifesting."

As a major hallucinogen, LSD also can produce *flashbacks,* in which disturbing false perceptions reappear several days, weeks, or even months later. This unpredictable result is related to the biochemical characteristics of the individual and of the ingested drug, rather than to any particular expectancy on the part of the user. Long-term psychological damage seems to be associated primarily with the stability of the personality, as well as the chemical properties of the drug.

We can sum up these observations on drug-induced states by pointing to four influential factors: the general psychological adjustment of the individual; the person's set or expectation as

a user, especially with the less powerful drugs; his or her biochemical condition; and the chemical makeup of the drug. When these factors are combined, it is not surprising that pychoactive drugs sometimes produce feelings of euphoria and sensory intensification and sometimes prompt violent, psychoticlike reactions. Even with mild stimulants the outcomes are unpredictable (Table 6–5).

We can note as well that drug abuse often begins in adolescence as issues of identity and indepedence emerge. It reaches its highest level in early adulthood. As these issues are resolved in the next decade, drug abuse may subside without drastic intervention.

• NORMAL CONSCIOUSNESS •

This survey of natural and induced variations offers an opportunity for a reminder about the fundamental nature of normal human consciousness, considered less directly in many other chapters, including those on sensation, perception, thought and language, motivation, emotion, personality, and adjustment. Presumably the result of an extraordinary evolutionary development, normal human consciousness provides us with our unique adaptive capacity, as well as our moments of greatest pleasure and deepest despair.

From the evolutionary perspective, this outcome occurred as natural selection favored those who could adjust most successfully to the environment. While other species developed stronger muscles, better vision, sharper teeth, and so forth, human beings developed the capacity to think about their surroundings and eventually to ponder events to which they were not immediately exposed. This expanded consciousness had an obvious survival value; it enabled our forbearers not only to obtain food and shelter and avoid predators in the vicinity but also to learn from the past, plan ahead, and contemplate circumstances that had not yet occurred. Innumerable adaptive problems could be solved by this broad consciousness and by the capacity for symbol making, shared with fellow creatures.

Today, normal human consciousness is regarded as active and exploratory, as emphasized in the chapters on sensation and perception. Human consciousness seeks information and attempts to impose an organization and interpretation on the events in our awareness, even those that are apparently meaningless. In these efforts to find out about the world and to understand it, human consciousness obviously has survival value.

William James was the first modern psychologist to emphasize the adaptive value of human consciousness, pointing to someone learning to ride a bicycle. While this skill is being developed, James explained, the person is clearly conscious of this activity. There is concentration on steering and balance, pedaling and braking. Slowly, as the habit approaches perfection, consciousness recedes. The bicycle rider pedals down the street planning for the day ahead, thinking about friendships, or simply enjoying to the fullest the sunshine and fresh air (James, 1890).

Similarly, a beginning artist, learning to mix paints, at first proceeds slowly and carefully, concentrating on each step. Eventually, after much practice, the action can be performed with little attention to it. Petra mixed paints without much thought, concentrating instead on the scene before her. Released from close attention to routine tasks, consciousness automatically moves to other matters.

Furthermore, James continued, consciousness is selective. It chooses among the objects and events of potential awareness. It welcomes some and rejects others, depending on their immediate interest.

This selectivity has been discussed in modern terms as partly productive, partly reflective. In the **productive mode,** awareness involves concerted mental activity, setting goals and developing procedures for achieving them. When a studio apartment became available in the old boarding house, Petra thought about moving, considered the financial aspect, and planned to visit, all part of the productive mode. We constantly look ahead, initiate an action, observe the results, and then continue or alter the plan, depending on the consequences (Hilgard, 1980). The productive mode clearly shows the adaptive function of normal human consciousness.

The **reflective mode** involves relaxation, enjoyment of one's own daydreaming, or simply openness to the environment, responding to it as a recipient rather than as a performer. This mode is largely unfocused and unrestrained. Petra often responded to her paintings this way. It may involve exploration of one's awareness, assigning the highest value to the present moment, the immediate experience in an aesthetic sense, detached from the past and future.

This distinction between the productive and reflective modes is imperfect, incomplete, and difficult to maintain, but it has been of value in theory and research on human consciousness (Hilgard, 1980). It reminds us that human consciousness is personal, ever-changing, and continuous and that it is defined as our awareness *at any given moment.*

As Petra lay awake in her new apartment, on that first morning—her daughter's birthday, normal human consciousness made her aware of her surroundings, her feelings, and herself as a unique being. We cannot know in what way it involved the productive and reflective modes, but we do know that she pondered a circumstance that perhaps was only imagined—her daughter's anger and feelings of betrayal at the adoption. In this sense, her normal human consciousness perhaps became maladaptive, producing needless moments of anguish and despair.

In the words of the poet John Milton, "The mind is its own place, and in itself/Can make a heav'n of hell, a hell of heav'n" (*Paradise Lost,* I).

It is entirely possible that Petra's daughter felt loved and secure in her adoptive family. She probably wondered about her origins but she may have felt little or no sense of abandonment.

• SUMMARY •

STUDY OF CONSCIOUSNESS

1. The study of consciousness began with Wilhelm Wundt's use of analytical introspection to identify the basic elements of consciousness. With the rise of John Watson's behaviorism, the study of consciousness was regarded as too subjective for psychological research. Successful investigations in memory, language, and dreaming led to a reemergence of interest in consciousness as part of cognitive psychology.

SLEEP AND DREAMS

2. The 24-hour alternation between activity and inactivity is called a circadian rhythm, which occurs in organisms ranging from insects to human beings. When the individual sleeps, several brain mechanisms induce quiescence; the neurotransmitter known as serotonin may play a role in sleep, apparently through activity in the reticular activating system.

3. Sleep is characterized by at least four stages that differ in depth and pattern of brain waves. The deepest sleep occurs in stages III and IV. Then, when stage I should reappear, rapid eye movements occur, usually a sign of dreaming.

4. Adult human beings dream for about two hours each night; babies spend more time dreaming. People dream about the commonplace in their lives. Stimuli that occur while people are asleep do not play a major role in the content of dreams.

5. Among several theories of dreaming, the psychoanalytic view states that the key issue is the latent content of the dream, which contains unconscious urges and memories. The Jungian approach focuses on all sorts of awareness that can be found in the manifest content. The information processing view regards dreaming as a means of sifting and sorting recent experiences, allowing the sleeper to awaken mentally refreshed.

MEDITATION AND HYPNOSIS

6. In concentrative meditation, there is a single focus; the aim is to fix attention on a specific stimulus, such as a soft light or tone. In mindfulness meditation, attention is directed to objects and events as they arise spontaneously in consciousness; the aim is full awareness of any and all contents of consciousness.

7. There are two dominant theoretical perspectives on hypnosis. One, with a social orientation, states that in hypnosis the individual is engaging in role enactment, simply trying to be a good subject. The other perspective, with a cognitive orientation, states that hypnosis involves a dissociation between two levels of consciousness.

ity of the central nervous system, thereby decreasing pain, anxiety, and related states. Stimulants, including amphetamines, arouse the central nervous system, increasing the individual's alertness and sense of well-being. Hallucinogens do not directly suppress or stimulate the central nervous system but rather produce alterations in perception.

DRUG-INDUCED STATES

8. Psychoactive drugs, which alter consciousness by influencing mood or perception, can be consumed in various ways, but the larger the amounts and the more directly they are brought into the bloodstream, the stronger the reactions.
9. Depressants, such as alcohol, serve to inhibit activ-

NORMAL CONSCIOUSNESS

10. Normal human consciousness appears in a productive mode, which includes setting goals and developing procedures for achieving them, and a reflective mode, in which the individual responds to the environment as a recipient rather than as a performer.

• WORKING WITH PSYCHOLOGY •

REVIEW OF KEY CONCEPTS

consciousness
altered states of consciousness

Study of Consciousness
analytical introspection
stream of consciousness
cognitive psychology

Sleep and Dreams
circadian rhythm
hypnagogic state
nocturnal myoclonia
reticular activating system
serotonin
electroencephalogram (EEG)
rapid eye movements (REMs)
REM rebound effect
insomnia
narcolepsy

sleep apnea
sleepwalking
dreams
lucid dreaming
activation-synthesis hypothesis
manifest content
latent content
dream interpretation
amplification of dreams
information processing viewpoint

Meditation and Hypnosis
meditation
concentrative meditation
mindfulness meditation
hypnosis
analgesia
regression
hypnotic amnesia

role enactment
dissociation view

Drug-Induced States
psychoactive substance
drug dependence
depressants
alcoholism
opiates
stimulants
amphetamines
cocaine
hallucinogens
marijuana
lysergic acid diethylamide (LSD)

Normal Consciousness
productive mode
reflective mode

CLASS DISCUSSION/CRITICAL THINKING

A NARRATIVE TWIST

Consider Petra's daughter years after the adoption, living as a teenager with her foster parents. Indicate the probable themes or contents of some of her dreams. In what ways, if any, might these themes have been similar to those of her birth mother? How might they have been different? Imagine the specific contents of one of her adolescent dreams and, by discussion of some details, show how it might be interpreted from a Freudian, Jungian, or information processing viewpoint.

TOPICAL QUESTIONS

• *Study of Consciousness.* "In the long run, the emphasis on objectiv- ity by the behaviorists was advanta- geous for the study of conscious- ness, which did not reemerge until the necessary advances had occurred in electronic research equipment." Overall, do you agree or disagree with this statement? Explain your reasons.

• *Sleep and Dreams.* Why might one depressed person sleep con- stantly and another experience acute insomnia? Explain your view. Explain why the dreams of men and women of the seventeenth century probably would show more sex dif- ferences than those of men and women today.

• *Meditation and Hypnosis.* Does the mere practice of meditation suggest stress in our current way of life? If lifestyles were more relaxed, would meditation become obsolete? If analgesia, regression, and amnesia are typical reactions in hypnosis, to what degree are pain, maturity, and memory learned responses? In what ways is a hypnotized human being like an animal?

• *Drug-Induced States.* How do the autobiographical accounts of drug use by intellectuals like Aldous Huxley and Samuel Coleridge influence drug use? Should their experiences be publicly ridiculed or ignored? Explain your view.

• *Normal Consciousness.* It has been stated that normal human con- sciousness, in certain respects, is no longer adaptive. Do you agree or disagree? State your reasons.

TOPICS OF RELATED INTEREST

In the brain, the reticular activating system plays a vital role in arousal and sleep (3). The experimental use of drugs can be compared with the therapeutic use (16). Normal human consciousness is revealed in the active and interrelated nature of the senses (4), selective and divided attention in perception (5), and all dimensions of thinking (9).

FUNDAMENTALS OF LEARNING

CONDITIONING AND LEARNING

❧

MEMORY

❧

THOUGHT AND LANGUAGE

❧

CLASSICAL CONDITIONING
Process of Classical Conditioning
Classical Conditioning Principles
Influence of Classical Conditioning

RESPONDENT AND OPERANT BEHAVIOR
Respondent Behavior
Operant Behavior

OPERANT CONDITIONING
Process of Operant Conditioning
Operant Conditioning Principles
Influence of Operant Conditioning

LEARNING COMPLEX RESPONSES
Concept of Chaining
Two-Factor Theory
Observational Learning
Learning and Cognition

7

CONDITIONING
AND LEARNING

THE BELLS HAD STOPPED RINGING. THE MEN HAD MOVED SILENTLY INTO THE GREAT HALL, AND THEY WERE STANDING AT THEIR PLACES IN FRONT OF oaken tables, burnished and smooth from scrubbing and use. Suddenly they filled the hall with a song of grace, in perfect unison, giving thanks and proclaiming their faith. A moment later, the scraping of benches, again in unison and without a word, signaled the start of the evening meal.

This scraping of benches evoked the attention of a very different element of monastic life, a society of scavenger cats. Sleeping and resting on the warm hearths, they were quick to raise their heads and twitch their tails at this familiar sound, which meant that a tender morsel might fall from the tables. Always hungry, they licked their chops in anticipation of raw fish or some other delicacy.

As the brothers consumed bean soup, fish cakes, and ale, Saint Ildefonso rose to make the evening announcements. Among them was a statement about Brother Mendo. A Latin phrase had burst from his lips during the silence of predawn prayers. For this transgression, Brother Mendo would receive the usual punishment in the kitchen, but no mention was made of its length. That would be announced later, leaving Brother Mendo and the reader to contemplate for a while his misdeed and its possible consequences.

During the silent meal, almost imperceptible movements occurred among the brethren in that dining hall: a slow nod here, a half-wink there, a seemingly inward smile. These acts almost seemed like the exchange of friendly greetings. In any case, along with their vows of poverty, chastity, and obedience, the brethren were bound together by thoughts and feelings about communal living.

Monastery life in the Renaissance has been depicted by many writers, but none with more flair for the serious and humorous than Lope de Vega, a seventeenth-century Spanish author recognized as one of the world's most eminent and productive dramatists. He wrote 1,500 plays, often completing one in merely a day. He also fell in love with many women, was imprisoned, then banished from Madrid, and on 29 May 1588 sailed with the Spanish Armada, composing poetry while heading into battle. Later, he briefly pursued the priesthood and, perhaps on this basis, described the forthcoming punishment for Brother Mendo in *El Capellán de la Virgen* (1615). The instructional value of this drama was first brought to attention by a pair of professors at the University of Connecticut, one in Spanish literature, the other in psychology (Bousefield, 1955).

They showed that Lope de Vega's work antedated by more than 300 years psychological concepts reported in this chapter.

With its focus upon life in a Spanish kitchen centuries ago, this narrative serves as a reminder of cultural differences, and it offers a comparison with a kitchen in twentieth-century America and the events that took place there, reported in a term paper by a young woman called Dolores (Pinto, 1992). The occupants of these kitchens lived on different continents, in different eras, with different goals and interests in life, and yet one can propose that their different behaviors, reported in the following pages, arose *in the same ways,* similarly shaped by their very different environments. These environmental influences are prominent in animal behavior as well, as illustrated by the cats in both settings.

In short, this narrative emphasizes that forces in the environment are fundamental factors in human behavior. Specifically, the process of **conditioning,** which is a relatively simple form of learning, arises through associations among stimuli and responses, either accidental or intentional. Conditioning stresses events in the environment, not thought processes inside the head. The term **learning,** much broader in scope, includes conditioning and cognitive processes; it refers to any enduring change in behavior that is the result of experience, rather than illness, maturation, or various physiological adjustments. We shall return to this broader concept of learning at the end of this chapter.

Conditioning processes, because they describe behavior as the function of stimulus–response associations, have been known as *S–R psychology.* Today they are more commonly regarded as part of **behaviorism,** noted for its concern with overt responses and external stimuli rather than internal processes. From this perspective, conditioning is the foundation of human learning, ranging across all cultures.

We begin this chapter with the study of classical conditioning, a relatively simple form of learning. Then, after defining two important concepts, respondent and operant behavior, we examine operant conditioning, which underlies the learning of basic habits and skills. At the close of the chapter, we focus on the learning of complex responses. Thus, the full discussion progresses from relatively simple to higher-level learning.

• CLASSICAL CONDITIONING •

Our modern understanding of classical conditioning began with a Russian physiologist interested in the study of gastric secretions. In fact, he received a Nobel Prize for his work on digestion. Does the name Ivan Pavlov ring a bell?

To study salivation in a live dog, Pavlov and his assistants made an incision in the dog's cheek and inserted rubber tubing, through which the saliva passed into a glass container. In this way, the amount of salivation could be measured in a precise, objective manner. When food was presented, the dog naturally salivated, and studies were made of these physiological processes.

Eventually something happened that caused Pavlov to redirect his interests. As these experiments progressed, the sight of the bowl, the sight of the experimenter, and eventually even the sound of the experimenter's footsteps produced salivation. Pavlov called these learned reactions in the dog *psychic*

secretions to distinguish them from the inborn physiological ones elicited by the food itself, and because they were interfering with his purpose, he felt they should be eliminated or studied directly. Deciding to study them, he changed the focus of his research from physiology to psychology. Today he and his numerous coworkers are generally regarded as psychologists in the Western world, although their work is considered part of physiology in the former Soviet Union (Windholz, 1990).

It had long been known that one's mouth waters at the sound of a dinner bell or some other stimulus related to food, but Pavlov saw in this circumstance a controlled method for investigating mental phenomena in live animals and perhaps human beings. The term *classical* means "in the established manner," which in this case refers to Pavlov's approach to these psychological processes. In **classical conditioning,** a previously neutral stimulus becomes capable of eliciting a certain involuntary response. This common definition serves adequately at this point, although closer inspection shows greater complexity (Rescorla, 1988, 1992). The function of classical conditioning, as will become evident later in the chapter, is primarily to assist the organism in preparing for some forthcoming important event (Kohn & Kalat, 1992).

PROCESS OF CLASSICAL CONDITIONING

Classical conditioning involves a relatively simple modification of involuntary behavior. This behavior is known as *respondent* behavior because the individual responds in an automatic, involuntary manner. Pavlov once referred to this conditioning process as "stimulus substitution": A previously neutral stimulus is substituted for a stimulus that originally elicited the response. The sound of the experimenter's footsteps became a substitute for the food; it too evoked the salivary response. This idea of stimulus substitution is helpful but not entirely accurate because the response to the new stimulus is not necessarily identical to the original response. It may be delayed, more abbreviated, less intense, or slightly different in other ways (Figure 7–1).

CONDITIONING PROCEDURES. In the laboratory, before the conditioning process begins, the new stimulus is tested to ensure that it is neutral. If, by itself, it elicits the response in question, then it is not a neutral stimulus for that response. Pavlov used the sound of a bell as a neutral stimulus for salivation. It did not elicit salivation but perhaps, through conditioning, it could develop the capacity to do so.

The conditioning process began when the bell was sounded on a number of occasions, each time followed by the appearance of food, which evoked the inborn, automatic salivary response. As this pairing was repeated, the sound of the bell developed the capacity to evoke salivation. Conditioning had occurred when this sound alone, a previously neutral stimulus, elicited the salivary response.

How might this process have influenced the monks at the monastery? At the sound of the bell for dinner, they experienced a mildly pleasant reaction, including salivation and other anticipatory responses. Over the years, the ringing of the bell had become a signal or temporary substitute for the food itself, evoking these reactions. For the scavenger cats, the scraping of the benches as the brethren sat down to dinner had become an even more powerful signal, for it immediately preceded a possible meal, intentionally or accidentally dropped from the table. On hearing this sound, they salivated, licked their lips, and twitched their tails in reflexlike fashion (Table 7–1).

A modern factory worker experienced this

FIGURE 7–1 IVAN PAVLOV AND ASSOCIATES. Third from the left, not counting the dog, Pavlov was a professor of physiology in a military school before his appointment to the Russian Academy of Sciences where he studied the principles of classical conditioning.

SUBJECTS	SIGNALS
Pavlov's dogs	Experimenter's footsteps
Monks in the monastery	Dinner bell
Scavenger cats	Scraping of benches

TABLE 7–1 LEARNING SIGNALS. The dogs, monks, and cats all learned different signals, but the process was the same. A previously neutral stimulus, immediately preceding the appearance of food, became a signal for that event.

outcome—with an unusual twist. A freight train went by his workplace each morning at 11:30, just before his lunch break, and eventually he felt the desire for lunch whenever he heard the train. Then he was transferred to a factory 80 miles north, alongside the same railroad track. The same train passed each day two hours earlier. Whenever he heard it, he felt hungry, although he had never considered eating lunch at 9:30 in the morning.

BASIC TERMS. Food automatically elicits salivation, and therefore Pavlov called this stimulus the *unconditional stimulus,* meaning that no learning, or conditioning, was required. It led naturally to the salivary response, which he called the *unconditional reflex.* But when the sound of the bell prompted the dog to salivate, he designated salivation as a *conditional reflex,* which emphasized that it depended on a certain process—the pairing of the neutral stimulus with an automatic or natural one (Pavlov, 1927).

In translation, the Russian word *ouslovny* became "conditioned" rather than "conditional," leading to widespread use of the adjective *conditioned.* In later research it became apparent that many conditioned reactions, strictly speaking, are not reflexes. For these reasons, the following terms have come into general usage today: There is the natural or **unconditioned stimulus** (US), which automatically evokes a certain response, without prior learn-

ing, and there is the **unconditioned response** (UR), elicited by the unconditioned stimulus. The unconditioned stimulus automatically evokes that response. No learning is required.

In addition, there is a neutral stimulus; it has no original capacity to elicit the response in question. Through pairing with the unconditioned stimulus, eventually it becomes a **conditioned stimulus** (CS), capable itself of eliciting the response. That response is then called the **conditioned response** (CR) because it is elicited by the newly developed conditioned stimulus.

One statement depicts this process: In classical conditioning, a previously neutral stimulus acquires the capacity to evoke a certain response.

An example should provide further clarification. Walking in the woods in a foreign country, you encounter this sign: SREGNITS. It means nothing to you. It is a neutral stimulus for anxiety or fear. Almost immediately, you are stung by a swarm of bees. The next day you pass this sign elsewhere, and again you are stung by bees. On the third day, you become anxious as soon as you see the sign, and yet you are stung again. Do you need more trials? No! That sign has changed from a neutral stimulus to a conditioned stimulus, and your anxiety on viewing it is a conditioned response.

The unconditioned stimulus in this instance is the bee sting. It automatically causes anxiety and discomfort, without learning of any sort.

Notice the timing. The neutral stimulus, the meaningless sign, appears first, *before* the sting of the bees. Thus, it becomes a signal for what will happen next, an attack by the insects. This process is normal or forward conditioning, and learning is often rapid. If the sign appeared instead at the moment when the bees began to sting, eventually you might become afraid of it, but learning would be slower. And if you encountered the sign only *after* being ravaged by the bees, it would hardly function as a signal!

CLASSICAL CONDITIONING PRINCIPLES

The early findings from Pavlov's laboratory have been amplified by modern research that focuses on how this form of learning originates, how it is modified, and how it disappears. The primary concern is with the principles in the learning process, not with salivation or any other response used for studying it. Pavlov's expectation, borne out in much subsequent research, was that many physiological and emotional reactions are acquired in this way (Pavlov, 1927; Figure 7–2).

Pavlov's dog learned to salivate to the sight of the bowl and to the experimenter's footsteps, but no conditioning was intended. These responses arose by chance, through accidental conditioning. Many such responses are acquired by human beings and animals in this way. It was partly through classical conditioning that the monks in the monastery, including Brother Mendo, experienced a pleasant reaction when they viewed the oaken tables. This furniture had been paired with many a happy feast. The garden gate, too, evoked a pleasant feeling. After passing through it, the monks each day enjoyed a half hour of warm sunlight and the chirping of birds in the beautiful flower garden. The table, gate, and other objects, presumably neutral stimuli before these pairings, thus became conditioned stimuli.

TIME SEQUENCES. Any one of three sequences can result in classical conditioning. In one, called **simultaneous conditioning,** the neutral and unconditioned stimuli are present only at the same time. For example, the bell is rung only when food is present. The stimuli commence and cease simultaneously.

In another sequence, **delayed conditioning,** the neutral stimulus appears first and continues to be present during the appearance of the unconditioned stimulus. The bell is rung, and while it is ringing the food is presented. This sequence is the most common form of classical conditioning.

In **trace conditioning,** the neutral stimulus does not appear with the unconditioned stimulus. It appears first, then disappears, and then the unconditioned stimulus appears. In Pavlov's laboratory and at the monastery, the bell was rung and then, some moments after it had stopped ringing, the meal was served. A memory or *memory trace* of the sound remained in the listener's mind when the meal became available, and the conditioning process depended on this trace.

Considerable research has shown that the delayed and trace procedures result in faster and stronger learning than does simultaneous conditioning. The most effective CS–US interval, measured from the onset of each stimulus, has been said to be approximately one-half second, though it varies considerably with different responses and different species (Hill, 1981; Tarpy, 1975). Among

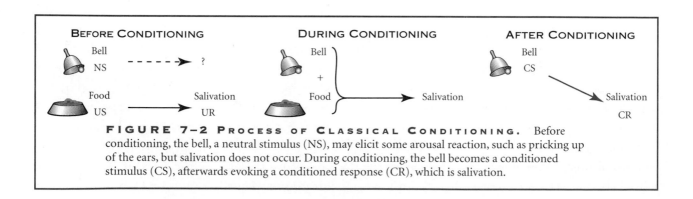

FIGURE 7–2 PROCESS OF CLASSICAL CONDITIONING. Before conditioning, the bell, a neutral stimulus (NS), may elicit some arousal reaction, such as pricking up of the ears, but salivation does not occur. During conditioning, the bell becomes a conditioned stimulus (CS), afterwards evoking a conditioned response (CR), which is salivation.

human beings the timing is not as important as among animals, for human beings have greater ability to make mental connections between temporally distant stimuli (Figure 7–3).

In this context, we should mention **backward conditioning,** in which the unconditioned stimulus precedes the neutral stimulus. The dog is fed and *then* the bell is rung. The bees sting you, and then the sign appears. This procedure does not produce significant conditioning, showing that the sequence of presentation is important. The primary factor in all conditioning is that the conditioned stimulus becomes a *signal* that the unconditioned stimulus is about to occur. In backward conditioning there is no signal.

STIMULUS GENERALIZATION. Suppose the monastery bell developed a crack. Would its slightly different sound evoke a salivary reaction among the brethren? Suppose Pavlov used a different bell? Would it still evoke this reaction? If so, stimulus generalization would have occurred. In **stimulus generalization,** a conditioned response is evoked by a stimulus that is not identical but merely similar to the conditioned stimulus.

In this case, the magnitude of the response depends on the characteristics of the new stimulus. The greater the similarity between the new and conditioned stimuli, the larger will be the response.

Pavlov found that a certain buzzer produced much the same reaction as the bell, and he attributed this reaction to a spread of effects from one region of the brain to other parts not previously excited.

A baby with a bladder ailment was taken regularly for painful medical treatments. She became quite fearful of doctors, especially those in long white coats, which she associated with the examinations and treatments. One day her sister took her to a restaurant where the busboys wore short white coats. As soon as she saw them, she began screaming and crying. She was too young to know about stimulus generalization and other psychological terms. She simply knew that she did not like white coats of any sort. That was the long and short of it.

DISCRIMINATION. In the process of **discrimination,** an individual learns the difference between two or more stimuli, responding only to the correct stimulus, not to others that may be similar. Pavlov taught his laboratory animals to make a discrimination between a large black *I*, the conditioned stimulus, and similar but not identical geometric patterns. When one of the similar patterns was presented, the dog at first salivated, but when this figure appeared several times without being followed by food, salivation gradually disappeared (Pavlov, 1927).

Discrimination eventually takes place whenever

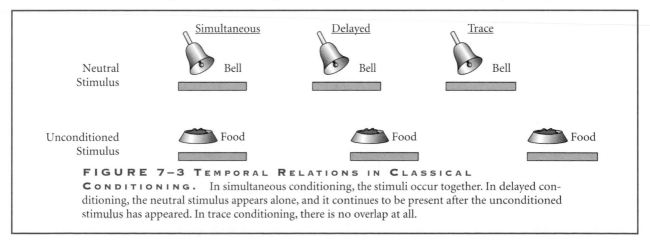

FIGURE 7–3 TEMPORAL RELATIONS IN CLASSICAL CONDITIONING. In simultaneous conditioning, the stimuli occur together. In delayed conditioning, the neutral stimulus appears alone, and it continues to be present after the unconditioned stimulus has appeared. In trace conditioning, there is no overlap at all.

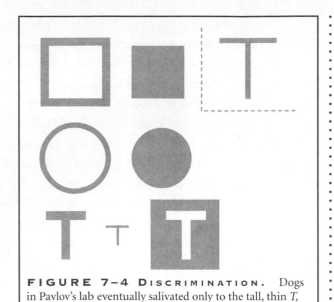

FIGURE 7–4 DISCRIMINATION. Dogs in Pavlov's lab eventually salivated only to the tall, thin *T*, the figure followed by the unconditioned stimulus.

the unconditioned stimulus always follows the conditioned stimulus but never follows other stimuli. After a while, the other stimuli cease to elicit a response (Figure 7–4). At the monastery, the brethren salivated to the dinner bell but not to the prayer bell, which was never followed by food. In other words, discrimination is essentially the opposite of stimulus generalization (Figure 7–5).

EXTINCTION AND SPONTANEOUS RECOVERY.
Once a conditioned response has been formed, how can it be eliminated? The most widely used method is to present the conditioned stimulus repeatedly without the unconditioned stimulus, a process called **extinction.** Gradually, the conditioned stimulus loses its acquired capacity. Pavlov's dog, after continued exposure to the bell without food, ceased to salivate to the bell. The conditioned response disappeared.

If the monks at the monastery became scrupulously careful about not dropping food, and yet the cats were exposed daily to their scraping benches, eventually this sound would lose its significance. The cats' reflexlike reactions of licking their chops and twitching their tails would not be elicited.

After a response has undergone extinction, it has not necessarily disappeared. Following an interval when the conditioned stimulus is not presented, the previously extinguished response may reappear, an outcome called **spontaneous recovery.** It is an inhibition, or forgetting, of extinction, showing that extinction is not necessarily permanent. For example, a child's fear of barking dogs may reappear after it has been extinguished if the child has not been in contact with dogs for an extended period. As Pavlov noted, however, spontaneous recovery grows weaker after each extinction. Continued extinction of a conditioned response produces less and less spontaneous recovery, until eventually the conditioned response fails to appear at all.

HIGHER-ORDER CONDITIONING.
In his laboratory, Pavlov found that a conditioned stimulus could serve as an "unconditioned stimulus." In this process, called **higher-order conditioning,** a neutral stimulus becomes a conditioned stimulus *without* ever being paired with an unconditioned stimulus; instead, it is paired with a conditioned stimulus.

In Pavlov's laboratory, the sound of a bell was paired with food, and it became a conditioned stimulus, leading to salivation in the dog. This procedure was *normal, first-order conditioning* because an *un*conditioned stimulus, the food, was used. In the next phase, called *second-order conditioning,* a light was employed as the neutral stimulus, and it was paired with the bell, which was not an unconditioned stimulus. Rather, it had just become a conditioned stimulus through pairing with the food. After being paired with the bell on several occasions, the light also became a conditioned stimulus sufficient to elicit the salivary response. Second-order conditioning had occurred, for a second conditioned stimulus had been developed, this one *without* the use of an unconditioned stimulus.

Suppose that a tap on the nose is then paired with the light. It too is *never* paired with food. If

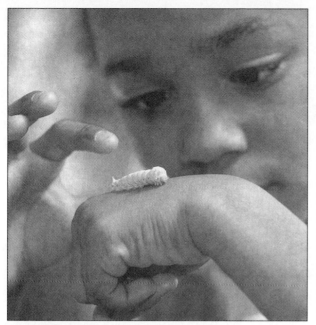

FIGURE 7–5 GENERALIZATION AND DISCRIMINATION. A child stung by a bee often fears other flying, buzzing insects. This outcome is efficient; through generalization, the child need not learn that the horsefly, for example may be dangerous. If the child fears all other insects, that response is inefficient. The child needs to develop a discrimination, learning that caterpillars and related creatures are not dangerous.

the tap eventually becomes effective in eliciting salivation, that process would be known as *third-order conditioning*, for it results in a third conditioned stimulus, again without using the unconditioned stimulus (Figure 7–6).

The key point in higher-order conditioning is that a neutral stimulus becomes a conditioned stimulus through pairing with a *previously conditioned stimulus* rather than with an unconditioned stimulus. Otherwise, the process is no different from first-order conditioning.

Pavlov experienced difficulty in obtaining more than second-order conditioning in dogs because the conditioned stimulus became extinguished after being used many times without the unconditioned stimulus. Pavlov believed that third-order, fourth-order, and higher levels of conditioning are possible with human beings. There is still debate on this issue, but most contemporary experts accept the concept of at least second-order conditioning in human beings and various animals (Barnet, Grahame, & Miller, 1991; Rescorla, 1988).

Higher-order conditioning also illustrates that a given stimulus cannot be identified as an unconditioned stimulus or a conditioned stimulus without reference to the way in which it is used. A bell can serve as a neutral stimulus in salivary conditioning; it can become a conditioned stimulus for salivation; and it can serve as an unconditioned stimulus for awakening someone.

ONE-TRIAL CONDITIONING. The conditioned response is usually built up gradually, but it also can develop through a single pairing of two stimuli, called **one-trial conditioning**. In these cases, the unconditioned stimulus may be of high intensity or prolonged, which is what happened in the case of Brother Mendo.

Saint Ildefonso finally announced his sentence: a week on the cold, hard kitchen floor. Apart from

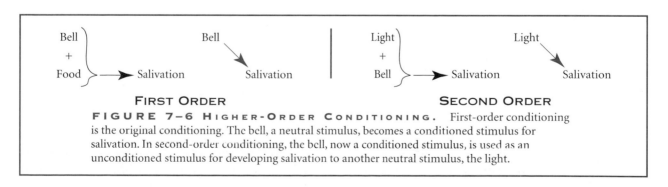

FIRST ORDER   **SECOND ORDER**

FIGURE 7–6 HIGHER-ORDER CONDITIONING. First-order conditioning is the original conditioning. The bell, a neutral stimulus, becomes a conditioned stimulus for salivation. In second-order conditioning, the bell, now a conditioned stimulus, is used as an unconditioned stimulus for developing salivation to another neutral stimulus, the light.

the humiliation of sitting at everyone's feet, the damp chill would make Brother Mendo shiver and shake constantly, and those unrelenting stones would make him ache and feel stiff. After his release from this one-trial conditioning, admittedly a long trial, just the sight of the floor would make him shiver and shudder a bit. All of the brothers punished in this manner detested that spot in the center of the floor.

Accidents commonly result in one-trial conditioning. In 20th-century America, a college student went for a drive in the country to celebrate the beginning of summer. While she was enjoying the fresh air and heavy fragrance of yellow jasmine, an oncoming car careened directly into her lane. There was a collision. The driver of the other car had fallen asleep, and the impact sent both cars into a field of yellow jasmine. Dazed and injured in the crash, for a long time afterward the young woman experienced a conditioned response. Her stomach tightened and she felt a bit queasy whenever she smelled yellow jasmine.

MULTIPLE CONDITIONED STIMULI. In his laboratory, Pavlov rang the bell to provide a specific stimulus, but he recognized that all sorts of stimuli can become conditioned, including the experimenter's footsteps and the dish containing the food. When we speak of *a* conditioned stimulus or *the* conditioned stimulus, we are simply citing a prominent stimulus that became conditioned. Modern research indicates that numerous associations can be formed in the conditioning process (Rescorla, 1988).

The ease with which certain stimuli become conditioned has interested experimental psychologists. Some become strongly conditioned on a single trial; others become conditioned weakly or not at all. According to this view, human beings and certain animals have a *biological preparedness* for certain instances and forms of conditioning (Seligman, 1970). For example, stimuli associated with

snakes are more fear-arousing and more resistant to extinction than stimuli associated with flowers (McNally, 1987). This difference in the acquisition and extinction of conditioned stimuli suggests that there is an evolutionary basis in the human predisposition to shun snakes and smell flowers.

To explore this hypothesis, several groups of water-deprived rats were treated in various ways, two of which deserve special attention. Both groups drank sweetened water from a spout that gave off a bright light and a clicking sound whenever it was licked. Thus, all rats drank "sweet, bright, noisy" water. Afterwards, the members of one group received an electric shock to the feet whenever they were drinking. The others received radiation poisoning that induced nausea an hour later.

The rats in each group were then tested with two different kinds of water. Some of those that received the shock were offered sweetened water, which they drank. Others were offered bright-noisy water, which they refused. Those that received the poison were tested in the same way, and they responded in the opposite manner, refusing the sweetened water and drinking the bright-noisy water (Figure 7–7). In other words, light and sound became conditioned when the stimulus was electric shock; the flavor became conditioned when the stimulus was nausea from the poison (Garcia & Koelling, 1966).

These outcomes confirmed the view that the associations in classical conditioning are not arbitrary. Some connections are more readily formed than others, perhaps because natural selection favors certain outcomes, as when wild rats become bait shy. They learn to avoid the poisoned food, but they do not avoid the place where they became poisoned. In other words, numerous stimuli may become conditioned stimuli, but we must also recognize a biological preparedness. When the unconditioned stimulus produces illness, flavors

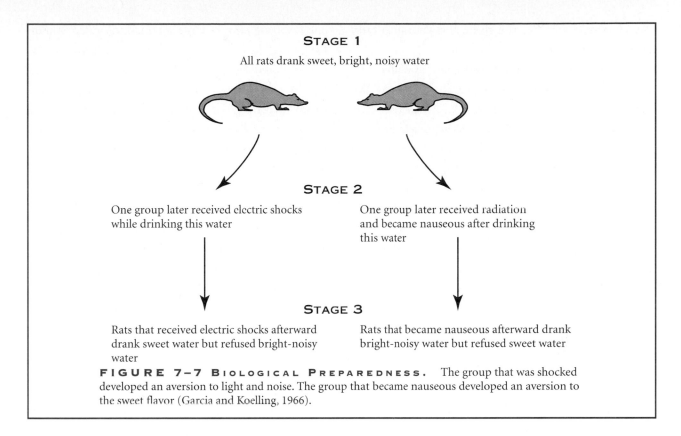

STAGE 1

All rats drank sweet, bright, noisy water

STAGE 2

One group later received electric shocks while drinking this water

One group later received radiation and became nauseous after drinking this water

STAGE 3

Rats that received electric shocks afterward drank sweet water but refused bright-noisy water

Rats that became nauseous afterward drank bright-noisy water but refused sweet water

FIGURE 7–7 BIOLOGICAL PREPAREDNESS. The group that was shocked developed an aversion to light and noise. The group that became nauseous developed an aversion to the sweet flavor (Garcia and Koelling, 1966).

and odors apparently become the conditioned cues. When the unconditioned stimulus produces pain, sights and sounds may become the important cues.

INFLUENCE OF CLASSICAL CONDITIONING

Ivan Pavlov's confidence in his studies led him to declare that "different kinds of habits based on training, education and discipline . . . are nothing but a long chain of conditioned reflexes" (1927). Most psychologists consider this statement oversimplified, although the influence of classical conditioning is widely recognized in a broad array of human activities. Practical applications have been found in such diverse problems as gambling, disease, and drug tolerance (Ban & Guy, 1985; Brown, 1986; Siegel, 1983). Probably the most common use occurs in advertising.

In the modern view, classical conditioning serves a broad signaling function. By this process, an organism learns about its environment; it prepares itself for some impending event (Kohn & Kalat, 1992).

In the monastery, the cats twitched their tails at the sound of the scraping benches. Formerly punished brethren, whenever they passed the kitchen floor, shuddered a bit, reliving their confinement. In our era, as just indicated, the sound of a train, the sight of busboys' coats, and the odor of yellow jasmine all have served in this same way, eliciting responses associated with an earlier event.

TESTING SENSORY ABILITIES. With this potential, classical conditioning procedures have been used to assess the sensory ability of infants, some handicapped people, and animals. In a clinic for hearing and speech disorders, suppose that an infant does not respond to certain sounds. How can we decide whether the child, too young to talk, has normal hearing?

While more modern methods are available, the use of classical conditioning is readily illustrated. We can gently prick the infant's foot and find that it is withdrawn. If so, the pinprick is an unconditioned stimulus for foot withdrawal. If we ring a bell in advance of the pinprick on each of several occasions, eventually the child with normal hearing withdraws the foot at the sound of the bell alone. We thus know that the infant's auditory mechanisms are functioning satisfactorily for this sound; some other factor must be causing its lack of reaction to certain sounds. There are, of course, certain constraints in using this procedure, but the conditioning process is successful even with very young infants.

TRAINING ANIMALS. To test for drugs after a horse race, for example, the animal must urinate, and yet no inspector wants to stand around, bottle in hand, waiting for that moment. Instead, at the horse trainer's whistle, the beast responds—usually. How does that happen? The answer lies in early conditioning. Soon after the animal's birth, the trainer whistles every time the newborn urinates naturally, and this practice of simultaneous conditioning is continued for months. As an adult, the horse cannot be made to urinate if it has no need to do so, but it can be helped to relax, and thereby to behave reflexively, by whistling the appropriate tune.

Classical conditioning is widely used for teaching animals the meaning of a verbal signal, such as "Bad Charlie." The words are spoken and then the dog perhaps is struck with a newspaper, causing it to cower and tremble. In the same manner, the animal learns "Good Charlie." The words are uttered and then the dog is fed and hugged. After several pairings, the dog wriggles or cowers at these previously neutral words. The dog does not understand language in any significant way; the hugging

and swatting simply serve as unconditioned stimuli following the vocal tone, which becomes a conditioned stimulus.

Many household animals also become trained unintentionally in this way, responding to the can opener, the sound of keys, or even the mail carrier's footsteps. Signal learning of this sort goes on throughout the lives of many domesticated animals.

DEVELOPMENT OF EMOTIONAL REACTIONS. The most widespread influence of classical conditioning lies in the development of attitudes and feelings among human beings. Conditioned responses of this sort pervade everyday life, as readily evident in the foregoing examples from Renaissance Spain and modern America.

Notice that these examples often involve negative emotional reactions. It is sad but true that there seem to be more instances of negative than positive emotional conditioning, surely because there are so many untoward events that befall all of us (Figure 7–8).

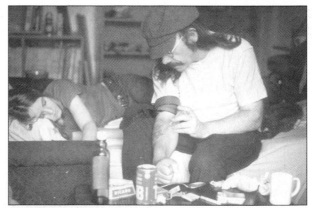

FIGURE 7–8 CONDITIONED DRUG REACTIONS.   The injection of a drug is an unconditioned stimulus for lowered blood pressure, increased respiration, and other compensatory reactions. When a drug is regularly injected in the same environment, that environment becomes a conditioned stimulus, evoking these compensatory reactions. When a customary high dose is used in novel surroundings, these compensatory responses are not activated. The body's conditioned countermeasures are not called forth, and the physiological effects of the drug are stronger than usual, increasing the chances of a fatality (Siegel, 1983).

It should be emphasized that positive feelings also can be acquired through classical conditioning. A student reported how she became fond of a cream-colored jeep in this way. Owned by her first boyfriend, it was associated with tasty dinners, hugging, fresh air, and a multitude of other good times. Seeing that car arriving and stopping at her house, she said, was enough to elicit a very definite feeling of excitement, of butterflies in the stomach. During that intense period of being in love, she experienced the same emotional reaction at the sight of any cream-colored jeep she happened to see in the street (Figure 7–9).

Through conditioning, even mildly aversive stimuli can evoke a positive response. Your author once entered an animal psychology laboratory and encountered what he considered to be the usual foul odor of animal research labs. His young daughter exclaimed, "Oh, I *love* that smell." Then she added, "It reminds me of Snoopy." Odors commonly become conditioned stimuli, and Snoopy had provided her with cuddliness and warmth in earlier days. Snoopy was her pet white rat.

FIGURE 7–9 CLASSICAL CONDITIONING IN ADVERTISING. Advertisers aim to develop positive emotional responses to their products. To achieve this goal, they use classical conditioning, associating the product—such as fishing gear, clothes, or a vacation tour—with a beautiful person, delicious food, peaceful nature scene, or all of these stimuli, thereby eliciting a positive emotional reaction.

Why do we love our mothers, according to Ivan Pavlov? The answer was partly in front of our baby faces. Mother was paired with milk, warmth, cuddliness, and support from our very first days. For most of us, this early pairing of mother with all sorts of comforts lasts quite a long time, augmented or diminished by events in subsequent years.

How do you make people fall in love with you, according to Pavlov? The answer is—by pairing yourself with appropriate stimuli. When you are with your target person, try to avoid smog, flat tires, and food poisoning, and certainly stay away from the income tax. Pair yourself with laughter, good food, warmth, and pleasant music. And if you have an opportunity, pair yourself with appropriate stimulation of free nerve endings in various parts of the body of your target person. Afterward, he or she may begin to tremble a bit and declare, "I'm in love with you." You'll know that this response is partly a conditioned emotional reaction—love, Pavlovian style.

• RESPONDENT AND OPERANT BEHAVIOR •

A careful distinction must be made at this point. We shall turn shortly to another form of conditioning, called operant conditioning, and therefore we must recognize another form of behavior, operant behavior. It differs significantly from respondent behavior, just discussed in the context of classical conditioning.

RESPONDENT BEHAVIOR

The cats licked their chops at the sound of the scraping benches; punished monks felt a bit anxious when confronted with the kitchen floor. Pavlov studied the acquisition of these emotional and physiological reactions through classical conditioning. He was interested in behavior automatically *elicited* by a stimulus. This behavior is called **respondent behavior** because it occurs as an automatic response to a specific stimulus. The individual responds involuntarily, without intending to do so.

In animals and human beings, we note responses that are inborn and puppetlike, called reflexes. A *reflex* is a relatively simple, involuntary reaction to some stimulus, typically involving a specific part of the body. A depressor applied to the back of the tongue produces the gagging reflex. A tap on the knee causes the patellar reflex, or knee jerk. The chill of winter made the brethren at the monastery shiver. All of these are respondent behaviors, inborn responses to specific stimuli.

The influence of classical conditioning is not restricted to these rather narrow, overt reactions, however. Other respondent behaviors are more subtle: The palms perspire; the pupils dilate; breathing becomes heavier. Still others are more diffuse, such as feelings of fear, hunger, love, and other emotions. A major part of everyday life, they are influenced not only by conditioning but also by cognitive processes, considered later.

The point to be appreciated here is that respondent behaviors, however broad or narrow, are "extracted," so to speak, by some specific stimulus in the environment. Goose bumps elicited by cold are an inborn reflex. Goose bumps elicited by the sight of a stone floor or the sound of an old school song are a conditioned response, acquired through classical conditioning. Regardless of how they originate and the stimulus by which they are elicited, respondent behaviors tend to be physiological and emotional, involving the smooth muscles and glands, as in perspiring, feeling nauseous, feeling elated, and so forth.

❧

OPERANT BEHAVIOR

How do we cope with these emotional reactions? What do we do about them? Poor Brother Mendo finally began his lengthy stay on the kitchen floor,

and he felt immediate discomfort. How would he cope with his distress?

Our coping behavior apparently emerges under circumstances quite different from those accompanying respondent behavior. This behavior is called **operant behavior** because the organism responds in a voluntary manner, operating on its environment, producing a certain outcome. This behavior is not elicited automatically by some stimulus; it is *emitted* voluntarily by the individual. Operant behavior was of special interest to B. F. Skinner, an active and eminent figure in psychology for 60 years (Lattal, 1992).

The forms of operant behaviors are endless. They include virtually all voluntary efforts at adjustment. A punished monk attempts to escape from the kitchen floor; scavenger cats want to satisfy their hunger. These responses usually involve the skeletal muscles, as the individual deals with the situation by praying, running, reading, writing, hiding, speaking, and so forth. These behaviors generally have an effect on the environment and, unlike respondent behavior, the individual is free to emit or not to emit them. Behavior of this sort is sometimes called a *free operant*. It is also known as *instrumental behavior*, for it is instrumental in achieving a certain outcome.

Operant behaviors are learned chiefly through their consequences. The individual does whatever works best in a given situation, at least at the moment. Sometimes this activity is intentional. Sometimes it occurs without full awareness. In both cases, the behavior may become a habit, depending on the effect it produces in the environment.

In summary, there are two broad classes of behavior, respondent and operant, and they differ in the degree to which they are under the individual's control. Respondent behaviors are essentially involuntary, concerning feelings and reflexive physiology. They are elicited by the environment. Operant behaviors are more voluntary, emitted by the individual as he or she deals with some event in the environment.

With this discussion of two kinds of behavior, we turn for a moment from the scavenger cats in the monastery to experimental cats in a psychologist's "puzzle box" at the turn of this century. Here we begin to consider operant conditioning.

The problem for these experimental cats, studied by an American psychologist named E. L. Thorndike, was to escape from the box and reach a nearby dish of food. Each food-deprived animal, tested individually, engaged in various random behaviors in the box, such as walking, scratching, pawing, stretching, and so forth, and eventually it pulled on a latch in the prescribed manner. Then the door opened; the cat escaped; and it consumed the food. On subsequent trials it pushed the latch correctly earlier and earlier.

The same result occurred when the cat was required to pull on a loop, bump a pole, or produce some other specific response to gain its release. The animal at first responded in various ways but eventually, immediately after it was placed in the box, it repeated the behavior it had emitted just prior to its escape. Thus the cat's behavior was molded by the environment. Such behaviors are said to follow the **reinforcement principle,** formerly called the *law of effect:* An organism tends to repeat those behaviors that bring about satisfaction, and it tends to discard those that bring about dissatisfaction or annoyance (Thorndike, 1898, 1911).

Later, B. F. Skinner began to study this process in detail, using rats and pigeons in laboratory experiments. He became a highly visible figure in the field of psychology, especially in studies of this form of learning, which he called operant conditioning (Iversen, 1992). Expressed simply, in **operant conditioning** behavior is determined by its consequences; an organism operates on its environment, and the probability of a given response depends on its prior consequences.

PROCESS OF OPERANT CONDITIONING

There are two basic differences between Pavlov's classical conditioning and Skinner's operant conditioning. The behavior is involuntary in classical conditioning, and the focus is on the meaning of a stimulus. The behavior is voluntary in operant conditioning, and the concern is with the consequences of the behavior (Table 7–2). This distinction between meanings and consequences will be considered again, in detail, later.

	CLASSICAL CONDITIONING	OPERANT CONDITIONING
Type of behavior	Involuntary responses; reflexes, glandular reactions.	Voluntary responses; reactions of the skeletal muscles.
Learning outcome	A formerly neutral stimulus signals a forthcoming event.	An operant response produces certain consequences, solving a problem.
Typical example	The scraping of benches elicited salivation in the cats.	The cats ran to find fallen food, thereby obtaining a meal.

TABLE 7–2 COMPARISON OF CLASSICAL AND OPERANT CONDITIONING. There are similarities and differences in these processes. Only the principal differences are indicated here.

The basic idea in operant conditioning is that behavior is determined *by its consequences.* We engage in operant behavior, and it has certain consequences. Behavior that produces positive consequences tends to be repeated.

Brother Mendo, in the early stages of his long confinement, alleviated his pain a bit by humming little tunes to himself. This behavior made him feel better, and so he continued to sing softly to himself. The monastery cats also emitted behaviors that produced positive consequences. At the proper moment, they scampered from their warm hearth to snatch a scrap of food dropped from the tables. Even an infrequent morsel was enough to keep them at this task.

In addition, operant behavior is sustained by eliminating negative consequences. A cook in any kitchen, after burning himself, adopts a different procedure. If he invariably is not burned using the new procedure, he is likely to repeat it. In the same way, a person trying to operate a keyboard, ride a bicycle, or solve some other problem also adopts behavior which gains positive outcomes or wards off negative outcomes. Operant behaviors are supported by their consequences.

Conditioning Procedures. In the laboratory, the experimental animal typically is placed in a *Skinner box,* more technically referred to as an *operant chamber,* which contains a lever and a device for dispensing food or water. There is no research interest in lever pressing per se but, as in Pavlov's work with salivation, this behavior is convenient for studying the conditioning process.

A food-deprived rat is free to move within the confined area, and eventually it presses the lever that triggers the food-delivery mechanism, producing a food pellet. After gaining this outcome, the subject continues its apparently random activity, but sooner or later it presses the lever again, obtaining another pellet. As time passes, the lever is pressed more and more frequently; finally, the rat, like the cats in the box, consistently operates the lever to obtain a favorable outcome, in this case food pellets (Figure 7–10).

The central concept here is **reinforcement,** which is any outcome following a response that increases the probability of a recurrence of that response. Whenever a person operates on the environment and obtains food, a smile, or a pat on the back, or avoids a spanking, a parking fine, or an illness, the probability increases that the individual will operate on its environment in this same way in the future. People sometimes speak of reward and punishment in these contexts, but these terms also have popular meanings and generally are not used in studies of conditioning processes.

To be more specific, in **positive reinforcement** the *appearance* of food, an *A* in school, or some comparable event increases the probability that a response will be repeated. Negative reinforcement, in contrast, involves the removal of an object or circumstance. In **negative reinforcement** the *disappearance* of extreme heat, confinement, or some comparable event increases the probability of a repetition of the response. All reinforcement, positive *or* negative, increases the likelihood that the preceding response will be repeated. The difference is this: In positive reinforcement, a satisfier appears; in negative reinforcement, an annoyer disappears.

The term *reward* is less precise, for it does not indicate whether the outcome involves the appearance or disappearance of a particular event. This lack of precision also occurs with punishment. In its popular use, *punishment* might refer to a spanking, which is the appearance of an event, or the loss of an allowance, which is the disappearance of some circumstance. For these reasons, many traditional behaviorists avoid the concept of punishment, as well as the practice of punishment, as noted later. The important point to note here is that negative reinforcement does *not* mean punishment. It is the *removal* of an aversive situation; it is a favorable event, a form of "reward" with many useful appli-

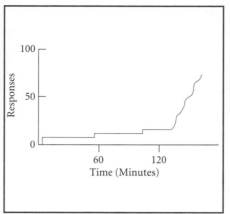

FIGURE 7–10 B. F. SKINNER AND OPERANT CONDITIONING.
When the rat presses the lever in this apparatus, food is delivered. As the graph shows, no lever presses occurred for the first 5 or 10 minutes; then they increased gradually; and after 2 hours they increased sharply.

cations, even in school, for it increases the probability of a certain response (Tauber, 1990; Table 7–3).

To simplify things, the term *reinforcement*, when used without a modifier, refers to a positive reinforcement, and we follow this use throughout these discussions. Remember, all reinforcement increases the probability of behavior.

BASIC TERMS. Other elements of operant conditioning are less specific than those for classical conditioning, primarily because in operant conditioning it is difficult to identify the original stimulus—the stimulus that first evoked the response. In lever pressing it may have been the sight of the lever, smells associated with the box, stimuli within the rat, or some combination

of these factors. The rat did press the lever, however, and this voluntary behavior, an **operant response,** had an effect on the environment. It produced a **reinforcing stimulus,** the food, thereby increasing the probability that this response will be repeated.

Sometimes another stimulus plays a role. Called a **discriminative stimulus,** it indicates when reinforcement is available. When the discriminative stimulus is present, a proper response will be reinforced. This stimulus does *not* automatically elicit the response, as in classical conditioning. Rather, it signals that reinforcement is available—if the response is emitted. In the Skinner box, perhaps food pellets are available only when a light is lit. Very quickly, the rat learns to press the lever when the light appears. Otherwise, it ignores the lever.

	DISPOSITION	
	Presentation	Removal
Positive	*Positive reinforcement.* Example: Receiving praise	*Deprivation.* Example: Losing a privilege
STIMULUS		
Negative	*Punishment.* Example: Receiving a spanking	*Negative reinforcement.* Example: Avoiding criticism

TABLE 7–3 CONSEQUENCES IN OPERANT CONDITIONING. Reinforcement, positive or negative, increases the probability of a response. Punishment and deprivation decrease the probability of a response.

This sequence tends to be repeated until the organism is no longer motivated to seek reinforcement (Figure 7–11).

It is not always possible to identify a discriminative stimulus, but one certainly seems evident in the plight of poor Brother Mendo, for his punishment was worse than yet described. He was required to eat his meals from the kitchen floor in the company of the monastery cats, and Saint Ildefonso forbade any punished monk to touch those fearless creatures. Accustomed to encountering one of the brethren in this predicament, they drove him wild by stealing his choicest morsels. For Brother Mendo, the kitchen floor was humiliating, painful, and frustrating, and it deprived him of his meals.

For the pesky scavenger cats, the operant cycle is readily evident. Brother Mendo's newly filled dish was a discriminative stimulus; stealing that food was their operant response; and having a meal was reinforcement.

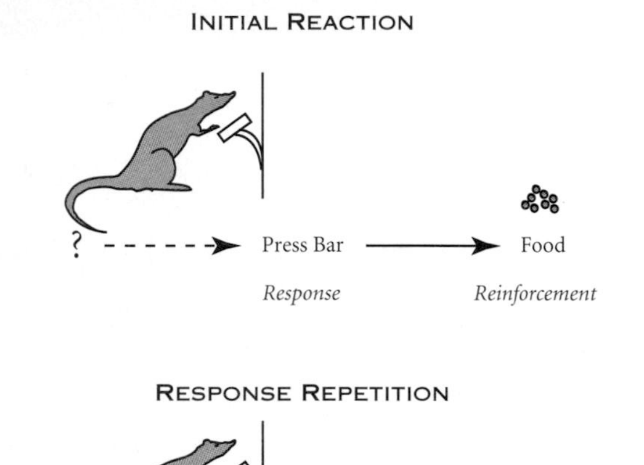

❧

OPERANT CONDITIONING PRINCIPLES

In operant conditioning, the acquisition of a response usually requires several trials, just as in classical conditioning. These two conditioning processes, classical and operant, also share other principles, specifically: stimulus generalization, discrimination, extinction, and spontaneous recovery. They also differ in certain respects.

Insofar as a discriminative stimulus can be identified, **stimulus generalization** occurs when a stimulus *not* used in the original conditioning evokes the response. For example, a rat that has learned to press a lever may press a similar handle or bar, demonstrating stimulus generalization. In **discrimination,** the subject learns to respond only to certain stimuli and not to others. Only the press of the lever is reinforced, not a press of other apparatus; thus, the rat develops discrimination.

These conditioning principles have been observed in numerous organisms. Horses, for example, when observing a circle 6.4 centimeters in size, learned to press a lever with their lips, for which they received food. With slightly smaller or larger circles, they still pressed the lever, displaying stimulus generalization. When the circles were very different in size from the original stimulus, lever pressing diminished, indicating discrimination. Later, some horses were

INITIAL REACTION

? - - - → Press Bar → Food
Response   *Reinforcement*

RESPONSE REPETITION

→ Press Bar → Food - - -
Response   *Reinforcement*

STIMULUS DISCRIMINATION

- - → Press Bar → Food - -
Response   *Reinforcement*
Light
Discriminative Stimulus

FIGURE 7–11 PROCESS OF OPERANT CONDITIONING. The initial stimulus is unknown; the rat presses the lever, an operant response, which produces food, a reinforcing stimulus. This outcome increases the probability that the response will be repeated. Eventually, some discriminitive stimulus, such as a light, may appear, indicating when food is available. The rat learns to press the lever only when the light is on, obtaining food.

trained to respond to the original circle but not to any of the others, for which no reinforcement was offered, and complete discrimination was promptly achieved (Dougherty & Lewis, 1991).

Similarly, **extinction** occurs in operant conditioning, meaning that after several trials without reinforcement, the conditioned response fails to appear. When food no longer follows a lever press, the horse or rat or other organism ceases this behavior (Figure 7–12).

When sufficient time has elapsed since extinction, **spontaneous recovery** may take place, in which a previously extinguished response reappears without further training. This outcome is most likely when the individual has been removed from the original conditioning situation for a considerable period. All of these principles were defined more fully earlier, in the context of classical conditioning.

USE OF REINFORCEMENT. It should be noted in passing that operant conditioning is not limited to the availability of food or water or some other necessity of life, called **primary**

reinforcement because it satisfies some inborn, physiological need. Some animals and most human beings respond for long periods of time to **secondary reinforcement,** which satisfies a learned or acquired need, arising through experience. Money is a good example of a secondary reinforcer. It does not satisfy any physiological need directly, and yet it is a powerful reinforcer. The words "Well done," the letter *A*, and countless other events or symbols constitute secondary reinforcement.

For all of us, the approval of parents, friends, colleagues, and other adults and children is a most important influence on behavior. We do not live by bread alone.

Primary or secondary, the reinforcement in operant conditioning is most efficient when it *immediately* follows the desired response. As a rule, the smaller the interval between response and reinforcement, the faster is the conditioning. Even a delay of a few seconds can retard the conditioning process.

Feeling very chilly, Brother Mendo pulled at the cord on his tunic, tightening the cloth around

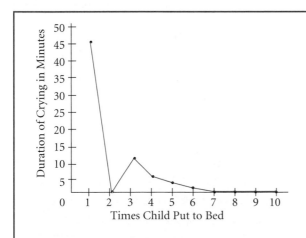

FIGURE 7–12 ELIMINATING AN OPERANT BEHAVIOR. A sick infant required much parental attention early in life. After he regained his health, his parents needed to stay with him at bedtime to prevent temper tantrums. When the parents were instructed to leave the child's bedroom immediately, his crying stopped. Lack of crying at the second bedtime perhaps was due to fatigue (Williams, 1959).

his body. Immediately, he felt a bit warmer. A few minutes later he pulled the cord again, once more obtaining immediate reinforcement.

In addition to immediate reinforcement, there are other considerations in developing an operant response. The first concerns shaping, used for learning complex responses. The second concerns schedules of reinforcement, used for strengthening an already established habit. The third involves a controversial issue, the use of punishment.

METHOD OF SHAPING. In conditioning a rat to press a lever, we can simply wait for this behavior to occur. At some point in its wanderings around the operant chamber the rat probably will press the lever, producing a food pellet. Some minutes, hours, days, or even weeks later, it will press the lever again and receive some more food. Eventually the rat will press the lever regularly, and the response will become well established.

But learning will occur more rapidly if we use a special operant principle. To avoid a long wait for the full response, we provide reinforcement for simpler behaviors that will lead to the full response. Thus, we begin by supplying a food pellet whenever the rat moves even a short distance in the direction of the lever. If we give a few more reinforcers, it will remain in this area, but then we give no more reinforcers until the rat moves still closer to the lever. The animal is thus brought to the wall containing the lever. Then it receives no more reinforcement until it touches the lever, perhaps sniffing it on the first occasion. Next, it must push the lever slightly to receive reinforcement; food is no longer given for merely touching the lever. Later, the rat must push the lever through a larger arc, for only these responses are reinforced. Finally, the rat must make the full response, pressing the lever through its complete arc to obtain a reinforcer.

This approach to learning is called **shaping,** for each successive step is slightly more demanding than the prior step, and reinforcement is contingent on success at that step. The learner gains mastery on a step-by-step basis. These intermediate tasks or steps, accomplished during the process of shaping, are known as **successive approximations.** For example, circus animals have been taught seemingly remarkable feats in this way (Figure 7–13).

Shaping can occur on an accidental basis. A child at dinner asks for the milk in a soft voice. The adults, engaged in conversation, pay no attention. The child asks in a louder voice, and someone passes the milk. As the days go by, the child continues to use this increased volume, but if he is ignored, he asks still more loudly. This behavior, if

FIGURE 7–13 SHAPING BEHAVIOR.
Many successive approximations were required to reach the final level of skill demonstrated by the airborne, water-skiing squirrel. Notice that the response is compatible with the animal's inborn behavior. Squirrels are accustomed to flying through the air.

reinforced, will continue, but if even this plea goes unattended later, eventually the child uses a very loud voice. As a result of these unintentional successive approximations, he shouts: "Please pass the milk." At that point, an adult may turn and say: "Try to speak more softly! Whoever taught you to speak like that?"

Used intentionally, shaping pervades our approach to the teaching-learning situation, not only in schools and business but also in the home, as the child, for example, learns to read letters, then words, then phrases and sentences, then easy books, and so forth. The steps are known as *successive* approximations to indicate that their sequence must be carefully arranged in order of difficulty. Mastery at each level prepares the learner for the next higher level.

REINFORCEMENT SCHEDULES. Acquisition of any habit is best accomplished by **continuous reinforcement,** or 100% reinforcement, in which each correct instance is reinforced, even in shaping. After the basic pattern is established, however, a different procedure is used to *increase the frequency of the response.* This procedure is known as *intermittent* or **partial reinforcement** because sometimes correct responses are reinforced and sometimes they are not. Under this condition, the response rate increases because more work is required to obtain each reinforcement and because, in some partial schedules, it is never clear when the next reinforcement will become available.

On a **fixed-ratio schedule** (*FR*), the subject is rewarded for only a certain proportion of correct responses. The subject might begin at FR 2, meaning one reinforcement for every two correct responses. After the subject has adapted to this schedule, then it might be changed to FR 3, in which reinforcement is available only after every third correct response. Gradually, over the course of days and weeks, the proportion of reinforcement

can be increased to FR 4, FR 6, FR 9, and so forth up to FR 30 or much more. With these changes, rats and pigeons and countless other animals can be made to perform at very high rates, pressing a bar, pecking a disc, and so forth. Among human beings, piecework in industry illustrates this schedule, especially when a bonus becomes available for pieces produced beyond a certain number. Rental agencies follow this principle more subtly when they offer dividends or reduced rates after each transaction of a certain amount.

To maintain a consistently high rate of responding, variable schedules are used, in which there is no indication when the next reinforcement will occur. On a **variable-ratio schedule** (*VR*), reinforcement is provided on an irregular basis but according to an overall proportion of correct responses. A VR 6 schedule, for example, involves *on the average* one reinforcement for every six responses, but the individual may emit eight responses and receive reinforcement, then three responses and receive reinforcement, and then seven responses before receiving reinforcement. The average is one reinforcement for every six responses, but there is no indication of when the next reinforcement will appear. Gambling establishments operate almost exclusively on this principle. The customer never knows when the next reinforcement will occur, producing a higher rate of response than would occur with a fixed-ratio schedule offering the same overall reinforcement (de Luca & Holborn, 1992).

Reinforcement on a **fixed-interval schedule** (*FI*) is available only after a certain interval of time has passed. Then reinforcement is available for the next correct response. For FI 30″ for example, a reinforcement is available every 30 seconds, and the rat receives it for the first correct response after that interval has passed, regardless of when the last previous reinforcement was obtained. Many organisms learn to discriminate this fixed interval between reinforcements quite accurately. Thus, the response rate increases just before the beginning of each new interval. At the human level, a fixed-interval schedule occurs in a wide variety of contexts, from college to Congress. When an assignment is due every Friday, homework rises to its highest level on Thursday, just before the next opportunity for reinforcement (Figure 7–14).

The **variable-interval schedule** (*VI*) varies around an overall average of time, rather than responses, and irregular intervals are used to achieve this average. On a VI 8′ schedule, reinforcement is available *on the average* of once every eight minutes. Thus, an individual might respond fifteen minutes before receiving reinforcement, then receive a reinforcement for the first response after just 1 minute, then after six minutes, then after ten minutes, and so forth, averaging one reinforcement every eight minutes. Under such conditions, pigeons have pecked for hours at the rate of five pecks per second; some have responded 10,000 times with a very low reinforcement rate (Skinner, 1953). Human beings act in much the same way, although without the pigeon's incredible persistence.

To summarize, we can say that continuous reinforcement is most effective during acquisition,

when the response is being learned. The schedules of partial reinforcement are most effective later in generating a high rate of response.

After a schedule of partial reinforcement, especially variable reinforcement, a response is highly resistant to extinction. The reason is that the partial schedule itself contains some *extinction* trials— meaning trials without reinforcement. This resistance to extinction after partial reinforcement is called, not surprisingly, the **partial-reinforcement effect.** After training on a variable schedule, for example, pigeons have responded thousands of times without reinforcement.

USE OF PUNISHMENT. Many psychologists, including Skinner, have spoken widely against the uses of punishment. For humanitarian and practical reasons, they find fault with **punishment,** defined as any outcome following a response that decreases the probability of a recurrence of that response.

Clearly, B. F. Skinner and Saint Ildefonso have very different views on this subject, and yet it would be inappropriate to decide that one is correct, the other wrong. Rather, they stress different

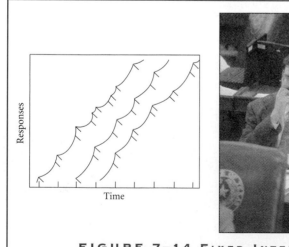

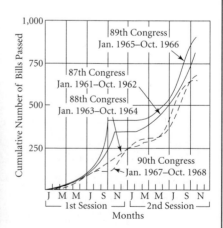

FIGURE 7–14 FIXED-INTERVAL SCHEDULES. A pigeon, rat, and monkey produced the curves on the left, obtaining food as reinforcement. Members of Congress produced those on the right. Their reinforcement was adjournment and vacation, after completing business (Weisberg & Waldrope, 1972). Fixed-internal schedules always yield scalloped curves.

aspects of the outcome. Saint Ildefonso would point out that punishment usually decreases the undesired response, at least for a while. Skinner would state that punishment is only temporarily effective and that the cost of suppressing the response is not worth the negative consequences it often generates.

The humanitarian reasons are obvious. Punishment can be cruel, and it can produce undesirable side effects in the punished individual, animal or human being, including anxiety, lethargy, conflict, illness, hyperactivity, and repetitive behavior. Animals have shown these reactions in experimental situations; clinical observations of severely punished children also provide evidence. Furthermore, punishment can lead to dislike of the punitive agent and the punished activity. These negative attitudes toward the home, school, or parent can remain for long periods, even a lifetime (Mathis & Lampe, 1991).

The punishment administered to Brother Mendo was rather severe, and it left him starving, except for the food that the finicky cats decided not to eat. According to the custom of that day, he might instead have been required to walk around all week with a stick in his mouth—perhaps to remind him not to stick his foot there. (Oh, Brother!) In any case, such punishments probably prompted low self-esteem among the brethren and unfavorable attitudes toward monastery life.

From a practical standpoint, Skinner argued that punishment is not effective in eliminating undesirable behavior; it simply suppresses that behavior. Also, punishment does *not* teach the desired behavior. It does not directly support a correct response. It may even be a stimulus to misbehavior through the attention it gains, relief from guilt feelings, or by serving some other subtle or latent purpose.

One critical factor is the immediacy with which punishment follows the response. Delayed and uncertain punishment, of whatever strength, is less effective than weaker punishment administered earlier (Figure 7–15).

Those who argue for the use of punishment point out that immediate suppression of the undesirable response may be very important, especially in the case of dangerous or threatening behavior.

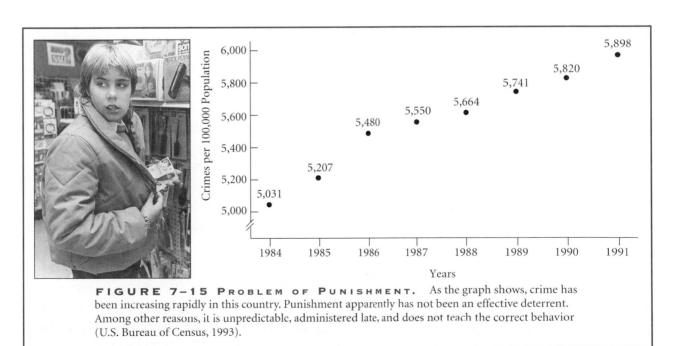

FIGURE 7–15 PROBLEM OF PUNISHMENT. As the graph shows, crime has been increasing rapidly in this country. Punishment apparently has not been an effective deterrent. Among other reasons, it is unpredictable, administered late, and does not teach the correct behavior (U.S. Bureau of Census, 1993).

Certain antisocial actions must be suppressed, even if punishment does not teach the person what to do. At least it indicates what not to do. Furthermore, during the period of suppression, rewards can be used to encourage more desirable behavior. In this context, it should be emphasized again that negative reinforcement is not punishment. Receiving high grades in a course and therefore becoming exempt from the final examination would be an instance of negative reinforcement.

In summary, there are three rules for punishment, if it must be used at all. (1) Administer punishment promptly and consistently. (2) Keep the level of punishment as mild as possible, making it largely informative. (3) Ensure that the correct response is known and available.

INFLUENCE OF OPERANT CONDITIONING

The procedures of operant conditioning are widely used today, knowingly or otherwise, within and outside psychology. Advocates of this approach to psychological issues believe that, if properly applied, it can make an enormous difference in the improvement of the human condition (Skinner, 1961, 1984; Thyer, 1991). In particular, it appears to be important in the theory and practice of shaping behavior of the young (Gewirtz & Peláez-Nogueras, 1992).

OPERANT CONDITIONING AS RECIPROCAL. In many situations, the response of one individual influences the response of the other. This situation is called **reciprocal conditioning,** for each individual's behavior is reinforcing to another. In the dining room, the hungry cats and monks were involved in reciprocal conditioning. The monks intentionally dropped the food, causing the cats to run, and the cats, by running, prompted the monks to drop food. Without fully realizing it, they kept one another dropping food or running to obtain it.

This reciprocity was depicted in a popular cartoon. "Wow! Have I got that guy conditioned," said one rat to another after some Skinnerian experiments. "Every time I push the lever, he gives me food."

In reciprocal conditioning, an individual operates on his or her environment and the environment, which includes the living organisms in it, operates on the individual as well. The parent controls the child, but as any parent knows, the child also controls the parent. A representative government creates and amends laws to control the people, but the people determine what laws the government will make. There are exceptions to this rule—including prisoners, the very elderly, and emotionally disturbed people, who sometimes have little control over their caretakers—but according to B. F. Skinner and others in operant conditioning, it applies in a broad way to most interpersonal relationships.

What is love, according to B. F. Skinner? It is an intricate pattern of reciprocal conditioning—or mutual reinforcement. Each partner supports behavior that the other partner emits. Suppose a man, for example, likes to wear expensive clothing and jewelry, and this style of dressing is admired by his significant other. Her admiration supports his dressing style; his manner of dress elicits her admiring remarks. Mutual reinforcement of desired behaviors—love, Skinnerian style.

LEARNING SKILLS AND SOLVING PROBLEMS. Operant conditioning has been widely used to teach animals tasks and tricks. Monkeys have been trained for assisting the handicapped, horses for crowd control, and dolphins for entertainment (Figure 7–16).

Pigeons have been trained as inspectors in a pill factory, a job for which they are well suited because of their high visual capacity. They identified defective pills with 99% accuracy, using their beaks to knock them off a slowly moving conveyor belt. Their performance was superior to that of human workers in the same role, and special safeguards were set up against possible errors, chiefly by requiring the birds to work in pairs or small groups, thus producing several judgments about the same pill (Verhave, 1966). They were never hired, however, apparently due to the fear of adverse publicity.

In fact, by training the monastery cats, Brother Mendo finally obtained a full meal. One night when Saint Ildefonso and all the other monks were asleep, he left the kitchen, found a big sack, rounded up all of the cats, and put them into the sack. Afterward, he crept out under an arch, found a big stick, and began this training, a procedure to which we shall return shortly.

At the human level, operant conditioning is employed for training in contexts too numerous to describe here, ranging from toilet training to pilot training. Later we shall note its role in personality, therapy, and weight control. In school, it has been used to increase reading skills (Brown, Fuqua, & Otts, 1986). At home, it has been used to eliminate fears and stuttering in children (Glasscock & MacLean, 1900; Onslow, Costa, & Rue, 1990). And it has all sorts of applications in health, ranging from promotion of dental care to use of safety belts (King & Fredericksen, 1984; Sowers-Hoag, Thyer, & Bailey, 1987).

People also employ operant conditioning in *self-management,* using the principles to change their own behavior. Individuals who want to exercise more, eat less, work harder, stop smoking, and so forth establish a set of behavioral objectives for themselves and then arrange a schedule of reinforcement contingent on meeting these objectives. Usually the schedule employs shaping, and therefore the objectives gradually become more demanding, day by day, week by week. The approach here,

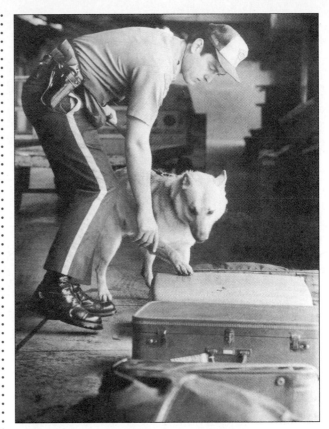

FIGURE 7–16 TRAINED ASSISTANCE BY DOGS. Through operant conditioning, dogs are trained to find drugs, capture suspects, help handicapped people, rescue victims and provide other forms of assistance.

however, is more cognitive self-regulation than it is operant conditioning, for the person is deciding in a purposeful, intended fashion how to change his or her behavior.

The reinforcement in these instances may be a bit of self-indulgence, such as a weekday movie or lunch-hour diversion. As the behavior continues to improve, it should become reinforcing in its own right, for the person is feeling healthier or becoming more productive. The behavior then becomes intrinsically satisfying; there may be no need for additional reinforcement.

CONDITIONING AND SOCIETY. In the novel *Walden Two* (1948), B. F. Skinner advocated careful use of operant conditioning for redesigning societies and improving human life. The issue is highly controversial, for it calls for reshaping human behavior through rearrangement of the environment by social scientists, but these views have found considerable support. One reason is that conditioning processes occur anyway as we interact with each other. Rather than leave them to chance, behaviorists prefer to apply the principles thoughtfully, with certain objectives in mind.

In another book, *Beyond Freedom and Dignity* (1971), B. F. Skinner emphasized that there is a selection process in the environment, and it pertains to behavior as well as to physical structure. Charles Darwin was concerned with the influence of the environment on the physical structure of the species over the millennia—the survival of the fittest organisms. B. F. Skinner was concerned with the influence of the environment on the behavior of the individual over the lifetime of the organism—the survival of reinforced responses. According to Skinner, virtually all of our major problems—overpopulation, energy depletion, pollution, and the nuclear threat—stem from reinforcement of inappropriate behaviors.

The difference between our present society and the one he proposes is that the reinforcement, or control, would be more carefully planned, rather than springing up haphazardly from the self-interests and political successes of many different people. The evolution of our present culture is the result of a massive but prescientific effort to control ourselves, others, and our environment. As Skinner said, we see what humanity under these circumstances has made of itself, but we have not yet discovered what scientific human beings, using a behavioral technology, can make of themselves. "A constantly experimental attitude toward everything—that's all we need" (Skinner, 1948).

• LEARNING COMPLEX RESPONSES •

For some, B. F. Skinner's view is not subversive or dangerous but rather impractical. Operant conditioning, opponents argue, does not apply to complex human behavior. Skinner's principles, if they are a plausible interpretation of basic habits, are insufficient to account for the broad range of human behavior. In training the cats, for example, Brother Mendo searched for a sack, the cats, and a big stick and then began the training. How do we explain this array of behaviors, comprising a sequence of events? In response, Skinner and his followers have pointed to further operant principles, including the concept of chaining.

CONCEPT OF CHAINING

A moment's reflection shows that human behavior does not occur in separate segments but in a more or less continuous flow, as just suggested. In a baseball game, the batter hits the ball, runs down the baseline, touches first base, and watches the coach for further signals, all in a rapid, integrated sequence. Similarly, the driver of an automobile emits a sequence of intricately interconnected behaviors. These acts cannot occur in a random order. Except for minor variations, only one sequence will achieve the goal. In this sequence, known as **chaining,** any given response in a series is connected to the preceding response and to the subsequent response, each in different ways.

In such a sequence, called a *behavior chain,* each response has two functions. It serves as reinforcement, usually secondary, for the previous response, and it serves as a cue to emit the next response in the chain. Brother Mendo's response of looking for a sack was reinforced when he found it, and it was a cue to look for the cats. Finding each cat was reinforced because then he could put it in the sack, and it was the cue to look for another cat or to creep off to the arch. Arriving under the arch was reinforced because then he could begin to use the stick, and so forth.

Each new condition in such a sequence is termed a *response-produced cue* because it arises from the prior response and also serves as a cue for the next response in the chain. In terms of operant conditioning, such a cue is a discriminative stimulus. These cues are usually visual or auditory, but some are kinesthetic, such as those that arise from turning the key in the ignition of a car, depressing the accelerator, or turning the wheel. The feel of these responses is satisfying because we know that we can move to the next response in the chain.

❦

TWO-FACTOR THEORY

How did Brother Mendo train the monastery cats to leave him in peace? A behavior chain was involved, but clearly there was something else too, which brings us to the question of the relationship between these two types of conditioning, classical and operant. How do they interact, if at all? One answer to this question involves the **two-factor theory** of conditioning, in which signs or signals are learned through the first factor, classical conditioning, and the responses for coping with these signals are acquired through the second factor, operant conditioning.

LEARNING SIGNALS AND SOLUTIONS. In one early experiment using the two-factor theory, guinea pigs were placed individually in a revolving drum. When a buzzer sounded, they received an electric shock. Through classical conditioning, pairing the buzzer and the shock on a number of trials, the buzzer became a conditioned stimulus, and the animals acquired a conditioned response, trembling at the sound of the buzzer. However, each animal in one group could avoid the shock by running at the beginning of the signal;

those in another group always received a shock regardless of their behavior. Eventually the guinea pigs in the first group began to run at the sound of the buzzer. For these subjects, operant conditioning had occurred, as well (Brogden, Lipman, & Culler, 1938).

According to this viewpoint, complex behavior involves a combination of classical and operant conditioning, wherein each form of conditioning makes a different contribution to the total learning situation. In classical conditioning, sometimes called *signal learning*, an organism learns the meaning of stimuli in its environment, at least in terms of positive or negative evaluation. It becomes prepared for what lies ahead (Kohn & Kalat, 1992). Operant conditioning is called *solution learning*, for here the organism learns about consequences—what to do about the desirable and undesirable events in its environment. Both components are involved in many learning situations.

In fact, it was through two-factor conditioning that Brother Mendo solved his problem. His solution, described with wit and wisdom by Lope de Vega, is a fictional part of this narrative and certainly cannot be condoned. The wit is obvious, and the wisdom is found in Lope de Vega's foreknowledge, depicting in light comedy two-factor theory three centuries before Pavlov, Skinner, and others provided scientific evidence.

As Brother Mendo explained: Standing there with the sack and stick on that dark night, first he would cough and then he would

> immediately whale the daylights out of the cats. They whined and shrieked like an infernal pipe organ. I would pause for a while and then repeat the operation—first a cough, and then a thrashing. I finally noticed that even without beating them, the beasts moaned and yelped like the very devil whenever I coughed (qtd. in Bousefield, 1955).

Afterward, he let the cats loose. Then he put away the sack and stick and sat down again.

This training served him well during the rest of his days on the floor. "If an animal approached my food," he pointed out, "all I had to do was cough, and my, how that cat did scat!"

The original training of the cats occurred in a classical framework. Coughing immediately preceded each beating, and eventually it signaled that the painful treatment was about to occur. When the animals heard the cough later, they fled, solving the problem through operant conditioning. They did not literally avoid a beating, but they removed themselves from an anxiety-producing situation, never discovering that the cough was really harmless.

Thus, the cats learned to be afraid through classical conditioning, for the cough was paired with the beating. They learned what to do about their fear through operant conditioning; they ran away.

And here we come to a very different kitchen—this one in twentieth-century America, mentioned at the outset of this chapter, inhabited by the college student named Dolores. One evening her whole family was in the kitchen, busy and harried with preparations for moving from Texas to Virginia. Then her mother became annoyed with her brother and scowled darkly. Immediately Dolores became anxious, just seeing her mother's expression, and suddenly moved to the dishwasher, attempting to fill it even though there were *no* dishes in the sink. Why did she do that?

This puzzling move, she decided later, was a habit. She had been unknowingly conditioned by her mother to do the dishes every time her mother scowled or became distressed (Pinto, 1992).

When Dolores was a child and did something wrong, her mother scowled in exasperation and then spanked her. The scowl was followed by a spanking. Eventually, through classical conditioning, Dolores became anxious simply upon seeing that scowl. Later, through operant condition-

ing, she learned what to do about her anxiety. She washed the dishes whenever her mother scowled. By this behavior, Dolores elicited praise for helping with housework, and at the same time she removed herself as a target for punishment, thereby further diminishing her anxiety (Figure 7–17).

TYPES OF TWO-FACTOR CONDITIONING. Dolores, the monastery cats, and the guinea pigs in the running wheel all exhibited a specific form of operant conditioning called avoidance conditioning. In **avoidance conditioning** the organism's response does not gain something positive, such as food, but rather prevents something negative, such as a shock, a beating, or a confinement. Another possibility in a negative situation is **escape conditioning,** in which the organism cannot completely avoid the noxious stimulus but instead can terminate the event once it has commenced. Both avoidance and escape are types of *aversive conditioning,* in which the organism eliminates a negative outcome. Thus, they involve negative reinforcement. Two-factor theory also applies when the organism gains a positive outcome, sometimes called *appetitive conditioning* because the organism gains something it wants. Here there is positive reinforcement.

For example, Dolores's family had three household cats. She was responsible for feeding them in the cellar, and she noted that they quickly became conditioned. At the sound of the dry food in the box, they mewed and smacked their lips. When the cellar door was open, they ran downstairs. Thus, they learned the signal for food, the rattle in the box, through classical conditioning. Then they learned what to do about it through operant conditioning; they ran into the cellar to obtain their meal.

At the human level, a man begins to like a certain cologne through its association with a loved one. Then he decides to do something about this preference. He purchases a bottle of the fragrance. Again, classical conditioning is a basis for learning

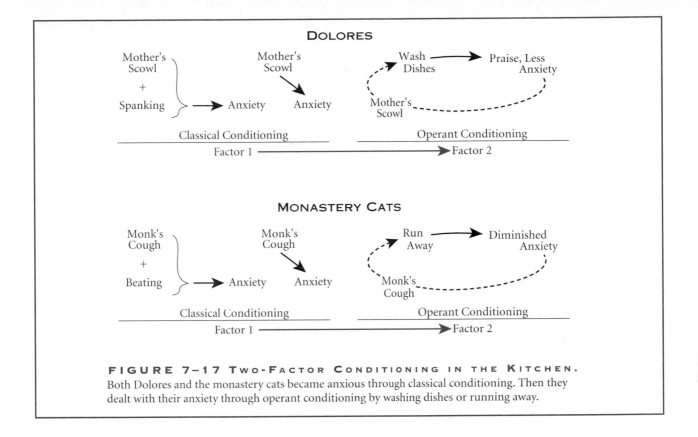

FIGURE 7-17 TWO-FACTOR CONDITIONING IN THE KITCHEN.
Both Dolores and the monastery cats became anxious through classical conditioning. Then they dealt with their anxiety through operant conditioning by washing dishes or running away.

the emotional response—in this case toward a particular odor—and operant conditioning is the basis for learning what to do about it—buying a certain cologne.

RESEARCH CHALLENGES. One purpose of theory is to provide an interpretation of research findings, and in this respect the two-factor approach has proven useful. Both the classical and operant views can be incorporated into a single framework. Two-factor theory presents an overall perspective, and it has suggested that both types of conditioning occur in every such incident.

Another purpose of theory is to stimulate further research on unresolved issues, and here again two-factor theory has been of value, raising the question of whether one or two processes are ultimately involved. For example, biofeedback experiments have suggested that apparently involuntary responses, which are the focus of classical conditioning, can be controlled by operant methods. In biofeedback, electronic devices measure a person's heart rate, brain waves, and so forth, and when this information is made available to the individual, the person often is able to modify his or her heart rate, brain waves, or other bodily processes. This feedback seems to constitute some type of reinforcement in the manner of operant conditioning.

Collectively, such studies suggest that there may be some crossover between the methods and responses in classical and operant conditioning, and some modification of the two-factor theory may be in order. Certain animal studies in avoidance conditioning also restrict application of this theory, for innate behavior sometimes proves resistant to conditioning. However, the two-factor view has maintained a prominent position in learning theory for over 40 years, and at this point there still seem to be two kinds of conditioning. Some version of this theory still appears warranted and useful (Stasiewicz & Maisto, 1993).

OBSERVATIONAL LEARNING

We should also recognize less traditional views of conditioning, including those that incorporate the concept of conditioning into a broader framework. Albert Bandura, in particular, has been influential in developing a perspective that combines elements of conditioning and cognition. The cognitive processes emphasize thinking and memory, which we shall consider shortly in this chapter and extensively in subsequent chapters. At the same time, Bandura's approach offers a practical outlook on the development of certain basic skills.

Imagine teaching a child to tie a shoe solely by operant conditioning. The process could be lengthy indeed, even with shaping. Supplying reinforcement after each correct behavior would be helpful, but the whole learning process could be greatly accelerated by one suggestion: "Watch me!" Then the teacher *shows* the child. In **observational learning**, also known as *social learning theory*, we learn by observing the responses of other people; they demonstrate various behaviors, and we can reproduce those behaviors at a later date. One important premise in this approach is that learning can occur through *observation alone*, without reinforcement. Someone watching another person tie a shoe or train a cat may learn the proper technique simply by observation. Later, when the proper occasion arises, this behavior will be emitted, and then the reinforcement will be obtained (Bandura, 1986, 1989).

PROCESS OF MODELING. In observational learning, the person demonstrating the correct performance is called a *model*. The process of reproducing that performance by watching someone who is competent is known as **modeling**. In this context, we should remark on Dolores's brother in Texas, an indolent adolescent. His behavior offers a good example of modeling.

His job each evening was to collect the three cats from outdoors, sometimes an irksome task, and he noticed Dolores's success with the box of dry food. When she shook it, the animals heard the noise and came running. So he merely modeled his behavior after that of his sister. He opened the back door, shook the box, and the cats came running home. His job was done, even without feeding them.

The brother also discovered some further principles of conditioning. After a while, the cats refused to enter the house when he shook the box. Too many shakings without feedings led to extinction. He also learned about discrimination. The cats continued to behave for his sister. They descended the stairs whenever *she* shook the box (Pinto, 1992).

It is through modeling, claim observational theorists, that children of fearful parents often become fearful, children of critical parents often become critical, and children of confident parents tend to be confident themselves. Even children of aggressive parents are likely to become aggressive, for an adult who punishes aggressive behavior is often demonstrating the very behavior that the child, when away from the punitive model, may imitate.

In one experiment, children three to five years of age were tested for fear of a dog, and then some of them observed a four-year-old child who showed no fear whatsoever. He happily patted the dog, scratched it, and fed it when confined alone with it in a pen. For other children, in a control group, there was no model. They simply observed the dog. After eight sessions under one of these conditions, all children again were measured individually for fear of a dog, and the findings were clear. Mere exposure to the animal made little difference. Instead, the children who observed the fearless model showed a markedly increased capacity to approach the dog, and when all children were exposed to an unfamiliar dog one month later, essentially the same results were found (Bandura, Grusec, & Menlove, 1967).

TYPES OF MODELS. The most effective models typically display characteristics admired by the observers. Dolores's brother, responsible for collecting the cats, watched his older sister. The children in the previous experiment observed a peer. They perhaps were influenced more by this fearless boy than they would have been by a fearless adult, for adults do many things that children know they should not do. In this case the **peer model,** close to the observer in age and background, probably was more influential then a **mastery model,** who demonstrates the behavior to perfection but is more distant socially (Figure 7–18).

In one instance some children watched a **symbolic model,** a person who is not actually present but appears only on television, on the radio, or in a story. This adult became aggressive and was rewarded, and later the children tended to behave aggressively in the same ways. Other children, in variations of this same film, saw the model being punished or ignored, and they did not adopt the model's aggressive style. But when these children were offered incentives for acting like the person in the movie, they too behaved in these aggressive ways (Bandura, 1965).

On such bases, observational learning makes a distinction between learning and performance. Learning, which is a change in behavior resulting from experience, can occur solely through observation; we learn simply by watching someone else. In these instances we can speak of *no-trial learning,* for the behavior has been acquired even without practice. The individual discovers what to do but does not necessarily emit that behavior. In performance, the individual emits the behavior in question if reinforcement is available.

Observational learning emphasizes physical reactions, but other responses can be learned too, including social behavior and emotional responses. One study showed that severe fear of spiders was most often acquired through observational learn-

ing, followed by conditioning and then cognitive processes (Merckelbach, Arntz, & de Jong, 1991). Even hypnotic suggestibility, which involves a mental set, is sometimes said to develop through modeling (Smyth, 1981). Observational learning occurs in numerous species, ranging from fish and octopuses to birds and mammals (Beulig & Dalezman, 1992; Fiorito & Scotto, 1992; Robert, 1990). Kittens, for example, learn to hunt by watching the mother. Those that have not observed an adult cat stalking prey are distinctly less successful in their early attempts (Sigel, 1992).

FIGURE 7–18 CHARACTERISTICS OF A MODEL. Typically, the most influential model for children is slightly older and moderately more skillful, as well as emotionally appealing. Thus a sibling may serve as a peer model and also a mastery model, as when a sister or brother is a skilled performer.

LEARNING
AND COGNITION

Human thought is the most outstanding development of psychological evolution. Hence, it is not surprising that many psychologists view memory, thinking, and associated processes, collectively referred to as **cognitive processes,** as playing a vital role in human learning. In fact, one of the strongest criticisms of the conditioning approach is that the contribution of the individual's mental activity is minimized or ignored.

Some cognitive psychologists point out that cognition occurs throughout conditioning phenomena. The conditioned individual develops an *expectancy* based on past experience, and this expectancy determines whether the behavior is repeated or discarded. Expectancy is a mental process, and therefore even in conditioning, the role of cognition must be considered.

In classical conditioning, the individual learns a new signal; in operant conditioning, the individual learns the relationship between a behavior and its consequences (Rescorla, 1992). Brother Mendo understood classical and operant conditioning in this fashion, and he was gratified that the cats had learned so quickly. In less than half an hour under the arch, they had learned the meaning of his cough, and he decided they would remember it if he were ever floored again.

LEARNING SIGNS AND RELATIONS. Cognitive learning emphasizes understanding, rather than a series of movements. Learned responses are not regarded as conditioned habits but rather as responses to relationships among stimuli. According to the cognitive view, a cat runs down to the cellar to obtain food because it has learned that the cellar and a dark area mean "food" and the upstairs and a light area mean "no food." The cat does not learn a series of specific, rote responses that bring it to the dark area and away from the light area; instead, it learns the significance of the signs.

In a classic experiment on this form of learning, a comparison was made among three groups of hungry rats in a maze. In one group, each subject received food each time it ran the maze, and a steady decrease in error scores was observed. In another group, each subject was given access to the maze without finding food, and there was little improvement in error scores. In a third group, also without food, there was little improvement until the eleventh trial. Then, when food was introduced as reinforcement, performance promptly approximated that of the group that had been rewarded continually. This sudden improvement suggested that the animals had acquired information about the maze that they did not utilize until it became advantageous for them to do so (Tolman & Honzik, 1930). They presumably learned spatial cues while roaming around the maze without reinforcement and then, when food became available, used these cues to find it (Figure 7–19). Such experiments are said to demonstrate **latent learning** because the subject develops a knowledge of the situation that becomes evident only at a later date, when reinforcement is available.

Differences of opinion on the underlying bases of latent learning have a long history, however. Modern experiments that systematically minimize or eliminate visual, auditory, or other cues have suggested that rats employ highly specific associative processes in learning place mazes, rather than forming some overall perceptual representation of the maze (Whishaw, 1991).

Studies of a different sort also support the cognitive perspective. They focus not on learning signs but rather on learning the difference between signs. Let us assume, for example, that the rat has been trained to discriminate between two gray stimuli, responding to the lighter one, which is reinforced with food. After this training, the rat is presented again with this lighter shade of gray, along with a still lighter gray. Which choice does the rat make? Does it choose the original light gray, which is now the darker shade? Or does it choose the new, still lighter gray? In fact, the rat makes its choice on the basis of *comparison* between the stimuli, choosing the still lighter gray in this case. Note that this stimulus is not the specific stimulus that was rewarded previously. Similarly, when the subject is trained to respond to the darker of the two gray stimuli in the original situation, it chooses the darker stimulus when a new pair is presented (Baker & Lawrence, 1951). The outcome in this type of experiment is called **transpositional learning** because the subject makes a comparison, crossing over to the lighter or darker stimulus. It does not maintain a fixed association to the original stimulus.

However, even these results have been interpreted from the conditioning viewpoint, using the concept of stimulus generalization. It is argued that the subject responds to the new *pair* of stimuli in the same way that it responded to the previous pair. The subject selects the lighter, or darker, portion of

each pair in each instance. And it is entirely possible that combinations of conditioning and cognitive components are involved in any such task.

A LEARNING CONTINUUM. Clearly, a number of functions are involved in human learning, regardless of the task to be mastered. The issue, therefore, is not conditioning *or* cognition. Rather, it is the *degree to which* the various processes are involved. Classical conditioning, for example, is not necessarily a low-level, mechanical process. Even in classical conditioning, the organism is an information seeker, alert to relationships among events in understanding the world (Rescorla, 1988). Similarly, cognitive theorists recognize the role of simple habits and reinforcement in most realms of human behavior.

Riding a bicycle, for example, emphasizes the integration of these different forms of learning. It

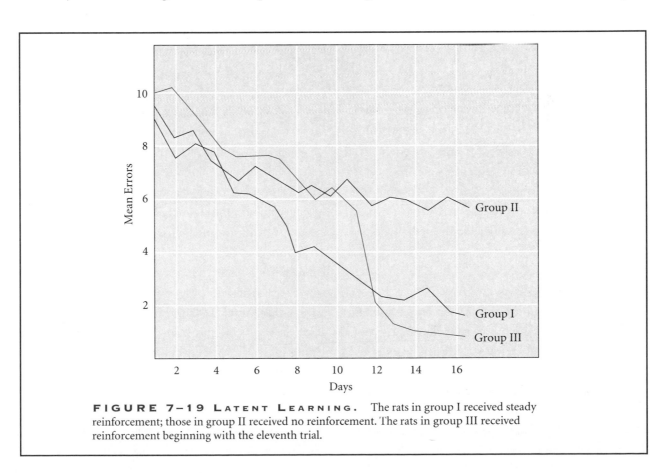

FIGURE 7–19 LATENT LEARNING. The rats in group I received steady reinforcement; those in group II received no reinforcement. The rats in group III received reinforcement beginning with the eleventh trial.

involves motor responses, acquired through conditioning, and also relevant cognitive abilities, such as knowing how to steer, when to brake, what to do to maintain balance, and so forth, all of which become almost automatic after extensive experience (Wierda & Brookhuis, 1991).

Most important in the cognitive tradition is the concept known as insight, sometimes regarded as the highest form of learning in human beings. In **insight,** the solution to a complex problem appears suddenly, not only on the basis of prior experience but also through some new way of perceiving the problem or new combination of earlier experiences. A student suddenly understands how to solve an algebra problem or comprehends the metaphor in a poem. By rearranging or reversing the sequence of letters, for example, you may have suddenly discovered the significance of that earlier sign: SREGNITS. Cognitive psychologists emphasize that insight requires fundamentally new ways of thinking or new combinations of thought, a view that has been prominent for some years, discussed later in the chapter on thought and language.

It thus appears that learning takes place on a continuum of increasing complexity. In this chapter, there is a gradual transition from the simpler forms of learning, emphasized in the conditioning processes, to observational learning, and to the solving of complex problems, of special interest from the cognitive viewpoint. These diverse forms of learning illustrate the multiple bases of behavior.

STUDY OF COGNITIVE PROCESSES.
Looking backward on that evening when she went to the sink with no dishes to be washed, Dolores thought about her behavior, the various factors involved, and developed an explanation with two-factor theory. Similarly, Brother Mendo thought about his problem with the pesky cats, and eventually he developed a scheme for training them. How do we understand these thoughts of Dolores and Brother Mendo in the context of conditioning?

As a rule, traditional behaviorists and other psychologists interested in conditioning do not study thought processes. Instead, they study overt responses, such as Dolores's dishwashing, her mother's scowl, Brother Mendo's coughing, the cats' running, and so forth. No psychologist can study everything, and those concerned with conditioning prefer to limit themselves in this way, utilizing the concepts of reinforcement, shaping, and chaining when referring to complex behavior. If Brother Mendo had previously employed his scheme for training the cats, its reappearance certainly would be explained on the basis of the reinforcement principle.

In recent years, there has been far greater recognition of internal or mental processes, even within the conditioning approach. From this viewpoint, our thoughts do not cause our behavior. They are regarded instead as responses that can be studied in much the same way as overt behavior. They take place inside us, presumably following the same laws as our external responses. The occurrence of each new thought, or response, is thus reinforcement for the preceding one and a cue for the next one. According to this view, Brother Mendo produced internal chains in this fashion, trying one response and then another, each symbolically, until he discovered a procedure for training the monastery cats. Dolores did likewise when she analyzed her behavior in the kitchen.

Some psychologists are content to speculate about thinking in this manner. Others adopt a dualistic approach, as in cognitive-behavioral psychology. They investigate cognitive and conditioning phenomena as separate entities. Still others study mental processes exclusively, which is the domain of cognitive psychology, the subject of the next chapters. Cognitive psychologists are convinced that memory, thought, and language are far too complex to be explained in the behavioristic tradition, and Skinner acknowledged that his view of language was not complete. Thus, psychologists studying these processes often find it convenient to specify these different types of learning (Table 7–4).

TYPE	PROCESS	IN THE KITCHEN
Classical conditioning	A neutral stimulus, after pairing with an unconditioned stimulus, elicits a response.	Dolores became fearful at her mother's scowl; her cats became aroused at the sounds of food.
Operant conditioning	A response is strengthened by satisfying consequences and weakened by annoying consequences.	Dolores washed dishes and escaped her mother's wrath; her cats ran downstairs and obtained food.
Observational learning	Another person's behavior is observed, remembered, and then, depending on its consequences, emitted later.	After watching Dolores, her brother collected the cats simply by shaking the box.
Cognitive learning	A problem is solved by mental processes; overt behavior is not necessarily involved.	Dolores thought about her behavior and then understood her conditioning in the kitchen.

TABLE 7–4 TYPES OF LEARNING

For most behaviorists, however, the emphasis remains on stimulus–response associations. Sometimes the association is between two stimuli, as in classical conditioning; sometimes it is between a response and a reinforcing stimulus, as in operant conditioning. For these reasons, conditioning is also known as *association learning*.

IN PERSPECTIVE. This narrative for conditioning phenomena came from the kitchen. We might ask why, for conditioning can occur anywhere. Of all the places around the the home, however, the kitchen offers the most potential, followed by the bedroom and bathroom. Think of all the opportunities for primary reinforcement in the kitchen: foods, drinks, odors, medications, and hugs and kisses, as well as scalding liquids, sharp knives, broken glass, and electric shocks—to say nothing of the potentially conditioned stimuli and secondary reinforcers: words, tones, gestures, facial expressions, television images, music, and so forth.

The cold, dark kitchen in the seventeenth-century Spanish monastery differed greatly from the bright, modern kitchen in Texas, but the same conditioning processes were at work in both places. Brother Mendo, Dolores, and the various cats were responsive to the reinforcing properties of their environments.

And that concludes our discussion of conditioning in the kitchen. You may remember it through association—with Brother Mendo on the cold floor, Dolores at the dishwasher, and the companionable cats in both kitchens.

• SUMMARY •

CLASSICAL CONDITIONING

1. In the simplest form of learning, called classical conditioning, a previously neutral stimulus develops the capacity to arouse some emotional or physiological response. It does so through association.

2. Some of the important principles of classical conditioning are stimulus generalization, discrimination, extinction, spontaneous recovery, and higher-order conditioning.

3. The most important role of classical conditioning lies in the development of diffuse emotional reactions and certain attitudes.

RESPONDENT AND OPERANT BEHAVIOR

4. Two types of responses are associated with conditioning processes. One type, called respondent behavior, usually involves the smooth muscles and glands; it is particularly amenable to the process of classical conditioning and typically occurs in emotional situations.

5. In operant behavior, the organism is more active, and its responses have more obvious consequences in the environment. These responses typically involve the skeletal muscles, as the organism emits behavior in a voluntary manner.

OPERANT CONDITIONING

6. Habits are acquired through operant conditioning, in which responses are followed by reinforcing stimuli. Primary reinforcement involves the satisfaction of physiological needs. Secondary reinforcement, such as money, a smile, or a high grade, involves the satisfaction of acquired needs.

7. In operant conditioning, an organism's response can be developed by shaping. The response can be increased in frequency by the use of partial reinforcement, including variable and fixed schedules.

8. Operant conditioning procedures are used extensively in childrearing, industry, education, and therapy. According to this view, many of our major social problems stem from lack of scientific control over human behavior, which could be achieved by more carefully planned reinforcements in the environment.

LEARNING COMPLEX RESPONSES

9. In conditioning theory, complex behavior is accounted for partly by chaining, the process of learning a series of related responses. Each response serves as reinforcement for the previous response and also as a cue for the next one.

10. Complex behavior is also accounted for partly by the two-factor theory, in which aspects of classical and operant conditioning are combined.

11. In observational learning, also known as social learning theory, learning can occur by watching a competent person, and the process is called modeling. The learned behavior will not necessarily be emitted, however, until an appropriate moment, usually when reinforcement is available.

12. In the cognitive view, the emphasis is on the organism's knowledge or understanding of the various elements in the learning situation. The cognitive viewpoint is illustrated in latent learning and relationship experiments. Given a complex problem, human beings and other higher organisms arrive at solutions that seem to involve elements of both approaches, conditioning and cognition.

• WORKING WITH PSYCHOLOGY •

❧ REVIEW OF KEY CONCEPTS ❧

conditioning
learning
behaviorism

Classical Conditioning
  classical conditioning
  unconditioned stimulus (US)
  unconditioned response (UR)
  conditioned stimulus (CS)
  conditioned response (CR)

simultaneous conditioning
delayed conditioning
trace conditioning
backward conditioning
stimulus generalization
discrimination
extinction
spontaneous recovery
higher-order conditioning
one-trial conditioning

Respondent and Operant Behavior
  respondent behavior
  operant behavior

Operant Conditioning
  reinforcement principle
  operant conditioning
  reinforcement
  positive reinforcement

negative reinforcement
operant response
reinforcing stimulus
discriminative stimulus
stimulus generalization
discrimination
extinction
spontaneous recovery
primary reinforcement
secondary reinforcement
shaping
successive approximations

continuous reinforcement
partial reinforcement
fixed-ratio schedule (FR)
variable-ratio schedule (VR)
fixed-interval schedule (FI)
variable-interval schedule (VI)
partial-reinforcement effect
punishment
reciprocal conditioning

Learning Complex Responses
chaining

two-factor theory
avoidance conditioning
escape conditioning
observational learning
modeling
peer model
mastery model
symbolic model
cognitive processes
latent learning
transpositional learning
insight

❧ CLASS DISCUSSION/CRITICAL THINKING ❧

A NARRATIVE TWIST

Imagine that Brother Enrique, another member of the monastery, committed a misdeed and found himself on the kitchen floor. In an act of friendship, Brother Mendo explained to him the coughing technique. Without training the cats again, would Brother Enrique have found the coughing procedure effective for controlling them? Argue both sides of the case, referring to a specific principle of conditioning in each instance. ❧

TOPICAL QUESTIONS

• *Classical Conditioning.* Using the process of classical conditioning and any stimuli you wish, how might you develop an aversion to drinking or smoking in an adolescent?

• *Respondent and Operant Behavior.* Imagine yourself as an electrician or a construction worker. Identify possible respondent and operant behaviors associated with this work and explain why you categorized them as such.

• *Operant Conditioning.* Using operant conditioning, explain how you would train your grandmother or granddaughter to complain less about your use of the telephone and to exercise regularly.

• *Learning Complex Responses.* Consider a child who has modeled the characteristics of a violent television personality. Discuss television censorship and free speech in this context. Suggest ways to modify television programming to induce more appropriate behavior.

❧ TOPICS OF RELATED INTEREST ❧

Using classical conditioning to reduce fear, often called systematic desensitization, is a mode of therapy (16). Studies in biofeedback (3) show how operant conditioning may be used to control presumably involuntary responses. Observational learning is influential in the development of gender identity (12). Approaches to personality are based on operant conditioning and observational learning (14).

ACQUISITION OF MEMORY
Sensory Stage
Short-Term Memory
Long-Term Memory
Levels of Processing

THE MEMORY TRACE
Measurement of Memory
Physiological Bases
Structure of the Trace

THEORIES OF FORGETTING
Decay Theory
Obliteration of the Trace
Interference Theory
Motivated Forgetting

PRINCIPLES OF MEMORIZING
Role of Motivation
Memory Systems

8

MEMORY

∾

BENJAMIN BURTT LIVED A NORMAL CHILDHOOD — EXCEPT FOR HIS STORY HOUR. EVERY DAY, BEGINNING WHEN THE BOY WAS 15 MONTHS OLD, HIS FATHER read aloud to him three short passages from a lengthy drama. Day after day, his father continued this practice until he had read each passage 90 times altogether. Then the father changed to another part of the same story, reading three more passages, again 90 times.

Imagine the scene. Harold Burtt, a professor at Ohio State University, reading aloud while his infant son sat, lay, or squirmed nearby. Still without mastery of language, Benjamin understood little, said less, and was not permitted toys or other playthings. Running around was not allowed either. Maybe his father, a college professor, was somewhat accustomed to an inattentive audience.

Every three months the father changed to three new passages, never, of course, with a word of complaint from his innocent little listener. After all, the drama his father recited was far too complicated for him to understand.

In fact, it was an adult story of symbolism and human destiny, Sophocles's *Oedipus Tyrannus.* And if that were not enough, the father always read it in the original Greek. For almost two years, the story of King Oedipus unfolded in this way for the unsuspecting child. When the sessions of this unusual story hour finally ended, Benjamin had reached his third birthday. Still learning the syntax and vocabulary of his native English, he had become a somewhat better listener.

The father had selected these passages carefully. They were fairly uniform in difficulty and were written in the same meter and dialogue form, all in iambic hexameter. No choruses were used, and each selection included approximately 20 lines. They were taken from diverse points throughout the play (Burtt, 1932).

What was Professor Burtt's purpose in all of this effort? He wanted to study **memory,** which is the capacity to utilize impressions from previous experience. Specifically, he wanted to discover how early in human life memories could be established. Little Benjamin was an excellent subject because the boy could not engage in extra practice with some-

one else; no other member of the family and no close friend knew Greek. He could test Benjamin's memory later, knowing just which passages had been read to him and at what ages.

The basic message in this chapter, demonstrated in Benjamin's exposure to Greek, is that memory involves three fundamental elements: **encoding,** which is the processing of incoming information; **storage,** the retention of information; and **retrieval,** the recovery of information at some later time. These three elements, which constitute the major topics in the study of memory, are sometimes known as the three *Rs: record, retain,* and *retrieve.* Employing a computer analogy, human memory requires data input, comparable to encoding; saving the information on a disk, comparable to storage; and using the menu to enter old files, comparable to retrieval.

We also approach the Burtts' work with the reader in mind, for the father had a second aim. He wanted to discover how long such memories might last. Today we can add a further question: What can be done to ensure that they last a long time? The outcome of this inquiry should be useful to anyone

taking courses or trying to pass examinations.

We begin this chapter with the acquisition of memory and then turn to its storage, represented in the memory trace. Afterward, we consider theories of forgetting, which attempt to explain why the trace is sometimes unavailable. Then we conclude with some principles of memorizing.

• ACQUISITION OF MEMORY •

When the first phase of Professor Harold Burtt's project was finally finished, he had read to his son 5,040 Greek syllables. Each one had been repeated 90 times, making 453,600 occasions on which he had recited one Greek syllable or another to the boy, testimony to his perseverance and perhaps his son's malleability (Table 8–1). Harold Burtt, incidentally, showed persistence in other matters as well, from handball to birdwatching. An amateur naturalist, he banded and recorded 164,054 birds. Whatever the endeavor, he was devoted to careful measuring and counting (Thayer & Austin, 1992).

His research with Benjamin reflects a long-standing controversy in the study of memory, one that has recently been rekindled. It concerns the relative values of two different types of investigations: experiments in the laboratory and observations in daily life. The advantage of the laboratory method lies in the opportunities for manipulation and con-

AGE (MONTHS)	PASSAGES FROM SOPHOCLES
15	I, II, III
18	IV, V, VI
21	VII, VIII, IX
24	X, XI, XII
27	XIII, XIV, XV
30	XVI, XVII, XVIII
33	XIX, XX, XXI

TABLE 8–1 BENJAMIN'S SCHEDULE.
The readings continued daily for almost two years. When they were finished, the little boy was just under three years old.

trol. People can be exposed to specific stimuli, and their memories can be precisely tested later (Banaji & Crowder, 1989). The case for naturalistic observation concentrates on the need to understand remembering and forgetting as they occur in daily life. This natural setting more than compensates for the reduced precision (Neisser, 1991). In searching for answers to the perplexing questions of memory, both approaches have proved useful. In fact, both are necessary for steady scientific advancement (Ceci & Bronfenbrenner, 1991).

Harold Burtt's investigation involved both dimensions. It was an experimental study, partly because it controlled the material to which the child was exposed, partly because in the later testing sessions it included some new passages, thereby permitting the precise comparisons essential in the experimental method. At the same time, an adult reading to a child was a naturally occurring event. The setting and even the activity were part of the daily routine for any normal child.

This investigation began 60 years ago, before the widespread use in psychology of the term **information processing,** which refers to the mental operations by which sensory experiences are converted into knowledge. It includes the ways in which we record, retain, and retrieve information; it implies that memory is an active process. Today, it also includes the concept of *parallel distributed processing,* which emphasizes that the brain manages several pieces of different information simultaneously in different brain regions. Most computers today, for example, process information sequentially, one piece after the other. In memory, the human brain not only responds to some eliciting stimulus but, at the same time, attempts to retrieve numerous bits of related information stored in different ways and different places. Human memory, therefore, is an exquisitely intricate and active system of simultaneous information processing.

Within the information processing viewpoint, two broad, complementary approaches to memory have been developed in recent years, one known as stage theory, the other as levels-of-processing theory. While they involve considerable overlap, research on the differences between them demonstrates the ways in which theories become modified, clarified, or rejected. As one view becomes outdated, it provides grounds for its successor. William James described this process in earthy terms: "Science feeds on its own decay" (1890).

We begin with the earlier view, the **stage theory of memory,** which depicts a sequence of three phases qualitatively different from one another: a sensory stage, short-term memory, and long-term memory (Figure 8–1). This three-stage view has been revised, but it forms an essential basis for later discussions (Atkinson & Shiffrin, 1968, 1971).

SENSORY STAGE

At 15 months of age, little Benjamin listened to his father read at a uniform rate, using approximately two seconds per line. Whatever he remembered was acquired through these sounds, for everything we know comes initially through the senses. Immediately after we experience anything, our nervous system contains very briefly an impression of that information. The term **sensory memory** refers to this momentary residual information within the nervous system, which has not been processed in any significant way.

A convincing demonstration of sensory memory was provided when adult subjects observed three rows of a few letters each for a fraction of a second. Then they were asked to recall them. About half of the letters were recalled in this way, but the investigator believed that virtually all of the letters had been in the subjects' sensory memory. The reason for the poor recall, it was hypothesized, lay in the delay between the disappearance of the letters and the time that elapsed before the subjects could recite all of them.

To test this hypothesis, the subjects were asked to observe briefly on a screen nine letters, appearing in three rows of three letters each. Then, alerted by a special tone that occurred immediately after the stimulation was removed, they were asked to recall one specific row of letters within the block. A high, medium, or low tone requested recall of the top, middle, or bottom row, respectively (Figure 8–2). In these instances the subjects were uniformly successful. They could recall any row of letters in the block, which suggested that after the pattern was withdrawn, the subjects, for a moment, had the

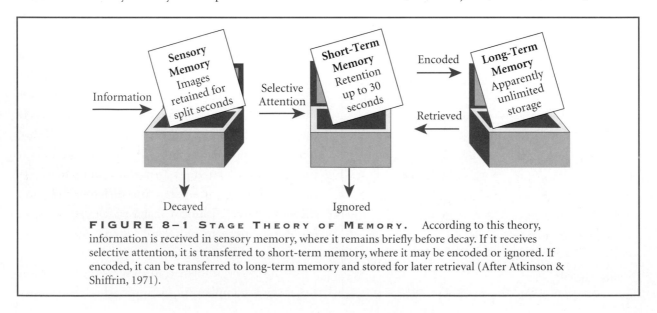

FIGURE 8–1 STAGE THEORY OF MEMORY. According to this theory, information is received in sensory memory, where it remains briefly before decay. If it receives selective attention, it is transferred to short-term memory, where it may be encoded or ignored. If encoded, it can be transferred to long-term memory and stored for later retrieval (After Atkinson & Shiffrin, 1971).

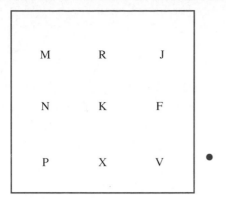

FIGURE 8-2 STUDY OF SENSORY MEMORY. When a low tone was sounded just after disappearance of the letters, it requested recall of the bottom row. The red dot did not appear; it is used here to illustrate the procedure (Sperling, 1960).

whole pattern of nine letters in sensory memory (Sperling, 1960).

In other words, sensory information must be processed immediately if it is to be retained. The speed with which it fades is indicated in these experiments. When the signal for recall was delayed by half a second or less, recall was significantly disrupted. When the delay was a full second, the subjects' success was no greater than it had been earlier, with no tone at all. On this basis, it is generally assumed that unanalyzed information in the visual realm lasts for one second or less. In auditory and other sensory modes, it may have longer or shorter durations.

Have you noticed, for example, that sometimes you can still remember a brief remark even though you were not paying attention a moment earlier? You can process it a split second afterward because the words are still in sensory memory, if not at the next stage, short-term memory. This brief auditory image is known as *echoic memory* because we hear something after the sound has disappeared. In the visual realm, the image is called *iconic memory*, meaning that it is a visual likeness. As might be expected, the stronger the stimulus, the longer the image lasts. The *haptic memory* concerns touch; it is the brief

impression still in your nervous system after a fly has left your forehead. Similarly, *kinesthetic memory* refers to memory for certain habitual movements—in the muscles, tendons, and joints. For example, you can still feel a good tennis shot for a moment after the ball has been hit. Presumably, there are such memories for all realms of sensory experience.

❧

SHORT-TERM MEMORY

The sensory image is unprocessed. It appears for a moment, an exact reproduction of the event as revealed by the sense organs, and then it disappears. If any of it is to be useful, it must be handled promptly, passing to another stage. This next stage, **short-term memory** (STM), involves temporary storage, defined in most studies as any interval less than 30 seconds, during which the information is processed or ignored. If ignored, it never becomes a long-term memory. If properly rehearsed, it can go into permanent storage. In either case, short-term memory is a temporary condition.

This early phase is also known as **working memory** because this label emphasizes active memory *processes*, rather than a seemingly static, brief storage. Working memory includes rehearsal of the new information, as well as its manipulation and evaluation (Baddeley, 1990). There is considerable debate about whether short-term memory and working memory refer to the same or different memory functions (Cantor, Engle, & Hamilton, 1991). Whatever the outcome, this research gives further attention to the concept of information processing in memory.

To use a metaphor, short-term memory has been regarded as a receiving platform at the warehouse. It has a limited area, and the workers have a limited time to move some newly acquired material into the warehouse for long-term storage. Something must be done in a hurry, for another shipment will be arriving soon.

LIMITED CAPACITY. The limited capacity of short-term memory was determined when adult learners were asked to memorize various amounts and types of information. It was found that the average person could manage approximately seven separate items. Some people could manage up to nine categories, which seemed to be the effective maximum, and almost all subjects could recall at least five items. The investigator was prompted to speak of the "magical number seven," adding that we should think of it as seven plus or minus two (Miller, 1956).

This limited capacity of short-term memory is both a drawback and an asset. The drawback is obvious, for information that cannot even be received certainly cannot be recalled a few hours, days, or years later. But imagine the difficulties if everything that passed through sensory memory remained in immediate awareness. Yesterday's lecture, today's essay, tonight's news, and the words on this page all would be swirling in our heads at the same time. Our minds would be overloaded with information from our environment, making it more and more difficult to receive and handle incoming information (MacGregor, 1987).

ENCODING: A BASIC PROCESS. To be retained in short-term memory, information must be manipulated or processed properly, as is evident when you ask someone for a telephone number. To be transferred and permanently stored in the vast warehouse of long-term memory, the number requires further processing. This data processing, as indicated earlier, is called *encoding* because it prepares information in a way that makes it likely to be remembered. Encoding is therefore the first component in memory (Figure 8–3).

One encoding process is simple **rehearsal**, in which the information is practiced, covertly or overtly. It is repeated several times, as in saying a telephone number again and again. The aim here is to keep the material available until it can be used, as

FIGURE 8–3 ENCODING THROUGH REHEARSAL. After dialing for information and obtaining a telephone number, the caller usually cannot afford the slightest diversion. Even a brief remark may disrupt encoding.

in dialing the number, or until it can be stored in some more integrated fashion.

The importance of rehearsal was demonstrated when experimental subjects attempted to remember nonsense syllables for a few seconds. The experimenter showed each subject a three-letter syllable followed by a number. The subject observed the syllable and then, to prevent rehearsal, counted backward by three or four from a randomly selected three-digit number. When asked the syllable three seconds later, the subject remembered it only about half the time. With successively more counting, recall continued to decline, and after 18 seconds, less than 10% of the syllables were recalled (Peterson & Peterson, 1959; Figure 8–4).

In terms of rehearsal, Harold Burtt worked under a handicap with his son. At 15 to 36 months, little Benjamin simply could not rehearse this material himself. To deal with this problem, his father recited each passage 90 times, which constituted prodigious rehearsal for him, although the boy could only sit and listen.

ROLE OF ORGANIZATION. In more complex encoding, there are three basic dimensions, or requirements, one of which is organization. The term *organization* carries its usual meaning, referring to some systematic or functional arrangement. For example, try to remember the following words: *gunners, door, a, floods, can, horrible, by, every.* It may be a difficult task, unless you employ an alphabetical organization—with each word larger than its predecessor.

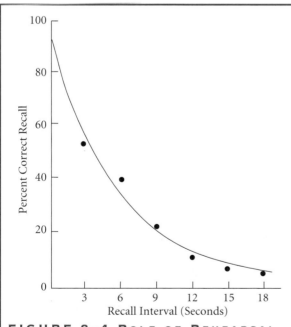

FIGURE 8–4 ROLE OF REHEARSAL. When subjects were prevented from rehearsal, short-term memory showed an almost immediate decline. After just five seconds, there was only about 40% correct recall.

The importance of organization has been demonstrated in experiments comparing free and serial recall. In *free recall* the learner is allowed to reproduce the list in any order; in *serial recall* the items must be remembered in a particular sequence, which requires some organization. When these types of recall are compared using tasks too difficult for success on the first trial, free recall is superior initially. The subject first responds with the last few words on the list, which are still available in short-term memory. Afterward, the subject reports the easiest words, wherever they appear in the list. In learning a complete list of several items, however, the subject almost invariably memorizes it more rapidly when using serial recall, which imposes its own organization (Earhard, 1967; Waugh, 1961). This superiority strongly suggests that memory is powerfully affected by organization, in this case imposed on the material by the sequence.

When there is no organization, the successful learner must develop one. The learner must create a **subjective organization,** a scheme or arrangement for viewing the material developed through personal experience. In memorizing a list of random dates, a woman thinks of them in terms of her eight cousins or the events in a novel. To remember certain facts a man wants to present in an interview, he organizes them around his favorite meal, using the different foods to form a rough framework. Many memory devices are most effective as a means of creating an organization, or order, for recall.

USE OF CHUNKING. Another encoding procedure becomes evident when you try to remember the following string of letters: *O-LDH-ARO-LDA-NDY-OUN-GBE-N.* There are 20 letters, well beyond your short-term memory capacity. If you succeeded, it was undoubtedly because you grouped them in a special way. If you forgot some, try reorganizing them into five words.

Read the immediately preceding sentence just once more, slowly, and then try to repeat it. If you were successful, grouping probably occurred again, despite the fact that the sentence contains not five words but ten, not 20 letters but 50. You probably grouped the elements somewhat like this: If you . . . forgot some, . . . try reorganizing them . . . into five words.

In one study, subjects were asked to sort a deck of cards into categories, with the aim of remembering the single word written on each card. Up to approximately seven, the larger the number of categories used, the better was the recall. Subjects using seven categories were approximately twice as successful as those using only two (Mandler, 1967). The reason: With few piles, there were too many items in each pile to be recalled. With many piles, considerably more than seven, the piles themselves could not be recalled.

This process is called **chunking,** which means combining separate pieces of information into groups, thereby forming fewer but broader categories, or chunks. Sometimes the chunks will be fairly obvious, sometimes not so apparent. With

extensive experience, chunks can be developed containing enormous amounts of information, as demonstrated when chess players viewed a board in the middle of a game. After five or six seconds, the board was emptied and they were asked to replace the pieces. Master chess players often reproduced the entire pattern of 32 pieces; novice players replaced only a half-dozen pieces. As the masters explained later, they could "chunk" the board—but only if it showed a real game in progress, consistent with the knowledge in their permanent memory (de Groot, 1965). With the pieces arranged randomly, chess masters could not remember them any better than beginners (Figure 8–5).

After various karate techniques were presented to 30 practitioners, those who were experts were distinctly superior to the novices in recalling them (Bedon & Howard, 1992). They did so by more successfully combining them into chunks or patterns.

NEED FOR CUING. In addition to organization and chunking, a third procedure for successful encoding involves the use of cues. Perhaps you

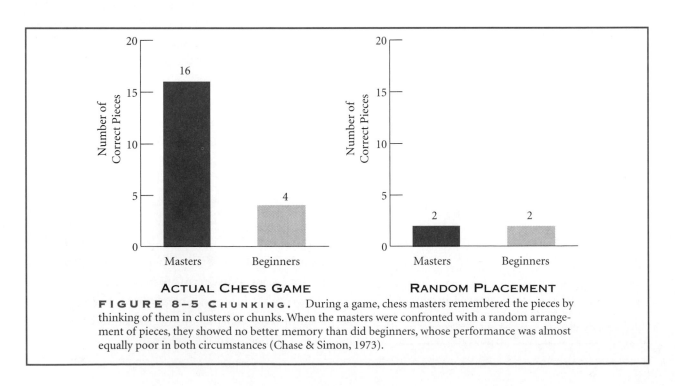

ACTUAL CHESS GAME

RANDOM PLACEMENT

FIGURE 8–5 CHUNKING. During a game, chess masters remembered the pieces by thinking of them in clusters or chunks. When the masters were confronted with a random arrangement of pieces, they showed no better memory than did beginners, whose performance was almost equally poor in both circumstances (Chase & Simon, 1973).

have taken a test in which you had learned the material but were unable to recall it. There was storage but no retrieval. Specifically, **cuing** is the identification or preparation of some signal, hint, or prompt which can be used to retrieve stored information. Cues can be verbal, visual, auditory, and so forth, ranging from key words to the image of a drawing in a psychology textbook.

In addition to intentional cues, there are spontaneous or unintentional cues, and the closer these are to the original situation, the more likely they are to enhance recall. In **context-dependent memory,** the details of the original setting, where the memory was encoded, can serve as retrieval cues. For example, retrieval may be aided by the presence of the classroom, a friend, or even a lunch box where the material was learned. In **state-dependent memory,** the individual's physical or mental condition may serve as a retrieval cue. If you learned something when you were sad, being in a sad mood may aid that memory. In other words, recall may be enhanced not only by use of the original external cues but also by a return to the original physical or mental state (Bower, 1981).

Not surprisingly, Benjamin was unable to use any such cues. In fact, his encoding of the Greek passages was dubious on all accounts—organization, chunking, and the preparation of cues. These three processes are the chief factors in most memory systems and, as noted at the end of this chapter, they pertain not only to encoding but to storage and retrieval as well.

LONG-TERM MEMORY

Short-term memory involves immediate awareness. The individual is conscious of these memories. The events in long-term memory have been stored, but they do not enter immediate consciousness until the retrieval process begins. In **long-term memory** (LTM) information is retained for *later* use, defined as any interval ranging from 30 or so seconds up to

the full life of the organism. It is final storage in the warehouse, not an interim processing stage. It was this aspect of memory that interested Harold Burtt.

Long-term memory differs from short-term memory in another way. It presumably has an unlimited capacity, or at least the limits are not known.

TRANSFER OF INFORMATION. If you listened to a novel list of unrelated words and were asked to recall them shortly thereafter, the outcome would be highly predictable. The first and last words would be most readily recalled. In the **primacy effect,** items at the beginning of a series are better remembered than later ones. In the **recency effect,** items at the end of the list show better recall scores than earlier items. This phenomenon is called the *serial position effect,* meaning that the location of a particular item in a list or passage plays a role in the likelihood that it will be remembered (Figure 8–6).

The serial position effect has several explanations, but two are most relevant to the transfer of information from short-term to long-term memory. First, items at the beginning of the list are

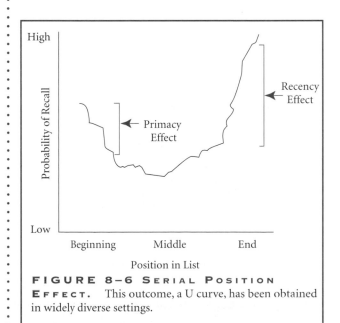

FIGURE 8–6 SERIAL POSITION EFFECT. This outcome, a U curve, has been obtained in widely diverse settings.

most rehearsed. They can be rehearsed until the list grows too long for individual items to be practiced. Second, items at the end of the list are presumably still in short-term memory at the time of recall. In fact, if recall is delayed, the recency effect is sharply diminished (Glanzer & Cunitz, 1966).

The rehearsal process thus plays a role in both instances. This process, incidentally, is sometimes *simple rehearsal,* involving not much more than regular repetition, and sometimes *elaborate rehearsal,* in which the information is processed with special attention to detail and meaning.

The serial position effect also has been obtained with animals. In one study, pigeons, monkeys, and people observed series of four images each. After each series, a test image was presented, and the subjects were trained to indicate whether or not it had appeared in the previous series. In all species, primacy and recency effects were observed. The first and fourth images were recognized with greater accuracy than the others. Furthermore, when the delay between exposure of images was brief, the primacy effect disappeared—apparently for lack of the usual rehearsal of early items. When the delay was lengthy, the recency effect disappeared—apparently because there was no longer any advantage in short-term memory (Wright, Santiago, Sands, Kendrick, & Cook, 1985). This research provides further evidence for the separation between short-term and long-term memory (Squire, Knowlton, & Musen, 1993).

TYPES OF LONG-TERM MEMORY. After decades of research, investigators have decided that long-term memory is not a single element or component. Rather, it consists of several different types, and these multiple kinds of memory appear to be mediated by different brain regions, as is evident in classical conditioning. Memory traces for generalized emotional responses, as in conditioned heart rate and blood pressure, appear to be signifi-

cantly related to activities in the amygdala. For highly specific conditioned reactions, such as the gagging reflex or eyeblink, another brain area, the cerebellum, plays a critical role (Lavond, Kim, & Thompson, 1993).

One major distinction among the types of long-term memory lies with memory for skills and habits, called *procedural memory,* and memory for facts and events, called *declarative memory.* In **procedural memory,** an individual remembers how to do something, how to perform some act, physical or mental. Procedural memory is involved in making a cup of cocoa, writing a computer program, and playing the trombone.

Most of these memories, especially if complex, are acquired slowly, practiced often, and repeated automatically. If you have learned to use a certain word processor, for example, you perhaps have noticed how much more rapidly and successfully you can do so than when you began, striking the right keys for retrieval, printing, storage, and so forth, often without much thought. There is considerable survival value in procedural memories; they enable us to perform daily habits automatically. And usually our procedural memories are accurate.

We err more often in another type of memory. Called **declarative memory,** it represents a statement of fact; it concerns ideas, dates, definitions, and an endless array of other factual information. The focus is on what, not how. And here two subtypes have been identified. There is, first, **episodic memory,** which involves specific events in the individual's past. There is a time-and-space dimension to episodic memory, directly experienced by the individual. A student says: "I remember that the rain began just as we were entering biology class."

Declarative knowledge of a more general sort, without restriction to time and place, is known as **semantic memory;** it includes mental representation of general ideas and a broad range of information:

the names of animals and plants never encountered directly, their habitats, their organs, their relationships, and countless other pieces of information in biology, for example, and elsewhere. As a rule, we do not remember when such information was acquired. It simply becomes part of our large storehouse of information (Tulving, 1985; Figure 8–7).

Procedural memory is not necessarily better than declarative memory. The outcomes depend on several factors, including prior experience, the number of repetitions, and the effort to remember. Tying shoes and riding a bicycle are well-practiced, well-remembered procedural events. Finding square roots and making Christmas pudding are also procedural memories, rarely practiced and therefore poorly remembered.

Procedural memory, incidentally, often illustrates **implicit memory,** meaning that it can be evoked without conscious effort. A person who has not ridden a bicycle for years simply mounts the vehicle and wheels away—or crashes. In either case, an effort to recall the principles of bicycle riding before attempting the task is of little value. Declarative memory more commonly illustrates **explicit memory,** for it typically involves an intentional, conscious effort to remember. It is formed and utilized with awareness, as when you recite a poem or the basic idea in a book.

STORAGE OF INFORMATION. Are different types of long-term memory stored in different ways? There is considerable speculation on this issue, and three modes of organization have been suggested: schemas and scripts, a conceptual hierarchy, and networks of associations.

Memories of all types are presumed to be stored in a **schema,** which is a general pattern or way of organizing information in a particular culture. For example, when students in England heard a myth told among Native Americans, many elements were foreign to them. When they attempted to recall the myth later, they did so in terms of their own schemas. The tale was organized or adapted to their own patterns of thought. It showed omissions, distortions, and additions reflecting an English way of thinking about things (Bartlett, 1932).

One type of schema often associated with procedural memory is called a **script,** meaning that it depicts a typical sequence of events in a particular setting. It may describe how a specific task is accomplished, or it may indicate more general steps in daily life. College students, for example, have restaurant scripts, dressing scripts, and test-preparation scripts. In the restaurant script there are certain procedures to be followed: obtaining a table, reviewing the menu, ordering a meal, consuming

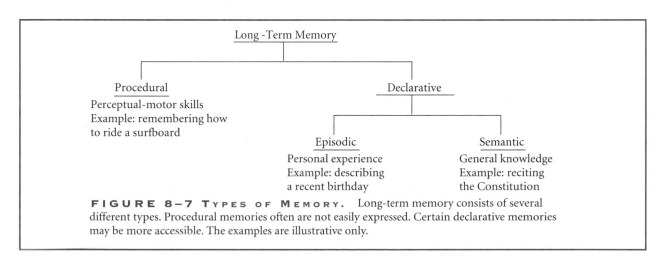

FIGURE 8–7 TYPES OF MEMORY. Long-term memory consists of several different types. Procedural memories often are not easily expressed. Certain declarative memories may be more accessible. The examples are illustrative only.

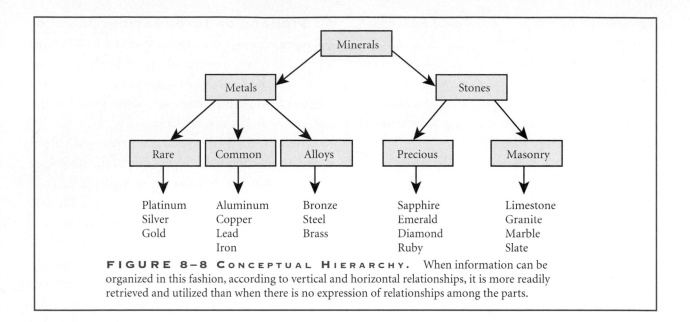

FIGURE 8–8 CONCEPTUAL HIERARCHY. When information can be organized in this fashion, according to vertical and horizontal relationships, it is more readily retrieved and utilized than when there is no expression of relationships among the parts.

the meal, asking for the bill, and so forth. When students were asked to recall procedures for dining in a restaurant, there was high agreement on the script, despite minor variations (Bower, Black, & Turner, 1979).

It is speculated that schemas operate for both input and output of information. Thus, they can be influential while an episodic memory is being constructed, during encoding, and while it is being reconstructed, during retrieval.

Declarative memory, especially, is often considered to be stored according to some hierarchy. In a **conceptual hierarchy,** items with a common property are arranged or classified in a graded order. Our memory of concepts in zoology, for example, includes kingdom, phylum, class, order, and so forth. Similarly, information about government, the church, geology, and other topics is organized this way (Figure 8–8).

In addition, there is considerable speculation about the ways in which semantic memories are reconstructed. The concept of a **network of associations** has been employed here, emphasizing that ideas are connected to each other in patterns, chains, or pathways, the recall of one idea leading to recall of another, that to another, that to still another, and so forth (Chang, 1986). This viewpoint has a long history, and modern theorists have confirmed it, emphasizing the "spread of activation" from one concept or idea to another. The concept of *red,* for example, is closely associated with the terms for some other colors. It is less closely associated with certain red fruits, such as *cherries* and *apples.* Still other concepts, such as *sunrise* and *sunset,* are even more distantly related (Collins & Loftus, 1975; Figure 8–9).

❧

LEVELS OF PROCESSING

In concluding this discussion of the development of memories, we take a step away from stage theory, which has been valuable in generating research and providing an overall conception of human memory. The stage approach involves considerable hypothesizing, however. Furthermore, the processing of information does not appear to be necessarily sequential. Tracing the flow of information through three stages may fractionate the problem, rather than

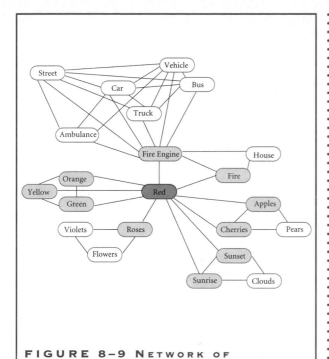

FIGURE 8–9 NETWORK OF ASSOCIATIONS. The word *red*, as the initiating stimulus, triggered thoughts of the concepts indicated in color, which in turn triggered thoughts of other concepts. The shorter lines indicate stronger associations.

give recognition to the presumably interactive and simultaneous processes underlying the memory system as a whole (Atkinson & Shiffrin, 1968, 1971).

A somewhat different view, emerging from stage theory, postulates a *single* memory stage or system. It has arisen because information processing seems to be involved at *all* phases of stage theory. The emphasis, therefore, is on the degree of information processing. According to the **levels-of-processing theory,** information that has been most thoroughly processed, through various cognitive activities on the part of the learner, is most likely to be remembered (Chaik & Lockhart, 1972).

EMPHASIS ON ENCODING. Any modern view of memory, whether or not it postulates stages, gives recognition to encoding, storage, and retrieval. Among levels-of-processing theorists, who

minimize the speculated stages, the emphasis is on the first of these, the encoding process.

In this approach, the short-term memory stage is regarded less as a hypothetical platform and more as a process. If the decision is to store rather than ignore, encoding must commence immediately. According to this view, the extent of encoding determines the level or strength of memory. Information processed only briefly and superficially is not well retained; that which is thoroughly and carefully processed goes into fuller and more permanent storage.

On this basis, the durability of little Benjamin's memory trace was questionable. He heard, perhaps inattentively, passages of a foreign language read aloud by a nearby adult. His father, in contrast, read Sophocles's works himself and probably enjoyed memorizing them, just as he enjoyed recording and remembering the birds in his neighborhood, facts about aviation, and techniques in advertising (Thayer & Austin, 1992). Several cognitive activities undoubtedly went into the formation of all of these memory traces.

DEPTH OF PROCESSING. One danger in the levels-of-processing viewpoint lies in the potential for circular reasoning. Events we remember are those that are fully processed, and when we process events completely, we remember them. It therefore behooves investigators to demonstrate as precisely as possible what is meant by levels of processing and their relationship to encoding.

In one study, subjects were shown a series of words one at a time, each preceded by one of four types of questions. These questions concerned the typeface in which the word appeared, the sound of the word, its category, or its contextual meaning. Believing that the questions constituted a reaction-time test, the subjects answered rapidly for all 36 words, and then an unexpected memory test was administered. It was predicted that memory would be a function of the type of question asked previously, with the question on typeface showing the poorest memory and that on meaning showing the best memory. This result was obtained in several experiments of this sort (Craik & Tulving, 1975).

When the questions merely concerned visual features of the letters, the subjects engaged in shallow processing. Questions about the word's rhyming characteristics prompted an intermediate level of processing. Questions about the word's use in a sentence required the deepest level of processing.

In related experiments, each subject was presented with a series of words and various questions, each question matched to a specific word. Sometimes the question concerned superficial characteristics of the word, such as its length or appearance. How many syllables did it have? Was it written in capital letters? For other words, the questions concerned meaning. Did the word refer to a tool? Was it a synonym for another word? Then the subjects were asked to recall the list of words, a task that they had not anticipated. As predicted, they recalled the words followed by questions about meaning more readily than those followed by superficial questions concerning form and length. Again, it was concluded that depth of processing was a central factor in recall (Parkin, 1984).

CONSTRUCTION AND RECONSTRUCTION. Encoding involves construction, and retrieval also seems to involve construction. It might be argued that both processes involve reconstruction, as well. In any case, the stage approach and the levels-of-processing view are both concerned with the details of these construction processes, although in different ways, and both have asked useful research questions.

In an extended series of studies involving stories and visual figures, reconstructive changes were of three types: simplification, elaboration, and con-

ventionalization. In *simplification,* parts of the original story or drawing did not appear in the reproduction. The general features and theme of a scene were retained, but certain details were omitted in telling the story or making the drawing. Certain other details were overemphasized, in the process called *elaboration,* presumably at the expense of the omitted details. A facial feature, mood, or weapon was recalled as larger, more intense, or more prominent than it had been in the original version, especially if it was important to the story. And finally, in *conventionalization,* strange or unfamiliar details were changed into more familiar forms. An unusual object was recalled in a more familiar design (Bartlett, 1932; Figure 8–10).

Reconstruction during the retrieval phase was also demonstrated when subjects watched a videotape of an automobile accident and later were questioned about it. One group was asked about the speed of the cars when they *hit* each other. The other group was asked about the speed of the cars when they *smashed into* each other. Some days afterward, all subjects were asked whether or not there was broken glass at the accident, and the results showed the expected, reconstructive pattern. Among subjects asked earlier what happened when the cars hit each other, 14% recalled broken glass. Among those asked earlier what happened when the cars smashed into each other, 32% recalled broken glass, although there was none at the scene of the accident (Loftus & Palmer, 1974).

Efforts to deal with these numerous facts and theories about the construction of memory have resulted in a **connectionist model** of the mind emphasizing associations among concepts, sensations, and other elements. Describing the workings of the mind in perception and thought, as well as memory, it has been useful in guiding research (Rumelhart, McClelland, & the PDP Research Group, 1986). In general terms, it assumes that the strength of associations among ideas, feelings, or

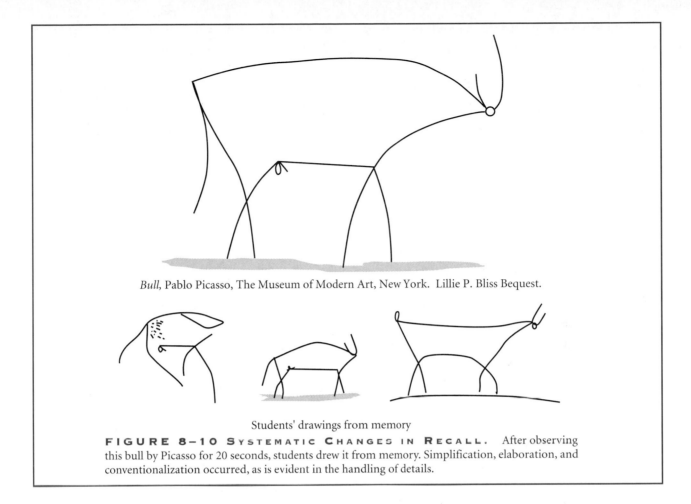

Bull, Pablo Picasso, The Museum of Modern Art, New York. Lillie P. Bliss Bequest.

Students' drawings from memory

FIGURE 8–10 SYSTEMATIC CHANGES IN RECALL. After observing this bull by Picasso for 20 seconds, students drew it from memory. Simplification, elaboration, and conventionalization occurred, as is evident in the handling of details.

memories reflects comparable associations among sets of neurons in the nervous system.

• THE MEMORY TRACE •

Five years after he had read and reread Sophocles's passages, Harold Burtt turned to the next phase in this research. It was time to find out what had transpired in the mind of little Benjamin. Harold remembered the passages. Did Benjamin remember them too?

When storage occurs, it must be based on some change within the individual. Sometimes called a **memory trace** or *engram,* this molecular change is presumed to lie in the nervous system, but we do not yet know with certainty what structures

or functions are modified or even whether the concept of a trace is an appropriate description of memory storage (Estes, 1991a). Therefore, some psychologists measure memory indirectly, focusing only on behavior. Others investigate the physiology of memory, focusing on its biochemical bases. One vital concern in memory research is the development of connections between these behavioral and neurological approaches (Hintzman, 1990).

❧
MEASUREMENT OF MEMORY

Psychologists who study memory by examining behavior have developed three methods for measuring memory: recall, recognition, and relearning.

METHOD OF RECALL. Harold Burtt began by using the method of recall, which is the most difficult memory task. In **recall,** the person is asked to reproduce a prior experience in any convenient manner, although the instructions may vary somewhat. In *free recall*, there is no significant prompting or cue. A common request is simply: "Tell what you remember" (Figure 8–11). Harold asked Benjamin to relate whatever he could of the original Greek passages, but the boy was completely puzzled. He had no idea that he had ever heard them previously. What did his father mean? What was this all about? Benjamin showed no recall whatsoever, perhaps a disappointing result in view of all the effort by his father.

When various signals or hints are offered, the procedure is called *cued recall.* In the courtroom, a witness might be asked: "Now tell me about the sounds. Do you remember any particular sounds or words?" Cued recall is sometimes called **redintegration,** from *re + integration,* for cues are given to make recall easier. One part is recalled or some prompt is given, and then another part is recalled from this information. Courtroom testimony typically begins with free recall, and when an

impasse is reached, cued recall is sometimes used. With eight-year-old Benjamin, even cued recall was of no help.

Especially when remembering visual stimuli, some people give exceptionally accurate testimony without any prompting. This phenomenon, most common in children, is known as **eidetic imagery,** or *photographic memory,* meaning a memory image that possesses the details of a photograph or hallucination. In hallucinations, the person believes the image represents something immediately present in the outer environment. People with eidetic imagery know that they are responding only to an image in the mind.

Sometimes recall is surprisingly accurate and automatic in many people. In **flashbulb memory,** certain details of an emotional experience are recalled with unusual ease and almost perceptual accuracy, as though the event was still in process (Brown & Kulik, 1977). Where were you when you learned of the space capsule *Challenger*'s explosion? Describe the circumstances at the birth of a sibling, death of a pet, or your first kiss. Events of deep personal significance, especially if they occur unexpectedly, often are very well remembered, as if a flash bulb had recorded every detail. The most responsible factors seem to be powerful emotional content and the uniqueness of the event (Sadowski & Quast, 1990).

METHOD OF RECOGNITION. Clearly easier than recall, in a test of **recognition** the previously encountered object or event is merely selected from a series of others not previously encountered. When a witness cannot recall any characteristics of a suspect, a lineup is prepared, and the witness tries to pick the correct person from the group. The information is available. The task is to identify it.

After it was clear that Benjamin had no recall, his father read to him some of the original Greek selections and asked if they seemed familiar. Again, the boy showed no memory whatsoever. Then he

FIGURE 8–11 RECALL TASK. In the space above this caption, draw or write a description of the illustration for the narrative at the beginning of this chapter, depicting the story of Benjamin Burtt and his Greek lessons. This task involves recall.

included some other passages, and still Benjamin showed no recognition.

Despite Benjamin's failure, recognition memory is remarkably successful. People who lament their poor memories are invariably referring to recall, not recognition, for research shows our tremendous capacity for this type of memory. In one instance, students were exposed to approximately 600 randomly selected visual stimuli, called an inspection series. Then some of the stimuli were paired with new stimuli, and the subjects were asked which member of the pair had been seen previously. The median correct recognition score was 88% for sentences, 90% for words, and 99% for pictures (Shepard, 1967). With 10,000 pictures, another researcher concluded that there is no recognizable limit for this type of visual memory (Standing, 1973).

Any recognition task depends heavily on the similarity of the alternatives, however. A teacher or experimenter can make up multiple-choice items that are extremely easy or difficult, depending on the information in the alternatives (Figure 8–12).

Occasionally, we find ourselves in the opposite situation, thinking that we recognize a certain person or place even though we know that cannot be possible. This feeling is referred to as a **déjà vu experience,** defined as an *incorrect* impression that the whole event has been encountered previously (Sno & Linszen, 1990). The French word *déjà* means "already." It *seems* we have already experienced a certain situation, and yet we realize that prior experience is impossible. This feeling arises because some specific part of the new situation—something as subtle as a slight odor, texture, rhythm, or color—is familiar, and then we make the incorrect assumption that the whole scene is familiar.

Sailing into a dozen Mediterranean seaports for the first time years ago, a man believed that he had visited each of them already, although that was impossible. Finally, he decided that this reaction arose because every seaport smelled of fish, seaweed, salt, and gasoline; otherwise, they were quite different. Odors perhaps mask the newness of the rest of a scene, resulting in a déjà vu experience, a view not yet fully confirmed (Sno, Schalken, & de Jonghe, 1992).

Reference to déjà vu is widely made and misused in daily life, as a dramatic way of stating that an event has occurred previously. On seeing the same unusual play twice in a baseball game, Yogi Berra exclaimed, only half-joking, "It's déjà vu all over again!" It was not déjà vu again; it was not even

FIGURE 8–12 RECOGNITION TASK. Without looking again, select the drawing that is most like the child in the opening narrative illustration for this chapter. This task is a test of recognition.

déjà vu. It was merely the same play happening twice.

METHOD OF RELEARNING. After Benjamin failed at both recall and recognition, Harold Burtt turned to relearning, the only remaining test of memory. As a method of measuring small amounts of memory, this approach is even more sensitive than recognition. In **relearning,** the individual learns the task again to the original level of success, and the effort required to relearn is compared with the original effort. If relearning is easier, presumably it is because some memory trace remains.

A bright, curious little boy now in elementary school, eight-year-old Benjamin cooperated with his father's request. He listened to his father reading aloud each of ten Greek passages once daily, day after day. The father read at a steady pace, always pausing for 15 seconds after each passage. After 18 days, the father changed to a procedure he called *prompting.* He read very slowly, requesting Benjamin to supply any words he could at the proper point. As these prompting trials continued, the father read less and less, paused more and more, and thereby allowed his son to supply more and more of the missing parts. Their mutual goal was that Benjamin, at some point, would be able to recite each passage in its entirety, from beginning to end, without any help from his father (Burtt, 1932).

Unknown to Benjamin, these passages included seven of the original 21 selections mixed with three new ones. Would he relearn the original selections more easily than the new ones?

This relearning procedure produces a **savings score,** which shows how much effort is saved from the original learning. If the subject demonstrates full memory on the first relearning trial, the memory is perfect and the savings score is 100%. If the number of relearning trials is the same as the original effort, there is no savings. The savings score is zero, and there is no memory. This procedure has been used effectively with a wide variety of subjects, ranging from insects to rhesus monkeys (Minami & Dallenbach, 1946; Swartz, Chen, & Terrace, 1991).

With Benjamin, the relearning procedure involved a deviation from the usual method, for at 15 months of age, when the research began, he certainly could not learn the passages by himself. For this reason, his father read them aloud 90 times each. Then, five years later, when Benjamin "relearned" these passages, his father read them again. We know of these efforts through Professor Burtt's report in a psychology journal, *An Experimental Study of Early Childhood Memory* (1932).

Finally, after more than a year and one-half, Benjamin reached the point of mastery. He had recited each of the passages once, entirely by himself, without error.

With considerable interest, Professor Burtt analyzed the results. He found that Benjamin had needed an average of 317 trials to relearn the original passages. For the new ones, he had required 435 trials. Benjamin thereby gave clear evidence, five years later, of memory for a significant portion of the earlier material. The overall savings score was 27% (Table 8–2).

Each of the seven passages Benjamin relearned came from a different period in his infancy, one of them from age 15 months, another from 18 months, and so forth, up to the last period, beginning at 33 months. Comparison of these results showed what one might expect. The passages presented at the earliest ages required the most relearning, but there were savings even for these passages. Harold Burtt had achieved his first aim. He had shown that human memories could be established as early as the first 15 months of life (Burtt, 1932).

☙

PHYSIOLOGICAL BASES

How do we explain Benjamin's 27% savings score, showing that he remembered material read to him

TYPE OF PASSAGE	TRIALS REQUIRED
Original	
1	382
2	253
3	385
4	379
5	328
6	226
7	265
Average	317
Control	
1	409
2	451
3	445
Average	435

Learning trials for control passages	435
Relearning trials for original passages	−317
Difference	118

$$\frac{435 - 317}{435} = \frac{118}{435} = 27\%$$

TABLE 8–2 RELEARNING AFTER FIVE YEARS. The figures show the average number of trials required for Benjamin to relearn seven original and three comparison passages, resulting in a savings score of 27%.

even before he had mastered language? What happened to Benjamin? What changes occurred in his underlying physiology? Attempts to locate the origins of memory in the nervous system, like the elusive sources of the Nile, have led to considerable speculation.

EVIDENCE IN BIOCHEMISTRY. Early investigations of ribonucleic acid (RNA), which is particularly influential in cell development, have shown the hope and frustration in this work. In these experiments, it was demonstrated that tiny flatworms learned and retained a classically conditioned response (Thompson & McConnell, 1955). Furthermore, when RNA was extracted from the tissues of the trained worms and injected into untrained worms, they learned the response more rapidly (McConnell, 1972). Such research suggested that memory might be transferred through chemistry, and RNA appeared to be *the* memory molecule.

However, there were several limitations in this research, the most important of which has been the difficulty in replicating it. Even the original investigators at times have been unsuccessful, even with larger animals, such as rats and fish. Instead, it appears that other chemical substances may have been involved. Furthermore, it seems that RNA molecules may simply enhance learning in some way, perhaps through protein production, rather than influencing memory per se (Guyette, Chavis, & Shearer, 1980). Quantitative changes in RNA and protein synthesis occur during learning, but there is little evidence that these changes are the fundamental bases of memory (Squire, 1987).

More promising findings have been obtained in recent clinical and experimental studies of neurotransmitter substances. As we saw in the chapter on the biological foundations of behavior, there are transmitters in the synapses for all sorts of human experiences, including sleep, pain, eating, emotion, and memory. For example, patients with Alzheimer's disease, who suffer from pronounced memory loss, show diminished synthesis of acetylcholine, important in cognitive functioning. Several other neurotransmitters, primarily norepinephrine and dopamine, also seem to modulate the development of memory (Morley & Flood, 1990).

The role of transmitter substances was supported when adults learned a 20-word list and a half hour later received either an intravenous infusion of one milligram of physostigmine, a substance that arouses diverse physiological activities, or one milligram of a saline solution, serving as a placebo. Eighteen minutes after the infusion and again 80 minutes afterward, the subjects attempted to recall as many words as possible. In the first recall trial, at 18 minutes, the subjects given physostigmine showed superior memory, and at 80 minutes the difference in favor of physostigmine was even greater (Davis, Mohs, Tinklenberg, Pfefferbaum, Hollister, & Koppell, 1978).

However, physostigmine is an energizer, and a mild dose of caffeine, nicotine, or another stimulant may temporarily increase performance. If we gave little Benjamin a stimulant, even he for a while might do better on something he already knew. It is unlikely that stimulants act only on memory per se, and thus the nature of the synaptic change, chemical or structural, is still uncertain.

One promising area of investigation concerns **long-term potentiation,** which is a sustained, permanent increase in the strength of a synaptic connection. The nerve pathway becomes more readily excitable on a long-term basis. This outcome was demonstrated by stimulating nerve tissue in the brain with a weak electric current and measuring the response. Afterward, when the same neural pathway was stimulated again, it gave a stronger response, and this greater response strength was observed again on later occasions. Highly complex biochemical reactions in the synapses, including protein synthesis, are presumed to be responsible for the increased excitability in long-term potentiation (Lynch & Baudry, 1984).

EVIDENCE IN BRAIN AREAS. For hundreds of years, the role of the brain in human memory has been recognized. But which parts play special roles? One answer to this question is the cerebral cortex, a massive mantle of cells discussed extensively in the chapter on biological foundations of behavior. The most advanced brain structure in an evolutionary sense, it is fundamentally involved in associative thinking and therefore in the retrieval of stored information.

Further studies have pointed to a smaller, subcortical organ, stimulated in studies of long-term potentiation. The **hippocampus** is a curved structure in the temporal lobes of the brain, named for the Latin word for "sea horse," in reference to its shape. Brain injuries from tumor, lack of oxygen, and surgery, as well as controlled studies with animals, cite functions of the hippocampus in memory (Macphail, 1986; Sutherland & McDonald, 1990). It seems to play a central role in *establishing* long-term memories, uniting separate pieces of information into an integrated, whole memory. Later, with the passage of time, this stored memory becomes relatively less dependent on the hippocampus and related structures (Squire & Zola-Morgan, 1991).

In one instance, H. M., a man in his twenties, underwent surgery for epileptic seizures that had beset him since childhood. Before the surgery he was above average in intelligence, as he was afterward, and his memory was normal. But following surgery and a hippocampal lesion, he experienced **anterograde amnesia,** in which no new memories can be established. H. M. could not remember new events in his life, a condition that enormously disrupted his social life. He could make no new friends, for he could not remember having met them. He was a social bore, not recalling what he had just said to anyone (Milner, Corkin, & Teuber, 1968).

Follow-up studies have shown that H. M. can learn *some new motor skills,* such as completing a puzzle or some other simple hand–eye coordination task. He cannot recall having mastered the new task, treating it later as though it were completely new, but he can perform it, even after a lapse of several weeks (Graf, Squire, & Mandler, 1984).

Another form of amnesia, **retrograde amnesia,** also experienced by H. M., involves a loss of memory for old experiences, especially those preceding the traumatic event. The afflicted individual is unable to recall the previous details, such as going to work, reaching the construction site, mounting the framework, reaching for a certain tool, and so forth. A similar form of forgetting may occur more briefly, and in a lesser degree, among people who have received electroconvulsive therapy. In both cases, if memory improves there is a gradual recovery of memory for events closer and closer to the traumatic episode; those immediately preceding it are the last to be remembered, if recovered at all (Figure 8–13).

MULTIPLE BASES OF MEMORY. It

appears that memory cannot be assigned to any particular biochemical element or brain area. The hippocampus may play a special role in the retention of factual information. Memories for procedures—on how to accomplish certain routine tasks—may be stored elsewhere in the brain (Squire, 1987). The site for a particular engram, or memory trace, appears to be partly specific, partly distributed. It may be specific in the sense that certain *sets* of neurons must be activated; it may be distributed in the sense that several brain areas—the hippocampus, cortex, cerebellum, amygdala, and other regions—also play a role (Rosenzweig, 1996) .

One fact seems certain: If memory is to occur, some new neural connections must be formed or some old ones must be functionally elaborated.

∽

STRUCTURE OF THE TRACE

In considering the physiological basis of memory, wherever its location, one might ask an equally compelling question: How does the trace work? What is its structure? Two basic hypotheses have been developed about the structure of the memory trace.

REAPPEARANCE HYPOTHESIS. Spec-

tacular events in brain surgery seem to support the view that memory in some way involves a permanent rearrangement of molecules, just as there is a lasting electromagnetic realignment of particles in a recording tape. This structural alteration, through prior experience, creates a trace that, if properly aroused, will reproduce the event in exact detail, just like the electromagnetic tape. According to this view, Benjamin Burtt would have a full memory of the earlier Greek passages if the proper traces were activated.

Patients' experiences in psychoanalysis, reporting long-forgotten childhood events, add further support to this view, popular for centuries. This outlook, the **reappearance hypothesis,** implies that a full memory will appear whenever the trace is properly retrieved. There is no memory loss; the complete experience is retained, somehow filed away in static fashion, waiting to be aroused. Forgetting is not a failure of storage but rather a failure to retrieve the existing information.

This possibility seemed all the more promising after some midcentury experiments by a well-known Canadian brain surgeon, Wilder Penfield. Patients often remain conscious during such surgery, with only a local anesthetic, for no pain is experienced in the brain itself. With the brain exposed, Penfield stimulated with a needle electrode various regions of the brain of an epileptic person, chiefly to identify possible areas of origin of the

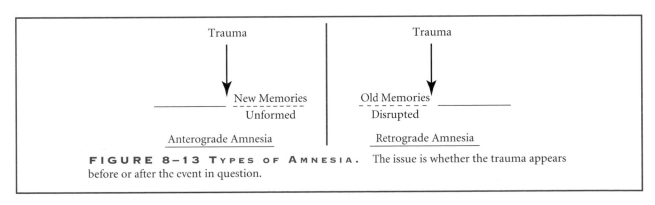

FIGURE 8–13 TYPES OF AMNESIA. The issue is whether the trauma appears before or after the event in question.

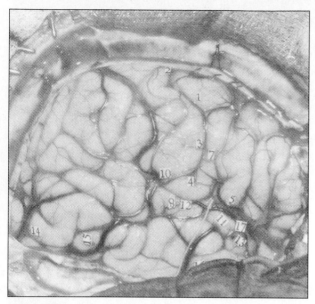

FIGURE 8-14 REAPPEARANCE HYPOTHESIS. Electrical stimulation at point 13 produced descriptions of hearing voices and seeing a circus wagon. The patient was told that the stimulation would be repeated. It was not, and she made no report. Then the same point was stimulated again, eliciting further details about the same voice (Penfield, 1958).

seizures. As he did so, the patient gave detailed reports of immediate experiences, such as seeing lights and hearing sounds. More important, with stimulation in other areas, the patient seemed to be reporting memories: circus wagons in childhood, prior work as a stenographer, and a play seen earlier (Penfield, 1958; Figure 8–14).

RECONSTRUCTION HYPOTHESIS. A contrasting hypothesis states that memories are not fixed images but rather reconstructions. A memory trace is a partial residue from the past, and current memories are built on these remnants. In the **reconstruction hypothesis,** bits and pieces of experience are used to assemble a memory (Neisser, 1967). To recall the Greek lessons, Benjamin would have to reassemble them and fill in the gaps with logic and expectations.

From this perspective, the surgical studies of brain stimulation have been criticized on several grounds. First, they provide no convincing evidence that the patient's report is a memory rather than a fantasy or even a dream. Furthermore, there is no evidence that the report is accurate or even complete. And finally, even if the reports do constitute accurate memories, there is still no evidence that all of our memories are retained permanently (Loftus & Loftus, 1980; Neisser, 1967).

In fact, if every experience remained in permanent storage, totally intact, life could become extremely difficult. Our retrieval system would constantly be overloaded, beset with major thoughts and insignificant matters.

William James advocated the reconstruction view, believing that a permanently existing memory image was highly unlikely. This perspective seems the more probable today, especially according to modern cognitive psychologists. In the levels-of-processing theory and even according to stage theory, memory is regarded as a dynamic process, not a passive experience, a view that has important implications for the ways in which we develop successful memory.

• THEORIES OF FORGETTING •

Around the time of Benjamin's thirteenth birthday, his father gave him a surprise— one the boy was likely to remember. He asked Benjamin to undertake his Greek lessons again. Would Benjamin memorize another ten passages?

So Harold Burtt devoted himself to this second follow-up study. This time, in recognition of Benjamin's greater maturity, he read the ten passages aloud twice daily, again using a rotated sequence. He began with a different passage each day in order to avoid devoting special attention to one passage or another.

Professor Burtt reported that his son's attitude was better than in the earlier tests "because he understood the scientific importance to a greater extent." And certainly Benjamin was a vastly improved learner. In addition, he knew that after he had mastered a certain passage, he would be through with it. On this basis, he required an average of only 149 trials to relearn the original selections. For the new ones, he needed 162 trials. This difference resulted in a savings score of 8%. The memory trace for the original passages was still there, but compared with the earlier savings of 27%, it was unquestionably weaker. Here again Benjamin had no idea which selections he had heard previously and which were new. His father noted all of these findings in a follow-up report, *A Further Study of Early Childhood Memory* (Burtt, 1937; Table 8–3).

This further loss on Benjamin's part brings us to the question of **forgetting,** defined as the inability to recall, to recognize, or to relearn at an improved rate. This condition may be due to storage failure, in which the information was not adequately maintained in the repository, or it may be due to retrieval failure, in which the trace was present but could not be evoked for lack of an appropriate cue. Also, it might have been an encoding failure, in which the information was never fully

TYPE OF PASSAGE	TRIALS REQUIRED
Original	
1	142
2	139
3	169
4	151
5	145
6	169
7	127
Average	149
Control	
1	169
2	151
3	166
Average	162

Learning trials for control passages	162
Relearning trials for original passages	−149
Difference	13

$$\frac{162 - 149}{162} = \frac{13}{162} = 8\%$$

TABLE 8–3 RELEARNING AFTER TEN YEARS. The figures show the average number of trials required for Benjamin to relearn seven original and three comparison passages, resulting in a savings score of 8%.

entered and never became a memory in the first place. Benjamin showed only 8% savings at age 13, partly because at age 3 he had been listening essentially to nonsense syllables, which show a rapid rate of forgetting.

We now turn to several theories that attempt to explain not the rate of forgetting but why memory failures occur at all. These theories of forgetting show once again that psychology is guided by diverse interpretations of its findings.

DECAY THEORY

Benjamin's latest savings score indicated that 92% of the original material had become inaccessible or lost. How did this happen?

According to the **decay theory,** which has much popular appeal, the memory trace deteriorates unless it is used. There is a storage failure, possibly a result of the continuous metabolic action of the cells of the nervous system. The lapse of time, according to this view, may be responsible for forgetting. When you memorize a telephone number and fail to remember it days later, it seems that the memory has just faded away.

Providing clear evidence for decay theory is extremely difficult because the processes postulated in the other theories of forgetting, such as interference and repression, presumably occur at the same time. Thus, the influence of decay alone cannot be readily demonstrated. Some evidence comes from a human adult who lost his sight at the age of two years. When he recovered it years later, he showed no memory of prior visual learning, behaving in the same fashion as someone who was born blind (Hebb, 1966). However, the force of this example is weakened by the fact that children seem to develop and organize their memories differently from adults.

Further claims come from short-term memory experiments, in which much information is lost in just a few seconds. Decay theorists stress that our capacity for processing information is limited and

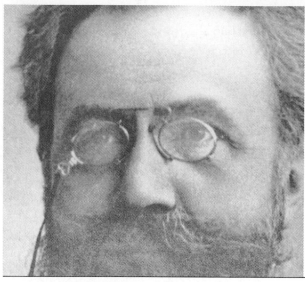

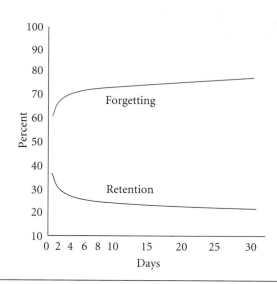

FIGURE 8–15 HERMANN EBBINGHAUS'S MEMORY CURVE.
Despite deficiencies in his work, Ebbinghaus inaugurated the use of quantitative methods in investigating memory. In these curves, obtained by using nonsense syllables, forgetting is the percentage lost; retention is the percentage retained.

that rehearsal prevents decay, chiefly by keeping the material active. When rehearsing stops, decay begins, independently of any outside interference. This theory lacks support, but it is also difficult to demonstrate that there is no deterioration of the memory trace with time.

Hermann Ebbinghaus, a significant figure in early studies of memory, served as his own subject, memorizing over 2,000 nonsense syllables altogether. Devised to provide a large quantity of unfamiliar material for memorization, each syllable was formed by placing a vowel between two consonants. Ebbinghaus memorized each list of several syllables until he could recite it perfectly, and then he tested himself on this material at several later dates. He found that about half of the material was forgotten after just 20 minutes, two-thirds after two days, and almost 80% by the end of the month. Forgetting was rapid at first and then slow (Ebbinghaus, 1913; Figure 8–15).

Later investigators, using many subjects and averaging the results, verified the general slope of the curve that Ebbinghaus found. However, this curve applies only to nonsense material, such as

Ebbinghaus's syllables and little Benjamin's foreign language passages and even here, there is no direct evidence for decay theory.

OBLITERATION OF THE TRACE

Another view that postulates a storage failure focuses on sudden destruction of a trace, presumably in its formative stages, rather than slow deterioration of a well-established trace simply through disuse. According to **obliteration theory,** the trace needs time to become firmly fixed. Certain conditions occurring soon after an experience can eradicate the memory before it becomes permanent.

Various experiments with rats, fish, and other animals have shown the importance of the time factor in obliteration of the memory trace. When rats were given electroconvulsive shocks at several later intervals following the original learning, a test of retention showed that the sooner the shock was administered, the larger was the disruption. When a shock occurred immediately after learning, forgetting was most pervasive (Pinel & Cooper, 1966).

This memory disruption apparently occurs by preventing protein synthesis, considered earlier as a possible chemical basis of memory through RNA. In one experiment, goldfish learned to avoid an electric shock by swimming to the darker end of the tank. Immediately after this learning, some of the fish were injected with puromycin, a substance that interferes with protein synthesis. These fish seemed to forget completely what they had just learned. When other fish were injected with puromycin an hour later, memory was unaffected, and injections approximately one half hour after the training resulted in an intermediate memory loss (Agranoff, 1967). As in electroconvulsive shock, the amount of memory loss seems to be closely related to the time of the obliterating stimulus.

In a very different, early experiment, college students, one by one, sat in a lighted room and learned a list of nonsense syllables. Then, to provide a brief rest, some were given simple jokes to read, and afterward they were asked to recall the syllables. For others, the rest period was no joke. Quite unexpectedly, the back of the chair collapsed; an electric shock occurred in the arms of the chair; scrap metal fell from the ceiling; a pistol shot rang out; and the lights went off, producing total darkness. When tested after this commotion, most subjects were in a state of collapse and shock themselves, and they forgot most of the list. One subject could not remember any syllables at all (Harden, 1930).

Take consolation in knowing that you did not participate in that research. According to the code of ethics of the American Psychological Association, it certainly would not be permitted today without the subjects' informed consent, however that might be defined. That investigator scared the nonsense out of those students.

In daily life, people often have amnesia for events immediately preceding or following an emotional upset, but investigators do not know how an emotional trauma interferes with retention. Nor do they fully understand the way in which electroconvulsive shock and lack of protein synthesis disrupt memory. It seems clear, however, that the trace needs time to consolidate or set and that immediate physical *or* emotional shock may disrupt the consolidation process (Squire, 1987).

INTERFERENCE THEORY

Aside from the encoding problem, Benjamin's memory loss might be explained on the basis of interference theory, and his father had been concerned about this possibility. According to **interference theory,** information is lost from memory because it is disturbed or displaced by other information. These disturbances can occur at any time, and therefore the memory problem can be either a storage failure or a retrieval failure (Tulving & Psotka, 1971).

PROACTIVE INTERFERENCE. When memory of earlier learning disrupts the recall of something learned later, the condition is called **proactive interference.** The disruptive events occur *before* the learning in question (Table 8–4).

Children are sometimes remarkable in their accurate recall of a holiday or birthday, often with far more details than the parents. Among the possible explanations, one lies with proactive interference. The child has experienced only a few such occasions before the most recent one. The parents may have been exposed to 40 or more, leaving significant opportunities for interference. When young adults and elderly subjects were compared for facial recognition, a relatively easy task, the results showed a

	LEARNING	LEARNING	RECALL
I	History	Sociology	Sociology
II	—	Sociology	Sociology

TABLE 8–4 PROACTIVE INTERFERENCE. For Group I, learning history disrupted recall of later learning, a sociology assignment.

memory deficit among the elderly, speculated to be the result of proactive interference from previously viewed faces (Flicker, Ferris, Crook, & Bartus, 1989).

Proactive interference is sometimes said to account for certain results obtained by Hermann Ebbinghaus, who found more rapid forgetting than is generally reported today. Since Ebbinghaus learned thousands of nonsense syllables during his experiments, it is quite likely that the earlier learning interfered with the later learning and memory.

RETROACTIVE INTERFERENCE. Another type of interference follows the opposite model. In **retroactive interference,** memories of later experiences disrupt the recall of something learned earlier. The disruptive events occur *after* the learning in question (Table 8–5).

In one instance, college students memorized lists of nonsense syllables and then engaged in various activities or went to sleep. Retention was tested one, two, four, and eight hours later, and it was found that memory was better after any amount of sleep than after a comparable amount of time spent while awake (Jenkins & Dallenbach, 1924; Figure 8–16).

Do these findings pertain to prose, as well as to nonsense syllables? When 391 university students attempted to recall prose passages after exposure to various types of intervening information, retroactive interference occurred just as reliably as it did with nonprose material (Dempster, 1988).

In one early investigation, cockroaches were selected for study because they can be made to remain motionless for long periods of time without the use of drugs or other agents that might disrupt the nervous system. They become completely still when their bodies are in extensive contact with an external object, producing a state of inactivity known as tonic immobility. After three groups of cockroaches learned a simple maze, one group was rendered immobile by inducing them to crawl into a box of tissue paper. A second group was allowed to run freely in their cages. The third group was more active than usual, for these roaches were placed on a moving treadmill. Like pedestrians in a modern airport, they had to keep moving to avoid falling off the treadmill or bumping into a wall. Memory was measured by relearning, and the savings scores clearly favored the motionless group. The normally active subjects performed at an intermediate level. Those trudging on the treadmill needed the most relearning trials. In fact, they showed no memory at all (Minami & Dallenbach, 1946).

These outcomes suggest that forgetting is caused by *what happens* during the passage of time. As we go back and forth on the subway, shuttle about in our cars, and run around town, are we literally losing our minds—or at least our memories? The potentially disruptive influence of such events makes interference theory a recurring issue and decay theory an elusive research topic (Hall, Bernoties, & Schmidt, 1995).

Benjamin's memory loss, if explained on the basis of interference theory, would not be significantly attributed to proactive interference. The original learning, so early in life, left relatively little chance for this type of interference. All sorts of subsequent activities could have disrupted later recall, providing a case for retroactive interference.

Interference theory, incidentally, offers an explanation for the *serial position effect* in long-term memory. If a student memorized Lincoln's Gettysburg Address and then tried to recite it years later, the best remembered parts would be the beginning and ending. Earlier, we noted that rehearsal could account for this outcome when the recall task occurs shortly after learning. But even for

	LEARNING	LEARNING	RECALL
I	Algebra	Chemistry	Algebra
II	Algebra	—	Algebra

TABLE 8–5 RETROACTIVE INTERFERENCE. For Group I, learning chemistry symbols disrupted recall of earlier learning, an algebra assignment.

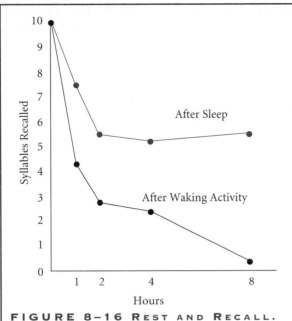

FIGURE 8–16 REST AND RECALL.
Many investigations show that the best preparation for an examination, *after* studying, is a good night's sleep (Jenkins & Dallenbach, 1924).

material learned years ago, the beginning and ending are the favored positions. For the first part of the contents, there can be no proactive interference due to prior material; for the end, there can be no retroactive interference due to subsequent material.

MOTIVATED FORGETTING

Our final view of forgetting, like obliteration theory, does not seem highly relevant in Benjamin's case. It did not emerge through laboratory studies of information processing but rather from Freud's clinical studies of people with adjustment problems. The memory problem is one of retrieval, not storage. In **motivated forgetting,** the full memory trace is presumably available, but the individual does not want to remember. Loss of memory is produced by an unconscious effort to forget, called *repression,* thereby ridding oneself of anxiety, frustration, or some other emotional concern.

Sigmund Freud once came across a name in his medical records and could not recall the patient at all, even though he had treated her for many weeks just six months earlier. Finally, information on his fees brought back all of the facts about the case. The patient was a 14-year-old girl who showed an anxiety reaction that was readily treated, although she still complained of stomach pains. Then, two months later, she suddenly died of sarcoma in the abdomen. Freud was deeply troubled, saddened, and embarrassed by the case, for while the obvious anxiety reaction held his attention, he had overlooked the first signs of the insidious physical ailment (Freud, 1914). Thus, it came to him as no surprise that he was motivated to forget that case.

According to modern psychoanalytic theory, repression can take place not only after the event has occurred but also while it is happening. In other words, repression may become a factor in the initial stages of memory formation, during encoding, and perhaps even in storage. If it takes place while a traumatic event is being encoded, that memory will be particularly inaccessible, for it will be poorly recorded in the first place (Bonanno, 1990).

Many psychologists are not satisfied with the concept of repression. Some point out that forgetting of negatively toned material may occur simply because there is no effort to remember the experience. Others prefer simpler explanations, especially interference theory.

The role of repression cannot be evaluated in Benjamin's case. The fact that Benjamin could not recall or even recognize the passages, but did show some memory through relearning, indicates that a partial trace remained from the earlier experience. No effort to stimulate that residue evoked a full, intact memory, however, as postulated in motivated forgetting.

• PRINCIPLES OF MEMORIZING •

The reader keeping track of Benjamin's efforts has perhaps surmised that he still had more work to do. His father had read

21 Greek passages in infancy, seven of which were relearned in childhood and seven in adolescence. The remaining seven, with three control passages, would provide one final test in adulthood, at 18 years of age. And they provide an opportunity for comparing the various theories of forgetting (Table 8-6).

This time Benjamin learned more slowly, perhaps because he was tired of this recurring task, every five years, and perhaps because he *was* experiencing some confusion with certain syllables learned earlier. Those from his effort at age 13 at times seemed to disrupt him. And this time, alas, he needed an average of 189 trials for the original passages and 191 for the new ones. The difference was negligible, producing a savings score of 1%. These results left no doubt about what had happened. No significant memory remained at all (Table 8–7).

The effects of the recitations in infancy, definitely manifest at age eight, still evident at age 13, had completely disappeared by age 18. Professor Burtt described this result with professional objectivity in his last report of this work, *An Experimental Study of Early Childhood Memory: Final Report* (1941).

In the last few years, all remaining traces of the stimulation in infancy had disappeared. But why? We have speculated about interference, decay, and even repression, all concerned with storage or retrieval, but something more can be said—about Benjamin's mode of encoding. When the syllables were read to Benjamin in his infancy, he had not mastered his own language, and language can play a vital role in memory. More important, Benjamin had no intention of remembering these syllables.

~

ROLE OF MOTIVATION

The acquisition of knowledge or a skill without the aim of mastering it is known as *incidental learning.* If you know the name of the city in which this book was published, that information is incidental learning—unless the instructor announced that you must know it for an examination. In contrast, *intentional learning* means that the memory has been acquired with effort, along the lines of the encoding procedures discussed earlier, so completely ignored by Benjamin. The intention to learn is usually vital for long-term storage.

What appears to be forgetting may occur simply because there was no impression, or an inadequate one, in the first place. We fail to remember names, and even passages from rituals recited hundreds of times, because we were inattentive when they were spoken. We do not remember certain details of an exciting event due to concentra-

THEORY	TYPE OF PROBLEM	REASON FOR MEMORY LOSS	EXAMPLE FROM BENJAMIN
Decay	Storage	Gradual deterioration of the trace due to the passage of time	No evidence either way
Obliteration	Storage	Eradication of a newly formed trace before consolidation	No report of this nature by Harold
Interference			
Proactive	Storage or retrieval	Disruption by events before the event in question	Unlikely; Benjamin's lessons took place early in life
Retroactive	Storage or retrieval	Disruption by events after the event in question	A plausible explanation for Benjamin's decreasing memory with increasing age
Motivated forgetting	Retrieval	A memory failure due to repression; the person unconsciously wants to forget	Difficult to evaluate; no clear evidence

TABLE 8–6 THEORIES OF FORGETTING. The decay, obliteration, and interference theories postulate a storage problem. Interference theory also postulates a retrieval problem, as does motivated forgetting.

TYPE OF PASSAGE	TRIALS REQUIRED
Original	
1	202
2	190
3	181
4	220
5	160
6	175
7	193
Average	189
Control	
1	205
2	193
3	175
Average	191

Learning trials for control passages	191
Relearning trials for original passages	−189
Difference	2

$$\frac{191 - 189}{191} = \frac{2}{191} = 1\%$$

TABLE 8–7 RELEARNING AFTER FIFTEEN YEARS. The figures show the average number of trials required for Benjamin to relearn seven original and three comparison passages, resulting in a savings score of 1%.

tion on other details with a higher attention value. Such outcomes do not constitute poor memory, for nothing was learned that might be forgotten later.

The significance of motivation is also evident from the opposite direction, in *overlearning*, which means learning beyond the point at which a task has merely been mastered. The value of this procedure was illustrated when adults learned lists of words beyond one perfect recall. Using half again as many practice trials as were required to reach the first perfect recall was designated 50% overlearning; using twice as many was called 100% overlearning. When these groups were compared with a third group that engaged in no additional practice trials, the results showed a distinct advantage for both amounts of overlearning (Krueger, 1929).

The idea of overlearning is misleading, suggesting that there has been too much practice. A highly motivated learner always passes beyond the point of initial mastery but has not learned the task too well. When college students and their tutors were tested several months after the course was over, the tutors retained more than the students they tutored, presumably because tutoring involved overlearning (Semb, Ellis, & Arauio, 1993).

MEMORY SYSTEMS

If motivation is influential in memory, perhaps sheer practice and determination can make a difference. Years ago, William James decided to answer this question by studying himself. Can memory be improved merely by exercise, just as one strengthens a muscle by exercising it?

James began by memorizing 158 lines from the works of Victor Hugo, applying himself to the task for eight consecutive days. Keeping a careful record of his time, he found that he required an average of 50 seconds to memorize each line. That was the "strength of his memory" before he began his program of memory exercise.

Next, he engaged in intensive memory exercise for 38 days. He attempted to strengthen his memory by memorizing Milton's poetry, spending 20 minutes each day in this effort. Afterward, was his memory stronger? The way to find out was to return to Victor Hugo's poetry. Could he memorize another 158 lines more easily than the earlier ones?

Using the same procedure as before, this time he required 57 seconds per line, just a bit slower than previously. The slightly poorer performance occurred, he said, because he had become "perceptibly fagged." He verified his finding by asking friends to serve as subjects, and they encountered the same result. One's basic memory capacity—or native retentiveness, as James called it—cannot be improved by exercise alone (James, 1890).

However, memory can be improved with **mnemonic devices,** systems designed to aid memory by efficient input and output. The encoding strategies mentioned earlier—organization, chunking, and retrieval cues—are the foundations of most mnemonic devices, which have existed since the time of ancient civilizations (Patten, 1990).

LOCI AND PEG WORDS. One of the more formal mnemonic devices is the **method of loci,** which uses a series of familiar places to aid recall. A locus is a place; loci are places. These places are parts of a well-established route to work, school, or somewhere else, and each item on the list to be remembered is associated with a specific place in this accustomed pathway. That place serves as a cue for recall, and imagery is used in each instance (Figure 8–17). This method illustrates the three basic factors in successful encoding. There is an organization, the accustomed pathway; there is the provision for chunking, accomplished by assigning a group of items at each stopping place; and there is opportunity for cuing, facilitated by creating distinct images at each location (Bower, 1970).

Giving more emphasis to the auditory realm, another approach is not based on a long-standing habit. The framework must be learned, and then it may play an almost irresistible role in recall, as is evident in so many television advertisements. A catchy jingle or simple poem promoting some product becomes unforgettable. In the **peg-word system,** the rhyming words are used as pegs for memorizing the new material. This method is especially useful for serial learning, for each place is numbered and can form a sharp image with the rhyme at that point (Table 8–8).

All mnemonic devices require practice. They do not work by themselves. When students were trained to use chunking, for example, their memory capacities for digits increased enormously. After extensive practice, they reached a level nine or ten times higher than their original level (Chase & Ericsson, 1982).

IN RETROSPECT. Looking backward, Benjamin's failure can be attributed significantly to inadequate encoding, the first element of

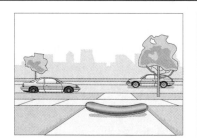

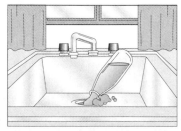

FIGURE 8–17 METHOD OF LOCI. Suppose a woman needs to remember a shopping list of hot dogs, cat food, tomatoes, bananas, and milk. On her habitual route home she encounters several familiar places—walking by the front path, checking the mail box, entering through the front door, hanging a coat in the closet, and going into the kitchen. To remember the shopping list, the person thinks of a large hot dog lying in the front pathway, a hungry cat having its supper in the mail box, tomatoes splattered on the front door, a bunch of bananas hanging in the coat closet, and a milk bottle bubbling its contents into the kitchen sink. To recall these items, she merely procedes mentally down the accustomed route, stopping in the pathway, by the mail box, at the door, and at other places to ask, "What did I put here?"

One is a bun; two is a shoe;
Three is a tree; four is a door;
Five is a hive; six is sticks;
Seven is heaven; eight is a gate;
Nine is wine; ten is a hen.

TABLE 8–8 PEG-WORD SYSTEM.
The verse must be learned first, a relatively easy task because of its rhyme and rhythm. Then each item on the list is put in its numbered place. Using the commuter's shopping list again, a learner might proceed as follows: one-bun would have a hot dog, a natural association; two-shoe might have cat food in the shoe; three-tree would have tomatoes among the branches, and so forth.

memory. He presumably did not cast the material into any systematic organization; he apparently did not use chunking, combining certain pieces of information into manageable subgroups; and he surely did not employ cuing, whereby he developed signals for retrieval of the stored information. Nevertheless, he and his father completed a very demanding scientific study revealing several important findings.

They showed, in the first place, the value of using relearning for measuring small amounts of memory. Compared with recall and recognition, relearning has the greatest sensitivity for detecting weak memories. Second, and more important, Professor Burtt accomplished his basic goal. He demonstrated that human memory can be established in infancy—as early as 15 months of age. Prior to this experiment, there was little compelling evidence that experiences at this early point of life could be retained in any amount. Third, the father

and son together provided support for Ebbinghaus's well-known curves of forgetting, except that they did so not for a few minutes, a few days, or one month—but for 15 years.

For these contributions to our understanding of memory, the Burtts are deserving of special recognition. It may be quite some time before another psychologist and partner are willing to examine memory in the dedicated manner of Harold and Benjamin. The father recognized his son, and the hundreds of hours Benjamin donated from infancy through early adulthood, by adding a footnote in one report: "To Benjamin P. Burtt, who served as subject in this rather tedious experiment" (Burtt, 1932).

By modern standards, the father is doubly deserving of our gratitude. He also served as a comparison subject in this research. Benjamin remained passive throughout the readings, and part of his forgetting may have been due to his developing brain structure. But his father became an active adult learner, reading every passage aloud, pronouncing each syllable slowly and carefully, 90 times each. Knowing Greek and the story of Oedipus, he had a context for remembering these lines, encoding them within this framework. On these bases, the drama of King Oedipus became available to him in memory not just through relearning or recognition for five years or ten years but even through recall into the very latest decades of his life.

That life was a long one, 101 years.

• SUMMARY •

ACQUISITION OF MEMORY

1. Immediately after we experience something, sensory memory provides a momentary residual stimulation. It involves largely unprocessed information, some of which can be transferred to short-term memory.

2. Short-term memory, the next stage, is also a temporary condition, sometimes known as working memory. During this period, a limited amount of information can be processed for permanent storage in long-term memory. Transfer to long-term memory requires successful encoding or recoding,

which involves: organization, chunking, and the use of cues to aid retrieval.

3. In the third phase, long-term memory apparently has an unlimited capacity and presumably involves different systems of storage for different types of memories—procedural, concerning how to do things, and declarative, concerning factual information.

4. Another approach, sometimes known as levels-of-processing theory, does not involve these hypothesized stages, separate from one another. It states instead that the permanence of a memory depends on the cognitive activities that go into its formation, especially encoding.

THE MEMORY TRACE

5. Memory can be measured by three basic methods: recall, recognition, and relearning. Redintegration is a variation of the method of free recall, for cues or hints are made available.

6. The biochemical nature of the trace is suspected to involve RNA, neurotransmitter substances, and perhaps long-term potentiation, which is a sustained, permanent increase in the strength of a synaptic connection. Several brain areas appear to be involved, especially the hippocampus and cerebral cortex.

7. According to the reappearance hypothesis, the memory trace remains intact in the brain as a structural alteration. In the reconstruction hypothesis, memories are not fixed and filed in the brain but rather reassembled, chiefly on the basis of remnants from past experience.

THEORIES OF FORGETTING

8. In decay theory, forgetting is presumed to involve a storage failure. Through disuse and the passage of time, the trace deteriorates.

9. According to obliteration theory, severe shock destroys the currently forming or newly formed trace before it is firmly established, causing forgetting through a storage failure.

10. There is also evidence that forgetting is produced by what happens over time, apart from some shock immediately after learning. Prior interference is known as proactive interference. Subsequent interference is called retroactive interference.

11. In motivated forgetting, it is hypothesized that unpleasant thoughts are unconsciously excluded from awareness, a process called repression. This problem is a retrieval failure.

PRINCIPLES OF MEMORIZING

12. Motivation is a most important aspect of successful memory. Forgetting may be very rapid when one has no desire to remember; overlearning shows that through extra effort, one can build up resistance to forgetting.

13. For successful encoding, storage, and retrieval, mnemonic devices are useful. The method of loci and the peg-word system illustrate these techniques.

• WORKING WITH PSYCHOLOGY •

❧ REVIEW OF KEY CONCEPTS ❧

memory	*Acquisition of Memory*	short-term memory (STM)
encoding	information processing	working memory
storage	stage theory of memory	rehearsal
retrieval	sensory memory	subjective organization

chunking
cuing
context-dependent memory
state-dependent memory
long-term memory (LTM)
primacy effect
recency effect
procedural memory
declarative memory
episodic memory
semantic memory
implicit memory
explicit memory
schema
script
conceptual hierarchy
network of associations

levels-of-processing theory
connectionist model

The Memory Trace
memory trace
recall
redintegration
eidetic imagery
flashbulb memory
recognition
déjà vu experience
relearning
savings score
long-term potentiation
hippocampus
anterograde amnesia
retrograde amnesia

reappearance hypothesis
reconstruction hypothesis

Theories of Forgetting
forgetting
decay theory
obliteration theory
interference theory
proactive interference
retroactive interference
motivated forgetting

Principles of Memorizing
mnemonic devices
method of loci
peg-word system

❧ CLASS DISCUSSION/CRITICAL THINKING ❧

A NARRATIVE TWIST

Assume that Harold Burtt, reciting to his 15-month-old son, had not read *Oedipus Rex* in the original Greek but had read rhyming poetry in English instead. He might have recited Longfellow's *Midnight Ride of Paul Revere*. By using poetry of this sort, would Harold have obtained different results in his study of infant memory? Why or why not? Suggest his reason for using the Sophocles's passages. Which approach seems preferable? Why? ❧

TOPICAL QUESTIONS

• *Acquisition of Memory.* Consider your preparation for an examination on the U.S. Civil War. Indicate in detail the strategies you might use, considering what you know about encoding. In your answer, include the concepts of organization, chunking, and cuing.

• *The Memory Trace.* Suppose your memory is malfunctioning and you are limited to one of its three capacities: recall, recognition, or relearning. Further, suppose you must select a different capacity for different occasions. Which might you choose if you were anticipating a routine day? Going to a high school reunion? Delivering a speech without the use of notes? Explain your reasons.

• *Theories of Forgetting.* Is forgetting a necessary condition for normal human functioning? Speculate on our lives if we could not forget. In this context, suggest a modification in memory capacity that might improve human adjustment.

• *Principles of Memorizing.* Think about a baseball team, a symphony orchestra, or the crew of a ship. Which mnemonic devices might be used to remember the membership in each instance? How would they be employed?

❧ TOPICS OF RELATED INTEREST ❧

Information processing is a central concept in perception (5), as well as in thought and language (9). Neurotransmitter substances, which presumably play an important role in memory, are discussed in the context of the biological bases of behavior (3). Repression, also called motivated forgetting, is the second phase in the three-stage approach in psychoanalysis (14).

COMPONENTS OF THINKING
Forming Concepts
Concepts and Language

ACQUISITION OF LANGUAGE
Nature of Language
Language Learning
Views of Language Learning

REASONING AND PROBLEM SOLVING
Computer Thought
Human Reasoning
Problem Solving

CREATIVE THINKING
Processes in Creativity
Creativity and Humor

9
THOUGHT
AND LANGUAGE

J UDITH ALMOST THOUGHT ABOUT BUILDING THE HOUSE HERSELF. THE CARPENTERS WERE SIMPLY TAKING TOO LONG TO BEGIN. A SMALL WOMAN WITH BIG IDEAS, Judith was a mother, psychologist, political activist, and environmentalist, but she could handle a hammer too.

Her husband had immense confidence in her abilities with people and tools. She *might* manage the task by herself. She was tired of living in their cramped quarters. She wanted a place of their own before their twins began school and she returned to her work in psychoneurology.

"What can I say? I can't build it any faster," replied Jim softly, laying down his tools, looking again at the architect's drawings, and shaking his head. He always spoke in a low voice with grammatically correct language. "I would like to do it sooner," he added (Kidder, 1985).

Jim knew a great deal about building houses. He had years of experience as a carpenter. As foreman of the group who would work on this job, he knew how much time it would take, that it was already April, and that the foundation had not been laid. Judith knew the kind of life she wanted to lead. She knew that houses shape our lives. In seeking a certain shelter, we seek a certain way of life.

Knowledge of any sort, together with the mental functions that lie behind it, is often referred to in psychology as **cognition.** This term includes all of the processes by which we know about the world, especially perception, memory, and thinking, as well as the use of language. We have already considered perception and memory; we now turn to thought and language. Here we are concerned with mental processes, not the structure of the brain, also considered earlier.

We begin this chapter with the components of thinking and then turn to the acquisition of language, for thought and language are intimately related. Afterward, we consider reasoning and problem solving and, as a special form of problem solving, creative thinking. The construction of Judith's house provides an everyday context for this discussion. It should enable most readers to apply these concepts to their own lives.

• COMPONENTS OF THINKING •

Judith described what she had in mind. "This New England farmhousey thing," she said, thinking about a tall, rectangular building with clapboard sides and porches, painted white. She wanted something compatible with the farmlands around the Connecticut River (Kidder, 1985). At the same time, she was concerned about function, remembering a fractured aphorism: A woman's home is her hassle.

Judith had the concept of a house. A **concept** is a general idea or category, a way of classifying things that have some common property. It refers to a class of objects or events considered equivalent in some way. The word *house* names a concept; it

refs to any structure that serves as a dwelling, a place of residence. A farmhouse is a subclass of *house,* and it too is a concept.

Thinking, whether by home owners, carpenters, or anyone else, is based on concepts. Concepts, in turn, are developed by thinking. The use of concepts therefore is a logical starting point in the study of thought and language.

❧

FORMING CONCEPTS

The words *carpenter, river,* and *mother* also refer to concepts. The word *mother,* for example, refers to all women who have given birth to a baby or who have adoptive responsibilities, regardless of other characteristics. In contrast, the word *Mother,* meaning your own mother, refers to just one person, and therefore it is not a concept. Similarly, the phrases *New England, Connecticut River,* and *Apple Corps* do not name concepts, for they too refer to unique particular instances, not a general category.

The Apple Corps, a construction company, included Jim and three other carpenters. Most outspoken among them was bearded Richard, a skillful, hardworking young man who kept one eye on their deadlines, the other on their progress. Apple Corps took their name from their town, Apple Valley, and we know about them from Tracy Kidder, nationally recognized author of a book about the building of Judith's farmhouse, which he succinctly titled *House* (1985).

Incidentally, *book* is a concept; *house* is too. But *House* is not.

Without concepts we could still have labels, such as names and comparable symbols, but we would have to treat every object as a completely separate event. Encountering a piece of paper, we would have to examine it to see if it contained writing or printing, indicating an agreement of some sort, and a place for the signatures of two or more parties. Having the concept of *contract* allows us to identify this document quickly and to assume that

it has the characteristics shared by other contracts.

Judith and her husband finally signed a contract with the Apple Corps, agreeing on a date for completion of the project: October 31. If the house remained unfinished after that Halloween night, the Apple Corps would turn into a pumpkin of sorts, paying a penalty of $100 for each additional day of work. This possibility unsettled Jim. He thought they might become the Apple Corpse.

TYPES OF CONCEPTS. Human beings use many types of concepts, ranging from simple to complex. The simplest concepts are identified by a single characteristic. For example, *round* is anything circular or ball-shaped; anything not judged as circular is not a member of this class. The word *taller* is a concept referring to a relationship. All things described this way have greater stature than things with which they are compared. The word *more* also involves a relationship, and here the comparison concerns mass. In fact, most words represent concepts of one sort or another.

The concepts used by adults typically have more than one attribute. Some *conjunctive concepts* have several attributes, and all must be present to satisfy the class. A *river,* for example, contains fresh water; it is large; it is longer than it is wide; and it flows in one direction. A river has at least these four attributes. Something similar but smaller is a brook. Something that does not flow in any direction is a pond or lake. And something that includes salt water may be an estuary.

Other complex concepts, known as *disjunctive concepts,* have several attributes, and any one of them, by itself, constitutes an instance of that event. In its modern sense, a *farm* may be an orchard for growing fruits, a garden for growing vegetables, land and buildings for raising animals, a body of water for cultivating edible sea creatures, or some combination of these events. Similarly, the concept of *brother-in-law* may mean the brother of one's wife or the brother of one's husband. The difficulty in forming disjunctive concepts is that, when there are several attributes and each of them alone can serve as an instance of that concept, the individual must discover whether any new event constitutes still another dimension (Bourne, 1966; Conant & Trabasso, 1964). For example, is the husband of one's sister also a brother-in-law?

In contrast, some concepts do not have a readily identifiable set of features. The concept *shelter* is easily understood, but what are its essential features? Must something have a roof to be a shelter? No—the side of a building provides shelter. Must it be constructed by human beings? Certainly not. Must it be attached to some relatively permanent structure? No again, for a newspaper held overhead provides shelter. Must it have a physical presence? No! Do not forget the tax shelter!

The concept of *clothing* is also readily acquired, but is a handbag a piece of clothing? A shirt surely is clothing, but what about the rest of your attire—your Mickey Mouse watch, earmuffs, and orthopedic sandals?

ACQUISITION OF CONCEPTS. Early laboratory studies and observations in daily life suggest two different processes by which we acquire concepts. The first is called the **features-based approach,** for it requires noting and remembering the essential features of an object or event. A person who acquires the concept *pencil* must observe that all such objects, regardless of how much they differ, have certain features in common. A pencil contains lead, is typically long and thin, is made of wood or metal or plastic, and is used for writing on paper or another flat surface. Someone may encounter for the first time a mechanical pencil with a pocket clip, an eraser, and other features. If this person decides that this object is also a pencil, he or she must have observed something of what pencils have in common. A crayon and pen, for example, use wax and ink, respectively, although they have the same shape (Figure 9–1).

Most modern researchers agree, however, that we do not form all concepts this way. We do not systematically identify the essential features of a

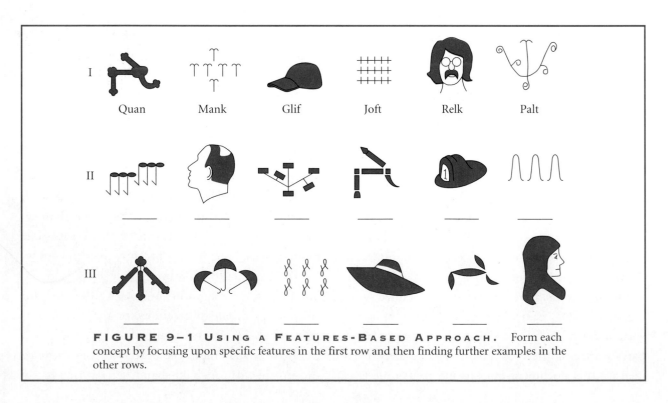

FIGURE 9–1 USING A FEATURES-BASED APPROACH. Form each concept by focusing upon specific features in the first row and then finding further examples in the other rows.

I Quan Mank Glif Joft Relk Palt

given concept, encounter some new object, and then carefully check to determine if the new object has each feature of the concept. Many concepts seem to be acquired more spontaneously, chiefly because they involve certain general characteristics about which most people agree. This quicker process is known as the **prototype-based approach,** which means that the person employs a good example of the concept and then compares each new instance with this example. If the match is close, the new instance is assumed to be part of the concept (Rosch, 1975). For instance, *furniture* is generally used for sitting, lying, eating, writing, reading, and so forth. A chair is a good example. We often base the concept *furniture* on this good model and then decide if new instances are sufficiently similar to be included (Murphy & Medin, 1985).

For a prototype of the concept *house,* you probably would use your own house, rather than an igloo, a tree hut, or a cave. For *bird,* you might use a robin—not a penguin or an ostrich, for these creatures do not fly. This outcome has been demonstrated in studies of the time it takes for people to classify objects as belonging to one concept or another. For example, when asked to decide if a robin is a bird, the subject's answer is immediate. When asked about the penguin, the response comes more slowly (Medin & Smith, 1984). As these results suggest, this approach has limitations because instances of a concept may vary widely from the prototype (Figure 9–2).

In forming an abstract concept, such as

contract—meaning an agreement—sometimes no clear prototype is available, and the specific features are not readily identifiable. The individual therefore may employ both approaches, noting the essential features and using an example. Not surprisingly, research shows that young children acquire such concepts only gradually, fitting examples into categories while ignoring the rules of adult logic (Strichartz & Burton, 1990).

CONCEPTS AND LANGUAGE

Toward the end of April, the Apple Corps began the first phase of construction, framing the house. The concept of *framing* means to build the skeleton of a house, giving it a basic shape, providing the supporting structures for the roof, floors, and walls. As this example shows, concepts and language are inextricably related.

"It strikes me as a bit holy to think you don't bargain, Jim," said Judith one day as they debated his fees. What does the concept *holy* mean? What does *bargain* mean? To be fully explained, all abstract concepts require extensive use of language.

CONCEPTS WITHOUT LANGUAGE.
Since language is unquestionably helpful in concept formation, there have been numerous attempts to discover whether animals can form concepts. In one experiment, rats were rewarded for selecting an upright triangle, as opposed to a circle or square. But after they succeeded regularly, the triangle was

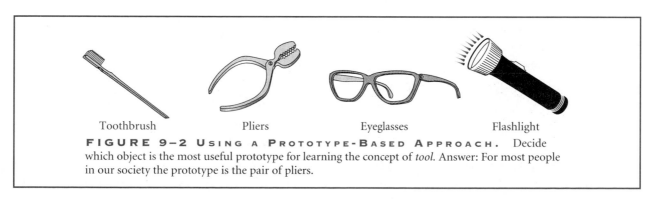

Toothbrush   Pliers   Eyeglasses   Flashlight

FIGURE 9–2 USING A PROTOTYPE-BASED APPROACH. Decide which object is the most useful prototype for learning the concept of *tool.* Answer: For most people in our society the prototype is the pair of pliers.

inverted, and then their success rate was no better than chance. Apparently they had not formed the concept of triangularity but rather were responding to a particular pattern of black and white. After all sorts of triangles were paired with other figures for 1,000 trials and the response to the triangle was always rewarded, some rats were successful on the first trial with a new triangle, one that was isosceles, colored, or different in some other way from the previous triangles. These animals, without language as far as we know, had abstracted and generalized. They were responding to the concept of triangularity, regardless of other characteristics (Fields, 1932, 1936).

There are clear differences among the species. Rats and pigeons, with much effort, can acquire concrete concepts like *triangularity* and *brightness,* in which the problem is basically a perceptual one, but they have difficulty with more complex concepts. Chimpanzees perform at a higher level. Even without a formal language, they can acquire abstract concepts, including *more, dirty, give,* and many others (Gardner & Gardner, 1969).

Normal human babies show the same reactions, and deaf children, deprived of a wealth of linguistic information, also can form abstract concepts. By 30 weeks of age, long before they have acquired language, human infants have the conceptual category of faces (Cohen & Strauss, 1979). From all these instances we conclude that concepts can be formed without language, even though words are enormously facilitating, especially with abstract concepts.

TEACHING LANGUAGE TO ANIMALS. Some psychologists interested in concept formation and language have accepted a special challenge: teaching a human language to animals. Chimpanzees, noted for their intelligence, have been selected for this work, which began in the 1920s with a young chimpanzee named Gua. She was brought up with a human baby, Donald. The two infants received the same attention, feeding, and toilet training from human adults. Donald's parents, Winthrop and Luella Kellogg, wanted to discover to what extent a chimpanzee reared like a child would develop like a human being.

The results were quite clear. At 16 months of age, Gua was superior in physical skills, such as strength and jumping, but she could only bark and screech in fear and pain and cry "oo-oo" when uncertain or anxious. Donald excelled in understanding simple concepts, and he even spoke a few words. The investigation was discontinued when Gua became too lively for the Kellogg household. Besides, Donald was missing out on birthday parties because the neighbors, knowing that the two infants had to be treated alike, did not want his "sister" along too (Kellogg & Kellogg, 1933).

Twenty years later, Vicki, a six-week-old chimpanzee, began her life in the household of Cathy and Keith Hayes—to be treated quite differently. Her "parents" devoted considerable effort to speech instruction. They rewarded her slightest vocalizations, moved her lips themselves, and served as models for her to imitate. They even took their chimp for a checkup at a college clinic, and then they went to a medical school for further consultations, all to no avail. After years of effort, their Vicki could only murmur "mama," "papa," and something like "k-p," for *cup* (Hayes, 1951).

Gua and Vicki learned very few concepts, and neither acquired any semblance of human language, perhaps because they were hampered by their speech mechanisms. Chimpanzees lack the mouth and throat coordination of even a very young child (Lenneberg, 1964). Thus, the next generation of investigators introduced still another approach.

Beginning when she was about one year old, a wild-born chimpanzee named Washoe was steadily exposed to American Sign Language (ASL), the gestural language system used among the hearing impaired in North America. She lived in a laboratory, not a household. Her chief tutors, Allen and Beatrice Gardner, were assisted by other team members, teaching ASL through conditioning, modeling, and the direct manipulation of her hands. On this basis, Washoe learned a number of concepts, including such abstract concepts as *more* and *funny*. She even employed these signs in sequence with others, asking for "More swinging" and "More drink" (Gardner & Gardner, 1969). Her vocabulary developed to more than 200 words, including action words and modifiers, as well as nouns, and she used them in many combinations and diverse situations (Gardner & Gardner, 1971).

But critics complained that Washoe's language ability was overestimated. It arose through imitation and reward training—as well as the Clever Hans effect, unconscious cuing on the part of the experimenter (Umiker-Sebeok & Sebeok, 1980). Further, her word combinations, a crucial feature of language competence, sometimes seemed arbitrary or incorrect. In short, although Washoe's accomplishments were surprising, especially in terms of concept formation, she had only achieved the language competence of a very young child.

To eliminate unconscious cuing, as well as imitation, another chimpanzee was not allowed to communicate directly with her trainers, Sue Savage-Rumbaugh and Duane Rumbaugh, or even with their assistants. Instead, Lana, named for the project, *Language Analogue*, communicated with a machine—a special computer equipped with a different geometric symbol on each key. To ask for a piece of bread, Lana used the *please* key, which turned on the computer, then the symbol for *give*, and then the one for *bread*. With this language system, she too has formed simple sentences, doing so essentially apart from human beings (Rumbaugh, 1977; Savage-Rumbaugh, Rumbaugh, & Boysen, 1980).

STATUS OF THE ANIMAL STUDIES.

Science is always unfinished business, and we can summarize the question of language learning in chimpanzees as follows. The current answer depends, in a large measure, on one's definition of language. If we concern ourselves with the acquisition of concepts and word combinations, there are reasons to defend their language ability. If, however, we require the rules of sentence structure, including the sequence in which words are used, chimpanzees have not yet demonstrated this grammatical competence. Most experts agree that the trained chimpanzee functions at a level below that of a three-year-old child.

Nevertheless, investigators have continued these painstaking efforts, pairing a young, untutored chimpanzee with wise old Washoe. Without any human beings in this teaching–learning situation, the youngster learned several signs (Fouts, Fouts, & Van Cantfort, 1989). Another investigator found that a chimpanzee reared with human beings comprehended some spoken sounds and produced some novel, symbolic combinations of words (Savage-Rumbaugh, 1990). However, even these efforts have not yet revealed accomplishments beyond the 3-year level.

So we are left with this question: Do chimpanzees say so little because they have so little to say? Research is turning in this direction, away from language and more directly toward concept formation and other cognitive abilities (Limber, 1977).

Among themselves, dolphins seem to have something to say, and in a cognitive sense they are close cousins to the chimpanzee. With a large, complex brain, they have shown an ability to master concrete concepts and follow simple directions. But there is no evidence that they can understand abstract concepts, exchange complex messages, or communicate about events not in their immediate environment (Chollar, 1989).

In summary, all such studies can be viewed from a different perspective—judged against the accomplishments of animals in the wild. Chimpanzees' highest cognitive capacities have been found in the forest: tool using, teaching, food sharing, cooperation in hunting, and avoiding predators. Animals' thinking, memory, and other

FIGURE 9–3 DOLPHIN COMMUNICATION. Dolphins communicate with each other by using a high-pitched whistle, presumably to identify themselves and perhaps to express basic emotions. To explore their environment, they employ a sonarlike click, listening for reflected sound. They can play simple games, but they cannot use language in a human manner.

symbolic processes probably are not well assessed when they live in a cage because a deprived environment limits opportunities for full development. Life in the wild exerts a strong, steady pressure on the learning processes necessary for survival. That environment thereby becomes a more powerful stimulant to overall cognitive development than does language learning in captivity (Boesch-Achermann & Boesch, 1993; Figure 9–3).

• ACQUISITION OF LANGUAGE •

Judith and the Apple Corps showed that human beings use at least two types of symbols in thinking: imaginal and propositional. In the **imaginal mode,** a symbol has the appearance of whatever it represents. A visual symbol looks like the object to which it refers; an auditory symbol sounds like the object to which it refers. Judith's mental image of her house looked the way she imagined the finished building, including the windows, chimney, and clapboard. In contrast, she also used the word *house,* a symbol that does not look like or sound like the building itself. It is an arbitrary symbol, having no obvious connection with whatever it represents. In the **propositional mode,** a symbol makes a declaration, usually in words. It proposes or asserts something. The words *Judith's* and *Judith's house* and *Judith's house must be finished on time* all have a propositional nature. Jim was ever mindful of that third proposition. He sometimes thought he never should have agreed to the penalty in the contract.

We construct these symbols of ourselves and our environments in order to think about the world. The difference between these symbols—images and abstractions—is readily illustrated in computer software. When a program uses images, the screen displays pictures of the different documents and procedures available. When a program uses propositions, the documents and procedures are indicated by words and numbers. The propositional mode is the chief concern in this chapter, most obviously reflected in language.

❧

NATURE OF LANGUAGE

Every human language can be organized into levels or systems, ranging from basic sounds and letters to the sequence and meaning of words and sentences. The first of these concerns sounds. All languages are surprisingly similar in the types of sounds they use, considering the wide variety of noises that human beings can make.

BASIC ELEMENTS OF LANGUAGE. The smallest functional sound unit in any language is a **phoneme,** of which there are about 40 in English.

Some languages have almost double that number, and some have fewer. The word *must* has four phonemes—*m, u, s,* and *t.* The word *on* has two—*o* and *n*—but the word *time* has only three—*t, i,* and *m.* As a very general rule, the phonemes in English are the different pronunciations for vowels and consonants in our language, as well as certain pairs of letters with a single sound, such as *ae, ei,* and a few other combinations.

In contrast, a **morpheme** is the smallest meaningful unit in a language, usually composed of several phonemes. The word *nail* is a morpheme because it has a distinct meaning. The words *hit, pull,* and *tack* are also morphemes, each composed of several phonemes.

At the next level of integration, words often consist of several morphemes, and many morphemes function only in the context of another morpheme. The word *nails* has two morphemes; there is the noun *nail* and the suffix *s,* signifying plural. The *s* gains its meaning by attachment to another morpheme. The word *screwdrivers* has four morphemes—the noun *screw,* the verb *drive,* the suffix *(e)r,* and the pluralization *s.* English-speaking adults of average ability learn about 80,000 morphemes (Miller & Gildea, 1987). They are either words or coherent parts of words.

Words, in turn, are arranged in appropriate ways to form phrases, clauses, and sentences, and these rules of meaningful organization are known as **syntax.** Syntax is one aspect of grammar, but it is not concerned with pronunciation or correctness of word choice. It is chiefly a matter of sequence. It is concerned with the ways in which words and series of words are organized into language.

The importance of syntax is illustrated in this improbable sequence: "Furiously sleep ideas green colorless." The word *furiously* is unlikely to be followed by *sleep,* which is unlikely to be followed by *ideas,* and so forth. Even the opposite sequence is improbable. *Colorless* is unlikely to be followed by *green,* and so forth. Yet the second expression is considerably closer to a meaningful English statement: "Colorless green ideas sleep furiously" (Chomsky, 1957). The organization of words contributes significantly to the overall meaning.

To summarize, the basic elements of any language are single sounds called phonemes, which are combined to form small units of meaning, known as morphemes. Some morphemes are words; others are combined into words. When words are organized according to certain rules, to make proper phrases and sentences, the condition is called syntax (Figure 9–4).

LANGUAGE AND SOCIETY. Sophisticated use of language includes two additional features: semantics and pragmatics. The term **semantics** con-

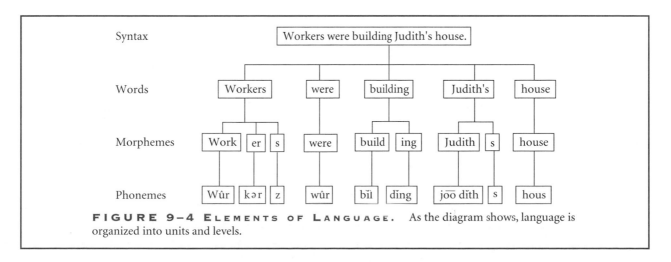

FIGURE 9–4 ELEMENTS OF LANGUAGE. As the diagram shows, language is organized into units and levels.

cerns meaning in its broadest sense, including the full range of social rules and customs that pertain to meaning. We now hear about *nail guns* and *gridlock;* something very good is sometimes referred to as *bad;* and four-letter words previously considered vulgar are now common. In semantics, words and other forms of communication are studied to discover and understand meanings and changes in meanings. When a breakdown in communication occurs, it may be attributed to a problem in semantics, in which the meaning is not clear, or to the presence of mixed messages, in which two or more signals are incompatible.

Breakdowns in communication between the sexes have received much public press, although they are not attributed to semantics per se and there is no evidence that differences are biologically driven. According to one view, language for men is a means of *report.* They talk as a way of presenting information, doing business, and maintaining independence. For women, language is more often a means of *rapport.* They commonly converse as a method of establishing and maintaining personal relationships. Such differences seem to arise in the ways boys and girls are socialized (Tannen, 1990).

Studies in semantics have identified two broad types of meaning, denotative and connotative. The **denotative meaning** points to something; it is the usual dictionary definition. The denotative meaning of the word *dog,* for example, is much the same for all of us—a domestic and carnivorous mammal of the canine family. The semantic system is largely concerned with these denotative meanings.

The **connotative meaning** involves abstract qualities, often with emotional implications, sometimes quite different for different people. Connotative meaning arises from the experiences people have with certain words—the associations words bring to mind, such as feelings of respect or disdain, pleasure or disgust. In its connotative meaning, the word *dog* implies that someone or something is contemptible, inferior, or nasty. The

Apple Corps would have resented the connotative meaning of *dog* applied to Brewster, their handsome Irish setter. In their opinion, Brewster displayed only admirable traits, such as loyalty and friendliness.

The relations between language and its users is known as **pragmatics,** which deals with the work that language does in a particular situation. Without sarcasm, it would be inappropriate to say to clean-shaven Jim: "I admire your beard." The sentence is linguistically correct, but the work of language in this instance is confusing or nonexistent. Someone might call Jim a dog, however, implying the connotative meaning. He might declare, "No way!" Or he might reject the insult more subtly: "Of course, you were not referring to yours truly!" These different responses serve different purposes. The choice of *me* or *yours truly* is a question of pragmatics; it involves the work of language in a specific interpersonal context.

The use of language becomes highly complicated and subtle when we turn to *figures of speech,* in which words are used apart from their literal sense. "I'm worried about a rainy day," Richard might say, urging his coworkers to keep up the pace. Rain did force the Apple Corps to take some days off, especially in April and May, and that was a legitimate concern. But the expression also served as a metaphor, referring to any occasion that might interfere with their progress. Figures of speech can become even more powerful than the direct use of language.

LINGUISTIC DETERMINISM. To what extent does language shape our thought about our world and the ways we perceive it? Some investigators have been led to a controversial hypothesis. Known as the Whorf hypothesis, or **linguistic determinism,** it states that language plays a fundamental role in the nature of a person's thinking. According to linguistic determinism, the Apple Corps's many words for saws—*crosscut saw, finish saw, ripsaw,* and *hacksaw*—greatly aid thinking about cut-

		English			
Red	Orange	Yellow	Green	Blue	Purple

	Shona		
Cipsᵚuka	Cicena	Citema	Cipsᵚuka

Bassa	
Zĩza	Hui

COLOR SPECTRUM IN THREE LANGUAGES

Black & White	Red	Yellow	Green & Blue	Brown
First Pair	Third Term	Fourth Term	Fifth & Sixth Term	Seventh Term

COLOR RECOGNITION IN MANY LANGUAGES

FIGURE 9–5 COLOR AND CULTURE. Different languages divide the color spectrum in different ways, as shown on the left, although they do not necessarily perceive them differently (Gleason, 1961). As shown on the right, when a language has only two terms for colors, they refer to black and white. If a third term is added, it designates red; when another is employed, it is for yellow, and so forth. Despite widely different vocabularies, cultures think about colors in the same sequence (Abramov & Gordon, 1994; Gleason, 1961).

ting something. Will they be cutting metal or wood, against the grain or with it, for a rough edge or finish work?

This hypothesis arose through studies of Native American languages. It was found that the Inuit, formally known as Eskimos, had more than 18 words for snow, not surprising in view of its prevalence in their lives. Natives of the upper Mississippi had a few adjectives, such as *powder* and *granular*, and Aztecs, in a hot climate, used the same basic words for ice, cold, and snow (Whorf, 1956). The Inuit words indicated how old the snow was, how wet, how large the flakes, and so forth. An individual whose language includes many terms for snow presumably can think about it in a greater variety of ways than a person who knows only a single word.

There is no doubt that the hypothesis of linguistic determinism holds to a limited degree, as shown in sexist language. Will Rogers said: "When a man does not have enough troubles, he buys himself a dog." Rogers was referring to anyone, male or female, using the noun *man* and the pronoun *he* in a generic sense. Research has shown, however, that the pronoun *he,* when intended as generic, is often interpreted as masculine, not neutral (Gastil, 1990).

Thus, today we often use *they* or *he or she,* a step toward equality for women.

However, language certainly does not restrict thought completely. When words are not available to accommodate new thoughts, they are invented. A child referring to ginger ale asks for "the drink that prickles." Not knowing a name for pliers, she speaks of "big tweezers." Today our language has been expanded to include bungie jumps, biofeedback, and boogaloo, including words and combinations of words presumably not used previously. Furthermore, the work with the Inuit may have been misrepresented, suggesting a greater vocabulary for snow and related terms than has been the case (Pullum, 1991).

Studies of the perception of color also have provided evidence against the hypothesis. These include research on the color spectrum and color recognition in different cultures (Figure 9–5).

In one instance, typical of several investigations, adults from the United States and New Guinea were compared for recognition of colors, a significant test because the Dani from New Guinea use only two words for colors, *warm* and *cold,* for bright and dark, respectively. In contrast, English offers eleven basic color terms: *red, orange, yellow, green, blue, violet, brown, black, white, gray,* and *pink.* The hypothesis of linguistic determinism would predict that the New Guinea subjects, with fewer words for colors, would have greater difficulty in discriminating among different hues. Yet the two groups showed no marked differences in recognizing and matching colors, despite the large differences in vocabulary (Heider, 1972; Rosch, 1973).

In summary, when stated in a weak form, there is some truth to this hypothesis. Language shapes thought—in restricted ways. For example, people have more favorable attitudes toward "assistance to the poor" than they do toward "welfare" (Rasinski, 1989). They are more likely to support a venture described as having an 80% chance of success than one described as having a 20% chance of failure (Kahneman & Tversky, 1984). And we know how often people try to use language to shape our thinking: Raising taxes becomes "revenue enhancement," seating first-class airline passengers ahead of everyone else becomes "preboarding," and so forth. In its strongest form, however, the hypothesis appears to be incorrect. Language does not determine our overall conception of reality, although its influence becomes more pronounced as thinking becomes more abstract.

~

LANGUAGE LEARNING

With this background, we turn to language learning in children, which has a lengthy history and has inspired thousands of studies (Suppes, Pavel, & Falmagne, 1994). Like other aspects of human development, language learning can be roughly characterized in terms of stages. The rate is not universal, but the sequence is essentially the same in all normal children.

EARLY VOCALIZATIONS. The first vocalizations include crying, gurgling, and a few other sounds, but the contented infant also emits cooing noises. This unpatterned **cooing** is simply a reflex

emission of air through the vocal cords. The infant's speech mechanisms continue to mature during this stage, perhaps partly as a result of this vocal activity.

During the stage of cooing, infants are listening to adults talking, and they begin to show a preference for a certain type of speech. Known as *caretaker speech,* it has a high-pitched intonation and a certain rhythm. In one study, infants of 4 months heard mothers at times talking to their own babies, using caretaker speech, and at times talking to adults. These sounds came from different directions, and typically the infants turned toward the caretaker speech, apparently confirming their interest in that high-pitched speech (Fernald, 1985). Infants in many cultures are responsive to this "baby talk" by men and women, even in the first days of life.

Around the fifth month there is a gradual transition from cooing to **babbling,** in which particular phonemes are repeated consistently, as in "da-da-da-da" and "lal-lal-lal-lal." This behavior represents greater control over the speech mechanisms, and these noises initially include all of the important sounds in adult speech. Babies throughout the world cannot be distinguished on this basis (Stott, 1967). Later, the Asian baby learns certain vowel sounds, the Spanish baby a rolling *r,* and the Norwegian baby guttural noises, none of which can be accurately reproduced by people who have not learned the language in childhood. This babbling appears to be a necessary prelude to speech. Infants who do not babble generally do not develop speech (Lieberman, 1984).

FIRST WORDS. Before the end of the first year, the typical human baby begins to distinguish the useful phonemes in his or her language. These phonemes are almost always words or parts of words. Therefore, the child gradually reaches the stage of **word recognition,** which shows understanding of the meaning of certain intonations and words. The child avoids things said to be hot, for example, without having any special sound or word to indicate that something is hot.

The infant's first spoken word, usually indistinguishable from babbling except by fond parents, is almost always a name of some sort. Hence, the next stage, appearing around the 12th month, is called the **one-word stage,** or first words, in which the infant uses labels for things. When something is hot the infant gives it a name, perhaps saying "ta" because consonants spoken at the front of the mouth, such as *p* and *t,* and *m* and *n,* are more read-

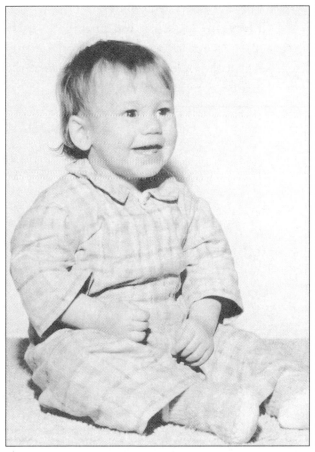

FIGURE 9–6 FIRST WORDS. The early production of front consonants and back vowels make it no accident that *mama* and *papa* are such universal names for parents around the globe, often uttered with a special enthusiasm when they first appear, around the end of the first year (Seigler, 1986).

ily produced than many other consonants. The back vowels, spoken at the back of the mouth, such as the *ä* in *father,* are the first to appear, however (Figure 9–6).

The exact meaning of the first words varies with the situation. Judith's son says, "House." This word might mean "That's a house" or "Where is the house?" The successful communicator is the parent who decodes the message, not the child, who transmits limited and ambiguous signals. A one-word phrase of this sort is sometimes called a **holophrastic expression,** meaning that a single word serves as a sentence, conveying a complex idea. There is still some debate, however, about just how much is intended (Dore, 1985).

"Architects!" howled one of the Apple Corps, looking up at the frame of Judith's house. By this holophrastic expression, he meant that the architect had planned the building improperly and that architects often make such mistakes (Kidder, 1985). He knew that the Apple Corps would be held accountable for any delay, although someone else might have made the error.

TELEGRAPHIC SPEECH. According to most experts, the beginning of language ability is not the individual's first word or first meaningful sound. Even Brewster, the Apple Corps's faithful setter, could bark "Woof, woof," meaning "I want food" or "Let me out." But sometime between the first and second years, the normal child achieves the developmental landmark of using words in combination. At this point, the child is beginning to use an active grammar or a language system. This point is therefore called the beginning of language development (Brown, 1973; Riley, 1987).

A two-year-old girl, just learning words in combination, extended toward her mother a slightly mangled finger. Her parent asked, "Oh, did Archie bite you?" A few days later, Archie did the deed again. This time the girl ran to her mother, displayed her little neighbor's toothwork, and exclaimed, "Bite you, bite you!" Combining a wrong pronoun with a wrong verb form, she gave the news: "I have been bitten" (Caldwell, 1991).

These early word combinations are known as **telegraphic speech** because, like telegrams, they are highly abbreviated word combinations but contain the most important elements. A woman says, "Dinner is ready." Her child responds, "Dinner ready."

SIMPLE SENTENCES. As the child's utterances become longer, they are organized into units. The expression "Go house" is expanded into the three-word sentence, "Let's go house." In the child's thinking, the word "let's" apparently is one unit, the phrase "go house" another, and the two are combined.

The child's speech hesitations reflect this hierarchical structure of language. Judith's child says, "Put . . . the big nail . . . in." The verb comes first, then the complete noun phrase, and then the isolated preposition. The child does not say, "Put the . . . big . . . nail in" or "Put . . . the big . . . nail in." Even in the first two or three years, the child somehow perceives the underlying grammatical elements (Brown & Bellugi, 1964; Riley, 1987).

COMPLEX CONSTRUCTIONS. Children's efforts to master word order are evident in their questions. They learn, for example, that the subject generally precedes the verb. They also learn that "wh" words, such as *what, why,* and *when,* come first in questions. Thus the first "wh" questions show both characteristics: "Where the house is?" and "What he can do?" Only gradually does the child learn to change the position of the subject and verb when asking a "wh" question: "Where is the roof?"

Interestingly, when the question does not begin with a "wh" word, the child readily reverses the subject and verb: "Is the roof done?" Apparently, the child can master one change or the other, the inclusion of the "wh" word or the change in

sequence, but not both together when first learning to form questions (Brown, 1973).

By four years of age, the typical child's expressions have increased considerably in length, and they generally show correct syntax. Improvements continue later, but at a slower rate (Figure 9–7).

By the age of six years, children have acquired a vocabulary of approximately 10,000 words and most of the basic constructions of their language (Carey, 1978; Miller, 1981). Vocabulary development and improvements in syntax of course continue for years. The average teenager can describe the framing of Judith's house in an interesting fashion: "The Apple Corps worked carefully, even though the whole frame would be covered over later by the walls and floors and ceilings."

Still later, the adult may use language to study language—discovering many expressions arising from carpentry. For example, "going against the grain" can be a mistake in any sphere of life. A

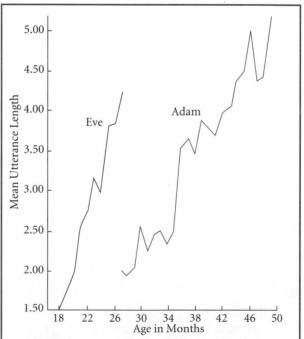

FIGURE 9–7 COMBINING WORDS. One indication of the child's progress in learning language is the mean length of utterance, measured in terms of morphemes. The occasional disruptions in progress are due to extraneous factors, such as the child's health and changes in the environment (Adapted from Brown, 1973).

"sore thumb" sticks out anywhere, especially in carpentry. And by using straight posts and level beams, the Apple Corps made square corners, giving Judith a "square deal."

VIEWS OF LANGUAGE LEARNING

How does any child learn language? When asked, many people will say that imitation is the crucial factor. The child copies what he or she hears, and in psychology this process is called *observational learning*. The child reproduces the behavior of competent speakers.

One child learns Chinese; another learns English. An Australian acquires a certain English accent, a Texan another. To indicate a 50:50 chance, an American child adopts the expression: "It's a tossup." The Canadian explains: "It's a matter of sixes." A child who speaks English learns to say, "I shall tell it to her." A child who speaks Spanish learns to use exactly the opposite sequence, "Se lo diré." The order here is: To her it tell shall I. Examples in support of imitation in learning language are endless (Kymissis & Poulson, 1990). But there is more involved.

CONDITIONING VIEWPOINT. According to B.F. Skinner and other behaviorists, adult speakers shape the infant's speech through *reinforcement.* They cuddle and smile when the baby begins cooing and babbling. The parents support the sounds made by the infant, and gradually the infant becomes aware of his or her capacity for speech. This aspect, the acquisition of verbal behavior, illustrates operant conditioning.

According to this viewpoint, classical conditioning is also involved. Someone uses the word *Daddy,* and after the father appears on several such occasions, the word comes to signify this person. Its meaning has been acquired through this process of pairing. Stimulus generalization, extinction, and secondary reinforcement are among the chief conditioning principles by which words are acquired (Skinner, 1957).

Two-word combinations, three-word combinations, and eventually whole sentences develop in these same ways. As reinforcement continues, together with chaining at higher levels of integration, the child's expressions appear in successively more complex units. And as intermittent reinforcement comes to play an increasing role, saying a whole sentence becomes reinforced merely by hearing a response from someone else. Largely through these extensions of conditioning principles, discussed in an earlier chapter, the child becomes increasingly capable in using language.

INNATE VIEWPOINT. If children learn only by imitation and conditioning, how do we account for their predictable errors, not found in adult language? The child says, "He hitted the nail." Further, how do we explain the fact that deaf children learn to speak? Helen Keller lost her capacity for vision and hearing when she was 18 months old, and yet she mastered English not as a series of mechanical signals but as an instrument of thought. Our steady mastery of language, perhaps the greatest achievement in human society, takes place at an astonishingly rapid rate and long before the child reaches maturity. The average child of six years, for example, learns more than a dozen words per day (Carey, 1978). According to the *innate viewpoint,* these outcomes are a function of the development of language areas in the brain, especially the growth that continues up to 24 months or more after birth (Goldman-Rakic, 1987).

On these bases, Noam Chomsky takes a distinct perspective. According to Chomsky and other linguists, language is learned so readily and uniformly because human beings have an inherited predisposition for language. We are "wired" for speech, born with a specific capacity for acquiring the rules of morphemes, syntax, and so forth. This postulated mechanism, called a **language acquisition device** (LAD), is composed of those parts of the human mind specifically and uniquely devoted to language learning (Chomsky, 1957, 1972). Presumed to be part of our biological inheritance, its adequate development requires a normal human environment in the early years.

Evidence for this view is also found in the fact that languages throughout the world are alike in significant ways. For example, the phonemes in all languages use only a fraction of the sounds that human beings are capable of making. There is also a similarity in hierarchical structure, for in all languages phonemes and morphemes are combined to form the larger units of full discourse (Lieberman, 1984). Further, there is no cultural group that does not have a fully developed language. African and Australian tribes use languages comparable in morphemes and syntax to those of ancient Greece and modern European communities (Hockett, 1960).

The innate approach focuses more on syntax and grammar than does the conditioning model. It is concerned with how human beings process or understand an infinite number of possible sentences, each of which can have a different meaning, and here the concern lies with two types of structure, reflected in any given sentence. First, there is the **surface structure,** which refers to the specific words and their organization in the sentence. It includes the relationships among parts of speech. In addition, there is the **deep structure,** also called the *underlying structure,* which refers to the meaning of or thought in the words. Consider this surface structure: "The architects are revolting." What is the deep structure? Are they repulsive or in rebellion? Similarly, one deep structure may be expressed by various surface structures: "Strike while the iron is hot." "Now is the time." "Just do it."

The operations that relate deep structure to surface structure are known as **transformational rules,** and according to the innate viewpoint, mas-tery of these rules is the chief accomplishment in language acquisition. They enable someone to begin with an idea, select appropriate words and sentences, and then produce the corresponding speech sounds, which is the process of speaking. They also enable someone to listen to these sounds, understand their specific meanings, and translate them into the overall deep structure, thereby comprehending the message. One basic aim in using the innate approach has been to develop a better understanding of transformational rules, how they govern these activities, and how they provide the enormous flexibility of human language.

COGNITIVE VIEWPOINT. A third approach argues that the conditioning model cannot account for the child's ability to produce or understand complicated sentences not encountered previously. The possibilities are too numerous and too complexly related to be explained in this manner, even with a broad interpretation of stimulus generalization. This approach also argues that the innate viewpoint does not focus on *how* we acquire language. It demonstrates that we do so rapidly and points to the complexity of this achievement. And neither approach successfully explains how adults and children monitor their own speech, often revising their words and syntax in midsentence, attempting to achieve a certain expression.

The cognitive approach stresses the role of *information processing,* focusing on the mental abilities involved in manipulating language, which is one aspect of mental development. It is a unique human capacity, but to study language by itself is to study it out of context. Language learning is inextricably related to the development of other mental abilities (Figure 9–8).

The most prominent spokesperson for this viewpoint has been Jean Piaget, a child psychologist whose work on cognitive development is discussed at length in a later chapter. He pointed out that

FIGURE 9–8 LANGUAGE LEARNING AND INFORMATION PROCESSING. After age six or so, when most children have acquired a sizeable vocabulary, information processing occurs more rapidly, apparently due to maturation of the brain. Growth of myelin, covering the nerve fibers, increases the speed of transmission of nerve impulses. Thus, children of this age can think faster than younger children.

language depends on thought and that its development proceeds only in this context. Without sufficient memory, the child cannot speak about an absent parent. Without some concept of pluralism, the child cannot talk about houses or carpenters. Knowledge of the rules of grammar is insufficient. In this respect, language is limited by thought (Piaget, 1959).

One advantage of the cognitive approach is that it provides a broad basis for research. Language development is studied in the context of the child's growing competence in perception, memory, reasoning, problem solving, and other symbolic processes. Suppose a child speaks of the future for the first time: "I will build it." Cognitive theorists would be less interested in the grammatical rules the child used in creating this expression than in the information processing that resulted in the child's perception of time, predictable behavior, personal responsibility, and so forth. Some understanding of

these concepts must have preceded the expression. Compared to the innate viewpoint, cognitive theorists place far more importance in the environmental input (Harkness, 1990; Morgan, 1990).

A COMBINED PERSPECTIVE. Viewed broadly, the basic ingredients of any language are the signals, composed of phonemes and morphemes, and a system for organizing these signals, known as syntax. When we consider mastery of these two aspects of language separately, a tentative resolution can be achieved among the conditioning, innate, and cognitive orientations.

In learning the basic signals of a language, such as vocabulary and tonal expressions, the conditioning principles seem most important. The child attaches meanings to words through their association with objects and events. Later, the child uses these words and, receiving reinforcement, uses them more and more often (Skinner, 1957). In terms of two-factor theory, word meanings are acquired essentially through classical conditioning and word usage is acquired through the operant process.

However, there is no evidence that conditioning processes change sharply at any point in the individual's life. How then can we explain the extremely rapid increase in vocabulary in the third and subsequent years? One reason is that the child is using words to acquire new words. A child might ask: "What means *stud*?" "What means *joist*?" A carpenter would explain that a stud is a post to hold up a wall; a joist is a beam to support the floor. The child's vocabulary thereby has been increased. The incorrect expression, using a "wh" word without changing the positions of the verb and noun, shows that the child is attempting to learn the rules of grammar, considered by some as evidence of a language acquisition device (Chomsky, 1975, 1986). These questions also show that the child is analyzing the environment to discover how it works. Language development, therefore, is part of a larger enterprise—the cognitive development of the child (Piaget, 1959).

In language learning, conditioning, an inherited predisposition, and cognitive development all appear involved. What has been said about research on human cognition also applies to language acquisition, which is part of cognitive psychology. The complexity of the overall problem demands approaches from different perspectives (Estes, 1991a). Controversies arising from diverse theories add vigor to the study of psychological questions (Salzinger, 1994; Table 9–1).

• REASONING AND PROBLEM SOLVING •

"This house is framed to a thirty-second of an inch, right to the ridge," Richard announced from the rooftop one day in mid-June. Then, standing among the rafters, he carefully attached the branch of a tree to the highest beam on the roof. With that brief ceremony, all four men celebrated the framing of Judith's house, paying homage to the forest, the source of their material. The house, in a symbolic sense, had become a tree once again.

At the same time, Richard worried openly about the Halloween penalty. "We're fussing with it a little bit," he added, thinking about the deliberate work of the rest of the crew.

On that late spring day, the Apple Corps turned promptly from the rapid and dramatic process of framing, which required teamwork, to the slower, more solitary finish work, making sashes and molding, cabinets and steps. In a display of good fellowship, and to speed up the work, Judith added her expertise as a carpenter, constructing a cabinet and then working on a closet. Her skill and determination won the admiration of the Corps, who thereby made her an honorary member (Kidder, 1985).

All of these tasks required a considerable degree of reasoning, and now we turn to this process. Thinking of diverse sorts, by human beings and computers, is based on **reasoning,** which is the logical manipulation of concepts. As opposed to fantasy and free association, reasoning is essentially controlled thinking. Reasoning is a very broad concept, so infiltrated into other cognitive processes that it is almost synonymous with cognition itself (Rips, 1990).

COMPUTER THOUGHT

We begin with the computer, a device for carrying out a sequence of operations in an explicitly defined manner. This sequence is usually known as a program. The computer does not yet operate at the level of human thinking, although it can accomplish marvelous feats with awesome speed and memory. Given the dimensions for each of the rooms in Judith's house, excluding halls, closets, and stairways, it could calculate almost instantaneously the total

SPOKESPERSON	VIEWPOINT	BASIC CONCEPT	EVIDENCE
B. F. Skinner	Conditioning	Reinforcement principle	Habitual expressions
Noam Chomsky	Innate	Language acquisition device	Speed of learning
Jean Piaget	Cognitive	Information processing	High-level syntax

TABLE 9–1 VIEWS OF LANGUAGE LEARNING. Several theories have been proposed for the development of language. Each theory offers a different basic concept and focuses on different evidence.

living and working space. Three general steps are involved: input of information, manipulation of information, and output of the solution.

ARTIFICIAL INTELLIGENCE. The broad and rapidly expanding field of **artificial intelligence** involves the development of computer programs that solve problems requiring rational, informed responses when accomplished by human beings. The aim is not to solve problems in a humanlike manner, just as animals are not designed to run like human beings, but rather to find efficient solutions. Specialists in artificial intelligence try to make machines do things that people currently do better, or to enable machines to do things that neither people nor machines currently do very well (Rich & Knight, 1991).

Through artificial intelligence, computers now assist with many routine tasks: correcting spelling, preparing menus, and recording numbers on bank checks. They can also assist with more abstract problems, such as medical diagnoses, mathematical computations, and the prescription of drugs. Success in such instances lies in the computer's focus on a specific, restricted topic. An enormous mass of information is collected on this topic and given to the computer. Then, by means of a program, the computer is instructed in a highly systematic way to solve the problem.

These narrowly focused programs are called **expert systems,** meaning that they function very effectively—like experts—in accomplishing highly specialized tasks. The oldest is MYCIN, a program for diagnosing infectious diseases. The physician presents to MYCIN the patient's personal characteristics, symptoms, and test results, and then the program makes recommendations. It considers the patient's general health, allergies, current medications, and related factors, just as your physician should do with you. Overall, it and similar medical systems appear to operate as well as or better than human medical experts confronted with the same problems (Perry, 1990).

Another expert system has an almost reproductive capacity. XCON was developed to determine the specifications for *new* computers. It follows more than 6,000 rules about how the parts should be combined in order to create a new computer system. In today's fast-changing world of electronics, simply keeping this expert system up-to-date has required eight full-time programmers at a cost of more than two million dollars per year. But it has saved five or six million annually, and now XCON knows more about developing computer systems than does any human expert (Harmon, Maus, & Morrissey, 1988).

Similarly, ART assists clerks in deciding whether to honor credit cards in doubtful cases; LISP helps scientists and engineers to solve mathematics problems; and GURU offers legal advice in international trading (Harmon et al., 1988). These systems are *not* intelligent in the human sense, however. They perform successfully only in an *extremely* confined context. Do not ask XCON, so capable in building computers, how to train a computer assistant, and do not query MYCIN about your black eye. They will not even understand these questions, much less give a useful answer.

USE OF ALGORITHMS. In some systems of artificial intelligence, the computer uses a method called an algorithm. An **algorithm** is any unambiguous procedure that, if used correctly, will solve a certain problem. It is essentially a recipe, a set of very well defined rules, that will lead to the solution in a careful series of finite steps. This prescription tells *exactly* what to do at any point in solving the problem, whether it involves adding numbers, building a staircase, or changing diapers.

The main staircase in Judith's house was a challenging piece of finish work for Jim. It would have two turns, many posts, and dozens of edges and

1. Place one number directly above the other and justify them at the right side.
2. Start with the rightmost column of numbers; consider it the current column.
3. Add the digits in the current column.
4. If the sum of the digits is less than 10, then record the sum under the current column below the line.
5. If the sum of the digits is greater than 10, record the remainder of the sum when 10 is subtracted from it. Place this remainder below the line in the current column, and record a 1 in the column to the left of the current column.
6. Let the column immediately to the left of the current column be the new current column.
7. If the current column is empty, stop. The result is available below the line.
8. If the current column is not empty, then go to step 3.

TABLE 9–2 AN ALGORITHM FOR ADDITION. This algorithm can be used to sum any two numbers greater than ten (Carberry, Khalil, Leathrum, & Levy, 1979).

joints. All treads had to be equal in width, all risers the same height, and each tread and riser together had to measure 17 or 18 inches. Even a minute error would cause endless stumbling on the stairs (Kidder, 1985).

Jim began by cutting the large posts. An algorithm for this task might begin as follows:

Step 1: *Specifying the Location of the Stairs.* Use a pencil and a 24-foot ruler made of metal. Place the left end of the marked edge of the ruler, showing distance in inches, at the point where you want the bottom of the post. Then extend the ruler and mark with the pencil . . .

In equally precise fashion, Step 2 would describe exactly how to cut the treads, Step 3 the risers, Step 4 the placement of these pieces, and so forth, step by step, until the staircase is finished.

An algorithm is also readily illustrated by showing what it is not, and here we can use a farcical example. A new father opens a box of diapers and reads the first step: *Place the baby on a flat surface.*

He presses the baby up against the wall and turns to the second step: *Unfold the diaper.* He unfolds the diaper until it is several square feet in size and thin as tissue paper. And so it goes. He reaches one of the later steps: *Bring the diaper up in front.* He pulls the diaper between his legs and tucks it under his belt, still holding the naked baby against the wall (Leitner, 1994).

The father is not fully at fault, for household instructions generally are not written as algorithms. They are prepared for human beings, who usually think in other ways. In a true algorithm, every condition is fully and clearly specified at each step. There is no ambiguity about which flat surface to use, how far to unfold the diapers, or who is to wear them (Table 9–2).

Algorithms have their limitations, however, as evident in the game of chess. There are 10^{120} possible moves in chess—more moves, so the saying goes, than there are atoms in the universe. It would take the fastest computer centuries to consider all of them, and therefore an algorithm would produce a very, very slow game of chess.

USE OF HEURISTICS. In the 1950s, a group of scientists led by Allen Newell and Herbert Simon became interested in developing a program of computer thought that would not rely on algorithms and therefore would not require vast amounts of computation. At the same time, it would not guarantee a solution. Newell and Simon wanted the computer to approach problem solving more in the manner of a human being—attempting to solve a problem even though, at the outset, the method is uncertain and the outcome unknown. Newell began working toward this goal as a graduate student, under Simon's direction, and together they constructed the pioneering Logic Theorist (LT), apparently the first computer program to solve problems by ignoring the less likely alternatives. This program provided proofs for 73% of the theorems in Newton's *Principia Mathematica* without considering all of the possibilities at each step, for a completely exhaustive search would have required hundreds of years. Afterward, Simon and others developed more advanced programs of this sort, thereby inaugurating a whole new approach to the study of mental processes (Newell, Shaw, & Simon, 1958).

They called this work *heuristics,* meaning that the problem solver uses the approaches most likely to yield a correct solution. A **heuristic** is a problem-solving technique that usually improves efficiency, a shortcut or rule of thumb that might work but offers no guarantee. Heuristics are efficient strategies; they can speed the solution—or lead to failure. The carpenter, lawyer, and truck driver consider the most plausible hypotheses first and proceed on that basis. If they did not, staircases would never be built, lawsuits would never end, and trucks would never get out of the city. In short, when there are many possibilities to be explored, the search becomes *selective*—which means that heuristics are involved (Simon, 1990).

In the 1960s, the Newell–Simon team advanced computer thought further by combining the LT with newer programs. They thereby developed the General Problem Solver (GPS), which included a broader problem-solving strategy, some-times called *means–ends analysis.* In this approach, each problem is considered in terms of a current state and goal state, and each question becomes: By what means does one move from the current state closer to the goal state? Problem solving is an attempt to identify and reduce the difference between the current state and the goal state by solving successive subproblems, each with a table of means to reach that particular subgoal (Newell & Simon, 1963; Table 9–3).

Considerable effort was required to fit all problems into this means–ends framework, however, and even then the GPS could not solve many problems easily managed by human beings. In the 1980s, Newell incorporated into the GPS a more effective memory system, one that could store and later utilize newly acquired knowledge to reason about future problems. This program, called Soar, is the first system in artificial intelligence to create its own subgoals and learn from its own experiences (Newell, 1990). Whenever Soar encounters a problem and subsequently surmounts it, that problem and its solution are retained in memory (Lindsay, 1991). In other words, Soar can use rules, solve problems, and *learn* from its mistakes. After solving a new problem, it remembers that procedure as a

---

THE PROBLEM		TABLE OF MEANS			
	DIFFERENCE	AIRPLANE	TRAIN	CAR	WALK
Suppose that we are in a car in downtown San Francisco and wish to go to some historic landmark in Boston. The following plan would evolve:	More than 1,000 miles	X			
1. The distance is considerably greater than 1,000 miles. The table says to take a plane, but first we must be at the airport. Thus going to the airport is a subproblem.	Less than 1,000 miles but more than 500 miles		X	X	
2. The distance from San Francisco to its airport makes taking a car appropriate. Since we are in the car already, we proceed to the airport parking lot.	Less than 500 miles but more than 1/2 mile			X	
3. We now need to arrive at the plane itself. The table suggests walking.					
4. We are now prepared to carry out the action in step 1. This action puts us at the Boston airport where similar steps will enable us to arrive at the desired location.	Less than 1/2 mile				X

TABLE 9–3 MEANS-ENDS ANALYSIS. In this simple problem, the place of origin is the current state; the destination is the goal state. The distance in miles between the two points is a convenient measure of the difference between the two states.

new rule. Some Soar systems operate with more than 10,000 rules (Adler, 1992).

Soar has not demonstrated human ability in problem solving, but it may be able to overcome several of its own deficits. More important, it may become a research model in cognitive science (Lindsay, 1991). It may stimulate the development of a unified theory of human cognition, one that brings together results from countless diverse investigations of human cognition and behavior (Adler, 1992).

COMPUTER SIMULATION. Psychologists and other scientists employ computers for another purpose besides artificial intelligence. Using heuristics, they program computers to represent or imitate human thinking, a condition called **computer simulation.** There is, of course, no effort to represent the physiological aspects of the human brain. Rather, the investigator can formulate highly precise hypotheses about the nature of thinking and then use the computer for an explicit test of these ideas.

Computers use both modes of thought, algorithms and heuristics, but one problem for scientists interested in the simulation of human thought is to program computers to use heuristics more flexibly. In comparison with human beings, they are still deficient in looking ahead, finding the best overall plan, and avoiding blind alleys. In other words, they are too stable, too willing to work on long problems without making adjustments.

Another problem is to improve information processing in the computer. Expressed in the language of modern cognitive psychology, **information processing** refers to the mental activities that human beings perform on information as it enters the brain, is stored in the brain, and is used in thinking. At this point, computer thought has not developed much beyond **serial processing,** in which instructions are followed in sequential fashion, one after another. Each bit of information relevant to

the problem is retrieved and acted on separately. One assumption about human thought is that the brain processes information simultaneously as well as sequentially. In **parallel distributed processing,** various operations are performed *at the same time* by different elements of the nervous system dealing with different but related pieces of information. In approaching Judith's staircase, for example, Jim looked at the allotted space, recalled his prior efforts with staircases, and thought about Judith's specifications. These diverse signals from perception, memory, and thought were handled at virtually the same moment in different parts of his nervous system. Efforts to induce parallel processing in computers are aimed at focusing computers simultaneously on different parts of the same problem, which of course creates the difficulty of merging these partial solutions.

In passing, we should note that human beings sometimes make very poor decisions. In comparison with computers, they are more readily distracted and, of course, emotional. Consequently, there have been attempts to include these characteristics in computer models (Colby, Weber, & Hilf, 1971).

We can conclude with a brief distinction. Artificial intelligence is primarily used instead of human thinking; computer simulation is used to study human thinking.

☙

HUMAN REASONING

Ancient writers referred to human beings as *the* reasoning species, suggesting that other forms of life do not reason, a view that we know today is incorrect. Nevertheless, the human capacity for reasoning seems to set us apart from all other species, including computers. We are far superior to computers in reasoning when information is lacking or confusing. As a rule, we use two general modes, inductive and deductive reasoning, although there are other forms as well.

INDUCTIVE REASONING. Sometimes we gather information and then try to develop a hypothesis or rule. After observing specific cases, we attempt to reach a conclusion about them. In **inductive reasoning,** we proceed from the particular facts to some general statement about those facts. Working on Judith's house, Richard finds that his sanding machine does not work. He looks at the old cord and socket, and worn places on the wires, and impatiently asks himself: "Is something wrong with the plug?" If he remembers using the machine for several long periods recently, he may ask: "Has it burned a fuse?" He has arrived at these hypotheses, or tentative conclusions, through inductive reasoning.

In inductive reasoning, thinking goes beyond the data to derive some broader statement. It might be called a *bottom-up approach,* for it goes from specific observations to a general conclusion. Clinical psychologists study their clients, attempting to understand their problems; carpenters examine their machines, trying to understand why they do not work; students think about their parents and professors, trying to understand them. Through inductive reasoning, they cannot be certain that they have arrived at a correct explanation. All they can do is generate possibilities.

DEDUCTIVE REASONING. On other occasions, out thinking moves in the opposite direction. In **deductive reasoning,** we begin with some general rule or rules and then examine their application in a particular instance. This form of reasoning can lead to conclusions that are logically necessary. If the initial propositions and mode of reasoning are correct, then the conclusion *must* follow. This thinking might be called a *top-down approach,* for it goes from the general statements to specific implications.

Richard decides through inductive reasoning that the machine does not work because there is no electricity. Through deductive reasoning, he can test this hypothesis. He reasons: "The machine will not work without electricity. Someone turned off the electricity. Therefore, the machine will not work." This method of formal reasoning, called a *syllogism,* is a three-part statement consisting of two premises and a conclusion. If the premises are true and the rules of logic are applied, then the conclusion must be true. An example, in abstract form, appears as:

> *X* is larger than *Y;*
> *Y* is larger than *Z;*
> Therefore, *X* is larger than *Z.*

In the same way, Richard can deduce other specifics. Through inductive reasoning, he may decide that the machine will not work because he has forgotten to plug it in, allowed it to become too hot, or created a short circuit. These hypotheses can be evaluated through deduction.

Solving problems in daily life usually involves a mixture of inductive and deductive reasoning. If our car stops, we may hypothesize that it is out of gas, which is inductive reasoning. Then we use deductive reasoning to test this hypothesis: If there is no gas, the gauge will be on empty; the gauge is not on empty; therefore, the car is not out of gas—or the gauge is broken. We use these forms of reasoning regularly and in various combinations without thinking very much about them.

FAULTY REASONING. Human beings also engage in another type of reasoning—faulty reasoning. The chief deficiency in the inductive approach occurs in not searching for disconfirming data. This tendency is so strong that it is called the **confirmation bias,** which is the inclination to look for and remember supporting rather than refuting evidence.

By including another number, find the simplest rule used in developing this series: 12, 15, 18, 21. . . . If you suggested 24, your number does illustrate the rule. Asked to state the rule, you might say: "Increasing numbers by increments of three." And you would be wrong. The rule here is simply increasing numbers. Rather than suggesting

SEVEN BALLS

The seven table-tennis balls are at the bottom of a 6-foot vertical pipe, diameter 4 inches, bolted securely to the floor. Remove the balls without destroying the pipe.

EIGHT COINS

All the coins are identical in appearance, but one is heavier than the others. Using a balance scale with two pans, find the odd coin by only two weighings.

NINE DOTS

Connect these dots by drawing four straight lines without taking the pencil from the paper and without retracing any lines.

FIGURE 9–9 PROBLEM SOLVING. In attempting to solve these problems, remember the importance of maintaining flexibility. *Answers:* For the balls, simply fill the pipe with water. For the coins, place three in each pan on the first trial. If the pans are even, weigh the two remaining coins to find the heavier one. If the pans are uneven, weigh two of the coins from the heavier pan. An uneven balance will show the heavier coin. If they are even, the remaining coin is the odd one. For the dots, think of the possibility that the lines may extend beyond the dots, as illustrated at the end of the chapter.

24, you might have tried 22 or 27 or something of that sort, thereby searching for disconfirming evidence for the hypothesis of increases by three. In testing hypotheses, we need to gather contradictory, discordant information (Hoch, 1986).

Charles Darwin was so aware of this tendency to forget disconfirming evidence and so intellectually honest that he made a point of jotting down immediately any observation that failed to support his views. Observations confirming them needed no special attention.

Mistakes in deductive reasoning often occur in the way the problem is interpreted. There is a tendency to distort or omit a statement. As a parent might say: "Children do not eat nutritious meals. Some foods they eat are actually toxic. Therefore, many children are likely to become ill." This conclusion is incorrect, for the substances eaten by children are not necessarily those that are toxic.

The parent distorted the second statement, thinking of *some* foods as *most* foods or *all* foods.

❧

PROBLEM SOLVING

As the August days grew shorter, the Apple Corps encountered a wide range of problems in the finish work. Jim's plan for the stairs ignited a lengthy discussion; Richard's kitchen required several new fixtures; those fixtures were several days late in arriving; and the tedious work of fitting trim in all sorts of places made thoughts of Halloween a bit scary for everyone. Then, almost without warning, the subcontractors appeared, solving problems concerned with plumbing, electricity, and so forth, just as all of us constantly solve problems (Figure 9–9).

Factors of accident and chance play a role in **problem solving,** in which some new response, or

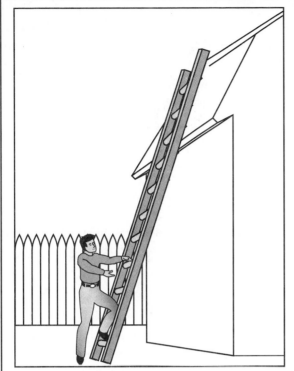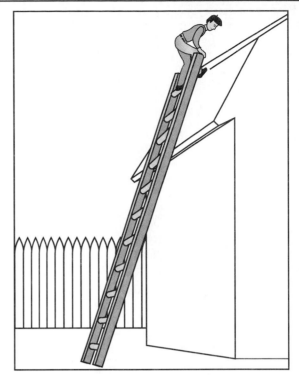

FIGURE 9–10 FRAMING THE PROBLEM (I). In one graphic approach, two ladders are drawn. Richard is at the bottom of one and the top of the other. These two Richards start to climb up and down, respectively, as their clocks begin to tick. With these images, it seems clear that they should meet somewhere.

some new combination of old responses, provides an answer to a question. If the process is successful, it usually involves three broad phases: depicting the problem, adopting strategies for a solution, and implementing the solution.

DEPICTING THE PROBLEM. In solving any problem, the old aphorism applies: "Well begun is half done." In building a house, the key process is framing, which means providing a basic structure. If the house is poorly framed—that is, if the skeletal structure is poor—all of the subsequent parts, including the walls, floors, ceiling, and certain fixtures, will be slightly or markedly wrong. In problem solving, framing also provides a basic structure. Specifically, **framing** in this sense is a way of presenting or representing the problem, stating

it in words or numbers or graphically. When framing is successful—representing the problem clearly and without distractions—problem solving is facilitated. When the problem is stated with too little or too much detail, the solution is hindered.

Richard one day climbed a tall ladder while balancing a heavy load on his shoulder. "You couldn't get a hoist, eh, Jim?" he complained (Kidder, 1985). He reached the top of the ladder, deposited his load, and rested briefly. Climbing down empty-handed later, he traveled more rapidly. While descending, did he ever reach a place on the ladder in the same number of seconds that he reached it on his upward trek? If so, can you identify that point?

These questions at first may seem overwhelming. The first step therefore is to frame the problem (Figure 9–10)—that is, to state it as accurately and

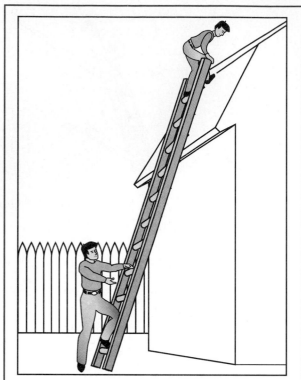

FIGURE 9–11 FRAMING THE PROBLEM (II). In another graphic approach, both Richards are drawn on the same ladder. Thus, only one clock is needed. With this drawing, it is quite clear that Richard climbing up must meet Richard going down the ladder. Also, the elapsed time must be the same for both of them, though they will not travel the same distance.

simply as possible, using the propositional or imaginal mode.

If you use words or numbers, framing is difficult. The problem still seems overwhelming. Using a graphic or imaginal mode frames the problem more clearly. It represents the essence of the problem without distractions. Then the first question is readily answered.

We cannot answer the second question, about the exact place on the ladder, without knowing the length of the ladder and the rates of speed. This question is a typical time-rate-distance problem, perhaps best framed in the propositional mode, using simple, round numbers at the outset.

However, a different graphic representation frames the problem even more clearly. It shows that the two Richards *must* encounter one another at the same time somewhere on the ladder (Figure 9–11).

The time spent in restating the problem or representing it in some other way is usually time well spent. Many people begin immediately to think of methods for solving the problem, an approach that may even retard the solution. In assisting other people in problem solving, help in framing it may be most important, especially when the problem is of a personal nature (Evans, Block, Steinberg, & Penrose, 1986).

DEVELOPING PROBLEM-SOLVING STRATEGIES. Once a problem has been framed, we typically do not have available a precisely outlined series of steps for the solution, as in an algorithm. Even if available, an algorithm sometimes takes much longer than necessary. Suppose Judith misplaced her earrings, leaving them on a post of the troublesome, slowly emerging staircase. To find them, knowing she had left them somewhere in her half-finished home, she would *not* begin the search by walking up and down the whole building, from one end to the other, each trip just beyond the unexplored edge of the previous one. If she continued in that fashion, and if the earrings were in the house, she would find them. The solution was guaranteed—but there was a better way.

Instead, human beings make decisions about likely outcomes. In **decision making,** the probabilities of relevant events are estimated and employed in selecting a strategy for solving a problem. For example, Judith should go immediately to the spot where she thought she left the earrings, a simple effort that might succeed. We all employ such heuristics automatically, but three are widely used: assessing availability, noting similarities, and creating subgoals.

1. **Assessing availability.** Especially with common problems, we often use the easiest strat-

FIGURE 9–12 CREATING SUBGOALS.
The problem of a car stalled in the snow is readily depicted: The car is stuck! However, even this problem can be approached in terms of subgoals: choosing the most experienced winter driver, ensuring that the wheels are not cramped, discovering where the snow is most densely packed, determining which wheel is spinning, recruiting pushers, deciding how to rock the vehicle, and so forth.

egy. In the **availability heuristic,** the problem-solving strategy is the one that comes to mind most readily, the first guess, chiefly because it is handy. Judith used the availability heuristic in finding her earrings. Later, one of the subcontractors was at the side of Judith's half-built house, where there was no door, and he wanted to enter quickly. He decided to use an unfinished window instead. The probability of success was indeterminate, but the cost of trying was low. This approach has an advantage; it is *readily* accessible and may prove useful (Kahneman, Slovic, & Tversky, 1982).

2. **Noting similarities.** In the **representative heuristic,** the problem-solving strategy is determined by the similarity between the new instance and a good model for a certain category of instances. The problem solver asks:

Does the new information match that of the model? If the new information appears to fit that category, the model or representative solution is attempted (Kahneman, Slovic, & Tversky, 1982). Provided that the fit is accurate, the solution may be readily achieved. If the new problem only *seems* similar but requires a different solution, use of the representative strategy may delay the solution.

3. **Creating subgoals.** Suppose the problem is complex, such as building the staircase. How can Jim make the staircase attractive and yet fit it into the limited space? A problem of this sort is typically approached by dividing it into parts and establishing subgoals. The first subgoal might be to determine the number of risers and treads needed to reach the second floor. The answer to this problem provides a partial answer to the larger problem. The second subgoal might be to determine how many large posts will be necessary to support the banister and railing, again providing part of the answer, and so forth. The difficulty with this heuristic lies in identifying useful, efficient subgoals (Figure 9–12). Such decisions are sometimes quite perplexing.

MAINTAINING FLEXIBILITY. If the solution cannot be implemented or if no solution can be found, then the problem solver needs flexibility, which is the hallmark of success across a wide range of problems. The single biggest obstacle in problem solving is that people often place unnecessary restraints on the way they depict the problem or the strategies they attempt to use in solving it. This tendency to approach a problem without regard for alternative solutions is known as a **set.** It may be a set in thinking, called a *thought set,* or a set in perceiving, called a *perceptual set.*

Consider this problem: Richard has it in front.

FIGURE 9–13 A PROBLEM IN FUNCTIONAL FIXEDNESS. In the classic two-string problem, the task was to tie together a pair of strings hanging from the ceiling, but one could not be reached without letting go of the other. Various tools were nearby; otherwise the room was empty. How could the problem be solved? **Answer:** The solution was to attach one of the tools to one string and set it in motion, like a pendulum. Then, with the other string in hand, the first string was grasped when it swung within range (Duncker, 1945; Maier, 1931).

Judith doesn't have it at all. Carpenters all have it. Wives never do. And Brewster, the dog, has it twice. What is it?

You probably directed your thoughts to these individuals, for you have learned something about them. Maybe you began thinking about Richard's beard or other personal characteristics. Experiencing no success, you perhaps turned to sex roles and gender differences, suggested by the group membership. You did not solve the problem, however, unless you broke the set of focusing on the people. The problem does not concern these individuals but the words used to represent them. The answer is the letter *r.*

A special case of an inhibiting set is called **functional fixedness,** in which an object is perceived as useful only for its original purpose. A pencil is regarded as a tool for writing and not as a

possible doorstop, window prop, or measuring instrument, depending on the occasion. When Jim needed a ruler, he simply spread his large right hand across a board and announced: "It's twelve inches." Years earlier he had overcome functional fixedness. He had measured his hands, for he found them useful as rulers (Kidder, 1985).

Jim's behavior in overcoming functional fixedness illustrates once again two types of symbols used in thinking. He imagined his hands as rulers, certainly an effort at problem solving in the imaginal mode. Then he measured them and discovered that they spanned 12 inches, thereby using the words and numbers of the propositional mode.

In a classic laboratory experiment on functional fixedness, the subjects were led to a room in which two strings were hanging from the ceiling, and they were asked to tie them together. The strings were long enough to be reached but too far apart to be grasped simultaneously. What did the subjects do to solve the problem? The room contained miscellaneous objects, and eventually a solution occurred to some subjects (Duncker, 1945; Maier, 1931; Figure 9–13).

In a variation of the two-string problem, one group of subjects was previously trained to use a switch to complete a circuit; another group was trained to use an electric relay; and a third group received no training with any apparatus. Then all subjects were presented with the two-string problem while the switch and relay lay nearby on the table. The question was not whether the subjects would solve the problem but how they might do so, for they were given a hint, if necessary. It was found that subjects trained with the relay used the switch for the pendulum; those trained with the switch used the relay; and those with no training were evenly divided. Using an object for one purpose apparently constituted a barrier to using it for another (Birch & Rabinowitz, 1951).

In many school programs, there has been renewed emphasis on solving such problems and achieving flexibility in thinking. Helping people to think in new ways is a fundamental challenge for all educators (Arnon & Kreitler, 1984).

• CREATIVE THINKING •

Another form of problem solving is not as obviously logical and controlled as reasoning. The aim in **creative thinking** is to produce a novel or highly original outcome with a useful or aesthetic purpose, rather than to solve a more common problem. Compared with ordinary problem solving, creative thinking has a more important basis in imagination; it requires a high degree of flexibility and the capacity to combine seemingly unrelated events.

With this focus, we arrive at Judith's concerns for form *and* function. She expected a completely efficient, up-to-date structure. At the same time, she wanted her house to express the character and history of its rustic New England community. A successful design of this sort, combining disparate elements, required creative thinking.

Inside the house, Jim's unfinished staircase posed a more specific problem. To make the stairs curved and continuous, the banister required taller posts at the bottom than at the top. To make the whole staircase consistent, all posts for the banister would have to be the same height—leaving the bottom of the banister apparently too low (Kidder, 1985). All around the house were problems of this sort, small and large, requiring creative solutions—and taking more time than expected.

❧

PROCESSES IN CREATIVITY

Two conditions hamper research on creativity. First, the behavior is infrequent, by definition. Second, it often takes place during lonely hours, as the works of Darwin, Einstein, Freud, and others bear testimony. Freud developed psychoanalytic theory during his years of "splendid isolation," as he called them, while he was almost completely isolated from the rest of his colleagues. For these reasons, and because creativity may be inhibited by the presence of an observer, investigators have been limited in scope.

PHASE THEORY. In early research, a retrospective approach was used. People were questioned *after* they had produced some significant, original work. Asked to think back on their effort, they gave an account of what had transpired, and four phases of the creative process were identified: preparation, incubation, illumination, and verification or revision (Wallas, 1926).

The preparation phase included training and hard work. As Thomas Edison said, much of his inspiration was perspiration. The incubation phase was characterized by no obvious progress. A problem remained latent in the person's mind for several days or weeks, without any conscious effort to work on a solution. According to many reports, the creative solution appeared unexpectedly, as a sudden illumination. The person was thinking about something else and—Aha!—the problem seemed solved. Finally, in verification, this solution was tested carefully, sometimes empirically, sometimes rationally.

ROLE OF TRIAL AND ERROR. Subsequent studies showed that many people who achieved creative outcomes, either slight or momentous, did not go through this sequence. Sometimes the stages were indistinct or did not appear at all. There was no incubation in one instance, a gradual solution in another. According to anecdotal reports, illumination often occurs during relaxation, without any prolonged incubation: immediately on awakening, in the shower, or while exercising. Perhaps at these times competing thoughts are at a low ebb. In any case, the four phases now appear oversimplified, although certain aspects are relevant to the creative process.

Creativity is currently believed to be more diffuse and less dramatic than phase theory indicated. There is considerable **trial and error,** which is random and exploratory activity, without a clear hypothesis. The subject uses one approach, discards it, tries another, and so forth. People who wish to be creative must accept the trial-and-error concept. They must be encouraged to take risks, to tolerate ambiguity, and to make mistakes (Sternberg & Lubart, 1992).

For example, still baffled by the staircase, Jim decided to make all of the posts equal in height, resigned to the fact that the bottom of the banister would look disconnected from the rest. One night, with the banister well underway, the architect secretly taped all of the smaller posts in place, thereby diminishing the disconnected look. Then he found an old can and placed it on top of one of the lower posts, simulating a cap. That cap appeared to correct the other problem, the difference in height. The next morning, satisfied with this solution, Jim made a cap, known as an easement, for each of the bottom posts. The problem was solved; the chief method was trial and error; and the Apple Corps still had a chance to meet the deadline.

CREATIVITY AND INSIGHT. The role of trial-and-error behavior was demonstrated in the earliest experiments with chimpanzees. When a stick was placed in their play cage, some of them poked it out between the bars and drew in some nearby bananas. When another stick was presented in two separate parts and the food was too far away to be obtained by only one part, a particularly bright chimpanzee named Sultan began to react to this problem in a random fashion. Then suddenly he seemed to see the relation between the two parts of the stick, collecting one, then the other, and joining them. He solved the problem with apparent suddenness, a reaction that is called **insight,** emphasizing some new way of perceiving the solution (Köhler, 1925).

Subsequent experiments afforded another interpretation, however. When chimpanzees were presented with an extremely simple stick problem, pulling on a hoe to rake in a banana, only two subjects, both with previous experience with sticks, solved this problem within the 30-minute period. Then all the animals were returned to their home cages, where they were permitted to play with dozens of sticks for three days, manipulating them for long periods of time with no obvious reinforcement. When reexamined on the stick problem later, all of them solved it within 20 seconds, and their success seemed attributable to the prior experience (Birch, 1945).

Human subjects, in fact, often use *covert trial and error,* in which various solutions are attempted implicitly, in the subject's mind, before overt behavior appears. Rarely do we solve a complex problem without making several attempts. The extent to which the solution seems to appear suddenly, through insight, depends partly on covert trial and error, partly on prior experience, and partly on the accuracy with which we recall the complete reasoning process later. Further studies of these underlying cognitive processes should gradually clarify the traditional, rather broad and vague concept of insight (Keane, 1989).

ROLE OF MOTIVATION. In addition, there usually is a strong sense of commitment or purpose. The creator is trying to solve a difficult problem by *any available means.* In the course of these persistent efforts, perhaps through trial and error, a creative solution appears. Or the creator has the specific *goal of being original,* trying to develop an original product. In both cases, motivation is the underlying issue (Perkins, 1981).

Commitment occurred in the architect's efforts with the banister. On his first night back after an absence of three weeks, he found a solution without disrupting Jim's work. His solution was useful in another sense too—it saved time, assisting the Apple Corps with the Halloween deadline.

Weeks earlier, with the chimney, Jim had the purpose of being creative. The architect had planned nothing new, expecting a square, well-built chimney, but Jim wanted something special. "I wonder," he said, "if we could do something to dress up the chimney." He discussed this goal with a bricklayer experienced in corbeling, in which various layers of brick extend outward from the vertical. They tried one design, then another, and settled on a plan. As testimony to Jim's creative effort, the bricklayer scrawled his name in the wet cement inside the chimney: GENTLEMAN JIM (Kidder, 1985).

CREATIVITY AND HUMOR

Creative people are commonly identified by a characteristic that does not necessarily contribute to creativity but is certainly a manifestation of it: a sense of humor. They tend to produce humor at a higher than average rate themselves, and they place a high value on humor in others. This interest in humor is not surprising, for much humor involves a novel way of looking at something. It requires a cognitive shift. An unexpected, worthwhile outcome is developed.

COGNITIVE RESTRUCTURING. Creativity and humor are commonly explained in this way—an unexpected solution that works. The chief principle is **restructuring,** in which the basic elements in a particular situation are reorganized or rearranged, providing it with a different meaning. The background material moves our thought in one direction; the punch line shows another way of looking at the situation.

A humble bricklayer, after building an excellent fireplace for a wealthy man, asked for his payment. Told he must wait for his money, the bricklayer asked his wealthy customer to wait, too. The fireplace was not to be used until the bill was paid. The customer agreed but shortly thereafter appeared at the bricklayer's door, complaining that his house was full of smoke. "I told you not to use that chimney," said the bricklayer. "When you pay

me, I'll fix it." The customer promptly paid, and then the bricklayer climbed to the roof of the house, carrying a brick. He dropped it down the chimney, breaking a plate of glass mortared across the flue (Kidder, 1985).

This story, well known to Judith and the Apple Corps, has several incongruities and surprises, each requiring a cognitive shift. An excellent chimney does not work; a rich man refuses to pay; he violates an agreement; suddenly the power shifts to the humble man, who has a very simple solution; and we laugh because he had outsmarted the rich man from the very beginning. The audience is propelled in one direction, then another, and another, with a surprising conclusion (Figure 9–14).

FIGURE 9–14 A COGNITIVE SHIFT. People who find humor in this cartoon experience a cognitive shift, especially if they focus first on the gun, presumably the most important element in the drawing. Then the viewer's gaze moves up the stems, and here restructuring occurs for the viewer. The victim is so terrified that his fear goes right up through the plant, like electricity. Or he is so frozen with fear that he cannot move, and the plant reacts instead.

INFLUENCES ON MOTIVATION
Inborn and Acquired Factors
Instinct and Human Behavior

SURVIVAL MOTIVES
Hunger and Thirst
Need for Sleep
Sexuality and Parenting

STIMULATION MOTIVES
Boredom and Curiosity
Affectional Stimulation

SOCIAL AND WORK MOTIVES
Desire for Affiliation
Achievement Motivation

THEORIES OF MOTIVATION
Biological Perspectives
Psychological Viewpoints
A Motivational Hierarchy

MULTIPLE BASES OF MOTIVATION

10
MOTIVATION

❧

R OBIN STOOD ON THE DECK OF HIS SAILBOAT AS IT ROCKED GENTLY IN ITS MOORINGS IN THE SERENE, SUN-KISSED MARINA AT SAN PEDRO, CALIFORNIA. Facing his father, he felt the awkwardness and tension of the moment.

Here was the man who bought him his first sailboat and gave him confidence as a sailor. Here was the man Robin admired as a boy, the man with whom he had struggled as a teenager—like so many fathers and sons. Here was the man Robin was now attempting to surpass by doing what his father had never done—sailing alone around the world. And this man, despite all of his silent pride in Robin, was ill at ease, wary about what lay ahead.

When his father finally extended his hand, Robin noticed it was trembling. The man mumbled something about a meeting in Hawaii and then went ashore.

Robin's mother never came aboard to bid him good-bye, and she never hid her worry. She had endless doubts about Robin's trip. He might be eaten by sharks, battered by storms, or beaten by strangers. She even consulted lawyers about legal opposition to his plan.

Robin Lee Graham was honestly and deeply embarrassed, partly by his parents' concerns, partly by the media at the marina. The swarms of reporters and television crews outnumbered his family and friends. Those from the *National Geographic* planned to publish periodic accounts of his endeavor, which might last for several years— if things went well. This publicity had produced a shower of farewell gifts, including a couple of kittens whose pictures appeared in newspapers from Los Angeles to London.

Even as he guided his 24-foot boat into the open ocean, reporters and spectators called to 16-year-old Robin over and over: "What makes you do it?" "Are you doing a stunt?" "Do you like school?" In one form or another, he was constantly asked: "Why do you choose to sail alone around the world?" (Graham, 1972).

Robin's goal raises the question of motivation, and even Robin did not know the answer. Why *was* he undertaking the voyage? He gave various replies, some evasive, some unclear even to himself.

His voyage is especially useful in this chapter on motivation because its length and complexity offer many different ways to examine this topic. The study of human motivation requires this diversity. How, for example, does a dieter manage to stay on his plan? Why does an athletic team become highly motivated for one game, lethargic for the next? What is the motivation behind needless gambling and low-altitude skydiving? Each of these questions poses its own special problems in motivation.

Psychologists have a long and special interest in solo voyagers, from sailor Joshua Slocum in 1895 through John Glenn and other solitary astronauts in more recent times. The constancy and loneliness of their environments appear contrary to our basic nature, raising questions about mental and physical health and our motivation for stimulation.

The significance of motivation can be understood by comparing a human being and a puppet.

The puppet is a static object, incapable of initiating its own activity. It moves only when its strings are manipulated; it is completely under external control. The concept of **motivation** refers to activation from within the organism; it is an internal state that activates and directs behavior.

We begin this chapter by studying the basic influences on motivation. Then we turn to survival motives, stimulation motives, and social and work motives. After a review of the theories of motivation, we conclude with a reminder of the basic theme in this book, the multiple bases of motivation.

• INFLUENCES ON MOTIVATION •

"Almost too easy," Robin wrote in his log, sailing toward Honolulu, his first port of call. Only one aspect of the voyage was certain. He would travel wherever he wished, spending weeks or months in any port that caught his fancy, especially those that differed from traditional Western ways. The voyage would be an endless adventure—on land as well as on sea (Figure 10–1).

Robin's oceangoing behavior, according to one explanation, was instinctive. The boy had an instinct for the sea, which prompted him to undertake the trip in the first place and helped him to respond properly at all times. Arriving in Hawaii ahead of schedule, he reported that the boat behaved well, the kittens did too, and he found no trouble of any sort. "I looked on this first leg . . . as a shakedown cruise," Robin added in the log (Graham, 1972).

This view of human behavior as sometimes instinctive is quite common and loosely applied in diverse situations. We hear that a gregarious man has an instinctive love of cocktail parties or that a woman possesses an instinct for handling horses. When asked about a new student center, a dean asserted: "My instincts tell me it will work."

The dean appears to be saying that certain inborn personal characteristics support his view. But it is highly unlikely that the dean has any instincts of this sort. He may have some deep feelings on the subject, and he may have considerable experience with college students, but he does not have any instincts about student centers if, indeed, he has any instincts at all.

As a rule, psychologists adopt a more precise view of instincts. An **instinct,** according to the traditional definition, is a relatively com-

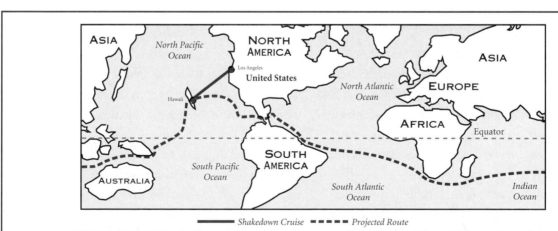

FIGURE 10–1 ROBIN'S PROPOSED ROUTE. The solid line to Hawaii shows the shakedown cruise, intended to ensure that the boat was in a fit condition. At one time, Robin planned to complete his trip by returning to Hawaii. The dashed line shows the proposed route for the full voyage around the world, without indicating specific ports.

plex, unlearned pattern of behavior that occurs in all normal, same-sex members of a given species. At the human level, therefore, a complex behavior must appear in *all* men or *all* women to be considered an instinct. We begin with this concept because it is so widely misused and because it emphasizes that motivation commonly arises through a combination of inborn and acquired factors.

∾

INBORN AND ACQUIRED FACTORS

To study the bases of instinct we begin at the animal level, with a situation that has been investigated extensively: the birth of the first litter of a female rat. Before the little ones are born, the mother shows a very clear pattern of responses, even when she has never observed maternal behavior in other rats. She builds a nest, usually of grass and twigs; then, after the birth, she bites the umbilical cord, licks the newborn, and eats the placenta. Afterward, she places the young in the nest one by one, and then she crouches over them in a protective posture.

This behavior qualifies as an instinct. It is complex; it appears without opportunity for learning; and it occurs in all female rats that have given birth.

What is behind this reaction? How does it take place? Something must occur *inside* the animal.

ROLE OF HORMONES. Most important are factors in the bloodstream, part of the individual's genetic inheritance. These inborn chemical substances, known as **hormones,** secreted by various glands, influence a wide variety of bodily activities, including maternal reactions, reproductive behavior, and responses in emergency situations.

In any adult rat or rabbit, one particular hormone, **prolactin,** plays a crucial role in maternal behavior, including nesting and the production of milk. Even a virgin rat injected with this substance displays maternal behavior when exposed to pups,

crouching over them, fixing a nest, and so forth. In female rabbits, injections of prolactin or a drug that causes false pregnancy prompts nest building (Zarrow, Sarwin, Ross, & Denenberg, 1962). There is no doubt about the significance of prolactin in maternal behavior among animals, including birds (Hall, 1991b).

Sexual behavior is similarly predictable. All male rats mate in the same way, whether or not they have observed mating in others; female rats also have a standard mating pattern. A necessary stimulus for mating behavior in many animals is the secretion of sex hormones, called **androgens** in the male and **estrogens** in the female. The former, found in both sexes but in greater amounts in the male, play a role in aggression. The latter are influential in maternal behavior. When the sex glands are removed a few days after birth, preventing these secretions, sexual behavior occurs infrequently. If the hormone is injected, sexual behavior returns. If a castrated male rat is injected with estrogen, it will exhibit female sexual responses, crouching and raising the hindquarters. When female rats are treated with androgen as adults, they display male sexual behaviors (Drickamer & Vessey, 1992).

Hormonal influences also occur at the human level, but they are distinctly less significant. They are also masked, complicated, and diminished by the enormous role of learning.

ROLE OF EXPERIENCE. On the basis of hormonal secretions, is there evidence that Robin Graham's oceangoing behavior was instinctive? The answer is clearly negative. No such inborn factors prompting someone to take to the sea have ever been identified. After three weeks in Hawaii, Robin sailed out of the harbor toward the vast, little-known areas of the South Pacific, and his throat was so tight with fear that he could hardly swallow. This reaction is clearly inconsistent with an instinct for sailing.

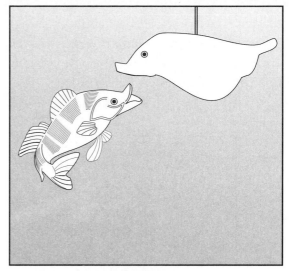

FIGURE 10–2 A RELEASER. In triggering the male stickleback's mating dance, the color and details of the female model are relatively unimportant, even the face and fins. The releaser is her highly visible visceral cavity—her swollen abdomen (Tinbergen, 1951, 1953).

In human beings and animals there is another consideration besides inborn factors. Experience is important too.

Prior to the birth of her litter, the mother rat behaves in a predictable way, licking herself extensively, especially in the vaginal region. One scientist observing this action wondered whether it had any significance for the later instinctive behavior. To test this hypothesis, he fitted some pregnant female rats with collars like Elizabethan ruffs, large enough to prevent them from licking the vaginal region. Each rat in another group wore a similar collar with a carefully placed notch that presented opportunities for the usual self-licking. All the collars were removed one or two hours before litters were produced, and all litters appeared normal at birth. Among the control mothers 95% of the pups survived weaning, but the experimental mothers, prevented from self-licking before the birth, ate most of their offspring. The few that survived initially were either not retrieved to the nest, retrieved and then eaten, or badly suckled, thereby expiring before the end of the usual nursing period (Birch, 1956).

Proper mothering is partly under the influence of the odors and tastes in the vaginal region. This stimulation prevents the mother rat from devouring her young, perhaps by sensitizing her to the chemical makeup of her own body, which bears a close resemblance to that of her offspring. However, instinctive behavior is not always perfect, and experience plays a role here too. With her first litter, even a normal mother rat sometimes consumes some of her babies. With later litters, this outcome is decidedly less likely. Similarly, a mother rabbit builds a nest for her first litter, but the nests for later litters are successively improved, again showing the influence of experience (Drickamer & Vessey, 1992).

In addition to prior experience, a certain form of present stimulation is usually necessary. This external stimulation, which initiates the instinctive pattern, is called a **releaser.** The male three-spined stickleback fish, for example, exhibits a complicated dancing pattern during the mating season (Figure 10–2). This elaborate behavior is alike in all these fish, and investigators wanted to know what specific detail in the environment served to release it. They built various models of a female about to lay eggs and presented them to the male. In this way, they found that a model that does not look like a fish but has a swelling in about the right place sets off this characteristic mating behavior (FitzGerald, 1993; Tinbergen, 1953).

These conditions do not require revision of our definition of instinct. The initial behavior is still unlearned, although a certain stimulus may be necessary to release it, and it may improve with practice. The basic pattern still occurs on the first trial. Altogether, instinctive behavior requires some internal stimulation, relevant prior experience, and contact with an appropriate releaser in the current environment.

INSTINCT AND HUMAN BEHAVIOR

If your parents or grandparents studied psychology in the 1920s, they read that human beings possess dozens of instincts, including instincts for good habits, disgust, retaliation, and altruism. Cleanliness was even said to be a human instinct.

Slowly, the pendulum swung in the other direction, and then a social psychologist published a book describing 5,648 usages of the concept *instinct*. With this publication, the unrestrained approach to instincts collapsed (Bernard, 1924). People realized that there are essentially no behaviors at the human level that fit the traditional definition. Human beings possess many reflexes, and they show inherited predispositions toward a variety of behaviors, including language use and social contact, but most psychologists today have strong reservations about attributing instincts to human beings, at least as traditionally defined in this book (Gal'perin, 1992).

The distinction between an instinct and a reflex is vital in understanding this viewpoint. An instinct is a *complex*, unlearned pattern of behavior. A **reflex** is a *simple*, unlearned response, usually involving some specific part of the body. A puff of air causes an eyeblink. A spray of cold water creates goose pimples. Robin Graham exhibited these reflexes when sailing toward his next port, the Samoan Islands. Like the knee jerk, salivation, and sneezing, these automatic responses are too simple and brief to be called instincts.

Robin showed learned reflexes in reacting to danger. In adverse seas he quickly pulled the tiller to one side and braced himself against the tilt of his boat. After fighting a severe storm, he used the term *instinct* incorrectly. "The instinct of survival takes over in the end," he wrote in his log (Graham, 1972). In fact, he was referring to reflexes and learning.

Even an instinct for survival appears unlikely in human beings, for legions of people engage in smoking, drinking, overeating, and similar behaviors that shorten their lives. Others, without intending to save themselves, walk into the ocean, lie down in the snow, jump off bridges, or take all sorts of unwarranted risks, as demonstrated by Robin himself. A true survival instinct, defined as a complex pattern of unlearned responses, presumably would have inhibited or interfered with his voyage.

We certainly can speak of an *urge* to live, which is present in most of us. We also can speak of reflexes that promote survival, such as gasping for air, blinking in a dust storm, and so forth.

Robin was talking about sailing, and sailing is learned. Otherwise, we all would know how to chart a course across the ocean, using celestial navigation to arrive at our destination. As a rule, when people speak of human instincts, they are referring to complex and subtle learning, often combined with reflexes.

There were some instinctive reactions in Robin's cats, such as mating and catching mice, but even at the animal level the concept of instinct is not particularly helpful in understanding the behavior. We say that the mother rat has a maternal instinct and therefore takes care of her babies, but we also say that she takes care of her babies because she has a maternal instinct. This reasoning is circular.

Many contemporary psychologists and ecologists prefer instead to speak of a **fixed action pattern** in animals, which means that a certain complex behavior appears to be innate, stereotyped, and independent of the organism's immediate control. This term includes no implication about how the behavior occurs. It simply indicates that certain animal species react in certain ways with members of their own kind. Such patterns are most striking in sexual behavior, care of the young, and territoriality (Drickamer & Vessey, 1992). Heredity and physiology, on the one hand, and the environment, on the other, play a role in an interactive fashion.

• SURVIVAL MOTIVES •

In turning to survival motives, we begin with *individual survival,* which is the capacity of an organism to reach a normal life span for its species. At the human level, the chief concerns, apart from respiration and safety, are obtaining adequate food, drink, and sleep. Sailing slowly among the hundreds of islands in the South Pacific, Robin had no problem here. In his leisurely travels, he found clams and squid, bought limes and papayas, and slept in the warm sun. He also met Patti Ratterree. They swam and sailed together and enjoyed the native foods.

Afterward, we turn to *species survival,* which is the preservation and continuation of a whole class or category of organisms. This survival is made possible by sexual and parental motivation, but if the species is to survive, the individual survival motives of course are essential too.

HUNGER AND THIRST

"A man seldom thinks of anything with more earnestness," said Samuel Johnson, "than he does of his dinner." What we want for dinner varies widely, however, showing the role of environmental factors in eating. The French and Arabs consume whole birds; Australian aborigines devour ants; and certain Indian societies consider cow urine in milk delectable. In the South Seas, Robin Graham sampled octopus in the Tonga Islands, spider conchs in the Yasawa Islands, and in the Viti Levu Islands he heard stories about the consumption of boiled human flesh.

REGULATION OF EATING. Some of the clearest signs of hunger are pangs in the stomach. Therefore, in early experiments, one subject swallowed a small balloon that could be inflated through an attached tube. When the tube was connected with appropriate apparatus, it gave indications of changes in pressure within the stomach. Contractions of the stomach were found to coincide with the gnawing feeling reported by the subject. On this basis, stomach contractions appeared to be the critical issue in the experience of hunger (Cannon & Washburn, 1912).

Later studies found that both stomach contractions and hunger pangs ceased with the administration of dextrose, a substance that raises the blood sugar level. Thus, the next research step was to examine the relationship between blood sugar level and hunger. Investigators injected blood from a starved dog into a normal dog and observed the contractions sometimes found in hunger. Injection of blood from a well-fed animal stopped these contractions (Luckhardt & Carlson, 1915). Such experiments supported the idea that blood sugar level is closely related to hunger, but again the answer is more complex. Blood sugar level is monitored by the brain.

Electrical stimulation of the side of the hypothalamus, called the **lateral hypothalamus,** activates and sustains eating in animals, even those presumably satiated. When this area is damaged or removed, experimental animals cease eating despite the availability of food, even though their normal needs have not been satisfied. Apparently they do not know when to start eating (Keesey, Corbett, Hirvonen, & Kaufman, 1984). Stimulation in the middle of this area, the **ventromedial nucleus** of the hypothalamus, promotes the opposite behavior: cessation of eating even among animals on a food deprivation schedule. When it is damaged or absent, experimental animals engage in overeating, sometimes reaching three times their normal weight (Mayer, 1956).

Earlier, these areas of the hypothalamus were thought to be highly specific centers for eating. The lateral hypothalamus seemed to be a start mechanism, the ventromedial nucleus a stop mechanism (Figure 10–3). However, similar outcomes have occurred with stimulation and lesions in other brain areas. Hence, the hypothalamus is considered a crucial factor, but not *the* factor, in eating. Among other influences, it seems to make the individual more sensitive to food-related stimuli (Berridge & Valenstein, 1991). Collectively, these studies show that eating is complexly determined, involving the mouth and throat, stomach, blood, and brain.

REGULATION OF BODY WEIGHT.

Extensions of this research suggest that the body monitors its intake of food to maintain a proper balance, called a *set point*. According to **set point theory,** each of us has a normal or natural weight, determined by inherited factors and maintained through automatic processes. Unless other conditions interfere, over the long term we adjust our eating habits and energy expenditure to keep the body weight at this point. Central to this theory is the concept of *metabolism,* a complex set of physical and chemical processes that convert food into energy, thereby consuming energy as well. Apparently our metabolic rate changes according to the caloric content available. When we go on a diet, the body compensates for the fewer calories by lowering its metabolic rate. When we gorge ourselves, it raises the rate, perhaps through the role of the ventromedial nucleus of the hypothalamus (Keesey & Pauley, 1986).

For these reasons, one approach to weight loss, by itself, usually is not effective. When

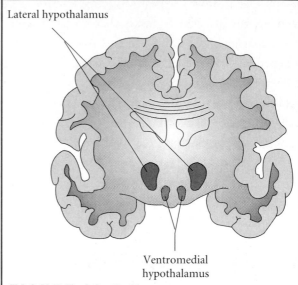

Lateral hypothalamus

Ventromedial hypothalamus

FIGURE 10–3 HUNGER AND THE HYPOTHALAMUS. The drawing shows a cross-section of the brain from the front. The terms *lateral* and *ventromedial* describe the location within the hypothalamus. *Lateral* means "to the side." *Ventro* indicates "lower" and *medial* means "situated in the middle." Both areas of the hypothalamus appear important in eating, though not exclusively in its onset or cessation.

dieters were studied, it was found, in accordance with set point theory, that their metabolic rates decreased. Yet some of these people raised their metabolic rates back to their normal levels, thereby losing weight. Who were these subjects? They were people who also engaged in extra exercise, which apparently was the crucial *additional* factor in energy expenditure (Wadden, Foster, Letizia, & Mullen, 1990).

In other words, body weight is determined by several factors and, among them, heredity sets some sort of overall potential. People born with a high set point have a predisposition to become overweight. Those with a low set point have a predisposition to become slender, even underweight. Environmental factors then determine how we develop within this potential. It seemed that Robin, for example, had a potential for low body weight, and his strenuous daily activities certainly fostered this outcome.

DEALING WITH OBESITY. In *obesity,* a person's body weight is at least 20–25% greater than the ideal weight, as determined by the height–weight ratio for that person, using tables for the two genders, different races, and various ages. The influential physical factors fall into two categories: food intake, by which we gain energy; and physical activity, metabolism, and thermogenesis, by which we spend it. In food intake, the amount of fat in the diet can be most important, contributing significantly to body weight. In spending energy, physical activity accounts for about 15–20% among average people. Metabolism usually accounts for 65–75% of our energy expenditure. A low metabolic rate is clearly a predisposing factor for obesity, apparently complicated by a deficiency in serotonin. Finally, thermogenesis is the process of producing heat in the body. Usually 10–15% of the body's total energy is spent in this manner, and even less may be required in obese individuals (Shah & Jeffery, 1991).

If a change is desirable, and the aim is to lose weight, the next steps emerge—more readily enumerated than followed. Collectively, they illustrate the multiple bases of behavior. First, it is useful to know the nutritional value of foods. An excess of blood sugar, also known as *glucose,* is stored as body fat. The chances of becoming overweight are increased by the consumption of foods high in glucose, such as cake and cookies, rather than those low in glucose but equivalent in caloric content, such as spinach and fish. Second, lasting weight loss is accompanied by a change in bodily processes related to metabolism; therefore, adequate exercise is essential. Twenty minutes may be the minimum to break a sweat, but a longer workout may be more useful for most people. Third, external conditions, such as watching television, prompt needless eating. The issue is partly mind over platter (Figure 10–4).

And finally, eat very s–l–o–w–l–y—for both physiological and psychological reasons. Physiologi-

FIGURE 10–4 DUAL VALUE OF EXERCISE. The potential weight gain from a chocolate sundae can be diminished or eliminated by exercise, which consumes calories. In addition, regular exercise can increase the normal metabolic rate. Thus, the body consumes calories at a faster rate even when the person is not exercising vigorously.

cally, a person begins to feel satisfied when food reaches the digestive tract, bloodstream, brain, and so forth. A person eating slowly will have consumed less food when that point is reached. On the psychological side, a person eating slowly will savor the food more and therefore consume less just for the taste.

ANOREXIA AND BULIMIA NERVOSA. Other eating disorders are almost the opposite of obesity. In **anorexia nervosa** a person eats barely enough to stay alive, producing physiological and psychological conditions associated with starvation: weakness, disruption of systemic functions, dizziness, and even hallucinations. Losses of 25% of the normal body weight are not uncommon. The most obvious precipitating cause of this disorder, almost ten times more prevalent in women than in men, is excessive dieting, prompted by a distorted body image. No matter how thin the person becomes, she still feels she is overweight and continues a semistarvation diet. In a seemingly related condition, **bulimia nervosa,** the individual eats regularly or even voraciously but then regurgitates the food. Some bulimic people eat constantly;

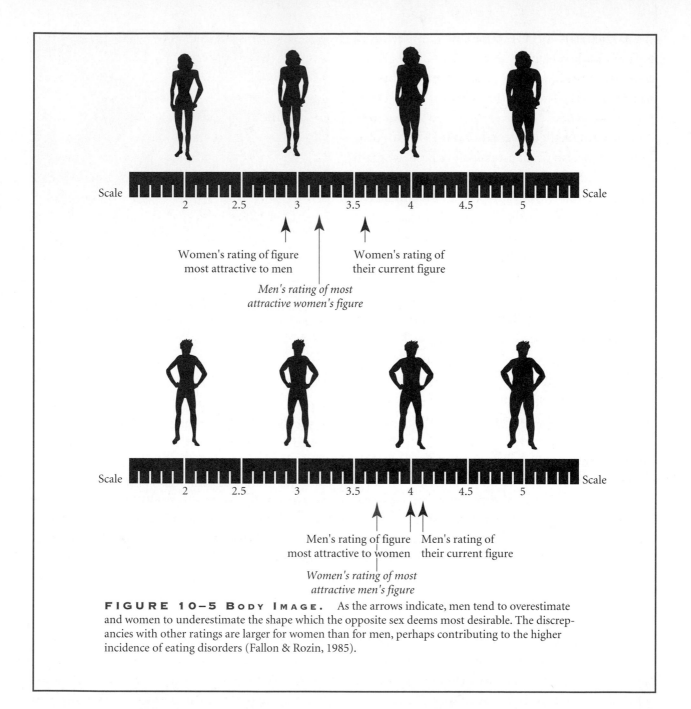

Scale   2   2.5   3   3.5   4   4.5   5   Scale

Women's rating of figure
most attractive to men

Women's rating of
their current figure

*Men's rating of most
attractive women's figure*

Scale   2   2.5   3   3.5   4   4.5   5   Scale

Men's rating of figure
most attractive to women

Men's rating of
their current figure

*Women's rating of most
attractive men's figure*

FIGURE 10–5 BODY IMAGE. As the arrows indicate, men tend to overestimate and women to underestimate the shape which the opposite sex deems most desirable. The discrepancies with other ratings are larger for women than for men, perhaps contributing to the higher incidence of eating disorders (Fallon & Rozin, 1985).

others engage in binges. If self-induced vomiting is not employed, laxatives may be used. People suffering from this disorder may be of normal weight and appear normal, if they can keep the regurgitation undetected (Varnado, Williamson, & Netemeyer, 1995).

Overall, for problems of body weight, health maintenance and, to some degree, body image, the preferred solution seems to lie in a program of regular, reasonable exercise.

With these conditions in mind, one key principle emerges for approaching the problem of body image. Determine whether it is a real or imagined problem. In the social context, studies show that both men and women hold misconceptions about the most desirable body shape (Figure 10–5). Men typically are trying to bulk up and women to slim down to reach what they feel is the ideal body image. And yet they are often wrong (Fallon & Rozin, 1985).

THIRST AND THE BRAIN. To survive, the human body also needs a constant supply of water. In fact, extreme thirst is more agonizing than extreme hunger—and more dangerous to health. Human beings can live without food for more than a week, but just a few days without water may be fatal. The depleted condition is called **cellular dehydration,** meaning loss of water in the cells of the body, which occurs constantly because the normal human being excretes about a quart of water each day through urination, exhalation, perspiration, and elimination.

Robin needed pure water at sea. Consuming sea water does not restore the body's water supply. It depletes it instead because sea water is almost 4% salt, much too salty for human consumption. To eliminate from the body the waste from one pint of sea water requires approximately one quart of body fluids—clearly a losing proposition. At sea, Robin caught rainwater in buckets and used it for showers only when he was certain that his physiological needs would be met.

The most obvious internal symptom of the need for water is dryness of the mouth and throat. But when people are subjected to different degrees of water deprivation, they drink water in proportion to the deficit. This accurate estimation is difficult to explain in terms of dryness of the mouth and throat because the first mouthful wets these areas, removing the condition that might provide a guide to the amount needed. To be effective in satisfying the body's need, water must enter tissue in other regions.

Parts of the hypothalamus are sensitive to a chemical agent in the blood called *angiotensin,* which indicates cellular dehydration. Angiotensin appears in greater quantities as the volume of blood

decreases, and the volume of blood depends partly on the volume of water in the body. These cells of the hypothalamus have been called **osmoreceptors,** meaning that they signal the passage of fluids through membranes, a process known as *osmosis.* Injections of salt solutions into osmoreceptors of the hypothalamus prompt dehydration and elicit drinking. Injections of plain water stop drinking only when they are placed in the anterior portion. Hence the anterior hypothalamus appears to be most closely related to drinking.

Environmental factors also influence the amount of drinking, as well as the types of beverages consumed. In the Vavau Islands, Robin drank kava, a slightly narcotic drink from shrub root, which made his lips and tongue feel as if he had just received a novocaine injection. "Kava is drunk by customers and staff," he said, speaking of the local shops, "the way that Americans use office water fountains" (Graham, 1972).

NEED FOR SLEEP

Twelve days after leaving the Solomon Islands, the sea churned up 20-foot swells and water poured into the cockpit as the tail of a hurricane kept Robin awake for 48 hours at a time, struggling for survival. When the winds finally subsided, Robin was completely exhausted. This extreme fatigue, he explained later, had a strange effect on him. At one point he had a spurt of energy, and then, a moment later, he felt totally unable to move at all—even to perform the simplest tasks (Graham, 1972).

Staying awake for long periods results in depression, extreme elation, anxiety, and other disorders. In an extensive two-year study, military personnel remained sleepless for 40, 65, or 90 hours; afterward, they showed hallucinations, loss of emotional control, and diminished intellectual functioning (Morris & Singer, 1961). Earlier, we noted similar deficits in sleep-deprived contestants in a tennis match (Edinger, Marsh, McCall, & Erwin, 1990).

Our need for sleep has been viewed from two theoretical positions, the first of which is a popular public view. According to the **restoration theory,** sleep replaces in the body biochemical and other factors depleted by the day's activities. During sleep we are repairing and recharging ourselves. Evidence for this view comes largely from studies of sleep deprivation (Horne, 1988).

From a different perspective, **adaptation theory** states that sleep evolved as an adjustment to a hostile environment, enabling human beings and other animals to avoid predators and, at the same time, to avoid expending useless energy. To serve both purposes, individuals went to sleep in safe places (Webb, 1974, 1983). For example, bats sleep in hiding places during the day, and they remain awake during the night, when their poor vision is not such a hazard. Most of their predators have poor night vision, too.

As so often is the case, the two theories are not incompatible. We need to recharge and repair ourselves periodically, as the restoration theory states. At the same time, adaptation theory recognizes the survival value of different patterns of sleep among the species. The human pattern is currently being subjected to modification by shift work, jet lag, artificial lighting, and the global economy. As noted earlier, these changes can lead to disruptions of normal physical and mental functioning.

❧

SEXUALITY
AND PARENTING

The survival of the species depends not only on individual survival but also on propagation. Here the limits of behavior among human beings, and even among apes, are so broad that no complex universal pattern can be identified. Survival of the species also depends on parental care, and again, the limits expand as one ascends the evolutionary scale.

SEXUAL MOTIVATION. There is little variation in sexual activity among rats and guinea pigs because this behavior depends chiefly, but not exclusively, on hormonal secretions, described earlier as androgens and estrogens in the male and female, respectively. Withdrawal of androgenic hormones in males distinctly alters sexual activity, as well as aggressive and scent-making behavior. When newborn and even prenatal males are deprived of these hormones, their sexual behavior in adulthood is like that of females (Drickamer & Vessey, 1992). The genetic constitution of young mammals is highly susceptible to early hormonal influences (Figure 10–6).

In human beings, the sex hormones are secreted by the **testes** in the male and **ovaries** in the female, collectively known as the *sex glands,* or *gonads.* If the testes are removed before puberty, sexual development is commonly disrupted. The effects of removing the ovaries before puberty are more difficult to predict, partly because the adrenal glands also secrete sex hormones. Castration after puberty usually does not result in complete cessation of sexual behavior in men or women, showing the influence of learning, although sexual behavior may appear at a reduced rate. In any case, the results are not nearly as significant as in lower animals.

Both men and women whose sex glands have degenerated late in life may continue to participate in sexual activities. Some women who have passed through menopause actually increase their sexual activity. When responsiveness does decrease in healthy, aging men, it appears to be related to diminished function in the pituitary gland as well as in the testes (Schiavi, Schreiner-Engel, White, & Mandeli, 1991).

Sexual behavior among human beings clearly illustrates the relationship between inborn and acquired factors in motivation. While there is no human sexual instinct, in the sense of a complex behavior pattern shared by all, there are genetically

FIGURE 10-6 SEXUAL BEHAVIOR IN ANIMALS. Mating patterns are much the same among members of the same species and same sex. Highly elaborate rituals are determined largely by hormonal and other inborn factors. Here the male peacock attempts to attract the female by an elaborate display of feathers.

driven sexual urges and various reflexes prompted by hormonal secretions. In addition, the pervasive influence of learning is evident in the wide variety of sexual behaviors of interest to some people but not to others. Even mouth kissing is learned. Once, after Robin was pulled from the surf by rescuers, he showed his interest in this activity (Graham, 1972). "And now," he gasped, turning to Patti, "what about some mouth-to-mouth resuscitation?"

SEXUALITY AND EVOLUTIONARY THEORY. A broad evolutionary perspective has implications for human sexuality. The aim in **evolutionary psychology** is to understand the ways in which human beings have developed solutions to their two overriding adaptive problems—survival and reproduction. The individuals who were successful at these tasks are our ancestors. Today, the subtasks for survival include learning a language, making friends, gaining competence at work, and so forth. The subtasks for reproduction include obtaining a mate, engaging in sex, offering parental care to offspring, and so forth.

Men and women are rather differently prepared for the reproduction task—at least in a biological sense. Healthy men have millions of sperm, readily available. Healthy women have a limited number of eggs, available only during periods of fertility. Furthermore, women who want to bear children must find a mate who will furnish the extensive resources necessary for this extremely demanding task. A promising candidate would be loyal, industrious, and assertive, a man capable of gaining status in the group. In contrast, men who want to rear children must find a mate capable of giving birth. Women who show this reproductive promise will be young, and they will be physically attractive to men. As a rule, women in our society generally prefer to marry successful, somewhat older, experienced men. Men are prompted to seek younger, sexually attractive women. These different mating preferences are presumably evolutionary outcomes of the different requirements for men and women in solving the reproduction problem (Buss, 1995; Simpson, 1995).

According to evolutionary psychology, sex differences in jealousy are also part of our biological inheritance. Among men, jealousy is elicited chiefly by evidence of sexual infidelity. Among women, it is also evoked by loss of attention and resources in the mating relationship (White & Mullen, 1989). In the same way, aggression in men and empathy in women may have their origins in the different reproductive tasks that confronted our male and female ancestors. These responses may be the evolved solutions of

FIGURE 10–7 MATERNAL BEHAVIOR. Patterns of mothering vary widely, showing the influence of learning. Some babies are bundled up in a procedure called swaddling, leaving them unable to reach, sit up, or crawl, yet they show no handicap in motor development.

the two genders for the task of reproduction (Buss, 1995).

Differences in sexual motivation appear to be related to these different reproductive tasks. For men, the dominant aim seems to be physical satisfaction; for women, it is more likely to involve love and a sense of personal commitment (Carroll, Volk, & Hyde, 1985). On these bases, it is not surprising that men's interest in sex is stimulated by direct, explicit communication, as in pornography; women are more motivated by the overall mood, style, and setting of the scene (Masters, Johnson, & Kolodny, 1982).

PARENTAL MOTIVATION. In many species, parental care is significantly influenced by

hormonal factors. Especially among animals, prolactin is the most basic condition for **maternal behavior,** meaning care of the young by the mother. Secreted by the pituitary gland, prolactin is also influential in sexual development. Guided somehow by these secretions, maternal behavior in lower animals is highly stereotyped. Without such influences, **paternal behavior,** care of the young by the father, is distinctly less predictable.

At the human level, despite the presence of prolactin, there is no worldwide pattern of mothering, unless it is feeding the child at the breast. Even breast-feeding is not universal, and in different cultures there are marked differences in weaning, both of which indicate the central role of learning (Figure 10–7). Hence, we cannot speak of a human maternal instinct, although this expression often appears, even in professional journals. The countless books and magazines on raising children show the overwhelming role of learning in human parental care.

Among human beings, a time comes when the offspring is ready to leave the parents. If kept too long under parental protection, children may never develop an adequate sense of independence and self-worth. If forced or permitted to leave too soon, they may encounter dangers that they cannot handle or may fail to develop certain skills. But when should a child, moving from infancy through adolescence, be allowed to do what? This question, the *universal parental dilemma*, can be answered only in terms of the readiness of the individual and the demands of the specific environment.

When Robin sailed from California, his parents received so much criticism that Robin's father published a letter explaining his view. It would have been easier to keep him home, he said, but he felt Robin could meet the challenges ahead.

• STIMULATION MOTIVES •

For Robin, sailing across the Coral Sea to New Guinea proved surprisingly difficult. Here he reached the doldrums, regions of the ocean near the equator where it is almost always calm, with only light winds.

Exposed to little more than the sky, the sea, and the sounds of his boat for days and days at a time, Robin began to "hate the bloody boat . . . her every creak, every bubble of her blistered paint." He decided that he would rather face hungry piranhas than go to sea alone again. "The calm began to get to me," he said. "I wanted to keep moving so I wouldn't go crazy."

The motivation for stimulation is typically considered in two categories, both essential for normal survival and development. First, there is the need for sensory variation, meaning that human beings need changes in stimulation. Second, there is the need, early in life, for affectional stimulation, meaning physical and emotional contact with other members of the species. Thus, **stimulation motives** appear to be biologically determined needs for excitation of some sort, not directly related to immediate survival. As yet, the underlying bases for such motives have not been established.

BOREDOM AND CURIOSITY

The need for sensory variation is particularly acute among solo, long-distance travelers. Especially on the high seas or in the skies, where there is little change in the surroundings, the traveler's mind can wander from the task at hand and even play tricks, apparently in an attempt to deal with the monotony.

Charles Lindbergh, flying the Atlantic alone, kept alert by singing, solving riddles, and doing mental exercises, but he still found himself upside down at one point, just a few feet above the water. Admiral Byrd, surrounded only by the wind, snow, and Antarctic darkness, imagined himself in a world of sunlight, full of green and growing things, surrounded by peaceful, kind people. Joshua Slocum, first to sail alone around the world, deliriously imagined a phantom helper who managed the helm while he was asleep, an experience that is common in such environments and perhaps an adaptive reaction (Suedfeld & Mocellin, 1987).

At the same time, these travelers undertook their trips to have new experiences, accomplish new feats, and try new procedures. The **sensory variation motive** includes both concerns, boredom *and* the need for a new form of stimulation, beyond that available in our normally changing environment.

PROBLEM OF SENSORY CONSTANCY.
In one study, human adults in a completely dark room were immersed in a tank of water, almost in a

suspended position. They could hear only their own breathing and some faint sounds from the piping; they later reported that this environment was the most even and monotonous they had ever experienced. After an hour or two, a tension developed that was described as desire for stimulation. Their muscles twitched at an increasing rate, and they used methods of self-stimulation, such as swimming slowly and stroking their fingers against one another. Longer periods in this environment brought intense concentration on a single aspect of the situation, such as slight noises, reveries, or visual hallucinations (Lilly, 1956).

The problem for these subjects was not lack of stimulation, which was admittedly low, but rather the constancy of the situation. Lying quietly in a tepid tub is not aversive initially, but after a while the subject seeks some change. Human beings, as noted in the earlier chapter on sensation, are responsive to *changes* in stimulation. In this aspect of the sensory variation motive, the **problem of sensory constancy,** people become disturbed due to lack of stimulus change. Basically, they are bored. There is no variety, no significant variation in their sensory experience. This problem is most common among people who are confined, such as the elderly, prisoners, and hospitalized patients (Corbin & Nelson, 1980; Grassian & Friedman, 1986; Rothblum, 1990).

Restricted to his 24-foot *Dove,* Robin tried various methods of gaining increased stimulation. Sometimes he made extra work out of daily chores. Sometimes he used his tape recorder extensively, speaking into it, recording other sounds, and then replaying what he had just heard. And sometimes Robin simply indulged in fantasies, which included thoughts of a reunion in Australia with Patti, who was making her own way through that part of the world (Graham, 1972).

DESIRE FOR NOVEL STIMULATION. The motivation for sensory variation also includes the need for *new forms* of stimulation.

In the **desire for novel stimulation,** there is a high degree of curiosity, an interest in exploration and manipulation in a normally changing environment. Human beings expend considerable effort simply trying to find out about things, as Robin's trip illustrates.

The problem here is not sensory constancy. Even if our surroundings change regularly in some way, at times we want to visit different restaurants, try new foods, and meet new people. City workers want a holiday in the country, and country folk want to visit the city. Robin wanted to visit foreign cultures and to test his skill as a sailor.

Monkeys are notorious for their curiosity. They stare endlessly at each other; they sniff and taste things constantly; and when a new object is presented, they investigate it thoroughly. When interest is satiated, another object prompts further manipulation and exploration (Van Lawick-Goodall, 1971).

There is an irony in Robin Graham's voyage. Ashore, he found much novel stimulation; at sea, he was sometimes bored to the point of becoming delirious. Illustrating many issues in motivation, his voyage shows that the human being is a "continually wanting animal."

❧

AFFECTIONAL STIMULATION

The desire for early physical and emotional contact with other members of the species and stimulation by them is called the motivation for **affectional stimulation.** It has been studied experimentally with animals and through observations of human infants. Like sensory variation, the satisfaction of this motive is not necessary for life, but apparently it is necessary for the full development of one's natural endowments. It too appears rooted in the organism's biological inheritance, although no clear physiological basis has been identified.

In one series of studies at the University of Wisconsin, Harry Harlow and his associates observed infant monkeys deprived of their mothers. Instead, the monkeys were provided with mechanical substitutes. One substitute consisted of a piece of wood covered with sponge rubber and terry cloth; the other substitute was made of wire mesh, thus lacking warmth and softness. Both models were the same size and shape, but the babies demonstrated a clear preference for the soft one, which provided contact comfort. In times of stress, they ran and clung to it as monkeys normally do to their real mothers, and when strange stimuli suddenly appeared, they were calmer with the soft model present (Figure 10–8).

The infants also preferred a rocking mother to one that was stationary and a warm one to a cool one. But *contact comfort*, consisting of touching, cuddling, and hugging, was clearly the most crucial maternal factor for infants. Even the features of the mother's face were unimportant. Further studies indicated that infant monkeys not only preferred cuddliness, warmth, rocking, and hugging but also *needed* such stimulation for normal development. Without it, they displayed deviant behavior. Infants reared with wire mothers eventually showed inadequate social, sexual, and even intellectual development in adulthood. Those reared with cloth-sponge mothers were better adjusted as adults (Harlow & Suomi, 1970).

The question of whether human infants require comparable types of affectional stimulation for normal development cannot be answered readily. However, separate studies of hospitalized children and orphans in Baltimore and Iowa indicate an apparently inborn need for this affectional stimulation. Infants in both groups, despite adequate physical care, developed illness, lost weight, and often died. Their nutritional and cleanliness needs were well met, but they received almost no adult attention. It was con-

FIGURE 10–8 CONTACT COMFORT.
Infant monkeys preferred the cloth model even though a comparable "mother," made of wire mesh, delivered milk.

cluded that they were retarded physically, intellectually, and emotionally because of a lack of this affectional stimulation (Bowlby, 1969; Skeels, 1966).

• SOCIAL AND WORK MOTIVES •

Earlier in this chapter, we examined *basic* or **primary motives,** biological conditions directly related to the organism's survival. They prompt us to seek food, water, stimulation, and so forth. Apart from these inborn needs, common to everyone, we live in different societies, possess different endowments, and encounter different opportunities in life. These conditions give rise to diverse learned motives, acquired in the course of our lifetimes, called *acquired* or **secondary motives.**

These motives may originate in our efforts to satisfy primary motives, but they develop through personal and social contacts. Hence, they are sometimes referred to as *personal* or *social motives*. They include, in particular, the motivations for affiliation and achievement.

↬

DESIRE FOR AFFILIATION

From time to time, the need for friendship or social support arises in most of us. This motivation for the company of other people is known as *gregariousness* or the **desire for affiliation.** On close scrutiny it is found in most, if not all, human beings.

For Robin, lack of companionship was a major problem. Finally reaching Darwin, Australia, his next port of call, he happily resumed a prospering romance with Patti, who had arrived by freighter, train, bus, and on foot. They spent many happy days together traveling, sailing, and enjoying the native foods and customs. When it came time for Robin to leave the harbor alone again, a desperate feeling of loneliness overcame him. Here his kittens proved indispensable, providing a semblance of the human companionship he so sorely missed.

AFFILIATION VERSUS AFFECTIONAL STIMULATION. This desire for affiliation is closely tied to affectional stimulation, but the difference is noteworthy. The previous discussion showed that we have a *need* for affectional stimulation that must be fulfilled, apparently *early* in life, to ensure adequate development. The need for physical contact seems to be part of our biological inheritance. In contrast, the desire for affiliation does not involve a biological need, as far as we know, and if it goes unfulfilled in adults, the result may be unhappiness but not necessarily disturbed adjustment.

Each of us goes through an extended period of infantile helplessness, and this dependency, longer than that of any other species, may lead to our later need for affiliation. In other words, our desire for affiliation may be a learned derivative of the need for affectional stimulation, extending into adult personal relationships. It may evolve partly as a vestige of childhood fears of abandonment, apart from whatever other satisfactions it may offer.

AFFILIATION AND ANXIETY. College students participated in an experiment in which they were exposed to different degrees of anxiety. Some were shown electrical testing apparatus and told that they would receive intense shock. Others, shown the same apparatus, were informed that the experiment would be enjoyable. Then each subject was asked to indicate a preference for waiting alone or with someone else before the research began. No shocks were given to anyone because the purpose of the research was to discover the subjects' companionship preferences while they awaited their fate. And indeed there were differences. People who were highly anxious, expecting a painful situation, wanted to be with other people. Those made less anxious were indifferent about affiliation.

This outcome prompted the investigators to wonder about the kind of affiliation desired by the anxious subjects. Did they just want to be with someone or did they have a preference for particular people? To answer this question a similar experimental procedure was used, except that the subjects were given the choice of being with people undergoing the same experiment or with people anticipating different experiences. Again, the results were decisive. The anxious subjects preferred to be with other anxious people, and the old saying may be in need of refinement. Misery loves not just company; it loves miserable company (Schachter, 1959).

To recapitulate briefly, we can say that our desire for the company of others seems to be related to early experiences; it increases when we become anxious; and when anxious, we generally prefer relationships with people in similar circumstances, although there are exceptions (Kulik & Mahler, 1990). This desire for companionship is

FIGURE 10–9 MEASUREMENT OF ACHIEVEMENT MOTIVATION.
The subject is asked to tell a story about each of several ambiguous pictures, similar to those illustrated here. Responses to the picture on the left are less likely to reflect achievement themes than are the stories to the more work-oriented picture on the right. A person with a high need for achievement may provide achievement-related responses to both pictures.

readily demonstrated in the practice of solitary confinement for prisoners and the despair of the elderly with no relatives and few friends.

Robin's morale reached its lowest point as he set sail alone for Cape Town, South Africa, a journey of 5,700 miles. "Loneliness again," he lamented into his tape recorder, thinking of another reunion with Patti. This loneliness, he explained, rode with him for a thousand days and throughout the longest nights (Graham, 1972).

∾
ACHIEVEMENT MOTIVATION

Another acquired motivation, more clearly derived from our efforts to satisfy basic needs, is readily evident in societies like the United States, which place greater emphasis on individuality and accomplishment than do many other contemporary cultures. This motive, the **achievement motive,** is present whenever someone is concerned with performing at a certain level or standard, set individually or by a group. Any standard implies a certain degree of excellence, so that the individual is pleased with competence and disappointed with incompetence (McClelland 1984; Figure 10–9).

FAMILY INFLUENCES. In modern American life, antecedents of the achievement motive appear in the earliest years, even among preschool children (Galejs, King, & Hegland, 1987). In this steady effort toward accomplishments, three significant family influences can be identified, one of which is the amount of independence training the child receives. Children who are encouraged to use their abilities constructively and to find out things for themselves, especially at early ages, are likely to be high in achievement motivation in later years. Another influential factor is the parents' occupational level, a condition to which the child is regularly exposed. The higher the level, the greater is the probable achievement motivation in the child. Third, birth order is a factor. The greater the number of children, the less attention the parents can give each child. The first-born child, alone with the parents for some time, usually receives the most attention and encouragement in the early years; this child has been found to have a higher need for achievement than the brothers and sisters (Breland, 1973; Pfouts, 1980; Sulloway, 1995).

Parental expectation can become excessive, however, or the child, for a variety of reasons, may lose interest in achievement. Too much parental pressure or too much *perceived* pressure may contribute to low achievement motivation.

Robin's father had high expectations for his son, and they were supported by Robin's actions. A sudden storm off the African coast, for example, almost destroyed Robin and his boat. Hours later, after reaching the shore, Robin went into the raging surf again, this time to save the *Dove,* which was dragging its anchor. Swimming against huge breakers in very cold water, he climbed into his boat, repaired its anchor, and came ashore in a life preserver. Jeopardizing his safety in these ways left no doubt about his achievement motivation.

INFLUENCE OF GENDER ROLES. For years in the United States and other countries, high achievement was synonymous with masculinity and regarded as incompatible with the traditional concept of the ideal woman. A psychologist named Matina Horner decided that some women therefore learned to underplay their abilities. In these instances, she hypothesized, there existed among women a **fear of success,** avoiding high achievement because it interfered with opportunities for affiliation, empathy, and personal relationships. Studying this concept in men and women, she found fear of success in both genders, as well as fear of failure. These investigations brought this phenomenon to broad public attention, and they contributed to changes in subsequent decades (Bremer & Wittig, 1980; Horner, 1970). Fear of success has decreased significantly among women, and men have become more concerned about the high cost of achievement (Fried-Buchalter, 1992; Sancho & Hewitt, 1990).

As gender stereotypes fade, men and women more readily adopt activities and personal styles previously characteristic of the opposite gender. When someone displays both sets of traits, the term *androgyny* is often used, meaning that the person possesses a balance of the qualities typically attributed to each. A more recent approach refers to *gender role transcendence,* emphasizing behavior that is not considered in terms of sex roles at all. The term *androgyny* includes *andro,* referring to men, and *gyny,* referring to women. In gender role transcendence, behavior is independent of gender roles.

In societies that strongly uphold traditional ideals, gender roles continue to be important. In others, such as Korea and Japan, gender roles have diminished in public life, but they remain a central part of private life, especially within the family (Yoo, 1994; Figure 10–10).

INTRINSIC AND EXTRINSIC MOTIVATION. Sometimes we strive to accomplish a task simply because we enjoy it. In **intrinsic motivation,** there is no obvious reward; the satisfaction is inherent in the task itself, a natural outcome of performance. Mastering the geography of a distant land simply to know about that country may involve intrinsic motivation. In **extrinsic motivation,** the satisfaction is external to performance of the task. Geography is studied to pass a test, conduct business, or for some other obvious gain.

FIGURE 10–10 LANGUAGE AND GENDER ROLES. In the Korean culture, the language indicates that men are expected to work outside the home and that women are expected to remain inside, managing the household and children. The term for husband literally means "outside person," the term for wife "inside person" (Yoo, 1994).

Does the availability of an extrinsic reward ever disrupt performance? It may. Monkeys have manipulated mechanical devices extensively for no reward whatsoever. When a food reward was introduced, they paid less attention to those devices (Harlow, Harlow, & Meyer, 1950). Schoolchildren have shown diminished interest in certain assignments after material rewards were introduced (Wilson, 1982). In these cases, the reward may appear as a bribe, suggesting that the task itself is distasteful, thus undermining interest.

For optimal motivation, the learner should begin with the smallest effective extrinsic reward. As mastery is gained, this reward is diminished, allowing satisfaction in doing the task correctly to become the dominant motivation. This satisfaction is intrinsic motivation.

• THEORIES OF MOTIVATION •

At this point, an overall perspective would be helpful, something that would organize the diverse aspects of human motivation into one encompassing scheme. Instead, as so often happens in the social and behavioral sciences, no one theory or approach is entirely satisfactory. Several viewpoints are possible, and each contributes something of value.

As Robin begins another long, lonely voyage, sailing this time from Cape Town, South Africa, across the Atlantic Ocean to South America, we turn to these viewpoints. We are prepared for much of this discussion because the psychological theories, in particular, have been traced intermittently throughout this book since the opening chapter.

BIOLOGICAL PERSPECTIVES

How do we meet all of the diverse biological requirements of the body? We have considered the need for food, drink, and sleep, but others, no less essential, perhaps are taken for granted, such as the need for oxygen and a certain body temperature. Even a few moments without proper oxygen, circulation of the blood, or other functions can endanger the entire individual.

CONCEPT OF HOMEOSTASIS. Some of these biological requirements must be satisfied voluntarily, as in eating and drinking. Others are met by complex processes that occur without direct effort on our part. Collectively, these biological processes are called **homeostasis,** the tendency of the body to maintain a proper internal environment, an equilibrium among its basic conditions. Clearly one of the most remarkable features of human physiology, homeostasis avoids disequilibrium in the body.

Homeostasis in the human body is much like a thermostat in the home. When the temperature is too low or too high, the thermostat sends a message for a change. Homeostasis is more complex but operates in much the same manner. One of the homeostatic processes for temperature maintenance, for example, involves the size of the capillaries that carry blood to different parts of the body. When the body is too hot, *vasodilation* occurs, meaning that the capillaries grow wider, sending more blood to the surface of the body, resulting in heat loss through radiation. When the body is too cold, *vasoconstriction* takes place, which retains the heat by restricting the flow of blood into peripheral body areas. Another homeostatic process for temperature maintenance involves perspiration, which occurs when the body is too hot; the body becomes water-cooled, losing heat through evaporation. When the body is too cold, it begins to shiver, maintaining or generating heat through muscular movements. All of these automatic changes are part of homeostasis.

An adequate oxygen supply is achieved by complex reflexes that increase respiration when there is an oxygen deficiency in the blood. The removal of damaged body cells also occurs automatically as a result of the action of white blood cells. We do not understand all of these stabilizing factors, but it is clear that this automatic control of temperature, oxygen, and certain conditions of nutrition gives the organism greater freedom to engage in higher-level activities. Human beings can write books, maintain friendships, and sail around the world because their vital organs can be maintained in a relatively constant environment.

DRIVE-REDUCTION THEORY. This regulation or balance is not achieved automatically in the case of hunger and thirst. Homeostasis indicates when the levels of glucose and other nutrients are too low and when the salt content of the body is too high, and then the individual must take the necessary action, consuming food or water, respectively. Our voluntary attempts to reduce this state of disequilibrium and tension are part of the homeostatic process, and here we encounter the concept of drive. A **drive** is a state of arousal in which the organism is ready to respond to any stimulus related to its physiological condition—that is, to homeostatic disequilibrium or bodily tension. This term came into widespread use when psychology turned away from the concept of instinct among human beings. A broader, more general concept, drive does not imply any specific pattern of complex behavior. It simply implies a readiness to respond to relevant stimuli.

On these bases, some psychologists study motivation in terms of **drive-reduction theory,** meaning that the behavior of organisms is directed toward dispelling bodily tension. Some tension or discomfort occurs, such as hunger, thirst, or the need for sleep, and the organism attempts to alleviate this condition. The satisfaction is the reduction of biological or even psychological tension.

This perspective has obvious merit for the survival motives just discussed, but it is not clearly relevant in the case of stimulation motives. In the context of drive-reduction theory, it is difficult to understand what disequilibrium prompts people to read ghost stories, ride roller coasters, or climb dangerous mountain peaks. It is not apparent what tension is reduced by these activities. It seems instead that they *create* tension. They cannot be explained by the problem of sensory constancy, for people who engage in these activities do not come from totally constant, unchanging environments. If they are interpreted as the desire for novel stimulation, then the question remains: What tension is being reduced?

The shortcomings of drive-reduction theory also have been demonstrated in studies of sexual behavior. In one instance, male rats in a two-choice maze invariably selected the route that led to a receptive female rather than to some nonsexual activity. However, they were always interrupted during copulation and thus never reached orgasm. Therefore, their choice increased rather than decreased sexual tension, but in repeated trials they continued to select this pathway. Drive-reduction theory does not have universal application, for it cannot explain the rats' continued behavior in this instance (Sheffield, Wulff, & Backer, 1951).

Today, the concept of drive reduction is applied only to motives with a clear biological basis and without the implication that it is the organism's purpose. This approach has the advantage of being broadly applicable, merely emphasizing a series of physiological events: need, drive, incentive, and reward. A **need** is any biochemical requirement for optimal adjustment. When it is not met, an imbalance occurs. This imbalance gives rise to a *drive,* described earlier. A specific stimulus relevant to this drive is called an **incentive,** for it initiates the action. Obtaining or consuming this incentive provides satisfaction or **reward** for the behaving organism.

Incentives are not goals. The organism's goal is to satisfy its need; the incentive is an appropriate object for doing so. With lack of water, for example, cellular dehydration creates the need; the thirst drive is the aroused state; water is the incentive; and consuming it is a reward. The term **goal-directed behavior** is now applied to this whole sequence of need, drive, incentive, and reward.

This sequence was readily illustrated when Robin reached Ascension Island, halfway across the Atlantic Ocean. He had a need for food, but it was too late to go ashore. In this state of arousal, called the hunger drive, he went fishing instead and caught a mackerel, which was the incentive. He never experienced any reward, however. Just after he hooked the fish, a large hammerhead shark came along and hooked it away from him (Figure 10–11).

If Robin had eaten the mackerel, he would not have remained fully adjusted or satisfied for long. Needs occur in cyclic fashion for all of us. Sooner or later another need arises, and the sequence is repeated.

EMERGENCE OF SOCIOBIOLOGY. This survey of biological motivation would not be complete without mention of still another perspective. A bold, controversial view called **sociobiology,** focusing on *altruism*—a concern for the welfare of others—and sexual behavior, states that these and certain other social behaviors are genetically driven and have survival value for the species, if not for the individual (Wilson, 1971, 1980). Arising through investigations of social interactions in ant colonies, it points out that the workers in these colonies pose a special evolutionary question, for they are sterile, playing no direct role in reproduction. Instead, they work out their lives in altruistic fashion, caring for others, particularly the queen and the newborn. In terms of evolutionary theory, what might be the gain for the individual? According to sociobiology, the gain lies in the survival of the genes of its species, for whom the sacrifice is made.

At higher evolutionary levels, the emphasis in sociobiology is on sexual behavior, where the males in many species are more polygamous than the females, seeking a wider variety of mates in the reproductive act. Redwing blackbirds, red deer, and baboons are among the many examples. This behavior, it is hypothesized, is also an evolutionary outcome of natural selection, increasing the chances of

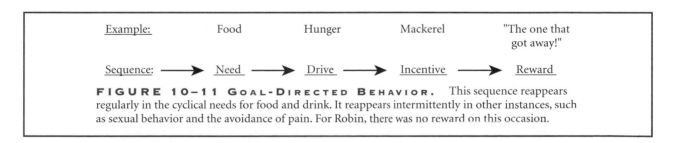

Example:	Food	Hunger	Mackerel	"The one that got away!"
Sequence: ⟶	Need ⟶	Drive ⟶	Incentive ⟶	Reward

FIGURE 10–11 GOAL-DIRECTED BEHAVIOR. This sequence reappears regularly in the cyclical needs for food and drink. It reappears intermittently in other instances, such as sexual behavior and the avoidance of pain. For Robin, there was no reward on this occasion.

survival of the male's genes. In contrast, survival of the female genes is increased in a more monogamous relationship focusing on parental care of the young. In short, staying at home favors the woman's genes; straying from home favors the man's. Sociobiology thus postulates genetic determinants in sexual behavior, as well as in altruism, selfishness, cowardice, and certain other social reactions (Wilson, 1980).

The concept of *genetic determinism* states that genes are influential in behavior, an idea that most people find acceptable in some form. But the issue posed by sociobiology is the *extent* to which human *social* behavior is genetically determined, especially altruism. Not widely debated at the levels of ants and animals, sociobiology becomes highly controversial when applied to human beings. Many individual motives are possible in human altruism, apart from genetic survival; these range from self-respect to public recognition (Figure 10–12). In human sexual behavior, despite the implications of evolutionary psychology, cultural factors result in extremely plastic and diverse gender roles. Aggression, achievement, and even the rates of homicide also differ massively from culture to culture, apparently under the influence of specific ecological and economic constraints (Nisbett, 1990).

In summary, sociobiology has been criticized as focused too narrowly on reproductive competition and on a specific interpretation of altruism. Opponents have stressed the great breadth of human social behavior, and they have proposed interpretations of altruism and sexual behavior based on social motives and group living, as well as pair bonding at different stages of personal relationships (Brewer & Caporael, 1990; Hendrick & Hendrick, 1991). Resistance to sociobiology undoubtedly will continue on these bases and also because this question, when approached in expanded form, becomes another dimension of the age-old heredity–environment

FIGURE 10–12 HUMAN ALTRUISM.
Among human beings, altruism is influenced by the degree of danger, presence of bystanders, time available, and various internal states. These conditions generally hold true for children, as well.

issue (Lieberman, Reynolds, & Friedrich, 1992; Sharp, 1986).

PSYCHOLOGICAL VIEWPOINTS

We have considered various systems or models of psychology throughout this book. Without further ado, we examine them here in the context of motivation, illustrated by Robin's voyage.

PSYCHOANALYTIC THEORY. Much of mental life, according to psychoanalysis, is influenced by unconscious psychological processes, especially in intimate relationships. These urges develop because people suffer disruptive emotional experiences in childhood that, long forgotten, retard later development. They influence us in various ways of which we are no longer aware, a condition called **unconscious motivation.** A three-stage process occurs in unconscious motivation: conflict or trauma, which the child cannot manage directly; repression, by which the conflict is unconsciously excluded from awareness; and symbolic behavior, which is the reappearance of the repressed experience in some disguised or indirect form.

One important, repressed early conflict reflects sexual and aggressive motives. In the Oedipus-Electra complex, the child seeks intimacy with the parent of the opposite sex and becomes resentful of the same-sex parent. This feeling provokes anxiety and cannot be managed at that early age. It is therefore repressed and reappears later in symbolic form. One likely solution later is identification with the adult rival, who is the father for the boy and the mother for the girl.

In sailing alone around the world, according to psychoanalysis, perhaps Robin identified with his father and also outdid him. Years earlier, Robin's father had wanted to make such a trip himself but decided that it was impossible. In fact, Robin's father purchased the *Dove*, helped him to prepare for the trip, and hoped all along that Robin would do it. When they met in the South Pacific after more than a year apart, Robin's father reported the home news and then immediately made plans for the next phase of Robin's journey, producing maps and charts, each marked with lines and dates for Robin's arrivals. "I should have understood his deep personal involvement in my voyage," Robin remarked later (Graham, 1972).

BEHAVIORAL PERSPECTIVE. In its traditional form, behaviorism has little to say about motivation, which is an internal state. Early behav-

iorism focused instead on observable acts. The study of internal conditions involved too much speculation.

Modern behaviorists have adopted a broader perspective, often approaching motivation from the standpoint of reinforcement. Behaviors that result in reinforcement tend to be repeated. Through these repetitions, behaviors are learned and become habits. This reinforcement process, known as *operant conditioning*, can have a long-lasting influence on behavior and therefore, by extension, on motivation.

Robin was given his first sailboat at age ten, and he sailed it every afternoon after school. Then, when he was 13, his father took him on an 11,000-mile voyage. These events, linking the sun, fresh air, and excitement with sailing, involved classical conditioning. And Robin's success in sailing involved operant conditioning. Looking back on these experiences, Robin said: "It is hard to believe that my parents, having allowed me to sail the South Seas at a most impressionable age, could ever have expected me to be a typical American school kid, to go to college and graduate to a walnut desk" (Graham, 1972).

In addition to well-formed sailing habits, Robin developed an aversion to school. He disliked the subjects, resented the homework, and wanted "the chance to escape from blackboards . . . from spelling words like 'seize' and 'fulfill.'" Robin had attended six different schools by his sophomore year in high school. His mother said, "I'm worried that he's such a loner." His first boat gave him the opportunity to be away from people, and the *Dove* gave him the same chance later.

When he began his solo voyage, Robin had learned to love the sea, to dislike school, to be self-reliant, and to be alone a great deal. This constellation of habits and interests certainly fits the behavioral perspective on such a voyage.

COGNITIVE VIEWPOINT. According to the cognitive viewpoint, motivation arises through appraisal of the situation. In **expectancy x value theory,** the motivation for any task or event depends on the individual's expectation of success or failure and the merit or worth of that outcome. In his effort to sail around the world, Robin apparently had a high expectation for success, based on his earlier lengthy cruises with his father, and he perceived the outcome as highly worthwhile, at least when he began the adventure. If he had seriously doubted the chances of success or if the outcome had not been valued, he would not have been motivated to undertake the voyage.

Acquired motives also are markedly influenced by our appraisal of ourselves. A critical factor here is the **self-concept,** the way a person thinks about himself or herself in a global sense. It includes a person's most important self-feelings and self-attitudes.

A practical observation on the role of the self-concept in achievement motivation dates to the 1930s and a series of investigations at the Hawthorne Works of the Western Electric Company, aimed at improving the output of factory workers responsible for assembling electrical relays. These workers were assigned to a certain area of a large room where they could be readily observed. Then, in systematic fashion, various changes were introduced into the setting. These included higher pay and shorter hours, which resulted in increased output. Improved lighting and better ventilation also had beneficial effects. Rest pauses and refreshments were examined, again with the same result. In short, whenever changes were introduced, many of which are part of the work environment today, production usually improved.

Eventually the investigators became doubtful about the remarkably positive effects of these successive changes, and they began restoring the original conditions, even turning down the lighting gradually, so that the workers did not notice it. Output improved nevertheless, and finally the investigators were forced to a different conclusion.

The workers were motivated to increase production not so much by the specific improvements in their environment, which did take place, but by their increased feeling of importance. They had been selected for a special investigation and apparently the company was interested in them as individuals, rather than as cogs in an industrial machine (Roethlisberger & Dickson, 1940).

The term **Hawthorne effect** now refers to any improvement in performance or outlook that occurs essentially because people receive attention, apart from any rewards. They are noticed. Their self-concept is enhanced. Informed teachers, coaches, managers, and administrators all show considerable respect for the Hawthorne effect, despite revisions and regular re-examinations of this classic research (Jones, 1992; Landy & Bittner, 1991).

❧

A MOTIVATIONAL HIERARCHY

A series of stages is postulated in the most widely recognized humanistic theory of motivation. According to Abraham Maslow's **motivational hierarchy,** human motives exist in a certain order or rank, with the most fundamental biological motives at the bottom. Psychological motives, usually of less immediate importance, are near the top. At different times in their lives, depending on their particular states, individuals are concerned with different levels in the hierarchy (Maslow, 1970).

MASLOW'S HIERARCHY. At the first level of Maslow's hierarchy are the *physiological needs,* pertaining to thirst, hunger, sleep, and other biological necessities for the maintenance of life. When motives at all levels are unsatisfied, the physiological needs are the strongest, as is evident with hunger in much of the world.

If these requirements are reasonably satisfied, then the motivation for *safety* emerges, such as the need for security, protection, and freedom from being tortured or otherwise threatened. Here the organism is concerned with being in a stable, secure environment. Although others disagreed, Robin assumed that his needs at both of these levels, physiological and safety, would be adequately met during his voyage. According to the theory, therefore, his concern would be focused at subsequent levels.

And it was. Robin experienced much deprivation at the next level. The motivation for *love and belonging* includes having friends, a family, or membership in a group. Even in our complex society, complete satisfaction at each level is not expected, but Robin clearly underestimated the difficulties in this aspect of his long voyage.

When the desire for love and belonging is satisfied to an acceptable to degree—or when circumstances prevent further efforts, as in Robin's case—then the individual is prompted to a still higher level, called *self-esteem*, a part of the self-concept which concerns attitudes toward oneself. Here the motivation is no longer to gain membership in a group but to have a favorable opinion of oneself. This opinion arises from personal experiences and through respect and admiration from other people. A perpetually wanting animal, however, the human being strives for a still higher level—if satisfied in terms of self-esteem.

In its original form, Maslow's hierarchy involves five levels, the highest of which is self-actualization, to which we shall turn in a moment. In revising his theory, Maslow postulated another two levels occurring just before self-actualization—*cognitive motives,* which include the desire for knowledge, understanding, and novelty, and *aesthetic motives,* based on the tendency to seek beauty and order in the world around us. The desire to sail around the world to meet people from other cultures is an example of the cognitive motives. Enjoying seascapes and landscapes illustrates the aesthetic motives. Like the other concepts in this hierarchy, these levels are sometimes regarded as imprecise and lacking in research support. Nevertheless, Maslow believed that our inborn nature,

modified by experience, determines their existence and order.

There is a special interest in the highest level of this hierarchy, called the *actualizing tendency,* or **self-actualization,** implying the fulfillment of one's talents and capacities to the utmost and the acceptance of oneself. At this level, which is not readily encountered, the individual is concerned about doing what he or she is best suited or intended to do, whether it is sailing alone around the world, caring for stray animals, or serving as a political activist. During his long voyage, Robin perhaps showed some elements of self-actualization (Table 10–1).

In the late stages of his career, Maslow emphasized the possibility of turning self-actualization in the direction of social interests, rather than toward one's own personal interests. He called this new focus *transcendence,* for it is directed away from egocentric needs toward the collective good.

CRITIQUE OF THE HIERARCHY. There are limitations in this hierarchy, which has been criticized, challenged, defended, and reformulated. In cultures

LEVEL	BEHAVIOR
Self-actualization	Completing the voyage, especially the return to California
Aesthetic needs	Enjoying the natural beauty in the Yasawa Islands
Cognitive needs	Learning about different cultures in the South Seas
Self-esteem	Managing his boat competently en route to Samoa
Love and belonging	Meeting Patti in New Guinea and Australia
Safety needs	Battling storms and tides along the African coast
Physiological needs	Catching fish for food, alleviating sensory constancy in the Coral Sea

TABLE 10–1 A MOTIVATIONAL HIERARCHY. The descriptions indicate that Robin was at various positions in the hierarchy during his voyage.

emphasizing group goals, for example, self-actualization appears inappropriately placed at the top of the hierarchy. For one group of Chinese, actualization *in service of society* was at the top (Nevis, 1983).

It is also argued that numerous individuals do not conform to the model; they bypass one or more levels of the hierarchy. A soldier risks his life to capture an enemy position, ignoring safety needs while satisfying the motive for belonging or self-esteem. Robin Graham sacrificed love and belonging in the course of his voyage. And he risked injury. After reaching the coast of South America and passing through the Panama Canal, he one day noticed an undernourished pelican with a torn pouch. Ignoring the dangers, he jumped into the ocean, captured the creature, and wired the broken bill with stainless steel. His satisfaction came the next day when he saw the pelican skillfully catching food (Figure 10–13).

Advocates of the hierarchy regard such behavior as minor exceptions to the general rule, which is still considered valid. In colloquial terms, when someone has nothing, the problem is food. When food is available, the problem is health. When food and health are available, the problem is sex—or love or recognition. If all of these needs are satisfied, then the concern may be with the afterlife or other, more abstract issues.

The hierarchy should not be regarded as a rigid sequence but rather as a general description of most people in our society, conveniently considered in just two broad divisions. At the bottom are the biological motives, including physiological and safety concerns; if they are reasonably well met, the various upper levels become important, involving psychological motives. As Robin's voyage illustrates, from time to time we find ourselves at very different levels of the hierarchy.

Possibly Robin Graham reached some sort of self-actualization during his voyage. As his father wrote, "Success or failure, he is fulfilling his destiny."

FIGURE 10–13 DEPRIVATION AND MOTIVATION. Vincent van Gogh continued his efforts at self-expression through art despite all sorts of adversities, including hunger, illness, and the lack of close personal support. In this sense, his career did not conform to Maslow's motivational hierarchy.

Early one April morning, five years after he began the voyage, Robin sailed the *Dove* up the California coast and into the Long Beach harbor, amid waves and toots and shouts of welcome from a fleet of yachts and shoreline spectators gathered to salute his return. A helicopter hovered overhead and Patti, in a launch, came alongside the *Dove* to hand Robin a breakfast tray complete with white linen and a bottle of champagne. Robin had circled the globe alone in a 24-foot sloop.

Robin sat on the cabin roof while reporters made inquiries. The basic question had not changed, except that it was worded in the past tense: "What made you do it?"

Robin wished he could have given better answers. But he consoled himself with the confession that he really did not know the answer himself (Graham, 1972). "I felt," he said, "it had something to do with fate and destiny. How could I phrase that? How could I tell these newsmen that I sailed across the world because I had to do so—because that was what I was meant to do?"

• MULTIPLE BASES OF MOTIVATION •

After the press conferences and articles for the *National Geographic*, Robin wrote a book about his journey, derived from the notes in his log and named after his little vessel, the *Dove* (Graham, 1972). Even in his book, Robin wondered how to explain the purpose of his long trip. He again decided that he had sailed around the world because it was something he had to do, an explanation that sounded like some form of self-actualization. And here we encounter the issue with which we began this chapter.

Instinct and self-actualization are strange bedfellows, but they have something in common. Like the concept of instinct, self-actualization has been criticized for its broad, unrestricted usage (Heylighen, 1993). Like instinct, self-actualization has wide appeal. When used to explain behavior, however, both concepts involve a fallacy to which many of us succumb from time to time. The **nominal fallacy** is the erroneous belief that giving something a name constitutes an explanation. However, labeling a behavior as an instinct, self-actualization, or something else usually does not contribute to our understanding. Instead, we typically should consider that behavior in the context of a wide array of factors, inborn and acquired. The complexity of human motivation sometimes causes us to seek easy answers, leaving us prone to the nominal fallacy.

Given this complexity, Robin's inability to answer is not surprising.

Numerous factors—some inherited predisposition, boredom with school, curiosity about other parts of the world, the achievement motive, an element of unconscious motivation, the force of the sailing habit, and even a provoking self-concept—all of these and other factors may have played a role in prompting Robin to travel 30,600 nautical miles alone. In deciding on *the* reason, the reader is reminded of the *fallacy of the single cause*. Behavior usually occurs for several reasons, and motivation, too, has its multiple bases. In all likelihood, no single factor can be identified.

Robin did have one final comment about motivation: "Life has to have some tension," he said, "the tension of making another port or finding a piece of gear to mend, or how to face a squall. Having no goal would be like sailing in the doldrums forever."

• SUMMARY •

∾

INFLUENCES ON MOTIVATION

1. Motivation is an internal condition that activates and directs behavior. An example is found in instinct, which is a complex, unlearned pattern of behavior occurring in all same-sex members of a given species. Instincts are influenced by a variety of factors.
2. As one proceeds up the evolutionary scale, there is decreasing evidence for instinctive behavior. In its traditional definition, the term is generally not applied to human beings.

∾

SURVIVAL MOTIVES

3. The biochemical basis of hunger involves conditions of the stomach, blood, and hypothalamus. The specific ways in which the hunger drive is satisfied are significantly influenced by learning.

4. Among the different views of sleep, restoration theory states that sleep repairs the body. Adaptation theory describes sleep as an evolutionary outcome of avoiding predators while conserving energy.

5. At the human level, sexual behavior readily illustrates the relationship between inborn and acquired factors in human motivation. It is stimulated by hormonal secretions, androgen and estrogen, but has an extremely important basis in learning.

❧

STIMULATION MOTIVES

6. Many organisms seek types of stimulation for which no physiological bases have been established, although the motives appear to be part of our biological inheritance. The sensory variation motive appears in two dimensions: the problem of sensory constancy and the desire for novel stimulation.

7. Animals and human beings also desire affectional stimulation, called contact comfort when the tactual element is emphasized. Life span studies suggest that it also plays an important role in ensuring normal physical, cognitive, and social development in human beings.

❧

SOCIAL AND WORK MOTIVES

8. The desire for affiliation is pervasive in virtually all cultures, so much so that it may seem to be based on inborn factors. However, the extended period of helplessness in human infancy could lead to the nearly universal desire to be with other people.

9. Achievement motivation develops during the individual's lifetime, influenced by opportunities for learning. Parental expectations and cultural influences appear to be most important in its development.

❧

THEORIES OF MOTIVATION

10. In the biological approach, the concept of drive reduction, although useful in understanding individual survival motives, is not readily applied to stimulation motives and sexual behavior.

11. Among the various psychological perspectives, the psychoanalytic view emphasizes unconscious motivation. In the cognitive view, motivation arises through an appraisal of the situation.

12. In the motivational hierarchy of the humanistic viewpoint, the physiological and safety needs appear first in order of importance. If these needs are satisfied, the individual becomes concerned with love and belonging, then self-esteem, then cognitive and aesthetic motives, and perhaps self-actualization, in that order.

❧

MULTIPLE BASES OF MOTIVATION

13. Several different factors usually are involved in the motivation to perform any complex act. This view is described as the multiple bases of motivation.

• WORKING WITH PSYCHOLOGY •

❧ REVIEW OF KEY CONCEPTS ❧

motivation

Influences on Motivation
instinct
hormones
prolactin
androgens

estrogens
releaser
reflex
fixed action pattern

Survival Motives
lateral hypothalamus

ventromedial nucleus
set point theory
anorexia nervosa
bulimia nervosa
cellular dehydration
osmoreceptors
restoration theory

adaptation theory
testes
ovaries
evolutionary psychology
maternal behavior
paternal behavior

Stimulation Motives
stimulation motives
sensory variation motive
problem of sensory constancy
desire for novel stimulation
affectional stimulation

Social and Work Motives
primary motives
secondary motives
desire for affiliation
achievement motive
fear of success
intrinsic motivation
extrinsic motivation

Theories of Motivation
homeostasis
drive
drive-reduction theory
need

incentive
reward
goal-directed behavior
sociobiology
unconscious motivation
expectancy x value theory
self-concept
Hawthorne effect
motivational hierarchy
self-actualization

Multiple Bases of Motivation
nominal fallacy

❧ CLASS DISCUSSION/CRITICAL THINKING ❧

A NARRATIVE TWIST

During his long voyage, Robin sat idly for days in an empty ocean, risked his life in raging storms, and visited cultures very different from his own. On these bases, did he achieve self-actualization, the highest level in Maslow's hierarchy? Explain your reasoning. Suppose instead that he had terminated his voyage in the South Seas, married a native woman, and raised their children with her. Would he have achieved self-actualization on this basis? Again, explain your answer. ❧

TOPICAL QUESTIONS

• *Influences on Motivation.* "Learning counteracts the gender-specific behaviors prompted by hormones and other internal factors." Support or dispute this statement for ani-

mals and human beings, emphasizing the idea of adaptation to the environment.
• *Survival Motives.* Think about the problem of anorexia nervosa. In what way does it raise questions about the human motive for survival? In what way may it reveal an attempt at survival? How does it illustrate the multiple bases of behavior? What recommendations can you make, at both the individual and national levels, to reduce its prevalence among college-age women and men?
• *Stimulation Motives.* Describe a community of people lacking the desire for novel stimulation. Include the positive and negative aspects. Would a heightened desire for novel stimulation be advantageous in this society? If so, propose ways of producing an increase. Explain.

• *Social and Work Motives.* Provide an explanation for why people in the United States are characteristically highly motivated, discussing the relationship between the self-concept and motivation. Is this characteristic desirable? To what extent does it involve detrimental consequences? Elaborate.
• *Theories of Motivation.* Identify someone who may have achieved self-actualization. Describe that person's characteristics and the setting. Does the description augment or diminish your interest in this concept? Explain.
• *Multiple Bases of Motivation.* Describe any reasonably complex behavior that seems to defy the principle of the multiple bases of motivation. Offer an explanation.

❧ TOPICS OF RELATED INTEREST ❧

Sexual motivation is discussed in the context of emotion (11). Unconscious motivation, a psychoanalytic concept, is considered in

relation to memory (8), personality (14) and therapy (16). Stimulation motives are related to sensory adaptation (4), and the need for affec-

tional stimulation involves the attachment of infants to their caretakers (12).

COMPONENTS OF EMOTION
Feelings in Emotion
Physiology of Emotion
Emotional Behavior
Cognition in Emotion

THEORIES OF EMOTION
Classical Views of Emotion
Arousal-Cognition Theory

LIKING AND LOVING
Developing Relationships
Love Relationships
Experiencing Sex
Sexual Behavior

ANGER AND AGGRESSION
Origins of Aggression
Reducing Aggression

STRESS IN DAILY LIFE
Stressful Events
Bodily Reactions to Stress
Coping with Stress

11
EMOTION
AND STRESS
❧

Dawn and Stephen enjoyed one another's company, and they shared some happy times in college. They even took the same psychology course and wrote their autobiographies as a class assignment. But they came from very different backgrounds.

When she was just a little girl, living with her family in affluent circumstances, Dawn awoke one night to loud noises and the shuffling of feet. This disturbance frightened her, for it formed no familiar pattern, such as the sounds from someone making a late snack or using the bathroom.

She heard a voice amid the commotion and thought it was her mother. Wriggling out of bed apprehensively, she opened the door a crack. Down the hallway, she saw her mother's back in the kitchen. When her mother turned around, she was a portrait of distress—biting her lower lip, her hair in disarray, her clothes disheveled, her eyes half closed and mournful. She began to shout in an incoherent jumble. "It was a raw scene," Dawn said later. "A drunken, miserable mother and a rather tongue-tied child."

At this same time, in a distant city, a little boy named Stephen shared his bedroom with an older brother. For Stephen, it was hardly a bedroom. He slept in a low chair converted into a couch at night, an arrangement made necessary by his unplanned birth, seven years after one brother, eleven years after another.

Stephen pestered his brothers in small ways—stealing their cookies and hiding their stamp collections. Stephen's older brother laughed and joked about such deeds, which pleased the little boy enormously. Stephen felt very happy whenever that brother played with him.

For the other brother, sharing his room with a child, Stephen was a nuisance—much too noisy and wrong about everything. These reactions made Stephen angry, as did his mother's attitude. She was reluctant to let her youngest child grow up. He did

anyway, asserting himself as a practical, rebellious adolescent (Goethals & Klos, 1976).

Living different lives in different parts of the country, Dawn and Stephen experienced moments of fear, joy, sadness, and anger, as well as the infinitely varied emotional states not so readily labeled. These diverse reactions, some from childhood, others in adulthood, provide a useful narrative for this chapter because they reflect the broad array of emotions we all experience with partners, family members, acquaintances, and even when alone.

This chapter begins with the basic components of emotion and then turns to theories of emotion. Afterward, we consider positive emotions, liking and loving, and then the negative side, anger and aggression. The chapter closes on a practical note, examining stress in daily life.

• COMPONENTS OF EMOTION •

After the encounter in the kitchen, Dawn found herself feeling afraid in almost every corner of their large house. Her heart pounded; she trembled; and her palms became moist. Sometimes she hid in her bedroom, out of harm's way, she hoped. In these events, we see the basic components of **emotion,** defined as a complex feeling state accompanied by physiological arousal and overt behaviors. Dawn felt afraid, the feeling component; her heart pounded and her palms became moist, the physiological component; and she hid in her room, the behavioral component.

Still another factor in emotion is the cognitive dimension. Merely thinking about an important event can make us emotional. Dawn explained later that just the thought of seeing her drunken mother caused her to become upset. Our thoughts often influence our feelings, but the other elements of emotion cannot be ignored.

FEELINGS IN EMOTION

Both motivation and emotion imply motion, coming from the Latin verb *movere,* which means "to move." Motivation is typically purposeful; a motivated person moves toward some goal. Emotion is primarily expressive; an emotional person is moved. Emotion can be motivating, however, to the extent that feelings prompt activity toward a goal. Certainly this was the case in Dawn's fearful retreat from her mother's alcoholic condition and Stephen's joyful approach to his older brother's games. Whenever we try to attain or dispel happiness, anger, disgust, and so forth, there is no doubt about the motivational significance of our feelings.

CLASSIFICATION OF FEELINGS. Human feelings are also characterized by their diversity. Consider the term **anxiety,** defined as a general state of uneasiness or apprehension. It can involve timidity, mistrust, dread, alarm, suspicion, terror, diffidence, and many further shades of meaning. In addition, it has different meanings in the different systems of psychology, such as psychoanalysis, behaviorism, and the humanistic viewpoint.

In dealing with this diversity, psychologists have attempted to identify the most basic or fundamental human feelings. Some of these classifications include a half-dozen feelings, others 15 or more (Table 11–1). Each basic feeling is assumed to have its own properties, but all can occur in combination, thereby influencing one another and accounting for the diversity in human emotional experience (Izard, 1971; Lazarus, 1991, 1993).

FEELINGS IN OPPOSITION. If we approach feelings as positive or negative, rather than through multiple classifications, modern theory and research can offer further insight. In this perspective, it is understood that the human nervous system is designed to oppose deviations from

NEGATIVE	MIXED	POSITIVE
Anger	Hope	Happiness
Anxiety (fear)	Compassion	Pride
Guilt (shame)		Relief
Sadness		Love
Envy (jealousy)		
Disgust		

TABLE 11–1 BASIC EMOTIONS. Among many attempts to identify our fundamental feelings, anger and anxiety or fear are universally included first, making a statement about the human condition. Some expression of happiness is often the third entry (After Lazarus, 1993).

normal or neutral, just as the human body, through homeostasis, automatically mobilizes itself to counteract injury or disease. In the same way, according to **opponent-process theory,** one set of feelings automatically initiates arousal of the opposite feelings, which appear later. In other words, positive feelings inevitably set the stage for negative feelings, and negative feelings eventually set in motion positive feelings (Solomon, 1980; Solomon & Corbit, 1974).

In school, Dawn was anxious and unhappy, totally unable to make friends. "I was impossibly silent in classes," she said, "by far the shyest and most afraid student in the school" (Goethals & Klos, 1976). When the bell rang, signaling the end of class, she experienced a rapid decline in these negative feelings. Her fear disappeared, but her emotional state did not return directly to neutral. Instead, Dawn felt joyful for a while. Then, later, even her joyfulness disappeared. Everything became quite normal again.

These sequential deviations from normalcy represent the usual pattern in our lives, according to opponent-process theory, and they occur whether the initial feeling is positive or negative. The first feeling, *A,* is aroused by its adequate stimulus, but after this stimulation ceases, a second or *B* state appears, which is in opposition to *A* and has been indirectly activated by *A.* After persisting for a while, the second feeling also disappears, and then there is a return to normal (Figure 11–1).

For example, intense intimacy, sexual or otherwise, is usually a very pleasant feeling, after which the sensation gradually diminishes, all constituting state *A*. As time passes, the feeling eventually changes to a slightly aversive state, a let-down feeling, the *B* state. And finally, the normal state returns. In contrast, the novice parachutist is apprehensive or terrified in state *A*, before jumping, and looks stunned even during the descent. Then, after a safe landing, in state *B*, the chutist is relieved, perhaps joyful. It is this pleasant after-feeling that keeps chutists jumping, joggers running, and sauna lovers bathing. According to opponent-process theory, having a baby, consuming drugs, winning a lottery, and innumerable other experiences involve this automatic reversal of feeling. On leaving the dentist's office, you do not feel merely okay. Even with minor physical discomfort, you feel elated, at least for a while.

A second postulate of this theory states: With repeated stimulation, the first or *A* state grows weaker and the second or *B* state grows stronger. As our love for someone continues, year after year, we become adapted to this *A* state. The love becomes less intense. Moreover, as it continues, the loss of this love becomes more and more stressful. This *B* state, the absence of love, has grown steadily more powerful because its opposite, the *A* state, has been regarded more and more as a normal part of life. The loss of something that is increasingly expected, or taken for granted, becomes increasingly disruptive.

The same phenomenon occurs when the initial state is negative. After a person has become an habitual jogger, the negative *A* state, in which the runner feels stiff and cold during the warm-up, is increasingly regarded as just part of the daily routine. It becomes less and less aversive. With continued jogging, moreover, the addictive aftereffect, or *B* state, increases. Continuing to run, year after year, the jogger becomes more and more dependent on this regular exhilaration (Table 11–2).

Thus, human beings seek to maintain emotional experiences of both types, initially positive

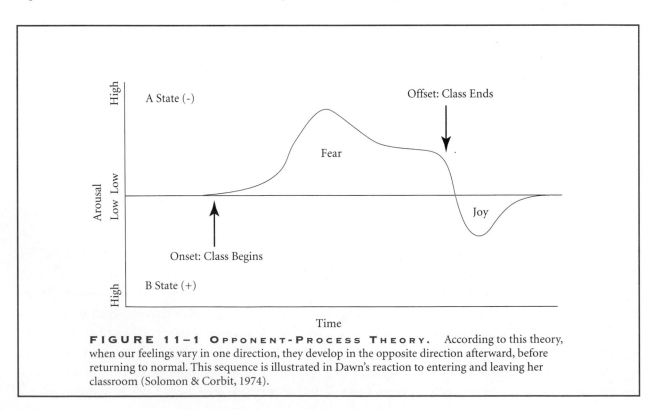

FIGURE 11–1 OPPONENT-PROCESS THEORY. According to this theory, when our feelings vary in one direction, they develop in the opposite direction afterward, before returning to normal. This sequence is illustrated in Dawn's reaction to entering and leaving her classroom (Solomon & Corbit, 1974).

EXAMPLE	EARLY STIMULATIONS		LATER STIMULATIONS	
	STATE A	STATE B	STATE A	STATE B
Parachutists	Terror, high arousal	Stunned, stony-faced	Tense, expectant	Jubilation
Persons in love	Ecstacy	Loneliness	Comfort	Grief
Dogs receiving shock	Terror, panic	Stealth, caution	Unhappiness	Joy
Drug users	Euphoria, rush pleasure	Craving	Normal feelings	Intense craving, agony

TABLE 11–2 CHANGES IN OPPONENT-PROCESS OUTCOMES. In the early and later stimulations, the *A* state induces its opponent process, the opposite or *B* state. However, repeated stimulations weaken the *A* state and strenghten the *B* state. After many jumps, the parachutist becomes less terrified and enjoys it more. Similarly, the habitual drug user experiences less euphoria and more withdrawal symptoms (Solomon & Corbit, 1974).

and initially negative. The immediately pleasant ones, such as eating and drinking, may become addictive due to the prompt and positive *A* state. The mildly unpleasant ones, such as jogging and skydiving, become habitual due to the increasingly powerful aftereffect, or *B* state. This viewpoint has been applied to all sorts of activities, including blood donation, breast-feeding, and bicycling for long distances. So sayeth the theory of opponent processes, which emphasizes the costs of pleasure and the benefits of pain (Solomon, 1980).

⁓

PHYSIOLOGY OF EMOTION

Whether or not some sort of homeostatic condition underlies our feelings, it is clear that widespread physiological changes take place in emotion. Even when we try to control our emotions, we often give ourselves away with hand tremors, sweating, excessive blinking, and other signs of arousal. All of these reactions depend on a highly complex network of nerve pathways throughout the human body. Among them, the two most important in emotion are the central nervous system and the autonomic nervous system.

ACTIVITIES IN THE CENTRAL NERVOUS SYSTEM. The major communications network in the human body is the central nervous system, comprised of the brain and spinal cord. As a coordinating system in emotion, it influences a wide variety of activities, directly or indirectly.

One region of the central nervous system, the **hypothalamus,** near the midbrain, plays a very large role in emotional and motivational behavior, including drinking, eating, fighting, fleeing, and sexual activity, as well as emotional expression. Impulses from the various receptors pass through or adjacent to the hypothalamus on their way to the upper brain regions. Impulses also come down into the hypothalamus from these regions, and the hypothalamus, in turn, relays them to the various muscles and viscera.

The outer covering and uppermost region of the brain, called the **cerebral cortex,** is instrumental in human thought and memory; therefore, it can influence emotion as well. We may become emotional or unemotional merely by the way we think about a particular situation. As Dawn explained, just thinking about the girl next door, who had many friends, made her feel lonely and upset (Goethals & Klos, 1976).

Recent experiments with animals suggest that fear can arise even without clear knowledge of the situation—that is, without the cerebral cortex. In these experiments, a tone or light was followed by a mild electric shock and eventually, through classical conditioning, rats learned to fear the tone alone. Whenever the tone was sounded, electrodes in the animals' brains showed complex neural activity in one particular brain site. A small almond-shaped region located close to the base of the brain, the **amygdala,** plays a significant role in motivation, emotion, and memory. In this case, the experiment went one step further. When the animals were deprived of information from the cortex by removal of that area, they nevertheless displayed the fear reaction. In other words, the animals were afraid without knowing the source of their fear (Le Doux, 1989). These findings may offer an explanation of those instances in which people react without really understanding the situation. Walking alone at night, you jump at the sound of footsteps behind you, and then afterwards you relax, realizing that a friend is running to catch up with you. Your initial fear perhaps arose through activities in the amygdala and then, moments later, the cortex had time to interpret the situation.

ACTIVITY IN THE AUTONOMIC NERVOUS SYSTEM.

Relatively independent of the central nervous system, the **autonomic nervous system** initiates and inhibits activities of diverse organs, thereby stimulating widespread, largely involuntary changes throughout the body during emotion.

The autonomic nervous system has two main branches, the sympathetic and parasympathetic divisions. As a rule, but not always, they work in opposition. If one division stimulates activity in an organ, the other inhibits it. The **sympathetic nervous system,** which plays the dominant role in emotion, accelerates the heart rate, increases the amount of adrenaline, inhibits activity in the intestines, activates the sweat glands, and prompts the pilomotor response—meaning goose bumps. The individual is emotionally aroused.

In fact, when a person is sufficiently aroused, one body part grows up to ten times its normal size. The enlargement of this organ, the pupil of the eye, is called dilation, and it has been known for centuries. It lies behind some familiar expressions:

"He became wide-eyed." "Her eyes grew big as saucers." In earlier days, women put a dilating fluid in their eyes, enlarging the pupils and thereby implying that their owner was emotionally aroused or at least attentive to the object of their gaze (Figure XI.1, Color).

When the event subsides the **parasympathetic nervous system** resumes control, for it becomes dominant in routine situations, reversing the changes that occur in an emergency. Heart rate and breathing become more normal, digestion begins again in the stomach, saliva reappears in the mouth, the pupils tend to constrict, and so forth. The individual begins functioning in a more routine fashion.

MEASURING PHYSIOLOGICAL ACTIVITIES.

Among the many measures of physiological activities in emotion, we have already considered the **electroencephalogram** (EEG), in which brain waves are recorded by a stylus on a moving sheet of paper. When the individual is resting a regular EEG rhythm appears, but in arousal other rhythms occur. For measuring the rate and rhythm of the heartbeat, electrodes are attached to the body and chest, and the tracings are called an **electrocardiogram** (EKG). The examiner looks for various patterns in this record, of which about a dozen have been established. Still another response of particular interest to psychologists is the activation of the sweat glands during emotional arousal. The resulting perspiration, especially on the palms of the hands, lowers the electrical resistance of the skin, called the **galvanic skin response** (GSR).

One instrument that measures several physiological responses simultaneously is the **polygraph,** a term that comes from *poly,* meaning "many," and *graph,* referring to writing. It records heart rate, breathing rate, blood pressure, and skin conductance, among other activities. It is called a *lie detector* because these responses change under arousal, and it is assumed that a person who is lying is highly aroused. Instead, it should be regarded as an emotion detector.

The subject is asked two types of questions, critical and neutral. The former concern the incident in doubt; the latter concern everyday events and are used to indicate the individual's typical or normal arousal level. The idea is that the guilty subject will show a higher emotional arousal to the critical questions (Figure XI.2).

But the body can be made to lie. Some subjects defeat the test by thinking about the same high-anxiety event in response to *every* question, critical and neutral, or they subtly tense their muscles as fully as possible, thereby portraying a uniformly high arousal level (Honts & Kircher, 1994). Others, accustomed to lying, can produce falsehoods with little anxiety. They may show uniformly low profiles. Still others, even when they have had no part whatsoever in the incident, may appear to be guilty simply because they are so worried about being found guilty. In one assessment of this device, polygraph experts studied 50 people known to be innocent and 50 who had confessed to a crime. Not knowing who was who, they made both types of errors—judging innocent people as guilty or guilty ones as innocent—in almost one-third of the cases (Kleinmuntz & Szucko, 1984; Saxe, Dougherty, & Cross, 1985).

. Most psychologists today have reservations about the use of polygraph tests. They feel that these tests, if permitted at all, should be employed only in narrowing a field of suspects (Steinbrook, 1992).

IDENTIFYING FEELINGS PHYSIOLOGICALLY. A question of theoretical interest has developed from the use of such instruments. Can our feelings be identified solely on the basis of these physiological conditions? By examining her physiological reactions, could we distinguish between Dawn's fear in school and her joy afterward? This capacity would have great significance for a theory of emotion, especially its physiological bases.

In a series of studies, records of heart activity and blood pressure were obtained from people exposed to various types of stress. Attempting to solve mental problems, they were criticized, given defective equipment, and administered mild electric shocks. Afterward, all subjects described their feelings, which were classified according to four categories: anxiety, anger directed toward the self, anger directed toward the experimenter, or no intense feeling. When these data were analyzed, physiological responses of low intensity were found to be associated with no intense feeling or with anger directed outward, toward the experimenter. Physiological responses of high intensity occurred with anxiety and anger directed inward, toward the self. In other words, the subjects with no anxiety or anger directed outward did not react physiologically in an emergency manner; the others responded physiologically as if there were in an emergency (Funkenstein, King, & Drolette, 1957; Schalling & Svensson, 1984).

However, a more convincing demonstration of physiological differences requires a prediction from one to the other. Knowing only a person's feelings, the investigator must be able to describe the pattern of physiological responses. Or knowing only the physiological reactions, the investigator must describe the person's feelings. Use of increasingly sophisticated equipment has facilitated progress toward this goal.

In one study, the subjects *imagined* past events in which they had become emotional—situations involving happiness, sadness, anger, or fear. Thinking about these situations reproduced the original feelings in abbreviated form. At the same time, the subjects' heart reactions were monitored by cardiovascular apparatus. Then it was discovered that certain cardiovascular patterns were associated with specific feelings (Schwartz, Weinberger, & Singer, 1981).

Studies with posed facial expressions also have yielded promising results. For this purpose, professional actors were videotaped as they produced emotional expressions and relived past emotional experiences. These contractions of facial muscles into the universal expressions of happiness, sadness, and so forth, perhaps combined with the cognitive arousal in reliving these states, generated specific changes in heart rate, stomach secretions, and other reactions. In the resulting autonomic nervous system activity, distinctions were made between positive and negative feeling states and, in several instances, among negative states (Ekman, Levenson, & Friesen, 1983). On such bases, there seems to be sufficient evidence for accepting the existence of physiological differences among emotions, however they may arise (Levenson, 1992).

~

EMOTIONAL BEHAVIOR

The emotional experience of another person is most readily evident in behavior. Fearful of her high school classmates, Dawn avoided them whenever possible. At a school dance, she was announced as the winner of the Most Studious Prize, but she did not dance. She stayed home, afraid to attend. Stephen became angry with his classmates, who taunted him with a derisive nickname. He responded by fighting and arguing.

All of us display our emotions on some occasions and try to hide them on others. To what extent do the behavioral aspects reveal the underlying emotion?

INTERPRETING EXPRESSIVE BEHAVIOR. Some emotional expressions are constant across different societies, and they provide cues about the emotion being experienced. Other emotional behaviors vary from culture to culture and even among people in the same culture. Sometimes we can identify the emotion; sometimes we are unsuccessful (Figure XI.3).

The universality of some facial expressions is evident when people turn the mouth up or down at the corners voluntarily, without some emotionally provoking event to stimulate them. These behaviors prompt subtle feelings of happiness and sadness, respectively. Such findings have increased speculation on the possible genetic bases of certain emotional expressions (Ekman, 1980).

Nevertheless, learning also plays a role—not only in when we express ourselves but also in how we do so. Among spectators at a European sporting event, whistling shows dissatisfaction with the performance. Among fans in the United States, whistling is more like cheering, a form of praise and encouragement. In some Asian societies, scratching the cheeks and ears is a sign of happiness. Clapping or rubbing the hands is a sign of happiness in this country.

When they win a lottery, some people clap, others cry, and still others show very little emotional expression. Therefore, we do not use just one set of cues in identifying an emotion in someone else. We consider what the person says, how the person looks and behaves, and also the circumstances, which can be very informative. We attempt to integrate all of these cues into one overall interpretation.

AROUSAL AND PERFORMANCE. When we speak of the magnitude of an emotional response, rather than the feeling involved, we are referring to the **arousal level,** which can be significantly related to behavior. If arousal is extremely high, the person may react wildly, as when Stephen, in a time of frustration about his tormentors in school, became rebellious and disruptive in class. Or the person may become unable to move at all. On that disturbing night when she discovered her mother's drunkenness, Dawn lay completely still in bed, hardly breathing (Goethals & Klos, 1976).

It has been suggested that maximum human performance is achieved with a moderate level of arousal. When arousal is very low, the individual is not sufficiently involved to perform successfully. When arousal is extremely high, the individual is too excited to maintain proper control, and again there is poor performance.

This statement about arousal level has been extended to include the nature of the task. According to the **Yerkes-Dodson law,** the optimal level of arousal depends on the complexity of the task to be performed. High arousal is appropriate for a relatively simple task, such as running away from something. Low arousal is appropriate when the task is more complex, such as learning a new computer program or writing poetry. This view seems reasonable and useful, but it has received only mixed support (Neiss, 1988; Teigen, 1994).

Studies of athletic contests offer impressive evidence that arousal can be too high. Common sense tells us, for example, that the home team usually has an advantage, which certainly is true in regular season games and even in early rounds of the World Series baseball and National Basketball Association playoffs. The home team wins more than 60% of the first games in a championship series. But in the *final* game of a seven-game playoff, when everything is on the line, the winning percentage of the home team drops to 39%. The speculated reason is that the home team performs in front of wildly cheering fans who expect and even demand a victory; these players experience more pressure than the visiting players and therefore do not perform up to their potential. Substantial evidence that the problem for the home team is choking under pressure appears in the fielding errors in baseball and the missed free throws in basketball, neither of which is significantly influenced by the play of the other team. In both sports these misplays by the home team are higher in game seven than in the earlier games (Baumeister & Steinhilber, 1984).

If a feeling of pressure is the critical factor, the same result should occur even when the home crowd is not demonstrative, as in golf championships. In one analysis of championship play, the performances of home-course favorites were compared with the performances of golfers from foreign courses. It was found that the play of the home golfers deteriorated more from the first to the last round than did the play of the visiting golfers (Wright, Jackson, Christie, McGuire, et al., 1991).

This finding, the home-field disadvantage, occurs only at the *end* of a long championship series, not at the beginning and not in a single-game championship. But do not bet on that.

COGNITION IN EMOTION

Among the diverse factors in emotion, the role of cognition is most widely debated. Feelings, physiological changes, and even behavior are inevitably involved, but is cognition also an inevitable component? Does it always play a role in emotion? According to some experts, the answer is "Yes." To experience an emotion, the individual must think about the stimulating circumstances. Why would Dawn lie frozen in bed without *any* understanding of the situation? The very different reactions of aroused animals also indicate some appraisal of the situation. According to the cognitive view, an evaluation of some sort is involved in *any* emotional reaction (Lazarus, 1993).

Other theorists argue that appraisal is not necessary. Different parts of the brain are involved in emotion and cognition, and everyday experience suggests that these responses are quite different. The alleged absence of cognition in extreme emotional states is indicated in familiar expressions: "I was so upset I couldn't think!" Cognition can cause emotion, and it can sustain emotion, but it is not a necessary or inevitable component of emotion (Plutchik, 1980; Weinrich, 1980).

FIGURE 11–2 COGNITION IN EMOTION. Overt behavior is not a good index of emotional arousal. Both the rabbit and the deer have determined that they are in danger, though they attempt to escape their predators by using opposite reactions, running away and standing motionless.

Psychologists adopting this view argue that some emotional behaviors occur even *before* the individual has appraised the situation. A calm, peaceful person suddenly recoils from something without knowing why, discovering the dangerous element later. We noted already that experimental animals may display fear without appraisal of the situation, apparently through activities in the amygdala, before the cerebral cortex has become involved (Le Doux, 1989, 1995).

A speculative attempt to reconcile these different views emphasizes that the two hemispheres of the brain serve somewhat different functions. Many studies suggest that the right hemisphere is more responsive to emotional stimulation than the left hemisphere. Damage to the right hemisphere causes greater difficulties in assessing emotional information than does comparable injury to the left hemisphere (Leventhal & Tomarken, 1986). Clinical patients with depressive reactions also show greater

than normal right hemisphere activity (Schaffer, Davidson, & Saron, 1983).

This approach, then, postulates two types of cognition in emotion. One, referred to as *analytic cognition,* is associated with the type of thinking commonly ascribed to the left hemisphere: verbal and direct. This cognition is essentially a logical understanding of something. The other, called *syncretic cognition,* is mediated by activities more closely associated with the right hemisphere: nonverbal and more holistic. It is characterized by spontaneity rather than intent, and it is presumed to be less logical and less conscious than analytic cognition (Buck, 1985).

In any case, there is agreement that cognition plays an important role in precipitating and sustaining emotional experiences—in animals and people (Figure 11–2). Dawn felt delighted merely thinking about her acceptance by several colleges. Stephen too was pleased to be going away to col-

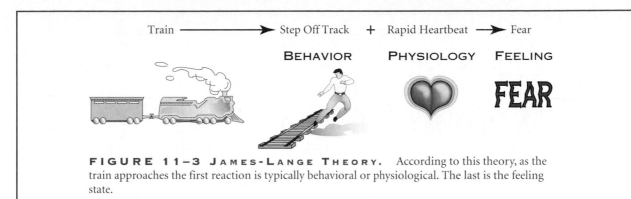

FIGURE 11–3 JAMES-LANGE THEORY. According to this theory, as the train approaches the first reaction is typically behavioral or physiological. The last is the feeling state.

lege. The prospect of escaping the confines of their hated schools made both of them happy indeed.

• THEORIES OF EMOTION •

In the fall of her junior year at college, Dawn gave a back-to-school party. Looking through a doorway, she saw Stephen for the first time, sitting on the stairs with friends, listening to someone's troubles. In her hostessing fervor, she did not have time to think more about that dark, appealing face.

Stephen remembered that first night differently. Sitting on the stairs, he met an old friend who was depressed. He felt a bit upset himself. Then he saw Dawn. She sat down next to him, waiting for his mood to change. It never did that night.

Later that week, Dawn and Stephen spent an evening together listening to music and discussing religion. The next day, they went to the beach. They swam, sat on the shore, and laughed a great deal. Dawn recalled, "I was truly happy for the first time in many months." Stephen thought to himself, "I have turned the corner and do not quite know where I am" (Goethals & Klos, 1976).

How would we attempt to explain these emotional reactions? What would we emphasize? Emotion is such a comprehensive concept that theories tend to focus on only one or two components, or they emphasize different components. Of all the major topics in psychology, understanding emotion seems to present the greatest challenge for an integrated approach (Oatley & Jenkins, 1992).

CLASSICAL VIEWS OF EMOTION

Among the major theoretical positions, the chief disagreement occurred between two classical viewpoints, the James-Lange and Cannon-Bard theories. At the time it appeared, the James-Lange theory promoted the opposite of what common sense suggests.

JAMES-LANGE THEORY. At the turn of this century, William James, in the United States, and Carl Lange, an eminent Danish scientist, came to a surprising conclusion. The behavioral and physiological reactions in emotion occur first, according to the **James-Lange theory,** and then they arouse the feelings. "We feel sorry because we cry, angry because we strike, afraid because we tremble," and not the other way around. Feelings are the result of feedback from bodily reactions, both muscular and glandular (James, 1890). Dawn felt happy that day at the beach because she smiled and laughed and because her heart palpitated.

James adopted this view largely on the basis of everyday situations. Standing in the path of an oncoming train, he claimed, you quickly step off the track and then you feel afraid (Figure 11–3). The feeling of fear is not truly experienced until you have retreated to the side and after the onset

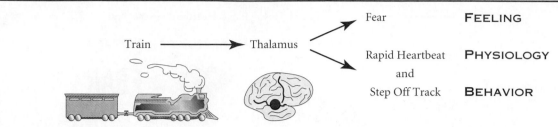

FIGURE 11–4 CANNON-BARD THEORY. The location of the thalamus is indicated by the colored dot on the cross-section of the human brain. By descending routes, according to the Cannon-Bard theory, it initiates physiological and behavioral reactions to the approaching train. By ascending routes, it also triggers mechanisms concerned with feelings about this event.

of physiological responses, such as rapid heartbeat, trembling, and increased breathing. When the results of this behavior and physiology reach the cerebral cortex, then you are truly afraid.

James's approach was the first modern theory of emotion and, despite its shortcoming, it set the direction for research for the next century (Mandler, 1990). In fact, one modern view reflects this position. The *facial feedback hypothesis* states that our facial expressions, through feedback from the controlling muscles, are partly responsible for the accompanying feelings (Izard, 1990).

In one test of this hypothesis, subjects were instructed to move their eyebrows down and together, raise their upper eyelids, narrow their lower lids, and press their lips together. This muscle-by-muscle instruction created the expression of anger in their faces, and physiological activities associated with anger occurred in the autonomic nervous system. Similar emotion-specific physiological reactions have been generated by using the instructions for expressions of fear, sadness, and disgust (Ekman, 1992).

Among the objections raised against the James-Lange theory, one concerns the timing of the events. Some physiological changes do not take place immediately, and yet our feelings appear rapidly. How can these feelings be explained on the basis of physiology? Our feelings sometimes continue even after the behavioral reaction has ceased. How can they be explained?

CANNON-BARD THEORY. One of those who took issue with the James-Lange theory was Walter Cannon, whose viewpoint was later extended by Philip Bard. Both physiologists, they produced the **Cannon-Bard theory,** sometimes called the *thalamic theory,* which emphasized that the thalamus plays a key role in stimulating the bodily arousal *and* the feelings of emotion. It sends signals to the autonomic nervous system, creating the bodily reactions, and also to the cerebral cortex, creating the feelings in emotion (Cannon, 1929).

According to this view, Dawn's happiness at the beach originated largely in the thalamus, which transmits *simultaneous* messages. The descending impulses, proceeding downward to the sympathetic division of the autonomic nervous system, activate the glands and skeletal muscles responsible for the physiology of emotion and the mechanisms for the behavioral reaction. Dawn's heart beat a bit faster, she laughed, and she danced around in a playful manner. The ascending impulses, relayed upward to the higher regions of the brain, initiate neural patterns responsible for the emotional experience. Dawn felt very happy. Through the thalamus, the sensations of bodily reactions and the feelings are combined almost simultaneously (Figure 11–4).

The Cannon-Bard theory was helpful in showing the importance of the thalamus, not considered in James's approach, but the neural anatomy of emotion is far more complicated. In the first place, the thalamus is not directly involved in activating

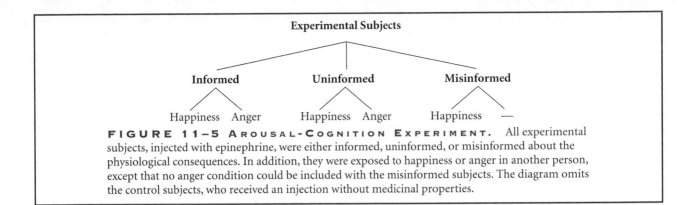

FIGURE 11-5 AROUSAL-COGNITION EXPERIMENT. All experimental subjects, injected with epinephrine, were either informed, uninformed, or misinformed about the physiological consequences. In addition, they were exposed to happiness or anger in another person, except that no anger condition could be included with the misinformed subjects. The diagram omits the control subjects, who received an injection without medicinal properties.

the muscles and glands. Second, the theory assumes that the thalamus, as a switchboard mechanism, prompts the emotional experience, but many other physiological structures are involved. Especially important is the hypothalamus, which plays a prominent role as a triggering mechanism. In addition, the limbic system and cerebral cortex are involved in emotion, as discussed earlier.

AROUSAL-COGNITION THEORY

The James-Lange theory ignored the role of the human brain in emotion, and the Cannon-Bard theory underestimated the role of the higher brain centers. Recent theorists have attempted to remedy these defects, focusing in particular on the cerebral cortex.

According to the **arousal-cognition theory,** emotional experience is a joint function of our degree of arousal, or physiological reactions, and our cognition, which is an interpretation of the situation. Initially, the arousal is simply nonspecific excitement; after cognition becomes involved, it is translated into a specific emotional experience. Aroused by a barking dog, a child interprets the condition as fear. Offended by a lack of consideration for the elderly, a senior citizen labels his aroused state as disgust. In these cases, the emotional experience arises through bodily feedback, and the reaction is brought into specific focus by an interpretation of the situation. Both factors, arousal *and* cognition, are important in the two-factor approach.

AROUSAL AND APPRAISAL. In an experiment by Stanley Schachter and associates, college students were injected with *epinephrine,* an adrenal hormone that induces an aroused state. The subjects in one treatment, called the informed subjects, were correctly informed that they would experience trembling hands, a pounding heart, and a flushed face. Others, the uninformed group, were told that they had received a vitamin compound with no immediate effects. The third group, the misinformed subjects, were led to expect symptoms that would not appear, such as numbness and itching. In addition, control subjects were injected with a saline solution that had no effect (Schachter & Singer, 1962).

All subjects were then exposed to one of two circumstances. In the euphoric or happy condition, they stayed in a waiting room with an accomplice of the experimenter who acted in a fun-loving, joking manner as he supposedly awaited his turn as a subject in the experiment. In the angry condition, the accomplice became highly irritated, complained about the questionnaire, made derisive comments, and stomped from the room. All subjects in both groups were observed through a one-way mirror and later were questioned about their feelings (Figure 11-5).

Schachter predicted that the misinformed and

uninformed subjects would be most susceptible to the mood in the environment and that the degree of susceptibility would be in proportion to the amount of epinephrine received. Having no explanation for their physiological arousal, which was readily apparent to them, they would interpret their feelings in terms of the circumstances. This prediction proved to be correct (Schachter, 1971).

According to this evidence, our interpretation of the situation determines the kind of feelings we experience, and the physiological changes determine the strength of this experience. In this view, also called *two-factor theory*, the cerebral cortex in particular plays a vital role in interpretation.

EVALUATION OF THE THEORY. A moment's introspection shows the powerful role of appraisal. Suppose you have just completed a term paper, and you are reviewing your accomplishment with joy and satisfaction. Suddenly you notice that you have used the wrong primary sources, and the paper is essentially worthless. Your ensuing response is disgust, fear, or shame. Your change in feeling has been produced solely by your reevaluation of your work.

The arousal-cognition view has focused attention on the role of cognition in emotional states, but it too has limitations. The subjects in the prior experiment, after being exposed to the different situations, were never asked to give their interpretation of those situations. We do not know about their cognitions. We only know that they were exposed to different stimulating conditions. Furthermore, our emotional reactions may be a function of cognition and physiological arousal, but all emotional states are not the same physiologically, differing *only* in cognitive factors. We need to know more about how the physiological factors are influential. Situational and physiological factors are relevant in all theories of emotion (Table 11–3).

This experiment has not been repeated with the same results, partly because there are now regulations against the use of epinephrine in this way (Leventhal & Tomarken, 1986). However, an experiment using incidental, unexpected exercise to induce arousal confirmed that people seek readily accessible explanations for their aroused states. When such cues are unavailable in the external environment, they look inward. By demonstrating the role of internal cues in emotional labeling, this research supported the arousal-cognition theory (Sinclair, Hoffman, Mark, Martin, & Pickering, 1994).

• LIKING AND LOVING •

"Stephen's entrance into my life was heralded by a joy . . . that quite surprised me," Dawn said. "I feel really protected and comforted by a PERSON."

"She is frank and open in what she wants and what she will give," Stephen said about Dawn. "Her smiling, which she has not shown before, makes me

THEORY	EXPLANATION	ILLUSTRATION
James-Lange	The behavioral and physiological reactions arouse the feeling.	Dawn became tongue-tied and trembled; which made her feel afraid.
Cannon-Bard	The thalamus stimulates bodily arousal and feelings.	Dawn became tongue-tied and trembled; simultaneously she felt afraid.
Arousal-cognition	The emotional experience depends on arousal *and* the interpretation of the situation.	Dawn interpreted her trembling as fear because she decided that the situation was dangerous.

TABLE 11–3 THEORIES OF EMOTION. A most important moment in Dawn's early life occurred when she encountered her drunken mother in the kitchen. These theories provide different interpretations of her emotional reaction.

feel like giving myself to her" (Goethals & Klos, 1976).

We often desire the company of someone *in particular*. We want to be with a specific person or group of people. Here we are speaking of liking and loving, topics that have aroused the poet and the philosopher, the cynic and the romantic. The feeling of *liking* someone involves enjoyment, appreciation, and common interests. It is not an abiding tie. In contrast, *loving* is a deep, enduring affection for another person, manifest in diverse ways.

One definition involves a love triangle—but not three people romantically inclined. Rather, the **triangular theory of love** describes three components, appearing in various amounts in any given love relationship: *intimacy*, which involves closeness and sharing; *commitment*, which is the devotion to the relationship; and *passion*, referring to the intensity of the feeling, often sexual. Intimacy alone, for example, is essentially friendship or liking. Commitment alone appears in a caretaker relationship. And passion, by itself, often emerges as the first state of a romantic relationship. The presence of all three components is called *consummate love*, although the theory speculates that this condition is unlikely to be maintained for an extended period (Figure 11–6). As time passes and passion subsides, intimacy and commitment become more ascendant (Sternberg, 1986).

How do we explain the origins of liking and loving? More specifically, how do we understand the development of such a relationship outside the family? From an investment perspective, adults develop or maintain a relationship with a partner according to what is gained from the association.

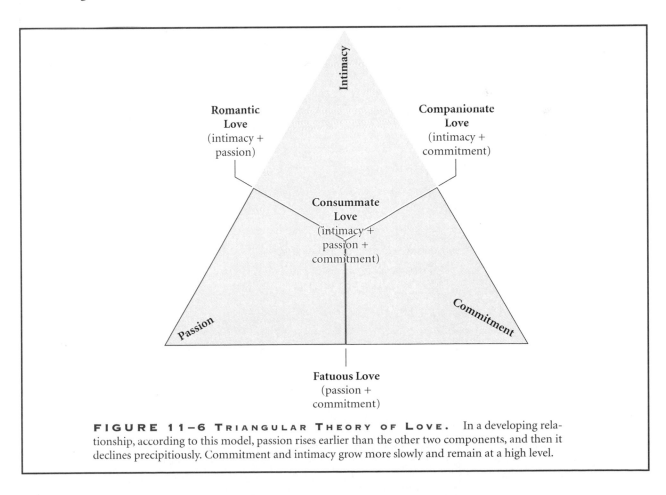

FIGURE 11–6 TRIANGULAR THEORY OF LOVE. In a developing relationship, according to this model, passion rises earlier than the other two components, and then it declines precipitously. Commitment and intimacy grow more slowly and remain at a high level.

DEVELOPING RELATIONSHIPS

The simplest explanation states that we like people associated with good times. Watching the ocean or enjoying a meal with someone can lead to liking that person. In the same way, through classical conditioning, a series of negative events with someone, such as shivering on a cold beach, becoming ill, or failing in school, can lead to an aversion.

Further, we prefer to be with people who support our actions, listen to our ideas, and provide physical comfort. Our response is a function of the outcome of our behavior, called the **reinforcement principle** in operant conditioning. In fact, B. F. Skinner has suggested that partnership love is simply mutual reinforcement. Each person gains something from the relationship. A man behaves in a humorous, playful style admired by his partner. He receives compliments; the partner enjoys the company of a light-hearted individual. The partner approaches the world in a practical, realistic manner that the man appreciates—and so forth.

EXCHANGE THEORY. Why then do people sometimes terminate a relationship from which they receive positive outcomes? During her sophomore year, Dawn stopped going out with Will, a handsome young man who was most attentive to her. According to **exchange theory,** maintaining a relationship depends not just on reinforcement but also on a gain that is greater than the overall expense. Crass as it may seem, this view states that an interpersonal relationship, like any other purchase or exchange, is judged in terms of profit and loss (Homans, 1974). Dawn's positive experiences with Will did not outweigh her effort and sacrifice—socializing only with Will's friends, tolerating his odd hours, and accepting his abuse. She broke off the relationship because the magnitude of the gain was not worth the cost.

Exchange theory is applicable even in abusive relationships and sexual harassment. An abused partner makes the decision to leave or remain on the basis of predictable decision rules regarding costs and benefits. The decision to stay may seem irrational to the outsider and may be irrational, but the decision process is not inherently abnormal or incompatible with exchange theory (Strube, 1991a).

In her emerging relationship with Stephen, Dawn was overjoyed by his attentiveness and willingness to help with her debts. These traits outweighed his tendency to drinking bouts and lack of academic focus. Stephen, in turn, found Dawn intellectually stimulating and physically attractive, characteristics more important to him than her emotional instability and financial problems. For both partners, the gain was greater than the cost.

EQUITY THEORY. According to another viewpoint, even relationships based on a gain greater than the cost are sometimes terminated, and here equity becomes the issue. Equity is concerned with fairness, and **equity theory** states that we maintain a relationship if the outcome is at least equal to what we feel we merit, weighing all of our social attributes against the norms of society. If Dawn and Stephen continued their relationship, it would be because each of them derived from it what he or she felt was merited, regardless of the cost–benefit margin. This viewpoint may seem even more calculating than exchange theory, but it has been demonstrated empirically that we tend to find partners of essentially our own social value, measured in terms of mental, physical, social, economic, and other indices. Mate selection, according to equity theory, is a compromise between our desire for an ideal partner and the realization that

THEORY	EXAMPLE
Conditioning: each partner gains something.	Dawn receives protection and comfort from a PERSON. Stephen gains the attention of someone who is open and smiling.
Exchange: each partner gains more than the relationship costs.	Dawn feels that Stephen's attentiveness and assistance with her debts outweigh his drinking bouts and lack of focus. Stephen finds Dawn's intellectual stimulation and physical attractiveness worth the problem of her emotional instability.
Equity: each partner gains what he or she feels is merited.	Dawn decides that Stephen, overall, is worth what she deserves. Stephen decides that Dawn is right for him, taking into account all their assets and limitations.

TABLE 11–4 MAINTAINING A RELATIONSHIP. The conditioning viewpoint merely considers the benefit. Exchange and equity theory consider the benefit in the context of cost and worth, respectively.

we probably must settle for what we seem to be worth (Walster & Walster, 1978; Table 11–4).

In one instance, support for equity theory was gathered from more than 300 college students, each engaged in a dating relationship. They were asked to make extensive observations about themselves, their partner, and the relationship. It was found that the students in the most equitable relationships were the most content with their partners and most committed to them (Winn, Crawford, & Fischer, 1991).

Equity theory does not maintain that all potential partners actively engage in a process of calculating their worth and then bartering for a mate on the open market, much as they might haggle over the purchase of an old picture frame at a garage sale. Rather, it states that an enduring relationship, within or outside marriage, often reflects some social assessment, intentionally or otherwise. As even the poet knows, "Everything must go to market." This search for equity has been found in physician–patient satisfactions and public interest transactions, as well as personal relationships (Koehler, Fottler, & Swan, 1992; Van Dijk & Wilke, 1993).

In contrast, the popular press strengthens a very different notion: romantic love, with its more idealized view of the participants and their alliance. Many partners regard their relationship in this manner. Their lives have been joined not through some vague assessment process but because they were destined for each other. According to this view, true love conquers all, even an assessment error.

❧

LOVE RELATIONSHIPS

During her high school years, Dawn made a promise to herself. Looking at her parents' marital problems and at other unsuccessful marriages, she decided that she would marry someone who would simply find her comfortable and socially convenient, in return for his very definite economic assets. Dawn here espoused a form of equity theory, assuming that each partner receives what he or she is worth. She also implied that there are degrees of liking and loving.

The bond between Dawn and Stephen began as simple liking, and then it changed to love, at least for Stephen. "I am now a newer person," he said. "I feel myself glowing to the people around the dark room" (Goethals & Klos, 1976).

Love, the subject of ballads and the object of research, is very difficult to define—along with intelligence, adjustment, creativity, and many other psychological concepts. Nevertheless, one approach has identified six basic *styles* of love. The three primary styles include erotic love, game-playing love, and friendship love; the three secondary styles include practical love, possessive love, and selfless love (Lee, 1973; Table 11–5).

The love styles of women tend toward friendship and practical love. Men engage in more erotic and game-playing love (Hendrick, Hendrick, Foote, & Slapion-Foote, 1984).

Love also has been considered from the viewpoint of *stages* rather than styles, and here two stages have received special attention: passionate and companionate love. When compared with the styles just mentioned, they are closest to erotic love and friendship love, respectively.

PASSIONATE LOVE. The highly aroused, somewhat confused state Stephen described is known as passionate love, erotic love, or sometimes romantic love. In **passionate love,** the partner is perceived in an idealized form, often with the expectation of complete and lasting fulfillment, and sexual attraction is a potent factor. The relationship is intense, sometimes volatile, and viewed with high hopes.

STYLE	ATTRIBUTE
Erotic	Instant physical attraction and passion
Game playing	Multiple partners, chasing and catching
Friendship	Long-standing relations, companionship
Practical	Careful assessment of specific traits
Possessive	Dependence on the relationship, lovesickness
Selfless	Spiritual, unselfish, concern for the partner

TABLE 11–5 STYLES OF LOVE. These styles also have Greek names. From top to bottom, they are: *eros, ludus, storge, pragma, mania,* and *agape* (Hendrick & Hendrick, 1986).

In this state of romantic love, Stephen proposed marriage. Dawn replied that she could not decide so quickly. A half hour later, she said simply: "Yes" (Goethals & Klos, 1976). In that interim, perhaps Dawn was pondering some dimension of equity theory. Stephen was having difficulty planning his life, and he came from a background quite different from hers. What were the long-range implications? What would her mother say?

In the United States, romantic or passionate love has been considered essential to a successful marriage and widely promoted in the mass media. Nevertheless, it is quite foreign to many contemporary cultures in which marriages are arranged, often early in life. Here the sexual aspects are considered less important than mutual interests and the exchange of ideas.

Passionate love is fleeting, despite the partners' fondest hopes. Inevitably, it must decline, not necessarily to end in pieces but at least in another form. One reason is that we cannot continue to receive increased pleasure from any form of stimulation, a phenomenon known as *adaptation.* Potato soup, a downhill ski run, and a partner's caresses all become less intensely satisfying with successive repetitions. A second reason concerns human development. We are always changing. Unless our partner, also changing, miraculously meets these new needs as well, we find that we are falling out of love, or in and out of love, or that our love is changing. It has been said that one difference between partners who decide to separate and those who stay together is the recognition of this fluctuating condition.

COMPANIONATE LOVE. If we stay in the relationship, this changed love often becomes **companionate love,** which is a deep affection for others with whom our lives are closely interwoven. It is less intense, more enduring, and more realistic than passionate love. In terms of the earlier triangular theory, companionate love can be considered a combination of intimacy and commitment. It is not true love any more than passionate love is true love. They are simply different forms of love.

Within long-term families there is companionate love between the spouses, between parents and children, and among brothers and sisters, but almost inevitably rivalries develop as well. Older people, as might be expected, place more emphasis on a companionate relationship, as opposed to a passionate one (Figure 11–7).

❧

EXPERIENCING SEX

And now for sex, a potent contributor to love at many ages, although far from indispensable. Sex can be involved at all stages of liking and loving, and it can be mixed with achievement and aggression.

Careful laboratory studies of the physiology of sex indicate two major changes in the body that underlie the great variety of sexual experiences in males and females alike. There is an increased flow of blood into the pelvic area, made possible by the dilation of the blood vessels. This extra blood supply, known as **vasocongestion,** has diverse repercussions, including engorgement of the sexual organs. In addition there is **myotonia,** which involves contractions of the muscles throughout the body, resulting in facial expressions, voluntary movements in the limbs, and involuntary spasms in the genital areas.

MALE SEXUAL RESPONSE. The reaction of the male is a continuous process best understood as four stages of a cycle: excitement, plateau, orgasm, and resolution. Physiological changes take place during each phase.

In the excitement phase, vasocongestion produces erection of the penis, possibly erection in the nipples, and perhaps reddening of the skin. There is a rise in pulse rate, respiration, and muscular tension until the plateau phase, during which the peak of sexual arousal is reached. The orgasm provides a release of this tension, and it occurs in two sub-

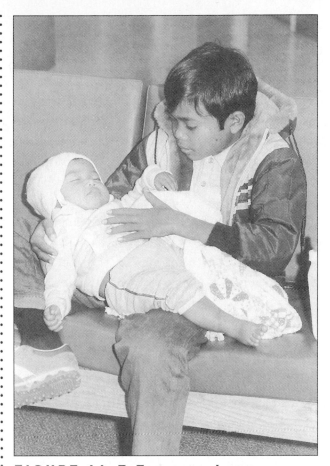

FIGURE 11–7 FAMILIAL LOVE.
Companionate love between siblings may be fostered by a significant age gap, enabling the older child to give and the younger to receive assistance. When children are closer in age, rivalries more often accompany familial affection.

stages. In the first, the inevitability of ejaculation is experienced in the contraction of the seminal vesicles, vas deferens, and prostate gland. The actual ejaculation, at intervals of .8 second, constitutes the second substage, and it is these contractions that are most closely associated with the pleasurable aspects of orgasm.

Following orgasm, there is a gradual return to the nonaroused state. This resolution phase, during which vasocongestion and myotonia disappear, involves a loss of sexual responsiveness. During this refractory period, the capacity for full sexual arousal, including erection, does not return immediately. The interval before its reappearance varies a great deal from one individual to another, lasting up to 24 hours or more in some instances.

FEMALE SEXUAL RESPONSE. Like the return of arousability in males, the whole cycle in females is highly variable from one person to another. Most females show the four-stage response, but in some women the excitement and orgasm stages are closely merged, as in a series of orgasms. In others there may be no discernible plateau. The four-step model is only representative of a typical sequence (Figure 11–8).

The important changes in the excitement phase include vasocongestion of the clitoris and seepage of vaginal fluid through the vaginal walls. This seepage, prompted by the blood engorgement of the genitals, furnishes the lubrication necessary for intercourse. It may be accompanied by the reddening sex flush and by swelling and erection of the nipples, resulting from vasocongestion and myotonia. These changes become intensified in the plateau phase, producing the tension necessary for orgasmic experience. Again, the rhyth-

mic contractions in orgasm occur at approximately .8-second intervals, but compared to the male's ejaculation, there is less external evidence of orgasm.

Afterward, there is no clear period of sexual inexcitability. With appropriate stimulation a woman can experience another orgasm during the resolution phase, but the reaction is diminished.

SEXUAL PROBLEMS. The chief sexual problems experienced by men are *erectile difficulties*, formerly known as impotence, and *premature ejaculation*, in which orgasm occurs too early. For women, the chief problems are *orgasmic difficulties*, traditionally known as frigidity. These newer terms reflect more tolerant attitudes toward sexual problems, including the view that they are often psychological. Many sexual problems reflect interpersonal factors *between* the partners, rather than the adjustment of one individual, and then they must be treated as such (Stravynski & Greenberg, 1990).

Sometimes there is no known physical or interpersonal problem, and then a straightforward pro-

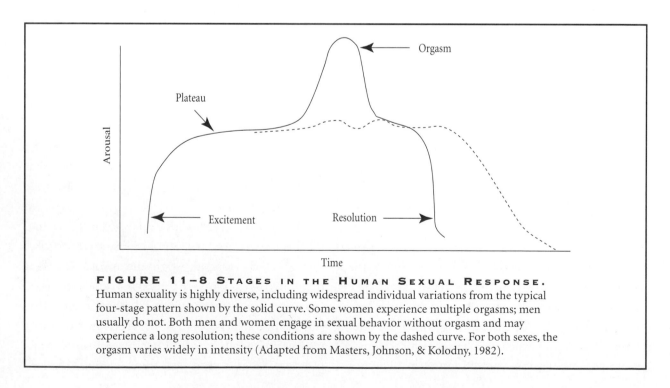

FIGURE 11–8 STAGES IN THE HUMAN SEXUAL RESPONSE.
Human sexuality is highly diverse, including widespread individual variations from the typical four-stage pattern shown by the solid curve. Some women experience multiple orgasms; men usually do not. Both men and women engage in sexual behavior without orgasm and may experience a long resolution; these conditions are shown by the dashed curve. For both sexes, the orgasm varies widely in intensity (Adapted from Masters, Johnson, & Kolodny, 1982).

cedure may be used. It begins with the couple in counseling sessions, aimed at the identification of negative attitudes toward sex and common causes of sexual problems, including unexpressed anger and guilt feelings. Then, in private, the couple starts to practice sexual exercises. In these activities, called the **sensate focus**, the partners take turns being the giver and receiver of sensual touching and pleasure—exploring the contours, textures, and odors of the partner's body, with no demands for performance. Relaxed closeness is the goal. Eventually, the couple moves toward increased sexual contact.

SEXUAL BEHAVIOR

Superimposed on these bodily responses are countless psychological dimensions arising through opportunities for learning. They can be enormously influential in sexual behavior and preferences. During high school, Dawn found masturbation pleasurable, and she practiced it in the imagined company of others. Stephen's early experiences took place on a bus with a female partner two years older than he. To the extent that these experiences were successful and gratifying, they played an important role in subsequent sexual interests.

MASTURBATION. The most common approach to sexual activity among adolescents and young adults is *masturbation,* in which satisfaction is obtained from direct stimulation of the genitals, usually self-stimulation. Our changing attitudes toward this practice, which occurs throughout adult life, illustrate the potent role of social forces in sexual expression. During the first half of this century, masturbation was strongly discouraged in many parts of the United States. Children were told that it was sinful, would damage the nervous system, and would make them unfit for business careers. Physicians stated: "Masturbation is one of the causes of insanity. To ascertain this fact it is only necessary to look over the reports of any of the

insane asylums of the land" (Whitehead & Hoff, 1929).

Today, with greater understanding of problems of personal adjustment, masturbation has been suggested in some treatment plans for sexual dysfunction. In reputable therapies, these exercises are presented along with activities for developing social skills, self-confidence, and healthy attitudes toward other adjustment issues (Stravynski & Greenberg, 1990).

HETEROSEXUAL PARTNERS. The wide variety in sexual behavior has been evident ever since the groundbreaking Kinsey surveys in the middle of this century. These studies showed that both men and women engaged in more diverse sexual outlets inside and outside marriage than even the experts would have predicted (Kinsey, Pomeroy, & Martin, 1948; Kinsey, Pomeroy, & Gebhard, 1953). These included *heterosexuality,* in which the attraction is toward a person of the opposite sex, and *homosexuality,* an attraction toward a person of one's own sex. In the immediately succeeding decades, with more liberal attitudes toward parenting, education, and lifestyles, together with birth control devices and treatments for sexual diseases, attitudes toward sexual behavior became even more liberal. But rather suddenly, in the early 1980s, a condition arose that ran counter to this sexual revolution—acquired immune deficiency syndrome (AIDS). The ease with which this disease can be transmitted has prompted the need for restraint in sexual activity.

Under the threat of AIDS, to what extent have heterosexual individuals actually changed their sexual practices? In an extensive study in the Netherlands, 512 heterosexual adults with multiple sexual partners were interviewed. Follow-up interviews were arranged every four months over a period of two years, attended by 340 of the subjects, 60% female and 40% male. The results indicated little change in genital, oral, and anal practices between heterosexual *private partners*. However, both men and women considerably reduced the number of private partners. There has been no apparent decline in the number of *commercial partners*—prostitutes and clients—but condom use among these partners has increased considerably (Hooykaas, Van der Linden, Van Doornum, & Van der Velde, 1991).

In the United States, one study focused on 101 dating couples rather than individuals with multiple sexual partners. Within these apparently monogamous relationships there was little change in sexual behaviors, although women reported themselves as more cautious than men (Sprecher, 1990).

HOMOSEXUAL PARTNERS. Attitudes toward homosexuality also have changed markedly over the course of human history. Among the ancient Greeks, homosexuality was encouraged. Beginning in the 1700s, when all forms of sexuality were seen as medical issues, homosexuality became greatly suppressed in the Western world. By the mid-twentieth century, slightly more than one of every three males reportedly had experienced an orgasm by homosexual contact, a figure considerably higher than was expected despite a possible bias in the sample (Kinsey, Pomeroy, & Martin, 1948). More recently, the American Psychiatric Association decided that homosexuality is not a psychiatric disorder and classified it as a disturbance only if the individual is in conflict about it. To prevent or diminish this conflict, the homosexual community has made efforts to assist gay and lesbian adolescents in understanding their sexuality and gaining a positive identity (Schneider, 1991).

In many parts of the world, including this country, there are more homosexual men than women, and investigators have tried to explain this difference. One hypothesis stresses the time of onset of the sex drive. Females begin puberty around age 11, but the sex drive does not appear for another three or four years. In males, puberty and the sex drive both begin around age 13. Until the early teens, friendships in both sexes are typically with members of the same sex. Males experience the onset of the sex drive in this context, whereas females experience it after the initiation of heterosexual contacts. On this basis, it is reasonable to expect more eroticization of homosexual cues among males and, insofar as fantasy is a component of sexual orientation, more homosexuality also (Storms, 1981).

From a very different perspective, one investigator compared the development of the hypothalamus in 41 human adults, many of whom had died from AIDS. The subjects included 19 homosexual men, 16 heterosexual men, and 6 heterosexual women. Prior studies with animals had shown that certain regions of the hypothalamus are larger in males than females and that this development depends in part on hormones, specifically in utero exposure to androgens. Among the men, one area of the hypothalamus in the heterosexual group was found to be approximately twice the size of this area in the homosexual subjects. For the women and homosexual men, the hypothalamic regions were approximately the same size. When comparisons were made between people who died of AIDS and those who died of other causes, no differences were found (Le Vay, 1991). Thus, it appeared that the cause of death probably was not a factor in the different sizes of the hypothalamus.

These results may be viewed in various ways. First, are they reliable? If so, does sexual orientation influence brain development or vice versa? Is there an interaction between sexual preference and development of the hypothalamus? To what extent, if any, are these differences related to hormonal conditions prior to birth? Whatever the outcome, these findings certainly do not rule out social factors, and again, the central message in the first chapter of this book is relevant: the multiple bases of behavior. Homosexuality, like creativity, alcoholism, heterosexuality, and artistic success, appears to be stimulated by a complex interplay of social, psychological, and physiological interactions, perhaps varying widely from one individual to another (Money, 1988).

SEX WITH AN OBJECT. Individuals are sometimes motivated to engage in sexual behavior in connection with a particular object. When this attachment is so strong that the presence of the object is essential for sexual gratification, the condition is called **fetishism.** Clothing, especially shoes, gloves, beads, and underwear, often becomes involved in fetishes. It is believed that the attachment is acquired through learning experiences in the early years, perhaps related to a neurological readiness for the conditioning of certain stimuli.

Within and across cultures, all sorts of objects and events are intended to augment sexual interest. These range from perfumes and cosmetics used in everyday life to hardware and apparel employed behind closed doors. The latter activities are discussed more fully in the chapter on adjustment.

• ANGER AND AGGRESSION •

Dawn was worried. Her mother opposed her approaching marriage for all sorts of reasons. In the first place, the bride and groom were too young. Worse yet, Stephen espoused a different religion, was an underachiever, and showed no clear job prospects. And Dawn had a promising career in arts and letters if she devoted herself extensively to those pursuits.

Dawn was worried because anger and aggression had been recurrent problems in their family; she argued loudly with her mother over the phone; and she wondered what would happen at the wedding. "There was always a battle," she said about her parents, who lived in bitterness on separate floors at opposite ends of the house.

Matters were little better for Stephen. His parents accepted the forthcoming marriage, but that was one of the few topics on which they agreed. Stephen's mother often insulted his father, and

eventually they became divorced. There was anger on both sides and actual aggression by his mother (Goethals & Klos, 1976).

Anger and aggression both involve hostility, but there is an important difference. In **anger,** *feelings* of hostility and displeasure are the chief characteristic. There may be angry behavior too, but there is no significant attack. In **aggression,** the *behavior* is dominant; there is an assault on another person or some object. However, angry feelings often underlie aggressive behavior.

❧
ORIGINS OF AGGRESSION

American society is an aggressive society. Football is not a contact sport—but a collision sport. Our television thrives on shootouts, war stories, and murder mysteries. The press widely publicizes crime and aggravated assault. With this problem so extremely prevalent, not just in the United States but elsewhere as well, the origins of aggression have become a controversial issue (Figure 11–9).

PREDISPOSITIONAL VIEW. According to some experts, human beings may have an inherited

FIGURE 11–9 AN ENVIRONMENT OF AGGRESSION. Aggressive acts dominate sports, films, and newspapers in the United States. Without doubt, a great deal of aggressive behavior is learned through these displays.

predisposition for aggressive behavior. These experts, typically from backgrounds in ethology and animal behavior, note the aggression in the animal kingdom. Iguanas butt heads; howler monkeys battle with deafening vocalizations; spiders and praying mantises eat their own kind. Animals fight to obtain food or a mate, to establish a territory, and to gain a position in a social hierarchy. Human beings have all of these concerns. Territorial rights, in particular, have been an object of warfare throughout human history (Lorenz, 1963; Morris, 1967).

Another view of aggression as innate comes from psychoanalysis and the work of Sigmund Freud, widely recognized for postulating two human instincts. One of these, the **life instinct,** or *eros,* motivates us to self-preservation, love, and sexual urges that result in the preservation of the species. The other, the **death instinct,** or *thanatos,* impels us toward the cessation of life's tensions. The ultimate aim of life, in this sense, is death, which is brought about partly by our destructive tendencies toward ourselves and others. Freud arrived at this conclusion through studies in evolutionary biology, experiences in World War I, and the military buildup before World War II. For him, the life and death instincts were constantly at odds, but the eventual winner was always the death instinct (Freud, 1915).

The chief objection to Freud's view is that there is no solid evidence in biology that a fundamental instinct in life aims to abolish all tension. This concept contradicts biological principles (Brun, 1953). However, the term *instinct* here reflects a lack of precision in translation from the German. Freud was not intending our modern definition of instinct—a complex, unlearned behavior pattern—but rather a broad urge, a *drive,* a motivational disposition. It is reasonable to postulate an aggressive drive much as one might postulate a sex drive, as a reservoir of energy to behave in a certain fashion. The two basic Freudian drives, sex and aggression, are regarded by many modern psycho-analysts and others as underlying a wide variety of behaviors, ranging from striving for power to conquests in love.

Both drives appear to be involved in **rape,** a violent sexual act based on physical assault or threats of harm. Rape is far more frequent than the crime statistics suggest, chiefly because many cases go unreported for fear of reprisal, embarrassment, or both. One form of rape, called *date rape,* involves acquaintances, not strangers, and in one large survey almost 10% of college women reported that they had been forced into sexual intercourse in this way (Koss, Gidycz, & Wisniewski, 1987). Sexual and aggressive elements are intertwined in rape of all kinds, making this behavior a highly complex problem.

ROLE OF LEARNING. For other investigators more compelling evidence on the origins of aggression is found in the environment. Learning theorists contend, for example, that if guns were more restricted, there would be less violence, and most studies favor this position—that aggressive behavior is increased by the presence of stimuli related to aggression. In typical research, subjects who experience frustration in the context of guns, clubs, and so forth show more aggressive reactions than do those who experience the same frustration in neutral circumstances (Berkowitz & LePage, 1967; Cahoon & Edmunds, 1984).

In addition to stimuli directly related to aggression, less obvious environmental conditions also are associated with aggressive behavior, such as crowdedness and even the weather. In one experiment with four rat colonies, conditions were arranged so that the first and last pens had only one entrance each. A dominant male controlled each of these pens, and the population stabilized at the expected level. The other two pens had two entrances each, and these colonies soon became extremely crowded. Social organization was markedly disrupted, with fighting and cannibalism among the males, neglect of the young by females, and aberrant sexual behavior in both sexes. The outcome in this environment was called a *behavioral sink,* referring to the destructive, pathological reaction that developed in the overcrowded conditions (Calhoun, 1962).

Still another factor involves observational learning. Children who are controlled by aggression become aggressive themselves (Bandura, 1986). There is some humor but no consolation in the cartoon showing an angry father spanking his child and saying: "There! That'll teach you not to hit your little brother!" There is, in fact, research evidence indicating that harsh parenting is transmitted across generations in this way (Simons, Whitbeck, Conger, & Wu, 1991). Investigations of televised aggression support this viewpoint. Most of the thousands of studies, reviewed in a massive report by the National Institute of Mental Health, indicate that watching aggression on television is a likely *cause* of aggression in children and adolescents (Figure 11–10).

REDUCING AGGRESSION

The argument over innate and learned factors in aggression arises partly because different definitions are involved. Sometimes aggression is defined as a vigorous pursuit of self-preservation, as when dispassionate animals kill merely for food. On this basis almost all organisms are potentially aggressive, for all of us have an innate desire to satisfy physiological needs. Aggression is also defined as the desire to inflict harm on another individual or object, even when there is no obvious gain. This behavior certainly seems learned, for it does not appear in animals or even in most human beings.

Regardless of the difficulties in definition, the important issue is this underlying question: How can we diminish whatever destructive predispositions exist among us?

CATHARSIS HYPOTHESIS. One view involves catharsis, which is a release of pent-up emotion. According to the **catharsis hypothesis,** the expression of anger, anxiety, or other feelings reduces

FIGURE 11–10 VIOLENCE IN FILMS. For most psychologists, the burden of proof has shifted. It now stands for film makers to demonstrate that the portrayal of violence does not stimulate aggression in viewers (Hoberman, 1990; Rubinstein, 1983).

the underlying drive, just as eating reduces the hunger drive. In this view, Dawn's ranting and raving after a disruptive phone conversation with her mother decreased her tendency to behave aggressively. Similarly, Stephen's expressions of anger diminished his inclination to behave aggressively against the furniture. However, the research points to a different conclusion. Opportunities for crying do not necessarily reduce depressive feelings (Kraemer & Hastrup, 1988). Opportunities for expressing anger have even sustained this feeling (Averill, 1982). Overall, the evidence is against the catharsis hypothesis (Bennett, 1991; Lewis & Bucher, 1992).

A variety of studies from the laboratory and clinic indicate another approach: talking and writing about the problem. This procedure can be helpful—up to a point. Reviewing what happened often brings a sense of completion. The person needs to confront the anger directly, make a confession, and then try to view it as a resolved matter.

FRUSTRATION-AGGRESSION HYPOTHESIS. A very different hypothesis points to the role of frustrating circumstances in the origins of aggression and therefore has implications for reducing it. In this view, called the **frustration-aggression hypothesis,** aggressive behavior always presupposes frustration, and frustration inevitably leads to some form of aggression. When the boss fails to negotiate a business deal, we are not surprised if she is a bit nasty (Dollard, Miller, Doob, Mowrer, & Sears, 1939).

Dawn was very happy with Stephen, unless her new world was ruptured by a phone call from her mother. After yelling over the telephone, frustrated by their inability to communicate, Dawn sometimes became aggressive with Stephen too. More respectful of his partner, Stephen bashed the furniture when he felt frustrated about his schoolwork (Goethals & Klos, 1976). The frustration-aggression hypothesis seems to be supported in these everyday examples.

The role of frustration in aggression also has been demonstrated in laboratory and field studies. In young children, the single best predictor of physical aggression is language immaturity—that is, an inability to express oneself well in words, clearly a source of frustration (Piel, 1990).

However, aggression sometimes occurs without frustration, and frustration does not always lead to aggression. A frustrated person may cry, complain, or withdraw instead. On these bases, the hypothesis has been revised: Frustration leads to a *readiness* to behave in an aggressive fashion. Then the appearance of aggressive behavior is significantly determined by environmental factors (Berkowitz, 1988, 1989). Even in this revised form, the hypothesis has implications for reducing aggression. These efforts must begin in the home, teaching children to deal more effectively with frustration, and they must include programs of assistance for underprivileged people who face overwhelming frustration daily.

This view, sometimes called the *cultural hypothesis,* states that aggression is learned through social or cultural patterns. The Zuni in North America have long been a pastoral, peaceful people. The

Comanche, in earlier years, had a tradition of aggressiveness and self-assertion. In New Guinea, the Arapesh regarded self-assertion and aggressiveness as abnormal. The Mundugumor fostered these behaviors and used aggressive methods to prepare the young for survival (Mead, 1939). It is clear that social conditions can mold aggressive, aggression-prone, or basically peaceful individuals, almost regardless of the ways their needs are satisfied.

• STRESS IN DAILY LIFE •

All cultures involve restrictions of some sort, and all of us are faced with the problem of satisfying physiological needs, as well as psychological motives. To the extent that we encounter difficulties in these respects, we experience stress. The condition of **stress** is a state of tension, strain, or conflict within an individual that has the potential to disrupt physical, mental, and behavioral functions. The person's normal balance or stability is threatened, requiring compensatory reactions or readjustments.

For Dawn, Stephen, and their families, the impending wedding brought forth various forms of stress and efforts at readjustment. Dawn's mother ordered the invitations and, in a moment of tension, forgot the RSVP cards. Aunts and uncles tried to find suitable gifts and make appropriate travel plans. The wedding couple faced last-minute chores and doubts. And both families made efforts to adjust to future in-laws.

STRESSFUL EVENTS

Stressful events can be chronic or fleeting, physical or psychological. Winning a scholarship, having a baby, and taking a vacation all require readjustment, as do divorce, loans, and retirement. In short, stressful events are changes of all sorts, positive or negative.

LIFE CHANGES. A popular approach to the measurement of stress emphasizes these changes in routines. Barriers and choices underlie many of them, but the chief issue in *life changes* is the extent to which they require readjustment by the individual. An instrument called the *Social Readjustment Rating Scale* presents 43 life changes in decreasing order of the readjustments they typically require. The sequence and numerical values assigned to these events were determined by asking many subjects to rate them for the degree of readjustment involved, regardless of its desirability. On this basis, death of a spouse and divorce were the most stressful events; Christmas and vacation were toward the bottom of the scale (Holmes & Rahe, 1967).

With their marriage, Dawn and Stephen would commence the life change ranked seventh on the scale. Both partners had already experienced trouble with their prospective in-laws, a problem ranked in the middle of the scale. With school over for the year, they were beginning a vacation, a mildly stressful occasion. As for their parents, they were having a son or daughter leave home, an event also ranked in the middle of the scale. For both families, the wedding was stressful beyond any bumbling or personal animosities that occurred (Table 11–6).

The wedding day also proved stressful. It rained the whole time. Dawn forgot her lines; the couple kissed too early in the ceremony; the reception was anything but jovial; and the crowd dwindled early. "The day . . . bestowed heroism on us all," observed Stephen wryly (Goethals & Klos, 1976).

CRITIQUE OF THE SCALE. People with high scores on the readjustment scale are considered to be under greater stress than those with low scores, especially if these scores are generated by negative events. The scale is not without its limitations, however. It omits events that may be highly significant for certain individuals, such as crime in the city and loneliness in the country. It also ignores how the person *feels* about that event. Earthquakes, surgical operations, and bankruptcy may be regarded very differently by different people.

RANK	LIFE EVENT	SCORE
1	Death of spouse	100
2	Divorce	73
3	Marital separation	65
4	Jail term	63
5	Death of close family member	63
6	Personal injury or illness	53
7	✓ Marriage	50
8	Fired at work	47
9	Marital reconciliation	45
10	Retirement	45
11	Change in health of family member	44
12	Pregnancy	40
13	Sex difficulties	39
14	Gain of new family member	39
15	Business readjustment	39
16	Change in financial state	38
17	Death of close friend	37
18	Change to different line of work	36
19	Change in number of arguments with spouse	35
20	Mortgage over $10,000	31
21	Foreclosure of mortgage or loan	30
22	Change in responsibilities at work	29
23	Son or daughter leaving home	29
24	✓ Trouble with in-laws	29
25	Outstanding personal achievement	28
26	Wife begin or stop work	26
27	Begin or end school	26
28	✓ Change in living conditions	25
29	Revision of personal habits	24
30	Trouble with boss	23
31	Change in work hours or conditions	20
32	Change in residence	20
33	Change in schools	20
34	Change in recreation	19
35	Change in church activities	19
36	Change in social activities	18
37	Mortgage or loan less than $10,000	17
38	Change in sleeping habits	16
39	Change in number of family get-togethers	15
40	Change in eating habits	15
41	✓ Vacation	13
42	Christmas	12
43	Minor violations of the law	11

TABLE 11–6 SOCIAL READJUSTMENT RATING SCALE. To determine the amount of stress someone is experiencing, the scores for all applicable events are summed. The checkmarks indicate events experienced by Dawn and Stephen at the time of their wedding. Note that the mortgage in item 20 depicts economic conditions 30 years ago (Holmes & Rahe, 1967).

Also, people who have suffered the death of a spouse or some other recent tragedy are especially vulnerable to other sources of stress. In fact, several of the life changes indicated on the stress scale may be the *result of stress*, rather than its cause. Divorce, disease, and dissatisfaction at work all may be exacerbated, if not caused, by the individual's reaction to some other major stressful event.

The readjustment scale also ignores hassles and minor problems, such as the late arrival of the mail, waiting lines for the bathroom, and poor service at the bus station. There is also routine but subtle stress in many jobs: the vigilance of the air traffic controller, the strain of the keyboard operator, and conflict with coworkers. In combination with other minor adversities, these events may be more stressful than some of those on the scale (De Longis, Coyne, Dekaf, Folkman, & Lazarus, 1982).

TYPES OF CONFLICT. Other stressful situations do not necessarily involve a life change but rather making a choice. In this circumstance, called a **conflict,** one choice or motive is opposed by one or more alternatives; all outcomes cannot be achieved. The conflict may be minor, as in selecting music for a wedding, or major, as in deciding whether or not to get married in the first place or choosing between two parents in a custody case. The latter conflicts clearly precede a life change.

Conflicts have been viewed in several categories. In the first, the **approach-approach conflict**, two or more equally attractive alternatives are incompatible. The fabled donkey, flanked by equally enticing and distant bales of hay, is said to have starved in the midst of plenty, a highly unlikely outcome. In contrast, two or more alternatives may be equally repellent, resulting in an **avoidance-avoidance conflict.** A man must work for a nasty boss or search for other employment.

Sometimes, rather than two or more alternatives, there is a single possibility with both positive and negative aspects, which is the **approach-avoidance** conflict. The use of alcohol is often a complex approach-avoidance conflict for college students (Schall, Kemeny, & Maltzman, 1992). Here we speak of *ambivalence*, meaning that the individual has positive and negative feelings about the same event. Sometimes, however, there are several possibilities, each with positive and negative features, resulting in a multiple approach-avoidance conflict. Contemplating a vacation, a woman wants to please her husband by visiting his family, but she finds them boring. She also wants to go to a conference on mountaineering, but it will be very expensive. One reason decisions are so difficult is that we experience opposed feelings about so many things (Lewin, 1935).

OUTCOMES OF CONFLICT. Compared to other conflicts, the approach-approach situation is easily resolved. When faced with two equally attractive choices, human beings will find a reason to select one of them. After all, they are *attractive.* A hungry man who likes lobster and steak will not let himself starve because he cannot make a choice. Even donkeys make choices, overcoming approach-approach dilemmas.

The avoidance-avoidance conflict presents more complications because the individual does not want to make any choice at all. A man must pay a large debt or run the risk of a lawsuit. Trying to avoid these *unattractive* alternatives, he may take a business trip, obtain another legal opinion, or decide that he must file for bankruptcy. In daily life, people often seek some escape from the whole situation.

Now what would happen if someone needing surgery, for example, viewed the hospital as having both positive and negative implications? That person would be in an approach-avoidance conflict, a troublesome situation because it involves ambivalence. This decision is made all the more difficult because, as shown in various experiments, when viewed from afar, the positive features of an approach-avoidance conflict often seem to outweigh the negative features. Viewed up close, the negative features seem more prominent. Thus, the person is brought into the conflict by the positive features, readily evident at a distance, and driven away by the negative features, more apparent at close range. For these reasons, the person vacillates, back and forth, and the approach-avoidance conflict may be prolonged.

Sitting in his living room, the prospective patient may have comforting thoughts about a clean and caring hospital with a friendly physician at his bedside. When he arrives at the hospital door, smells the medicinal odors, and hears the screeching ambulance at the emergency dock, he may promptly reject the idea of hospitalization. The approach-avoidance conflict often ends when another factor becomes involved, upsetting the balance between the approach and avoidance tendencies. A friend accompanies the patient to the hospital, and with this new element the balance is shifted and a decision is reached (Figure 11–11).

In resolving these conflicts, flexibility is most important. Nevertheless, it is difficult to inculcate flexibility—inducing chronic "avoiders" to approach a problem and chronic "approachers" to ignore some situations (Roth & Cohen, 1986).

❧ BODILY REACTIONS TO STRESS

Response to stress involves all of the basic dimensions of emotion previously noted: feelings, physiological processes, behavior, and cognitive factors. Each of these topics is considered later in the chapter on adjustment, but certain physiological reactions should be noted here as well.

GENERAL ADAPTATION SYNDROME. Whether it arises from a wedding, an infection, or bankruptcy, stress can produce bodily changes. These physiological reactions to stress, known as the **general adaptation syndrome,** are characterized by three phases: alarm, resistance, and exhaustion. A syndrome is a pattern or organization of symptoms, and here they occur in a sequence (Selye, 1976).

The first phase is the **alarm reaction,** which is the organism's initial defense, an overall bodily

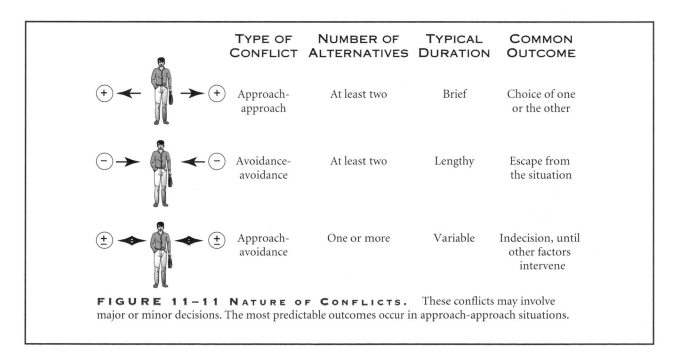

	TYPE OF CONFLICT	NUMBER OF ALTERNATIVES	TYPICAL DURATION	COMMON OUTCOME
(+) ← → (+)	Approach-approach	At least two	Brief	Choice of one or the other
(−) → ← (−)	Avoidance-avoidance	At least two	Lengthy	Escape from the situation
(±) → ← (±)	Approach-avoidance	One or more	Variable	Indecision, until other factors intervene

FIGURE 11–11 NATURE OF CONFLICTS. These conflicts may involve major or minor decisions. The most predictable outcomes occur in approach-approach situations.

response to any stress. Among these defensive forces are increased secretions from the pituitary and adrenal glands, producing the adrenocorticotropic hormone and cortisone. Combined with other stress-reducing changes, these responses enable the organism to sustain the second stage, called **resistance,** which is an emergency reaction requiring much energy. However, the individual's psychological and physiological resources cannot cope endlessly with constant tension; they gradually become depleted, and the person runs the risk of illness. With no diminution of stress, the third and final stage is reached, called **exhaustion,** for the organism's earlier reactions have been repeated until they are no longer possible. If the stress continues, death occurs.

On other occasions, the stress may be brief and beneficial for the individual, facilitating completion of a difficult task, and then it is called **eustress.** In all forms of human existence, stress is inevitable and a certain amount of eustress enhances our lives. The purpose of life is not to avoid all stress; some stress makes us feel good and enables us to engage in athletic competitions, climb mountains, and write term papers.

PSYCHOPHYSIOLOGICAL DISORDERS.

Extended, adverse stress contributes to headaches, sinus problems, skin disorders, allergies, kidney damage, high blood pressure, and many other malfunctions in the individual. Stephen believed that several puzzling physical ailments experienced by his parents were influenced by the stress in their lives. Some years ago these problems were called *psychosomatic disorders,* for they involved psychological influences on the body, or *soma,* but this term was misunderstood. People erroneously decided that there was no bodily problem in a psychosomatic reaction. Today when physical illness or disease is caused or increased by psychological stress, the reaction is known as a **psychophysiological disorder.**

The first clear evidence that ulcers in human beings can be influenced by emotional stress came from observations of a man whose stomach was partially exposed because of injury. While it was being repaired through surgery, it was possible to observe the gastric activities directly and to collect samples of the stomach's contents. When the subject was under stress, his stomach became red and turgid and the production of acid increased sharply. This sequence of events seemed to illustrate the origin of peptic ulcers in human beings (Wolf & Wolff, 1943; Figure 11–12).

Earlier, we noted the relationship between the type A personality and vulnerability to coronary heart disease. The **type A personality** is character-

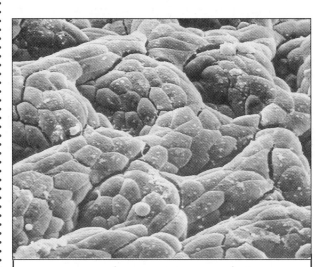

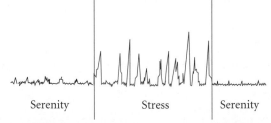

Serenity   Stress   Serenity

FIGURE 11–12 EMOTION AND THE STOMACH. The photo shows the lining of the stomach enlarged 500 diameters. During a period of stress, the patient's stomach activities increased markedly. Amid this overactivity, the stomach tried to digest itself, resulting in hemorrhaging and perforation of ulcers (Wolf & Wolff, 1943; Davenport, 1972).

ized by a sense of urgency, time pressure, and often hostility. Over a period of eight years, the Framingham Heart Study, in Massachusetts, examined more than 1,500 adults classified as type A or as *type B personality,* more relaxed and dispassionate. The incidence of heart disease among type A men was found to be almost triple the incidence among type B men. Among women, the incidence was twice as high for the type A personality (Haynes, Feinleib, & Kannel, 1980).

Related studies have shown the role of extended stress in infectious diseases (Barker, 1987), heart disorders (Taylor, 1991), asthma and arthritis (Friedman & Booth-Kewley, 1987), and even the common cold. In the last study, approximately 400 subjects were administered a cold virus and then, during a seven-day quarantine, they were assessed for cold symptoms. It was discovered that subjects experiencing high levels of stress displayed a rate of cold symptoms twice that of subjects experiencing low levels of stress (Cohen, Tyrrell, & Smith, 1991).

COPING WITH STRESS

Whatever the problem and the physical reaction to it, the individual usually has available a variety of potential coping responses. These have been depicted in several categories, based on the reports of many people coping with stressful events over a period of several weeks (Stone & Neale, 1984). They can be usefully considered with respect to the stressor, stress reaction, and outside assistance.

DEALING WITH THE STRESSOR. In approaching any stressful situation, the first task is to identify the source of the problem. If the problem can be resolved, then the action should deal with the **stressor,** the event in the environment most directly responsible for

the stress. After the wedding, Dawn took direct action against an event that could be changed. She asked her mother to stop calling her with problems, making it quite clear that she had new priorities and that Stephen was at the top of the list. "I have my own family now," she said, and her mother responded with silence (Goethals & Klos, 1976).

Sometimes the problem cannot be resolved directly or the cost is too great. Then the best plan may involve a less direct approach. Two such strategies, at times quite effective, include reframing and distraction. In **reframing,** the person thinks about the problem in a new way, viewing it as more tolerable, as a temporary disruption, or perhaps even as a good learning experience. Also known as *restructuring,* the procedure basically involves a transformation of meaning (Bandler & Grinder, 1982).

In counseling situations, reframing has been used with all sorts of personal problems, including divorce. For women in midlife, divorce can mean the loss of social contacts, a small remarriage pool, and possibly discriminatory practices in the labor market, as well as the stresses of aging. In the reframing technique, divorced people are encouraged to regard the experience differently—as an opportunity for growth, independence, and perhaps renewed contacts with their adult children (Bogolub, 1991). Evidence for the beneficial effects of positive thinking has been mounting steadily. A hopeful outlook is good for people (Scheier & Carver, 1993).

The other strategy, **distraction,** focuses attention on some other activity instead. It is commonly useful with children, for they have a short attention span and therefore are readily distracted.

Following the stress of the wedding, Dawn and Stephen left for the seashore and found themselves booked with a middle-aged tour group with whom they were not compatible. They solved the problem by reframing. After all, they *were* at the beach and Dawn's mother had paid for the trip. They also used distraction, making friends with a couple on the islands—who gave Dawn the feeling that a responsive, open-minded marriage was possible.

Another prominent method, hardly a coping strategy, is to accept the situation. In fact, the survey on coping with stress showed acceptance to be the second-most common coping response. Here the individual takes no significant action, direct or indirect, to decrease the stress. Presumably, it seems that nothing can be done, that no action is worth the effort, or that any action would only make matters worse.

After the honeymoon, Stephen went looking for work and found it impossible to obtain any respectable job. "So I turned my sights toward the less respectable," he reported, and his new boss precipitated another problem. The man phoned Dawn and invited her to dinner—secretly. When Stephen found out, he made no secret of his displeasure. "We never got along very well after that," he confided about his boss. But he accepted the situation, working every day for an employer he actively disliked (Goethals & Klos, 1976).

MODIFYING THE STRESS REACTION.

Other approaches involve the physical dimension, rather than the cognitive, and the focus is on the stress reaction, not the stressor. The aim here is to reduce bodily tension which, if chronic, might lead to ulcers, backache, or other psychophysiological disorders. Now widely recognized, these methods include biofeedback and meditation, discussed in earlier chapters, and also systematic desensitization, considered later in the context of therapy.

In addition, modern *relaxation techniques* include methods for control of breathing, muscle relaxation, and visualization. Some people employ this method before going to work or even on the job, using long, slow exhalations, progressively relaxing the muscles from head to toe, and imagining themselves in a green forest or beside a gentle stream, warm and quiet. At the other end of the continuum, vigorous *physical exercise* includes running, aerobics, weight training, and other activities. Among people experiencing stress and then assigned to various exercise programs, including a no-exercise condition, numerous studies show the value of physical exercise for reducing the stress reaction (Folkins & Sime, 1981).

SEEKING OUTSIDE ASSISTANCE.

Eventually, like all couples, Dawn and Stephen began to experience some problems with each other. She decided that Stephen's interest in sex had diminished distinctly during the summer. "A point of great delicacy between us," she noted. She tried not to be demanding, but her requests made them both uneasy.

Stephen quit his job in September, pleased to be finished, but then there were school problems. By this time his "lazy way of life," as he called it, apparently had exerted an undesirable effect on Dawn, diminishing her sense of control and energy. She found herself unable to work around the house and lost a writing routine that previously had produced publishable poetry and prose (Goethals & Klos, 1976).

In coping with these problems, the couple might have sought outside assistance—specifically *support from friends or peers,* obtaining advice or encouragement. As an alternative, they might have sought *support from experts,* consulting a marriage counselor, career counselor, or other professional person. Rejecting both approaches, they might have done nothing significant and the problems might have diminished or vanished. Problems sometimes disappear as spontaneously as they have arisen.

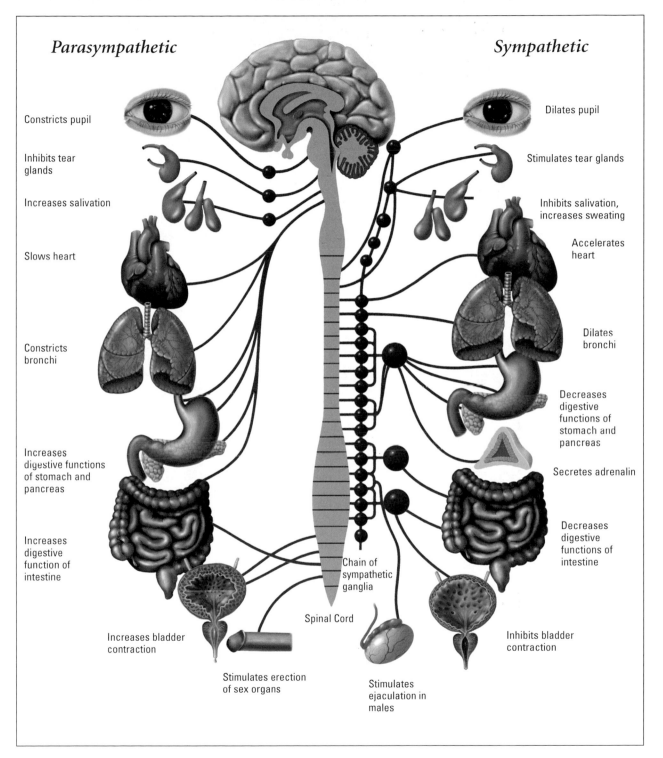

FIGURE XI.1 SYMPATHETIC AND PARASYMPATHETIC SYSTEMS. As shown, the sympathetic and parasympathetic systems may influence the same organs, but they do so in different ways. The sympathetic system serves for the release of energy; the parasympathetic serves for its restoration.

FIGURE XI.2 USE OF THE POLYGRAPH. The examination begins with neutral questions, establishing the individual's general level of arousal. Then critical questions are intermittently included, and the examiner searches for sudden changes in the person's physiological reactions. Even with current safeguards, this procedure is not highly reliable (Lykken, 1991).

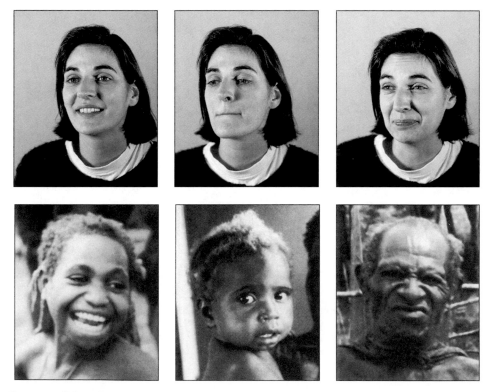

FIGURE XI.3 FEELINGS AND FACIAL EXPRESSIONS. In most cases, the pleasant-unpleasant dimension is readily discernible. It is more difficult to determine which photographs show fear, happiness, and disgust. Try to do so with these photos. Answers: for the woman, these reactions were elicited by the arrival of a friend, a sharp reprimand, and a raw egg dropped in her hand. For the man and boys, they were elicited a friend, by a stranger from another culture, and the sight of someone eating canned food, respectively (Ekman, 1980).

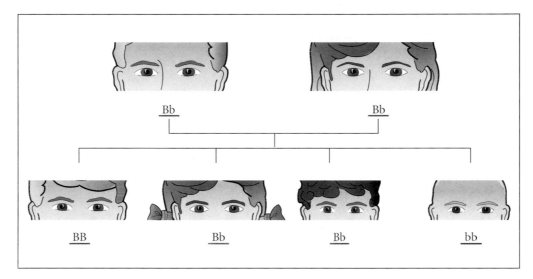

FIGURE **XII.1** DOMINANT AND RECESSIVE GENES. The child receives one member of each pair of genes from each parent. With these parents, brown eyes will be more prevalent than blue because *B* is dominant over *b*. In this case, the ratio is 3:1. While this example illustrates the transmission process, physical and behavioral traits typically are determined in a far more complex manner.

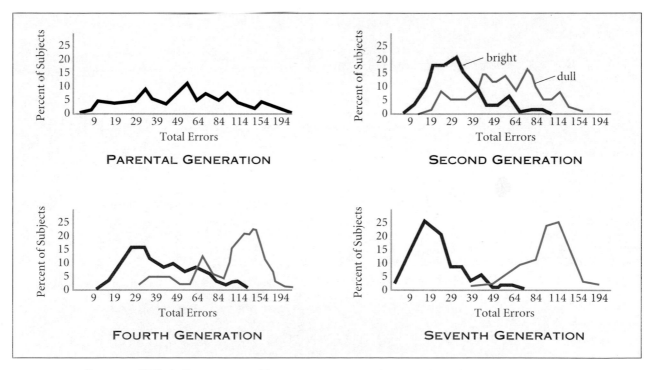

FIGURE **XII.2** POLYGENIC TRAIT. Beginning with a normal population, shown in black, the brightest rats were bred with the brightest rats and the dullest with the dullest rats. In the second generation, two separate groups began to appear, shown in red and green. By the seventh generation, the difference in error scores between the bright-bred and dull-bred groups was indeed marked (Tryon, 1940).

THREE-MONTH-OLD FETUS

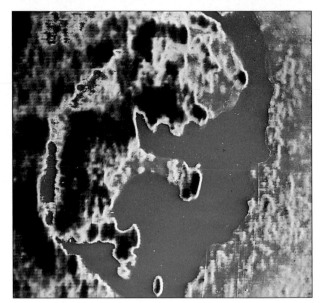

THREE-MONTH-OLD FETUS

FOUR-MONTH-OLD FETUS

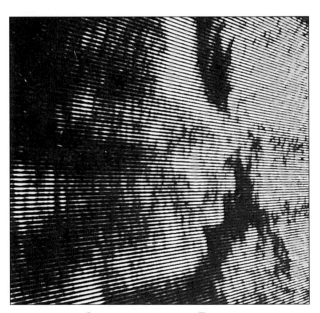

SIX-MONTH-OLD FETUS

FIGURE XII.3 THE HUMAN FETUS. In the upper row, on the left, a three-month-old fetus is shown from above by using a very fine, plastic viewing fiber; on the right, it is shown from the side in an ultrasound image. In the lower row, a four-month-old fetus is seen from above through fiberoptics; a six-month-old fetus is seen from the side by ultrasound.

Instead, they wrote about their problems, each composing an autobiography during their senior year. Writing these reports may have been therapeutic—a way of coping. They were published under the title *Experiencing Youth: First-Person Accounts* (Goethals & Klos, 1976).

IN PERSPECTIVE. These methods of coping with stress are often combined. In dealing with school, Stephen used family support, obtaining assistance from his new wife, as well as a tutor, and reframing, comparing school with his summer job, which left him working for a disagreeable boss with questionable ethics. He *could* have taken direct action by going to the library a few hours each day.

For both Dawn and Stephen, relaxation became most important. "Laughing is what makes us happy," said Stephen. "We are incredibly foolish with each other" (Goethals & Klos, 1976).

Looking at her new life, Dawn felt optimistic. "It makes me feel very lucky," she said. Perhaps she was thinking about how much she had changed since the time of her resolution in high school—to marry only for comfort and money.

Amid this optimism, certain facts must be recognized. Dawn was the daughter of separated parents, Stephen the son of divorced parents. Dawn and Stephen both experienced considerable family strife during their childhoods, and they married immediately after adolescence. People coming from these circumstances—family strife in childhood, parental unions terminated by law or choice, and youthful marriages of their own—tend to become divorced or separated themselves (Amato & Keith, 1991).

We know nothing more of Dawn and Stephen. Their separate autobiographies conclude at this point, leaving the reader to decide whether they reached the next phase of their relationship—the stage of companionate love.

• SUMMARY •

COMPONENTS OF EMOTION

1. The basic components of emotion are feelings, physiological reactions, behavior, and cognitive factors. For the individual, the most obvious aspect of emotion is the feeling. According to opponent-process theory, the onset of a positive or negative feeling automatically sets in motion the opposite feeling before there is a return to the normal state.

2. The physiological components of emotion include widespread excitatory and inhibitory reactions that occur through stimulation of the hypothalamus and cerebral cortex in the central nervous system and subsequent arousal of the sympathetic division of the autonomic nervous system. There has been some success in differentiating feelings on the basis of physiological reactions alone.

3. Emotional experience in others is most evident in the behavioral component. Efforts to identify feelings through behavior, focusing on facial expression and postural-gestural reactions, have indicated similarities and differences across cultures.

4. In emotion, the role of cognition is most widely debated. According to some experts, an emotional reaction cannot occur without some appraisal of the situation. According to others, an evaluation of the situation may produce an emotional state, but it is not a necessary component of emotion.

THEORIES OF EMOTION

5. The James-Lange theory states that feelings are the result of bodily responses and behavior. The Cannon-Bard theory emphasizes the role of lower brain centers, especially the thalamus, which activates the various dimensions of emotion simultaneously.

6. According to the arousal-cognition view, also called two-factor theory, physiological changes determine the strength of the feelings, and our interpretation of the circumstances determines what kinds of feelings we experience.

LIKING AND LOVING

7. The reinforcement principle, in operant conditioning, states that a relationship is maintained if it leads to positive outcomes for both parties. According to exchange theory, maintaining a relationship depends on achieving a gain greater than the overall expense. According to equity theory, the partners maintain the relationship if they feel they are deriving from it what they merit or deserve.

8. Compared to liking, love is more intense and appears in two basic forms. Passionate or romantic love often involves fantasy, is likely to be negative as well as positive, grows weaker with the passage of time, and includes sexual involvement. Companionate love is affection among people whose lives are deeply intertwined; it is friendlier, less intense, and more stable than passionate love.

9. The basic physiological changes in sexual behavior in males and females include vasocongestion, which is dilation of the blood vessels, and myotonia, which involves muscle contractions throughout the body. The associated psychological processes in both sexes occur in four stages: excitement, plateau, orgasm, and resolution.

10. Sexual behavior among human beings is significantly influenced by learning. The origins of sexual orientation, toward a homosexual or heterosexual preference, are still unknown, but there is potential evidence for both biological and social factors.

ANGER AND AGGRESSION

11. Aggression has been considered by some experts as universal among human beings. This view arises chiefly from research on aggressiveness in the animal kingdom and from psychoanalysis, which postulates a human predisposition for destructive tendencies. According to another view, the environment plays a crucial role, providing opportunities for learning aggressive or peaceful behavior.

12. The catharsis hypothesis, that the expression of anger reduces the underlying drive, has not been impressively supported. The frustration-aggression hypothesis, in revised form, states that frustration leads to a readiness to behave aggressively. The cultural hypothesis states that different cultures can mold people into aggressive, aggression-prone, or peaceful peoples.

STRESS IN DAILY LIFE

13. Stress is produced by life events, positive and negative, requiring readjustment. These events have different meanings for different individuals, and therefore subcultural and individual norms must be considered. There are three general types of conflicts: approach-approach, avoidance-avoidance and approach-avoidance.

14. The general adaptation syndrome, a pattern of symptoms in response to chronic stress, is characterized by three broad phases: the alarm reaction, resistance, and exhaustion. These processes also may contribute to psychophysiological disorders.

15. In managing stress, if the problem cannot be solved directly or if the cost is too great, then indirect coping strategies may be useful: reframing, distraction, relaxation, exercise, and outside assistance.

❧ REVIEW OF KEY CONCEPTS ❧

Components of Emotion
  emotion
  anxiety
  opponent-process theory
  hypothalamus
  cerebral cortex
  amygdala
  autonomic nervous system
  sympathetic nervous system
  parasympathetic nervous system
  electroencephalogram (EEG)
  electrocardiogram (EKG)
  galvanic skin response (GSR)
  polygraph
  arousal level
  Yerkes-Dodson law

Theories of Emotion
  James-Lange theory
  Cannon-Bard theory

arousal-cognition theory

Liking and Loving
  triangular theory of love
  reinforcement principle
  exchange theory
  equity theory
  passionate love
  companionate love
  vasocongestion
  myotonia
  sensate focus
  fetishism

Anger and Aggression
  anger
  aggression
  life instinct
  death instinct
  rape

catharsis hypothesis
frustration-aggression hypothesis

Stress in Daily Life
stress
conflict
approach-approach conflict
avoidance-avoidance conflict
approach-avoidance conflict
general adaptation syndrome
alarm reaction
resistance
exhaustion
eustress
psychophysiological disorder
type A personality
stressor
reframing
distraction

❧ CLASS DISCUSSION/CRITICAL THINKING ❧

A NARRATIVE TWIST

Consider the relationship between Dawn and Stephen from a social assessment perspective. Stephen embraced a religion different from Dawn's and, while she achieved academic success easily, he was doing poorly in school. From Dawn's viewpoint, were these characteristics of Stephen costs or benefits for her? Argue both sides of the case. Imagine that Stephen became a prominent political figure on the campus. Would this development have been a cost or benefit, or both, for Dawn? Why? ❧

TOPICAL QUESTIONS

• *Components of Emotion.* Does identifying the components of emotion through modern research diminish romance today? Or does it incite romance by teaching people what they are feeling and how to manage their feelings? Explain.
• *Theories of Emotion.* Using the arousal-cognition theory, explain one onlooker's rescue of a child from a burning building and another onlooker's immobility at the scene. Compare them in terms of both arousal and cognition.
• *Liking and Loving.* You must choose whether to live on an island

where there is only passionate love or only companionate love. Which would you select? Why? What personal consequences does your choice involve? How would you compensate for unfilled needs?
• *Anger and Aggression.* What would you do to reduce aggressive behavior in prisons?
• *Stress in Daily Life.* To what degree is our culture responsible for our personal level of stress? Would changes in American society significantly alleviate your own stress? Is stress largely a matter of the ways in which you think about things? Present your view.

Physiological mechanisms in emotional arousal and relaxation are discussed in the context of the biological bases of behavior (3). In psychoanalytic theory, aggression is an expression of the id (14). Violence on television is an issue in observational learning (7).

PATTERNS OF GROWTH

HUMAN DEVELOPMENT

INTELLIGENCE AND TESTING

DEVELOPMENTAL ISSUES

AT CONCEPTION
Determiners of Heredity
Genetic Processes

PRENATAL PHASE AND INFANCY
Early Neural Growth
Sensorimotor Development
Social-Emotional Development

CHILDHOOD AND ADOLESCENCE
Physical Development
Cognitive Development
Moral Development
Social Development

ADULTHOOD AND OLD AGE
Physical Changes
Cognitive Abilities
Social Relations

INDIVIDUAL DIFFERENCES

12

HUMAN DEVELOPMENT

THE PLAINS OF IOWA WERE SPARED THE BATTLES OF OUR CIVIL WAR, BUT A CLUSTER OF BUILDINGS REMAINED AS A MONUMENT TO THAT GREAT STRUGgle. By the 1930s, the hospital and barracks were housing instead a small army of children, residents of the Iowa Soldiers' Orphans' Home. Neglected or rejected by their next of kin, they were wards of the state.

The Home from the outside had a deserted look because the children were rarely allowed outdoors for unrestricted play. Instead, they spent most of the time inside, a procedure that facilitated their care. The infants lived together in the nursery, little girls in one dormitory, little boys in another, the older girls in a cottage, and so forth. These confinements further simplified the management of these bereaved little citizens.

C.D., a baby of 13 months, lay inert most of the time. She did not even try to pull herself into an upright position in her crib. She showed no interest in playthings and uttered few spontaneous sounds. Her little neighbor, B.D., three months older, also ignored the few toys in the nursery, and she too lay mute or cried, without babbling. In short, both babies appeared to be retarded.

Neither infant came from a promising background. The mother in both cases was reportedly retarded, and there was no information on the father. Examinations by a psychologist, pediatrician, and nurses made dire predictions. "C.D. will be unable to make her way outside the care and protection offered by an institution." For B.D., the prognosis was equally unfavorable (Skeels & Dye, 1939).

Indeed, for these children, life's prospects were dim. If they could leave, where would they go?

At this time, the Iowa Board of Control of State Institutions had just introduced new psychological services. For this purpose, the Board appointed to its first position Harold M. Skeels, who was recently finished with his clinical training. Skeels' work at this orphanage tells a remarkable story, for it includes much of the life span and shows how these little girls led psychologists to a new view of human development.

The study of **human development** concerns the ways in which people change as they grow older. It emphasizes the patterns that occur for most people throughout the life span. In this chapter, after a brief consideration of developmental issues and hereditary influences at conception, we progress to each of the major life stages—the prenatal phase and infancy, childhood and adolescence, adulthood and old age. The chapter concludes with a comment on individual differences.

In approaching these stages, William Shakespeare's celebrated description is helpful. It begins:

> *At first the infant,*
> *Mewling and puking in the nurse's arms.*
> *And then the whining school-boy, with his satchel*
> *And shining morning face, creeping like snail*
> *Unwillingly to school. And then the lover,*
> *Sighing like a furnace, with a woeful ballad*
> *Made to his mistress' eyebrow. . . .*
> —*As You Like It*, 2:7

These words illustrate an important procedural question: Should our discussion proceed chronologically, from infancy to childhood, then adolescence, and so forth, as Shakespeare suggests? Or should it proceed topically, focusing on physical, cognitive, and then social development, the chief topics in human development today? Grounds for the latter approach are also evident in Shakespeare's words: The infant, mewling and puking, demonstrates physical development; the whining schoolboy, creeping like a snail to school, is en route to further cognitive development; and the lover, sighing unto his mistress' eyebrow, certainly displays social and emotional development. In fact, all three areas of development occur at *all* chronological stages (Table 12–1).

Both approaches are used here. The chronological approach forms the basic structure, as revealed in the chapter outline, which begins with conception and continues through old age. Within each chronological stage, the discussion proceeds essentially from physical to cognitive and then to social development.

• DEVELOPMENTAL ISSUES •

At the outset, however, certain developmental issues deserve our attention. Emerging in many areas of human development, they have precipitated considerable research and theory in the field.

The first issue concerns the **critical period,** a brief interval in the life span during which the individual is unusually responsive to certain forms of stimulation. The question here is not whether such periods exist but rather for which areas of development, and when, and how long, and with what outcomes? It is quite clear, for example, that ingestion of certain drugs during a woman's first weeks of pregnancy can damage the brain and heart of the unborn child. For the use of drugs, these early weeks are a critical period. Ingestion of the same drugs at the end of the pregnancy will have a lesser effect (Overholser, 1990).

In contrast, the importance of cognitive and social stimulation for the infant is widely debated, prompted in part by the story of the orphans in Iowa. If an environment is negative, does it create irreversible cognitive damage? Research in language acquisition suggests that there may be a critical period for this task, after which language cannot be readily or normally mastered (Curtiss, 1977; Itard, 1807).

Many experts consider adolescence a critical period in human development, especially for sexual stimulation. The individual may become almost irreversibly attached to some other person or event, even by chance. According to some, the roots of impotence, cross-dressing, and sexual fixations have been traced to this period (Money, 1986). For others, the significance of adolescence is overestimated. The instability is not as universal and the period not as critical as popular accounts suggest (Galambos, 1992). In any case, the question of critical periods extends from conception through the adolescent years.

A second issue, with a long history in psychology, concerns the roles of heredity and environ-

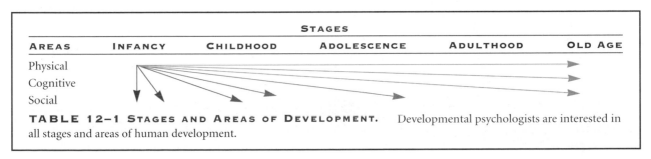

	STAGES				
AREAS	INFANCY	CHILDHOOD	ADOLESCENCE	ADULTHOOD	OLD AGE
Physical					
Cognitive					
Social					

TABLE 12–1 STAGES AND AREAS OF DEVELOPMENT. Developmental psychologists are interested in all stages and areas of human development.

ment in human development. Called the **heredity–environment issue,** it arises over the relative contributions of each set of factors, inborn and acquired, in the different spheres of human development. Years ago, when C.D. and B.D. were living in the orphanage, the usual answer cited heredity, and these children seemed to be retarded on that basis. Today we recognize that both factors are always present and contribute in complex ways to human development (Figure 12–1). Also known as the *nature–nurture issue,* this controversy has been lengthy and vigorous (Mealey, 1990; Rushton, 1991).

Nature has provided some help in assessing these influences. Pairs of **identical twins,** who develop from a single fertilized ovum and therefore have exactly the same heredity, sometimes have been adopted into different homes. In a collection of extensive searches in Europe and North America, such twins were brought together and compared. They were found to be much more alike in physical characteristics and appearance than were comparable pairs of **fraternal twins,** who share no more inheritance than other brothers and sisters. In height, the identical twins showed a close resemblance (Erlenmeyer-Kimling & Jarvik, 1963). In intelligence there was an average difference in IQ of about 8 points, but an important factor here is

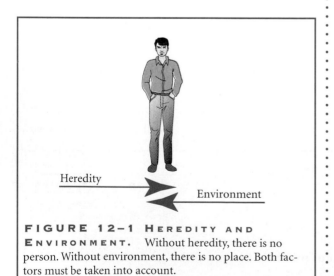

FIGURE 12–1 HEREDITY AND ENVIRONMENT. Without heredity, there is no person. Without environment, there is no place. Both factors must be taken into account.

whether the twins had received comparable schooling. Differences in educational opportunity can produce significant differences in intelligence (Anastasi, 1988). Finally, in personality traits, the separately reared identical twins were sometimes similar and sometimes as different as fraternal twins (Gottesman, 1963; Newman, Freeman, & Holzinger, 1937).

These findings permit some generalizations about the relative influence of heredity and environment, provided that we ignore extreme circumstances. Environmental factors influence physical appearance, but they are comparatively more influential in cognitive and social development, in which one's parents, friends, and cultural milieu play decisive roles. The opposite statement might be made for heredity. Under normal conditions, heredity is highly influential in physique and less influential but certainly still important in cognitive and social development.

One ongoing study, known as the *Minnesota Twin Study,* has involved 402 sets of twins, identical and fraternal, reared together or apart. The debate continues, for recent results suggested that about 50% of personality diversity is attributable to genetic factors, an estimate considerably higher than that expected by many psychologists (Tellegen, Lykken, Bouchard, Wilcox, Segal, & Rich, 1988).

Through such investigations, it has become apparent that the heredity–environment debate is not an either-or issue. The result of any given inherited potential inevitably depends on the environment and vice versa, a condition known as the **interaction principle.** The current concern is with the relationships between these two sets of factors, an interplay of forces that can be extremely complex and intermixed (Magnusson & Törestad, 1993; Scarr, Weinberg, & Levine, 1986).

The interaction principle has been most clearly demonstrated in laboratory manipulations with animals. In one instance, newborn rats selectively bred for brightness or dullness were maintained for forty days in one of three environments: restricted, neutral, or enriched. Later, they were tested for learning ability. It was found that the bright and dull groups differed by fewer than nine points when they came from either the restricted or enriched environment. However, there was a difference of 47 points between the bright and dull groups from the neutral environment. Heredity had a marked influence in that setting but not in the others (Cooper & Zubek, 1958; Figure 12–2).

This same principle applies to other species. In the production of beef, Galloway cattle fare better than Aberdeen Angus in poor grazing areas, but Angus produce more beef in good grazing areas (Haldane, 1946). Whether the Galloway or Aberdeen Angus cattle have the more favorable heredity for beef production depends on the area in which they are grazing—that is, on the environment. Among African cichlids, heredity enables a male fish to defeat the others in combat. It thereby gains ascendancy in its enviroment. Then, *after it* attains the dominant position in this particular setting, it shows rapid growth of brain cells and gonads. In other words, the environment then influ-

ences its physical development. (Davis & Fernald, 1990). Once again, heredity and environment are intricately connected in a feedback system in which they influence one another.

Similarly, a human being does not inherit a specific behavioral trait but rather a tendency or predisposition that becomes manifest in one way in one situation, differently in another, and perhaps remains latent in a third. Except in highly unusual instances, neither heredity nor environment is omnipotent (Plomin & Rende, 1991).

Like the rest of us, the development of the Iowa orphans was influenced by both heredity and environment, inevitably in interaction. On the hereditary side, they and we began life in a very small way, as a single cell. The fertilized cell, resulting from the union of the father's sperm and the mother's egg, is but half the size of the dot over this *i*, and yet *all* the inborn influences on our physical, mental, and even social development are set at this miraculous moment of conception.

❧

DETERMINERS OF HEREDITY

Within the fertilized cell, complex organizations of chemical materials called **chromosomes** carry the information about an individual's inheritance. They received this name because they were first seen by scientists as colored strands. Microscopic studies have shown that there are 46 chromosomes in every human cell, and on the basis of size and form, they can be arranged into 23 pairs.

One pair consists of the sex chromosomes, and one member of this pair, *X* or *Y*, results in the development of a male or female. The male receives an *X* from the mother and a *Y* from the father, resulting in *XY*. The female receives an *X* from each parent. Therefore, the orphan girls, like all girls, had

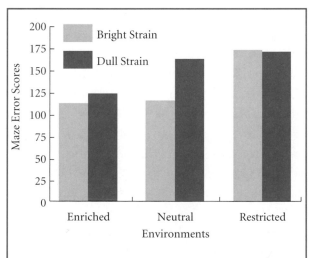

FIGURE 12–2 INTERACTION EFFECT. Maze learning by rats showed the influences of heredity only in a neutral environment. They were obscured by environmental influences in the highly restricted and enriched conditions (Pettigrew, 1964).

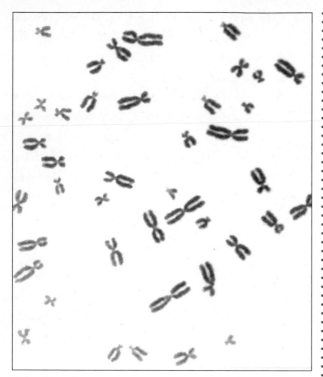

FIGURE 12–3 HUMAN CHROMOSOMES. Chromosomes are not located in pairs, side by side. Rather, each chromosome can be matched to another according to size and structure.

an *XX* combination (Figure 12–3).

Within the chromosomes are the fundamental determiners of heredity, called **genes,** which contain the basic hereditary blueprint, specifically directing the development of most physical characteristics and certain behavioral traits. The numbers of genes is still a matter of guesswork, with estimates varying from 1,000 to 100,000 per chromosome. In a series of continuing studies, it has been discovered that *deoxyribonucleic acid* (DNA) is the basic genetic substance of all kinds of living organisms, including human beings. All genes are comprised of DNA molecules. The structure of this molecule has been established and it is possible to study genes at the molecular level.

Whenever a cell divides, its chromosomes and their thousands of genes are duplicated. As the cells multiply, the complete genetic code is passed on to each of the resulting cells, giving all cells except the reproductive cells an identical inheritance.

Beginning at puberty, the reproductive cells, the **sperm** cells in the male and the **ova,** or egg cells, in the female, undergo a division different from that just described. As they split and become duplicated, they receive *only one member of each pair* of chromosomes. Ova receive half of the female's chromosomes; sperm receive half of the male's chromosomes. Different ova produced by the same individual receive different chromosomes, and the same is true for sperm.

Thus, there are millions of possible combinations of chromosomes among the reproductive cells of any one female. There are also millions of possible combinations in the male. Taken together, the potentially different inheritances for any given individual, with chromosomes from the male *and* female, rise into the billions. They become even higher when, during the cell division process, chromosomes occasionally split apart, and a segment of one chromosome is exchanged with a segment of another split chromosome.

&

GENETIC PROCESSES

By inheriting pairs of chromosomes, human beings also inherit pairs of genes, again one member of each pair from each parent. These genes may be dominant or recessive for any given trait. A **dominant gene** takes precedence over the other member of the pair. It is expressed when two members of a gene pair are alike *or* different. A **recessive gene,** in contrast, is influential only when it is paired with another recessive gene of the same type. Otherwise, it has no influence.

These conditions are readily illustrated in the determination of eye color. For example, one of the orphan children had brown eyes and, because genes come in pairs, let us refer to these genes as *BB*. The capital *B* is used because the gene for brown eyes is dominant. Another child might have had *Bb;* if so, she also would have had brown eyes because of the dominant *B.* The lowercase *b* denotes the gene for blue eyes, a recessive gene. It will not exhibit any effect unless it appears with another recessive gene for this trait.

If someone with *BB* marries someone with *bb*, all of the offspring will be brown-eyed, *Bb*, receiving one gene from each parent. But if both parents are *Bb*, in a sufficiently large sample three-fourths will be brown-eyed, as *BB* or *Bb*, and only one-fourth blue-eyed, as *bb* (Figure XII.I, Color).

Today it is understood that few human characteristics are controlled by a single-gene pair. One exception is Huntington's chorea, an inherited nervous condition with involuntary twitching and convulsions, as well as mental deterioration. In this case the *H* or abnormal gene is dominant, and the *h* for the normal condition is recessive. A union of *Hh* parents would produce the same distribution seen for *Bb* parents, and the offspring would have a 75% chance of manifesting the disease, but fortunately this dominant gene is rare.

POLYGENIC TRAITS. Most human characteristics show countless differences. Therefore they are thought to be influenced by multiple pairs of genes with *no* dominance. Whenever any characteristic appears in varying degrees or forms, such as physique or intelligence, it is known as a **polygenic trait,** meaning that it has been influenced by multiple pairs of genes.

Human subjects cannot be bred in accordance with scientific research. Thus, investigators often use animals to study the ways in which multiple pairs of genes seem to operate. In one instance 142 rats were tested for their capacity to learn a maze. The differences were remarkable. For example, one rat made only 5 errors and another made 214 before learning the maze. Those rats making few errors were designated bright, and those making many errors were designated dull. Keeping the environment constant, the investigator then mated the brightest rats in each generation with one another. He also mated the dullest rats in each generation

with one another. At first, in the early generations, there was not much difference between the offspring in the two groups, suggesting that maze learning is not controlled by a single dominant gene. If a single gene had been dominant, a more pronounced difference in learning would have appeared in the first generations. Instead, seven generations were required before two distinct types of rats—maze-bright and maze-dull—were produced by this process of selective breeding (Tryon, 1940; Figure XII.2).

The genetic backgrounds of human beings cannot be manipulated in this manner, but sometimes hereditary influences appear overwhelming anyway. For example, there seemed little doubt about the inheritance of the two little girls at the orphanage. Weak and frail, clearly slow in development, C.D. and B.D. spent their days rocking and whining, although no organic problem could be identified.

By chance, when Harold Skeels went to the orphanage to offer psychological services in 1932, he observed them on one of his early visits. At 13 and 16 months of age, they should have been in the dormitories with the other children. Skeels could not help but notice their physical and mental retardation. They behaved more like the newborn babies in the cribs, making almost no effort to play with anything or anyone. He called them "pitiful little creatures" (Skeels & Dye, 1939).

BEHAVIORAL GENETICS. At both the animal and human levels, a field of study called **behavioral genetics** aims to discover the hereditary foundations of the ways organisms respond in their environment. This research is often misunderstood, for it has the capacity to demonstrate not only genetic but also environmental influences on behavior, depending on the design of the research (Plomin & Neiderhiser, 1992; Rose, 1995).

In behavioral genetics, an individual's full genetic makeup can only be assumed. Thus, the sets of genes assumed to underlie any given trait are referred to as the **genotype.** For blue eyes, the genotype is *bb*, referring to the postulated genetic structure. The observable trait, blue eyes, is the **phenotype,** derived from the stem *pheno*, meaning "showing" or "displaying." The phenotype is blue eyes; the genotype is *bb*.

With animals, research may begin with the phenotype, or performance, as just illustrated with maze learning among rats. Those that were most successful were mated with one another, as were those least successful. For research beginning instead with the genotype, males and females from the *same* litter are mated over and over for many generations, producing a *pure* strain, meaning that the animals have essentially the same genetic background. Then, when two or more different inbred strains are exposed to the same environment, any difference in behavior between them can be attributed to the difference in genetic makeup.

At the human level, the obvious control for genetic makeup involves members of pairs of identical twins. In later chapters, on intelligence and adjustment disorders, we shall consider the merits of such studies.

• PRENATAL PHASE AND INFANCY •

One principle of development applies even before birth. Called **differentiation,** it states that human development proceeds from simple to complex and from the general to the specific. In biology, this process refers to the steady development of many specialized organs, emerging out of an originally undifferentiated mass of tissue. In psychology, it indicates that our behavior becomes increasingly specific and complex as we progress from infancy to adulthood. Our use of the hands, acquisition of language, expression of feelings, and virtually all other human capacities develop in this way, from a generalized response to highly specific reactions.

EARLY NEURAL GROWTH

Expressed as stages, the prenatal changes appear in three periods. The period of the fertilized ovum, or **zygote,** lasts for about ten days after conception, characterized by rapid cell division. The period of the **embryo,** from the second week to the end of the second month, is marked by the beginning of the heartbeat at three weeks and by some developing sensory and motor mechanisms, such as the eyes, hands, and feet. And finally, beginning at the third month and extending until birth, the period of the **fetus** shows all sorts of dramatic developments, including the bulk of neuronal development, between 10 and 20 weeks, and the first sensitivity to stimulation, which occurs in the head region (Figure XII.3).

Researchers in neurology study malformations in the nervous system during these periods, arising from many sources. Collectively, these sources are called **teratogens,** meaning environmental or chemical factors that disrupt normal development, producing birth defects. In a pregnant woman, the disease known as *rubella*, a form of measles, is a teratogen. It can cause retardation and deafness in the offspring. Alcohol consumption can cause growth deficiencies and mental retardation, a condition known as *fetal alcohol syndrome* (Overholser, 1990). Even maternal malnutrition has detrimental effects, producing babies more susceptible to diseases. Teratogens, moreover, are most influential during embryonic and early fetal development, rather than just before birth. These first weeks are therefore a critical period.

No significant teratogens occurred in the prenatal life of the two orphan girls, as far as we know. No birth injuries or glandular dysfunctions were observed. Their retardation could not be explained on these bases.

The transition from the human womb to our immeasurably complex outside world has been called the *birth trauma*. The newborn is suddenly confronted with diverse social and nonsocial stimuli. Its sensory and motor immaturity and the absence of relevant past experience render it relatively unresponsive at first, making the transition easier.

At birth, the individual begins *infancy*, a term derived from Latin, referring to the first one or two years of postnatal human life. Literally, it means "unable to speak."

At this point the infant's brain is only about one-fourth of its adult size, but it soon increases enormously in complexity and interconnections. Six months later, the brain achieves half of its full size.

Initially, the areas below the brain's surface, or cortex, control most of the infant's reactions. These subcortical structures are most important in automatic responses, such as breathing and reflexes. The grasping reflex of the newborn infant is well known. When stimulated in the palm, the infant involuntarily makes a fist, grasping the stimulating object. About a month after birth, this reflex disappears, and then it returns three or four months later. It is speculated that this dormant interval, which occurs in other reflexes as well, allows time for development of the neural structures underlying voluntary responses.

SENSORIMOTOR DEVELOPMENT

At the Orphans' Home, all newborn babies lived in the nursery, sleeping in individual cribs without toys or mobiles. Instead, they gazed at protective coverings on the sides of the cribs. Later, they were moved to small dormitories, where two caretakers cleaned, fed, and clothed them.

In newborn babies, it is not possible to identify physical, cognitive, and social developments as distinct from one another because differentiation has not proceeded to this point. These functions have not yet emerged as separate entities. Hence, rather than speaking of physical development, the focus in the prior discussion was on the development of the nervous system, which underlies *all* behavior and

experience. Similarly, in the following discussion we are concerned with sensory and motor development, for the infant's capacities have not yet developed to the point where we can speak easily of cognition—apart from sensory and motor ability. In fact, to measure the cognitive ability of C.D. and B.D., we would measure vision, hearing, general activity, and so forth, for these are the means by which an infant eventually becomes intelligent about its environment.

When psychologist Harold Skeels assessed the mental development of these two orphans, C.D. demonstrated an IQ of 46 and B.D. an IQ of 35. It seemed that B.D., under optimal circumstances, might have performed up to 10 points higher. At these young ages, further evidence was needed, and therefore a second test was used. It yielded essentially the same results.

The girls performed so poorly that foster placement could not be anticipated. With the orphanage at Davenport already overcrowded, adoption unlikely, and the prognosis dismal, Skeels recommended early transfer to an institution for mentally retarded people, where they were destined anyway. Two months later, this transfer was made to the institution at Woodward. These tearful little creatures, 15 and 18 months of age, were sent off to new lives (Skeels & Dye, 1939). Their runny noses, poor muscle tone, and lack of responsiveness would be someone else's problem.

SENSORY DEVELOPMENT IN EARLY INFANCY. The infant's visual world is largely colorless, at least initially, but color vision improves rapidly during the first month. By six months of age, the infant's capacity approaches the adult level. There is currently no satisfactory explanation for the young infant's color deficiency, but it may be related to an overall insensitivity to differences in light intensity (Brown, 1990).

In one series of studies, 43 infants ranging in age from two days to six months were tested in a special apparatus. It consisted of a large frame for holding visual stimuli over the infant's bed, a series of stimuli, and a peephole through which the investigator could observe the direction and length of fixation of the infant's gaze. Each infant was exposed to various patterned and unpatterned stimuli up to eight times. The results showed considerably more visual attention to the patterned surface than to plain but colored ones and most attention to an outline of a human face. This finding indicates that the visual world of even the very young infant is not entirely formless (Fantz, 1961).

Hearing also appears quickly after birth. The newborn is responsive only to loud noises, but soon pitch, quality, and other aspects of sound are discriminated. Sensitivity to temperature and other stimuli, and the capacities for taste and smell, although present in the fetus, continue to increase in the following weeks.

MOTOR DEVELOPMENT IN INFANCY.

During the prenatal and early postnatal years, there is a universal tendency in vertebrates to develop faster at the head than at the tail. The head of a human fetus has reached a greater proportion of its ultimate size than the lower body parts, and the same condition holds for a young child. Since the direction of the head is referred to as *cephalic* and the direction of the tail as *caudal*, this head-to-tail growth is known as **cephalocaudal development.** Similarly, structures close to the center of the body develop faster than those at the extremes. A comparison of the body parts shows that early in life the trunk grows more; later, the arms and legs grow more. This center-to-extremities growth is known as **proximodistal development,** meaning from near to far. In summary, in our early years we grow downward from the top, outward from the center.

The most obvious postnatal developments pertain to the muscles. The baby learns to control the head before the legs, illustrating the cephalocaudal sequence. The baby moves the arms as a whole

before gaining effective control of the hands and fingers, demonstrating proximodistal development.

As its muscles grow, and especially as neural development continues, the normal infant progresses to successive stages in *locomotion,* which is the capacity to move oneself from place to place. In the first year, this progression goes from lying to sitting to standing and finally to walking with assistance. These stages are essentially predictable, and ages have been identified at which they often occur, although there are distinct variations in the rates at which even normal children reach them.

At the time they were recommended for transfer, C.D. and B.D. were well behind the usual rate of development. C.D., 13 months of age, made no attempts to sit or stand unaided. B.D., at 16 months, was unable to walk, even with assistance. In normal development, the younger baby would have been crawling up and down stairs; the older one would have been standing and walking alone (Figure 12–4).

Compared with later development, these early physical changes take place with remarkable speed. The only comparable period of physical development—less dramatic but remarkable in its own way—is the adolescent growth spurt.

❧

SOCIAL-EMOTIONAL DEVELOPMENT

Six months after the transfer of the two little girls, Harold Skeels's responsibilities were expanded beyond the orphanage to include two state institutions for the mentally retarded. One day while visiting the wards at Woodward, he noticed "two outstanding little girls." They were healthy, playful children, toddling about like most others of their age. He hardly recognized them as the hopelessly retarded pair transferred to the institution a half year earlier. In disbelief, he tested them again and found that they were approaching the lower level of normal development. After another 12 months, he

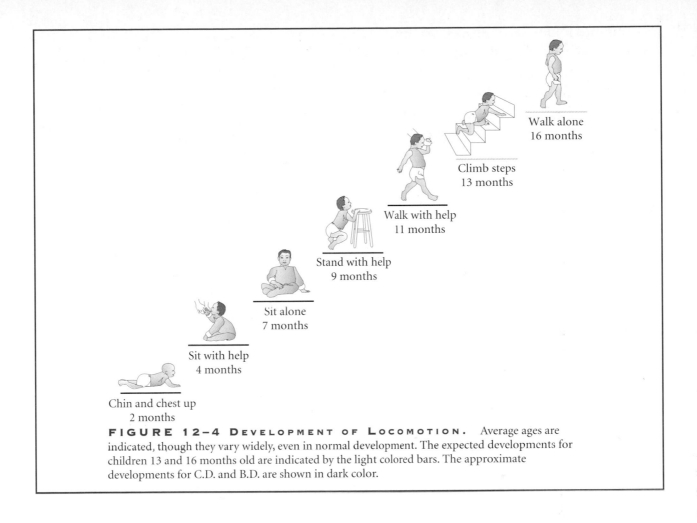

FIGURE 12–4 DEVELOPMENT OF LOCOMOTION. Average ages are indicated, though they vary widely, even in normal development. The expected developments for children 13 and 16 months old are indicated by the light colored bars. The approximate developments for C.D. and B.D. are shown in dark color.

Walk alone
16 months

Climb steps
13 months

Walk with help
11 months

Stand with help
9 months

Sit alone
7 months

Sit with help
4 months

Chin and chest up
2 months

tested them once more, obtaining still higher results, within the normal range. Finally, when the little girls were 40 and 43 months of age, Skeels obtained IQs of 95 and 93, respectively, just slightly below average (Skeels & Dye, 1939).

These physical and cognitive developments were truly remarkable, but the girls also showed noticeable social development. They seemed happier and more stable emotionally. Skeptical of the tests and of the permanence of these improvements, Skeels suggested no change in their lives. The children would stay in the institution, and he would return later to check their progress (Skeels & Dye, 1939).

The principle of differentiation, just as it holds for physical and cognitive development, also applies to social development. There is no identifiable social responsiveness in newborn infants, as clearly distinct from emotional, sensory, or motor behavior. The baby looks for its mother and perhaps reaches for her. Later it smiles, cries in anger, coos, and learns to express affection. Only gradually does the behavior of the newborn become differentiated into the many different social and emotional reactions of the child and adult.

IMPRINTING AND ATTACHMENT. In the early decades of this century, the role of early experience in human development was not understood as we know it today. It had been described by poets and philosophers, and Alexander Pope had written: "Just as the twig is bent, the tree's inclin'd" (*Moral*

Essays, I, 1734). However, it had not yet come under careful scrutiny by scientists, who were just beginning studies of social behavior in animals.

Under normal circumstances, for example, newborn ducklings and goslings follow their mother soon after hatching, perhaps because they are stimulated initially by her movements or vocalizations. This learned attachment of young animals to members of their own species is called **imprinting,** and it is acquired during a certain *optimal* time for learning. This period varies for different species. In geese, it is up to 16 hours after birth. Afterward, readiness to learn to follow declines rapidly. The young bird is so ready during these early moments—a critical period—that this behavior can be elicited by almost any perceptible object that moves, living or inanimate. Furthermore, once this attachment has been established, it is essentially irreversible (Lorenz, 1958; Figure 12–5).

Most researchers refuse to speculate regarding any fixed interval for human social responsiveness. The first 3 days after birth, for example, may be sufficient for initiating in the human infant a special responsiveness to the mother's voice (DeCasper & Fifer, 1980). Within 30 weeks, infants acquire the concept of a human face (Cohen & Strauss, 1979). Some investigators therefore speak of a *sensitive period,* implying its importance but not its irreversibility.

Through their regular interactions, an intense and enduring emotional relationship often develops between an infant and its human caretaker, called **attachment.** It begins by three months of age, perhaps earlier, when the baby takes special note of the caretaker and develops a special affection for that particular person. By six months, this attachment becomes an important source of security as the child begins to investigate the world around it. Any disruption in this relationship produces stress and even depression in either or both individuals.

The observations of imprinting in animals

FIGURE 12–5 IMPRINTING. Immediately after birth of these goslings, Konrad Lorenz waddled and quacked his way around a meadow for two hours, occasionally glancing back at the piping little creatures marching obediently behind him. Lorenz was the first moving object in their lives, and they developed a learned attachment to him, called imprinting, shown here in later days.

foretold in a rough manner the later scientific interest in attachment among human beings, but the findings are hardly comparable. Imprinting in animals is essentially predictable, remarkably firm, and not highly variable from one individual to another. Attachment is a more elusive concept, not yet supported by substantial evidence or clearly distinguished among the many different terms for early human social support (Newcomb, 1990).

EMERGING EMOTIONAL REACTIONS. Investigations of early emotional development have fostered a wide array of techniques. In one instance, infants were systematically stimulated by toys, parents, and food. A panel of judges, not informed of the circumstances, identified the infant's reaction only on the basis of its facial expression. The results indicated that the expression of interest is present shortly after birth, along with the startle pattern and distress. These are followed by a true social smile at about one to two months, then anger at three to four months, fear at six months, and so forth (Izard, Huebner, Risser, & Dougherty, 1980). As in earlier studies, negative emotional reactions generally were identified earlier than positive expressions.

At six or seven months, the infant becomes afraid with unfamiliar people, a condition called **stranger anxiety.** The baby cries, turns away, hides, or clings to the parent. These responses typically disappear sometime after the first year. Around this same period, occasionally lasting for many months, a related concern arises. In **separation anxiety,** the child shows great distress on being away from the parent. Both types of anxiety appear to be significantly influenced by biological factors in maturation, for they are common in many cultures.

Among theoretical explanations for these anxieties, the Darwinian view postulates that the various emotions have survival value or at least had this capacity in earlier evolutionary history. The negative emotions, in particular, are viewed in this way: Fear stimulates flight from predators; anger prompts retaliation; and the startle pattern provides a reflex withdrawal from an unexpected stimulus. Smiling and crying also have survival value, eliciting the attention of adults.

CARETAKER–CHILD INTERACTION.

When Harold Skeels reexamined the two orphan girls again and again, they showed unmistakable development, eventually reaching the normal range. There seemed little doubt that the original evaluations had given a reasonably accurate assessment of their functioning at the orphanage, and yet each

successive examination showed more normal development. What had happened?

Attention had happened—good old tender, loving care. In the institution for the mentally retarded, each child had been placed separately on a ward for older girls and women ranging in age from 18 to 50 years old. One of these women spontaneously became the adoptive mother of each child. The others served as adoring aunts. Equally important, the ward attendants became attracted to C.D. and B.D., the only preschool children in the area. The setting was abundant in affection and interesting stimulation for them, although most of their caretakers had no more mental ability than a nine-year-old child (Skeels & Dye, 1939).

Back at the orphanage, these children would have lived in an overcrowded, underfurnished dormitory. With only one or two caretakers for every 12 to 18 children, sustained contacts with adults for these boys and girls were rare, limited chiefly to physical care.

The difference between life at the orphanage and life at the institution for the mentally retarded lay not in the satisfactions of biological needs, which were approximately equal in the two institutions. One difference was the availability of toys and other equipment. More important was the difference in **caretaker–child interaction,** which refers to attention and responsiveness to a child on the part of adults, including diverse opportunities for play and support. It was in the context of these games and related experiences with women and older girls that the two younger ones showed such marked changes, including improved emotional development.

The two little girls of course differed from one another, and many differences in infant behavior cannot be attributed to environmental influences (Kagan, Snidman, Julia-Sellers, & Johnson, 1991). One task of the caretaker is to recognize early the baby's temperament and to respond accordingly.

At some point during the second year, normal babies use words in combinations. This cognitive-motor development represents the beginning of speech and therefore the transition from infancy to childhood.

The stage of childhood lasts about ten to twelve years, until adolescence, which is defined differently in different cultures and even for the two sexes. In the United States, the stage of adolescence today it is often considered to span the years 11 to 18 in girls and 13 to 20 in boys. Especially in adolescence, the three areas of development—physical, cognitive, and social—occur at very different rates in different people, meaning that some developments may not be complete until the twenties. Both childhood and adolescence are considered in three phases: early, middle, and late.

The two orphans, C.D. and B.D., were in early childhood when they received the abundant attention and affection from the retarded girls and women. After slightly more than two years, Skeels decided that they were behaving in an essentially normal manner. It was unlikely that life with retarded people would meet their future developmental needs, and so the girls were returned to the orphanage to await adoption. This adoptive placement occurred a year later, when they were about four years old.

This totally unexpected development, especially in such an unlikely place as an institution for the mentally handicapped, so impressed Harold Skeels that he made another radical proposal. A whole group of orphans should be transferred to live with the mentally retarded. Little could be lost, he pointed out, because those who did not attain normal development would simply remain where they were destined anyway. Naturally, the Board of Control of State Institutions responded to this plan with grave misgivings, fearing damage to the children and to the reputation of their institutions.

A compromise was reached. To escape the stigma of being committed as mentally retarded at an earlier age than usual, the children would be considered house guests at the institution, their names remaining on the orphanage roster. Each child would be placed singly on a ward, or in some cases in pairs, and there would be periodic reevaluations. All of these arrangements were described in Skeels's report on this procedure, *A Study of the Effects of Differential Stimulation on Mentally Retarded Children* (Skeels & Dye, 1939).

Under this plan, 11 children were transferred to the state institution at Glenwood, making a total of 13 who went earlier than usual to live with the mentally retarded. Their average age was 19 months, and reevaluation was scheduled to take place within two years.

~

PHYSICAL DEVELOPMENT

Human **physical development** involves the growth of all structures of the body. These structures underlie all behavior and experience; therefore, physical, cognitive, and social development are interrelated.

PHYSICAL CHANGES IN CHILDHOOD. Biological inheritance manifests itself not only in physical characteristics but also in a certain sequence of physical development. When this sequence is universal among all normal members of a given species and depends almost solely on biological factors, it is called **maturation**. This shared unfolding of structure and behavior, which takes place almost automatically and inevitably, suggests a common inheritance among the group members. Even among retarded and precocious individuals, the *sequence is the same* as it is for normal or average individuals. It simply occurs at a different rate.

Maturational influences also appear in the

changes in body proportions. In length, the ratio of the head to the total body at birth is 1:4. By age six years, it becomes 1:6. After twelve years, it remains approximately 1:8. A similar change occurs in the ratio of the head to the limbs. The newborn infant can hardly reach the top of its head, for its arms, legs, and head are almost the same length. These proportions change steadily until, at adolescence, the limbs are more than twice the length of the head (Figure 12–6).

Increases in physical size continue until approximately the eighteenth year, and they can be considered in stages. During infancy, they are more rapid than at any other time in life. In early childhood, ages two through five, the rate decreases but remains rapid. Then the years of middle and late childhood, from five to eleven or so, bring a marked change. Growth is so slow that it sometimes seems there is none at all.

ADOLESCENT GROWTH SPURT. The second spurt of physical growth in the human life cycle marks the stage of **adolescence,** a time when girls and boys reach reproductive capacity and also experience marked intellectual and emotional changes. Some of the physical changes are obvious, such as the increasingly feminine and masculine proportions in physique and the rapid increases in height and weight in both sexes, but they are not synchronized among or within adolescents. Girls generally mature earlier than boys, some much sooner than their friends of both sexes. Others are late. Boys, too, mature at very different rates, as do the separate body parts. The chin, nose, neck, and feet may grow early and rapidly, leaving many adolescent boys gawky and awkward—out of step with themselves, as well as with their peers.

The most significant of these changes are less obvious, arising from hormonal secretions beginning at about the tenth year. A marked rise in the production of **estrogens,** the female sex hormone, is partly responsible for the girl's changing figure and increasing interest in the opposite sex. The secretion of **androgens,** the male hormone, begins a bit later, stimulating the male sex characteristics. The beginning of reproductive capacity, called **puberty,** occurs with the onset of menstruation in girls, sometime after age 11, and the presence of sperm cells in boys, approximately one or two years later.

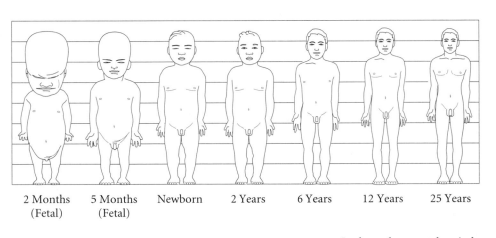

| 2 Months (Fetal) | 5 Months (Fetal) | Newborn | 2 Years | 6 Years | 12 Years | 25 Years |

FIGURE 12–6 PROCESS OF MATURATION In the early prenatal period especially, the head is very large in proportion to the body, a characteristic which continues in the first weeks of postnatal life. After age six, the head-to-body ratio is close to that of the adult.

FIGURE 12–7 ADOLESCENCE AS A CRITICAL PERIOD. One major task is the acceptance of sexual impulses and their integration into the personality.

Two generations ago the average British girl reached puberty at 15, and centuries earlier she reached it at 16 or later. This trend toward earlier onset of menstruation has been found throughout developed parts of the world. A most likely contributor is improved nutrition throughout the growth period. Comparisons of well-nourished and poorly nourished populations support this idea, showing a sharp difference in the median age at first menstruation (Tanner, 1971). Still another possibility is the increased stimulation and stress in developed countries, brought about by the automobile, telephones, television, and other complexities of modern urban life (Adams, 1981). The adolescent spurt is a universal inheritance, but the time of its occurrence depends partly on the interplay of environmental factors, especially nutrition and social changes (Hamburg & Takanishi, 1989).

PROBLEMS OF ADOLESCENT SEXUALITY. Attracted to sexual experience by earlier puberty and sexually oriented mass media, adolescents are engaging in intercourse at younger and younger ages. This activity, unless guided by principles of safe sex, involves two dangers: sexually transmitted disease and unwanted pregnancy. The chief concern in both cases is prevention (Turkington, 1992; Figure 12–7).

Instances of AIDS among teenagers have been increasing precipitously, and the other hazard, adolescent pregnancy, can become an enormous handicap for adolescent girls—and boys too. And yet, among teenagers who are sexually active, less than one-third employ contraceptives regularly; approximately one million girls become pregnant each year (Dryfoos, 1990).

On these bases, the need for sex education seems paramount. But who should offer it? How should it be presented? What should it contain? With these questions largely unanswered, teenage pregnancy in this country is markedly higher than in other industrialized countries, such as Sweden, where sex education is part of the school curriculum. Teenage sexual activity is approximately the same in both places, and therefore the responsible factor seems to be effective sex education (Figure 12–8). Surveys of adolescents in this country and abroad have shown that even without extensive sex education in school, instruction from parents is extremely limited, reported by only 14% in some cases (Finkel & Finkel, 1983; Mayekiso & Twaise, 1993).

❧

COGNITIVE DEVELOPMENT

As the child matures, its mental capacities become more prominent and varied, and these changes are known as **cognitive development.** The term *cognition* means knowing or understanding; it includes not only intelligence but also such complementary or component processes as perceiving, recognizing,

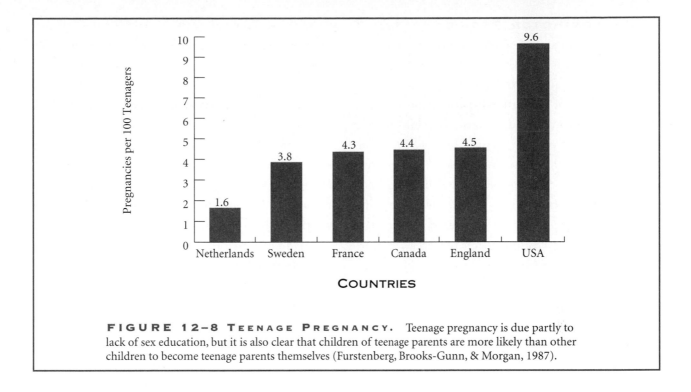

FIGURE 12–8 TEENAGE PREGNANCY. Teenage pregnancy is due partly to lack of sex education, but it is also clear that children of teenage parents are more likely than other children to become teenage parents themselves (Furstenberg, Brooks-Gunn, & Morgan, 1987).

recalling, and interpreting information, as well as all forms of reasoning.

One of the foremost figures in this area has been a Swiss psychologist, Jean Piaget. Early in his research, he turned to a difficult question: What is the nature of knowledge? In search of answers, he decided to talk with children, who are in the early stages of acquiring it.

Through his studies on thought, morality, and language in the child, Piaget made an enduring contribution to developmental psychology, fostering experiments unrivaled in the history of the field (Beilin, 1992). Eventually, he came to the view that the child's thinking is not just a simpler version of adult thought. It is *qualitatively* different, based on a different understanding of reality, one that slowly changes according to maturation and experience as the child actively develops new mental processes.

Two processes underlie these changes, according to Piaget. The first, **assimilation,** is the process of fitting new information into our current understanding of the world. Encountering a new event, we use an old way of interacting with it. The child's first footwear includes stockings and booties; through assimilation, the child learns that shoes, slippers, and similar objects also go on the feet. However, when young children begin dressing themselves, they often put their shoes on the wrong feet. When corrected, or through experience, the child learns that shoes, unlike stockings and booties, are shaped to fit a specific foot. This response, **accommodation,** is the process of altering our current understanding, or cognitive structure, to make it more consistent with the new experience. In accommodation, we modify our old way of thinking to fit the new facts.

Adults behave similarly, for example, when they learn computer programs. They approach a program on the basis of what they already know and then modify their knowledge appropriately. This process is cyclical, moving from assimilation to accommodation, back to assimilation, and so forth, whether the problem is understanding how clothes fit or how computer programs work.

SENSORIMOTOR PERIOD. The first of Piaget's four stages occurs from birth to approximately 18 to 24 months of age, at which time infants do not think in the sense that older children do. This stage of cognitive development is called the **sensorimotor period** because the child merely senses things and acts on them.

At this stage, infants do not seem to conceive of objects as having any permanent, independent existence apart from their own experience with them. They do not carry around in their heads the symbols or images of objects. Or at least they show no awareness of an object when not looking at it, handling it, or otherwise acting on it. When Piaget dangled a rattle in front of his daughter's face, Jacqueline wriggled with delight. But when he hid it under a blanket as she watched, she immediately lost interest.

A few months later, Jacqueline behaved differently, as did her cousin Gerard when his ball rolled under an armchair. He retrieved it with difficulty, and later, when it rolled under the sofa, he looked there, too. When he could not find it, he crossed the room and explored under the armchair, where the ball was previously found. Gerard had acquired **object permanence,** which is the understanding that an object continues to exist even when it is not directly available to the senses (Piaget, 1954).

This understanding of object permanence is one of the accomplishments that mark the end of the sensorimotor period, a step that is enormously important because it permits children to represent objects to themselves. They need not act on something for it to exist in their minds. They have memories. They can carry images of rattles, balls, and other things in their heads, which is perhaps the beginning of thinking.

It was during the sensorimotor period that the two orphans, C.D. and B.D., were transferred to live with retarded people. This early action took place essentially by chance. However, the subsequent transfer of 11 more children was intentionally arranged to coincide with the end of the sensorimotor period, as we know it today, a time at which mental developments are rapid and dramatic.

PREOPERATIONAL THOUGHT. In this new stage, called the **preoperational period,** children can represent things to themselves, but they still do not readily understand the use of symbols, cannot perform logical manipulations with information, and cannot readily change the direction of their thinking. Children are preoperational throughout most of the preschool and early school years, from age 18 or 24 months to age six or seven years (Piaget & Inhelder, 1969).

One prominent characteristic of preoperational thought is its egocentrism. In **cognitive egocentrism,** for example, children do not realize that their thoughts are not necessarily shared by other people. Asked what happened at school, one child said, without further explanation, "Tommy did it." In **perceptual egocentrism,** children do not realize that their perceptions are not necessarily shared by other people. A three-year-old girl, playing hide-and-seek, shut her eyes and said, "Ha, ha! Can't see me!" (Clinchy, 1975).

In a test of perceptual egocentrism, each child was seated at a table that held a model of three mountains. Seated at this same table but in a different chair was a doll, and the child's task was to select from a series of pictures the one that represented the way the mountains looked from the doll's viewpoint. The child could walk around and observe the model from any position at the table but had to return to his or her own seat to select the picture. Preschoolers had little success with this task. Not understanding how the operation of changing location gave a different view, they consistently selected the picture that matched the mountains as seen from their own vantage point (Piaget & Inhelder, 1967).

Another characteristic of preoperational thought is evident when an object is changed in some way. The child is impressed with how it appears, rather than with less striking characteristics, such as how it was made. The aim in the **conservation task** is to discover whether a child recognizes that certain basic properties of something remain constant when only its appearance is changed.

Among many forms of the conservation task, one involves two identically shaped, tall jars containing equal amounts of liquid. After the child asserts that the contents are equal, the contents of one jar are poured into a third jar, which is low and wide. The amount of liquid has not changed; it is conserved. But the preoperational child, attending to the height of the tall column of liquid, typically maintains that there is more liquid in that tall, thin beaker than in the short, wide one. This thought is called *preoperational* because the child reasons in terms of the dominant perceptual experience rather than the logical operations involved (Figure 12–9).

CONCRETE OPERATIONS. Around age six, the child begins to master conservation problems. One six-year-old girl and an experimenter dropped marbles, one by one, into different beakers. The child's fell into a short, wide beaker and the experimenter's into a tall, thin one. The child, who could count to 30, counted the marbles as they dropped, and at first she maintained that she and the experimenter had the same number.

"How do you know?" she was asked. "Because I counted 'em. You've got ten and I've got ten." As the column of marbles mounted more impressively in the tall beaker, she began to hesitate. Finally, even though she counted 20 in each, she decided that the experimenter had more. Then she became confused: "You've got more, 'cause they're spread out more. No . . . I don't know" (Clinchy, 1975). This confusion is a sign of cognitive growth because the child considers other factors besides the dominant perceptual features.

During the stage of concrete operations, which lasts until age 11 or perhaps longer, the child becomes capable of reversing the procedure. One examiner made two straight clay "worms" of equal length and then formed the child's into a curly worm, testing the conservation of length. When asked if they were still the same length, the child said: "Acourse. If you pull my worm straight, he'll look like yours. They were both the same to start" (Clinchy, 1975). This capacity to use logic to solve problems when the physical objects are directly available is called **concrete operations.**

At the close of this stage, the individual can solve problems requiring classification, ordering, and sequencing, but only in specific situations, with the materials present. The child can arrange a series of sticks from tallest to shortest without making errors. The child can think of a given stick as both shorter than the preceding one and longer than the

FIGURE 12–9 CONSERVATION TASK WITH MARBLES. Sometimes marbles are used instead of water. The child agrees that the two tall vessels contain approximately the same number of marbles. After watching the contents of one tall vessel emptied into a lower vessel, the child who does not understand conservation states that the other tall vessel has more marbles.

next one. Children at this stage have mastered the operations required in solving such problems, which is why we speak of concrete operations (Piaget, 1950).

FORMAL OPERATIONS. Suppose, however, that we asked the child to solve for the first time the lily-pad problem. A frog sits on the only lily pad on a pond. The pad reproduces itself, doubling every 24 hours; the next day there are two pads, the following day four, and so fourth. At the end of a month, the pond is covered completely. At what point in the month will the frog find the pond half covered?

In thinking about this problem, regardless of the solution, the adult uses **formal operations,** which is the capacity for reasoning apart from concrete situations. It is abstract reasoning, Piaget's final level of cognitive development. Around age 11 or older, the average child, entering adolescence, begins to engage in this type of thinking, although at a less sophisticated level than most adults. The adolescent well into formal operations may think of different approaches to the lily-pad problem and then realize that it is most readily solved by working backward from the end of the month, rather than forward from the beginning. If the pads double each day, then the pond must be half covered on the next-to-last day of the month.

In the previous stage, the child was able to classify, enumerate, and place objects and events in time and space, but in formal operations the child can *imagine* the possibilities inherent in a problem. Probably the most important feature of formal operations is that reality is seen as just one aspect of what might be. The adolescent generates hypotheses and tests them to find which one seems most valid and can even leave reality altogether, reasoning entirely in abstract terms. Not all adolescents and adults do so, however. Many never leave concrete operations (Figure 12–10).

The capacity for formal operations means that the cognitive world of the adolescent and adult is very different from that of the child, who lives largely a here-and-now existence. Adolescents, in particular, begin to imagine other worlds, especially ideal ones. They imagine worlds with better governments, better economic systems, better schools, better health care and even—ah, yes—better parents. Some of these things are not hard for any of us to imagine. Then they make comparisons with their current circumstances and often rebel or change their lifestyles. As formal operations develop, adolescents move beyond conventional standards of morality toward the construction of their own moral principles (Elkind, 1967).

It has been hypothesized, incidentally, that this

Formal operations, 11–
Logical, abstract reasoning; developing and testing hypotheses

Concrete operations, 7–11
Conservation and logical reasoning with concrete objects and events

Preoperational, 2–7
Perceptual and cognitive egocentrism; lack of conservation

Sensorimotor, 0–2
Lack of object permanence; response only to immediate environment

FIGURE 12–10 STAGES OF COGNITIVE DEVELOPMENT.
The ages are approximate; only the chief features are indicated.

mental growth contributes to certain fallacies adolescents may have about themselves. Self-conscious about their new and uncontrollable physical and psychological developments, they may imagine that they are under special scrutiny by others. This *imaginary audience*, it is speculated, partly accounts for teenagers' extreme concern about looking alike, thereby increasing peer support and diminishing the chances of being noticed. In the *personal fable*, the adolescent decides that his or her surprising new thoughts are unique. No one else has had them. The adolescent may think: "My parents never understood love the way I do." "No disaster will happen to me." Only gradually do they realize that their newly discovered mental abilities are shared by their mother and father, who at one time also questioned *their* parents' childrearing, business, religion, and other practices (Elkind, 1967, 1984).

A clear illustration of formal operations is apparent in Harold Skeels's work. He made an extraordinary proposal: to transfer mentally retarded children to a ward for mentally retarded girls and women in order to make the children normal. At face value, the proposal was preposterous. However, Skeels had reasoned from the preliminary findings with C.D. and B.D. He imagined a similar outcome—or rather hoped "that possibly 50 percent of the cases might show at least some improvement" (Skeels & Dye, 1939).

CRITIQUE OF PIAGETIAN THEORY. One process underlies many of the changes in all stages, according to Piaget. It is *overcoming* egocentrism, which in this instance does not refer to personal interests or selfishness. Rather, **egocentrism** means that the individual's view of the world is self-centered. The individual assumes that the only understanding of the world is the one he or she possesses. Experience plays a vital role in enabling the individual to diminish egocentrism as the child discovers that objects exist even when not immediately present, that other people have thoughts different from his or her own, that there are agreed-upon systems for ordering and classifying things, and that the reality one experiences is just one of many possibilities. Needless to say, even adults never completely overcome this egocentrism.

How does the child make these advances? Piaget pointed to assimilation and accommodation, but his work is largely a description of what the child can and cannot do. There is a large difference in thought, for example, between a child in the preoperational stage and a child in concrete operations, but how does the child move to successive stages? How do these changes occur? How does the child overcome egocentrism? These questions remain to be answered. Several factors, external and internal, presumably influence the child's performance and hence, to a lesser degree, placement at a particular stage.

According to critics, differences in children's constructions of reality are influenced not only by differences in the various tasks they can perform but also by differences in information processing. In focusing on stages, which are somewhat arbitrary classifications, Piaget underestimated the *continuity* in cognitive development, which becomes manifest especially in the study of individual children (Niaz, 1991). Piaget's contribution to our understanding of children's thoughts has been enormous, yet its influence in the context of our advancing knowledge is regularly debated (Beilin, 1992; Halford, 1990).

INFORMATION PROCESSING VIEWPOINT. Foremost among the other approaches to cognitive development is the **information processing viewpoint,** which emphasizes *how* the individual obtains and utilizes information, focusing on the mental operations by which the child converts sensory experience into knowledge. Perception, memory, and thinking are the basic concerns in the information processing approach. More inferential than Piaget's original work, this approach is also more directly concerned with the operations that go on inside the "black box," a metaphor referring to the fact that mental functions cannot be observed directly. They take place inside the skull and can only be inferred.

In the information processing viewpoint, the idea of task specificity is important. It means that the performance on a particular problem or task pertains only to *that* task. The results are not generalizable; they cannot be applied beyond the immediate, specific situation.

The most widely cited Piagetian tasks are the conservation experiments, and follow-up studies show that the outcomes are often task specific. A child at age six or so may successfully manage conservation of liquid or solids, with water or marbles transferred from one container to another, but may be unable to solve a problem in conservation of length, in which a piece of string laid out straight is judged to be longer than one of equal length rolled into a ball. The solution to the conservation problem depends not only on the child's age, or stage, but also on the type of conservation task involved (Figure 12–11).

Similarly, the three-mountain problem allegedly shows the child's inability to put herself perceptually in someone else's place, but this same child may perform successfully on a simpler test of perceptual egocentrism, hiding a doll from the experimenter while viewing it herself. This less complex task is still a test of perceptual egocentrism (Flavell, Shipstead, & Croft, 1978).

The steady unfolding of the child's intellect is not an automatic process, as Piaget himself pointed out. It requires appropriate stimulation. The child becomes a little scientist or explorer, seizing opportunities to twist and pull, pick and drop, poke and rub, shake and break, trying to understand our world. In this context, Piagetians speak of "growledge"—meaning that children somehow grow their knowledge. However, the ways in which they achieve this development remain largely unknown, for studies in information processing and neural science are still far apart. To understand these processes, a bridge between these two fields will be necessary (Simon, 1990).

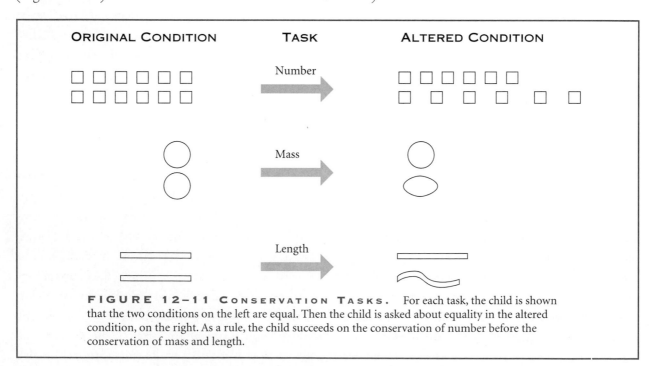

ORIGINAL CONDITION   **TASK**   **ALTERED CONDITION**

Number

Mass

Length

FIGURE 12–11 CONSERVATION TASKS. For each task, the child is shown that the two conditions on the left are equal. Then the child is asked about equality in the altered condition, on the right. As a rule, the child succeeds on the conservation of number before the conservation of mass and length.

MORAL DEVELOPMENT

As children develop increased responsiveness to the environment, they begin to learn how society works—what is right, wrong, expected, and so forth. Gradually they learn the rules of their social group and the world at large, a process called **moral development.**

KOHLBERG'S APPROACH TO MORAL REASONING.

The concept of moral development includes two basic dimensions: moral reasoning and moral behavior. Human beings need to learn what is appropriate, and then they need to guide their behavior in these ways. In this respect, moral development occupies a position midway between cognitive and social development.

One of the earliest modern theories of moral reasoning was presented by an American psychologist, Lawrence Kohlberg, who viewed moral development from a cognitive perspective. His work provided evidence for six levels of moral reasoning, occurring in pairs. Therefore three basic levels were identified: preconventional, conventional, and postconventional.

In **preconventional morality,** characteristic of children ages four or five through ten, the basis for a moral judgment is the *physical consequences* of an act. Children of these ages judge misbehavior by the amount of damage someone does or by the amount of punishment that the person receives.

Two boys at the orphanage had a fight, but only one, with telltale bruises on his face, was caught and punished. In the preconventional view, the boy who was never punished was not such a bad child.

Around age ten, the approximate time for reaching **conventional morality,** there is a broader social concern, an effort to *maintain the social order,* but only in a stereotypical "good child" manner.

The laws are still fixed, and conformity is the goal; the aim is to avoid disapproval.

Even if one boy in the fight is being severely beaten, the bystander who does not intervene is a good child—according to conventional morality. The moral aim is to be a good boy or good girl, and not entering the fight achieves this goal. It gains the approval of authority.

The major difference between the second and third levels lies in the awareness of independent moral principles. Recognizing that there is an almost inevitable conflict of interests within a large group, the person at the level of **postconventional morality** understands the relativism of personal values and standards. According to Kohlberg, only a minority of the population reach this stage which, if entered at all, begins no earlier than age 13. At this level, there is a concern for human rights in the broadest sense and respect for the dignity of *people as individual human beings* (Kohlberg, 1969).

A bystander at the fight may decide to ring the fire alarm, not because there is a fire but because he or she feels that all physical hostility is immoral and wants the fire department to intervene. The law or rule of not ringing a false alarm is disobeyed because fighting violates a personal moral principle. This individual—according to postconventional morality—is responding to his or her own conscience.

MORAL BEHAVIOR.

The other issue is moral behavior, and the question here concerns the correlation between ways of thinking and ways of behaving. Does the child who shows high moral reasoning also display high moral behavior?

In one early study, children were assessed for honesty in a wide variety of situations, ranging from recreational activity to school work. For example, they tried to identify some interesting objects. Then they were asked to go alone to the next room to return them, but a special observer could detect whether they kept any of these objects. After many tests of this sort, the most pronounced finding was that stealing, lying, or any other form of dishonesty occurred unpredictably from one situation and one child to another (Hartshorne & May, 1928). Some years later, these findings were reexamined, chiefly because they gave so little support for any persistent traits. Again, however, the evidence for moral behavior in young children was not impressive (Rushton, Brainerd, & Pressley, 1983; Rushton, Jackson, & Paunonen, 1981).

Moral reasoning is a necessary but not sufficient condition for moral behavior. The task of teaching moral reasoning and moral behavior in diverse situations lies before us, especially in the home and school. One problem in American society today, many contend, is a decline in moral instruction (Bok, 1988).

CRITIQUE OF KOHLBERG'S THEORY. The first effort to demonstrate empirically and in detail that morality can be viewed in stages, Kohlberg's theory is a pioneering effort. There is some doubt, however, about its applicability across cultures. The upper levels do not appear in certain societies, and they are found only on rare occasions in others. Further, it has been argued that Kohlberg's theory contains a political bias; it offers implicit support for people who believe in principles that may conflict with established laws. They should reach the upper levels of postconventional morality more readily than those who adhere to laws approved by the governing bodies.

A limitation of a different sort arises because Kohlberg's work was based essentially on studies of boys. These all-male samples reflected an assumption that gender differences may exist, and yet the morality of girls, as a separate issue, has not been investigated extensively. Using boys, Kohlberg's view of morality focuses on respecting others' rights. It stresses justice. Carol Gilligan has pointed out that girls develop moral reasoning along different lines.

Their focus is on developing personal relationships, caring for others, and becoming attached to them. It stresses care. Gilligan's approach states that the issues of intimacy, nurturance, and affiliation should be reflected in any view of morality (Gilligan, 1982). The difference in these views is sometimes known as the *justice–care debate*, reflecting the emphasis in each instance. Various theoretical and practical proposals have been made to resolve these differences (Brown & Tappan, 1991; Puka, 1991).

∿

SOCIAL DEVELOPMENT

Morality had been an issue back at the orphanage in Iowa. Harold Skeels had prematurely transferred 13 children to the wards for mentally retarded women. According to what he had learned from C.D. and B.D., that transfer was morally defensible. Then, rather suddenly, he came to an important realization. The tests administered to those children before their transfer also had been administered routinely to *all* children who stayed at the orphanage. He could conduct an empirical study, comparing the scores of children who were transferred with those of children who stayed at the orphanage. And he could do so without any concerns about morality or any resistance from the Board of Control. He would simply look at the old records.

Examining the orphanage files, Skeels identified 12 *non*transferred children who might serve as a comparison group. One of the boys in this group suffered from mild deafness, but otherwise the transferred and comparison groups were similar in age, and their average time with the retarded women or at the orphanage spanned about two years.

Skeels's purpose was to detect any differences in scores that had occurred during that time. And his findings were remarkable. The transferred group had achieved an average gain in IQ of 28 points. Among the comparison group, there was an average loss of 26 points. The mean IQ of the transferred children was close to normal, and the comparison

	TRANSFERRED GROUP				COMPARISON GROUP		
CASE	FIRST IQ	LAST IQ	CHANGE	CASE	FIRST IQ	LAST IQ	CHANGE
1	89	113	+24	1	91	62	−29
2	57	77	+20	2	92	56	−36
3	85	107	+22	3	71	56	−15
4	73	100	+27	4	96	54	−42
5	46	95	+49	5	99	54	−45
6	77	100	+23	6	87	67	−20
7	65	104	+39	7	81	83	+2
8	35	93	+58	8	103	60	−43
9	61	80	+19	9	98	61	−37
10	72	79	+ 7	10	89	71	−18
11	75	82	+ 7	11	50	42	−8
12	65	82	+17	12	83	60	−23
13	36	81	+45				
Average	64	92	+28	Average	87	61	−26

TABLE 12–2 CHANGES IN IQ OF SKEELS'S CHILDREN. C.D. is case 5, and B.D. is case 8. Their gains were the largest among all the transferred children.

group had fallen into the retarded range (Skeels & Dye, 1939; Table 12–2).

This positive outcome for the transferred children, according to Harold Skeels, was due to the stimulation and caretaker–child interaction they had received in the institution for the mentally retarded. In contrast, the overworked matrons at the orphanage made their young charges stand up, sit down, and do most other things in unison. There was little time for interactions and activities with other children or adults, thereby fostering **social development,** a person's growing capacity for successful relations with other people.

GENDER IDENTITY. Social development is often closely linked to gender identity; they can have considerable significance for one another. The term **gender identity** means that people recognize themselves as belonging to one sex or the other; they have confidence in themselves as male or female. This outcome is prompted by adult expectations, social stereotypes, and the more subtle ways in which the sexes are treated differently.

The concepts of male and female are among the earliest that young children acquire. Formed in a rudimentary sense in the first two years, they play

a crucial role in further development, even into adulthood and the workplace (Ely, 1995).

Long-term studies show a decrease in traditional sex roles for men and women, but the change is substantially greater for women (McBroom, 1987). In this regard, gender theory approaches the study of sex roles from either of two directions. Some investigators maximize the differences by contrasting the sexes; others minimize them by stressing the equality or similarity between the sexes (Hare-Mustin & Marecek, 1988). Still others, especially psychoanalysts, raise fundamental questions about the function of gender identity in people's lives. For personal adjustment, the capacity to tolerate ambiguity in gender categories may be as important as achieving a single sex-appropriate view of oneself (Goldner, 1991).

PSYCHOSOCIAL STAGES: CHILD-HOOD. At various points in this book, the works of stage theorists are noted: Freud, concerned with sexual development; Piaget, with emphasis on cognitive development; and Kohlberg, who investigated moral development. Each examined development in the early years rather than across the life span.

Erik Erikson, a psychoanalyst who acknowledged a debt to Sigmund Freud, has been responsible for much of the current interest in the entire life cycle, and he decided that human development occurs in eight stages. These are called **psychosocial stages** because many aspects of psychological and social functioning are interrelated and show consistent changes during the life cycle. At each stage, the focus is on a specific crisis in our relationships with other people (Erikson, 1963). The ways in which these crises are managed play a major role in the individual's capacity to respond successfully to personal and social problems at later stages. In childhood, these successive stages are four in number: trust, autonomy, initiative, and industry.

The newborn's first awareness is of physical needs, most obviously the need for nourishment. If the caretaker fulfills these needs consistently, the infant develops trust. In this crisis of **trust versus mistrust,** the infant acquires a sense of reliance on and confidence in its environment or, through early deprivation of these needs, it becomes unresponsive and distrustful. It was just after this stage that Skeels's transferred group was sent from the orphanage to live with the retarded women and girls. Developmental psychologists would point out that the chances for a positive outcome would have been decidedly diminished if the transfer had occurred later.

By the second year of life, the muscular and nervous systems have developed markedly. The child is no longer content to sit and watch, but judgment develops more slowly. The caretaker's decisions about how much freedom to allow are therefore very important in the crisis of **autonomy versus doubt,** from which the child emerges with a sense of independence or with feelings of fear and dependence.

Once a sense of independence has been established, the child wants to try out various possibilities. It is during this crisis of **initiative versus guilt,** from age three to six years, that the child's willingness to try new things is facilitated or inhibited. If the caretaker responds to the child's creative effort in attempting to paint the bathroom, for example, rather than to the resulting mess, the crisis tends to be resolved in a favorable direction.

From six to twelve years the child develops a greater attention span, needs less sleep, and gains rapidly in strength. Therefore, he or she can expend much more effort in acquiring skills. Eager to learn real skills, rather than pretend to have them, the child reaches a new stage. In this crisis, **industry versus inferiority,** the fortunate child is guided to tasks that are appropriate for him or her at the given moment, developing a sense of accomplishment, rather than feelings of failure (Figure 12–12).

THE IDENTITY CRISIS. Adolescence means growing up, which often includes the well-known adolescent–parent conflict. The adolescent at times demands considerable freedom, borrowing the car and staying out late. At other times, the adolescent shows sustained dependence, needing assistance with school or personal relationships. In nonindustrialized countries, the adolescent rebellion is moderate or nonexistent. The apparent reason is that

FIGURE 12–12 SOCIAL DEVELOPMENT THROUGH PLAY. Children's play includes constructive, imaginary, and rough-and-tumble activities, all influential in social development.

entrance into an agricultural or hunting-and-gathering society is far easier than finding a place in a highly developed culture. Young people in our country need a temporary place for themselves while they search for a more permanent place in the larger social context (Elkind, 1984; Galambos, 1992).

In the crisis of **identity versus role diffusion,** the adolescent gradually develops a sense of self as a consistent and unique person or instead begins to experience a fragmented, disconnected, and unclear sense of self. Through Erikson's work, the period of adolescence is regarded as involving an **identity crisis,** a search for self-understanding marked by emotional upheaval and difficulties in establishing a consistent personality. However, uncertainty about attitudes, values, ethics, career opportunities, and religious beliefs appears at later stages too.

• ADULTHOOD AND OLD AGE •

With the full life cycle in mind, Harold Skeels one day began a highly improbable task. Almost a quarter of a century after his original work, he set out to find all 25 of his former subjects, 13 from the transferred group and 12 from the comparison group. What had become of the little girls and boys who lived for a while with the mentally retarded women? What about those who stayed at the orphanage? Now about 30 years old, where were all of these people? What places had they taken for themselves in society?

Some of them still lived in Iowa, not far from the orphanage site, but others had moved to the farthest corners of the country, including Florida and California, and efforts to contact them were time-consuming and frustrating. Once located, each subject was interviewed, along with the adoptive parents whenever possible, and these findings were presented in another report, *Adult Status of Children with Contrasting Early Life Experiences: A Follow-up Study* (Skeels, 1966).

Among the 12 people in the comparison group, four were still institutionalized, and one had died in an institution. The state had cared for these people for a combined total of 273 years. In the transferred group, *none* of the 13 members was institutionalized, and the state had cared for them for only 72 years. The maintenance costs for the comparison group were five times greater than those for the transferred group.

An equally impressive difference appeared in the work records for both groups. All members of the transferred group worked inside or outside the home. Only half of the comparison group were so employed, sometimes intermittently. The transferred group also appeared to be in better physical health. In all respects, that group had become more firmly established in adulthood.

The stage of adulthood, the longest in human life, has been least studied in psychology. For many years it was thought that adulthood contained no significant developmental changes, but now it is regarded as a period with numerous important transitions—from the intermittent dependency of late adolescence to the intermittent or total dependency of old age. It is basically divided into three stages: young adulthood, from the twenties to 45 or so; middle adulthood, from 45 to 65; and old age, from 65 onward.

PHYSICAL CHANGES

One reason that adulthood was ignored in earlier research is that the physical changes are slower and less obvious than those that occur during childhood and adolescence. Moreover, after the twenties, the basic process is decline.

From this perspective, two generalizations should be kept in mind, for they summarize the findings on physical decline and aging. First, it is not readily apparent whether diminished physical functions are due to aging or to disease. It has been very difficult to demonstrate that decreased ability is a natural result of aging per se. Second, differences in physical ability among individuals of the same age are generally less pronounced at midlife than in the later years. The elderly show wider variations than do younger adults (Jones, 1987).

PHYSICAL DECLINE IN ADULTHOOD. Maximum physical growth occurs around ages 18 to 20. Certainly by age 30, power, agility, and endurance are at their peaks and, except in highly trained athletes, the decline has commenced. Skeels's subjects were around this age when he commenced his follow-up studies.

Athletes who continue to improve their performance later do so chiefly by increasing their knowledge about competitive situations and by restricting themselves to certain roles, such as the designated hitter in baseball or the field goal kicker in football, or by restricting themselves to certain sports, such as golf, in which strength and endurance are not prime factors. Even for the average person, the environment plays a role in physical condition, always in the context of a given heredity. Men and women in their sixties, through careful programs of exercise, rest, nutrition, and avoidance of stress, can maintain a better physical condition than those in their thirties who ignore these factors.

By the late forties and fifties, as muscle strength and capacity more clearly decline, there is an increase in body weight, a decrease in hair on the head—especially in men—and the appearance of wrinkles in the skin. Body fat tends to accumulate in the trunk and to decrease on the limbs, and therefore physical appearance sometimes changes without any marked change in weight. The need for assistance in daily routines, such as seeing and chewing, becomes evident in the use of eyeglasses and dental crowns.

PHYSICAL CONDITION OF THE ELDERLY. As the late years in the full life cycle are approached, hearing aids, canes, and pill boxes accompany the crowns and eyeglasses. Old age, indeed, is not for sissies. Posture, stature, and locomotion also change noticeably. The bent or stooped look occurs through alterations in bone structure, a decrease in muscle mass, and loss of elasticity in the tendons and ligaments. Elderly people *have* shrunk. They are stiffer and shorter than they were in earlier years, even if they can stand up straight.

These exterior changes reflect changes in the interior, not only in the heart and lungs but also in the brain. After midlife, the brain begins to decrease in volume at the rate of one or two percent each decade, chiefly through the slow loss of neurons in physical deterioration (Miller, Alston, & Corsellis, 1980). This rate of change is less than that elsewhere in the body and by itself represents no significant loss of mental ability. Redundancy in the nervous system apparently prevents any appreciable decline in abilities, and it is clear that certain brain areas can take over functions of other areas. It has also been suggested that the brain may prune some synapses to achieve its proper adult organization. In other words, efficient networks for performing certain tasks may require a reduction in the potential for performing others (Greenough & Juraska, 1979).

With our increasingly older population, experts in this field now have begun to speak of the young-old, referring to people in the first decade after retirement, and the old-old, who range upward from 75. Again, individual differences are important. Many old-old function better than young-old.

❧

COGNITIVE ABILITIES

When physical and cognitive development in adulthood are compared, one difference is readily apparent. Unlike physical development, there is no inevitable decline in cognitive ability beginning in early adulthood. In fact, there may be no decline until middle adulthood or much later, depending to a significant degree on the type and extent of mental activity in the adult's life. In other words, exercise, rest, and nutrition may help slow the inevitable physical decline beginning in the late twenties, keeping the body in its best possible physical condition, but various mental activities during these same years may even increase cognitive ability.

The difference in mental ability between the two groups in Harold Skeels's research remains essentially unknown in adulthood, despite the large difference in childhood and the different employment histories. Out of respect for these adults, Skeels did not administer mental tests. However, he did obtain information on their educational levels, finding that the transferred group was far superior here, too (Table 12–3).

COGNITIVE DEVELOPMENT IN ADULT-HOOD. While progressing in a career and certain hobbies, a person's activities often demand more and more attention to mental tasks, and with this practice and experience, mental capacity typically increases. As indicated in the next chapter on intelligence, there may be a gradual improvement in

intellectual ability even into the sixth and seventh decades of life. A key factor, perhaps *the* key factor, is the extent to which the individual engages in stimulating and challenging mental activity.

In this regard, we can speak of **metacognition,** meaning the extent to which an individual understands his or her own cognitive processes. Metacognition is knowing what one knows, thinking about one's own thinking. To improve our thinking, we need to become aware of how our thinking works, evaluating its successes and failures, regulating it according to the problem. Without conscious effort, many adults commonly develop increased metacognition over the years (Powell & Whitlaw, 1994). The process of teaching people to think about their thinking may hold special promise in education.

COGNITION IN THE ELDERLY. The most obvious change among the old-old, and even in many young-old, is a *decline in speed* in mental functions, including perception, recall, problem solving, and other forms of information processing. Like physical movement, mental activity becomes slower through changes in the nervous system. There is abundant evidence for diminished speed in almost every cognitive task in which speed has been measured (Light, 1991; Birren & Fisher, 1995).

There is also a *decline in learning,* but if learning is defined as the rate of acquiring new information, the underlying problem is still the speed of processing new information. This decline also may arise through decreasing confidence, lack of exposure to contemporary educational opportunities, and a diminished attention span (Botwinick, 1984).

The *memory problems* of the elderly are legion, and apparently they arise in two general ways, apart from the possible changes in neurophysiology. First, perception may be part of the problem. With decreased sensory abilities, elderly people do not obtain new information in an efficient, well-organ-

TRANSFERRED GROUP		COMPARISON GROUP	
CASE	GRADE	CASE	GRADE
1	11	1	2
2	5	2	2
3	15	3	4
4	15	4	3
5	10	5	0
6	12	6	13
7	12	7	8
8	12	8	2
9	6	9	3
10	14	10	6
11	16	11	2
12	12	12	3
13	13		
Average	12	Average	4

TABLE 12–3 LEVEL OF EDUCATION OF SKEELS'S ADULTS. Only two of the transferred children failed to attend high school. Only one of the comparison children reached that level.

ized fashion. Second, these problems should be understood not as storage problems but as problems in retrieval, for laboratory studies have shown that the elderly perform quite differently on tests of recognition and recall. When young adults and the elderly are compared on recognition of well-learned material, their scores are almost equal; when compared on recall, the elderly do more poorly (Mitrushina & Satz, 1989; Poon, 1985).

Failing memory is especially evident in **Alzheimer's disease,** a progressive brain disorder in the later years characterized not only by forgetting but also by disorientation, slowness of speech, and general apathy. A fatal disease, Alzheimer's eventually results in total mental and emotional deterioration. In this respect, the caregiver becomes a patient too, experiencing the consequences of coping with an important problem that has no immediate solution (Ehrlich & White, 1991; Parks & Pilisuk, 1991).

In normal health, verbal abilities are often maintained or even improved until well past the middle of life. People engaged in scholarly tasks, working at jobs that require special attention to words, or simply practicing language skills, show no diminution in verbal ability in the sixth and seventh decades or later (Schaie & Willis, 1986; Figure 12–13). They approach new problems with a vast background, and this wisdom or experience may compensate for deficits in speed and perceptual-motor abilities.

❧

SOCIAL RELATIONS

Since the middle of this century, the highly complex social environment of the adult has received increasing research attention, and several points of transition have been identified. These developmental tasks do not occur with the regularity of childhood changes, but they occur for most adults: joining the labor force, getting married, becoming a parent, raising an adolescent, reaching mid-career in

FIGURE 12–13 MAINTAINING COGNITIVE ABILITY. Mental challenges play a vital role in maintaining intellectual ability in the later decades, just as they are essential to mental development in the earlier years.

work, adjusting to life without dependent children, and so forth.

SOCIAL CONCERNS: ADULTHOOD. For young adults, an enormous challenge is posed by *career planning,* which means preparing a satisfying and productive vocational path. A major part of the identity crisis, this problem is complicated by the fact that careers planned today may not even exist in another decade. Moreover, our changing physical, intellectual, and social makeup require constant career adjustment and readjustment during our working lives.

The aim in career planning is to make optimal use of one's talents, but ultimately the career must be a compromise between what one would like to do and what reality offers. In the future, with constant and rapid change in the workplace, the diagnosis and treatment of work-related problems may become a major specialty in psychology (Handy, 1990; Lowman, 1993).

Around the forties or later, men and women often experience a tension or lack of fulfillment in their lives, called the **midlife crisis** or midlife transition. These years may reveal that certain things cannot be accomplished in life, that there can be no new start, and that the end is approaching (Levison, Darrow, Klein, Levinson, & McKee, 1978). In this respect, the midlife crisis—which is *highly* variable in age and intensity, if it appears at all—marks a transition from young adulthood to middle adulthood.

The responsibilities of young adulthood, according to Erik Erikson, can create tensions and frustrations. They are therefore accompanied by an attempt to develop an intimate relationship, physical or psychological, with someone else. If this crisis of **intimacy versus isolation** is adequately resolved, the adult feels personal support in the culture; otherwise he or she feels alienated. But a commitment to someone else, especially in the context of childrearing, requires abandoning one's own goals to some degree, something that is not readily undertaken. Hence Erikson emphasizes that true intimacy is not possible without first achieving identity and gaining confidence in oneself.

If intimacy is reflected in marriage, then the results of Skeels's follow-up study were again dramatic. Of the 13 transferred children, 11 were married. Of the 12 comparison children, only two had married, and one of these marriages ended in divorce. Intimacy is not requisite for matrimony and certainly is not absent among unmarried people, but the very large difference in this traditional measure of becoming partners suggests an overall difference in interpersonal relationships between the two groups (Skeels, 1966).

Erikson has pointed out that the demands of intimacy are often in conflict with those of work. In fact, Sigmund Freud defined mental health in adults as the capacity to love and to work. It is noteworthy, therefore, that all of Skeels's transferred group were employed in some way, while only half of the comparison group were employed. Hence, by both criteria, love and work, the transferred group had found a much firmer place in the community, supporting family members as well as themselves (Table 12–4).

In middle adulthood, Erikson continued, there may be a broadening concern, beyond intimacy. In this crisis, called **generativity versus stagnation,**

TRANSFERRED GROUP		COMPARISON GROUP	
CASE	OCCUPATION	CASE	OCCUPATION
1	Staff sargeant	1	Institutional inmate
2	Housewife	2	Dishwasher
3	Housewife	3	Deceased
4	Nursing instructor	4	Dishwasher
5	Housewife	5	Institutional inmate
6	Waitress	6	Compositor/typesetter
7	Housewife	7	Institutional inmate
8	Housewife	8	Dishwasher
9	Domestic service	9	Floater
10	Real estate sales	10	Cafeteria worker
11	Vocational counselor	11	Gardener's assistant
12	Gift shop sales	12	Institutional inmate
13	Housewife		

TABLE 12–4 TYPE OF OCCUPATION OF SKEELS'S ADULTS. These differences in occupation also were reflected in the spouses. The occupations of the spouses of the transferred group ranged from dental technician to flight engineer to advertising copywriter. The one spouse in the comparison group was employed in the home.

there is an expansion of one's interests to include the next generation, or else there is a rather restrained and exclusive focus on one's personal goals. The concern in generativity is not just bearing children, for the biological parent is not necessarily interested in future generations. The positive solution to this crisis is manifested in working, teaching, and caring for the young, in nurturing the products and ideas of the culture, and in a more general "belief in the species." This response reflects a desire to leave something of benefit to humanity rather than an exclusive concern with one's own well-being.

SOCIAL CONCERNS: OLD AGE.

If the criterion for entering old age is the generally accepted retirement age of 65, then every day more than 4,000 people in the United States enter this life stage. For many adults, a central part of the self-concept is the vocational self, regardless of the type of work in which one is engaged. Thus, retirement from a formal work setting is a most important transition among the elderly.

According to Erikson, in the final life crisis, **integrity versus despair,** a person finds meaning in memories or instead looks back on life with dissatisfaction. Integrity implies emotional integration; it means accepting one's life as one's own responsibility. It is based not so much on what has happened as on how one feels about it. If a person has found meaning in certain goals, or even in suffering, then the crisis has been satisfactorily resolved. If not, the person experiences dissatisfaction, and the prospect of death brings despair.

With their infirmities, the elderly remind us of the young. As they become more and more limited, the earlier issues of industry, initiative, autonomy, and even trust arise again. With fewer and fewer friends and sometimes no family, loneliness is the critical psychological problem, often managed by maintaining a sense of humor about one's predicament.

CRITIQUE OF ERIKSON'S THEORY.

For many critics, Erikson's later stages seem vague, and there is a reason. The biological changes in adulthood are not nearly as sudden and marked as those in childhood and adolescence, and they are not accompanied by such obvious behavioral changes as the child's first steps, the adolescent's first shave, and the young mother's first lactation. As a result, Erikson's stages for adulthood become more philosophical, less biological. His theory has been criticized for these reasons: What are the operational definitions of intimacy, generativity, and integrity? And what is the evidence that people in adulthood behave in these ways? There is a need for greater precision in these later stages (Hamachek, 1990).

Other critics, on the grounds that self-knowledge can be achieved only after intimacy with someone else, maintain that the stage of intimacy should appear before that of identity. Still others argue that the order may be one way for men and the other way for women. These arguments suggest that these two developmental tasks influence one another, continue throughout adulthood, and are closely related. In fact, advanced stages of identity formation have been found to be associated with increased levels of intimacy formation (Kacergius & Adams, 1980).

In adulthood, the points of change instead seem to be determined more by social factors, especially socioeconomic status. Among people in the lower class, the prime of life is considered to be the late twenties and early thirties, and middle age begins at 40; people in the upper middle class regard 40 as the prime of life and 50 as the onset of middle age (Neugarten, 1968). Education, financial resources, and occupational status all create more opportunities for upper-class and middle-class people and therefore prolong the midlife stages (Hopson & Scally, 1980).

In the context of these criticisms, Erikson's theory has made three special contributions. The first major developmental theory to emphasize the full life span, it has called attention to the phases or periods in adulthood. Second, it has focused on social development, as distinct from other areas of development. Third, it has emphasized the adolescent identity crisis, an expression now so popularized that it is used throughout the adult life cycle. It is particularly relevant in our highly technical, rapidly changing society, one in which lifestyles and career paths may be disrupted without notice (Figure 12–14).

DEATH AND DYING. The subject of death, long taboo or ignored in Western research, has been studied in investigations with terminally ill patients, suggesting that dying also can be viewed in stages.

Five in number, these include: denial, in which the individual, responding to the shock, feels that a mistake has been made; anger, when the patient, accepting the evidence, feels unfairly treated; bargaining, a relatively short period during which the individual promises better behavior in exchange for a longer life; then depression, involving a feeling of hopelessness and grief at the separation from loved ones; and finally acceptance, if there is sufficient time, wherein the person is neither depressed nor angry but resigned to the final outcome of the life cycle (Kübler-Ross, 1969).

The response to this conception has been mixed and sometimes strongly disputed. While it concerns an important and neglected issue in

ELDERLY
Integrity vs. despair
Fulfillment in life

MIDDLE ADULTHOOD
Generativity vs. stagnation
Future generations

YOUNG ADULTHOOD
Intimacy vs. isolation
Personal and career commitments

ADOLESCENCE
Identity vs. role diffusion
Sense of self

LATE CHILDHOOD, 6–12
Industry vs. inferiority
Competence, ability

 MIDDLE CHILDHOOD, 3–6
Initiative vs. guilt
Effort, willingness

EARLY CHILDHOOD, 1–3
Autonomy vs. doubt
Self-control

 INFANCY, 0–1
Trust vs. mistrust
Dependence on others

FIGURE 12–14 PSYCHOSOCIAL STAGES. This sequence shows an expanding social context. Concerns at any stage may reappear later (Erickson, 1963).

American psychology, there is a need for further empirical support, precise definitions, and an overall theoretical structure. It does not apply when death is sudden, and it appears more relevant to cases of early, prolonged illness than to dying at a much later age.

With increasing research interest, there is now emphasis on *healthy death,* which is not a self-contradictory expression. Death, an inevitable conclusion to the developmental process, can be approached in ways that are appropriate and meaningful, resulting in healthy attitudes among the dying person, the family, and the support person (Smith & Maher, 1991). The prospects for a healthy death are most likely following a purposeful, healthy life.

Whether one accepts these psychological stages of death or Erikson's stages of life, there is no doubt that human beings are always in the process of developing. In one way or another, the life of every human being is shaped and reshaped every day.

• INDIVIDUAL DIFFERENCES •

Developmental psychologists sometimes study the ways in which people are alike, as illustrated in the stage theories of Erikson, Freud, Kohlberg, and Piaget. And sometimes they focus on the ways in which they differ, called the psychology of individual differences.

All of the adults in Skeels's comparison group differed from one another, but one person was special. He had achieved an education not only the highest in his group but also equal to or higher than that of all but four members of the transferred group. Through his work in printing, he had earned higher wages than the rest of the comparison group combined. Perhaps this surprising outcome was due in part to his disability, for he was the boy with the mild hearing loss. After leaving the orphanage, he went to a school for the deaf, where he received considerable individual attention. This personal support and careful instruction could have been a significant factor in his later favorable development.

The printer's position in the comparison group prompts us to recognize differences among us. The concept of **individual differences** states that all of us are unique; each of us deviates in one way or another from the average and from all other people in physical, cognitive, social, and other characteristics. Even identical twins are not exactly alike. The aim, in concluding this chapter, is to remind the reader about such variations. Psychologists study them to understand more fully and accurately the complexities of human behavior and experience, thereby according to all individuals greater respect and human dignity (Betz & Fitzgerald, 1993).

When compared with the people in his group, as well as with those in the transferred group, the printer's success also illustrates the interaction principle. It shows that a particular heredity can interact with a particular environment, producing unexpected results.

In addition, the success of the printer demonstrates possible shortcomings in Harold Skeels's research. No investigator can take into account all potentially relevant factors, and in this instance all children were first tested at approximately 18 months of age, when the scores are unreliable predictors of adult intelligence. The capacity of the printer, and indeed of all the subjects in these relatively small samples, might have been quite different from that indicated at the early age. Moreover, the rate of adoption for the transferred children was higher than that of the orphanage children. It could have influenced later adult status considerably. But of course adoption, in turn, was significantly influenced by the earlier gains.

Ideally, the Skeels research should be repeated with larger groups of subjects, more precise measures of early development, and greater control over adoption procedures. But unless we lose sight of what has been learned already, such studies should never take place. Orphanages like those of the 1930s are now prohibited by state law. Infants and young children awaiting adoption today, in hospitals and elsewhere, usually receive considerable individual attention, largely through the efforts of temporary foster families.

This approach to adoption, and indeed our modern view of effective day care for all children, owes much of its origin to two frail, runny-nosed, little orphans. They led Harold Skeels to a group of loving, retarded women.

• SUMMARY •

DEVELOPMENTAL ISSUES

1. The study of human development concerns changes that take place throughout the life span, and certain fundamental issues have arisen. One of these concerns the nature and duration of critical periods, during which the individual is unusually responsive to certain forms of stimulation. The heredity–environment issue concerns the contribution of each factor in human development. Today it is recognized that both heredity and environment are always present and always in interaction.

AT CONCEPTION

2. At conception, our biological inheritance is determined by 23 pairs of chromosomes or, more specifically, by the almost countless genes within the chromosomes. The genes contain the basic hereditary blueprint; they direct the development of many physical characteristics and behavioral traits.

3. Most human traits seem to depend on an interaction of multiple pairs of genes. Through controlled studies of animals, using genotypical and phenotypical perspectives, as well as studies of identical twins, the field of behavioral genetics attempts to discover the hereditary and environmental foundations of behavior.

PRENATAL PHASE AND INFANCY

4. The first three months of prenatal life are particularly susceptible to the influence of teratogens,

meaning factors that disrupt normal development, producing birth defects. Neural development continues after birth, at which time the brain is only about one-fourth of its adult size.

5. The principle of differentiation indicates that development proceeds from the simple to the complex, from general reactions to highly specific responses, and it is evident in both sensory and motor development. The normal human infant, for example, progresses from lying to sitting to standing and to walking on a predictable basis.

6. The phenomena of imprinting and critical periods in animals suggest that the timing of early experiences can be influential in human development as well. These so-called sensitive periods in human beings are not as sharply defined as those in animals, but they can play an influential role in learning and social development.

CHILDHOOD AND ADOLESCENCE

7. When developmental responses appear in a given sequence at about the same age in all members of a species, they are said to be due to maturation, as in cephalocaudal and proximodistal development. In postnatal life, human beings show very rapid physical development for the first two years. A second period of rapid physical development occurs during adolescence, when hormonal secretions produce physiological changes having wide repercussions.

8. Stages of cognitive development have been identified by Jean Piaget. In the sensorimotor stage, the child is simply acting on and experiencing the environment. In the preoperational stage, the child slowly overcomes certain aspects of egocentrism,

perceiving the world from others' viewpoints. As concrete operations are achieved, the child becomes capable of solving concrete problems. Formal operations, not necessarily achieved by all adolescents or adults, involve the capacity for solving abstract problems.

9. The development of morality is studied in two dimensions, moral reasoning and moral behavior. One view of moral reasoning postulates three basic stages: preconventional morality, conventional morality, and postconventional morality. Correlations between moral reasoning and moral behavior have not been substantial.

10. According to Erikson's life span theory of psychological stages, human development involves a series of eight crises, four of which occur in childhood: trust, autonomy, initiative, and industry. The psychosocial crisis during adolescence is that of establishing a personal identity, which means developing a sense of self as a consistent yet unique person.

❧

ADULTHOOD AND OLD AGE

11. Maximum physical growth and ability are achieved by the late twenties, after which a slow but steady decrease begins in strength, quickness, and size. Throughout young adulthood and middle adult-hood, the rate of change depends partly on environmental circumstances. The elderly can vary sharply in physical ability, a condition partly responsible for references to the young-old and old-old.

12. There is no inevitable decline in cognitive ability in young and middle adulthood and sometimes even into the early years of old age. There may even be steady improvements, depending significantly on the type and extent of intellectual activity in the individual's adult life. Among the elderly, the inevitable decline is most obvious in the speed of mental functions.

13. Healthy adults, according to Erikson, can find satisfaction in relations with others. The psychosocial crises in adulthood involve intimacy, which occurs with another person, and generativity, which concerns future generations. Elderly people are confronted with the eighth and last psychosocial crisis, achieving integrity, which means developing a sense of meaning in one's life.

❧

INDIVIDUAL DIFFERENCES

14. The concept of individual differences states that everyone is unique. We all differ from one another in physical, cognitive, and social dimensions.

• WORKING WITH PSYCHOLOGY •

❧ REVIEW OF KEY CONCEPTS ❧

human development

Developmental Issues
critical period
heredity–environment issue
identical twins
fraternal twins
interaction principle

At Conception
chromosomes
genes

sperm
ova
dominant gene
recessive gene
polygenic trait
behavioral genetics
genotype
phenotype

Prenatal Phase and Infancy
differentiation
zygote
embryo

fetus
teratogens
cephalocaudal development
proximodistal development
imprinting
attachment
stranger anxiety
separation anxiety
caretaker–child interaction

Childhood and Adolescence
physical development
maturation

adolescence
estrogens
androgens
puberty
cognitive development
assimilation
accommodation
sensorimotor period
object permanence
preoperational period
cognitive egocentrism
perceptual egocentrism
conservation task
concrete operations
formal operations

egocentrism
information processing
  viewpoint
moral development
preconventional morality
conventional morality
postconventional morality
social development
gender identity
psychosocial stages
trust versus mistrust
autonomy versus doubt
initiative versus guilt
industry versus inferiority

identity versus role
  diffusion
identity crisis

Adulthood and Old Age
metacognition
Alzheimer's disease
midlife crisis
intimacy versus isolation
generativity versus stagnation
integrity versus despair

Individual Differences
individual differences

❧ CLASS DISCUSSION/CRITICAL THINKING ❧

A NARRATIVE TWIST

Assume that the transferred orphans in Skeels's study had been sent to live with women in prison, rather than with mentally retarded women. Would this circumstance have produced for the children outcomes different from those obtained with the retarded women? What might have been the chief differences, if any? From the opposite perspective, would the presence of the children have influenced the prisoners? If so, how? If not, why not? Explain your views. ❧

TOPICAL QUESTIONS

• *Developmental Issues.* Suppose you are allowed to study human development from only one perspective, either chronological for just one area of development throughout the life span *or* topical for all three areas at just one stage of life. Which

approach would you choose? Why? Describe the specific chronological stages or topics to which you would give most emphasis.
• *At Conception.* Is it possible that a grandparent may make no contribution to the genetic inheritance of his or her grandchild? Explain the reason for your answer, referring to the matter of chance in the assortment of chromosomes within the sperm and ovum and in the association of a particular sperm and ovum at fertilization.
• *Prenatal Phase and Infancy.* The concept of imprinting is typically applied to the attachment of offspring to the mother shortly after birth. To what extent might this concept be applied to teenage lovers in middle adolescence? Discuss the question of readiness. Point out the defects and limitations in this speculation.

• *Childhood and Adolescence.* Is the development of morality primarily a problem in cognitive psychology or social psychology? Pick one side and develop an argument. Then defend the other side of the argument.
• *Adulthood and Old Age.* In which decade of adulthood—the thirties, forties, fifties, or sixties—will you be most gratified with your life? Give specific reasons for your choice and indicate the reasons why you do not choose the other decades.
• *Individual Differences.* Consider the question of individual differences at the various life stages. Are they larger in infancy, childhood, adolescence, middle adulthood, or old age? Defend your answer.

❧ TOPICS OF RELATED INTEREST ❧

Freud's views of sexual development constitute a stage theory (14). The nature–nurture issue reappears in

the context of intelligence (13). Individual differences are relevant to discussions of intelligence (13),

personality (14), and variability in statistics (18).

THE TESTING MOVEMENT
Intelligence Testing
Evaluating Tests
Tests as Tools

EXTREMES OF INTELLIGENCE
Mental Retardation
Mental Giftedness

THEORIES OF INTELLIGENCE
Psychometric Approach
Cognitive Approach

NATURE–NURTURE ISSUE
Studies of Group Differences
Methods of Assessment
Nature–Nurture Interaction

INTELLIGENCE AND AGING
Cross-Sectional Studies
Longitudinal Studies
Importance of Experience

13
INTELLIGENCE
AND TESTING

RENEE LIVED IN NORWICH WITH HER FAMILY. IT MIGHT HAVE BEEN CALLED AN EXTENDED, NO-PARENT FAMILY, FOR SHE LIVED WITH HER GRANDMOTHER AND two cousins.

The Grants, along with 30 other families, had been selected for study by a team of research psychologists from a nearby university, examining influences on the literacy of children in low-income communities. The team members were interviewing the families, observing the children, and administering various tests.

"Renee will do my homework if I sweep the kitchen floor for her," Tanya announced proudly to their visitor from the university, perhaps without fully appreciating the difference between housework and homework. They do *sound* alike. The visiting psychologist, on the lookout for the school dropout, was interested in all members of the household, including the grandmother.

Granny was virtually illiterate. In her late sixties, she was learning to read in a class held at the building where she cleaned offices every weekday evening. Granny looked forward to these classes. "The teacher is understanding," she explained.

"The best person I look up to is my grandmother," Renee declared, "because when I want something, I get it. When I'm sick, she takes care of me. When I want to talk to her about something, she'll listen. She is like a mother to me."

Renee arrived at her grandmother's house almost ten years earlier, at age two. She was followed by her younger cousins, Tanya and Sharon. These three schoolgirls and Granny formed a close family unit, organizing their lives around the television set to a large extent. They shared their home with two long-term boarders and an intermittent stream of relatives who appeared and disappeared at a moment's notice. These transient kin seemed to have no more in common with one another, or with the Grant family, than people at a motel.

For more than 20 years, Granny had lived in the neighborhood, a low-income community, ethnically and linguistically mixed. She even lived in the same house, sent her children to the local school, and was sending her grandchildren there. She enjoyed watching them set out for school each day. That school was quite adequate as far as she was concerned.

Robin Henderson lived in the same neighborhood. As 12-year-old classmates in Mr. Barasch's sixth-grade class, she and Renee maintained a special friendship, although they came from quite different

BEIRCE SCHOOL ROOM 20 1990–91

homes. Robin shared a meticulously neat and clean three-bedroom apartment with her nuclear family: both parents, two older brothers, and a younger sister. For economic reasons, they had immigrated from Trinidad, and both parents held jobs outside the home.

In the Henderson household, furnished with books and magazines, schoolwork was considered most important. Ms. Henderson, in particular, held high educational aspirations for her children, an outlook that prompted her to criticize the Norwich schools from time to time. Robin was bright, and Ms. Henderson had committed herself to long-term career goals for all of her children (Snow, Barnes, Chandler, Goodman, & Hemphill, 1991).

The different intellectual abilities of Renee and Robin, the school dropout problem, and the learning activities in Mr. Barasch's classroom offer a useful narrative about intelligence, testing, and related research questions. Renee, for example, caused some concern among her teachers. Her low scores on intelligence tests and her background in a largely nonliterate household placed her at risk for leaving school early. Would that happen? What might be done to prevent this outcome?

Amid these practical questions, one long-standing abstract problem for psychologists and teachers alike has been the definition of intelligence. Today **intelligence** is most commonly defined as the capacity to learn from experience and to adapt to new situations. This definition has the advantage of being applicable at various levels of the animal kingdom, but it does not show the complexity of the concept or the differences of opinion about it. Our discussion is therefore organized around four related controversies, presented in the context of the Grant family and their neighbors, the Hendersons.

First, we look at the testing movement. It began with the measurement of intelligence, still disputed today. Second, we consider extremes of intelligence, especially the question of appropriate schooling for children with retardation and giftedness. It has had a remarkably stormy history. Third, we examine diverse theories of intelligence, noting that psychologists themselves have been unable to agree on the basic nature of this concept. The fourth great controversy concerns the nature-nurture issue. Here we note the complex roles of heredity and environment in human development. In conclusion, we consider current views on a question that no longer appears controversial, at least for the moment: intelligence and aging. What happens to us intellectually as we grow older?

• THE TESTING MOVEMENT •

At the time of Granny's birth, in the first decade of this century, there were no significant psychological tests of any sort. Psychological characteristics were considered immeasurable. Intelligence, aptitude, and personality could not be measured in physical terms and therefore could not be measured at all—or so it was believed. No one would have seriously considered measuring Granny's intelligence, except a young Frenchman, Alfred Binet.

INTELLIGENCE TESTING

As director of the first psychological laboratory in France, Binet had been asked by the Ministry of Education to solve a practical problem. Which Parisian schoolchildren had insufficient ability to profit from normal classroom instruction? Decisions based solely on teachers' judgments were inap-

propriate because they could be influenced by extraneous factors: the child's conduct, appearance, family, and so forth. Binet therefore began to construct an **intelligence test,** broadly defined as an instrument for measuring a wide range of mental and some physical abilities, especially verbal, numerical, and social competence.

BINET'S EARLY SCALES. The fundamental idea in Binet's approach, which had not been attempted previously in any precise fashion, was to arrange a series of questions or problems in everyday life in order of increasing difficulty. He and his collaborator, Theophile Simon, therefore devised a number of different questions involving memory, attention, and visual discrimination. Then, by experimenting with children who were making normal progress at home and in school, they determined the difficulty of these tasks, discovering which of them could be performed by average children at each of the various age levels.

At the lowest level, for example, Binet moved around a dimly lit room with a lighted candle. No question was asked. Did the child follow the candle with its gaze, moving the eyes and head as necessary? In the intermediate range, a somewhat older child was asked to imitate gestures and obey brief requests: "Touch your nose." "Put this box on the table." At a still higher level, the child was asked to define words, remember numbers, and think abstractly. "Tell me what *pretend* means." "Say these numbers after me: 7, 4, 5, 2." Binet and Simon tested normal schoolchildren in these ways and then in 1905 published this collection of items (Binet & Simon, 1905).

Immediately, this test became a target of criticism. Detractors objected that it had an arbitrary zero point. A child who could not answer any questions nevertheless had *some* intelligence. Binet agreed, replying that his scale was not intended to be like physical measurement. His goal was merely to classify children according to ability, not to measure intelligence in absolute amounts. His test showed which children were most capable, least capable, of average ability, and so forth.

Others objected that the test did not assess inborn ability, apart from experience. Again Binet replied that his purpose had been misunderstood. His focus was on current intellectual performance, not its origins.

Psychiatrists and teachers also had grave doubts. How could a 40-minute test be more accurate than a longer interview or extended classroom experience? Binet's response was to ask them how they formed their conclusions, and it was clear that they also resorted to tests. But their tests were awkwardly applied, involved inconsistent scoring standards, and varied from one instance to another (Tuddenham, 1962).

To dispel further resistance, Binet devised an improved instrument, the 1908 scale, eliminating the weakest items and adding a variety of new ones. All of these items were identified according to age levels from 3 to 12 years. An item was included at the 5-year level, for example, because the average five-year-old child could pass it. It was too difficult for the average four-year-old and too easy for the average six-year-old. With this procedure the 1908 scale could be used to determine a child's mental age. The **mental age** (MA) is the level of mental ability of the average child at any given chronological age. All five-year-old children who are average in intelligence have a mental age of 5 years.

STANFORD-BINET SCALE. The Binet scales soon found advocates in the United States, especially at Stanford University in California. By discarding certain items, developing others, and changing the age levels, psychologists there in 1916 prepared a massive adaptation of this scale for the American population (Terman, 1916). This well-constructed test, the **Stanford-Binet Intelligence Scale,** became the leading intelligence test in the

AGE	SAMPLE ITEM
2	"Point to your toes."
6	"Tell me what's next: A minute is short; an hour is ___."
10	"Try to repeat these numbers: 8–9–4–2–6–1."
14	"How are 'begining' and 'end' alike?"
Adult	"What does this mean? 'The watched pot never boils?'"

TABLE 13–1 STANFORD-BINET INTELLIGENCE SCALE. As these illustrations show, test items for young children typically involve concrete activities, such as building with blocks or pointing to things. Those for older subjects are generally more abstract.

world. Now there are standard versions, adaptations, and short forms for different groups all over the globe (Prewett, 1992; Table 13–1).

A refinement to the concept of mental age was adapted from Germany. The child's cumulative age since birth, called the **chronological age** (CA), is also considered. Using the conventional formula, the mental age is divided by the chronological age to yield an **intelligence quotient** (IQ), which is simply a ratio of these two ages: IQ = MA/CA (100). A child with a chronological age of 10 and a mental age of 10 has an IQ of 100, for the result is always multiplied by 100 to remove the decimal point. Tests that yield intelligence quotients are constructed so that the average IQ is 100.

The advantage of the IQ is that it can be used to compare children of different ages, such as Renee, Tanya, and Sharon, all with different levels of ability. For example, a six-year-old child with a mental age of 8 would have an IQ of 133. Compared to age peers, this six-year-old child and a nine-year-old child with a mental age of 12 are equally bright (Table 13–2).

THE WECHSLER SCALES. Not long after the Stanford-Binet Intelligence Scale appeared, a group of psychologists at Bellevue Psychiatric Hospital in New York City experienced its shortcom-

IQ	= MA/CA × 100
	= 8/6 × 100 = 133
	= 12/9 × 100 = 133

TABLE 13–2 COMPUTATION OF IQ. The conventional method of computing the IQ provides a rapid, close approximation to the modern deviation method, developed from statistical tables.

ings for work with their particular population, largely adults. These psychologists, in a hospital setting, under the direction of David Wechsler, began developing a test more suitable for clinical work. They focused on adults; they developed procedures for identifying different types of intellectual abilities; and in doing so, they recognized the disruptive role of adjustment problems, including psychiatric difficulties (Wechsler, 1939).

Appearing in 1939, this test became the forerunner of several revisions and extensions downward for younger subjects, now collectively called the **Wechsler Intelligence Scales.** The adult edition, used for people from the late teens to the mid-70s, is called the *Wechsler Adult Intelligence Scale (WAIS)* (1981). There is an edition for children, the *Wechsler Intelligence Scale for Children (WISC-III)* (1991). Another edition serves preschool children. In addition, there are Spanish versions, *Escala de Inteligencia Wechsler para Adultos (EIWA)* and another for children, *Escala de Inteligencia Wechsler para Niños (EIWN-Revisada)*, referred to later with respect to culturally sensitive testing.

In contrast to the Stanford-Binet, the Wechsler items are grouped into two large categories: verbal and nonverbal. The nonverbal category assesses intelligence without using words, an essential approach in cases of language handicaps. Then the items in these two major categories are divided into subtests. For example, the verbal subtests measure memory, vocabulary, verbal reasoning, and so forth. The nonverbal items measure capacity for spatial relations, perceptual speed, nonverbal reasoning, and the like (Figure 13–1).

Administration of a full Wechsler test provides an overall measure of intelligence, or IQ, including a *verbal IQ* and a *nonverbal IQ,* the latter also called *performance IQ,* In addition, scores on the separate subtests, when examined as a group, provide a profile of the individual's intellectual strengths and weaknesses. The capacity to generate these different profiles is an important characteristic of the Wechsler tests (Burgess, 1991).

❧

EVALUATING TESTS

All children in Renee's sixth-grade class had been administered the vocabulary subtest of the Wechsler Intelligence Scale for Children. Renee never did well on these tests, a concern for her teachers, as well as members of the university research team. Some students, when tested once and then again

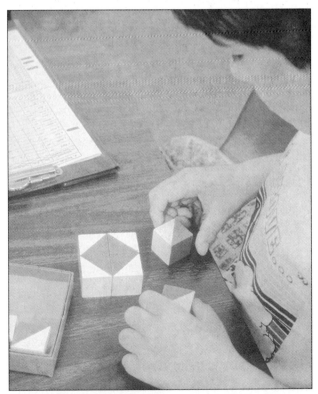

FIGURE 13–1 WECHSLER NONVERBAL ITEMS. The subject here is arranging colored blocks to form various patterns.

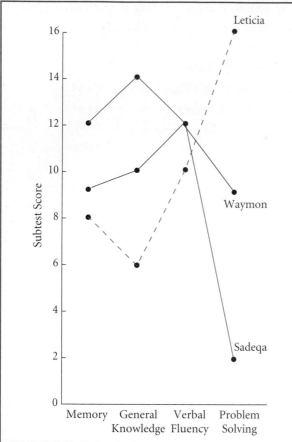

**FIGURE 13-2 DIFFERENCES IN
MENTAL ABILITIES.** Each person achieved an
average score of ten on four Wechsler subtests. However,
their results form very different profiles, indicating that
each overall IQ may represent diverse mental abilities.

four years later, actually obtained lower scores on
the second occasion. These outcomes might have
been influenced by the tendency of Mr. Barasch to
use low-level textbooks. In any case, the scores were
used for decisions about grade promotion and
placement in reading groups (Snow et al., 1991).

Such tests can yield useful information about
individuals (Figure 13-2). But they need adequate
reliability, validity, and norms.

THE QUESTION OF RELIABILITY. Consider a man who is worried about his weight. Stepping on a scale, he notes that he weighs 160
pounds, an unexpected loss of 10 pounds. After
stepping off the scale, he decides to weigh himself

a second time. The scale reads 158. Then, he tries
his neighbor's scale, which is another version of his
own model, and it gives a reading of 161. There is
still some doubt in his mind, however. So he asks
his neighbor to read the dial, and the neighbor
reports a reading of 160.

This example illustrates the question of **reliability,** which concerns the consistency of test
results—that is, the agreement among scores whenever the test is administered to the same people on
several occasions.

One of Binet's early items asked the child
which would be better to eat, a piece of wood or a
piece of cake. If the child chose correctly on some
trials and incorrectly on others, the item had low
reliability. Assuming that the characteristic being
measured remains constant, the answer should be
the same on every occasion. Thus, **test-retest reliability** is determined by administering the test to a
group of subjects, repeating the procedure later
with the *same* subjects, and then comparing the two
sets of scores. The test is reliable to the extent that
each subject achieves the same score on both occasions.

Subjects taking a psychological test for the second time may recall their earlier answers, thereby
generating an erroneously high measure of reliability. The approach here is to use **equivalent-form
reliability,** which involves different versions of the
same test, similar in content and structure but containing different questions. If the subjects achieve
similar scores on the two versions, the test has high
equivalent-form reliability.

To be useful, the answers must be scored. The
issue here, called **interjudge reliability,** concerns
consistency among examiners in scoring the same
response. If two or more examiners award the same
score to the same answer, the test item has high
interjudge reliability. If not, it has low reliability
and is of doubtful value.

These three types of reliability were illustrated
by the man checking his weight. He stepped on his

scale a second time, test-retest reliability. He tried his neighbor's version of the same scale, equivalent-form reliability. And he asked his neighbor to read the scale, a matter of interjudge reliability.

THE QUESTION OF VALIDITY. In evaluating any test, validity is the key issue. The concern in **validity** is whether a test measures what it purports to measure. A valid test accurately assesses the characteristic in question. For example, a valid test of sales ability measures sales ability, not something else.

There are many forms of validity but, among them, **face validity** is not true validity. It merely indicates that a test *seems* appropriate for its alleged purpose. The test looks like it works. In World War I, when aircraft pilots first engaged in warfare, it was decided that a good pilot would be calm and unperturbed in the face of the unexpected. Thus, it seemed that the gunshot-and-cold-cloth test would be useful. A pistol suddenly was fired near the unsuspecting candidate; later, a cold cloth was flung in his face. Hundreds of men were thereby rejected as pilots, for their reactions were judged to be too slow or too prolonged for good pilots. Later, during World War II, this test was studied further and found to be worthless. The startle pattern and hand tremors did not predict success or failure as a pilot. The cold-cloth-in-the-face test had nothing more than face validity (National Research Council, 1943).

Among the true types of validity, **predictive validity** makes a statement about the future; it attempts to forecast the performance of subjects at a later date, after they have received some form of training or other preparation. A test with significant predictive validity for aircraft pilots would identify candidates likely to profit most from pilot training.

In contrast, **concurrent validity** is concerned with the present; it indicates which subjects are best suited to perform a certain task right away, without further training. A test with high concurrent validity, for example, would identify the best person for immediate work as a translator of foreign languages or consultant in computer technology.

To determine the validity of a test, apart from face validity, it is necessary to have a *criterion*, which is a standard for judging the value of something. For a test of sales ability, sales records might be useful as a criterion. Many people would be administered the test of sales ability, and these results would be compared with their sales records. Did the people with high sales records earn high scores on the test? Did those who made few sales make low scores? If so, the test has some degree of validity for sales ability. It can identify or predict this characteristic.

However it is determined, validity generally is the most important characteristic of a test. If validity is reasonably high, ranging at least in the upper half of a scale from 0.00, meaning no validity, to 1.00, indicating perfect validity, then the test can be regarded as having some capacity for measuring what it claims to measure. Reliability coefficients are typically higher, but they do not provide any direct evidence of the validity of a test.

As a rule, a test that is valid, accurately measuring what it purports to measure, is also reliable—providing the same results on each occasion. In contrast, a test can be reliable, giving the same result each time, without measuring what it purports to measure. Requesting schoolchildren to race around the playground may produce much the same results each time, demonstrating reliability, but this test is not a valid measure of intelligence.

THE NEED FOR NORMS. The other concern is **norms,** which are standards or guidelines for interpreting a test score, developed from previous test scores. Norms are collections of prior scores that serve as reference points for determining what is normal, high, or low on a particular test or test item. Any score can be judged against this collection of scores.

When using a test, there may be a need for *national norms,* meaning scores that are representative of the population throughout the country. On other occasions, it may be more appropriate to use *local norms,* obtained from a specific group, such as the pilots for just one airline.

Using the national norms on a reading test, Renee was found to be more than a year below her expected grade level. Using the local norms for the Norwich public schools, she was closer to average. In decisions about schooling, hiring, and promotion, local norms may prove more helpful than scores from the general population (Darou, 1992).

TESTS AS TOOLS

Psychological tests are instruments for solving a problem. They provide a sample of behavior for making decisions about selection and placement. Is Ms. Henderson a promising candidate for a certain job at the bank? Is her oldest son in a school environment suited to his interests and abilities?

TYPES OF TESTS. Literally hundreds of new tests appear each year in our society, designed for all sorts of purposes. Their profusion is so great that catalogues of thousands of pages are needed to describe them, containing information on the publisher, price, and purpose, as well as on reliability, validity, and norms. The oldest of these catalogues, now in its eleventh edition, is the *Mental Measurements Yearbook* (Kramer & Conoley, 1992). It lists 18 categories of tests, summarized as five types, the first of which has been described already: intelligence, achievement, aptitude, interest, and personality.

The reader is perhaps all too familiar with the **achievement test,** which measures a person's current level of accomplishment in a particular field, ranging from Latin to landscaping. There are many national tests of this type, such as the *Wide Range Achievement Test,* used in Renee's school. When her

class was tested for word recognition, the students scored on the average 1.6 years below the national norms. In other words, their achievement was 1.6 years lower than that of the average student of their age throughout the country. Renee's level was still lower. She was a year and a half behind even her own classmates.

The capacity to learn is known as *aptitude.* An **aptitude test** measures probable accomplishment at some future date, after training. A test of flying aptitude should have high predictive validity. A test of flying achievement indicates a person's current ability as a pilot—right now, as the plane sits on the runway, ready for takeoff. It should have high concurrent validity. Electronic, mechanical, and clerical workers are the largest labor groups in the United States, and tests of these aptitudes are widespread (Figure 13–3).

There are no right or wrong answers on a vocational **interest inventory** because here people merely indicate their *preferences* for work-related activities.

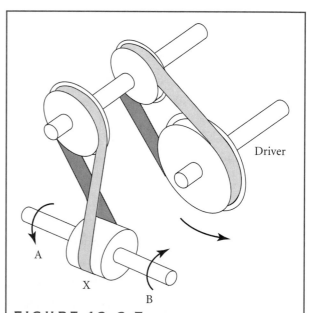

FIGURE 13–3 TEST OF MECHANICAL APTITUDE. With the driver moving in the indicated direction, determine the direction of rotation of axle *X*. In evaluating an answer, the examiner may consider the amount of time required and the probability of guessing correctly.

On the *Strong-Campbell Interest Inventory,* for example, a person reads a list of diverse occupations, school subjects, and hobbies and then for each item marks "Like," "Indifferent," or "Dislike." In vocational counseling, this information is used with a great deal of other background material, for it does not consider ability in any significant manner.

Finally, the **personality test** aims to provide a broad description of an individual, measuring characteristic habits, interests, attitudes, and other qualities, including forms of adjustment and maladjustment. Discussed at length in the next chapter, these tests tend to be broad and diverse, ranging from multiple-choice items to highly ambiguous stimuli, such as vague pictures and inkblots.

USING TESTS. All types of tests may be improperly used. The intention may be good but the practice poor. A test *must* be administered, scored, and interpreted appropriately. The misinterpretation of test scores is a most significant factor in the controversy over intelligence testing (Snyderman & Rothman, 1987; Figure 13–4).

Mr. Barasch used the Wide Range Achievement Test to establish reading groups of different levels, and Renee's performance on one test illustrates the potential danger. Her score was low, and in an interview with one of the psychologists studying the Norwich schools, she gave various explanations. She had been sick the day of the test. Moreover, she had forgotten her glasses. How could she answer the questions if she could not read them? She even recruited Granny to plead her case—so determined was she that the score should be ignored or the test administered again (Snow, 1991).

To summarize the testing movement in a positive way, at least three uses of psychological tests can be recommended without significant reserva-

FIGURE 13–4 USING TESTS. These pictures involve a test of reasoning. Arrange them in a meaningful sequence. *Answer:* The arrangement considered correct is *D, F, C, A, E,* and *B.* However, *D* is sometimes placed last instead of first. The man is seen taking his coat and hat off the hook rather than hanging them up before eating. His dinner has been stolen, and he wants to leave before losing anything else. This reasoning lessens the joke, but the careful examiner is aware that the answer is not contradicted by evidence in the drawings.

tions. They appear to avoid most, if not all, of the limitations. First, individual tests can be useful for diagnosis. They can assist in any detailed study and understanding of one person. Second, group tests can be an efficient technique in research, useful for collecting large masses of data from many subjects. And third, group tests can be useful for identifying people with special talents. The reason is that high scores are typically more valid than low scores. People may perform below their level of ability for many reasons, but they can hardly perform above it. The superior scores can be noted and the others ignored (Jensen, 1980).

• EXTREMES OF INTELLIGENCE •

"You've got your assignment; it's time to start," Mr. Barasch said, beginning a classroom project on the computation of fractions.

"I don't like yellow paper," objected Renee, leaving her desk.

Borrowing some white sheets from classmates, she distributed them to her neighbors and kept one for herself. Then she raised her hand: "Hey, Mr. Barasch. I need help on number 16."

"Okay," he said, assisting her for a moment. As soon as he left, Renee and her neighbors began talking and giggling again.

Mr. Barasch became increasingly exasperated as the lesson continued, attempting to deal with too many students at one time, each with different needs and different abilities. Concerned that his students might be disruptive, he planned activities that were simple to supervise. One method was to ask students to read aloud. This approach of course failed to take into account their different abilities (Snow et al., 1991).

Mental abilities, and most other human characteristics, are distributed across a wide range, often according to the **normal distribution,** meaning a bell-shaped curve in which most scores cluster near the center and the rest taper off uniformly to the extremes. On intelligence tests, the average IQ is 100, and the extremes of intelligence refer to people at the very ends of the intelligence continuum, comprising the upper and lower 2% of the general population (Figure 13–5).

Those in the lower 2%, with an IQ below 70, are people with **mental retardation** or *mental disability.* As a result, they learn more slowly than others and need more support in the learning environment. The intelligence of those in the upper 2%, with an IQ above 130, is called **mental giftedness.** Compared to others, they learn rapidly and easily, often by themselves. Whenever possible, special provisions are made for the education of both groups.

It should be noted that some people with normal or even high intelligence may have a **learning disability,** meaning a difficulty with some specific mental skill, such as reading, spelling, or mathematics. Some of these disabilities appear to be caused by perceptual deficits, others by defects in memory, many of which are not noticeable in daily life and therefore remain undetected for years, as claimed for Thomas Edison, among others. These disabili-

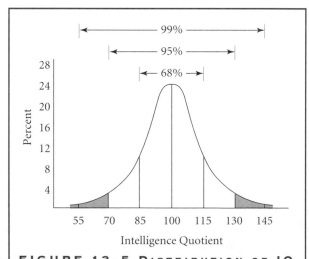

FIGURE 13–5 DISTRIBUTION OF IQ.
The graph shows the approximate percentage of the general population at different points within the full range of IQs. The shaded areas represent the extremes of intelligence.

ties also may appear and disappear inexplicably, emphasizing the need for regular reevaluation of schoolchildren.

Mr. Barasch had made one provision for the differences in ability among his students. When the ten-o'clock bell rang, the six students at the highest reading level remained in his classroom—to use books with a restricted vocabulary, designed for sixth graders of *average* ability. Those in the middle and lowest groups filed into the hall, Renee included, and headed for the remedial classroom, although none of them had mental retardation. In the Norwich schools, there were special classes for those students (Snow et al., 1991).

MENTAL RETARDATION

An individual with mental retardation is described as having a handicap that ranges from mild to moderate to profound, depending on the IQ and other factors. In all cases, the focus is on treatment, not custodial care (Figure 13-6). However, before turning to that issue we should consider the causes of retardation, emphasizing that although the following factors are considered separately, they often act in combination (Scott & Carran, 1987).

GENETIC FACTORS. When retardation occurs extensively along family lines, it seems to be inherited. In such cases parents, children, and even grandchildren have received custodial care in the same institution. It should be noted, incidentally, that *incest,* sexual relations between people closely related in kinship, can be a cause of mental handicap. In these unions, the potential influence of detrimental recessive genes is sharply increased. It is no accident that the fear and stigma of incest have deep roots in human history (Jancar & Johnston, 1990).

Some instances of genetic retardation occur in **phenylketonuria** (PKU), transmitted by a recessive gene in both parents. This disorder can be diagnosed at an early age by testing the urine of new-

FIGURE 13-6 EDUCATION OF PERSONS WITH MENTAL RETARDATION. The instructor is using role playing to teach a student how to clean the floors. After demonstrating the correct procedure, the instructor asks the student to repeat this behavior using the same equipment.

born babies for the presence of phenylpyruvic acid, which interferes with brain functioning, producing mental sluggishness. If detected, the baby receives a controlled diet, removing the phenylpyruvic acid, and the disorder is alleviated. The symptoms also may be managed by ingestion of a phenylalanine-free dietary supplement (Hoskin, Sasitharan, & Howard, 1992).

The defect known as **Down's syndrome** is usually a condition of moderate retardation, due to a chromosomal disorder. A person with Down's syndrome has an extra twenty-first chromosome, and therefore the defect is sometimes called *trisomy 21.* The incidence of Down's syndrome increases sharply among the offspring of older mothers.

Still another form of genetic retardation, fragile X syndrome, is more common in males, accounting for 5–7% of all of their retardation, but it can also occur in females. So called because it is associated with a fragile site on the X chromosome, the **fragile X syndrome** involves difficulties in information processing, defective language, and deficits in social skills. Down's syndrome and fragile X syndrome are the most common forms of genetically based mental retardation (McEvoy, 1992; Zigler & Hodapp, 1991). Pharmacological treatment with folic acid often suppresses fragile X syndrome; it may even have a beneficial effect on cognitive and behavioral development (Curfs, Wiegers, & Fryns, 1990).

HEALTH FACTORS. In other cases, low intelligence is caused by some physical damage or disease in the pregnant woman or infant. These health problems include intoxication, brain injury, and malnutrition, and when a treatment is available, it is essentially medical. In one such disorder, **cretinism,** the individual is characteristically dwarfed, overweight, and lethargic, with an IQ that usually does not exceed 50. This problem may be related to underactivity of the thyroid gland in the mother or to nutritional deficiencies in her diet. If cretinism is diagnosed early and thyroxin is administered, sometimes this condition too can be alleviated.

A more widespread cause of mental retardation, perhaps a leading cause in the United States, is **fetal alcohol syndrome** (FAS), a cluster of traits including low birth weight, sleep disturbances, poor coordination, and low intelligence, found among infants born to mothers who consumed alcohol during the pregnancy. At one time, it was believed that this syndrome arose only through alcoholic mothers. It now appears that even very mild alcohol intake places the baby at risk (Phelps & Grabowski, 1992).

CULTURAL DEPRIVATION. Lack of normal learning experiences early in life, called **cultural deprivation,** can contribute to mental retardation. We saw this condition in the case of orphanage children left unattended and isolated for most of their childhood. They showed significantly less mental ability in adulthood than did a comparison group of children who, living in an institution with many older women, received considerable attention, stimulation, and learning opportunities (Skeels, 1966).

Over half of the children in Norwich, a small city in the northeastern United States, lived in deprived circumstances, as defined by eligibility for the free-lunch program. Only three towns in the state reported lower household incomes. Almost 25% of the students did not speak English as their native language, and many of the adults did not use literacy—reading and writing—to any significant degree. To learn to read, Renee and her cousins had to rely on a school system in which the dropout rate was increasing steadily (Snow et al., 1991).

The child deprived of early learning experiences not only fails to acquire certain necessary skills—and the conjectured brain development— but is also deprived of the intellectual tools for developing additional skills. Recognition of this "snowball effect" has prompted educational programs such as Head Start, designed to enable underprivileged children to develop to the best of their potential.

EMOTIONAL FACTORS. Intellectual functioning also can be disrupted by adjustment disorders, and many people with mental retardation experience emotional problems. The original handicap leads to frustration, which causes emotional upset, in turn engendering a further mental handicap.

One student in Mr. Barasch's class was handicapped for several reasons, including emotional factors. Very shy, he avoided his teachers and school assignments. Exposed to the frequent arguments of his parents, he was often ill or tardy at school. Assessing his chances of completing high school, his fifth-grade teacher called them "doubtful" (Snow et al., 1991).

EDUCATION OF PEOPLE WITH RETARDATION. Among several problems in educating people with retardation, one concerns children who simply have some specific difficulty in a normal classroom. They are learning disabled, not mentally retarded, and usually have abilities too high for placement in special programs. In most schools, the aim is **mainstreaming,** which avoids complete separation of special-needs children and instead integrates them with other children through special provisions in the typical classroom. These provisions include greater structure, highly concrete materials, and a slower pace, including extra practice on specific tasks (Simpson & Myles, 1993; Springer & Coleman, 1992).

Children with mental retardation are often considered in three groups. The child who is *educable* is able to profit from instruction at some level of elementary school—learning academic, social, and occupational skills to the point of total or partial independence as an adult. The *trainable* child is not educable in the sense of achieving significant academic skills or social and occupational independence. This child can learn self-help skills, however, and can make limited contributions to work at home. For the *totally dependent* person, custodial care is required to fulfill personal needs and for survival.

MENTAL GIFTEDNESS

Popular belief in earlier days promoted the stereotype of a person with mental retardation as almost totally helpless, a myth that hopefully has been dispelled. Popular belief also gave a picture of the genius as physically weak and socially inferior, inept in almost everything except purely intellectual activity. Was this belief also a myth?

CHARACTERISTICS OF GIFTED PEOPLE. Lewis Terman, using Binet's instrument and others like it, decided to study this question. In fact, Terman, at Stanford University, was the chief force behind the development of the Stanford-Binet, and he identified over 1,000 schoolchildren with IQs ranging from 135 to 200. This group of

boys and girls, affectionately known as Termites, ranged from 3 to 19 years of age at the time. Terman hoped to determine the mental, physical, and personality characteristics of these intellectually gifted children.

Another purpose of this study was to observe human development throughout these people's lives, sometimes called *life span research.* The Termites were examined several times as children; they were examined again at 30 years of age; and altogether they have been studied intermittently for six decades. The oldest of all life span research, it has contributed significantly to developmental psychology and our understanding of gifted people.

Terman's findings completely contradicted the idea of the genius as a misfit. Compared with unselected children of the same age, the Termites were above average in popularity, cheerfulness, generosity, and fondness for being with large groups of people. In addition, they seemed healthier and had less mental illness. The deviation from the norm was upward in nearly all instances, a striking contrast to the popular stereotype of the socially inept child prodigy (Terman & Oden, 1947; Table 13–3).

At 30 years of age, the intellectual performance of the Termites was again in the upper 2% of the population, as much above the general adult level as it had been above the general child level earlier. Success in education and employment was much

TRAIT	PERCENT
Sense of humor	74
Cheerfulness	64
Self-confidence	81
Generosity	58
Leadership	70
Popularity	56
Fondness for groups	52

TABLE 13–3 TRAITS OF GIFTED PEOPLE. The table shows the percentage of gifted subjects who equaled or exceeded the mean for comparison subjects on each trait (Terman & Oden, 1947).

greater than one would expect in a random sample of adults of that same age (Terman, 1954).

PROBLEMS OF THE GIFTED. Experts also thought that gifted children were prone to certain problems in school, and Terman studied this question. He found that the traditional learning environment sometimes created a hardship for the gifted child, who must develop some tolerance for more typical learning rates and performance. But society must make adjustments, too. John Stuart Mill began to study Greek at age three. Charles Dickens wrote a tragedy before he was seven. Albert Einstein, at sixteen, discovered the paradox from which his theory of relativity was developed. With this precocity, tendencies to be independent and outspoken are likely.

Today we recognize that gifted people are a diverse group possessing special talents. Compared with other students, gifted individuals show a wider and less predictable range of abilities (Malone, Brownstein, von Brock, & Shaywitz, 1991; Sternberg, 1985). In particular, there is a need for programs to identify and assist gifted minority children. Given the unpredictability of special talents, these programs require precise multicultural assessment procedures (Ford & Harris, 1990).

EDUCATION OF THE GIFTED. Most students in Mr. Barasch's classroom regarded schoolwork as something to do when there were gaps in their conversations and entertainment. Robin Henderson was different.

"Oh, I know what 'puny' is," she said to Mr. Barasch, looking up from her work. "Very small."

"I want to start the story now," said Mr. Barasch. "Is everyone open to page 186?"

"Do we have to read aloud?" Kerry asked.

"Yes," announced Mr. Barasch firmly. "Robin, why don't you begin?"

Robin began the reading that day. Compared to the others, Robin read very well. She also finished assignments quickly and, on occasion, helped others with their work. Otherwise, there were no accommodations for her high level of ability (Snow et al., 1991).

Public education in the United States has concentrated largely on the typical student, aiming at mass education. There have been comparatively few large-scale programs for the gifted, who often go unattended. One argument against such programs lies in the diversity of American public school curricula, which allegedly provide the necessary enrichment opportunities already. Another states that gifted children will learn on their own, which is true to a substantial degree.

Those who promote special opportunities for the gifted raise a counterargument. They state that only by this procedure can we make the fullest use of human abilities, our most precious natural resource. It is also argued that special education for the gifted is in keeping with the basic American premise: Every student has the right to an education appropriate to his or her interests and abilities (Griggs, 1984).

As a rule, programs for the gifted involve enrichment, acceleration, or special classes, and each has its assets. In *enrichment* the child is encouraged to engage in additional schoolwork in related areas beyond the usual assignments. In *acceleration,* the child progresses to higher grades as rapidly as possible, according to mental age, not chronological age. And in *special classes,* the gifted child follows a curriculum that is faster in pace and less structured than that for the average child. Robin's school apparently did not have any extensive program of special classes for the gifted (Figure 13–7).

A rapid learner, Robin had a calmness and self-possession not evident among other students. Occasionally she showed real interest in schoolwork, asking questions, tutoring classmates, and so forth. Typically, however, she simply put her head down and slept at her seat. Mr. Barasch did not

FIGURE 13–7 EDUCATION OF GIFTED PERSONS. In this special class, gifted students worked together, learning from one another. They conducted their own investigations of reflexes and instincts and shared their findings with their peers.

understand this lack of interest in school (Snow et al., 1991).

Two years earlier, in Ms. Pasquale's fourth-grade class, Robin had been distinctly more engaged in schoolwork. Ms. Pasquale was open, flexible, and challenging as a teacher. Her classroom included an extensive collection of books, maps, and teacher-constructed charts, guided by the needs of her students.

• THEORIES OF INTELLIGENCE •

Robin Henderson had lived in Norwich for six years, half of her life. Her father, a quiet man, held two jobs outside the home. He left decisions about the house and family to his wife, who worked in a savings bank. She was critical of the Norwich schools, complaining that they underestimated Robin's abilities (Snow et al., 1991).

We speak of Robin's mental abilities, for she had several talents—playing the clarinet, reading poetry, writing stories for pleasure—and in the long-standing controversy over the nature of human intelligence, distinct types of intelligence have been increasingly recognized, especially in recent years. In the course of this controversy, psychologists have pursued two quite different paths, one older and more statistical, the other newer, broader, and more speculative.

PSYCHOMETRIC APPROACH

The first, known as the **psychometric approach,** aims to understand the mind, or *psyche,* through measurements of mental characteristics. It is based on the analysis of test results, dating back to Binet's early work.

Binet's effort produced a test far more widely acclaimed than he ever imagined, and it inaugurated the psychometric movement. Psychological tests became the means for discovering the nature of intelligence. This approach produced an efficient, simple, and broad definition—which is also circular: Intelligence is what intelligence tests measure.

THE *G* AND *S* FACTORS. After the Stanford-Binet and several other tests had been administered to many subjects, it was observed that the scores correlated with one another and that even the subtest scores were correlated. On this basis, an English psychologist, Charles Spearman, hypothesized that the different test items measured some common factor, called **general intelligence,** or *g,* and that many different skills involve this common factor. Mechanical ability, musical ability, mathematical ability, and others show a correlation with one another because certain amounts of *g* are required in all instances.

In addition to *g,* early theorists argued that each capacity calls for at least one **specific ability,** or *s,* which pertains to a particular field or skill. Facility in mathematics, for example, requires a certain amount of *g* and also specific mathematical abilities, such as ability to subtract, ability to multiply, and so forth, which would be the various *s*'s in mathematical performance. Similarly, mechanical ability would require several mechanical *s*'s, as well as a certain amount of *g* (Spearman, 1927).

PRIMARY MENTAL ABILITIES. This view raised the possibility of some intermediate factors in intelligence, not as broad as *g* or as narrow as *s.* In mathematics, for example, perhaps a factor like number ability stood between general intelligence and the ability to subtract, to multiply, and so forth. If so, several such factors might account for most human intellectual capacity.

Analyses of many test scores can indicate which abilities are associated with one another and which are relatively independent. This statistical technique, called *factor analysis,* identifies the basic, irreducible factors in sets of test scores and it also reflects the psychometric approach. According to the *factorial approach,* intelligence is composed of a discrete number of factors, distinguishable because they do not correlate highly with one another.

Following this reasoning, two American psychologists, Louis and Thelma Thurstone, attempted to identify these intermediate factors. Through factor analysis, they defined seven *primary mental abilities,* readily measured by their tests. These were word fluency, number ability, verbal comprehension, memory, reasoning, spatial relations, and perceptual speed (Thurstone & Thurstone, 1941).

THEORY OF MULTIPLE INTELLIGENCES. A more recent and controversial approach has been developed by Howard Gardner. He has postulated seven different kinds of intelligence, but his seven are *not* that seven—the seven primary mental abilities just mentioned. This approach is based on extensive research with people of special abilities, and it is controversial because it goes beyond mental functions. Stating that our traditional conception is too narrow, the theory of **multiple intelligences** addresses the broad spectrum of human abilities, including the arts, social relations, self-expression, and physical skills, as well as the traditional language and numerical abilities (Gardner, 1983).

These seven kinds of intelligence are: *linguistic,* evident in prose and poetry; *logical-mathematical,* demonstrated in mathematics, science, and philosophy; *spatial,* required in art, architecture, engineering, navigation, and related fields; *musical,* as in musical performance and composition; *bodily-kinesthetic,* essential in athletics, dance, and dramatic productions; *interpersonal,* shown in relations with other people; and *intrapersonal,* displayed in self-understanding, awareness of self, and so forth (Gardner, 1983). Clearly, these factors represent a much wider array of skills than do the older, more traditional tests of intelligence, even those in the factorial mode (Table 13–4).

One interesting difference among these factorial approaches concerns social intelligence. This

TYPE	OCCUPATION	EDUCATIONAL ACTIVITIES
Linguistic	Script writer	Storytelling, learning foreign languages
Logical-mathematical	Scientist	Playing chess, programming computers
Spatial	Sculptor	Designing tools, using a camera
Musical	Saxaphonist	Singing, listening to discs
Kinesthetic	Skater	Using athletic equipment, dancing
Interpersonal	Salesperson	Leading discussions, social activities
Intrapersonal	Self-knowledge	Keeping a journal, introspection

TABLE 13–4 MULTIPLE INTELLIGENCES. According to the theory of multiple intelligences, there are seven kinds of intelligence, each associated with certain occupations and educational activities, as illustrated by these samples. Traditional education focuses on linguistic and mathematical intelligence; the others are frequently overlooked in formal schooling (Armstrong, 1990).

ability holds a prominent place in the theory of multiple intelligences, especially in the interpersonal and intrapersonal domains, and yet it is ignored in other views. To ignore the social skills of someone like Renee Grant is to ignore her chief strength. As she reported to a member of the university research team, she began the study of Spanish by herself, not as a school subject but as a means of achieving better communication with friends (Snow, 1991). In the classroom, she was highly effective with peers, certainly a group leader, and maintained an almost collegial relationship with teachers. According to the theory of multiple intelligences, this ability should be considered a special factor in intelligence, along with linguistic ability, spatial ability, and so forth. Such views have become an important new line of inquiry among research psychologists (Riggio, Messamer, & Throckmorton, 1991).

One obvious problem with the psychometric or factorial approaches is the lack of agreement. Which are the basic factors? How many are there? Even after factor analysis, there is always some unexplained residue, perhaps because there is still some *g* factor present. Debate over the presence and significance of *g* in school and on the job continues even today (Ree & Earles, 1993; Sternberg & Wagner, 1993). Still another problem is that factors identified on a statistical basis must be labeled or otherwise designated, a procedure that is sometimes arbitrary. In short, the factorial approach has failed to yield the specific factors of intelligence, even when the most sophisticated tests are used (Zachary, 1990).

COGNITIVE APPROACH

Modern investigations also have produced a new approach to theories of intelligence, one that arose through developments in cognitive psychology. Called the **cognitive approach,** or sometimes the *information processing approach,* it stresses how information is obtained, stored, and used—the mental operations in intelligent behavior. The focus is more on thought processes, less on test scores. The basic question is this: What cognitive processes, or strategies, do we employ when we behave in an intelligent fashion?

STRUCTURE-OF-INTELLECT MODEL. Our discussion begins with an approach that falls between the factorial and information processing views. Developed and regularly modified by J. Paul Guilford over the course of his career, this comprehensive theory considers intellectual ability in three dimensions: how information is processed, called *operations;* what information is processed, called *contents;* and the results of this processing, called *prod-*

ucts. These dimensions are subdivided into six, five, and six parts, respectively, making a cubic model with 180 potential intellectual abilities, which define the **structure-of-intellect model** of intelligence (Guilford, 1988).

Characteristics of the operations dimension have been considered already in the chapters on perception, memory, and also thought and language. More than the others, this dimension focuses on information processing and presents the model as a cognitive theory. For example, one operation, *convergent thinking,* involves a search for a particular answer to a specific question. Which are the two largest rivers in Europe? The aim is to discover the solution generally recognized as the correct or best answer. This type of thinking is often assessed on standard tests of general information. Another operation, *divergent thinking,* procedes in different directions, seeking alternatives. What are several ways to travel around Europe without much money? The goal here is to create a number of alternatives. This form of thinking is commonly required on tests of creativity.

The contents dimension, closer to the psychometric approach, involves the various kinds of information that might be dealt with intellectually. It might include symbolic information, such as the letters and numbers in language and mathematics. It might involve behavioral information, colloquially called "body language," expressing unverbalized feelings. A very bright mathematician, for example, is not necessarily astute in understanding people.

Finally, the products dimension is concerned with results. What happens when someone performs certain mental operations on certain contents? One outcome is classes, in which two or more things are grouped together, as in concept formation. Another is systems, in which two or more things are organized in a special way, such as phrases in a sentence or postulates in a scientific theory. The products dimension is the form in which information is cast by the responding individual. Theoretically, all of the outcomes in any sort of problem solving should be found somewhere in this three-dimensional model (Guilford, 1975, 1988; Figure 13–8).

These studies have prompted the hypothesis that mental ability, like personality, shows increasing differentiation from birth through the most formative years. There may be a proportionately greater *g* factor in infants and more specific abilities in adulthood. This differentiation occurs partly on the basis of maturation, but it seems to be particularly sensitive to experience, as well.

CRYSTALLIZED AND FLUID INTELLIGENCE. By comparison, a very different theory illustrates the divergence among these views. Rather than 180, it identifies only two potential abilities, which at this point must come as a relief to the reader.

The first, **crystallized intelligence,** is based on an accumulation of knowledge about the world and an ability to apply it in solving *daily* problems. It includes facts, vocabulary, and expressive capacity. The individual with high crystallized intelligence generally is recognized as an expert in at least one field. Crystallized intelligence develops in everyday life, through learning in school, at work, around the house, and elsewhere.

The second type, **fluid intelligence,** is the capacity to solve *novel* problems not encountered previously, using rapid and accurate reasoning. These problems cannot be readily solved through prior experience; thus crystallized intelligence is not essential. Rather, fluid intelligence provides a rapid analysis of the novel problem and accurate processing of new information. In a word, fluid intelligence provides flexibility when dealing with novelty.

When you use a map successfully, solve an arithmetic problem, or spell *crystallized* correctly, crystallized intelligence is involved. Experience is a most significant factor. Fluid intelligence is required when you form an hypothesis about some

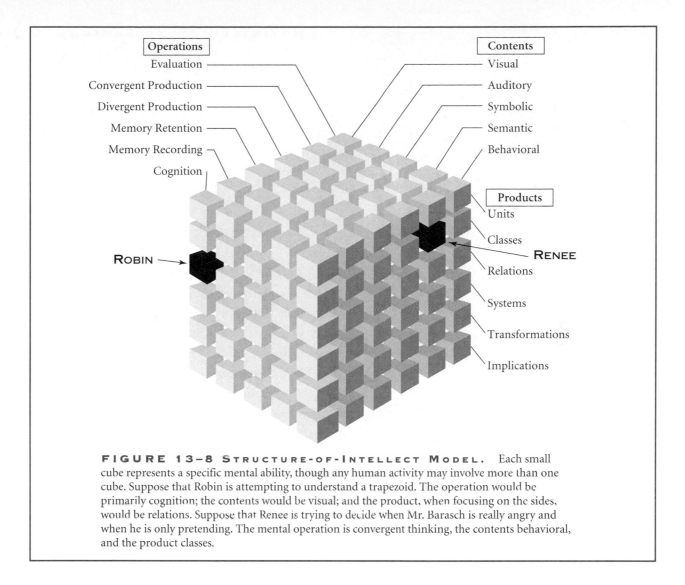

FIGURE 13–8 STRUCTURE-OF-INTELLECT MODEL. Each small cube represents a specific mental ability, though any human activity may involve more than one cube. Suppose that Robin is attempting to understand a trapezoid. The operation would be primarily cognition; the contents would be visual; and the product, when focusing on the sides, would be relations. Suppose that Renee is trying to decide when Mr. Barasch is really angry and when he is only pretending. The mental operation is convergent thinking, the contents behavioral, and the product classes.

novel problem or invent a new product. Flexibility is essential (Cattell, 1971).

TRIARCHIC THEORY. A final cognitive approach has gained attention because it is extremely broad and, at the same time, highly applicable to daily life. Developed by Robert Sternberg, the **triarchic theory** describes intelligence in three domains: componential, experiential, and contextual (Sternberg, 1985). The *componential* domain emphasizes the cognitive processes involved in typical intellectual pursuits, including school. This domain appears whenever someone answers the questions on standard tests of intelligence. Its name refers to such traditional components as perception, memory, and thinking.

The *experiential* domain turns in a different direction, focusing on the capacity to combine unique experiences in creative ways. Intelligence in this domain enables an individual to deal successfully with new situations and new tasks. To do so, the person must manage routine problems readily and easily, recognizing them as such and solving them almost without thought. This capacity leaves the individual with the interest, energy, and creativity necessary for success with novel problems.

Finally, there is the *contextual* domain, which, more than the others, is culturally or situationally

FIGURE 13-9 INTELLIGENCE AND KNOWLEDGE. The sailor is intelligent at sea, the cook in the kitchen, and the bee keeper around the hives. Knowing the habits of bees is a component of intelligence in this situation. But contextual intelligence is more than knowledge. It includes the capacity to find or create situations favorable to one's special abilities.

defined. It focuses on specific settings, ranging from the great outdoors to the boardroom, from the home to the street. Individuals with high contextual intelligence are able to place themselves in situations that require their particular talents, or they can modify settings to create a better match with their talents. Resourcefulness is vital (Figure 13–9).

The triarchic theory of intelligence aims to describe the intellectual abilities of all sorts of people in terms of these three domains, possessed in varying amounts. The students in Mr. Barasch's classroom, for example, could be approached in these ways. Robin's strength clearly lay in componential intelligence, despite her lack of interest in school. Renee was most capable in the contextual realm. With relatively little academic ability, she functioned very well in all sorts of situations outside school, especially social settings.

NONINTELLECTUAL FACTORS. As implied in the triarchic theory, intelligence should not be equated solely with mental operations. Nonintellectual factors are also involved, such as motivation, adjustment, and emotion. Intelligence, from this perspective, involves a value judgment; it is not only rational and purposeful but also directed to goals which are worthwhile (Scarr, 1981; Wechsler, 1975). For example, in the Norwich schools Robin lacked academic goals and values. In that sense, she did not have high functional intelligence in school (Snow et al., 1991).

These nonintellectual factors broaden the concept of intelligence a great deal. They also show the imposing problem of developing an adequate theory of intelligence. Fortunately, a concept can be quite useful even without a theory or a universally accepted definition.

In summary, we can conclude that the concept of *general* intelligence, prevalent at the turn of this century, perhaps has outlived its theoretical usefulness (Thorndike, 1990). Research today is guided along two complementary paths: the factorial approach, derived from psychometric studies, and the information processing approach, arising through cognitive psychology. Both approaches have been useful and are currently employed in further explorations of the nature of intelligence.

• NATURE-NURTURE ISSUE •

Parents provide our heredity *and* our early environment, quite a responsibility. There are exceptions, of course, as in the Grant family. Almost nothing is known about Renee's father, who was never mentioned around the house. After Renee's mother left the extended family years earlier, Renee rarely saw her (Snow, 1991).

Robin's mother, much involved in her children's schooling, had little formal education herself. Nevertheless, Ms. Henderson made rapid career advancement in a very short time. Her oldest son, after just a year in the United States, was a good student, reading well beyond his grade level. Ms. Henderson was concerned about her children's schooling because she knew that the roots of intelligence lie in the environment, as well as in heredity. Closed doors and a silent television during homework hours testified to this outlook (Snow et al., 1991).

Ideas on the origins of intelligence have prompted a long line of controversy dating back to Sir Francis Galton, a very bright Englishman, free from financial worries, who pondered the origins of his own high intelligence as he strolled the streets of London in 1882. He founded the first laboratory for studying mental abilities (Figure 13–10). Then he coined a phrase for the ensuing controversy. The **nature–nurture issue** refers to the debate over the contributions of heredity and environment, respectively, in the development of human abilities, especially intelligence, a controversy that continues even among experts today (Rushton, 1991; Vanderwolf & Cain, 1991).

Adding to the controversy have been mistakes, overzealous claims, and fraud on both sides. Sir Cyril Burt, an Englishman knighted for his research with identical twins, concocted data on behalf of the hereditarian view. Dr. Rick Heber, awarded several million dollars to augment intelligence among underprivileged children in Milwaukee, claimed massive changes in IQ, never issued a final report, and then was convicted of misusing federal funds (Page, 1986). These irregularities stand in marked contrast to the extensive and honest efforts that normally characterize scientific research throughout the world.

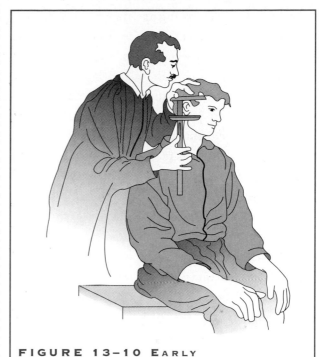

FIGURE 13–10 EARLY MEASUREMENT OF HUMAN CHARACTERISTICS. Sir Francis Galton established his first laboratory beside a fairgrounds but behind a trellis that merely allowed curious visitors to the fair to peek at the laboratory activities. He charged threepence for admission and did a thriving business. His assistants measured thousands of people for all sorts of physical and psychological traits.

꽃

STUDIES OF GROUP DIFFERENCES

Attempts to study the nature–nurture issue in large groups of human beings began most obviously in the United States during World War I, when more than 1,750,000 men were tested as they entered military service. The aim was twofold: to exclude those who were intellectually unfit and to place the others in positions most appropriate to their abilities. For these purposes, two group tests were developed: one verbal, known as the *Army Alpha,* and one nonverbal, the *Army Beta.* The outcome was a heated debate with political overtones, chiefly in the context of immigration laws.

THE POLITICAL ISSUES. One analysis of the Alpha scores echoed not only across the land but throughout the halls of Congress. Men from 16 countries were involved, and their scores showed sharp differences in intellectual ability. Those from countries in Northern and Western Europe were at the top of the scale, and those from nations in

Southern and Eastern Europe were toward the bottom. It was concluded, quite erroneously, that these national differences were due to hereditary factors (Kamin, 1974).

Subsequent inquiry disclosed that test performance was related to length of residence in the United States. Recent immigrants made low scores; those who had been here for 20 years made scores comparable to those of native-born American citizens, regardless of national background. The environmentalists, stressing the role of learning and experience in behavior, hailed this finding. It suggested that nurture, not nature, was the crucial factor.

But the hereditarians had another explanation. The Army Beta, a nonverbal test, constructed for people who did not speak English, also showed low scores for immigrants, and they were arriving in the United States in increasing numbers, much to the consternation of some observers. Again the environmentalists resisted this interpretation, claiming that exposure to the American culture was the crucial factor, even with a nonverbal test.

These data and interpretations from World War I began a long line of debate on group differences in intelligence, focusing on nationalities, racial groups, social classes, and the like. The history of this research is too long and political for inclusion here. The issue has been revived in contemporary form, however, with publication of *The Bell Curve*, a statistically based review of intelligence, genetics, and enthnicity in the context of social policy. It raised political as well as psychological questions about welfare procedures, affirmative action, and Head Start programs, provoking considerable controversy within and outside psychology (Hernstein & Murray, 1994).

Politics aside, most psychologists agree that intelligence has a genetic component and that, on conventional tests of IQ, certain subgroups score higher or lower than others. The interpretation of these differences is another matter. It seems clear that heredity contributes to within-group differences, but it is not yet apparent in what way, if at all, heredity contributes to among-group differences.

In either case, research findings alone cannot dictate social policy because political action requires judgments about goals and values. However, research findings may provide useful guidelines about the potential outcomes of various social policies (Arvey et al., 1994).

In Norwich and the surrounding area, for example, class differences were evident in the schools and homes. Towns less than 50 miles away, with the highest school budgets in the state, obtained the best, most inspirational teachers available. The low-level, uninspired approach characterizing Mr. Barasch's teaching occurred in other Norwich classrooms, resulting in a dropout rate of 25% among high school students. Whatever the sources of intelligence, in Norwich they generally were not nurtured at home or at school.

The Henderson home, however, seemed to provide some hope. Robin began the Norwich school system ahead of her grade level—although by the sixth grade she was showing a decline relative to national standards (Snow et al., 1991).

SEX DIFFERENCES. The question of sex differences in intelligence has not yet become controversial, partly because journalists have not focused on the small differences that do exist—magnifying them, debating them, or attributing them to various sources, biological or environmental. This question can be dispatched summarily because there is no significant difference between the sexes in *overall* intellectual capacity. This finding, suggested in small samples of women during World War II, has been corroborated in hundreds of studies of subjects ranging from grammar school children to psychiatric patients and college students (Kimura, 1992; Matarazzo, 1972).

There are, nevertheless, specific test items on which males and females perform differently. Binet and Terman, at the beginning of the testing movement, attempted to include in their tests an equal number of male-biased and female-biased items, or they tried to exclude such items entirely. This trend in test construction has continued, making it not surprising that large random samples of males and females score similarly on measures of general intelligence. Thus, there has been no controversy—yet.

These differences in specific abilities fit the popular notions. Women tend to perform slightly higher than men on tests of verbal fluency and perceptual speed; men tend to show somewhat greater success on tests of spatial relations and mathematical reasoning (Figure 13–11). It is not yet known whether these small but reliable findings for *specific* abilities reflect cultural or biological differences or both sets of factors in interaction (Hyde & Linn, 1988; Rosen, 1995). The influence of sex hormones on brain development begins very early in life, and during this sensitive period they may per-

manently alter brain function in ways yet to be understood (Kimura, 1990, 1992).

PROBLEMS IN MEASUREMENT. What can we say about these disparate efforts to identify hereditary and environmental factors in intelligence, whether they pertain to national, racial, social, or other characteristics? Beset with innumerable problems in measurement and testing, they leave us with respect for the complexities of this research.

In the first place, despite hopeful efforts with the Army Beta, it is virtually impossible to construct a **culture-free test** one in which the items do not favor any particular society. Some cultural factors inevitably become involved, even with the most carefully constructed nonverbal items. Robin, who spent her early years in Trinidad, came from a home that stressed reading and writing. Renee, born in the United States, lived in a home stressing work and social skills. Any test might favor one back-

---

TASKS FAVORING WOMEN

Perceptual Speed
Find the house that exactly matches the one on the left.

Verbal Fluency
Indicate another word that begins with the same letter, not included in the list.

L _ _ _

Limp, Livery, Love, Laser, Liquid, Low, Like, Lag, Live, Lug, Light, Lift, Liver, Lime, Leg, Load, Lap, Lucid

Answers:
The house at the far right; Life or any other word beginning with L.

TASKS FAVORING MEN

Spatial Relations
A hole has been punched in the folded sheet. How will the sheet appear when unfolded?

 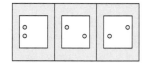

Mathematical Reasoning
In the space at the left, write the answer to the following problem.

If only 60% of seedlings will survive, how many must be planted to obtain 660 trees?

Answers:
The middle sheet; 1,100 seedlings.

FIGURE 13–11 GENDER DIFFERENCES IN MENTAL ABILITIES. On most tests of intelligence, men and women perform similarly. These tasks illustrate some of the differences.

ground more than another. It might also favor one gender more than another, suggesting the need for a *gender-free* test as well.

Creating a test that is devoid of culture, gender, and other potential sources of bias appears to be an impossibility. For this reason, there have been attempts to eliminate all items influenced more by one culture than by another, thereby constructing a **culture-fair test** (Figure 13–12). As any test approaches the culture-fair ideal, however, it loses its capacity to predict performance in a specific situation, which is often the purpose of testing. A test equally appropriate for Trinidadians and New Englanders probably is not highly predictive of behavior in either culture.

The difficulties in developing culture-fair tests are also illustrated with the Escala de Inteligencia Wechsler para Adultos (EIWA). The Spanish Wechsler, mentioned earlier, is not merely a translation of the English version; it is an adaptation, involving many new items. However, Hispanic cultures are diverse, ranging from the Iberian peninsula to the South Pacific. This particular edition, developed in Central America, is not completely suitable for Spaniards or South Americans. Further, the test results are hardly comparable to those of the English version, even for highly bilingual people. When the two versions are used with the same bilingual subjects, the English version leads to an underestimation and the Spanish version to an overestimation of intelligence (Lopez & Taussig, 1991). Collectively, these findings point once again to the importance of **culturally sensitive testing,** meaning assessment procedures designed specifically to measure abilities and interests in a particular population or subgroup.

Still further, there is the inevitable problem of the confounded or mixed result. Highly intelligent parents provide their children with enriched environments, not only with reading materials and games but also in conversation. These children have a double advantage, a favorable heredity *and* a stim-

FIGURE 13–12 CULTURE-FAIR TEST. Fill in the blank space in the lower right corner. People from some cultures would be at a disadvantage in attempting this task. For this reason, such tests are often called *culture-reduced tests. Answer:* The solution is one cross above one wavy line.

ulating environment. Duller parents typically rear children in an impoverished environment. These children have a double disadvantage. Thus, the investigator cannot be certain of the influence of either factor.

Amid these difficulties, it appears virtually impossible to demonstrate conclusively the genetic basis of group differences in intelligence. Contemporary studies with sophisticated research designs have not shown any significant differences between groups that might be attributed solely to underlying genetic factors (Mackenzie, 1984; Weinberg, Scarr, & Waldman, 1992). Performance differences exist, but at this time there is no way of establishing sufficiently controlled conditions to determine the role of genetic factors in producing them.

❧

METHODS OF ASSESSMENT

Today the basic question is no longer heredity *or* environment. Sometimes it is a question of emphasis, weighing the two sets of influences, and sometimes it is a question of interaction. How do heredity and environment unite to produce a certain outcome?

STUDIES OF IDENTICAL TWINS. Sir Francis Galton also inaugurated the study of identical twins, who have the same genetic makeup; therefore, these studies provide a control for hereditary factors. In many parts of the world, investigators have shown a relationship between the scores for members of twin pairs (Figure 13–13).

These results are commonly reported as a correlation coefficient, which provides a numerical indication of the degree of association between two variables. This coefficient, or numerical index, can vary from 0, meaning no relationship, to ±1.00, the maximum relationship. Overall, the correlations for numerous sets of identical twins are in the vicinity of .80, indicating a close relationship, or high agreement, between the scores, even when the two people have been reared apart. Correlations among fraternal twins, other brothers and sisters, and cousins are successively lower (Bouchard & McGue, 1981; Segal, 1985; Table 13–5).

This finding seems to support the hereditarian viewpoint, but there are two general objections. First, the correlation of .80 is less than perfect, demonstrating the influence of environmental factors as well. In fact, the impact of heredity in these

FIGURE 13–13 STUDIES OF IDENTICAL TWINS. When pairs of identical twins are studied for any characteristic, the research can accommodate both perspectives: heredity, looking for similarities, and the environment, looking for differences.

instances is estimated as the square of the correlation. Hence, the hereditary influence is assumed to account for about 64% of overall intelligence: .8 × .8 = .64. Second, this correlation of .80 is about equally distant between the approximately .60 correlation for fraternal twins, with no more common inheritance than ordinary siblings, and a perfect 1.00 correlation, which would occur if heredity were the only influence (Bouchard & McGue, 1981; Gottesman, 1963). Thus, even with identical twins, the environmental factor is clearly present.

When identical twins have been reared apart, generally one has not lived as a prince and the other as a pauper. Adoption agencies try to place foster children with adoptive parents who have comparable IQs. Hence, the environments of separated identical twins have not been very different. Under these circumstances, identical twins reared apart have shown greater similarity in intelligence than other siblings reared together (Bouchard, Lykken, McGue, Segal, & Tellegen, 1990).

RELATIONSHIP	GENETIC SHARING	CORRELATION
Identical twins, together	100%	.86
Identical twins, apart	100%	.72
Fraternal twins, together	50%	.60
Siblings, together	50%	.47
Siblings, apart	50%	.24
Cousins, apart	12½%	.15

TABLE 13–5 FAMILY CORRELATIONS IN INTELLIGENCE. The role of genetic factors is apparent in the higher correlations for identical twins than for any other relationship. The role of the environment is evident in the lower correlations for identical twins reared apart rather than together and for ordinary siblings reared apart rather than together. The table shows weighted average correlations (Bouchard & McGue, 1981).

HERITABILITY ESTIMATES. Studies in quantitative genetics have added some further understanding of the contribution of heredity, developing a concept known as the heritability estimate. The **heritability estimate** is a proportion or ratio representing the extent to which any given characteristic can be attributed to genetic factors, as opposed to *all* factors that might contribute to that characteristic. People exposed to *exactly* the same environment all of their lives would have a heritability estimate of 100% for all traits, meaning that all differences among them would be due to heredity. This condition of course is impossible.

In practice, heritability of intelligence is very difficult to estimate, and the figures vary widely. It is not surprising to find them ranging upward from 30% or so to as high as 80%. They are derived by studying similarities in intelligence, or any other characteristic, among subjects known to have the same or similar genetic backgrounds. Identical twins are a prime source of data. Other investigations have included brothers and sisters, parents and offspring, and even grandchildren, cousins, and other relatives.

STUDIES OF SIBLINGS. Investigations of family size and birth order have shed light on environmental influences. As a very *general* rule, the larger the family, the lower the *average* IQ among the siblings. The usual explanation focuses on the quality of the intellectual environment in the family, assuming that hereditary differences are randomized across birth order for the hundreds of thousands of subjects in these studies. When there is only one child or two siblings, each child can receive considerable stimulation from the parents. As the number increases, especially when there are more than four siblings, it becomes more and more difficult for the parents to provide special opportunities for mental development in each child (Pfouts, 1980).

The older children in a large family tend to have somewhat higher IQs than the younger children, a condition that has been substantiated in studies around the world (Wilson, Mundy-Castle, & Panditji, 1990; Zajonc & Markus, 1975). In their earliest years, the oldest siblings have early intellectual stimulation from parents more to themselves. Later-born children must share it from the beginning, sometimes with several siblings. On reading these words, do not swagger or thump your chest as a first-born, and do not slump in despair as a later-born child. You are no different than you were moments ago. Remember, too, that the average differences are *very* small and that, with the vicissitudes of life, there are countless exceptions.

Another advantage of being an older child lies with the opportunity to teach younger ones. We learn partly by instructing others, as Renee sometimes did with Tanya and Sharon. Renee also profited from the exclusive attention of her grandmother before Tanya and Sharon arrived in the household.

There are, of course, advantages for later-born children. One seems to lie in the social realm. Compared to older siblings, younger ones may be more skillful in managing interpersonal situations. Another advantage lies in the opportunity for learning physical skills, provided that the older siblings are willing to share their expertise. Younger children are also more likely to be independent, even rebellious (Sulloway, 1995). In addition, there is evidence that birth-order effects of all sorts diminish in adulthood, not a surprising outcome when we think of the profound influences of marriage, career, and other responsibilities in adult life (Schooler, 1972).

STUDIES OF COMPENSATORY EDUCATION. Another effort to study the nature–nurture issue has occurred in **compensatory education,** which attempts to provide early learning opportunities and an enriched environment for disadvantaged children. Some well-known programs of this sort include Head Start and A Better Chance

(ABC). They were founded with the expectation that an early enriched or remedial education would prove useful for disadvantaged children, compensating for even earlier environmental deficits.

Long-term follow-up studies of Head Start, one of the earliest and largest equal-opportunity programs in the United States, show several areas of favorable development among the graduates. The evidence for mental growth remains mixed, but these advantages are sometimes delayed (Figure 13-14). If the interventions continue, they may have a lasting effect (Besharov & Hartle, 1987; Kotelchuck & Richmond, 1987).

~

NATURE–NURTURE INTERACTION

Today we realize that children can appear retarded and become retarded from being reared in deprived circumstances. The role of the environment, under-estimated in many early studies of intellectual deficit, was apparent in the Grant family. Granny left school in the third grade. "I had to raise myself," she declared, an orphan early in life. Renee, already in danger of leaving school, was exposed to Granny's largely nonliterate household (Snow et al., 1991).

Considering all of the findings on identical twins, family constellations, and special education, what can we say about the contributions of heredity and environment to the intelligence of a given *individual?* Most psychologists would answer somewhat in this fashion: Heredity sets certain broad limits of potential intelligence, and environment determines the extent to which we achieve this potential. These limits are sometimes called the **reaction range,** referring to the genetically based limits or range of any inherited capacity, including intelligence. In a favorable environment, children should develop close to the peak

FIGURE 13–14 EARLY INTERVENTION. The intellectual developments produced by Head Start and similar programs are still debated. Personal and social gains have been well established, however, and these capacities are critical to successful functioning in adulthood.

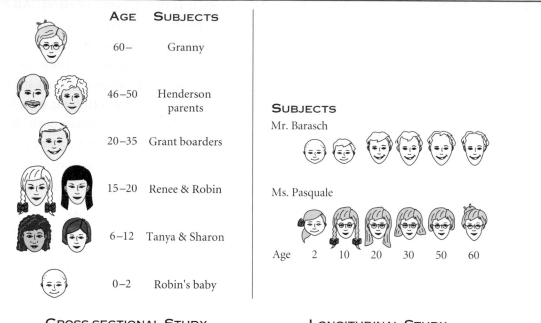

AGE	SUBJECTS
60–	Granny
46–50	Henderson parents
20–35	Grant boarders
15–20	Renee & Robin
6–12	Tanya & Sharon
0–2	Robin's baby

SUBJECTS

Mr. Barasch

Ms. Pasquale

Age   2   10   20   30   50   60

CROSS-SECTIONAL STUDY   LONGITUDINAL STUDY

FIGURE 13–16 DEVELOPMENTAL RESEARCH METHODS. In the cross-sectional study, different people are tested at different ages, all at the same time. In the longitudinal study, the same people are tested over and over again at different ages throughout their lives. In both procedures, many subjects are used at each age level.

tudinal subject at a younger and an older age is due to the general impact of aging per se, but subjects at the older ages are also benefiting from our expanding fund of knowledge and vastly improved methods of disseminating it (Emanuelsson & Svensson, 1990). Furthermore, there is a steady loss of the less healthy and less adjusted subjects, who no longer participate further in the research. In short, the advantage of the longitudinal study— avoiding a cohort effect by studying the same subjects throughout the developmental process—is offset by significant expenditures of time and money, as well as the potential for a biased sample of higher scores through improved education.

Thus, estimates are too low with the first approach, too high with the second. Each method has its assets and limitations (Figure 13-16).

One correctional procedure involves the use of comparison subjects with the longitudinal approach. These comparison subjects are tested at the same age as the longitudinal subjects were when they began the research or when they reached any later age under investigation. The difference in performance, if any, between the comparison subjects and the longitudinal subjects *at that same age*, years earlier, represents the amount of cultural change during that period. When this amount is subtracted from the performance of the longitudinal subjects, it corrects the data for cultural improvements. More sophisticated methods are also available, for one of the goals of developmental research is to take advantage of the longitudinal method while minimizing its drawbacks (Farrington, 1991; Verhulst & Koot, 1991).

This procedure was used in a longitudinal study of 96 male students who were tested as freshmen in 1919, again as alumni in 1950, and then once more in 1961. On the occasion of the final testing, 101 male freshmen at the same university were also tested, and the difference between their

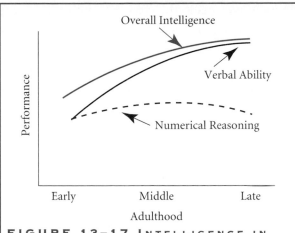

FIGURE 13-17 INTELLIGENCE IN ADULTHOOD. This graph illustrates findings in various studies. With adjustments for cultural change, the smooth lines indicate general trends, not specific patterns.

scores in 1961 and those of the earlier freshmen in 1919 represented the amount of cultural change. Thus, the gain of the alumni after 42 years was adjusted by this score, and overall, there was still an improvement in total ability. Verbal ability, in particular, increased markedly, remaining high at least through the fifties (Owens, 1966; Figure 13-17).

Other investigations have added confirmation, suggesting that intelligence may not reach its peak until the sixties or even later (Hertzog & Schaie, 1986). Then the different abilities show different rates of decline, with the major loss lying in the speed of response, followed by numerical ability (Honzik & MacFarlane, 1973; McCrae & Costa, 1987). However, the age of onset of this decline is significantly influenced by the person's intellectual interests and activities (Owens, 1966; Schaie, 1993).

IMPORTANCE OF EXPERIENCE

The subjects in the previous studies were college graduates, generally in vocations or avocations demanding a high level of mental activity. Among these individuals, a steady increase in intelligence

can be expected for six or seven decades, especially in intelligence as a repository of information, skills, and problem-solving techniques acquired in daily life. As in all areas of human development, people exposed to a less favorable environment will experience an earlier peak ability and a slow but steady decline thereafter. One's occupation and mental activity are vital factors for continued mental growth in later adulthood (Owens, 1966; Schaie, 1993).

We leave the Grants and Hendersons with this finding in mind. Challenging mental activity is the critical factor in continued mental growth in the adult years.

The low expectation of her teachers was not the only reason Robin Henderson left school. The multiple bases of behavior suggest that other factors probably were involved as well. Clearly, her sexual activity played a role. Apparently another factor was her relationship with her mother, whom she described as "picky . . . not very nice, and impossible to please." Robin became resentful of her mother's attempts to encourage greater scholastic effort. With these factors in mind, there is considerable doubt that Robin, as a teenage mother, will ever complete a traditional high school program. Her definite intellectual potential may lie fallow or, in fact, begin to decline early in life. These doubts were expressed by the investigators who studied the children in 31 Norwich families. The influence of the home, they concluded, is the most powerful predictor of student achievement in school. The findings in many households are implicit in the title of their book on this research, *Unfulfilled Expectations: Home and School Influences on Literacy* (Snow et al., 1991).

There may be futher opportunities for Robin, however. Some programs for teenage parents have been highly successful, reducing the failure-to-finish rate from 80% to 38% (Clinchy, 1991). Robin certainly possesses the necessary componential intelligence, described earlier as an academic domain in the triarchic theory. For Robin, school assignments and tests were always easy—perhaps too easy. In a teenage parenting program she would pursue two courses of study: a traditional high school curriculum and instruction in parenting.

Participating in the same Norwich classrooms, Renee too had been assigned academic tasks below the average level but, with less capacity, she was less hindered by this lack of encouragement. While she drew meager academic assistance from her nonliterate grandmother, she obtained help from other students, joined an after-school program, and phoned a cousin across town when no other support was available. In these ways, Renee advanced through the Norwich system, and one day she graduated from high school, much to the delight of her very proud Granny. Afterward, she began looking for work for which she knew she was suited: "A people type of job" (Snow et al., 1991).

At some level, Renee understood her contextual intelligence, although she perhaps never encountered triarchic theory. Despite limited scholastic ability, Renee made the classroom into a favorable setting for herself, one that recognized her social competence. Almost brash with teachers on occasion, she nevertheless was selected as a teacher's aide and recognized as a class leader. In life after graduation, she should make the most of this practical intelligence, finding work situations in which it can be exercised or modifying a work setting to permit it to flourish.

And finally, we leave Granny, in her late sixties. She never graduated from elementary school, but she too had a practical intelligence, not unlike Renee. With common sense and a buoyant style, she had become an excellent model for her grandchildren, especially by going to class at night. This activity had two important benefits. First, she was demonstrating an attitude for all of her family: Learning never ends. Second, by providing herself with a challenging intellectual climate, she was forestalling a more rapid decline in her own mental abilities. In Granny's effort, all of us can find some inspiration.

• SUMMARY •

❧

THE TESTING MOVEMENT

1. Intelligence is difficult to define, but most definitions generally refer to some aspect of flexibility or versatility of adjustment. Its measurement is often accomplished by individual intelligence tests: the Stanford-Binet and the Wechsler scales.
2. Well-constructed tests show high reliability, which refers to the consistency of subjects' scores. Successful tests must have high validity, which means that the test measures what it purports to measure. Norms are compilations of test scores that serve as guidelines for interpreting any particular score.
3. Tests are best understood as human tools, possessing assets and limitations. They can be useful for diagnosis, research, and screenings. Most important, the test user must exercise caution in the interpretation of test scores.

❧

EXTREMES OF INTELLIGENCE

4. People with mental retardation, comprising the lower 2% of the population in measured intelligence, are classified as totally dependent, trainable, or educable. Causal factors in mental retardation include genetic factors, health factors, cultural deprivation, and emotional factors, which can accompany any sort of mental retardation.
5. Mentally gifted people comprise the upper 2% of the population in mental ability; generally they are more physically fit, socially adept, and traditionally

moral than the general population. Educational programs are less structured and proceed more rapidly than those for other children.

❧

THEORIES
OF INTELLIGENCE

6. In the psychometric approach to a theory of intelligence, the results of traditional intelligence tests are used to speculate on the nature of intelligence. The theory of multiple intelligences has identified seven kinds of intelligence: linguistic, logical-mathematical, spatial, musical, bodily-kinesthetic, interpersonal, and intrapersonal.

7. The cognitive approach stresses how information is obtained, stored, and used—the mental operations in intelligent behavior. The structure-of-intellect model postulates many distinct intellectual abilities. Crystallized and fluid intelligence stress the accumulation of knowledge and the capacity to solve novel problems, respectively. And the triarchic theory identifies three domains: componential, experiential, and contextual.

❧

NATURE-
NURTURE ISSUE

8. The nature–nurture controversy has a long history, extending through many studies of group

differences. The question of the genetic basis of group differences is impossible to answer for several reasons, chiefly the absence of satisfactory tests.

9. Research on the nature-nurture issue involves comparison of identical twins reared apart; these studies have shown the influences of both heredity and environment, including a hereditability estimate.

10. The influences of heredity and environment are always present, and they depend upon one another. Heredity sets broad limits, and environment determines the extent to which this intelligence is achieved. The key issue is their interaction.

❧

INTELLIGENCE
AND AGING

11. In studies of human development at different ages, two research methods are available. Cross-sectional investigations use different subjects at different ages. They are relatively quick and efficient, but they include the risk of a cohort effect.

12. Longitudinal investigations study the same subjects as they grow older. They avoid a cohort effect, but they are costly in terms of time and money.

13. When control procedures are used to correct for cultural changes, it is found that mental growth may continue into the sixth decade or later, providing that the individual is engaged in stimulating mental activities.

• WORKING WITH PSYCHOLOGY •

❧ REVIEW OF KEY CONCEPTS ❧

intelligence

The Testing Movement
  intelligence test
  mental age (MA)
  Stanford-Binet Intelligence Scale
  chronological age (CA)
  intelligence quotient (IQ)
  Wechsler Intelligence Scales
  reliability

test-retest reliability
equivalent-form reliability
interjudge reliability
validity
face validity
predictive validity
concurrent validity
norms
achievement test
aptitude test

interest inventory
personality test

Extremes of Intelligence
  normal distribution
  mental retardation
  mental giftedness
  learning disability
  phenylketonuria (PKU)
  Down's syndrome

fragile X syndrome
cretinism
fetal alcohol syndrome (FAS)
cultural deprivation
mainstreaming

cognitive approach
structure-of-intellect model
crystallized intelligence
fluid intelligence
triarchic theory

culturally sensitive testing
heritability estimate
compensatory education
reaction range
interaction principle

Theories of Intelligence
  psychometric approach
  general intelligence (*g*)
  specific ability (*s*)
  multiple intelligences

Nature-Nurture Issue
  nature–nurture issue
  culture-free test
  culture-fair test

Intelligence and Aging
  cross-sectional studies
  cohort effect
  longitudinal studies

❧ CLASS DISCUSSION/CRITICAL THINKING ❧

A NARRATIVE TWIST

Suppose that Renee, with her particular inheritance, had lived in the Henderson household. Suppose Robin, with her genetic makeup, had been a member of the Grant family. Speculate on the intellectual, social, and educational development of each girl at two stages, first as a student in Mr. Barasch's sixth-grade class and then four years later, when they would have been approximately 16 years old. Discuss the probable developmental changes experienced by each girl. Discuss the likely differences between the girls at each age. ❧

TOPICAL QUESTIONS

• *The Testing Movement.* You have been chosen to devise a nonverbal test identifying mentally gifted. Describe three sample items from your test.

• *Extremes of Intelligence.* Suppose typical students were educated as mentally gifted students. Would their intelligence be enhanced? Would it be diminished? Explain your reasons.

• *Theories of Intelligence.* Consider the factorial approach to intelligence. Develop a set of basic mental abilities that you feel encompasses the whole range of intelligence. Defend your selection.

• *Nature-Nurture Issue.* To what extent is a culture-fair test possible? Write questions that might be considered for a culture-fair test.

• *Intelligence and Aging.* You are about to read an article on intelligence and aging among people with exceptional intelligence. Among which group, those with retardation or those who are gifted, would you expect to find the most variable changes in middle adulthood and old age? Why?

❧ TOPICS OF RELATED INTEREST ❧

The technique of correlation, which underlies the concepts of validity and reliability, is discussed in the chapter on statistical methods (18). The operations dimension of the structure-of-intellect model concerns memory (8) and thinking (9). The Skeels research in human development provides evidence for environmental influences on intelligence (12).

THE
INDIVIDUAL

PERSONALITY

ADJUSTMENT AND DISORDER

THERAPY

PSYCHOANALYTIC THEORY
Structure of Personality
Personality Development
Unconscious Motivation
Psychodynamic Views

CONSTITUTIONAL THEORY
Biological Approach
Personality Traits

BEHAVIORAL AND COGNITIVE THEORY
Operant View of Personality
Social Learning and Personality
Consistency Controversy

HUMANISTIC THEORY
Free Will and Uniqueness
Person-Centered Approach

PERSONALITY IN PERSPECTIVE
Personality Testing
The Eclectic Approach

14
PERSONALITY

ɞ

HER ATTRACTIVE FACE LINED WITH ANGER, JENNY ANNOUNCED TO ROSS THAT SHE WOULD HAVE HIM ARRESTED IF HE APPEARED AT HER DOOR AGAIN. Ross then turned and left without a word.

In the midst of her anger, Jenny's heart ached.

Could he have married without telling her? Why did he not share this vital part of his life? Oh, if only Ross would change his ways.

As mother and son, they had enjoyed a happy earlier life. From Ross's first years, they had visited museums, exchanged stories, and walked in the park together. They had lived for a time in a small, windowless apartment; she found work as a librarian; and she made certain that her son had the best food and clothing available. Ross went to the very best schools; no sacrifice was too great for Jenny. After graduation, he entered an excellent university—and then went off to war overseas.

When Ross returned two years later, he was a different person. He stayed home less, enjoyed his female companions more, and spent much money entertaining them. For one reason or another, Jenny found fault with all of these women, girl friends and girlfriends.

Then, one day, Jenny made a fateful discovery. Ross had lied to her. He was secretly married. This deception prompted that outburst at her doorway, and it permanently changed their lives.

A tall, sturdy, slightly rugged person with gray-green eyes and jet black hair, Jenny Masterson was a physically striking woman in her late fifties, and she spoke with conviction. "My whole life has been wasted," she declared dramatically. It would be impossible, she continued, ever again to believe a word that left the lips of her handsome son.

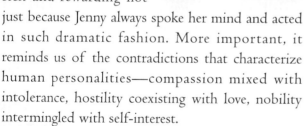

This tale of love and alienation in the lives of Jenny and Ross is one of the poignant stories in modern studies of personality. Assembled by the renowned Gordon Allport, a pioneer in the development of personality theory, it remains rich and rewarding not just because Jenny always spoke her mind and acted in such dramatic fashion. More important, it reminds us of the contradictions that characterize human personalities—compassion mixed with intolerance, hostility coexisting with love, nobility intermingled with self-interest.

We know Jenny through her many letters, most of which she wrote to Glenn, her son's former college roommate. Jenny and Glenn maintained only a distant, pen-pal relationship, but he saved her letters, later gave them to Allport, and then they were published under the title *Letters from Jenny* (Allport, 1965). Through these letters, we also know Ross. They provide a study in personality of special interest, for they depict a fundamental family relationship.

The term **personality** refers to the characteristic and unique ways in which an individual responds to the environment. It emphasizes consistent patterns of behavior, but uniqueness is also stressed. All of us have some patterns of behavior in common with other people, even with Jenny. But in each of us these are combined in special ways and united with less common patterns to form a set of behaviors and experiences that are distinct from all others.

But how do we go about understanding the whole individual, the entire personality? We cannot examine every detail of a person's past and present

behavior and experience. Instead, we use selected viewpoints, each giving emphasis to a special psychological process. These viewpoints—psychoanalytic theory, constitutional theory, behavioral and cognitive theory, and humanistic theory—are the most fundamental psychological approaches to the study of personality (Liebert & Spiegler, 1987). At the end of the chapter, we consider personality in perspective, noting that each theory makes a special contribution to our understanding of personality.

• PSYCHOANALYTIC THEORY •

Contrary to popular thought, Sigmund Freud, founder of psychoanalysis, was not particularly interested in therapy. "I have never really been a doctor in the proper sense," he said. Then he added: "Nor did I ever play the doctor game." He practiced therapy for two reasons— to earn a living, which he could not do by research, and to gather the information necessary to build a theory. That information came from people who sought his therapeutic assistance. His basic goal in life was "to understand something of the riddles of the world in which we live . . . perhaps even to contribute something to their solution" (Freud, 1927).

As its founder, Freud spoke of psychoanalysis in two major ways. First, **psychoanalysis** is a theory of personality stating that unconscious conflict, usually from childhood, is a major force in the adult personality. This conflict arises largely through early sexual development and the individual's effort to deal with the resulting anxiety. In addition, psychoanalysis is a method of therapy based on Freud's theory and discussed in a later chapter (Figure 14–1).

Conflict was a central theme in Jenny's life, not only in day-to-day events but also in three dramatic instances. Jenny's father died when she was 18, leaving her as the chief source of support for six siblings. After they left home, Jenny left too, engaged to a man whom her father had disliked. Amid a quarrel with her mother and aunts and uncles, she married this man anyway, a divorced citizen from another country and a different religion. Following this upheaval, she broke connections with her family.

Two years later, when Jenny was pregnant with their first child, her young husband suddenly died. Once again, she became the head of a household, this time of her own family. After five years as a widow with a young son, Jenny returned to her sisters and brother. Once more a quarrel broke out, this one over her approach to childrearing. Jenny ended the conflict by severing relations again, this time for 25 years.

This pattern of conflict and rupture was repeated still again in her confrontation with Ross. Jenny disowned her only offspring. "The idea of my holding out the olive branch to Ross," she declared emphatically after that moment in her doorway, "is too disgusting for words" (Allport, 1965).

At that point in her life, Jenny had no close

FIGURE 14–1 FOUNDER OF PSYCHOANALYSIS. Often feeling like an outcast and isolate in his work, Sigmund Freud sometimes took solace in the company of his dogs. A man of habit, he took a walk and had his beard trimmed daily. An intrepid adventurer in the world of ideas, he revised or extended his theory of personality on several occasions.

family relationships and no friends, for minor emotional breakups occurred regularly. As always, Jenny attributed them to the other person. She had no insight into her own behavior and how it might have contributed to the problem. According to psychoanalysis, Jenny lacked this insight because the earlier conflicts, responsible for precipitating this quarrelsome behavior, had been forgotten. They had been pushed into an unconscious realm, although they still influenced her behavior.

☙

STRUCTURE OF PERSONALITY

In psychoanalytic theory, the building blocks of personality consist of three systems or psychic forces:

the id, ego, and superego. They are called psychic forces because they are mental processes that influence the ways we think and behave. Sometimes they are said to represent, in a very loose way, the biological, psychological, and social elements of personality, respectively. Collectively, they constitute the basic structure of personality (Freud, 1923).

INBORN NATURE OF THE ID. The new baby is activated purely by innate impulses. It strives for physical satisfaction and nothing more. These inborn biological urges, present in all human beings, are collectively referred to as the **id.**

The id has complete disregard for anything except biological satisfaction, and it includes two fundamental impulses: sex and aggression. The sex impulse, called **eros** or the *life instinct,* concerns survival. It is love directed toward oneself and others. The needs for sustenance and sleep, as well as the desire for love and sexual experience, are all part of the life instinct. The other impulse, called **thanatos** or the *death instinct,* was a late addition to psychoanalytic theory and not as fully developed. Operating in a more subtle fashion, it involves aggression and destructive behavior toward the self and others. These two forces, eros and thanatos, are inseparable, one seeking creation, the other destruction. In referring to each of them as an instinct, however, Freud was not using the term in its conventional sense today. He was speaking instead of a broader, less well defined tendency, more like an inborn motivational or emotional disposition.

The newborn is "all id," wanting food right away when hungry, urinating without consideration of time or place, and so forth. The id follows the **pleasure principle,** which requires the immediate satisfaction of needs, regardless of the circumstances or consequences. The primary concern, in fact the only concern, is immediate gratification.

EMERGENCE OF THE EGO. As the growing infant learns to react to its environment, the expression of the id becomes modified. Partly out of the energy provided by the id, and partly from experiences in the environment, there emerges a new dimension called the ego. The **ego,** which in Latin means "I" or "self," becomes the executive or problem-solving dimension of the personality, operating in the service of the id. It assists the id in achieving its ends, taking into account the conditions of the external environment.

The ego follows the **reality principle,** which is the capacity to delay gratification in order to avoid an unpleasant outcome or to obtain a better outcome later. In the words of psychoanalysis, it requires a suspension of the pleasure principle according to the circumstances in the environment. Most infants soon discover that sucking on clothes does not satisfy hunger and that wet diapers are uncomfortable. As the baby calls for the mother and finds other ways to solve its problems, the ego emerges, especially through such psychological processes as perceiving, learning, remembering, and reasoning—all aspects of the ego. Under these influences, the child gradually refrains from acting solely according to biological impulses.

The relation between the ego and id has been compared with that between a rider and horse. All of the locomotive energy is provided by the id, or horse, while the rider, or ego, has the opportunity to determine the goal and guide his or her powerful mount toward it. But in these relations the picture all too often changes. The rider is obliged to direct the steed toward the goal that the animal itself wishes to pursue (Freud, 1933).

DEVELOPMENT OF THE SUPEREGO. Throughout life, the ego is confronted with another force in the personality, one that develops a bit later, through contact with various people. Especially through the influence of parents and teachers, the child acquires certain values and standards of behavior, known as the **superego.** These standards are learned. They represent the internalized values of the parents and, through them, of society.

One part of the superego, roughly comparable to a **conscience,** is critical and involves prohibitions; it discourages behavior deemed undesirable by parents and elders. It develops primarily under the influence of scorn and threats of punishment. The gradual development of the conscience is illustrated by the little girl who was dropping eggs from her high chair, one by one, observed surreptitiously by her mother. "Mustn't dood it," said the child, shaking her head before each release. "Mustn't dood it." *Splat!* At that point in her life, the result was more intriguing than the strength of her conscience.

Another part of the superego, the **ego ideal,** has positive values, encouraging the goals of the parents and other elders. It too develops through experience, guilt, and the support of elders, as well as through imitation of them. Together, the conscience and ego ideal, formed early in life, make up the superego, the third basic dimension of personality.

THE EGO'S TASKS. As the self, or director of the personality, the ego is responsible for enabling the individual to take his or her place in society. In doing so, it operates in the service of the id, meeting the individual's biological requirements under the watchful eye of the superego. The id and superego, with their very different concerns, usually make separate demands on the ego, but they are not necessarily opposed to one another and the ego is not a referee. For example, a highly aggressive, despotic leader may decide that it is his duty to destroy a certain sect or group of people. Here the destructive impulses of the id and the conscience of the superego have the same goals, placing heavy pressure on the ego.

The ego must meet these demands in a particular context—that is, in a given reality, one that may not offer ready satisfactions for the id or superego. The ego is therefore beset with demands on all sides: biological urges, social prescriptions, and the limitations of the environment. A strong, effective ego is the essential ingredient in a mature personality.

Did Jenny possess a strong, well-formed ego? In some respects she did, for early in life she supported several sisters and a brother. Later, she alone supported her son, providing him with extensive care (Figure 14–2). In some respects she did not, for she was unable to manage her life to her own satisfaction. She was without friends, separated from all of her family, and without any meaningful activity.

PERSONALITY DEVELOPMENT

In the words of the poet John Milton: "The childhood shows the man, / As morning shows the day" (*Paradise Lost, IV*). After many years of studying adult men and women in his consulting room, Sigmund Freud agreed. A person's early experiences exert a profound influence on later behavior.

There are two reasons for the powerful influence of early experiences. First, the child is relatively helpless in the face of conflicts—too weak to fight, too small to flee, too mute to explain, too ignorant to understand, too immature even to ask useful questions. At the mercy of his or her environment, the child must simply endure whatever happens. Second, the outcomes of these early conflicts set patterns that, once underway, are difficult

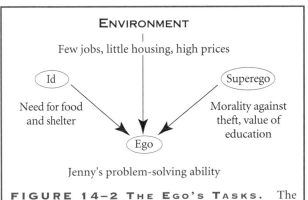

FIGURE 14–2 THE EGO'S TASKS. The id and superego make demands upon the ego. Often, the ego attempts to meet these demands in the context of a difficult environment, as was the case with Jenny.

to change. For better or worse, they become fixed or permanent.

What are these conflicts? They are the ego's struggles with the biological demands of the id, the social standards of the superego, and the constraints of the environment. When the ego cannot manage these pressures readily and directly, which is often the case for a child or even an adult, the conflict is resolved indirectly. Through the process of **repression,** the objectionable experience is excluded from awareness, banished from consciousness. It becomes *unconscious, seemingly* forgotten, as noted in further detail shortly. Certain cases of childhood sexual abuse seem to lend support to this view (Briere & Conte, 1993; Clark, 1993).

PSYCHOSEXUAL STAGES. In the childhood years, there is a steady physical unfolding in several areas. In locomotion, for example, the infant first raises its head, then sits with support, then without support, then stands with help, and so forth, until the child is able to run, skip, and move about in other complex ways. In grasping, the infant first waves the arms, then palms things using the whole hand, then opposes all of the fingers to the thumb, then just the index finger, and so forth. In sexual development, broadly defined to include sensual as well as explicitly sexual experiences, there is also a predictable sequence of unfolding. This growth of sensitivity occurs first in the mouth, then the anus, and finally the genitals.

These phases of sexual development are called **psychosexual stages,** meaning that psychological development is influenced by unfolding sexual interests. These sexual interests can become the source of exquisite pleasure and profound frustration. Thus, the child's early conflicts develop in the context of these stages (Freud, 1933).

ORAL STAGE. The infant's first concern is to obtain food, and the body area of greatest sensitivity at this time is the mouth, especially the lips and tongue. Thus, this early task of ingesting food, together with the sensitivity of the mouth, prompted Freud to call this initial period the **oral stage.** If the caretaker regularly satisfies the infant's food requirements during this period, along with sucking and other oral needs, the experience is pleasurable and an optimistic view of life begins to emerge. The child develops a trusting, confident outlook. Most important, this first relationship with a caretaker sets a pattern or model for all subsequent relationships. If the infant's needs are not met, feelings of uncertainty and dissatisfaction are likely outcomes and, if repressed, they may become manifest later, in the adult personality (Figure 14–3).

An adult with unresolved problems in this first stage may develop into an *oral character,* prone to excessive eating and drinking, sarcasm and arguing, or depression and pessimism. Dissatisfied with the love, food, and attention received in the first stage of life, the individual's psychological growth has been arrested at that point. The person uncon-

FIGURE 14–3 ORAL BEHAVIOR. According to psychoanalytic theory, thumb sucking among older children often reflects a desire to return to the earlier security of feeding from the nipple and protection by the mother. The so-called oral child is typically passive, withdrawn, and dependent.

sciously attempts to resolve the earlier problems by seeking extra love, attention, food, knowledge, and so forth, or perhaps through some less obvious fixation, such as gossip, argument, or biting remarks. This condition is known as a **fixation** because normal gratification has been blocked at an earlier stage and the individual remains preoccupied with achieving the pleasure denied earlier.

When we consider Jenny Masterson from the psychoanalytic perspective, we note immediately her adversarial, unfriendly relationships with essentially everyone she encountered. Even when she liked someone initially, she had a predictable tendency to turn against that person eventually: her lawyer, physician, landlords, employers, postal clerks, sales clerks, a friend here, another there, and so forth, to say nothing of her parents, siblings and, alas, even her son. Looking backward in a psychoanalytic vein, we would speculate that Jenny's disrupted love relationships with Ross and virtually all other adults, including her family, reflected conflict and frustration in the very earliest stage of life, the oral stage, which set the pattern for later relationships.

ANAL STAGE. In the second and even the third year, the **anal stage,** a new sensitivity appears, in the anus, and the child is confronted with a very difficult task: toilet training. It can become a special problem because the child, perhaps for the first time, is expected to oppose or deny the demands of the id. Toilet training therefore plays a role in ego development. If the training is smooth and successful, the child takes further pleasure in himself or herself and develops further confidence. But if the demands are too harsh, fixation may again occur.

In adulthood, the *anal character* may be incurably messy and disobedient, perhaps in continued defiance of an overly strict parental approach in earlier years. Or this person may be scrupulously neat, clean, prompt, and precise, attempting to make amends for childhood slips. Consider the once popular play and television show about a pair of mismatched bachelors who decide to live together, *The Odd Couple.* Dirty, rumpled Oscar uses his napkin to clean his shoes and his sleeve to wipe his mouth. Squeaky-clean Felix wears plastic baggies on his hands when touching his own door knobs and incessantly sprays his home with disinfectant. These two men, so much at odds with one another, have the same underlying problem, according to psychoanalytic theory—an unresolved anal problem. As infants, they received toilet training that was too strict for their readiness at the time. As adults, they are fixated; their difficult earlier days are still with them.

These stereotyped descriptions of personality are regarded with skepticism by many modern psychologists, but many believe in the broader principle—that adult life brings a symbolic re-enactment of childhood problems. In calling attention to the importance of childhood experiences in adult behavior, apart from these hypothesized outcomes, Freud made a most significant contribution to the study of personality.

PHALLIC STAGE. The period from three to six years is the **phallic stage,** a term that Freud used for both boys and girls, during which the child discovers pleasures associated with the genitalia, including various forms of masturbation. But more important for personality development is an increasing awareness of sex roles and an emerging interest in the parent of the opposite sex. Freud described this reaction with reference to King Oedipus, a figure in early Greek drama who unknowingly murdered his father and married his mother. In the **Oedipus complex,** a son regards his father as a rival and seeks intimate relations with his mother. Freud referred to the daughter's family position in the same way; she strives in particular for the love of her father and regards her mother as an obstacle to this goal. Other psychologists have labeled this condition of the daughter the **Electra complex** (Powell, 1993).

This rivalry with the same-sex parent causes anxiety, for that parent is big and powerful. The normal child therefore handles the Oedipus problem by a shift in outlook. In this process, called **identification,** the child adopts the manner, attitudes, and interests of the same-sex parent, attempting in this way to avoid the rivalry with that parent and, at the same time, to win the love and respect of the other parent. This process is assumed to be particularly important for developing appropriate sex roles.

LATER STAGES. At the conclusion of the phallic stage, there is an apparent absence of sexual interests. They are still present, Freud claimed, but he called this period of late childhood the **latency stage** because sexuality is not an overt concern. This stage, from age six to the onset of adolescence, may be a cultural artifact, however. In certain societies, including ours, there may be no decrease in sexual interests in late childhood.

With the beginning of adolescence and the **genital stage,** there is a reawakening of sexual interests and a search for people to provide sexual satisfaction. The individual becomes other-oriented as well as self-oriented, seeking to combine self-concerns with those of other people. Insofar as the earlier conflicts have been adequately resolved, the individual settles into the task of establishing mature relationships with other people, a stage that lasts throughout the adult years (Figure 14–4).

UNCONSCIOUS MOTIVATION

In psychoanalysis, the fundamental concept is the unconscious—or unconscious motivation—discussed in prior chapters on consciousness, memory, and motivation. In **unconscious motivation,** traumatic events earlier in life, seemingly forgotten, continue to influence behavior, but they do so without the individual's full awareness. Too difficult for the ego to manage, they never fully disappear.

To review earlier discussions succinctly, unconscious motivation can be viewed as developing in these stages: conflict, repression, and symbolic behavior. A *conflict* in the early years cannot be managed by the immature ego, thereby causing anxiety. To deal with this anxiety, the ego uses *repression,* by which memory of

Genital (12–Adult): Intimacy.
The adolescent begins to develop intimate love relationships and to work as a member of society.

Latency (6–12): Repression.
The child identifies with the parent of the same sex; Oedipal/Electra impulses are repressed.

Phallic (3–6): Masturbation.
The child obtains pleasure from genital stimulation and desires the parent of the opposite sex.

Anal (1–3): Elimination.
The infant learns to control the expulsion of waste, a major task in emerging ego development.

Oral (0–1): Sucking.
The infant receives food and comfort from a caretaker and learns to expect these satisfactions.

FIGURE 14–4 PSYCHOSEXUAL STAGES. Biologically determined, these stages appear through normal maturation, stimulating related erotic activity. Conflict can interfere with these erotic outcomes and therefore disrupt psychological development at any stage, especially the first three, producing a fixation that may continue into adulthood.

the conflict is pushed into the unconscious realm. Repression requires energy, however, and at various points in later life, especially when the individual is tired, annoyed, or ill, the repressed conflict reappears in *symbolic behavior,* as an expression but also a disguise of the underlying conflict. The disguise is part of the ego's work, keeping unwanted, repressed thoughts and feelings out of consciousness (Freud, 1900, 1938).

According to Freud, mental life actually occurs at several levels. The first, the *conscious,* consists only of an individual's current thoughts and feelings at any given moment. It is transitory. The next, the *preconscious,* can become conscious with some simple, direct effort at recall. For example, describe your first kiss. That should be possible, provided it was not *too* traumatic. If it were, then that experience should be buried in the third level, the unconscious. The contents of the *unconscious* have been repressed and cannot become conscious through ordinary efforts at recall. The special techniques of psycho-analytic therapy are necessary to retrieve these memories (Figure 14–5). Otherwise, the contents of the unconscious are revealed only occasionally and in disguise through symbolic behavior—in the form of dreams, errors in everyday life, defense mechanisms, maladjustment, and even lifestyle.

ERRORS IN EVERYDAY LIFE. The symbolism in dreams has been considered already, in the chapter on consciousness, and it is still debated today. However, Freud's view of errors in everyday life has become so popular that a minor error in speech, writing, memory, or the performance of some task is often called a **Freudian slip,** meaning that it is a symbolic expression of some unconscious motive. The slip partially reveals some repressed impulse or conflict. A man contemplating a diet asked a woman for a good seducing plan. A woman, not wanting her daughter to leave home, injured herself in a highly unusual manner, requir-

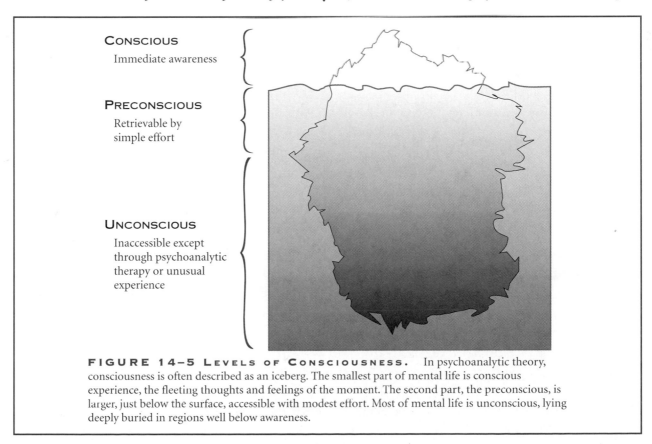

FIGURE 14–5 LEVELS OF CONSCIOUSNESS. In psychoanalytic theory, consciousness is often described as an iceberg. The smallest part of mental life is conscious experience, the fleeting thoughts and feelings of the moment. The second part, the preconscious, is larger, just below the surface, accessible with modest effort. Most of mental life is unconscious, lying deeply buried in regions well below awareness.

ing her daughter to stay home and assume the burden of care. Freud noticed such mistakes in his own and others' lives, speculated on their origins, and wrote at length about their significance in *The Psychopathology of Everyday Life* (1914), a book that played an enormous role in the acceptance of Freud's initially shocking theories (Gay, 1990).

At a party, Freud once surprised himself in offering his hand to his hostess, as a polite greeting. Aware of no dishonorable intent, he suddenly found that he had untied the bow at the front of her gown "with the dexterity of a conjurer" (Freud, 1914).

Carl Gustav Jung on several occasions had forgotten to mail a particular letter lying on his desk. Then he tried to mail it, and he discovered that it had no address. One day, he finally did mail it, and the post office sent it back—for it had no stamp (Freud, 1914). It seemed to Jung that he had a strong unconscious resistance to sending that letter.

The evidence for Freudian slips is largely anecdotal because it is difficult to study small mistakes in everyday life, but experimental studies have provided some support. In a typical investigation, two groups of men performed the same simple task, reciting pairs of words. This task was explained to one group by a male experimenter who attached electrodes to their bodies in preparation for unpredictable electric shocks—which were never administered. The task was explained to the other group by a seductive female experimenter dressed in a distinctly provocative manner. Word pairs were then flashed on a screen for one second each, such as *sham–dock* and *brood–nests.* At the sound of a buzzer, the men spoke aloud whatever pair had just appeared on the screen. The men in the fear-arousal condition showed a tendency to pronounce the first pair as *damn shock;* those in the sexual-arousal condition, if they made a mistake on the second example, were most likely to say *nude breasts.* Similarly, *worst–cottage* became *cursed wattage* for the first group; *past–fashion* became *fast passion* in the second group. Still further, the men most anxious about sexual issues in general made a distinctly higher number of sex-related slips than others in the second group (Motley, 1987).

Of course, not all slips and bungled actions seem to involve unconscious urges. Many of them can be more reasonably explained on the basis of habit or faulty thinking. In January, for example, we often write the date incorrectly, referring to the old year. In these instances, habit seems to be the primary factor, not unconscious motivation.

DEFENSE MECHANISMS. Another manifestation of symbolic behavior, popular in the public domain, is the **defense mechanism,** a method used by the ego in dealing with anxiety aroused by the id or the superego. The primary defense mechanism is *repression,* for that is the ego's basic defense against overwhelming anxiety. Then, to aid the repression and often to disguise further the real problem, the ego may use additional mechanisms. In the defense mechanism of **rationalization,** for example, the individual is not only unaware of repressed thoughts but also substitutes false reasons for real ones. A man applies unsuccessfully for a job and responds with a sour-grapes attitude: "Who'd want to work for *that* so-and-so anyway?" He offers an alibi for a situation that he finds threatening to his self-esteem—being rejected for the position.

Throughout adulthood, Jenny engaged in confrontations with almost everyone she met. She failed to understand her constant fighting stance and its detrimental effects, apparently because its origins in childhood conflict had been pushed into the unconscious. The ego, through repression, had rejected awareness of this conflict and, through rationalization, had cast the resulting hostile impulses into a favorable light instead, claiming that they produced a useful outcome: "They clear the air." This rationalization served a dual purpose.

It allowed Jenny to go on picking fights and also enabled her to avoid rejection, for she spurned others before they might reject her.

In another defense mechanism, called **reaction formation,** the individual adopts attitudes and behaviors that are the opposite of those judged to be unacceptable. These opposed reactions, it is hypothesized, also aid repression. After a narrow escape on one of his missions, a wartime flyer declared that he never feared anything. He fainted, however, after each of his next two flights. Later, following administration of sodium pentothal, the so-called truth drug, he revealed more basic feelings. He said, "I was scared. Me scared! I didn't think I'd ever be scared" (White, 1964).

Rather than adopting false reasons or reasons that are the opposite of our repressed feelings, we sometimes attribute the unwanted feelings, behavior, or problem to someone else, in which case we may be engaging in **projection.** Again, there are two phases: repressing unacceptable thoughts and, in this case, ascribing them to others, which promotes the repressive process.

In a classic study of projection as a defense mechanism, college men rated themselves and others on four socially undesirable traits: stinginess, obstinacy, disorderliness, and bashfulness. Some students gave themselves high ratings on traits for which they received high ratings from their friends. Other students gave themselves low ratings on traits for which they received high ratings from friends; furthermore, they rated other people higher on these undesirable traits than did the rest of the group (Sears, 1936). These students lacked insight into their own undesirable qualities and falsely saw them in others instead. They engaged in projection, one of the predominant defense mechanisms in late adolescence (Cramer, 1991).

Other behaviors often considered symbolic, and therefore evidence of unconscious motivation, include adjustment disorders, many of which Freud

called neuroses, and various lifestyles. A *lifestyle* is a way of living which reflects certain attitudes, motives, values, or other personal concerns. According to psychoanalysis, repressed childhood conflict may become manifest not only in the lifestyles of oral and anal characters but also, for example, in the behavior of a *Don Juan,* a man obsessed with the seduction of women, presumably owing to a fixation at the phallic stage. Extreme fears, addictions, hostilities, and other preoccupations, including excessive hobbies and pleasures, also may be regarded in this way (Figure 14–6).

This assumption, that long-forgotten childhood trauma may be responsible for unusual adult behav-

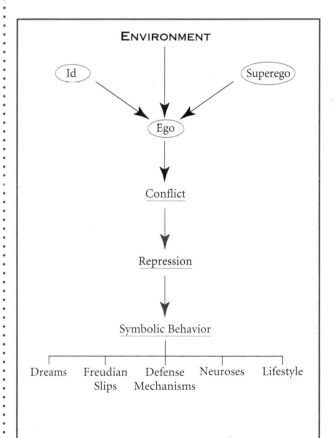

FIGURE 14–6 UNCONSCIOUS MOTIVATION. According to psychoanalysis, the roots of Jenny's disruptive personal relationships lay in unresolved childhood *conflict.* Pushed into the unconscious by *repression,* signs of this conflict emerged in *symbolic behavior,* especially her use of defense mechanisms and constantly combative lifestyle.

ior, has become increasingly accepted in modern research, especially in investigations of amnesia, phobias, psychophysiological disorders, and aggressive behaviors. It shows Freud's unquestionable influence not only on our ideas about adjustment and psychological disorders, the topics of the next chapter, but also on the formulations of other leading theorists.

∽

PSYCHODYNAMIC VIEWS

Under Freud's leadership, psychoanalysis was a unified system of psychology, but eventually its followers separated into subgroups, each reflecting different assumptions and emphases. However, all of them share the belief that human behavior is influenced by conscious and unconscious forces.

For example, while Freud focused on the overwhelming significance of the first six years in human life, **object-relations theory,** for example, concentrates on the first two years, especially the infant's relationship with the primary caretaker. The idea is that from the child's immature, naive perspective in the very first years, his or her caretaker is not a parent or even a person. It is a *something,* an object that intermittently appears and disappears, makes noise, provides comfort, and so forth.

From the object-relations viewpoint, the first object in our lives, usually the mother, is extremely crucial in personality development. On this basis, the adjustment problem in later life is inevitably more difficult for males than for females, for little boys, in forming an identity, must break away from that first love object (Chodorow, 1978). The long-term outcome is that men may have a more difficult time developing subsequent relationships (Westen, 1991).

Object-relations theory is an example of a recent departure from orthodox psychoanalysis. Some of the most important deviations occurred earlier, however, during Freud's lifetime. All of them are loosely described as psychodynamic theo-

ries. A **psychodynamic theory** is a modification of traditional psychoanalytic doctrine, as developed by Sigmund Freud, often with greater emphasis on conscious motivation—but with attention to unconscious processes as well.

ANALYTIC PSYCHOLOGY. The heir apparent to Freud's work was Carl Gustav Jung. However, he rejected Freud's emphasis on sex as the primary energizing force in personality (Figure 14–7). The two men also differed in their conception of the unconscious. Freud postulated an individual unconscious, containing the unknown conflicts of a particular individual. Jung in addition hypothesized a **collective unconscious,** which is

FIGURE 14–7 CARL GUSTAV JUNG (1875–1961). This Swiss psychoanalyst traveled with Sigmund Freud to the United States, where they gave lectures on their work. With a third traveler, they discussed their dreams during the voyage, conducting what they called the first group analysis. Jung decided that Freud's resistance to these activities foreshadowed their later personal difficulties.

universal among us, containing all of the human traits and cultural characteristics inherited by all of us from earlier ancestors, not only in human history but also in the evolutionary stages of animal life (Jung, 1928). The underlying similarities among different cultures are regarded as support for this idea. Hence, Jung's approach, called *analytic psychology,* is of special interest in anthropology, religion, literature, and art, as well as other fields (Johnson, 1991).

The collective unconscious includes **archetypes,** which are not specific thoughts or behaviors but rather unconscious tendencies and images inherited from human experience throughout the ages. They include such symbols as the *good mother,* the *evil beast,* and the *divine being,* central to the belief systems of almost all cultures. Two core archetypes are the feminine side of the male personality, the *anima,* and the masculine side of the female personality, the *animus.* While they arise partly through hormones and human physiology, they are also shaped by the experiences of men and women living together throughout countless centuries. As men associate with women, they become feminized in outlook and values. As women share life and work with men, they become masculinized. In all spheres, balance is the key. In Jenny's case, Jungians would speculate that the animus was overdeveloped, prompting a somewhat masculine lifestyle, evident in her independence and resistance to authority, as well as her inability to understand and relate successfully to those of her own sex. Freud, incidentally, emphasized that each sex possessed both male and female hormones, although at the time there was no known way to verify this viewpoint.

Jung also was responsible for two expressions widely popularized outside psychology. The *introvert* is someone whose interests and thoughts are directed primarily inward, toward the self. The *extravert* is a person who is outgoing and highly responsive to the environment.

INDIVIDUAL PSYCHOLOGY. Another early analyst who diverged from Freud's views was Alfred Adler. Just as Freud considered human beings to be motivated by pleasure, Adler regarded them as motivated by a desire for power. He did not regard sex as the basic motivating force in life, placed little emphasis on unconscious processes, and eventually turned Freud's attention to the issue of aggression (Figure 14–8).

In Adler's *individual psychology,* striving for success and superiority played an important role. Today the term **sibling rivalry** refers to a child's competition with brothers and sisters for the parents' love and attention. It is one of Adler's most influential ideas. Many contemporary psychologists argue that this rivalry among children for the love of the parents is far more influential in personality development than the Oedipus/Electra rivalry between a child and the same-sex parent for the love of the parent of the opposite sex. Adler also developed a related term, the **inferiority complex,** which refers to an individual's feeling of being less competent than others. Both concepts imply an effort to overcome

FIGURE 14–8 THE ADLERS. An ophthalmologist by training, Alfred left orthodox psychoanalysis following his outspoken criticism of Freud's theory of sexuality. Raissa, an emancipated Russian, gained a reputation as an outspoken political activist, espousing socialist causes. Together, the Adlers were an exceptional Viennese couple.

personal deficiencies, real or imagined (Adler, 1927).

As the oldest of seven siblings, Jenny for a brief time had her parents all to herself, but then she was displaced by more and more siblings, given increasing responsibility for their care, and received less and less attention herself. In the Adlerian view, these conditions led to resentment and sibling rivalry, exemplified later in Jenny's poor relations with adults. In a symbolic sense, Jenny became a sibling among Ross's girlfriends, fighting with them for his love and attention.

A NEO-FREUDIAN PERSPECTIVE. Other followers who disagreed with Freud maintained a closer overall allegiance. Called *neo-Freudians,* they revised or modified his theory rather than breaking away in the manner of Jung and Adler. An earlier chapter described Erik Erikson's psychosocial stages, developed from Freud's psychosexual stages; on this basis, Erikson is a neo-Freudian. Another neo-Freudian, Karen Horney (pronounced *Horn-eye*), grew up in Berlin with a Dutch mother and a Norwegian father (Figure 14–9). With this diverse background, she too challenged Freud's emphasis on sexual motivation and conflicts with the parents. Her fundamental concept is **basic anxiety,** which arises in the helplessness and insecurity of childhood. This early dependency leaves an enduring uncertainty about relationships with other people, even in adult life.

According to Horney, there are three **response strategies,** or *neurotic trends,* by which human beings cope with their basic anxiety about personal relationships. In *moving toward people,* they seek love and approval by being compliant and submissive. In *moving against people,* they deny their desire for support and acceptance, behaving in a competitive, domineering style instead. When *moving away from people,* they withdraw from others, establishing themselves as independent and separate. Horney's

FIGURE 14–9 KAREN HORNEY (1885–1953). Arriving in the United States in mid-career, Horney challenged Freud's emphasis on biological factors in personality development, focusing instead on social influences. She also resisted Freud's male chauvinism, viewing the male achievement motive as an unconscious effort to compensate for a subordinate role in the reproductive process.

major point is that overreliance on any one trend results in maladjustment. The individual becomes too submissive, hostile, or isolated to derive satisfaction from interpersonal relationships. The most adequate adjustment is a balance among them (Horney, 1937).

TRAUMA THEORY. As a traditional psychoanalyst who reflects the Freudian concern with childhood and the Oedipus myth, and yet has a decidedly revised interpretation, Alice Miller has become especially popular with laypersons. She points out that Freud produced a *guilt interpretation* of the myth, faulting the son for the tragedy of killing his father and marrying his mother. In opposing this view, Miller notes that earlier the father had tried to kill his infant son, that years later he provoked Oedipus into their fight, and that Oedipus really did not desire his mother. He became her husband primarily to save the city of Thebes. The emphasis on these events, holding the parents accountable, is called the *innocent interpretation,* for the child is not held responsible for the problems.

In modern life, according to Miller, the parents are often at fault. The child's frustrated instinctual drives, resulting in pathological disturbances, are not due to wishes or fantasies. They are attributable to actual events, as in incest, and also to other sorts of physical and psychological abuse, intentional or otherwise. This theory, focusing on real and highly disruptive childhood events, is called **trauma theory,** which is essentially child-abuse theory (Barclay, 1991; Lowen, 1980; Miller, 1983, 1984a).

PSYCHOANALYSIS AND PSYCHODYNAMIC THEORY. These refinements of psychoanalysis are testimony to its influence. Experts and laypersons do not modify or extend inconsequential work. They have resisted Freud on several points: placing too much emphasis on human sexuality, a stress more appropriate in his time than today; his view of dreams as repressed childhood wishes, a claim that can hardly be proved or disproved; narrow and negative attitudes toward women, which appeared in several writings; and a speculative, unscientific approach to other topics in psychology. A gifted writer who gave free reign to his imagination, Freud argued by style, example, and analogy, rather than by empirical data, a serious limitation in his work. Much of psychoanalytic theory is untestable by any known methods, for it contains urging and check-ing forces that can be construed as operating in diverse ways, resulting in a theory with low predictive capacity.

These limitations should not obscure Freud's many extraordinary achievements. He became *the* pioneer in several areas of research: sex and sex education, the study of dreams, and the clinical approach to psychological problems. His method of psychotherapy, also called psychoanalysis and discussed extensively in a later chapter, became the model for many forms of therapy.

Despite these accomplishments, his biggest contribution lay in a new way of looking at the adult personality, seeking its origins in the child's early years. His idea that repressed childhood conflict can influence adult behavior is accepted today by experts and laypersons around the world, although psychoanalysis is constantly re-evaluated and reinterpreted in the context of social changes (Warren, 1990). While modern theorists disagree with Freud on specific points, there is no doubt about the overall significance of his work. It has exerted a profound influence on our modern view of humanity (Emde, 1992; Kaley, 1993).

• CONSTITUTIONAL THEORY •

Most people, when asked to describe Jenny Masterson, would not refer to psychoanalytic concepts. Instead, they would describe her as a certain personality type or according to certain personality traits, emphasizing the way she was at the moment, without speculating about her earlier years. This approach, depicting people as certain types or possessing certain traits, is popular among laypeople because it is efficient to apply and readily understood.

After his mother's rejection, Ross wrote to Glenn, his former roommate, and described his mother as self-centered, sentimental, and depressed. "I am afraid there is little one can do" (Allport,

1965). Two months later, he wrote again. This time he depicted himself as apprehensive, intelligent, witty—and frustrated. In both cases, Ross was describing personality according to a set of specific characteristics.

In the fifth century B.C. a Greek physician, Hippocrates, developed the first recorded approach to personality types. He decided that there were four basic fluids, or humors, in the human body: black bile, yellow bile, phlegm, and blood. The proportions among these fluids influenced a person's behavior (Figure 14–10).

This theory was a constitutional theory, meaning that it was based on the individual's physical makeup. A **constitutional theory** states that personality arises through genetically determined predispositions and early environmental influences. Certain physiological conditions are inborn; certain psychological experiences occur early in life; as a result, personality is constant and stable over the lifetime of the individual.

BIOLOGICAL APPROACH

Among the constitutional theories, two can be classified as biological in the sense that they focus on inherited characteristics. One of these points to the stability of temperament over the life span. The other continues along the lines initiated by Hippocrates, identifying categories or types of people.

STABILITY OF TEMPERAMENT. Almost immediately after a child's birth, parents notice differences among singly born children. The concept of **temperament** refers to the typical or usual patterns of *emotionally toned reactions* appearing in an individual's early years and remaining throughout most of the lifetime. These include level of activity, readiness to interact, range of feeling, and amount of tension. Temperament is part of personality, an apparently inherited emotional dimension.

One dimension of temperament that has received considerable attention in recent decades is **shyness,** the tendency to feel tension in social situations and therefore to withdraw from them. Its genetic origins are suggested by the differences even in infants. Some are obviously *inhibited,* others quite *uninhibited* in response to a stranger (Figure 14–11). Furthermore, a majority of children retain their characteristic style at least through the eighth year of life. Also, relatives of the shy children show a greater preponderance of social anxiety than do relatives of the more social children. These findings indicate the stability of the shy–sociable temperament and suggest a genetically mediated condition (Kagan, Snidman, Julia-Sellers, & Johnson, 1991).

How would we rate Jenny on shyness? Very low,

MELANCHOLIC

CHOLERIC

PHLEGMATIC

SANGUINE

FIGURE 14–10 HIPPOCRATES'S HUMORS. According to this theory, a person with too much black bile might be downcast with depression. Too much yellow bile made a person impulsive and angry. An excess of phlegm caused a lethargic and unresponsive style, rejecting even invitations for games or love. And a dominance of blood brought forth a cheery, hearty approach to life.

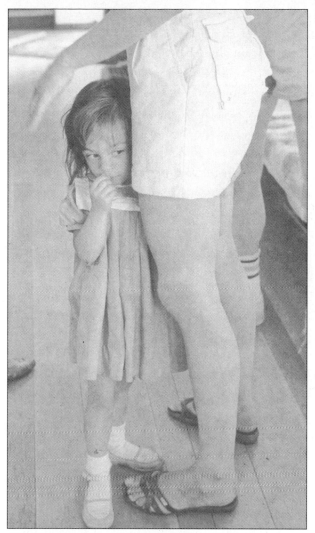

**FIGURE 14–11 SHYNESS AS TEMPERA-
MENT.** From the very earliest years, a child may be consistently timid and emotionally restrained in the presence of
unfamiliar events. Another child may display
minimal uncertainty and even spontaneous pleasure (Kegan,
Snidman, Julia-Sellers, & Johnson, 1991).

the extent to which personality is determined by
heredity. While estimates vary, they generally
ascribe no more than 40% or 50% to genetic factors (Plomin, Chipeur, & Loehlin, 1990; Plomin &
Rende, 1991).

If hereditary estimates vary upward to 50%,
then at least half of the influences on personality
arrive through the environment. And yet comparisons of identical and even fraternal twins show
that the members of pairs reared apart are no more
or less alike in personality than those reared
together. At first glance, this finding seems to indicate that environment plays little or no role in personality development—a conclusion that we know
is incorrect. Rather, it points to subtle but important environmental differences for children within
the same family. These differences are referred to as
the *nonshared environment,* indicating factors within a
family which are important to the development of
one or more siblings and yet are not shared by all
siblings or are shared by them but interpreted differently (Plomin, 1990; Plomin & Rende, 1991).
Birth order, gender differences, and disparities in
abilities and interests are all part of the nonshared
environment. Each sibling, with his or her special
characteristics, is a *vital* element in the lives of other
siblings, as are the parents' differential responses to
their children. Collectively and individually, these
differences and comparisons, intentional or otherwise, among siblings living in close proximity, may
exert profound influences on personality development.

Jenny grew up in the same family as her brother
and sisters, but for her this environment was
very different from that of her younger siblings.
Jenny was thrust into her mother's caretaker role,
responsible for her siblings' safety while her
mother worked outside the home. Later, Jenny was
thrust into her father's support role, significantly
responsible for their financial welfare. These early,
heavy responsibilities, part of her nonshared environment, could have greatly augmented what-

indeed. She certainly was not backward about stepping forward—and the limited evidence suggests
that she had acted this way since her youth.

Another line of evidence is found in studies of
twins. From the genetics viewpoint, identical twins,
regardless of where they have been reared, should
show greater similarity than fraternal twins, and
these results have been obtained in numerous studies of personality. A subsequent question concerns

ever constitutional tendencies toward arousability and rivalry existed on an inherited basis.

EVIDENCE FOR TYPOLOGY. The other major biological approach has pursued Hippocrates's early efforts in ways he probably never imagined, resulting in mixed support. A personality **typology** is a system for classifying people according to a few broad dimensions, each of which involves a characteristic style of behavior. In contrast to temperament, there is no special emphasis on emotional reactions.

In an ambitious attempt at midcentury, a group of investigators studied the physiques of approximately 4,000 male college students. This procedure produced three **somatotypes,** a term coming from the Greek root *soma,* meaning "body," classifying a person according to physical structure: the **endomorph,** characterized by prominence of the abdomen and softer body parts; the **mesomorph,** characterized by a muscular build; and the **ectomorph,** characterized by a lean body, with a minimum of flesh (Figure 14–12). Then the subjects were rated for temperament, and again three types

emerged: *viscerotonia,* meaning jovial and relaxed; *somatotonia,* displaying an energetic, competitive, and perhaps aggressive style; and *cerebrotonia,* with a thoughtful, restrained approach to life. Afterward, the association between the somatotypes and temperaments was determined, and it was found to be quite high (Sheldon, Stevens, & Tucker, 1940).

Despite these findings, the relationship between body type and personality has little overall empirical support today in subsequent studies of the general population. When 300 college men were assessed by fully independent body and personality typing, a decidedly smaller relationship was obtained (Hood, 1963). Investigations with children also have shown a lower correlation (Walker, 1962). Cross-cultural results do not support the theory (Lester, 1986). Nevertheless, the possibility of some association between body type and personality continues to intrigue investigators (Lester & Wosnack, 1990; Shubs, 1985).

More recently, a British psychologist with a German background, Hans Eysenck, developed and tested a theory of personality that demonstrates genetic factors and, at the same time, adds unexpected support for Hippocrates's typology. Eysenck began with *introversion–extraversion,* the typology first brought into prominence by Carl Gustav Jung, focusing on physiological differences between these types, especially in the central nervous system. Eysenck decided that *introverts,* whose personality orientation is marked by interest in their own thoughts and feelings, possess a nervous system that is readily aroused. Introverts therefore avoid further stimulation. At the other end of the continuum, *extraverts* are interested in social and other activities in the outer environment. Their central nervous system is more often underaroused and therefore searches for further stimulation (Eysenck, 1990).

In one investigation, subjects indicated their preferences for noise level while they were studying. As predicted, the introverted subjects preferred a

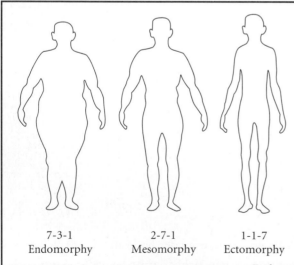

| 7-3-1 | 2-7-1 | 1-1-7 |
| Endomorphy | Mesomorphy | Ectomorphy |

FIGURE 14–12 SOMATOTYPES. Each subject was rated on all three physical dimensions, using a scale from 1 to 7. Then he was described in terms of his dominant dimension (Sheldon, 1942).

lower level of stimulation than did the extraverted people (Campbell & Hawley, 1982). Another study investigated differences between introverts and extraverts in response to the same noise. Using electrodes measuring skin conductance and activity in the auditory cortex, introverts showed greater responsiveness to sensory stimulation than extraverts and also a faster reaction (Bullock & Gilliland, 1993; Stelmack, 1990; Figure 14–13).

Using factor analysis, Eysenck identified a second basic dimension, *stable–unstable,* which focuses not on the need for arousal but on the speed and extent of arousal. Stable people are generally calm and slow to become aroused; unstable people respond more quickly and sharply. When these two dimensions are combined, with introversion–extraversion on one axis and stable–unstable on the other, they provide a modern version of Hippocrates's typology. The stable and introverted person is phlegmatic, the stable-extraverted is sanguine. The unstable-introverted is melancholic, and the unstable extravert is choleric.

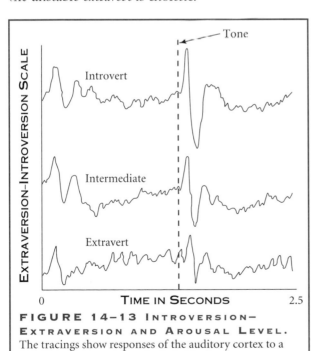

FIGURE 14–13 INTROVERSION– EXTRAVERSION AND AROUSAL LEVEL. The tracings show responses of the auditory cortex to a low-frequency tone of 80 decibels. The introvert was more aroused and the extravert less aroused than the subject rated intermediate on the introversion–extraversion scale.

In passing, further evidence for a biological background in personality has emerged from an extension of Eysenck's ideas on arousability. The basic concept is called **sensation seeking,** which indicates a preference for novel, thrilling, even dangerous stimulation (Zuckerman, 1979, 1990). People of this sort are likely to enjoy sky diving, scuba diving, and bungee jumping. People low on sensation seeking prefer to chat with old friends, smell the flowers, and listen to familiar music. According to this view, sensation seekers are underaroused and therefore seek excitement through gambling with their health, money, and so forth more readily than people who are easily aroused.

PERSONALITY TRAITS

For most psychologists, the type approach is too simple to express the uniqueness and complexity of human personality. People are more differentiated from one another and far more complicated than can be indicated in a typology. In contrast, **personality traits** describe a person in terms of a series of specific, relatively enduring characteristics, thereby offering special potential for depicting uniqueness. A trait is regarded as long-standing but not necessarily permanent; the personality type presumably endures for the individual's lifetime.

Jenny was often suspicious and independent— at home, on the street, and among acquaintances. These persistent characteristics might be considered traits. She was properly suspicious in one respect, for Ross *had* secretly married. In breaking off all relations with him too, leaving herself completely alone, Jenny further demonstrated her independence. Consistency is the key in the trait approach.

SEARCHING FOR BASIC TRAITS. One goal in trait research has been to find the primary characteristics common to most individuals, called **basic traits.** This task appears impossible at first

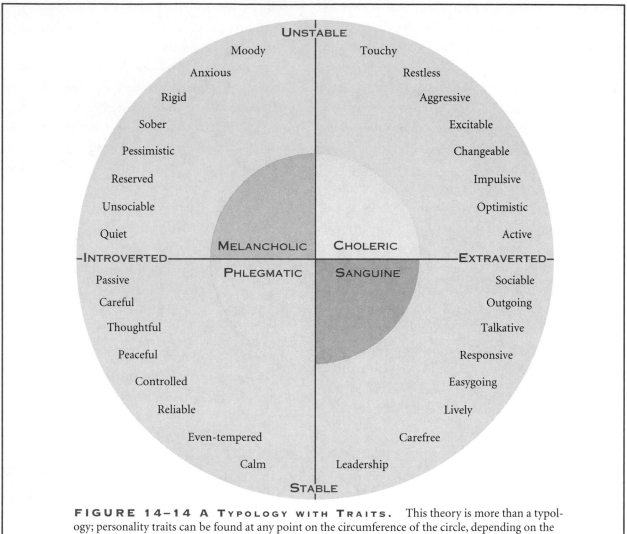

FIGURE 14–14 A TYPOLOGY WITH TRAITS. This theory is more than a typology; personality traits can be found at any point on the circumference of the circle, depending on the contributions from each dimension.

glance because of the complexity of personality. One preliminary review of all pertinent adjectives used in everyday life revealed almost 18,000 terms, some of which had similar meanings, such as *fearful, apprehensive, troubled,* and *worried.* Thus, one term, *anxious,* might represent many of them (Allport & Odbert, 1936).

When the statistical procedure known as *factor analysis* came into wide use, hopes were high that it would show, on a statistical basis, which traits were most closely associated with one another, thus revealing the fundamental clusters or factors. One early investigation revealed seven basic trait clusters.

More recent studies reflected Hippocrates' four types with gradations among them, yielding 32 traits (Eysenck, 1967; Figure 14–14). Still, others produced different lists of basic traits or factors. Some of the traits in the list of seven, for example, seemed to be combinations of those in a later list of 16 basic traits (Cattell, Eber, & Tatsuoka, 1970; Figure 14–15).

Investigators continued to accept this challenge nevertheless, and within the last two decades separate strands of research have resulted in a surprising conclusion: tentative agreement on five basic traits. Called the **Big Five,** they include extraversion,

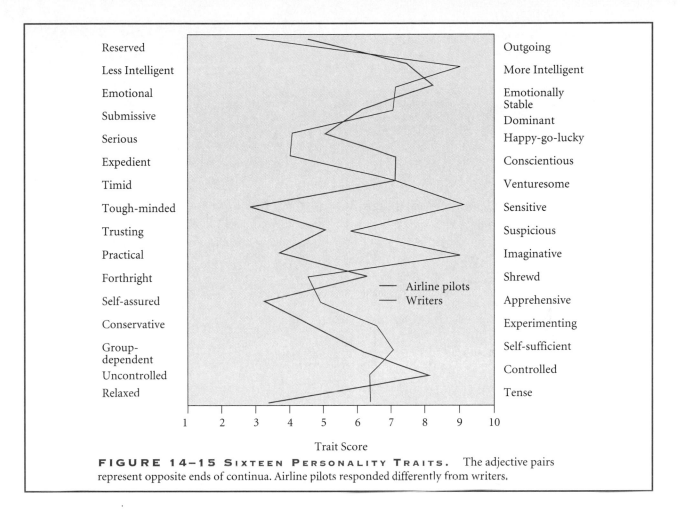

Reserved											Outgoing
Less Intelligent											More Intelligent
Emotional											Emotionally Stable
Submissive											Dominant
Serious											Happy-go-lucky
Expedient											Conscientious
Timid											Venturesome
Tough-minded											Sensitive
Trusting											Suspicious
Practical											Imaginative
Forthright											Shrewd
Self-assured											Apprehensive
Conservative											Experimenting
Group-dependent											Self-sufficient
Uncontrolled											Controlled
Relaxed											Tense

—— Airline pilots
—— Writers

1   2   3   4   5   6   7   8   9   10

Trait Score

FIGURE 14–15 SIXTEEN PERSONALITY TRAITS. The adjective pairs represent opposite ends of continua. Airline pilots responded differently from writers.

friendliness, conscientiousness, emotional stability, and openness to experience. Each of these traits can be thought of as representing a separate continuum ranging from high to low. Thus, the first trait can vary from extreme extraversion to extreme introversion without necessarily placing a value on either end of the continuum. People simply differ in this way. On the second trait, some people are almost always friendly; others are intermediate or vary a great deal from time to time; and still others are usually hostile or unfriendly. Collectively, these five dimensions provide a comprehensive framework for describing any personality.

Less fundamental, more specific patterns of behavior, regarded as **subtraits,** can be located within these basic traits. For example, consider these characteristics: dependable, careless, cautious,

and fussy. In one way or another, they are all subsumed under conscientiousness, the third of the Big Five traits. Another subtrait, sentimentality, apparently is a blend of friendliness, emotional stability, and openness to experience. Studies of cultures from the Far East to Western Europe have found these five factors to be relatively stable and representative of people ranging in age from the twenties to the nineties (Costa & McCrae, 1980, 1988). Evidence for a five-factor structure is substantial, especially in view of the skepticism surrounding factor-analytic research in the last half century (Digman, 1990; Wiggins & Pincus, 1992).

TRAITS IN THE INDIVIDUAL. Apart from the number and identification of basic traits in all human beings, there has been considerable interest

FIGURE 14–16 THE BIG FIVE.
Each trait exists on a continuum. Thus Jenny can be rated from high to low on each trait and its subtraits. Trait theories with more factors are more descriptive but also more cumbersome.

In the figure:

EXTRAVERSION
Sociable, talkative

OPENNESS
Imaginative, broad interests

FRIENDLINESS
Good-natured, cooperative

EMOTIONAL STABILITY
Calm, composed

CONSCIENTIOUSNESS
Dependable, careful

in the way traits are arranged or organized in each of us, giving everyone a unique personality (Allport, 1961). For Jenny, lack of friendliness was a dominant basic trait. Her suspiciousness was an important variation of that basic trait. On the extraversion scale, she is toward the middle, at times one way, at times the other. This basic trait is not a dominant characteristic for Jenny. It does not describe her as succinctly as does the friendliness dimension (Figure 14–16).

In making these distinctions among individuals, it must be remembered that a trait is not some concrete entity. Rather, it is an abstract concept, useful for explaining certain phenomena and for making predictions. The traits of suspiciousness and extraversion, for example, have no independent reality, separate from a person's behavior and experience.

How did Jenny become this way? How did she acquire these traits? Trait theory is largely a descriptive approach. It does not explain how traits are combined or clustered within the individual. And it does not yet explain how they emerge—how we develop these highly specific characteristics.

"Hunting a job is not a pleasant occupation when one is past 30," Jenny wrote. "My luck in quest of a job is something to be either laughed about, or wept about."

Day after day she tramped the streets, wearing a hole in her shoe and a blister on her heel. "However, I'm not grumbling—not kicking—not wholly discouraged, *yet*. There must be a turn in the Lane somewhere," she concluded (Allport, 1965).

According to learning theory, Jenny's persistence in the face of these difficulties was determined largely by events in her environment. Specifically, learning theory offers two broad views of personality, both stressing the role of environmental factors.

OPERANT VIEW OF PERSONALITY

On several occasions we have considered the first perspective, known as **operant learning** or *operant conditioning*, which emphasizes the role of environmental influences on behavior. It stresses that what happens in the environment is *the* critical factor in learning and therefore for the development of personality. Thinking, reasoning, and other inner states are recognized, but they are not of significant concern in this approach. An effort is made instead to understand human behavior in terms of directly observable events—overt behavior and its consequences—and therefore this view is called the *behavioristic* or behavioral perspective.

According to this approach, responses that are supported by the environment tend to be repeated, a phenomenon known as the **reinforcement principle.** Those responses that are not reinforced tend to be discarded. Thus, certain responses grow stronger and stronger, depending on their consequences. Personality is composed of these reinforced responses, which in lay terms are known as habits. From the viewpoint of operant conditioning, especially as portrayed by B. F. Skinner, personality is largely a constellation of habits.

Even a response that has been supported only intermittently may be repeated frequently. In *partial reinforcement,* occasionally the response results in reinforcement and at other times it does not; the individual adapts to this situation by emitting the response regularly, even though it is reinforced only irregularly. For example, until their breakup, Jenny had devoted an enormous amount of attention to Ross because this behavior had been continuously and then partially reinforced (Figure 14–17). Operant conditioning shapes personality just as the sculptor shapes clay (Chance, 1988; Staats, 1993).

When her father died, Jenny was left as the financial head of a family. In her late twenties, after her husband's death, she again found herself in this situation, this time with her own child to support. The behavioral theorist would point to the consequences of Jenny's hard work in both instances. In the first instance, she obtained food and shelter for herself, as well as

gratitude from six siblings. In the second, she earned the affection and growing responsiveness of the baby.

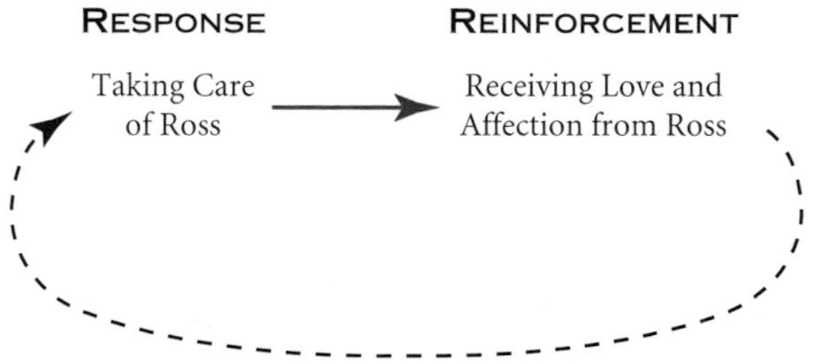

When her husband was alive, Jenny complained that she was confined to the home. After he died, she held several jobs, and self-sufficiency was further reinforced. Jenny became a highly assertive individual. But all of these efforts at survival, acquired early in life, left little time for developing a friendlier, more cooperative way with others. Jenny's social skills diminished. As she became less sociable, other people perhaps were less friendly to her, interpreting her behavior as a sign of indifference, if not hostility. She thus became more socially isolated and more and more combative in her attempts to make a place for herself and her son (Allport, 1965).

According to operant learning theory, Jenny was assertive because assertive responses were reinforced. She continued to hunt for a job, despite lack of success, because this behavior had been reinforced on earlier occasions.

Ross, in contrast, eventually learned to become evasive with his mother, even to the point of lying, fearing Jenny's abusive response to his financial status and his relations with women. He did not disclose his marriage for this same reason. Jenny unintentionally reinforced secrecy, evasiveness, and even lying on Ross's part. In complete ignorance of what she had wrought, or at least contributed to, Jenny announced: "Ross is the *greatest liar* I have ever known" (Allport, 1965).

SOCIAL LEARNING AND PERSONALITY

Another approach to personality through learning theory also recognizes reinforcement, but its role is less central. This view, called **social learning theory,** emphasizes social and cognitive processes in the development of personality. One of its most

FIGURE 14–17 PERSISTENCE AND REINFORCEMENT. The operant learning theorist would explain Jenny's relationship with Ross on the basis of reinforcement. In earlier days, she received steady love and affection from Ross for taking care of him. In later years, when it was no longer appropriate, she continued to behave in this way, presumably because of the earlier regular reinforcement and later partial reinforcement.

RESPONSE — Taking Care of Ross

REINFORCEMENT — Receiving Love and Affection from Ross

important concepts is *observational learning,* wherein an individual develops or changes behavior simply on the basis of observing others, without direct reinforcement. A child's personality develops partly by watching other people.

The chief advocate of this approach has been Albert Bandura, whose research took him from the clinic and laboratory to daily life. As noted in an earlier chapter, this approach combines elements of operant learning, particularly the concept of reinforcement, and elements of cognitive psychology, especially the processes of attending and memory. Much of Bandura's work has been devoted to understanding the role of these factors in fostering aggressive personalities (Bandura, 1977, 1986; Rubinstein, 1983).

MODELING. The person being observed is known as a *model,* and the learning process is called *modeling.* It emphasizes that an individual can acquire knowledge and potential behavior without making any overt response, simply by observing and thinking about what has been observed. Learning is facilitated by reinforcement but, in contrast to the operant view, learning can occur without any reinforcement at all (Figure 14–18).

An important concept here is *vicarious reinforcement,* in which the observer gains satisfaction indirectly, through imagined participation in the model's experience. Only the model receives reinforcement. A girl observes her mother working as a school principal and notes the satisfaction that her

FIGURE 14–18 LEARNING THROUGH MODELING. For children observing their elders, the words of Ralph Waldo Emerson are appropriate: "What you are speaks so loudly, I cannot hear what you say." The older person's actions may exert a powerful influence; the child learns by observing and emulating the model.

mother derives from this administrative work. After this vicarious experience, the girl models her personality after her mother's behavior, working outside the home and gaining reinforcement herself.

RECIPROCAL DETERMINISM. Social learning theory in many respects stands in a middle ground between operant learning and the cognitive approach. According to Bandura, exclusive emphasis on one or the other leads to an incomplete analysis of the response. A former behaviorist, Bandura now includes mental processes in his studies of personality.

Another important principle in Bandura's work is the concept of **reciprocal determinism,** which means that cognition, overt behavior, and environmental factors all influence one another in an interlocking system. Each element partly determines and is determined by the others. The human personality, according to reciprocal determinism, is not one of complete free will or complete determinism. We are somewhere in the middle; we control and we are controlled (Bandura, 1986, 1990).

Jenny knew that she needed a job to support herself. Her social security benefits were not enough. This *cognition,* or belief, influenced her behavior, stimulating her to look for work, and it made the environment appear threatening. In turn, her *behavior,* tramping the streets unsuccessfully, increased her angry and suspicious thoughts. It also led to a hostile environment, for when she spoke disrespectfully to prospective employers, they became angry and did not offer her a job. This hostile *environment* elicited more angry thoughts and more aggressive reactions on Jenny's part (Figure 14–19).

LOCUS OF CONTROL. An even more cognitive approach is appropriately considered a limited-domain theory, or mini-theory, because it is not as broad as the others in this chapter. The con-

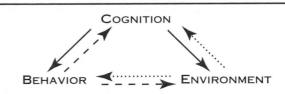

FIGURE 14–19 RECIPROCAL DETERMINISM. The concept of reciprocal determinism involves mutual influences. Jenny's thoughts, behavior, and environment all influenced one another as she angrily and unsuccessfully searched for a job.

cept known as **locus of control** concerns the extent to which people perceive the influential forces in their lives as lying within or outside of themselves (Rotter, 1966, 1990). For example, despite the limited opportunities, Jenny still assumed she would find a job if she only kept hunting. We would say that Jenny had an *internal locus of control,* for she believed that she had a significant degree of control over the situation and its outcomes. She believed she determined her own fate.

Ross, in contrast, at least as he viewed his mother's situation, had decided that there were forces over which he had no control. In this respect, he had an *external locus of control,* believing that there was nothing he could do to change the situation. Fate and luck, not personal qualities, are perceived as the vital factors in an external locus of control.

People assessed for locus of control generally show one tendency or the other to varying degrees. However, Ross's reaction to his mother's situation illustrates two important points. First, people may have an external locus of control regarding some events in their lives, such as the behavior of their parents, and a more internal view concerning others, such as performance in school and relations with friends. Second, locus of control for any given event is not necessarily fixed and permanent. Ross may decide later that there *is* something he can do. As a rule, successful adjustment is more closely associated with internal locus of control (Findley & Cooper, 1983; Lefcourt, 1982).

CONSISTENCY CONTROVERSY

In past years, advocates of learning theory have challenged trait theorists on the constancy of traits. Learning theorists state that behavior is determined by the situation or event in question, not by some inner characteristic of the individual. One reason that the trait view persists, according to learning theorists, is that we tend to see people only in one situation or another—going to work, in the classroom, in church, or on the athletic field. Since there is regularity in each of these conditions, we infer that certain traits are responsible for the individual's consistency.

However, when we examine a group of people together in any context, we know that the situation is also important. Each person behaves somewhat differently from the others, but they all show certain similarities. This view, that behavior is a function of personal traits and also of the situation, promotes once again the *interaction principle.* The idea is that both factors are important, but they combine in different ways in different people.

In the context of the interaction principle, one further point should be made. If we want to predict a person's behavior in a highly specific situation, such as the way she eats when alone, then the learning approach seems appropriate. We ask: What are the reinforcers in that situation? If our interest lies in predicting how she will act in less specific circumstances, such as meeting new people or finding an apartment, then trait theory appears to be more useful. In other words, each approach makes its own contribution. In many respects, this controversy has come full circle, establishing trait theory once again as a viable approach to personality and providing greater insight into the circumstances in which the different approaches to personality are most valid (Kenrick & Funder, 1988; Wiggins & Pincus, 1992).

• HUMANISTIC THEORY •

Ross did not stay married for long. Following his divorce, he went to the seashore with his latest girlfriend. After three weeks, he returned with an ear infection that caused him to be hospitalized. The abscess spread to the brain, and medications were administered—too late. Ross died in the hospital unexpectedly.

The funeral was simple. The only mourners in attendance were Jenny, Glenn, and Ross's girlfriend. At one point, with her sense of the dramatic, Jenny announced that she was bored. After the ceremony, she criticized Ross's girlfriend. Everyone was glad to go home—separately.

Jenny carried Ross's ashes with her and stored them on her closet shelf. In a symbolic sense, Ross was *hers* again. With his death, Jenny had lost her focus in life but not her usual ways. "Nobody can injure Ross now," she declared. "I don't have to share him with anybody" (Allport, 1965).

How are we to understand Jenny in these situations? How should we approach her feelings about herself, her deceased son, and his girlfriend? And why did she adopt these views of herself and others in the first place?

More than the other theories, the humanistic approach is concerned with people's feelings and views about themselves. Jenny is a sensitive individual who has experienced many severe difficulties in life, and she must be understood on this basis. The **humanistic viewpoint,** compared with the others, emphasizes free will and the uniqueness of every human being.

FREE WILL AND UNIQUENESS

All personality theories are based on certain conceptions of human nature. The psychoanalytic approach regards personality as determined by unconscious conflict. The behavioral and social learning approaches consider personality to be determined by reinforced and modeled behavior, respectively. These views involve **determinism,** which states that behavior follows certain natural laws; any action is the inevitable result of preceding causes. All events, physical and psychological, are attributable to antecedent events. The constitutional approach, although it does not take a clear position on personality development, is based on the notion of genetic determinism, an unfolding of inborn patterns.

In opposition to these views, which have been dominant forces in personality theory for years, the humanistic approach is based on the concept of **free will,** which states that the causes of behavior lie in the voluntary decisions and actions of the individual. Among all the species, human beings have a special capacity for self-direction and choice.

Within the philosophy of free will, humanistic psychology focuses on the uniqueness of each human being, expressed in three dimensions. First, we are not simply at a higher level of evolution than animals. Rather, each of us has many extraordinary capacities, including reasoning, remembering, and so forth. This *complexity* means that people cannot be successfully studied in segments, as happens in laboratory experiments focusing on isolated aspects of behavior. Instead, humanistic psychologists advocate a broader, more imaginative approach to personality research. In its sharpest form, this criticism states that many psychologists concentrate on minor questions for which there are adequate research methods, rather than addressing more important issues with less precision.

Another aspect of this uniqueness is our *subjectivity,* meaning our capacity for diverse sensations and feelings about ourselves, other people, and aspects of our physical environment. We do more than respond to the environment in an overt manner. We have feelings, and we respond to them, too. They sometimes upset us and confuse us as we try to understand ourselves and others. We often make the wrong inferences from a person's behavior, not knowing that person's feelings. "Externals don't portray insides; Jekylls may be masking Hydes" (Jourard, 1964).

In particular, humanists believe that Western psychology underestimates the role of private experience in personality. They suggest that Western psychology has much to learn from Eastern societies emphasizing meditation and introspection (Chang & Page, 1991; Rhee, 1990).

A third characteristic of human uniqueness is the *capacity for growth,* meaning that each of us has a tendency to seek expression and achieve goals. We can develop in ways that are important to us. These concerns have been largely overlooked among other theories of personality (Table 14–1). Here we find one of the most obvious outcomes of the humanistic approach to personality—extensions into daily life. The effort to foster personal growth has led to the human potential movement among laypersons, including encounter groups, support groups, and other explorations of one's own personality.

PERSON-CENTERED APPROACH

The humanistic tradition is most clearly illustrated in Carl Rogers's **person-centered approach,** which

---

Complexity: Jenny had a high degree of intelligence, and yet she was ignorant about social skills. She was fiercely independent, and yet she wanted closer personal relationships.

Subjectivity: Jenny experienced love for her son, hostility toward authority, jealousy toward Ross's girlfriends, and compassion for mistreated children.

Capacity for growth: At an early age, Jenny became a highly reliable provider, supporting six siblings and later Ross. However, she never developed satisfactory relations with other adults, and she never showed an interest in understanding her problem.

TABLE 14–1 HUMAN UNIQUENESS. Jenny's personality illustrates the three fundamental characteristics emphasized in humanistic theory. According to this perspective, these characteristics are the basic dimensions of human uniqueness.

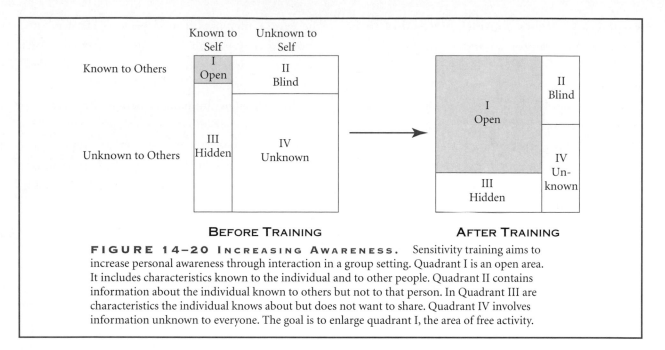

FIGURE 14–20 INCREASING AWARENESS. Sensitivity training aims to increase personal awareness through interaction in a group setting. Quadrant I is an open area. It includes characteristics known to the individual and to other people. Quadrant II contains information about the individual known to others but not to that person. In Quadrant III are characteristics the individual knows about but does not want to share. Quadrant IV involves information unknown to everyone. The goal is to enlarge quadrant I, the area of free activity.

stresses that each individual plays a major role in shaping his or her own destiny. Broader and more speculative than the personality theories discussed earlier, it places each of us at the center of our own existence, stressing our capacity for awareness and for increasing that awareness, as well as deciding about our own lives (Figure 14–20).

For example, with Ross's ashes still in her closet, Jenny worried about his remains. If she died unexpectedly, they would be left to someone else. "To be thrown into the garbage box," she declared. Faced with this possibility, Jenny reached a difficult decision, one not readily explained on the basis of unconscious motivation, constitutional factors, the reinforcement principle, or modeling. Jenny looked at herself, pondered her future, and then decided that she should promptly dispose of her son's ashes.

One rainy morning she took them to Coney Island, met a man carrying an umbrella, and requested his help while climbing out to the end of the breakwater. The man gravely agreed, provided that Jenny gave her word not to commit suicide.

Amid a sudden downpour, Jenny stepped from one slippery rock to another while the man shouted directions about which rock to use. Blown by the wind, splashed by the waves, encumbered by her precious burden, Jenny finally reached the end of the jetty, and suddenly it was done! The ashes were in the sea. Jenny came ashore, shook hands with her supporter, and then, with a sense of the absurdity of the moment, took off her shoes and ceremoniously dumped the water out of them. Later, she said to herself with satisfaction: "He was gentleman enough not to ask my name, or a thing about me" (Allport, 1965).

The person-centered approach rests on the philosophical position of *phenomenology*, which states that behavior is determined by the way the individual perceives and experiences the world, rather than by objective reality per se. It was not only the presence of Ross's ashes that determined Jenny's reaction. Equally important was her distrust of most human beings, her perception of her own future, and her thoughts about the man with the umbrella. The emphasis in phenomenology is on each individual's unique view of the world.

ACTUALIZING TENDENCY. The only motive postulated in the person-centered approach is the **actualizing tendency,** also called *self-actualiza-*

tion, an inborn predisposition to develop and use all the capacities that maintain, enhance, and fulfill the organism. The most fundamental concept in the person-centered approach, and the third characteristic of human uniqueness, just mentioned, it includes not only biological drives but also drives toward competence and mastery. As described by Abraham Maslow, who developed this concept, actualization is exclusively a positive force, and it appears in all sorts of ways, large and small, throughout life. It is the basic force in life. Inappropriate sexual and aggressive behaviors occur only when the actualizing tendency is adversely influenced by environmental circumstances (Maslow, 1970).

The actualizing tendency, discussed in the chapter on motivation, is present in everyone, and it is the basic force in psychotherapy. In people entering therapy, it has somehow become blocked or restrained. The function of the counselor is to create an empathetic interpersonal climate, allowing this inborn tendency to emerge in the individual and to become influential once again (Bozarth & Brodley, 1991).

CONGRUENCE AND INCONGRUENCE. Children provided with love and understanding develop in accordance with the actualizing tendency. A little girl explores and expresses her developing abilities, and her experiences are included in her concept of self. There is *congruence,* for the child's personal experience and self-concept are compatible.

Even the best-intentioned parents cannot provide love and understanding consistently. Most parents, and the culture as well, establish some conditions of worth, meaning that love is contingent on certain behavior. A little girl says to her sister, "I hate you." The child is chastised, and her parent responds with a condition of worth. "You are a bad girl to hate." In an effort to regain the parent's love, the child says, "I *am* bad when I hate."

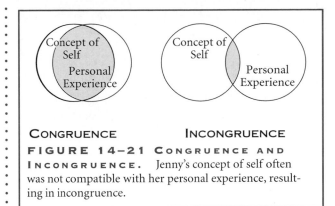

CONGRUENCE INCONGRUENCE

FIGURE 14–21 CONGRUENCE AND INCONGRUENCE. Jenny's concept of self often was not compatible with her personal experience, resulting in incongruence.

She denies her hate, no longer including it as part of her self, and yet she inevitably runs into situations that arouse this feeling. When this negative feeling is denied, the outcome is *incongruence;* the child's concept of self and her personal experience are disparate. They do not coincide.

A little boy is told, "Boys do not feel frightened." This condition of worth leads the boy to distrust his own experience. Compelled to live according to this standard, the child no longer acknowledges fear and helplessness, even when such feelings are appropriate.

Jenny found fault with virtually everyone—her mother, her sisters, her son, his friends, her friends, and even a mourner at her son's funeral. This fault finding arose through Jenny's phenomenological view, the way she perceived the world. Things did not fit. Jenny's self-concept was that of a good, honest, hard-working person who starved to help others. Her experiences were those of being rebuffed and rejected by everyone. The outcome was incongruence (Figure 14–21). Jenny simply did not see herself in reasonably realistic terms.

• PERSONALITY IN PERSPECTIVE •

Jenny was right in her premonition. She left this world with the same decisiveness and display that characterized her life. One day as she was entering a crowded dining room, she suddenly expired, falling dead on the spot, just as she had predicted.

Sensing the value of her letters, Glenn had already asked Jenny if she would be willing to have them published. Surprised by the request, Jenny's response was characteristically assertive: "Yes," she replied, "if you think they would do anybody any good!"

Glenn forwarded more than 300 of Jenny's letters to Harvard University, where they were edited and prepared for publication by Gordon Allport, the country's leading personality theorist at the time. The task for the psychologist or lay reader, Allport declared, is to explain Jenny—in one way or another (Allport, 1965). Jenny pins the reader down with this unspoken challenge: "And what do you make of *me?*"

In accepting this challenge, most psychologists would want to include in their study various personality tests. A **personality test** is a set of questions used to measure the enduring characteristics of any individual, including habits, motives, interests, thoughts, feelings, attitudes, values, and personal style. The aim is a broad description of an individual. More than any other type of test, a personality test attempts to assess the *whole* individual, rather than some specific dimension, such as intelligence, aptitude, and so forth.

༄

PERSONALITY TESTING

In form and structure, personality tests range widely, not a surprising condition when one considers the range of characteristics they attempt to assess. Some are highly structured, with standard questions and specific answers. Others are unstructured; the task is ambiguous, and no specific answers are expected. Within this range of tests, it is useful to identify four types of assessment, partly because they illustrate the diversity of these instruments and partly because each type of test can be loosely linked with a particular theory of personality. No one test is inevitably or exclusively used with one theory, however. These tests include projective techniques, personality inventories, and situational tests, as well as personal documents.

PROJECTIVE TECHNIQUES. Many psychologists today, within and outside psychoanalysis, use tests containing incomplete sentences, inkblots, and other ambiguous stimuli. A test of this sort, called a **projective technique,** is often considered useful in understanding the deeper aspects of personality, for the subject is asked to respond to some vague stimulus. It is assumed that these responses reveal the subject's underlying concerns—feelings, desires, fears, and so forth. After all, the stimulus itself provides little direction in how to respond. This act of perceiving one's own characteristics elsewhere is known as *projection.* According to Freud, a projective response always represents energy, sexual or aggressive, pressing for discharge.

Consider this sentence fragment: "As a child, I always liked to go to the _____." A man might respond with the word *store* or *park.* These responses only indicate that he, like most of us, was interested in enjoying himself as a child. The incomplete sentence is not sufficiently ambiguous to elicit a significant projective response. Suppose the man were asked to complete this shorter fragment: "As a child, _____." He might answer, "I wanted my father to pay more attention to me." A friend might reply, "I often thought about running away." Jenny might say, "Mother made me do all the work." Someone else might declare, "I can't answer this one." Even when a person refuses to answer this incomplete sentence, the response may tell more about that person than a stereotyped answer to the first item.

The same rationale is present in the use of inkblots. In the **Rorschach inkblots** test, named after Hermann Rorschach, the young Swiss psychi-

FIGURE 14–22 AN INKBLOT. This configuration illustrates the stimuli used in the Rorschach test. A person responding to this inkblot might perceive a bug, creatures about to kiss, private parts, or other details.

atrist who developed this technique, there are ten cards, each containing a black or colored inkblot. The person taking the test is asked to state what he or she sees in these blots, purposely selected because they do not depict anything in particular. Thus, the subject's response must be directed, at least in a large part, by underlying personal concerns (Figure 14–22).

In some cases, the subject is asked to tell stories about ambiguous scenes. The **Thematic Apperception Test** (TAT) includes 20 pictures ranging from landscapes to human figures, all intended to suggest prominent themes. Stimulated by these pictures, the subject's stories are analyzed for recurrent ideas, fantasy, logic, and so forth (Figure 14–23).

Responses to projective tests are not judged solely on the basis of what is perceived. The subject's style, explanation, timing, effort, and other characteristics are also part of the scoring. Many psychologists therefore feel that these tests are uniquely useful for understanding the deeper aspects of personality (Piotrowski, Keller, & Ogawa, 1993). Opponents argue that projective techniques often lack evidence of validity

or show only limited validity (Viglione, Brager, & Haller, 1991; Vincent & Harman, 1991).

PERSONALITY INVENTORIES. Other tests are designed to measure specific, typical characteristics, rather than underlying themes in personality. The **personality inventory** is a printed form containing a series of statements, questions, or adjectives about human behavior, and the person completing the inventory indicates whether they apply to him or her. For each item or question, the usual alternatives are: "Yes," "No," and "Uncertain." A person's overall performance is often compared with the scores of other people who have taken the same inventory.

Inventories are most compatible with the trait and other constitutional approaches but they, in particular, are used in all sorts of contexts. The underlying rationale is that most people, when given an appropriate opportunity, can provide a reasonably accurate self-report.

One such form is the **California Personality Inventory** (CPI), used for assessment of characteristic traits in the general population. It includes scales measuring such traits as dominance,

FIGURE 14–23 AN AMBIGUOUS SCENE. Responding to this image, the subject makes up a story, indicating what occurred earlier, what is happening at the moment, and how events will turn out in the future. Examine this drawing and then tell yourself your own story.

sociability, self-control, and so forth. When taken seriously and interpreted properly, it is one of the most useful tests for the general population (Van Hutton, 1990). For each person completing the inventory, the results can be expressed as a *personality profile*, which is a graphic or numerical representation of the scores on separate traits, facilitating a comparison among them (Table 14–2).

A similar technique, generally used for a different purpose, is known as the **Minnesota Multiphasic Personality Inventory-2** (MMPI-2), originally developed a half-century ago to identify people with specific disorders. It is used today for all kinds of people, with and without obvious adjustment problems (Helmes & Redden, 1993; Butcher & Rouse, 1996).

The original version, with a decidedly psychiatric slant, was developed by presenting hundreds of test items to different populations, psychiatric and otherwise. Then the psychologists who constructed them determined which items were answered in which manner by which psychiatric and comparison groups. Depressed people answered certain items in a certain way, and that pattern became the profile for depression. Hypochondriacs showed a different pattern. In other words, the items were originally included in the trial version of the test on the basis of what *might* be appropriate. Then they were retained later on the basis of what

actually *worked* with certain groups of subjects. Many items served no purpose. They did not discriminate among any of the groups and therefore were discarded.

The test items concerned attitudes, moods, and behaviors of all sorts. How would you answer these items?

I like the sight of unpaved roads.
People should remember their dreams.
I am always self-confident.

There are no right or wrong answers, but beware. The MMPI-2 includes several items to catch people trying to make a good impression. These constitute a *lie scale,* used to detect faking or dishonesty, for most people answer them in a predictable way. The third item above, about self-confidence, might be included in the lie scale. For almost everyone, even Abraham Lincoln, the honest answer would be "False." Thus, a person can create a false impression on the MMPI-2, but that effort may be detected—and surely defeats the purpose of taking the inventory, now used in dozens of different countries for assessing people in all walks of life (Hathaway & McKinley, 1989; Table 14–3).

SITUATIONAL TESTS. With an emphasis on the environment, operant learning theorists are less inclined to use projective tests or even

Sample Items	Trait Scales	
I liked *Alice in Wonderland* by Lewis Carroll.		
	H Dominance	Communality
	Capacity for status	Achievement via
	L Sociability	conformity
I would never play cards (poker) with a stranger.	Social presence	H Achievement via
	Self-acceptance	independence
	Well-being	Intellectual
	H Responsibility	efficiency
	Socialization	Psychological
	Self-control	mindedness
	L Tolerance	Flexibility
	Good impression	

TABLE 14–2 CALIFORNIA PERSONALITY INVENTORY. In taking this inventory, the subject answers "True" or "False" to many items. Two sample items are shown. Among the trait scales, possible high scores for Jenny are indicated by *H*, low score by *L*.

TRAIT	DESCRIPTION
Hypchondriasis	Exaggerated concern with health
H Depression	Pessimism, despondency
H Hysteria	Emotional instability, repression
Psychopathic deviation	Antisocial style, rebelliousness
Masculinity-femininity	Reflecting traditional sex roles or interests
Paranoia	Poor reality contact
H Hypomania	Energetic, impulsive, grandiose
Introversion	Reserved, inhibited

TABLE 14–3 MINNESOTA MULTIPHASIC PERSONALITY INVENTORY-2. The interpretation of individual scores requires considerable experience. Traits indicated by *H* are those on which Jenny might receive high scores.

personality inventories. The former reveal internal states, of little interest to traditional learning theorists, and the latter indicate only what subjects say about themselves, not what they actually do. To predict how a person will behave in a certain context, many learning theorists use a **situational test,** which is as similar as possible to the real-life setting in which the person must perform later. Sometimes this situation is simply part of everyday life (Figure 14–24).

While hunting for a job, Jenny was involved in a situational test of sorts. After a desperate search, she finally found a position in a child-care center. "Everything is all right if I can only remain here for at least six months," she wrote to Glenn. A month later she wrote again: "I would rather be dead than work in this place. . . . It's too shameful for words." In this *temporary* work assignment, Jenny proved a failure. She was not the right person and did not earn the permanent position. She kept her sense of humor, however, declaring on her departure: "Too much is enough" (Allport, 1965).

Years ago, situational tests were used to select young men for secret and difficult wartime missions. Naturally, actual war situations could not be

used. Instead, the men were taken in small groups to different locations, one of which was a brook— regarded as a raging torrent so fast and deep that nothing could rest on the bottom. Their task was to transport heavy equipment across it. As the men built a bridge, an overhead cable, or some other device for transportation, the examiners observed their behavior. Some of them became leaders; others followers, still others showed resistance to working with the group (OSS Assessment Staff, 1948).

Situational tests are extremely time-consuming to construct and administer because the subjects must be observed continuously. Use of videotapes has simplified the procedure, for here the subjects observe a film of a specific event. Then they use a

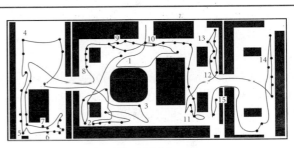

First Child

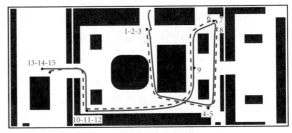

Second Child

FIGURE 14–24 A SITUATIONAL TEST. Two children were brought separately to the entrance of a museum. The dark areas indicate exhibits; the white areas indicate hallways. The solid colored lines show each child's route, and the dots and numbers indicate each child's location at the end of each minute of observation. One child refused to move without the presence of the observer, whose path is indicated by the dashed line (After Marston, 1925).

checklist to indicate the ways they would respond to that particular situation (Stricker & Rock, 1990).

PERSONAL DOCUMENTS. Personality assessment also can be approached from a different direction, using spontaneous rather than reactive measures. The personality tests discussed previously are reactive measures because the subject is presented with a test and asked to react—that is, to answer the questions. The task is not a routine part of everyday life.

In contrast, spontaneous measures of personality emerge in the course of the subject's daily functioning. At the beginning of this book, measures of this sort were described as *archival data,* available in public files and records, such as marriage certificates, employment histories, deeds of ownership, and so forth. Archival data are especially useful for investigating the behavior of groups. For studying an individual, more detailed information can be found in **personal documents,** such as journals, tapes, letters, diaries, essays, pictures, poetry, and so forth, composed by that person. These documents are not personality tests as such, but they can be used for personality assessment, as evident in the letters from Jenny (Figure 14–25).

Assessment through personal documents is most consistent with humanistic theory. Just as this theory emphasizes human uniqueness, the use of personal documents provides for a full range of individual expression. Spontaneous productions by the individual are the chief concern, rather than reactions to formal tests.

&

THE ECLECTIC APPROACH

Jenny Masterson has been considered from four theoretical perspectives, each making a special contribution to our study of personality. This examination of her life has shown that each approach has assets and limitations. No one theory can take all factors into account.

TABLE 14–25 PERSONAL DOCUMENT.
This excerpt from one of Jenny's letters shows her handwriting and power of expression. Her signature reveals a playful title bestowed by Glenn: Lady B. Her "prison" is a nursing home (Allport, 1965).

Even collectively, these theories do not give *the* answer. Instead, they show how psychologists think about personality.

These theories differ, for example, in the attention they give to past and present events in the formation of personality. Psychoanalysis stresses past experience; behavioral and cognitive theories and the humanistic viewpoint give greater consideration to present circumstances; and the time factor is not a significant consideration in constitutional theory.

Similarly, the theories differ in the attention given to the basic psychological processes. Motivation is an important theme in psychoanalysis, evident in the unconscious factors assumed to influence Jenny's relations with women and Ross. Perception is stressed in the humanistic viewpoint, illustrated in the difference between Jenny's self-concept and personal experience. Learning processes are fundamental in behavioral theory, and in constitutional theory, the inborn, biological factors receive special emphasis (Table 14–4).

For these reasons, many psychologists employ an **eclectic approach** in the study of personality,

THEORY	INTERPRETATION
Psychoanalysis	Jenny's difficult personal relations with almost everyone reflected unconscious conflict, a fixation perhaps dating back to the oral stage.
Constitutional theory	Jenny was a highly independent person who resisted domination by everyone, including her husband, parents, and siblings.
Behavioral theory	Jenny had been reinforced for depending on herself—first as a child in a fatherless family and later as a single mother.
Humanistic view	Jenny's self-concept was not congruent with her personal experience when she was with her parents, her son, and other adults.

TABLE 14–4 PERSONALITY THEORIES. The major personality theories provide four views of Jenny's discord with family members.

meaning that they select any aspect of any theory that seems most appropriate in a given circumstance. The eclectic theorist works apart from any exclusive system, using the advantages of all approaches. Eclecticism also occurs in personality assessment. Many psychologists use several of the tests discussed previously. No one personality test or theory incorporates all that is beneficial in the other procedures.

These different perspectives show enormous breadth in the study of personality. They also show some of the many issues to be considered if psychologists are to achieve a more complete understanding of human personality (Revellen, 1995).

Like the rest of us, Jenny struggled to understand her own personality, as well as those of others, and perhaps she was vaguely aware of the problems she created for herself and Ross. In any case, she sensed a potential for difficulty in mother–son relationships. "Have you read *The Magnificent Andersons . . . ?*" she once wrote to Ross's roommate (Allport, 1965). "If not, get it, it's about an only son, and how his mother *ruined* him."

PSYCHOANALYTIC THEORY

1. Personality is generally defined as the unique and characteristic ways in which an individual reacts to his or her surroundings. The fundamental elements in the structure of personality in psychoanalytic theory are the id, ego, and superego.

2. Early experiences are emphasized in psychoanalytic theory, particularly the psychosexual stages: oral, anal, and phallic. The oral stage involves the first love relationship. The anal stage concerns the formation of habits. The phallic stage emphasizes interpersonal relations and the Oedipus–Electra complex.

3. According to psychoanalytic theory, early conflicts and frustrations may be repressed and later reappear in symbolic form, often sexual or aggressive in nature. This sequence of conflict, repression, and symbolic behavior is known as unconscious motivation.

4. Carl Gustav Jung postulated a collective unconscious, which is a common inheritance among all human beings from earlier evolutionary stages. Alfred Adler regarded aggression as more important than sex as a basic motivating force in life, expressing the ideas of sibling rivalry and inferiority complex. Karen Horney emphasized basic anxiety, arising from the helplessness of early childhood, and became a pioneer in feminizing psychoanalysis. Alice Miller has reversed the interpretation of the Oedipus myth, pointing to child abuse and the par-

ents' early role in many of the problems in the adult personality.

❧

CONSTITUTIONAL THEORY

5. Constitutional theory states that personality arises through genetically determined predispositions and early environmental influences. Two constitutional theories that can be considered biological include studies of temperament, which refers to emotionally toned reactions, and studies of typologies, which are systems of classifying people according to a few broad dimensions.

6. According to trait theory, the elements of personality are a cluster of basic traits presumed to be comprehensive, irreducible, and more or less universal. A five-factor model has recently been presented: extraversion, friendliness, conscientiousness, emotional stability, and openness to experience.

❧

BEHAVIORAL AND COGNITIVE THEORY

7. According to operant learning, the basic elements of personality are reinforced responses, acquired through environmental factors. They follow the principle of reinforcement, but partial reinforcement and other concepts are also important.

8. Social learning theory states that behavior is acquired not only through direct reinforcement but also on the basis of observation and vicarious reinforcement. When another person is observed, the model's behavior may be reproduced later by the observer.

9. To predict behavior in a specific situation, learning theory seems most useful; to predict across several situations, the trait approach appears most efficient.

❧

HUMANISTIC THEORY

10. The humanistic viewpoint stresses free will and the uniqueness of each human being. This uniqueness is described in terms of complexity, subjectivity, and potential for growth.

11. Person-centered theory emphasizes the role of the individual in shaping his or her own destiny. Maladjustment and dissatisfaction occur when one's self-concept is at odds with one's experiences in the environment—that is, when the self and personal experience lack congruence.

❧

PERSONALITY IN PERSPECTIVE

12. For measuring the subject's underlying motives and attitudes, projective tests are assumed to be especially useful. Personality inventories are printed forms containing questions about behavior that subjects answer about themselves. In situational tests, the subject is observed in a typical or unusual environment. Assessment procedures throughout psychology sometimes involve personal documents, such as diaries, essays, journals, letters, poetry, and so forth.

13. All theories of personality have assets and limitations. The eclectic psychologist selects whichever views seem most appropriate at a given moment.

• WORKING WITH PSYCHOLOGY •

❧ REVIEW OF KEY CONCEPTS ❧

personality	thanatos	repression
	pleasure principle	psychosexual stages
	ego	oral stage
Psychoanalytic Theory	reality principle	fixation
psychoanalysis	superego	anal stage
id	conscience	phallic stage
eros	ego ideal	Oedipus complex

Electra complex
identification
latency stage
genital stage
unconscious motivation
Freudian slip
defense mechanism
rationalization
reaction formation
projection
object-relations theory
psychodynamic theory
collective unconscious
archetypes
sibling rivalry
inferiority complex
basic anxiety
response strategies
trauma theory

Constitutional Theory
    constitutional theory
    temperament
    shyness
    typology
    somatotypes
    endomorph
    mesomorph
    ectomorph
    sensation seeking
    personality traits
    basic traits
    Big Five
    subtraits

Behavioral and Cognitive Theory
    operant learning
    reinforcement principle
    social learning theory

reciprocal determinism
locus of control

Humanistic Theory
    humanistic viewpoint
    determinism
    free will
    person-centered approach
    actualizing tendency

Personality in Perspective
    personality test
    projective technique
    Rorschach inkblots
    Thematic Apperception Test
    personality inventory
    California Personality Inventory
    Minnesota Multiphasic Person-
       ality Inventory-2 (MMPI-2)
    situational test
    personal documents
    eclectic approach

❧ CLASS DISCUSSION/CRITICAL THINKING ❧

A NARRATIVE TWIST

Ross lived exclusively with his mother from birth through high school. Then he broke away during his college years. After this separation, which theory of personality would Ross most likely have used in describing Jenny: psychoanalytic, constitutional, behavioral, or humanistic? Why? In forming and defending an answer, take into account not only Jenny's interests and behaviors but also the ways Ross reacted to them. ❧

TOPICAL QUESTIONS

• *Psychoanalytic Theory.* Among all of the concepts in psychoanalysis, which one seems most important in our culture today? Support your choice.

• *Constitutional Theory.* You have just developed a theory of personality that identifies six primary traits, three social and three nonsocial. What are they? Are they all source traits? Explain the reasons for your choices.

• *Behavioral and Cognitive Theory.* Suppose you are applying for a scholarship and need to ask a psychology instructor for a letter of reference. Would you try to find a behaviorist or a cognitive theorist? Explain your answer.

• *Humanistic Theory.* Does person-centered theory project onto people too much responsibility for determining their own destiny? Could this condition appear to be overwhelming and stimulate guilt rather than initiative? Explain your view.

• *Personality in Perspective.* Consider some historical figure, such as Abraham Lincoln or Joan of Arc. Or consider a mythical figure, such as Santa Claus or Snow White. Try to show how psychoanalysis, trait theory, behaviorism, and humanistic theory all might be useful in describing one of these individuals.

❧ TOPICS OF RELATED INTEREST ❧

Principles of Freudian theory are described in the context of memory (8) and motivation (10). Defense mechanisms are considered in the chapter on adjustment (15). Prior discussions have considered operant conditioning (7) and observational learning (7). The concept of interaction is relevant in discussions of intelligence (13) and research methods (2). The issues of reliability and validity, underlying personality assessment, were discussed in connection with psychological testing (13).

15
ADJUSTMENT
AND DISORDER

THE PAIR SAT BEHIND CLOSED DOORS. FINALLY, THE PSYCHIATRIST SPOKE AGAIN. "WHAT ELSE CAN YOU TELL ME?" SHE ASKED THE YOUNG MAN. "IS THERE anything else?"

"No, they just say 'Empty.' "

"Anything . . . anything more?"

"Well, sometimes they say—'Empty!' 'Hollow!' 'Thud!' "

Resigning herself to this impasse, the psychiatrist made some further notes, then tried to ask more productive questions. She asked the man about his home life. How was everything there? He described his wife and children affectionately and spoke of his parents in the same way.

When asked about his job, he explained that he was a pediatrician, expressing the pleasures of that work, as well as its burdens. Then he chatted about his hobbies.

Once more the psychiatrist inquired about the voices. Were they still there? The man nodded emphatically, "Yes!" Did they say the same things? He repeated: "Empty!" "Hollow!" "Thud!"

These remarks left the psychiatrist puzzled. The young man showed signs of a serious adjustment problem. He seemed to be suffering from hallucinations. At the same time, he appeared to be reasonably happy and living a productive life. He did not mention that he had been referred to the hospital by David Rosenhan. He was there seeking admission, which was all that mattered at that point.

After more questions and further doubt, the psychiatrist finished the interview and then led the young man down the hall to the nurse's station. He was admitted to the psychiatric ward, thereby initiating a surprising story about human adjustment useful in this chapter.

This chapter begins by examining the process of adjustment and then turns to the perplexing problem of determining abnormality. Afterward, the focus shifts to the major types of disorders. The chapter concludes with a discussion of adjustment and culture, for any view of adjustment must take into account cultural standards.

Throughout this chapter, beware of the *medical student syndrome.* Students in medicine and psychology often see themselves as displaying the symptoms they are studying. All of us have physical and psychological difficulties of some sort, and some of them may seem similar to topics discussed in this text. If you begin to think, as a result of this reading, that you have a particular adjustment problem not noticed previously, you are probably wrong. But

if something has been bothering you and the following discussion increases your concerns, do not try self-diagnosis and do not ignore the problem any longer. Seek assistance.

• PROCESS OF ADJUSTMENT •

Adjustment is a continuous process, not a fixed or static state. Specifically, **adjustment** is the constant process of satisfying one's needs and desires as they emerge and reemerge throughout life. On this basis, no one achieves complete adjustment, at least not for long. Eventually, some need or desire arises, physical or psychological, and the individual seeks ways to deal with it. These concerns may be distinct and immediate, as in hunger or fear, or they may be difficult and lengthy, as in developing a vocational path in today's continuously changing society (Slee, 1993). As noted by Marcus Aurelius, an early Roman philosopher: The art of living is sometimes more like wrestling than dancing (*Meditations,* 7:61).

Many of us, dealing with our own adjustment problems, may overestimate the adjustment of others throughout the world. As we look around, there are people who seem to maintain a *normal adjustment,* healthy and free of conflict, acting within the acceptable standards of some group, without significant difficulty (Wolman, 1989). However, they are often people we do not know well. If we knew them better, we might decide that they too are wrestling, rather than waltzing through life (Figure 15–1).

DAVID ROSENHAN

FIGURE 15–1 THE ART OF LIVING. The psychology of adjustment attempts to assist people with problems of living and to understand why life for so many often becomes so difficult. The greatest of all arts, according to sages throughout the centuries, is the art of living appropriately.

THE ADJUSTMENT CONTINUUM

Adjustment is a continuous process and, in a general sense, it exists on a continuum. At one end there is the so-called adjusted person, who in many respects is ever-changing and ever-adapting, coping with problems and disappointments in life without excess stress and in a way that promotes progress. At the other end is the poorly adjusted person. In the extreme, this person may show signs of anxiety, aggression, or disordered thinking, perhaps like the young pediatrician just mentioned. He reported hearing unspoken voices, which were hallucinations, having no basis in reality, and he was admitted to the hospital. A person in this condition is less adaptive, responding in much the same way regardless of the circumstances, with the result that his behavior is often inappropriate.

However, the line between adjustment and maladjustment—normal and abnormal or functional and dysfunctional—is vague and variable. It depends on a number of factors, including the setting, culture, and era in which the individual lives, as well as the person's age, sex, and outlook on life. This idea appears intermittently throughout our discussion, as we examine various points on this continuum and consider the underlying factors.

Where on this continuum, for example, do we place Mahatma Gandhi? What about Joan of Arc, Florence Nightingale, Albert Einstein, Edgar Allan Poe, Wolfgang Amadeus Mozart, and countless others? What sort of medicine, government, law, education, literature, and music would be available if all of these and similar individuals were clearly at the adjusted end of the continuum?

VIEWS OF MENTAL HEALTH. Successful adjustment is sometimes referred to as mental health, another concept that is difficult to define. Insofar as adjustment is a continuous process, maintaining mental health is also a more or less constant process. Expressed the other way around, mental health is not a permanent state. All of us become a *bit* depressed from time to time. In a broad sense, criteria for **mental health** include feelings of well-being and accomplishments appropriate to one's abilities (Wolman, 1989).

Theorists of all sorts have offered more specific definitions. In the midst of his work with maladjustment, Sigmund Freud was asked to describe mental health. He quickly replied: "The capacity to love and to work." This response has been expanded by others into books and articles. Freud simply meant that the well-adjusted person finds fulfillment in both respects (Jones, 1957).

Abraham Maslow described the mentally healthy person in terms of self-actualization. Human beings constantly seek expression of their potential. Those developing and utilizing their capacities to the fullest are said to be self-actualizing (Maslow, 1970). Another humanistic psychologist, Carl Rogers, cited two dimensions of mental health: openness to experience and trust in oneself. These characteristics are not fixed and permanent; they are transient and fluid processes. With openness and trust, an individual may become a fully functioning person (Rogers, 1980). Clearly, Maslow and Rogers recognize the importance of feelings and also the realization of one's potential.

More recent conceptions of mental health focus on cognitive elements, including optimism and self-esteem. A person's outlook on life is not only an important characteristic but also a determinant of mental health (Scheier & Carver, 1992).

Recent research also has overturned earlier findings about the traditional male gender role in relation to mental health. There are positive features in the traditional masculine role, such as taking an active, achievement-oriented approach to life's challenges. There are also positive features in the traditional feminine role, such as experiencing satisfaction through intimate personal relationships. It now appears that androgynous people, possessing positive elements of traditional male and female response styles, are most likely to be regarded as mentally healthy (O'Heron & Orlofsky, 1990).

CRITERIA FOR MALADJUSTMENT.
Consider the question of adjustment from a different context. Suppose a person becomes extremely depressed on being diagnosed with cancer. Is this response a normal reaction to a life-threatening illness? Or is it a psychological disorder? Could it be both?

In thinking about psychological disorders, there are many perplexing decisions, but in most societies two criteria define this end of the continuum. The first concerns personal discomfort, and sometimes this discomfort is obvious. The individual is clearly unhappy, unable to work, and unsuccessful with others. The complaints and demeanor loudly proclaim personal distress.

Sometimes this discomfort is not at all obvious, as when someone hears unspoken voices, suffers disturbing thoughts, or simply feels wretched. We are shocked to discover that a person who seems happy and successful has committed suicide, needed psychiatric assistance, become divorced, or simply confessed to a deep dissatisfaction with life, not evident to the casual observer. In the poet's words, Richard Cory was a gentleman, clean favored, schooled in every grace, and richer than a king: "And Richard Cory, one calm summer night, / Went home and put a bullet through his head" (Robinson, 1921).

The second criterion involves socially disruptive behavior. The maladjusted person disturbs other people, causing suffering of some sort. This outcome is obvious in a sudden rampage of destruction, but it also occurs in lesser forms. A person at the bus station regularly accosts anyone available, asking demanding, insulting, or incoherent questions. An adolescent sets fire to buildings with the intention of destroying property. Such people are not necessarily discontent with themselves; they may be judged as maladjusted or dysfunctional on the basis of the consequences for others.

All of us have experienced discomfort, and most of us have disrupted others in one way or another. Hence, it is the intensity and frequency of these conditions that define any point on the continuum. The psychiatrist in the mental hospital was faced with these questions during the interview with the pediatrician. Where did he stand on this continuum?

STATISTICAL AND CLINICAL APPROACHES.
In making judgments about personal discomfort and disruptive behavior, psychologists tend to proceed along two lines. The first, a *statistical approach,* is concerned with the probabilities

of various reactions. How rare is the feeling or behavior? How far does it deviate from the norm? Running naked in New York and fasting for weeks—statistically rare events—may reflect some psychological disturbance. However, they may not be signs of maladjustment at all. Madame Curie and Harry Houdini were statistically rare individuals, and they participated in statistically rare events in science and magic, but they would not be considered abnormal (Figure 15–2). The statistical approach does not take into account the usefulness or desirability of the behavior.

From the other perspective, the person is not judged merely on the basis of statistical probabili-

FIGURE 15–2 A STATISTICALLY RARE INDIVIDUAL. Born a slave and raised amid abject poverty, George Washington Carver became a renowned agricultural chemist, widely respected for literally hundreds of discoveries concerning uses and products of the peanut and potato. By these means, he greatly assisted poor farming communities in the South.

ties or usual behavior. In the *clinical approach,* the decision rests on the qualitative judgment of a professional psychologist, psychiatrist, or group of such people. The premise here is that careful, well-trained clinicians can arrive at a more sensible, accurate conclusion than that obtained on the basis of sheer numbers. Fasting is statistically deviant, but it may serve a useful purpose, as part of a protest movement for social change, bringing attention to some form of injustice. Similarly, people who run naked in the street must be viewed in a given context. A rapid, public display of nudity, called streaking, has been a popular diversion on occasion in the last decades of this century. Some interpretation of each event is needed, and it can be accomplished by an experienced, conscientious professional.

These two approaches, statistical and clinical, are often used together, each with its special assets and limitations. In fact, the pediatrician was admitted to the mental hospital because hearing unspoken voices is a statistically rare event, and it is considered a serious clinical matter. Still another approach raises the issue of the lawfulness of the individual's behavior. Not of concern here, it offers a legal definition of abnormality.

෴

COPING EFFECTIVELY

We solve many adjustment problems in completely routine fashion, so much so that we may not realize we have surmounted a problem. Several basic ways of coping with personal problems were enumerated in the chapter on emotion and stress. They are relevant here. In this review, it should be remembered that these are normal and generally satisfactory adjustment reactions, although some are more useful than others.

The most effective approach is *to deal directly with the problem,* taking some direct action to change or eliminate it. In fact, direct action is the only method of really solving the problem. The pediatrician apparently went to the hospital to take direct action on the problem of unspoken voices. Once in the hospital, he was faced with a different problem—adjusting to that institutional setting.

Deprived of many conveniences, the hospitalized patients found ways to deal with their barren environment, making it more comfortable and interesting. One patient used a heating unit on the ward as a personal clothes dryer. Another requested a second serving at lunch—to be consumed later as "afternoon tea." Still another urinated into the laundry bin to save a trip to the toilet: "Those clothes were dirty anyway" (Rosenhan, 1973). The latter habit, a dubious practice from the viewpoint of health standards, illustrates socially disruptive behavior.

If the problem is insoluble, then indirect methods must be used, and there are several indirect, positive methods of coping. One such method is *to think about the problem differently.* In reframing the problem, also called *cognitive restructuring,* the individual looks at the problem from a new perspective. It is defined as more tolerable, less disruptive, or simply unimportant. A hospitalized person might decide that the institution is really not so bad after all—offering free food, shelter, and a chance to do some extensive thinking without disruptive telephone calls. Besides, the state pays some of the bills.

Another problem for the patients involved relations with the hospital staff. In doing their work, the staff often behaved in ways that rejected the patients, ignoring their attempts to make contact (Table 15–I). For the patients, one means of dealing with this rejection was to think about it differently. They might have decided that they should only expect routine assistance from the overworked staff. They might have looked forward instead to personal relations with family, friends, and other patients.

In addition, the individual can attempt *to relieve the stress reaction.* These techniques include two rather opposite approaches—complete relaxation and vig-

TYPE OF RESPONSE	PSYCHIATRISTS	NURSES
Moves on, averts head	71%	88%
Makes eye contact	23%	10%
Pauses and chats	2%	2%
Stops and talks	4%	1%

TABLE 15–1 RESPONSE TO PATIENTS BY HOSPITAL STAFF. These results, obtained from several hospitals, show the reaction of 13 psychiatrists and 47 nurses when a patient tried to initiate contact with them. Altogether, there were 185 attempts to contact the psychiatrists and 1,283 attempts to contact the nurses (Rosenhan, 1973).

orous exercise. The former includes muscle relaxation, breathing control, and visualization techniques in which one imagines relaxing scenes. The latter involves weight training, aerobics, and athletic competition, all of distinct value for reducing stress. They not only relax the body and relieve tension but also, by restoring normal balance, they offer the individual greater opportunity for using cognitive methods (Figure 15–3). The rested and controlled individual may think of a new plan.

One of the most common and useful indirect methods of handling problems is employed by almost everyone at one time or another. A *sense of humor* keeps one's problems in perspective—or at least puts them into the context of circus music, which seems to play in the background of all of our lives. Humor permits a person to acknowledge and to deal with events that are otherwise too difficult to be borne directly (Vaillant, 1992). People who can laugh at their troubles have in part mastered those troubles.

❧

INEFFICIENT COPING

We respond to everyday problems of adjustment in diverse ways. Most of these reactions are not statistically rare or clinically prominent, and they typically do not involve significant personal discomfort or disruption of others. They are routinely employed by all of us from time to time.

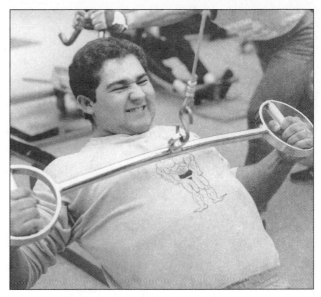

FIGURE 15–3 REDUCING STRESS. Complete relaxation and vigorous exercise can regulate disrupted biological processes and provide a refreshed mental state; they are often recommended for use in coordinated fashion.

But they may be inefficient. They may drain our energy, cause needless expenditure of time, prevent us from finding better solutions, and even make us more troubled. To what extent are they inefficient and damaging? The answer of course depends on their degree and duration.

DEFENSE MECHANISMS. Redefining the situation and using exercise, relaxation, and humor are conscious efforts to deal with an insoluble problem. According to many psychologists, we also use a method of which we are less aware. A **defense mechanism** is an unconscious means of dealing with anxiety, based on self-deception. As noted in the previous chapter, the basic defense mechanism is **repression,** a process of forgetting by which unpleasant thoughts are excluded from awareness, without the intention to do so. An individual who has seriously embarrassed, offended, or harmed someone else may be completely unable to remember that event, no matter how hard he or she tries. And certainly an individual who has been molested may be unable to remember it (Briere & Conte, 1993; Clark, 1993). This reaction differs from

suppression, which is a *conscious* attempt to avoid certain thoughts or actions and therefore not a defense mechanism in the traditional sense. The individual, aware of the offensive act, simply tries to think about something else, thereby blocking out the memory.

Since Sigmund Freud developed the concept, lists of defense mechanisms have become many and varied, depending on the strictness of the definition, especially the role of repression. However, certain defense mechanisms appear on all lists: rationalization, reaction formation, and projection, discussed in the previous chapter, as well as displacement, denial, and sublimation.

In **displacement,** an emotional reaction intended for a certain person or object is shifted to some other target. An adult frustrated in love with another adult may lavish extraordinary affection on a niece or nephew. A child, angered by parental restrictions, may break a toy. When the feelings and behavior are hostile, this reaction is often called *displaced aggression,* meaning that the attack is directed to a less threatening object rather than the source of its origin, which may be too threatening to confront. For such behavior to be considered a defense mechanism, rather than simply misdirected retaliation, the motives for aggression must be unconscious.

When some event is too difficult to confront, the mechanism may be **denial,** which is a refusal to recognize certain aspects of reality. An alcoholic person may deny his addiction or refuse to believe that extensive drinking can produce certain physical ailments.

Anxiety is often most successfully managed by **sublimation,** for here unacceptable impulses are directed toward socially approved targets. An aggressive person might become a crime fighter or trial lawyer. A sexually frustrated person might develop a program of sex education for teenagers or create sensuous art forms (Table 15–2).

Using any defense mechanism, especially repression, requires a constant expenditure of energy because the unconscious thoughts are always seeking expression. According to psychoanalysis, so much energy goes into the effort of excluding unwanted thoughts from awareness that repressed people are often stiff, inflexible, tired, and readily upset. They have relatively little energy left over for the tasks of daily life, to say nothing of unusual tasks, such as creativity. In other words, the process of repression occurs at the cost of considerable energy and flexibility.

Nevertheless, the use of defense mechanisms may be advantageous in two respects. Through repression, we may forget some of our most difficult problems and traumatic experiences. Through other defense mechanisms, especially sublimation, we may find partially effective ways of dealing with them.

DECREASED RESPONSIVENESS. After coping ineffectively with problems, human beings sometimes abandon their efforts, displaying lethargy and helplessness instead. They give up

MECHANISM	DEFINITION	ILLUSTRATION
Repression	Unconsciously excluding anxiety-provoking thoughts from awareness	A man who was sexually abused as a child cannot recall the traumatic incidents.
Rationalization	Finding false reasons to justify one's own behavior	A rejected author declares that he would not cooperate with that publisher anyway.
Reaction formation	Counteracting an unconscious impulse with the opposite reaction	Resenting her responsibility for elderly parents, a woman nurtures them intensely.
Projection	Attributing to others one's own unacceptable traits	A reckless auto racer declares that he drives well; other drivers are dangerous.
Displacement	Transferring an emotional reaction onto a less threatening target	Forsaken by his father, a boy directs his admiration and respect to a teacher.
Denial	Refusing to accept reality; rejecting evidence	A teenager decides that pregnancy is impossible, even without contraception.
Sublimation	Channeling basic impulses into more useful, creative expressions	An aggressive, defiant man devotes himself to the war on poverty.

TABLE 15–2 TRADITIONAL DEFENSE MECHANISMS. All defense mechanisms involve unconscious processes. Sublimation is generally considered more effective than the others because the repressed impulses are directed into socially useful activities.

hope, too defeated even to express resentment. In a hospital or jail, at work or in school, a person may feel overwhelmed and cease responding.

We do not know if the pediatrician reacted this way during his hospitalization. We do know that immediately after admission, he no longer claimed to hear voices and began taking notes on what he observed. He found that most patients sat or dozed in the lounge area, partly because of the medication they were given, partly because they had become dispirited (Rosenhan, 1973). If sufficiently frustrated by any uncontrollable circumstance, a person may display this adjustment reaction—some form of decreased responsiveness, becoming listless or apathetic.

In an experimental study, dogs were placed in a suspension harness that allowed some freedom of movement, and they all received a brief, mild shock. Some could not terminate it, but others could do so by pressing a nearby panel. Then each dog was placed individually in an open compartment without a harness, where another electric shock occurred. It was found that the dogs that had previously learned to escape the shock by pressing the panel readily jumped a barrier and thereby escaped the new shock. The others, although they could move about freely, usually whined and settled into a position to endure the shock, making no escape movements. Their earlier **learned helplessness,** in which they could do nothing to alleviate a stressful situation, apparently induced them to become lethargic later (Seligman, 1975; Seligman & Maier, 1967).

Certain ghetto situations may be analogous to the conditions of learned helplessness among animals. Poverty-stricken people may seem too lazy to do anything about their situation, but perhaps, like the dogs in harness, they have learned—rightly or wrongly—that there is nothing they can do to change it. After years of learned helplessness, they have stopped trying. The concept of laziness is inappropriate, just as it is in so many cases of homelessness (Goodman, Saxe, & Harvey, 1991; Olson & Schober, 1993).

RESORTING TO FANTASY. The inactive individual has not necessarily ignored the problem. Sometimes the problem is solved inwardly, by wishful thinking and dreams called **fantasy.** In imagination, a person may accomplish all sorts of feats, finding true love, vanquishing a rival, and overcoming an insurmountable obstacle (Figure 15–4). In *The Secret Life of Walter Mitty* a meek, ineffective man becomes a ship's captain in a raging storm, a brilliant surgeon directing an unprecedented operation, a courageous wartime hero, and so forth, all merely in his own thoughts while standing in the rain, caught in heavy traffic, or otherwise running errands for his mother (Thurber, 1983).

FIGURE 15–4 ENGAGING IN FANTASY.
In fantasy play, a child may be trying out adult roles not readily available. Fantasy in this context represents a constructive force in personality development.

FIGURE 15-5 DISPLACED AGGRESSION. This tennis player throwing his racquet clearly illustrates displaced aggression. The tennis racquet did not cause the problem. He has just missed a crucial point.

Everyone engages in fantasy. Such activities are not necessarily deviant. In fact, fantasy is often a major step in creative problem solving. It is a sign of maladjustment only when it becomes a persistent substitute for reality.

AGGRESSION AND REGRESSION. Unsuccessful coping may result in aggressive behavior. People sometimes become abusive, break rules, argue, or criticize others. Or they assault someone physically. Aggression may be directed toward the source of frustration, toward an object or innocent person—as in displaced aggression—or even toward oneself (Figure 15–5).

As emphasized in the chapter on emotion and stress, aggression may be provoked by a variety of causes, and it is associated with many forms of maladaptive behavior, including substance use, impulse-control disorders, and the antisocial personality. Serious forms of aggression are discussed later in this chapter.

When other responses prove inadequate, people sometimes engage in **regression,** meaning that they move backward, repeating behavior that was satisfying or more appropriate at an earlier stage of development. Regression is childish behavior. Following the birth of a new brother or sister, an older child may revert to crying, baby talk, or bedwetting, and may even strike the newcomer, attempting to regain parental attention. Such behavior is not limited to children. Husbands sometimes attempt to dominate their wives, and wives their husbands, by sulking, weeping, and threats of harm to themselves if they do not get their way. If not directly aggressive, the regressed individual may be passively so, refusing to do something until his or her wish is granted.

As we turn to the question of abnormality, we should note again that adjustment lies on a continuum and is a continuous process. Aggression, regression, and the other previously discussed reactions, if chronic and extreme, would be considered abnormal. Similarly, some of the reactions to be considered next, although generally more deviant, are not completely debilitating.

• DETERMINING ABNORMALITY •

In the more disruptive adjustment disorders, we encounter less direct, less efficient problem solving. The individual is approaching abnormality, or mental disorder, a most important and complex issue in psychology. Its complexity is readily evident when even experts acknowledge that they have no adequate definition for the various boundaries of *mental disorder* (American Psychiatric Association, 1994).

Regardless of what definition we use, the pediatrician was a fraud. He *was* a pediatrician, one of eight people entering mental hospitals on the East Coast or West Coast, but he did not hear unspoken voices and experienced no psychiatric symptoms. He and the others sought admission under false pretenses, as part of a secret plan to investigate psychiatric hospitals. These five men and three women included a student, painter, housewife, psychiatrist, and three psychologists, as well as the pediatrician. David Rosenhan, a psychologist at Stanford University, was among them. Prior to their attempts to gain admission, all had been judged normal in an independent clinical evaluation. During the admissions interview, they gave only a false name, a false occupation when necessary, and the false complaint of hearing voices. Otherwise, there were no further alterations of any facts.

They entered 12 hospitals altogether, for some were admitted to more than one institution. All of them sought admission for the purpose of discovering whether expert clinicians could distinguish normal from abnormal behavior. In addition, they wanted to investigate conditions in mental hospitals. These pseudopatients were members of a research program called the *Rosenhan study*, after the chief investigator (Rosenhan, 1973).

This well-known research immediately demonstrated its major point: Experts can be fooled; they may make mistakes. It also suggested that psychiatric diagnosis is a complex process.

∾

THE DIAGNOSTIC CHALLENGE

When the Rosenhan deception was announced, it caused a titanic uproar. The press, always in search of a story, applauded this mischief, for it ridiculed psychiatry, clinical psychology, and the whole process of diagnosis. Psychiatry was quackery. Imagine! Hospitalizing perfectly normal people.

The professionals were outraged, naturally. This research, if it could be called that, revealed absolutely nothing new. It merely confirmed what everyone knows: Careful, hardworking experts in any field can be tricked by unscrupulous people.

And sober-minded folk saw in this duplicity certain defects and something of merit. Honest professionals had been treated fraudulently and perhaps unfairly, but this ruse clearly pointed to shortcomings in the diagnostic process. Rosenhan emphasized this point in his report, entitled *On Being Sane in Insane Places* (1973). If people are sane but in a place for the insane, even the experts may regard them as insane.

SELF-REPORT IN DIAGNOSIS. The hospitalization of the Rosenhan pseudopatients showed an important characteristic of the diagnostic process. It can be significantly influenced by what the patient says about his or her life. If the individual is not socially disruptive, the decision about abnormality rests with the patient's self-report of personal discomfort: "I am unhappy." "I hear voices." Clinical psychologists and psychiatrists have long known how dependent they are on the patient's self-report, and the Rosenhan research confirmed this view.

The same condition applies whenever someone seeks assistance in physical health, law, education, or any other field. A person wishing to obtain poor advice or a wrong diagnosis simply supplies false information. The Rosenhan study showed nothing new about fraud, although it did highlight the difficulty of diagnosis and did demonstrate the need for care in taking a patient's self-report at face value.

The fact that allegedly normal individuals were diagnosed as abnormal does *not* deny the validity of the diagnostic process or the relevant concepts, just as our difficulty in defining these terms does not repudiate our use of the ideas. Hot differs from cold, beautiful from ugly, and day from night, though there is no critical event of separation in any case. We argue about the distinction between life and death, and yet the value of these concepts is not refuted. In short, useful distinctions can be made between normal and abnormal, sanity and insanity, though clinicians can be fooled and certainly there are difficult cases.

LIMITATIONS OF THE DIAGNOSTIC PROCESS. Our lack of knowledge of the causes of mental disorder is an obvious limitation in the diagnostic process. As recently as the early twentieth century, people showing deviant behavior were thought to be possessed by the devil and described as *mad*. Later they were called *insane* and *abnormal*, but these terms were detrimental to the individual. When the concept of **mental illness** was introduced, it indicated a mental disorder of physical or psychological origin sufficiently severe to require professional assistance (Wolman, 1989). It also implied that the disturbed person has some disease analogous to physical illness.

By the middle of the twentieth century, this interpretation of the problem was criticized by an outspoken, dissident psychiatrist, Thomas Szasz. Calling disturbed people ill merely justified medical practice, he claimed. He popularized a new expression: "the myth of mental illness." It resisted the idea that psychological disorders are no different from physical disorders and that professional intervention is necessary to provide a cure. Szasz's replacement term, *problems in living*, has not been adopted, partly because it is more cumbersome (Szasz, 1974). Nevertheless, his assault on psychiatric practices became the early roots of movements for patients' rights and changes in the field (Smith, 1986).

In addition, the diagnostic labels focus on symptoms rather than causes. It is for this reason that the Rosenhan study provided such uniform results: The pseudopatients simply matched their behavior to the diagnostic symptoms. Claiming to hear nonexistent voices, they were admitted to a psychiatric ward. After they stopped reporting the voices, they were discharged. This focus on symptoms persists because it is useful in organizing clinical knowledge and in treating certain patients, but it does not further our understanding of the underlying psychological processes (Fernald & Gettys, 1980; Persons, 1986).

Sooner or later, the diagnostic label becomes a stigma, branding the individual as a social misfit or malcontent, but here the problem is in society. It is the culture, not the diagnosis or the label per se, that stigmatizes the person, as evident in the violent portrayal of psychological disorders on television. Most people with severe disorders are not dangerous but rather socially isolated and inept. The enormously detrimental effects of this portrayal are seen in the fear it arouses in the family, friends, neighbors, and coworkers of the individual.

One demonstration of the power of psychiatric labeling employed videotaped interviews of people said to be attending a mental health center. On the tapes, they were introduced as normal, undiagnosed, or schizophrenic—meaning a serious abnormal behavior. Each label was applied to each person in one context or another, and the tapes were rated by three groups of college students. It was found that a person labeled as schizophrenic was inevitably rated as deviant in social skills. Individuals not so labeled were not described as deviant. Some consolation was found among 30 trained social workers. They did not succumb to the labels, making their ratings without this potential bias influencing their judgments (O'Connor & Smith, 1987).

There are no simple solutions to these problems. Forms of maladjustment have been conceptualized in many ways, none of which has been highly successful. Earlier in this century a psychoanalytic concept, **neurosis,** was widely used to indicate a broad array of disorders characterized primarily by anxiety, experienced directly or indirectly. Except in psychoanalysis, the concept of neurosis has been largely abandoned, chiefly because it is too broad, lacking a clear definition. Moreover, psychoanalysis is only one of several major perspectives on psychological disorders.

DIAGNOSTIC MANUAL FOR MENTAL DISORDERS.

Today the most definitive diagnostic source is the fourth edition of the *Diagnostic and Statistical Manual of Mental Disorders (DSM-IV)*, published in 1994 by the American Psychiatric Association. This edition, like its predecessors, includes a wide range of diagnostic categories (Table 15–3).

Any conception of mental disorders has social and professional significance. The *Diagnostic and Statistical Manual* is a social document with implications for health status, legal competence, disability payments, and so forth. Furthermore, the diagnostic labels may influence people's perception of a person's worth. Thus, the debate continues over just which patterns of behavior belong in the manual and how they should be presented (Nathan, 1991; Wilson & Walsh, 1991).

Disorders in Infancy, Childhood, or Adolescence
Delirium, Dementia, and Amnesic Cognitive Disorders
Mental Disorders Due to a General Medical Condition
Substance-Related Disorders
Schizophrenia and Other Psychotic Disorders
Mood Disorders
Anxiety Disorders
Somatoform Disorders
Factitious Disorders
Dissociative Disorders
Sexual and Gender Identity Disorders
Eating Disorders
Sleep Disorders
Impulse-Control Disorders
Adjustment Disorders
Personality Disorders

TABLE 15–3 MAJOR DIAGNOSTIC CATEGORIES. This table shows the major categories in the *Diagnostic and Statistical Manual, IV.* All categories include numerous subcategories.

In its almost 900 pages, the *DSM-IV* ignores **insanity,** a legal term indicating that someone is not of sufficiently sound mind to be responsible for his or her conduct. Insanity is a critical legal concept because it means someone does not know right from wrong and therefore is not responsible for wrongdoing. For corrective action, this person is referred to the mental health system rather than the prison system.

DIAGNOSTIC PERSPECTIVES

The focus in *DSM-IV* is on symptoms, but clinicians inevitably become concerned about origins of mental disorders. As they formulate treatment plans, they recognize several theoretical perspectives on causal factors, reflecting systems of psychology considered earlier: the biological, psychoanalytic, behavioral, and cognitive. Many clinicians adopt an eclectic perspective, using diverse elements from each of these and other viewpoints.

For example, one section of the *DSM-IV* describes impulse-control disorders, such as *kleptomania* and *pyromania,* an inability to resist stealing for pleasure and setting fire for pleasure, respectively. Still another impulse-control disorder involves **pathological gambling,** a persistent tendency to take risks with money, leaving the outcome largely to chance. This habit can cause more than loss of money and disruption of family and vocational life. It can result in forgery, fraud, embezzlement, and related illegal acts. This problem is especially disastrous for people with marginal incomes. Unfortunately, those who can least afford to lose the money—with the least education and least secure employment—are most likely to gamble it away (Volberg & Steadman, 1988, 1989). As the race-horse gambler said, "I'm going to the track today and hope I come out even—because I really need the money."

Pathological gambling may or may not begin

with some inherited predisposition, but according to the *biological view,* changes may take place within the nervous system as gambling continues. Initially, the gambler seeks action, an aroused state. Casino gamblers often report euphoria as the dice are rolled for a bet. Racetrack bettors describe a heart-stopping excitement when the announcer calls: "They're off!" The pathological element apparently arises in the need to maintain or increase this excitement, which is produced by increasingly greater risks, presumably associated with changes in brain chemistry. There is biological evidence that in some people the central nervous system is under-aroused and therefore highly responsive to further stimulation (Eysenck, 1990). In sensation-seeking behavior, discussed in the previous chapter, people search for thrilling, even dangerous stimulation (Zuckerman, 1990).

A very different perspective is adopted in the *psychoanalytic view,* which regards pathological gambling as symbolic of some underlying, unconscious problem, a symptom of earlier, unresolved personal issues. For many psychoanalysts, pathological gambling is a regression to the powerlessness of childhood. The hoped-for fortune is the parental figure to which the childlike gambler appeals for love, protection, and other forms of assistance (Cordery, 1987). In fact, loss of a parent in the early years and inconsistent discipline are characteristics associated with pathological gambling.

In the *behavioral view,* any response intermittently reinforced is difficult to extinguish. The gambler keeps betting because every so often there is a payoff. This occasional reinforcement is sufficient to maintain the behavior. Or the act itself may be reinforcing, apart from the payoff. The individual gambles because this behavior relieves feelings of helplessness, anxiety, or depression (American Psychiatric Association, 1994).

Modern social science is characterized by a widespread concern with information processing.

On this basis, the *cognitive view* of pathological gambling focuses on the gambler's fallacy, which is an overestimation of the odds of winning. The individual erroneously decides that after ten consecutive losses, for example, the odds of winning on the very next chance are increased. Regardless of the fallacy, if gambling continues an increasingly risky pattern is likely to develop, with larger and larger bets, attempting to undo the series of losses. The mental processes responsible for this behavior involve various thought distortions, including denial, superstitions, and even over-confidence (American Psychiatric Association, 1994).

Pathological gambling is distinguished from social gambling, which occurs with colleagues, lasts for a specific period, and is based on predetermined, acceptable losses. It also differs from professional gambling, in which calculated risks are taken under a strict code of discipline. Cultural variations in the type and extent of gambling are observed throughout the world.

• TYPES OF DISORDERS •

After entering the hospitals, the Rosenhan pseudopatients immediately stopped claiming to hear unspoken voices. Instead, they behaved normally, engaging the real patients and staff in conversation and, according to plan, taking notes on what took place in the hospital. This note-taking was a primary research goal, and it showed, among other results, that the real patients recognized normality better than did the professional staff. At least they were more suspicious of the Rosenhan pseudopatients (Table 15–4).

The hospital environment included patients with all sorts of backgrounds and diagnoses, but relatively few of them would be classified according to the first two or three categories in the following sequence of psychological disorders. As a rule, anxiety and somatoform disorders do not require hospitalization, or at least extensive hospitalization.

ANXIETY DISORDERS

The predominant feature in an anxiety disorder is, of course, anxiety. Among all of the disorders in the *DSM-IV,* these occur most frequently, and they most closely represent what used to be called *neurosis.* The most common forms include generalized anxiety, phobia, posttraumatic stress, and the obsessive-compulsive disorder.

GENERALIZED ANXIETY DISORDER. When a person experiences excessive worry for no apparent reason, and this condition has existed for at least six months, it may be referred to as a **generalized anxiety disorder.** This intense concern about circumstances that do not appear to warrant such anxiety is also accompanied by irritability, disturbed sleep, or some other related symptom. The person may say, "I'm really worried, but I don't know why. I have no reason to be, but I am."

Muscle tension is one of the prominent symptoms, evident in trembling, twitching, fatigue, and restlessness. In addition, there may be sweating and hot flashes or chills. At work or in moments of relaxation, the individual may feel irritable or keyed up or may have difficulty concentrating (American Psychiatric Association, 1994). However, this diagnosis does not apply if the anxiety seems to be due to some other mental disorder or to some organic factor, such as a thyroid condition or caffeine intoxication.

SPECIFIC PHOBIA. Unreasonable fear of some clearly discernible object or event, sufficient to interfere with an individual's work or social endeavors, is known as a **specific phobia.** Unlike the individual experiencing generalized anxiety, the phobic person knows what he or she fears and avoids that object or event. These reactions often involve animals: dogs, cats, insects, snakes, and rodents (Figure 15–6). Other specific phobic reactions involve strangers, blood, closed spaces, and air travel. They do not include fear of humiliation in social situations, referred to as *social phobia,* which involves difficulty speaking to strangers, using public places, and engaging in group behavior.

FIGURE 15–6 ORIGINS OF PHOBIAS. Phobias involving wild animals, insects, darkness, and heights are interpreted from various theoretical perspectives. In the behavioral approach, the phobia arises through association with some anxiety-provoking situation. In the psychoanalytic tradition, the phobic reaction is a symbolic expression of unconscious conflict. In the biological or evolutionary perspective, the phobia reflects a genetic predisposition from earlier times in which such events represented real dangers.

Sigmund Freud's case of Little Hans is a classic description of a specific phobia. A healthy five-year-old boy one day began to cry and refused to go for his usual walk. The next day he cried and refused again. Finally, he explained to his mother that he was afraid of horses, a fear that was inexplicable because the boy had never been kicked, bitten, or otherwise harmed by a horse. Eventually he could not go outside at all and complained that a horse might come into his room (Freud, 1909).

For any phobia, the degree of impairment depends partly on the environment. Little Hans was highly incapacitated because horses appeared throughout Vienna in his day. Snake phobias generally are not a problem for city dwellers; elevator phobias are of little significance in the country. Phobias in the general population range from agoraphobia, fear of open spaces, to zoophobia, fear of animals. However, people seldom seek treatment—perhaps because their avoidance reaction has become an accepted habit, part of everyday life, while therapy is an unknown condition and therefore even more threatening.

POSTTRAUMATIC STRESS DISORDER.

Another form of anxiety is not confined to a specific context. It can appear almost any place. Whenever someone re-experiences a severely disturbing event, thereby becoming intensely anxious again, the condition is called **posttraumatic stress disorder.** It is initiated by a memory, nightmare, flashback, or some other reminder of the original, terrifying incident. Rape victims, disaster survivors, and military personnel with wartime experiences have all reported this syndrome. Often it includes an insensitivity or numbness to people and events reminiscent of the painful experience, thereby disrupting the individual's capacity for intimacy, sexual desire, and close relationships.

The puzzling part of this disorder is that the memories do not fade. The brain's capacity for forgetting seems somehow disrupted. Speculation concerns the role of the amygdala in anxiety, apparently the most fundamental human emotion (Davis, 1992). There is also speculation that traumatic memories may be more readily stored in the right hemisphere, presumably involved in processing affect (Schiffer, Teicher, & Papanicolaou, 1995).

OBSESSIVE-COMPULSIVE DISORDER.

Most people experience some thoughts and actions of a recurring nature. We may think about an embarrassing experience over and over, unable to forget it, or we may expend too much effort writing and rewriting an inconsequential letter. When such ritualistic behavior requires considerable expenditure of time or its omission causes marked distress, it may be considered an **obsessive-compulsive disorder.** The essential feature is some persistent yet useless thought or action, consuming more than an hour daily (American Psychiatric Association, 1994).

The recurrent thought is called an *obsession,* and it causes pronounced anxiety. A repetitive thought of contamination, perhaps through eating improperly washed food, is an example. A recurrent act, such as constantly arranging and rearranging a linen closet, is known as a *compulsion,* and it serves to reduce anxiety. Excessive drinking and gambling are sometimes referred to as compulsive, but this usage is not in accordance with diagnostic standards. There is an obvious purpose in these repetitive behaviors; they are not completely useless activities.

Compulsive people often emerge as checkers or cleaners. Checkers ensure that the doors are locked, the clothes hung properly, the faucets turned off, or the plants watered, and then they check on their checking, again and again. Cleaners endlessly wash their hands, polish their shoes, sweep the floor, and rinse the sink, scrubbing and cleansing everything to the point where daily life is significantly disrupted. All of us check and clean in limited ways.

In obsessive-compulsive cases, these behaviors become overpowering habits, experienced in adult life by slightly over 2% of the population (American Psychiatric Association, 1994).

~

SOMATOFORM DISORDERS

The essential feature in a **somatoform disorder** is a physical symptom, a malfunction of the body, or *soma*, which cannot be fully explained by any medical condition. The symptom appears instead to be related to psychological stress, particularly inappropriate social learning and family problems (Ader & Cohen, 1993; Mullins & Olson, 1990). There is no faking or false claim, as with the Rosenhan pseudopatients.

In one form, called *somatization disorder*, the individual has multiple somatic complaints extending over several years, usually beginning in the teens, rarely later than the twenties. Without any identifiable physiological defect to account for the symptoms, the afflicted individual may seek medical care from several sources, sometimes simultaneously, with complaints about gastrointestinal, reproductive, cardiopulmonary, and other problems, as well as assorted aches and pains. The individual always has a series of *vague physical ailments*, if not of one sort, then of another.

In contrast, the *conversion disorder* is more specific, involving a persistent loss or alteration of a certain physical function. There is an inexplicable loss of muscle control or sensitivity in a *specific organ* of the body (Figure 15–7).

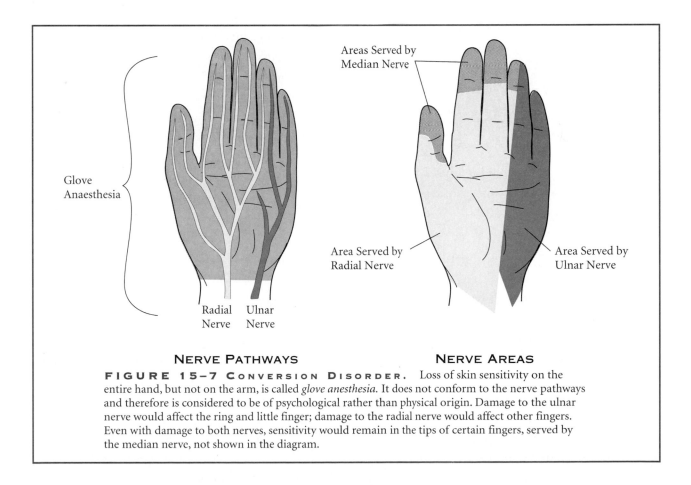

Glove Anaesthesia

Radial Nerve Ulnar Nerve

Areas Served by Median Nerve

Area Served by Radial Nerve

Area Served by Ulnar Nerve

NERVE PATHWAYS   **NERVE AREAS**

FIGURE 15–7 CONVERSION DISORDER. Loss of skin sensitivity on the entire hand, but not on the arm, is called *glove anesthesia*. It does not conform to the nerve pathways and therefore is considered to be of psychological rather than physical origin. Damage to the ulnar nerve would affect the ring and little finger; damage to the radial nerve would affect other fingers. Even with damage to both nerves, sensitivity would remain in the tips of certain fingers, served by the median nerve, not shown in the diagram.

By definition, there is no known neurophysiological basis for these physical ailments, but two psychological mechanisms are suggested to account for them. There is the *primary gain,* which is the alleviation of anxiety from some other source. The underlying psychological disturbance, which is the real problem according to psychoanalysis, is kept out of awareness. The *secondary gain* involves some additional advantage, apart from disguising the fundamental problem. This gain may be achieved in the form of sympathy or gifts from others, or it may enable the afflicted individual to avoid some distasteful task.

The concept of secondary gain is central to the behavioral interpretation of somatoform disorders. According to the reinforcement principle, the individual's symptoms are maintained through the attention and support offered by people in the environment. The psychoanalytic interpretation focuses on repression and conversion of the earlier problem into some symbolic form, in this case a physical symptom. Nausea, for example, may be related to unconscious oral concerns. The biological perspective points out that the somatization disorder appears in 10–20% of all first-degree biological female relatives of a woman with this disorder (American Psychiatric Association, 1994). And the cognitive view stresses diverse mental events possibly responsible for this maladaption (Dodge, 1993). As expected, the different viewpoints stress different factors, although they demonstrate overlapping concerns.

In a related problem, *hypochondriasis,* there is no marked physical disorder but rather an excessive concern over one's health. Everyday coughs and cramps are considered symptoms of a dreaded disease. The person has an "illness phobia," constantly worried about health problems despite medical opinion to the contrary. This reaction appears to be partly by secondary gain.

DISSOCIATIVE DISORDERS

Some reactions to stress are characterized by forgetting or blocking out pervasive portions of one's life. In the dissociative disorder, there is a disruption of memory, consciousness, perception, or identity. Two or more aspects of the personality no longer appear connected. They seem to function independently, and yet they coexist, as in amnesia, fugues, and the dissociative identity disorder.

AMNESIA AND FUGUE. Loss of memory too pervasive to be considered ordinary forgetting is called *amnesia.* A case of **dissociative amnesia** involves extensive memory loss, presumably on a psychological basis, with no observable physical cause. This memory failure may pertain to any traumatic event in the individual's lifetime, and it may involve a specific setting, such as the workplace, or it may be more general. In either case, the individual remains in familiar surroundings and is otherwise reasonably adjusted.

Sometimes an individual cannot remember his or her name, family, or friends, and no one within hundreds of miles seems to know this person. This condition is known as a *fugue,* meaning a "flight." In a typical **dissociative fugue,** which also has no known organic basis, the person has experienced extreme memory loss and has moved some distance from home. In a sense, he or she has done in a serious and dramatic way what many of us may want to do occasionally—just go away and forget everything for a while.

DISSOCIATIVE IDENTITY DISORDER. A more popularized form of forgetting involves the **dissociative identity disorder,** in which a person seems to have two or more personality states. Previously called *multiple personality,* it is fictionally depicted in *Dr. Jekyll and Mr. Hyde* by Robert Louis Stevenson. A real-life account appeared in the book

The Three Faces of Eve, describing a woman with three personalities: Eve White, an unhappy housewife; Eve Black, a high-spirited, sexy young woman; and Jane, a dignified, cultured person (Thigpen & Cleckley, 1954). In her autobiography about these personalities, Chris Sizemore described several traumatic incidents with dead people in early childhood, from which she retreated in horror. It seemed to her at the time that someone else was viewing these scenes, not her. After an extensive course of therapy, during which one of the personalities sometimes displaced another in the middle of the treatment session, she eventually developed into an integrated adult with a single personality (Sizemore & Pittillo, 1977).

Many cases have been cited recently, including people accused of crimes who report that the deed was committed by their "other personality." Such claims raise perplexing legal questions about competence to stand trial, the insanity plea, and even malingering (Lewis & Bard, 1991). In forensic settings, it may be almost impossible to distinguish this disorder from clever deceit (Dinwiddie, North, & Yutzy, 1993).

Hypotheses about the origins of the dissociative identity disorder have ranged from childhood trauma to family disorders, but some form of self-hypnosis may be involved. To deal with severe conflict, such as sexual abuse or parental suicide, the child perhaps develops separate selves or personalities, each with its own awareness and memories (Confer & Ables, 1983; Figure 15–8).

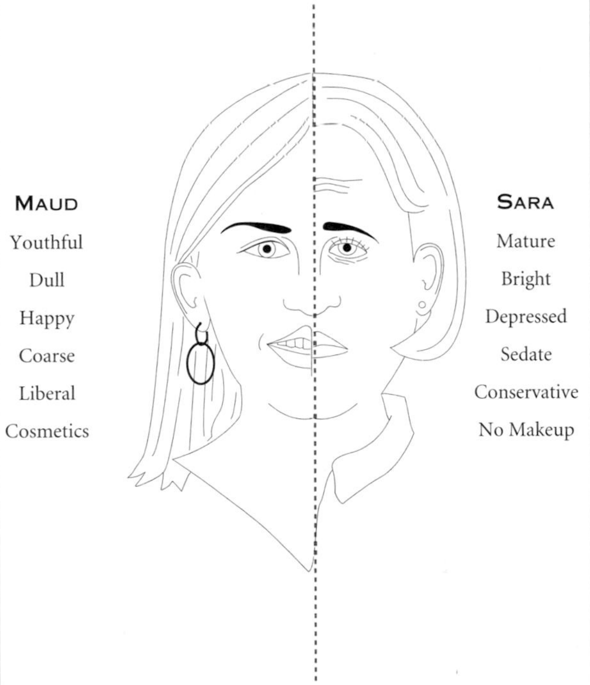

FIGURE 15–8 DISSOCIATIVE IDENTITY DISORDER. Maud and Sara were two different personalities in one woman's life. They alternated control of the same body (From Lipton, 1943).

MAUD
Youthful
Dull
Happy
Coarse
Liberal
Cosmetics

SARA
Mature
Bright
Depressed
Sedate
Conservative
No Makeup

MOOD DISORDERS

On the hospital wards, the Rosenhan pseudopatients soon discovered that no one cared what they did, provided that they caused no problem. Hence, most of them made their observations and completed their records openly, writing on standard tablets in dayrooms and elsewhere, describing how patients and staff dealt with crowding, medical procedures, and work routines. In some cases, the conditions were good and the staff laudable. In others, the situation was deplorable (Rosenhan, 1973).

Many of the patients on the ward suffered from one of two different disorders, both of which deserve careful consideration. The essential characteristic of the first, a mood disorder, is a prolonged, very deep feeling that influences one's entire outlook on life. The second, schizophrenia, involves primarily disordered thought. Alterations in thinking and mood are present in virtually all serious maladjustment, but exaggerated or inappropriate emotions are most obvious in mood disorders.

MAJOR DEPRESSIVE DISORDER. When feelings of intense disappointment and helplessness about life continue for at least two weeks, or there is a loss of pleasure in virtually all activities for an equal period, the condition may be a **major**

depressive disorder. However, these feelings must be accompanied by other symptoms, such as weight loss, fatigue, insomnia, agitation, a feeling of guilt, inability to concentrate, and so forth.

Extreme depression may result in complete loss of hope and, in dire cases, suicide. Women are more than twice as likely as men to attempt suicide, not a surprising condition inasmuch as they are more prone to depression (Strickland, 1992). Men are three or four times more likely to commit the act, however, partly because they use more potent weapons, such as guns and ropes, rather than poison or pills.

Suicide rates are highest among older people with little money, no friends, and poor health, but they are also high, and on the rise, among adolescents, especially those maintaining high aspirations or using illegal drugs. Recognition of these characteristics, particularly quiet depression, is essential in suicide prevention (Shneidman, 1981). Prescriptions on how to commit suicide, intended for terminally ill people, have raised further controversy in this area.

BIPOLAR DISORDER. Other mood disorders are characterized by sharp mood swings or up-and-down feelings. When an extremely excited or manic episode is preceded or followed by depression, the condition is called a **bipolar disorder.** The emotions may fluctuate rapidly from one pole to the other, or they may stay for some time at one extreme.

In the *manic episode* the individual may be extremely happy, singing at the top of his voice, or irritable, moving quickly in unrestrained fashion. Sometimes there is a flight of ideas; the individual goes off rapidly on one tangent, then another, and then another, as each idea occurs. In the *depressive episode* the person loses interest in life, including eating and other pleasurable activities, shows a loss of energy, and complains of worthlessness. Self-destructive acts and suicidal thoughts also may be present.

The manic and depressive conditions may alternate in a variety of ways, but the manic episode is usually sudden in onset, commonly the first phase of a bipolar disorder. The depressive episode is characteristically more prolonged, and recovery is more gradual. Today extreme mania and depression are seldom seen in mental hospitals because medications are used to stabilize the patient's emotional condition. But not all who suffer this condition are responsive to medication, and symptoms sometimes appear in spite of this treatment.

VIEWS OF DEPRESSIVE DISORDERS. Heredity is a major consideration in the biological view of depressive disorders. Studies of identical twins and adopted children support this outlook. Identical twins show similarity in depression. Neither or both members tend to be susceptible. Adopted children who display mood disorders tend to have biological parents with these disorders (Wender, Kety, Rosenthal, Schulsinger, Ortmann, & Lunde, 1986). Evidence for a neuropsychological factor is found in the rhythms of the bipolar disorder. When people suddenly become depressed or euphoric for no apparent reason, internal factors are believed to be at work, linked to brain chemistry. Norepinephrine and serotonin are neurotransmitters involved in arousal, awareness, and cognitive functions, and therefore it is hypothesized that depression may involve a depletion of these substances. In fact, medications that enhance the supply of norepinephrine and serotonin have been found to diminish depression (Schildkraut, Green, & Mooney, 1985).

From the psychoanalytic perspective, a major contributor to the depressive disorder is unconscious anger. This resentment, which cannot be openly expressed, has been turned toward the self, complicating the problem because then the individual experiences anger in both directions, outward and inward. The outward targets of this anger may be responsible for real or imagined rejection in childhood, or they may be deceased people, prompting resentment and anger over the loss (Fenichel, 1982).

The behavioral view is more parsimonious, attributing the reaction to changes in the environment, which no longer offers support for habitual behaviors. Divorce, death, retirement, being fired, reaching menopause, and countless other events result in a loss of reinforcement. The individual ceases to respond, and the related behaviors gradually disappear (Lewinsohn, 1974). The outcome is that other people cease even their normal reactions or they express sympathy, both of which augment a vicious cycle, resulting in less and less responsiveness on the part of the individual. Depression, in the behavioral view, arises through a lack of reinforcement in the environment.

Cognitive theorists also have interpretations of these disorders, especially mood disorders. Focusing on attributional style, one view states that people become depressed because they engage in self-blame, searching for evidence to confirm their worthlessness (Beck, 1976; Beck & Freeman, 1990). In another view, cognitive theorists suggest that the key factor is the individual's perception that events are out of his or her control, a view consistent with the principle of learned helplessness. A depressed person decides that nothing can be done about the situation. These two views are hardly compatible. People should not engage in self-blame, which is the basis of the first theory, if events are uncontrollable, as stated in the second interpretation. As so often happens in psychology, there are research findings to support both views (Benassi, Sweeney, & Dufour, 1988; Sweeney, Anderson, & Bailey, 1986).

Such findings are not surprising for two reasons. There are different types of depression, and different thought processes may be associated with each. Expectation, self-esteem, and explanatory style—optimism or pessimism—are important determinants of mental health, and they may even contribute significantly to physical health (Adler & Matthews, 1994).

SCHIZOPHRENIA

All of the Rosenhan pseudopatients, amid their bold research and note-taking, eventually gained a discharge. Their hospitalizations ranged from 7 to 52 days, with an average of 19 days (Rosenhan, 1973).

Here we find a lesson in the Rosenhan study that is just the opposite of what was intended. It was not evidence against clinical practice. Rather, it was further proof that the diagnostic system works, at least for apparently serious cases (Spitzer, 1975). When the patients feigned abnormality, they were incarcerated. When they abandoned their symptoms, they were discharged. The average hospitalization was 19 days, and the decision to discharge was made some days earlier in each case. When one considers the unpredictability of symptoms in almost any psychiatric disorder, slightly more than two weeks seems to be a reasonable period for a change in diagnosis (Farber, 1975).

Nevertheless, one of the fraudulent patients was hospitalized for almost two months. For someone behaving in a normal fashion, hospitalization for this period could have seemed quite a while.

The pseudopatients faked a disorder known as **schizophrenia**, which includes any of these symptoms: hallucinations, delusions, disorganized speech, disorganized behavior, and lack of responsiveness to the surroundings. Fundamentally it is a distortion of reality. The *hallucinations* are false perceptions, such as seeing images or hearing voices that have no objective basis. The Rosenhan subjects succeeded in their strategy because they made such a firm claim about this characteristic of the schizophrenic condition. They pretended to be having hallucinations. The *delusions* are false beliefs. The delusional person may think that he is the head of the institution in which he is a patient or that he has detected poison in his food. Inappropriate emotional responses also may appear, and incoherent speech is a common characteristic.

However, most schizophrenic people are not wildly crazy, despite suggestions in the mass media. Their condition may not even be noticeable on superficial contact, and it often fluctuates. Sometimes only close observation shows the deficits in thinking (Taylor & Abrams, 1984).

For the pseudopatients in the Rosenhan study, the diagnosis in every case was the same, a psychotic disorder, specifically schizophrenia. This general term, **psychotic disorder,** or *psychosis,* has several different definitions, all indicating a very serious, highly incapacitating mental state, includ-

ing loss of contact with reality, as well as delusions, hallucinations, and other fundamental disturbances (American Psychiatric Association, 1994). In a legal context, this condition is insanity. From a lay perspective, the person is crazy. Schizophrenia is the most widely publicized psychotic reaction, but there are others, including pure delusional disorders, substance-induced psychotic disorders, and those due to a general medical condition, such as thyroid malfunction, infection, or brain injury (Figure 15–9).

SIGNIFICANCE OF THE SYMPTOMS. Schizophrenic symptoms are likely to appear first in adolescence or early adulthood, and they may develop over a long period. This condition is called *chronic schizophrenia,* for the individual has been maladjusted for years, in minor or major ways, and eventually the condition is recognized as schizo-

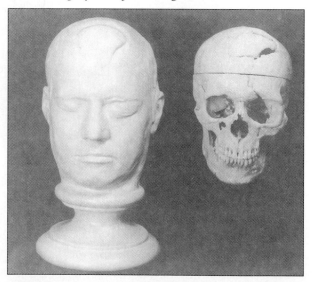

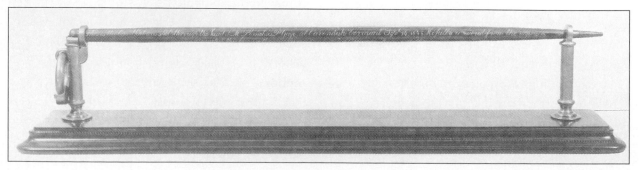

FIGURE 15–9 BRAIN DAMAGE AND PSYCHOTIC DISORDER. On the unlucky 13th of September 1848, an explosion sent a 13-pound, 4-foot crowbar completely through the head of Phineas Gage, a railroad foreman in Vermont. Miraculously, he recovered physically, but afterwards he was extremely obstinate, unrealistic, and emotional. Known earlier as a well-controlled, successful man, his friends simply said he was "no longer Gage" (Harlow, 1869). The crowbar, preserved in a museum, entered under the left cheekbone and exited from the left frontal lobe.

phrenic. In *acute schizophrenia*, the condition appears abruptly, apparently in response to some sudden stress, such as losing one's spouse, job, or life savings. While the origins of schizophrenia are uncertain, the prognosis is most favorable when the symptoms develop suddenly, over a short term.

Schizophrenic symptoms can be described in another twofold category that has significance for prognosis. These categories are positive and negative, which in this context do not indicate good and bad. Instead, **positive symptoms** are behavioral excesses: hallucinations, delusions, incoherent speech, and aggressive behavior. The **negative symptoms** are behavioral deficits: loss of interest in the world, absence of emotional expression, inattention, and lack of speech. Among schizophrenic people, those with positive signs are regarded as having more promise for treatment and recovery than those with negative signs (Andreasen, Flaum, Swayze, Tyrrell, & Arndt, 1990; Fenton & McGlashan, 1991; Figure 15–10).

SUBTYPES OF SCHIZOPHRENIA. In earlier days, classifications included certain subtypes of schizophrenia, now not widely emphasized. Some people show the *disorganized type,* displaying disorganized behavior, disorganized speech, and inappropriate feelings in certain situations. When not completely immobile for long periods of time,

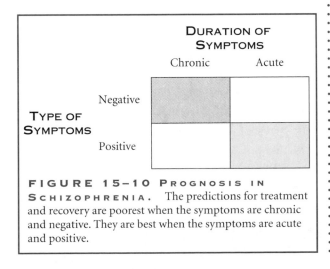

FIGURE 15–10 PROGNOSIS IN SCHIZOPHRENIA. The predictions for treatment and recovery are poorest when the symptoms are chronic and negative. They are best when the symptoms are acute and positive.

the *catatonic type* may endlessly repeat certain gestures, facial expressions, or words, often in a highly excitable, even violent manner. Today the catatonic condition is viewed as a motor dysfunction occurring in diverse psychiatric problems, sometimes associated with medications prescribed for other symptoms (Rogers, 1991). For many people with schizophrenia, the diagnosis is *undifferentiated type* because the symptoms cannot be readily classified or represent some mixture of other types.

The *paranoid type* of schizophrenia is usually the most difficult to diagnose because there is no disorganization or catatonia; instead, the individual speaks quite lucidly and convincingly, often about a central theme. On closer inspection, it may become clear that the theme is based on irrational premises. These premises may involve delusions of persecution, in which the person wrongly believes that people are trying to harm him. Or they may involve delusions of grandeur, in which he believes himself to be an extraordinarily important person.

Regardless of the specific symptoms and subtypes of schizophrenia, the Rosenhan research demonstrated a humanitarian dimension in our psychiatric services. *All* of the pseudopatients were hospitalized. When someone requests or seems to need hospitalization, that condition is taken very seriously. Hence, the admitting officers in the Rosenhan study cannot be judged too harshly. The appearance of the pseudopatients at the hospital door was certainly an implicit sign that they were seeking help. Things are as they should be—proof of a condition dangerous to oneself or others normally is not required for admission to a hospital (Blair, 1973).

DANGER OF LABELS. In all instances except one, the Rosenhan pseudopatients were discharged with the diagnosis *schizophrenia in remission,* indicating that the symptoms somehow had disappeared without treatment. This label, contrary to what one might hope, does not mean that the person is cured or has recovered. It simply indicates that no schizophrenic symptoms are currently present, and here we encounter another lesson from the Rosenhan study: the dangers of psychiatric labeling.

The most disconcerting finding in this research is that this label would have stayed with the patients, indicating that they were or had been schizophrenic, psychotic, or whatever label one prefers. It undoubtedly would have influenced others' reactions to them in their later lives had they not used pseudonyms. Sometimes it was significant on the ward, where normal behavior was wrongly interpreted to coincide with the diagnostic label. One would hope instead that the early diagnosis would have been modified in accordance with later evidence or that it might have been a deferred diagnosis, recognizing that the early symptoms were unclear (Farber, 1975).

In fairness to the professionals in the Rosenhan study, schizophrenia in remission is relatively rare as a discharge diagnosis. Most patients are still disturbed when released from the hospital, allowed to go home under outpatient care, with the use of medication, accompanied by family or friends. Being disturbed does not necessarily require further hospitalization, just as physical illness does not imply that hospitalization is necessary. In this sense, the discharge diagnosis of schizophrenia in remission is more understandable.

SEARCH FOR CAUSES. What makes people suddenly leave the world of accepted reality and enter one of their own making? The frank answer is that we do not yet know. This question is one of the most puzzling of all in clinical psychology. Significant progress may occur only when it is recognized that schizophrenia, as the term is currently employed, may represent not one but a wide variety of brain disorders. On this basis, different investigators, all studying different aspects of schizophrenia, may in fact be studying quite different illnesses (Heinrichs, 1993).

To describe how various factors interact in psychotic disorders, psychologists often refer to a *diathesis-stress model.* This rather imposing label can be readily understood, for *diathesis* simply means an inherited predisposition to a certain disease. The meaning of *stress* is obvious. Thus, the **diathesis-stress model** states that the origins of schizophrenia, or other *serious* mental disorders, lie in a combination of factors including, on the one hand, a genetic predisposition and, on the other hand, stressful environmental conditions that cause this predisposition to become manifest. An individual with a marked hereditary predisposition may show a schizophrenic reaction under relatively mild environmental pressures; a person without this genetic potential may not show schizophrenia even in highly adverse circumstances. In a favorable setting, neither person will manifest the disorder (Monroe & Simons, 1991).

In this model, the genetic factors are specific to the disorder; the environmental factors are not specific. The environmental stress is common to many types of adjustment problems (Fowles, 1992).

There is substantial evidence that heredity plays a role, especially in schizophrenia, as supported by studies of identical and fraternal twins. Since identical twins have the same inheritance, schizophrenic reactions, if based on heredity, should show a higher correspondence than in fraternal twins. A number of studies support this conclusion. When one twin experiences a schizophrenic condition, the chances of the other twin becoming schizophrenic are approximately five times greater for identical than for fraternal twins (Gottesman & Shields, 1966; Table 15–5). In schizophrenic and nonschizophrenic twins, there are also marked differences in the development of subcortical brain areas (Torrey, Bowler, Taylor, & Gottesman, 1994).

COUNTRY	IDENTICAL TWINS		FRATERNAL TWINS	
	NUMBER OF PAIRS	PERCENT BOTH SCHIZOPHRENIC	NUMBER OF PAIRS	PERCENT BOTH SCHIZOPHRENIC
United States	174	69	296	11
United Kingdom	37	65	60	13
Sweden	11	64	27	15
United States	41	61	53	13
Japan	55	60	11	18
Germany	19	58	13	0
United Kingdom	24	42	33	9
Denmark	7	29	31	6
Norway	8	25	12	17
Weighted average		62		12

TABLE 15–5 TWINS AND SCHIZOPHRENIA. This investigation summarized the results of many twin studies throughout the world. For all countries, the percentage of instances in which both twins were schizophrenic was much larger for identical than for fraternal pairs, showing the influence of genetic factors (Gottsman & Shields, 1966, 1982).

Further hereditary evidence comes from foster children adopted shortly after birth, some having a biological parent diagnosed as schizophrenic and others with apparently normal parents. In these cases, the rate of schizophrenia or borderline schizophrenia is significantly higher for the children having a biological parent diagnosed as schizophrenic. Since both groups have foster parents with apparently comparable childrearing methods, the difference in schizophrenic reactions seems to suggest an inherited condition (de Marchi, 1991). However, the mode of inheritance of schizophrenia is still not understood (Baron, 1986; Knight, Knight, & Unguari, 1992).

From a neurophysiological perspective, it is postulated that dopamine, a neurotransmitter involved in brain arousal and motor activity, may play a key role in schizophrenia. According to the **dopamine hypothesis,** a schizophrenic condition is caused by unusually high levels of dopamine or is the result of a brain unusually responsive to normal amounts of this neurotransmitter. Evidence for this hypothesis is found in cases of overdoses with amphetamines, which stimulate dopamine activity. Even in normal individuals, sufficient quantities of amphetamines can provoke a psychoticlike reaction. Similarly, minimal injections of a stimulant that produces dopamine have prompted temporary but increased schizophrenic symptoms in people who are mildly schizophrenic already (Davis, 1974). Drugs known to block dopamine have been effective in reducing schizophrenic symptoms (McGeer & McGeer, 1980). In addition, postmortem studies and brain scans support the dopamine hypothesis (Davis, Kahn, Ko, & Davidson, 1991). Collectively, these investigations have resulted in steady progress in understanding the neurobiology of dopamine systems, but it still has not been demonstrated that dopamine itself is a fundamental cause of schizophrenia (Healy, 1991).

Brain scans and imaging techniques capable of revealing brain structure and function have added biochemical evidence (Andreasen, 1988). With regard to structure, they show a degeneration of neural tissue in the cerebral cortex of people diagnosed with schizophrenia, most prominent in those with long-standing schizophrenic symptoms (Jernigan et al., 1991). In function, they show diminished activity in the brains of people with schizophrenia, compared with normal brains, especially in the frontal lobes (Weinberger & Kleinman, 1986). Whether a cause or a consequence, such defects coincide with what might be expected in this disorder.

Investigators concerned with environmental influences regard many of these studies quite differently. In the identical-twin studies, for example, they point out that when one twin is schizophrenic, the other is not inevitably schizophrenic, although their inherited structures are exactly the same. Similarly, some foster children born to normal parents develop borderline schizophrenic reactions. Schizophrenia may occur through recessive genes, but child-rearing practices and the context of the schizophrenic behavior also may be highly influential factors.

Within the family, difficulties arise when the child and parents are unsuccessful in communicating with one another. This problem is viewed broadly as **communicative deviance,** in which the parents criticize or ignore the child, contradict themselves, or otherwise communicate in an unintelligible fashion. A review of almost three decades of research on the family environment and psychopathology has provided some support for this viewpoint, showing that disturbances among family members are associated with schizophrenic and affective disorders in the offspring (Goldstein, 1988).

Research has shown, furthermore, that relapse into a schizophrenic condition is distinctly related to emotion in a family. The degree to which the family expresses hostility to and overinvolvement with a former patient is called **expressed emotion** (Hooley, 1985). Patients who return to a home with high expressed emotion are several times more likely to relapse than those who return to a home without critical or overly involved family members (Leff & Vaughn, 1981).

Poverty is a related condition. Many studies have demonstrated that the greater the poverty and population density, the greater is the incidence of schizophrenia. Two causal interpretations seem involved. According to one view, lower-class com-munities engender schizophrenia through frustration and social disorganization. According to another, schizophrenic individuals migrate to impoverished urban areas as part of a process of social selection. In either case, poverty involves stress, and exposure to stress is regarded by many investigators as an important contributor to this disorder (Coyne & Downey, 1991).

In summary, hereditary, biochemical, and environmental factors all appear influential, again illustrating the theme of the multiple bases of behavior. Diverse factors *combine* in various ways to produce a psychotic condition (Gallagher, Jones, & Barakat, 1987). The current view is that genetic factors may play a significant predisposing role while environmental or biological factors serve as precipitating events.

❧

PERSONALITY DISORDERS

The pseudopatients in the Rosenhan study attempted to portray a schizophrenic condition. They succeeded in this deceit because their chief symptom was a concern about another reality, a claim that could not be contradicted by objective evidence. They heard voices that no one else could hear. For most people in our society, such voices would be a source of serious personal discomfort.

At the beginning of this chapter, two criteria were cited as defining maladjustment: personal discomfort and socially disruptive behavior. We now turn to socially disruptive behavior, which also exists on a continuum.

The **personality disorder** is a persistent and inflexible pattern of behavior that deviates from cultural expectations and, stable over the years, results in distress for colleagues and associates, as well as for the afflicted individual. People with this disorder wear out their relationships with others by their relentless and excessive demands. They are recognized for the havoc and exasperation they cause others, more than for their own sense of distress.

They are considered in several subcategories, three of which illustrate the inflexibility of the established pattern.

ANTISOCIAL PERSONALITY DISORDER.

The essential feature of the **antisocial personality disorder** is a chronic disregard for social order and legal restraints. The individual tends to violate the rights of others in some significant way. In earlier days, this individual was called a *psychopath* or *sociopath*. For this diagnosis, the individual must be at least 18 years of age. Otherwise the problem is considered a chronic disorder of childhood, or it is not yet of sufficient duration to be regarded as a personality disorder.

Among men, in whom the antisocial personality disorder is more common, the typical early signs include persistent lying, thefts, vandalism, fighting, truancy, and low school achievement. In adult life, an important symptom is the inability to sustain a consistent work record, evident in unemployment, absenteeism, and departure from the job without notice, much like the truancy and poor school performance of earlier years. Antisocial personalities may be likable on superficial contact and may hold important positions at work. In such cases, the problem usually has not been sufficiently severe to interfere with the necessary schooling.

BORDERLINE PERSONALITY DISORDER.

An individual with the diagnosis of **borderline personality disorder** usually demontrates instability in self-image, mood, and personal relationships, sometimes showing characteristics close to schizophrenic and mood disorders, prompting the term *borderline*. For brief periods the person may seem out of contact with reality, but the hallmark is instability—sudden, dramatic shifts in regard for others. A new acquaintance is viewed as a supportive, caregiving person and then abruptly considered cruelly punitive. An old lover or friend is idealized and romanticized one moment, criticized and slandered the next. Often the intense emotional displays have no obvious external cause.

People with this disorder are potentially self-damaging. They may impulsively engage in pathological gambling, unsafe sex, careless driving, or binge eating. Recurrent suicidal gestures or self-mutilation may occur, initiated as an effort to avoid separation or abandonment, real or imagined, from someone perceived as important to them.

NARCISSISTIC PERSONALITY DISORDER.

According to a Greek myth, Narcissus fell in love with himself (Figure 15–11). Unable to fall in

FIGURE 15–11 NARCISSISTIC PERSONALITY DISORDER. Gazing too fondly at his own reflection, Narcissus thereby gave his name to a personality disorder. It is characterized by a sense of self-importance and a strong need for admiration from others.

love with the beautiful nymph Echo, he fell in love instead with his own image reflected in a pool of water. Individuals with a **narcissistic personality disorder** have experienced a similar fate; they are intensely focused on themselves. Unable to take the perspective of another person, they have instead a sense of entitlement, demanding privileges yet denying them to others. As a result, they fail to form mature and satisfying relationships with coworkers and other colleagues.

A key element in the narcissistic personality disorder is an exaggerated concern over how one appears to others. Guided by their wish to impress others, such persons are more concerned with their image and importance than with how they and others feel. Even with a distinguished record of achievements and successes, they persistently seek attention and approval from others (Lowen, 1983).

Among all psychiatric classifications, personality disorders of all types are commonly misdiagnosed, partly because they are not well understood, partly because the subtypes may overlap. Furthermore, the characteristics central to personality disorders clearly exist on a continuum, from mild expressions to pathological extremes. The gentler expressions are present in normal or slightly eccentric individuals. The clinician's judgment of the duration, frequency, and intensity of impairment is a critical factor in the diagnosis.

VIEWS OF CAUSAL FACTORS. As in schizophrenia, one set of causal factors may lie in the individual's genetic background. Adopted children whose mothers have been diagnosed as antisocial personalities, in comparison with adopted control children, show a significantly higher rate of antisocial behavior, despite leaving the mother in infancy (Crowe, 1974). Underactivity of the nervous system may be involved. Antisocial personalities, in terms of brain function, apparently are not as readily aroused as more normal individuals. They are uniformly slower in all sorts of reaction time, which is a mea-

sure of arousability (Pfeiffer & Maltzman, 1974). Consequently, such people may engage in actions that yield more than normal excitation.

Family structure may be an influential factor, especially when no other adequate social attachments are available to the developing personality. If the parents and others are rejecting or neglecting, sometimes the young person uses antisocial behavior to gain attention (Loeber & Dishion, 1983).

Delinquent and criminal behaviors are not confined to antisocial personalities. People in any condition may transgress against society.

The causes of the borderline and narcissistic disorders are also far from understood. Learning appears to be significantly involved in the former condition because fears of abandonment or rejection by others are so prominent. For the latter, the environment also may play a significant role, for this disorder seems to be increasing in recent years. Some writers have suggested that Western culture, with its emphasis on success, individualism, and power, encourages the narcissistic personality disorder (Lasch, 1978; Lowen, 1983).

• ADJUSTMENT AND CULTURE •

After the pseudopatients were released from the hospital, all was not quiet for long in psychiatric admissions offices. David Rosenhan announced another investigation. Within three months, fraudulent people would try again to gain admission to one of the twelve hospitals in the original research. This time Rosenhan was giving the staffs a clear warning. Could they detect the frauds? Rosenhan called this part of his research the "challenge study."

Like their predecessors, these pseudopatients would feign certain symptoms. Clearly, they needed to display behaviors deemed abnormal or deviant in our culture, and here we return to the issue considered at the beginning of this chapter: What is abnormal? There we considered statistical and clinical judgments and the dual criteria of personal discomfort and socially disruptive behavior. Here, at the close of this chapter, we recognize a broader determining factor—the influence of culture.

Suppose the pediatrician in the admissions office claimed intense anxiety about his penis receding into his body, thereby causing his death. Would he have been accepted for psychiatric treatment? The answer probably would depend on the amount of anxiety expressed—unless the examiner were someone with experience in Asian cultures. This condition, not considered a mental disorder in this country, is included in the *Chinese Classification of Mental Disorders*. Called *koro*, it is known by various local terms throughout southern and eastern Asia (American Psychiatric Association, 1994).

Suppose the pseudopatient who was a college student claimed that her brain was fatigued. This malady, *brain fag*, arising from too much thinking, might well elicit psychiatric attention in West Africa but perhaps not so readily in the United States. Similarly, *taijin kyofusho* is a distinctive Japanese phobia that one's body parts are offensive in form, odor, or movement. Included in the Japanese diagnostic system, it resembles our social phobia in certain ways; at the same time, this comparison shows that concepts of normal and abnormal are inevitably culture bound.

∾

ASSESSING ADJUSTMENT

Suppose you are in a restaurant and someone nearby protests against the food. He complains loudly and then hurls his fork across the room. Still upset with the menu, he throws himself on the floor, pounding his fists. Tears come to his eyes, and he begins to shout. What do you think of *his* behavior? You regard it as abnormal—until you find out that this patron is two years old.

When a clinician ponders any psychological disorder, two questions came immediately to mind: What is the person's age? And gender? No

statement about diagnosis or prognosis can ignore these factors.

Today, with greater awareness of cultural diversity, a third characteristic becomes relevant immediately: cultural background. To understand the significance of all of these factors—culture, age, and gender—the following discussion considers two additional psychological disorders. The aim is to show that what is deviant in one culture, at one age, or for one gender is not necessarily deviant for another.

SUBSTANCE-RELATED DISORDERS. Cultures around the world vary widely in the degree to which the consumption of psychoactive substances is regarded as abnormal or illegal. A **psychoactive substance** alters the mental processes in some marked way, chiefly by depressing or stimulating activity in the central nervous system or by producing alterations in perception.

The chief feature in *substance dependence* is the chronic inability to regulate consumption of a drug, medication, or toxin—resulting in disturbances in thought, behavior, and biological functioning. Caffeine dependency is not included, chiefly because few heavy coffee drinkers have difficulty switching to substitutes (Figure 15–12).

SOURCE	CAFFEINE	
Coffee, brewed, 6 oz	100 mg	
Coffee, instant, 6 oz	65 mg	
Soda, caffeinated, 12 oz	45 mg	
Tea, 6 oz	40 mg	
Analgesic, 1 tablet	35 mg	
Chocolate, 1 bar	5 mg	

FIGURE 15–12 CULTURE AND CAFFEINE. Throughout the world, caffeine is the most widely consumed psychoactive drug. The average intake in developing countries is less than 50 milligrams per day, but in Sweden and England the average exceeds 400 milligrams per day.

All other substance-related disorders fall into the category of *substance abuse,* a residual category that does not involve dependency. Someone binges wildly on a particular substance every few weekends; someone else continues drinking alcohol despite a warning about damage to the liver. Both are symptoms of substance abuse but there is no clear dependency (American Psychiatric Association, 1994).

Some social groups, such as Muslims, show a low incidence of alcoholism because this substance is forbidden in their society; others, including large populations in Western nations, show high rates. In Asian cultures, alcohol-related disorders are relatively infrequent, due partly to physiological factors. In Chinese, Japanese, and Korean populations, a biochemical predisposition sometimes operates against alcohol consumption by producing adverse physiological reactions, such as heart palpitations and a flushed skin condition (American Psychiatric Association, 1994).

Age plays a role in alcoholism throughout the world. Consumption is highest among people between 18 and 30 to 40 years old, a condition that holds for all mood-altering substances. After middle age, and especially among elderly people, biological changes result in decreased consumption. Greater susceptibility to alcohol's depressant effects causes more severe intoxication, thereby creating related physiological problems (American Psychiatric Association, 1994).

Gender differences in alcoholism are readily evident among young people. In the United States, they show a ratio of males to females reaching 5 to 1. However, the ratio changes substantially at older ages, for women begin drinking more heavily later in life. Incidentally, due to their lower percentage of body water and lower metabolic rate for alcohol, they tend to acquire a higher blood alcohol concentration than do men and therefore are at greater risk for health-related consequences (American Psychiatric Association, 1994).

SEXUAL DISORDERS. Sexual activities also vary widely depending on culture, age, and gender. Certain modes of satisfaction, infrequent in one population, may become highly significant in another or for subgroups or individuals.

Disturbances in the normal sexual response cycle, including sexual desire and psychophysiological changes, are the defining characteristics of **sexual dysfunction.** Typically, there is a disturbance in both respects, the sense of pleasure and the physiological activities. This disruption is most evident in men in the form of erectile disorder and premature ejaculation. The chief problem for women is an orgasmic disorder or general lack of responsiveness (Bhugra, 1987).

Judgments about these disorders must consider the person's background. In some societies, sexual responsiveness in the female is considered relatively insignificant; the main concern is fertility. In other cultures, males experience problems which are less frequently encountered in the United States. In India, *dhat* refers to severe anxiety and somatic concerns associated with ejaculation, accompanied by a fear of complete loss of semen (American Psychological Association, 1994). In all cultures, diminished sexual interests are associated with aging, although there are wide individual differences.

The essential feature of a **paraphilia** is sexual attraction to some object or event not normally associated with sexual arousal. The term is derived from *para,* meaning "beyond," and *philia,* indicating a tendency or attraction toward something. There are intense sexual urges or fantasies concerning nonhuman objects, nonconsenting partners, and the suffering or humiliation of some human being. The individual may engage in a variety of these behaviors with a variety of people (Abel & Osborn, 1992). This problem is extremely serious when a nonconsenting partner is involved, adult or child.

When the attachment is to an object, arousing sexual urges or fantasies, the condition is called *fetishism.* Leather items and underwear are common fetishes, although sometimes the attraction is to a smell, sound, or other stimulus. In two paraphilic practices, *sadism* and *masochism,* sexual excitement is attained from delivering and receiving punishment, respectively. Sexual arousal apparently is derived from the total control, or lack of control, over another person, thereby facilitating the expression of various sexual fantasies. The critical legal issue here is the consent or willingness of another adult.

Paraphilic practices that figure prominently in the press involve the display or observation of sex organs, usually by men. In *exhibitionism,* a person obtains sexual gratification by showing his or her organs to others, including strangers. This behavior, is considered an offense in the street. Its counterpart, *voyeurism,* involves sexual pleasure from observing others' sex organs or sexual behavior. Again, peeking without consent invites arrest as a Peeping Tom.

Here again, adjustment is on a continuum, for these reactions clearly relate to normal behaviors. Seeing and being seen are natural aspects of sharing between sexual partners; exhibitionism and voyeurism expand these responses. The dominance and submission of sadists and masochists are outgrowths of the give-and-take basic to sexual intercourse. Even a fetish is an extension of normal behavior, for the focus of the sexual response is broadened to include something in addition to or other than the individual's partner.

For these reasons, the diagnosis of paraphilias across cultures is decidedly complicated. A behavior considered abnormal in one setting may be acceptable elsewhere (Figure 15–13). Gender differences are quite stable, however. Paraphilias everywhere are far more common in men than in women (American Psychiatric Association, 1994).

For the sake of completeness, it should be noted that the *DSM-IV* also includes the extremely rare **gender identity disorder,** a strong desire to be, or insistence that one is, of the opposite sex, apart from any perceived cultural advantage, and a persistent distress about one's own sex or gender role.

FIGURE 15–13 SUBCULTURAL NORMS.   Decisions about abnormality and maladjustment are complicated by subcultural norms. Each year 16 men in this college club, producing a highly regarded musical show, dress in and act the parts of women. This cross-dressing is not considered a paraphilia, called *transvestism,* unless the men obtain sexual excitement from wearing women's clothes. Former club members include John F. Kennedy and Franklin Delano Roosevelt.

Adults with this disorder are preoccupied with the wish to be a member of the other sex. Men with this disorder are three times more common than women and seem to suffer more from peer rejection (Shane & Shane, 1995).

CULTURAL RELATIVISM

During the period of the challenge study offered by David Rosenhan, 193 patients were admitted to the psychiatric ward of the selected teaching and research hospital. Of these, approximately 20% were judged with high confidence by at least one staff member to have been feigning schizophrenic symptoms. How successful was this staff in meeting Rosenhan's challenge? Not very—no Rosenhan pseudopatient sought admission during this interval (Rosenhan, 1973).

This further deception showed once again that assessing psychological disorder is a complex, challenging task. When factors of culture are included, it becomes even more so.

All societies must deal with psychological disorders, and certain behaviors are unacceptable throughout most of the civilized world. These include homicide, rape, theft, arson, treason, and assault and battery, all destructive to the social order. Other behaviors, less aggressive, are regarded quite differently in different societies. Polygamy has been the custom in certain Middle Eastern societies; nakedness is accepted in diverse cultures; and prostitution is practiced openly in many parts of the globe. All these behaviors are considered deviant, if not illegal, in much of contemporary Western society.

The term **cultural relativism** indicates that there are no universal standards for judging many social phenomena. The standards for virtue, beauty, justice, and adjustment are culture-bound; they have a particular meaning in a particular environment.

Behavior considered normal in one society may be regarded as abnormal in another (Figure 15–14).

DIFFERENCES AMONG SUBCULTURES. The marked differences among subcultures, even in the same society, are illustrated by a man from the Ozark Mountains. He received a call from God to preach in his community, and his efforts were received with considerable enthusiasm. Soon he was called by God to a neighboring community, and then to another, and he was warmly received on each occasion. His growing reputation eventually prompted him to accept a call to St. Louis. There he was received with less enthusiasm—and a call by the police, who arrested him for disturbing rush-hour traffic (Slotkin, 1955). Lauded and encouraged in one environment, he was considered deviant and socially disruptive in another.

Hearing voices that no one else can hear, like the Rosenhan pseudopatients, is not a sign of disturbed behavior in all cultures. In some, it may even

FIGURE 15–14 CULTURAL RELATIVISM. The culture plays a critical role in decisions about deviance. Nakedness is not cricket during a match.

be regarded as an honor. A delusion in one society may be a belief in another, and the trance state is regarded very differently in different cultures (Westermeyer, 1987). Such differences emphasize once again that there can be no universal definition of good adjustment and poor adjustment. Anyone stating such a definition is simply expressing a preference for a particular social or ethical order (Smith, 1986; Szasz, 1970).

DIFFERENCES AMONG ERAS. Standards also change from one era to the next within a given culture, especially a highly developed one. Our ideas about nakedness, nonmarital cohabitation, and homosexuality have changed a great deal from those of two generations ago. When compared with the first part of this century, ours seems a very different world indeed. Similarly, our views about what constitutes rape, child abuse, and discrimination are constantly being revised, and there have been continuous efforts to change the grounds for divorce and the insanity plea in legal issues. All such classifications must be tentative, reflecting cultural standards and the tentative nature of knowledge (Sue & Sue, 1987).

The *DSM-IV* is simply a momentary point in an ongoing process, indicating the criteria for our particular era. There is relativity across cultures and also within the same culture over time.

At some future date, the Rosenhan study should be of interest to historians, for the observations of the pseudopatients provided considerable information on life in a twentieth-century mental hospital—the crowded conditions, inadequate medical procedures, and sometimes good, sometimes poor staff–patient relations (Rosenhan, 1973). They showed that many responses of the patients were normal or reasonable reactions to confinement, as they tried to avail themselves of any small opportunity to improve their circumstances: pilfering biscuits from the dining hall, making friendships with the staff, and feigning illness to receive special treatment. Frequent trips to the gymnasium did not necessarily indicate an interest in vigorous exercise. More commonly, they offered a chance for a surreptitious snooze on the soft mats.

The Rosenhan study also may seem a bit puzzling to historians, for it contends that the sane cannot be distinguished from the insane. To demonstrate this point, Rosenhan selected eight accomplices, all allegedly normal. He then selected symptoms that would realistically portray them as abnormal, the voices saying "Empty!" "Hollow!" and "Thud!" Finally, he asserted that all of these accomplices behaved in a normal fashion once they gained admission to the ward. These claims about normal and abnormal may seem a bit incongruous in a study attempting to demonstrate that the two conditions cannot be distinguished from one another.

• SUMMARY •

∾

PROCESS OF ADJUSTMENT

1. Adjustment is a continuous process; individuals constantly strive to satisfy physiological or psychological motives. Adjustment also exists on a continuum from well adjusted to poorly adjusted.
2. An individual can attempt to cope with an adjustment problem in many ways: direct action, cognitive restructuring, relaxation techniques, vigorous exercise, and a sense of humor.
3. Inefficient coping responses include defense mechanisms, which are unconscious means of dealing with anxiety: repression, displacement, denial, and sublimation. Other reactions include lethargy, fantasy, aggression, and regression.

DETERMINING ABNORMALITY

4. The labels for poorly adjusted people have changed considerably with the passage of time, reflecting greater acceptance of the problem, but eventually any label becomes derogatory. The latest diagnostic manual, *DSM-IV*, includes a wide range of classifications.

5. Four common views of maladjustment include: the biological, giving attention to the neurophysiological bases of behavior; the psychoanalytic, emphasizing unconscious processes; the behavioral, focusing on reinforcement in the environment; and the cognitive, pointing to the mental processes responsible for maladaptive behavior.

TYPES OF DISORDERS

6. The various anxiety disorders include: generalized anxiety disorder, in which there are no specific symptoms except anxiety; specific phobia, which involves an incapacitating fear of a harmless object; posttraumatic stress disorder, a reminder of some terrifying event; and obsessive-compulsive disorder, with recurrent thoughts and/or actions.

7. In the somatoform disorder, it is assumed that psychological stress has played a role in producing bodily symptoms. The somatization disorder involves multiple complaints often vaguely identified. In the conversion disorder, there is a more specific loss or alteration of a physical function.

8. The various dissociative disorders include: amnesia, which involves pervasive forgetting with no evidence of brain damage; fugue, in which the individual may be discovered far from home with no memory of his or her past; and dissociative identity disorder, a dramatic form of forgetting in which the individual demonstrates various personalities.

9. The mood disorder is associated with emotional turmoil, especially a deep feeling of elation or depression. One form, the major depressive disorder, involves intense feelings of helplessness and disappointment; another is the bipolar disorder, characterized by extreme elation or alternating periods of elation and depression.

10. The chief characteristics of schizophrenia, a psychotic reaction, include hallucinations, delusions, and incoherent speech. The person is out of contact with reality and usually requires hospitalization. Heredity, biochemical, and environmental factors all seem involved in these disorders.

11. In a personality disorder, some trait or set of traits prevents the individual from fulfilling expected social roles. These include the antisocial personality disorder, violating others' rights; the borderline personality disorder, characterized by instability; and the narcissistic personality disorder, preoccupied with the self.

ADJUSTMENT AND CULTURE

12. Substance-related disorders involve the consumption of psychoactive materials in a fashion that interferes with daily life. Sexual disorders are of three types. Sexual dysfunction involves an inhibition of interest or performance in the full sexual response. Paraphilias involve attraction to stimuli not normally part of sexual arousal. In gender identity disorder, a person strongly desires to be a member of the opposite sex.

13. The concept of cultural relativism indicates that certain abstract concepts have meaning only in relation to the standards of a given society. Behavior considered normal in one culture may be regarded as abnormal in another.

• WORKING WITH PSYCHOLOGY •

❧ REVIEW OF KEY CONCEPTS ❧

Process of Adjustment
adjustment

mental health
defense mechanism

repression
suppression

displacement
denial
sublimation
learned helplessness
fantasy
regression

Determining Abnormality
mental illness
neurosis
insanity
pathological gambling

Types of Disorders
generalized anxiety disorder

specific phobia
posttraumatic stress disorder
obsessive-compulsive disorder
somatoform disorder
dissociative amnesia
dissociative fugue
dissociative identity disorder
major depressive disorder
bipolar disorder
schizophrenia
psychotic disorder
positive symptoms
negative symptoms
diathesis-stress model

dopamine hypothesis
communicative deviance
expressed emotion
personality disorder
antisocial personality disorder
borderline personality disorder
narcissistic personality disorder

Adjustment and Culture
psychoactive substance
sexual dysfunction
paraphilia
gender identity disorder
cultural relativism

❧ CLASS DISCUSSION/CRITICAL THINKING ❧

A NARRATIVE TWIST

Imagine that the Rosenhan study were repeated today using the same symptoms. Would the rate of admission to the hospitals be the same or different? Why? In reaching a decision, consider the current practices in mental health centers, role of the insurance industry, and possible influence of Rosenhan's research on subsequent psychiatric admissions. Then imagine that today's pseudopatients might falsely claim instead to be victims of childhood sexual abuse. Would this approach influence the outcome of the study? Explain the reasons for your answer. ❧

TOPICAL QUESTIONS

• *Process of Adjustment.* Should

political and social activists, leading marches and sit-ins and organizing dissent, be considered maladjusted for their socially disruptive behavior? Explain your view. Think about Walter Mitty, who regularly resorted to fantasy simply to make daily life a bit more pleasant, imagining himself in all sorts of heroic situations while accomplishing mundane tasks. Does this response solve problems, obscure them, or in fact create problems? Explain how it may play a role in any of these outcomes.

• *Determining Abnormality.* Suppose a woman snores mildly at night, but it significantly disrupts the sleep of her bedtime companion. If she seeks treatment for this problem, which does not disturb her, should

she be eligible for insurance coverage? Is her snoring a significantly abnormal condition to warrant medical reimbursement?

• *Types of Disorders.* Speculate on some specific diagnostic problem underlying the development of the *DSM-IV*, such as the criteria for a certain phobia or somatoform disorder. Which criteria of maladjustment should be regarded as most significant? Why? In view of social biases and cultural norms, which interest groups, if any, should be given special consideration?

• *Adjustment and Culture.* How does cultural relativism play a role in the ratings of films as PG, R, and X? Are some criteria universal, pertaining to all cultures? Explain your view.

❧ TOPICS OF RELATED INTEREST ❧

Methods of dealing with stress are described in connection with emotion (11). Repression is discussed in several other contexts: memory

(8), motivation (10), personality (14), and therapy (16). Aggression is considered with regard to emotion (11). The systems of psychol-

ogy relevant to diagnostic perspectives have been presented on several occasions, beginning in the opening chapter (1).

ENTERING THERAPY

INSIGHT THERAPIES
Traditional Psychoanalysis
Humanistic Approach
Cognitive Therapy
The Group Context

BEHAVIOR THERAPIES
Classical Conditioning Methods
Operant Conditioning Methods
Observational Learning

BIOMEDICAL THERAPIES
Natural Body Therapies
Electroshock and Psychosurgery
Psychotherapeutic Drugs

EVALUATING THERAPY
Problems in Evaluation
Effectiveness of Therapy

MENTAL HEALTH MOVEMENTS
Institutional Treatment
Preventive Mental Health

16
THERAPY

❧

MACK GREETED THE GUESTS IN HEARTY FASHION—
SHAKING HANDS, SMILING, AND MAKING SMALL
TALK, BEHAVING WITH THE CONFIDENCE THAT
suited his role for the evening, master of ceremonies. The annual school
banquet was a celebration for all, including city officials, leaders from
rival institutions, and other dignitaries.

Mack's school achievements made him a natural choice for this honor.
Admired as a scholar and athlete, he was known to everyone.

The hall filled slowly at first, and Mack chatted easily. As the crowd
increased, he felt a bit warm, perhaps because of the increased heat in
the room. While talking and shaking hands, he began to perspire.
After another ten minutes, he suddenly found himself feeling very hot
indeed. In fact, he could not stop the sweat dripping from his forehead and
chest.

As master of ceremonies, he was extremely embarrassed. A few moments
later he left the hall—and his sweating stopped almost immediately.

Mack could not remember the rest of the evening in any detail. He returned to the banquet and somehow managed his part adequately. But he certainly did remember his sweating, which first became a problem that night when he was sixteen years old. Afterward, he sweated profusely on almost every formal social occasion.

Mack considered this problem a personal failing. He felt that others, if they knew, would regard it in the same way. He decided to deal with it directly, just as he had done with other challenges in his life. Determined that sweating would not deter him from whatever he wanted to do, Mack involved himself in more and more formal social situations, playing a prominent role, wearing coat and tie, even taking courses in public speaking (Moylan & Dadds, 1992).

Mack's story serves well as the narrative for this chapter because it represents many people who enter therapy, so often concerned with social issues. But there are other reasons too. His effort to deal with this problem in therapy took some surprising turns. Furthermore, it required more than one form of therapy, which is often the nature of effective treatment. Finally, it offers comparisons with other people who sought treatment for the same problem.

In psychology, **therapy** includes any procedure for alleviating a personal problem, whether that problem is emotional, behavioral, or physical, and it also includes any procedure for achieving personal growth. Therapy is a growth-oriented process, and growth can occur in many ways. There are now over 300 different kinds of therapy in the United States (Karasau, 1986; May, 1987).

These highly diverse methods can be considered in three broad categories, evident in the chapter outline: insight therapies, behavior therapies, and biomedical therapies. Before turning to them, we begin with the question of entering therapy. At the end of the chapter, we conclude with the issues of evaluating therapy and mental health movements.

Through *insight therapies,* troubled people alleviate personal problems by discussing the ways they think and feel about them. The first noted consumer of this kind of therapy, Anna O., working with Sigmund Freud and a colleague, accidentally inaugurated this method by chatting with her therapist after her usual hypnotherapy session. At first she referred to it as *chimney sweeping,* a metaphor expressing the idea that she was entering deep, dark, inaccessible places, trying to clear up things. Later, she and Freud gave it a more dignified colloquial name, the *talking cure,* meaning that discussing problems seemed to aid in their solution.

The *behavior therapies* include methods for changing emotional reactions and bad habits through principles of classical and operant conditioning. In colloquial terms, these therapies are called the *carrot-and-stick approach,* for they are loosely described as involving rewards and punishments. More accurately, reinforcement principles are used to develop desirable responses and eliminate undesirable ones.

The premise in the *biomedical therapies* is that disease or psychological maladjustment can be treated by altering the person's physiological makeup. This approach is largely the traditional medical perspective. It brings about a change in the person's body, often an electrochemical change, and therefore is sometimes called the *body cure.*

What, then, is psychotherapy? The term **psychotherapy** is a loose reference to a variety of treatments for mental and physical disorders (Wolman, 1989). Changes in therapy over the years have produced this vague definition. Does it refer only to the insight therapies, its original meaning? Does it now include behavior therapies, which generally developed later? Should it include any treatment with a psychological intent? With these unanswered questions in mind, its usage is generally avoided in this chapter.

• ENTERING THERAPY •

Despite his direct efforts to cope with his excessive sweating, Mack's problem did not disappear or even diminish appreciably. Four years later, during his third year in college, it was still very much with him, and Mack decided it might hinder his future career. Thus, 20-year-old Mack took what was for him a bold step in a different direction. He entered therapy (Moylan & Dadds, 1992).

All sorts of people enter therapy for all sorts of day-to-day problems—advancement at work, embarrassing habits, family matters, and lack of self-confidence, as well as more serious difficulties. It is surprising how many people think they are all alone with a problem that so many others, in their private lives, also share.

At the time, Mack thought his difficulty was merely extensive sweating. In fact, he was experiencing an anxiety disorder, as described in the previous chapter. These disorders are the most common emotional problems in the United States and the chief reason people enter therapy (Robins & Regier, 1991). Specifically, Mack was experiencing a *social phobia*, which is a fear of embarrassment or humiliation in the presence of other people, usually beginning in adolescence, when the young person becomes more aware of interpersonal interests.

In selecting a therapist, people may choose among professionals with different specializations.

Therefore, it is wise to engage in some exploratory effort first, just as you would in buying an automobile. People who are successful in treatment often consult and work with a few different therapists before making a successful connection with one of them. These therapists may include clinical psychologists, psychiatrists, and social workers, as well as counselors of all sorts. Mack entered therapy through the health services at his university.

Insurance companies may play a role in the selection process, deciding which activities will be insured, whom the patient may seek as a therapist, and how many sessions will be approved for reimbursement. The company may approve only a few visits—the number deemed adequate to deal with an emergency—although the person might derive long-term preventive benefit from many more sessions. However, compared with 20 years ago, more policies today cover *some* therapy sessions. With these new policies and the desire for efficiency in our fast-paced society, briefer treatment is becoming popular. In **brief therapy**, the therapist and person seeking assistance plan on a sequence of no more than a half dozen sessions.

Before entering therapy, two characteristics of the therapeutic process should be understood. First, the individual in therapy can say whatever comes to mind, whatever seems helpful, without fear of reprisal. This condition, **confidential communication,** means that the therapist will not reveal the contents, or even the general nature of the topics, to anyone. They are private matters, strictly between therapist and patient. Except when criminal or suicidal behavior may be involved, the therapist has the obligation to withhold this information from everyone.

This condition, deemed essential for the treatment process, may place an unusual burden on the therapist. A patient with the potential for sexual abuse, for example, raises a difficult ethical issue. The therapist has an allegiance to that patient and also a responsibility to society. Guidelines have been developed to assist therapists in dealing with the complexities of such cases (Somberg, Stone, & Claiborn, 1993; Woody, 1990).

Eventually, a person in therapy considers terminating the process—because the problem has been alleviated, the procedure is unsuccessful, or further expenditures are impossible. But more complex reasons for terminating therapy involve the concept of resistance.

Especially in the psychoanalytic sense, **resistance** is any interference with the progress of treatment by the patient. In various ways, the patient undermines efforts to reach the goal for which he or she entered therapy in the first place. The person avoids discussing important topics, misses appointments, ignores homework assignments, forgets to take medication, and so forth. According to the concept of resistance, now recognized in all sorts of therapies, the person is evading the real issues and their solutions because confronting them seems more threatening than the discomfort of day-to-day living. Dealing with the patient's resistance is therefore a major therapeutic task.

Mack's therapist eventually showed special skill in this regard, for Mack was highly resistant to the behavior therapy with which his treatment began. Mack's lack of success with that treatment underscores a basic theme in this chapter: Different treatments may be effective with different people, even among those experiencing similar problems. That failure, discussed later, lasted throughout the first five weeks of Mack's treatment, after which his therapist turned from behavior therapy to an insight therapy.

• INSIGHT THERAPIES •

The basic processes in **insight therapy** are conversations aimed at enabling the troubled individual to achieve increased self-

understanding and thereby to deal more effectively with these problems. These therapies involve different kinds of insight, intellectual and emotional, but the common theme is that increased awareness obtained through verbal interactions can contribute to beneficial changes in adjustment. The person's interaction with the therapist is therefore the critical factor.

Throughout all of the early therapy sessions, Mack explained that the perspiration appeared only on his body, neck, and forehead. He stoutly denied experiencing any anxiety. That arose, he explained, only *after* he started sweating. Then he did feel anxious because he was out of control.

Mack also explained that he always wanted to be in *complete* control. He feared being vulnerable or dependent; these feelings were a weakness he could not accept. Instead, he aimed to excel in all spheres, a goal that certainly contributed to his distinguished career in school. Mack was in good health, and a checkup showed no obvious physical reason for his problem. His most outstanding traits were a highly rational style and some difficulty discussing emotionally toned topics (Moylan & Dadds, 1992).

TRADITIONAL PSYCHOANALYSIS

Among all forms of psychological therapy, the most renowned is probably psychoanalysis. Its founder, Sigmund Freud, confessed that his real interest in therapy lay not in curing patients but in understanding their problems. Through private practice, he earned a living and satisfied his curiosity (Freud, 1927).

His method of therapy, called **psychoanalysis,** is an attempt to help the patient discover and reinterpret unconscious conflicts, usually dating from childhood, chiefly through three processes—free association, transference, and interpretation. All aim at achieving insight by lifting the veil of repression, thereby helping the person to deal more effectively with long-forgotten emotional concerns.

FREE ASSOCIATION. In traditional psychoanalysis, the person lies on a couch while the therapist, called an *analyst,* remains unobtrusively nearby, encouraging that person to say anything that comes to mind, just as it occurs. The basic idea is that the patient is more relaxed when lying down and therefore more likely to express deeper thoughts and feelings, rather than to discuss topics of daily conversation. In this unrestrained flow of ideas, known as **free association,** the patient attempts to reveal all thoughts, no matter how trivial, embarrassing, disrespectful, or illogical they may seem (Figure 16–1).

Through this unrestrained process, with one thought connected to another, the patient is brought to an awareness of his or her unconscious mental life. Recalled and communicated with great difficulty, these intimacies are assumed to be connected in some way with early childhood conflicts.

This task of lying on a couch and saying whatever comes to mind sounds easy, but the person is hard at work attempting to uncover the very thoughts that are most painful. While Mack never entered psychoanalysis, a man called Mr. G did because he too suffered from excessive sweating. It appeared all over his body, including his palms. In daily life, he was a fastidious person, but eventually, lying on an analyst's couch, he talked at length about repugnant ideas—unclean toilets, dirty underclothes, and lice. At one point he suddenly recalled awakening at age five with the fear of having defecated in bed. Instead he discovered that the dark object was a shoe. Soiling himself in any way, he reported, was a constant fear, even as a young man (Dosuzkov, 1975).

TRANSFERENCE. In addition, the analyst encourages **transference,** in which the patient reacts emotionally to the analyst as though the analyst

FIGURE 16–1 FREUD'S COUCH. The couch included a blanket for warmth and a pillow for comfort. Freud sat in the stuffed chair at the head of the couch, out of the person's field of vision.

were someone else, usually a parent or other significant adult in the patient's earlier life. When the patient becomes angry or disappointed with the analyst, and the latter has done nothing to provoke this reaction, these feelings may be the result of transference. The analyst has become a substitute for someone else. The patient's feelings and behavior are appropriate to the other person.

At an emotional point in one psychoanalytic session, a patient told her analyst that she was glad he was not wearing a certain pearl necklace. The analyst suddenly realized that a strong transference was occurring; the patient was responding to this bearded, pipe-smoking figure as though he were her mother. In this emotionally driven, highly distorted view, the woman was behaving as though the conversation were actually taking place with her mother at that moment. According to modern analysts, transference is the most powerful technique in psychoanalysis (Grotstein, 1990).

In the presence of a friendly businessman whom he wanted to impress, Mr. G became anxious and perspired a great deal. He reacted as though this older man were his father, an example of transference outside therapy (Dosuzkov, 1975). By remaining neutral and by avoiding personal biases as far as possible, the analyst facilitates transference. Then, by examining the patient's feelings and behavior in these instances, both the patient and analyst can gain insight into the patient's earlier relations with certain people (Table 16–1).

USE OF INTERPRETATION. In a third technique, called **interpretation,** the analyst provides clarification and suggestions, helping the

---

Patient: I should say what I've got to say and get out of here. I shouldn't be taking up your time. I feel like you couldn't be interested in me if I don't have something important to say. I become very anxious when I can't say something important. I figure you're probably angry with me when I don't keep you interested.

Therapist: But I'm not angry with you for not keeping me interested, and although I'm busy, I enjoy spending the hour with you.

Patient: Well . . . Well, why do I feel this way then? It's the way I always feel . . . like no one is interested in me. I'm always afraid to talk with my teachers for fear that they aren't interested in what I have to say. That's the way it always was with my father. Being a doctor, he was continually on call. If we ever started talking, which was seldom, the phone would always ring and he would have to leave.

Therapist: Then you are reacting to me and your teachers as if we were like your father?

Patient: I guess that's so . . . you know, that's just what I'm doing.

TABLE 16–1 TRANSFERENCE. Note that the therapist's final comment takes the form of a question, not a declaration (Fernald, 1993).

---

patient to evaluate or reconsider the possible significance of events within and outside therapy. The aim is to assist the patient in self-discovery.

Among all the possibilities for interpretation, Freud was most interested in dreams. The actual events of the dream, as noted in the chapter on consciousness, are the *manifest content,* only of minor interest in psychoanalysis. This dream story is regarded as a disguise, hiding the underlying meaning of the dream, the *latent content,* which is unconscious. The aim of dream interpretation is to discover this hidden meaning, usually involving a childhood conflict or wish.

On several occasions Mr. G had a brief dream: "Someone in gray says that a caesarean section will have to be performed." Through dream interpretation in psychoanalysis, it seemed that the latent content of this dream was related to incidents of punishment by his father, represented symbolically as the surgeon. The unconscious issue was the Oedipus complex.

Later, it appeared that Mr. G's sweating was perhaps related to bedwetting, which occurred a great deal during his childhood. By this uncontrollable behavior he disappointed his mother, and he believed he thereby lost her love, again raising the Oedipus issue. In adulthood, his profuse sweating first appeared after his fiancée abruptly left him for another man. Her act perhaps symbolized the perceived loss of his mother's love. He became gloomy and troubled, and then he entered therapy. He spent a relatively short time in psychoanalysis, and his problem of sweating disappeared during this treatment (Dosuzkov, 1975).

In any therapy, information supplied by the patient is given careful consideration. Mack at first described his childhood as very happy. In a later session, he gave quite a different impression. He was a shy child, had difficulty playing with other children, and was enormously embarrassed one day when adults openly commented on his shyness and then left him alone, feeling abandoned. His mother urged him to present himself well to others, and subsequently she enrolled him in speech therapy, drama classes, and debating teams. He described her as someone "upright and strong . . . who never talks of emotions" (Moylan & Dadds, 1992).

INFLUENCE OF CONTEMPORARY PSYCHOANALYSIS. Traditional psychoanalysis is a long process, sometimes requiring three to five sessions per week for several years. It is also a strenuous process, for the patient is struggling to confront traumatic experiences that presumably he or she wants most to avoid. Many practitioners therefore view psychoanalysis as the *only* means for bringing about a thorough personality reorganization, chiefly because it focuses on *unconscious* conflicts, rather than events in conscious awareness. Thus, it is claimed that psychoanalysis can induce changes achieved in no other form of therapy (Brenner, 1987; Richard-Jodoin, 1991).

Partly because of its length, many contemporary practitioners adopt a different approach to this therapy. These modified psychoanalytic procedures, called *psychodynamic therapy*, emphasize drives and motives, but there is less interest in unconscious conflicts dating from childhood and greater concern for current social relationships. Many of these methods are short-term therapies (Pedder, 1990).

In our very different world, one can easily underestimate the magnitude of Freud's accomplishments *in his time.* For many changes in modern life, including those in sex education, childrearing, and clinical practice, as well as attitudes toward criminal behavior and emotional disturbance, Sigmund Freud's contribution was monumental. Particularly when reading secondary reports and English translations of his work, we overlook the highly conservative social, medical, and ethnic practices that defined science in Austria during his life-time (Leupold-Lowenthal, 1991). To have developed his views in that climate of opinion was indeed a singular achievement.

HUMANISTIC APPROACH

In humanistic therapy, the individual rests in a comfortable chair, rather than on a couch. He or she is considered a person, not a patient, and the therapist does not try to use free association, transference, or interpretation. Instead, the events in therapy are determined largely by the person seeking assistance.

The goal of **humanistic therapy** is to assist the individual in achieving personal growth, realized through insights developed by self-confrontation. In normal daily life, personal development is obstructed by encounters with people so occupied with their own desires and frustrations that they hamper one another's ability to gain self-understanding. The appropriate solution, according to humanistic therapy, is to enter an environment fostering greater personal awareness.

CHARACTERISTICS OF PERSON-CENTERED THERAPY. In the United States, the leading approach to humanistic therapy was developed by Carl Rogers. In the early phases of his career, he developed a therapy called *nondirective counseling,* meaning that the counselor did not exert any influence on the therapeutic process. Gradually he realized that the therapist or counselor, simply by personal manner, inevitably influenced the counseling session. He therefore changed the name to *client-centered therapy,* indicating that the therapeutic effort was controlled by the client. And finally, to dispel the suggestion that the individual in therapy was a client and therefore under the direction of someone who renders professional services, Rogers changed the name to *person-centered therapy.*

In **person-centered therapy,** the individual seeking help is regarded as capable of solving his or her own personal problems and therefore of determining the course of therapy. It is the counselor's task to provide a favorable climate for this growth process. Within this climate, the person's *actualizing tendency*—that is, the person's capacity for growth and self-understanding—is released (Rogers, 1961, 1977, 1980).

In creating this therapeutic environment, three characteristics are essential. First, the therapist must be able to sense accurately the individual's feelings and thoughts, a quality known as *empathy.* Empathy means apprehending the state of

mind of someone else but, unlike sympathy, without necessarily feeling the way the other person feels (Figure 16–2). The person-centered counselor also shows *genuineness* of feelings, openly expressing thoughts and attitudes. The opposite of an actor or salesperson, who sometimes must maintain a façade, the person-centered counselor may even demonstrate genuineness through self-disclosure about a highly personal issue such as sweating. The third characteristic is *unconditional positive regard,* which means that the counselor accepts the person no matter how that person thinks, feels, or behaves. Unconditional positive regard is an attitude of warmth and no-strings-attached caring. This coun-

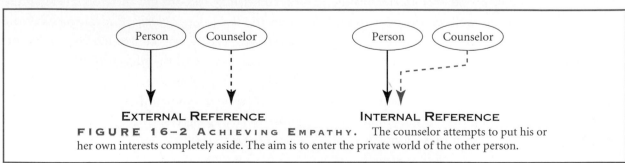

FIGURE 16–2 ACHIEVING EMPATHY. The counselor attempts to put his or her own interests completely aside. The aim is to enter the private world of the other person.

seling climate communicates a belief about the innate capacity and dignity of all human beings (Zimring, 1990).

If Mack had entered person-centered therapy, the effective counselor would have communicated full acceptance of Mack, regardless of how much Mack became embarrassed, odorous, or sweaty. The person-centered counselor would have assumed that Mack, in this emotional climate, could find his own solutions to his problems.

PERSON-CENTERED COUNSELING TECHNIQUES. In addition to these personal qualities, there are several techniques by which this therapeutic environment can be established. For example, the counselor sometimes uses *restatement of content,* rephrasing the person's statements in somewhat different words. In the following session, a 28-year-old man considered himself an outcast, feeling that no one wanted his company:

P (Person)   No, I just ain't no good to anybody, never was, and never will be.

C (Counselor)   Feeling that now, hm? That you're just no good to yourself, no good to anybody . . .

P: Yeah (muttering in low, discouraged voice). That's what this guy I went to town with just the other day told me.

C: This guy that you went to town with really told you that you were no good? Is that what you're saying? Did I get that right? (Rogers, 1967)

Note that the counselor twice simply restated the person's expression, making no effort to interpret the feeling or analyze the problem. His purpose was to show that he understood and accepted the person's reaction.

Similarly, the counselor may assist the person in the *clarification of feelings,* expressing the person's emotional reactions in somewhat clearer form. By this technique, the person learns to identify and accept his feelings more readily. For example, the man described above expressed his feeling of worthlessness. The counselor remarked on this feeling, and the man replied:

P (Person):   I don't care though.

C (Counselor):   You tell yourself you don't care at all, but somehow I guess some part of you cares because some part of you weeps over it (Rogers, 1967).

Note here that the man talked in one way, saying he did not care, and yet behaved in another, by weeping. The counselor merely brought these two manifestations of feelings to the man's attention.

The counselor also uses brief vocalizations as a sign of *active listening,* uttering almost inaudibly "umm-hmm" and "m-hm" to indicate that all is understood and that he or she is thinking *with* the person. This approach was evident in the following session, even when the young man expressed seriously depressive thoughts:

P (Person):   I ain't no good to anybody, or I ain't no good for nothin' . . .

C (Counselor):   M-hm . . . (Waiting for some further response.) (Rogers, 1967)

In summary, the person-centered counselor believes that people have the capacity to solve their own problems. The counselor's primary aim is to honor this self-authority, creating an atmosphere in which people can become the "architects of their own lives" (Bozarth, 1991).

EXISTENTIAL THERAPY. Some humanistic therapists are even more philosophical. They follow an approach known as **existential therapy,** which stresses the need to understand human existence and focuses on the problem of finding meaning in life. This problem of finding meaning arises for several reasons. When our values are challenged, as happens in a fast-changing society, cherished ways must be abandoned, leading to anxiety and uncertainty. Also, every normal adult is aware that he or she will no longer exist at some future time, and this understanding causes anxiety and despair. Furthermore, most of us have the potential to accomplish many things in life, and we must choose among them. In choosing what we want to become, we choose not to become something else, and this awareness brings further anxiety (May, 1981).

The goal in therapy is not to avoid anxiety altogether. Anxiety is part of life; it cannot be eliminated. Instead, existential therapists assist people in accepting anxiety, coping with it directly, and finding meaning through the pain it involves (Figure 16–3).

What meaning do you find in life? Think about the following italicized sentence: *Opportunity is nowhere.* What can you do about this problem? Create a small space after the *w.* Existentialists argue that you have a responsibility to do so: *Opportunity is now here.*

EXISTENTIAL THERAPEUTIC TECHNIQUES. Existential therapists are not clear on the techniques to be used in achieving this goal. For the most part they employ methods from other therapies, especially psychoanalysis. One exception is Viktor Frankl. His fundamental therapy procedure is *paradoxical intention,* which encourages the person to assume, as strongly as possible, the very attitude or feeling that is troublesome. By confronting that feeling directly and regularly in a controlled setting, the person is assisted in gaining control over it (Hill, 1987). Other therapies use this procedure, called **flooding,** in which the individual is continually exposed to an anxiety-producing situation until the feeling finally becomes extinguished.

In flooding, or paradoxical intention, Mack would not struggle against sweating. Rather, he would give it the fullest possible expression, thinking about sweating as much as possible in formal social situations. Eventually this direct effort to sweat should bring about a change of attitude. Mack would cease to fear sweating. He could think of himself as having control over it, and the symptom should disappear.

INFLUENCE OF THE HUMANISTIC APPROACH. The person-centered view contributed significantly to the development of insight therapies during the second half of this century. With its emphasis on the release of growth potential, it has been extended beyond therapy to all sorts of human relationships: athletic endeavors, business negotiations, and creativity as well as classroom instruction (Fernald, 1995). This approach is less effective with people seeking specific advice, reassurance, or even constructive criticism. The

FIGURE 16–3 FINDING MEANING IN LIFE. A prominent, early existentialist, as well as a prisoner in concentration camps in World War II, Viktor Frankl, noted that the prison inmates who found meaning in their suffering most readily endured the hardship. He then formulated this fundamental principle of existentialism: The most basic of all human freedoms is the capacity to "choose one's attitude in a given set of circumstances."

person-centered counselor will not enter into the relationship in these ways.

Existential therapy is chiefly the product of a loosely organized group of European philosophers, some of them therapists. Many have been trained in psychoanalysis, but others have their own viewpoints, with the result that existentialism is not highly systematic. The common bond is a resistance to the highly doctrinaire approach of other methods. The popularity of the person-centered approach is one reason why existentialism has not become a more dominant force among American insight therapies. Another reason is the comparative lack of special methods in existential therapy.

COGNITIVE THERAPY

A person's therapy may begin with one approach and then shift to another; effective therapy often operates in this fashion, as happened in Mack's case. In the early sessions, Mack reported no anxiety prior to his excessive sweating. In his opinion, the key factor was increased body heat. If he could diminish his body temperature at the right time, he might eliminate the problem. Ultimately, however, certain events helped Mack to realize that anxiety *was* involved; then he and his therapist turned to cognitive therapy.

In **cognitive therapy,** it is assumed that adjustment disorders are caused by misunderstandings and misperceptions and that these problems can be resolved by helping people to abandon their erroneous ways of thinking. This approach to insight provides a sharp contrast to the previous therapies. The basic premise is the opposite of that of psychoanalysis, and the basic method is contrary to that of person-centered therapy.

Regarding the premise, psychoanalysis and cognitive therapy both recognize an interaction between thoughts and feelings, but each has a different starting point. Psychoanalysis begins with feelings. The concern is with emotional experiences from childhood that disrupt adult thoughts and behavior. Cognitive therapy begins with illogical thoughts, which cause upset feelings. One cognitive approach in particular, **rational-emotive therapy,** emphasizes that irrational thinking causes emotional disruption and that the solution lies in learning to think logically. In this approach, the therapist participates actively and directly as an instructor, a method that is quite contrary to person-centered therapy, in which the therapist remains in the background as a facilitator.

CONSEQUENCES OF ILLOGICAL THINKING. Rational-emotive therapy was developed by Albert Ellis, a former analyst who decided that psychoanalysis required too much time. After his own difficult early years, Ellis decided that he had to figure things out for himself, which he did, developing a set of prescriptions for everyday life. Basically, Ellis and his followers believe in the rigorous application of the rules of logic, straight thinking, and the scientific method to problems in everyday living. The therapist's first task is to uncover irrational thinking in the patient's experience. Then the therapist urges the patient to adopt more reasonable ways.

A young man came to rational-emotive therapy complaining that he was unhappy because other people did not like him. But the therapist insisted that there was another reason:

P (Patient): Well, why was I unhappy then?

T (Therapist): It's very simple—simple as *A, B, C,* I might say. *A,* in this case, is the fact that these men didn't like you. Let's assume that you observed their attitude correctly and were not merely imagining they didn't like you.

P: I assure you that they didn't. I could see that very clearly.

T: Very well, let's assume they didn't like you and call that *A.* Now *C* is your unhappiness—which we'll definitely have to assume is a fact, since you felt it.

P: Damn right I did!

T: All right then: *A* is the fact that the men didn't like you. *C* is your unhappiness. You see *A* and *C* and you assume that *A*, their not liking you, caused your unhappiness, *C*. But it didn't.

P: It didn't? What did, then?

T: *B* did.

P: What's *B*?

T: *B* is what you said to yourself while you were . . . with those men.

P: What I said to myself? But I didn't say anything.

T: You did. You must have. Now think back to your being with these men; think what you said to yourself; and tell me what it was.

P: Well . . . I . . .

T: Yes?

P: Well, I guess I did say something.

T: I'm sure you did. Now what did you tell yourself when you were with those men?

P: I . . . well, I told myself that it was awful that they didn't like me, and why didn't they like me, and how could they not like me and . . . you know, things like that.

T: Exactly. And that, what you told yourself, was *B*. And it's always *B* that makes you unhappy in situations like this. Except as I said before, when *A* is a brick falling on your head. That, or any physical object, might cause you real pain. But any mental or emotional onslaught against you—any word, gesture, attitude or feeling directed against you—can hurt you only if you let it. And your letting such a word, gesture, attitude, or feeling hurt you, your telling yourself that it's awful, horrible, terrible—that's *B*. And that's what you do to you (Ellis, 1962).

The aim in rational-emotive therapy is to educate the person in the *ABCs* of life. In the *ABC approach*, the activating event, *A*, contributes to emotional and behavioral consequences, *C*, largely because of the person's belief, *B*, about the event. In this therapy, the person learns these *ABC's*, concentrating in particular on how the interpretation of

events—the *B* factor—can lead to adjustment difficulties (Ellis, 1991).

In approaching the problem of sweating, Mack's therapist adopted the *ABC* viewpoint. For Mack, the activating event, *A*, was feeling warm; the consequence, *C*, was sweating; and *B* was Mack's belief that any sign of sweating was unacceptable, showing that he was out of control. The critical factor therefore was *B*, Mack's belief, what he said to himself about sweating.

TEACHING LOGICAL THINKING. Mack's denial of anxiety prior to sweating prevented use of this therapy in the early weeks. Then, in his sixth session, Mack explained that he had felt a bit nervous during an accidental meeting with a young woman a few days earlier. Those feelings, he said, were all "locked inside." The next week, he failed a course examination for the first time in his life. Despite careful preparation, he was unable to answer many questions, explaining that his "nerves were all shot." It was therefore agreed that the following week Mack's therapist would give him a letter to his dean, requesting permission to postpone all further examinations.

In that next session, Mack read the therapist's letter, which explained that he was in treatment for an anxiety disorder. Immediately after reading the word *anxiety*, Mack laughed nervously. He said it made him realize that he had a "big problem." Then perspiration began pouring from his face and body. His therapist, realizing the importance of the moment, gently encouraged him to express his feelings aloud. Mack said that he felt like exploding, that he had a furnace in his heart, that he was acutely aware of the sweat dripping from his face and body. After ten minutes, the episode subsided, and then Mack viewed his sweating from a different perspective. He understood that anxiety *was* involved (Figure 16–4).

In the following session, the therapist supported Mack's new thoughts and challenged his old beliefs about his need for full control. Specifically, Mack was encouraged to question the silent but

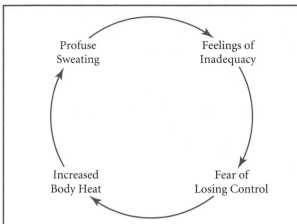

FIGURE 16-4 CYCLE OF EXCESSIVE SWEATING. Profuse sweating led to feelings of inadequacy and these feelings, through fear of losing control and subsequently increased body heat, led to more sweating (Adapted from Moylan & Dadds, 1992).

powerful sentences he said to himself about avoiding anxiety completely. Some anxiety was inevitable, a natural condition of life.

Over the following weeks, Mack adopted this new approach. Whenever he began to feel warm in social situations, he told himself:

"It's perfectly normal to feel mildly anxious when meeting new people."

"It is okay to be myself—I don't always have to perform."

"My blood is not boiling."

"I'm not going to explode."

These statements reduced the intensity of his reaction. Although he still felt a bit anxious, the initial feeling did not escalate into a full-blown sweating episode (Moylan & Dadds, 1992).

COGNITIVE THERAPY FOR DEPRESSION. Another cognitive therapist, Aaron Beck, left psychoanalysis not because it was taking too much time but because his patients were making too many negative statements about themselves—and hardly knew they were doing so. Beck decided to do something about their statements. His cognitive therapy has proved valuable partly because it is aimed directly at depression and partly

because it has offered a useful blend with other techniques.

Inaugurated well after Ellis taught his *ABCs* for the first time, Beck's cognitive therapy is less direct, less demanding, and less confrontational. Founded on the same principle, that irrational thinking causes people to become upset and behave inappropriately, it gives more responsibility to the client for identifying and discarding illogical thoughts. The idea is that people are more likely to act on these findings if they discover them for themselves in their own lives.

ENCOURAGING ADAPTIVE THINKING. Consider the following statements, characteristic of the thinking of depressed people:

"My colleagues do not like me."

"I do not have talent for anything."

"Things never work out for me."

A therapist using Beck's approach would not challenge the person, declaring those statements to be wrong. Rather, the therapist would work more gently, encouraging the person to look for the evidence, which is often never questioned (Beck, 1991).

In examining maladaptive thinking, the person is alerted to common categories rather than to a system of *ABCs*. In one category, *overgeneralizing,* the person's thinking extends beyond what is warranted by the facts. "Nobody ever tells me anything," a woman declares on hearing a certain piece of news belatedly. She would be asked to cite solid evidence that she is regularly excluded from information. In *selective attention,* the individual ignores contrary evidence. Noticing the heating bill in their home, a spouse exclaims, "This place is too expensive for us." She would be asked to take into account the family's overall income and expenses. There are no intermediate positions in *polarized thinking,* which regards events only in terms of extremes. "Going on a picnic will be terrible," a person exclaims, thinking only of the possibility of insects. She would be asked to consider the more promising aspects as well, such as the sunshine, flowers, and fresh air. In all of these maladaptive responses, there is a common feature: The importance of a single element is overdramatized.

People in Beck's therapy are encouraged to monitor their ways of thinking: writing down maladaptive thoughts, figuring out why they occurred, and coming up with solutions. During therapy, these findings are discussed, and commonly there is not much evidence to justify this extreme thinking.

RISE OF COGNITIVE-BEHAVIORAL THERAPY.

The rational-emotive therapist often develops homework assignments carefully prepared in order of gradually increasing difficulty. They must be followed by practice, practice, practice. People must *learn* their *ABCs* (Ellis, 1991, 1993).

As part of this education, rational-emotive therapists also use humor, making patients laugh even at themselves. Mack might be told, "It's impossible to live without some anxiety. Don't sweat it so much." In fact, all of us would be encouraged to use the services of a readily available therapist who asks no fee: Seymour Humor (Goodman, 1994).

Homework and self-reinforcement are also fundamental in Beck's approach. First promoted in behavior therapy, to be considered shortly, they have resulted in **cognitive-behavioral therapy**, a combination of cognitive and behavioral techniques focusing on thoughts *and* habits, especially useful with various anxiety disorders, depression, and lack of assertiveness (Brewin, 1996).

For example, in *assertiveness training* the aim is to assist people in dealing with interpersonal situations, helping them to avoid being overly shy or overly aggressive. A person wanting to become more assertive would be given very simple assignments at first, such as telephoning businesses and asking about their products. After success is achieved in these anonymous calls, the homework might require face-to-face contact—asking directions from people in the street or offering assistance to them. At a still higher level, the person might be requested to talk with a fellow employee, then with the boss, and so forth. Rather than becoming critical of themselves after these events, people in therapy are encouraged to reward their behavior by doing something pleasant—taking a swim, watching a film, or sampling a pie.

The concern with thoughts of course comes from the cognitive realm; the interest in habits arises from behavior therapy. A man who wants to avoid sweating is encouraged to examine his thoughts *and* behavior. This dual focus makes cognitive-behavioral therapy widely applicable to adjustment problems (Michelson & Marchione, 1991; Morin, Kowatch, Barry, & Walton, 1993; Wilson & Fairburn, 1993).

THE GROUP CONTEXT

Many people bring interpersonal problems to therapy—difficulties with family members, fellow employees, the opposite sex, friends, acquaintances, and even strangers. Group therapy thus serves a dual purpose. With several members participating simultaneously, it is more economical than individual therapy. In addition, **group therapy** offers a live setting in which people can share interpersonal problems, benefitting from these interactions in the problem-solving process. Group therapy often includes an implicit statement about psychological disorders: By the crowd they have been broken; by the crowd they shall be healed.

Members of *spontaneous groups* enter therapy for their own individual purposes, although they may have a common concern. A leader facilitates progress, following whatever theoretical orientation seems appropriate, but otherwise there is no expectation that people will adopt certain roles. They discuss problems in whatever ways they wish (Figure 16–5).

FIGURE 16–5 GROUP THERAPY. Spontaneous groups usually range in size from 6–12 members, including one or two leaders. No roles are assigned, except to a leader.

In other modes, members of *pre-formed groups* know one another and attempt to assist one another in solving a shared problem. In **family therapy,** the family meets as a group and treats all problems of the group and individual members as family problems (Minuchin, 1974, 1984). Amid the intimate emotional life of the family, its members do not fully understand how they influence one another. The therapist observes them in interaction, develops interpretations of these family processes, and shares them with the members.

From this perspective, Mack's problem was not *his* problem; it was a family problem, developed and maintained in that context. In his early years, Mack's mother was determined that he would perform well in public and avoid emotional expression. She exerted vigorous efforts to achieve this goal. As a result, Mack had a strong underlying fear of mis-

behaving. In this respect, his problem was a family problem or at least an issue with his mother.

In **marital therapy,** lack of harmony in the marriage, or the maladjustment of one partner, is considered the couple's problem, stemming from their mutual concerns. Attempts to change only the person displaying the symptoms, called the *identified patient,* are regarded as fruitless because the problem is maintained by the members' interactions. The marriage partners must be treated as a unit. When the marital partners enter therapy together, as a couple, the prospects for the marriage are more favorable than when they enter individual therapy separately (Cookerly, 1980).

Finally, *structured groups* approaches involve roles. The individuals in the group act out certain parts or adopt the characteristics of certain people, thereby revealing how they think and feel about them. A shy person might try to negotiate a contract with someone who plays the role of a boss. One role-playing approach, stressing verbal and physical expression, is **Gestalt therapy,** used with individuals or groups. The group leader attempts to maintain a strong, creative relationship with each person (Jacobs, 1992).

The unique element of group therapy is the potential for constructive interaction with people other than the therapist. In this respect, group therapy occupies an important place among the various insight therapies (Table 16–2).

• Behavior Therapies •

Mack began to achieve dramatic success in cognitive therapy but, as previously noted, that treatment occurred after an unsuccessful experience with behavior therapy. In **behavior therapy,** the focus is on the symptom, some undesirable emotional response or bad habit, and the treatment involves principles of conditioning. The problem is considered the result of environmental or situational factors, not faulty thinking. The term *behavior modification* is broader, referring not only to therapy but to all instances in which behavioral techniques are used, including programs for driving safely, teaching tricks to circus animals, and effective parenting.

During Mack's first two sessions, which were largely orientation sessions, he was administered tests to assess the nature and extent of his problem. Mack's scores on these self-report inventories were within the usual range except in one minor instance, but the therapist's attention was caught by the manner in which Mack responded to the questions. Although there were no instructions to do so, he crossed out on the answer sheet such words as *worry,* *distress,* and *anxiety.* At the top of the sheet he wrote that he never experienced these feelings at all. Thus, the therapist decided that there was little value at that point in discussing the possible role of anxiety

Type	Basic Goal
Psychoanalysis	To assist Mack in bringing repressed childhood experiences into awareness
Person-centered approach	To enable Mack to utilize his potential for growth and thereby to solve his own problems
Existential approach	To help Mack tolerate anxiety and sweating and to find meaning in these reactions
Rational-emotive therapy	To teach Mack to think differently—to change the messages he sends to himself
Cognitive therapy (Beck)	To encourage Mack to question his maladaptive ways of thinking
Group therapy	To aid Mack and other family members in understanding their interactions with one another

TABLE 16–2 TYPES OF INSIGHT THERAPY. These therapies aim to achieve different kinds of insight. The techniques are directed to these different aims.

in Mack's problem. Instead, Mack acknowledged a feeling of body heat immediately preceding his sweating, and the behavior therapy began on that basis.

Behavior therapy emerged from a controversial experiment in the early decades of this century. It showed how classical conditioning might be involved in anxiety reactions.

CLASSICAL CONDITIONING METHODS

An 11-month-old boy, Little Albert, served as the subject, partly because he was so fearless, reaching out to explore any new object, including a white rat, fire, blocks, and so forth. One day a white rat was placed on the edge of his blanket, and when he reached to touch it, a loud noise was made. All normal babies are afraid of loud noises, and Little Albert was startled. When the rat appeared the next day, Albert reached to touch it again, and once more the loud noise occurred. This time Albert whimpered a bit, and after similar pairings for five more days, the boy began to cry as soon as the rat appeared. Classical conditioning had occurred. The child had become fearful of the rat, previously a neutral or even a positive stimulus (Watson & Rayner, 1920).

Thirteen months later, the investigators prepared to begin removal of this conditioned emotional reaction, pairing the white rat with ice cream, toys, or other pleasant stimuli, but they were prevented from doing so. Little Albert's family moved from the vicinity. We know nothing more about Albert, the subject in the first recorded experimental demonstration of the acquisition of a phobia, an investigation that might not be permitted today, at least not without special permission from a review board, owing to the potentially disruptive influence on the subject.

A few years later, a three-year-old boy was discovered who seemed like Little Albert but just a bit older. Peter was afraid of small furry animals, thereby offering an opportunity to test the proposed therapy procedure—pairing the feared object with some pleasant stimulus. When Peter was seated in his high chair, a caged rabbit was placed some distance away, far enough so that Peter was not afraid, and immediately he received a piece of candy. On each successive trial, the presence of the rabbit preceded the appearance of candy, ice cream, or a friend. Through these pairings, as the rabbit was gradually brought closer to Peter, his fear was replaced with a positive emotional response (Figure 16–6). Eventually he enjoyed having the rabbit in his lap. He said, "I like the rabbit" (Jones, 1924, 1974).

When classical conditioning is used in this way, to reverse or dissipate an unwanted emotional response, the process is sometimes called *counterconditioning.* A strong positive stimulus is paired with a weaker negative stimulus, and the reaction to the positive stimulus becomes the dominant response. However, the negative stimulus must be introduced gradually. If the food or other reinforcer is only mildly positive, and the rabbit is presented too directly and too openly, a very different outcome may occur. We may have instead a fearful boy with an eating disorder.

SYSTEMATIC DESENSITIZATION. Since the days of Little Albert and Peter, behavior therapists have improved this counterconditioning technique in various ways, making it more precise and efficient. In one method, **systematic desensitization,** classical conditioning procedures are used with deep muscle relaxation and a carefully graded series of steps to eliminate unwanted emotional reactions. The person's emotional response is systematically diminished. In this process, the negative stimulus may not even be present. Therapy can be successful even when it is merely imagined.

Preparation of the series of graded steps is a joint responsibility of the therapist and client. Called an **anxiety hierarchy,** it is a carefully sequenced list of all disturbing events in a certain

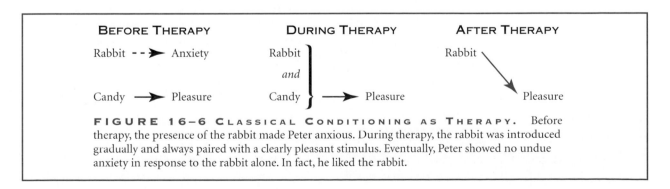

FIGURE 16–6 CLASSICAL CONDITIONING AS THERAPY. Before therapy, the presence of the rabbit made Peter anxious. During therapy, the rabbit was introduced gradually and always paired with a clearly pleasant stimulus. Eventually, Peter showed no undue anxiety in response to the rabbit alone. In fact, he liked the rabbit.

class or category, ranked from most to least threatening, top to bottom.

Mack was responsive to the idea of developing a list of situations likely to evoke his sweating. Insisting that anxiety was not involved, he and the therapist prepared an ordered list of ten situations. At the bottom of the list, as the first step, was this scene: making polite conversation with new people.

After constructing the hierarchy, the therapist teaches the person techniques for relaxation, used to counteract the negative stimulus. The patient receives training in *deep muscle relaxation,* a state that is incompatible with anxiety. In this training the patient learns the locations and better control of all muscle groups in the body (Wolpe, 1961).

Using the least anxiety-arousing scene in the person's list, and with the incompatible relaxation response well established, the counterconditioning begins. Closing the eyes, the patient leans back, fully relaxed, and the therapist instructs him or her to visualize the scene at the bottom of the list. If this image produces no anxiety, the therapist and patient move up to the next item, and then the next, and so forth, until anxiety is encountered. At this point, further training in relaxation is administered or, if necessary, the therapist and patient together move back down the list to the prior item, where no significant anxiety was encountered. Still further relaxation is encouraged and, when the patient is ready, upward progress begins again (Figure 16–7). This mode of therapy has been notably effective with phobias of all types, as well as with broader emotional problems, ranging from test anxiety to urinary disorders (Hudesman, Loveday, & Woods, 1984; Nicolau, Toro, & Perez-Prado, 1991).

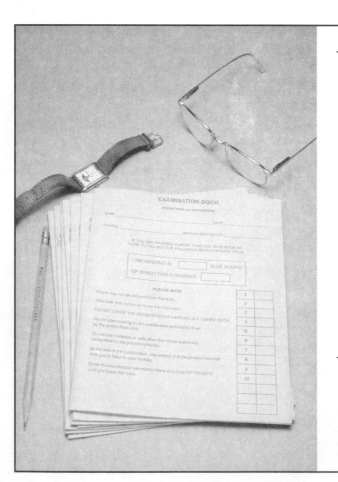

I am now going to ask you to imagine a number of scenes. You will imagine them clearly. . . . If, however, at any time you feel disturbed or worried and want to attract my attention, you will be able to do so by raising your left index finger. First I want you to imagine that you are standing at a familiar street corner on a pleasant morning watching the traffic. . . . *(Pause of about 15 sec.)*

Now imagine that you are at home studying in the evening. It is the 20th of May, exactly a month before your examination. *(Pause of 5 sec.)*

Now again imagine that you are studying at home a month before your examination. *(Pause of 5 sec.)*

If you felt any disturbance whatsoever to the last scene raise your left index finger now. *(Patient raises finger.)* If the amount of disturbance decreased from the first presentation. . . . again raise your finger. *(Patient does not raise finger.)* Just keep on relaxing. *(Pause of 15 sec.)*

Imagine that you are sitting on a bench at a bus stop. . . .

FIGURE 16–7 SYSTEMATIC DESENSITIZATION. The therapist proceeded slowly with a student who was anxious about taking college examinations. This scene in the photograph with the exam booklets, pencil, and watch, at the top of her list, would be the last one to be imagined (Wolfe, 1969).

Mack showed an ability to relax, and he was able to imagine vividly the weakest scene on his list. Nevertheless, he stopped the procedure after imagining the first scene—making polite conversation with new people. He explained that he felt uncomfortable but was unable to offer a reason. He also declared that he could not do his therapy homework that week. It required participation in two social events, and he did not have time for them. In addition, his university examinations would interfere with therapy. Clearly, Mack was displaying resistance. Little did he realize that certain events, discussed previously in conjunction with his therapy—meeting the young woman, failing the examination, and reading the letter to his dean—would prompt him to take a very different view of his adjustment difficulty. After those events, he decided that his problem involved anxiety; then he and his therapist approached his treatment on that basis, using a cognitive therapy. Under other circumstances, however, Mack or someone else might have achieved success through further behavior therapy. The outcome of any particular treatment with any individual is difficult to predict.

AVERSION THERAPY. Systematic desensitization is used to eliminate a negative emotional response, such as fear of an animal, social situations, or an examination. In contrast, **aversion therapy** uses conditioning techniques to eliminate unwanted positive emotional responses, including addictions and attachments, as in smoking and transvestism, respectively.

To eliminate alcoholism, for example, a nauseating drug may be included with the liquor. Shortly after drinking, the person becomes quite ill, vomiting extensively. With several repetitions of these events, the taste of the alcohol becomes aversive, for it precedes or accompanies the vomiting. In one review of this procedure, alcohol abstinence of at least one year was found in approximately 60% of the cases (Elkins, 1991). However, addictions are

uniquely resistant to therapy, even in this form, and many people are reluctant to enter such therapy, which is intrusive, costly, and controversial (Wilson, 1991). Moreover, simply creating a negative reaction to an undesirable stimulus is not the most effective solution. It is also desirable to develop a positive reaction to more appropriate stimuli, such as health foods and health drinks, which also may be accomplished by classical conditioning.

❧

OPERANT CONDITIONING METHODS

Some undesirable reactions are more voluntary. Rather than simply fearing dental treatment, for example, children may actively resist, pushing the dentist away and refusing to cooperate. These more voluntary behaviors are the focus of operant methods, aimed at the development of desirable habits and the elimination of undesirable ones. The therapist looks for something in the environment that sustains the behavior, a condition called *reinforcement*, for it increases the probability that the response will appear.

In one instance, six children were selected for behavior therapy, examined and screened by dentists as distinctly disruptive patients. On observing them in the dental office, the behavior therapist immediately realized that their disruptive reactions were followed by reinforcement. When Heidi, age three, became too disruptive, the dentist ceased his efforts. Heidi thereby escaped further dental treatment (Allen & Stokes, 1987).

CONTINGENCY MANAGEMENT. To change Heidi's response to the dentist, the therapist changed the consequences of good and poor patient behavior. Good behavior, defined as sitting still, was no longer followed by further treatment, as on earlier occasions. Instead, it was followed by cessation of treatment and congratulations from the dentist. This behavior was developed gradually in practice sessions. If Heidi was quiet for just three seconds, the dentist immediately stopped the sound of the drill, or removed the needle from view, and told Heidi that she was being a very big helper. By being quiet for just three seconds, Heidi escaped the anxiety-provoking stimulus and received praise for her behavior. Very gradually, longer periods of sitting quietly were required—five seconds, ten seconds, and so forth—until Heidi could remain quiet for a half-minute (Figure 16–8).

Other reinforcers were also used. Following cooperative behavior, small, decorative stickers were pasted on a colored index card attached to the dental light, where it could be readily observed by Heidi. In other words, if Heidi stuck to her task, being a big helper, and the dentist stuck to his, using short treatment intervals, both were rewarded with stickers: the dentist employing his needle, the child observing her decorations. In addition, if Heidi remained cooperative for the whole session, she could take home the toy on the counter.

If Heidi was disruptive, all talk and other interactions with her ceased immediately. The therapist avoided eye contact, and he and the dental assistant turned their backs to Heidi. In short, the whole environment in the dentist's office was carefully arranged to support cooperative dental behavior and to discourage disruptive behavior.

This procedure, when used in therapy, is known as **contingency management,** for it means that reinforcement principles are employed on a regular basis, usually by a team or group of people, all aimed at changing some specific behavior. For Heidi and the other five children, the outcome was positive in every case. They all became excellent dental patients (Allen & Stokes, 1987).

In contingency management with many subjects, poker chips or stickers are used as reinforcers, or tokens, and the program is called a **token economy.** In this way, reinforcement can occur promptly

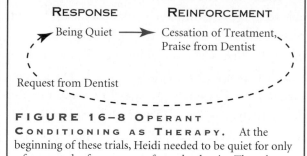

FIGURE 16–8 OPERANT CONDITIONING AS THERAPY. At the beginning of these trials, Heidi needed to be quiet for only a few seconds after a request from the dentist. Then the dental procedure was discontinued and she received praise from the dentist. Gradually, she was required to remain quiet for longer and longer periods in order to receive this reinforcement.

and the subjects can continue their behavior without significant disruption simply by collecting the tokens, rather than taking time out to eat something, hug someone, or play with a doll.

Less tangible than tokens, feedback is also considered a form of reinforcement. In psychology, **feedback** is any direct information about one's own behavior. Simply informing people about the frequency or consequences of their behaviors may change their response rate. For this purpose, Mack's therapist requested him to record the frequency and intensity of his sweating throughout the period of therapy. This procedure also provided a means of assessing Mack's progress (Table 16–3).

USING PUNISHMENT. The leading figure in operant conditioning, B. F. Skinner, resisted the use of punishment in any form, as do many behavior therapists today. Nevertheless, others believe that the end justifies the means.

Effective punishments are usually immediate and mild. Being made to stay after school typically is not immediate; a spanking is not mild; both punishments are likely to result in resentment of the punitive person. Timeout generally avoids these problems. In **timeout,** the misbehaving individual is left alone immediately, a procedure that involves mild punishment and extinction too, for no rein-

1. Feeling warm on the face, slightly uncomfortable.
2. Feeling the body become warm, uncomfortable.
3. Experiencing beaded sweat, feeling intense heat.
4. Sweating profusely, feeling out of control.

TABLE 16–3 RECORDING SWEATING.
To evaluate his progress in therapy, Mack was asked to keep weekly records of his sweating. He noted each incident and the amount of sweating, using this 4-point scale (Moylan & Dadds, 1992).

forcement is possible under this condition. The person in charge leaves promptly after the misbehavior, ensuring that there are no objects in the room that might provide reinforcement. The time-out interval usually lasts only a few minutes, rarely more than half an hour, but the immediacy and message of rejection can be highly effective.

In some cases, punishment may be warranted even when the behavior appears involuntary. For example, an infant less than a year old was unable to keep food in its stomach. The baby always vomited within ten minutes after eating, and medical investigations revealed no organic basis for the problem. With no obvious alternatives and the infant's health in serious jeopardy, the hospital staff decided to try punishment. A one-second electric shock was administered to the legs as soon as vomiting commenced, and it was repeated at one-second intervals during the vomiting. After the second session the electric shock was rarely required, and after the fifth session the vomiting disappeared completely. The infant gained weight steadily and showed increased interest in its surroundings (Lang & Melamed, 1969).

This same procedure was used with four adults who sought therapy for excessive sweating. When the amount of perspiration increased above a certain level, the subjects were administered electric shock. Under these rather disagreeable conditions, all of them learned to decrease their sweating markedly (Kuypers & Cotton, 1972).

OBSERVATIONAL LEARNING

Learning can take place without direct reinforcement, as indicated at earlier points in this text. In this view, called **observational learning** the individual acquires new ways of behaving by watching others. The person demonstrating the correct behavior is known as a model. He or she may be a *peer model,* close to the learner in age and background, or a *mastery model,* highly skillful but more distant in age, background, or social context. The model displays the behavior in question, showing no fear when confronted by a dentist, a group of people, a large dog, and so forth.

Reproducing someone else's behavior is called **modeling.** Modeling tends to increase when there is an opportunity for reinforcement. In therapy, a model can demonstrate the correct response, and reinforcement can be used to maintain the behavior, especially in the early stages. This approach might have been employed with Heidi at the dentist's office, using a child three or four years old to demonstrate good behavior as a dental patient. It has been especially effective in overcoming phobias and developing confidence in children (Greer, Dorow, Williams, & McCorkle, 1991; Malgady, Rogler, & Constantino, 1990; Mullare & Fernald, 1971).

This form of learning emphasizes *self-efficacy,* which is an individual's sense of being able to do something—the feeling of capability in a given situation. The expectation of success or failure underlies self-efficacy, and therefore modeling therapy includes a cognitive component.

• BIOMEDICAL THERAPIES •

Sweating cools the body. It is a normal response when body temperature rises. Excessive sweating is known as *hyperhidrosis,* for *hyper* is a prefix indicating an excess and *hidro* comes from the Greek word signifying water. Early research identified two types of excessive sweating: one largely confined to the palms, soles of the feet, and armpits, the other more generalized across the face, neck, and trunk. Mack's sweating conformed to the latter pattern.

In both cases, anxiety appears to be the initiating factor. The hypothalamus, monitoring body temperature, responds to arousal and body heat, activating the sweat glands by means of the sympathetic nervous system. Mack was totally unaware of the underlying anxiety in the early stages of his therapy, as indicated in the report of his treatment, entitled *Hyperhidrosis: A Case Study and Theoretical Formulation* (Moylan & Dadds, 1992).

Inasmuch as Mack's problem involved an obvious physical symptom, he might have sought assistance from a therapist with medical training or a biological orientation. This form of therapy is called *biological* or **biomedical therapy,** for it uses manipulation of physiological conditions to alleviate symptoms of psychological disorder. It is also known as *somatic therapy* because tissues of the body, or *soma,* are altered for the purpose of diminishing problems that are partly psychological in origin.

❧

NATURAL BODY THERAPIES

Over the years, mental and physical health in the United States has generally been approached through the treatment of illness and disease, rather than prevention. The focus is on hospital care, more than health care (Kiesler, 1992). This approach has been very expensive and awesomely effective in treating health crises and emergencies of various sorts. It has been less impressive in dealing with certain forms of mental illness, cancer, degenerative diseases, and other conditions in which the mind can be influential in susceptibility to the disease (Weil, 1990).

For these reasons, there has been growing interest in less technical, less expensive approaches, variously called alternative, or unconventional health care. Also known as **natural body therapies,** they seek to utilize the body's innate tendency to recover and achieve a balanced state, chiefly through normal daily activities. They include physical exercise, breathing exercises, massage and muscular therapy, programs of nutrition, rest and relaxation, as well as meditation and even biofeedback, all aimed at releasing chronic tension and restoring the balance of the body. The basic procedure is to take advantage of the wisdom of the body in curing itself, mentally and physically, by using natural, nontechnical methods (Brown, 1973a; Stanway, 1987).

These therapies share two characteristics. First, they are *noninvasive,* meaning that there is no intrusion into the body by surgery, electrical impulses, manufactured chemicals, or any other means. Second, they generally have a *holistic orientation,* directed to the body *and* mind, rather than just the presenting symptom. The rationale here is that emotional factors can play a vital role in physical health, just as physical well-being can influence mental health. Generally, they would not be used alone in cases of major mental disorder. They may complement the insight and behavior therapies, as well as other biomedical therapies; therefore they are sometimes called *complementary therapies.* Diverse studies have shown their contribution in treating certain stress-related illnesses, especially hypertension and depression (Benson & Stuart, 1993).

In one instance, biofeedback was employed with 14 adults suffering from hyperhidrosis. Using electronic recording equipment, they were provided with precise visual cues indicating their amounts of sweating. Of the 14 patients, 11 suffered from sweating confined to the hands, feet, and armpits; after treatment, they reported less tension and had visibly reduced their sweating. The other three patients, who did not respond to the biofeedback treatment, suffered from diffuse sweating all over the body (Dullier & Gentry, 1980). The reasons for these very different reactions by the two groups remain unknown.

ELECTROSHOCK AND PSYCHOSURGERY

The orthodox biomedical methods are almost invariably prescribed by physicians for serious psychological disorders. They require extremely conscientious application, for they may have damaging outcomes, as shown in historical studies in the United States and England in the last 50 years (Endler, 1988; Rollin, 1990).

ELECTROCONVULSIVE THERAPY. A physician in Vienna during Sigmund Freud's era noticed that an accidental overdose of insulin produced a moment of unconsciousness in a patient with psychiatric symptoms. Moreover, the patient seemed better adjusted afterward. An Italian physician, Hugo Cerletti, then tried electric shock to pro-

duce brief unconsciousness in a schizophrenic patient whose speech had been incomprehensible for many years. After the second 110-volt discharge for one-half second, the patient sat up in bed. When asked what had happened, he replied: "I don't know; perhaps I have been asleep" (Cerletti, 1950).

Today in **electroconvulsive therapy** (ECT) a convulsion lasting for a few seconds is induced by passing a weak electrical current through the brain, and this procedure sometimes diminishes certain symptoms of mental illness, especially severe depression. Electrodes placed at the temples transmit the current while the patient is under sedation. A period of unconsciousness follows, but recovery is rapid. The patient usually leaves the office within an hour after arrival, allegedly without much discomfort during the actual treatment. There are sharp differences of opinion here, however. A patient often receives a series of treatments, perhaps six to twelve. The number of visits, their length, and the outpatient procedure make them in some ways like appointments for other medical or dental problems (Figure 16–9).

After extensive use in the middle decades of this century, electroconvulsive therapy diminished for two reasons. First, it is often accompanied by

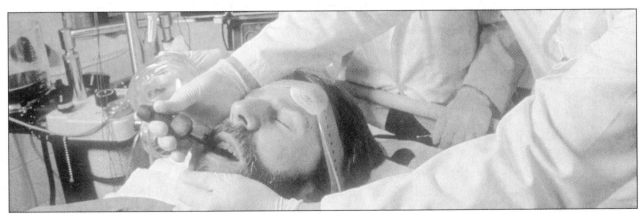

FIGURE 16–9 ELECTROCONVULSIVE THERAPY. The use of electroconvulsive therapy for psychological disorders remains highly controversial. Its mild resurgence today is due to the use of anesthesia and chemical methods for reducing the convulsive reaction.

memory loss, usually temporary, sometimes permanent. Second, in the early years, before the widespread use of therapeutic drugs, the procedure was dangerous, resulting in broken bones and dislocations from the convulsions. With the advent of psychotherapeutic drugs it remains a last-resort therapy, limited chiefly to people with severe, chronic depression, particularly those with suicidal tendencies for whom antidepressants have not been effective.

The treatment process is not understood. Electroconvulsive therapy has been compared to shaking or hitting a radio to eliminate static; sometimes the mechanism works better afterward, but for unknown reasons. In any case, renewed interest also arises from the technique of inducing the electrical current in only half of the brain, the nondominant hemisphere. This procedure reduces memory impairment, apparently without loss of therapeutic effectiveness. The reasons for its advantage over the bilateral method are unclear (Sackeim, 1991).

PSYCHOSURGERY. Another somatic procedure falling into disuse is *psychosurgery,* which is surgery performed to alleviate mental disorder. In the first half of this century, two methods were employed: *lobectomy,* in which parts of the frontal lobe were removed, and **lobotomy**, in which the connections between this lobe and other parts of the brain were destroyed. Lobotomy became the preferred approach because of its greater simplicity and precision (Freeman & Watts, 1950).

Psychosurgery was developed largely by a Portuguese physician, Antonio Egas Moniz, after observing some experimental monkeys. They had received this operation, and to Moniz it seemed that they had joined a "happiness cult." He decided to try the procedure on allegedly hopeless human patients and, regarding it a success, continued the procedure with many other patients. Eventually, in

1949, he was awarded a Nobel Prize for this work, but not everyone considered it a success. One of his disgruntled patients returned and shot Moniz, leaving him permanently disabled (Moniz, 1944).

Psychosurgery is extremely serious, for the change in the patient is irreparable. When it is successful, the patient becomes less depressed but may lose the zest for life too. In the book and film *One Flew Over the Cuckoo's Nest,* a mental patient called McMurphy was humorous and unrestrained until he received a lobotomy. Afterward, he was more restrained and less impulsive but also showed the lack of responsiveness characteristic of a lobotomized patient. For these reasons, and because drug treatments appear much more effective, psychosurgery is also a last-resort therapy, largely of historical interest. With severe epilepsy it has eliminated seizures, but sometimes at the cost of deterioration in other functions (Stevens, 1990).

Psychosurgery of a very different sort was attempted in early medical treatment of hyperhidrosis. One effort included removal of certain nerve fibers in the sympathetic nervous system. This obviously drastic procedure brought brief relief but severe compensatory reactions—hyperhidrosis in other areas of the body (Cloward, 1969).

❧

PSYCHOTHERAPEUTIC DRUGS

Compared with electroshock and psychosurgery, drugs represent a true revolution, but they too must be used with caution. For psychological reasons, the drug may become essential for day-to-day living, and dangerous side effects may appear. A **side effect** is a secondary outcome of the treatment, completely unintended, often unpredictable, and usually unwanted. These range from itchiness of the skin and a dry mouth to major physical disorders, such as incoordination and chronic tremors. In rare cases, a side effect can be beneficial, alleviating some other health problem.

Sometimes drug therapy can be almost miraculous, yet critics complain that drugs today are promoted like cosmetics and candy, with too little regard for the consumer and too much emphasis on marketing. Claims are inflated, dangers ignored, and countless patients overmedicated (Karon, 1991).

TYPES OF THERAPEUTIC DRUGS. The drugs commonly used to alleviate psychotic symptoms, specifically hallucinations and disturbed thinking, are known as **antipsychotic drugs.** These medications include Thorazine, the trade name for chlorpromazine, Haldol, and Stelazine. Directed primarily to schizophrenia, they are a prime reason for the diminished populations in hospitals in the last several decades. With a chemical structure much like that of dopamine, cited in the previous chapter as a likely factor in schizophrenia, they relieve the symptoms by blocking the release and reception of dopamine in the synapses. They often do so, however, at the cost of various side effects, including dizziness, dry mouth, and disturbances of muscular control, reflected in an impeded gait, involuntary movements, and other disruptions of body functions (Kane, 1987).

The treatment of depression includes three different categories of **antidepressant drugs,** all providing the user with an emotional lift, stimulating increased activity and greater interest in the world. The *tricyclic drugs* and *serotonin reuptake blockers* both block the reuptake of certain neurotransmitters, thereby increasing their presence at the synaptic site. These naturally occurring chemicals thus remain in the synapses longer than usual. On these bases, it appears that the depletion of serotonin, norepinephrine, and other neurotransmitters in the synapses may be a factor in depression. The third

category of antidepressant drugs, *monoamine oxidase inhibitors,* sustains the action of neurotransmitters in a different manner, chiefly by inhibiting substances that neutralize them.

Known by the trade names Tofranil and Elavil, antidepressant medications act more slowly than antipsychotic drugs, apparently creating gradual changes at the receptor sites. They may take two weeks or so to become effective. Common side effects include dizzy spells, dry mouth, and disrupted vision. Prozac, a serotonin reuptake blocker, was once widely prescribed because it seemed to work without side effects for most patients. However, there have been accounts of its implication in suicidal impulses, bringing into serious question its freedom from complications (Teicher, Glod, & Cole, 1990).

Once described as a miracle drug, lithium today is in a category of its own. The reason is that **lithium,** a naturally occurring salt substance also manufactured for therapeutic purposes, has proved extraordinarily successful in eliminating the chief symptoms of bipolar disorder, acting primarily on the manic, or euphoric, side. Its exact mode of operation remains unknown, although the sites may be somewhere other than the synapses. It typically takes effect within four to six days, proving successful with approximately 80% of the population, but again there are side effects. More important, an underdose will be ineffective and a steady overdose can have serious health implications. Thus, the lithium level in the blood must be monitored regularly.

The most common psychotherapeutic drugs, with millions of prescriptions each year, are neither antipsychotics, antidepressants, nor lithium. Called **antianxiety drugs** or *minor tranquilizers,* they diminish the nervousness, unhappiness, sleeplessness, and tension experienced by so many people in modern life. Major drugs in this category are known by the

TYPE	PURPOSE
Antipsychotic	To diminish hallucinations, delusions, and withdrawal
Antidepressant	To alleviate feelings of depression
Lithium salt	To eliminate symptoms of a manic state
Antianxiety	To reduce tension and anxiety

TABLE 16-4 COMMON PSYCHOTHERAPEUTIC DRUGS. The potential side effects vary considerably.

trade names Valium, Librium, and Xanax. Acting promptly at receptor sites, they diminish anxiety by suppressing neural activity and therefore reducing the level of excitation. However, their impact disappears within a few hours. The dominant side effect is relaxation to the point of drowsiness or sluggishness, experienced by a sizable minority of users. Other side effects include constipation, dry mouth, and sometimes nausea. Virtually all of these drugs act as sedatives. Some forms are even used as sleeping pills (Table 16-4).

INFLUENCE OF DRUGS. Overall, drug therapy has proved to be a widespread means of control rather than cure. Drugs generally do not eliminate a mental problem; they do suppress the symptoms. If the drug is withdrawn, the disturbance often reappears. Also, drug dependency may be induced, and serious side effects may occur. For these reasons, drugs should be reserved for crises as far as possible, making people more amenable to other treatments, including insight therapy and behavior therapy (Kendall & Lipman, 1991).

Drug therapy has also been used with hyperhidrosis. One woman experienced profuse sweating in the palms of her hands, quickly and extensively; this reaction was blocked by an anticholinergic agent inhibiting the action of acetylcholine at the receptor site. Using this medication, she readily engaged in systematic desensitization, imagining successful inhibition of sweating during the therapy sessions. This desensitization played an important role in her recovery. It enabled her to develop a sense of mastery over the problem that she could not have gained by taking the drug alone (Drimmer, 1985).

• EVALUATING THERAPY •

Amid these diverse therapies, the question of outcome remains. Are therapies effective? With whom? In what way? Is some particular form of therapy more beneficial than simply waiting for the disorder to disappear spontaneously, as the recuperative powers of nature take their course? Such questions are answered empirically by seeking objective, direct evidence, a theme that has recurred throughout this book (Table 16-5).

PROBLEMS IN EVALUATION

Mack's therapy ended after 20 sessions. In his therapist's opinion, and in Mack's own judgment, the procedures had been successful. Mack's weekly reports showed that the frequency and intensity of his sweating had diminished markedly. Incidents occurred on the average only once per week, and their intensity was rated at the lowest possible level. Mack also stated that he was more at ease in social situations and with himself. Moreover, on the one self-report item that suggested a pretreatment difficulty, his posttreatment performance was in the normal range. He no longer believed that every problem had *a perfect solution* (Moylan & Dadds, 1992).

CHOOSING THE CRITERIA. Mack's case shows some of the problems in evaluating the out-

TYPE OF THERAPY	FOCUS	TECHNIQUES
Insight		
Psychoanalysis	Unconscious conflicts	Free association, transference, interpretation
Humanistic approach	Actualization, meaning	Restatement, clarification, active listening
Cognitive approach	Irrational thinking	Education, confrontation, homework
Group therapy	Social interactions	Spontaneous groups, family and marital
Behavior		
Classical conditioning	Attitudes, feelings	Systematic desensitization, aversion therapy
Operant conditioning	Habits, overt acts	Contingency management, token economy
Observational learning	Diverse behaviors	Peer and mastery models
Biomedical		
Natural body therapy	Innate capacity for health	Exercise, massage, nutrition, relaxation
Electroshock/surgery	Physiological malfunction	Electroconvulsive therapy, lobotomy
Psychotherapeutic drugs	Electrochemical imbalance	Antipsychotic, antidepressant, antianxiety

TABLE 16–5 SUMMARY OF MAJOR THERAPIES. Each therapy has its own focus, arising from assumptions about the origins of the disorder. The various techniques have been developed to pursue each focus.

comes of therapy. The first problem lies in choosing the criteria for success or improvement. With Mack, how much sweating is acceptable? In what circumstances? For someone else, should success in therapy be discharge from the clinic, going to work, or a satisfactory report from the family? Note, for example, the difference between humanistic therapy and psychoanalysis in this regard. The person-centered counselor aims to assist the individual in achieving self-actualization. The psychoanalyst, if following Freud's more pessimistic dictum, simply aims to help the patient achieve a normal level of human unhappiness.

Many of the obvious or positive symptoms of schizophrenia, such as bizarre behavior and disordered thinking, can be treated with drugs. However, the negative or deficit symptoms—social isolation and lack of interest in the world—are less responsive to the usual dopamine-blocking agents (Kay & Lindenmayer, 1991). Some symptoms disappear with treatment; others do not. Which ones should be the criteria for success?

ASSESSING LATER ADJUSTMENT.

Even with adequate criteria, another difficulty arises: assessing later adjustment. If changes occur during or after therapy, are they temporary or relatively enduring? If they do not appear immediately, will they occur later? In either case, were they the result of therapy?

Attempts to answer questions about subsequent adjustment are called *follow-up studies* because former patients are re-examined at a later date. Do they show any improvement? Have they regressed? Are they experiencing new difficulties? In many such studies, the issue of symptom substitution arises. In **symptom substitution,** a new symptom replaces those removed by therapy. The therapy perhaps has been unsuccessful, for example, if Mack develops headaches or asthma attacks instead.

There is evidence on both sides of this question, but it now seems that replacement symptoms do not *necessarily* appear in regular fashion. For behavior therapy, the research typically shows no substitute symptoms (Azrin & Peterson, 1990; Kazdin, 1982). For the insight and relationship therapies especially, symptom substitution may depend on the therapist's expectations. If the therapist believes that substitution is inevitable, a compliant patient may develop a new symptom in conformance with this expectation (Caldwell, 1990).

DETERMINING SPONTANEOUS REMISSION. Still another major difficulty arises because some people seem to get well on their own, without therapy. This phenomenon was brought to attention 30 years ago when an English psychologist found that, among people receiving treatment, the rate of recovery or distinct improvement was about 67%. However, the rate of recovery for people with comparable illnesses, yet *without* treatment, was also found to be 67% (Eysenck, 1952, 1965). The implications of this report, particularly among psychologists in clinical practice, continue even today (Kazdin, 1990).

This research prompted a closer look at the no-treatment cases. When symptoms disappear without any formal treatment, the outcome is known as **spontaneous remission,** and some psychologists believe that the early findings on spontaneous remission are essentially correct. Others believe that the rate is far below 67%. A review of several studies found it to be in the vicinity of 30% (Bergin, 1971). Still other experts believe that the recovery rates both with and without treatment have yet to be effectively demonstrated (Mariezcurrena, 1994). In any case, a reanalysis of the original data on spontaneous remission, together with the results from a contemporary program of therapy, showed that half of the therapy patients had improved after eight weeks compared with only 2% of the original untreated individuals during an equal interval (McNeilly & Howard, 1991).

THE PLACEBO ISSUE. Another important issue is the treatment of no-treatment cases. Historically, it has been assumed that control subjects should receive some form of attention, usually nontherapeutic social interaction. This procedure is called a placebo, for it aims to give the control subjects an experience comparable to that of the experimental subjects without the critical ingredient—the therapy itself. They might participate in educational opportunities, recreational programs, or other activities with a personal-social dimension but no therapy. These placebo comparisons are essential in studies of drug therapy, for the aim is to assess the influence of the chemical or medical elements alone, excluding psychological factors as artifacts (Figure 16–10).

The issue is not so clear among insight and behavior therapies. Should the no-treatment cases in these investigations also participate in some form of social interaction, apart from therapy? If they do, then the personal-social dimensions in therapy have been somewhat discounted, though they are widely recognized as major components of the treatment process in these therapies (Strupp, 1986; Wilkins, 1986). Sometimes even the control subjects—if they meet regularly about the problem, without therapy—show clear signs of improvement (Elkin et al., 1989). This long debate over spontaneous remission and the definition of no-treatment cases shows few signs of abatement (Kirsch, 1990).

❧

EFFECTIVENESS OF THERAPY

Despite these obstacles, hundreds of studies have been conducted evaluating the effectiveness of therapy. Patients have been located and examined years after treatment, and multiple criteria have been established as measures of effectiveness. Control groups, composed of people on clinic waiting lists, have been used, involving placebo and no-treatment conditions.

OUTCOMES OF THERAPY. Overall the findings have been clearly positive. In comparisons of behavior therapy and various insight therapies,

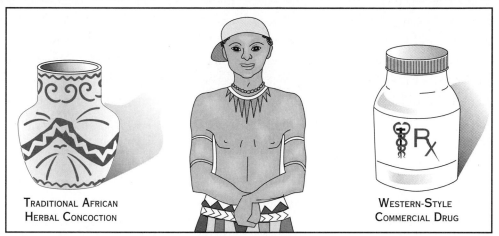

FIGURE 16–10 DEMONSTRATING THE PLACEBO EFFECT.
Malawian students were administered a placebo that appeared to be a traditional African concoction. On another occasion, they consumed a placebo that resembled a Western-style commercial drug. Neither placebo contained medicinal properties, but the subjects were told to expect an increase in their oral temperature. This response occurred in both cases (Zimba & Buggie, 1993).

and in investigations of different types of insight therapy and drug therapy, all therapy groups have been found significantly more improved than the control groups (Devine & Fernald, 1973; DiLoreto, 1971; Elkin et al., 1989; Miller & Berman, 1983). One extensive analysis examined 375 studies of the effectiveness of therapy, and it was concluded that the typical therapy patient was more improved than 75% of the people who, for various reasons, did not receive therapy but needed or sought it (Smith & Glass, 1977). Another extensive review also concluded that about 80% of the research showed largely positive results (Luborsky, Singer, & Luborsky, 1975). In fact, few important differences in outcome have been found among many forms of insight and behavior therapy (Bentler, 1991; Stiles, Shapiro, & Elliott, 1986). When more than 300 investigations of therapy, education, and related procedures were evaluated, they showed a dramatic pattern of positive effects (Lipsey & Wilson, 1993).

Overall, it appears that forms of insight ther-apy are most useful with unfocused concerns of mild or moderate intensity. Uncertainty or confusion about personal relationships, identity, and work situations may be approached in these therapies, which aim at increased self-understanding. More specific problems, such as phobias, assertiveness, bad habits, addictions, sexual problems, eating disorders, and sleeping disorders, may be usefully treated by behavior therapies. The biomedical therapies, especially drug therapies, appear most appropriate for alleviating severe symptoms, diffuse or specific, and for enabling people with such symptoms to take advantage of other forms of therapy. Thus, it follows that for many people, particularly those with significantly disabling personal problems, some sort of combined therapy, including insight or behavioral therapy *and* biomedical treatment, may be most appropriate.

INTERACTION PRINCIPLE. The method of therapy does not operate independently of the therapist or the problem, however. We must conclude that the important aspect of any therapeutic situation is the **interaction principle,** meaning the mutual influences of the patient, therapist, and method on one another—how they combine to determine the overall outcome.

For example, classical conditioning has been used to prevent hyperhidrosis. One woman was taught to shiver whenever she said the word *cold* to herself. Shivering reduced her body temperature. Thus, she thought about the word *cold* in anxiety-provoking social situations and thereby reduced her body temperature, preventing excessive perspiration (King & Stanley, 1986). Mack was taught the same procedure in therapy. In fact, rather than simply thinking about the word *cold* and making himself shiver, he was asked to take a cold shower every day, ensuring that the cold water sprayed on his forehead and trunk. Simultaneously, he repeated aloud the word *cold* (Moylan & Dadds, 1992). Nevertheless, this procedure did not prove effective for Mack in social situations, partly because it was used along with the anxiety hierarchy, which he actively resisted.

Many therapists therefore employ an **eclectic approach,** choosing from the various methods the ones that seem most appropriate for a given patient and problem. Others use combined techniques. In the **multimodal approach,** several therapy methods are employed simultaneously with the same individual or group of individuals. The eclectic approach stresses the use of *any* potentially helpful therapy; the multimodal approach emphasizes combinations. In the treatment of depression, for example, cognitive therapy *and* drug therapy appear to be more effective together than either of these treatments administered separately (Elkin et al., 1989; Kendall & Lipman, 1991).

THE THERAPEUTIC ALLIANCE. In studies of the interaction principle, all three factors emerge as important: the patient, therapist, and

method (Kazdin, 1990). Each accounts for some of the success in therapy; no one of them alone accounts for the full outcome. However, if one interaction is to emerge as more potent than the others, it may be the therapist–patient interaction.

It should be remembered that the patient's expectation in therapy is a crucial factor in therapy outcomes. Much of this expectation may lie in the therapist's capacity to communicate hope, to instill confidence in the therapeutic process, and to motivate the patient. According to contemporary experts, therefore, the best single predictor of the outcome of therapy is the presence of a **therapeutic alliance,** in which the patient feels that the therapist truly cares and understands, is truly an ally, and is truly connected to his or her problems and personal welfare (Grotstein, 1990; Karon, 1991; Smith & Thompson, 1993; Figure 16-11).

Mack's therapist had a special opportunity to foster this alliance during the eighth therapy session, through the letter to his dean. For the first time, Mack suffered profuse sweating in front of someone who totally accepted the problem, encour-

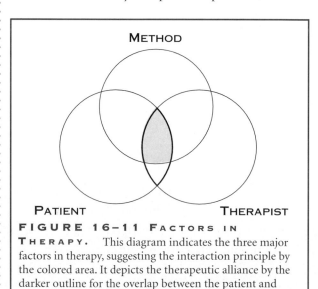

FIGURE 16–11 FACTORS IN THERAPY. This diagram indicates the three major factors in therapy, suggesting the interaction principle by the colored area. It depicts the therapeutic alliance by the darker outline for the overlap between the patient and therapist variables (Karon, 1991).

aging him to discuss his fears openly, without concern about humiliation or rejection. This unexpected episode in the midst of Mack's therapy went a *long* way toward establishing a therapeutic alliance.

• MENTAL
HEALTH MOVEMENTS •

Attempts to deal with mental disorders in the United States show a history of gains and setbacks. Benjamin Rush, a signer of the Declaration of Independence and generally acknowledged as the founder of American psychiatry, was instrumental in promoting the view that mental illness arose from conditions within the individual, a perspective that fostered the mental health movement. His terrifying methods of treatment are considered less enlightened, however (Figure 16–12).

A half-century later, Dorothea Dix inaugurated a broader movement, focusing on living conditions. She successfully persuaded the government to construct hundreds of institutions, called asylums, solely for housing mentally disturbed people. The word *asylum* means a refuge, an isolated place, where people with psychological disorders could be properly treated. These more humane conditions resulted in somewhat better care and greater respect for afflicted people.

INSTITUTIONAL TREATMENT

Nevertheless, this isolation became an obstacle to mental health. People transferred to asylums tended to undergo **institutionalization,** adapting their behavior to the organization or setting in which they lived, adjusting to the requirements of *that*

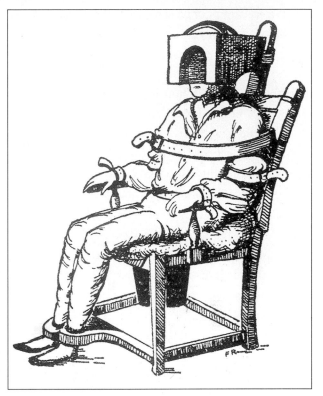

FIGURE 16–12 EARLY TREATMENT OF MENTAL DISORDERS. Benjamin Rush assumed that mentally ill people had lost the normal physiological balance of the body. To restore this balance, his patients were strapped into a special chair or bed and whirled rapidly in a circle, immersed in cold water, or swung from a beam. There is no evidence that these harsh methods were productive.

community. In these large, isolated hospitals, typically without sufficient staff or funds, patients were required to do little more than eat, sleep, and attend occasional therapy sessions. The challenges of daily life—meeting new people, accepting new work responsibilities, entertaining oneself, and so forth—were not readily available, leaving them unprepared to return to their earlier lives. Rather than preparing them for the outside world, life in an asylum was preparing them for life in an asylum. Some of these issues were considered in the Rosenhan study, described in the previous chapter (Rosenhan, 1973).

DEINSTITUTIONALIZATION. With the advent of drug therapy beginning in the middle of this century, the pendulum has swung back again—but not to the same place. Society is again faced with the problem of housing for the mentally ill, as in the days before Dorothea Dix, but this time it is *after* treatment and after discharge. The process of discharging or transferring former mental patients into the community is called **deinstitutionalization,** which commonly takes place about two weeks after admission. This relatively short period of hospitalization for severe mental disorders, made possible by drug therapy, avoids institutionalization for a lengthy stay. It is also less expensive and prepares the person for additional treatment, often forms of insight and behavior therapy. That is the bright side.

The dark side of deinstitutionalization is evident on the streets of almost any city in the United States: homelessness. Despite plans and promise, the facilities for deinstitutionalization have not been made widely available. Communities are not well prepared to receive discharged patients. One major reason is that insurance programs, including national health policies, simply are not directed to outpatient care for mentally ill people (Kiesler, 1982). Lacking supervision and adequate halfway house facilities, former patients discontinue their therapy and must be regularly readmitted for treatment. This cycle, repeated for more than half of all psychiatric admissions, is called the *revolving door outcome,* meaning that many patients are constantly in and out of the hospital. Many others simply remain homeless (Figure 16–13).

INVOLUNTARY COMMITMENT. A very different issue arises with involuntary hospitalization. When a person seems seriously disturbed and is placed in a mental institution against his or her will, the procedure is called *involuntary commitment,* and it raises an ethical question. Should the law permit someone to commit someone else to a hospital? If so, what standard should be used in making this commitment? Even experts disagree about the definition of mental disorder.

According to one viewpoint, mental disorder alone, assuming that it can be accurately identified, is sufficient to permit confinement of an individual to a mental institution. The argument is that the individual, when improved, will be thankful for the commitment. The opposite position is that involuntary commitment should not be permissible under any circumstance. In fact, it is argued that modern psychiatry practices a two-directional coercion of individuals regarded as mentally ill. Involuntary commitment commences treatment, and deinstitutionalization—from a place that has become the individual's home—occurs when insurance benefits cease or other factors become ascendant (Szasz, 1977, 1990, 1991).

☙

PREVENTIVE MENTAL HEALTH

The major focus of the previous discussion has been on the alleviation of mental disorders. A very different approach follows an old slogan: An ounce of prevention is worth a pound of cure. The stress is on prevention, rather than treatment.

This relatively new concept, **preventive mental health,** emphasizes that many mental disorders can be avoided by identifying and meeting the needs of the individual *before* or during stressful events. One aim is to provide immediate support for people at risk, such as abused and battered children, families of alcoholic individuals, members of minority groups, and homeless people. These programs include counselors with special sensitivity to cultural issues (Malgady, Rogler, & Constantino, 1990).

Whether preventive mental health would have assisted Mack, we cannot know. Prevention often

FIGURE 16–13 HOMELESSNESS AND PSYCHOLOGICAL DISORDER. A representative shelter for the homeless in Boston was studied on a typical evening. All 78 overnight guests were interviewed by mental health professionals. Most of them were found to be suffering from major psychological disorders (Bassuk, Rubin & Lauriat, 1984).

takes the form of education for parents and spouses, as well as children, and Mack's mother suffered from much the same personal style that he displayed, although without the symptom of excessive sweating. She too was extremely preoccupied with her presentability, typically quite tense, and unable to express her feelings. An effort at therapy on her part in earlier years might have constituted preventive mental health for Mack.

An unexpected event at the end of therapy enabled Mack to observe this rigid quality in himself. He gave a public address quite successfully and, unknown to him, the occasion had been videotaped. Afterward, as he watched the videotape, he noted his very controlled, almost aloof manner, which he felt did not fit his inner self. This observation increased his desire to change his image and to let others know him as he had come to know himself. As he left therapy, he continued to express these new ideas about his changing sense of self (Moylan & Dadds, 1992).

MODELS OF MALADJUSTMENT. Preventive measures, and the various therapies, are based on conceptions or models of maladjustment. Three such models have been prominently identified, one associated with the devil, another with medicine, and the third with culture.

Centuries ago, the **devil model** stated that a person became disturbed because the devil had taken up residence in his or her body. The proper treatment for any bedeviled person was punishment that might cause the intruder to leave: beating, starving, dunking, bleeding, whirling, or some similar procedure. Even so, the devil often stayed. For prevention, the chief suggestion was to stay away from the devil.

Earlier in this century, the **medical model** became the dominant view, suggesting that mental illness, like physical illness, reflects a diseased condition of the body. Some adjustment disorders are of this nature, and the medical model has been successful in certain of these instances. Other disorders do not seem to be medical, and yet their treatment sometimes falls into this domain. The concept of mental illness may send us off in the wrong direction in these instances (Engel, 1992).

Today the **sociocultural model** is becoming increasingly popular, emphasizing the role of the environment in maladjustment. The special value of this model lies in its relevance for preventive mental health. It includes a variety of workers not found in formal medical practice: the *substance abuse counselor, marriage counselor, physical abuse counselor,* and others. The *hotline* is a telephone number that, when dialed at any time of night or day, provides a willing, supportive listener, usually a layperson but sometimes a professional.

At the same time, the **support group** or *self-help group* is a collection of lay people facing similar problems, and they provide one another with emotional support and some technical assistance. Sometimes patterned after Alcoholics Anonymous, the basic idea is that people sharing a problem can help each other, whether the issue is parenting, physical illness, coworkers, or some other life crisis (Grief & Kristall, 1993; Miller, 1992; Wegener, 1992).

The other major aim of the preventive mental health movement, besides providing immediate support, is educating the public. Part of this task is a research problem, obtaining answers to numerous persistent questions about mental health. Another part lies in communicating to laypersons what is already known about mental disorders, their prevention, and their treatment. This communication can be accomplished partly through the specialty of **community psychology,** which aims to educate and support people in deprived circumstances.

A word about Mack is appropriate in this context, for it provides one further bit of instruction concerning preventive mental health and the research process that underlies the movement. Approximately ten months after Mack left formal treatment, his therapist located him once again and requested that he resume his weekly recordings. The aim was a follow-up study, assessing Mack's subsequent adjustment. For three weeks, Mack recorded the frequency and intensity of excessive sweating, which turned out to be a very simple task. The results showed rare instances of sweating, all at very low intensity, clearly within the normal range. We cannot be certain that therapy solved Mack's problem; we can say that the excessive sweating disappeared while he was undergoing this treatment process (Figure 16-14).

CULTURAL AND GENDER ISSUES. Like other areas of psychology, the mental health movement is increasingly recognizing the issues of culture and gender. Studies of cultural differences range from self-appraisal to modes of communication. Therapists who work with people from diverse cultural backgrounds, or any culture other than their own, will profit from a deeper understanding of these issues (Shweder & Sullivan, 1993).

In surveys of physical health, for example, Latin American populations in the United States generally believe themselves to be in significantly

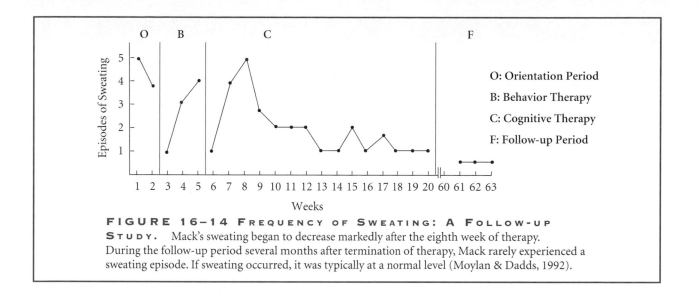

FIGURE 16–14 FREQUENCY OF SWEATING: A FOLLOW-UP STUDY. Mack's sweating began to decrease markedly after the eighth week of therapy. During the follow-up period several months after termination of therapy, Mack rarely experienced a sweating episode. If sweating occurred, it was typically at a normal level (Moylan & Dadds, 1992).

poorer health than that determined by independent medical examinations. European-American populations in the United States, on the average, describe themselves as slightly healthier than the rating obtained by standard biomedical assessments (Angel & Guarnaccia, 1989; Angel & Idler, 1992). Clearly there are cultural differences in experiencing physical disorders, reporting them, or both conditions. These and comparable findings in other areas contain obvious implications for all caregivers.

Gender differences are evident in participation in therapy, as noted in the next chapter. Men are distinctly less inclined than women to enter into a therapeutic relationship. The traditional male role is not consistent with the demands for a favorable outcome in therapy: willingness to engage in self-disclosure and emotional intimacy (Betz & Fitzgerald, 1993).

Mack showed this resistance in several respects. For four years, he endured the problem of sweating without sharing it with anyone. Then, when he began therapy, he was still unable to confront the feeling behind his sweating. He felt he had to "rise above it." After five weeks of treatment, he changed.

He decided that expressing emotion was not necessarily a weakness. His confrontations with the young woman, college examination, and letter to his dean, as well as the therapy sessions, helped him to reach this decision and to discover the real issue: a subtle, underlying anxiety.

An incident at the very end of the follow-up study suggested that Mack had overcome this problem. His family and friends had gathered at a large dinner party, and they were joking that Mack had no girlfriend. Mack began to feel himself growing warmer and therefore pulled off his sweater, an act that prompted more laughter and kidding. Mack, however, interpreted the event very differently. He explained to his therapist afterward that he felt comfortable revealing to the guests that he indeed felt warm (Moylan & Dadds, 1992). The act of taking off his sweater was a statement to himself. He had faced his anxiety without concern for what others thought.

Previously, Mack would have worn the sweater, felt himself growing warm, and tried unsuccessfully to regain control. He would have sweated it out under his sweater. Instead, by discarding the garment, he had demonstrated acceptance of himself.

ENTERING THERAPY

1. Confidential communication means that the therapist will not reveal information about the therapy session. In resistance, the patient unconsciously avoids progress because the present discomfort appears less painful than the anticipated discomfort of confronting the real problems directly.

INSIGHT THERAPIES

2. The insight therapies involve a series of interviews between a person seeking assistance and a therapist who listens, questions, or otherwise creates an atmosphere conducive to self-understanding. In psychoanalysis, three techniques are emphasized: free association, transference, and interpretation.

3. In person-centered therapy, the major humanistic approach, the emphasis is on the person's ability to solve his or her own problems in a climate that provides empathy, genuineness, and unconditional positive regard. In existential therapy, it is assumed that anxiety is an inevitable aspect of human life; people must learn to accept it and deal with it effectively.

4. Cognitive therapists generally take the view that the therapist should control the sessions. The basic assumptions in rational-emotive therapy are that the therapist knows best and that the person's thinking must be improved by understanding the *B* element of the *ABC*s. Cognitive therapy for depression is less confrontational.

5. Many therapies take place in spontaneous groups. In other group therapies, the members know one another and attempt to solve a shared problem. As in family and marital therapy, one member's problem is the group's problem.

BEHAVIOR THERAPIES

6. The behavior therapies are based on principles from the laboratory. Those arising from classical conditioning are of two types: systematic desensitization, which is concerned with reducing negative emotional responses, as in phobia; and aversion therapy, which is concerned with reducing positive emotional responses, as in alcoholism.

7. The operant methods are based on the systematic use of rewards and mild punishments. When reinforcement procedures are employed on a regular basis, the process is known as contingency management. When punishment is employed, it should be as immediate and mild as possible.

8. Observational learning is based on the principle that people can acquire new ways of behaving by watching others. The person demonstrating the behavior is known as a model, and the process of reproducing it is called modeling.

BIOMEDICAL THERAPIES

9. Biomedical therapies attempt to change mental functioning by altering conditions of the body. The natural body therapies seek to utilize the body's innate tendency to recover and achieve a balanced state. They are noninvasive and holistic in orientation, directed to the mind–body connection.

10. In electroconvulsive therapy, sometimes used with depression, a coma or convulsion is produced by a brief, weak electric shock. Psychosurgery involves cutting nerve pathways in the frontal area of the brain, after which some depressive patients seem more adjusted. Except as a last resort, these procedures have been largely discontinued.

11. With the advent of psychotherapeutic drugs, people are less frequently institutionalized. Under medication, they may be able to maintain jobs and appear at a clinic on an outpatient basis. The use of drugs generally suppresses rather than eliminates symptoms; therefore, drug therapy is commonly used with other treatments.

EVALUATING THERAPY

12. There are numerous problems in evaluating the effectiveness of therapy. These include: establishing adequate criteria for measuring cure or improvement; maintaining continuous, long-term follow-up studies to detect changes in adjustment; and obtaining accurate data on spontaneous remission in the general population.

13. Studies of therapy outcomes have found all therapy groups significantly more improved than control groups. However, the method, therapist, and patient all influence the outcome, a condition called the interaction principle.

MENTAL HEALTH MOVEMENTS

14. Deinstitutionalization is the process of discharging or transferring former mental patients to the community. It is often unsuccessful because appropriate support procedures are unavailable, necessitating rehospitalization, a condition known as the revolving door outcome.

15. The sociocultural model of mental disorder recognizes the role of the environment in contributing to maladjustment and therefore places increased emphasis on preventive mental health.

• WORKING WITH PSYCHOLOGY •

REVIEW OF KEY CONCEPTS

therapy
psychotherapy

Entering Therapy
brief therapy
confidential communication
resistance

Insight Therapies
insight therapy
psychoanalysis
free association
transference
interpretation
humanistic therapy
person-centered therapy
existential therapy
flooding
cognitive therapy
rational-emotive therapy
cognitive-behavioral therapy
group therapy
family therapy

marital therapy
Gestalt therapy

Behavior Therapies
behavior therapy
systematic desensitization
anxiety hierarchy
aversion therapy
contingency management
token economy
feedback
timeout
observational learning
modeling

Biomedical Therapies
biomedical therapy
natural body therapies
electroconvulsive therapy (ECT)
lobotomy
side effect
antipsychotic drugs
antidepressant drugs

lithium
antianxiety drugs

Evaluating Therapy
symptom substitution
spontaneous remission
placebo
interaction principle
eclectic approach
multimodal approach
therapeutic alliance

Mental Health Movements
institutionalization
deinstitutionalization
preventive mental health
devil model
medical model
sociocultural model
support group
community psychology

A NARRATIVE TWIST

Concerned about his sweating, Mack initially entered behavior therapy. Later, deciding that another approach might be more helpful, he changed to cognitive therapy. Mack instead might have tried other forms of insight therapy. Make a recommendation for him to enter either psychoanalysis or person-centered therapy. Then provide reasons for your choice, referring to specific therapeutic techniques and the ways they might be used in working with Mack's problems. ❧

TOPICAL QUESTIONS

• *Entering Therapy.* Consider the caution *Caveat emptor,* meaning "Let the buyer beware." Should a troubled person be held responsible for seeking proper treatment? What role should insurance regulations play? Within this context, make some recommendations for empowering the consumer.

• *Insight Therapies.* Compare person-centered therapy and its near opposite, rational-emotive therapy. Is empathy or education more useful in helping people to deal with adjustment problems? Explain your view.

• *Behavior Therapies.* Is behavior modification involved in certain forms of insight therapy? Make an argument for the presence of operant conditioning in verbal behavior and classical conditioning in the formation of positive attitudes.

• *Biomedical Therapies.* Almost 50 years ago, Antonio Egas Moniz won a Nobel Prize for his implementation of psychosurgery, a procedure largely ignored today, if not disparaged. Was his work a useful step forward, merely supplanted by psychotherapeutic drugs? Was it a step backward, one for which the prize was too hastily rewarded? Take a position that considers his contribution from both perspectives.

• *Evaluating Therapy.* In *Alice's Adventures in Wonderland* the Dodo bird says: *"Everybody* has won." How can this conclusion be correct for the outcomes of therapy when the different therapies involve different techniques? In your answer, refer to the interaction principle.

• *Mental Health Movements.* How will the revolution involving psychotherapeutic drugs be regarded in 2005, a half century after its origin? Will the use of drugs have become even more massive? Will community resources be aimed more directly at alleviating mental health problems? What developments may occur to influence the historical perspective on the drug revolution of the 1950s?

❧ TOPICS OF RELATED INTEREST ❧

Further background for understanding psychoanalysis as a therapy appears in discussions of memory (8), motivation (10), personality (14), and adjustment (15). Behavior therapy is based on the principles of classical and operant conditioning (7). The multiple bases of behavior is a fundamental theme throughout this book; it raises the question of the interaction principle, also discussed with respect to human development (12), intelligence (13), and personality (14).

SOCIETY
AND CULTURE

SOCIAL BEHAVIOR

❧

ATTITUDES
Forming Attitudes
Consistency in Attitudes
Techniques of Persuasion

SOCIAL COGNITION
Forming Impressions
Using Stereotypes
Attribution Theory

INTERPERSONAL ATTRACTION
Factors in Attraction
Long-Term Relationships

SOCIAL INFLUENCE
Tendency to Conform
Compliance and Obedience
Altruistic Behavior

GROUP PROCESSES
Status in the Group
Cooperation and Competition
Making Decisions
Group Leadership

17
SOCIAL
BEHAVIOR

STACY CRAWLED OUT OF HER SLEEPING BAG BEFORE DAWN AND JOINED HER COMPANIONS AT THE SIX-FOOT STONE ALTAR. THE SHERPAS WERE ALREADY THERE sprinkling rice, chanting softly, and burning branches of juniper. They certainly were not going to miss the ceremony. After all, they had built the altar to assist them in challenging Chomolungma, the mightiest mountain in the world.

The dozen or so Americans laid on the shelf of that altar their most precious possessions at the moment—chocolate candies, raisins, flags and pennants, and bottles of whiskey. The Sherpas offered up sampas, which are balls of barley flour, standard fare at the Pujah, a Buddhist blessing ritual.

Although the Americans did not understand the Pujah, they were taking no chances. It *might* help—when they faced the towering masses of ice and snow, the shrill whistle of blizzard winds, and the sudden roar of an avalanche. Appealing to Buddha and the mountain gods for a safe passage up Mount Everest, the Western name for Chomolungma, seemed like quite a good idea. Moreover, this ceremony reminded everyone that they were a team. Especially when they entered the Khumbu Ice Fall, 2,000 feet of sheer, vertical ice, the success of any one climber would depend on the cooperation of all. Of those who attempt this passage, many do not return.

Meanwhile, an American research group of psychologists and physiologists from the University of Washington went about its own business, preparing to assess the climbers on this expedition. People at high altitudes quickly lose control of mental and physical capacities, due to lack of oxygen, and the research team wanted to investigate these conditions. Knowing they would not ascend Everest beyond the second base camp, they were generally less concerned about satisfying the mountain gods.

While the climbers in the American expedition reflected on the challenge ahead, the Sherpas chanted and chanted, at times in wild crescendos, at times in low murmurs, like quiet prayers. Occasionally, they called to the Americans, asking them to throw handfuls of rice into the sky, as further offerings to Buddha.

When the ceremony was over, the American climbers frivolously tossed barley flour at one another, producing billowy white clouds suggestive of the blizzards ahead. Then they smeared flour on their hair and faces. The white streaks symbolized a long, happy life, and they were eager to do whatever might contribute to that outcome. Afterward, they posed for a photograph. Seemingly happy and confident, their smiles and besmirched faces belied the dangers that lay ahead (Allison, 1993).

The Sherpas were more reserved. They knew the mountains well, living in Nepal, among the Himalayas, between the borders of China and India. Often hired as porters and guides for climbing, they also knew the importance of teamwork on these expeditions.

What would happen on this expedition as friendships formed and personal difficulties arose? Who would climb with whom on the summit teams? Would Stacy Allison reach the top of the

world? Would she be the first American woman to do so? Would cultural differences emerge?

Behaviors of this sort, and the related interactions, are the substance of social psychology. Simply defined, **social psychology** is the study of individuals in groups, specifically the ways in which human beings interact with one another. The Everest expedition provides a helpful background for this discussion because it includes interactions among men and women from two cultures and three groups: the American climbers, the Sherpa guides and porters, and the Washington research team.

We begin this chapter by examining attitudes, considered by some psychologists as a first principle in social behavior. Then we study a more exclusively social issue, social cognition. How do we interpret information about other people? At the next stage, we consider interpersonal attraction, our preferences for relationships with specific people.

The discussion then turns from the individual to the group, focusing on the conditions and outcomes of social influence: conformity, compliance, obedience, and altruism. Finally, we consider fundamental group processes, as individuals interact within the group setting.

• ATTITUDES •

One of the most widely used concepts in social psychology, an *attitude* is difficult to define. For this reason, and because attitudes cannot be observed directly, some psychologists ignore them. They study only overt behavior rather than make assumptions about inner states that allegedly influence behavior. The position adopted in this text, and by many social psychologists today, is that attitudes are important and can be usefully defined (Dillard, 1993). An integral part of an individual's interactions with others, an **attitude** is a tendency to make an evaluation,

reflected in three basic components: thinking, feeling, and acting (Olson & Zanna, 1993).

Thinking, the first component, obviously involves a thought or belief about something. Stacy Allison believed that mountaineering is a healthy, inspiring activity, especially if pursued with proper knowledge and caution. What about her feelings?

Stacy immediately became excited by any opportunity to climb challenging mountains. This general excitement also became differentiated into more specific feelings, such as enthusiasm, confidence, and anticipation. And third, what about her actions? She reacted in a predictable, consistent manner. At the first opportunity, she signed on for an Everest expedition. In fact, she signed up twice, for her first effort proved to be a bitter, wrenching failure.

A year earlier, with three other American climbers, she had almost reached the peak of Mount Everest. After spending seven nights in an atmosphere too thin to support sustained life, they remained pinned down by an autumn blizzard, the worst on Mount Everest in 40 years. At that altitude, the human digestive system cannot readily utilize nourishment, and the climber's muscles begin to atrophy. At dawn the next day, the team members asked themselves: "One more day?" One member, barely able to eat breakfast, shook his head. "If I don't go down today," he said, "I'm not going to get down." As the climbers began their descent, they hid their anguish, and for Stacy that disappointment was acute. The others were men. If the team had advanced those last 3,000 feet, she would have been the first American woman to reach the peak of Mount Everest (Allison, 1993).

Clearly, Stacy Allison had a positive attitude toward mountaineering, even in the face of this disappointment. It showed in her thinking, feeling, and acting. These three components are also described as cognitive, affective, and behavioral components.

FIGURE 17–1 COMPONENTS OF ATTITUDE. The behavioral component of an attitude often is not readily displayed, especially in comparison with the cognitive and affective components. Among people with favorable attitudes toward mountaineering, only a few regularly climb mountain peaks.

FORMING ATTITUDES

How do attitudes develop? The obvious answer is that they arise initially through contacts with our parents, early teachers, and other adults. Later, peers and friends influence the various components (Figure 17-1). But the basic question still stands: By what processes do attitudes develop?

DIRECT INSTRUCTION AND MODELING. In the most obvious instances, attitudes are formed by direct instruction. A small girl was informed that she would have tapioca for lunch. She replied: "I don't like that." Then she asked, "What is it?" She had been told by her older sister that tapioca has a disagreeable taste, a form of direct instruction. Attitudes toward mountaineering, religious ceremonies, and social psychology develop in the same way. Direct instruction can play a significant role, as it did for Stacy in her adolescent years, but it is far from the whole story.

Sometimes the instruction is indirect. People teach one another merely by what they do. Siblings, parents, friends, public figures, and total strangers can influence our attitudes in this way—by acting as models. A *model* is someone who demonstrates the proper performance, intentionally or otherwise. During college, Stacy observed a park ranger nimbly scaling the summit of a rocky ledge. Watching her, Stacy decided that being a mountaineer was "everything I wanted to be" (Allison, 1993).

Children who observe their elders happily eating grasshoppers want to eat grasshoppers too. Those who notice adults befriending strangers tend to develop positive attitudes toward strangers. In this process, called *modeling*, discussed in the chapter on learning, one person learns by following the example of another.

CLASSICAL AND OPERANT CONDITIONING. Suppose a parent who wears a certain cologne is also kind and helpful to his child. Through the pairing of this odor with kindness, food, play, and so forth, the child eventually develops a positive attitude toward the cologne. Associated with good outcomes, this event becomes favorable too. You may recognize this process as classical conditioning.

An early study of this process used the names

for various nationalities—German, Swedish, French, and Dutch. They were paired with positive, negative, or neutral words. Later, after many pairings, an attitude questionnaire was administered regarding these nationalities. It was found that each nationality was perceived as positive, negative, or neutral, depending on its previous associations (Staats & Staats, 1958). Today there is abundant evidence of this sort (Kuykendall & Keating, 1990).

Suppose the child wore the cologne one day, and his family complimented him on it. If so, this behavior of wearing perfume was reinforced, and it was likely to reappear. The process here is operant conditioning, for behaviors that produce positive consequences tend to be repeated. While Stacy was mountaineering in Yosemite National Park one summer during college, her behavior certainly produced positive consequences. She felt the rhythm of the climb, the whispering of mountain breezes, and the sun on her back. She felt as free as a hawk that happened to be riding an updraft of air above her. As she expressed it, "The world was in harmony" (Allison, 1993).

ROLE OF COGNITION. Attitudes also can be developed or changed through the way we think about things—without direct instruction, modeling, or any significant conditioning. Thought is involved in all of those processes, and sometimes thought alone is the basis for attitude formation.

Suppose a young man receives a grade of 40 on a mathematics exam. Thinking that 44 is the maximum score, he regards his work favorably. Then he discovers that 60 is the maximum score, and his attitude toward his score promptly becomes unfavorable. Both attitudes are developed simply on the basis of reasoning, as he compares himself with an absolute standard and perhaps with other students, as well. Cognitive processes can be fundamentally involved in the development of attitudes (Chaiken & Stangor, 1987).

MEASUREMENT OF ATTITUDES. Regardless of their origins, how can we measure attitudes toward mountaineering or mathematics? A common method involves a *Likert rating scale,* in which printed statements concerning the issue are each accompanied by a scale of three to seven intervals, ranging from extremely negative to extremely positive. The subjects indicate their attitude toward each statement by marking a position on the scale. Likert scales are relatively easy to construct and score, but they can be readily faked (Table 17-1).

A very different approach employs modern electronic equipment for assessing heart rate, skin conductance, and even pupillary changes. Less subject to fabrication, physiological reactions are becoming more important as measures of attitudes (Tesser & Shaffer, 1990).

But there are problems here, too. First, a pounding heart and increased rate of breathing indicate that the reaction is a strong one, but we do not know whether it is positive or negative. Second, there are large individual differences in emotional expression. Some people, when aroused, experience a pounding heart; others develop sweaty palms; and still others show neither response, but their voices rise instead. Third, many measures, such as pupillary changes, require highly controlled conditions or elaborate apparatus. And finally, to the

---

1. Mountaineering is a worthwhile activity.
   SA   A   (MA)   MD   D   SD
2. Climbing mountains builds character.
   SA   (A)   MA   MD   D   SD
3. For an experienced person, climbing Mount Everest can be a safe form of recreation.
   SA   A   MA   MD   (D)   SD

SA = Strongly agree   MD = Mildy disagree
A = Agree   D = Disagree
MA = Mildly agree   SD = Strongly disagree

TABLE 17–1 AN ATTITUDE SCALE. A full attitude scale would include many items of this sort. The subject's reponse to each item is assigned a value ranging from +3 to −3, excluding 0. The scores for the circled responses here would be +1, +2, and −2. Hence, the total score is +1.

extent that the person being tested can concentrate on something else, the results may be misleading. Altogether, several physiological, psychological, and behavioral measures must be combined for the most effective measurement of attitudes.

CONSISTENCY
IN ATTITUDES

Ralph Waldo Emerson remarked: "A foolish consistency is the hobgoblin of little minds." Most of us develop and maintain attitudes that are in agreement with one another, however. Several theories of attitude formation and change are based on this principle of consistency.

EARLY VIEWPOINTS. Among these theories, the oldest is called **balance theory** because it stresses that people seek a balanced or harmonious state among their attitudes. In college, Stacy met a young woman named Evelyn, and they became friendly. Both of them were learning mountaineering and enjoying it immensely. There were positive relationships all around; a balanced state existed. As this friendship developed, they discovered that neither of them liked their college studies. A balanced state still existed, for they liked each other and both disliked college.

Suppose a husband favors gun control and his wife does not, and yet they have a very satisfying marital relationship. Here there is imbalance. Neither person's attitude is supported by the other,

whom he or she likes (Alessio, 1990; Heider, 1946; Figure 17–2).

Another approach goes a step beyond balance or harmony. It regards attitudes as changeable and considers the probable outcome of these changes. Specifically, **congruity theory** states that attitude shifts occur in the direction of increased consistency (Osgood, Suci, & Tannenbaum, 1957). A woman mildly against day care finds that a lawyer she much admires is in favor of day care. It is hypothesized that her attitude toward him will become less positive and her attitude toward day care less negative. The degree of change should not be equal, however, unless the different attitudes are of the same strength. A greater shift is expected in the milder attitude. If she is not particularly concerned about day care and feels strongly about the lawyer, then her attitude toward day care should undergo the greater change in strength and direction.

In one study, 604 people from the general population were interviewed by telephone and asked their views on the quality of clothes available for purchase at various places of business. These places ranged from major department stores to off-price discount warehouses. As predicted by congruity theory, perception of the wearing apparel was decidedly influenced by the type of business with which it was associated. When offered for sale by department stores, brands of clothing were rated significantly higher than when available at discount and chain stores (Morganosky, 1990).

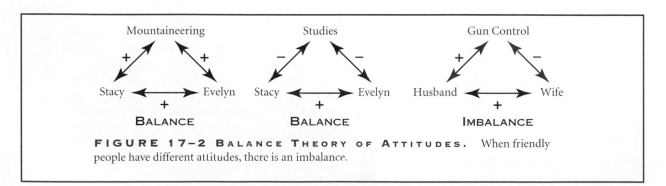

FIGURE 17–2 BALANCE THEORY OF ATTITUDES. When friendly people have different attitudes, there is an imbalance.

DISSONANCE THEORY. The third approach, dissonance theory, goes beyond the degree or direction of attitude change within an individual. It emphasizes instead the psychological processes by which inconsistency is resolved. This theory is called **cognitive-dissonance theory** because the individual's cognitions are dissonant or inconsistent, and the person is motivated to dispel this state of tension in various ways.

Consider what happened when people opposed to the use of electric shock agreed to administer shocks to others as part of a research project. Before the experiment, they experienced directly the amount of shock that the subjects would receive and rated its painfulness. After the experiment, in which they shocked other people, they again rated the painfulness of the shock. Can you make a prediction based on dissonance theory? In the second rating, did they increase or decrease their estimate of the painfulness of the shock? It had been anticipated that the subjects, after administering the shock to other people, would then rate it as less painful, and this prediction was supported (Brock & Buss, 1962).

More recently, householders in one group were informed about the inconsistency between their attitudes toward conservation and their high consumption of electricity. Those in a second group were simply informed that they were high consumers of electricity. Still others were sent information on how to conserve electricity. After two weeks, energy consumption was measured once again in all groups. It was found that among the 272 subjects, those in the first group, with high dissonance, conserved more electricity than those in any of the other groups (Kantola, Syme, & Campbell, 1984).

According to this research, dissonance can be reduced through rationalizing, perceiving selectively, changing one's behavior, or seeking new information. The subjects in the first experiment apparently were rationalizing or engaging in selective perception when rating the second shock as less painful. Those in the study on energy consumption changed their behavior. There is, of course, no dissonance if the individual does not perceive any inconsistency (Table 17-2).

TECHNIQUES OF PERSUASION

Apart from theory, everyday life in this country includes many practical techniques for developing and changing attitudes, especially through the mass media. They are vital not only to salespersons and swindlers but also to educators, counselors, health officials, and people concerned with public welfare. They urge us to drive safely, avoid drugs, dispose of litter and, of course, mail holiday gifts early.

THEORY	EMPHASIS	EXAMPLE
Balance	Harmony among an individual's attitudes	Wendy loves her sister Stacy, who enjoys mountaineering. Wendy mildly disapproves of mountaineering. There is imbalance.
Congruity	Attitude shift within an individual	Wendy feels strongly about her sister. She is only mildly against mountaineering. Thus, her attitude toward mountaineering will shift in a positive direction.
Cognitive dissonance	Resolving inconsistency among attitudes	Wendy feels some tension because her attitudes are inconsistent. She decides that she needs more information on the dangers of mountaineering.

TABLE 17–2 THEORIES OF ATTITUDE CONSISTENCY. Wendy maintained a loving relationship with her sister Stacy, and yet she had a mild dislike of mountaineering. Each of the three major theories of attitude consistency approaches Wendy's situation somewhat differently.

Mountaineers cannot finance major expeditions themselves, as Stacy soon discovered. They must persuade individuals and manufacturers to donate supplies, equipment, and funds. For this purpose, both Everest teams, based in Seattle, used an assortment of techniques addressing the three basic elements in communication: the source, audience, and message.

SOURCE CHARACTERISTICS. It has been almost 20 centuries since Aristotle wrote in his *Rhetoric* that the *ethos*, or credibility, of the communicator is the most important single factor in the persuasiveness of a communication, and most subsequent research supports this view (McGuire, 1985; Zimbardo & Lieppe, 1991). The crucial elements in credibility are trust and expertise. Don Goodman, organizer of the second expedition, had both of these qualities. Using his good-natured integrity and experience in climbing Everest, he gained considerable financial support from private corporations and public appeals (Allison, 1993).

Credibility also came from the University of Washington, which assembled the research group accompanying the expedition. High-altitude mountaineering is of special interest to investigators in psychology and physiology because the environment is extreme, yet natural. Learning and other thought processes are impaired at high altitudes due to the lack of oxygen in vital brain areas (Nelson, Dunlosky, White, Steinberg, Townes, & Anderson, 1990). One aim of the Washington research team was to study human thought under hypoxia, a condition of oxygen deficiency sometimes resembling alcohol intoxication.

The importance of source credibility is clearly recognized by television advertisers. They hire professional athletes to endorse sneakers, movie stars to endorse skin creams, and sedentary types to promote hemorrhoid treatments. An integral factor in the acceptance of the message, however, is the perceived intent of the communicator. Therefore, unsolicited common folk actually outstrip sports heroes and other celebrities in popularity for endorsement of products. These neighborly individuals presumably have no ulterior motives! And they ask for a lower endorsement fee.

AUDIENCE CHARACTERISTICS. A second concern, after the credibility of the communicator, is the participation of the audience. Here again, early studies established a principle that is still accepted today: Audiences tend to have the most positive attitudes toward events in which they have become most involved—through discussions, clapping, singing, and so forth. Sports teams, musical shows, and political speakers all utilize this principle, as did the Everest expeditions. The members involved the press in question-and-answer sessions, held rallies, and encouraged interested individuals to participate in fund-raising (Allison, 1993).

The importance of participation was demonstrated in a classic study during World War II. Choice cuts of meat were scarce, and attempts were made to persuade people to use less-preferred meat products. In one research program, some shoppers listened to a lecture on using these products. Other shoppers were involved in a group discussion about the problems they might experience in using such foods and how they might overcome them. At a later date, the investigators checked to discover the effectiveness of the two presentations. They found the discussion method far superior for promoting a change in attitude and behavior (Lewin, 1947).

Modern investigators have taken this question one step further, assessing the importance of the audience's predisposition to become active or passive. Hence, a dozen commercials were presented to 252 undergraduates serving as subjects. Each commercial was either open-ended, in which some issues were left to be considered by the interviewer, or closed-ended, raising no unanswered points. As predicted, when the audience was predisposed to be active and involved, the open-ended commercials stimulated more favorable reactions than the closed-ended ones. With uninterested audiences, there was little difference between the two appeals (Sawyer & Howard, 1991).

MESSAGE CHARACTERISTICS. The importance of message characteristics depends on the source and audience, and vice versa, as implied already. Nevertheless, a fundamental question arises in nearly all efforts at persuasion: To change an audience's attitude, should the message give the full story, telling both sides, or not? To persuade someone to accept viewpoint *A*, should viewpoint *B* be included or ignored?

Except in the case of very simple messages, such as those merely promoting a common product, the most lasting effect is achieved by presenting the desired view, the opposite view, and then counterarguments against the opposite view. In this way, the audience is inclined toward *A* and prepared against future propaganda on behalf of *B*, the opposing viewpoint. A *two-sided presentation*, in which the speaker discusses both the pros and cons of each side, can provide immunization against later exposure to opposing viewpoints. This balanced approach appears to be particularly important for audiences of high intelligence and for hostile or neutral audiences, who need to hear both sides of the issue (McGuire, 1985).

From another perspective, most messages can be divided roughly into two types. Those that appeal to thought and reason use a central route; they go directly to the point and substance of the issue. Those that employ extraneous appeals, such as songs and celebrities and slogans, follow a peripheral route; the approach is roundabout and more emotional. Which route is favored? Research has shown that an enduring attitude change is most likely fostered by the central route. To develop or change a *complex* attitude, we need to think about the proposition, elaborate on it, and consider the details. This finding supports the *elaboration-likelihood model* of persuasion, which states that when the audi-

ence is intelligent and motivated, a direct appeal to thought, reason, and mulling things over will be the better route to persuasion. When the audience is less able and willing, rules of thumb and short cuts will be more effective (Petty & Cacioppo, 1986).

Many messages include both approaches. In her fund-raising efforts, Stacy stressed the specific facts of the expedition and used an emotional appeal, trying to make the prospective giver "feel the poetry of the climb" (Allison, 1993).

FEAR-AROUSING MESSAGES. Among all the questions about message characteristics, the use of fear has received the most research attention (Olson & Zanna, 1993). One form of common sense states that warnings about dangers should aim to instill a high level of fear. An announcement might show alcohol, a crashed car, and a graveyard. Another might show a cocaine addict describing her broken life. A competing form of common sense states that unpleasant messages are rejected or ignored; only positive appeals are heeded. A message low in fear arousal might show an animated embryo thanking its mother for not using alcohol or cigarettes (Reeves, Newhagen, Maibach, Basil, & Kurz, 1991).

This debate has a long history with mixed results, for several factors are influential, one of which is the subjects' initial level of fear. If it is high, a further increase may produce an immobilized state or an avoidance reaction, thus impeding change. If it is low, arousing fear may stimulate action in the desired direction. Hence, campaigns against AIDS and drug abuse, for example, must take into account the original level of anxiety in the target population (Sherr, 1990).

A related vital factor is the extent to which the message contains instructions on the correct or desired behavior. Messages low in fear arousal generally contain more detailed instructions and advice than those high in fear arousal. Therefore, other things being equal, they may be more likely to lead to constructive behavior (Reeves et al., 1991).

In summary, these techniques of persuasion reflect the basic theme of this book: the multiple bases of behavior. An audience may be persuaded by the credibility of the source, participation in the presentation, balance of the presentation, and arousal of fear, which in turn depends on the initial level of fear and the amount of instruction in the message. Behavior is influenced by many factors within and outside the individual.

• SOCIAL COGNITION •

After the Pujah blessing ceremony, the camp alarms went off at 2:00 A.M., and the ascent began that day, August 29. The climbers wanted to complete most of the day's work before the sun heated and loosened the ice. Donning boots and head lamps, they began setting a zigzag route through the ice fall. Jim Frush, leader on the mountain, encouraged group efforts and team spirit. Working together under the constant threat of avalanches, the members became more and more aware of one another.

This awareness brings us to a prominent topic in social psychology, **social cognition,** concerned with how people interpret information about other people, their relationships, social events, and social institutions. Social cognition is the inner, individual dimension of social behavior and experience.

FORMING IMPRESSIONS

The expedition included two hard-working physicians, Steve Ruoss and Geoff Tabin, both in their early thirties, quick-witted, and experienced at high altitudes. Steve was a bit taller; Geoff was bearded; and they both wore the usual climber's garb (Allison, 1993).

What do we think about these members of the expedition? What are they like? We have only their clothes, physical appearance, and occupations on which to make a judgment. This problem, called *person perception,* refers to the ways in which we perceive and understand another individual. Part of social cognition, it appears to be an extremely complex activity, raising questions about unconscious as well as conscious processes (Figure 17–3).

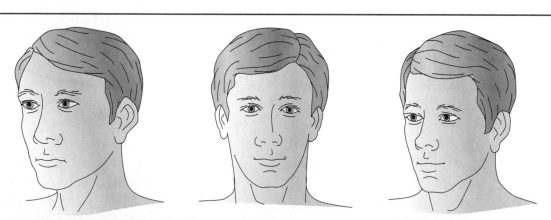

FIGURE 17–3 AWARENESS AND PERSON PERCEPTION. Decide which face is most attractive and indicate the reasons for your choice. Subjects performing this task typically prefer the center face, with normal proportions, rather than the one on the left or right, with the eyes too high or too low, respectively. In repeating this task with many different faces and explaining the reasons for their choices, subjects commonly select the normal face but do not refer to the proportions. In other words, they seem to utilize information about the faces that is not immediately accessible to their awareness (Hill & Lewicki, 1991).

INFLUENCE OF CENTRAL TRAITS.

Especially when dealing with strangers, we dislike ambiguity. We try to resolve the uncertainty as soon as possible, and therefore we sometimes form an impression based on little evidence. If we arbitrarily decide, for example, that one of these mountaineers is cold and aloof and that the other is warm and personable, then we may soon find ourselves jumping to other conclusions about them.

This characteristic, degree of social warmth, also called the *warm–cold dimension,* is highly influential in our estimates of other personal traits; therefore, in social psychology it is called a **central trait.** Central traits are instrumental in the way we perceive other people; they are *not* necessarily the *basic traits* of the individual, discussed in the chapter on personality. Research on central traits has shown that a person described as intelligent, skillful, industrious, cold, determined, practical, and polite is considered significantly different from one described in exactly the same way, except with the substitution of *warm* for *cold.* The warm–cold dimension greatly influences our judgment about whether the person is generous, happy, good-natured, and even important. Other traits have not shown this effect. The substitution of *blunt* for *polite,* for example, does not change the overall rating significantly (Asch, 1946).

Another characteristic that is certainly central and therefore influences other people's reactions is *insane, schizophrenic,* or *crazy.* Once a person has been so labeled, even normal behaviors tend to be perceived as deviant (Rosenhan, 1973).

A perceptual error of this sort is known as the **halo effect,** meaning that a favorable or unfavorable judgment about one characteristic prompts similar judgments about other characteristics of this same person, regardless of the objective situation. Suppose Geoff proves to be highly intelligent, an admirable quality. The halo effect prompts us to assume that he possesses other esteemed traits. The halo effect even operates with beauty. Beautiful people tend to be judged as more intelligent than people of the same intelligence who are less attractive (Hatfield & Sprecher, 1986).

OUT-OF-ROLE BEHAVIOR.

Another way of forming impressions relies on unusual or unexpected behavior. For example, some members of the Everest expedition, those with the most experience, signed on as summit climbers. They expected or hoped to make the last stage of the ascent, reaching the very top of the mountain. Others joined as support climbers; with less experience, they agreed to stay at the lower levels, assisting the summit teams. Besides Stacy, clearly a summit aspirant, there were two other women on the expedition. One of them, Peggy Luce, was inexperienced. "I don't mind being a support climber," she said, acknowledging her background. "I just want to go" (Allison, 1993).

Scaling Mount Everest is not a straightforward task. It begins when support climbers and summit climbers establish a large base camp at the bottom of the mountain, followed by four or so intermediate camps partway up the mountain. After the fourth camp has been set, two or three summit climbers attempt to reach the top of the mountain.

Suppose, instead, that one of the support climbers decides to make a sprint for the summit. What would be your impression of this person? You might decide that this person is bold and unruly. Why? The reason is that this response would involve out-of-role behavior. A role is a pattern of behavior associated with a particular position, and *out-of-role behavior* is a response not expected from someone in that position. A support climber should not suddenly ignore agreements and behave instead like a summit climber. If this behavior occurred, it would seem to be a characteristic of that individual.

In one experiment, the subjects listened to a tape in which people sometimes showed the behavior expected of a job applicant and sometimes showed out-of-role behavior, making irrelevant comments and asking inappropriate questions. When these people acted contrary to the expected role, the judges perceived them as showing their true colors (Jones, David, & Jergen, 1961). Not called forth by any obvious aspect of the external situation, out-of-role behavior is assumed to be a function of underlying personal characteristics.

∾

USING STEREOTYPES

A major reason for the interest in attitudes among early social psychologists was their relevance for stereotypes and prejudice. Recently, with greater sensitivity to cultural differences, there has been a resurgence of research interest in these topics (Olson & Zanna, 1993).

The attempt to climb Mount Everest involved two major cultural groups, North Americans and Sherpas. Among the Americans, there were subgroups of summit climbers and support climbers, and they differed in age, experience, and the goal of climbing to the top of the world. Also, there was the research team, distinguished by its academic interests.

The Sherpas, people of Tibetan stock, live on the southern side of the Himalaya Mountains. They are dark-skinned, possess powerful lungs, and demonstrate considerable mountaineering ability. Knowing that Karma was a Sherpa, in fact manager of the Sherpas on this expedition, we might decide that he too was an agile climber.

A view of this sort, based on an oversimplified perception or rigid generalization, is known as a stereotype. In a **stereotype,** certain traits are assigned to an individual simply because that person is a member of a particular social group—an occupational group, race, nationality, or other category of people. According to stereotypes, Italians are passionate; the upper class is snobbish; librarians are prim and proper; and psychologists . . . well . . . er . . . they like to write about stereotypes. In

fact, as the head Sherpa on this expedition, Karma was regarded as overweight, sloppy, and too dedicated to Nepalese beer to be a notable climber (Allison, 1993). He did *not* fit the stereotype.

What characteristics are used in forming stereotypes? Just as you would expect, they are immediately accessible: gender, age, and race. On this basis, one would expect physical appearance to be an important basis for stereotypes, and such is the case (Fiske, 1993).

STEREOTYPES AND PREJUDICE. In addition to stereotypes, our ideas about people are sometimes based on considerable emotion without much thought. This reaction is known as a **prejudice,** which is an attitude, usually negative, toward something or some members of a group, developed without objective evaluation. The topic in question has been prejudged. Like other attitudes, a prejudice has three components—cognitive, affective, and behavioral—but the latter two dominate, especially the affective component. Also, like other attitudes, a prejudice may be formed through modeling, conditioning, and direct instruction. We can be prejudiced for or against people who drink beer, become physicians, or pursue any other lifestyle.

Stereotypes and prejudices differ in at least two related ways. The former are more cognitive, concerned with thinking; the latter are more affective, concerned with feelings. Consequently, and this is the second difference, stereotypes can be relatively neutral; prejudices are essentially positive or negative, usually negative (Hilton & von Hippel, 1996).

STEREOTYPES AS FACILITATING. A great deal has been written about stereotypes, and there has been considerable reluctance among educated people to think in terms of these categories. Nevertheless, we all use them in dealing with people. We make generalizations about adolescents, used-car dealers, scientists, and kings—all from the perspectives of our different subcultures. Without some generalizations, life would be difficult indeed; we would have to start from the zero point in each new situation (Figure 17-4).

The psychologists on the Washington research team, for example, behaved according to occupational stereotypes. They administered questionnaires to climbers at different altitudes, aiming to discover the ways in which oxygen deprivation influenced climbers' memories and judgments about their memories.

If you are to be a host for the weekend, you want to know whether your guest is a child, a guide from the Maine woods, or a city lawyer. Then you plan to bob for apples, serve apple strudel, or visit the Big Apple. These decisions are also based on stereotypes.

Thirty people serving as judges were asked to predict the occupational interests of six strangers. In one instance, the predictions were based on the information that each person was a typical male or female undergraduate at a certain university. In

FIGURE 17–4 USING STEREOTYPES. Make some guesses about this man's favorite activities. Select two: reading fairy tales, watching football games, going to sewing class, playing with his dog. Generalizations about truck drivers *may* aid in first impressions, but the observer must be prepared to revise them on the basis of contrary evidence.

another instance, predictions were made after each stranger appeared separately before the judges and completed simple tasks, such as drawing on the blackboard, building a house of cards, and describing the room. When the two predictions were compared, it was found that those based on the stereotypes were significantly more accurate than those based on observations of each individual's expressive behavior. The clues provided by the behavior were either ignored or misunderstood by the judges (Gage, 1952).

These results suggest that in forming first impressions, knowledge of a stereotype may be superior to brief observation. The crucial factor, of course, is the accuracy of the stereotype. If you are seeking porters and climbers to assist in an Everest expedition, you would be wise to search among the Sherpas.

STEREOTYPES AS DEBILITATING. Despite the possible advantage of stereotypes in forming first impressions, their limitations must be kept firmly in mind. First, their accuracy may be overrated or unknown. Second, although a stereotype may have some validity for a group of people, the chances are considerably less that it applies to a given individual. Contrary to a popular stereotype, not every psychologist is a bearded fellow with rumpled clothes and a foreign accent. And many are only mildly eccentric. Not all Sherpas are able mountaineers, as Karma demonstrated.

Third, and most important, some stereotypes involve **ethnocentrism,** the belief that other cultures are necessarily odd, immoral, or inferior because they do not share the standards of one's own culture. For many years, people living in the United States described countries with fewer technological developments as backward. The damaging consequences of such a viewpoint need not be elaborated. As a native of one of these countries wryly explained to a missionary, in a popular cartoon: "It's not that my country is underdeveloped but perhaps that yours is overdeveloped."

Furthermore, as stereotypes become increasingly affective, they become prejudices. In *sexism*, for example, one gender is considered inferior to the other, rather than different from it. In *ageism*, it is considered better to be young than old. The elderly are not valued for their experience but rejected for their lack of strength and quickness, both mental and physical. Cultures differ widely in ageism, as is evident in comparisons among China, Nepal, and the United States.

CULTURAL PLURALISM. The term **culture** refers to the totality of beliefs and behavior patterns characteristic of a particular group. These may include language, customs, and religion, as well as age, racial background, and other factors.

The difficulty of cross-cultural understanding is evident in a comparison between common aphorisms in the United States and Japan. One well-known piece of advice in this country states: "The squeaky wheel gets the oil." The Japanese have a different saying: "The nail that stands out gets pounded down." In the collectivist cultures of Eastern societies, individual differences are minimized. In many Western societies, people take pride in being distinguished (Triandis, McCusker, & Hui, 1990). In the United States, people tend to develop an *individual self*, in which personal traits are more important than group memberships. Japanese commonly develop a *relational self*, identifying themselves as group members first and then as individuals.

Cultural differences in the United States are heightened by differences among our ancestors, including Native Americans, African-Americans, and European colonists, as well as the enormous diversity among later immigrants. According to the melting pot theory, it was assumed that features of these subcultures would melt away, becoming assimilated into a new, unique, and homogeneous culture, that of the United States. This outcome has not occurred, partly because people are proud of their heritage and partly because some subcultures were denied ready assimilation into the dominant society. Instead, the new metaphor is a mosaic. The social ideal is *cultural pluralism*, in which differences among subcultures are recognized, accepted, and valued (Figure 17-5).

Faced with this challenge, our society is encouraging **multicultural awareness,** meaning sensitivity to and acceptance of differences among subgroups or subcultures, regarding them as equally viable approaches to human civilization. Multicultural awareness is essentially the opposite of ethnocentrism. As we move toward a global economy, culturally sensitive research becomes essential to the integrity of psychology (Graham, 1992).

As it turned out, awareness of other cultures was inevitable on the south side of Mount Everest

FIGURE 17–5 CULTURAL DIFFERENCES. Necessity is the mother of invention, prompting certain skills in one culture not found in another.

during Stacy's second expedition. Groups from several nations sought or built routes to the summit. A team of Koreans cooperated with the Americans. The French became three parties, traveling together but climbing separately. The Czechs and New Zealanders formed a joint team, and the Spaniards struggled to find their place among these diverse groups.

❧

ATTRIBUTION THEORY

The third woman climber on the American expedition was Diana Dailey, a very athletic person in her mid-forties and ever mindful of her fitness. Popular opinion pointed to her as most likely to become the first American woman to reach the peak of Mount Everest. Overflowing with energy, Diana rarely stopped training and spoke in a friendly manner to everyone (Allison, 1993).

How did the other members of the expedition *decide* about her personality? What thought processes did they use? Here we are concerned not with impressions of other people but rather with how they are formed.

The aim of **attribution theory** is to understand how people explain others' and their own behavior. Behavior can be attributed to dispositions within the individual, to factors in the environment, or to both conditions (Kelley, 1967; Zuckerman & Feldman, 1984).

ASSIGNING CAUSES. Let us look at the fact that Diana trained incessantly. The expedition members might have decided that this behavior occurred because she had high standards and was conscientious. In a **dispositional attribution,** the causes of behavior are assigned to traits or dispositions within the individual. Diana behaved that way because she was that way; she was simply and naturally energetic.

Alternatively, her teammates might have decided that she exercised constantly because she was new to the expedition and uncertain of her place in it. After becoming established, she would be more relaxed. Then, too, perhaps she wanted to be the first American woman to scale Everest, an opportunity that might come her way. In a **situational attribution,** the causes of behavior are assigned to the circumstances, not to the individual.

In making this decision, three factors are influential. The first, consistency, concerns the regularity with which the behavior occurs. If Diana exercised intensely every day, which she did, then we would be inclined to maintain the dispositional attribution. A second factor, consensus, raises the question of whether other people behave the same way. If no other member of the expedition engaged in such extensive exercise, including newcomers, then there is further evidence for the dispositional attribution. And finally, the concern in distinctiveness is whether or not this behavior occurred in other contexts (Kelley, 1967). If Diana trained constantly back in Seattle and elsewhere, even before the expedition became possible for her, then the dispositional attribution would have still further confirmation.

OVERATTRIBUTION EFFECT. It would be nice to say that when the evidence is mixed, people carefully weigh all factors and arrive at a wise decision, but such is not the case. In judging *other people's behavior,* we tend to overestimate the importance of personality characteristics. This tendency to overlook the influence of the situation in judging other people's behavior, and to overemphasize personal traits instead, is sufficiently pervasive in our culture that it has been called the **overattribution effect**—also known as the *fundamental attribution error.* Observing Diana's strenuous efforts at physical conditioning on the mountain, her teammates might have assumed that she had received financial inducements to become the first American woman to climb Mount Everest, that she was trying to impress other climbers, or that she had been threatened with dismissal if she did not do well. As a rule, we do not make these sorts of assumptions because we have not observed the relevant background factors. Rather, we note the individual's behavior and assume that she is invariably that way. We decide that Diana is always highly energetic and conscientious (Table 17–3).

Evidence for the overattribution effect has been obtained in many ways. In one instance, college men were asked to cite the reasons for selecting their major fields of study and for being attracted to their girlfriends. They tended to use slightly more situational explanations, referring to factors outside themselves. They explained: "Investment banking pays well" or "She's affectionate." Quite different attributions were made, however, when they were asked to explain why a *friend* chose a particular major and girlfriend. The reasons here were much in favor of the dispositional attributions, meaning factors within the individual. They cited their friend's need for this or that job or girlfriend (Nisbett, Caputo, Legant, & Mareck, 1973).

In an industrial setting, 36 managers of various businesses evaluated themselves and their employees on the job, and these ratings also gave evidence of the overattribution effect. The managers used more dispositional attributions in explaining their employees' behavior than in evaluating their own performances (Martin & Klimoski, 1990). According to the managers, the employees behaved that

way because they *were that way* rather than because of the circumstances.

As always, a caution is necessary, and in this case it concerns the matter of culture. Research has indicated that people from cultures stressing *in*dependence, such as the United States and England, are more likely to engage in overattribution than are people from cultures stressing *inter*dependence and group relations, such as Hong Kong, Japan, and India (Markus & Kitayama, 1991; Smith & Whitehead, 1984). In other words, dispositional attributions are more typical in Western cultures; situation attributions are somewhat more typical in Eastern cultures (Lee, Hallahan, & Herzog, 1996; Miller, 1984b; Schuster, Fosterling, & Weiner, 1989).

SELF-SERVING PERCEPTIONS. Knowing a great deal about their own personal circumstances, people in independent cultures tend to explain *their own* behavior from the opposite perspective. They often attribute their reactions to the circumstances, displaying a situational bias, especially in unfavorable circumstances. In situations of spouse abuse, for example, the aggressors tend to attribute their behavior to external causes. The spouse was irresponsible, unfaithful, or hostile, and the beating was administered for that reason (Overholser & Moll, 1990).

Suppose a new employee criticized his boss and

CONCEPT	PROCESS	EXAMPLE
Dispositional attribution	Assigning the causes of behavior to the individual	Diana trains constantly because she is that way, always energetic.
Situational attribution	Assigning the causes of behavior to the situation	Diana trains constantly because she is new to the expedition.
Overattribution effect	Underestimating the influence of the situation in judging others' behavior	Diana trains constantly because she is very energetic; there are no significant situational factors.

TABLE 17–3 BASIC CONCEPTS IN ATTRIBUTION THEORY. The overattribution effect occurs when we attend only to the most dominant cues available—in this case, Diana's energetic training efforts.

then was fired. Falling prey to the overattribution effect, he might report that his boss was ignorant, unfair, and dishonest. Similarly, falling prey to the self-serving bias concerning his own behavior, he would likely explain that his criticism of his boss was called forth by the circumstances. He probably would not conclude that he was an argumentative, fault-finding individual, as might his coworkers.

When husbands and wives estimated how much each of them contributed to several household chores, the combined totals for each pair usually exceeded 100% because the partners overestimated their own contributions. They were not around when the spouse took out the trash, cleaned out the closet, and worked out the budget. They knew very well when they did these tasks themselves (Ross & Sicoly, 1979). This response is not an attribution bias, for the concern is not with the causes of someone's behavior. Rather, it has been called an *egocentric bias,* showing once again that we have our own self-centered perceptions about the trash, the closets, the budgets, and other details of this world.

• INTERPERSONAL ATTRACTION •

With this background in attitudes and social cognition, we now consider our preferences for living and working with certain people, a condition called **interpersonal attraction.** Among the diverse members of the Everest expedition, who might be attracted to whom? What factors might be involved in these preferences? How do they operate?

FACTORS IN ATTRACTION

On a cold, dark, windswept mountain, most of us would be at least mildly attracted to a strong, experienced mountaineer, but in more routine circum-
stances other factors are prominent. We generally seek health, beauty, wisdom, and wit; they are obvious determinants of attraction. We cannot always have what we want, however, and with this reservation in mind, there are two basic determinants of attraction: similarity and familiarity.

DEGREE OF SIMILARITY. When a large, outspoken woman marries a small, quiet man, people say, "Opposites attract!" Here we encounter a commonsense view that does not make sense. It usually ignores many basic similarities between the partners. Indeed, the members of this couple probably speak the same language, have a similar level of intelligence, and share ideas about ethics, religion, and politics. If they are going to continue to be compatible, they should have similar ideas about handling money and avocational interests, as well. They may even have a common concern about physical size, each finding some consolation in the other's dimensions. When one considers all the marriages and friendships one knows, and all possible dimensions of individual differences, it is clear that opposites do *not* attract.

A fun-loving but slightly anxious man may enjoy the company of a confident but reserved woman. The expression about opposites attracting perhaps notes some exceptions, or it refers to less important characteristics. If not, there would be many more marriages and friendships between elderly, sophisticated intellectuals and youthful, uneducated peasants from other cultures.

According to the **matching hypothesis,** the members of a couple are usually about equal in physical attractiveness, whatever their individual standards of beauty. This hypothesis has been supported in research with both dating and married couples (Wong, McCreary, Bowden, & Jenner, 1991). In one study, the photographs of members of 99 married couples were rated individually for physical attractiveness by a panel of judges. Then the two scores for each couple were compared. Afterward, the photographs for each sex were mixed and then paired on a random basis, creating 99 randomly matched couples from the same photographs. When the ratings for these randomly paired couples were compared, they showed much less similarity than the ratings for the married couples. The marital partners were also more similar in other ways, apart from appearance (Murstein, 1972).

If the members are not approximately equal in attractiveness, then the less attractive person usually offers some compensating quality. This trade-off, discussed previously in the context of equity theory, states that in the marketplace of interpersonal relations we develop and maintain a relationship only if the outcome is at least what we feel we deserve, weighing all of our attributes against the norms of society.

Members of a couple also tend to be similar in intelligence. Highly intelligent and marginally intelligent people generally do not seek one another's company. Common interests also play a vital role. All told, it is likely that in any marriage, friendship, or even social gathering, there are many more important similarities than differences in attitudes, interests, and abilities (Figure 17–6).

On the lower slopes of Everest, the expedition scientists—psychologists and physiologists—tended to associate with one another, just as the mutual interests of the climbers, struggling to extend a route up the mountain, caused them to be attracted to one another. Although rivals in one sense, Stacy and Diana maintained a closer relationship with each other than they did with the scientists.

DEGREE OF FAMILIARITY. Our preference for certain people is indisputably related to another major factor: familiarity. Among occupants of an apartment complex, for example, a pronounced relationship was found between friendship patterns and distances between apartments, even when the distances were no more than ten yards (Festinger, Schachter, & Back, 1950). In other words, presence makes the heart grow fonder, despite Shakespeare's famous line about absence.

In modern society, familiarity is not necessarily a function of proximity. With the telephone, magazines, videos, and television, familiarity can be gained even at a distance. To improve their chances for election, political candidates seek almost any sort of exposure. There is so much evidence that attraction increases with familiarity that this finding has been called a general law of human behavior. If you want someone to like you, hang around as much as possible. It should help.

In one instance, a mixed list of the names of 200 public people and 40 nonexistent people were rated on a like–dislike scale, and a marked direct relationship was discovered between the familiarity of the figure and the favorability of the ratings (Harrison, 1969). In another instance, the mere anticipation of familiarity increased liking for another person. College students in this study met in groups,

FIGURE 17–6 SIMILARITY AND ATTRACTION. Your friends generally share your interests, as well as your intelligence, age, and background. Similarity is an extremely powerful factor in interpersonal attraction.

expecting to work afterward with some students and not with others. Although exposure was equal, the ratings for likability of anticipated partners were significantly higher than those for anticipated nonpartners (Darley & Berscheid, 1967).

This general law extends even to events and ideas. People exposed frequently to certain passages of music liked those passages more than others to which they had been exposed less frequently (Zissman & Neimark, 1990). College students exposed to situations requiring negotiations rated the most familiar situations as most likely to be settled by agreement (Druckman & Broome, 1991).

It has been said that women fall in love by way of their ears and men by way of their eyes. By whatever means, we usually fall in love with our neighbors, or at least with people we know well.

❧
LONG-TERM RELATIONSHIPS

Similarity and familiarity are vital factors in attraction. In long-term relationships, other factors become prominent, especially psychological characteristics. Styles of loving were discussed in the chapter on emotion; the focus here is on the continuation and dissolution of relationships.

SELF-DISCLOSURE IN THE RELATIONSHIP. In a two-person, loving relationship, the passionate dimension declines relatively early, as noted already, often replaced by other forms of love, most notably companionate love. What fosters this development? One critical issue is successful communication. It is often the foundation of a long-term relationship (Brehm, 1992).

Within this communication, self-disclosure is perhaps the foremost issue. When people communicate intimate thoughts, desires, and memories about themselves, the process is called **self-disclosure.** Efforts to study self-dis-

closure constitute a prominent research theme in current studies of interpersonal relationships (Kelley, 1991).

One of the major findings is the *reciprocity* in self-disclosure. The amount of information disclosed *to* a friend, colleague, parent, or partner is closely related to the amount of information disclosed *by* that person. As one person makes disclosures, the other is prompted to react similarly. This process strengthens their familiarity with one another, a fundamental dimension of attraction (Miller, 1990; Figure 17-7).

Timing is important. Self-disclosure will not invariably strengthen a relationship. Especially at the outset, a person engaging in much self-disclosure may appear lacking in discretion and thereby disrupt the developing friendship (Levin & Gergen, 1969). The longer the relationship exists, and the more it is based on significant mutual events rather than trivial ones, the more likely it is that self-disclosure will strengthen the personal bond.

"I wasn't the easiest woman to get to know," Stacy said of herself. Eventually she met a man named David Shute; he made it easier. "He moved slowly," she said of their conversations, "and waited for me to catch up." Then she added, referring to self-disclosure: "Sometimes it took a while for me to get up the courage to round the corner, but

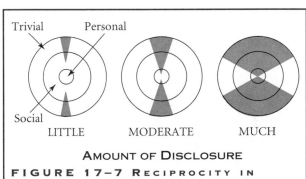

AMOUNT OF DISCLOSURE
FIGURE 17-7 RECIPROCITY IN SELF-DISCLOSURE. As self-disclosure continues, it increases in depth and breadth. In reciprocal fashion, each partner stimulates the other to react in this way (Adapted from Brehm, 1992).

when I did I usually found him there smiling gently" (Allison, 1993).

DISSOLUTION OF THE RELATIONSHIP.
One obvious but limited measure of marital dissatisfaction is *divorce*, which does not include separated or unhappily married couples. Over the next decade or so, almost two-thirds of the new marriages in this country will result in divorce and these divorces are most likely to occur within the first few years after marriage (Cleek & Pearson, 1985; Huston & Vangelisti, 1991).

This rising divorce rate is due not so much to an increase in marital unhappiness as to a decrease in the barriers to a separation of some sort (White & Booth, 1991). Among other factors, the less the shared time, the weaker the support network, and the younger the partners at the time of marriage, the greater is the likelihood of divorce (Felmlee, Sprecher, & Bassim, 1990; White, 1990).

One puzzling finding concerns *cohabitation,* in which a couple lives together in a sexual union before marriage. Cohabitation would seem to provide a test for marriage and also a practice period, thereby lowering the divorce rate. However, a very different result has been found. Among married couples, those who cohabited previously divorce sooner than those who did not cohabit (Halli & Zimmer, 1991; Newcomb, 1987). What is the explanation? The answer seems to lie in the nature of cohabitation, which is apparently much like the marital state. When divorce rates have been compared for previously cohabiting and noncohabiting married couples, and the length of their relationship is determined from the date the couple first began living together, there is no significant difference in the rate of divorce (Teachman & Polonko, 1990). A noteworthy phenomenon, cohabitation has not yet had a significant impact on the divorce rate or marriage rate.

What interaction patterns develop among couples who divorce? This question returns to the issue of communication and self-disclosure. One partner's effort to discuss a certain matter often is met with resistance by the other, resulting in a *demand–withdraw pattern* of interaction (Berscheid, 1994). The demander is typically the female partner, the withdrawer the male partner, and various interpretations have been offered for this gender difference. It may arise from traditional differences between men and women in communicative style; it may be due to differences in status and power, wherein men have less to gain than women (Christensen & Heavey, 1990).

An attempt to prevent the demand–withdraw pattern began with engaged couples measured for probability of marital satisfaction and then assigned randomly to a premarital intervention program or a control condition. This program trained the couples in communication skills, as well as problem solving, and 18 months later these couples were found to be significantly happier in their relationship than the couples in the control condition. After another 18 months, similar differences were found, again in favor of the intervention group (Markman, Floyd, Stanley, & Storaasli, 1988).

GENDER DIFFERENCES IN SOCIAL BEHAVIOR.
There are gender differences not only in the demand–withdraw pattern but also in emotional expression. When the interaction includes conflict, men are likely to become angry and women are likely to feel sad or fearful (Gottman & Levenson, 1986). It has been hypothesized but not yet demonstrated that these differences are related to gender differences in the activation of the autonomic nervous system.

Gender is also related to self-disclosure, self-destruction, self-esteem, and many other social behaviors (Banaji & Prentice, 1994). With close friends, women engage in much more self-disclosure than men (Dindia & Allen, 1992). Thus, it is not surprising that men are decidedly less interested in participating in therapy. To be successful, the person must become emotionally responsive and engage in self-disclosure (Betz & Fitzgerald, 1993).

This masculine resistance to therapy is especially significant because masculinity is hazardous to health. Under conditions of stress, the socialization of men tends to restrict their responses to consuming drugs, driving rapidly, acting aggressively, and other self-destructive behaviors. Greater readiness to engage in a therapeutic relationship presumably would reduce these physical and psychological risks (Eisler & Blalock, 1991).

Men and women traditionally develop self-esteem in different ways. Men commonly do so through competition, outdoing their peers. Women more often obtain self-esteem through personal relations (Joseph, Markus, & Tafarodi, 1992). But conditions are changing. Stacy prided herself on building her own home, and she clearly gained self-esteem from her success in mountaineering. Gender differences in gaining esteem are rapidly diminishing in many parts of the United States (Fried-Buchalter, 1992; Sancho & Hewitt, 1990).

Gender differences should not be expected to disappear, however. Gender is the most basic of all human categories (Banaji & Prentice, 1994).

• SOCIAL INFLUENCE •

At this point, we should be explicit about the transition taking place in this chapter. We have been moving steadily away from the individual toward people in interaction. Our earlier emphases were on attitudes, social cognition, and interpersonal attraction—how people think about and perceive others. The forthcoming emphases are on social influence and group processes—how people interact with one another in a group setting.

Interactions among members of the Everest team changed markedly after the four inter-mediate camps had been set, for then it was time for the big push to the summit, a dangerous trek in that rarefied air. Only two or three members could climb together, and Jim, as leader, selected these smaller summit teams. He chose Steve and Stacy to accompany him on the first team, much to their irrepressible joy. Diana did not hide her displeasure over her assignment to the second team. Geoff was one of a pair of climbers on the third. Except for the first team and Peggy, who knew she belonged on the fourth team, these results were a widespread source of dissatisfaction. As Stacy acknowledged, "Any leader who puts himself on the first summit team, no matter the circumstances, is bound to face criticisms" (Allison, 1993).

The term **social influence** refers to the ways in which people modify one another's behavior or experience, intentionally or otherwise. These actions range from the unspoken expectations of group membership to an explicit request from an individual. Jim's assignment of climbers to summit teams resulted in reluctant compliance by those involved, an instance of very direct social influence.

TENDENCY TO CONFORM

In established groups, there is agreement on many behaviors, such as patterns of dress, speech, religious outlook, sexual behavior, and so forth. Even in spontaneously formed groups, this agreement is evident and the pressure toward conformity can be significant. In **conformity,** an individual adopts the thoughts or behaviors of a social group *without* any direct pressure to do so.

On the Everest expedition, a plastic pink flamingo was used to mark the entry of the meeting area at base camp, perhaps because it provided such a clear contrast to its surroundings. Moreover, all members of the American party carried a tiny toy flamingo in their packs. This trinket served no

FIGURE 17–8 CONFORMITY IN DAILY LIFE. Acceptance by others is a fundamental goal at all ages. It is achieved partly by adherence to group customs and interests.

obvious purpose. No one was explicitly asked to carry it; the members did so spontaneously. In these ways, they displayed conformity. They voluntarily adopted an implicit social code (Figure 17-8).

Conformity is influenced by **social norms,** which are unstated expectations indicating what social behavior is usual or typical. People generally do not wish to violate a norm or standard, even when there is no direct pressure to behave like others.

In a series of experiments some years ago, conducted by a social psychologist, Solomon Asch, American college students were asked to make judgments about the length of vertical lines. Seven men made these simple judgments aloud, one by one, in a group setting, but the sixth person in the sequence was the only true subject. The other people were Asch's accomplices and, without the true subject's knowledge, on many trials they all intentionally made the same incorrect guess. Perhaps for the first time in his life, the true subject suddenly found the evidence from his senses contradicted by the unanimous opinion of the majority (Figure 17–9).

The results were impressive. Even in this simple task, only about one-fourth of the subjects completely resisted the others' answers, making no errors, and they remained doubt-ridden throughout the investigation. Among those who yielded, some were influenced occasionally. Others followed

the unanimous but incorrect opinion on every trial, showing complete acquiescence to group pressure. Later, it was found that they grossly underestimated their degree of conformity (Asch, 1956).

Experiments with French and Norwegian subjects supported these findings, although the two groups performed somewhat differently. Subsequent studies showed these same results among Arabian and British students. On these bases, the powerful influence of a unanimous group on the behavior of an individual, resulting in conformity, is now known as the *Asch effect.* Some mixed results have appeared in recent years, perhaps owing to social change, making the Asch effect a topic of continued interest in contemporary psychology (Amir, 1984; Friend, Rafferty, & Bramel, 1990; Larsen, 1990).

These results should not suggest that conformity is undesirable. Think of the impossibility of maintaining any social group if people did not conform to certain standards. Nonconformity, furthermore, does not necessarily indicate independence. Some people adopt the contrary view regardless of the issue. They are called *counterdependent* because their views are determined by the norm, although in the opposite direction.

Uncertainty may play a role in a special type of conformity. In a crowd or mob scene, people sometimes lose their sense of individual responsibility,

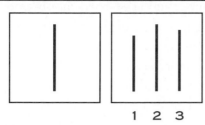

FIGURE 17–9 CONFORMITY IN THE LABORATORY. The task was to match the single line on the left with the line of the same length from the card at the right, some distance away.

engaging in behaviors they would otherwise resist, a condition called **deindividuation.** The focus instead is on the present environment, as in mass looting or taunting or even physical aggression. The group setting offers anonymity, and deindividuated people may act in uncharacteristically hostile ways, quite different from their usual behavior.

COMPLIANCE AND OBEDIENCE

As we turn now to compliance and obedience, the social influence changes. It is no longer unintentional. It is direct and purposeful. In **compliance,** people yield to pressure to think or behave in a certain way, responding to a direct request by someone else. One party does not have complete authority over the other, however. The relationship involves negotiation or persuasion.

When the three Americans on the first summit team began their trek toward the top of the world, Pasang Timba, the most experienced of three Sherpas, climbed with them. Two assistants, Appa and Pemba, each carrying an extra bottle of oxygen, brought up the rear, some 100 yards behind. But as the ascent continued across steep terrain, the gap grew larger and larger. Then, for the third or fourth time, Jim stopped to wait for them and, as he peered through the morning darkness, a stream of profanity erupted from his lips: Appa and Pemba

were *descending* the mountain. They had turned around; they were traveling down steadily and quickly, not like injured men, who would have moved more slowly. Money was no longer an issue; they were interested in safety (Allison, 1993).

For Appa and Pemba, compliance was out of the question. And the situation did not involve obedience, for Jim had no physical, legal, or even substantial financial control over them. So the three Americans watched most of their oxygen disappear down the mountainside.

This issue of compliance commonly occurs in small groups or one-to-one relationships, as between spouses, a salesperson and a potential customer, or among friends. In these situations, pressure toward compliance is often exerted in one of two ways, each with a sales-pitch emphasis: the foot-in-the-door and door-in-the face techniques.

OBTAINING COMPLIANCE. The idea behind the **foot-in-the-door technique** is that after complying with a smaller request, a person is more likely to comply with a larger one. The first step is to get your foot in the door—*then* ask for more.

In one study, homemakers were requested to support safe driving by signing a petition or placing a small sign in a window of their home. That was the small beginning. After two weeks, a different investigator asked all subjects to place a large, attention-getting sign on their lawns. As expected, compliance with this almost unreasonable request was related to prior compliance. Among householders who had agreed to the smaller request, 55% agreed to display the new sign. Among a control group, who had not been approached previously, only 20% agreed to do so (Freedman & Fraser, 1966).

After complying with the first request, people apparently regard themselves as "doing that sort of thing." Thus they continue, complying with the next request (Wagener & Laird, 1980).

A different technique begins with an unreasonably large request. Called the **door-in-the-face** technique, the person is confronted with a request that almost certainly will be refused; then, when the second and real request is made, the likelihood of acceptance is increased. When college students were asked to donate two hours per week for two years working with juvenile delinquents, none agreed to do so. But afterward, approximately 50% were willing to take juvenile delinquents to the zoo one afternoon for two hours. Among students who were asked merely to accompany juvenile delinquents to the zoo, only 17% complied (Cialdini, Vincent, Lewis, Catalan, Wheeler, & Danby, 1975).

Here again, speculation follows self-perception theory. The subjects who refused the first request perhaps viewed themselves as uncooperative and uncongenial. Thus, they complied more readily with the second opportunity, redeeming themselves and enhancing their self-image (Cialdini, 1993).

OBEDIENCE TO AUTHORITY. Obedience involves even more direct pressure than compliance. In **obedience**, people respond to a demand, not a request, and the conditions of the relationship are not negotiable. The power, through physical strength or circumstances, lies with one party, and the other is expected to be submissive and dutiful. The relationship between a salesperson and a customer raises the issue of compliance; the relationship between a boss and the salesperson involves obedience (Table 17–4).

One investigation of obedience became known as the *Milgram study*, owing to its controversial nature and the name of the chief investigator, Stanley Milgram. As explained in the chapter on research methods, each subject, serving as a teacher, was required to punish a learner's incorrect responses by administering electric shocks to that person. The learner made errors regularly, and the research question was: How much shock would the subject administer before refusing to follow the experimenter's requests?

When this experiment was completed with 40 subjects, the results were totally unexpected. Altogether, 65% of the subjects obeyed *all* of the experimenter's orders, punishing the learner with 450 volts, the maximum shock available. They did so even when the learner no longer responded to the task and therefore was being punished for doing nothing. In the remaining cases, the experiment was discontinued when the subject refused to administer a stronger shock, but *no one* refrained from administering 300 volts, labeled "intense shock," at which point the learner pounded on the wall and then became silent (Figure 17–10).

The learner, an accomplice of the experimenter, never received any shocks at all. He simply disconnected the generator.

Further studies with different subjects in different settings gave the same result, demonstrating the overwhelming significance of the social setting.

TYPE	DESCRIPTION	EXAMPLE
Conformity	Without direct pressure, people adopt the behavior or thoughts of others; there is no coercion.	All Everest expedition members carried a toy pink flamingo in their packs.
Compliance	In response to a direct request, people behave in a certain way; the conditions may be negotiable.	Appa and Pemba climbed with the first summit team, until they changed their minds.
Obedience	People respond to an order or command in the expected way; the conditions are not negotiable.	Expedition members followed Jim's order, building the lower route before making summit attempts.

TABLE 17–4 TYPES OF SOCIAL INFLUENCE. Social influence results in a range of specific responses. Conformity, compliance, and obedience are the most prominent outcomes.

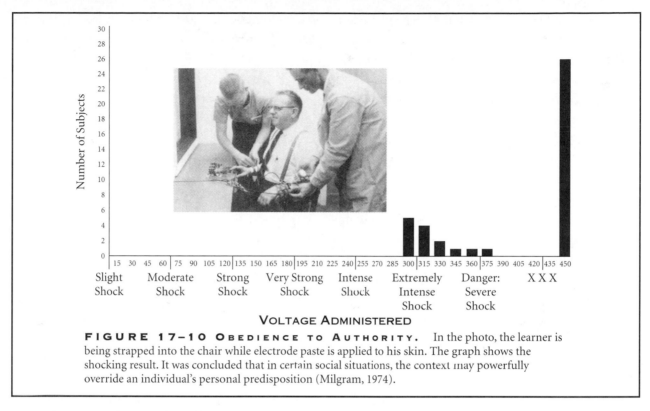

FIGURE 17–10 OBEDIENCE TO AUTHORITY. In the photo, the learner is being strapped into the chair while electrode paste is applied to his skin. The graph shows the shocking result. It was concluded that in certain social situations, the context may powerfully override an individual's personal predisposition (Milgram, 1974).

According to Milgram, the setting was *the* crucial factor in determining obedience (Milgram, 1974). Social pressure can be more influential than character and personality in determining behavior in certain situations (Blass, 1991). Looking back on this research, Milgram pointed out that people in daily life often must obey orders about which they have some doubt. The physician requests a certain medicine; a lieutenant orders a certain training procedure. The person receiving such an order typically obeys, but there may be moments when doubt or opposition should be expressed.

After the Everest expedition established camps high on the mountain, Jim asked Geoff to examine the eyes of each climber, searching for retinal hemorrhaging, often a symptom of more serious problems caused by high altitude. Then Jim said: "Don't tell anyone the results." Geoff resisted this order. He decided that his teammates deserved to know about the condition of their own bodies. Eventually Jim withdrew his order, but news of his plan swept through the camp, causing distrust and dis-

sension among the members. Geoff was lauded for his refusal to obey.

&

ALTRUISTIC BEHAVIOR

Pasang and the three Americans struggled upward for two more hours, until the first morning light revealed their progress and the distance from the summit. At that point, Jim calculated their remaining oxygen and dejectedly shook his head. With a tone of finality, he announced: "That's it, then. We go back and try again tomorrow."

Stacy resisted. Noting the perfect weather, thinking of their enormous efforts, and well aware of commitments to other team members and people back home, she opposed the idea.

"Look," she insisted, gesturing to the clear skies. "One of us should go."

Steve immediately agreed, and then Jim did too. Thus, at that point, opportunities for altruism were open to all three climbers.

In the behavior known as **altruism,** for no obvious reward someone assists another person needing help. Altruism is a selfless act, a sacrifice for the welfare of others. Each of the climbers could have suggested that one of the others be allowed to achieve the goal all three of them so deeply desired. But none of them displayed this altruism.

Instead, Jim turned to Pasang and said, "Choose a number between one and ten." Pasang did so, not fully understanding the purpose, and the three American climbers guessed. Stacy announced, "Four." The number was *three*, and she was the winner.

Accepting this outcome and looking at the oxygen supply, Jim then said to Pasang: "You can come down with us if you want to."

"No," replied Pasang, perhaps displaying altruism. "I go up."

"You'll run out of oxygen," Jim countered.

"I go up," repeated Pasang, knowing his stronger lungs could function with distinctly less oxygen than that required by the Americans. Nevertheless, he was clearly placing himself in danger (Allison, 1993).

Altruism has long interested philosophers and scientists, for it appears to be a sacrificial act, performed as an end in itself, without any obvious gain to the helper. From an evolutionary perspective, this behavior promotes the species' genes. From a psychological perspective, altruism may satisfy personal motives. For many observers, therefore, the concept of altruism still lacks substantial evidence (Krebs, 1991; Sorrentino, 1991).

TEMPORARY STATES. In one early study, students in divinity school walked alone through a back alley, passing a slumping figure in a doorway. Shabbily dressed, he coughed and groaned as each student opened the door to the building. Some of the students were on their way to give a brief talk about the Good Samaritan, a tale of a good deed. Others were planning to speak on careers after divinity school. Some in each group were in a hurry; others were just about on time; still others had time to spare. Of all these people, less than half offered aid to the person slumped in the doorway. Which ones were they?

Those who offered help were not necessarily the students with the Good Samaritan in mind, and they were not those thinking about careers after graduation. The students most likely to help were those with a few minutes to spare. Those least likely to stop were in great haste. In later interviews, it was found that the hurried subjects experienced some emotional upset after their encounter in the alleyway, but to stop and help would have meant a delay in proceedings that other people had carefully arranged. Another loyalty, rather than insensitivity, seemed responsible for their failure to offer assistance (Darley & Batson, 1973).

Behavior is complex, however, and having time to spare is not the only facilitating state. Being in a good mood is also important (Isen & Levin, 1972).

SITUATIONAL FACTORS. In addition, situational factors can be influential. These findings have emerged from research studies and real-life incidents in which people have observed muggings or property damage without making any effort to assist. Collectively, they point to a **bystander intervention effect,** which states that the larger the group observing someone apparently needing help, the less likely it is that any one of them will offer aid. A lone bystander is more apt to help.

When several people are present, there is a perceived *diffusion of responsibility,* in which each bystander may decide that action can be taken or should be taken by others. For example, when college students overheard someone having an epileptic seizure, their efforts to help were decidedly slower and less frequent when they believed that another person also heard the victim's cries, although neither the victim nor anyone else was in sight. The innocent bystander apparently feels much more innocent when others are present too.

When a bystander is alone, the feeling of personal responsibility makes the person more likely to assist (Latané & Darley, 1968; Latané & Nida, 1981).

Another reason for lack of assistance is that among a crowd the situation sometimes is not regarded as an emergency. The result is *pluralistic ignorance,* in which many observers, well aware of one another but not fully understanding the situation, wait for someone else to make an interpretation. They think that the situation might be a prank or that the person can manage without assistance (Krebs, 1970).

Still another situational factor is the amount of *personal risk* to the helper. People are less inclined to intervene when they may incur harm themselves. In other words, the nature of the commitment is clearly a factor (Clary & Orenstein, 1991).

Whether people help depends significantly on how these situational factors interact with their temporary states at the time. What influenced Pasang on that desolate ridge of Mount Everest? Maybe it was the financial gain for assisting Stacy to the very top. Maybe it was his mood at the moment or a desire to reach the summit himself. Maybe it was all of those factors. And maybe it included altruism.

PERSONALITY FACTORS. We cannot dismiss personality completely. Other things being equal, some people are more likely to help than others. What can be said about these people?

In a field study of altruism, 34 people who had assisted victims of traffic accidents were assessed for personality. They were compared with 36 witnesses of accidents who had not provided assistance. The two groups were matched for age, sex, and socioeconomic status, and both groups completed a personality questionnaire. Compared to the witnesses, the altruistic subjects had a stronger belief in a just world, more concern for social responsibility, and greater empathy (Bierhoff, Klein,

& Kramp, 1991). They did not differ with respect to competence in administering first aid.

In summary, we can say that there seem to be few consistently all-around Good Samaritans among us (Gergen, Gergen, & Meter, 1972). Situational factors and temporary personal states play an important role in this behavior, but personal traits cannot be totally discounted (Bierhoff, Klein, & Kramp, 1991; Rushton, 1991).

• GROUP PROCESSES •

In social psychology, a **group** is two or more individuals who are united by some common characteristic and whose actions are interrelated. This relationship can be temporary and incidental, as strangers in an elevator, or relatively enduring and fundamental, as family members. Stacy and Pasang, standing high on that cold, steep mountain, were clearly a group, for they had climbed together, shared nourishment, and called out advice to one another.

Far below them, the University of Washington research team formed a very different group with different goals. They confronted this question: If climbers' memories are faulty at high altitudes, do the climbers know it? Are they aware of their deficits? Knowledge about one's knowledge, called *metacognition,* has vital implications throughout our lives, especially on mountain tops and in other dangerous situations (Nelson Dunlosky, White, Steinberg, Townes & Anderson, 1990). We now look more closely at the interactions among members of groups, referred to as group processes.

STATUS IN THE GROUP

In any group, each member has a **role,** which is a pattern of behavior expected of that member. A role typically is associated with a certain **status,** which is the respect or standing one has among the group members. On an Everest expedition, support climbers have the least experience, and therefore they are low in the hierarchy. The climber with the most experience is usually the expedition leader, at the top of the hierarchy.

Within a group, a person may have more than one role, and these roles may be formal or informal. In addtion, roles are often complementary. The role of a mother is defined with respect to the child. A team member has no role without other team members.

In the animal world, status and role seem to be functions of power, a condition called to scientific attention years ago by a Norwegian investigator who observed barnyard chickens. The most dominant chicken pecked all others and was pecked by none in return. Another chicken pecked all others except the most dominant one, which of course pecked it. This social order extended down to the bottom of the hierarchy, where one chicken was pecked by every other chicken and pecked none in return. This dominance hierarchy among members of a group, known as a **pecking order,** has been verified in many modern studies (Schjelderup-Ebbe, 1935). Research with mice, dogs, monkeys, and many other species shows dominance relations based on fighting, but the perfect, straight-line dominance seen in chickens is rare.

Usually a person's status is based on something other than physical domination, such as money, knowledge, social skills, verbal ability, or the interaction of many such characteristics.

Studies of two-person and three-person groups have shown that a dominance hierarchy begins to develop just seconds after strangers meet, evident in talking the most, successfully interrupting others, avoiding interruptions by others, receiving glances from others, and gesticulating in a dominant manner. Subtle nonverbal signals, such as the other person's appearance and level of activation, apparently serve as early cues for the assess-

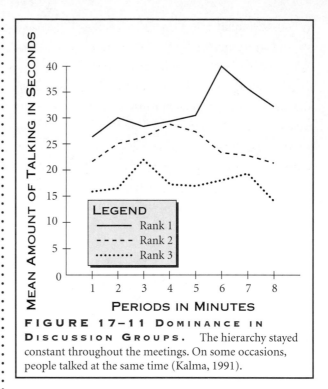

FIGURE 17–11 DOMINANCE IN DISCUSSION GROUPS. The hierarchy stayed constant throughout the meetings. On some occasions, people talked at the same time (Kalma, 1991).

ment of dominance in these discussions (Kalma, 1991; Figure 17-11).

On the basis of physical ability and knowledge of mountaineering, Stacy had moved to the top of the hierarchy of the Everest expedition, selected for the first summit team. Then, through luck in the lottery, she won first place on that summit team. And finally, through sheer determination, she and Pasang clambered across one icy wall after another, ridge upon ridge, until they reached a place where there was nowhere else to climb. They stood on the top of the world.

"We really did it," Stacy cried into the wind, which immediately swept her hat from her head. As she watched it sail down thousands of feet into Tibet, her eyes became hot and cloudy. She *was* the first American woman to climb Mount Everest, and she felt a blinding wave of emotion (Allison, 1993).

Pasang pumped his ice axe overhead, hooting and exulting with whatever air he had left in his lungs. After all, he was the first man, Sherpa or otherwise, to accompany an American woman to the peak of Chomolungma! And he did so without supplementary oxygen. Besides, Stacy might recognize his heroic effort with a very large tip.

❧

COOPERATION AND COMPETITION

As a rule, a group setting engenders a higher degree of responsiveness to a particular task than when the same individuals are alone, an outcome known as **social facilitation.** The necessary condition for social facilitation is the presence of someone else, or several people (Levine, Resnick, & Higgins, 1993). This increased activity—in working or eating or whatever—occurs even among animals, and the reason apparently lies in the increased arousal of the individual in the presence of others. Among human beings, for example, there is a strong positive correlation between the number of people present and the size of the meal consumed by each person (de Castro, 1991; Redd & de Castro, 1992).

When people are working in groups and told that their output will not be compared, the facilitating effect fails to appear. When they are working individually and told that they will be compared with others working in separate rooms, their performance is comparable to that in the group situation. Experiments of this sort, dating from the earliest days of social psychology, suggest that social facilitation is the result of some sort of rivalry or competitive effort, or perhaps simply an effort to keep pace rather than to outdo others (Dashiell, 1935; Levine, Resnick, & Higgins, 1993).

Human behavior is highly complex, however, and therefore we occasionally find almost the opposite response. People in groups sometimes engage in **social loafing,** expending less energy and producing less in the group than when by themselves.

In fact, the output of the individual seems to decrease in proportion to the size of the group (Geen, 1991; Levine, Resnick, & Higgins, 1993).

What causes this change in behavior or prompts such different behaviors in a group? The critical factor is *recognition.* If an individual's specific contribution probably will be noted or acknowledged, social facilitation is likely. Otherwise, social loafing will occur (Gabrenya, Wang, & Latané, 1985; Hardy & Latané, 1986).

Most group situations engender some form of striving to do well, with or against other group members. On Everest, all of the American summit teams were striving to reach the top of the mountain. Stacy and Diana vied to become the first American woman. And the international teams were competing for access to the lower routes or to win a "first" on the summit in some new category. One daredevil Frenchman wanted to become the first person to jump *off* Mount Everest, using a contraption that was partly a parachute, partly a hang glider. Another wanted to be the fastest person *on* the mountain, hoping to set a world speed record, climbing without supplemental oxygen.

Here we ask: What factors typically determine whether individuals or groups, striving to perform well, will become cooperative or competitive?

CHILDREARING PRACTICES. In daily life, two factors stand out as engendering cooperation or competition, one of which is childhood training. Earlier, we noted that cultural practices can mold aggressive or cooperative patterns.

In the United States, childrearing generally fosters competition and individuality, especially in school systems that stress high achievement. In certain other cultures, such as those of China and Israel, different habits are emphasized, and the child's identity is more involved with the group of which he or she is a member. Young children are taught to clean the table together or to calculate the

FIGURE 17-12 EDUCATION FOR COOPERATIVE BEHAVIOR. For children in elementary school in China, cooperating with classmates may be even more important than grades on examinations (Filstrup & Filstrup, 1983).

classroom budget together, an approach that fosters cooperative attitudes and behavior (Figure 17–12).

SUPERORDINATE GOALS. The second basic factor engendering cooperation or competition pertains to the setting, as illustrated in an investigation known as the *Robbers' Cave experiment,* so named for the state park in Oklahoma where it was conducted. At a summer camp, 12-year-old boys who did not know one another previously were separated into two groups. A tournament of games was then arranged between the two groups: touch football, tug of war, baseball, and a treasure hunt, and eventually what commenced as good sportsmanship became extremely rivalrous. The opposing groups began name calling, planned raids on opponents' territory, destroyed property, and engaged in scuffles.

The experimenters then attempted to change this situation, testing the hypothesis that pleasant social contacts would reduce the friction. When these contacts were provided, the procedure was sometimes successful, but at other times it merely provided greater opportunities for conflict. In the dining hall, individuals from the two groups shoved and pushed one another, called each other names, and threw food and utensils.

A second hypothesis was then tested. The experimenters created a series of problems producing **superordinate goals,** which are goals shared by all community members and having a higher priority than any others. Solutions would benefit both groups, but neither group could achieve them alone. A break in the water supply required close inspection of the terrain for one mile, and a breakdown in the truck that was to take both groups on a picnic required that everyone pull together on the same rope used previously in the tug of war. Eventually, new relationships developed to the point at which the boys sought opportunities to mingle with the other group, had best friends there, held a joint campfire, and went home together (Sherif, 1956).

It was more than proximity that reduced the tension; it was working together toward overriding goals, important to all concerned. Responding to an *outside* threat can make an enormous difference in overcoming rivalries.

Jim, as leader of the Everest expedition, made a concerted effort to establish *group* goals. Before leaving the United States, all expedition members agreed that no one would make a spontaneous summit bid, attempting a dash to the peak without regard for other members. The aim for all climbers and all backers in Seattle would be for the *expedition* to reach the summit. Stacy stressed this condition in her detailed account of this adventure, *Beyond the Limits* (Allison, 1993).

A META-ANALYSIS. One group of psychologists decided to review all of this research on cooperation and competition by a procedure called meta-analysis. The aim of **meta-analysis** is not to contribute further empirical research but rather to examine carefully a large number of completed investigations, comparing their findings and thereby drawing some overall conclusion about the preponderance of evidence. In other words, meta-analysis is a technique for summarizing the results from many studies, viewing them as a population of subjects or items to be combined and analyzed (Lipsey & Wilson, 1993).

In this case, the meta-analysis was performed on the outcomes of research on cooperative, competitive, and individual efforts in groups. Altogether, 122 studies were compared, involving almost 300 separate findings. The results showed that cooperation is significantly more effective than competition or individual efforts in promoting achievement and productivity (Johnson, Maruyama, Johnson, Nelson, & Skon, 1981).

&

MAKING DECISIONS

Eventually all groups with any sort of cohesion must make at least two fundamental decisions, explicitly or implicitly. A goal must be established—whether it is purely social, work-oriented, or both—and some means of pursuing that goal must be identified.

How do groups reach these decisions? What are the processes? In a dictatorship or other autocracy, these decisions are made by the leader, benevolent or malevolent. The group members do not participate; there is little group process. The following discussion concerns open, democratic groups, ones that encourage an exchange of ideas.

GROUPTHINK. An obviously critical factor in any group decision is the cohesiveness of the group—the extent to which it functions *as a group.* The stronger such ties among members, the more readily group decisions are reached, but sometimes agreement is reached too easily.

We cannot be certain what occurred among the members of the Czech summit team, but they reached a tragic decision. After three days seeking the summit, all without food, they decided to keep moving upward, rather than descend. By the fourth morning, Dusan and Jaroslav were losing their vision; Peter was dehydrated and starved; Josef was fatigued. Then, as darkness fell, a storm ripped the top of the mountain. The next day, the Czechs had vanished, presumably blown off the face of Chomolungma by the 150-mile-per-hour winds.

Perhaps the desire for group cohesion stifled individual challenges and critical thought. Perhaps the capacity to think had been diminished by the altitude, as suggested by the findings of the University of Washington research team. At higher and higher altitudes, with less and less oxygen, climbers become increasingly less certain about their intellectual capacities.

When all group members are reluctant to criticize or challenge one another, the group decision may not be the most effective response. The concept of **groupthink** occurs when a group places such a high value on cohesion and morale that decision-making ability is limited; the members suspend critical thinking to maintain group morale (Park, 1990).

Consider these presidential decisions in the last thirty years: Kennedy supported the disastrous invasion of Cuba at the Bay of Pigs; Johnson escalated the war in Vietnam; and Nixon and his advisors, when the Watergate break-in was discovered, attempted a cover-up. All of these decisions, according to the groupthink concept, arose because the effort to maintain group cohesion outstripped the concern for reaching a sound decision (Janis,

FIGURE 17–13 CONSEQUENCES OF GROUPTHINK. The Challenger explosion offers an example of the dangers of groupthink. In January 1986, a space engineer advised against the flight owing to hazards of subfreezing temperatures. To prevent groupthink outcomes, selected group members are sometimes assigned to play the role of gadfly or devil's advocate.

1982). Even in the Challenger explosion, one member of the group declared that the spaceship should not be launched. In the context of group solidarity and a certain leadership style, this sole dissenter was ignored, and the results were disastrous (Moorhead, Ference, & Neck, 1991; Figure 17-13).

How can we avoid groupthink? Some investigators claim there is not much to avoid, believing that the problem has been overemphasized in the public press and undersupported in the research laboratory (Aldag & Fuller, 1993). For others, the basic procedure is to point out the dangers in placing a high value on compatibility. Group members, instead, are urged to understand that dissenting opinions and a slower pace may be essential to long-term success (Neck & Moorhead, 1995).

GROUP SHIFTS. When problems are solved by a group, another outcome is likely besides the groupthink solution. The group decision may be more extreme than the average decision of all the individual members.

Early research showed that when college students solved problems in a group, they tended to reach riskier decisions than when working alone, an outcome called the *risky shift.* They took greater chances when companions shared the risk. Later, when other problems were used, a conservative shift was noted (Knox & Safford, 1976). In both cases, there was a shift away from moderation. On this basis, the concept of **group polarization** emerged, meaning that the group decision is frequently closer to one pole or the other than it is to the average position of the individuals. The reasons, still unclear, appear related to persuasive statements by group members holding extreme views and to the process of social comparison, in which we obtain guidance by observing what others do (Levine & Moreland, 1990).

BRAINSTORMING. Groupthink and group polarization are unexpected, potentially limited outcomes when groups make decisions. Positive outcomes can occur too, provided that group processes are held in check in the early momemts.

The aim in **brainstorming** is to generate as many creative ideas as possible, chiefly by suspending temporarily all criticism of these ideas. Each group member is first instructed to adopt a free-wheeling attitude toward the problem, thinking without restraint about *any possible solutions.* All members are encouraged to build on others' efforts, advancing any ideas in any way possible. Afterward, a critical attitude is adopted; all of these ideas are evaluated. Here the thought processes become more realistic and less fanciful than earlier. At the end, the group may vote on the most promising solutions that have emerged, perhaps ranking them in order of feasibility, cost, or related criteria.

When people engage in brainstorming in

an interactive group, the first person's suggestion often directs the thinking of the next person, and that member's response channels the thoughts of the next, and so forth. This interaction typically generates fewer and less creative ideas than those developed by people working separately (Paulus & Dzindolet, 1993).

The solution is relatively simple. The brainstorming session should begin with each person working alone, generating as many ideas as possible. Then, after this individual work, the group should assemble for brainstorming, using one another's ideas as springboards.

~

GROUP LEADERSHIP

Even in an initially leaderless group, one or more people eventually assume a dominant role. This leadership, whether it is imposed from the outside or emerges through interactions among the members, of course can have a significant influence on the performance of the group.

On the Everest expedition, Jim was the leader, consulting occasionally with Don. His decisions seemed fair but sometimes unwise. For instance, he placed unwarranted trust in Karma as head of the Sherpas. His plan for the secret eye exams diminished morale. By choosing himself for the first summit team, he disrupted team spirit. And finally, Jim told news reporters that he and Steve *chose* Stacy to try for the summit with the last oxygen bottle. He suggested that they did so for the good of the team and to give her the chance to become the first American woman to scale Mount Everest.

Hearing this remark, Stacy objected, and Steve shook his head, smiling crookedly. They saw Jim, at that moment, trying to enhance his image as expedition leader. If he could not make the summit himself, then he would settle for the suggestion of altruism on his part and a superordinate goal held by the team, putting an American *woman* on top.

Jim was a capable leader on the mountain, but in making personnel decisions he showed less sagacity (Allison, 1993).

LEADERSHIP ROLES. What is leadership? It is persuasion; it is not domination. As defined in psychological research, leadership involves persuading people to ignore their individual concerns and devote themselves instead to a common goal, one that is important for the welfare of the group (Hogan, Curphy, & Hogan, 1994).

Just how and when a person is suited for leadership has been difficult to determine. For many years, investigators attempted to discover the essential traits of an effective leader.

Intelligence, flexibility, and strength of character were prominently mentioned, and it was assumed that the leader was the best-liked, most active, and most able member of the group, a view known as the *great-person theory* of leadership. The idea here is that each person has a single status, and an all-around great person is at the top.

As this research continued, the hope of discovering a highly prescriptive, invariant set of characteristics faded for two reasons. First, it was found that different situations usually require somewhat different traits in a leader. If a hierarchy could be established for one situation, it would have to be re-established for another, depending on the situation and the traits of the group members. Second, even within one situation, there seem to be at least two different leadership roles, each making its own contribution to the group process.

There is a **task specialist,** or *instrumental leader,* who is concerned with identifying the problem, discovering methods of dealing with it, and implementing the best solution. This person is oriented to a specific obstacle or threat in the group, and usually he or she ranks highest on activity and best ideas. In addition, there is a **social specialist,** or *expressive leader,* who is the central figure in maintaining group cohesion and morale (Bales, 1951). Also called the maintenance specialist, this person often has a good sense of humor, ranks highest on likability, and encourages others (Hogan, Curphy, & Hogan, 1994).

On rare occasions, the two roles are held by the same person. But especially as the group continues to function, different individuals emerge in these capacities.

LEADER–FOLLOWER INTERACTION. In most group situations, there are a few general characteristics of enduring leadership. The individual who assumes primary control is usually above average in intelligence, although not the most brilliant individual in the group. There is some truth in the old political maxim: The best-qualified person, in terms of ability, is not popular enough to be elected. Any enduring leader also must be close to the group members in attitudes and interests.

Certain situational factors also are influential. A task leader is more likely to be suitable if the morale of the group is unusually good or if the group has deteriorated almost to the point of disintegration. When conditions are neither extremely favorable nor extremely unfavorable, a social specialist may be more effective. The primary need here is to maintain solidarity (Fielder, 1964).

The study of leadership today therefore focuses on characteristics of the followers, as well as those of the leader, for followers certainly can influence leaders. In this sense, leadership is a shared and fluid process. Charisma, for example, is not simply a quality possessed by a leader—it is something accorded by followers, as part of the leadership process. Our understanding of leadership is incomplete if we fail to recognize leader–follower interactions (Wakefield, 1992).

As the group goals change, a leader may become a follower, especially in a very large group,

such as a whole nation. Different situations require different leadership abilities, as illustrated by Jim's leadership, which was highly effective on the mountain but disparaged at base camp. Here again we encounter the interaction principle. The type of leadership that proves most effective depends on the followers, the situation, the level of development of the group, and its goals (Figure 17-14).

IN PERSPECTIVE. As we close this chapter, the reader may wonder about the other summit climbers. When it came time for her attempt, Diana's team was driven down the mountain by a severe storm, a bitter disappointment for her. Geoff reached the summit alone with great satisfaction, for it was his third attempt. The 209th person to climb to the top of Mount Everest, he celebrated by depositing there a pink flamingo and the American flag (Tabin, 1993). Peggy summited too, prompting admiration among some expedition members, animosity among others.

The admiration came from Jim and Don. As the least experienced climber on the expedition, Peggy fell twice, started to roll down the mountain, and stopped herself by digging her ice axe into the snow. Her success spoke for itself, as well as for Dawa Tsering, the Sherpa who accompanied her (Tabin, 1993).

Others had a very different view of Peggy's accomplishment. The American expedition, Steve pointed out, was based on teamwork and team goals. Members were to take only measured risks and to remain responsible for their own safety. By taking unnecessary risks, inexperienced Peggy had broken the agreement and been disloyal to everyone in the group. "And success in the face of stupidity," he declared, "is still stupidity" (Allison, 1993).

A few days earlier, Narayan Shrestha, a Sherpa in the Spanish expedition, had been swept to his death by an avalanche. Michel Parmentier, from the

FIGURE 17–14 LEADERSHIP AND THE SITUATION. Winston Churchill was voted into the highest positions in England in times of war. When peace returned, he was twice immediately voted out of office. Even while in prison, Nelson Mandela maintained a powerful leadership in South Africa. Released from prison, he continues to maintain that role.

French team, was found frozen in the snow, apparently a victim of exhaustion and altitude sickness. They were among nine climbers who died on the slopes of Mount Everest during these three months. Only the American and Korean expeditions suffered no fatalities (Nelson et al., 1990). On the average, for every trek up Mount Everest, two people fail to survive (West, 1986).

Peggy was grateful to be alive, and she leaves us with several questions. Should her bold dash to the summit be explained by situational factors? Or might it be better explained by dispositional attributions? Or, more accurately, to what extent were each of these factors involved? In answering these questions, remember that people in Eastern cultures are often inclined to find the causes of behavior in the setting or situation. In Western societies, they are more likely to cite factors within the individual, as personal traits or dispositions (Lee, Hallahan, & Herzog, 1996).

Other things being equal, which they rarely are, we can sum up the cultural issue in this fashion. If we were to ask Dawa Tsering why Peggy sprinted to the summit, he would be likely to give reasons external to Peggy. She had fine weather, a prepared route, perfect timing, and even his presence as a support climber. If we were to ask Steve Ruoss, he would be more likely to explain Peggy's act on the basis of personal traits, including out-of-role behavior. In fact, he did, declaring that Peggy's dash to the peak, especially by a support climber, showed only ignorance and selfishness. Rescue efforts, if needed, would have endangered many members of the American expedition.

From a broader viewpoint, we must remember that we all have a cultural perspective, whether we look at the world from the top of Mount Everest or from a less lofty location. The contents of this book come largely from the Western world, and therefore the possible cultural bias of even this psychology is not to be taken lightly.

ATTITUDES

1. An attitude is defined as a tendency to make an evaluation, and it is considered to have three components: thinking, feeling, and acting. Attitudes are formed through direct instruction, modeling, and classical and operant conditioning, and the same processes are involved in changing attitudes.

2. Several theories of attitude formation and change are based on the principle that human beings try to avoid or eliminate inconsistencies. These approaches include: balance theory, which deals with harmony among attitudes in one or more individuals; congruity theory, concerned with attitude shifts; and cognitive-dissonance theory, which stresses that individuals can dispel inconsistency through rationalization, selective perception, and the acquisition of new information.

3. A most important factor in persuasion is the credibility of the communicator, who must be perceived as trustworthy and expert if the communication is to be persuasive. The use of fear depends on the initial level of fear in the audience and on the extent to which the message includes instructions on what to do, as well as what to avoid.

SOCIAL COGNITION

4. Person perception, which is part of social cognition, refers to the ways we understand another individual. In forming impressions of people, the warm–cold dimension often outweighs all other traits, partly because of the halo effect.

5. Stereotypes sometimes may facilitate first impressions, but it is extremely difficult to determine the accuracy of such generalizations. Many stereotypes are negative or ethnocentric, and they ignore individual differences. Prejudices are almost always harmful because the issue, by definition, has been prejudged.

6. Attribution theory is concerned with how people explain others' behavior, as well as their own. In general, they use a disposition attribution for others. Conversely, they use a situational attribution for themselves.

INTERPERSONAL ATTRACTION

7. Several factors seem influential in interpersonal attraction, but two are primary. These include similarity—of interests, intelligence, and even physical appearance—and familiarity with the other person.

8. In self-disclosure, one person communicates to another details of his or her personal life. Reciprocal self-disclosure is an important characteristic of a long-term relationship. In unsuccessful long-term relationships, a demand–withdraw pattern may develop in which one partner attempts to discuss a certain issue and the other withdraws from this interaction.

SOCIAL INFLUENCE

9. In conformity, an individual adopts the thoughts or behaviors of a social group without any direct pressure to do so. Individuals sometimes conform simply because they do not want to be different. Conformity also arises when people are uncertain about what to do.

10. In compliance, people are encouraged or induced to behave in certain ways; there is some direct pressure. Studies have shown two ways in which compliance can be obtained in negotiations: the foot-in-the-door technique and the door-in-the-face technique. In obedience, there is a demand, not a request. The Milgram study of obedience demonstrated that social pressure may be more influential than personality in determining behavior in certain situations.

11. Altruism seems generally less attributable to a particular type of personality than to the individual's temporary personal states, such as haste and mood, and to characteristics of the situation, especially the number of bystanders and degree of personal risk.

GROUP PROCESSES

12. A group member is usually assigned or adopts a role, which is a pattern of expected behavior. Status, which is closely related to role, refers to a person's position in the group hierarchy.

13. When people work in the presence of others, they often accomplish more than when working alone, an outcome called social facilitation. Two factors that seem important in inducing cooperation in natural settings are early childhood training and the existence of superordinate goals, which benefit all group members. According to a meta-analysis, cooperation is more effective than competition in promoting achievement and productivity.

14. In groupthink, a group places such a high value on cohesion and maintenance of morale that critical thinking is suspended and decision-making ability is thereby limited. The concept of group polarization indicates that a group decision is likely to be more extreme, in any direction, than the average decision of the individual members.

15. The emergence of a leader is dependent partly on intelligence and partly on congruence in leader–follower characteristics. Even within the same group, two prominent leadership styles may be required, one involving a task specialist and the other a social specialist. In any case, leadership is a process, a function of leader-follower interactions and the group context.

• WORKING WITH PSYCHOLOGY •

❧ REVIEW OF KEY CONCEPTS ❧

social psychology

Attitudes
  attitude
  balance theory
  congruity theory
  cognitive-dissonance
    theory

Social Cognition
  social cognition
  central trait
  halo effect
  stereotype
  prejudice
  ethnocentrism
  culture
  multicultural awareness

attribution theory
dispositional attribution
situational attribution
overattribution effect

Interpersonal Attraction
  interpersonal attraction
  matching hypothesis
  self-disclosure

Social Influence
  social influence
  conformity
  social norms
  deindividuation
  compliance
  foot-in-the-door technique
  door-in-the-face technique

obedience
altruism
bystander intervention effect

Group Processes
  group
  role
  status
  pecking order
  social facilitation
  social loafing
  superordinate goals
  meta-analysis
  groupthink
  group polarization
  brainstorming
  task specialist
  social specialist

❧ CLASS DISCUSSION/CRITICAL THINKING ❧

A NARRATIVE TWIST

The Sherpas assisted the Americans in reaching the peak of Mount Everest. Using the concepts of ethnocentrism and multicultural awareness, suggest some ways that each group might have perceived the other in seeking this goal. Then

suppose that the conditions were reversed. The Americans assisted the Sherpas in achieving a goal, such as establishing and maintaining fast-food restaurants in Nepal. Show how the issues of ethnocentrism and multicultural awareness might arise in this context as well. ❧

TOPICAL QUESTIONS

• *Attitudes.* Ms. Zing takes a pro-life position on abortion. What position is she likely to take on capital punishment? Explain the reasons for your choice, referring to the consistency principle.

• *Social Cognition.* In the overattribution effect, too much emphasis is placed on dispositional factors, too little on situational factors. If a friend and a stranger both observe a young man behaving in an unusual manner, such as wearing no shirt on a cold day, who is more likely to display this effect, the friend or the stranger? Why?

• *Interpersonal Attraction.* Ms. Able and Mr. Baker are single, live near each other, and share certain characteristics—such as high intelligence, a certain religious outlook, and financial concerns—and yet they have different careers, hobbies, physical appearances, and geographic backgrounds. Discuss the possibility that they will become longtime companions.

• *Social Influence.* The foot-in-the-door and door-in-the-face techniques are somewhat opposite approaches for obtaining compliance. For eliciting compliance from a small child, which technique seems more promising? To obtain a large donation to a charity, which technique appears more useful? Explain the reasons for your answers.

• *Group Processes.* Does groupthink occur more often in public life today than two centuries ago? Or are the media simply more adept at gaining details of incidents of groupthink? Explain your answer, using an example from politics or business.

❧ TOPICS OF RELATED INTEREST ❧

In many respects, psychotherapy is concerned with attitude formation and change (16). Interpersonal attraction, especially the development of intimate relationships, is viewed in the context of reinforcement theory (7) and emotion (11). The Milgram study was considered in the context of research methods (2).

IN THE
WORKPLACE

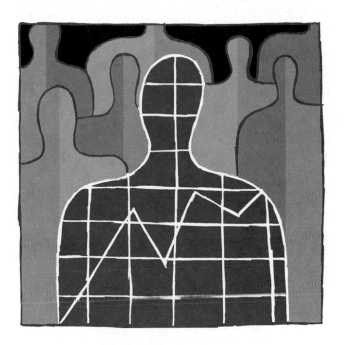

STATISTICAL METHODS

QUANTIFICATION IN PSYCHOLOGY
Statistics in Research
Misuse of Statistics

DESCRIPTIVE STATISTICS
Graphs and Numbers
Measures of Central Tendency
Measures of Variability
Describing Sets of Scores

CORRELATIONAL STATISTICS
Types of Correlation
Determining Relationships

INFERENTIAL STATISTICS
Sampling Procedures
Point Estimation
Study of Differences

STATISTICS AS A TOOL

18
STATISTICAL METHODS

EXAMINE THE KEYS ON YOUR COMPUTER OR TYPE-
WRITER KEYBOARD. NOTICE THAT *E*, THE MOST COM-
MON LETTER IN ENGLISH, HAS AN INCONVENIENT
location. It requires a s–t–r–e–t–c–h.

The letter *A*, also frequently used, is a bit hard to reach. With small hands or short fingers, that must be exasperating.

The consonants, alphabetized in the home row, are not alphabetical elsewhere. And the vowels are scattered unpredictably throughout the keyboard. Why?

This keyboard is one of the most important tools in modern society. Could it be improved? Should it be redesigned for today's high-tech workplace?

Back in the 1930s, a pair of brothers-in-law, August Dvorak and William Dealey, decided to study typing behavior. Both psychologists, they began by observing people using the early typewriting machines. Then they filmed typists in action and viewed these films in slow motion. Convinced by these films that further studies would be worthwhile, they planned hundreds of statistical tests of various letter and finger combinations. To accomplish this goal, they added other psychologists to their team (Dvorak, Merrick, Dealey, & Ford, 1936).

Without knowing it, this group at the University of Washington, working partly under the auspices of the U.S. Navy, had entered a race against time, for the winds of World War II had already swept across parts of Western Europe. And without knowing it, they were in competition with corporate America, which had its own interests to protect.

We shall follow their surprising, bittersweet story throughout this chapter, for it shows how statistics can be used to answer research questions. It also illustrates the human-factors approach in psychological investigations.

These psychologists, men and women, worked in **human-factors psychology,** a specialty devoted to the design of tools and procedures well suited to human use, especially in the work environment. Employing diverse research techniques, including statistical methods, human-factors psychologists have studied jobs of all sorts, from bricklaying to using the computer keyboard. This interdisciplinary field today is composed largely of psychologists and engineers (Howell, 1994). As our society continues to evolve, human-factors psychologists will face many challenges,

including those posed by the new technologies, our longer life span, and their interactions (Nickerson, 1992).

In Europe, where this specialty has an industrial background, it is known as *ergonomics,* meaning the study of work or energy expenditure. In both instances, the concern is not only with physical equipment, such as tools and machines, but also with the psychological environment, including personnel and management policies (Page, 1995).

Especially in the design of computer equipment, there is a growing awareness of human-factors issues, most evident in the popular label *user friendly.* Manufacturers' failure to attend to this issue today usually results in the loss of sales. Sometimes it becomes the basis of litigation in liability for health and safety. As a lure for buying countless products, advertisers now proclaim that their products have an *ergonomic design* (Howell, 1994).

This chapter begins by illustrating quantification in psychology, using examples from human-factors research. Then it turns to three major topics: descriptive statistics, which characterize a group of scores; correlational statistics, which indicate relationships among scores; and inferential statistics, used to make guesses about scores that are not available. The chapter closes with a statement about statistics as a tool in science.

For hundreds of years, progress in science has been closely linked to developments in mathematics and statistics. Tremendous advances in astronomy occurred in the eighteenth century after the mathematical laws of celestial motion were established. Developments in probability theory played an indispensable role in the growth of physics. The potential uses of statistical procedures in sociology and anthropology were first realized in the nineteenth century. And Sir Francis Galton, late in that century, brought statistical methods into psychology through his studies of physical and psychological differences among people. These successive developments reflect Galton's view, shared by many scholars: Until the observations in any field of study have been quantified, that branch of knowledge cannot be considered science.

❧

STATISTICS IN RESEARCH

The term **statistics** refers to the collection and evaluation of numerical information, including methods for demonstrating facts and the relations among them. This meaning, emphasizing methods, is intended throughout this chapter. The term also has a second meaning; it refers to the results of using these methods—the numerical values themselves. This second meaning is implied whenever someone says: "Statistics show that . . ."

PRODUCTIVITY AT WORK. Early in this century, a young college dropout found work in the coal mines and a place for himself in the history of psychology—by using simple statistical methods. Shortly after his arrival at the Bethlehem Steel Company, Frederick Taylor noticed that most of the workers shoveled heavy iron ore, up to 38

pounds per shovelful, and they tired quickly. Or they shoveled rice coal, with less than 4 pounds in each shovelful, and they exerted themselves relatively little, even after several hours. Intrigued with this information, Taylor decided to find out the most appropriate load for a worker shoveling all day—that is, the poundage per shovelful that would permit him to do the most work.

Assigning shovelers to different parts of the yard, Taylor appointed observers to study them with watches and weighing scales. At the outset, all of these workers used shovels with large blades, and the weight of the material they shoveled each day was carefully noted. Then part of the blade was cut off, making a smaller load and, after another period of shoveling, the total weight of the shoveled material was noted once more. By this process, cutting the blade again and again, making the loads lighter and lighter, Taylor discovered the optimal shovelful: 22.5 pounds. That amount enabled the average man to do the most work per day.

That finding prompted Bethlehem Steel Company to change its procedures. Thereafter, the company distributed each day to each worker a shovel of a certain size, depending on the material that worker would be lifting. Respect for that new policy enabled Taylor to receive a promotion, and respect for that investigation, demonstrating the value of statistics in research, helped inaugurate the field of human-factors psychology (Taylor, 1911).

The workplace has changed considerably since Frederick Taylor's day, but human factors psychologists still study lifting of all sorts. They measure strain, fatigue, and energy expenditure, all to make the work easier and more productive (Gallagher, 1991; Mital, 1992).

COMFORT IN THE HOME. Human-factors psychology is not limited to the work environment. On awakening in the morning, you look at the clock, fill the bathtub, check the thermometer, and seat yourself in a chair for breakfast. The shape, size, and design of each of these devices have been influenced by human-factors psychologists.

In the bathroom, if the tub is too small, you are uncomfortable. If it is too big, it requires unnecessary space and hot water. What is the preferred shape and size for most people? Here human-factors psychologists have been interested in comfort rather than work, and they answer such questions by modifying bathtubs in various ways, asking subjects to bathe, and then assessing their comfort. But despite their findings, bathtubs today often use conventional designs (Figure 18–1).

HEALTH AND THE KEYBOARD. In most settings, productivity and comfort are dual considerations, accompanied by another factor, health. These three issues, readily evident in the use of the computer keyboard, account in a general way for most of the specific goals in human-factors psychology.

When the typewriter was invented almost 125 years ago, little thought was given to productivity. Rather, it was believed that the machine would give a neater, cleaner result than the usual handwriting, which certainly has been the case. Workers might use the machine with one finger, two fingers, or whatever way they wished. Hand movements were not an issue.

By the time the human-factors team from the University of Washington entered the scene, touch typing had become the predominant mode of operation and hand movements had become a concern. The University of Washington, incidentally, is known around Seattle as UW or, more colloquially, U Dub. When the UW team examined its films of typists at work, these pictures showed the hands

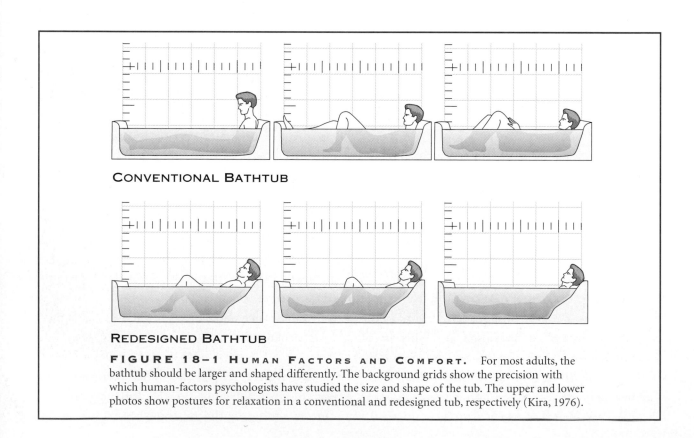

CONVENTIONAL BATHTUB

REDESIGNED BATHTUB

FIGURE 18–1 HUMAN FACTORS AND COMFORT. For most adults, the bathtub should be larger and shaped differently. The background grids show the precision with which human-factors psychologists have studied the size and shape of the tub. The upper and lower photos show postures for relaxation in a conventional and redesigned tub, respectively (Kira, 1976).

moving far more than appeared necessary. The rhythm essential for fast typing often seemed disrupted by awkward movements.

Today, with still greater speed and massive use of the keyboard throughout the workplace, operators using the standard electronic keyboard are producing many hand movements and finger movements per hour. In short, they are overtaxing themselves, resulting in a dramatic rise in injuries (Figure 18–2). Caused by constant, similar movements, *repetitive strain injuries* from the keyboard include pain in the wrist, fingers, and elbows, accompanied sometimes by swelling or numbness in the hands. The data entry operator, who may stroke the keys up to 200,000 times per day, is especially prone to this disorder. In terms of movement, this work is perhaps the equivalent of walking with the fingers across the keyboard for about 10 miles (Jones, Burnsed, & Marquardt, 1991).

What can be done about this problem? The answer to that question appears later in this chapter, derived largely through statistical methods. The UW team of course never anticipated this problem, although its members did their unknowing best to offer a solution based on statistical analyses.

MISUSE OF STATISTICS

Responsibility for the successful use of statistical information lies largely with the producer, but it also falls to the consumer, who must develop statistical literacy. A major approach to knowledge, **statistical literacy** is the ability to make sound judgments about the quality and usefulness of numerical information. It is acquired slowly, but the appropriate attitude—a cautious interpretation of the evidence—is readily illustrated.

In 1936, at just the time the UW team was conducting investigations of typing behavior, the *Literary Digest*, a national magazine, was conducting the first major poll in a national presidential election. Over two million voters were sampled from lists in telephone directories and automobile registrations, and the results predicted an overwhelming victory for the Republican candidate, Alfred Landon. However, Franklin Delano Roosevelt, the Democratic candidate, won easily in almost every state. Then it was discovered that in those years of the Great Depression the lists did not represent Republicans and Democrats equally. Far more

FIGURE 18–2 HAND MOVEMENTS ON THE KEYBOARD. As this photo indicates, the hands must move rapidly into many different positions while typing on the standard keyboard. If continued for extended periods, these movements can result in tendinitis and other repetitive strain injuries.

Republicans owned cars and telephones, and shortly after this massive, embarassing error, the *Literary Digest* became defunct.

Although telephones may be more equally distributed among members of the political parties today, this problem has not disappeared. Many households now have unlisted telephones; others have no telephones. Telephone directories still do not include the entire population. Mail surveys have a low response rate because people do not want to take the time or trouble to answer. Even in-person surveys have limitations, due chiefly to the potential for interviewer bias.

In viewing the results of any poll or survey, a statistically literate person will be cautious. He or she will ask how the subjects were chosen, how the data were collected, by whom, with what instrument, and so forth. If these procedural details are not available, then the results themselves must be regarded with considerable skepticism.

Even when the information is correct, the presentation may give a wrong impression. Consider further examples, again from very different settings.

During World War II, the Office of Strategic Services carried out an elaborate series of tests for selecting men and women to serve as spies, counter-spies, and undercover agents. In one of many tests, groups of four to seven candidates were assembled separately beside a secluded brook that was to be regarded as a raging torrent so fast and deep that nothing could rest on the bottom. The task was to transport equipment and personnel to the other side as quickly as possible within one hour. In this situation, the examiners looked for signs of cooperation, resistance, leadership, impulsive behavior, and so forth (OSS Assessment Staff, 1948).

The candidates required, on the average, about 30 to 45 minutes to solve the problem. But this statement gives an incomplete, distorted picture of what really happened. Many groups failed to solve the problem at all. A few did so very rapidly, one in just four minutes (OSS Assessment Staff, 1948).

Thus, the average time required for the solution does not provide a satisfactory understanding of the overall performances.

Statistical findings are also presented visually. Misleading graphs are sometimes created by using pictures to distort the real differences between quantities (Figure 18–3).

One broad aim of this chapter is to encourage a critical attitude toward statistics. Even without impressive statistical literacy, we can still be cautious about the interpretation of numerical information.

• DESCRIPTIVE STATISTICS •

After reviewing their films of the typing process, the UW team decided that the standard keyboard was the typist's "first difficult problem . . . a crazy patchwork put together long ago" (Dvorak, Merrick, Dealey, & Ford, 1936). Hence, this human-factors team abandoned their investigation of the learning process to confront more directly the problem of fitting the machine to the worker. Here the first step was simply to measure the efficiency of the standard keyboard. If this efficiency was found to be low, as expected, then the team would pursue a second goal, the development of an improved design.

To assess the standard keyboard, the UW team needed information on two sets of variables—the work to be performed and the workers' capabilities. The work to be performed is a transcription skill; visual or auditory signals must be accurately and rapidly transformed into letters on a screen or page. The capabilities of the worker are chiefly finger and hand dexterity, as well as knowledge of the language.

For presenting such information, descriptive statistics are extremely useful. In **descriptive statistics,** the aim is to describe or characterize a set of scores, usually by indicating the typical score and differences among the scores. Descriptive statistics

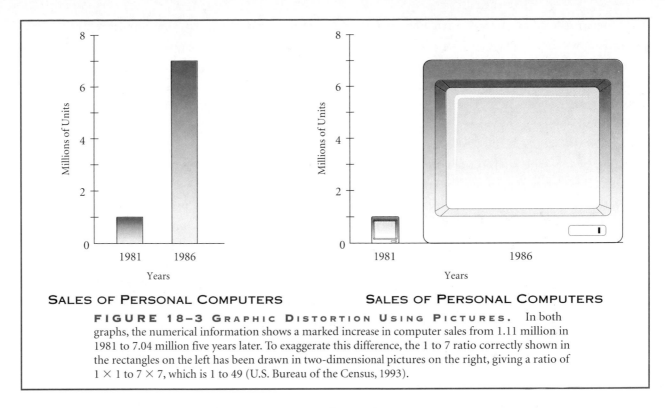

FIGURE 18-3 GRAPHIC DISTORTION USING PICTURES. In both graphs, the numerical information shows a marked increase in computer sales from 1.11 million in 1981 to 7.04 million five years later. To exaggerate this difference, the 1 to 7 ratio correctly shown in the rectangles on the left has been drawn in two-dimensional pictures on the right, giving a ratio of 1×1 to 7×7, which is 1 to 49 (U.S. Bureau of the Census, 1993).

show in a relatively simple manner the overall trends in a group of scores.

GRAPHS AND NUMBERS

The UW team commenced with the question of letter frequencies. Which letter of the alphabet is most commonly used in English? Which is next, and so forth? Which letter is least used? Samples of written English from diverse sources revealed the frequencies for the 26 letters and four punctuation marks: the period, comma, colon, and semicolon.

A	B	C	D	E	F	G	H
684	160	231	261	1,000	102	99	402
I	J	K	L	M	N	O	P
484	23	41	349	198	469	561	158
Q	R	S	T	U	V	W	X
10	423	486	685	223	66	132	20
	Y	Z	.	,	:	;	
	175	9	86	115	11	16	

The following scores were obtained:

These scores are called **raw scores** because they are original scores, just as they were obtained from the original measurement. In other words, raw scores are untreated; they have not been submitted to any statistical analysis. But with a large number of raw scores, as in this case, the major characteristics cannot be readily perceived. The scores are too numerous. Some *general* description is needed, and here we turn to two ways of summarizing results: graphs and numerical values.

USE OF GRAPHIC DISPLAYS. One method for presenting any group of scores is to construct a **graph**, which is a visual display of numerical values made by connecting lines or geometric figures. Graphs are pictures of a sort.

They show the frequency with which scores or other items occurred, or they display the relationship between sets of scores. Generally, the scores or items appear on the horizontal axis, and the frequencies or performances are indicated on the vertical axis. The vertical axis should begin at zero and accomodate all possible scores. These conventions in constructing

One graph constructed with bars, the **bar graph**, shows the frequency of the different scores or items by using rectangles of appropriate heights. The width of the rectangle is arbitrary, but the height is proportional to the frequency of the scores it represents.

When the scores for all 26 letters are displayed in a bar graph, the differences become readily apparent. The letter *E* is by far the most frequently used letter, outscoring not only its nearest rivals but almost half of the alphabet. It occurs more often than the 12 least-used letters combined (Figure 18–4).

Which finger of a trained keyboard operator types the letter *E?* The left middle finger, which is not as agile as the left index finger. And for most people, the left is not as agile as the right. So *E* does not appear to be well assigned. And where is it placed? It is not even in the home row—but we are getting ahead of ourselves.

Using this graph, an observer can tell at a glance the most common scores, least common scores, and those of intermediate frequency. Graphs truly provide a quick picture. Here it can be readily observed that the letters *J, X, Q,* and *Z* are rarely used. In all such cases, an old saying must be modified: A well-constructed graph is worth a thousand numbers.

USE OF NUMERICAL VALUES. The second major method for describing a group of raw scores is the use of numerical values. A few such values can summarize the performance of the whole group, commonly by providing two types of information: the typical scores and the extent to which all scores differ from the typical scores.

For example, the frequency counts for the 26 letters show that scores of 198 and 223 are in the middle of the distribution. In this respect, they are typical scores. The letters *E* and *Z* include the highest and lowest scores, 1,000 and 9, respectively. They are extreme scores. Collectively, these numerical values give some idea of the full distribution,

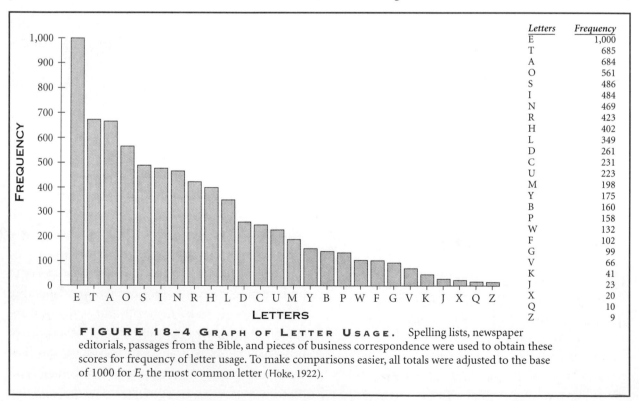

Letters	Frequency
E	1,000
T	685
A	684
O	561
S	486
I	484
N	469
R	423
H	402
L	349
D	261
C	231
U	223
M	198
Y	175
B	160
P	158
W	132
F	102
G	99
V	66
K	41
J	23
X	20
Q	10
Z	9

FIGURE 18–4 GRAPH OF LETTER USAGE. Spelling lists, newspaper editorials, passages from the Bible, and pieces of business correspondence were used to obtain these scores for frequency of letter usage. To make comparisons easier, all totals were adjusted to the base of 1000 for *E*, the most common letter (Hoke, 1922).

but they can be supplemented by other values, to which we now turn.

MEASURES OF CENTRAL TENDENCY

The most obvious values for describing a group of scores indicate the central tendency. They are called **measures of central tendency** because they indicate the performance of typical subjects or items, near the *center* of the group. For the letters of the alphabet, inspection suggests that the central or typical score is around 200 or so, but this answer is just a guess. To be more precise, three different measures are available.

MODE, MEDIAN, AND MEAN. One measure of central tendency is called the **mode** because it is the score that occurs most frequently. It can be remembered by thinking of pie à la mode, which literally means "pie in the current fashion." The score most in fashion, or most frequent, is the mode. Among the 26 raw scores tabulated for the letters, no score occurred more than once. Thus, there is no mode, or modal score.

Another measure of central tendency, the **median,** is the middle point in a distribution when all scores have been ranked according to size. It has half of the scores above it and half below it. The meaning of this term can be remembered by thinking of a highway where the sign says: "Keep Off the Median Strip." This strip divides the highway in half, just as the median divides the ranked scores in half.

When there is an odd number of cases, the median is the middle of the ranked scores; with even-numbered groups, it is that point equidistant between the two middle scores. In the group of 26 raw scores, the median is halfway between the scores for *M* and *U*, as evident when all 26 scores are ranked in order of magnitude. These middle scores are 198 and 223, giving a median of 210.5.

The most useful measure of central tendency is generally the **mean,** which is remembered simply as the arithmetic average. It is obtained by adding all of the scores and dividing by the number of scores. For the 26 raw scores, the sum is 7,451 and the mean is 286.6.

INTERPRETATION OF MODE, MEDIAN, AND MEAN. For practice, consider the following scores made by ten male keyboard operators in a typing pool. They show typing speed expressed as words per minute:

58 42 52 40 59 46 54 50 41 58

What is the mode? It is the most frequent score, which is 58. Two operators made this score.

What is the median? It is the middle point when all ten scores are ranked by size. In this case, it is 51.

What is the mean? It is the average for all scores. The sum of the scores is 500. When divided by 10, it gives a mean of 50.

When comparisons are made among these measures of central tendency, certain conclusions can be drawn. The mode is the least reliable measure, particularly when the number of scores is small. It may change markedly when just one score is added, subtracted, or altered in any way because it represents only the most frequent score. If one of the keyboard operators who achieved 58 words per minute had been ill on the day of the test and scored 41, the mode for the whole group would have become 41, decreasing by 17 points.

The median is more reliable, or stable, because it represents the ranks of all scores. Changing one score from 58 to 41 would lower the median by only 3 points because only the position of that one score in the ranked group would be changed. It would move from the high end of the distribution to the low end, making the median 48 instead of 51. The median is a better measure of central tendency because the *ranks* of all scores are considered.

The mean, based on the *values* of all scores, not just the ranks, is generally the most reliable measure of central tendency. It is the only measure that takes into account all of the information about each score. If any score is changed at all, the mean is always changed somewhat. For this reason, the mean is a basic point of departure for further statistical analysis. In the change just mentioned, the mean would have been altered by less than two points, from 50 to 48.3.

One caution is in order. When some scores are quite deviant, the mean is more affected than either the median or mode. In these instances, the median may be the most useful measure of central tendency.

Suppose an eleventh keyboard operator, for some reason, typed only six words per minute. Including this score lowers the mean by 4 points, making it 46. The mode remains unchanged at 58, and the median is changed by only one point, decreasing from 51 to 50. Thus, the three measures vary in stability depending on the distribution of scores in the group. *Usually* the mean is most descriptive, or most stable, but its use in unusual distributions may be debatable.

THE NORMAL DISTRIBUTION. When the distribution is completely symmetrical, these three measures of central tendency all have the same value. For example, when the scores for 100 typists in a pool are presented in graphic form, they accumulate in the center and decline on both sides at a decreasing rate. Whenever many factors act in a complex, often unknown, way to determine a single event, the symmetrical, bell-shaped distribution, with moderate variation among the scores, is called a *normal curve* or **normal distribution**. With large samples, many human characteristics, such as height, weight, intelligence, and typing speed, appear as approximately normal distributions (Figure 18–5).

All normal distributions are symmetrical and bell-shaped, but all symmetrical distributions are not necessarily normal. Sometimes the symmetrical distribution does not look much like a bell. The scores are too tightly clustered, making the distribution too tall, or they are too spread out, making it too flat to constitute a normal, bell-shaped distribution.

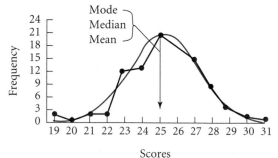

FIGURE 18–5 NORMAL DISTRIBUTION. The black figure presents 100 typing scores according to the number of typists who made each score. If more scores were obtained, this figure would approach even more closely the symmetrical, bell-shaped pattern of the normal curve, shown in color.

Skewed Distributions. At other times, the scores pile up at one end or the other, and the distribution is clearly not normal. In a **skewed distribution,** which has a spread of exceptionally high scores, or low scores, the three measures of central tendency provide different indications of the typical score. With a skewed distribution, care must be taken in selecting any measure of central tendency as representative of the entire group.

A number of unusually low scores produces a **negatively skewed distribution,** observed in arrival times at concerts, ball games, and similar events. A few people may arrive an hour or more before the performance, enjoying the players' warm-up and one another's company. Others arrive well ahead; most appear just before the show begins; and there are always a few latecomers, usually by only a few minutes. The latecomers are rarely as tardy as the early arrivals are ahead of the starting time.

In a **positively skewed distribution,** a spread of scores extends in the direction of high scores. For example, the distribution of departure times after a theatre performance or athletic contest produces a positive skew. Most people leave promptly, but a number linger for varying lengths—chatting, resting, reminiscing, or simply waiting for the crowd to disappear (Figure 18–6).

In both skewed distributions, the spread of extreme scores always pulls the mean in its own direction. Thus, in comparison to the other measures of central tendency, a negative skew lowers the mean; a positive skew raises the mean.

MEASURES OF VARIABILITY

In addition to the average or typical score for the letters of the alphabet, the UW team was interested in differences among them. Were the scores for the various letters much alike, or did they vary markedly? The mean score for all letters and punctuation marks was 286.6. Were the scores for the individual letters clustered nearby, or did they range widely?

Similarly, were the typing scores much like one another? The mean typing score for ten men was 50 words per minute. Were most scores close to 50 or did they differ markedly?

To understand any group of scores, we need not only some measure of central tendency but also some measure of difference or dispersion. These latter measures, called **measures of variability,** indicate the degree to which the scores in a group *differ* from some typical score. The usual measures of variability are the range and standard deviation.

Range and Standard Deviation. The simplest indicator of variability is the **range,** which is the difference between the lowest and

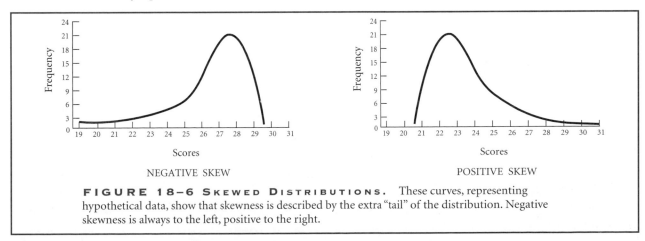

NEGATIVE SKEW

POSITIVE SKEW

FIGURE 18–6 Skewed Distributions. These curves, representing hypothetical data, show that skewness is described by the extra "tail" of the distribution. Negative skewness is always to the left, positive to the right.

highest scores. The range for letter frequencies was calculated in this way, as noted already. The score of 1,000, for *E*, minus 9, for *Z*, gave a range of 991. Like the mode, the range is unstable, for it takes into account only two scores in the group. Without the *E*, the highest score would have been for *T*, at 685, and the range would have been reduced to 676, a difference of over 300 points.

Another measure of variability, less well known and more complex, is preferred in science because, like the mean, it is based on *every* value in the group. It is therefore more reliable than the range. Called the **standard deviation** (SD), it indicates the degree of deviation of all the scores from the mean. In a sense, it is a sort of average deviation except that squaring and a square root are involved. Addressing the question of dispersion or variability, it shows whether the scores are close to the mean or widely dispersed.

For ease of understanding, consider two sets of hypothetical scores. For the Reds, they are: 2, 14, 25, 39, and 45. The mean of these scores is 25. For the Blues, they are: 109, 109, 110, 111, and 111. The Blues' mean is 110. Obviously, the scores for the Reds are more widely dispersed than those for the Blues. Thus, the standard deviation for the Reds will be larger than that for the Blues. This fact can be confirmed by noting the deviation of each score from its mean:

	Reds				
Raw Scores	2	14	25	39	45
Deviations	−23	−11	0	+14	+20

	Blues				
Raw Scores	109	109	110	111	111
Deviations	−1	−1	0	+1	+1

One might hastily conclude that the standard deviation is simply the mean of these deviations, but that is not the case. The rules of mathematics

and the intricacies of the standard deviation require one further step, partly because the sum of the positive deviations is always equal to the sum of the negative deviations, giving an overall sum of zero. For this reason, among others, we square the deviations. Then we sum them and divide by their number, obtaining the average of these squared deviations. Finally, we take the square root of that number because earlier, we squared the deviations. As the last step, they must be unsquared. This procedure returns the standard deviation to the same units as the original scores.

In summary, the standard deviation is calculated in the following manner. Find the deviation of each score from the mean. Square each deviation. Find the average of these squared deviations by adding them and dividing by their number. Then obtain the square root.

As a further illustration of the range and standard deviation, consider once again the scores from the typing pool, this time involving ten women as well as the ten men. The lowest score for the women is 45 and the highest is 56, giving a range of 11 words per minute. For the men, the range is from 40 to 59, or 19 words per minute. On this basis, the men differed from one another more than did the women, although both groups achieved a mean score of 50 words per minute:

Women	51 48 45 49 53 52 50 47 49 56
Men	58 42 52 40 59 46 54 50 41 58

The standard deviation provides a similar conclusion but on a much firmer and more precise basis. For the ten women's scores, the sum of the squared deviations from the mean is 90. Hence, the standard deviation is the square root of 90/10, which is the square root of 9, or 3. For the ten men's scores, the sum of the squared deviations is 490. Thus, the standard deviation is the square root of 490/10, which is the square root of 49, or 7 (Figure 18–7).

		WOMEN				MEN	
SUBJECT	SCORE	DEVIATION (D)	DEVIATION SQUARED (D²)	SUBJECT	SCORE	DEVIATION (D)	DEVIATION SQUARED (D²)
1	51	+1	1	1	58	+8	64
2	48	−2	4	2	42	−8	64
3	45	−5	25	3	52	+2	4
4	49	−1	1	4	40	−10	100
5	53	+3	9	5	59	+9	81
6	52	+2	4	6	46	−4	16
7	50	0	0	7	54	+4	16
8	47	−3	9	8	50	0	0
9	49	−1	1	9	41	−9	81
10	56	+6	36	10	58	+8	64
Sums	500	0	90	Sums	500	0	490

Mean = 50
Computation:

$$SD = \sqrt{\frac{\text{sum } D^2}{N}} = \sqrt{\frac{90}{10}} = \sqrt{9} = 3$$

Mean = 50
Computation:

$$SD = \sqrt{\frac{\text{sum } D^2}{N}} = \sqrt{\frac{490}{10}} = \sqrt{49} = 7$$

FIGURE 18–7 COMPUTATION OF STANDARD DEVIATION.
Calculation of the standard deviation (SD) involves the number of scores (N) and the deviation of each score from the mean (D). It is simply the average deviation of the scores from the mean—except that squaring and a square root are involved. These examples illustrate use of the formula.

INTERPRETATION OF STANDARD DEVIATION. The standard deviation of 7, compared with 3, indicates more variability among the men than among the women. In this instance, as in all others, the larger the standard deviation, the greater is the variability.

Boxes of cereal seem to be highly variable in the amounts they contain. When newly opened, some are almost half empty. Others are moderately full. A few are filled to the top. In contrast, dollar bills are minted with extremely little variation in size, color, and so forth, partly to prevent counterfeiting. People on the street show more variability in dress than people in church. There is more variability in sexual behavior among human beings than among animals. All of these differences are most accurately and usefully reflected in the standard deviation.

In personality, one individual may be steady and impassive, showing little emotion of any sort. Another person may be sometimes calm, sometimes highly emotional, openly displaying markedly positive and negative feelings. If we were to quantify the degree of expressed emotion in these two people, they would produce very different standard deviations. The first individual would show a distinctly lower mean and a smaller standard deviation than the second person.

The standard deviation is useful in several ways, especially in a *normal* distribution. With large samples of subjects, the scores for most human characteristics are distributed approximately according to the normal distribution. In these distributions, the standard deviation identifies a certain proportion of the scores and even the positions of individual scores within the group.

The scores between one standard deviation below the mean and one standard deviation above the mean always comprise 68% of all scores in the group. Similarly, 95% of the scores are included between two standard deviations below the mean and two standard deviations above the mean. Finally, the distance between three standard deviations below and three standard deviations above the mean includes approximately 99% of all the scores. This relationship between standard deviation units and percentage of cases under the normal distribu-

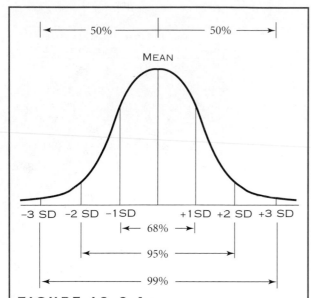

FIGURE 18–8 AREAS OF THE NORMAL DISTRIBUTION. As indicated above the figure, a normal distribution has half of the scores on each side of the mean. The percentages below the figure show the proportion of scores between the mean and various standard deviations. These properties of the normal distribution play a central role in estimating probabilities.

tion is basic to inferential statistics, which we shall consider later (Figure 18–8).

❦

DESCRIBING SETS OF SCORES

With the information about letter usage in English, the UW human-factors team turned to the next question, the capability of the worker. Their aim was to discover the dexterity of the different fingers. For this purpose, they studied several groups of subjects, male and female, all potential typists. In one instance, investigators measured finger dexterity by requesting 54 subjects to tap with each finger separately as rapidly as possible on a table. The wrist and nontapping fingers were held stationary, using a 30-second interval for each finger (Hoke, 1922).

To describe these scores, measures of central tendency and variability are needed. Together they indicate the typical performance and deviations from the typical performance.

For central tendency, the mean was employed, calculated separately for each finger, excluding the thumb, and separately for each hand. In this way, it was found that the right index finger was most capable, followed by the left index finger. Next were the middle fingers, then the little fingers, and finally the ring fingers, again right and left, respectively (Hoke, 1922). It appears no accident that the two index fingers are used in the hunt-and-peck method of typing.

Then came the question of variability. How consistent were the different fingers? Did the index finger vary more in its performance than the middle finger or ring finger? These data could be influential in designing a new keyboard.

As it turned out, consistency was not an issue. The standard deviations among the fingers were similar. No one finger was markedly less predictable than the others. They all displayed about the same amount of variability in performance (Table 18–1).

Examples of the value of taking into account both measures, means and standard deviations, are evident throughout human behavior. One golfer,

FINGER	MEAN	STANDARD DEVIATION
Right index	161.2	25.0
Left index	149.9	24.6
Right middle	134.3	25.9
Left middle	120.8	26.0
Right little	114.8	27.5
Left little	105.9	29.7
Right ring	101.4	29.9
Left ring	98.6	25.5

TABLE 18–1 FINGER ABILITIES. When ranked from fastest to slowest according to mean rate of tapping, there were marked differences among the fingers. However, the fingers did not differ significantly in variability, as shown by the standard deviations (Hoke, 1922).

with an average score of 82, is *always* in the low eighties. The other, a far better player, often comes close to par, but on bad days he becomes upset and scores in the nineties. He too has an average score of 82, but these two golfers are very different types of players.

With this information on finger ability, the human-factors team then turned to finger workload. What was the workload for each finger? These workloads were determined by noting the keys assigned to each finger and the frequencies with which they were typed. When these frequencies were summed for all keys for each finger, the left index finger scored highest, the left middle next, then the right index, and so forth (Table 18–2).

The total workload for each finger was the only concern. Hence, there was no calculation of central tendency or variability.

• CORRELATIONAL STATISTICS •

The first recorded typewriter patent was registered in London in 1714, and for the next century and a half inventors attempted to build a machine that would work. All sorts of contraptions were tried, including typewriters for use on horseback. All sorts of keyboards were designed, intended for use by the hunt-and-peck method. But all of these early machines failed. One major difficulty was the constant jamming of the keys. These failures were widely ridiculed, and attempts to modify the keyboard to present jamming were regularly ineffective.

Finally, in 1873, Christopher Sholes and his coworkers in Milwaukee solved the problem. They developed a successful machine, chiefly by constructing a keyboard on which the keys did not interfere with one another. This keyboard became widely popular. Universally accepted as the *QWERTY* or *standard keyboard*, it was the design investigated by the UW human-factors team 60 years later. *QWERTY* refers to the first letters in the upper row.

The UW team knew about the work to be performed on this keyboard. It had been determined by the frequencies of letter usage in English. This team also knew about the abilities of the fingers, discovered by the tapping test. The next step was to discover whether the most work was assigned to the most capable fingers, a critical issue in typing efficiency.

To achieve this goal, they turned to a second major method, **correlational statistics,** describing the *relationship between two sets* of scores. The concern was no longer with describing one or several sets of scores. The team was interested instead in determining the *association between pairs* of scores, each pair generated by the same subject or source. This association is referred to as *correlation.*

The term **correlation,** coming from *co-relation,* indicates the extent to which two variables are related.

FINGER	KEYS TYPED: LETTERS AND PUNCTUATION						WORKLOAD
Left index	r 423	f 102	v 66	t 685	g 99	b 160	1,535
Left middle	e 1000	d 261	c 231				1,492
Right index	y 175	h 402	n 469	u 223	j 23	m 198	1,490
Right ring	o 561	l 349	. 86				996
Left little	q 10	a 684	z 9	shift 100			803
Left ring	w 152	s 486	x 20				658
Right middle	i 484	k 41	, 115				640
Right little	p 158	; 16	: 11	? 11	shift 100		296

TABLE 18–2 FINGER WORKLOADS. The workload for each finger was determined by adding the frequencies of the letters and punctuation marks it typed. Responsibilities for the shift key were divided equally between the left and right little fingers (Hoke, 1922).

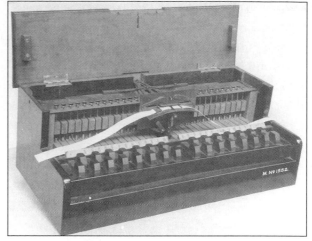

FIGURE 18–9 EARLY TYPEWRITERS. These early machines developed mechanical failures of all sorts, including the persistent problem of a workable keyboard.

Among adults, age and illness are related. Older adults are more likely than younger adults to have physical disorders. Typing speed and hat size are not correlated. Fast typists do not wear larger or smaller hats than slow typists. Temperature and aggression are mildly related. The higher the temperature, the greater are the chances of a riot or mob reaction.

❧

TYPES OF CORRELATION

Specifically, the UW team was confronted with this question: What was the correlation between finger ability and workload? Were the strongest, most capable fingers doing the most work? Were the weakest, least capable fingers doing the least work? If the most capable fingers were carrying the heaviest loads, the correlation would be high, and the keyboard was reasonably well designed. If not, if some of the less capable fingers were carrying heavy loads and vice versa, then the correlation would be low. The keyboard would be laid out poorly (Figure 18–9).

Correlations have two characteristics, size and direction. In size, they can range from high to low; in direction, they can be positive or negative. If the standard keyboard is efficient, the correlation

between finger ability and finger workload should be high *and* positive.

SIZE OF CORRELATION. In numerical value, or size, the correlation can range from 0 to +1.00 or from 0 to -1.00. No correlation can exceed a value of 1.00, which indicates a perfect relationship, something rarely found in psychological studies. A statistical computation that yields a larger result must be in error.

Correlations close to 1.00, positive *or* negative, are regarded as high; those near 0 are described as low; and those in between are considered mild or moderate. Among adult human beings, the relationship between weight and height is moderate to high, perhaps in the vicinity of .60 to .80, depending on the composition of the group. The relationship between weight and intelligence is low, essentially 0. And the relationship between weight and strength is intermediate, the exact value varying with the individuals in the sample.

DIRECTION OF CORRELATION. The direction of correlation can be positive or negative. When it is positive, both scores in each pair tend to go in the same direction, increasing together or decreasing together. Among older adults, age and illness are said to be positively correlated. When age is high, the probability of illness is high. When age is low, the probability of illness is low. The pairs of scores increase or decrease together in a **positive correlation.** For a given individual, *both* scores tend to be low or moderate or high. Expressed differently, we can say that there is a direct relationship between the two variables.

In negative correlation, a high score on one variable is associated with a low score on the other. The two members of each pair of scores go in opposite directions in a **negative correlation;** if one score is high, the other tends to be low, and vice versa. Among adults, age and health are negatively correlated. As they grow older, adults tend to be less healthy. Among children, interest in reading and the tendency to drop out of school are also negatively correlated. The higher the interest in reading, the lower is the dropout problem. There is an inverse, or negative, relationship between these variables (Figure 18–10).

Provided that the variables are understood, no particular merit is attached to a positive or negative correlation. Both indicate a relationship. Among adults, the correlation between exercise and health is positive; the correlation between exercise and disease is negative. This issue is the way the second variable is expressed, as health or illness.

DETERMINING RELATIONSHIPS

Earlier, we saw that raw scores can be presented visually, as a graph, or numerically, by indicating an overall score or value. These same two approaches can be used for correlation, but two sets of scores are involved. For the keyboard, these scores describe finger ability and finger workload.

Finger ability was determined by tapping tests, as indicated earlier. The right index finger scored highest, the left index finger next, and so forth through the left ring finger, which ranked lowest in ability.

The scores for finger workload were developed by noting the letters for which each finger was responsible and the frequency with which these letters were typed. Thus, the next task was to depict the relationship between these two sets of scores, using a graphic display or numerical calculation.

USE OF SCATTERGRAMS. In a graphic display, each entry is shown according to both scores. One score is plotted on the horizontal axis, the other on the vertical axis. The result, when all pairs of scores have been plotted, is called a **scattergram,** which shows the distribution, or scatter, among the plotted points. It gives some idea of the relationship between the two sets of scores.

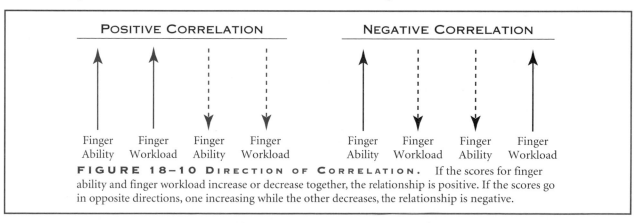

FIGURE 18–10 DIRECTION OF CORRELATION. If the scores for finger ability and finger workload increase or decrease together, the relationship is positive. If the scores go in opposite directions, one increasing while the other decreases, the relationship is negative.

The less the scatter, the stronger the relationship. In fact, if the correlation is perfect, the points fall in a straight diagonal line, and this condition is called a straight-line or **linear relationship.** If the points are widely scattered, the relationship is close to zero. Furthermore, if the slope of the scatter is upward, left to right, the relationship is positive. If it is downward, left to right, the relationship is negative (Figure 18–11).

In constructing the scattergram for finger ability and finger workload, the ability score for each finger was plotted on the horizontal axis and the workload score on the vertical axis. Inspection of the resulting scatter showed that the plotted points did not form a straight line. They fell in a mildly diffuse pattern, indicating only a moderate positive relationship (Figure 18–12).

OBTAINING A COEFFICIENT. The scattergram gives a visual representation, not a numerical value. For greater precision, and for use with further statistical methods, a coefficient is calculated.

This **coefficient of correlation** is a numerical value between 0.00 and ±1.00 showing the degree of relationship between two sets of scores. The closer the coefficient is to 1.00, the higher is the relationship between the sets of scores.

There are several methods for finding the coefficient of correlation. One frequently used procedure, the *product-moment method,* takes into account the deviations of scores from the mean of each variable. Developed by an Englishman, Karl Pearson, and therefore called the Pearson product-moment, the resulting numerical value, or coefficient, is symbolized as *r.* In another method, called the *rank-difference method,* the basic procedure is to find the difference in ranks for each pair of scores. Also called the Spearman rank-difference, after another Englishman, Charles Spearman, the resulting numerical value is *rho.*

Using the scores indicated earlier, the ranks for finger ability and finger workload were entered into the rank-order formula. The result was a coefficient of correlation of +.43.

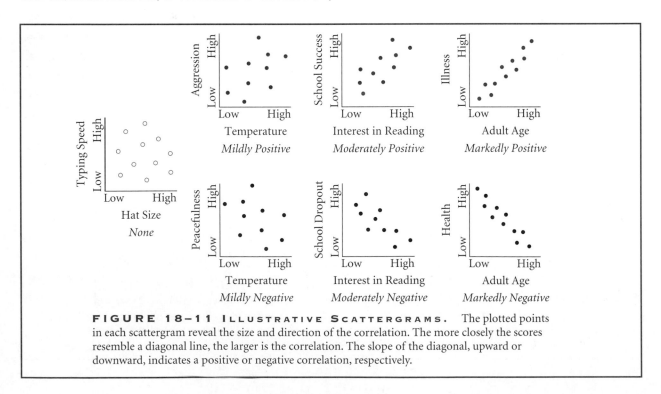

FIGURE 18–11 ILLUSTRATIVE SCATTERGRAMS. The plotted points in each scattergram reveal the size and direction of the correlation. The more closely the scores resemble a diagonal line, the larger is the correlation. The slope of the diagonal, upward or downward, indicates a positive or negative correlation, respectively.

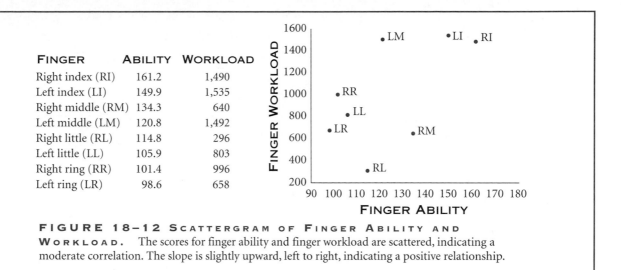

FINGER	ABILITY	WORKLOAD
Right index (RI)	161.2	1,490
Left index (LI)	149.9	1,535
Right middle (RM)	134.3	640
Left middle (LM)	120.8	1,492
Right little (RL)	114.8	296
Left little (LL)	105.9	803
Right ring (RR)	101.4	996
Left ring (LR)	98.6	658

FIGURE 18–12 SCATTERGRAM OF FINGER ABILITY AND WORKLOAD. The scores for finger ability and finger workload are scattered, indicating a moderate correlation. The slope is slightly upward, left to right, indicating a positive relationship.

INTERPRETATION OF THE COEFFICIENT. In evaluating this finding, note first that the correlation is positive, meaning that high scores on one variable are associated with high scores on the other; low scores on one variable are associated with low scores on the other. But note also the size of the coefficient. It shows only a moderate relationship between finger ability and workload. Considering the extremely wide usage of this standard keyboard, this relationship of +.43 is not impressive. In several instances, less capable fingers do more work than more capable ones. The middle finger of the right hand is third in ability, yet it has the next to lowest workload of all eight fingers.

This correlation, or any other, does not indicate that one variable causes the other. It does not mean that finger ability causes workload or vice versa. Among children, weight and memory are positively correlated, but one would not reasonably conclude that gaining weight improves a child's memory or that improvement in memory causes weight gain. Both conditions increase with a third variable, age. The influence of age becomes evident when we correlate weight and memory in children of the same age, for then the relationship is negligible. In short, a correlation merely shows a relationship; it does *not* demonstrate a causal relationship.

Although one may exist, cause and effect cannot be assumed.

Furthermore, a correlation does not indicate a percentage. A coefficient of +.43 does *not* mean that one variable accounts for 43% of the other variable. And it does not mean that these two variables have 43% in common. Rather, the mutual dependence between them is considerably less than might be expected from a casual glance. If the correlation coefficient is .40, for example, then squaring it gives: $.40 \times .40 = .16$. Only 16% of the variability on one measure can be explained by variations in the other (Evans & Waites, 1981). Similarly, a correlation of +.50 indicates only 25% interdependence. In other words, correlation shows the degree of agreement between two variables, not their common properties.

This relationship between finger workload and finger ability suggests that the standard keyboard is not well designed. It could be more efficient. Ask any of today's million keyboard operators to type the word *million*. Imagine typing it yourself, if you know this keyboard.

As the UW team pointed out, this word is typed entirely with the right hand. Such a discovery was disappointing. Imagine typing: *Afterwards we were sadder.* Like that italicized phrase, thousands of

Row												
Upper	Q	W	E	R	T	Y	U	I	O	P	¼ ½	
Home	A	S	D	F	G	H	J	K	L	;	"	
Lower	Z	X	C	V	B	N	M	,	:	?/		

FIGURE 18–13 STANDARD KEYBOARD. The hands are positioned on the home row with the index fingers on *F* and *J*. Most typing occurs in the upper row.

words are typed entirely with the left hand, which does the most work. The standard keyboard is not the *greatest*, overtaxing the left hand (Figure 18–13). There are many one-handed sequences, in which one hand types several consecutive letters while the other remains idle, thereby limiting typing speed to one-half its maximum pace. Without alternation of the hands, efficiency is at a *minimum*.

• INFERENTIAL STATISTICS •

One early supporter of the new "type-machine," as he called it, was Mark Twain. In fact, he claimed to be the first person ever to write a book with it, using it for the last half of the manuscript for *The Adventures of Tom Sawyer*. Nevertheless, he found it full of devilish defects (Figure 18–14).

These defects included the keyboard design, which later offered a subtle benefit for crafty salespersons. Using just the index fingers, as was the habit in those earlier days, they could readily demonstrate to prospective customers the promise of their product. Perhaps the keyboard was planned this way—so that they could type the name of the machine in the upper row: T Y P E W R I T E R (Gould, 1987).

With clear evidence of the inappropriate workload for the different fingers and the numerous one-handed sequences in English, August Dvorak

took a strong stand against the standard keyboard: "This 'universal keyboard' tosses the typing into an upper row of keys. . . . overburdens the lesser fingers and . . . forces frequent idling of one hand while the other types entire words" (Dvorak, Merrick, Dealey, & Ford, 1936). Faced with this discouraging design after two years of evaluation, the UW team took a new direction. They began to prepare an improved keyboard.

To achieve this purpose, they gathered more statistical information on letter usage; they experimented with many different locations for the keys; and they studied the relationships among finger movements. They assessed error rates, speed of typing, and even the rhythms reported by experienced typists. Gradually, they developed a completely new keyboard, known as the *Dvorak* or *simplified keyboard*.

To assess the effectiveness of this simplified keyboard, they used typing speed as the chief criterion of success, measuring words per minute. There were thousands of keyboard operators in the United States, however, and all of these people could not be included in their various tests. Here they were faced with the third and final major problem in statistics, the problem of statistical inference.

In *descriptive statistics*, a group of scores is described, and all of them are available. Certain values, such as the mean and standard deviation, indicate the performance of the whole group. In

FIGURE 18–14 ACCEPTANCE OF THE TYPEWRITER. Mark Twain used the typewriter in 1874 and then ignored it for 30 years, until he wrote his autobiography in 1904. At the beginning of this interval, he noted, the machine was a curiosity, and people who used it were a curiosity, too. But by the turn of the century, he decided, the situation had been reversed. People who did *not* own it were a curiosity (Twain, 1906).

correlational statistics, the purpose is to discover the relationship between two sets of scores. The aim is to show the degree of association, if any, between one variable and another. In **inferential statistics,** an inference, or educated guess, is made about the probability of obtaining the observed scores and scores *not* observed. Inferential statistics concern *probability,* meaning the chances that a certain event will occur. In the case of the keyboard, the scores of a sample of typists using the simplified keyboard can be used to make an inference or statement of probability about the scores that might be obtained from all typists using this simplified keyboard.

SAMPLING PROCEDURES

In studying their keyboard, the human-factors psychologists selected a **sample** of subjects, which is only a portion of all possible subjects. A sample is a subgroup; it is part of a larger group. The sample of typists might have included 10, 100, or 1,000 subjects, depending on the ease of obtaining them and the sampling method employed. All possible subjects in the larger group comprise the **population,** a term that does not refer exclusively to animals or human beings. A population includes *all* possible cases in any particular class or category: aggressive behaviors, athletic shoes, abdominal pains, or albino rats, as well as typists using the simplified keyboard. All typists using the simplified design could not be tested; therefore, estimates about the whole population were made by testing just some of them—a sample.

It should be emphasized that the larger the sample—that is, the more subjects from the population included in the sample—the greater is the probability that the sample will reflect the characteristics of the population. In other words, increasing the size of the sample increases the chances for reaching correct conclusions about the population.

When a sample reflects the characteristics of the population from which it has been selected, it is called a **representative sample.** It accurately depicts the population; it shows what is fundamentally true about that larger group. When it does not, it is a *biased sample,* meaning that it is prejudiced or inclined in one way or another. The usual way of obtaining a representative sample is through random sampling. In a **random sample,** every person or item in the population has an equal chance of being included. This condition is often achieved by using random numbers, assigning one number to each subject, and then drawing the numbers in such a way that no number is more likely to be chosen than any other number.

In studies of the simplified keyboard, samples of various sizes were obtained. One sample included 44 college students and adults. Another included 83 college students. After testing these beginning typists on the simplified keyboard, the investigators inferred how the *whole population of beginning typists* might perform while typing the same material on this same keyboard. The mean score for one sample was approximately 41.5 words per minute after 45 hours of instruction. Thus, it might be inferred that the whole population would perform at this speed after the same instruction.

POINT ESTIMATION

One form of inferential statistics is called **point estimation** because a score obtained with a few subjects is used to estimate a score that might be obtained with many subjects. Forty people might be tested on the simplified keyboard, for example, and their mean score might be used to estimate the mean for all simplified keyboard users. This procedure involves point estimation because the purpose is to estimate one point or value in a population—such as the mean—by using information from a sample.

Point estimation is widely used in political polls. A few voters are questioned, and these results are used to predict the winner. In all such cases, the accuracy of the estimate depends significantly on which subjects are included in the sample. Sampling techniques are now so sophisticated that predictions can be highly accurate, even with relatively small samples.

THE STANDARD ERROR. But with the beginning typists, no one could be certain that the sample mean, 41.5 words per minute, truly represented the mean of the whole population of people beginning to use the simplified keyboard. The only

way to know for certain would have been to test all beginning operators, but that was impossible. Thus, steps were taken to deal with the uncertainty, using a procedure for estimating the probable error. This procedure is possible because *chance errors* in sampling, in the long run, tend to be distributed according to the normal distribution. As noted earlier, many factors acting in a complex, unknown way on a single event often produce a normal distribution.

The sample mean for the typing test was 41.5 words per minute. For other samples, the means might have been higher, lower, or the same. We simply do not know. But if the investigators continued taking samples from the entire population of beginning simplified keyboard users and continued finding their means, eventually they would have discovered that this distribution of sample means was nearly a normal distribution. Furthermore, the *mean of these sample means* would have been close to the population mean. It would have reflected the true mean of the population of all beginning simplified keyboard operators.

The problem was that these investigators, like others, could not take endless samples. In fact, they had only a few samples. But fortunately, statisticians have developed a method for determining how much any one sample mean may be in error. This measure, called a **standard error,** is used in determining the amount of error likely in a sample statistic. An extension of the concept of standard deviation, the standard error provides an estimate of the amount that a sample mean varies by chance from the true mean of the population.

FACTORS INFLUENCING THE STANDARD ERROR. By now, you may be approaching the standard error with some shortness of breath and moist palms. Relax. It is not necessary to calculate the standard error here, and this statistic does not involve any new concepts. The aim in this context is simply to understand how it operates, and you can be assured that it is essentially a function of just two factors, both encountered already. The standard error depends on the size of the sample and the standard deviation of that sample.

The larger the sample, the smaller is the standard error. A moment's reflection shows why this is true. Suppose an entire population consisted of 1,500 people using the simplified keyboard. A sample of 1,499 subjects would contain very little error, for only one keyboard operator would be missing. That person's typing score, even if by chance it were extremely high or low, would have little influence on the mean score made by 1,499 other people. But if the sample were 150 typists, constituting just 10% of the whole population, chance factors in that sample might give a false impression of the population. And if the sample included only three or four subjects, chance factors probably would give a wrong impression (Figure 18-15).

The other factor influencing the standard error, besides the size of the sample, is its standard deviation. For samples of at least moderate size, such as 30 or more entries, the smaller the standard deviation, the smaller is the standard error. In other words, the more closely the scores cluster around the sample mean, the more likely it is that the sample mean adequately represents the population mean.

In summary, when there are many scores, and when the deviation among them is small, the standard error is small. Under these conditions, the sample mean is likely to reflect the population mean.

When the standard error was obtained for one sample of simplified keyboard operators, it was found to be 1.5 words per minute. When this value was applied to the sample mean of 41.5 words per minute, probability statements

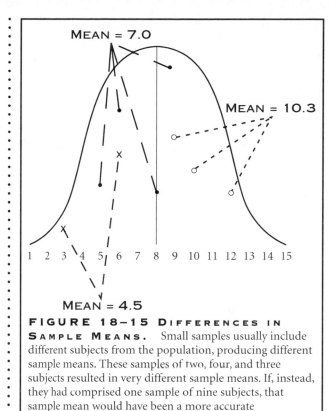

FIGURE 18-15 DIFFERENCES IN SAMPLE MEANS. Small samples usually include different subjects from the population, producing different sample means. These samples of two, four, and three subjects resulted in very different sample means. If, instead, they had comprised one sample of nine subjects, that sample mean would have been a more accurate representation of the population mean, which is eight.

could be made about the population mean. One standard error subtracted from the mean was equal to 41.5 minus 1.5, or 40. One standard error added to the mean was equal to 41.5 plus 1.5, or 43. Hence, the true mean score for the population of beginning Dvorak typists probably lay somewhere in the interval from 40 to 43 words per minute. The chances of the true mean falling within this interval, as evident in our earlier discussion of the standard deviation and the normal distribution, were approximately 68 out of 100. This statement of probability was the best estimate of the performance of the whole population of simplified keyboard users. For a higher degree of confidence, a still wider interval would have been necessary. For example, the chances were 95 out of 100 that it fell approximately between 38.5 and 44.5 and 99 out of 100 that it falls between 37.0 and 46.0. Stated in more general terms, it appeared likely that the population mean was a value close to 41.5 words per minute.

❧

STUDY OF DIFFERENCES

All normal keyboards have three rows of letters, and obviously it is easier to use the home row, where the fingers are stationed initially, than to use either of the other rows. With the QWERTY or standard keyboard, more than half of the work is done on the row *above* the home row, which includes the letters *E* and *T,* two of the most frequently used letters. Slightly less than one-third of the work occurs in the home row.

For the Dvorak simplified keyboard, the human-factors psychologists placed the most common letters in the home row. They assigned the moderately used letters to the top row and the least-used letters to the bottom row, for it is easier to reach above than below the home row. This design distinctly favored the home row, where almost three-quarters of all typing is accomplished (Table 18–3).

To compare this model with the standard keyboard, we must go beyond point estimation. Instead, we want to know about the *difference* between two sample means, comparing the simplified keyboard with the standard keyboard. Thus, we want to estimate two points, one in each popula-

	KEYBOARD	
ROW	STANDARD	SIMPLIFIED
Upper	52	22
Home	32	70
Lower	16	8

TABLE 18–3 ROW WORKLOADS. The table shows the percent of typing in each row. With the typist's fingers so often in the home row of the simplifed keyboard, it almost seems that the hands are not moving at all.

tion. This question, determining whether a difference between two or more sample means represents a difference between the population means, is called the **study of differences** or *testing an hypothesis.*

The essential feature of much psychological research, evident in the study of differences, is a comparison between experimental and control groups. The question here is: Which subjects type faster, those with the simplified keyboard or those with the standard keyboard? At this point, in this last portion of the last chapter in this book, we encounter once again a recurrent theme: the effort to answer psychological questions through empiricism rather than by speculation, common sense, or even pure reasoning.

TESTING AN HYPOTHESIS. Answering this question empirically requires an appropriate experimental design. In the traditional approach, the experimental and control groups are as equal as possible in all relevant respects—age, experience, intelligence, motivation, and so forth—except one. This factor, the independent variable, is present or manipulated for the experimental group but not for the control group. In the case at hand, the independent variable is the keyboard design. If a difference in performance is found between the two groups, it is attributed to this variable.

On these bases, the UW group formed and tested their hypothesis: Operators using the experimental or simplified keyboard would learn faster than those using the standard design.

STATISTICAL SIGNIFICANCE. In early studies of the standard keyboard using hundreds of beginning operators, the mean score was 25.0 words per minute after one course of instruction. For two dozen beginning operators learning the simplified keyboard during less than half that period, the mean score was approximately 41.5

words per minute. The length of instruction was markedly shorter with the simplified design, and yet there was a difference of 16.5 words per minute in favor of that keyboard (Dvorak, Merrick, Dealey, & Ford, 1936).

This difference between samples of typists using the standard or simplified keyboard seems large, but would it have appeared if both populations had been tested instead? In other words, does this difference between the sample means reflect a true difference between the population means? Would another test, with different samples of subjects drawn from the same populations, have produced a similar difference?

The statistic of interest here is partly familiar, for it is again a standard error—this time the standard error of the *difference* between the means, rather than the standard error of just one mean. As we approach this new concept, there is again no need for heart palpitations and knocking knees. Calculations are not important. It is sufficient merely to appreciate that the procedure goes one step beyond the calculation of the standard error for a single mean. It is the difference between two sample means divided by the probable error in determining that difference. Once more, the normal distribution is relevant, and the probability again is expressed in terms of chances out of 100.

When the probability is low that a finding is due to chance, it is considered to have statistical significance. It might have occurred through chance factors, but the investigator is confident at a high level that it was due instead to the influence of the specific factor under investigation, in this case the keyboard design. As a rule, **statistical significance** is considered to be present when the probability of obtaining a certain result by chance is very small, typically less than 5 chances out of 100.

With statistical significance, if the experiment were repeated 100 times, for example, in only 5

instances would a difference of this magnitude be due to chance. This result is described as $p < .05$, which means that the probability of finding a difference this large or larger on the next trial, if there is really no difference between the populations, is less than 5 in 100.

To be even more stringent, the standard could be raised to $p < .01$, meaning that the probability of finding a difference this large on a chance basis, when there really was no difference, is 1 in 100, or less. In studies of difference, just as in point estimation, the true difference cannot be known for certain because all members of both populations cannot be tested. The conclusion remains a statement of probability.

In the case of the two keyboards, it was very unlikely that the difference of 16.5 words per minute between the sample means occurred on a chance basis ($p < .01$). In short, we are quite confident that it was due instead to the simplified design.

• STATISTICS AS A TOOL •

This difference of 16.5 words per minute, when calculated for a workday of seven or eight hours, represented a difference of several thousand words each day. It demonstrated rather clearly the advantage of the simplified keyboard. More important in the present context, it showed the value of statistical methods. They served as tools for the evaluation of the old keyboard and later for developing a new, simplified design.

Statistical methods are no different from other human tools. They can be used improperly; just like a hammer, violin, or ice skates, they are no better than their users. Whether statistics are beneficial or harmful, or whether a particular potential is achieved, depends in a large measure on who compiles and interprets them.

In constructing this simplified keyboard, the UW psychologists first placed the most frequently used letters in the home row. Then they assigned the most work to the most capable fingers. Finally, and most important, they assigned the letters for alternate use by the two hands, thereby diminishing one-handed sequences. To achieve this alternation, the UW team assigned the five vowels to the left hand and the five most common consonants to the right hand. Since consonants typically follow vowels and vice versa in English, alternation is maximized, and the amount of typing is approximately balanced between the two hands. On the simplified keyboard, one hand moves down to strike a letter while the other moves up into position to strike the next letter (Figure 18–16).

With this new keyboard, typists won seven first places in an international typing contest; the UW team achieved their research goal; and the members published their findings in a book entitled *Typewriting Behavior* (Dvorak, Merrick, Dealey, & Ford, 1936). Shortly thereafter, their keyboard was banned as unfair competition in typing contests, much like a curved stick in ice hockey or a deep pocket in lacrosse, making high scoring too easy. This decision did not deter Barbara Blackburn, who could barely type 50 words per minute on the standard keyboard. At the suggestion of her typing instructor, she turned to the Dvorak simplified model and has been listed in the *Guinness Book of World Records* as typing 150 words per minute for 50 consecutive minutes (Larsen, 1985). Unofficially, she has exceeded 200 words per minute (Cassingham, 1986).

If the simplified keyboard becomes widely accepted, the diminished effort of the operators may become a decisive factor, not only for increasing speed and comfort but also for decreasing the risk of repetitive strain injuries. The distance traveled by the fingers on the standard keyboard is 10 to 16 times greater than on the simplified design (Katzeff, 1983; Lamb, 1983). Many people who are not data entry personnel spend three or four hours per day at the keyboard, becoming susceptible to these injuries, including carpal tunnel syndrome, a painful disorder that can lead to permanent damage of the hand. It is caused by pressure on the nerve extending through the passage formed among the carpal bones of the wrist; more than 700,000 cases were diagnosed in 1988 (Oransky, 1994).

The increase in these injuries presents a challenging problem for human-factors psychologists (Howell, 1993). Even with the standard keyboard, this problem can be diminished by very different keyboard designs, including chorded keyboards, on which combinations of keys are pressed simultane-

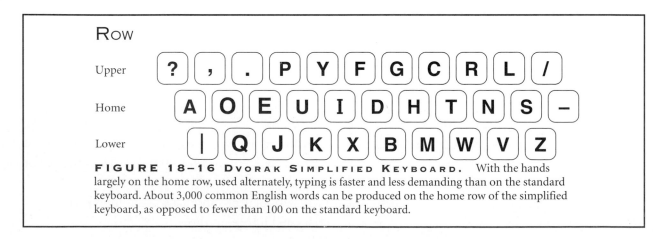

FIGURE 18–16 DVORAK SIMPLIFIED KEYBOARD. With the hands largely on the home row, used alternately, typing is faster and less demanding than on the standard keyboard. About 3,000 common English words can be produced on the home row of the simplified keyboard, as opposed to fewer than 100 on the standard keyboard.

ously, or by a split keyboard, with the two halves comfortably apart, providing each hand with its own, spatially separate set of keys (Gopher & Raij, 1988; Kroemer, 1992).

Statistics will be used in this research, just as they were employed in the design of the simplified keyboard. There they served to describe data, such as letter frequencies and typing speeds; to determine the association between sets of data, such as the correlation between finger ability and finger workload; and to test hypotheses about the success of the new keyboard. In the latter case, typists using the simplified design were much faster than those using the standard model.

This quantification of data does not provide incontestable evidence of any general phenomenon. It merely indicates in objective fashion what was found in a particular set of circumstances and the probability of obtaining the same findings in the future. The concept of **probability** concerns the likelihood that a particular event will appear or reappear, as opposed to a different event. It is a comparison of alternatives. All scientific statements are, in the last analysis, probability statements.

And at this point, with a head full of statistics, you may wonder why the standard keyboard was so poorly designed in the first place. There are two competing explanations. According to one, the so-called *random explanation*, the standard keyboard arose haphazardly, with no thought of touch typing until almost a quarter of a century later. Placement of the keys was determined by a random selection of the letters as they were taken from the printer's font, partly alphabetized. While the hunt-and-peck method prevailed, placement of the keys was relatively unimportant. The standard keyboard was satisfactory.

According to the other view, sometimes known as the *intentional explanation*, the standard keyboard was purposely scrambled in the early machines. The aim was to prevent collisions among the long levers on which the letters were mounted. If the typist worked rapidly, the keys jammed. An awkward keyboard design impeded typing speed, thereby offering a machine that worked. Intentionally scrambling the letters solved a nasty problem, one that baffled typewriter manufacturers at the time.

We do not know which explanation is correct, but we do know that the simplified keyboard was developed at the wrong time for its acceptance. The Great Depression, followed by World War II, and then the quickly formed habits in the rising economies of the 1950s and 1960s all became obstacles to change. There may have been another reason too—a commercial concern, less widely recognized. The potential manufacturers of the new keyboard were diverted from their usual commercial goals during World War II and became munitions manufacturers instead. After the war, one of them purchased the rights to this design and yet did nothing with them, perhaps because by that time the standard model was selling so well (Dvorak, 1985). Manufacturers generally do not make significant changes in products with brisk sales.

The simplified keyboard has been approved by the American National Standards Institute, an endorsement that provides official recognition (Lamb, 1983). It is faithfully employed by a number of private citizens and institutions but rarely found in the broader commercial world.

Statistical methods showed its success. Statistics also show that most keyboard operators today continue to use the old model. That model is something like an irregular verb. People may dislike it, but no one can seem to change it. Observing this neglect of his work, August Dvorak recalled the words of Ralph Waldo Emerson: "If a man builds a better mousetrap, the world will beat a path to his door." Then he added with a wry smile, "Emerson never said how long it would take."

QUANTIFICATION IN PSYCHOLOGY

1. Throughout its history, scientific progress has been closely linked with advances in statistical methods. The field of psychology is no exception. Use of statistical methods in psychological research is readily evident in human-factors psychology, a specialty devoted to the design of tools and procedures well suited to human use.

2. When properly employed, statistics can demonstrate certain facts more accurately than words. When misused in the collection and presentation of data, statistics can create a distorted impression.

DESCRIPTIVE STATISTICS

3. The aim of descriptive statistics is to present a group of scores clearly and simply. One approach involves pictorial methods, especially the use of graphs. They illustrate the results but do not permit further statistical analyses.

4. A more common approach is based on two numerical values, measures of central tendency and measures of variability. The three widely used measures of central tendency are: the mode, median, and mean. These measures are identical in a normal distribution.

5. Measures of variability indicate the extent to which scores in a group differ from one another. The simplest measure is the range, which includes only the lowest and highest scores and therefore is unreliable. The standard deviation, based on the values of all the scores, is used in most statistical analyses.

6. A group of scores can be analyzed and summarized by descriptive statistics, usually by presenting the mean and standard deviation.

CORRELATIONAL STATISTICS

7. Statistics also can be used to study the relationship between two sets of scores. In this case, a coefficient of correlation is computed; it can be positive, meaning that high scores on one trait are associated with high scores on the other, or negative, meaning that high scores on one trait are associated with low scores on the other.

8. The magnitude of this relationship can be indicated by plotting all the entries on a scattergram. When this relationship is indicated by computing a coefficient of correlation, which gives a numerical result, it does not indicate a percentage, and it does not imply causality.

INFERENTIAL STATISTICS

9. For practical purposes, an investigator generally cannot study all potential subjects. Instead, a sample is selected and studied and, by use of this information, estimates are made about characteristics of the larger population. This process is called inferential statistics.

10. One form of inferential statistics is known as point estimation because a score obtained with a sample of subjects is used to estimate a score that might be obtained from the larger population.

11. In the study of differences, an inference is made about the difference between two or more population values, judging from the difference between sample values. These samples might represent experimental and control groups in research.

STATISTICS AS A TOOL

12. Statistical methods are important research tools, but like any other human tool they can be misused. The quantification of data can be used to describe findings in an objective fashion and to determine the probability of obtaining the same findings in the future.

❧ REVIEW OF KEY CONCEPTS ❧

human-factors psychology

Quantification in Psychology
statistics
statistical literacy

Descriptive Statistics
descriptive statistics
raw scores
graph
bar graph
measures of central tendency
mode
median
mean

normal distribution
skewed distribution
positively skewed distribution
negatively skewed distribution
measures of variability
range
standard deviation (SD)

Correlational Statistics
correlational statistics
correlation
positive correlation
negative correlation
scattergram
linear relationship

coefficient of correlation

Inferential Statistics
inferential statistics
sample
population
representative sample
random sample
point estimation
standard error
study of differences
statistical significance

Statistics as a Tool
probability

❧ CLASS DISCUSSION/CRITICAL THINKING ❧

A NARRATIVE TWIST

Rather than investigating the keyboard and developing a new design, the UW team might have studied the bathroom shower or bathroom sink instead, making one or the other more useful and pleasant for most people. Indicate the people they might have studied, variables they might have examined, statistical data they might have obtained, and some of the changes in the shower or sink they might have suggested as a result of their investigations. ❧

TOPICAL QUESTIONS

• *Quantification in Psychology.* Suggest a topic for a one-hour lesson to promote statistical literacy in elementary school. Describe how this lesson will develop an interest in

statistics, rather than competence in statistical calculations.

• *Descriptive Statistics.* To obtain an approximate measure of children's height in a remote school district without measuring every child, a researcher lined them up in order, from tallest to shortest, and then noted the height of each child at the end of the line and the one in the middle. Discuss the descriptive statistics obtained in this instance. Describe the reliability of these measures.

• *Correlational Statistics.* In discussing diet and health, Mr. Black says there is a high positive correlation; Mr. White says the correlation is high but negative; and Mr. Brown says the correlation is not just high but also causal. Who is right? Must

someone be wrong? Explain your reasons in each case.

• *Inferential Statistics.* Imagine that you are investigating racial attitudes among students at a city high school. You conduct the study with a sample of subjects and conclude that there is no racial tension. A week later, several interracial disruptions occur. Explain this apparent contradiction, using the concept of inferential statistics.

• *Statistics as a Tool.* Investigators point out that their results *show* or *demonstrate* such-and-such. Rarely do they claim that their results *prove* such-and-such. Why do they take this position? Explain your answer in the context of probability.

Sampling techniques are discussed in the context of research methods (2). Statistical methods are essential in the construction and use of psychological tests, especially the concept of correlation (13). The topic of experimental design is closely tied to testing hypotheses and using inferential statistics (2).

EPILOGUE

IT HAS BEEN WRYLY NOTED THAT PSYCHOLOGY HAS A LONG PAST BUT ONLY A SHORT HISTORY. THE LONG PAST REFERS TO SPECULATIONS about human behavior dating to classical antiquity. The short history emphasizes that scientific psychology is little more than a century old.

Early in its development, at the close of the nineteenth century, modern psychology was most clearly associated with philosophy. Productive relations between the two disciplines were sought and praised. At the universities, both in Europe and America, psychologists held appointments as philosophers. Few people realized that psychology one day would emerge as a separate scientific enterprise.

By the turn of this century, the influence of philosophy had lessened in favor of a second element—experimentalism. The president of the American Psychological Association at that time observed: "Psychological theory is influenced to a large, and perhaps at times to an embarrassing, extent by points of view and forms of expression derived from the physical sciences" (Sanford, 1903). A growing number of psychologists were not embarrassed; they continued this trend, emulating the methods of the natural sciences. A few years later, a new president of the Association noted that psychologists were meeting that year in affiliation with naturalists, rather than philosophers. In the grand style of his era, he declared: "We are off with our old love, and on with a new" (Marshall, 1908).

A third clear trend in psychology's short history is its diversity, of which this book is a prime example. Beginning in midcentury, contemporary psychology has been marked by the steady development of specialized branches. Today the field is so diverse that it sometimes seems unlikely to continue as a whole. Psychological inquiry now takes place in all aspects of human endeavor, and as new needs arise, diversity and specialization will increase (Hilgard, Leary, & McGuire, 1991).

The most dominant figure in early American psychology represented all three of these trends. William James was a philosopher, at times an experimentalist, and certainly a man of diverse interests. A man for all seasons, James influenced enormously the psychologists under his tutelage and those who came after him.

One of them, Mary Calkins, cherished pleasant memories of studying with James, a relationship that was especially significant because she was the only woman in his course. In looking back on that first seminar, she wrote: "The other members of his seminary in psychology dropped away in the early weeks of the fall of 1890; and James and I were left not . . . at either end of a log but quite literally at either side of a library fire" (Calkins, 1930).

The log to which Mary Calkins refers is Mark Hopkins's metaphor for education. The teaching-learning process, he said, involves a log with a teacher on one end and a student on the other.

It is now my moment to step off that log. I have enjoyed this experience. Best wishes to you at both ends in the future.

LDF

GLOSSARY

Within the following definitions, the terms appearing in italic typeface are entries elsewhere in this glossary. Those that may be phonetically unfamiliar to the reader include a pronunciation guide.

absolute threshold   The lowest level of intensity at which a certain form of stimulation can be detected, resulting in *sensation.* When a *stimulus* reaches this threshold, the nerve fiber fires.

accommodation   A form of *adaptation* to new or existing conditions. (1) In *cognitive development,* the process of altering one's current understanding to make it more consistent with a new experience. (2) In *visual sensitivity,* the process of focusing, in which the *lens'* curvature increases for nearby objects and decreases for distant objects.

acetylcholine (uh-seed'-l-koe'-leen)   A *neurotransmitter substance* that plays a prominent role in muscular activity, acting chiefly at muscular synapses. It can be either excitatory or inhibitory.

achievement motive   A *secondary motive* in which the individual is concerned with performing at a certain level or standard, set individually or by a *group.*

achievement test   A test for measuring the current level of accomplishment in a particular field.

achromatic vision   See *monochromat.*

action potential   A brief shift in electrical energy in a nerve fiber, called the neural impulse. When a *stimulus* reaches a certain level of intensity, a part of the nerve fiber is momentarily activated. In this activated state, the fiber is said to be depolarized because it briefly has the same poles or charges on either side of the cell membrane.

activation-synthesis hypothesis   A *biological approach* to the study of *dreams,* proposing that neural impulses are initiated in the *reticular activating system,* responsible for basic arousal, and that this information then is synthesized with data already stored in the *cerebral cortex,* resulting in the dream experience.

actualizing tendency   In *humanistic psychology,* a fundamental, inborn predisposition for growth and fulfillment. Human beings have a special capacity for controlling their actions, making choices, and growing through experience, which culminates in *self-actualization.*

adaptation   Changes in behavior or experience according to conditions in the environment, as the organism adjusts to the situation. For example, *visual sensitivity* increases or decreases in response to dim or bright illumination, respectively. Various types of adaptation include: *accommodation, assimilation, general adaptation syndrome, institutionalization.*

adaptation theory   In *evolutionary psychology,* the view that sleep evolved as an adjustment to a hostile environment, enabling individuals to avoid predators and to conserve energy. See *restoration theory.*

additive color mixture   The phenomenon that occurs when colored lights are mixed, in which each light adds a different reflectance or *wavelength* to the outcome, resulting in a given *hue.*

additive effect   In *multifactor studies,* an outcome in which the total influence of all factors is simply cumulative, equal to the sum of their separate influences.

adjustment   The continuous process of satisfying one's *needs* and desires as they emerge and reemerge throughout life. A condition of successful adjustment is called *mental health;* severe maladjustment is considered *mental illness.*

adolescence   In *human development,* the stage that begins with *puberty* and is characterized by marked physical growth and biological changes, as well as intellectual and emotional changes.

adrenal glands   A pair of *endocrine* glands located in the back of the abdomen below the rib cage, just above the kidneys. They secrete adrenaline (*epinephrine*) and other *hormones.*

affectional stimulation   Physical and emotional contact with other members of the species and stimulation by them. Desire for this type of contact is a *stimulation motive.*

afferent neuron   See *sensory neuron.*

affiliation   See *desire for affiliation.*

afterimage   In *visual sensitivity,* the existence of a color experience after the *hue* is no longer observed. A positive afterimage is the same hue; a negative afterimage is complementary.

aggression   Behavior involving assault, physical or verbal, upon another person or some object, often arising from the *feeling* of anger.

alarm reaction   The first of three phases in the *general adaptation syndrome;* it is the organism's initial defense, an overall bodily *response* to any *stress.* Among these defensive forces are increased secretions from the *adrenal glands* and *pituitary gland.*

alcoholism   A form of *drug dependence* involving the inability to take only one or two drinks or to go a day or two without alcohol. An alcoholic, or problem drinker, as defined clinically, is anyone who is unable to stop using this *depressant* for at least a month, despite signs of disease or disorder.

algorithm   Any unambiguous procedure that, if used correctly, will solve a certain problem; a set of very well defined rules, describing the solution in a careful series of finite steps. Algorithms are used in some *artificial intelligence* systems.

all-or-none law   The principle stating that a nerve fiber responds at its full strength or not at all.

altered states of consciousness   Modes of awareness characterized by changes in *perception* and in the capacity for self-control and logic. Normal altered states of *consciousness* include: *dreams, hypnagogic state,* sleep. Other altered states can be elicited by *hypnosis, meditation,* or a *psychoactive substance.*

altruism   Consideration for the welfare of others; selflessness, manifested in assisting someone else when there is no obvious benefit to oneself.

Alzheimer's disease (ältz'-hye-murz) A progressive *brain* disease that occurs during old age and is characterized by loss of *memory,* disorientation, slowness of speech, and general apathy, eventually resulting in total mental and emotional deterioration.

amnesia A form of forgetting. See *anterograde amnesia, dissociative amnesia, hypnotic amnesia, retrograde amnesia.*

amphetamines Drugs, classified as *stimulants,* that are used to stay awake and increase alertness; they may cause euphoria and health hazards.

amplification of dreams A *psychodynamic* technique for understanding a person's *dreams* by expanding their contents in any way possible, such as through an interior dialogue, in which the dreamer has an imaginary conversation with the dream elements and enacts any and all of them.

amygdala A small, almond-shaped structure near the base of the *brain* that plays a significant role in *motivation, emotion,* and *memory.* It is part of the *limbic system.*

anal stage In *psychoanalysis,* the second of five *psychosexual stages;* it occurs in childhood in the second and third year, during which the chief sexual pleasure is derived from stimulation of the anus, and the child is confronted with toilet training.

analgesia Insensitivity to painful stimulation, induced by such factors as injury, drugs, or *hypnosis.*

analytical introspection A systematic effort to observe and classify the basic elements of one's experience, to measure *consciousness* by looking inward under standard conditions. The basic approach in Wundt's laboratory.

androgens Male sex *hormones,* found in both sexes but in greater amounts in the male, where they are produced by the *testes.* Significantly increasing with the onset of *puberty,* they stimulate male sex characteristics as well as sexual behavior.

anger The feeling of hostility and displeasure. There may be angry behavior too, but it is not considered *aggression* unless an assault is made.

anorexia nervosa A disorder in which a person eats barely enough to stay alive, producing physiological and psychological conditions associated with starvation.

anterograde amnesia A *memory* defect in which no new memories can be established.

antianxiety drugs In *biomedical therapy,* medications used to alleviate *anxiety,* diminishing nervousness, unhappiness, sleeplessness, and tension.

antidepressant drugs In *biomedical therapy,* medications used to alleviate depression, providing an emotional lift and stimulating increased activity and greater interest in the world.

antipsychotic drugs In *biomedical therapy,* medications used to alleviate symptoms of *psychotic disorder,* specifically hallucinations and disturbed thought patterns.

antisocial personality disorder A *personality disorder* in which the individual disregards social order and legal restraint, often violating the rights of others in some significant way.

anxiety A general state of uneasiness or apprehension. This *emotion* can involve timidity, mistrust, dread, alarm, suspicion, terror, diffidence, and so forth. Anxiety disorders include: *generalized anxiety disorder, obsessive-compulsive disorder, posttraumatic stress disorder, specific phobia.*

anxiety hierarchy A clear, carefully sequenced list of all disturbing events in a certain class or category, ranked from most to least threatening, used in *systematic desensitization.*

aphasia (uh-fay'-zhuh) Literally, "without language." Any *brain* disorder involving language functions.

applied psychology The utilization of psychological principles to solve practical problems and to improve the human condition. Also called applied research, the aim is to apply the findings of *basic research* in *psychology* to specific areas of human endeavor. Major specialization include: *clinical psychology, community psychology, counseling psychology, educational psychology, environmental psychology, health psychology, legal psychology, media psychology, social psychology.*

approach-approach conflict See *conflict.*

approach-avoidance conflict See *conflict.*

aptitude test A test for measuring probable accomplishment at some future date, after training.

archetypes Elements of the *collective unconscious* that are not specific thoughts or behaviors but rather unconscious tendencies and images inherited from human experience through the ages. This *psychodynamic* concept includes the animus, anima, good mother, evil beast, divine being, and so forth.

arousal-cognition theory A *two-factor theory,* combining a *biological approach* and *cognitive approach,* that views *emotion* as a joint function of *arousal level,* or physiological reactions, and *cognition,* by which the situation is interpreted. The arousal is simply nonspecific excitement; through cognition, it is translated into a specific emotional experience. Aroused by a barking dog, a child interprets the condition as fear.

arousal level The magnitude of a *response.*

artificial intelligence Computer programming that solves problems requiring rational, informed responses when accomplished by human beings. The aim is not to imitate human *intelligence* but rather to find efficient solutions.

assimilation A form of *adaptation.* In *cognitive development,* the process of fitting new information into one's current understanding of the world.

association cortex Major areas of the *cerebral cortex* not directly involving motor or sensory functions. Concerned with integrating and analyzing information, the association cortex seems most significantly involved in *memory,* language, and other complex *cognitive processes.*

attachment In infancy, an intense and enduring emotional relationship between the baby and the parent or caretaker.

attending A readiness to perceive; an active orientation toward *perception* of certain forms of stimulation, often involving an adjustment of the *sense organs.*

attitude A tendency to make an evaluation, which is reflected in thoughts, feelings, and actions.

attribution theory An approach to *social cognition* that aims to understand how people explain others' and their own behavior, focusing on the procedures or implicit rules used in making inferences about behavior and personal characteristics. In a dispositional attribution, the causes of behavior are assigned to traits or dispositions within the individual. In a situational attribution, they are assigned to the circumstances, not the individual. The overattribution effect is the tendency to overlook the influence of the situation in assigning the causes of other people's behavior.

auditory localization See *binaural cues.*

auditory sensitivity One of the five *traditional senses;* the experience of hearing; responsiveness to the energy of sound waves, including *frequency.*

autokinetic effect (aw-toe-kuh-ned'-ik) The *perception* of movement when both the *stimulus* and viewer are stationary. In a totally dark room, a small, fixed spot of light will appear to move by itself; this *illusion* of motion immediately ceases when another light is displayed.

autonomic nervous system One of two divisions of the *peripheral nervous system;* it initiates and inhibits diverse physiological activities, stimulating widespread and largely involuntary changes in muscles and glands throughout the body. The autonomic *nervous system* is further divided into the *parasympathetic nervous system* and *sympathetic nervous system.*

autonomy versus doubt The second of eight *psychosocial* crises; it occurs in childhood after the first year of age, during which the child gains a sense of independence or instead develops feelings of fear and dependence.

availability heuristic The *heuristic,* or strategy for *problem solving,* that comes to mind most readily, chiefly because it is handy.

aversion therapy A method of *behavior therapy* employing *classical conditioning* to eliminate unwanted positive emotional *responses* by pairing them with some negative condition.

avoidance-avoidance conflict See *conflict.*

avoidance conditioning A form of *two-factor conditioning* in which the organism prevents an aversive event, such as confinement. Compare with *escape conditioning.*

axon Part of the *neuron;* a fiber that characteristically carries impulses away from its *cell body* toward other neurons.

babbling In language development, the consistent repetition of particular *phonemes,* such as "da-da-da-da," appearing about the fifth month of normal human infancy. It involves increased control over the speech mechanisms, but as yet no comprehension.

backward conditioning A sequence of *classical conditioning* in which the *unconditioned stimulus* precedes the neutral *stimulus.*

balance See *sense of balance.*

balance theory A *cognitive approach* to *attitude* formation and change, stressing that people seek a balanced or harmonious state among their attitudes.

bar graph In descriptive statistics, a *graph* made with rectangular bars showing the frequency of different scores or items. The height of the rectangle is proportionate to the frequency of the score it represents.

basic anxiety The helplessness and insecurity of childhood, influencing the *personality* and often leaving an enduring uncertainty about interpersonal relationships, even in later life.

basic ethical question In *research,* the question of whether any possible discomfort incurred by all subjects collectively outweighs the gain in alleviation of human and nonhuman problems. Other questions concern *informed consent,* confidentiality, and the *debriefing* interview.

basic research Scientific search for increased understanding of the world, employing various *scientific methods: case study, experimental method, naturalistic observation, survey method.* Compare with *applied psychology.*

basic traits Primary *personality traits;* broad, fundamental characteristics common to most individuals. In one approach, called the Big Five, they are: extroversion, friendliness, conscientiousness, emotional stability, openness to experience. Each trait represents a separate continuum ranging from high to low, and each encompasses several *subtraits.*

basilar membrane (ba'-suh-lur) A tissue in the *cochlea* of the *inner ear* that contains tiny hair cells that are the *receptors* for *auditory sensitivity.*

behavior therapy A form of *therapy* that focuses exclusively on the symptom, some undesirable emotional *response* or bad habit, and employs principles of *conditioning* in treatment. Behavioral methods include: *aversion therapy, cognitive-behavioral therapy, contingency management, systematic desensitization, timeout, token economy.*

behavioral genetics A field of study that aims to discover the hereditary foundations of behavior. This essentially *biological approach* can demonstrate not only genetic but also environmental influences, depending upon its design.

behaviorism A *system of psychology* stating that overt behavior is the only suitable topic in psychology. In this approach, *conditioning* is considered the foundation of *learning.*

bias A preference or inclination that inhibits an objective observation, resulting in an inaccurate judgment. A bias is a type of inhibiting *set,* or expectancy.

Big Five See *basic traits.*

binaural cues In *auditory sensitivity,* the *depth perception* cues provided by both ears, including time difference, intensity difference, and phase difference, all helpful in determining direction. Locating the direction of a sound by hearing alone is called auditory localization.

binocular cues In *visual sensitivity,* the *depth perception* cues that require both eyes, including convergence and retinal disparity.

biofeedback A procedure for making available to the *brain* information about body functions. It is often used as a relaxation technique, usually employing some sort of measuring or monitoring device that indicates, for example, heart rate or blood pressure; this *feedback* then can be used for self-regulation of these normally involuntary functions.

biological approach A *system of psychology* that studies behavior, experience and mental processes in terms of the structure and function of underlying physical and biochemical mechanisms.

biomedical therapy Any form of treatment involving manipulation of physiological conditions to alleviate psychological disorder, also known as somatic therapy. Biomedical methods include: drug therapy (*antianxiety drugs, antidepressant drugs, antipsychotic drugs, lithium, psychoactive substances*), electroconvulsive therapy, lobotomy, *natural body therapies.*

bipolar disorder A mood disorder in which an extremely excited or manic episode is preceded or followed by depression. The emotions may fluctuate rapidly from one pole to the other, or they may stay for some time at one extreme.

blind spot The point in the visual field where *visual sensitivity* is completely absent because the *optic nerve* takes up this space on the *retina,* leaving no room for *rods* and *cones.*

body therapies See *natural body therapies.*

borderline personality disorder A *personality disorder* characterized by instability in self-image, mood, and personal relationships; the individual experiences sudden, dramatic shifts in regard for others. This disorder is so named because, for brief periods, the person may seem out of contact with reality, a characteristic of schizophrenic and mood disorders.

bottom-up approach A view of *perception* that begins at the level of the sense organs, focusing on the basic features of the incoming message rather than on information in the higher-level mental functions of the brain. See *top-down approach.*

brain An intricate concentration of nerve tissue within the skull; the primary *organ* of the *nervous system.* The central transmitting and receiving station for *neural coding,* in an evolutionary sense it has three divisions: *forebrain, hindbrain, midbrain.* The outer covering of the brain is the *cerebral cortex,* under which lie the *subcortical structures.* The brain and *spinal cord* form the *central nervous system.*

brainstorming A *group* approach to *problem solving* that emphasizes *creative thinking.* The aim is to generate as many ideas as possible, chiefly by suspending all criticism at the outset.

brief therapy A *therapy* procedure, often used by *insight* therapists, in which the therapist and person seeking assistance plan a sequence of no more than six sessions.

brightness constancy A type of *perceptual constancy* in which the brightness of an object is not perceived to change appreciably with changes in illumination. A black belt can be illuminated until the amount of light entering the eye is greater than that received from a white shirt, and yet the belt will still appear black and the shirt white.

bulimia nervosa A disorder in which the individual eats regularly or even voraciously but then regurgitates the food.

bystander intervention effect A condition in which the larger the *group* observing someone apparently needing help, the less likely it is that any one of them will offer aid. A lone bystander is more apt to help.

California Personality Inventory (CPI) A *personality inventory* for assessing characteristic traits in the general population, such as dominance, sociability, self-control, and so forth.

Cannon-Bard theory A theory of *emotion,* also called the thalamic theory, emphasizing the key role of the *thalamus* in stimulating both the bodily arousal and the feelings.

caretaker-child interaction Attention and responsiveness on the part of adults toward a child, including diverse opportunities for play and exploration, as well as support.

case history A comprehensive study of a particular person, *group,* or event. A chief procedure in the *case study,* it includes information not only from interviews and tests but also from family, friends, *personal documents,* and other sources.

case study A *research* method employing diverse psychological techniques— chiefly interviews, *case histories,* and psychological tests—with individuals or *groups,* for studying people or events in considerable detail.

catharsis hypothesis The view that expressing an *emotion* reduces its underlying *drive,* just as eating reduces the hunger drive.

cell body The central part of the *neuron,* containing the nucleus.

cellular dehydration Loss of water in the cells of the body, occurring constantly through urination, exhalation, perspiration, and elimination. Certain nerve cells in the *hypothalamus,* called *osmoreceptors,* monitor this activity.

central nervous system The primary integrating and control center in the human body, composed of the *brain* and *spinal cord.* One of the two primary divisions of the *human nervous system,* it receives impulses from the other primary division, the *peripheral nervous system,* and from its own subdivisions.

central tendency See *measures of central tendency.*

central trait In *social cognition,* any personal characteristic, such as degree of social warmth, that is highly influential in the estimate of an individual's other traits.

cephalocaudal development (sef′-uh-loe-kaw′-dul) In *physical development,* growth from head to tail, especially prominent in the prenatal phase and early infancy in vertebrates.

cerebellum The most prominent structure of the *hindbrain,* a major mechanism in maintaining posture and coordination. It plays a role in the capacity to repeat well-practiced movements.

cerebral cortex The outer covering of the *brain,* with many folds or convolution in human beings, providing a large neural surface for higher-level *cognitive processes,* voluntary movement, and emotional behavior. Underneath the cortex are the *subcortical structures.*

chaining In *operant conditioning,* a series of interconnected *responses.* Each response serves as *reinforcement* for the previous response, and as a *stimulus* or cue to emit the next response.

chromosomes Complex organizations of chemical materials in an organic cell; each chromosome contains thousands of *genes,* which carry the information about an individual's inheritance.

chronological age (CA) Cumulative age since birth, used in calculating an *intelligence quotient.*

chunking For *encoding a memory,* a strategy in which the learner, confronted with a large number of items, arranges them into categories or subgroups, thereby making them more manageable.

circadian rhythm (sur-kay′-dee-un) Regular alternation between greater and lesser activity in *consciousness,* physiology, *sensation,* and behavior. It typically refers to a 24-hour period, during which human beings complete a full wake-sleep cycle.

classical conditioning The process of association by which a previously neutral *stimulus,* through association with an *unconditioned stimulus,* is made capable of eliciting a certain involuntary *response.* Classical *conditioning* thus modifies *respondent behavior,* concerned with physiological reactions and feelings.

classical experiment The fundamental research procedure of the *experimental method,* in which all potentially influential factors are controlled or held constant except one, called the *independent variable,* which is manipulated to discover its influence.

Clever Hans effect Communication through subtle, unintentional, nonverbal cues. In research, this process may signal to the subject the *response* the investigator desires. It is named for the Berlin horse that tapped out answers by observing such cues from people around him.

clinical psychology A specialization that deals with maladjustment of all sorts, including the diagnosis and treatment of *mental illness.*

closure See *principle of closure.*

cocaine A drug, classified as a *stimulant,* that is obtained from the coca plant and consumed via needle, pipe, or pill to induce a state of bliss. Its effects are so euphoric that dependency can arise quickly and so stimulating that it can cause cardiac arrest.

cochlea (käk′-lee-uh) A snail-shaped canal in the *inner ear* that includes the *basilar membrane,* which contains the *receptors* for *auditory sensitivity.*

coefficient of correlation In *correlational statistics,* a numerical value between 0.00 and ±1.00 showing the degree of relationship between two sets of scores. The closer the coefficient is to 1.00, the higher is the *correlation.*

cognition Knowledge of any sort, together with the mental functions that lie behind it. This term includes all of the *cognitive processes* by which we understand or know about the world—*memory, perception,* thinking, and so forth—as well as *intelligence* and the use of language.

cognitive approach A view of behavior and experience, also called the information processing viewpoint, focusing on the *cognitive processes* by which information is obtained, stored, and used. In the study of intelligence, the emphasis is on mental functions, in contrast to the *psychometric approach,* a view of intelligence which is more concerned with test scores.

cognitive-behavioral therapy A treatment technique aimed at altering both thinking and habits, and which is especially useful with *anxiety* disorders, depression, and lack of assertiveness. The concern with thinking is from *cognitive therapy,* the interest in habits from *behavior therapy.*

cognitive development The aspect of *human development* that involves increasing mental capacities. It progresses through four stages, according to Jean Piaget: *sensorimotor period, preoperational period, concrete operations, formal operations.* Piaget emphasized the task of overcoming *egocentrism* in thinking at each stage.

cognitive-dissonance theory A theory of *attitude* formation and change, stating that when an individual's *cognitions* are dissonant or inconsistent, the person seeks to dispel this state of tension by rationalizing, perceiving selectively, changing his or her behavior, or seeking new information.

cognitive egocentrism See *egocentrism.*

cognitive processes The mental activities by which an organism obtains, stores, and uses information—*memory, perception,* thinking, and so forth.

cognitive psychology A *system of psychology* concerned with knowledge or understanding. The focus is on the *cognitive processes* by which we understand our world, as well as the various states of *consciousness.*

cognitive therapy An approach to *insight therapy* assuming that mental disorders are caused by irrational thinking and that they can be resolved by helping people to abandon maladaptive thinking. Specific methods employing

this approach are *Beck's cognitive therapy, cognitive-behavioral therapy* and *rational-emotive therapy.*

cohort effect A difference in behavior or experience among generations that is not attributable to aging, but rather to some other factor shared by the *group,* such as education or disease.

collective unconscious A realm of inaccessible thought, universal among human beings, according to Carl Jung's *psychodynamic* approach to *personality.* It contains all of the traits and cultural characteristics inherited by every person from all ancestors, including the evolutionary stages of animal life.

collector mechanisms Those parts of the *sense organs* that gather and channel information in some way but do not record it.

color constancy A type of *perceptual constancy* in which the normal *hue* is perceived despite changes in lighting. For example, a white rabbit in the setting sun reflects orange rays, but it is perceived as white.

communicative deviance The view that *schizophrenia* is caused by unsuccessful communication within the family. The caretakers criticize or ignore the child, contradict themselves, or otherwise communicate in an unintelligible fashion.

community psychology A specialization that offers diagnostic and therapeutic services to nearby people in deprived circumstances, as well as formal instruction through the mass media.

companionate love Deep affection for others with whom one's life is closely interwoven. It is less intense, more enduring, and more realistic than *passionate love.*

compensatory education Programs that provide early *learning* opportunities and an enriched environment for the education of disadvantaged children.

compliance A yielding to *social influence* in which an individual submits to pressure to think or behave in a certain way, responding to a direct request by someone else.

computer simulation Computer programming that represents or imitates human thinking, using *heuristics.* These techniques serve as a means for investigating the process of *problem solving.*

concentrative meditation Any *meditation* technique in which attention is directed toward a single source of stimulation, such as the breath or a point of light.

concept A general idea or category; a way of classifying things according to some common property. The process of thinking is based on concepts.

conceptual hierarchy A method of *storage* of *long-term memory,* especially *declarative memory,* in which items with a common property are arranged or classified in a graded order. For example, in zoology the hierarchy includes: kingdom, phylum, class, order, and so forth.

concrete operations The third of Piaget's four stages of *cognitive development;* it appears in childhood from about six or seven years of age to the eleventh year or later, during which children gain the capacity for using logic to solve problems when the physical objects are directly available—a form of *reasoning.*

concurrent validity A form of *validity* concerned with the present. A test with high concurrent validity accurately indicates which subjects are best suited to perform a certain task right away, without further training.

conditioned response (CR) In *classical conditioning,* a *response* elicited by a *conditioned stimulus.*

conditioned stimulus (CS) In *classical conditioning,* a previously neutral *stimulus,* with no original capacity to elicit a certain *response,* which has become capable of eliciting that response through pairing with an *unconditioned stimulus.* That response thus becomes a *conditioned response.*

conditioning An elementary form of *learning* that arises through the association of a *stimulus* and *response,* accidental or intentional. The two primary types of conditioning are *classical conditioning* and *operant conditioning;* both are employed in *two-factor theory.*

cones Specialized *receptors* for *visual sensitivity,* located in the *retina* of the eye, that mediate color vision, or the experience of *hue.*

confidential communication A standard condition of *therapy* in which the therapist will not reveal the contents, or even the general nature of the topics, to anyone, except when criminal or suicidal behavior may be involved.

confirmation bias The inclination to look for and remember supporting rather than refuting evidence when *testing an hypothesis.*

conflict A situation in which one choice or motive is opposed by one or more alternatives and all outcomes cannot be achieved. In an approach-approach conflict, two or more equally attractive alternatives are incompatible; if one is selected, the other must be relinquished. An avoidance-avoidance conflict involves two or more equally repellent alternatives. An approach-avoidance conflict occurs whenever the outcome of a particular decision has both positive and negative aspects.

conformity A yielding to *social influence* in which an individual adopts the thoughts or behaviors of a *group* without any direct pressure to do so; it is influenced by *social norms.*

confounding variable In a *classical experiment,* an extraneous *variable,* any factor that exerts an unwanted influence on the *dependent variable,* giving the experiment an uninterpretable result.

congruity theory A largely *cognitive approach* to *attitude* formation and change, stating that attitude shifts occur in the direction of increased consistency.

connectionist model An approach to thought and memory emphasizing associations among *concepts, sensations,* and other elements; it assumes that the strength of associations among ideas, feelings, or *memories* reflects comparable associations among neural pathways.

connotative meaning In *semantics,* the type of meaning that involves abstract qualities, often with emotional implications. For example, the word *dog* may be used to imply that someone is contemptible, inferior, or nasty.

conscience The part of the *superego* that involves prohibitions, discouraging behavior deemed undesirable by the individual, ideas typically acquired from the parents and elders.

consciousness Awareness of one's own existence and surroundings at any given moment. Normal consciousness is sometimes experienced in the *productive mode,* sometimes in the *reflective mode.*

conservation task A test to discover whether a child recognizes that certain basic properties of something remain constant when only its appearance is changed.

constancy See *perceptual constancy, problem of sensory constancy.*

constitutional theory A primarily *biological approach* stating that *personality* arises through genetically determined predispositions and early environmental influences. Certain physiological conditions are inborn; certain psychological experiences occur early in life; as a result, personality is constant and stable over the lifetime.

context-dependent memory A *memory* in which the details of the original setting during the *encoding* of the memory later serve as *retrieval* cues for that memory.

contingency management A method of *behavior therapy* in which a team of people employ *operant conditioning* to change some specific behavior by regularly controlling *reinforcement* for that behavior.

continuity See *principle of good continuity.*

continuous reinforcement In *operant conditioning,* the condition of 100-percent *reinforcement,* in which each correct *response* is reinforced.

control condition In a *classical experiment,* the condition that is equivalent to the *experimental condition* except for the *independent variable,* which is absent or held constant under its normal, nonexperimental circumstances.

conventional morality The second of Kohlberg's three major stages of *moral development,* beginning around age ten, during which the individual is concerned with pleasing authority figures and winning approval. Moral judgment is based on maintaining the social order.

cooing A *reflex* emission of air through the vocal cords, resulting in unpatterned vocalizations. In language development, it is among the first vocal activities in normal human infancy.

corpus callosum (koar′-pus kuh-loe′-sum) A bundle of nerve fibers joining the hemispheres of the *cerebral cortex.* It is highly instrumental in coordinating memories and other functions in both sides of the body.

correlation In *correlational statistics,* the extent to which two numerical values are related. In negative correlation, increasing values for one factor are associated with decreasing values for the other factor. In positive correlation, increasing values for one factor are associated with increasing values for the other factor.

correlational statistics In *statistics,* numerical values or procedures that describe the relationship, or *correlation,* between two sets of scores, often expressing measures of *reliability* and *validity.*

counseling psychology A specialization that deals with personal problems in the normal range of behavior, such as vocational problems, adjusting to retirement, school progress, and so forth.

covert observation A form of *naturalistic observation* in which the investigator conceals the research. The individuals being studied do not know they are part of a research project.

creative thinking A form of *problem solving* that aims to produce a novel outcome with a useful or aesthetic purpose, rather than to solve a common problem. Creative thinking is not as logical and controlled as *reasoning;* it relies heavily on imagination, flexibility, and the capacity to combine seemingly unrelated events.

cretinism (kreet′-n-iz-m) A form of *mental retardation* in which the individual is characteristically dwarfed, overweight, and lethargic, with an IQ that usually does not exceed 50.

critical period In *human development,* any of several intervals during which the individual is highly responsive to certain forms of stimulation or has an unusual readiness for *learning.*

cross-sectional studies Investigations of development in which subjects of different ages are compared and studied simultaneously; the purpose is to identify changes across different ages or eras.

crystallized intelligence An accumulation of knowledge about the world and an ability to apply it in daily life. This type of *intelligence* develops through *learning* and includes facts, vocabulary, and expressive capacity.

CT scan Computerized tomography (tuh-mäg′-ruh-fee) scan, also called CAT scan. A computerized cross-sectional image of the *brain;* also the process of producing the image, in which a series of X-rays, each from a slightly different angle, are synthesized.

cuing For *encoding* a *memory,* a strategy in which the learner identifies or prepares some signal, hint, or prompt for later *retrieval* of the information.

cultural deprivation Lack of the early *learning* experiences that are common to a given *culture,* a condition that can contribute to *mental retardation.*

cultural relativism The view that there are no universal standards for many social phenomena. Standards for virtue, beauty, justice, and *adjustment* have particular meanings in a particular environment. Behavior considered normal in one *culture* may be seen as abnormal in another.

culturally sensitive testing Assessment procedures designed specifically to measure abilities and interests in a particular *culture* or subculture. In a

culture-fair test, attempts have been made to eliminate all items influenced more by one culture than another. In a culture-free test, virtually impossible to construct, the items would not reflect or favor any culture.

culture The totality of beliefs and behavior patterns characteristic of a particular *group:* language, customs, religion, age, racial background, occupation, prior experience, and so forth.

culture-fair test See *culturally sensitive testing.*

culture-free test See *culturally sensitive testing.*

cutaneous sensitivity One of the five *traditional senses;* responsiveness to stimulation of the skin, referred to imprecisely as the sense of touch, resulting in the experience of pressure, temperature, and pain. It is the external form of *somesthesis* or body feeling.

death instinct See *thanatos.*

debriefing interview In *research,* an interview conducted at the completion of a project to ensure the maximum benefit for the subject and to obtain any further information that might be useful in research.

decay theory A view of *forgetting* as a *storage* failure due to deterioration of the *memory trace* when it is not used.

decision making Estimating the probabilities of relevant events and using them to select a strategy for *problem solving.*

declarative memory A type of *long-term memory* that represents a statement of fact; it concerns ideas, dates, definitions, and an endless array of other factual information.

deductive reasoning A form of *reasoning* that begins with some general rule or rules and then examines their application in a particular instance. In this form of thinking, if the initial propositions and mode of reasoning are correct, then the conclusion *must* follow.

deep structure In language, the underlying structure in a sentence; the meaning or thought in the words.

defense mechanism A form of symbolic behavior resulting from *unconscious motivation,* and thus based on self-deception, often used to deal with *anxiety* or *stress.* The fundamental defense mechanism is *repression;* to aid the repression, and often to disguise further the real problem, the individual may use additional defense mechanisms: *denial, displacement, projection, rationalization, reaction formation, sublimation.*

deindividuation Loss of normal self-restraint, apparently precipitated by a loss of personal identity due to *social influence.* In a crowd or mob, people can lose their sense of responsibility, engaging in behaviors from which they would refrain if not in the *group.*

deinstitutionalization The process of discharging or transferring former mental patients from the institution to the outside community.

déjà vu experience (day-zha voo) An incorrect impression that a whole event has been encountered previously, although prior experience with the whole event is impossible.

delayed conditioning A sequence of *classical conditioning* in which the neutral *stimulus* appears first and continues to be present during the appearance of the *unconditioned stimulus.*

dendrite Part of the *neuron;* a fiber with innumerable branches that receives impulses and carries them toward its own *cell body.*

denial A *defense mechanism* in which the individual refuses to recognize some aspect of reality.

denotative meaning In *semantics,* the type of meaning that points to something specific; the usual dictionary definition. The denotative meaning of the word *dog* is a domestic and carnivorous mammal of the canine family.

dependent variable In a *classical experiment,* a *variable* that changes in accordance with the manipulation of the *independent variable.* Its presence or intensity depends on the independent variable.

depolarized See *action potential.*

depressants The *psychoactive substances* that inhibit activity in the *central nervous system,* thereby decreasing *anxiety,* pain, and related states; the basic effect is sedation. Also called downers, these drugs include *alcohol* and *opiates.*

depth perception The aspect of *perception* involving awareness of distance, space, or the size of objects. Depth cues include: *binaural cues, binocular cues, monaural cues, monocular cues.*

descriptive statistics In *statistics,* numerical values or procedures that aim to describe or characterize a set of scores, using *measures of central tendency* and *measures of variability.*

desire for affiliation A *secondary motive* in which the individual seeks the company of others for friendship or social support.

desire for novel stimulation A *sensory variation motive* in which the individual seeks not merely changes in stimulation but also new forms of stimulation.

determinism The philosophical view that behavior follows certain natural laws; according to determinism, any event, physical or psychological, is the inevitable result of preceding causes.

devil model An early view of *mental illness* stating that a person became maladjusted because the devil had taken up residence in his or her body.

Diagnostic and Statistical Manual of Mental Disorders (DSM-IV) The fourth edition of a manual for the diagnosis of psychiatric disorders.

diathesis-stress model (dye-ath′-uh-sus) A theory stating that *schizophrenia,* mood disorders, and other severe forms of *mental illness* arise from a combination of genetic factors and environmental conditions. A diathesis is an inherited predisposition to a certain disease, and *stress* causes it to be manifested.

dichromat An individual whose color sensitivity is limited to two hues, usually yellow and blue.

difference threshold In the process of *sensation,* the smallest perceptible difference between two *stimuli* of the same type, also called a just noticeable difference (**j.n.d.**).

differentiation The process by which the development of an organism proceeds from simple to complex, from general to specific. (1) In *physical development,* it involves the steady growth of specialized organic structures from an undifferentiated mass of tissue. (2) In *personality* development, behavior becomes increasingly specific and complex throughout most of one's life.

discrimination In the *conditioning* process, a condition in which an individual is sensitive to the difference between stimuli, making a *response* only to one specific *stimulus* and not to others that may be similar.

discriminative stimulus In *operant conditioning,* a *stimulus* that indicates when *reinforcement* is available; when it is present, a correct *response* will be reinforced.

displacement A *defense mechanism* in which an emotional response intended for a certain person or object is shifted to some other target.

dispositional attribution See *attribution theory.*

dissociation view A theory of *hypnosis* stressing a separation between different levels of awareness in the hypnotized individual. According to this cognitive viewpoint, a consciousness beyond immediate awareness assumes control. See *role enactment*.

dissociative amnesia Extensive *memory* loss, presumably on a psychological basis; a form of *amnesia* with no observable physical cause. In this *dissociative* disorder, the individual remains in familiar surroundings and is otherwise reasonably adjusted.

dissociative fugue (fyoog) A *dissociative* disorder in which the individual is found far from home with no *memory* of his or her name, family, friends, and so forth. A fugue is a "flight."

dissociative identity disorder A *dissociative* disorder, previously called multiple personality, in which the individual seems to have two or more *personality* states; during the experience of each *identity*, the individual has no *memory* of the other identities.

distal stimulus A *stimulus* as it occurs at its physical source, such as light waves from a lamp.

distraction A strategy for *stress* reduction that focuses attention upon some nonstressful activity instead.

divided attention The condition of *attending* simultaneously to two or more events.

dominant gene A *gene* that takes precedence over the other member of its pair in directing the inheritance of a trait. A dominant trait is manifested whenever both genes are of the dominant type; it is also manifested when one is a dominant gene and the other a *recessive gene*.

door-in-the-face technique A method of obtaining *compliance* by beginning with an unreasonably large request. After being confronted with a request too large to accept, a person is more likely to comply with a smaller one.

dopamine (doe′puh-meen) A *neurotransmitter substance* that affects *emotions, learning,* and *memory.* It also influences the control of voluntary movements.

dopamine hypothesis The view that *schizophrenia* is caused by unusually high levels of *dopamine* or by an unusual responsiveness to it in normal amounts.

double-blind design In an experiment, a situation in which neither the investigator nor subjects know to which group any subject belongs. A third party

decides which subjects receive which treatment and codes them for the investigator.

Down's syndrome A moderate, inherited form of *mental retardation* resulting from an extra twenty-first *chromosome.*

dream interpretation A highly complex and speculative form of psychoanalytic *interpretation* that aims to understand the underlying psychological significance, or *latent content,* of a *dream* by examining the dream story, or *manifest content,* and *free association.*

dreams Images, thoughts, and feelings experienced during sleep, typically occurring four or five times throughout a normal sleeping period and indicated by *rapid eye movements,* prompting the term REM sleep. Dreaming is a normal *altered state of consciousness.*

drive In *goal-directed behavior,* a state of arousal arising from a biological *need.* A drive is not an *instinct,* although sometimes referred to loosely as such, nor is it a *reflex;* a drive is a *motivation.*

drive-reduction theory A view of *motivation,* based on the *biological approach,* postulating that motivated behavior is directed toward dispelling bodily tension and achieving *homeostasis.*

drug dependence Continued use of a *psychoactive substance* resulting in increased need for that drug. Also called substance dependence or drug addiction, it can be physical or psychological.

eardrum Part of the *outer ear,* also called the tympanic membrane, located at the end of the auditory canal. In *auditory sensitivity,* the vibrations of the eardrum activate the mechanisms of the *middle ear.*

eclectic approach The selection of any aspect of any *theory* that seems most appropriate in a given circumstance; in *therapy,* the use of whatever treatment method seems most appropriate.

ectomorph See *somatotypes.*

educational psychology A specialization that seeks to expand knowledge and concern about the teaching-*learning* process and to apply this knowledge in school and work settings.

EEG See *electroencephalogram.*

effect See *reinforcement principle.*

effectors The muscles and glands; the *organs* that enable the organism to take some action—that is, to have an effect on the environment.

efferent neuron See *motor neuron.*

ego Latin for "I" or "self." In *psychoanalysis,* one of three psychic forces that make up the *personality;* it is the executive or *reasoning* dimension that assists the id in satisfying biological urges. However, the ego follows the *reality principle,* taking into account the conditions of the external environment.

egocentrism A self-centered view of the world, in which the individual assumes that the only understanding of the world is the one he or she possesses. During the *preoperational period,* children display *cognitive egocentrism,* in which they do not realize that other people may have thoughts different from theirs, and *perceptual egocentrism,* in which they do not realize that other people perceive things from a viewpoint different from theirs.

ego ideal The part of the *superego* that involves positive values, encouraging the goals of parents and elders. It develops through experience and through the support and imitation of elders.

eidetic imagery (eye-ded′-ik) An instance of *recall* of a *memory* in which the image possesses the details of a photograph or hallucination. Often called photographic memory, it is most common in children.

EKG See *electrocardiogram.*

Electra complex A condition in which a daughter strives for the affection of her father and regards her mother as an obstacle to this goal, arising during the *phallic stage* and managed through the process of *identification* with the mother. See *Oedipus complex.*

electrocardiogram (EKG) A record of the rate and rhythm of the heartbeat. Electrodes are attached to the body and chest and the examiner looks for various patterns.

electroconvulsive therapy (ECT) A *biomedical therapy* in which a convulsion of a few seconds is induced by passing a weak electrical current through the *brain.* The aim is to diminish certain symptoms of mental disorder, especially severe depression.

electroencephalogram (EEG) A record of *brain* waves, in which spontaneous regular and irregular rhythms may be observed. The device used to record these patterns is an electroencephalograph (EEG).

embedded messages Any *stimuli* that are purposely indistinct or hidden, presumably influencing *perception* either without the perceiver's awareness or by eliciting increased attention.

embryo An organism in the early prenatal phase. In human beings, this stage lasts from the second week through the end of the second month of the pregnancy.

emotion A complex feeling state accompanied by physiological arousal, mental activity, and overt behaviors. Emotions and related conditions commonly dealt with in psychological contexts include: *aggression, anger, anxiety, love, stress.*

empiricism From the Greek "experience;" the concept that all knowledge is gained through the senses, directly from experience. Empiricism stresses observable phenomena.

encoding The processing of *memory;* it is the acquisition of information or a skill for *storage* and later *retrieval.* Successful encoding often involves three basic strategies: *chunking, cuing, organization.*

endocrine system A series of interlocking glands that secrete *hormones* directly into the bloodstream: *adrenal glands, gonads, pituitary gland, thyroid gland.* This *system* is primarily concerned with maintenance functions, pertaining to growth, general vigor, and other long-range developments.

endomorph See *somatotypes.*

endorphins From "endogenous morphine;" natural anesthetics apparently secreted by certain *brain* cells and released in abnormal levels during times of *stress.*

environment The sum total of external conditions. See *heredity-environment issue.*

environmental psychology A specialization that aims to design physical settings to be functional and comfortable in a mental, physical, and ecological sense.

epinephrine (ep-uh-nef'-reen) A *hormone,* also called adrenaline, secreted by the *adrenal glands;* it stimulates the *sympathetic nervous system,* affecting *arousal level* and increasing energy in emergencies and other emotional situations.

episodic memory A subtype of *declarative memory* involving specific events in the individual's past. This type of *memory* has a time-and-space dimension; a specific episode is remembered.

equity theory A view stating that human beings maintain an *interpersonal* relationship if the outcome is at least equal to what they feel they merit, weighing all of their attributes against prevailing standards. Equity theory is primarily a *cognitive approach* to interpersonal relationships.

equivalent-form reliability Agreement among scores whenever different versions of a test are administered to the same people. A test or test item has equivalent-form *reliability* to the extent that each subject makes the same score on each version.

eros In *psychoanalysis,* the life instinct, one of the two fundamental impulses of the *id.* It involves desire for survival, including the sex impulse, and *love* of oneself and others.

escape conditioning A form of *two-factor conditioning* in which the organism cannot completely prevent an aversive condition but instead terminates it after it has commenced. Compare with *avoidance conditioning.*

ESP See *extrasensory perception.*

estrogens Female sex *hormones,* produced by the *ovaries.* Significantly increasing with the onset of *puberty,* they stimulate female sex characteristics as well as sexual behavior.

ethical question See *basic ethical question.*

ethnocentrism In *social cognition,* the belief that other *cultures* are necessarily odd, immoral, or inferior because they do not share the standards of one's own *group.*

eustress (yoo-stress) A form of *stress* that is brief and beneficial for the individual, facilitating completion of a difficult task.

evolutionary psychology An approach to psychology that attempts to understand the ways in which human beings have developed solutions to two overriding problems of *adaptation*—survival and reproduction. It assumes that the individuals who were successful at these tasks are our ancestors.

exchange theory A view stating that human beings maintain an *interpersonal* relationship if the gain is greater than the overall expense; like any other exchange or purchase, it is judged in terms of profit and loss. Exchange theory is primarily a *cognitive approach* to interpersonal relationships.

exhaustion The third and final phase of the *general adaptation syndrome;* it occurs when the organism's earlier *responses* have been repeated until they are no longer possible. If the *stress* continues, death occurs.

existential therapy A form of *humanistic therapy* that emphasizes each person's need to understand his or her existence. Existential therapists assist people in accepting *anxiety,* coping with it directly, and finding meaning through the pain it involves.

expectancy x value theory A *cognitive approach* stating that the *motivation* for any task depends upon the individual's expectation of success or failure and the worth of that outcome.

experiment See *classical experiment, experimental method.*

experimental condition In a *classical experiment,* the condition in which the *independent variable* is present or manipulated to some degree.

experimental method A fundamental research method in which *variables* are manipulated or controlled in precise ways, often in the *classical experiment.* It provides the most promising answers to cause-and-effect questions, and thus it is often considered foremost among the various *scientific methods* in psychological inquiry.

experimenter effects Any factors originating from an investigator that influence the results of research without the investigator's knowledge, such as the investigator's expectations, habits, and personal characteristics. Such effects include unconscious signals in posture, gesture, and vocal tone emitted by all of us in speaking. This unintentional *cuing* is known as the *Clever Hans effect.*

expert systems Narrowly focused computer programs, employing *artificial intelligence,* that function very effectively—like experts—in accomplishing highly specialized tasks, such as diagnosing infectious diseases.

explicit memory A type of *long-term memory* that usually involves an intentional, conscious effort to remember; the *memory* is formed and utilized with awareness, as when the individual recites a poem.

expressed emotion The degree to which the family of a patient recovering from *schizophrenia* expresses hostility and overinvolvement toward him or her. Patients who return to a home with high expressed *emotion* are several times more likely to relapse than those without critical or overly involved family members.

extinction In the *conditioning* process, the disappearance of a *response* to a given *stimulus.* Extinction is not necessarily permanent; the response can reappear, a condition called *spontaneous recovery.*

extrasensory perception (ESP) An awareness with no sensory basis; a psychic phenomenon in which *perception* allegedly occurs without use of the normal modes of *sensation.*

extrinsic motivation The *motivation* to succeed at a task in which the satisfaction is external to performance of the task, as in studying geography to pass an exam or to impress others.

face validity Seeming to possess *validity*. A test with face validity appears appropriate for its alleged purpose, but may not be.

fallacy of the single cause The often erroneous belief that just one condition or factor leads to a certain outcome.

falsifiable The potential of a *theory* or explanation to be proven incorrect. Such an explanation is not so broad and all-encompassing that it covers all possibilities or so vague that it cannot be examined by some *scientific method.*

family therapy A form of *group therapy* in which a family constitutes the group. All problems of the group and individual members are treated as family problems. The therapist observes the family interactions, develops interpretations of these processes, and shares them with the family.

fantasy Wishful thinking and daydreaming, sometimes used as a means of coping with *stress.* In imagination, a person may accomplish all sorts of feats, find true love, vanquish a rival, and overcome an insurmountable obstacle. It is often a major step in *creative thinking.*

fear of success Avoiding high achievement because it may interfere with opportunities for affiliation, empathy, and personal relationships.

feature detectors Highly specialized cells in the visual cortex that respond only to a specific feature or characteristic of a visual *stimulus,* such as a straight edge, an angle, brightness, or movement of a spot.

features-based approach One of two chief methods of *concept* formation; it requires noting and remembering the essential features of an object or event. A person who acquires the concept of a pencil must observe that all such objects, regardless of how much they differ, have certain features in common.

feedback Any direct information about one's own behavior. Feedback is used as a therapeutic technique and as an instructional procedure.

fetal alcohol syndrome A condition characterized by low birth weight, sleep disturbances, poor coordination, and *mental retardation.* It is found among babies born to mothers who consumed alcohol during the pregnancy.

fetishism A condition in which the presence of a certain object is essential to sexual gratification. It is a form of *paraphilia*—sexual attraction to anything not normally associated with sex.

fetus An organism in the late prenatal phase. In human beings, this stage begins with the third month and extends until birth and includes all sorts of dramatic neural developments.

figure-ground relationship The form of *primitive organization* in which a figure or pattern is perceived as having a certain contour that stands out against a background, or ground; the *perception* of a certain theme and its surroundings, such as a bird seen against the sky.

fixation In *psychoanalysis,* a state of arrested psychological growth, resulting when normal gratification has been blocked at an earlier *psychosexual stage* and the individual remains preoccupied with achieving the denied outcome.

fixed action pattern In animals, a complex behavior that appears to be innate, stereotyped, and independent of the organisms immediate control; sometimes called an *instinct.* Such patterns are most striking in sexual behavior, care of the young, and territoriality.

fixed-interval (FI) schedule In *operant conditioning,* a *partial reinforcement* schedule in which *reinforcement* for correct *responses* is available only after a certain interval of time. Each reinforcement becomes available following a fixed period since the prior reinforcement.

fixed-ratio (FR) schedule In *operant conditioning,* a *partial reinforcement* schedule in which *reinforcement* is provided only for a certain proportion of correct *responses.* The ratio refers to the number of reinforced responses in comparison with the total number of responses.

flashbulb memory An instance of *recall* of a *memory* in which details of an emotional experience are remembered with unusual ease and almost perceptual accuracy, as though the event was still in process.

flooding A method of therapy in which the individual who becomes distressed in a certain situation is continually exposed to that situation until the *anxiety* finally becomes extinguished.

fluid intelligence The capacity to solve novel problems, using rapid and accurate *reasoning.* These problems require flexibility in *intelligence* and cannot be readily solved through prior *learning.*

foot-in-the-door technique A method of obtaining *compliance* by beginning with a very small request. After complying with a small request, a person is more likely to comply with a larger one.

forebrain One of three divisions of the *brain;* it is fundamentally involved in *cognitive processes* and *emotion.* The most recently developed, in an evolutionary sense, it is also the uppermost, farthest from the *spinal cord.* Its most prominent structure is the *cerebral cortex.*

forgetting The inability to engage in *recall* or *recognition,* or in *relearning* at an improved rate; the loss of a *memory.*

formal operations Piaget's fourth and final stage of *cognitive development;* it may appear around the eleventh year or later, evident in the capacity for abstract *reasoning* apart from concrete situations.

forming an hypothesis The first of three steps in the *scientific method;* in this step, an educated guess or prediction is made. The investigator develops a tentative statement to be tested.

form perception The aspect of *perception* that determines what is being observed. The object usually has some familiar qualities; thus, the task is often called pattern recognition, indicating a comparison of incoming information with stored information.

fovea (foe′-vee-uh) The area of heaviest concentration of *cones* in the *retina* of the eye. In *visual sensitivity,* the fovea is responsible for the clearest images and fullest experience of color.

fragile X syndrome An inherited form of *mental retardation* associated with a fragile site on the X *chromosome;* it is more common in males.

framing Any way of presenting or representing a problem, stating it in words or numbers or graphically. When framing is successful—representing the problem clearly and without distractions—*problem solving* is facilitated.

fraternal twins Siblings resulting from the same pregnancy but from different *zygotes.* In contrast to *identical twins,* they share no more inheritance than siblings born at different times.

free association In *psychoanalysis,* a chief technique in which the patient attempts to reveal all thoughts, just as they occur, in random fashion, no matter how trivial, embarrassing, disrespectful, or illogical they may seem.

free will The capacity for self-direction and choice. In the *humanistic viewpoint,* the causes of behavior lie in the voluntary decisions and actions of the individual.

frequency Number of occurrences. The number of vibrations per second in *auditory sensitivity.* Low, regular frequencies produce a tone of low pitch; high, irregular frequencies produce a noise of high pitch.

Freudian slip A minor error in speech, writing, *memory,* or the performance of some task. It is assumed to be a form of symbolic behavior resulting from *unconscious motivation;* the slip partially reveals some repressed impulse.

frontal lobes One of four divisions of the hemispheres of the *cerebral cortex,* the lobes located at the front of the *brain,* over the eyes; they are involved in motor control and *cognitive processes.*

frustration-aggression hypothesis An assumption that aggressive behavior is always preceded by frustration and that frustration inevitably leads to some form of *aggression.*

fugue See *dissociative fugue.*

functional fixedness An inhibiting *set,* or expectancy, in which an object is considered useful only for its original purpose, as when a pencil is regarded as a tool for writing and not as a possible doorstop, window prop, or measuring instrument, depending upon the task.

functionalism An early *system of psychology* emphasizing the functions rather than the contents of mental life—its purpose rather than its nature, what it does rather than what it is.

GABA Gamma amino butyric acid (gam'-uh uh-mee'-noe byoo-tir'-ik). The most widespread inhibitory *neurotransmitter substance.* It apparently plays a role in epilepsy.

galvanic skin response (GSR) The lowering of electrical resistance of the skin caused by perspiration, resulting from activation of the sweat glands during emotional arousal. It is one of the *responses* measured by a *polygraph.*

gate control theory An attempt to explain pain, postulating that impulses traveling along certain nerve fibers in the *spinal cord* act as a barrier to pain impulses. The gate gives priority to nonpain impulses arriving at the same time, traveling the same nerve pathways that the pain impulses would have used.

gender identity The recognition of oneself as one sex or the other. Also called sex *role,* it is closely linked to *social development;* it implies confidence in oneself as male or female.

gender identity disorder An extremely rare form of maladjustment involving a strong desire to be, or insistence that one is, of the opposite sex—apart from any perceived cultural advantage—and a persistent state of distress about one's *gender identity.*

general adaptation syndrome The physiological *responses* to *stress,* characterized by three phases of *adaptation: alarm reaction, resistance* (1), *exhaustion.*

general intelligence (g) In a *psychometric approach* to *intelligence* suggested by Charles Spearman, a factor that pertains to many different skills. Mechanical ability, musical ability, mathematical ability, and other abilities show a *correlation* with one another because a certain amount of general intelligence is required in all instances.

generalized anxiety disorder An *anxiety* disorder in which the individual experiences excessive worry for several months for no apparent reason, accompanied by irritability, disturbed sleep, or some other related symptoms.

generativity versus stagnation The seventh of eight *psychosocial* crises; it occurs in middle adulthood, during which there is an expanding of one's interests to include the next generation or instead there is a rather restrained and exclusive focus on one's personal goals.

genes Within the *chromosomes,* the fundamental determiners of heredity. Pair of genes, passed on at the moment of conception, direct the development of traits in the organism; these traits include most physical characteristics and certain behavioral traits.

genital stage In *psychoanalysis,* the fifth and final *psychosexual stage;* it appears with the onset of *adolescence.* During this period, there is a reawakening of sexual interests and a search for people to provide sexual satisfaction. This stage involves the capacity for mature relationships.

genotype The sets of *genes* assumed to underlie an observable trait, called the *phenotype.* For example, the genotype is designated *bb* when the phenotype is blue eyes.

Gestalt therapy (guh-stält') In *group therapy* or individual *insight therapy,* a role-playing approach stressing verbal and physical expression.

goal-directed behavior According to *drive-reduction theory,* a sequence of *motivation: need, drive, incentive, reward.* For example, lack of water creates a need; the thirst drive is the aroused state; water is the incentive; and consuming it is a reward.

gonads Sex glands; the *endocrine* glands influential in sexual behavior; the *ovaries* in women and *testes* in men.

graded potential A small change in polarization in the membrane of a receiving nerve fiber. The size of the shift can vary, depending upon the amount and type of information in the incoming message. When the graded potential reaches a certain level of intensity, called the *absolute threshold,* it stimulates the nerve fiber to fire, producing an *action potential.*

graph In *statistics,* a visual display of numerical values, showing the relationship between scores, made by lines or geometric figures of certain shapes.

group Two or more individuals who are united by some common characteristic and whose actions are interrelated. This relationship can be temporary and incidental, as in *group therapy,* or relatively enduring and fundamental, as in a *culture.*

group polarization A condition in which the outcome of *decision making* in a *group* is closer to one pole or the other than it is to the average position of the individual members. The group is *not* split into opposing factions, as the term might suggest.

group tests Instruments of measurement administered to many people simultaneously. These tests are scored by machine.

group therapy A form of *insight therapy* in which people can share questions and concerns with one another and a therapist. These interactions, which may include spontaneous groups, pre-formed groups, and structured groups with role-playing methods, aim to assist the individuals in achieving personal growth or solving personal problems. Types of *group therapy* include: *family therapy, marital therapy, support groups.*

groupthink A condition in which a *group* places such a high value on cohesion and morale that the contributions of dissenting individuals and capacity for *decision making* are limited.

gustatory sensitivity One of the five *traditional senses;* the experience of taste; responsiveness to nongaseous chemical energy.

hallucinogens The *psychoactive substances* that primarily produce alterations in *sensation* and *perception,* heightening or distorting awareness of oneself or the environment. Usually included in this category are *lysergic acid diethylamide* and *marijuana.*

halo effect In *social cognition,* the result that occurs when a favorable or unfavorable judgment about one characteristic prompts similar judgments about other characteristics of the same person, regardless of the objective situation.

Hawthorne effect Any improvement in *motivation* and performance that occurs essentially because people receive recognition, apart from any material benefits.

health psychology A specialization that concerns not only diagnosis, treatment, and prevention of illness but also the issue of health education.

hemispheric specialization The normal condition of the *cerebral cortex* in which its two hemispheres, connected by the *corpus callosum,* have somewhat different but largely overlapping capacities. For most people, the left hemisphere is more dominant in using words, numbers, and especially spoken language. The right hemisphere appears to be more dominant in synthesizing and utilizing spatial and other nonverbal information.

heredity The genetic transmission of characteristics from the parents to their offspring.

heredity-environment issue The long debate over the relative contributions of inborn and acquired factors in the developmental process; also called the **nature-nurture issue.**

heritability estimate In *behavioral genetics,* a proportion or ratio representing the extent to which any given characteristic can be attributed to genetic factors, as opposed to *all* factors that might contribute to that characteristic.

heuristic In *problem solving,* any technique using a short cut or rule of thumb that might work but offers no guarantee. As efficient strategies, heuristics are selective and thus speed success—or failure. Two common heuristics are the *availability heuristic* and the *representative heuristic.*

higher-order conditioning A *classical conditioning* procedure by which a neutral *stimulus* becomes a *conditioned stimulus* without ever being paired with an *unconditioned stimulus;* it is paired instead with an already conditioned stimulus.

hindbrain One of three divisions of the *brain;* it plays a significant role in vital functions, such as waking, sleeping, balance, and coordination. The oldest, in an evolutionary sense, it is also the lowest, closest to the *spinal cord.*

hippocampus A curved *subcortical structure* near the *temporal lobes* of the *brain,* named for the Latin word for sea horse, in reference to its shape. It seems to play a vital role in *memory.*

holophrastic expression (hä-luh-frass'-tik) A single word used to convey a complex idea. In language development, this ability appears after the first year of normal human infancy.

homeostasis (hoe-mee-oe-stay'-sus) A state of balance within the body. In every living organism, there is a tendency to maintain a proper internal environment, to attain equilibrium among its basic biological processes.

hormones Glandular secretions of the *endocrine system* that ensure fundamental chemical activities within the whole organism, influencing virtually every bodily function—body growth, utilization of food, energy expenditure, reproductive reactions, and so forth. Significant hormones include: *androgens, epinephrine, estrogens, prolactin.*

hue Color. In *visual sensitivity,* the *wavelengths* of light energy are registered in the *cones,* responsible for the experience of hue, called color vision.

human development An area of study that concerns the ways in which people change as they grow older, emphasizing the patterns that occur for most people throughout the life-span. It is often approached chronologically, beginning with conception and following the major life stages: prenatal phase, infancy, childhood, adolescence, adulthood, old age.

human-factors psychology A subspecialty within the field of *psychology* devoted to the design of tools and procedures well suited to human use, especially in the work environment. In Europe, it is known as ergonomics, meaning the study of work or energy expenditure.

humanistic psychology A *system of psychology* that arose in the 1960s as a protest against *behaviorism* and *psychoanalysis.* Based on the philosophical position of free will, it emphasizes complexity, subjectivity, and the capacity for growth in human beings.

humanistic therapy A broad, unstructured approach to *insight therapy* based on *humanistic psychology;* it attempts to assist a person in achieving personal growth or in solving a personal problem through self-confrontation. The aim is greater personal awareness, chiefly by focusing upon immediate experience. Two humanistic approaches are *existential therapy* and *person-centered therapy.*

humanistic viewpoint An approach to *personality* that emphasizes *free will* and the uniqueness of every human being. In contrast, most other approaches are based on *determinism.*

hypnagogic state (hip'-nuh-gä'-jik) The interval of drowsiness between wakefulness and sleep. It is a normal *altered state of consciousness* and includes vivid images that lack the narrative, unfolding, and sometimes bizarre quality of normal *dreams.*

hypnosis An interaction in which one person, responding to suggestions by someone else, experiences involuntary changes in *memory, perception,* or behavior, and sometimes even changes in physiology. Classic hypnotic effects include: *analgesia, hypnotic amnesia, regression.* An *altered state of consciousness.*

hypnotic amnesia A form of *retrograde amnesia* induced by *hypnosis.* The individual, following the hypnotist's instruction, has no *memory* afterward of the events that occurred during the session.

hypothalamus A small *subcortical structure* of the *brain,* located just below the *thalamus,* that plays a large role in *motivation* for many behaviors, including *aggression,* sexual behavior, and expression of *emotion.* Certain parts of the hypothalamus help to regulate eating (*lateral hypothalamus, ventromedial nucleus*) and drinking (*osmoreceptors*).

hypothesis See *forming an hypothesis, testing an hypothesis.*

id In *psychoanalysis,* one of three psychic forces that make up the *personality;* it is a collection of inborn biological urges present in all human beings. The id follows the *pleasure principle,* with complete disregard for anything except immediate gratification of biological urges; it includes two fundamental impulses: *eros* and *thanatos.*

identical twins Siblings resulting from the same *zygote.* Because they have identical *genes,* they are considerably more alike than *fraternal twins.*

identification The process by which a child adopts the manner, *attitudes,* and interests of an older person, usually the same-sexed parent, attempting in this way to avoid rivalry with that parent and to win the love and respect of the other parent. This process is assumed to be particularly important for developing *gender identity.*

identity crisis A *critical period* in *adolescence* during which the individual experiences emotional upheaval and uncertainty regarding his or her *role* in life. It may occur at other times too.

identity disorder See *dissociative identity disorder, gender identity disorder.*

identity versus role diffusion The fifth of eight *psychosocial* crises; it occurs in *adolescence,* during which the person develops a sense of self as a consistent and unique person or instead begins to experience a fragmented, disconnected, and unclear *self-concept.*

idiographic research (i-dee-oe-graf'-ik) An intensive *case study* of just one person, group, or event, attempting to describe the special "lawfulness" of that individual. Uniformities among people or events are of lesser concern; *individual differences* are emphasized.

illusion A false *perception.* There are many common optical illusions, such as the widely experienced moon illusion, in which the moon when low in the sky appears up to one-third larger than the same moon when overhead. Other visual illusions include: *autokinetic effect, phi phenomenon.*

imaginal mode A way of thinking based on a symbol that has the appearance of whatever it represents. A visual symbol looks like the object to which it refers; an auditory symbol sounds like the object to which it refers. Different from the *propositional mode.*

implicit memory A type of *long-term memory* evoked without conscious effort. This type of *memory* occurs when a person who has not ridden a bicycle for years is able to do so without any specific effort.

imprinting In infancy, the process by which babies acquire *attachment* to members of their own species, particularly to a caretaker.

incentive A specific *stimulus* that initiates action to satisfy a *drive.*

incidental sample A *sample* that is drawn from whatever subjects in the *population* happen to be available and willing to respond. See *inferential statistics*

independent variable In a *classical experiment,* the *variable* that is manipulated in accordance with the research purpose—to discover its effect. The purposeful changes in this variable are independent of any other aspect of the experiment. Any factor that changes as a result of this manipulation is called a *dependent variable.*

individual differences The unique qualities of each organism. In *human development,* each person deviates in one way or another from what is aver-age or typical and from all other people. Uniqueness is emphasized in the study of *personality.*

individual tests Instruments of measurement administered to only one person at a time. Such tests may include *projective techniques* as well as traditional questions.

induced movement The *perception* of a stationary *stimulus* as moving, as in the *impression* that the moon is moving behind the clouds when it is the clouds that are actually moving.

inductive reasoning A form of *reasoning* that proceeds from the particular facts to a general statement about those facts. This form of thinking goes beyond the data to derive some broader view. It does not necessarily lead to correct explanations; all it can do is generate possibilities.

industry versus inferiority The fourth of eight *psychosocial* crises; it occurs in childhood from about age six to age twelve, during which the child gains a sense of accomplishment or instead develops a sense of inferiority and incompetence (*inferiority complex*).

inferential statistics In *statistics,* the use of numerical values in a sample to make predictions or guesses about the *probability* of obtaining the same scores in a population; used in *point estimation* and the *study of differences.*

inferiority complex An individual's feelings of being less competent than others. In *psychodynamic theory,* dealing with this crisis is influential in *personality* development.

information processing The ways in which information is obtained, retained, and utilized. In the functions of *cognition—memory, perception,* thinking, and so forth—and *sensation,* human beings and other species process many pieces of information simultaneously (*parallel distributed processing*). Most computers only process one piece of information at a time (*serial processing*).

informed consent In *research,* the condition in which the general nature, risks, and benefits of research participation are explained to all subjects before the procedures begin. They are told what will be expected of them; if they agree to participate, they are giving informed consent.

initiative versus guilt The third of eight *psychosocial* crises; it occurs in childhood from about three to six years of age, during which the child's willingness to try new things is either facilitated or inhibited.

inkblots See *Rorschach inkblots.*

inner ear One of the three regions of the human ear; it is the converting system of *auditory sensitivity,* changing the mechanical motions of sound waves into electrochemical impulses. The vibrations of the *oval window* exert pressure on a liquid in the *cochlea,* which surrounds the *basilar membrane* and stimulates the *receptors* for hearing. Also in the inner ear, the *nonauditory labyrinth* contains the mechanisms that mediate balance and motion.

insanity A legal term for *mental illness* indicating that someone is not of sufficiently sound mind to be responsible for his or her conduct.

insight A sudden understanding, as when a solution to a complex problem appears abruptly. It occurs not only through prior experience but also through new ways of thinking or new combinations of thought.

insight therapy A form of *therapy* employing conversations aimed at enabling the troubled individual to achieve increased self-understanding and to use this *insight* to deal more effectively with personal problems. Originally called *psychotherapy,* this approach is employed in *cognitive therapy, humanistic therapy,* and *psychoanalysis.*

insomnia A sleep disorder characterized by chronic inability to go to sleep or to remain asleep.

instinct A complex, unlearned pattern of behavior, apparently inborn, that occurs in all normal, same-sexed members of a given species, such as nest building in pregnant rabbits.

institutionalization The *adaptation* of incarcerated people to the organization or setting in which they live, whereby they adjust to the requirements of *that* situation rather than to those of the outside world.

integrity versus despair The eighth and final *psychosocial* crisis; it occurs in old age, during which the person finds meaning in memories or instead looks back on life with dissatisfaction.

intelligence Overall mental ability. The capacity for *learning* from experience and adapting to new situations. See *multiple intelligences* and *triarchic theory.*

intelligence quotient (IQ) A measurement of mental ability. Using the conventional formula, *mental age* is divided by *chronological age* and multiplied by 100: IQ = MA/CA (100).

intelligence test A test for measuring a wide range of mental and some physical abilities, especially verbal, numerical, and social competence: *Stanford Binet Intelligence Scale, Wechsler Intelligence Scales.*

interaction principle The influence of two or more factors upon one another. In the *heredity-environment issue,* the impact of any particular heredity or any particular environment occurs only within the context of the other, and therefore they are mutually influential.

interactive effect In *multifactor studies,* an outcome in which the total influence of all factors is different from the sum of their separate influences, due to the relationships among the various influences. The result is not merely cumulative; the separate influences are interdependent.

interest inventory An instrument in which people merely indicate their preferences, usually for work-related activities. It is not a test in the strict sense; there are no right or wrong answers.

interference theory A view of *forgetting* postulating that information is lost from *memory* because it is disturbed or displaced by some other information. Interference can occur at any time, and therefore the problem can be a failure in *storage* or *retrieval.* In proactive interference, memory of earlier experiences disrupts the retrieval of something learned later. In retroactive interference, memory of later experiences disrupts the retrieval of something learned earlier.

interjudge reliability An agreement among scores whenever the same test is graded by different examiners. A test or test item has interjudge *reliability* to the extent that each examiner awards the same answers with the same score.

interneuron A *neuron* that transmits messages from *sensory neurons* to *motor neurons* and also to other interneurons. Interneurons complete certain *reflex arcs,* enable most impulses to ascend the *spinal cord,* stimulate innumerable circuits within the *brain,* and eventually prompt other impulses that descend the spinal cord.

interpersonal attraction In *social psychology,* preferences for living and working with certain individuals. Interpersonal attraction is an aspect of any human relationship.

interpretation In *psychoanalysis,* a chief technique in which the analyst provides clarification and suggestions, helping the patient to evaluate or reconsider the possible significance of events within and outside the treatment session, including the patient's *dreams.*

intersensory perception The simultaneous *perception* of information from several sources of *sensation,* and the integration of this new information with current information.

intimacy versus isolation The sixth of eight *psychosocial* crises; it occurs in early adulthood, during which the individual feels personal support from others or instead feels alienated.

intrinsic motivation The *motivation* to succeed at a task in which the satisfaction is inherent in the task itself, as in studying the geography of a distant land just to know about that country.

inventory See *interest inventory, personality inventory.*

IQ See *intelligence quotient.*

iris The muscular disc that gives color to the eye and serves a regulatory function by dilating or constricting the *pupillary opening.*

James-Lange theory (Län´-guh) A view of *emotion* postulating that the behavioral and physiological reactions in emotion occur first, and then they arouse the feelings.

just noticeable difference See *difference threshold.*

kinesthesis (kin-us-thee´-sus) The *proprioceptive sense* that provides information about the position and movement of body parts, made possible by special *receptors* in the muscles, tendons, and joints. It is an internal form of *somesthesis* or body feeling.

language acquisition device (LAD) An inborn mechanism for language development, composed of those parts of the human mind specifically and uniquely devoted to the *learning* of language, according to the innate view of language learning.

latency stage In *psychoanalysis,* the fourth of five *psychosexual stages;* it begins in childhood around age six and lasts until *adolescence;* during this period, there is an apparent absence of sexual interests.

latent content In *dream interpretation,* the underlying significance of a *dream;* the forbidden impulses, rendered unconscious through the process of *repression,* that are transformed by the dream work into the obvious story, or *manifest content,* of the dream.

latent learning A type of *learning* in which knowledge becomes evident only at a later date, when *reinforcement* is available.

lateral hypothalamus The side of the *hypothalamus.* Stimulation of this area activates and sustains eating in experimental animals, even those presumably satiated; when it is damaged or removed, they cease eating despite the availability of food, even when hunger is not satisfied.

law of specific nerve energies The principle stating that an organisms experience or *sensation* is a function of the particular nerves that are stimulated, not *how* they are stimulated. A person may see flashes of light because visual nerves have been stimulated directly, not because light waves have entered the eye.

learned helplessness A condition in which the individual responds to *stress* with apathy and feelings of inadequacy, a reaction resulting from former stressful situations that the person was unable to change.

learning Any lasting change in behavior resulting from experience, rather than solely from a physiological change, such as fatigue or illness. Learning incorporates both *cognitive processes* and *conditioning.*

learning disability A *learning* deficit in a specific mental skill, such as reading, spelling, or mathematics, sometimes occurring in people with otherwise normal or even high *intelligence.*

legal psychology A specialization that uses knowledge of human behavior to improve our system of laws, making them more humane and just.

lens The transparent structure near the front of the eye that gives an image a sharp focus in *visual sensitivity* by automatically altering its shape or curvature, a reaction called *accommodation (2).*

levels-of-processing theory A *view of memory* which states that the information most thoroughly processed is the most likely to be remembered.

life instinct See *eros.*

limbic system A *subcortical structure* of the *brain,* comprised of certain portions of the *thalamus, hypothalamus,* and several other organs, including the *amygdala.* The limbic system plays a key role in *emotion.*

linear relationship An association. In *correlational statistics,* the association between sets of scores, represented in a *scattergram* by plotted points tending toward the shape of a straight line.

linguistic determinism The hypothesis stating that a person's language plays a fundamental role in shaping his or her thinking.

lithium A naturally occurring salt substance used as a medication in *biomedical therapy* to alleviate the chief symptoms of *bipolar disorder,* acting primarily in the manic episode.

lobotomy A *biomedical therapy* in which connections in the *frontal lobes* of the *brain* are destroyed. The aim is to diminish certain symptoms of mental disorder, especially severe depression.

loci See *method of loci.*

locus of control The extent to which people perceive the influential forces in their lives as lying within or outside of themselves. An internal locus of control is a belief in a significant degree of control over one's own life. An external locus of control is a belief that there is little one can do to change the condition of one's life.

longitudinal studies Investigations of development in which the same subjects are studied over and over again, at different ages, compared with themselves as they grow older; the purpose is to identify changes across different ages or eras.

long-term memory (LTM) The final *storage* of a *memory,* not an interim processing stage; it is the third phase in the *stage theory of memory.* In this stage, defined as any interval from 30 or so seconds up to the full life of the organism, information is retained for later use.

long-term potentiation A sustained, permanent increase in the strength of a synaptic connection. With repeated use, the nerve pathway becomes more readily excitable on a long-term basis, strengthening the *memory trace.*

love See *companionate love, passionate love, triangular theory of love.*

LSD See *lysergic acid diethylamide.*

lucid dreaming A state in which the individual is sound asleep and also aware of dreaming. In such *dreams,* the individual presumably possesses a conscious mind in a sleeping body.

lysergic acid diethylamide (LSD) (li-sur'-jik, dye-eth'-il-uh-myde) A drug that may produce symptoms similar to those of *psychotic disorder,* such as hearing unspoken voices and seeing nonexistent events. It is usually classified as a *hallucinogen.*

mainstreaming An educational procedure that avoids separate schooling for children with *mental retardation* and instead integrates them with other children, through special provisions for *learning* in the typical classroom.

major depressive disorder A mood disorder in which the individual experiences feelings of intense disappointment and helplessness about life lasting at least two weeks, or loss of pleasure in virtually all activities for an equal period. It is typically accompanied by *insomnia,* weight loss, fatigue, agitation, or other symptoms.

manifest content In *dream interpretation,* the obvious *dream* story as recalled by the dreamer. It is the symbolic manifestation of the dream's underlying significance, called the *latent content.*

marijuana A drug derived from the hemp plant; it usually produces a sense of exhilaration and intoxication when ingested. It is considered by some a mild *hallucinogen.*

marital therapy A form of *group therapy* in which a married couple constitutes the group. Lack of harmony in the marriage, or the maladjustment of one partner, is considered the couple's problem, stemming from their mutual concerns.

mastery model See *modeling.*

matching hypothesis A view of *interpersonal attraction* stating that the members of a couple are usually about equal in physical attractiveness, or other characteristics, and when the members are not approximately equal, the less attractive person usually offers some compensating factor.

maternal behavior Care of the young by the mother, which may be significantly influenced by the hormonal secretion *prolactin.*

maturation A certain sequence of *physical development* that is universal among all normal members of a given species and depends almost solely upon inherited biological factors.

mean In *descriptive statistics,* one of the three usual *measures of central tendency;* it indicates the arithmetic average of a group of scores. The mean is obtained by adding all of the scores and dividing by the number of scores.

measures of central tendency In *descriptive statistics,* numerical values that indicate typical scores, near the center of a group of scores. The usual measures are *mean, median,* and *mode.*

measures of variability In *descriptive statistics,* numerical values that indicate the degree to which the scores in a group differ from some average or typical score. The usual measures of variability are *range* and *standard deviation.*

media psychology A specialization that attempts to understand how electronic and printed information can be used for the public good.

median In *descriptive statistics,* one of the three usual *measures of central tendency;* it indicates the middle point in a distribution of scores. When all scores have been ranked in numerical order, the median has half of the scores above it and half below it.

medical model A *biological approach* to maladjustment suggesting that *mental illness,* like physical illness, reflects a diseased condition of the body.

meditation A method of achieving an *altered state of consciousness,* such as deep relaxation or increased awareness, chiefly by restricting incoming *stimuli.* Two types of meditation are *concentrative meditation* and *mindfulness meditation.*

medulla The part of the *hindbrain* that controls digestion, breathing, and blood circulation. In the lowest part of the *brain,* it contains numerous neural tracts, connecting many brain areas.

memory The capacity to utilize impressions from previous experience. The three basic steps in this process are *encoding, storage,* and *retrieval.* A stage theory postulates three phases: *sensory memory, short-term memory, long-term memory.*

memory trace A molecular change presumed to lie in the *nervous system* and postulated as the basis of *memory,* according to the *biological approach;* it is also called an engram.

mental age (MA) The level of a person's mental ability at any given *chronological age.* It is determined by an *intelligence test* and used in calculating an *intelligence quotient.*

mental giftedness Mental excellence; high *intelligence* as indicated by an IQ above 130, occurring in the upper 2 percent of the general population.

mental health Successful *adjustment,* involving feelings of well-being and the realization of one's potential. Absence of adjustment disorder.

mental illness An *adjustment* disorder; a state of mental dysfunction of physical or psychological origin sufficiently severe to require professional assistance, sometimes called abnormality. Types of disorders include: eating disorders (*anorexia nervosa, bulimia nervosa*), *anxiety* disorders, *dissociative* disorders, substance-related disorders (*drug dependence*), mood disorders (*bipolar disorder, major depressive disorder*), impulse-control disorders (*pathological gambling*), *personality disorders, psychotic disorders,* sexual disorders (*gender identity disorder, paraphilia, sexual dysfunction*), sleep disorders (*insomnia, narcolepsy, sleep apnea, sleepwalking*), *somatoform disorders.*

mental retardation Mental disability; low *intelligence* as indicated by an IQ below 70, occurring in the lower 2 percent of the general population.

mesomorph See *somatotypes.*

meta-analysis A technique for examining the results from many studies, thereby yielding some overall summary about the evidence.

metacognition The understanding of one's own *cognitive processes;* thinking about one's own thinking. Without conscious effort, many people develop increased metacognition throughout adulthood.

method of loci A *mnemonic device* that employs a series of familiar places in a well-established path. A locus is a place; loci are several places. Each item on the list to be memorized is associated with a specific place in the pathway.

midbrain One of three divisions of the *brain;* it serves a vital role in processing information for the upper brain regions, especially information from the eyes and ears.

middle ear One of the three regions of the human ear; it is the amplifying system for *auditory sensitivity,* containing the *ossicles,* three small bones that are activated by the *eardrum* of the *outer ear* and in turn activate the *oval window* of the *inner ear.*

midlife crisis A period in adulthood during which the individual experiences a tension or lack of fulfillment in life. It is highly variable in its intensity and the age at which it occurs.

mindfulness meditation A *meditation* technique in which attention is directed toward a broad awareness of objects and events as they arise spontaneously.

Minnesota Multiphasic Personality Inventory-2 (MMPI-2) A *personality inventory* originally developed a half-century ago to identify people with specific psychological disorders. It is used today to assess all sorts of traits in all kinds of people, with and without maladjustment.

mnemonic devices (nee-män´-ik) Systems designed to aid memorization by efficient input and output. Most mnemonic devices are based on strategies for the *encoding* of *memory.*

mode In *descriptive statistics,* one of the three usual *measures of central tendency;* it indicates the score that occurs most frequently in a group of scores.

modeling In *observational learning,* the process of reproducing the behavior, and often the *attitudes,* of a person competent in some role, called a model. A peer model is close to the observer in age and background; a mastery model demonstrates the behavior to perfection but is more distant socially; a symbolic model is not actually present but appears only on television, the radio, or in a story.

monaural cues In *auditory sensitivity,* the *depth perception* cues available to one ear alone, including loudness, complexity, and volume, all helpful in determining distance.

monochromat An individual who is color blind, with no experience of *hue,* seeing only degrees of gray. The term achromatic vision means seeing "without color."

monocular cues In *visual sensitivity,* the *depth perception* cues observable by just one eye, including interposition, shadows, linear perspective, texture gradient, relative size, relative movement, and *accommodation (2).*

moral development The aspect of *human development* that involves learning the rules of the social *group* and the world at large; it takes place primarily during childhood, and it may occur in three stages: *preconventional morality, conventional morality, postconventional morality.*

morpheme The smallest meaningful unit in a language, usually composed of several *phonemes.* The word *nail* is a morpheme. Words often consist of several morphemes, and many morphemes function only in the context of another morpheme. The word *nails* has two morphemes: the noun *nail* and the suffix *s.*

motivated forgetting A type of *forgetting* in which the full *memory* is presumably available, but the individual does not want to remember; it is a *retrieval* failure produced by an unconscious effort to forget, called *repression.*

motivation Activation from within the organism; an internal state, or *drive,* that energizes and directs behavior. Types of motives include: *primary motives, secondary motives.*

motivational hierarchy A *humanistic viewpoint* stating that human motives exist in a certain order or rank, with the most fundamental, biological motives at the bottom, and psychological

motives, usually of less immediate importance, near the top. Abraham Maslow's original motivational hierarchy described five levels of *motivation:* physiological needs, safety, love and belonging, self-esteem, *self-actualization.* His revised theory proposed two more levels, just before self-actualization: cognitive motives and aesthetic motives.

motor cortex One of the major areas of the *cerebral cortex;* it is a narrow strip at the rear of the *frontal lobes.* The motor cortex is the primary area for controlling body movements.

motor neuron A *neuron* that transmits impulses from the *central nervous system* to the *effectors*—muscles and glands, enabling the organism to initiate actions and to create effects.

MRI scan Magnetic resonance imaging scan. A cross-sectional image of the *brain;* also the process of producing the image, in which an intense magnetic field is used to generate several views of the brain, which are then combined and analyzed by a computer.

multicultural awareness In *social cognition,* a sensitivity to and acceptance of differences among *groups* and subgroups, regarding them as equally viable approaches to human *culture.*

multifactor studies Research projects that examine two or more *independent variables* together. Interest in multifactor studies lies in their greater efficiency than the *classical experiment* and also in the capacity to discover what happens when two or more factors are combined.

multimodal approach The combination of several *theories* or viewpoints in studying a given circumstance; in *therapy,* the combined use of several treatment methods.

multiple bases of behavior The premise that behavior is typically influenced by many factors, both within and outside the individual, often interacting with one another.

multiple intelligences A *psychometric approach* to *intelligence* that addresses the broad spectrum of human abilities. This approach identifies seven kinds of intelligence: linguistic, logical-mathematical, spatial, musical, bodily-kinesthetic, interpersonal, intrapersonal.

myelin sheath (mye´-uh-lun) A white, fatty substance covering certain *axons,* serving chiefly to insulate one axon from the electrical activities of other axons. It prevents interference among adjacent *neurons* and also speeds the transmission of the impulse.

myotonia (mye-uh-toe'-nee-uh) Contractions of the muscles throughout the body; during sexual arousal, it includes involuntary spasms in the genital areas.

narcissistic personality disorder A *personality disorder* involving exaggerated self-importance. Like the Greek mythical character Narcissus, who fell in love with his own image, individuals with this condition are intensely preoccupied with themselves. Unable to take the perspective of another person, they expect special treatment and recognition without showing mutual respect.

narcolepsy A severe form of the sleep disorder hypersomnia, which is the inability to stay awake. A narcoleptic individual undergoes sudden uncontrollable episodes of falling asleep.

natural body therapies Methods of *biomedical therapy* that utilize the body's innate tendency to recover and achieve a balanced state, or *homeostasis,* chiefly through normal daily activities: physical exercise, massage and muscular therapy, programs of nutrition, rest and relaxation, and so forth. One such method is the *sensate focus,* used to treat certain sexual problems.

naturalistic observation A *research* method in which behavior is studied in its usual setting, without questioning or testing the subjects. Forms of observation include: *covert observation, nonparticipant observation, overt observation, participant observation.*

nature-nurture issue See *heredity-environment issue.*

need Any biochemical requirement for an organisms optimal *adjustment.* An unsatisfied need causes an imbalance, giving rise to a *drive.*

negative correlation See *correlation.*

negative reinforcement The disappearance of an aversive event. Following a *response,* any outcome that increases the probability of that response by preventing or terminating an aversive *stimulus,* such as a spanking, a parking ticket, or confinement. Negative *reinforcement* is not a negative event, but instead the *removal* of a negative event. Therefore, it is not *punishment,* for punishment *is* a negative event.

negative symptoms Behavioral deficits associated with *schizophrenia:* loss of interest in the world, absence of emotional expression, inattention, lack of speech.

negatively skewed distribution See *skewed distribution.*

nervous system A coordinating network that regulates internal activities and responds to external stimulation, transmitting information throughout the body. It is the major integrating *system* in animals and human beings, consisting of the *brain, spinal cord,* and numerous *neurons.* The two primary divisions of the human nervous system are the *central nervous system* and *peripheral nervous system.*

network of associations A method of *storage* of *long-term memory,* usually employed with *semantic memory,* emphasizing that ideas are connected to one another in patterns, chains, or pathways. During *retrieval* of the information, remembering one idea leads to remembering another, which in turn leads to remembering the next, and so forth.

neural coding The ways in which neural impulses are distributed throughout different areas of the *brain.*

neuron The basic element of the human *nervous system,* a simple cell specialized for transmitting electrochemical messages. Commonly called a nerve, it is composed of a *cell body* and two types of fibers called *axons* and *dendrites.* Types of neurons include: *interneuron, motor neuron, sensory neuron.*

neuropsychology A broad *biological approach* emphasizing the role of the *nervous system* in relation to behavior and experience.

neurosis A condition involving a wide variety of symptoms emphasizing *anxiety,* bodily disorders, and compulsive behavior. Except in traditional *psychoanalysis,* this term has been largely abandoned, chiefly because it is too broad, lacking a clear definition.

neurotransmitter substance Any chemical that is discharged into a *synapse,* acting on the membrane of an adjacent *neuron* in either an excitatory or inhibitory manner. Important neurotransmitters include: *acetylcholine, dopamine, GABA, norepinephrine, serotonin.*

nocturnal myoclonia (mye-uh-kloe'-nee-uh) A pronounced muscle spasm, much more than a twitch, that occurs during the *hypnagogic state.* Also called a hypnagogic jerk, it is sometimes so violent that it awakens the individual for a brief, painful instant.

nominal fallacy The erroneous belief that giving something a name constitutes an explanation for it.

nomothetic research (noe-muh-thed'-ik) Studies attempting to discover general laws of behavior, applicable to all human beings in varying degrees.

nonauditory labyrinth The delicate, mazelike structure in the *inner ear* that is not related to hearing; it is filled with fluid and has two types of chambers—*semicircular canals* and the *vestibular system*—concerned with *passive motion* and the *sense of balance.*

nonparticipant observation A form of *naturalistic observation* in which the investigator merely observes. He or she does not live with, work with, or otherwise join the subjects being studied.

norepinephrine (nor-ep-uh-nef'-reen) A *neurotransmitter substance,* also called noradrenaline, that affects general arousal, *emotion, learning,* and *memory* by producing excitatory reactions at *synapses* for the heart, blood vessels, and genitals. It promotes an alert, active state and can result in a highly pleasurable reaction.

normal distribution In *descriptive statistics,* a symmetrical distribution with moderate variation among the scores, represented graphically as a bell-shaped curve. Whenever it occurs, the three *measures of central tendency* all have the same value.

norms Test scores or other data that serve as standards or guidelines for interpreting the performance of an individual who has completed the same task. They serve as reference points for determining what is common or rare for a given group.

novel stimulation See *desire for novel stimulation.*

obedience A yielding to *social influence* in which an individual responds to a demand, not simply a request, to behave in a certain way; the conditions are not negotiable.

object permanence The understanding that an object may continue to exist even when it is not directly available to the senses. It is one of the accomplishments that mark the end of the *sensorimotor period,* the transition from infancy to childhood, and the beginning of thinking.

object-relations theory A *psychodynamic theory* that concentrates on the first two years of life, especially the baby's relationship with the primary caretaker. From the baby's immature, naive perspective, the caretaker is not a parent or even a person but an object that intermittently appears and disappears. In this viewpoint, the first object in one's life, usually the mother, is crucial in *personality* development.

obliteration theory A view of *forgetting* as a *storage* failure based upon sudden destruction of the *memory* *trace,* presumably in its formative stages. The trace needs time to become firmly fixed, and certain events occurring soon after an experience can eradicate the trace before it becomes permanent.

observational learning In *social learning theory,* a form of *learning* in which an individual develops or changes behavior simply by observing the behavior of others, without *reinforcement.* This process is called *modeling.*

obsessive-compulsive disorder An *anxiety* disorder in which the individual engages in some persistent yet useless thought or action, consuming more than an hour daily. The recurrent thought is called an obsession. A recurrent act is known as a compulsion.

occipital lobes One of four divisions of the hemispheres of the *cerebral cortex,* the lobes located at the extreme back of the *brain;* they process visual information.

Oedipus complex (ed′-uh-pus) A condition in which a son regards his father as a rival and seeks sexual intimacy with his mother, arising during the *phallic stage* and managed through the process of *identification* with the father. See *Electra complex.*

olfactory epithelium A thin layer of tissue at the top of the nasal cavity; it contains long threadlike structures that are the *receptors* for *olfactory sensitivity.*

olfactory sensitivity One of the five *traditional senses;* the experience of smell; responsiveness to gaseous chemical energy.

one-trial conditioning An instance of *classical conditioning* in which a *conditioned response* develops through just a single pairing of a neutral *stimulus* with an *unconditioned stimulus.*

one-word stage In language development, the phase during which the individual first uses labels for things. It appears about the twelfth month of normal human infancy.

operant behavior Voluntary behavior by which an organism operates on its environment: running, writing, hiding, speaking, and so forth. Such behaviors are not inborn, but learned, chiefly through their consequences. The process of modifying operant behavior is called *operant conditioning.*

operant conditioning The process of association by which an organism learns to respond to its environment in accordance with the consequences of that behavior. Behavior, from the standpoint of operant *conditioning,* follows the *reinforcement principle.* The association is between a response and reinforcement.

operant learning Basically, *operant conditioning,* stressing that what happens in the environment is *the* critical factor in *learning.* It involves directly observable events—overt behavior and its consequences—and therefore is also called the behavioristic or behavioral view.

operant response Some voluntary *response* that has an effect on the environment.

operational definition A description of something in highly explicit, usually quantifiable terms. It indicates the specific procedures by which something is measured or otherwise clearly defined.

opiates Drugs, classified as *depressants,* that come from the opium poppy and include not only opium but also its derivatives, morphine and heroin. They are also called narcotics because they can produce not only a rush of pleasure but also a sleeplike state.

opponent-process theory A view that opposing forces stimulate one another. (1) In *emotion,* the view postulating that arousal of one set of feelings automatically initiates arousal of the opposite feelings, which appear later. (2) In *visual sensitivity,* the view of color vision postulating three different pairs of *receptor* mechanisms, with the members of each pair working in opposition: red-green, yellow-blue, black-white. Excitation of one *hue* in a pair stimulates excitation of the other.

optic nerve Nerve fibers that carry impulses for *visual sensitivity* from the *retina* of the eye to the *brain.*

oral stage In *psychoanalysis,* the first of five *psychosexual stages;* it occurs in the first year of infancy, during which the chief sexual pleasure is derived from stimulation of the mouth.

organ In biology, a distinct and specific body part, specialized to perform a particular function. The *sense organs* are concerned with the intake of information. Other organs are concerned with output, such as the muscles; they are called *effectors.* Still others, such as the *brain,* are concerned with activities within the body, including management of information, maintenance, and integration functions.

osmoreceptors Certain *receptors* in the *hypothalamus* that signal the passage of fluids through membranes, a process known as osmosis. They are sensitive to angiotensin, a chemical agent in the blood that indicates *cellular dehydration* and therefore signals thirst.

ossicles Three small bones of the *middle ear,* called the hammer, anvil, and stirrup. In *auditory sensitivity,* the vibrations of sound from the *eardrum* pass through these bones in succession, each one pressing on the next; the stirrup, in turn, presses against the *oval window.*

outer ear One of the three regions of the human ear; it is comprised of mechanisms for *auditory sensitivity:* the folds of skin outside the head, the auditory canal, and the *eardrum.*

ova The reproductive cells in the female, produced by the *ovaries.*

oval window The beginning of the *inner ear,* located adjacent to the stirrup in the *middle ear.* The vibrations of the oval window activate the *receptors* for *auditory sensitivity.*

ovaries The *gonads,* or sex glands, in the female, which produce *ova.* They also produce sex *hormones,* primarily *estrogens.*

overattribution effect See *attribution theory.*

overt observation A form of *naturalistic observation* in which the subjects are aware that they are being studied; the research purpose is acknowledged.

parallel distributed processing A form of *information processing* in which various mental operations are performed simultaneously. See *serial processing.*

paraphilia Sexual attraction to an object or event not normally associated with sexual arousal. Sexual attraction to a physical object is called a *fetishism;* other paraphilic sexual behaviors include masochism and sadism.

parasympathetic nervous system One of two subdivisions of the *autonomic nervous system;* it becomes dominant in ordinary states, providing for normal body functioning and the conservation of energy. It acts as a routine system, reversing the changes that occur during arousal: the heart rate and breathing become more normal, digestion begins again in the stomach, saliva reappears in the mouth, and so forth.

parietal lobes One of four divisions of the hemispheres of the *cerebral cortex,* the lobes located at the top and back of the *brain;* they are concerned with body feeling, or *somesthesis.*

Parkinson's disease A disease of the *nervous system* characterized by muscular tremors, rigidity, and loss of voluntary control, resulting in slowness and inability to move. It occurs primarily in men during old age.

partial reinforcement In *operant conditioning,* intermittent *reinforcement,* in which some correct *responses* are reinforced and some are not reinforced.

partial-reinforcement effect In *operant conditioning,* resistance to *extinction* after *partial reinforcement,* especially on a variable schedule.

participant observation A form of *naturalistic observation* in which an investigator joins the people being studied and takes part in their activities.

passionate love An intense form of *love,* in which the partner is perceived in an idealized form, often with the expectation of complete, lasting fulfillment. A potent factor in passionate love is sexual attraction. Also called erotic or romantic love, it is less realistic than *companionate love.*

passive motion The *proprioceptive sense* that occurs whenever an individual is traveling from one place to another but not actively moving, such as in elevators and automobiles. It can be rotary or linear, mediated by the *semicircular canals* and *vestibular system,* respectively.

paternal behavior Care of the young by the father. It lacks the physiological influences associated with *maternal behavior* and is less predictable.

pathological gambling A persistent tendency to take risks with money, leaving the outcome to chance. It is an impulse-control disorder; the individual cannot resist this urge.

pattern theory A view of *gustatory sensitivity* postulating that the taste conveyed by any given fiber depends on the activity in other fibers.

pecking order A dominance hierarchy within a *group;* it is a form of *status.*

peer model See *modeling.*

peg-word system A *mnemonic device* that employs a catchy jingle or simple poem. The rhyming words are used as pegs or cues for recall of the items to be memorized.

perception The process by which organisms select, organize, and interpret *stimuli,* combining sensory information with prior *learning.* The experience of *sensation* is a more basic, direct experience; perception, which includes *memory,* is a higher level *cognitive process.*

perceptual constancy The aspect of *perception* in which objects are recognized under differing conditions of stimulation. Types of perceptual constancy include: *brightness constancy, color constancy, shape constancy, size constancy.*

perceptual egocentrism A form of *egocentrism,* most pronounced during the *preoperational period,* in which children do not realize that other people perceive things from a viewpoint which is different from theirs.

perceptual grouping The form of *primitive organization* in which the parts of a figure are perceived according to various patterns, depending upon their specific properties. Parts are grouped according to the *principle of closure, principle of good continuity, principle of proximity,* or *principle of similarity.*

perceptual set See *set.*

peripheral nervous system Almost all of the nerves outside the *brain* and *spinal cord.* One of the two primary divisions of the human *nervous system,* it serves to transmit messages to and from the other primary division, the *central nervous system.* The peripheral nervous system is in turn divided into the *autonomic nervous system* and *somatic nervous system.*

personal documents Journals, tapes, letters, diaries, essays, pictures, poetry, and so forth. They can serve as a means for psychological assessment of the owner or composer.

personality The characteristic and unique ways in which an individual responds to his or her environment. The study of consistent patterns of behavior, emphasizing *individual differences.*

personality disorder A persistent and inflexible pattern of behavior that deviates from *social norms;* if it remains stable over the years, it results in distress or impairment. People with this form of *mental illness* are recognized for the problems they cause others, rather than for their own sense of discomfort. Types of personality disorders include: *antisocial, borderline, narcissistic.*

personality inventory A printed form containing a series of statements, questions, or adjectives about human behavior. In this type of *personality test,* the person simply indicates whether the items apply in his or her experience. Two popular inventories are the *California Personality Inventory* and *Minnesota Multiphasic Personality Inventory.*

personality test A set of questions or other materials used to measure the enduring characteristics of any individual, including habits, motives, interests, thoughts, feelings, attitudes, values, and personal style. Types of tests and other items used to assess *personality* include: *personal documents, personality inventory, projective technique, situational test.*

personality traits Long-standing personal dispositions that describe an individual's *personality* in terms of specific, relatively enduring characteristics, not necessarily permanent. A given trait is classified as either a *basic trait* or *subtrait.*

person-centered approach The *humanistic viewpoint* of Carl Rogers, stressing *free will* and the *actualizing tendency,* which involves the role each individual plays in shaping his or her own destiny. Emphasis is given to each individual's capacity for determining his or her own life and making decisions about it, based on that person's unique view of the world.

person-centered therapy A prominent form of *humanistic therapy* in which the individual is considered capable of solving his or her own problems and therefore of determining the course of treatment. The counselor provides a favorable atmosphere for releasing the person's capacity for growth, self-understanding, and self-management that is, for *self-actualization.*

PET scan Positron emission tomography scan (tuh-mäg′-ruh-fee). A cross-sectional image of the *brain* at work; also the process of producing the image, in which the subject ingests a glucose compound utilized in the brain, then engages in various activities. The brain areas most activated utilize the most glucose, revealing the function in which they are involved.

phallic stage In *psychoanalysis,* the third of five *psychosexual stages;* it occurs in childhood from age three through age six, during which the child discovers pleasures associated with the genitalia, including various forms of masturbation. Freud applied this term to both sexes. There is also an emerging interest in the parent of the opposite sex.

phenotype The observable trait resulting from a particular set of *genes,* called the *genotype.* For example, when the phenotype is blue eyes, the genotype is designated *bb.*

phenylketonuria (PKU) (feen′-l-kee-tuh-noo′-ree-uh) An inherited form of *mental retardation* transmitted by a *recessive gene* in both parents, in which a substance called phenylpyruvic acid interferes with *brain* functioning.

pheromones Odorous substances that serve a communication function among members of the same species and sometimes even between species. Animal pheromones provide signals about sexual readiness, food sources, territorial boundaries, and so forth.

phi phenomenon The *perception* of movement suggested by a rapid sequence of slightly different still images, as in the advertising *illusion* of a lighted neon arrow that seems to move when there are in reality two or several arrows, each in a different location, going on and off alternately.

phobia See *specific phobia.*

phoneme The smallest functional sound unit in any language. There are about 40 phonemes in English. The word *must* has four phonemes—*m, u, s,* and *t,* but the word *time* has only three—*t, i,* and *m.* Phonemes are used to compose units of meaning called *morphemes.*

physical development The aspect of *human development* that involves the growth of all structures of the body, including the *organs* and *systems* that enable the individual to respond to the environment.

pituitary gland A pea-sized *endocrine* gland located just below the center of the *brain,* attached to the *hypothalamus.* Called the master gland, it secretes a variety of *hormones,* including *prolactin,* and influences the secretions of several other endocrine glands.

place theory A view of *auditory sensitivity* postulating that different frequencies of vibration arouse different regions of hair cells on the *basilar membrane,* and the resulting impulses go to different regions of the auditory cortex. Pitch depends on the place in the membrane that is most activated and also the place in the auditory cortex receiving the resulting neural impulses.

placebo (pluh-see′-boe) An object or event without any intrinsic value used to control subjects' expectations in research. In an experiment, this pill or other treatment gives the subjects in the *control condition* the same expectation, or *set,* as those in the *experimental condition,* receiving the real treatment, presumably with therapeutic or other properties

pleasure principle The basis of operation of the *id,* requiring immediate gratification of a biological *need,* regardless of the circumstances.

point estimation In *inferential statistics,* a method by which a mean or other score obtained with a *sample* is used to estimate the probability of obtaining the same score with the *population.*

polarized See *resting potential.*

polygenic trait A characteristic that has been influenced by multiple pairs of *genes.* It therefore appears in varying degrees or forms, as in physique or mental ability.

polygraph An instrument that measures several physiological *responses* simultaneously, including heart rate, breathing rate, blood pressure, and skin conductance, called the *galvanic skin response.* It is sometimes called a lie detector because these responses change under emotional arousal and it is assumed that a person who is lying is highly aroused.

population All possible cases in any particular class or category. In *inferential statistics,* data obtained from a *sample* are used to estimate characteristics of the population.

positive correlation See *correlation.*

positive reinforcement Following a *response,* any outcome that increases the probability of a recurrence of that response; a satisfier, a *stimulus* such as food, a smile, or a good grade. The term *reinforcement* without a modifier generally refers to positive reinforcement.

positive symptoms Behavioral excesses associated with *schizophrenia:* hallucinations, delusions, incoherent speech, aggressive behavior.

positively skewed distribution See *skewed distribution.*

postconventional morality Kohlberg's third and final major stage of *moral development,* beginning around age 13, if entered at all, during which the individual becomes aware of independent moral principles, recognizing the almost inevitable conflict of interests within a large group, and understands the relativism of personal standards. Moral judgment is based on the concepts of human rights and the dignity of people as individuals.

posttraumatic stress disorder An *anxiety* disorder in which the individual re-experiences a severely disturbing event. It is initiated by some reminder of the original incident.

pragmatics The relationships between language and its users; the work that language does in a particular situation. For example, the choice of words often depends on the context; formal and informal settings may call for different language to convey the same point.

preconventional morality The first of Kohlberg's three major stages of *moral development,* from age four or five to around age ten, during which the individual considers misbehavior in terms of the amount of damage someone does or the amount of *punishment* the person receives. Moral judgment is based on the physical consequences of an act.

predictive validity A form of *validity* that makes a statement about the future. A test with high predictive validity accurately forecasts the performance of subjects at a later date, after they have received some form of training or other preparation.

prejudice In *social cognition,* a belief about something or some members of a *group,* developed without objective evaluation. In this type of *bias,* the topic in question has been prejudged.

preoperational period The second of Piaget's four stages of *cognitive development;* it appears in childhood from approximately 18–24 months of age to the sixth or seventh year, during which children can represent things to themselves but cannot readily understand the use of symbols, perform logical manipulations, or change the direction of their thinking.

preventive mental health An approach to *mental health* emphasizing that many mental disorders can be avoided by identifying and meeting the needs of the individual before or during stressful events.

primacy effect In the *retrieval* of a *memory,* the serial position effect in which items at the beginning of a series are better remembered than items in the middle of the series.

primary motives The biological urges directly related to the organism's survival, arising from biological *needs* and prompting it to seek food, water, and other necessities for life. Also called survival motives or basic motives.

primary reinforcement A reinforcer that satisfies a necessity of life; *reinforcement* that satisfies some inborn, physiological *need.*

primitive organization Those aspects of *perception* that are determined by the fundamental, inborn characteristics of the *sense organs* and *nervous system.* Two forms of primitive organization are the *figure-ground relationship* and *perceptual grouping.*

principle of closure The tendency in *perceptual grouping* to make assumptions about the undetected parts of a partially perceived *stimulus.* A person standing partly behind a tree is still perceived as a human being, provided enough of the person is visible.

principle of good continuity The tendency in *perceptual grouping* to perceive a *stimulus* as continuing in its established direction, making an obvious or "good" figure. When several balloons are clustered together, we decide which contours belong to which balloons on the basis of the natural continuity of the lines.

principle of proximity The tendency in *perceptual grouping* to perceive *stimuli* near one another as belonging together.

principle of similarity The tendency in *perceptual grouping* to perceive *stimuli* that are alike as belonging together.

proactive interference See *interference theory.*

probability The likelihood that a particular event will appear or reappear, as opposed to a different event. See *inferential statistics.*

problem of sensory constancy Lack of *stimulus* change; when there is no significant variation in a particular form of *sensation,* an experience common among prisoners and the elderly. The desire to overcome this problem is a *sensory variation motive.*

problem solving A form of *reasoning* in which some new response, or some new combination of old responses, provides an answer to a question. The problem-solving process involves depicting the problem, called *framing; decision making;* and following a strategy or *heuristic.*

procedural memory A type of *long-term memory* in which the individual remembers how to do something, how to perform some act, physical or mental.

productive mode An awareness that involves concerted mental activity, setting goals and developing procedures for achieving them. This type of *consciousness* involves both short-term and long-term planning.

projection A thrusting outward. A *defense mechanism* in which the individual attributes unacceptable thoughts, feelings, or behavior to someone else. More broadly, the *perception* of one's own traits or underlying concerns in other, typically unstructured stimuli.

projective technique A *personality test* employing incomplete sentences, inkblots, or other ambiguous *stimuli.* It is assumed that the subject's *responses* to vague stimuli will reveal, through the process of *projection,* his or her underlying feelings, desires, fears, and so forth. Projective techniques include the *Rorschach inkblots* and *Thematic Apperception Test.*

prolactin (proe-lak′-tun) A *hormone* secreted by the *pituitary gland* that plays a crucial role in *maternal behavior,* especially in animals, including nesting and the production of milk.

propositional mode A way of thinking based on a symbol that makes a declaration, usually in words. It proposes or asserts something by using language. Different from the *imaginal mode.*

proprioceptive senses The modes of *sensation* that provide information about conditions within the body: *kinesthesis, passive motion, sense of balance, visceral sensitivity.*

prototype-based approach One of two chief methods of *concept* formation; it begins with a good example of the concept and then compares each new instance with this example. If the match is close, the new instance is assumed to be an instance of the concept. A chair is a good example of the concept of furniture.

proximal stimulus A *stimulus* as it occurs at the *receptors,* such as the light waves at the *retina.*

proximity See *principle of proximity.*

proximodistal development (präk′-suh-moe-diss′-tul) In *physical development,* growth from near to far, from center to extremities, especially prominent in the prenatal phase and early infancy in vertebrates.

psychoactive substance Any drug that produces an *altered state of consciousness.* Some of these drugs are also used in *biomedical therapy;* others are used only for the altered state they produce, sometimes so violent that unprescribed use is illegal. They include: *depressants, hallucinogens, stimulants.*

psychoanalysis A *system of psychology* and theory of *personality,* originating with Sigmund Freud, that focuses upon *unconscious motivation* and internal *conflict,* usually from childhood. Also, a form of *insight therapy* aimed at resolving these conflicts, chiefly through three processes: *free association, interpretation,* and *transference.* Adaptations of psychoanalysis are referred to as *psychodynamic theory.*

psychodynamic theory Any modification of *psychoanalysis* that emphasizes *unconscious motivation* but not in the traditional manner. Psychodynamic perspectives, while recognizing the significance of the individual's past experiences, place more stress on current *interpersonal* relationships.

psychology The *science* of human and animal behavior, experience, and mental processes. Its goals are to under-stand why organisms behave, feel, and think as they do, called *basic research,* and to apply this knowledge in diverse situations, called *applied psychology.*

psychometric approach The study of *intelligence* through measurements of mental characteristics. Also called the factorial approach, it aims to identify the discrete factors of intelligence. In contrast to the *cognitive approach,* the focus is more on test scores than on thought processes.

psychophysiological disorder Physical illness or disease that is caused or increased by psychological *stress.*

psychosexual stages In *psychoanalysis,* a series of five phases in psychological development as it is influenced by unfolding sexual interests. The *personality* develops in accordance with these experiences, affecting *interpersonal* relationships at each stage. In sexual development, broadly defined to include sensual as well as explicitly sexual experiences, there is a predictable sequence: *oral stage, anal stage, phallic stage, latency stage, genital stage.*

psychosocial stages Eight phases of *social development,* identified by Erik Erikson, involving many aspects of psychological and social functioning that are interrelated and show consistent changes throughout the life cycle: *trust versus mistrust, autonomy versus doubt, initiative versus guilt, industry versus inferiority, identity versus role diffusion, intimacy versus isolation, generativity versus stagnation, integrity versus despair.* In this *psychodynamic theory* each stage focuses on a specific crisis in *interpersonal* relationships.

psychotherapy Loosely, any of several forms of *therapy* for mental and physical disorders. Originally, what is now called *insight therapy.*

psychotic disorder A form of *mental illness* involving a distortion of reality. It is a very serious, highly incapacitating state, including delusions, hallucinations, and other fundamental disturbances; *schizophrenia* is a psychotic disorder.

puberty The beginning of reproductive capacity, which is a characteristic of *adolescence.* In human *physical development,* it occurs with the onset of menstruation in females, sometime after age 11 or so, and the presence of *sperm* cells in males, one or two years later.

punishment Following a *response,* any outcome that decreases the probability of a recurrence of that response. Punishment is not *negative reinforce-*

ment; it is the opposite of *any* type of *reinforcement,* which supports a response rather than weakens it.

pupillary opening The aperture in the *iris* of the eye, which varies in size automatically, depending partly upon the amount of light available.

questionnaire A printed form with questions of all sorts, often administered by mail or telephone, sometimes in a direct interview. The primary tool of the *survey method,* it is intended to be answered by many people.

random sample In *inferential statistics,* a *sample* in which every person or item in the *population* has an equal chance of being included, often achieved by assigning random numbers.

range In *descriptive statistics,* one of the *measures of variability;* it indicates the difference between the lowest score and highest score in a group of scores.

rape A violent act of sex and *aggression,* based on physical assault or threats of harm. One form of rape, called date rape, involves acquaintances, not strangers.

rapid eye movements (REMs) Quick motions of the eyes associated with deep sleep, in which the eyes dart in one direction and another, in coordinated fashion, under the closed lids. During REM sleep, breathing becomes heavy and irregular, blood pressure increases, muscles begin twitching, and *dreams* are most common.

rational-emotive therapy A form of *cognitive therapy* emphasizing that irrational thinking causes disruption of *emotions.* The treatment is to educate the person in rational thinking.

rationalization A *defense mechanism* in which the individual is not only unaware of repressed thoughts but also substitutes false reasons for real ones.

raw scores In *descriptive statistics,* original scores, just as they have been obtained from measurement, not yet submitted to any statistical analysis.

reaction formation A *defense mechanism* in which the individual adopts attitudes and behaviors that are the opposite of those judged to be unacceptable.

reaction range In *behavioral genetics,* the genetically based limit or range of an inherited capacity; in turn, development within that range depends upon the environment. For example, individuals raised in a favorable environment should develop near the peak of their intellectual reaction range; those in less fortunate circumstances should reach a lower point.

reality principle The basis of operation for the *ego,* involving the capacity to delay gratification—to suspend the *pleasure principle*—in order to avoid an unpleasant or to obtain a more pleasant outcome later.

reappearance hypothesis A view postulating that a full *memory* will appear whenever the *memory trace* is properly stimulated. There is no memory loss; the complete experience is retained, somehow filed away in static fashion, waiting to be aroused.

reasoning The logical manipulation of *concepts.* In contrast to *fantasy* and *free association,* it is controlled thinking. A very broad concept, it is sometimes synonymous with *cognition* itself.

recall One of three methods of measurement of a *memory;* in recall, the individual reproduces information with no significant prompts or cues. In cued recall, known as *redintegration,* retrieval relies on *cuing.*

recency effect In the *retrieval* of a *memory,* the serial position effect in which items at the end of a series are better remembered than items in the middle of the series.

receptors Highly specialized *neurons* within the *sense organs,* sensitive to specific types of physical stimulation, converting it to neural impulses.

recessive gene A *gene* that does not take precedence over the other member of its pair for a given trait. A recessive trait is manifested only when both genes are of the recessive type; it is not manifested when one gene is a *dominant gene.*

reciprocal conditioning An *operant conditioning* situation in which the *response* of one individual supports the response of the other, and vice versa. Each individual's behavior provides *reinforcement* for the other's behavior, affecting the overall *interpersonal* relationship.

reciprocal determinism In *social learning theory,* the principle stating that mental functions, overt behavior, and environmental factors all influence one another in an interlocking system. Each element partly determines and is determined by the others. The human *personality,* in this approach, is not one of complete *free will* or complete *determinism,* but involves both.

recognition One of three methods of measurement of a *memory;* in recognition, the previously encountered object or event is selected from among others not previously experienced.

reconstruction hypothesis A view postulating that memories are not fixed images but rather reconstructions. A *memory trace* is a partial residue from the past, and a current *memory* is assembled from such bits and pieces of experience.

redintegration (ree-dint-uh-gray'-shun) Cued *recall,* in which prompts are given to make *retrieval* of a *memory* easier.

reflective mode An awareness that involves relaxation, enjoyment of one's own daydreaming, or simply an openness to the environment, responding to it as a recipient, rather than a performer. This type of *consciousness* is largely unfocused and unrestrained.

reflex A simple, unlearned *response,* usually involving some specific part of the body, as when a puff of air causes an eyeblink or a spray of cold water creates goose pimples.

reflex arc The simple connection between a *sensory neuron* and *motor neurons* comprising the basic pattern of the spinal *reflex.*

refractory period A waiting or restoration period necessary before a nerve fiber is ready to respond to another impulse.

reframing Viewing, or *framing,* a problem differently, also called *restructuring.* In reframing as a strategy for *stress* reduction, the individual thinks about the problem in a new way, viewing it as more tolerable, a temporary disruption, or a good learning experience.

regression Engaging in behavior that was satisfying or more appropriate at an earlier stage of development.

rehearsal The process of repeating or practicing new information, covertly or overtly, as an aid to *encoding* a *memory.* Rehearsal keeps the material available until it can be used or stored.

reinforcement In the *conditioning* process, any outcome that follows a *response* and increases the probability of a recurrence of that response.

reinforcement principle The guiding rule of *operant conditioning,* formerly called the law of effect, which states that the probability of any given *response* is a function of the consequences of that behavior. In *operant behavior,* responses resulting in *reinforcement* tend to be repeated; those not supported by the environment tend to be discarded.

reinforcing stimulus In *operant conditioning,* a *stimulus* that results in *reinforcement* for a given *response,* increasing the likelihood of that response being repeated.

relearning One of three methods of measurement of a *memory;* in relearning, the individual learns a task again to the original level of success and the *savings score* reveals the amount of memory.

releaser Any external *stimulus* that initiates an *instinct.*

reliability Consistency, repeatability. The extent of *correlation* among scores from tests conducted under comparable conditions. Types of reliability include: *equivalent-form reliability, interjudge reliability, test-retest reliability.*

REM rebound effect A phenomenon that results when a person is deprived of REM sleep—during which *dreams* occur—and later compensates by dreaming more than usual.

REMs See *rapid eye movements.*

replicating the result The third and final step in the *scientific method;* in this step, an investigation is repeated and the finding re-examined to confirm its presence. The essence of a scientific finding, according to many authorities, is that the same result is obtained over and over again in every repetition of the original research.

representative heuristic Any *heuristic,* or strategy for *problem solving,* that is determined by the similarity between the new problem and a good model for a certain category of problems. If the new problem appears to fit that category, the representative solution—the one that worked previously—is attempted.

representative sample In *inferential statistics,* a *sample* that accurately depicts the characteristics of the *population* from which it has been selected. A *random sample* is more likely to be representative than is an *incidental sample.*

repression The fundamental *defense mechanism;* it is a form of *motivated forgetting* by which unpleasant thoughts are unconsciously excluded from awareness.

research See *basic research, idiographic research, nomothetic research.*

resistance Opposition. (1) In physiology, the second of three phases in the *general adaptation syndrome;* it is the organism's *response* of sustained defense against *stress,* requiring much energy. (2) In *therapy,* any interference with the progress of treatment by the patient.

respondent behavior Any involuntary *response;* behavior that is automatically elicited by a specific *stimulus,* such as shivering in response to cold; a *reflex* is the simplest form of respondent behavior. Such behaviors are inborn, not learned.

response Any activity or event resulting from a *stimulus.*

response bias A predetermined tendency to react in a certain way; a reaction that is influenced by factors apart from the stimulating condition.

response strategies In *psychodynamic theory,* three methods by which human beings can cope with their *basic anxiety* regarding *interpersonal* relationships: moving toward people, moving against people, moving away from people.

resting potential The unactivated state of a nerve fiber, without stimulation. It awaits a *stimulus* of certain minimum intensity, called the *absolute threshold,* to activate the fiber. In this resting state, the fiber is said to be polarized because it has opposite poles or charges on either side of the cell membrane.

restoration theory A *biological approach* to sleep, postulating that it allows the body to replace biochemical and other factors depleted by the day's activities. See *adaptation theory.*

restructuring Thinking in which the basic elements in a particular situation are rearranged, providing it with a different meaning. Also called *reframing,* it is a shift in thought that provides a novel solution to a problem. Restructuring is an integral part of *creative thinking* and humor.

reticular activating system (RAS) (ri-tik′-yuh-lur) A *subcortical structure* of the *brain* that influences arousal and plays a prominent role in sleep by ceasing the transmission of certain neural impulses.

retina The light-sensitive surface at the inside rear of the eye that contains the *receptors* for *visual sensitivity,* called *cones* and *rods.*

retrieval The recovery of information or a skill after prior *encoding* and *storage.* Methods of retrieval include: *recall, recognition, relearning.*

retroactive interference See *interference theory.*

retrograde amnesia A loss of *memory* in which the afflicted individual is unable to remember prior experiences; a condition of extensive *forgetting,* often brought on by a traumatic event.

reward In *goal-directed behavior,* obtaining or consuming an *incentive.*

The term reward is often mistaken to mean *reinforcement;* however, *reinforcement* can be positive or negative and, in either case, strengthens a given *response.* In contrast, *punishment* weakens the response.

rods Specialized *receptors* for *visual sensitivity,* located in the *retina* of the eye toward the periphery, that are sensitive only to the brightness of light. They reveal patterns of black, white, and gray, often in extreme peripheral vision, which also serves best for night vision.

role A pattern of behavior expected of a *group* member, typically associated with a certain *status.* Two important roles in most groups are *social specialist* and *task specialist.*

role enactment A theory of *hypnosis* stressing that the hypnotized individual is trying to fill a *role.* According to this social viewpoint, the hypnotized person is behaving like a "good subject." See *dissociation view.*

Rorschach inkblots (roar′-shäk) A *projective technique,* named after Hermann Rorschach, using ten cards, each containing a black or colored inkblot. The subject is asked to state what he or she sees in the blots, purposely selected because they do not depict anything in particular.

rule of one variable In a *classical experiment,* the practice of studying only one *variable* at a time. Just one factor is manipulated at any given moment, in order to determine its influence.

saccadic movements (sa-käd′-ik) Tiny involuntary eye movements that occur whenever we look at the world. Seemingly related to the *sensory variation motive,* they take place several times per second, moving the image onto the *fovea,* which gives the clearest vision.

sample In *inferential statistics,* a portion of all possible subjects from a *population.* Types of samples include: *incidental sample, random sample, representative sample.*

savings score In *relearning,* the amount of effort saved from the original *learning;* if relearning is easier, the individual demonstrates *memory,* presumably because a *memory trace* remains.

scattergram In *correlational statistics,* a *graph* plotted on a horizontal axis and vertical axis showing the relationship between two sets of scores, indicated by the distribution, or scatter, among plotted points.

schema A method of *storage* of *long-term memory* based on a general pattern or way of organizing information in a particular society. Schemas can be influential during *encoding* as well as *retrieval,* particularly with *episodic memory.*

schizophrenia A *psychotic disorder* that includes any of these symptoms: hallucinations, delusions, disorganized speech, disorganized behavior, lack of responsiveness to the surroundings.

science Knowing or knowledge. More accurately, it means that careful, systematic procedures have been followed in obtaining knowledge. Science is not a particular field of study, like *archeology;* rather, it is a system for making discoveries.

scientific method A process of obtaining verifiable knowledge, characterized by the attitude of demanding evidence, traditionally obtained in three steps: *forming an hypothesis, testing an hypothesis, replicating the result.* The expression "scientific method" can be misleading because there are many such methods.

script A method of *storage* of *long-term memory,* often associated with *procedural memory,* that depicts a typical sequence of events in a particular setting; it may describe how a specific task is accomplished, or it may indicate more general steps in daily life.

secondary motives Learned desires that energize and direct behavior; *motivation* not directly related to survival, such as the *achievement motive* and *desire for affiliation.* They may arise from efforts to satisfy *primary motives,* but they develop through personal and social contacts.

secondary reinforcement A reinforcer that satisfies a learned or acquired need. Money is a good example of secondary *reinforcement;* it does not satisfy any physiological *need* directly.

selective attention The condition of *attending* exclusively to something, focusing upon one aspect of the environment and shutting out others.

self-actualization The highest level of Abraham Maslow's *motivational hierarchy,* involving fulfillment of one's talents and capacities to the utmost and acceptance of oneself. At this level of *motivation,* not readily achieved, the individual is concerned about doing what he or she is best suited or intended to do. In this view, all motivation arises from the *actualizing tendency.*

self-concept The way a person thinks about himself or herself in a global sense. According to cognitive and

humanistic theories especially, it is central to *personality* development, including a person's most important self-feelings and self-attitudes.

self-disclosure In an *interpersonal* relationship, the communication of intimate thoughts, desires, and memories about oneself.

semantic memory A subtype of *declarative memory* involving general ideas and a broad range of information: names, meanings, relationships, and countless other pieces of information. Semantic *memory* does not involve a specific time or place.

semantics In language, the study of meaning in its broadest sense, including the full range of social rules and customs that pertain to meaning.

semicircular canals In the *inner ear,* the part of the *nonauditory labyrinth* responsible for sensitivity to rotary motion, a form of *passive motion.*

sensate focus A *natural body therapy* used to alleviate certain *sexual dysfunctions.* It involves a series of exercises in which partners take turns being the giver and receiver of sensual touching and pleasure—exploring the contours, textures, and odors of the partner's body with no demands for performance. Relaxed closeness is the goal.

sensation The process of becoming aware of a *stimulus;* receiving information from the environment via the *sense organs.* Sensation can be considered in four phases, each performed by different types of structures: *collector mechanisms, receptor* mechanisms, transmission mechanisms (*sensory neurons*), *neural coding* mechanisms.

sensation seeking A preference for novel, thrilling, even dangerous stimulation, such as sky diving or mountain climbing. It may be an extension of the normal *desire for novel stimulation.*

sense of balance The *proprioceptive sense* that maintains the body's position or equilibrium relative to gravity. The mechanism primarily concerned with balance is called the *vestibular system.*

sense organs The eyes, ears, nose, tongue, skin, and other *organs* that provide information about an organism's environment, resulting in *sensation.*

sensorimotor period The first of Piaget's four stages of *cognitive development;* it appears from birth to approximately 18–24 months of age, during which babies do not think in the sense that older children do; they merely sense things and act upon them, eventually acquiring *object permanence.*

sensory constancy See *problem of sensory constancy.*

sensory cortex One of the major areas of the *cerebral cortex;* it is the primary area for receiving incoming information in the process of *sensation.* The primary areas for sight, called the visual cortex, are in the *occipital lobes.* Impulses for hearing are received by the auditory cortex, located chiefly in the *temporal lobes.* The primary area for body feeling, or *somesthesis,* is the somatosensory cortex, at the front of the *parietal lobes.*

sensory memory Momentary, residual information within the *nervous system,* not yet a processed *memory,* not in memory *storage;* it is the first of three phases in the *stage theory of memory.* It is assumed that unanalyzed information in the visual realm lasts for one second or less; in other modes of *sensation,* it may have longer or shorter durations.

sensory neuron A *neuron* that transmits messages to the *central nervous system* from the *sense organs*—eyes, ears, and so forth—enabling the organism to see, hear, and have other experiences.

sensory variation motive A *stimulation motive* in which the individual seeks to alleviate boredom by obtaining some change in stimulation, thus overcoming the *problem of sensory constancy.* When an altogether new form of stimulation is sought, this motive is called the *desire for novel stimulation.*

separation anxiety A form of *anxiety,* appearing in infancy at about six or seven months of age, in which the baby shows great distress upon being away from the parent or caretaker.

serial processing A form of *information processing,* used by most computers, in which directions are followed in sequential fashion. Each bit of information is acted upon separately, one after another. See *parallel distributed processing.*

serotonin (sir-uh-toe'-nun) A *neurotransmitter substance* associated with drowsiness, sleep, and food metabolism. It plays a role in food intake and appetite, especially the ingestion of protein, carbohydrates, and even alcohol.

set A tendency to respond in a predetermined way; an expectancy. A perceptual set is a readiness to perceive something in particular or to perceive it in a particular way.

set point theory A *biological approach* to eating, postulating that the body monitors its normal weight, called a set point, determined by inherited factors and maintained through automatic processes. Over the long term, unless other conditions interfere, human beings adjust their eating habits and energy expenditure to keep the body weight at this point.

sexual dysfunction Any disturbance in the normal sexual *response* cycle, including sexual desire and *psychophysiological* changes. Common sexual problems include erectile difficulties (impotence) and premature ejaculation in men, and orgasmic difficulties (frigidity) in women.

shape constancy A type of *perceptual constancy* in which something is perceived as having the same shape regardless of the perceiver's vantage point. For example, a circle is perceived as circular even when it is viewed from an angle, making the retinal image oval in shape.

shaping An *operant conditioning* procedure for learning complex *responses,* using a step-by-step sequence called successive approximations, in which *reinforcement* is provided for simpler behaviors that will eventually lead to the full response. Each step is slightly more demanding than the prior one, and reinforcement is contingent upon success at that step, then the next, and so forth.

short-term memory (STM) Temporary *storage* of a *memory,* less than 30 seconds, during which the information is ignored, and therefore lost to full memory, or processed, going into more permanent storage. Also called *working memory,* it is the second of three phases in the *stage theory of memory.*

shyness A dimension of *temperament* involving the tendency to feel tension in social situations and therefore withdraw from them.

sibling rivalry In *psychodynamic theory,* competition among brothers and sisters for the parents' love and attention.

side effect Any secondary outcome of a therapeutic treatment, physical or mental, completely unintended, often unpredictable, and usually unwanted.

signal detection theory The view of *sensation* postulating that the detection of stimulation depends not only upon the intensity of the stimulus and sensitivity of the organism but also upon the conditions for making the judgments; *set,* or expectancy, and *motivation* are also involved.

similarity See *principle of similarity.*

simultaneous conditioning A sequence in *classical conditioning* in which the neutral *stimulus* and *unconditioned*

stimulus are present only at the same time.

single-blind design In an experiment, a situation in which the subjects do not know to which group they belong, *or* in which the investigator does not know to which group any subject belongs.

situational attribution See *attribution theory.*

situational test A *personality test* used to predict how a person will behave in a certain context. The individual is assessed in a situation as similar as possible to the setting in which he or she must perform later.

size constancy A type of *perceptual constancy* in which the perceived size of an object does not change a great deal under different viewing conditions. For example, people far away have a smaller retinal image than those closer, but they look about the same size.

skewed distribution In *descriptive statistics,* an asymmetrical distribution with many unusually low scores, called a negatively skewed distribution, or many unusually high scores, called a positively skewed distribution. Whenever it occurs the three *measures of central tendency* provide different indications of the typical score.

sleep apnea A sleep disorder in which an individual awakens briefly several times during the night because breathing is interrupted. The muscles controlling the air passages become relaxed during sleep, and surrounding tissues block the passages; waking restores breathing.

sleepwalking A sleep disorder in which an individual walks around without awakening, sometimes engaging in other activities as well, such as eating, dressing, using the bathroom, and so forth. It typically does *not* occur during the dreaming state.

social cognition Individuals' *perceptions* and *attitudes* regarding other people. It involves the ways in which individuals interpret information about others, their relationships, and social events and institutions.

social development Acquiring the capacity for successful relations with other people.

social facilitation A condition in which *group* members expend more energy and produce more than when working individually. This condition is likely whenever individuals' specific contributions are expected to be acknowledged; otherwise, *social loafing* will occur.

social influence The ways in which people modify one another's behavior or experience, intentionally or otherwise. These actions range from unspoken expectations to explicit demands.

social learning theory A view of *learning* that emphasizes *social cognition* and *cognitive processes.* A central concept in this approach is *observational learning,* by which an individual acquires behavior by observing the behavior of others. Social learning theory in many respects stands in a middle ground between *operant learning* and the *cognitive approach.*

social loafing A condition in which *group* members expend less energy and produce less than when working individually. The output of the individual seems to decrease in proportion to the size of the group or chance of being noticed. See *social facilitation.*

social norms Unstated expectations indicating what behavior is usual or typical in a given *group.* People generally do not wish to violate *norms,* even when there is no direct pressure to behave in any certain way.

social psychology A specialization concerned with the study of individuals in *groups,* specifically the ways in which human beings interact with one another.

social specialist A *group* leader who is the central figure in cohesion and morale. A person in this *role* is also called an expressive leader.

sociobiology A *biological approach* to *motivation* that focuses on *altruism* and sexual behavior. These and certain other social behaviors, even in human beings, are viewed as genetically driven. They are considered to have survival value for the species, if not for the individual.

sociocultural model A view of *mental illness* emphasizing the role of the environment in maladjustment. The value of this model lies in its relevance for *preventive mental health.*

somatic nervous system One of two divisions of the *peripheral nervous system;* it provides motor control and body feeling, or *somesthesis.* This part of the *nervous system* transmits incoming information from the sense organs and outgoing information to the muscles; it is therefore responsible for the regulation of voluntary behavior.

somatoform disorder A malfunction of the body, or *soma,* which cannot be fully explained by any medical condition. The physical symptom appears instead to be psychologically based.

somatotypes   A *typology* that classifies individuals according to physical structure; from the Greek for "body." The endomorph is characterized by prominence of the abdomen and softer body parts; the mesomorph has a muscular build; and the ectomorph is lean in appearance, with a relatively large surface area in relation to body weight.

somesthesis   (soe-mess-thee′-sus)   The body feeling, involving *sensations* of pressure, temperature, and pain. It has two divisions: external, involving *cutaneous sensitivity*, commonly called the sense of touch; and internal, concerned with feeling in the muscles, tendons, and joints (*kinesthesis*) and in the internal organs (*visceral sensitivity*).

specific ability(s)   In a *psychometric approach* to *intelligence* suggested by Charles Spearman, a factor that pertains to a particular field or skill. Facility in mathematics, for example, requires specific mathematical abilities, such as ability to subtract, ability to multiply, and so forth.

specific nerve energies   See *law of specific nerve energies*.

specific phobia   An *anxiety* disorder in which the individual experiences unreasonable or excessive fear of some clearly discernible object or event, sufficient to interfere with an individual's work or social endeavors.

sperm   The reproductive cells in the male, produced by the *testes*.

spinal cord   An intricate bundle of nerve fibers extending down the spinal column in organisms with a backbone. This major part of the *nervous system* contains the nerve fibers for *reflexes*, our most primitive and automatic *responses*, and it conveys messages to and from the *brain*, providing the basis for much more complex responses. The brain and spinal cord form the *central nervous system*.

spontaneous recovery   In the *conditioning* process, the reappearance of a previously extinguished *response*, following a period of time when the *stimulus* that evoked the response has not been presented. It is an inhibition, or *forgetting*, of *extinction*.

spontaneous remission   The disappearance of symptoms without any formal *therapy*.

stage theory of memory   An approach that depicts *memory* in three sequential phases of *information processing*, qualitatively different from one another: *sensory memory, short-term memory, long-term memory*.

standard deviation (SD)   In *descriptive statistics*, one of the usual *measures of variability*; it indicates the degree of deviation of all scores from the *mean*. If the scores tend to be close to the mean, the standard deviation is small; if they tend to be widely dispersed, it is large.

standard error   In *inferential statistics*, an estimate of the amount of error likely in a given statistic. An extension of the concept of *standard deviation*, the standard error is a measure of the *probability* that, for example, a sample *mean* represents the *population* mean.

Stanford-Binet Intelligence Scale   A leading individual *intelligence test*, with standard versions, adaptations, and short forms for various groups worldwide.

state-dependent memory   A *memory* in which the individual's physical or mental condition during the *encoding* of the memory may serve as a *retrieval* cue.

statistical literacy   The capacity to understand and use numerical information; the ability to make judgments about the quality and usefulness of *statistics*.

statistical significance   In *inferential statistics*, a low *probability* of obtaining a certain result by chance, typically less than 5 chances out of 100.

statistics   The collection and evaluation of numerical information, including methods for demonstrating facts and the relationships among them; also, the data resulting from the use of these methods. See *correlational statistics, descriptive statistics, inferential statistics*.

status   The respect or standing an individual has in a *group*, typically associated with a certain *role*.

stereochemical theory   A view of *olfactory sensitivity* postulating that an odor is experienced when airborne molecules of various shapes fit into similarly shaped sockets in the *receptors*.

stereotype   In *social cognition*, an oversimplified or rigid generalization, in which certain traits are assigned to an individual simply because that person is a member of a particular occupational *group*, race, nationality, or other category of people.

stimulants   The *psychoactive substances* that arouse the *central nervous system*, heightening its action and increasing related bodily activities. Also called uppers, these drugs include *amphetamines* and *cocaine*.

stimulation motives   Certain apparently inborn motives that do not directly

aid biological *needs*, as do *primary motives*, but seem to be necessary for normal survival and development. This type of *motivation* includes the desire for *affectional stimulation* and *sensory variation motive*.

stimulus   Latin for "spur." Any factor that initiates some activity or event, called a *response*.

stimulus generalization   In the *conditioning* process, a condition in which the *stimulus* that evokes a *response* is not identical but merely similar to the original stimulus.

storage   The processing of *memory*; it is the retention of information or a skill after prior *encoding*, available for later *retrieval*. Methods of *long-term memory* storage include: *conceptual hierarchy, network of associations, schema, script*.

stranger anxiety   A form of *anxiety*, appearing in infancy from about six or seven months to one year of age, in which the baby becomes afraid with unfamiliar people, crying, turning away, hiding, or clinging to a parent or caretaker.

stream of consciousness   The view that *consciousness* is continuous, always changing, and personal as it flows from one experience to the next.

stress   A state of tension, strain, or *conflict* within an individual that has the potential to disrupt physical, mental, and behavioral functions. The physiological reactions to stress are known as the *general adaptation syndrome*. Some methods of coping deal with the cause of stress, or *stressor*, such as *distraction or reframing*, and some methods modify the stress reaction, such as relaxation techniques or exercise.

stressor   The event in the environment most directly responsible for the *stress*.

structuralism   An early *system of psychology* emphasizing the contents rather than the functions of mental life—its nature rather than its purpose, what it is rather than what it does.

structure-of-intellect model   An approach to *intelligence*, intermediate between the *cognitive approach* and *psychometric approach*, that considers how information is processed (operations), what information is processed (contents), and the results of this processing (products). These three dimensions are further divided into 180 potential intellectual abilities.

study of differences   In *inferential statistics*, a method of determining the probability that a difference between two or more *sample* scores, such as *means*, represents a difference between the *population* means.

subcortical structures The lower regions of the *brain,* at the very center, beneath the *cerebral cortex.* They include: *hippocampus, hypothalamus, limbic system, reticular activating system, thalamus.* These structures play an important role in regulating basic bodily functions.

subjective organization For *encoding* a *memory,* a strategy in which the learner uses personal experience to develop a scheme or arrangement for approaching the material to be mastered.

sublimation A *defense mechanism* in which unacceptable impulses are directed toward socially approved targets. For example, an aggressive person might be a crime fighter or trial lawyer.

subliminal advertising A method of presenting information in which a message is presented so quickly or at such a low level of intensity that it cannot be detected, presumably just below the *absolute threshold,* and yet it allegedly influences *perception.*

subtractive color mixture The phenomenon that occurs when pigments or colored inks are mixed, in which the resultant *hue* depends upon the light that is absorbed from the spectrum.

subtraits Secondary *personality traits;* less fundamental, more specific patterns of behavior within the broader *basic traits.* For example, dependability, carelessness, cautiousness, and so forth represent varying levels in the basic dimension of conscientiousness.

successive approximations See *shaping.*

superego In *psychoanalysis,* one of three psychic forces that make up the *personality;* it is concerned with the values and standards of behavior learned through contact with various people, especially parents and teachers. Comprised of the *conscience* and *ego ideal,* the superego represents the internalized standards of the parents and, through them, of society.

superordinate goals Goals shared by everyone in a *group* and having a higher priority than any other goals.

support group A collection of laypersons with similar problems. In this form of *group therapy,* the individuals provide one another with emotional support and some technical assistance, too.

suppression A mental process in which the individual deliberately attempts to avoid certain thoughts or feelings, usually by thinking about something else. In contrast to *repression,* suppression is conscious rather than unconscious.

surface structure In language, the specific words and their organization in a sentence, including the relationships among the parts of speech.

survey method A *research* method in which many people are questioned about their attitudes, knowledge, or behavior, often by mail, telephone, or in an interview. This technique has the advantage of including a large number of subjects.

symbolic model See *modeling.*

sympathetic nervous system One of two subdivisions of the *autonomic nervous system;* it plays the dominant role in *emotions* and other states of arousal. It acts as an emergency system, accelerating the heart, increasing *epinephrine,* inhibiting activity in the intestines, and activating the sweat glands, all in an integrated fashion.

symptom substitution The occurrence of a new symptom in place of symptoms removed by *therapy.*

synapse (sin'-aps) The small space between adjacent neurons, where the nerve impulse is transmitted from the end of an *axon* to the *dendrite* or *cell body* of an adjacent *neuron.*

syntax The rules of meaningful organization of words to form phrases, clauses, and sentences—that is, to form language. It is one aspect of grammar, but it is not concerned with pronunciation or correctness of word choice; it is chiefly a matter of sequence.

system In biology, a series of interacting *organs* and connecting links, making a functional whole, such as the *endocrine system* and *nervous system.* See *system of psychology.*

system of psychology A broad perspective that guides research and *theory* in *psychology.* A system defines the particular field, identifying its problems and developing methods of inquiry and application. Contemporary systems include: *behaviorism, biological approach, cognitive psychology, humanistic psychology, psychoanalysis,* in addition to *evolutionary psychology.*

systematic desensitization A method of *behavior therapy* employing *classical conditioning* to eliminate *anxiety* or other unwanted emotional *responses,* using deep muscle relaxation and a carefully graded series of steps.

task specialist A *group* leader who is concerned with identifying the group goal or problem, discovering methods of dealing with it, and implementing the best solution. A person in this *role* is also called an instrumental leader.

telegraphic speech Highly abbreviated word combinations containing the most important elements of meaning. In language development, this ability typically appears between the first and second year of age.

temperament In *constitutional theory,* the typical or usual patterns of emotionally toned reactions appearing in an individual's early years and remaining throughout most of the lifetime, such as *shyness.* It is part of *personality,* an apparently inherited dimension involving *emotion.*

temporal lobes One of four divisions of the hemispheres of the *cerebral cortex,* the lobes located at the sides of the *brain,* near the ears; they process auditory information.

teratogens (tuh-rad'-uh-junz) Environmental or chemical factors disrupting normal development in the prenatal phase, producing birth defects, such as *cretinism* and *fetal alcohol syndrome.*

terminal threshold The point at which normal *sensation* changes to pain, produced by strong light, loud sound, extreme heat, or any other *stimulus.*

test-retest reliability The degree of agreement among scores whenever the same test is administered to the same people on more than one occasion. A test or test item has test-retest *reliability* to the extent that each subject makes the same score on each occasion.

testes The *gonads,* or sex glands, in the male, which produce *sperm.* They also produce sex *hormones,* primarily *androgens.*

testing an hypothesis The second of three steps in the *scientific method;* in this step, evidence is collected in support or refutation of a prediction, with an emphasis on objectivity. An hypothesis is tested by obtaining information in a laboratory, clinic, or any other place where the behavior occurs.

thalamus A *subcortical structure,* at the very center of the *brain,* that serves as a switchboard for various brain regions. It manages input from all forms of *sensation* except smell.

thanatos In *psychoanalysis,* the death instinct, one of the two fundamental impulses of the *id.* It involves *aggression* and destructive behavior toward oneself and others.

Thematic Apperception Test (TAT) A *projective technique* in which the subject is asked to tell stories about ambiguous scenes—landscapes, human figures, and so forth—all suggesting prominent themes. The stories are then analyzed for recurrent ideas, logic, and so forth.

theory A set of principles with explanatory value. In contemporary usage, "theory" and "system" are often interchanged. Psychoanalysis, for example, is a *system of psychology,* a framework for approaching the whole field. Within psychoanalysis, there is a theory of dreams, a theory of neurosis, a theory of childhood sexuality, and so forth, all part of the larger system.

theory of evolution A conception of biological development presented by Charles Darwin, postulating that any given plant or animal species has developed through modifications of preexisting species, all of which have under gone the process of natural selection.

therapeutic alliance In *therapy,* a bond, tie, or relationship between the patient and therapist positively influencing the overall outcome. In a therapeutic alliance, the patient feels that the therapist truly cares and understands, is truly an ally, and is truly connected to his or her problems and welfare.

therapy Any procedure for alleviating personal problems, whether behavioral, emotional, or physical, ranging from *adjustment* problems to severe *mental illness;* also, any procedure for achieving personal growth. Therapy is generally considered in three broad categories: *behavior therapy, biomedical therapy, insight therapy.*

threshold See *absolute threshold, difference threshold, terminal threshold.*

thyroid gland An *endocrine* gland at the base of the neck beside the windpipe, just above the upper chest, that influences general body vigor. Lack of its *hormone,* thyroxin, early in life can result in inactivity and *cretinism.* Undersecretion at later ages often produces lethargy; oversecretion seems to result in tension.

timeout A form of *punishment* in which the individual is left alone for a short time. As an *operant conditioning* technique, it is used in *behavior therapy.*

token economy A therapeutic technique in which tokens, such as poker chips or stickers, are used as *secondary reinforcement,* which can be exchanged later for some desirable object or event.

top-down approach A view of *perception* emphasizing the higher-level *cognitive processes*—including *set,* or expectancy, and *motivation.* It begins with information in the brain, rather than with incoming information at the sense organs. See *bottom up approach.*

trace conditioning A sequence of *classical conditioning* in which the neutral *stimulus* does not appear with the *unconditioned stimulus;* it appears first, then disappears, and then the unconditioned stimulus appears.

traditional senses The five modes of *sensation* that typically provide information about conditions outside the body: hearing, touch, taste, smell, sight—*auditory sensitivity, cutaneous sensitivity, gustatory sensitivity, olfactory sensitivity, visual sensitivity.*

trait See *central trait, personality traits (basic traits, subtraits), polygenic trait.*

transference In therapy by *psychoanalysis,* a chief technique in which the patient responds emotionally to the analyst as though the analyst were someone else, usually a parent or other significant adult in the patient's earlier life.

transformational rules The mental operations that relate the *deep structure* of a sentence to the *surface structure.* Mastery of these rules relies heavily on *syntax* and is a major achievement in language development, usually appearing in childhood by the age of four or five.

transpositional learning A type of *learning* that takes place when an individual makes a comparison, successfully responding to a relationship among stimuli, rather than maintaining a fixed association to the original *stimulus.* For example, a subject learns always to choose the lighter of two shades of gray, even when that shade is lighter than the original, training stimulus in some trials and the darker than the original stimulus in other trials.

trauma theory A *psychodynamic theory* that focuses upon real and highly disruptive childhood events that influence *personality* development, especially child abuse.

trial-and-error Random and exploratory activity, without a clear hypothesis. In *problem solving,* the individual uses one approach, discards it, tries another, and so forth. Human beings often engage in covert trial-and-error, in which various solutions are attempted implicitly, in the subject's mind, before any overt attempt at a solution.

triangular theory of love A view of *interpersonal* relationships that postulates three components appearing in various amounts in any given *love* relationship: intimacy, which involves closeness and sharing; commitment, which is the devotion to the relationship; and passion, referring to the intensity of the feeling, often sexual. The presence of all three factors is called consummate love.

triarchic theory A *cognitive approach* that describes *intelligence* in three domains: componential, referring to such traditional components as *memory, perception,* and thinking; experiential, which focuses upon the capacity to combine unique experiences in creative ways, enabling the individual to deal successfully with novel situations and new tasks; and contextual, which is culturally or situationally defined, focusing upon specific settings.

trichromatic theory In *visual sensitivity,* the view of color vision postulating three types of *cones,* especially responsive to long, intermediate, and short *wavelengths.* A mixture presumably takes place in the *brain* on the basis of these diverse signals, making possible the experience of any *hue.*

trust versus mistrust The first of eight *psychosocial* crises; it occurs in infancy, during which the baby gains a sense of reliance and confidence about its environment or instead becomes unresponsive and distrustful.

two-factor theory Any approach combining two views. Two-factor *conditioning* considers *learning* in two domains. The first is signal learning (*classical conditioning*), by which the organism learns the meaning of signs or signals in its environment. The second is solution learning (*operant conditioning*), by which the organism learns what to do about those events. In *emotion,* the two factors are: *arousal,* which is the physiological response, and *cognition,* by which the situation is interpreted.

type A personality A personal style characterized by ambition, a sense of urgency, and rapid performance of tasks. The type A *personality* often involves high levels of *stress* and is sometimes associated with heart disease.

typology A system for classifying people according to a few broad dimensions or categories. For example, *somatotypes* are based on physical structure. In a *personality* typology, each category involves a characteristic style of behavior, inherited and lifelong.

unconditioned response (UR) In *classical conditioning,* a relatively simple, inborn *response* to a specific stimulus. It is automatically elicited by an *unconditioned stimulus;* no *learning* is required. The knee jerk is an unconditioned response to a tap on the patellar tendon.

unconditioned stimulus (US) In *classical conditioning,* a *stimulus* that automatically evokes a certain *response,* called an *unconditioned response.* A tap on the patellar tendon is an unconditioned stimulus for the knee jerk.

unconscious motivation Any *motivation* arising from the influence of seemingly forgotten traumatic events, usually from childhood; these events continue to influence later behavior, but without the individual's full awareness. Unconscious motivation is the fundamental principle of *psychoanalysis* and involves three stages: *conflict* or trauma; *repression,* by which the conflict is unconsciously excluded from awareness; and symbolic behavior, which is the reappearance of the repressed experience in some disguised or indirect form.

unobtrusive measures A research method in which the investigator collects information about people without disturbing them in any way or, in most cases, even observing them directly. The investigator simply examines traces of their behavior, such as effects on the environment, public records, and so forth.

validity The extent to which a test measures what it purports to measure. Two types of validity are *concurrent validity* and *predictive validity.* Apparent validity is called *face validity.*

variability See *measures of variability.*

variable Any changeable factor or element. It is some condition that the investigator wishes to study.

variable-interval (VI) schedule In *operant conditioning,* a *partial reinforcement* schedule in which *reinforcement* for correct *responses* is provided at irregular intervals but according to an overall average of the time between reinforcements. The intervals are variable, but collectively they conform to a predetermined average.

variable-ratio (VR) schedule In *operant conditioning,* a *partial reinforcement* schedule in which *reinforcement* for correct *responses* is provided on an irregular basis but according to an overall proportion of correct responses. The ratio refers to the number of reinforced responses in comparison with the total number of correct responses.

vasocongestion (vay'-zoe-kun-jess'-chun) Increased flow of blood; during sexual arousal, it includes engorgement of the sex organs.

ventromedial nucleus (ven'-troe-mee'-dee-ul) The central portion of the *hypothalamus.* Stimulation of this area promotes cessation of eating in animals, even among those on a food-deprivation schedule; when it is damaged or absent, experimental animals engage in overeating.

vestibular system (ve-stib'-yuh-lur) In the *inner ear,* the part of the *nonauditory labyrinth* concerned with the *sense of balance* and linear motion, a form of *passive motion.*

visceral sensitivity (viss'-uh-rul) The *proprioceptive sense* that provides information about feelings in the internal *organs* and glands. Visceral *sensations* include: thirst, hunger, nausea, bladder tensions, sexual tensions, suffocation, the feeling of fullness, and varieties of body feeling, or *somesthesis.*

visual sensitivity One of the five *traditional senses;* the experience of sight; responsiveness to the energy of light waves. It includes the experience of *hue,* or color.

volley theory A view of *auditory sensitivity* postulating that nerve fibers work in groups, producing successive, simultaneous discharges. Pitch depends on the *frequency* of volleys rather than the frequency carried by the individual fibers.

wavelength The distance between the crests of two adjacent waves. In *visual sensitivity,* the human eye is attuned only to a narrow range of light wavelengths; the experience of *hue,* called color vision, is largely a function of wavelength.

Weber's law (vay'-bur) The principle, named for physiologist E. H. Weber, stating that the *difference threshold* is a constant fraction of the standard *stimulus.*

Wechsler Intelligence Scales (wek'-slur) A series of individual *intelligence tests* with several subscales grouped into two large categories, verbal and nonverbal.

word recognition In language development, the first understanding of the meaning of certain intonations and words. Before the end of the first year of human infancy, the baby usually begins to distinguish the useful *phonemes* in his or her language.

working memory A term for *short-term memory* that emphasizes active *memory* processes rather than static, brief *storage.* It includes *rehearsal* of the new information and also its manipulation and evaluation.

Yerkes-Dodson law (yur'-kees) The principle stating that the optimal *arousal level* for performance depends on the complexity of the task involved. High arousal is appropriate for a relatively simple task; lower arousal is more appropriate when the task is complex.

zygote (zye'-goat) A fertilized *ovum,* resulting from the union of the ovum with a *sperm;* an organism at the beginning of the prenatal phase. In human beings, this stage lasts for about ten days after conception and is characterized by rapid cell division.

REFERENCES

Abel, G. G., & Osborn, C. (1992). The paraphilias: The extent and nature of sexually deviant and criminal behavior. *Psychiatric Clinics of North America, 15,* 675–687.

Abramov, I., & Gordon, J. (1994). Color appearance: On seeing red—or yellow, or green, or blue. *Annual Review of Psychology, 45,* 451–485.

Adair, J. G., Sharpe, D., & Huynh, C. L. (1990). The placebo control group: An analysis of its effectiveness in educational research. *Journal of Experimental Education, 59,* 67–86.

Adams, C. F. (1991). Explanation and social change: How the scientific establishment's acceptance of ESP and PK would influence contemporary society. *Journal of the American Society for Psychical Research, 85,* 43–66.

Adams, J. F. (1981). Earlier menarche, greater height and weight: A stimulation-stress factor hypothesis. *Genetic Psychological Monograph, 104,* 3–22.

Ader, R., & Cohen, N. (1993). Psychoneuroimmunology: Conditioning and stress. *Annual Review of Psychology, 44,* 53–85.

Adler, A. (1927). *The practice and theory of individual psychology.* New York: Harcourt, Brace & World.

Adler, N., & Matthews, K. (1994). Health psychology. *Annual Review of Psychology, 45,* 229–259.

Adler, T. (1992). Researchers win national medals. *APA Monitor, 23* (1), 16.

Agranoff, B. W. (1967). Memory and protein synthesis. *Scientific American, 216,* 115–122.

Akers, R. L. (1992). *Drugs, alcohol and society.* Belmont, CA: Wordsworth.

Albert, M. S., & Lafleche, G. (1991). Neuroimaging in Alzheimer's disease. *Psychiatric Clinics of North America, 14,* 443–459.

Albright, T. D. (1992). Form-cue invariant motion processing in primate visual cortex. *Science, 255,* 1141–1143.

Aldag, R. J., & Fuller, S. R. (1993). Beyond fiasco: A reappraisal of the groupthink phenomenon and a new model of group decision processes. *Psychological Bulletin, 113,* 533–552.

Alessio, J. C. (1990). A synthesis and formalization of Heiderian balance and social exchange theory. *Social Forces, 68,* 1267–1286.

Allen, K. D., & Stokes, T. F. (1987). Use of escape and reward in the management of young children during dental treatment. *Journal of Applied Behavior Analysis, 20,* 381–390.

Allison, S. (1993). *Beyond the limits.* Boston: Little, Brown.

Allport, G. W. (1961). *Pattern and growth in personality.* New York: Holt, Rinehart, & Winston.

Allport, G. W. (1965). *Letters from Jenny.* New York: Harcourt, Brace & World.

Allport, G. W., & Odbert, H. S. (1936). Trait-names: A psycholexical study. *Psychological Monographs, 211.*

Amato, P., & Keith, B. (1991). Parental divorce and the well-being of children: A meta-analysis. *Psychological Bulletin, 110,* 26–46.

Ambady, N., & Rosenthal, R. (1992). Thin slices of expressive behavior as predictors of interpersonal consequences: A meta-analysis. *Psychological Bulletin, 111,* 256–274.

Ambady, N., & Rosenthal, R. (1993). Half a minute: Predicting teacher evaluations from thin slices of nonverbal behavior and physical attractiveness. *Journal of Personality and Social Psychology, 64,* 431–441.

American Psychiatric Association. (1994). *Diagnostic and statistical manual of mental disorders* (4th ed.). Washington, DC: American Psychiatric Press.

American Psychological Association. (1990). Ethical principles of psychologists. *American Psychologist, 45,* 390–395.

Amir, T. (1984). The Asch conformity effect: A study in Kuwait. *Social Behavior and Personality, 12,* 187–190.

Amoore, J. E., Johnston, J. W., & Rubin, M. (1964). The stereochemical theory of odor. *Scientific American, 210*(2), 42–49.

Anastasi, A. (1988). *Psychological testing* (6th ed.). New York: Macmillan.

Anderson, D. B., & Pennebaker, J. W. (1980). Pain and pleasure: Alternative interpretations for identical stimulation. *European Journal of Social Psychology, 10*(2), 207–212.

Andreasen, N. C. (1988). Brain imaging: Applications in psychiatry. *Science, 239,* 1381–1388.

Andreasen, N. C., Flaum, M., Swayze, V. W., Tyrrell, G., & Arndt, S. (1990). Positive and negative symptoms in schizophrenia. *Archives of General Psychiatry, 47,* 615–621.

Angel, R., & Guarnaccia, P. J. (1989). Mind, body, and culture: Somatization among Hispanics. *Social Science Medicine, 28,* 1229–1238.

Angel, R., & Idler, E. L. (1992). Somatization and hypochondriasis: Socio-cultural factors in subjective experience. *Research in Community Mental Health, 7,* 71–93.

Appel, P. R. (1990). Clinical applications of hypnosis in the physical medicine and rehabilitation setting: Three case reports. *American Journal of Clinical Hypnosis, 33,* 85–93.

Arnon, R., & Kreitler, S. (1984). Effects of meaning training on overcoming functional fixedness. *Current Psychological Research and Reviews, 3,* 11–24.

Arvey, R. D. *et al.* (1994). Mainstream science on intelligence. *Wall Street Journal,* December 13.

Asch, S. E. (1946). Forming impressions of personality. *Journal of Abnormal Social Psychology, 41,* 258–290.

Asch, S. E. (1956). Studies of independence and submission in group pressure. *Psychological Monographs, 70,* 416.

Aserinsky, E., & Kleitman, N. (1953). Regularly occurring periods of eye motility, and concomitant phenomena during sleep. *Science, 118,* 273–274.

Atkinson, J. W. (1965). The mainsprings of achievement-oriented activity. In J. D. Krumboltz (Ed.), *Learning and the educational process.* Chicago: Rand-McNally.

Atkinson, R. C., & Shiffrin, R. M. (1968). Human memory: A proposed system and its control processes. In K. W. Spence & J. T. Spence (Ed.), *The psychology of learning and motivation* (Vol. 2). New York: Academic Press.

Atkinson, R. C., & Shiffrin, R. M. (1971). The control of short-term memory. *Scientific American, 225,* 82–90.

Averill, J. R. (1982). *Anger and aggression.* New York: Springer.

Azrin, N. H., & Peterson, A. L. (1990). Treatment of Tourette Syndrome by habit reversal: A waiting-list control group comparison. *Behavior Therapy, 21,* 305–318.

Baddeley, A. D. (1990). *Human memory.* Boston: Allyn & Bacon.

Baird, J., & Wagner, M. (1991). Transformation theory of size judgment. *Journal of Experimental Psychology: Human Perception and Performance, 17,* 852–864.

Baker, R. A., & Lawrence, D. H. (1951). The differential effects of simultaneous and successive stimuli presentation on transposition. *Journal of Comparative and Physiological Psychology, 44,* 378–382.

Baker, T. B., Morse, E., & Sherman, J. E. (1986). The motivation to use drugs: A psychobiological analysis of urges. *Nebraska Symposium on Motivation, 34,* 257–323.

Bales, R. F. (1951). *Interaction process analysis.* Chicago: University of Chicago Press.

Ban, T. A., & Guy, W. (1985). Conditioning and learning in relation to disease. *Activitas Nervosa Superior, 27,* 236–245.

Banaji, M. I., & Prentice, D. A. (1994). The self in social contexts. *Annual Review of Psychology, 45,* 297–332.

Banaji, M. R., & Crowder, R. G. (1989). The bankruptcy of everyday memory. *American Psychologist, 44,* 1185–1193.

Bandler, R., & Grinder, J. (1982). *Reframing.* Moab, Utah: Real People Press.

Bandura, A. (1965). Influence of models' reinforcement contingencies on the acquisition of imitative responses. *Journal of Personality and Social Psychology, 1,* 589–595.

Bandura, A. (1977). *Social learning theory.* Englewood Cliffs, NJ: Prentice Hall.

Bandura, A. (1986). *Social foundations of thought and action: A social cognitive theory.* Englewood Cliffs, NJ: Prentice Hall.

Bandura, A. (1989). Regulation of cognitive processes through perceived self-efficacy. *Developmental Psychology, 25(5),* 729–735.

Bandura, A. (1990). Some reflections on reflections. *Psychological Inquiry, 1,* 101–105.

Bandura, A. Grusec, J. E., & Menlove, F. L. (1967). Vicarious extinction of avoidance behavior. *Journal of Personality and Social Psychology, 5,* 16–23.

Banks, W. P., & Krajicek, D. (1991). Perception. *Annual Review of Psychology, 42,* 305–331.

Barber, T. X., Wilson, S. C., & Scott, D. S. (1980). Effects of a traditional trance induction on response to "hypnotist-centered" test suggestions. *International Journal of Clinical Experimental Hypnosis, 28,* 114–125.

Barclay, M. W. (1991). The return of trauma theory: Implications for hermeneutic psychotherapy. *Humanistic Psychologist, 19,* 134–157.

Barker, G. H. (1987). Invited review: Psychological factors and immunity. *Journal of Psychosomatic Research, 31,* 1–10.

Barnet, R. C., Grahame, N. J., & Miller, R. R. (1991). Comparing the magnitudes of second-order conditioning and sensory preconditioning effects. *Bulletin of the Psychonomic Society, 29,* 133–135.

Baron, M. (1986). Genetics of schizophrenia: I. Familial patterns and mode of inheritance. *Biological Psychiatry, 21,* 1051–1066.

Bartlett, F. C. (1932). *Remembering.* New York & London: Cambridge University Press.

Basow, S. A. (1992). *Gender: Stereotypes and roles.* (3rd ed.). Pacific Grove, CA: Brooks/Cole.

Bassuk, E. L., Rubin, L. & Lauriat, A. (1984). Is homelessness a mental health problem? *American Journal of Psychiatry, 141,* 1546-1550.

Batchelor, R. A. (1986). The psychophysics of inflation. *Journal of Economic Psychology, 7,* 269–290.

Baumeister, R. F., & Steinhilber, A. (1984). Paradoxical effects of supportive audiences on performance under pressure: The home field disadvantage in sports championships. *Journal of Personality and Social Psychology, 47(1),* 85–93.

Baumrind, D. (1964). Some thoughts on ethics of research: After reading Milgram's "Behavioral study of obedience." *American Psychologist, 19,* 421–423.

Bayley, N., & Oden, M. H. (1955). The maintenance of intellectual ability in gifted adults. *Journal of Gerontology, 10,* 91–107.

Beck, A., & Freeman, A. (1990). *Cognitive theory of personality disorders.* New York: Guilford Press.

Beck, A. T. (1976). *Cognitive therapy and emotional disorders.* New York: International Universities Press.

Beck, A. T. (1991). Cognitive therapy: A thirty-year retrospective. *American Psychologist, 46,* 368–375.

Bedon, B. G., & Howard, D. V. (1992). Memory for the frequency of occurrence of karate techniques: A comparison of experts and novices. *Bulletin of the Psychonomic Society, 30,* 117–119.

Beier, E. G. (1974, October). Nonverbal communication: How we send emotional messages. *Psychology Today,* pp. 52–56.

Beilin, H., (1992). Piaget's enduring contribution to developmental psychology. *Developmental Psychology, 28,* 191–204.

Bem, D. J., & Honorton, C. (1994). Does psi exist? Replicable evidence for an anomalous process of information transfer. *Psychological Bulletin, 115(1),* 4–18.

Benassi, V. A., Sweeney, P. D., & Dufour, C. L. (1988). Is there a relation between locus of control orientation and depression? *Journal of Abnormal Psychology, 97(3),* 357–367.

Benjamin, L. T., Durkin, M., Link, M., Vestal, M., & Acord, J. (1992). Wundt's American doctoral students. *American Psychologist, 47,* 123–131.

Bennett, J. C. (1991). The irrationality of the catharsis theory of aggression as justification for educators' support of interscholastic football. *Perceptual and Motor Skills, 72,* 415–418.

Benson, H., Malhotra, M. S., Goldman, R. F., Jacobs, G. D., et al. (1990). Three case reports of the metabolic and electroencephalographic changes during advanced Buddhist meditation techniques. *Behavioral Medicine, 16,* 90–95.

Benson, H., & Stuart, E. M. (1993). *The wellness book.* New York: Simon & Schuster.

Bentler, L. E. (1991). Have all won and must all have prizes? Revisiting Luborsky et al.'s verdict. *Journal of Consulting and Clinical Psychology, 59,* 226–232.

Berecz, J. M. (1992). *Understanding Tourette syndrome, obsessive compulsive disorder, and related problems.* New York: Springer.

Bergamini, D. (1971). *Mathematics.* New York: Time-Life Books.

Bergin, A. (1971). The evaluation of therapeutic outcomes. In A. Bergen & S. Garfield (Eds.). *Handbook of psychotherapy and behavior change.* New York: Wiley.

Berkowitz, L. (1988). Frustrations, appraisals, and aversively stimulated aggression. *Aggressive Behavior, 14,* 3–11.

Berkowitz, L. (1989). Frustration-aggression hypothesis: Examination and reformulation. *Psychological Bulletin, 106,* 59–73.

Berkowitz, L., & LePage, A. (1967). Weapons as aggression-eliciting stimuli. *Journal of Personality and Social Psychology, 7,* 202–207.

Bernard, L. L. (1924). *Instinct: A study in social psychology.* New York: Holt.

Berridge, K. C., & Valenstein, E. S. (1991). What psychological process mediates feeding evoked by electrical stimulation of the lateral hypothalamus? *Behavioral Neuroscience, 105,* 3–14.

Berscheid, E. (1994). Interpersonal relationships. *Annual Review of Psychology, 45,* 79–129.

Besharov, D. J., & Hartle, T. W. (1987). Head Start: Making a popular program work. *Pediatrics, 79,* 440–441.

Betz, N. E., & Fitzgerald, L. F. (1993). Individuality and diversity: Theory and research in counseling psychology. *Annual Review of Psychology, 44,* 343–381.

Beulig, A., & Dalezman, J. (1992). Observational learning of imprinting behavior in Japanese quail (*Coturnix coturnix japonica*). *Bulletin of the Psychonomic Society, 30,* 209–211.

Bhugra, D. (1987). A retrospective view of a sexual dysfunction clinic, 1980–83. *Sexual and Marital Therapy, 2,* 73–82.

Bierhoff, H., Klein, R., & Kramp, P. (1991). Evidence for the altruistic personality from data on accident research. *Journal of Personality, 59,* 263–280.

Binet, A., & Simon, T. (1905). Applications des méthods nouvelles au diagnostic du niveau intellectuel chez des enfents normaux et anormaux d'hospice et d'école primaire. *Anee Psychologique, 11,* 245–336.

Birch, H. G. (1945). The relation of previous experience to insightful problem-solving. *Journal of Comparative Psychology, 38,* 367–383.

Birch, H. G. (1956). Sources of order in the maternal behavior of animals. *Journal of Orthopsychiatry, 26,* 279–284.

Birch, H. G., & Rabinowitz, H. S. (1951). The negative effect of previous experience on productive thinking. *Journal of Experimental Psychology, 41,* 121–125.

Birren, J. E. & Fisher, L. M. (1995). Aging and speed of behavior. *Annual Review of Psychology, 46,* 329–353.

Blair, S. M. (1973). [Letter to the editor]. *Science, 180,* 362–363.

Blass, T. (1991). Understanding behavior in the Milgram obedience experiment: The role of personality, situations, and their interactions. *Journal of Personality and Social Psychology, 60,* 398–413.

Block, P. (1904, August 15). Der kluge Hans. *Berliner Tageblatt,* p. I.

Blume, S. B. (1991). The problems of quantifying alcohol consumption. *British Journal of Addiction, 86,* 1059–1060.

Boesch-Achermann, H., & Boesch, C. (1993). Tool use in chimpanzees: New light from dark forests. *Current Directions in Psychological Science, 2,* 18–21.

Bogolub, E. B. (1991). Women and mid-life divorce: Some practice issues. *Social Work, 36,* 428–433.

Bok, D. (1988). Ethics, the university and society. *Harvard Magazine, 90,* 39–50.

Bonanno, G. A. (1990). Repression, accessibility, and the translation of private experience. *Psychoanalytic Psychology, 7,* 453–473.

Bonate, P. L. (1991). Serotonin receptor subtypes: Functional, physiological, and clinical correlates. *Clinical Neuropharmacology, 14,* 1–16.

Bond, C. T., Francis, R. C., Fernald, R. D., & Adelman, J. P. (1991). Characterization of complementary DNA encoding the precursor for gonadotropin-releasing hormone and its associated peptide from a Teleost fish. *Molecular Endocrinology, 5,* 931–937.

Boneau, C. A. (1990). Psychological literacy: A first approximation. *American Psychologist, 45,* 891–900.

Borbely, A., Achermann, P., Trachsel, L., & Tobler, I. (1989). Sleep initiation and initial sleep intensity: Interactions of homeostatic and circadian mechanisms. *Journal of Biological Rhythms, 4*(2), 149–160.

Borgeat, F., Elie, R., & Castonguay, L. G. (1991). Muscular response to the therapist and symptomatic improvement during biofeedback for tension headache. *Biofeedback and Self-Regulation, 16,* 147–155.

Boring, E. G., Langfeld, H. S., & Weld, H. P. (1948). *Psychology, a factual textbook.* New York: Wiley.

Botwinick, J. (1984). *Aging and behavior* (3rd ed.). New York: Springer.

Bouchard, T., Lykken, D., McGue, M., Segal, N., & Tellegen, A. (1990). Sources of human psychological differences: The Minnesota study of twins reared apart. *Science, 250,* 223–228.

Bouchard, T. J., & McGue, M. (1981). Familiar studies of intelligence: A review. *Science, 212,* 1055–1059.

Bourne, L. E. (1966). *Human conceptual behavior.* Boston: Allyn & Bacon.

Bousefield, W. A. (1955). Lope de Vega on early conditioning. *American Psychologist, 10,* 828.

Bower, G. H. (1992). Reviewing the basics. *APS Observer, 5,* 2.

Bower, G. H. (1970). Analysis of a mnemonic device. *American Scientist, 58,* 496–510.

Bower, G. H. (1981). Mood and memory. *American Psychologist, 36,* 129–148.

Bower, G. H., Black, J. B., & Turner, T. J. (1979). Scripts in memory for text. *Cognitive Psychology, 11,* 177–220.

Bowlby, J. (1969). *Attachment and loss. I: Attachment.* New York: Basic Books.

Boynton, R. M. (1982). Spatial and temporal approaches for studying color vision. *Documenta Ophthalmologica Proceedings Series, 33,* 1–14.

Bozarth, J. D. (1991). Person-centered assessment. *Journal of Counseling and Development, 69,* 458–461.

Bozarth, J. D., & Brodley, B. T. (1991). Actualization: A functional concept in client-centered therapy. *Journal of Social Behavior and Personality, 6,* 45–59.

Brehm, S. S. (1992). *Intimate relationships* (2nd ed.). New York: McGraw-Hill.

Breland, H. M. (1973). Birth order effect: A reply to Schooler. *Psychological Bulletin, 80,* 210–212.

Bremer, T. H., & Wittig, M. A. (1980). Fear of success: A personality trait or a response to occupational deviance and role overload? *Sex Roles, 6,* 27–46.

Brenner, C. (1987). Working through: 1914–1984. *Psychoanalytic Quarterly, 56,* 88–108.

Brewer, M. B., & Caporael, L. R. (1990). Selfish genes vs. selfish people: Sociobiology as origin myth. *Motivation and Emotion, 14,* 237–243.

Brewin, C. R. (1996). Theoretical foundations of cognitive-behavioral therapy for anxiety and depression. *Annual Review of Psychology, 47,* 33–57.

Briere, J., & Conte, J. R. (1993). Self-reported amnesia for abuse in adults molested as children. *Journal of Traumatic Stress, 6,* 21–31.

Brock, T. C., & Buss, A. H. (1962). Dissonance, aggression, and evaluation of pain. *Journal of Abnormal Social Psychology, 65,* 197–202.

Brockhaus, A., & Elger, C. E. (1990). Hypalgesic efficacy of acupuncture on experimental pain in man: Comparison of laser acupuncture and needle acupuncture. *Pain, 43,* 181–185.

Brogden, W. J., Lipman, E. A., & Culler, E. A. (1938). The role of incentive in conditioning and extinction. *American Journal of Psychology, 51,* 109.

Bromley, D. B. (1990). Academic contributions to psychological counseling: I. A philosophy of science for the study of individual cases. *Counselling Psychology Quarterly, 3,* 299–307.

Brown, A. M. (1990). Development of visual sensitivity to light and color vision in human infants: A critical review. *Vision Research, 30,* 1159–1188.

Brown, D. M., Fuqua, J. W., & Otts, D. A. (1986). Helping reluctant readers "stick" to it. *Academic Therapy, 21,* 599–604.

Brown, L. M., & Gilligan, C. (1992). *Meeting at the crossroads: Women's psychology and girls' development.* Cambridge, MA: Harvard University Press.

Brown, L. M., & Tappan, M. B. (1991). "Interpretive experiments: Probing the care-justice debate in moral development": Commentary. *Human Development, 34,* 81–87.

Brown, M. (1973a). The new body psychotherapies. *Psychotherapy: Theory, Research and Practice, 10,* 98–116.

Brown, R. I. (1986). Arousal and sensation-seeking components in the general explanation of gambling and gambling addictions. *International Journal of the Addictions, 21,* 1001–1016.

Brown, R. W., & Kulik, J. (1977). Flashbulb memories. *Cognition, 5,* 73–99.

Brown, R. W. (1973b). *A first language: The early stages.* Cambridge, MA: Harvard University Press.

Brown, R. W., & Bellugi, U. (1964). Three processes in the child's acquisition of syntax. *Harvard Educational Review, 34,* 133–151.

Brown, R. W., Galanter, E., Hess, D. & Mandler, G. (1962). *New directions in psychology.* New York: Holt.

Brun, R. (1953). Uber Freud's Hypotheses vom Todestrieb. *Psyche,* 81–111.

Bruner, J. S. (1958). Social psychology and perception. In E. E. Maccoby, T. M. Newcomb, & E. L. Hartley (Eds.), *Readings in social psychology* (3rd ed.). New York: Holt.

Bruner, J. S. (1986). *Actual minds, possible worlds.* Cambridge, MA: Harvard University Press.

Bruner, J. S. (1990). *Acts of meaning.* Cambridge, MA: Harvard University Press.

Bruner, J. S., & Goodman, C. C. (1947). Value and need as organizing factors in perception. *Journal of Abnormal and Social Psychology, 42,* 33–44.

Buck, R. (1985). Prime theory: An integrated view of motivation and emotion. *Psychological Review, 92,* 389–413.

Bullock, W. A., & Gilliland, K. (1993). Eysenck's arousal theory of introversion-extraversion: A converging measures investigation. *Journal of Personality and Social Psychology, 64,* 113–123.

Burgess, A. (1991). Profile analysis of the Wechsler intelligence scales: A new index of subtest scatter. *British Journal of Clinical Psychology, 30,* 257–263.

Burtt, H. E. (1932). An experimental study of early childhood memory. *Pedag. Sem. Journal of Genetic Psychology, 40,* 287–295.

Burtt, H. E. (1937). A further study of early childhood memory. *Journal of Genetic Psychology, 50,* 187–192.

Burtt, H. E. (1941). An experimental study of early childhood memory: Final report. *Journal of Genetic Psychology, 58,* 435–439.

Butcher, J. N. & Rouse, S. V. (1996). Personality: Individual differences and clinical assessment. *Annual Review of Psychology, 47,* 87–111.

Buss, D. M. (1995). Evolutionary psychology: A new paradigm for psychological science. *Psychological Inquiry, 6,* 1–30.

Cahoon, D. D., & Edmunds, E. M. (1984). Guns/no guns and the expression of social hostility. *Bulletin of the Psychonomic Society, 22,* 305–308.

Caldwell, D. F. (1991, October). Personal communication.

Caldwell, F. (1990). Symptom substitution: The reification of a metaphor? *Australian Journal of Clinical Hypnotherapy and Hypnosis, 11,* 29–32.

Calhoun, J. B. (1962, February). Population density and social pathology. *Scientific American,* p. 139–148.

Calkins, M. W. (1905). A reconciliation between structural and functional psychology. *Psychological Review, 13,* 61–81.

Calkins, M.W. (1930). Mary Whiton Calkins. In C. Murchison (Ed.), *A history of psychology in autobiography* (Vol. I). Worcester, MA: Clark University Press.

Campbell, J. B., & Hawley, C. W. (1982). Study habits and Eysenck's theory of extraversion-introversion. *Journal of Research in Personality, 16,* 139–146.

Campbell, S. S., & Tobler, I. (1984). Animal sleep: A review of sleep duration across phylogeny. *Neuroscience & Biobehavioral Reviews, 8,* 269–300.

Cannon, W. B. (1929). *Bodily changes in pain, hunger, fear and rage* (2nd ed.). New York: Appleton-Century-Crofts.

Cannon, W. B., & Washburn, A. L. (1912). An explanation of hunger. *American Journal of Physiology, 29,* 441–454.

Cantor, J., Engle, R., & Hamilton, G. (1991). Short-term memory, working memory, and verbal abilities: How do they relate? *Intelligence, 15,* 229–246.

Cappon, D., & Banks, R. (1960). Studies in perceptual distortion: Opportunistic observations on sleeping deprivation during a talkathon. *Archives of General Psychiatry, 2,* 346–349.

Carberry, M. S., Khalil, H. M., Leathrum, J. F. & Levy, L. S. (1979). *Foundations of computer science.* Potomac, MD: Computer Science Press.

Carey, S. (1978). The child as a word learner. In M. Halle, J. Bresnan, & G. A. Miller (Eds.), *Linguistic theory and psychological reality.* Cambridge, MA: MIT Press.

Carroll, J. L., Volk, K. D., & Hyde, J. S. (1985). Differences between males and females in motives for engaging in sexual intercourse. *Archives of Sexual Behavior, 14,* 131–139.

Cassara, B. B. (1990). *Adult education in a multicultural society.* London: Routledge.

Cassingham, R. (1986, Summer). Flying fingers. *Dvorak Developments,* No. 46, p. 7.

Cattell, R. B. (1971). *Abilities: Their structure, growth, and action.* Boston: Houghton Mifflin.

Cattell, R. B., Eber, H. W., & Tatsuoka, M. M. (1970). *Handbook for the sixteen factor personality questionnaire.* Champaign, IL: Institute for Personality Ability and Testing.

Ceci, S. J., & Bronfenbrenner, U. (1991). On the demise of everyday memory. *American Psychologist, 46,* 27–31.

Cerletti, U. (1950). Old and new information about electroshock. *American Journal of Psychiatry, 107,* 87–94.

Chaik, F. I., & Lockhart, R. S. (1972). Levels of processing: A framework for memory research. *Journal of Verbal Learning and Verbal Behavior, 11,* 671–684.

Chaiken, S., & Stangor, C. (1987). Attitudes and attitude change. *Annual Review of Psychology, 38,* 575–630.

Champlain, F. C., & Kopelman, R. E. (1991). Hinrichs revisited: Individual evaluations of income increments. *Journal of Psychology, 125,* 359–373.

Chance, P. (1988). *Learning and behavior* (2nd ed.). Belmont, CA: Wadsworth.

Chang, R., & Page, R. (1991). Characteristics of the self-actualized person: Visions from the East and West. *Counseling and Values, 36,* 2–10.

Chang, T. M. (1986). Semantic memory: Facts and models. *Psychological Bulletin, 99,* 199–220.

Chase, M. H., & Morales, F. R. (1990). The atonia and myoclonia of active (REM) sleep. *Annual Review of Psychology, 41,* 557–584.

Chase, W. G., & Ericsson, K. A. (1982). Skill and working memory. In G. H. Bower (Ed.), *The psychology of learning and motivation* (Vol. 16). New York: Academic Press.

Chase, W. G. & Simon, H. A. (1973). The mind's eye in chess. In W. G. Chase (Ed.) *Visual information processing.* New York: Academic Press.

Cherry, E. C. (1953). Some experiments on the recognition of speech with one and two ears. *Journal of the Acoustical Society of America, 25,* 925–979.

Cheung, B. S., Howard, I. P., & Money, K. E. (1991). Visually induced sickness in normal and bilaterally labyrinthine-defective subjects. *Aviation, Space, and Environmental Medicine, 62,* 527–531.

Chodorow, N. (1978). *The reproduction of mothering: Psychoanalysis and the sociology of gender.* Berkeley: University of California Press.

Chollar, S. (1989, April). Conversations with the dolphins. *Psychology Today,* pp. 52–56.

Chomsky, N. (1957). *Syntactic structures.* The Hague: Mouton.

Chomsky, N. (1972). *Language and mind.* New York: Harcourt, Brace, Jovanovich.

Chomsky, N. (1975). *Reflections on language.* New York: Pantheon.

Chomsky, N. (1986). *Knowledge of language.* New York: Praeger.

Christensen, A., & Peavey, C. L. (1990). Gender and social structure in the demand/withdrawal pattern of marital conflict. *Journal of Personality and Social Psychology, 59,* 73–81.

Cialdini, R. B. (1993). *Influence: Science and practice* (3rd ed.). New York: Harper Collins.

Cialdini, R. B., Vincent, J. E., Lewis, S. K., Catalan, J., Wheeler, D., & Danby, B. L. (1975). Reciprocal concessions procedure for inducing compliance: The door-in-the-face technique. *Journal of Personality and Social Psychology, 31,* 206–215.

Clark, D. L. (1985). The vestibular system: An overview of structure and function. *Physical and Occupational Therapy in Pediatrics, 5,* 5–32.

Clark, K. R. (1993). Season of light/season of darkness: The effects of burying and remembering traumatic sexual abuse on the sense of self. *Clinical Social Work Journal, 21,* 25–43.

Clary, E. G., & Orenstein, L. (1991). The amount and effectiveness of help: The relationship of motives and abilities to helping behavior. *Personality and Psychology Social Bulletin, 17,* 58–64.

Cleek, M. B., & Pearson, T. A. (1985). Perceived causes of divorce: An analysis of interrelationships. *Journal of Marriage and the Family, 47,* 179–191.

Clinchy, B. (1975, February). Piaget [Lecture]. Wellesley, MA: Wellesley College.

Clinchy, E. (1991). No reason to be educational failures. *Equity and Choice, 7,* 65–70.

Cloward, R. B. (1969). Hyperhidrosis. *Journal of Neurosurgery, 30,* 545–551.

Cohen, D. B. (1973). Sex, role orientation and dream recall. *Journal of Abnormal Psychology, 82,* 246–252.

Cohen, J. B., & Chakravarti, D. (1990). Consumer psychology. *Annual Review of Psychology, 41,* 243–288.

Cohen, L. B., & Strauss, M. S. (1979). Concept acquisition in the human infant. *Child Development, 50*(2), 419–424.

Cohen, S., Tyrrell, D. A., & Smith, A. P. (1991). Psychological stress and susceptibility to the common cold. *New England Journal of Medicine, 325,* 606–612.

Coke, M. M. (1992). Correlates of life satisfaction among elderly African Americans. *Journal of Gerontology, 47,* 316-320.

Colby, K. M., Weber, S., & Hilf, F. D. (1971). Artificial paranoia. *AI, 2,* 1–26.

Coleman, R. M. (1986). *Wide awake at 3:00 A.M.* Philadelphia: W. H. Freeman.

Coles, R. (1989). *The call of stories: Teaching and the moral imagination.* Boston: Houghton Mifflin.

Collins, A. M., & Loftus, E. F. (1975). A spreading-activation theory of semantic processing. *Psychological Review, 82,* 407–428.

Commons, M., Nevin, J. A., & Davison, M. (1991). *Signal detection: Mechanism, models, and applications.* Hillsdale, NJ: Erlbaum.

Comstock, G., & Paik, H. (1991). *Television and the American child.* San Diego, CA: Academic Press.

Comstock, G., & Strasburger, V. (1990). Deceptive appearances: Television violence and aggressive behavior. *Journal of Adolescent Health Care, 11,* 31–44.

Conant, M. B., & Trabasso, T. (1964). Conjunctive and disjunctive concept formation under equal-information conditions. *Journal of Experimental Psychology, 67,* 250–255.

Confer, W. N., & Ables, B. S. (1983). *Multiple personality: Etiology, diagnosis, and treatment.* New York: Human Sciences Press.

Conway, M. A. (1991). In defense of everyday memory. *American Psychologist, 46,* 19–26.

Cookerly, J. R. (1980). Does marital therapy do any lasting good? *Journal of Marital and Family Therapy, 6,* 393–397.

Cooper, R. M., & Zubek, J. P. (1958). Effects of enriched and restricted early environments on the learning ability of bright and dull rats. *Canadian Journal of Psychology, 12,* 159–164.

Corbin, S., & Nelson, T. (1980). Using Angels and Devils: A board game developed for play in nursing homes. *International Journal of Aging & Human Development, 2,* 243–250.

Cordery, G. (1987). The gambling grandfather in *The Old Curiosity Shop. Literature and Psychology, 33,* 43–61.

Cornsweet, T. M. (1970). *Visual perception.* New York: Academic Press.

Costa, P. T., & McCrae, R. R. (1980). Still stable after all these years: Personality as a key to some issues in aging. In P. Baltes & O. Brim (Eds.), *Life span development and behavior* (Vol. 3). New York: Academic Press.

Costa, P. T., & McCrae, R. R. (1988). Personality in adulthood: A six-year longitudinal study of self-reports and spouse ratings on the NEO personality inventory. *Journal of Personality and Social Psychology, 54,* 853–863.

Cowart, B. J. (1989). Relationships between taste and smell across the adult life span. *Annals of the New York Academy of Sciences, 561,* 39–55.

Coyne, J. C., & Downey, G. (1991). Social factors and psychopathology: Stress, social support, and coping processes. *Annual Review of Psychology, 42,* 401–425.

Craik, F. I. M., & Tulving, E. (1975). Depth of processing and the retention of words in episodic memory. *Journal of Experimental Psychology: General, 104,* 268–294.

Cramer, P. (1991). Anger and the use of defense mechanisms in college students. *Journal of Personality, 59,* 39–55.

Crick, F., & Mitchison, G. (1983). The function of dream sleep. *Nature, 304,* 111–114.

Crowe, R. R. (1974). An adoption study of antisocial personality. *Archives of General Psychiatry, 31,* 785–791.

Curfs, L. M., Wiegers, A. M., & Fryns, J. P. (1990). Fragile-X syndrome: A review. *Brain Dysfunction, 3,* 1–8.

Curtiss, S. (1977). *Genie: A psycholinguistic study of a modern-day "wild child."* New York: Academic Press.

Darley, J. M., & Batson, C. D. (1973). "From Jerusalem to Jericho": A study of situational and dispositional variables in helping behavior. *Journal of Personality and Social Psychology, 27,* 100–108.

Darley, J. M., & Berscheid, E. (1967). Increased liking as a result of the anticipation of personal contact. *Human Relations, 20,* 29–40.

Darou, W. G. (1992). Native Canadians and intelligence testing. *Canadian Journal of Counselling, 26,* 96–99.

Daruna, J. H., & Morgan, J. E. (1990). Psychosocial effects on immune function: Neuroendocrine pathways. *Psychosomatics, 31,* 4–12.

Darwin, C. (1859). *The origin of the species by means of natural selection* (6th ed., 1872). New York: Appleton.

Darwin, C. (1872). *The expression of the emotions in man and animals.* Chicago: University of Chicago Press, 1965.

Dashiell, J. F. (1935). Experimental studies of the influence of social situations on the behavior of individual human adults. In C. Murchison (Ed.), *Handbook of social psychology.* Worcester, MA: Clark University Press.

Davenport, H. W. (1972). Why the stomach does not digest itself. *Scientific American, 220,* 87–93.

Davidson, R. A., & Smith, B. D. (1991). Caffeine and novelty: Effects on electrodermal activity and performance. *Physiology and Behavior, 49,* 1169–1175.

Davis, J. M. (1974). A two-factor theory of schizophrenia. *Journal of Psychiatric Research, 11,* 25–29.

Davis, K. L., Kahn, R. S., Ko, G., & Davidson, M. (1991). Dopamine in schizophrenia: A review and reconceptualization. *American Journal of Psychiatry, 148,* 1474–1486.

Davis, K. L., Mohs, R. C., Tinklenberg, J. R., Pfefferbaum, A., Hollister, L. E., & Koppell, B. S. (1978). Physostigmine: Improvement of long-term memory processes in humans. *Science, 201,* 272–274.

Davis, M. (1992). The role of the amygdala in fear and anxiety. *Annual Review of Neuroscience, 15,* 311–327.

Davis, M. R., & Fernald, R. D. (1990). Social control of neuronal soma size. *Journal of Neurobiology, 21,* 1180–1188.

Davis, P. J. (1987). Repression and the inaccessibility of affective memories. *Journal of Personality and Social Psychology, 53,* 585–593.

Davis, P. J., & Schwartz, G. E. (1987). Repression and the inaccessibility of affective memories. *Journal of Personality and Social Psychology, 52,* 155–162.

De Carvalho, R. J. (1991). The humanistic paradigm in education. *Humanistic Psychologist, 19,* 88–104.

DeCasper, A. J., & Fifer, W. P. (1980). Of human bonding: Newborns prefer their mothers' voices. *Science, 208,* 1174–1176.

de Castro, J. M. (1991). Social facilitation of the spontaneous meal size of humans occurs on both weekdays and weekends. *Physiology and Behavior, 49,* 1289–1291.

de Groot, A. D. (1965). *Thought and choice in chess.* The Hague: Mouton.

Delmonte, M. M. (1990). Meditation and change: Mindfulness versus repression. *Australian Journal of Clinical Hypnotherapy and Hypnosis, 11,* 57–63.

Delmonte, M. M. (1995). Silence and emptiness in the service of healing. *British Journal of Psychotherapy, 11,* 368–378.

De Longis, A., Coyne, J., Dekaf, G., Folkman, S., & Lazarus, R. (1982). Relationship of daily hassles, uplifts, and major life events to health status. *Health Psychology, 1,* 119–136.

de Luca, R. V., & Holborn, S. W. (1992). Effects of a variable-ratio reinforcement schedule with changing criteria on exercise in obese and nonobese boys. *Journal of Applied Behavioral Analysis, 25,* 671–679.

de Marchi, N. (1991). The genetics of schizophrenia. *Developmental Medicine and Child Neurology, 33,* 452–458.

Dement, W. C. (1960). The effect of dream deprivation. *Science, 131,* 1705–1707.

Dement, W. C. (1992). *The sleepwatchers.* Stanford, CA: Stanford Book Series.

Dement, W. C., & Wolpert, E. A. (1958). The relation of eye movements, body motility, and external stimuli to dream content. *Journal of Experimental Psychology, 55,* 543–553.

Dempster, F. N. (1988). Retroactive interference in the retention of prose: A reconsideration and new evidence. *Applied Cognitive Psychology, 2,* 97–113.

Dennett, M. R. (1985). Firewalking: Reality or illusion. *Skeptical Inquirer, 10,* 36–40.

Devine, D. A., & Fernald, P. S. (1973). Outcome effects of receiving a preferred, randomly assigned, or nonpreferred therapy. *Journal of Consulting and Clinical Psychology, 41,* 104–107.

Digman, J. M. (1990). Personality structure: Emergence of the five-factor model. *Annual Review of Psychology, 41,* 417–440.

Dillard, J. P. (1993). Persuasion past and present: Attitudes aren't what they used to be. *Communication Monographs, 60,* 90–97.

Dillbeck, M. C., & Orme-Johnson, D. W. (1987). Physiological differences between transcendental meditation and rest. *American Psychologist, 42,* 879–881.

Dillman, D. A. (1991). The design and administration of mail surveys. *Annual Review of Sociology, 17,* 225–249.

DiLoreto, A. O. (1971). *Comparative psychotherapy: An experimental analysis.* Chicago: Aldine-Atherton.

Dindia, K., & Allen, M. (1992). Sex differences in self-disclosure: A meta-analysis. *Psychological Bulletin, 112,* 106–124.

Dinwiddie, S. H., North, C. S., & Yutzy, S. H. (1993). Multiple personality disorder: Scientific and medicological issues. *Bulletin of the American Academy of Psychiatry and the Law, 21,* 69–79.

Dodge, K. A. (1993). Social-cognitive mechanisms in the development of conduct disorder and depression. *Annual Review of Psychology, 44,* 559–584.

Dollard, J., Miller, N. E., Doob, L. W., Mowrer, O. H., & Sears, R. R. (1939). *Frustration and aggression.* New Haven, CT: Yale University Press.

Dore, J. (1985). Holophrases revisited. In M. D. Bartlett (Ed.), *Children's single-word speech.* New York: Wiley.

Dorr, A. (1986). *Television and children.* Beverly Hills, CA: Sage.

Dosuzkov, T. (1975). Idrosophobia: A form of pregenital conversion. *Psychoanalytic Quarterly, 44,* 253–265.

Dougherty, D., & Lewis, P. (1991). Stimulus generalization, discrimination learning, and peak shift in horses. *Journal of the Experimental Analysis of Behavior, 56,* 97–104.

Drickmer, L. C., & Vessey, S. H. (1992). *Animal behavior* (3rd ed.). Dubuque, IA: W. C. Brown.

Drimmer, E. K. (1985). Desensitization and benztopine for palmer hyperhidrosis. *Psychosomatics, 26,* 888–889.

Druckman, D., & Broome, B. J. (1991). Value differences and conflict resolution: Familiarity or liking? *Journal of Conflict Resolution, 35,* 571–593.

Dryfoos, J. G. (1990). *Adolescents at risk: Prevalence and prevention.* New York: Oxford.

Dullier, P., & Gentry, W. (1980). Use of biofeedback in treating chronic hyperhidrosis: A preliminary report. *British Journal of Dermatology, 103,* 143–146.

Duncker, K. (1945). On problem solving. *Psychological Monographs, 58* (Whole No. 270).

Dvorak, A., Merrick, N. L., Dealey, W. L., & Ford, G. C. (1936). *Typewriting behavior.* New York: American Book Company.

Dvorak, H. (1985, July). Personal communication.

Earhard, M. (1967). Subjective organization and list organization as determinants of free-recall and serial-recall memorization. *Journal of Verbal Learning and Verbal Behavior, 6,* 501–507.

Ebbinghaus, H. (1913). *Memory* (H. A. Ruger & C. E. Bussenius, Trans.). New York: Teacher's College, Columbia University. (Original work published 1885)

Edinger, J. D., Marsh, G. R., McCall, W. V., & Erwin, C. W. (1990). Daytime functioning and nighttime sleep before, during, and after a 146-hour tennis match. *Sleep, 13,* 526–532.

Ehrlich, P., & White, J. (1991). TOPS: A consumer approach to Alzheimer's respite programs. *Gerontologist, 31,* 686–691.

Eisler, R. M., & Blalock, J. A. (1991). Masculine gender role stress: Implications for the assessment of men. *Clinical Psychology Review, 11(1),* 45–60.

Ekman, P. (1980). *The face of man: Expressions of universal emotions in a New Guinea village.* New York: Garland STPM Press.

Ekman, P. (1992). Facial expressions of emotion: New findings, new questions. *Psychological Science, 3,* 34–38.

Ekman, P., Levenson, R. W., & Friesen, W. V. (1983). Autonomic nervous system activity distinguishes among emotions. *Science, 221,* 1208–1210.

Elkin, I., Shea, M. T., Watkins, J. T., Imber, S. D., Sotsky, S. M., Collins, J. F. Glass, D. R., Pilkonis, P. A., Leber, W. R., Docherty, J. P., Fiester, S. J., & Parloff, M. B. (1989). NIMH treatment of depression collaborative research program: General effectiveness of treatments. *Archives of General Psychiatry, 46,* 971–982.

Elkind, D. (1967). Egocentrism in adolescence. *Child Development, 38,* 1025–1034.

Elkind, D. (1984). *All grown up and no place to go.* Reading, MA: Addison-Wesley.

Elkins, R. L. (1991). An appraisal of chemical aversion (emetic therapy) approaches to alcoholism treatment. *Behavior Research and Therapy, 29,* 387–413.

Ellis, A. (1962). *Reason and emotion in psychotherapy.* New York: Lyle Stuart.

Ellis, A. (1991). The revised ABC's of rational-emotive therapy. *Journal of Rational-Emotive and Cognitive-Behavior Therapy, 9,* 139–172.

Ellis, A. (1993). Reflections on rational-emotive therapy. *Journal of Consulting and Clinical Psychology, 61,* 199–201.

Elms, A. (1972). *Social psychology and social relevance.* Boston: Little, Brown.

Elwork, A. Sales, B. D., & Alfini, J. J. (1977). Juridic decisions: In ignorance of the law or in light of it? *Law and Human Behavior, 1,* 163–189.

Ely, R. J. (1995). The power of demography: Women's social constructions of gender identity at work. *Academy of Management Journal, 38,* 589–634.

Emanuelsson, I., & Svensson, A. (1990). Changes in intelligence over a quarter of a century. *Scandinavian Journal of Educational Research, 34,* 171–187.

Emde, R. N. (1992). Individual meaning and increasing complexity: Contributions of Sigmund Freud and René Spitz to developmental psychology. *Developmental Psychology, 28,* 347–359.

Emmons, W., & Simon, C. W. (1956). The non-recall of material presented during sleep. *American Journal of Psychology, 69,* 76–81.

Endler, N. S. (1988). The origins of electroconvulsive therapy (ECT). *Convulsive Therapy, 4,* 5–23.

Engel, B. T. (1972). Operant conditioning of cardiac function: A status report. *Psychophysiology, 9,* 161–177.

Engel, G. L. (1992). The need for a new medical model: A challenge for biomedicine. *Family Systems Medicine, 10,* 317–331.

Epstein, S. (1994). Integration of the cognitive and psychodynamic unconscious. *American Psychologist, 49,* 709–724.

Erikson, E. (1963). *Childhood and society* (2nd ed.). New York: Norton.

Erikson, M. (1968). The inhumanity of ordinary people. *International Journal of Psychiatry, 6,* 278–279.

Erlenmeyer-Kimling, L., & Jarvik, L. F. (1963). Genetics and intelligence: A review. *Science, 142,* 1477–1479.

Estes, W. K. (1991a). Cognitive architectures from the standpoint of an experimental psychologist. *Annual Review of Psychology, 42,* 1–28.

Estes, W. K. (1991b). Introduction: Principles of psychology 1890–1990. *Psychological Science, 1,* 149–150.

Evans, B., & Waites, B. (1981). *IQ and mental testing: An unnatural science and its social history.* Atlantic Highlands, NJ: Humanities Press.

Evans, D. A., Block, M. R., Steinberg, E. R., & Penrose, A. M. (1986). Frames and heuristics in doctor-patient discourse. *Social Science and Medicine, 22,* 1027–1034.

Eysenck, H. J. (1952). The effects of psychotherapy: An evaluation. *Journal of Consulting and Clinical Psychology, 16,* 319–324.

Eysenck, H. J. (1965). The effects of psychotherapy. *International Journal of Psychiatry, 1,* 97–144.

Eysenck, H. J. (1967). *The biological basis of personality.* Springfield, IL: Charles C. Thomas.

Eysenck, H. J. (1990). Biological dimensions of personality. In L. A. Pervin (Ed.), *Handbook of personality theory and research.* New York: Guilford Press.

Fabrega, H. (1989). Cultural relativism and psychiatric illness. *Journal of Nervous and Mental Disease, 177,* 415–425.

Fallon, A. E. & Rozin, R. (1985). Sex differences in perceptions of desirable body shape. *Journal of Abnormal Psychology, 94,* 102–105.

Fancher, R. E. (1990). *Pioneers of psychology* (2nd ed.). New York: Norton.

Fantz, R. (1961). The origin of form perception. *Scientific American, 204*(5), 66–72.

Farber, I. E. (1975). Sane and insane: Constructions and misconstructions. *Journal of Abnormal Psychology, 84,* 589–620.

Farrington, D. P. (1991). Longitudinal research strategies: Advantages, problems, and prospects. *Journal of the American Academy of Child and Adolescence Psychiatry, 30,* 369–374.

Felmlee, D., Sprecher, S., & Bassim, E. (1990). The dissolution of intimate relationships; a hazard model. *Social Psychology Quarterly, 53,* 13–30.

Fenichel, O. (1982). Reflections on training and theory. *International Review of Psycho-Analysis, 9*(2), 155–161.

Fenton, W. S., & McGlashan, T. H. (1991). Natural history of schizophrenia subtypes: II. Positive and negative symptoms and long-term course. *Archives of General Psychiatry, 48,* 978–986.

Fernald, A. (1985). Four-month-old infants prefer to listen to motherese. *Infant Behavior and Development, 8,* 181–195.

Fernald, C. D., & Gettys, L. (1980). Diagnostic labels and perceptions of children's behavior. *Journal of Clinical Child Psychology, 9,* 229–233.

Fernald, L. D. (1984). *The Hans legacy.* Hillsdale, NJ: Erlbaum.

Fernald, L. D. (1987). Of windmills and rope dancing: The instructional value of narrative structures. *Teaching of Psychology, 14,* 214–216.

Fernald, P. S. (1993). Unpublished case materials. Portsmouth, NH.

Fernald, P. S. (1995). Preparing psychology graduate students for the professoriate. *American Psychologist, 50,* 421–427.

Festinger, L., Reicken, H. W., & Schachter, S. (1956). *When prophecy fails.* Minneapolis: University of Minnesota Press.

Festinger, L., Schachter, S., & Back, K. (1950). *Social pressures in informal groups.* Palo Alto, CA: Stanford University Press.

Fielder, F. E. (1964). A contingency model of leadership effectiveness. In L. Berkowitz (Ed.), *Advances in experimental social psychology* (Vol. 1). New York: Academic Press.

Fields, P. E. (1932). Studies in concept formation: I. The development of the concept of triangularity in the white rat. *Comparative Psychology Monograph, 9.*

Fields, P. E. (1936). Studies in concept formation: IV. A comparison of white rats and raccoons with respect to their visual discrimination of certain geometrical features. *Journal of Comparative Psychology, 21,* 341–355.

Filstrup, C. & Filstrup, J. (1983). *China: From emperors to communes.* Minneapolis, MN: Dillon.

Findley, M. J., & Cooper, H. M. (1983). Locus of control and academic achievement: A literature review. *Journal of Personality and Social Psychology, 44,* 419–427.

Finkel, M. L., & Finkel, D. J. (1983). Male adolescent sexual behavior, the forgotten partner. *Journal of School Health, 53,* 544–547.

Fiorito, G., & Scotto, P. (1992). Observational learning in *Octopus vulgaris. Science, 256,* 545–547.

Fiske, S. T. (1993). Social cognition and social perception. *Annual Review of Psychology, 44,* 155–194.

FitzGerald, G. J. (1993). The reproductive behavior of the stickleback. *Scientific American, 268,* 80–85.

Flavell, J. H., Shipstead, S. G., & Croft, K. (1978). Young children's knowledge about visual perception: Hiding objects from others. *Child Development, 49,* 1208–1211.

Flicker, C., Ferris, S., Crook, T., & Bartus, R. (1989). Age differences in the vulnerability of facial recognition memory to proactive interference. *Experimental Aging Research, 15,* 189–194.

Flynn, T. M. (1991). Development of social, personal and cognitive skills of preschool children in the Montessori and traditional preschool programs. *Early Child Development and Care, 72,* 117–124.

Folkins, C. H., & Sime, W. E. (1981). Physical fitness training and mental health. *American Psychologist, 36,* 373–389.

Ford, D. Y., & Harris, J. J. (1990). Black students: "At promise" not "at risk" for giftedness. *Journal of Human Behavior and Learning, 7,* 21–29.

Fossey, D. (1983). *Gorillas in the mist.* Boston: Houghton Mifflin.

Fouts, R., Fouts, D., & Van Cantfort, T. (1989). The infant Louis learns signs from cross-fostered chimpanzees. In R. A. Gardner, B. T. Gardner, & T. E. Van Cantfort (Eds.), *Teaching sign language to chimpanzees.* New York: State University of New York Press.

Fowles, D. C. (1992). Schizophrenia: Diathesis-stress revisited. *Annual Review of Psychology, 43,* 303–336.

Fraenkel, P. (1995). The nomothetic-idiographic debate in family therapy. *Family Process, 34,* 113–121.

Freedman, J. L., & Fraser, S. C. (1966). Compliance without pressure: The foot-in-the-door technique. *Journal of Personality and Social Psychology, 4,* 195–202.

Freeman, W., & Watts, J. W. (1950). *Psychosurgery in the treatment of mental disorders and intractable pain.* Springfield, IL: Charles C. Thomas.

Freeman, W. J. (1991). The physiology of perception. *Scientific American, 264,* 78–85.

Freud, S. (1900). The interpretation of dreams. In *Standard edition of the complete works of Sigmund Freud* (Vols. 4–5). London: Hogarth Press, 1953.

Freud, S. (1909). Analysis of a phobia in a five-year-old boy. In *Standard edition of the complete works of Sigmund Freud* (Vol. 10). London: Hogarth Press, 1953.

Freud, S. (1914). *Psychopathology of everyday life.* New York: Macmillan.

Freud, S. (1915). Instincts and their vicissitudes. In *Collected papers* (Vol. 4). London: Hogarth Press, 1946.

Freud, S. (1923). The ego and the id. In *Standard edition of the complete works of Sigmund Freud* (Vol. 19). London: Hogarth Press, 1961.

Freud, S. (1927). *The question of lay analysis.* New York: Norton, 1959.

Freud, S. (1933). New introductory lectures on psycho-analysis. In *Standard edition of the complete works of Sigmund Freud* (Vol. 22). London: Hogarth Press, 1964.

Freud, S. (1938). An out-line of psycho-analysis. In *Standard edition of the complete works of Sigmund Freud* (Vol. 23). London: Hogarth Press, 1964.

Fried-Buchalter, S. (1992). Fear of success, fear of failure, and the imposter phenomenon: A factor analytic approach to convergent and discriminant validity. *Journal of Personality Assessment, 58,* 368–379.

Friedman, H. S., & Booth-Kewley, S. (1987). The "disease-prone personality": A meta-analytic view of the construct. *American Psychologist, 42,* 539–555.

Friend, R., Rafferty, Y., & Bramel, D. (1990). A puzzling misinterpretation of the Asch "conformity" study. *European Journal of Social Psychology, 20,* 29–44.

Fry, W. F. (1986). Humor, physiology, and the aging process. In L. Nahemow, K. A. McCluskey-Fawcett, & P. E. McGhee (Eds.), *Humor and aging.* Orlando, FL: Academic Press.

Funkenstein, D. H., King, S. H., & Drolette, M. E. (1957). *Mastery of stress.* Cambridge, MA: Harvard University Press.

Furstenberg, F. F., Brooks-Gunn, J. & Morgan, S. P. (1987). *Adolescent mothers in later life.* Cambridge, England: Cambridge University Press.

Gabrenya, W. K., Wang, Y., & Latané, B. (1985). Social loafing on an optimizing task: Cross-cultural differences among Chinese and Americans. *Journal of Cross Cultural Psychology, 16,* 223–242.

Gackenbach, J., & LaBerge, S. (1988). *Conscious mind, sleeping brain.* New York: Plenum Press.

Gage, N. L. (1952). Judging interests from expressive behavior. *Psychological Monographs, 66* (18, Whole No. 350).

Galambos, N. L. (1992). Parent-adolescent relations. *Current Directions in Psychological Science, 1,* 146–149.

Galejs, I., King, A., & Hegland, S. M. (1987). Antecedents of achievement motivation in preschool children. *Journal of Genetic Psychology, 148*(3), 333–348.

Gallagher, B. J., Jones, B. J., & Barakat, L. P. (1987). The attitudes of psychiatrists toward etiological theories of schizophrenia: 1975–1985. *Journal of Clinical Psychology, 43,* 438–443.

Gallagher, S. (1991). Acceptable weights and physiological costs of performing combined manual handling tasks in restricted postures. *Ergonomics, 34,* 939–952.

Gal'perin, P. I. (1992). Human instincts. *Journal of Russian and East European Psychology, 30,* 22–36.

Garcia, J., & Koelling, R. A. (1966). Relation of cue to consequence in avoidance learning. *Psychonomic Science, 4,* 123–124.

Gardner, B. T., & Gardner, R. A. (1971). Two-way communication with an infant chimpanzee. In A. M. Schrier & F. Stollmitz (Eds.), *Behavior of nonhuman primates.* New York: Academic Press.

Gardner, H. (1983). *Frames of mind.* New York: Basic Books.

Gardner, R. A., & Gardner, B. T. (1969). Teaching sign language to a chimpanzee. *Science, 165,* 664–672.

Gastil, J. (1990). Generic pronouns and sexist language. *Sex Roles, 23,* 629–643.

Gay, P. (1990). *Reading Freud: Explorations and entertainments.* New Haven, CT: Yale University Press.

Gazzaniga, M. S., Bogen, J. E., & Sperry, R. W. (1965). Observations on visual perception after disconnexion of the cerebral hemispheres in man. *Brain, 88,* 221–236.

Geen, R. G. (1991). Social motivation. *Annual Review of Psychology, 42,* 377–399.

Gergen, K., Gergen, M., & Meter, K. (1972). Individual orientations to prosocial behavior. *Journal of Social Issues, 28,* 105–130.

Gewirtz, J. L., & Peláez-Nogueras, M. (1992). B. F. Skinner's legacy to human infant behavior and development. *American Psychologist, 47,* 1411–1422.

Gibson, E. J., & Walk, R. D. (1960). The "visual cliff." *Scientific American, 202,* 64–71.

Gilligan, C. (1982). *In a different voice: Psychological theory and women's development.* Cambridge, MA: Harvard University Press.

Gissurarson, L. R. (1990). Comments on feedback in the literature of psi training. *Journal of the Society for Psychical Research, 56,* 91–96.

Glanzer, M., & Cunitz, A. (1966). Two storage mechanisms and free recall. *Journal of Verbal Learning and Verbal Behavior, 5,* 351–360.

Glasscock, S. E., & MacLean, W. E. (1990). Use of contact desensitization and shaping in the treatment of dog phobia and generalized fear of the outdoors. *Journal of Clinical Child Psychology, 19,* 169–172.

Gleason, H. A. (1961). *An introduction to descriptive linguistics.* New York: Holt.

Goethals, G. W., & Klos, D. S. (1976). *Experiencing youth: First-person accounts* (2nd ed.). Boston: Little, Brown.

Goldman-Rakic, P. S. (1987). Development of cortical circuitry and cognitive function. *Child Development, 58,* 601–622.

Goldner, V. (1991). Toward a critical relational theory of gender. *Psychoanalytic Dialogues, 1,* 249–272.

Goldstein, M. J. (1988). The family and psychopathology. *Annual Review of Psychology, 39,* 283–299.

Goodman, J. (1994). *Laughing matters.* Saratoga Springs, NY: The Humor Project.

Goodman, L., Saxe, L., & Harvey, M. (1991). Homelessness as psychological trauma: Broadening perspectives. *American Psychologist, 46,* 1219–1225.

Gopher, D., & Raij, D. (1988). Typing with a two-hand chord keyboard: Will the QWERTY become obsolete? *IEEE Transactions on Systems, Man, and Cybernetics, 18,* 601–609.

Goteborgs, U. (1990). Schizophrenia: A subcortical neurotransmitter imbalance syndrome? *Schizophrenia Bulletin, 16,* 425–432.

Gottesman, I. I. (1963). Heritability of personality. *Psychological Monographs, 77* (9, Whole No. 572), 1–21.

Gottesman, I. I., & Shields, J. (1966). Schizophrenia in twins: 16 years' consecutive admissions to a psychiatric clinic. *British Journal of Psychiatry, 112,* 809–818.

Gottman, J. M., & Levenson, R. W. (1986). Marital processes predictive of later dissolution. *Journal of Personality and Social Psychology, 53,* 221–233.

Gould, S. J. (1987, January). The panda's thumb of technology. *Natural History,* pp. 14–23.

Graf, P., Squire, L. R., & Mandler, G. (1984). The information that amnesic patients do not forget. *Journal of Experimental Psychology: Learning, Memory, and Cognition, 10,* 164–178.

Graham, R. L. (1972). *Dove.* New York: Harper & Row.

Graham, S. (1992). "Most of the subjects were white and middle class": Trends in published research on African Americans in selected APA journals, 1970–1989. *American Psychologist, 47,* 629–639.

Grassian, S., & Friedman, N. (1986). Effects of sensory deprivation in psychiatric seclusion and solitary confinement. *International Journal of Law and Psychiatry, 8,* 49–65.

Green, D., & Swets, J. (1966). *Signal detection theory and psychophysics.* New York: Wiley.

Greenough, W. T., & Juraska, J. M. (1979, July). Synaptic pruning. *Psychology Today,* p. 120.

Greenwald, A. G. (1992). New look 3: Unconscious cognition reclaimed. *American Psychologist, 47,* 766–779.

Greenwald, A. G., Spangenberg, E. R., Pratkanis, A. R., & Eskenazi, J. (1991). Double-blind tests of subliminal self-help audiotapes. *Psychological Science, 2,* 119–122.

Greer, R. D, Dorow, L., Williams, G., & McCorkle, N. (1991). Peer-mediated procedures to induce swallowing and food acceptance in young children. *Journal of Applied Behavior Analysis, 24,* 783–790.

Grief, G. L., & Kristall, J. (1993). Common themes in a group for noncustodial parents. *Families in Society, 74,* 240–245.

Griggs, S. A. (1984). Counseling the gifted and talented based on learning styles. *Exceptional Children, 50,* 429–433.

Grotstein, J. S. (1990). The contribution of attachment theory and self-regulation theory to the therapeutic alliance. *Modern Psychoanalysis, 15,* 169–184.

Guilford, J. P. (1975). Factors and factors of personality. *Psychological Bulletin, 82,* 802–814.

Guilford, J. P. (1988). Some changes in the structure-of-intellect model. *Educational and Psychological Measurement, 48,* 1–4.

Guyette, C. A., Chavis, D. M., & Shearer, D. H. (1980). The effect of ribonucleic acid injections upon the maze learning ability of rats. *Physiology & Behavior, 24(5),* 971–974.

Guze, B. H., & Barrio, J. C. (1991). The etiology of depression in Parkinson's disease patients. *Psychosomatics, 32,* 390–395.

Halbrook, B. (1995). Integrating contemplative psychotherapy and counseling. *TCA Journal, 23,* 21–27.

Haldane, J. B. S. (1946). The interaction of nature and nurture. *Annals of Eugenics, 13,* 197–205.

Halford, G. S. (1990). Is children's reasoning logical or analogical? Further comments on Piagetian cognitive developmental psychology. *Human Development, 33,* 356–361.

Hall, C., Bernoties, L. & Schmidt, D. (1995). Interference effects of mental imagery on a motor task. *British Journal of Psychology, 86,* 181–190.

Hall, C. S., & Van de Castle, R. L. (1966). *The content analysis of dreams.* New York: Appleton-Century-Crofts.

Hall, D. (1991a). The research imperative and bureaucratic control: The case of clinical research. *Social Science and Medicine, 32,* 333–342.

Hall, E. T. (1966). *The hidden dimension.* New York: Doubleday.

Hall, M. R. (1991b). Endocrinological and behavioral changes associated with the onset of incubation in the duck. *Physiology and Behavior, 50,* 311–316.

Halli, S. S., & Zimmer, Z. (1991). Common law union as a differentiating factor in the failure of marriage in Canada, 1984. *Social Indicators Research, 24,* 329–354.

Hamachek, D. (1990). Evaluating self-concept and ego status in Erikson's last three psychosocial stages. *Journal of Counseling and Development, 68,* 677–683.

Hamburg, D. A., & Takanishi, R. (1989). Preparing for life: The critical transition of adolescence. *American Psychologist, 44,* 825–827.

Handy, C. (1990). *The age of unreason.* Boston: Harvard Business School Press.

Harden, L. M. (1930). Effect of emotional reactions upon retention. *Journal of General Psychology, 3,* 197–221.

Hardy, C., & Latané, B. (1986). Social loafing on a cheering task. *Social Science, 71,* 165–172.

Hare-Mustin, R. T., & Marecek, J. (1988). The meaning of difference: Gender theory, postmodernism, and psychology. *American Psychologist, 43,* 455–464.

Harkness, S. (1990). A cultural model for the acquisition of language: Implications for the innateness debate. *Developmental Psychobiology, 23,* 727–739.

Harlow, H. F., Harlow, M. K., & Meyer, D. R. (1950). Learning motivated by a manipulation drive. *Journal of Experimental Psychology, 40,* 228–235.

Harlow, H. F., Harlow, M. K., & Suomi, S. J. (1971). From thought to therapy: Lessons from a primate laboratory. *American Scientist, 59,* 538–549.

Harlow, H. F., & Suomi, S. J. (1970). Nature of love—simplified. *American Psychologist, 25,* 161–168.

Harlow, J. M. (1869). *Recovery from the passage of an iron bar through the head.* Boston: David Clapp & Son.

Harmon, P., Maus, R., & Morrissey, W. (1988). *Expert systems: Tools and applications.* New York: Wiley.

Harris, V. A., & Katkin, E. S. (1975). Primary and secondary emotional behavior: An analysis of the role of autonomic feedback on affect, arousal, and attribution. *Psychological Bulletin, 82,* 904–916.

Harrison, A. A. (1969). Exposure and population. *Journal of Personality, 37,* 359–377.

Hartmann, E., Bernstein, J., & Wilson, C. (1967, April). *Sleep and dreaming in the elephant.* Report to the Association for the Psychophysiological Study of Sleep.

Hartshorne, H. & May, M. A. (1928). Studies in the nature of character. In *Studies in deceit* (Vol. 1). New York: Macmillan.

Hatfield, E., & Sprecher, S. (1986). *Mirror, mirror . . . : The importance of looks in everyday life.* Albany: State University of New York Press.

Hathaway, S. R., & McKinley, J. C. (1989). *MMPI-2: Minnesota Multiphasic Personality Inventory-2. Manual for administration and scoring.* Minneapolis: University of Minnesota Press.

Hayes, C. (1951). *The ape in our house.* New York: Harper & Row.

Haynes, S. G., Feinleib, M., & Kannel, W. (1980). The relationship of psychosocial factors to coronary heart disease in the Framingham study: III. Eight-year incidence of coronary heart disease. *American Journal of Epidemiology, 111,* 37–58.

Healy, D. (1991). D-sub-1 and D-sub-2 and D-sub-3. *British Journal of Psychiatry, 159,* 319–324.

Hebb, D. O. (1966). *A textbook of psychology* (2nd ed.). Philadelphia: Saunders.

Heider, E. R. (1972). Universals in color naming and memory. *Journal of Experimental Psychology, 93,* 10–20.

Heider, F. (1946). Attitudes and cognitive organization. *Journal of Psychology, 21,* 107–112.

Heinrichs, R. W. (1993). Schizophrenia and the brain: Conditions for a neuropsychology of madness. *American Psychologist, 48,* 221–233.

Hellige, J. B. (1990). Hemispheric asymmetry. *Annual Review of Psychology, 41,* 55–80.

Hellige, J. B. (1993). Unity of thought and action: Varieties of inter-action between the left and right cerebral hemispheres. *Current Directions in Psychological Science, 2,* 21–25.

Helmes, E., & Redden, J. R. (1993). A perspective on developments in assessing psychopathology: A critical review of the MMPI and MMPI-2. *Psychological Bulletin, 113,* 453–471.

Hendrick, C., & Hendrick, S. (1991). Dimensions of love: A socio-biological interpretation. *Journal of Social and Clinical Psychology, 10,* 206–230.

Hendrick, C., Hendrick, S., Foote, F., & Slapion-Foote, M. (1984). Do men and women love differently? *Journal of Social and Personal Relationships, 1,* 177–195.

Herrnstein, R. J., & Murray, C. (1994). *The bell curve: Intelligence and class structure in American life.* New York: Free Press.

Herskovits, M. J., Campbell, D. T., & Segall, M. H. (1969). *A cross-cultural study of perception.* Indianapolis: Bobbs-Merrill.

Hertzog, C., & Schaie, K. W. (1986). Stability and change in adult experience. *Psychology and Aging, 1,* 159–171.

Herzog, H. A. (1988). Naturalistic observation of behavior: A model system using mice in a colony. *Teaching of Psychology, 15,* 200–202.

Herzog, H. A. (1991). Conflicts of interests: Kittens and boa con-strictors, pets and research. *American Psychologist, 46,* 246–247.

Heylighen, F. (1992). A cognitive-systemic reconstruction of Maslow's theory of self-actualization. *Behavioral Science, 37,* 39–58.

Hilgard, E. R. (1973). A neodissociation interpretation of pain reduction in hypnosis. *Psychological Review, 80,* 396–411.

Hilgard, E. R. (1980). Consciousness in contemporary psychology. *Annual Review of Psychology, 31,* 1–26.

Hilgard, E. R. (1993). Which psychologists prominent in the second half of this century made lasting contributions to psychological theory? *Psychological Science, 4,* 70–80.

Hilgard, E. R., Leary, D. E., & McGuire, G. R. (1991). The history of psychology: A survey and critical assessment. *Annual Review of Psychology, 42,* 79–107.

Hill, K. A. (1987). Meta-analysis of paradoxical interventions. *Psychotherapy, 24,* 266–270.

Hill, T., & Lewicki, P. (1991). The unconscious. In V. J. Derlega, B, A, Winstead, & W. H. Jones (Eds.), *Personality. Contemporary theory and research.* Chicago: Nelson-Hall.

Hill, W. F. (1981). *Principles of learning: A handbook of applications.* Sherman Oaks, CA: Alfred.

Hilton, J. L. & von Hippel, W. (1996). Stereotypes. *Annual Review of Psychology, 47,* 237–271.

Himelein, M. J., Nietzel, M. T., & Dillehay, R. C. (1991). Effects of prior juror experience on jury sentencing. *Behavioral Sciences and the Law, 9,* 97–106.

Hintzman, D. L. (1990). Human learning and memory. Connections and dissociations. *Annual Review of Psychology, 41,* 109–139.

Hoberman, H. M. (1990). Study group report on the impact of tele-vision violence on adolescents. *Journal of Adolescent Health Care, 11,* 45–49.

Hobson, A. (1988) *The dreaming brain.* New York: Basic Books.

Hoch, S. J. (1986). Counterfactual reasoning and accuracy in pre-dicting personal events. *Journal of Experimental Psychology: Learning, Memory, and Cognition, 11,* 719–731.

Hockett, C. F. (1960). The origin of speech. *Scientific American, 203,* 89–96.

Hogan, R., Curphy. G. J., & Hogan, J. (1994). What we know about leadership: Effectiveness and personality. *American Psychologist, 49,* 493–504.

Hoke, R. E. (1922). *The improvement of speed and accuracy in typewriting.* The Johns Hopkins University Studies in Education, No. 7.

Holmes, D. S. (1984). Meditation and somatic arousal reduction. *American Psychologist, 39,* 1–10.

Holmes, T. H., & Rahe, R. H. (1967). The social readjustment rat-ing scale. *Journal of Psychosomatic Research, 11,* 213–218.

Holyoak, K. J., & Spellman, B. A. (1993). Thinking. *Annual Review of Psychology, 44,* 265–315.

Homans, G. C. (1974). *Social behavior: Its elementary forms* (Rev. ed.). New York: Harcourt, Brace, Jovanovich.

Honts, C. R., & Kircher, J. C. (1994). Mental and physical counter-measures reduce the accuracy of polygraph tests. *Journal of Applied Psychology, 79,* 252–259.

Honzik, M. P., & MacFarlane, J. W. (1973). Personality development and intellectual functioning from 21 months to 40 years. In L. F. Jarvik, C. Eisdorfer, & J. Blum (Eds.), *Intellectual functioning in adults: Psychological and biological influences.* New York: Springer.

Hood, A. B. (1963). A study of the relationship between physique and personality variables measured by the MMPI. *Journal of Personality, 31,* 97–107.

Hooley, J. M. (1985). Expressed emotion: A review of the critical lit-erature. *Clinical Psychology Review, 5,* 119–139.

Hooykaas, C., Van der Linden, M., Van Doornum, G., & Van der Velde, F. (1991). Limited changes in sexual behavior of heterosex-ual men and women with multiple partners in the Netherlands. *AIDS Care, 3,* 21–30.

Hopson, B., & Scally, M. (1980). Change and development in adult life: Some implications for helpers. *British Journal of Guidance Counsel, 8,* 175–187.

Horgan, J. (1993). Eugenics revisited. *Scientific American, 268,* 122–131.

Horne, J. A. (1988). *Why we sleep.* Oxford, UK: Oxford University Press.

Horner, M. (1970). Femininity and successful achievement: A basic inconsistency. In J. Bartwick, E. Bouvan, M. Horner, & D. Gutmann (Eds.), *Feminine personality and conflict.* Pacific Grove, CA: Brooks/Cole.

Horney, K. (1937). *The neurotic personality of our time.* New York: Norton.

Hoskin, R. G., Sasitharan, T., & Howard, R. (1992). The use of a low phenylalanine diet with amino acid supplement in the treatment of behavioral problems in a severely mentally retarded adult female with phenylketonuria. *Journal of Intellectual Disability Research, 36,* 183–191.

Howard, G. S. (1991). Culture tales: A narrative approach to think-ing, cross-cultural psychology, and psychotherapy. *American Psychologist, 46,* 187–197.

Howard, G. S. (1993). Why William James might be considered the founder of the scientist-practitioner model. *Counseling Psychologist, 21,* 118–135.

Howell, W. C. (1993). Engineering psychology in a changing world. *Annual Review of Psychology, 44,* 231–263.

Howell, W. C. (1994). Human factors and the challenges of the future. *Psychological Science, 5*(1) 4–7.

Hubel, D. H., & Wiesel, T. N. (1962). Receptive fields, binocular interaction and functional architecture in the cat's visual cortex. *Journal of Physiology, 160,* 106–154.

Hubel, D. H., & Wiesel, T. N. (1979). Brain mechanisms of vision. *Scientific American, 241,* 150–162.

Hudesman, J., Loveday, C., & Woods, N. (1984). Desensitization of test anxious urban community-college students and resulting changes in grade point average: A replication. *Journal of Clinical Psychology, 40,* 65–67.

Hughes, T., & Helling, M. (1991). A case for obtaining informed consent from young children. *Early Childhood Research Quarterly, 6,* 225–232.

Huntingford, F. A. (1984). Some ethical issues raised by studies of predation and aggression. *Animal Behavior, 32,* 210–215.

Hurvich, L. M., & Jameson, D. (1957). An opponent-process theory of color vision. *Psychological Review, 64,* 384–404.

Huston, T. L., & Vangelisti, A. L. (1991). Socioemotional behavior and satisfaction in marital relationships. *Journal of Personality and Social Psychology, 61,* 721–733.

Hyde, J. S. (1991). *Half the human experience* (4th ed.). Lexington, MA: Heath.

Hyde, J. S., & Linn, M. C. (1988). Gender differences in verbal ability: A meta-analysis. *Psychological Bulletin, 104,* 53–69.

Innis, N. K. (1992). Tolman and Tryon: Early research on the inheritance of the ability to learn. *American Psychologist, 47,* 190–197.

Isen, A. M., & Levin, P. F. (1972). Effects of feeling good on helping: Cookies and kindness. *Journal of Personality and Social Psychology, 21,* 384–388.

Itard, J. M. G. (1801). *De l'education d'un homme sauvage.* Paris: Goujon.

Itard, J. M. G. (1807). *Rapports et mémoires sur le sauvage de l'Aveyron.* Paris: Alcan. (G. Humphrey & M. Humphrey, Trans.). The wild boy of Aveyron. Englewood Cliffs, NJ: Prentice Hall, 1962.

Ivancevich, J. M. (1986). Life events and hassels as predictors of health symptoms, job performance, and absenteeism. *Journal of Occupational Behavior, 7,* 39–51.

Iversen, I. H. (1992). Skinner's early research: From reflexology to operant conditioning. *American Psychologist, 47,* 1318–1328.

Izard, C. (1971). *The faces of emotion.* New York: Appleton-Century-Crofts.

Izard, C. (1990). Facial expressions and the regulation of emotions. *Journal of Personality and Social Psychology, 54,* 487–498.

Izard, C., Huebner, R., Risser, D., & Dougherty, L. (1980). The young infant's ability to produce discrete emotion expressions. *Developmental Psychology, 16,* 132–140.

Jacobs, L. (1992). Insights from psychoanalytic self-psychology and intersubjectivity theory for Gestalt therapists. *Gestalt Therapy, 15,* 25–60.

James, W. (1890). *The principles of psychology.* New York: Holt.

Jancar, J., & Johnston, S. J. (1990). Incest and mental handicap. *Journal of Mental Deficiency Research, 34,* 483–490.

Janis, I. L. (1982). *Groupthink: Psychological studies of foreign-policy decisions and fiascos* (2nd ed.). Boston: Houghton Mifflin.

Jenkins, J. G., & Dallenbach, K. M. (1924). Oblivscence during sleep and waking. *American Journal of Psychology, 35,* 605–612.

Jensen, A. R. (1980). *Bias in mental testing.* New York: Free Press.

Jensen, M. P., & Karoly, P. (1991). Motivation and expectancy factors in symptom perception: A laboratory study of the placebo effect. *Psychosomatic Medicine, 53,* 144–152.

Jernigan, T. L., Zisook, S., Heaton, R. K., Moranville, J. T., Hasselink, J. R., & Braff, D. L. (1991). Magnetic resonance imaging abnormalities in lenticular nuclei and cerebra cortex in schizophrenia. *Archives of General Psychiatry, 48,* 881–890.

Johnson, D. W., Maruyama, G., Johnson, R., Nelson, D., & Skon, L. (1981). Effects of cooperative competitive, and individualistic goal structures and achievement: A meta-analysis. *Psychological Bulletin, 89,* 47–60.

Johnson, N. B. (1991). Primordial image and the archetypal design of art. *Journal of Analytical Psychology, 36,* 371–392.

Johnston, D. W. (1991). Behavioral medicine: The application of behavior therapy to physical health. *Behavioral Psychotherapy, 19,* 100–108.

Jones, E. (1957). *Life and work of Sigmund Freud* (Vol. 3). New York: Basic Books.

Jones, E. E., David, K. E., & Jergen, K. J. (1961). Role playing variations and their informational value for person perception. *Journal of Abnormal Social Psychology, 63,* 302–310.

Jones, F. N. (1987). Ageing: Sensory and perceptual changes. In R. L. Gregory (Ed.), *The Oxford companion to the mind.* New York: Oxford University Press.

Jones, J. R., Burnsed, G. M., & Marquardt, J. S. (1991). *Preventing repetitive strain.* San Bruno, CA: Kranes Communications.

Jones, M. C. (1924). A laboratory study of fear: The case of Peter. *Pedag. Sem., 31,* 308–315.

Jones, M. C. (1974). Albert, Peter, and John B. Watson. *American Psychologist, 29,* 581–583.

Jones, S. R. (1992). Was there a Hawthorne effect? *American Journal of Sociology, 98,* 451–468.

Joseph, R. A., Markus, H. R., & Tafarodi, R. W. (1992). Gender and self-esteem. *Journal of Personality and Social Psychology, 63,* 391–402.

Jourard, S. (1964). *The transparent self: Self-disclosure and well-being.* (2nd ed., 1971). New York: Van Nostrand.

Jung, C. G. (1928). *Contributions to analytical psychology.* New York: Harcourt.

Jung, C. G. (1963). *Memories, dreams, reflections.* London: Routledge & Kegan Paul.

Jung, C. G. (1964). *Man and his symbols.* London: Aldus Books.

Kacergius, M. A., & Adams, G. R. (1980). Erikson stage resolution: The relationship between identity and intimacy. *Journal of Youth and Adolescence, 9,* 117–126.

Kagan, J., & Snidman, N. (1991). Infant predictors of inhibited and uninhibited profiles. *Psychological Science, 2,* 40–44.

Kagan, J., Snidman, N., Julia-Sellers, M., & Johnson, M. O. (1991). Temperament and allergic symptoms. *Psychosomatic Medicine, 53,* 332–340.

Kahneman, D., Slovic, P., & Tversky, A. (1982). *Judgment under uncertainty: Heuristics and biases.* New York: Cambridge University Press.

Kahneman, D., & Tversky, A. (1984). Choices, values, and frames. *American Psychologist, 39,* 341–350.

Kaley, H. (1993). Psychoanalysis in education: Attitude and process. *Psychoanalytic Psychology, 10,* 93–103.

Kalma, A. (1991). Hierarchisation and dominance: Assessment at first glance. *European Journal of Social Psychology, 21,* 165–181.

Kamin, L. J. (1974). *The science and politics of I.Q.* New York: Wiley.

Kane, J. M. (1987). Treatment of schizophrenia. *Schizophrenia Bulletin, 13,* 133–156.

Kantola, S. J., Syme, G. J., & Campbell, N. A. (1984). Cognitive dissonance and energy consumption. *Journal of Applied Psychology, 69,* 416–421.

Kanwisher, N., & Driver, J. (1992). Objects, attributes, and visual attention: Which, what, and where. *Current Directions in Psychological Science, 1,* 26–31.

Karasu, T. (1986). The specificity versus non-specificity dilemma: Toward identifying therapeutic change agents. *American Journal of Psychiatry, 143,* 687–695.

Karon, B. P. (1991, August 18). Psychotherapy: Treatment of choice for schizophrenia. American Psychological Association Convention, San Francisco, CA: [Address].

Katzeff, P. (1983, February 14). *Boston Business Journal, 2,* pp. 1, 22–23.

Kay, S. R., & Lindenmayer, J. P. (1991). Stability of psychopathology dimensions in chronic schizophrenia: Response to clozapine treatment. *Comprehensive Psychiatry, 32,* 28–35.

Kazdin, A. (1982). The token economy: A decade later. *Journal of Applied Behavior Analysis, 15,* 431–445.

Kazdin, A. E. (1990). Psychotherapy for children and adolescents. *Annual Review of Psychology, 41,* 21–54.

Keane, M. (1989). Modelling problem solving in Gestalt "insight" problems. *Irish Journal of Psychology, 10,* 201–215.

Keesey, R. E., Corbett, S. W., Hirvonen, M. D., & Kaufman, L. N. (1984). Heat production and body weight changes following lateral hypothalamic lesions. *Physiology and Behavior, 32,* 309–317.

Keesey, R. E., & Pauley, T. L. (1986). The regulation of body weight. *Annual Review of Psychology, 37,* 109–134.

Kelley, H. H. (1967). Attribution theory in social psychology. In D. Levine (Ed.), *Nebraska Symposium on Motivation.* Lincoln: University of Nebraska Press.

Kelley, H. H. (1991). Research on interpersonal relationships. *Japanese Journal of Experimental Social Psychology, 30,* 259–267.

Kelley, H. H. (1992). Common-sense psychology and scientific psychology. *Annual Review of Psychology, 43,* 1–23.

Kellogg, W. N., & Kellogg, L. A. (1933). *The ape and the child.* New York: McGraw-Hill.

Kelman, H. C. (1967). Psychological research on social change: Some scientific and ethical issues. *International Journal of Psychology, 2,* 301–313.

Kendall, P. C., & Lipman, A. J. (1991). Psychological and pharmacological therapy: Methods and modes for comparative outcome research. *Journal of Consulting and Clinical Psychology, 59,* 78–87.

Kenrick, D. T., & Funder, D. C. (1988). Profiting from controversy: Lessons from the person-situation debate, *American Psychologist, 43,* 23–34.

Kenshalo, D. R. (1986). Somesthetic sensitivity in young and elderly humans. *Journal of Gerontology, 41,* 732–742.

Kidder, T. (1985). *House.* Boston: Houghton Mifflin.

Kiesler, C. A. (1982). Mental hospitals and alternative care: Noninstitutionalization as a potential public policy for mental patients. *American Psychologist, 37,* 349–360.

Kiesler, C. A. (1992). U.S. mental health policy: Doomed to fail. *American Psychologist, 47,* 1077–1082.

Kihlstrom, J. F. (1985). Hypnosis. *Annual Review of Psychology, 36,* 385–418.

Kihlstrom, J. F., Barnhardt, T. M., & Tataryn, D. J. (1992). The psychological unconscious: Found, lost, and regained. *American Psychologist, 47,* 788–791.

Kimura, D. (1990). Profile: Vive la difference. *Scientific American, 263,* 40–42.

Kimura, D. (1992). Sex differences in the brain. *Scientific American, 267,* 119–125.

King, A. C., & Fredericksen, L. W. (1984). Low-cost strategies for increasing exercise behavior: Relapse preparation training and social support. *Behavior Modification, 8,* 3–21.

King, M. G., & Stanley, A. V. (1986). The treatment of hyperhidrosis: A case report. *Australian Journal of Clinical and Experimental Hypnosis, 14,* 61–64.

Kinoshita, T. (1990). Current trends in health psychology. *Japanese Psychological Review, 33,* 3–34.

Kinsey, A. C., Pomeroy, W. B., & Gebhard, P. H. (1953). *Sexual behavior in the human female.* Philadelphia: Saunders.

Kinsey, A. C., Pomeroy, W. B., & Martin, C. E. (1948). *Sexual behavior in the human male.* Philadelphia: Saunders.

Kira, A. (1976). *The bathroom.* New York: Bantam Books.

Kirsch, I. (1990). *Changing expectations: A key to effective psychotherapy.* Pacific Grove, CA: Brooks/Cole.

Kleinman, A. (1987). Anthropology and psychiatry: The role of culture in cross-cultural research on illness. *British Journal of Psychiatry, 151,* 447–454.

Kleinmuntz, B., & Szucko, J. (1984). Lie detection in ancient and modern times: A call for contemporary scientific study. *American Psychologist, 39,* 766–776.

Knight, J., Knight, A., & Unguari, G. (1992). Can autoimmune mechanisms account for the genetic predisposition to schizophrenia? *British Journal of Psychology, 160,* 533–540.

Knox, R. E., & Safford, R. K. (1976). Group caution at the race track. *Journal of Experimental Social Psychology, 12,* 317–324.

Koehler, W. F., Fottler, M. D., & Swan, J. E. (1992). Physician-patient satisfaction: Equity in the health services encounter. *Medical Care Review, 49,* 455–484.

Kohlberg, L. (1969). Stage and sequence: The cognitive-developmental approach to socialization. In D. A. Goslin (Ed.), *Handbook of socialization theory and research.* Chicago: Rand McNally.

Köhler, W. (1925). *The mentality of apes.* New York: Harcourt, Brace.

Kohn, A., & Kalat, J. W. (1992). Preparing for an important event: Demonstrating the modern view of classical conditioning. *Teaching of Psychology, 19,* 100–102.

Korn, J. H. (1988). Students' roles, rights, and responsibilities as research subjects. *Teaching of Psychology, 15,* 74–78.

Koss, M., Gidycz, C., Wisniewski, N. (1987). The scope of rape. *Journal of Consulting and Clinical Psychology, 55,* 162–170.

Kotelchuck, M., & Richmond, J. B. (1987). Head Start: Evolution of a successful comprehensive child development program. *Pediatrics, 79,* 441–445.

Kotre, J. (1992). Experiments as parables. *American Psychologist, 47(5),* 672–673.

Kraemer, D. L., & Hastrup, J. L. (1988). Crying in adults: Self-control and autonomic correlates. *Journal of Social and Clinical Psychology, 6,* 53–68.

Kramer, J. J., & Conoley, J. C. (1992). *The eleventh mental measurements yearbook.* Lincoln, NE: Buros Institute of Mental Measurements.

Krebs, D. L. (1970). Altruism: An examination of the concept and a review of the literature. *Psychological Bulletin, 73,* 258–302.

Krebs, D. L. (1991). Altruism and egoism: A false dichotomy? *Psychological Inquiry, 2,* 137–139.

Krener, P. K. & Mancina, R. A. (1994). Informed consent or informed coercion? *Journal of Child and Adolescent Psychopharmacology, 4,* 183-200.

Kroemer, K. H. (1992). Performance on a prototype keyboard with ternary chorded keys. *Applied Ergonomics, 23,* 83–90.

Krueger, W. C. F. (1929). The effect of overlearning on retention. *Journal of Experimental Psychology, 12,* 71–78.

Kübler-Ross, E. (1969). *On death and dying.* New York: Macmillan.

Kuhn, T. S. (1962). *The structure of scientific revolutions.* Chicago: University of Chicago Press.

Kulik, J. A., & Mahler, H. I. (1990). Stress and affiliation research: On taking the laboratory to health field settings. *Annals of Behavioral Medicine, 12,* 106–111.

Kunz, P. R., & Fernquist, R. M. (1989). Opinions on abortion as measured by the lost-letter technique. *Psychological Reports, 65,* 1343–1346.

Kuykendall, D., & Keating, J. (1990). Altering thoughts and judgments through repeated association. *British Journal of Social Psychology, 29,* 79–86.

Kuypers, B. R., & Cotton, D. W. (1972). Conditioning of sweating, a preliminary report. *British Journal of Dermatology, 87,* 154–160.

Kymissis, E., & Poulson, C. L. (1990). The history of imitation in learning theory: The language acquisition process. *Journal of the Experimental Analysis of Behavior, 54,* 113–127.

Laird, A. (1932). How the consumer estimates quality by subconscious sensory impressions. *Journal of Applied Psychology, 16,* 241–246.

Lamb, G. M. (1983, May 25). Goodbye to QWERTY—new typing keyboard is faster. *Christian Science Monitor,* p. 4.

Lamiell, J. T. (1991). Valuation theory, the self-confrontation method, and scientific personality psychology. *European Journal of Psychology, 5,* 235–244.

Landy, F., & Bittner, K. (1991). The early history of job satisfaction. In C. J. Cranny (Ed.), *Job satisfaction: Advances in theory and research.* Lexington, MA: Lexington Books.

Lane, H. (1979). *The wild boy of Aveyron.* Cambridge, MA: Harvard University Press.

Lang, P. J., & Melamed, B. G. (1969). Avoidance conditioning therapy of an infant with chronic ruminative vomiting. *Journal of Abnormal Psychology, 74,* 1–8.

Larsen, D. (1985, January 10). Battle of the typewriter keyboards. *Los Angeles Times,* p. 1.

Larsen, K. S. (1990). The Asch conformity experiment: Replication and transhistorical comparisons. *Journal of Social Behavior and Personality, 5,* 163–168.

Larson, D. E. (1990). *Mayo Clinic family health book.* New York: Morrow.

Lasch, C. (1978). *The culture of narcissism.* New York: Norton.

Laszlo, J. I., & Bairstow, P. J. (1983). Kinesthesis: Its measurement, training and relationship to motor control. *Quarterly Journal of Experimental Psychology: Human Experimental Psychology, 35A,* 411–421.

Latané, B., & Darley, J. M. (1968). Group inhibition of bystander intervention in emergencies. *Journal of Personality and Social Psychology, 10,* 215–221.

Latané, B., & Nida, S. (1981). Ten years of research on group size and helping. *Psychological Bulletin, 89,* 308–324.

Lattal, K. A. (1992). B. F. Skinner and psychology. *American Psychologist, 47,* 1269–1272.

Lavond, D. G., Kim, J. J., & Thompson, R. F. (1993). Mammalian brain structures of aversive classical conditioning. *Annual Review of Psychology, 44,* 317–342.

Lazarus, R. S. (1991). Progress on a cognitive-motivational-relational theory of emotion. *American Psychologist, 46,* 819–834.

Lazarus, R. S. (1993). From psychological stress to the emotions: A history of changing outlooks. *Annual Review of Psychology, 44,* 1–21.

Leaf, P. J., Weissman, M. M., Myers, J. K., Tischler, G. L., & Holzer, C. E. (1984). Social factors related to psychiatric disorders: Yale epidemiologic catchment area study. *Social Psychiatry, 19,* 53–61.

Le Doux, J. E. (1989). Cognitive-emotional interactions in the brain. *Cognition and Emotion, 3,* 267–289.

LeDoux, J. E. (1995). Emotion: Clues from the brain. *Annual Review of Psychology, 46,* 209-235.

Leahey, T. N. (1992). The mythical revolutions of American psychology. *American Psychologist, 47,* 308–318.

Lee, F., Hallahan, M., & Herzog, T. (1996). Explaining real life events: How culture and domain shape attributions. *Personality and Social Psychology Bulletin, 22,* 732–741.

Lee, J. A. (1973). *The colors of love: An exploration in the ways of loving.* Ontario: New Press.

Lefcourt, H. M. (1982). *Locus of control: Current trends in theory and research.* Hillsdale, NJ: Erlbaum.

Leff, J. P., & Vaughn, C. E. (1981). The role of maintenance therapy and relatives' expressed emotion in relapse of schizophrenia: A two-year follow-up. *British Journal of Psychiatry, 139,* 102–104.

Leikind, B. J., & McCarthy, W. J. (1985). An investigation of firewalking. *Skeptical Inquirer, 10,* 23–34.

Leitner, H. (1994, September 21). Introduction to computing [Lecture]. Cambridge, MA: Harvard University.

Lenneberg, E. H. (1964). The capacity for language acquisition. In J. A. Fodor & J. J. Katz (Eds.), *The structure of language.* Englewood Cliffs, NJ: Prentice Hall.

Lester, D. (1986). A cross-cultural test of Sheldon's theory of personality. *Journal of Social Psychology, 126,* 695–696.

Lester, D., & Wosnack, K. (1990). An exploratory test of Sheldon's theory of personality in neonates. *Perceptual and Motor Skills, 71,* 1282.

Leupold-Lowenthal, H. (1991). The impossibility of making Freud English: Some remarks on the Strachey translation of the works of Sigmund Freud. *International Review of Psycho-Analysis, 18,* 345–350.

Le Vay, S. (1991). A difference in hypothalamic structure between heterosexual and homosexual men. *Science, 253,* 1034–1037.

Levenson, R. W. (1992). Autonomic nervous system differences among emotions. *Psychological Science, 3,* 23–27.

Leventhal, H., & Tomarken, A. J. (1986). Emotion: Today's problems. *Annual Review of Psychology, 37.*

Levin, F. M., & Gergen, K. J. (1969). Revealingness, ingratiation, and the disclosure of self. *Proceedings of the Annual Convention of the American Psychological Association, 4,* 447–448.

Levine, J. M., & Moreland, R. L. (1990). Progress in small group research. *Annual Review of Psychology, 41,* 585–634.

Levine, J. M., Resnick, L. B., & Higgins, E. T. (1993). Social foundations of cognition. *Annual Review of Psychology, 44,* 585–612.

Levine, M., Toro, P. A., & Perkins, D. V. (1993). Social and community interventions. *Annual Review of Psychology, 44,* 525–558.

Levinson, D., Darrow, C., Klein, E., Levinson, M., & McKee, B. (1978). *The seasons of a man's life.* New York: Knopf.

Levinson, K. S., Pesina, M. D., & Rienzi, B. M. (1993). Lost letter technique: Attitudes toward gay men and lesbians. *Psychological Reports, 72,* 93–94.

Lewin, K. (1935). *A dynamic theory of personality.* New York: McGraw-Hill.

Lewin, K. (1947). Group decision and social change. In E. E. Maccoby, T. M. Newcomb, & E. L. Hartley (Eds.), *Readings in social psychology* (3rd ed.). New York: Holt.

Lewinsohn, P. M. (1974). A behavioral approach to depression. In R. J. Friedman & M. M. Katz (Eds.), *The psychology of depression: Contemporary theory and research.* New York: Halsted.

Lewis, D. O., & Bard, J. S. (1991). Multiple personality and forensic issues. *Psychiatric Clinics of North America, 14,* 741–756.

Lewis, W. A., & Bucher, A. M. (1992). Anger, catharsis, the reformulated frustration-aggression hypothesis, and health consequences. *Psychotherapy, 29,* 385–392.

Lieberman, L., Reynolds, L. T., & Friedrich, D. (1992). The fitness of human sociobiology: The future utility of four concepts in four subdisciplines. *Social Biology, 39,* 158–169.

Lieberman, P. (1984). *The biology and evolution of language.* Cambridge, MA: Harvard University Press.

Liebert, R. M., & Spiegler, M. D. (1987). *Personality: Strategies and issues* (5th ed.). Chicago: Dorsey Press.

Liebes, T. (1994). Narratization of the News: An introduction. *Journal of Narrative and Life History, 4,* 1-8.

Light, L. L. (1991). Memory and aging: Four hypotheses in search of data. *Annual Review of Psychology, 42,* 333–376.

Lilly, J. C. (1956). Mental effects of reduction of ordinary levels of physical stimuli on intact, healthy persons. *Psychiatric Research Reports, 5,* 1–28.

Limber, J. (1977). Language in child and chimp? *American Psychology, 32,* 280–295.

Lindsay, R. K. (1991). Symbol-processing theories and the SOAR architecture. *Psychological Science, 2,* 294–302.

Linschoten, M. R., & Kroeze, J. H. (1991). Spatial summation in taste: NaCl thresholds and stimulated area on the anterior human tongue. *Chemical Senses, 16,* 219–224.

Lipsey, M. W., & Wilson, D. B. (1993). The efficacy of psychological, educational, and behavioral treatment: Confirmation from meta-analysis. *American Psychologist, 48,* 1181–1209.

Livingstone, M., & Hubel, D. (1988). Segregation of form, color, movement, and depth: Anatomy, physiology, and perception. *Science, 240,* 740–749.

Locke, E. A. (1992). There can be no balance between animal and human rights. *Psychological Science, 3,* 143.

Loeber, R., & Dishion, T. (1983). Early predictors of male delinquency: A review. *Psychological Bulletin, 94,* 68–99.

Loftus, E. F., & Loftus, G. R. (1980). On the permanence of stored information in the human brain. *American Psychologist, 35,* 409–420.

Loftus, E. F., & Palmer, J. C. (1974). Reconstruction of automobile destruction: An example of the interaction between language and memory. *Journal of Verbal Learning and Verbal Behavior, 13,* 585–589.

Lopez, S. R., & Taussig, I. M. (1991). Cognitive-intellectual functions of Spanish-speaking impaired and nonimpaired elderly: Implications for culturally sensitive assessment. *Psychological Assessment, 3,* 448–454.

Lorenz, K. Z. (1958). The evolution of behavior. *Scientific American, 199*(6), 67–78.

Lorenz, K. Z. (1963). *On aggression.* New York: Harcourt, Brace & World.

Lowen, A. (1980). *Fear of life.* New York: Macmillan.

Lowen, A. (1983). *Narcissism: Denial of the true self.* New York: Macmillan.

Lowman, R. L. (1993). *Counseling and psychotherapy of work dysfunction.* Washington, DC: American Psychological Association.

Luborsky, L., Singer, B., & Luborsky, L. (1975). Comparative studies of psychotherapies. *Archives of General Psychiatry, 32,* 995–1008.

Luck, S. J., Hillyard, S. A., & Mangun, G. (1989). Independent hemispheric attentional systems mediate visual search in split-brain patients. *Nature, 342,* 543–545.

Luckhardt, A. B., & Carlson, A. J. (1915). Contributions to the physiology of the stomach, XVII. On the chemical control of the gastric hunger mechanism. *American Journal of Physiology, 36,* 37–46.

Lykken, D. T. (1991). Why (some) Americans believe in the lie detector while others believe in the Guilty Knowledge Test. *Integrative Physiological and Behavioral Science, 26,* 214–222.

Lynch, G., & Baudry, M. (1984). The biochemistry of memory: A new and specific hypothesis. *Science, 224,* 1057–1063.

MacGregor, J. N. (1987). Short-term memory capacity: Limitation or optimization? *Psychological Review, 94,* 107–108.

Mackenzie, B. (1984). Explaining race differences in IQ: The logic, the methodology, and the evidence. *American Psychologist, 39,* 1214–1233.

MacNichol, E. F., Jr. (1964). Three-pigment color vision. *Scientific American, 211,* 48–56.

Macphail, E. M. (1986). Animal memory: Past, present, and future. *Quarterly Journal of Experimental Psychology: Comparative and Physiological Psychology, 38,* 349–364.

Madigan, S., & O'Hara, R. (1992). Short-term memory at the turn of the century: Mary Whiton Calkins's memory research. *American Psychologist, 47,* 170–174.

Magnusson, D., & Törestad, B. (1993). A holistic view of personality: A model revisited. *Annual Review of Psychology, 44,* 427–452.

Maier, N. R. F. (1931). Reasoning in human beings. II. *Journal of Comparative Psychology, 12,* 181-194.

Malgady, R. G., Rogler, L. H., & Constantino, G. (1990). Hero/heroine modeling for Puerto Rican adolescents: A preventive mental health intervention. *Journal of Consulting and Clinical Psychology, 58,* 469–474.

Malone, P. S., Brownstein, P. J., von Brock, A., & Shaywitz, S. S. (1991). Components of IQ scores across levels of measured ability. *Journal of Applied Social Psychology, 21,* 15–28.

Malson, L. (1972). *Wolf children.* London: NLB.

Mandler, G. (1967). Organization of memory. In K. W. Spence & J. T. Spence (Eds.), *The psychology of learning and motivation* (Vol. I). New York: Academic Press.

Mandler, G. (1990). William James and the construction of emotion. *Psychological Science, 1,* 179–180.

Mandler, J. M. & Johnson, N. S. (1977). Remembrance of things parsed: Story structure and recall. *Cognitive Psychology, 9,* 111-151.

Mariezcurrena, R. (1994). Recovery from addiction without treatment: Literature review. *Scandinavian Journal of Behavior Therapy, 23,* 131-154.

Markman, H. J., Floyd, S. J., Stanley, S. M., & Storaasli, R. D. (1988). Prevention of marital distress: A longitudinal investigation. *Journal of Consulting and Clinical Psychology, 56,* 210–217.

Markus, H. R., & Kitayana, S. (1991). Culture and the self: Implications for cognition, emotion, and motivation. *Psychological Review, 98,* 224–253.

Marshall, H. R. (1908). The methods of the naturalist and psychologist. *Psychological Review, 15,* 1–24.

Marston, L. R. (1925). The emotions of young children: An experimental study of introversion and extraversion. *University of Iowa Studies in Child Welfare, 3,* No. 3.

Martin, S. L., & Klimoski, R. J. (1990). Use of verbal protocols to trace cognitions associated with self- and supervisor evaluations of performance. *Organizational Behavior and Human Decision Processes, 46*(I), 135–154.

Maslow, A. H. (1970). *Motivation and personality* (2nd ed.). New York: Harper.

Massaro, D., & Cowan, N. (1993). Information processing models: Microscopes of the mind. *Annual Review of Psychology, 44,* 383–425.

Masters, W. H., Johnson, V. E., & Kolodny, R. C. (1982). *Human sexuality.* Boston: Little, Brown.

Matarazzo, J. D. (1972). *Wechsler's measurement and appraisal of adult intelligence* (5th ed.). New York: Oxford University Press.

Mathis, J. O., & Lampe, R. E. (1991). Corporal punishment: A TACD issue. *TACD Journal, 19,* 27–32.

Maturana, H. R., Lettvin, J. Y., McCulloch, W. S., & Pitts, W. H. (1960). Anatomy and physiology of vision in the frog (*Rana pipien*). *Journal of General Physiology* (2nd Suppl.), *43,* 129–175.

Maury, L. F. A. (1861). *Le sommèil et les rêves [Sleep and dreams].* Paris: Didier.

May, R. R. (1981). *Freedom and destiny.* New York: Norton.

May, R. R. (1987). Therapy in our day. In J. K. Zeig (Ed.), *The evolution of psychotherapy.* New York: Brunner Mazel.

Mayekiso, I. V., & Twaise, N. (1993). Assessment of parental involvement in imparting sexual knowledge to adolescents. *South African Journal of Psychology, 23,* 21–23.

Mayer, J. (1956). Appetite and obesity. *Scientific American,* Nov., 108–116.

Mazur, J. E. (1986). *Learning and behavior.* Englewood Cliffs, NJ: Prentice Hall.

McBroom, W. H. (1987). Longitudinal change in sex role orientations: Differences between men and women. *Sex Roles, 16,* 439–452.

McCallum, R. S., & Glynn, S. M. (1979). Hemispheric specialization and creative behavior. *Journal of Creative Behavior, 13,* 263–273.

McClelland, D. C. (1984). *Human motivation.* Glenview, IL: Scott, Foresman.

McClelland, D. C., & Atkinson, J. W. (1948). The projective expression of needs (I): The effect of different intensities of hunger drive on perception. *Journal of Psychology, 25,* 205–222.

McClelland, D. C., Atkinson, J. W., Clark, R. A., & Lowell, E. L. (1953). *The achievement motive.* New York: Appleton-Century-Crofts.

McConnell, J. V. (1972). The biochemistry of memory. In R. C. Teevan (Ed.), *Readings in introductory psychology.* Minneapolis, MN: Burgess.

McCrae, R. R., & Costa, P. T. (1987). Validation of the five factor model of personality across instruments and observers. *Journal of Personality and Social Psychology, 52,* 81–90.

McDonald, W. M., & Nemeroff, C. B. (1991). Neurotransmitters and neuropeptides in Alzheimer's disease. *Psychiatric Clinics of North America, 14,* 421–442.

McEvoy, J. (1992). Fragile X syndrome: A brief overview. *Educational Psychology in Practice, 8,* 146–149.

McGeer, P. L., & McGeer, E. G. (1980). Chemistry of mood and emotion. *Annual Review of Psychology, 31,* 273–307.

McGuire, W. J. (1985). Attitudes and attitude change. In G. Lindzey & E. Aronson (Eds.), *Handbook of social psychology* (3rd ed.). New York: Random House.

McMaster, N. L. (1990). The courts and hypnotically refreshed memory: A review of the literature. *Australian Journal of Clinical Hypnotherapy and Hypnosis, 11,* 1–9.

McNally, R. J. (1987). Preparedness and phobias: A review. *Psychological Bulletin, 101,* 283–303.

McNeilly, C. L., & Howard, K. I. (1991). The effects of psychotherapy: A reevaluation based on dosage. *Psychotherapy Research, 1,* 74–78.

McPherson, M. W. (1992). Is psychology the science of behavior? *American Psychologist, 47,* 329–335.

Mead, M. (1939). Sex and temperament. In *From the South Seas.* New York: Morrow.

Mealey, L. (1990). Differential use of reproductive strategies by human groups. *Psychological Science, 1,* 385–387.

Medin, D. L., & Smith, E. E. (1984). Concepts and concept formation. *Annual Review of Psychology, 35,* 113–138.

Mees, C. E. K. (1934). Scientific thought and social reconstruction. *Electrical Engineering, 53,* 383–384.

Meeus, W. H. J., & Raaijmakers, Q. A. W. (1986). Administrative obedience: Carrying out orders to use psychological-administrative violence. *European Journal of Social Psychology, 16,* 311–324.

Meltzer, H. (1930). Individual differences in forgetting pleasant and unpleasant experiences. *Journal of Educational Psychology, 21,* 399–409.

Melzack, R. (1987). Pain. In R. L. Gregory (Ed.), *The Oxford companion to the mind.* New York: Oxford University Press.

Mendelson, W. B. (1990). The Stony Brook 600: The experience of a sleep disorder center. *Annals of Clinical Psychiatry, 2,* 277–283.

Merckelbach, H., Arntz, A., & de Jong, P. (1991). Conditioning experiences in spider phobias. *Behavioral Research and Therapy, 29,* 333–335.

Michelson, L. K., & Marchione, K. (1991). Behavioral, cognitive, and pharmacological treatments of panic disorder with agoraphobia. *Journal of Consulting and Clinical Psychology, 59,* 100–114.

Middlebrooks, J. C., & Green, D. M. (1991). Sound localization by human listeners. *Annual Review of Psychology, 42,* 135–159.

Milgram, S. (1974). *Obedience to authority: An experimental view.* New York: Harper & Row.

Milgram, S. (1992). *The individual in a social world: Essays and experiments* (2nd ed.). New York: McGraw-Hill.

Miller, A. (1983). *For your own good.* New York: Farrar, Straus, Giroux.

Miller, A. (1984a). *Thou shalt not be aware.* New York: Farrar, Straus, Giroux.

Miller, A. K., Alston, R. L., & Corsellis, J. A. (1980). Variation with age in the volumes of grey and white matter in the cerebral hemispheres of man: Measurements with an image analyzer. *Neuropathology and Applied Neurobiology, 6,* 119–132.

Miller, G., & Gildea, P. (1987). How children learn words. *Scientific American, 257,* 94–99.

Miller, G. A. (1956). The magical number seven, plus or minus two. Some limits on our capacity for processing information. *Psychological Review, 63,* 81–97.

Miller, J. (1984b). Culture and the development of everyday social explanations. *Journal of Personality and Social Psychology, 46,* 961–978.

Miller, L. (1992). When the best help is self-help; or, Everything you always wanted to know about brain injury support groups. *Journal of Cognitive Rehabilitation, 10,* 14–17.

Miller, L. C. (1990). Intimacy and liking: Mutual influence and the role of unique relationships. *Journal of Personality and Social Psychology, 59,* 50–60.

Miller, N. S., & Ries, R. K. (1991). Drug and alcohol dependence and psychiatric populations: The need for diagnosis, intervention, and training. *Comprehensive Psychiatry, 32,* 268–276.

Miller, R. C., & Berman, J. S. (1983). The efficacy of cognitive behavior therapies: A quantitative review of the research evidence. *Psychological Bulletin, 94,* 39–53.

Miller, S. A. (1976). Nonverbal assessment of conservation of number. *Child Development, 47,* 722–728.

Milner, B., Corkin, S., & Teuber, M. L. (1968). Further analysis of the hippocampal amnesic syndrome. *Neuropsychobiology, 6,* 215–234.

Minami, H., & Dallenbach, K. M. (1946). The effect of activity upon learning and retention in the cockroach. *American Journal of Psychology, 59,* 1–58.

Minuchin, S. (1974). *Families and family therapy.* Cambridge, MA: Harvard University Press.

Minuchin, S. (1984). *Family kaleidoscope.* Cambridge, MA: Harvard University Press.

Mital, A. (1992). Psychophysical capacity of industrial workers for lifting symmetrical and asymmetrical loads symmetrically and asymmetrically for 8-hour work shifts. *Ergonomics, 35,* 745-754.

Mitrushina, M., & Satz, P. (1989). Differential decline of specific memory components in normal aging. *Brain Dysfunction, 2,* 330–335.

Money, J. (1986). Lovemaps: Clinical concepts of sexual/erotic health and pathology, paraphilia, and gender transportation of childhood, adolescence, and maturity. New York: Irvington.

Money, J. (1988). Sin, sickness, or status? Homosexual gender identity and psychoneuroendocrinology. *Annual Progress in Child Psychiatry and Child Development,* pp. 41–76.

Moniz, Egas. (1944). *A expansão da angiografia e da leucotomia préfrontal.* Lisboa: Bertrand.

Monroe, S. M., & Simons, A. D. (1991). Diathesis-stress theories in the context of life stress research. *Psychological Bulletin, 110,* 406–425.

Moore, T. E. (1985, July). Subliminal delusion. *Psychology Today,* pp. 10–11.

Moore, T. E. (1992). Not so subliminal [Letter to the editor]. *APA Monitor, 23*(1), 3.

Moorhead, G., Ference, R., & Neck, C. (1991). Group decision fiascoes continue: Space shuttle Challenger and a revised groupthink framework. *Human Relations, 44,* 539–550.

Morgan, J. L. (1990). Input, innateness, and induction in language acquisition. *Developmental Psychobiology, 23,* 661–679.

Morganosky, M. A. (1990). Store and brand type influences on the perception of apparel quality: A congruity theory approach. *Clothing and Textiles Research Journal, 9,* 45–49.

Morin, C. M., Kowatch, R. A., Barry, T., & Walton, E. (1993). Cognitive-behavior therapy for late-life insomnia. *Journal of Consulting and Clinical Psychology, 61,* 137–146.

Morley, J. E., & Flood, J. F. (1990). Neuropeptide Y and memory processing. *Annals of the New York Academy of Sciences, 611,* 226–231.

Morris, D. (1967). *The naked ape.* New York: Dell.

Morris, G. O., & Singer, M. T. (1961). Sleep deprivation: Transactional and subjective observations. *Archives of General Psychology, 5,* 453–461.

Motley, M. T. (1987). What I meant to say. *Psychology Today, 21,* 24–28.

Moylan, A., & Dadds, M. R. (1992). Hyperhidrosis: A case study and theoretical formulation. *Behavior Change, 9,* 87–95.

Mullare, S., & Fernald, P. S. (1971). *Influences of experimentally induced expectation upon elimination of a fear response.* Unpublished study, Durham, NH: University of New Hampshire.

Mullins, L. L., & Olson, R. A. (1990). Familial factors in the etiology, maintenance, and treatment of somatoform disorders in children. *Family Systems Medicine, 8,* 159–175.

Munley, P. H. (1991). Confidence intervals for the MMPI-2. *Journal of Personality Assessment, 57,* 52–60.

Murphy, G. L., & Medin, D. L. (1985). The role of theories in conceptual coherence. *Psychological Review, 92,* 289–316.

Murray, J. B. (1991). Nicotine as a psychoactive drug. *Journal of Psychology, 125,* 5–25.

Murstein, B. I. (1972). Physical attractiveness and marital choice. *Journal of Personality and Social Psychology, 22,* 8–12.

Nardi, P. M. & Sherrod, D. (1994). Friendship in the lives of gay men and lesbians. *Journal of Social and Personal Relationships, 11,* 185-199.

Nathan, P. E. (1991). Substance use disorders in the DSM-IV. *Journal of Abnormal Psychology, 100,* 356–361.

National Institute of Mental Health. (1991). *Psychiatric services and the changing scene.* Washington, DC: Government Printing Office.

National Institute of Mental Health. (1992). *New developments in the pharmacological treatment of schizophrenia.* Washington, DC: National Institute of Health.

National Research Council. (1943). *An introduction to aviation psychology* (Research Bulletin No. 4, Committee on Selection and Training of Air-Craft Pilots). Civil Aeronautics Administration.

Neck, C. P. & Moorhead, G. (1995). Groupthink remodeled: The importance of leadership, time pressure, and methodical decision-making procedures. *Human Relations, 48,* 537-557.

Neher, E., & Sakmann, B. (1992). The patch clamp technique. *Scientific American, 266,* 44–51.

Neiss, R. (1988). Re-conceptualizing arousal: Psychobiological states and motor performance. *Psychological Bulletin, 103,* 345–366.

Neisser, U. (1967). *Cognitive psychology.* New York: Appleton-Century-Crofts.

Neisser, U. (1991). A case of misplaced nostalgia. *American Psychologist, 16,* 34–36.

Neisser, U., & Becklen, K. (1975). Selective looking: Attending to visually specific events. *Cognitive Psychology, 7,* 480–494.

Nelson, T. O., Dunlosky, J., White, T. M., Steinberg, J., Townes, B., & Anderson, D. (1990). Cognition and metacognition at extreme altitudes on Mount Everest. *Journal of Experimental Psychology: General, 119,* 367–374.

Neugarten, B. L. (1968). Adult personality: Toward a psychology of the life cycle. In B. L. Neugarten (Ed.), *Middle age and aging: A reader in social psychology.* Chicago: University of Chicago Press.

Nevis, E. C. (1983). Using an American perspective for understanding another culture: Toward a hierarchy of needs for the People's Republic of China. *Journal of Applied Behavioral Science, 19,* 249–264.

Newcomb, M. D. (1987). Cohabitation and marriage: A quest for independence and relatedness. *Applied Social Psychology Annual, 7,* 128–156.

Newcomb, M. D. (1990). Social support by many other names: Towards a unified conceptualization. *Journal of Social and Personal Relationships, 7,* 479–494.

Newell, A. (1990). *Unified theories of cognition.* Cambridge, MA: Harvard University Press.

Newell, A., Shaw, J. C., & Simon, H. A. (1958). Elements of a theory of human problem solving. *Psychological Review, 65,* 151–166.

Newell, A., & Simon, H. A. (1963). GPS: A program that simulates human thought. In E. A. Feigenbaum & J. Feldman (Eds.), *Computers and thought.* New York: McGraw-Hill.

Newman, H. H., Freeman, F. N., & Holzinger, K. J. (1937). *Twins: A study of heredity and environment.* Chicago: University of Chicago Press.

Niall, K. K. (1988). On the trichromatic and opponent-process theories: An article by E. Schrodinger. *Spatial Vision, 3,* 79–95.

Niaz, M. (1991). Correlates of formal operational reasoning: A neo-Piagetian analysis. *Journal of Research in Science Teaching, 28,* 19–40.

Nickerson, R. (1992). *Looking ahead: Human factors challenges in a changing world.* Hillsdale, NJ: Erlbaum.

Nicolau, R., Toro, J., & Perez-Prado, C. (1991). Behavioral treatment of a case of psychogenic urinary retention. *Journal of Behavior Therapy and Experimental Psychiatry, 22,* 63–68.

Nisbet, J. D. (1957). Symposium: Contributions to intelligence testing and the theory of intelligence: IV. Intelligence and age: Retesting with twenty-four years' interval. *British Journal of Educational Psychology, 27,* 190–198.

Nisbett, R. E. (1990). Evolutionary psychology, biology, and cultural evolution. *Motivation and Emotion, 14,* 255–263.

Nisbett, R. E., Caputo, G. C., Legant, P., & Mareck, J. (1973). Behavior as seen by the actor and the observer. *Journal of Personality and Social Psychology, 27,* 154–164.

Nissani, M. (1990). A cognitive reinterpretation of Stanley Milgram's observations on obedience to authority. *American Psychologist, 45,* 1384–1385.

Oatley, K., & Jenkins, J. M. (1992). Human emotions: Function and dysfunction. *Annual Review of Psychology, 43,* 55–85.

O'Connor, T., & Smith, P. (1987). The labeling of schizophrenics by professionals and lay-persons. *British Journal of Clinical Psychology, 26,* 311–312.

O'Heron, C. A., & Orlofsky, J. L. (1990). Stereotypic and non-stereotypic sex role trait and behavior orientations, gender identity, and psychological adjustment. *Journal of Personality and Social Psychology, 58,* 134–143.

Ohzawa, I., DeAngelis, G. C., & Freeman, R. D. (1990). Stereoscopic depth discrimination in the visual cortex: Neurons ideally suited as disparity detectors. *Science, 249,* 1037–1041.

Olds, J. (1956). Pleasure centers in the brain. *Scientific American, 195,* 105–116.

Olds, M. E., & Forbes, J. L. (1981). The central basis of motivation: Intracranial self-stimulation studies. *Annual Review of Psychology, 32,* 523–574.

Oles, K. S. (1992). Parkinson's disease and the elderly. *Journal of Geriatric Drug Therapy, 6,* 41–71.

Olson, G. I., & Schober, B. I. (1993). The satisfied poor: Development of an intervention-oriented theoretical framework to explain satisfaction with a life in poverty. *Social Indicators Research, 28,* 173–193.

Olson, J. M., & Zanna, M. P. (1993). Attitudes and attitude change. *Annual Review of Psychology, 44,* 117–154.

O'Neill, R. M. (1990). Case study: The illustrative nightmare of a young borderline woman. *American Journal of Psychoanalysis, 50,* 71–74.

Onslow, M., Costa, L., & Rue, S. (1990). Direct early intervention with stuttering: Some preliminary data. *Journal of Speech and Hearing Disorders, 55,* 405–416.

Oppenheim, A. N. (1992). *Questionnaire design, interviewing, and attitude measurement.* New York: St. Martin's Press.

Oransky, I. (1994, May 3). Student injuries on rise. *Harvard Crimson,* pp. 1–3.

Osgood, C. E., Suci, G. J., & Tannenbaum, P. H. (1957). *The measurement of meaning.* Urbana, IL: University of Illinois Press.

OSS Assessment Staff. (1948). *The assessment of men.* New York Rinehart.

Oswald, I. (1987). Dreaming. In R. L. Gregory (Ed.), *The Oxford companion to the mind.* New York: Oxford University Press.

Overholser, J. C. (1990). Fetal alcohol syndrome: A review of the disorder. *Journal of Contemporary Psychotherapy, 20,* 163–176.

Overholser, J. C., & Moll, S. H. (1990). Who's to blame: Attributions regarding causality in spouse abuse. *Behavioral Sciences and the Law, 8,* 107–120.

Owens, W. A. (1966). Age and mental abilities: A second adult follow-up. *Journal of Educational Psychology, 57,* 311–325.

Page, E. B. (1986). The disturbing case of the Milwaukee Project. In H. H. Spitz and E. R. Johnstone, *The raising of intelligence: A selected history of attempts to raise retarded intelligence.* Hillsdale, NJ: Erlbaum.

Page, M. R. (1995). Human factors: A user's view of ergonomics. *Ergonomics, 38,* 539-545.

Park, W. (1990). A review of research on groupthink. *Journal of Behavioral Decision Making, 3,* 229–245.

Parkin, A. J. (1984). Levels of processing, context, and the facilitation of pronunciation. *Acta Psychologica, 55,* 19–29.

Parks, S., & Pilisuk, M. (1991). Caregiver burden: Gender and the psychological costs of caregiving. *American Journal of Orthopsychiatry, 61,* 501–509.

Parsons, H. M. (1992). Hawthorne: An early OBM experiment. *Journal of Organizational Behavior and Management, 12,.* 27-43.

Pashler, H. (1990). Do response-modality effects support multi-processor models of divided attention? *Journal of Experimental Psychology: Human Perception and Performance, 16,* 826–842.

Pashler, H. (1992). Attentional limitations in doing two things at the same time. *Current Directions in Psychological Science, 1,* 44–48.

Patten, B. M. (1990). The history of memory arts. *Neurology, 40,* 346–352.

Patterson, G. (1990). Freud's rhetoric: Persuasion and history in the 1909 Clark Lectures. *Metaphor and Symbolic Activity, 5,* 215–233.

Paulus, P. B., & Dzindolet, M. T. (1993). Social influence processes in group brainstorming. *Journal of Personality and Social Psychology, 64,* 575–586.

Pavlov, I. P. (1927). *Conditional reflexes.* (G. V. Anrep, Trans.). New York: Oxford University Press.

Pedder, J. R. (1990). Lines of advance in psychoanalytic psychotherapy. *Psychoanalytic Psychotherapy, 4,* 201–217.

Pelham, B. W. (1993). The idiographic nature of human personality: Examples of the idiographic self-concept. *Journal of Personality and Social Psychology, 64,* 665–677.

Penfield, W. (1958). *The excitable cortex in conscious man.* Springfield, IL: Charles C. Thomas.

Pepler, D. J. & Craig, W. M. (1995). A peek behind the fence. *Developmental Psychology, 31,* 548-553.

Perkins, D. N. (1981). *The mind's best work.* Cambridge, MA: Harvard University Press.

Perry, R. B. (1935). *The thought and character of William James. Vols. I and II.* Boston: Little, Brown.

Perry, C. A. (1990). Knowledge bases in medicine: A review. *Bulletin of the Medical Library Association, 78,* 271–282.

Persons, J. B. (1986). The advantages of studying psychological phenomena rather than psychiatric diagnoses. *American Psychologist, 41,* 1252–1260.

Peterson, L. R., & Peterson, M. J. (1959). Short-term retention of individual verbal items. *Journal of Experimental Psychology, 58,* 193–198.

Petty, R. E., & Cacioppo, J. T. (1986). *Communication and persuasion: Central and peripheral routes to attitude change.* New York: Springer-Verlag.

Pfeiffer, K., & Maltzman, I. (1974). Warned reaction times of sociopaths. *Journal of Research in Personality, 8,* 64–75.

Pfouts, J. H. (1980). Birth order, age-spacing, IQ differences, and family relations. *Journal of Marriage and the Family, 42,* 517–531.

Pfungst, O. (1911). *The horse of Mr. von Osten.* (C. L. Rahn, Trans.). New York: Holt. See also R. Rosenthal (Ed.), *Clever Hans: The horse of Mr. von Osten* (C. L. Rahn, Trans.). New York: Holt, 1965.

Phelps, L., & Grabowski, J. (1992). Fetal alcohol syndrome: Diagnostic features and psychoeducational risk factors. *School Psychology Quarterly, 7,* 112–128.

Piaget, J. (1950). *The psychology of intelligence.* New York: Harcourt, Brace.

Piaget, J. (1954). *The construction of reality in the child.* (M. Cook, Trans.). New York: Basic Books.

Piaget, J. (1959). *Language and thought of the child.* London: Routledge & Kegan Paul.

Piaget, J., & Inhelder, B. (1967). *The child's conception of space.* (F. J. Langdon & J. L. Lunzer, Trans.). New York: Norton.

Piaget, J., & Inhelder, B. (1969). *The psychology of the child.* New York: Basic Books.

Piel, J. A. (1990). Unmasking sex and social class differences in childhood aggression: The case for language maturity. *Journal of Educational Research, 84,* 100–106.

Pinel, J. P. J., & Cooper, R. M. (1966). Incubation and its implications for the interpretation of the ECS gradient effect. *Psychonomic Science, 6,* 123–124.

Pinto, S. (1992). [Term paper on conditioning]. Wellesley, MA: Wellesley College.

Piotrowski, C., Keller, J. W., & Ogawa, T. (1993). Projective techniques: An international perspective. *Psychological Reports, 72,* 179–182.

Plomin, R. (1990). The role of inheritance in behavior. *Science, 248,* 183–188.

Plomin, R., Chipeur, H. M., & Loehlin, J. C. (1990). Behavioral genetics and personality. In L. A. Pervin (Ed.), *Handbook of personality theory and research.* New York: Guilford Press.

Plomin, R., & Neiderhiser, J. (1992). Genetics and experience. *Current Directions in Psychological Science, 1,* 160–163.

Plomin, R., & Rende, R. (1991). Human behavioral genetics. *Annual Review of Psychology, 42,* 161–190.

Plutchik, R. (1980). A general psychoevolutionary theory of emotion. In R. Plutchik & H. Kellerman (Eds.), *Emotion: Theory, research, and experience.* New York: Academic Press.

Plutchik, R., & Ax, A. F. (1967). A critique of "Determinants of emotional state" by Schachter and Singer (1962). *Psychophysiology, 4,* 79–82.

Poon, L. W. (1985). Differences in human memory with aging: Nature, causes, and clinical applications. In J. E. Birren & K. W. Schaie (Eds.), *Handbook of the psychology of aging* (2nd ed.). New York: Van Nostrand.

Pope, K. S., & Vetter, V. A. (1992). Ethical dilemmas encountered by members of the American Psychological Association: A national survey. *American Psychologist, 47,* 397–411.

Powell, D. H., & Whitlaw, D. K. (1994). *Profiles in cognitive aging.* Cambridge, MA: Harvard University Press.

Powell, S. (1993). Electra: The dark side of the moon. *Journal of Analytical Psychology, 38,* 155–173.

Prentiss, C. W. (1901). The otocyst of dicapod crustacea: Its structure, development and functions. *Bulletin of the Museum of Comparative Zoology, Harvard College, 36(7),* 165–251.

Prewett, P. N. (1992). Short forms of the Stanford-Binet Intelligence Scale: Fourth edition. *Journal of Psychoeducational Assessment, 10,* 257–264.

Prieto, J. M., Fernández-Ballesteros, R., & Carpintero, H. (1994). Contemporary psychology in Spain. *Annual Review of Psychology, 45,* 51–78.

Puka, B. (1991). Interpretive experiments: Probing the care-justice debate in moral development. *Human Development, 34,* 61–80.

Pullum, G. K. (1991). *The great Eskimo vocabulary hoax.* Chicago: University of Chicago Press.

Rachlin, H. (1991). *Introduction to modern behaviorism* (3rd ed.). New York: Freeman.

Randi, J. (1982). *Flim-flam!: Psychics, ESP, unicorns, and other delusions.* Buffalo, NY: Prometheus.

Rasinski, K. A. (1989). The effect of question wording on public support for government spending. *Public Opinion Quarterly, 53,* 388–394.

Ray, O. (1983). *Drugs, society, and human behavior.* St. Louis: Mosley.

Redd, M., & de Castro, J. (1992). Social facilitation of eating: Effects of instruction on food intake. *Physiology and Behavior, 52,* 749–754.

Ree, M. J., Earles, J. A. (1993). *g* is to psychology what carbon is to chemistry: A reply to Sternberg and Wagner, McClelland, and Calfee. *Current Directions in Psychological Science, 2*(1), 11–12.

Rees, L. (1961). Constitutional factors in abnormal behaviour. In H. J. Eysenck (Ed.), *Handbook of abnormal psychology.* New York: Basic Books.

Reeves, B. R., Newhagen, J., Maibach, E., Basil, M., & Kurz, K. (1991). Negative and positive television messages: Effect of message type and context on attention and memory. *American Behavioral Scientist, 34,* 679–694.

Reid, T. R. (1985, May 1). It may be taps for the QWERTY keyboard. *Washington Post,* pp. 1, 4.

Reimann-Marcus, B. (1992). Antecedents and incidence of divorce: Changing mores in a rural community. Unpublished master's thesis, Harvard University, Cambridge, MA.

Rescorla, R. A. (1988). Pavlovian conditioning: It's not what you think it is. *American Psychologist, 43,* 151–160.

Rescorla, R. A. (1992). Hierarchial associative relations in Pavlovian conditioning and instrumental training. *Current Directions in Psychological Science, 1,* 66–70.

Revelle, W. (1995). Personality processes. *Annual Review of Psychology, 46,* 295-328.

Rhee, D. (1990). The Tao, psychoanalysis and existential thought. *Psychotherapy and Psychosomatics, 53,* 21–27.

Rhine, J. B. (1974a). A new case of experimenter unreliability. *Journal of Parapsychology, 38,* 215–225.

Rhine, J. B. (1974b). Security versus deception in parapsychology. *Journal of Parapsychology, 38,* 99–121.

Rich, E., & Knight, K. (1991). *Artificial intelligence* (2nd ed.). New York: McGraw-Hill.

Richard-Jodoin, R. M. (1991). How analytic is psychoanalytic psychotherapy? *Journal of the American Academy of Psychoanalysis, 19,* 339–351.

Riggio, R. E., Messamer, J., & Throckmorton, B. (1991). Social and academic intelligence: Conceptually distinct but overlapping constructs. *Personality and Individual Differences, 12,* 695–702.

Riggs, L. A., Ratliff, F., Cornsweet, J. C., & Cornsweet, T. N. (1953). The disappearance of steadily fixated visual test objects. *Journal of the Optical Society of America, 43,* 495–501.

Riley, L. R. (1987). *Psychology of language development.* Toronto: Hoegrefe.

Rips, L. J. (1990). Reasoning. *Annual Review of Psychology, 41,* 321–353.

Robert, M. (1990). Observational learning in fish, birds, and mammals: A classified bibliography spanning over 100 years of research. *Psychological Record, 40,* 289–311.

Robins, L. N., & Regier, D. A. (Eds.). (1991). *Psychiatric disorders in America: The epidemiologic catchment area study.* New York: Free Press.

Robinson, E. A. (1921). *Collected Poems.* New York: Macmillan.

Rock, I. (1975). *An introduction to perception.* New York: Macmillan.

Roediger, H. L. (1991). They read an article? A commentary on the everyday memory controversy. *American Psychologist, 46,* 37–40.

Roethlisberger, F. J., & Dickson, W. J. (1940). *Management and the worker.* Cambridge, MA: Harvard University Press.

Roffwarg, H. P., Munzio, J. N., & Dement, W. C. (1966). Ontogenetic development of human sleep-dream cycle. *Science, 152,* 604–609.

Rogers, C. R. (1961). *On becoming a person: A therapist's view of psychotherapy.* Boston: Houghton Mifflin.

Rogers, C. R. (1967). A silent young man. In C. R. Rogers (Ed.), *The therapeutic relationship and its impact.* Madison: University of Wisconsin Press.

Rogers, C. R. (1977). *Carl Rogers on personal power.* New York: Delacorte Press.

Rogers, C. R. (1980). *A way of being.* Boston: Houghton Mifflin.

Rogers, D. (1991). Catatonia: A contemporary approach. *Journal of Neuropsychiatry and Clinical Neurosciences, 3,* 334–340.

Rollin, H. R. (1990). The dark before the dawn. *Journal of Psychopharmacology, 4,* 109–114.

Rosch, E. (1973). On the internal structure of perceptual and semantic categories. In T. E. Moore (Ed.), *Cognitive development in the acquisition of language.* New York: Academic Press.

Rosch, E. (1975). Cognitive representations of semantic categories. *Journal of Experimental Psychology: General, 104,* 192–233.

Rosen, M. (1995). Gender differences in structure, means, and variances of hierarchically ordered ability dimensions. *Learning and Instruction, 5,* 37-62.

Rosenhan, D. L. (1973). On being sane in insane places. *Science, 179,* 250–258.

Rosenman, R. H., Brand, R. J., Jenkins, C. D., Friedman, M., Straus, R., & Wurm, M. (1975). Coronary heart disease in the Western Collaborative Group Study. *Journal of the American Medical Association, 233,* 872–877.

Rose, R. J. (1995). Genes and human behavior. *Annual Review of Psychology, 46,* 625-654.

Rosenzweig, M. R. (1996). Aspects of the search for the neural mechanisms of memory. *Annual Review of Psychology, 47,* 1-32.

Ross, M., & Sicoly, F. (1979). Egocentric biases in availability and attribution. *Journal of Personality and Social Psychology, 37,* 322–336.

Roth, S., & Cohen, L. J. (1986). Approach avoidance, and coping with stress. *American Psychologist, 41,* 813–819.

Rothblum, E. D. (1990). Psychological factors in the Antarctic. *Journal of Psychology, 124,* 253–273.

Rotter, J. B. (1966). Generalized expectancies for internal versus external control of reinforcement. *Psychological Monographs, 80* (Whole No. 609).

Rotter, J. B. (1990). Internal versus external control of reinforcement: A case history of a variable. *American Psychologist, 45,* 489–493.

Rubinstein, E. A. (1983). Television and behavior: Research conclusions of the implications. *American Psychologist, 38,* 820–825.

Ruffin, C. L. (1993). Stress and health: Little hasslers *vs.* major life events. *Australian Psychologist, 28,* 201-208.

Rumelhart, D. E., McClelland, J. L., & the PDP Research Group. (1986). *Parallel distributive processing.* Cambridge, MA: MIT Press.

Rushton, J. P. (1991). Is altruism innate? *Psychological Inquiry, 2,* 141–143.

Rushton, J. P., Brainerd, C. J., & Pressley, M. (1983). Behavioral development and construct validity: The principle of aggregation. *Psychological Bulletin, 94,* 18–38.

Rushton, J. P., Jackson, D. N., & Paunonen, S. V. (1981). Personality: Nomothetic or idiographic? A response to Kenrick and Stringfield. *Psychological Review, 88,* 582–589.

Russell, R. W. (1988). Behavioral effects of the chemical environment. *Pharmacopsychoecologia, 1,* 1–13.

Saariluoma, P. (1992). Do visual images have Gestalt properties? *Quarterly Journal of Experimental Psychology: Human Experimental Psychology, 45A,* 399–420.

Sabin, J., & Silver, M. (1992). Preface to the second edition. In S. Milgram, *The individual in a social world: Essays and experiments* (2nd ed.). New York: McGraw-Hill.

Sackeim, H. A. (1991). Optimizing unilateral electroconvulsive therapy. *Convulsive Therapy, 7,* 201–212.

Sacks, O. W. (1987). *The man who mistook his wife for a hat.* New York: Harper & Row.

Sadowski, M., & Quast, Z. (1990). Reader response and long-term recall for journalistic test: The roles of imagery, affect, and importance. *Reading Research Quarterly, 25,* 256–272.

Saks, M. M. (1992). Obedience versus disobedience to legitimate versus illegitimate authorities issuing good versus evil directives. *Psychological Science, 3,* 221–223.

Salzinger, K. (1994). The LAD was a lady, or the mother of all language learning. *Journal of the Experimental Analysis of Behavior, 62,* 323–329.

Samson, S., & Zatorre, R. J. (1991). Recognition memory for text and melody of songs after unilateral temporal lobe lesion: Evidence for dual coding. *Journal of Experimental Psychology: Learning, Memory, and Cognition, 17,* 793–804.

Sancho, A. M., & Hewitt, J. (1990). Questioning fear of success. *Psychological Reports, 67,* 803–806.

Sanford, E. C. (1903). Psychology and physics. *Psychological Review, 10,* 105–119.

Sanson, A. & di Muccio, C. (1993). The influence of aggressive and neutral cartoons and toys on the behaviour of preschool children. *Australian Psychologist, 28,* 94-99.

Sarbin, T. R. (1986). *Narrative psychology: The storied nature of human conduct.* New York: Praeger.

Sarbin, T. R. (1991). Hypnosis: A fifty-year perspective. *Contemporary Hypnosis, 8,* 1–15.

Satin, M. (1990, September/October). Nine ideas to improve the schools. *Utne Reader,* pp. 78–83.

Savage-Rumbaugh, E. S. (1990). Language acquisition in a nonhuman species: Implications for the innateness debate. *Developmental Psychobiology, 23,* 599–620.

Savage-Rumbaugh, E. S., Rumbaugh, D. M., & Boysen, S. (1980). Do apes use language? *American Science, 68,* 49–61.

Sawyer, A. G., & Howard, D. J. (1991). Effects of omitting conclusions in advertisements to involved and uninvolved audiences. *Journal of Marketing Research, 28,* 467–474.

Saxe, L., Dougherty, D., & Cross, T. (1985). The validity of polygraph testing: Scientific analysis and public controversy. *American Psychologist, 40,* 355–366.

Scarborough, E., & Furumoto, L. (1987). *Untold lives.* New York: Columbia University Press.

Scarr, S. (1981). Testing for children: Assessment and the many determinants of intellectual competence. *American Psychologist, 36,* 1159–1166.

Scarr, S. , Weinberg, R. A., & Levine, A. (1986). *Understanding development.* New York: Harcourt, Brace, Jovanovich.

Schachter, S. (1959). *The psychology of affiliation.* Palo Alto, CA: Stanford University Press.

Schachter, S. (1971). *Emotion, obesity, and crime.* New York: Academic Press.

Schachter, S., & Singer, J. (1962). Cognitive, social, and physiological determinants of emotional state. *Psychological Review, 69,* 379–399.

Schaffer, C. E., Davidson, R. J., & Saron, C. (1983). Frontal and parietal electroencephalogram asymmetry in depressed and nondepressed subjects. *Biological Psychiatry, 18,* 753–762.

Schaie, K. W. (1958). Rigidity-flexibility and intelligence: A cross-sectional study of adult life span from 20 to 70. *Psychological Monographs, 72*(9).

Schaie, K. W. (1993). The Seattle longitudinal studies of adult intelligence. *Current Directions in Psychological Science, 2,* 171–175.

Schaie, K. W., & Willis, S. L. (1986). *Adult development and aging* (2nd ed.). Boston: Little, Brown.

Schall, M., Kemeny, A., & Maltzman, I. (1992). Factors associated with alcohol use in university students. *Journal of Studies on Alcohol, 53,* 122–136.

Schalling, D., & Svensson, J. (1984). Blood pressure and personality. *Personality and Individual Differences, 5,* 41–51.

Schank, R. C. (1990). *Tell me a story: A new look at real and artificial memory.* New York: Scribner's.

Scheflen, A. E. (1964). The significance of posture in communication systems. *Psychiatry, 27,* 316–331.

Scheier, M. F., & Carver, C. S. (1992). Effects of optimism on psychological and physical well-being. *Cognitive Therapy Research, 16,* 201–228.

Scheier, M. F., & Carver, C. S. (1993). On the power of positive thinking: The benefits of being optimistic. *Current Directions in Psychological Science, 2,* 26–30.

Schiavi, R. C., Schreiner-Engel, P., White, D., & Mandeli, J. (1991). The relationship between pituitary-gonadal function and sexual behavior in healthy aging men. *Psychosomatic Medicine, 53,* 363–374.

Schiffer, F., Teicher, M. H. & Papanicolaou, A. C. (1995). Evoked potential evidence for right brain activity during the recall of traumatic memories. *Journal of Neuropsychiatry, 7,* 169-175.

Schildkraut, J. J., Green, A. I., & Mooney, J. J. (1985). Affective disorders: Biochemical aspects. In H. I. Kaplan & B. J. Sadock (Eds.), *Comprehensive textbook of psychiatry.* Baltimore: Williams & Wilkins.

Schjeldrup-Ebbe, T. (1935). Social behavior of birds. In C. Murchison (Ed.), *Handbook of social psychology.* Worcester, MA: Clark University Press.

Schneider, M. (1991). Developing services for lesbian and gay adolescents. *Canadian Journal of Community Mental Health, 10,* 133–151.

Schneidman, E. S. (1981). Suicide. *Suicide and Life Threatening Behavior, 11,* 198-220.

Schooler, C. (1972). Birth order effects: Not here, not now! *Psychological Bulletin, 78,* 161–175.

Schuster, B., Fosterling, F., & Weiner, B. (1989). Perceiving the causes of success and failure: A cross-cultural explanation of attributional concepts. *Journal of Cross-Cultural Psychology, 20,* 191–213.

Schwartz, G. E., Weinberger, D. A., & Singer, J. A. (1981). Cardiovascular differentiation of happiness, sadness, anger, and fear following imagery and exercise. *Psychosomatic Medicine, 43,* 343–364.

Scott, K. G., & Carran, D. T. (1987). The epidemiology and prevention of mental retardation. *American Psychologist, 42,* 801–804.

Sears, R. R. (1936). Experimental studies of projection: I. Attributions of traits. *Journal of Social Psychology, 7,* 151–163.

Sebeok, T. A. (1985). A scientific quibble. *Semiotica, 57,* 117–124.

Sechrest, L., & Figueredo, A. J. (1993). Program evaluation. *Annual Review of Psychology, 44,* 645–674.

Segal, N. L. (1985). Monozygotic and dizygotic twins: A comparative analysis of mental profiles. *Child Development, 56,* 1051–1058.

Seligman, M. E. P. (1970). On the generality of the laws of learning. *Psychological Review, 77,* 406–418.

Seligman, M. E. P. (1975). *Helplessness: On depression, development, and death.* San Francisco: Freeman.

Seligman, M. E. P., & Maier, S. F. (1967). Failure to escape traumatic shock. *Journal of Experimental Psychology, 74,* 1–9.

Selye, H. (1976). *The stress of life* (2nd ed.). New York: McGraw-Hill.

Semb, G., Ellis, J., & Arauio, J. (1993). Long-term memory for knowledge learned in school. *Journal of Educational Psychology, 85,* 305–316.

Shah, M., & Jeffery, R. (1991). Is obesity due to overeating and inactivity, or to a defective metabolic rate? A review. *Annals of Behavioral Medicine, 13,* 73–81.

Shane, M. & Shane, E. (1995). Clinical perspectives on gender role/identity disorder. *Psychoanalytic Inquiry, 15,* 39-59.

Shapley, R. (1990). Visual sensitivity and parallel retinocortical channels. *Annual Review of Psychology, 41,* 635–658.

Sharp, H. S. (1986). Darwin and sociobiology: A reply to Turke. *American Anthropologist, 88,* 155–156.

Sheffield, F., Wulff, J., & Backer, R. (1951). Reward value of copulation without sex drive reduction. *Journal of Comparative and Physiological Psychology, 44,* 3–8.

Sheldon, W. H., Stevens, S. S., & Tucker, W. B. (1940). *The varieties of human physique.* New York: Harper.

Shepard, R. N. (1967). Recognition memory for words, sentences and pictures. *Journal of Verbal Learning and Verbal Behavior, 6,* 156–163.

Sherif, M. (1956). Experiments in group conflict. *Scientific American, 195,* 54–58.

Sherr, L. (1990). Fear arousal and AIDS? Do shock tactics work? *AIDS, 4,* 361–364.

Shneidman, E. (1985). *Definition of suicide.* New York: Wiley.

Shopland, C., & Gregory, R. (1964). The effects of touch on a visually ambiguous three-dimensional figure. *Quarterly Journal of Experimental Psychology, 16,* 66–70.

Shubs, C. H. (1985). Empirical research in bioenergetic analysis. *Bioenergetic Analysis, 1,* 196–205.

Shweder, R. A., & Sullivan, M. A. (1993). Cultural psychology: Who needs it? *Annual Review of Psychology, 44,* 497–523.

Siegel, S. (1983). Classical conditioning, drug tolerance, and drug dependence. In R. G. Smart, F. B. Glaser, Y. Isreal, H. Kalant, R. Popham, & W. Schmidt (Eds.), *Research advances in alcohol and drug problems.* New York: Plenum Press.

Siegler, R. S. (1986). *Children's thinking.* Englewood Cliffs, NJ: Prentice Hall.

Sigel, M. (1992). *The Cornell book of cats.* New York: Villard.

Silliman, E. R. (1992). Three perspectives of facilitated communication: Unexpected literacy, Clever Hans, or enigma? *Topics in Language Disorders, 12,* 60–68.

Simon, H. A. (1990). Invariants of human behavior. *Annual Review of Psychology, 41,* 1–19.

Simons, R. L., Whitbeck, L. B., Conger, R. D., & Wu, C. (1991). Intergenerational transmission of harsh parenting. *Developmental Psychology, 27,* 159-171.

Simpson, J. A. (1995). A paradigm whose time has come. *Psychological Inquiry, 6,* 71-75.

Simpson, R. L., & Myles, B. S. (1993). Successful integration of children and youth with autism in mainstreamed settings. *Focus on Autistic Behavior, 7,* 1–13.

Sinclair, R. C., Hoffman, C., Mark, M. M., Martin, L. L., & Pickering, T. L. (1994). Construct accessibility and the misattribution of arousal: Schachter and Singer revisited. *Psychological Science, 5,* 15–19.

Sizemore, C. C., & Pittillo, E. S. (1977). *I'm Eve.* New York: Doubleday.

Skeels, H. M. (1966). Adult status of children with contrasting early life experiences: A follow-up study. *Monographs of the Society for Research in Child Development, 31* (3, Whole No. 105).

Skeels, H. M., & Dye, H. B. (1939). A study of the effects of differential stimulation on mentally retarded children. *Proceedings & Addresses of the American Association on Mental Deficiency, 44,* 114–136.

Skiba, R. J., & Raison, J. (1990). Relationship between the use of timeout and academic achievement. *Exceptional Children, 57,* 36–46.

Skinner, B. F. (1948). *Walden two.* New York: Macmillan.

Skinner, B. F. (1953). *Science and human behavior.* New York: Macmillan.

Skinner, B. F. (1957). *Verbal behavior.* New York: Appleton-Century-Crofts.

Skinner, B. F. (1961). The design of cultures. *Daedalus, 90,* 534–546.

Skinner, B. F. (1971). *Beyond freedom and dignity.* New York: Knopf.

Skinner, B. F. (1984). The evolution of behavior. *Journal of the Experimental Analysis of Behavior, 41,* 217–221.

Skinner, B. F. (1990). Can psychology be a science of mind? *American Psychologist, 45,* 1206–1210.

Slee, P. T. (1993). Children, stressful life events, and school adjustment: An Australian study. *Educational Psychology, 13,* 3–10.

Slotkin, J. S. (1955). Culture and psychopathology. *Journal of Abnormal Social Psychology, 51,* 269–275.

Small, M. A. (1993). Advancing psychological jurisprudence. *Behavioral Sciences and the Law, 11,* 3–16.

Smith, D. C., & Maher, M. F. (1991). Healthy death. *Counseling and Values, 36,* 42–48.

Smith, M. B. (1990). Humanistic psychology. *Journal of Humanistic Psychology, 30,* 6–21.

Smith, M. L., & Glass, G. V. (1977). Meta-analysis of psychotherapy outcome studies. *American Psychologist, 32,* 752–760.

Smith, R. G. (1986). Classics revisited: Thomas S. Szasz. *Issues in Radical Therapy, 12,* 12–15.

Smith, S., & Whitehead, G. (1984). Attributions for promotion and demotion in the United States and India. *Journal of Social Psychology, 124,* 27–34.

Smith, T. C., & Thompson, T. L. (1993). The inherent, powerful therapeutic value of a good physician-patient relationship. *Psychosomatics, 34,* 166–170.

Smyth, L. D. (1981). Towards a social learning theory of hypnosis: I. Hypnotic suggestibility. *American Journal of Clinical Hypnosis, 23*(3), 147–168.

Sno, H. H., & Linszen, D. H. (1990). The déjà vu experience: Remembrance of things past? *American Journal of Psychiatry, 147,* 1587–1595.

Sno, H. H., Schalken, H. F., & de Jonghe, F. (1992). Empirical research on déjà vu experiences: A review. *Behavioural Neurology, 5,* 155–160.

Snow, C. E. (1991, May 23). Personal communication.

Snow, C. E., Barnes, W. S., Chandler, J., Goodman, I. F., & Hemphill, L. (1991). *Unfulfilled expectations: Home and school influences on literacy.* Cambridge, MA: Harvard University Press.

Snyderman, M., & Rothman, S. (1987). Survey of expert opinion on intelligence and aptitude testing. *American Psychologist, 42,* 137–144.

Solomon, R. L. (1980). The opponent-process theory of acquired motivation. *American Psychologist, 35,* 691–712.

Solomon, R. L., & Corbit, J. D. (1974). An opponent-process theory of motivation. *Psychological Review, 81,* 119–145.

Somberg, D. R., Stone, G. L., & Claiborn, C. D. (1993). Informed consent: Therapists' beliefs and practices. *Professional Psychology Research and Practice, 24,* 153–159.

Sorrentino, R. M. (1991). Evidence for altruism: The lady is still waiting. *Psychological Inquiry, 2,* 147–150.

Sowers-Hoag, K. M., Thyer, B. A., & Bailey, J. S. (1987). Promoting automobile safety belt use by young children. *Journal of Applied Behavior Analysis, 20*(2), 133–138.

Spearman, C. (1927). *Abilities of man.* New York: Macmillan.

Sperling, G. (1960). The information available in brief visual presentations. *Psychological Monographs, 74,* 1–29.

Sperry, R. W. (1968). Hemisphere deconnection and unity in conscious awareness. *American Psychologist, 23,* 723–733.

Sperry, R. W. (1984). Consciousness, personal identity and the divided brain. *Neuropsychologia, 22,* 661–673.

Spitzer, R. L. (1975). On pseudoscience, logic in remission, and psychiatric diagnosis: A critique of D. L. Rosenhan's "On being sane in insane places." *Journal of Abnormal Psychology, 84,* 442–452.

Sprecher, S. (1990). The impact of the threat of AIDS on heterosexual dating relationships. *Journal of Psychology and Human Sexuality, 3,* 3–23.

Springer, J., & Coleman, K. B. (1992). The ACCESS Educational Leadership Team: A teacher-student advocacy group. *Special Services in the Schools, 6,* 51–65.

Squire, L. R. (1987). *Memory and the brain.* New York: Oxford University Press.

Squire, L. R., Knowlton, B. & Musen, G. (1993). The structure and organization of memory. *Annual Review of Psychology, 44,* 452–495.

Squire, L. R., & Zola-Morgan, S. (1991). The medial temporal lobe memory system. *Science, 253,* 1380–1386.

Staats, A. W. (1993). Personality theory, abnormal psychology, and psychological measurement: A psychological behaviorism. *Behavior Modification, 17,* 8–42.

Staats, A. W., & Staats, C. K. (1958). Attitudes established by classical conditioning. *Journal of Abnormal Social Psychology, 57,* 37–40.

Standing, L. (1973). Learning 10,000 pictures. *Quarterly Journal of Experimental Psychology, 25,* 207–222.

Stanway, A. (1987). *The natural family doctor.* New York: Simon & Schuster.

Stasiewicz, P. R. & Maisto, S. A. (1993). Two-factor avoidance theory: The role of negative affect in the maintenance of substance use and substance use disorder. *Behavior Therapy, 24,* 337-356.

Steinbrook, R. (1992). The polygraph test: A flawed diagnostic method. *New England Journal of Medicine, 327,* 122–123.

Stelmack, R. M. (1990). Biological bases of extraversion: Psychophysiological evidence. *Journal of Personality, 58,* 293–311.

Sternberg, R. J. (1985). *Beyond IQ.* New York: Cambridge University Press.

Sternberg, R. J. (1986). A triangular theory of love. *Psychological Review, 93,* 119–135.

Sternberg, R. J., & Lubart, T. I. (1992). Buy low and sell high: An investment approach to creativity. *Current Directions in Psychological Science, 1,* 1–5.

Sternberg R. J., & Wagner, R. K. (1993). The *g*-ocentric view of intelligence and job performance is wrong. *Current Directions in Psychological Science, 2(1),* 1–5.

Stevens, J. C. (1989). Food quality reports from noninstitutionalized aged. *Annals of the New York Academy of Sciences, 561,* 87–93.

Stevens, J. R. (1990). Psychiatric consequences of temporal lobectomy for intractable seizures: A 20–30–year follow-up of 14 cases. *Psychological Medicine, 20,* 529–545.

Stiles, W. B., Shapiro, D. A., & Elliott, R. (1986). Are all psychotherapies equivalent? *American Psychologist, 41,* 165–180.

Stokols, D. (1992). Establishing and maintaining healthy environments. *American Psychologist, 47,* 6–22.

Stone, A. A., & Neale, J. M. (1984). New measure of daily coping: Development and preliminary results. *Journal of Personality and Social Psychology, 46,* 892–906.

Stoppers, P. J., & Waller, P. E. (1993). Using the free fall of objects under gravity for visual depth estimation. *Bulletin of the Psychonomic Society, 31,* 125–127.

Storms, M. D. (1981). A theory of erotic orientation development. *Psychological Review, 88,* 340–353.

Stott, L. H. (1967). *Child development: An individual longitudinal approach.* New York: Holt.

Strathman, A., Baker, S. M., & Kost, K. A. (1991). Distinguishing the psychologies of the sociophysical and the natural environment. *American Psychologist, 46,* 164–165.

Stravynski, A., & Greenberg, D. (1990). The treatment of sexual dysfunction in single men. *Sexual and Marital Therapy, 5,* 115–122.

Strichartz, A. F., & Burton, R. V. (1990). Lies and truth: A study of the development of the concept. *Child Development, 61(1),* 211–220.

Stricker, L. J., & Rock, D. A. (1990). Interpersonal competence, social intelligence, and general ability. *Personality and Individual Differences, 11,* 833–839.

Strickland, B. R. (1992). Women and depression. *Current Directions in Psychological Science, 1,* 132–135.

Strober, M. (1991). Family-genetic studies of eating disorders. *Journal of Clinical Psychiatry, 52,* 9–12.

Strube, M. J. (1991a). A rational decision-making approach to abusive relationships. *Revista Intercontinental de Psicologia y Educación, 4,* 105–120.

Strube, M. J. (1991b). *Type A behavior.* Newbury Park, CA: Sage.

Strupp, H. H. (1986). Psychotherapy: Research, practice, and public policy (How to avoid dead ends). *American Psychologist, 41,* 120–130.

Sturgis, E., Tollison, C., & Adams, H. (1978). Modification of combined migraine-muscle contraction headaches using BVP and EMG feedback. *Journal of Applied Behavior Analysis, 11,* 215–223.

Sudzak, P., Glowa, J., Crawley, J., Swartz, R., Skolnick, P., & Paul, S. (1986). A selective imidazohenzodiazepine antagonist of ethanol in the rat. *Science, 234,* 1243–1247.

Sue, D., & Sue, S. (1987). Cultural factors in the clinical assessment of Asian Americans. *Journal of Consulting and Clinical Psychology, 55,* 479–487.

Suedfeld, P., & Mocellin, J. S. (1987). The "sensed presence" in unusual environments. *Environment and Behavior, 19,* 33–52.

Sulloway, F. J. (1995). Birth order and evolutionary psychology: A meta-analytic overview. *Psychological Inquiry, 6,* 75-80.

Sundstrom, E., Bell, P. A., Busby, P. L. & Asmus, C. (1996). Environmental psychology, 1989-1994. *Annual Review of Psychology, 47,* 485-512.

Supa, M., Cotzin, M., & Dallenbach, K. M. (1944). Facial vision: The perception of obstacles by the blind. *American Journal of Psychology, 57,* 133–183.

Suppes, P., Pavel, M., & Falmagne, J. U. (1994). Representations and models in psychology. *Annual Review of Psychology, 45,* 517–544.

Sutherland, R. J., & McDonald, R. J. (1990). Hippocampus, amygdala, and memory deficits in rats. *Behavioral Brain Research, 37,* 57–79.

Swartz, K. B., Chen, S., & Terrace, H. S. (1991). Serial learning by rhesus monkeys: I. Acquisition and retention of multiple four-item lists. *Journal of Experimental Psychology: Animal Behavior Processes, 17,* 396–410.

Sweeney, P. D., Anderson, K., & Bailey, S. (1986). Attribution style in depression: A meta-analytic review. *Journal of Personality and Social Psychology, 50,* 974–991.

Sweet, M. J., & Johnson, C. G. (1990). Enhancing empathy: The interpersonal implications of a Buddhist meditation technique. *Psychotherapy, 27,* 19–29.

Sweller, J., & Gee, W. (1978). Einstellung, the sequence effect, and hypothesis theory. *Journal of Experimental Psychology: Human Learning and Memory, 4,* 513–526.

Szasz, T. (1970). *The manufacture of madness.* New York: Harper & Row.

Szasz, T. (1974). *The myth of mental illness.* New York: Harper & Row.

Szasz, T. (1977). *Psychiatric slavery: When confinement and coercion masquerade as cure.* New York: Free Press.

Szasz, T. (1990). Law and psychiatry: The problems that will not go away. *Journal of Mind and Behavior, 11,* 557–563.

Szasz, T. (1991). Noncoercive psychiatry: An oxymoron. *Journal of Humanistic Psychology, 31,* 117–125.

Tabin, G. (1993). *Blind corners: Adventures on seven continents.* New York: ICS Books.

Tannen, D. (1990). *You just don't understand: Women and men in conversation.* New York: Morrow.

Tanner, J. M. (1971). Sequence, tempo and individual variation in the growth and development of boys and girls aged twelve to sixteen. *Daedalus, 100,* 907–930.

Tarpy, R. M. (1975). *Basic principles of learning.* Glenview, IL: Scott, Foresman.

Tauber, R. T. (1990). Changing teachers' attitudes toward punishment. *Principal, 69,* 28, 30.

Taylor, F. W. (1911). *Principles of scientific management.* New York: Harper Brothers.

Taylor, M. A., & Abrams, R. (1984). Cognitive impairment in schizophrenia. *American Journal of Psychiatry, 141,* 196–201.

Taylor, S. E. (1991). *Health psychology* (2nd ed.). New York: McGraw-Hill.

Teachman, J. D., & Polonko, K. A. (1990). Cohabitation and marital stability in the United States. *Social Forces, 69,* 207–220.

Teicher, M., Glod, C., & Cole, J. (1990). Emergence of intense suicidal preoccupation during fluoxetine treatment. *American Journal of Psychiatry, 14,* 207–210.

Teigen, K. H. (1994). Yerkes-Dodson: A law for all seasons. *Theory and Psychology, 4,* 525-547.

Tellegen, A., Lykken, D. T., Bouchard, T. J., Wilcox, K. J., Segal, N. L., & Rich, S. (1988). Personality similarity in twins reared apart and together. *Journal of Personality and Social Psychology, 54,* 1031–1039.

Terman, L. M. (1916). *The measurement of intelligence.* Boston: Houghton Mifflin.

Terman, L. M. (1954). Scientists and nonscientists in a group of 800 gifted men. *Psychological Monographs, 68*(7).

Terman, L. M., & Oden, M. II. (1947). *Genetic studies of genius: IV. The gifted child grows up: Twenty-five years' follow-up of a superior group.* Palo Alto: Stanford University Press.

Tesser, A., & Shaffer, D. R. (1990). Attitude and attitude change. *Annual Review of Psychology, 41,* 479–523.

Thayer, P. W., & Austin, J. T. (1992). Harold E. Burtt (1890–1991). *American Psychologist, 47,* 1677.

Thayer, S. (1988). Close encounters. *Psychology Today, 22,* 30–36.

Thigpen, C. H., & Cleckley, H. (1954). A case of multiple personality. *Journal of Abnormal and Social Psychology, 49,* 135–151.

Thompson, R., & McConnell, J. J. (1955). Classical conditioning in the planarian (*Dugesia dorotocephaea*). *Journal of Comparative Psychology, 48,* 65–68.

Thorndike, E. L. (1898). Animal intelligence: An experimental study of the association process in animals. *Psychological Monographs, 2*(8).

Thorndike, E. L. (1911). *Animal intelligence.* New York: Macmillan.

Thorndike, R. M. (1990). Origins of intelligence and its measurement. *Journal of Psychoeducational Assessment, 8,* 223–230.

Thurber, J. (1983). *The secret life of Walter Mitty.* Mankato, MN: Creative Education.

Thurstone, L. L. (1950). The factorial description of temperament. *Science, 111,* 454–455.

Thurstone, L. L., & Thurstone, T. G. (1941). Factorial studies of intelligence. *Psychometric Monographs, 2.*

Thyer, B. A. (1991). The enduring intellectual legacy of B. F. Skinner: A citation count from 1966–1989. *Behavior Analyst, 14,* 73–75.

Timberlake, W. (1993). Animal behavior: A continuing synthesis. *Annual Review of Psychology, 44,* 675–708.

Tinbergen, N. (1953). *Social behavior in animals.* New York: Wiley.

Tinbergen, N. (1965). *Animal behavior.* New York: Time, Inc.

Tolaas, J. (1980). Dreams, dreaming, and recent intrusive events. *Journal of Altered States of Consciousness, 5,* 183–210.

Tollefson, G. D. (1991). Anxiety and alcoholism: A serotonin link. *British Journal of Psychiatry, 159,* 34–39.

Tolman, E. C., & Honzik, C. H. (1930). Introduction and removal of reward, and maze performance in rats. *University of California Publications in Psychology, 4,* 257–275.

Torrey, E. F., Bowler, A. E., Taylor, E. H., & Gottesman, I. I. (1994). *Schizophrenia and manic-depressive disorder.* New York: Basic Books.

Triandis, H. C., McCusker, C., & Hui, C. H. (1990). Multimethod probes of individualism and collectivism. *Journal of Personality and Social Psychology, 59,* 1006–1020.

Tries, J. (1990). The use of biofeedback in the treatment of incontinence due to head injury. *Journal of Head Trauma Rehabilitation, 5,* 91–100.

Tryon, R. C. (1940). Genetic differences in maze-learning ability in rats. *Thirty-ninth Yearbook, National Society for Studies in Education,* Part I, 111–119.

Tuddenham, R. D. (1962). The nature and measurement of intelligence. In L. Postman (Ed.), *Psychology in the making: Histories of selected research problems.* New York: Knopf.

Tulving, E. (1985). How many memory systems are there? *American Psychologist, 40,* 385–398.

Tulving, E., & Psotka, J. (1971). Retroactive inhibition in free recall: Inaccessibility of information available in the memory store. *Journal of Experimental Psychology, 87,* 1–8.

Turkington, C. (1992). US can, should do more to prevent AIDS. *APA Monitor, 23*(1), 8–9.

Twain, M. (1906). *The $30,000 bequest and other stories.* New York: Harper Brothers.

Ulrich, R. E. (1991). Animal rights, animal wrongs and the question of balance. *Psychological Science, 2,* 197–201.

Umiker-Sebeok, J., & Sebeok, T. A. (1980). Introduction: Questioning apes. In T. A. Sebeok & J. Umiker-Sebeok (Eds.), *Speaking of apes.* New York: Plenum Press.

U.S. Bureau of the Census. (1993). *Statistical abstract of the United States: 1993* (113th ed.). Washington, DC: Author.

Vaillant, G. E. (1992). *Ego mechanisms of defense: A guide for clinicians and researchers.* Washington, DC: American Psychiatric Press.

Valenstein, E. S. (1973). *Brain control.* New York: Wiley.

Vanderwolf, C. H., & Cain, D. P. (1991). The neurobiology of race and Kipling's cat. *Personality and Individual Differences, 12,* 97–98.

Van Dijk, E., & Wilke, H. A. (1993). Differential interests, equity, and public good provision. *Journal of Experimental Social Psychology, 29,* 1–16.

Van Hutton, V. (1990). Test review: The California Psychological Inventory. *Journal of Counseling and Development, 69,* 75–77.

Van Lawick-Goodall, J. (1971). *In the shadow of man.* New York: Dell.

Varnado, P. J., Williamson, D. A., & Netemeyer, R. (1995). Confirmatory factor analysis of eating disorder symptoms in college women. *Journal of Psychopathology and Behavioral Assessment, 17,* 69-79.

Vega, L. de (1615/1934-35). El capellán de la virgen. In *Obras Dramaticas Escogidas,* Madrid: Hernando.

Verhave, T. (1966). The pigeon as a quality control inspector. *American Psychologist, 21,* 109–115.

Verhulst, F. C., & Koot, H. M. (1991). Longitudinal research in child and adolescent psychiatry. *Journal of the American Academy of Child and Adolescent Psychiatry, 30,* 361–368.

Viglione, D., Brager, R., & Haller, N. (1991). Psychoanalytic interpretation of the Rorschach: Do we have better hieroglyphics? *Journal of Personality Assessment, 57,* 1–9.

Vincent, K. R., & Harman, M. J. (1991). The Exner Rorschach: An analysis of its clinical validity. *Journal of Clinical Psychology, 47,* 596–599.

Vitz, P. (1990). The use of stories in moral development. *American Psychologist, 45,* 709-720.

Vokey, J. R., & Read, J. D. (1985). Subliminal messages: Between the devil and the media. *American Psychologist, 40,* 1231–1239.

Volberg, R. A., & Steadman, H. J. (1988). Refining prevalence estimates of pathological gambling. *American Journal of Psychiatry, 145,* 502–505.

Volberg, R. A., & Steadman, H. J. (1989). Prevalence estimates of pathological gambling in New Jersey and Maryland. *American Journal of Psychiatry, 146,* 1618–1619.

Wadden, T. A., & Anderton, C. H. (1982). The clinical use of hypnosis. *Psychological Bulletin, 91,* 215–243.

Wadden, T. A., Foster, G. D., Letizia, K. A., & Mullen, J. L. (1990). Long-term effects of dieting on resting metabolic rate in obese outpatients. *Journal of the American Medical Association, 264,* 707–711.

Wagener, J., & Laird, J. (1980). The experimenter's foot-in-the-door: Self-perception, body weight, and volunteering. *Personality and Social Psychology Bulletin, 6,* 441–446.

Wagner, M. W., & Monnet, M. (1979). Attitudes of college professors toward extra-sensory perception. *Zeletic Scholar, 5,* 7–16.

Wakefield, J. C. (1992). The concept of mental disorder: On the boundary between biological facts and social values. *American Psychologist, 47,* 373–388.

Walker, R. N. (1962). Body build and behavior in young children. *Monographs of the Society for Research in Child Development, 27* (Whole No. 84).

Wallace, R. K., & Benson, H. (1972, February). The physiology of meditation. *Scientific American, 226,* 85–90.

Wallas, G. (1926). *The art of thought.* New York: Harcourt, Brace.

Walls, G. L. (1942). Eye movements and the fovea. In G. L. Walls (Ed.), *The vertebrate eye and its adaptive radiation.* Bloomfield Hills, MI: Cranbrook Institute of Science.

Walsh, C., & Cepko, C. (1992). Widespread dispersion of neuronal clones across functional regions of the cerebral cortex. *Science, 255,* 343–440.

Walsh, R., & Vaughn, F. (1992). Lucid dreaming: Some transpersonal implications. *Journal of Transpersonal Psychology, 24,* 193–200.

Walster, E., & Walster, G. W. (1978). *A new look at love.* Reading, MA: Addison-Wesley.

Walther, E. (1986). Telepathy: A testable hypothesis. *Journal of the Society for Psychical Research, 53,* 201–209.

Wand, B. (1993). The unity of the discipline: A challenge for the profession. *Canadian Psychology, 34,* 124–134.

Warren, B. (1990). Psychoanalysis and personal construct theory: An exploration. *Journal of Psychology, 124,* 449–463.

Warren, R. M. (1984). Helmholtz and his continuing influence. *Music Perception, 1,* 253–275.

Watkins, J. G., & Watkins, H. H. (1990). Dissociation and displacement: Where goes the "ouch"? *American Journal of Clinical Hypnosis, 33,* 1–10.

Watson, J. B. (1930). *Behaviorism.* New York: Norton.

Watson, J. B., & Rayner, R. (1920). Conditioned emotional reactions. *Journal of Experimental Psychology, 3,* 1–14.

Waugh, N. (1961). Free versus serial recall. *Journal of Experimental Psychology, 62,* 496–502.

Webb, W. B. (1974). Sleep as an adaptive response. *Perceptual & Motor Skills, 38,* 1023–1027.

Webb, W. B. (1983). Theories in modern sleep research. In A. Mayes (Ed.), *Sleep Mechanisms and Functions.* Wokingham, UK: Van Nostrand, Rheinhold.

Webb, W. B., & Agnew, H. W. (1974). Sleep and waking in a time-free environment. *Aerospace Medicine, 45,* 617–622.

Webb, W. B., & Cartwright, R. D. (1978). Sleep and dreams. *Annual Review of Psychology, 29,* 223–252.

Wechsler, D. (1939). *The measurement of adult intelligence.* Baltimore: Williams & Wilkins.

Wechsler, D. (1958). *The measurement and appraisal of adult intelligence* (4th ed.). Baltimore: Williams & Wilkins.

Wechsler, D. (1975). Intelligence defined and undefined: A relativistic appraisal. *American Psychologist, 30,* 135–139.

Wedderburn, A. A. (1992). How fast should the night shift rotate? A rejoinder. *Ergonomics, 35,* 1447–1451.

Wegener, N. (1992). Support group services in the workplace: The practice and the potential. *Social Work with Groups, 15,* 207–222.

Weil, A. (1990). *Natural health, natural medicine.* Boston: Houghton Mifflin.

Weinberg, R., Scarr, S., & Waldman, I. (1992). The Minnesota transracial adoption study: A follow-up of IQ test performance at adolescence. *Intelligence, 16,* 117–135.

Weinberg, S. L., & Goldberg, K. P. (1990). *Statistics for the behavioral sciences.* New York: Cambridge University Press.

Weinberger, D. R., & Kleinman, J. E. (1986). Observation on the brain in schizophrenia. In A. J. Frances & R. E. Hales (Eds.), *American Psychiatric Association: Annual Review* (Vol. 5). Washington DC: American Psychiatric Press.

Weinrich, J. D. (1980). Toward a sociobiological theory of the emotions. In R. Plutchik & H. Kellerman (Eds.), *Emotion: Theory, research, and experience.* New York: Academic Press.

Weisberg, P., & Waldrop, P. B. (1972). Fixed-interval work habits of Congress. *Journal of Applied Behavioral Analysis, 5,* 93–97.

Wender, P. H., Kety, S. S., Rosenthal, D., Schulsinger, F., Ortmann, J., & Lunde, I. (1986). Psychiatric disorders in the biological and adoptive families of adopted individuals with affective disorders. *Archives of General Psychiatry, 43,* 923–929.

Wertheimer, M. (1938). Laws of organization in perceptual forms. In W. D. Ellis (Ed.), *A source book of Gestalt psychology.* New York: Harcourt, Brace, Jovanovich.

West, J. B. (1986). Do climbs to extreme altitude cause brain damage? *Lancet, 2,* 387–388.

West, L. (1967). Vision and kinesthesis in the acquisition of typewriting skill. *Journal of Applied Psychology, 51*(21), 161–166.

Westen, D. (1991). Social cognitions and object relations. *Psychological Bulletin, 109,* 429–455.

Westermeyer, J. (1987). Cultural factors in clinical assessment. *Journal of Consulting and Clinical Psychology, 55,* 471–478.

Wever, E. G. (1949). *Theory of learning.* New York: Wiley.

Whishaw, I. Q. (1991). Latent learning in a swimming pool task by rats: Evidence for the use of associative and not cognitive mapping processes. *Quarterly Journal of Experimental Psychology: Comparative and Physiological Psychology, 43,* 83–103.

White, G., & Mullen, P. (1989). *Jealousy: Theory, research, and clinical strategies.* New York: Guilford Press.

White, L. K. (1990). Determinants of divorce: A review of research in the Eighties. *Journal of Marriage and the Family, 52,* 904–912.

White, L. K., & Booth, A. (1991). Divorce over the life course. *Journal of Family Issues, 12,* 5–21.

White, R. W. (1964). *The abnormal personality.* New York: Ronald.

Whitehead, C. S., & Hoff, C. A. (1929). *Ethical sex relations or the new eugenics: A safe guide for young men—young women.* Chicago: Hertel.

Whitlock, F. A. (1987). Addiction. In R. L. Gregory (Ed.), *The Oxford companion to the mind.* New York: Oxford University Press.

Whorf, B. L. (1956). *Language, thought and reality.* Cambridge, MA: MIT Press.

Wickremasinghe, W. (1991). *Handbook of world education.* Houston, TX: American Collegiate Service.

Wierda, M., & Brookhuis, K. A. (1991). Analysis of cycling skill: A cognitive approach. *Applied Cognitive Psychology, 5,* 113–122.

Wiggins, J. S., & Pincus, A. L. (1992). Personality: Structure and assessment. *Annual Review of Psychology, 43,* 473–504.

Wilkins, W. (1986). Placebo problems in psychotherapy research: Social-psychological alternatives to chemotherapy concepts. *American Psychologist, 41,* 551–556.

Wilkinson, R. T. (1992). How fast should the night shift rotate? *Ergonomics, 35,* 1425–1446.

Williams, C. D. (1959). The elimination of tantrum behavior by extinction procedures. *Journal of Abnormal and Social Psychology, 59,* 269.

Wilson, D., Mundy-Castle, A., & Panditji, L. (1990). Birth order and intellectual development among Zimbabwean children. *Journal of Social Psychology, 130,* 409–411.

Wilson, E. O. (1971). *The insect societies.* Cambridge, MA: Harvard University Press.

Wilson, E. O. (1980). *Sociobiology: The new synthesis* (abr. ed.). Cambridge, MA: Harvard University Press.

Wilson, G. T. (1991). Chemical aversion conditioning in the treatment of alcoholism: Further comments. *Behavioral Research and Therapy, 29,* 415–419.

Wilson, G. T., & Fairburn, C. G. (1993). Cognitive treatments for eating disorders. *Journal of Consulting and Clinical Psychology, 61,* 261–269.

Wilson, G. T., & Walsh, B. T. (1991). Eating disorders in the DSM-IV. *Journal of Abnormal Psychology, 100,* 362–365.

Wilson, J. T. (1990). Significance of MRI in clarifying whether neuropsychological deficits after head injury are organically based. *Neuropsychology, 4,* 261–269.

Wilson, S. J. (1982). Influence of social class, sex, and type of feedback on children's motivation to solve cognitively challenging tasks. *Genetic Psychology Monographs, 105,* 235–254.

Windholz, G. (1990). Pavlov and the Pavlovians in the laboratory. *Journal of the History of the Behavioral Sciences, 26,* 64–74.

Winn, K. I., Crawford, D. W., & Fischer, J. L. (1991). Equity and commitment in romance versus friendship. *Journal of Social Behavior and Personality, 6,* 301–314.

Wise, R. A., & Rompre, P. P. (1989). Brain dopamine and reward. *Annual Review of Psychology, 40,* 191–225.

Wolf, S., & Wolff, H. G. (1943). Evidence of the genesis of peptic ulcer in man. In S. S. Tompkins (Ed.), *Contemporary psychopathology.* Cambridge, MA: Harvard University Press.

Wolman, B. B. (1989). *Dictionary of behavioral science* (2nd ed.). New York: Academic Press.

Wolpe, J. (1961). The systematic desensitization treatment of neurosis. *Journal of Nervous and Mental Disease, 132,* 189–203.

Wong, F. Y., McCreary, D. R., Bowden, C. C., & Jenner, S. M. (1991). The Hing hypothesis: Factors influencing dating preferences. *Psychology: A Journal of Human Behavior, 28,* 27–31.

Wood, J. M., Bootzin, R. R., Kihlstrom, J. F., & Schacter, D. L. (1992). Implicit and explicit memory for verbal information presented during sleep. *Psychological Science, 3,* 236–239.

Woody, J. D. (1990). Resolving ethical concerns in clinical practice: Toward a pragmatic model. *Journal of Marital and Family Therapy, 16,* 133–150.

Wright, A. A., Santiago, H. C., Sands, S. F., Kendrick, D. F., & Cook, R. G. (1985). Memory processing of serial lists by pigeons, monkeys, and people, *Science, 229,* 287–289.

Wright, E. F., Jackson, W., Christie, S. D., McGuire, G. F., et al. (1991). The home-course disadvantage in golf championships: Further evidence for the undermining effect of supportive audiences on performance under pressure. *Journal of Sport Behavior, 14*(1), 51–60.

Wundt, W. (1912). *An introduction to psychology.* London: Allen.

Wu, K. K. & Lam, D. J. (1993). The relationship between daily stress and health: Replicating and extending previous findings. *Psychology and Health, 8,* 329–344.

Yoakum, C. S., & Yerkes, R. M. (1920). *The Army mental tests.* New York: Holt.

Yoo, L. (1994). Understanding the "brick ceiling": Investigations of the relationships among gender, sex-role, and attitude toward women managers in Korea. Unpublished honors thesis, Harvard-Radcliffe Colleges, Cambridge, MA.

Zachary, R. A. (1990). Wechsler's intelligence scales: Theoretical and practical considerations. *Journal of Psychoeducational Assessment, 8,* 276–289.

Zajonc, R. B., & Markus, G. B. (1975). Birth order and intellectual development. *Psychological Review, 82,* 74–88.

Zangwill, O. L. (1987). Experimental hypnosis. In R. L. Gregory (Ed.), *The Oxford companion to the mind.* New York: Oxford University Press.

Zani, B. & Kirchler, E. (1991). When violence overshadows the spirit of sporting competition. *Journal of Community and Applied Social Psychology, 1,* 5-12.

Zanot, E. J., Pincus, J. D., & Lamp, E. J. (1983). Public perceptions of subliminal advertising. *Journal of Advertising, 12,* 39–45.

Zarrow, M. X., Sarwin, P. B., Ross, S., & Denenberg, V. H. (1962). Maternal behavior and its endocrine basis in the rabbit. In E. L. Bliss (Ed.), *The roots of behavior.* New York: Hafner.

Zepelin, H., & Rechtschaffen, A. (1974). Mamalian sleep, longevity, and energy metabolism. *Brain, Behavior, and Evolution, 10,* 425–470.

Zhang, H. (1988). Psychological measurement in China. *International Journal of Psychology, 23,* 101–117.

Zigler, E., & Hodapp, R. M. (1991). Behavioral functioning in individuals with mental retardation. *Annual Review of Psychology, 42,* 29–50.

Zimba, C. G., & Buggie, S. E. (1993). An experimental study of the placebo effect in African traditional medicine. *Behavioral Medicine, 19,* 103–109.

Zimbardo, P. G. (1992). Foreword. In S. Milgram, *The individual in a social world: Essays and experiments* (2nd ed.). New York: McGraw-Hill.

Zimbardo, P. G., & Leippe, M. R. (1991). *The psychology of attitude change and social influence.* New York: McGraw-Hill.

Zimring, F. (1990). A characteristic of Rogers's response to clients. *Person-Centered Review, 5,* 433–448.

Zissman, A., & Neimark, E. (1990). The influence of familiarity on evaluations of liking and goodness of several types of music. *Psychological Record, 40,* 481–490.

Zuckerman, M. (1979). *Sensation seeking: Beyond the optimal level of arousal.* Hillsdale, NJ: Erlbaum.

Zuckerman, M. (1990). The psychophysiology of sensation seeking. *Journal of Personality, 58,* 313–345.

Zuckerman, M., & Feldman, L. S. (1984). Actions and occurrences in attribution theory. *Journal of Personality and Social Psychology, 46,* 541–550.

ACKNOWLEDGMENTS

Photos and art:

Chapter 1   Page 6 Dodge Fernald; p. 8 Hulton Deutsch Limited; p. 9 Bettman Archives; p. 10 Dodge Fernald; p. 11 Harvard University Collection of Historical Scientific Instruments; p. 12 Harvard University Archives; p. 13 (left) Partridge, Wellesley College Library; p. 13 (right) The Schlesinger Library, Radcliffe College; p.15 D.W. Fawcett/Komuro/Science Source, Photo Researchers, Inc.; p. 16 UPI, Bettman; p. 17, Harvard University Archives; p. 18, Bettman; p. 19, Wayne Behling; p. 22 (right) James King-Holmes, Science Photo Library/Photo Researchers, Inc.; p. 22 (left) Lawrence Migdale, Photo Researchers, Inc.; p. 24 Susan Woog Wagner, Photo Researchers, Inc.

Chapter 2   Page 36 Peter Veit, DRK Photo; p. 41 Dodge Fernald; p. 49 Ken Karp; p. 54 Prof. Philip G. Zimbardo

Chapter 3   Page 72 E.R.Lewis/Omikron, Photo Researchers, Inc.; p. 78 A. Glauberman, Photo Researchers, Inc.; p. 88 Will & Deni McIntyre, Photo Researchers, Inc.

Chapter 4   Page 99 Bayer, Monkmeyer Press; p. 101 Patrick Ward, Stock Boston; p. 105 Omikron, Photo Researchers, Inc.; p. 114 Omikron/Science Source, Photo Researchers, Inc.; p. 118 Peter Simon, Stock Boston; p. 121 Tony Tickle, Tony Stone Images.

Chapter 5   Page 132 Tim Davis, Photo Researchers, Inc.; p. 134 © American Association of Advertising Agencies; p. 139 Aaron Siskind (1903-1991) *Feet* 133, 1958. Courtesy of The Harvard University Art Museums. The Aaron Siskind Foundation, Inc. Gift of Mrs. Phyllis Lambert.; p. 143 David Rigg, Tony Stone Images; p. 144 Spencer Grant, Monkmeyer Press; p. 145 William Vandivert, Scientific American; p. 148 Globus Studios, The Stock Market; p. 150 Hillel Burger, Peabody Museum, Harvard University. Courtesy of the President and Fellows of Harvard College, All rights reserved; p. 152 From *Perception* by Irvin Rock. Copyright 1984 by Scientific American Books and from *Visual Illusions* by Richard L. Gregory. Copyright 1968 by Scientific American, Inc. All rights reserved.

Chapter 6   Page 165 Michael Siluk, The Image Works; p. 174 Tibor Hirsch, Photo Researchers, Inc.; p. 176 Bettman; p. 177 Barbara Alper, Stock Boston; p. 180 Peter Menzel, Stock Boston

Chapter 7   Page 196 Bettman; p. 201 Russell D. Curtis, Photo Researchers, Inc.; p. 204 David Stoecklein Terry, The Stock Market; p. 205 Alan· Mercer, Stock Boston; p. 209 (left) Harvard University Archives; (right) Will Rapport, B.F. Skinner Foundation; p. 211 M. Neveux, Westlight; p. 212 Gerald Davis, Woodfin Camp & Associates; p. 214 Bob Daemmrich, Stock Boston; p. 216 Gale Zucker, Stock Boston; p. 217 Michael Grecco, Stock Boston

Chapter 8   Page 236 Michael Dwyer, Stock Boston; p. 252 From W. Penfield, *The Excitable Cortex in Conscious Man.* Thomas, 1958, p. 27; p. 254 Bettman

Chapter 9   Page 272 Maurice E. Landre/National Audubon Society, Photo Researchers, Inc.; p. 277 Dodge Fernald; p. 281 Nita Winter, The Image Works; p. 292 Lynn McLaren, Photo Researchers, Inc.; p. 295 Pantheon Books

Chapter 10   Page 311 Harvard Crimson; p. 313 Pierre Burger/ National Audubon Society, Photo Researchers, Inc.; p. 315 (left) Diane Rawson, Photo Researchers, Inc.; (right) Lionel DeLevingne/ Stock Boston; p. 317 Harry F. Harlow, University of Wisconsin, Harlow Primate Laboratory; p. 320 Dodge Fernald; p. 321 D.H. Hessel, Stock Boston; p. 324 Michael Hayman, Photo Researchers, Inc.; p. 328 Giraudon, Art Resource

Chapter 11   Page 342 (left)Alan Carey, Photo Researchers, Inc.; (right) John Griffin, The Image Works; p. 351 Miro Vintoniv, Stock Boston; p. 355 Michael Hayman, Stock Boston; p. 357 Neal Peters Collection; p. 362 Professor P. Motta, Dept. of Anatomy, University La Sapienza, Rome, Science Photo Library/Photo Researchers, Inc.

Chapter 12   Page 376 Dr. James L. German, III; p. 382 Thomas McAvoy, Time-Life Picture Agency/ Time, Inc.; p. 386 Photo Researchers, Inc.; p. 396 David S. Strickler, Monkmeyer Press; p. 400 Michael Kagan, Monkmeyer Press

Chapter 13   Page 413 Bob Daemmrich, The Image Works; p. 421 Paul Conklin, Monkmeyer Press; p. 423 Monkmeyer Press; p. 428 Lewis P. Watson, Monkmeyer Press; p. 433 Elizabeth Crews, Stock Boston

Chapter 14   Page 447 Bettman; p. 450 Elizabeth Crews, Stock Boston; p. 456, 457 Dodge Fernald; p. 458 UPI, Bettman; p. 461 Stock Boston; p. 468 Lawrence Migdale, Photo Researchers, Inc.; p. 475, 476 Dodge Fernald

Chapter 15   Page 487 PH College Archives; p. 489 (left) Monkmeyer Press; (right) Stock Boston; p. 492 Elizabeth Crews, The Image Works; p. 493 Yann Arthus-Bertrand, Peter Arnold, Inc.; p. 497 Stock Boston; p. 504 (both) Warren Anatomical Museum; p. 510 Bettman; p. 513 Harvard Crimson; p. 514 (left) Stock Boston; (right) AP/Wide World Photos

Chapter 16   Page 523 Reuters, Bettman; p. 526 Steve Goldberg, Monkmeyer Press; p. 528 UPI, Bettman; p. 533 Michael Newman, PhotoEdit; p. 536 Teri Stratford, Stock Boston; p. 541 Will & Deni McIntyre, Photo Researchers, Inc.; p. 549 Bettman; p. 551 Ulrike Welsch, Photo Researchers, Inc.

Chapter 17   Page 562 Michael Dwyer, Stock Boston; p. 571 Michael C. Hayman, Stock Boston; p. 572 Dodge Fernald; p. 576 Frank Siteman, Picture Cube, Inc.; p. 580 Trevor, Inc., Monkmeyer Press; p. 583, Alexander Milgram copyright 1965 by Stanley Milgram. From the film "Obedience," distributed by the N.Y.U. Film Library. p. 588 Tomas D.W. Friedman, Photo Researchers, Inc.; p. 590 Steve Halber, AP/Wide World Photos; p. 593 (left) UPI, Bettman; 593 (right) Reuters, Bettman

Chapter 18   Page 603 Teri Stratford; p. 608 Dodge Fernald; 614 (left & right) Bettman; p. 619 Bettman

Color inserts

Figure III-1, Figure III-2 Dartmouth Publishing, Inc.; Figure III-3 Mazziotta Et, Photo Researchers, Inc.; Figure IV-1 Fritz Goro, Life Magazine, Time Warner, Inc.; Figure IV-2 Dann Coffey, The Image Bank; Figure IV-4 Douglas Faulkner, Photo Researchers, Inc.; Figure XI-1 Alexander & Turner; Figure XI-2 David Frazier/Photo Researchers, Inc.; Figure XI-3 (top) Teri Stratford; Figure XI-3 (bottom) Paul Ekman/ Garland STPM Press, reproduced by permission.; Figure XII-3a Lennart Nilsson/Bonnier Fakta; Figure XII-3b Photo Researchers, Inc.; Figure XII-3c Lennart Nilsson/Bonnier Fakta; Figure XII-3d Photo Researchers, Inc.

The following works have been excerpted or referenced in this text and are acknowledged as follows:

Chapter 2   Excerpts from Stanley Milgram, *THE INDIVIDUAL IN A SOCIAL WORLD*, 1977, 1992. New York: McGraw-Hill.

Chapter 3   Excerpts adapted with the permission of Simon & Schuster from *THE MAN WHO MISTOOK HIS WIFE FOR A HAT: and other clinical tales* by Oliver Sacks. Copyright © 1970, 1981, 1983, 1984, 1985 by Oliver Sacks.

Chapter 9   Excerpts from *HOUSE* by Tracy Kidder. Copyright © 1985 by John Tracey Kidder. New York: Houghton-Mifflin.

Chapter 10   Excerpts from *DOVE* by Robin Graham. New York: HarperCollins.

Chapter 13   Excerpts from *UNFULFILLED EXPECTATIONS* by Catherine Snow et al. Copyright © 1991 by the President and Fellows of Harvard College. Cambridge, MA: Harvard University Press.

Chapter 11   Excerpts from George Goethals & Dennis S. Klos *EXPERIENCING YOUTH*. 1976, 1970. Boston: Little Brown. (Courtesy of Natalie Goethals)

Chapter 14   Excerpts from *LETTERS FROM JENNY* by Gordon W. Allport, copyright © 1965 by Harcourt Brace & Company and renewed 1993 by Robert P. Allport, reprinted by permission of the publisher.

Name Index

A

Abel, G.G., 512
Ables, B.S., 501
Abramov, I., 275
Abrams, R., 504
Achermann, R., 167
Acord, J., 11
Adair, J.G., 51
Adams, C.F., 124
Adams, G.R., 402
Adams, H., 87
Adams, J.F., 386
Adelman, J.P., 66
Ader, R., 499
Adler, A., 458
Adler, N., 503
Adler, T., 286
Agnew, H.W., 163
Agranoff, B.W., 255
Akers, R.L., 185
Albert, M.S., 81
Albright, T.D., 148
Aldag, R.J., 590
Alessio, J.C., 564
Alfini, J.J., 26
Allen, K.D., 537, 538
Allen, M., 578
Allison, S., 560, 561, 562,
   563, 566, 567, 568, 569,
   570, 573, 578, 579, 581,
   584, 586, 589, 591, 592
Allport, G.W., 446, 447,
   459, 464, 466, 467, 470,
   472, 474, 477, 478, 479
Alston, R.L., 398
Amato, P., 365
Ambady, N., 21, 22, 152
American Psychiatric Associ-
   ation, 23, 168, 183, 492,
   496, 497, 498, 499, 504,
   511, 512, 513
Amir, T., 580
Amoore, J.E., 112
Anastasi, A., 374
Anderson, C.H., 179
Anderson, D.B., 153
Anderson, D., 566, 585

Anderson, K., 503
Andreasen, N.C., 505, 507
Angel, R., 553
Appel, P.R., 178
Arauio, J., 259
Arndt, S., 505
Arntz, A., 223
Aron, R., 293
Arvey, R.D., 430
Asch, S.E., 569, 580
Aserinsky, E., 167
Asmus, C., 24
Atkinson, J.W., 153
Atkinson, R.C., 234, 243
Austin, J.T., 243
Austin, T.J., 233
Averill, J.R., 357
Azrin, N.H., 545

B

Back, K., 576
Backer, R., 323
Baddeley, A.D., 235
Bailey, J.S., 217
Bailey, S., 503
Baird, J., 143
Baker, R.A., 225
Baker, S.M., 24
Baker, T.B., 182
Balenstein, E.S., 80
Bales, R.F., 592
Ban, T.A., 203
Banaji, M.I., 57, 233, 578,
   579
Bandler, R., 363
Bandura, A., 222, 223, 357,
   468, 469
Banks, R., 162
Banks, W.P., 141
Barakat, L.P., 508
Barber, T.X., 179
Barclay, M.W., 459
Bard, J.S., 501
Barker, G.H., 363
Barnes, W.S., 410, 414, 419,
   420, 422, 423, 428, 429,

430, 435, 439, 440
Barnet, R.C., 201
Barnhardt, T.M., 136
Baron, M., 507
Barrio, J.C., 74
Barry, T., 532
Bartlett, F.C., 241, 244
Bartus, R., 256
Basil, M., 567
Bassim, E., 578
Bassuk, E.L., 551
Batchelor, R.A., 101
Batson, C.D., 584
Baudry, M., 250
Baumeister, R.R., 341
Baumrind, D., 53
Bayley, N., 437
Beck, A.T., 503, 531
Becklen, K., 135
Bedon, B.G., 238
Beier, E.G., 22
Beilin, H., 387, 391
Bell, P.A., 24
Bellugi, U., 278
Bem, D.J., 124
Benassi, V.A., 503
Benjamin, L.T., 11
Bennett, J.C., 357
Benson, H., 87, 175, 540
Bentler, L.E., 547
Berecz, J.M., 79
Bergamini, D., 124
Bergin, A., 546
Berkowitz, L., 356, 358
Berman, J. S., 547
Bernard, L.L., 306
Bernoties, L., 256
Bernstein, J., 167
Berridge, K.C., 308
Berschied, E., 577, 578
Betz, N.E., 404
Betz, N.E., 553, 579
Beulig, A. 223
Bhugra, D., 512
Bierhoff, H., 585
Binet, A., 411
Birch, H.G., 292, 294, 305
Birren, J.E., 399

Black, J.B., 242
Blair, S.M., 505
Blalock, J.A., 579
Blass, T., 59, 583
Block, M.R., 290
Block, P., 5, 14
Blum, S.B., 184
Boesch, C., 272
Boesch-Achermann, H., 272
Bogen, J.E., 84
Bogolub, E.B., 363
Bok, D., 394
Bonanno, G.A., 257
Bonate, P.L., 74
Bond, C.T., 66
Boneau, C.A., 58
Booth, A., 578
Booth-Kewley, S., 363
Bootzin, R.I. 27
Borbely, A., 167
Borgeat, F., 88
Boring, E.G., 101
Botwinick, J., 399
Bouchard, T.J., 374, 433
Bourne, L.E., 268
Bousefield, W.A., 194, 219
Bowden, C.C., 575
Bower, G.H. 21, 239, 242,
   260
Bowlby, J., 317
Bowler, A.E., 506
Boynton, R.M., 107
Boysen, S., 271
Bozarth, J.D., 473, 527
Brager, R., 475
Brainerd, C.J., 394
Bramel, D., 580
Brehm, S.S., 577
Brehm, S.S., 577
Breland, H.M., 320
Brener, T.H., 320
Brenner, C., 525
Brewer, M.B., 324
Brewin, C.R., 532
Briere, J., 450, 489
Brock, T.C., 565
Brodley, B.T., 473
Brogden, W.J., 219

Piotrowski, C., 475
Pittillo, E.S., 501
Pitts, W.H., 105
Plomin, R., 375, 377, 461
Plutchik, R., 341
Polonko, K.A., 578
Pomeroy, W.B., 353, 354
Poon, L.W., 400
Pope, K.S., 36
Poulson, C.L., 279
Powell, D.H., 399
Powell, S., 451
Pratkanis, A.R., 99
Prentice, D.A., 578, 579
Prentiss, C.W., 119
Pressley, M., 394
Prewett, P.N., 412
Psotka, J., 255
Puka, B., 394
Pullum, G.K., 275

Q

Quast, Z., 246

R

Raaijmakers, Q.A.W., 49, 58
Rabinowitz, H.S., 292
Rachlin, H., 17
Rafferty, Y., 580
Rahe, R.H., 359
Raij, D., 625
Raison, J., 41
Randi, J., 123
Rasinski, K.A., 39
Ratliff, F., 106
Ray, O., 184
Rayner, R., 535
Read, J.D., 135
Rechtshaffen, A. 162
Redd, M., 587
Redden, J.R., 476
Ree, M.J., 425
Reeves, B.R., 567, 568
Regier, D.A., 521
Reicken, H.W., 37
Reimann-Marcus, B., 48
Rende, R., 375
Rende, R., 461
Rescorla, R.A., 195, 201, 202
Rescorla, R.A., 224, 225
Resnick, L.B., 587

Resnick, L.B., 587
Revelle, W., 479
Reynolds, L.T., 324
Rhee, D., 471
Rhine, J.B., 123
Rich, E., 283
Rich, S., 374
Richards-Jodoin, R.M., 525
Richmond, J.B., 435
Rienzi, B.M., 42
Ries, R.K., 184
Riggio, R.E., 425
Riggs, L.A., 106
Riley, L.R., 277, 278
Rips, L.J., 282
Risser, D., 383
Robert, M., 223
Robins, L.N., 521
Robinson, E.A., 486
Rock, D.A., 478
Roediger, H.L., 37
Roethlisberger, F.J., 326
Roffwarg, H.P., 170
Rogers, C.R., 486, 526, 527
Rogers, D. 505
Rogler, L.H., 539, 550
Rollin, H.R., 541
Rompre, P.T., 80
Rosch, E., 269, 276
Rose, R.J., 377
Rosen, M., 431
Rosen, R., 310, 311
Rosenhan, D.L., 488, 491, 493, 501, 503, 513, 515, 549, 669
Rosenhan, D.L., 501, 503, 513, 515, 549, 56
Rosenman, R.H., 25
Rosenthal, D., 502
Rosenthal, R., 21, 22, 152, 502
Rosenzweig, M.R., 251
Ross, M., 575
Ross, S., 304, 361
Rothblum, E.D., 316
Rothman, S., 417
Rotter, J.B., 469
Rouse, S.V., 476
Rubin, L., 551
Rubin, M., 112
Rubinstein, E.A., 468
Rue, S. 217
Rumbaugh, D.M., 271
Rumelhart, D.E., 244
Rushton, J.P., 374, 394, 429, 585
Russell, R.W., 100

S

Saariluoma, P., 139
Sabin, J., 59
Sackeim, H.A., 542
Sacks, O.W., 64, 67, 72, 77, 80, 82, 86, 90
Sadowski, M., 246
Safford, R.K., 590
Sakmann, B., 70
Saks, M.M., 55
Sales, B., 26
Salzinger, K., 282
Samsun, S., 85
Sancho, A.M., 320, 579
Sands, S.S., 240
Santiago, H.C., 240
Sarbin, T.R., 179
Saron, C., 342
Sarwin, P.B., 304
Sasitharan, T., 419
Satin, M., 25
Satz, P., 400
Savage-Rumaugh, E.S., 271
Sawyer, A.G., 567
Saxe, L., 339, 491
Scally, M., 402
Scarborough, E., 12
Scarr, S., 374, 428, 432
Schachter, S., 37, 318, 345, 346
Schacter, B.L., 27
Schacter, S., 576
Schaffer, C.E., 342, 400, 437, 439
Schalken, H.F., 247
Schall, M., 360
Schalling, D., 339
Scheflen, A.E., 21
Scheier, M.F., 363
Scheier, M.F., 486
Schiavi, R.C., 312
Schiffer, F., 498
Schiffrin, R.M., 243
Schildkraut, J.J., 502
Schjelderup-Ebbe, T., 586
Schmidt, D., 256
Schneider, M., 152
Schneider, M., 354
Schneidman, E.S., 502
Schober, B.I., 491
Schooler, C., 434
Schreiner-Engel, P., 312
Schulsinger, F., 502
Schuster, B., 574
Schwartz, G.E., 339
Scott, J.P., 179

Scott, K.G., 419
Scotto, P., 223
Sears, R.R., 358, 455
Sears, R.R., 455
Sebeok, T.A., 24
Sebeok, T.A., 271, 374
Segal, N.L., 433
Segall, M.H., 150
Selligman, M.E.P., 202, 491
Selye, H., 361
Semb, G., 259
Shaffer, D.R., 563
Shah, M., 309
Shane, E., 513
Shane, M., 513
Shapiro, D.A., 547
Shapley, R., 105
Sharp, H.S., 324
Sharpe, D., 51
Shaw, J.C., 285
Shaywitz, S.S., 422
Shearer, D.H., 249
Sheffield, F., 323
Sheldon, W.H., 462
Shepard, R.N., 247
Sherif, M., 588
Sherman, J.B., 182
Sherr, L., 567
Shields, J., 506, 507
Shiffrin, R.M., 234
Shipstead, S.G., 392
Shopland, C., 138
Shubs, C.H., 462
Shweder, R.A., 24, 552
Sicoly, F., 575
Siegel, S., 203, 204
Sigel, M., 223
Silliman, E.R., 24
Silver, M., 59
Sime, W.E., 364
Simon, C.W., 27
Simon, H.A., 238, 285, 392
Simon, P., 411
Simons, A.D., 506
Simons, R.L., 357
Simpson, J.A., 313
Simpson, R.L., 421
Sinclair, R.C., 346
Singer, B., 547
Singer, J.A., 339, 345
Singer, M.T., 311
Sizemore, C.C., 501
Skeels, H.M., 317, 372, 377, 379, 381, 383, 384, 391, 395, 397, 401, 420
Skiba, R.J., 41
Skinner, B.F., 17, 216, 217,

SUBJECT INDEX

A

Abnormality, 492-496
and DSM IV, 495
maladjustment, defined, 486
mental disorder, 492
mental illness, 494
neurosis, 494-495
See also Adjustment
Absolute threshold. *See* Threshold
Accommodation, 104, 387
Accretion measures. *See* Unobtrusive measures
Acetylcholine, 74
Achievement motive, 319-321
Achievement tests. *See* Testing
Achromatic vision, 108
Activation-synthesis hypothesis, dreaming, 171-172
Actualizing tendency. *See* Self actualization
Adaptation
in love, 350
in vision, 105-106
Adaptation theory of sleep, 312
Adaptation, visual, 105-106
Additive effect, 52
Adjustment, 483-515
assessment of, 511-513
continuum of, 485-487
coping effectively, 487-488
culture and gender, 511-513
disorders, types of, 496-510
and cultural relativism, 513-515
inefficient coping, 488-492
and personality testing, 474-478
See also Abnormality
Adler, Alfred, 457-458

Adolescence
cognitive development in, 390-391
defined, 385
growth spurt, 385-386
identity crisis, 396-397
sexual problems of, 386
Adrenal glands, 89
Affectional stimulation, 316-317. *See also* Affiliation
Affiliation, desire for, 318-319
Afterimage, visual, 107-108
Aggression, 355-358, 392
versus anger, 355
catharsis hypothesis 357
frustration-aggression hypothesis, 357-358
and learning, 356-357
predispositional view, 355-356
AIDS, 353-354, 386
Alarm reaction, 361
Algorithm, 283-284
All-or-none law, 70
Altered states of consciousness, 160, 162-168
Altruism, 323-324, 583-585
Alzheimer's disease, 74, 400
American Sign Language (ASL), 270-271
Amnesia, 500
anterograde, 250
retrograde, 250-251
Amplification of dreams, 173
Amygdala, 79, 337-338
Anal stage, 451
Analytical introspection, 160-161
Androgens, 304, 312, 385
Anger. *See* Aggression
Animals
ethics in research, 54
and human language, 270-272
imprinting in, 381-382,

instincts in, 303-306
observation of, 36
training of, 204, 216-217
Anorexia nervosa, 309
Antianxiety drugs, 543-544
Antidepressant drugs, 543
Antipsychotic drugs, 543
Antisocial personality disorder, 509
Anxiety
and affiliation, 318-319
as a conditioned reaction, 204-205
and defense mechanisms, 454-456, 489-490
disorders, 497-499
hierarchy, 535-536
stranger, 383
separation, 383
See also Autonomic nervous system
Anxiety disorders, 497-499
generalized, 497
obsessive-compulsive, 498-499
specific phobia, 497-498,
posttraumatic stress, 498,
Anxiety hierarchy, 535-536
Aphasia, 83
Appetitive conditioning, 220
Applied psychology, 20, 24-26
Approach-approach conflict, 360
Approach-avoidance conflict, 360
Aptitude tests. *See* Testing
Archetypes, 457
Archival data. *See* Unobtrusive measures
Arousal level, 340-341
Arousal-cognition theory, 345-346
Artificial intelligence, 283
Assertiveness training, 532
Assimilation, 387
Association cortex, 82-84

Attachment, 381-382
Attending, 132
adjustments in, 132-133
divided, 135-136,
embedded messages, 134-135
modalities in, 135-136
selective, 132-135
stimulus, characteristics of, 133-134
Attitudes, 561-565
consistency, 564-565,
dissonance theory, 565
measurement of, 563-564,
Attribution theory
defined, 152, 573
dispositional, 573
overattribution effect, 573-574
situational, 573
Auditory localization, 146
Autokinetic effect, 118
Autonomic nervous system, 66-67, 86-88, 338
Autonomy versus doubt, 396
Availability heuristic, 290-291
Aversion therapy, 537
Aversive conditioning, 220
Avoidance conditioning, 220
Avoidance-avoidance conflict, 360
Axon, 68

B

Babbling, 276
Backward conditioning, 199
Balance theory, attitudes, 564
Balance, sense of, 118-119
Basic anxiety (Horney) 458
Basic ethical questions, 54-55
Basic research. *See*, Research, basic
Basilar membrane, 109

Behavior therapy
  aversion, 536-537
  contingency management, 537-538
  defined, 534,
  desensitization, systematic, 535-537
  modeling, 539
  with punishment, 538-539
  token economy, 538
Behavioral genetics, 377-378
Behavioral medicine. *See* Health psychology
Behaviorism, 16-17, 325
Bias
  control of, 51-52
  and ethnocentrism, 571-572
  in observation, 37-38
  and prejudice, 570
  in sampling, 619
Big Five, traits, 464-465
Binaural cues to depth, 146
Binet, Alfred, 411-412
Binocular cues to depth, 145
Biofeedback, 87-88
Biological approach
  bases of behavior, 63-90
  and brain, 76-86
  to personality, 460-463
  as a system, 14-15
  and therapy, 540-544
Biomedical therapy, 540-544
Bipolar disorder, 502
Blind spot, 104, 105
Borderline personality disorder, 509
Boredom. *See* Stimulation motives
Bottom-up approach, perception, 140-141
Brain fag, 511
Brain, 76-86
  amygdala, 79
  cerebellum, 76
  cerebral cortex, 80-84
  forebrain, 77-78
  hindbrain, 76
  midbrain, 76-77
  hypothalamus, 78-79
  limbic system, 79-80,
  medulla, 76
  reticular activating system, 77
  septal area, 80
  thalamus, 78

Brainstorming, 590-591
Brief therapy, 521
Broca's area, 83-84
Bulimia nervosa, 309-310

C

California Personality Inventory (CPI) 475-476
Calkins, Mary W., 12-13
Cannon-Bard, 344
Caretaker-child interaction, 383
Case histories, 45
Case study, 42-45
  interview, 43
  tests, 43-44
  case history, 45
Catatonic type, schizophrenia, 505
Catharsis hypothesis, 357
Cawkins, Mary C., 12-13
Cell body of neuron, 68
Cellular dehydration, 311
Central nervous system, 67, 337-338. *See also* Brain, Cerebral cortex, Spinal cord
Central tendency, measures of, 607-609
Central traits, 569
Cephalocaudal development, 380
Cerebellum, 76
Cerebral cortex, 80-84
  association cortex, 82-83
  in emotion, 337
  lobes of, 81
  motor cortex, 82
  sensory cortex, 82
  study of, 81
Chaining, 218-219
Charcot, Jean-Martin, 8
Childhood
  cognitive development, 386-392,
  language development, 277-279
  moral development, 393-394
  physical development, 384-385
  psychosicial stages of, 396
  social development, 394-397
Chromosomes, 375-376

Chunking, in memory, 237-238
Circadian rhythm, 125
Circadian rhythm, 163
Classical conditioning, 195-205
  basic process, 195-197
  biological preparedness, 202-203
  and emotional reactions, 204-205
  principles of, 198-203
  testing sensory ability, 203-204
  training animals, 204
Classical experiment. *See* experimental method
Classical versus operant conditioning, 207, 219
Clever Hans effect, 21, 51
Clinical psycholgy, 27
Cochlea, 109
Coefficient of correlation, 616-617
Cognition
  defined, 266
  in emotion, 341-343
  and language, 280-282
  and learning, 224-227
  and motivation, 325-326
  See also Memory, Perception, Thinking
Cognitive approach, intelligence, 425-428
Cognitive development
  in adulthood, 399
  in childhood, Piaget, 387-391
  defined, 386
  in the elderly, 399-400
  in infancy, 379-380
  as information processing, 391-392
Cognitive psychology, 18-20, 162
Cognitive therapy, 529-532
Cognitive-behavioral therapy, 532
Cohabitation, 578
Collective unconscious, 456-457
Collector mechanisms in sense organs, 97
Color mixture,106-107
  additive, 107
  subtractive, 106-107
Color vision

afterimage, 107-108
  opponent-process theory, 107
  theories of, 107-108
  trichromatic theory, 107
Communicative deviance, schizophrenia and, 508
Community psychology, 552
Companionate love, 350-351
Compensatory education, 434-435
Competition, 587-589
Compliance
  defined, 581
  door-in-the-face technique, 581-582
  foot-in-the-door technique, 581
Computer
  keyboard, 618, 624
  simulation of thought, 286
  thought, 282-286
  See also Artificial intelligence
Concepts, 266-272
  features-based approach, 268
  prototype-based approach, 269
  without language, 269-270
Conceptual hierarchy, memory, 242
Concrete operations, 389-390
Conditioned response, 197
Conditioned stimulus, 197
Conditioning and language learning, 279, 281
Conditioning, 195-221
  classical, 195-205
  operant, 207-218
  reciprocal, 216
  two-factor, 219-221
Cones, 104
Confidential communication, 521-522
Confirmation bias, 287-288
Conflict
  in psychoanalysis, 324-325, 452-453
  types of, 360-361
Conformity, 579-581
Confounding variable, 50
Congruence, in personality, 473

and behavior, 340-341
and cognition, 341-343
defined 334
feelings, 335-337
liking and loving, 346-351
physiology of, 337
and sex, 351-355
and stress, 358-365
theories of, 343-346

Empiricism
in assessing treatment, 544
defined, 5-7
in evaluating the keyboard, 622
in intercranial self-stimulation, 80
in science, 6-7
in studies of illusions, 154

Rehearsal, 236-237
chunking, 237-238
cuing, 238-239
organization, 237

Endocrine system, 88-90
adrenal glands, 89
gonads, 89
hormones, 88
pituitary glands, 88-89
thyroid glands, 89

Encoding, memory, 232, 236-237, 243
Endomorph, 462
Endorphine, 75-76
Endorphins, 125
Environment
and aggression, 355-358
deprived, 420
and intelligence, 430, 434, 435-436
nonshared, 461
and schizophrenia, 508
Environmental psychology, 24
Epinephrine, 89, 345
Episodic memory, 240
Equity theory, love, 348-349
Erikson's psychosocial stages, 395-397, 401-403
Eros, 448
Erosion measures. *See* Unobtrusive measures
Escape conditioning, 220
Estrogens, 304, 312, 385
Ethics in research and practice, 26-28, 53-56

Ethnocentrism, 571-572
Evolution, theory of, 7-8
Evolutionary psychology
and altruism, 323-324
and sexual behavior, 313-314.
See also Evolution, theory of
Exchange theory, love, 348
Exhibitionism, 513
Existential therapy, 527-528
Expectancy x value theory, 326
Experimental method, 45-53
classical, 46-48
confounding variable, 50
control condition, 49-50
design, 49-52
experimental condition 49-50
rule of one variable 46
Experimenter effects, 51
Explicit memory, 241
Expressed emotion and schizophrenia, 508
Extinction, 200, 211
Extrasensory perception (ESP) 123-124
Extrinsic motivation, 320-321
Eye, parts of, 103-104

F

Facial-feedback hypothesis, 344
Fallacy of single cause, 28, 329
Fallacy, in adolescent thought, 391
Falsifiable claims, 27
Familiarity and attraction, 576-577
Family
and schizophrenia, 508
and intelligence, 433-434, 435-436
and nonshared environment, 461.
See also Parents
Fantasy, 491
Fear of success, 320
Fear, in persuasion, 567-568
Feature detectors, 105
Feedback, in therapy, 538
Feelings, in emotion, 335-337

Fetal alcohol syndrome, 378, 420
Fetishism, 512-513
Fetus, 378
Figure-ground relationships, 137-138
Figures
impossible, 137
reversible, 137-138
Fixed-action pattern, 307. *See also* Reflex
Fixed-interval reinforcement, 213-214
Fixed-ratio reinforcement, 213
Flashbulb memory, 246
Flooding, in therapy, 528
Fluid intelligence, 426-427
Follow-up studies, therapy, 545
Forebrain, 77
Forgetting
decay theory, 253-254
defined, 253
interference, 255-257
motivated, 257
obliteration theory, 254-255
Formal operations, 390-391
Fovea, 104
Fragile X syndrome, 419-420
Framing, in problem solving, 289-290
Fraternal twins, 374
Fraud
in clinical practice, 27
Rosenhan study, 488-515
Free association, 523
Free will, 470-471
Freud, S. , 15-16, 172-173, 257, 446-456, 489-490, 522-523
Freudian slips, 453—454
Frontal lobe, 81,
Frustration-aggression hypothesis, 357-358
Fugue, 500
Functional fixedness, 292
Functionalism, 11-12

G

GABA, (gamma amino butyric acid), 75
Galvanic skin response (GSR) 338

Gambling, pathological, 495-496
Gate-control theory, 116
Gender
alcoholism, 512
communication and, 578
differences in therapy, 553
identity, 395
mental abilities 430-431
mental health, 486
moral development, 394
roles, 320
and sexual disorders, 512-513
Gender differences
adjustment, 552-553
social behavior, 578-579
Gender identity disorder, 513
Gender issues, adjustment, 552-553
General adaptation syndrome, 361-362
General intelligence, 424
Generalization, stimulus, 199, 210
Generalized anxiety disorders, 497
Generativity versus stagnation, 401-402
Genes, 376-378
Genes, modifiability of, 65-66
Genital stage, 452
Genotype, 378
Gestalt principles. *See* Grouping principles
Giftedness. *See* Mental giftedness
Goal-directed behavior, 323
Gonads, 89
Graphs, 605-606
Group polarization, 590
Group processes, 585-593
brainstorming, 590-591
cooperation and competition, 587-589
group shifts, 590
groupthink, 589-590
leadership, 591-592
pecking order, 586
role and status, 585-586
superordinate goals, 588-589
Group tests, 43-44
Group therapy
defined, 532
family therapy, 533

multiple bases, 329
species survival, 312-315
for stimulation, 315-317
theories of, 321-329
Motivational hierarchy, 326-329
Motor cortex, 82
Motor neuron, 68
Movement, perception of, 146-148
illusory, 148-149
induced, 147
MRI (magnetic resonance imaging) 81
Muller-Lyer illusion, 150-151
Multicultural awareness, 572-573
Multifactor study, 52-53
additive effect, 52
interactive effect, 52-53
Multimodal approach, in therapy, 548
Multiple bases of behavior
defined, 28, 29
in firewalking, 125
and hunger, 309
in memory, 251
and motivation, 329
in persuasion, 568
in schizophrenia, 508
and sexual behavior, 354
Multiple intelligences, 424-425
Myelin sheath, 68

N

Narcissistic personality disorder, 509-510
Narcolepsy, 168
Natural body therapy, 540-541
Naturalistic observation, 35-38
covert observation, 36
nonparticipant observation, 37
overt observation, 35-36
participant observation, 37
Nature-nurture issue. *See* Heredity-environment issue
Need, 323
Negative symptoms, schizophrenia, 505

Nervous system
autonomic, 86-87
central, 67
parasympathetic, 87
peripheral, 66-67
somatic, 66-67
sympathetic, 87
Network of associations, memory, 242
Neural coding, 97-98
Neural communication
chemical foundations, 72-76
neural message, 70-72
neuron, 68-69
Neuron, 68-69
action potential of 70
excitatory reaction of, 73
graded potential of, 72
inhibitory reaction of, 73
polarized, 70
refractory period, 71
resting potential, 70
structure of, 68
types of, 68-69
Neuropsychology, 15
Neurotransmitter substance, 73-76
acetylcholine, 74
debate over, 75-76
dopamine, 74
endorphine
GABA (gamma amino butyric acid),75,
norepinephrine, 74
Nocturnal myoclonia, 164
Nominal fallacy, 329
Nomothetic research, 45
Nonauditory labyrinth, 118-119
Nonshared environment, 461
Norepinephrine, 74,
Normal distribution, 418, 608
Norms, 39-40
Novel stimulation, 316

O

Obesity, 309
Object permanence, 388
Object relations theory, 456
Obliteration theory, 254-255
Observation. *See* Naturalistic observation
Observational learning, 222-223, 539

Obsessive-compulsive disorder, 498-499
Occipital lobe, 81
Oedipus complex, 451-452
Old age
Alzheimer's disease, 74
cognitive changes, 399
Parkinson's disease, 74
physical changes, 398
social concerns, 402
Olfactory epithelium, 112
One-trial conditioning, 201-202
One-word stage, 277
Operant learning. *See* Operant behavior, Operant conditioning, Operant view of personality
Operant behavior, 206-207
Operant conditioning, 207-218
basic process, 207-210
chaining, 218-219
defined, 207
influence of, 216-218
principles of, 210-216
reinforcement principle, 207
skills and problem-solving, 216-217
and society, 217-218
Operant response. *See* Operant behavior
Operant view of personality, 466-467
Operational definition, 48-49
Opponent-process theory
drugs, 182
emotion, 335-337
Oral stage, 450-451
Organization, in memory, 237
Organs, biological, 64-65
Osmoreceptors, 311
Out-of-role behavior, 569-570
Oval window, 109
Ovaries, 312
Overattribution effect, 573-574

P

Pain sensitivity. *See* Cutaneous sensitivity

Parallel distributed processing, 104, 140, 147, 233, 286
Paranoid type, schizophrenia, 505
Paraphilia, 512
Parasympathetic nervous system, 87, 338
Parents and parenting
caretaker attachment, 382
caretaker speech, 276
caretaker-child interaction, 383
influences on achievement, 319-320
as models, 222
Oedipus-Electra complex 451-452
and motivation, 314-315
superego, 448-449
trauma theory, 458-459
Parietal lobe, 81
Parkinson's disease, 74
Partial-reinforcement effect, 213
Passionate love, 350
Patch clamp technique, 70
Paternal behavior, 314
Pattern theory. *See* Taste
Pavlov, Ivan, 195-200, 203, 205
Pecking order, 586
Perception versus sensation, 131
Perception, 129-155
constancy, 141-143
defined, 131
depth, 144-146
form, 140-141
illusion, 148-151
influences on, 152-155
interpretation in, 143-152
movement, 146-148
organization in, 136-143
of people, 151-152.
unconscious, 136
versus sensation, 121,131
See also Sensation
Perceptual grouping. *See* Grouping principles
Perceptual processes. *See* Perception
Perceptual set, 153
Peripheral nervous system, 66-67
autonomic nervous system, 66

Stage theory of memory, 234-242
Standard deviation (SD), 610-611
Standard error, 620
Stanford-Binet Intelligence Scale, 412
Statistical literacy, 603-604
Statistical significance, 622-623
Statistics, 56-57, 599-625
  correlational, 613-618
  descriptive, 604-613
  inferential, 618-623
  misuse of, 603-604
  in research, 601-603
  as a tool, 623-625
Status, 585-586
Stereochemical theory. See Smell, sense of
Stereotypes
  cultural pluralism, 572-73
  as debilitating, 571-572
  defined, 570
  as facilitating, 570-571
  and prejudice, 570
Stimulation motives, 315-317
Stimulus
  defined, 21
  distal, 143
  proximal, 143
Storage, memory, 232
Stranger anxiety, 383
Stream of consciousness, 161
Stress reduction, 363-365
  distraction, 363-364
  physical exercise, 364
  reframing, 363
  relaxation, 364
  seeking assistance, 364
Stress, 358-365
  bodily reaction in, 361-363
  conflict and, 360-361
  coping with, 363-365
  defined, 358
  life changes and, 358-360
Stressor, 363
Structuralism, 10-11
Structuralism vs functionalism, 13
Structure-of-intellect model, 425-427
Study of differences, 622
Sublimation, 490

Subliminal advertising, 98-99,134
Successive approximations, 212-213
Superego, 448-449
Support group, 552
Suppression, 489
Survey method, 38-42
  questionnaires, 38-40
  sampling, 40
  unobtrusive measures, 40-42
Survival motives. See Hunger, Parenting, Sexual behavior, Sleep, Thirst
Sympathetic nervous system, 87, 338
Symptom substitution, 545
Synapse, 71-72
Syntax, 273
Systematic desensitization, 535-537
Systems of psychology, 14-20 See Behaviorism, Biological approach, Cognitive psychology, Evolutionary psychology, Humanistic psychology, Psychoanalysis
Systems, biological. See Nervous system, Endocrine system

T

Taste, 113-114
Telegraphic speech, 277-278
Television
  advertising, 566
  and aggression, 357
  and media psychology, 25-26
Temperament, 460-462
Temperature sensitivity. See Cutaneous sensitivity
Temporal lobe, 81
Teratogens, 378
Terminal threshold. See Thresholds
Testes, 312
Testing
  achievement, 416
  aptitude, 416
  intelligence, 411-416
  interest, 416-417
  norms, 415-416

personality 417, 474-478
  reliability, 414-415
  validity, 415
Tests, psychological, 43-44
  group, 43-44
  individual, 44
Thalamus, 78
Thanatos, 448
Thematic apperception test (TAT), 475
Theory
  defined, 14
  opponent-process, 107, 335-337
  two-factor, 219-221, 345-346
  See Attitudes, Consciousness, Dreaming, Emotion, Evolution, Forgetting, Hypnosis, Intelligence, Language, Memory, Motivation, Sensation. See also Systems of Psychology
Therapeutic alliance, 548
Therapy, 519-553
  entering, 521-522
  insight, 522-532
  group, 532-534
  behavioral, 535-539
  modeling, 539
  natural body, 540-541
  biomedical, 540-544
  evaluation of, 544-546
  effectiveness of, 546-548
  therapeutic alliance, 548
Thinking, 265-296
  and cognition, 266
  and concepts, 267-272
  creative, 293-296
  imaginal mode, 272
  language, 272-282
  propositional mode, 272
  reasoning, 282-293
Third-force psychology, 18
Thirst, 311
Thresholds, 98-102
  absolute threshold, 98
  terminal threshold, 99-100
  difference threshold, 100-101
Thyroid gland, 89
Timeout, in therapy, 538-539
Top-down approach, perception,141

Touch. See Cutaneous sensitivity
Tourette's syndrome, 79
Trace conditioning, 198
Traits, personality
  basic traits, 463-464
  Big Five, 464-465
  defined, 463
  subtraits, 465
Transference, 523-524
Transformational rules 280
Transpositional learning, 225
Trauma theory, 458-459
Trial-and-error in creativity, 293-294
Triangular theory of love, 347
Triarchic theory, intelligence, 427-428
Trust versus mistrust, 396
Two-factor theory. See Theory
Type A personality, 24-25, 362-363

U

Unconditioned response, 197
Unconditioned stimulus, 197
Unconscious
  collective, 456-457
  motivation, 16, 325, 452-456
  perception, 136
Unconscious motivation, 16
Unconscious motivation, 325
Unconscious motivation, 452-456
Unconscious, collective, 456-457
Unobtrusive measures, 40-42

V

Validity, 415
  face validity, 415,
  predictive validity, 415,
  concurrent validity, 415,
  norms, 415-416
Variability, measures of, 609-612
Variable, 46
Variable-interval reinforcement, 214

Variable-ratio reinforcmeent, 213
Ventromedial nucleus, 307-308
Vestibular system, 118-119
Visceral sensitivity, 118
Vision, 103-108
   operation of the eye, 103-104,
   vision and the brain, 104-105,
   adaptation, 105-106
   stimulus change, 106,
color vision, 107-108
Visual sensitivity, defined, 103
Volley theory of hearing, 111
Voyeurism, 513

W

Wave
   alpha, 164
   amplitude, 103, 109
delta, 165
   mixture, 103, 109
   wavelength, 103, 109
Weber's law, 101
Wechsler Intelligence Scales, 412-413
Wernicke's area, 84
Word recognition, 276-277
Working memory. *See* Short-term memory
Wundt, 160-161
Wundt, Wilhelm, 10-11
Wundt, Wilhelm, 10-11, 160-161

Y

Yerkes-Dodson law, 341

Z

Zygote, 378

NARRATIVE INDEX

This index shows the chapters in which the various narratives appear, indicated according to the chief characters, objects, or activi-